Street by Stree

KENT

Enlarged areas **ASHFORD, CANTERBURY, CHATHAM, DOVER, FOLKESTONE, GILLINGHAM, MAIDSTONE, MARGATE, RAMSGATE, ROCHESTER, ROYAL TUNBRIDGE WELLS, SEVENOAKS**
Plus Broadstairs, Bromley, Croydon, Dartford, East Grinstead, Gravesend, Herne Bay, Lewisham, Orpington, Rye, Tilbury, Tonbridge, Whitstable, Woolwich

3rd edition March 2008
© Automobile Association Developments Limited 2008

Original edition printed May 2001

This product includes map data licensed from Ordnance Survey® with the permission of the Controller of Her Majesty's Stationery Office. © Crown copyright 2008. All rights reserved. Licence number 100021153.

The copyright in all PAF is owned by Royal Mail Group plc.

Published by AA Publishing (a trading name of Automobile Association Developments Limited, whose registered office is Fanum House, Basing View, Basingstoke, Hampshire RG21 4EA. Registered number 1878835).

Produced by the Mapping Services Department of The Automobile Association. (A03563)

A CIP Catalogue record for this book is available from the British Library.

Printed by Oriental Press in Dubai

The contents of this atlas are believed to be correct at the time of the latest revision. However, the publishers cannot be held responsible or liable for any loss or damage occasioned to any person acting or refraining from action as a result of any use or reliance on any material in this atlas, nor for any errors, omissions or changes in such material. This does not affect your statutory rights. The publishers would welcome information to correct any errors or omissions and to keep this atlas up to date. Please write to Publishing, The Automobile Association, Fanum House (FH12), Basing View, Basingstoke, Hampshire, RG21 4EA. E-mail: streetbystreet@theaa.com

Ref: ML103y

Key to map pages	ii-iii
Key to map symbols	iv-1
Enlarged map pages	2-23
Main map pages	24-347
Index – towns & villages	348-350
Index – streets	351-409
Index – featured places	410-421
Acknowledgements	422

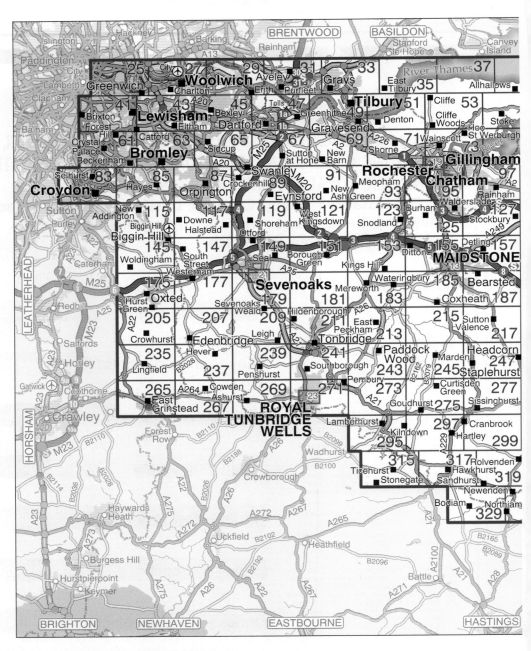

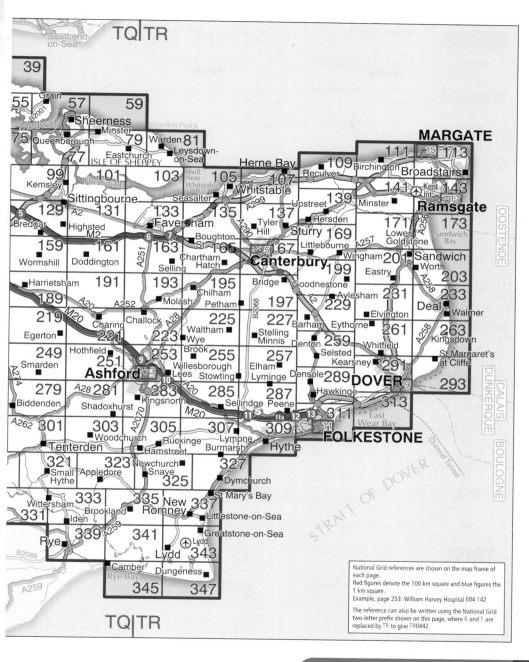

TQ|TR

Southend-on-Sea

39

55 Grain
57
59

B2001

75 Queenborough
Medway
Sheerness
Minster
Warden Point

77 Eastchurch
ISLE OF SHEPPEY
79 Warden
81 Leysdown-on-Sea

99 Kemsley
101
The Swale
103
Shell Ness
Whitstable Bay
105
Herne Bay
107
Reculver
109 Birchington

MARGATE

111
115
113

Broadstairs

Whitstable
Seasalter
Upstreet
139 Minster
141
Kent Int.
143
117

129 Bredgar
A2
131
Sittingbourne
133 Faversham
135
137 Tyler Hill
Sturry 169
Littlebourne
Wingham 201
Worth
Sandwich

Ramsgate

171 Lower Goldstone
173
Sandwich Bay

159 Wormshill
Highsted
M2
161 Doddington
163
Boughton St
Chartham Hatch
Selling
A251
165
167
Canterbury 199
Eastry
231
Elvington
233 Deal
203
Walmer

189 Harrietsham
191
193
Molash
195 Chilham
Petham
B2068
197
Goodnestone
229 Aylesham
Eythorne
261
Whitfield
263 Kingsdown

219 Egerton
M20
221 Charing
Challock
A28
223 Wye
225 Waltham
Stelling Minnis
227 Barham
Denton
259 Selsted
Kearsney
291 St Margaret's at Cliffe

249 Smarden
Hothfield
251 Ashford
253 Lees
Willesborough
Stowting
255 Brook
Elham
Lyminge
257 Densole
289 DOVER
313
293

279 Biddenden
A28
281
283 Kingsnorth
285 Sellindge
Peene
287
Hawkinge
East Wear Bay
FOLKESTONE

301 Tenterden
303 Woodchurch
Shadoxhurst
305 Ruckinge
Hamstreet
307 Lympne
Burmarsh
309
Hythe
Channel Tunnel

321 Small Hythe
Appledore
323 Newchurch
Snave
325
327 Dymchurch
St Mary's Bay

333 Wittersham
Brookland
Iden
335 New Romney
337 Littlestone-on-Sea
Greatstone-on-Sea

331
339 Rye
A259
341 Lydd
343
STRAIT OF DOVER

345 Camber
Rye Bay
Dungeness
347

A259
B2089
B2089

OOSTENDE
CALAIS DUNKERQUE BOULOGNE

National Grid references are shown on the map frame of each page.
Red figures denote the 100 km square and blue figures the 1 km square.
Example, page 253: William Harvey Hospital 604 142

The reference can also be written using the National Grid two-letter prefix shown on this page, where 6 and 1 are replaced by TR to give TR0442.

TQ|TR

2.5 inches to 1 mile   **Scale of main map pages**   1:25,000

0   1/2   miles   1   1 1/2

0   1/2   kilometres   1 1/2   2

Junction 9	Motorway & junction
Services	Motorway service area
	Primary road single/dual carriageway
Services	Primary road service area
	A road single/dual carriageway
	B road single/dual carriageway
	Other road single/dual carriageway
	Minor/private road, access may be restricted
← ←	One-way street
	Pedestrian area
	Track or footpath
	Road under construction
	Road tunnel
P	Parking
P+	Park & Ride
	Bus/coach station
	Railway & main railway station
	Railway & minor railway station
⊖	Underground station
⊖	Light railway & station
+++++++++	Preserved private railway

LC	Level crossing
●—●—●	Tramway
-----------	Ferry route
....	Airport runway
—·—·—·—	County, administrative boundary
▼▼▼▼▼▼▼▼▼	Mounds
17	Page continuation 1:25,000
3	Page continuation to enlarged scale 1:10,000
	River/canal, lake, pier
	Aqueduct, lock, weir
465 ▲ Winter Hill	Peak (with height in metres)
	Beach
	Woodland
	Park
	Cemetery
	Built-up area
	Industrial/business building
	Leisure building
	Retail building
	Other building

City wall	Castle
A&E	Hospital with 24-hour A&E department		Historic house or building
PO	Post Office	Wakehurst Place NT	National Trust property
	Public library	M	Museum or art gallery
i	Tourist Information Centre		Roman antiquity
i	Seasonal Tourist Information Centre		Ancient site, battlefield or monument
	Petrol station, 24 hour Major suppliers only		Industrial interest
†	Church/chapel		Garden
	Public toilets		Garden Centre Garden Centre Association Member
	Toilet with disabled facilities		Garden Centre Wyevale Garden Centre
PH	Public house AA recommended		Arboretum
	Restaurant AA inspected		Farm or animal centre
Madeira Hotel	Hotel AA inspected		Zoological or wildlife collection
	Theatre or performing arts centre		Bird collection
	Cinema		Nature reserve
	Golf course		Aquarium
▲	Camping AA inspected	V	Visitor or heritage centre
	Caravan site AA inspected		Country park
	Camping & caravan site AA inspected		Cave
	Theme park		Windmill
	Abbey, cathedral or priory		Distillery, brewery or vineyard

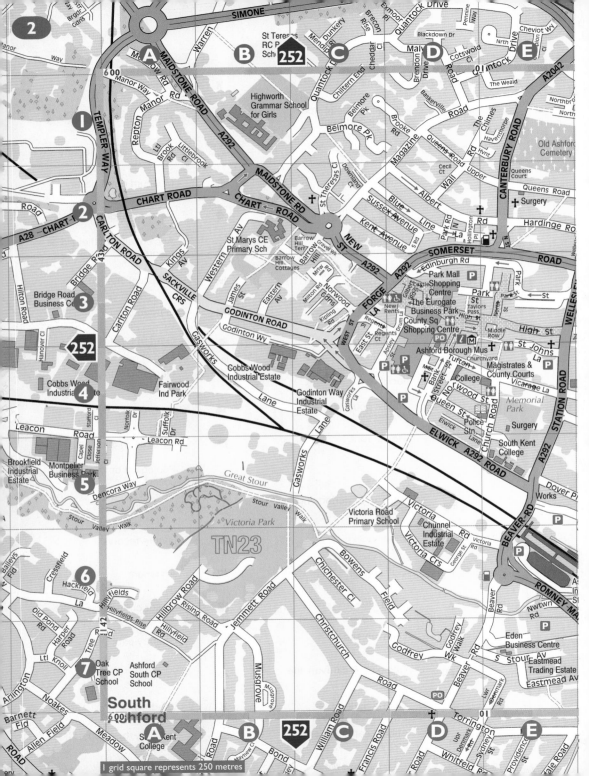

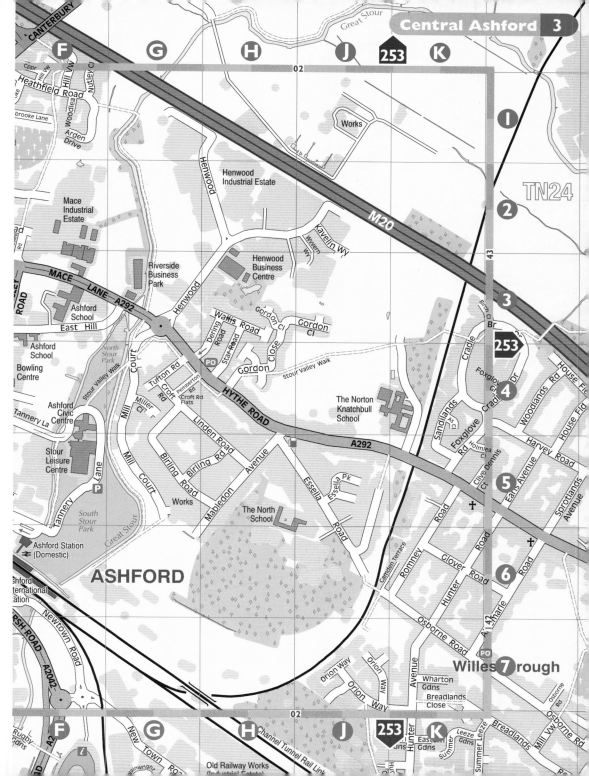

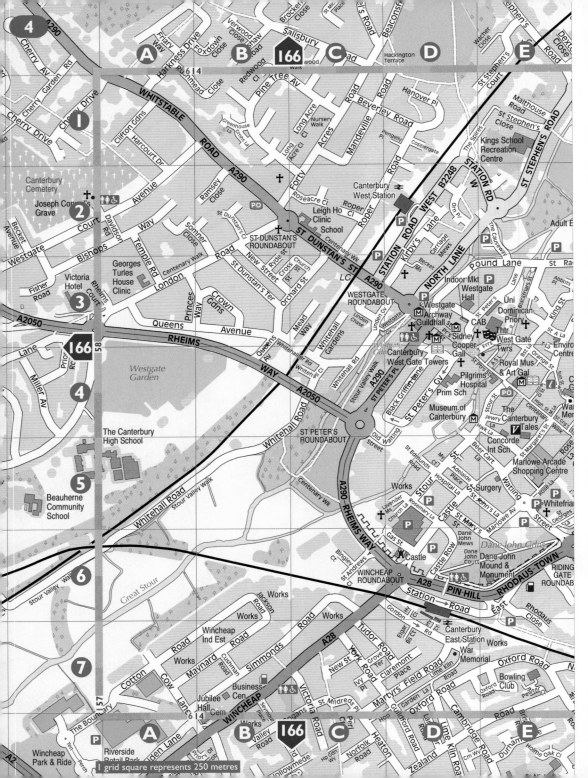

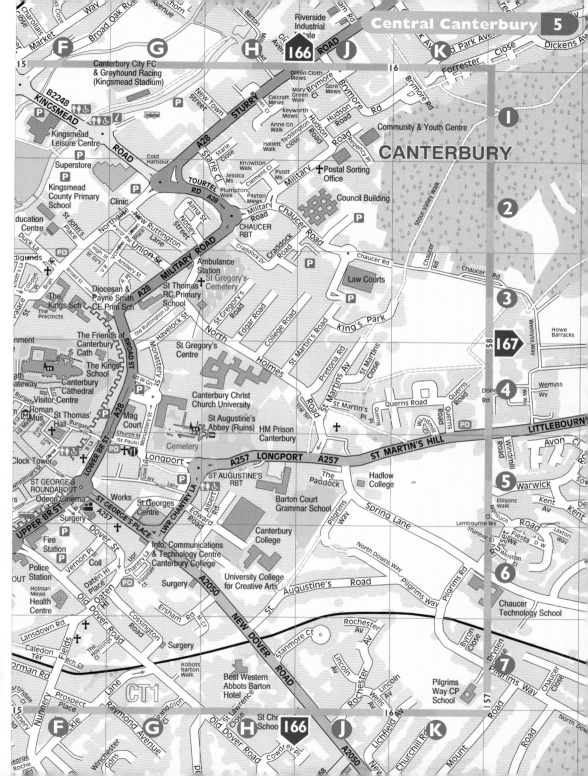

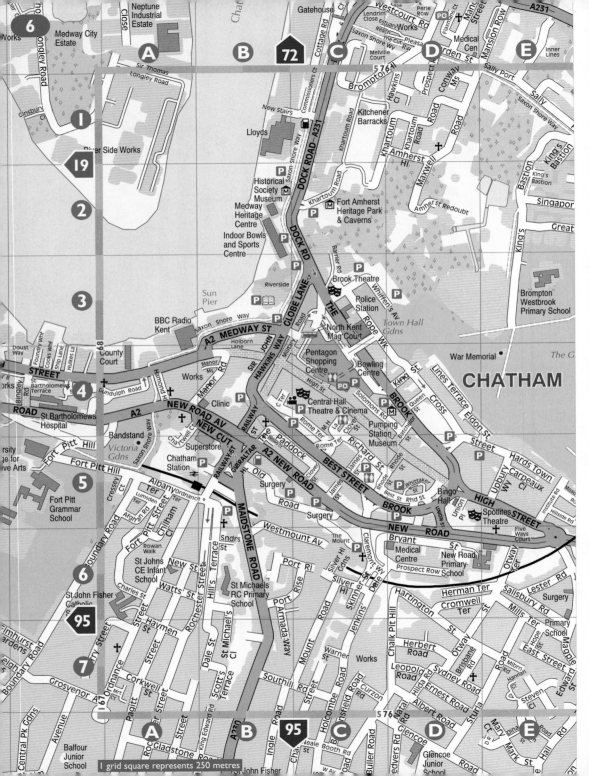

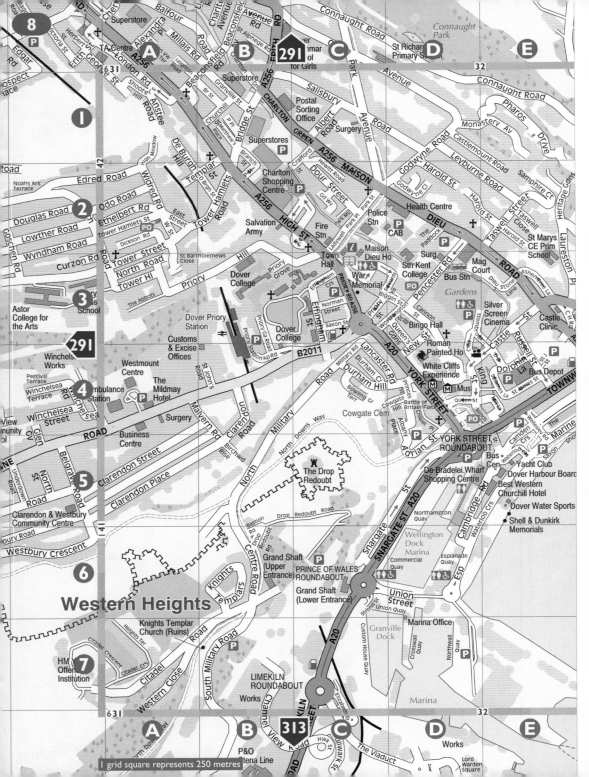

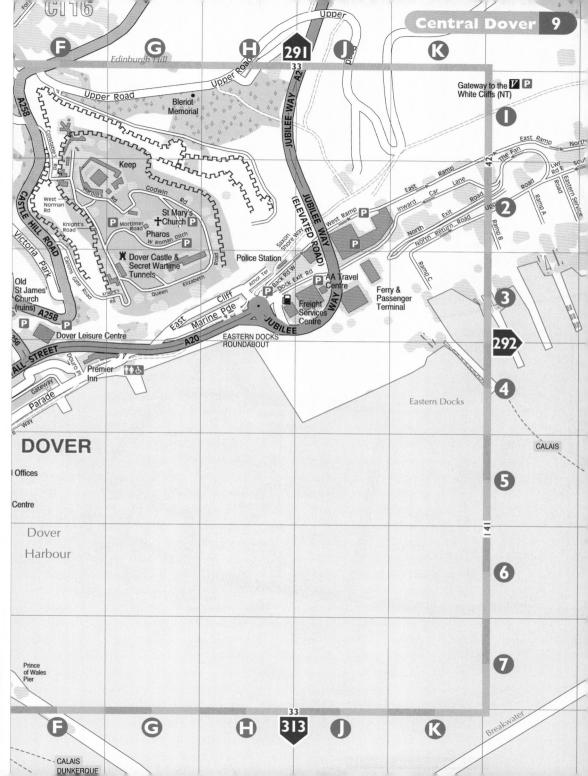

CT16

F G H **291** 33 J K

Edinburgh Hill

Upper Road

Upper Road

A258

Bleriot Memorial

Gateway to the **V** **P**
White Cliffs (NT)

I

JUBILEE WAY A2

East Ramp
North

The Fan

42

Keep

West Norman Rd

Constable's Rd

Harold's Rd

Godwin Rd

Knight's Road

Mortimer Road

St Mary's
Church

P

Pharos

W Roman Ditch

P

East Ramp
Inward

Car Lane

Upper Road

Lwr
Rd E

Road

Ramp A

Eastern Road

2

North

Exit

Road

Ramp B

North Return Road

JUBILEE WAY (ELEVATED ROAD)

Saxon Shore Way

West Ramp

P

P

Ramp C

3

Castle Hill Road

Victoria Park

Canons Gate Road

Knight's Rd

Queen Elizabeth Road

Police Station

P

Athol Ter

Back Rd W

Dock Exit Rd

Dover Castle & Secret Wartime Tunnels

Old St James' Church (ruins)

A258

P

Dover Leisure Centre

A356

ALL STREET

Douro Pl

Premier Inn

Gateway

Parade

Way

East Cliff Marine Pde

A20

JUBILEE

WAY

EASTERN DOCKS ROUNDABOUT

Freight Services Centre

P

AA Travel Centre

Ferry & Passenger Terminal

292

4

Eastern Docks

CALAIS

5

141

DOVER

Offices

Centre

Dover

Harbour

6

Prince of Wales Pier

7

F G H **313** 33 J K

Breakwater

CALAIS
DUNKERQUE

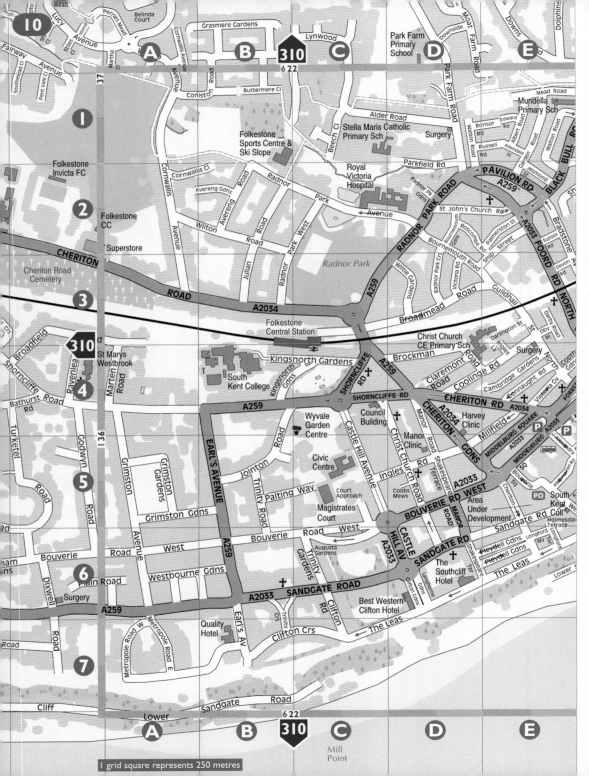

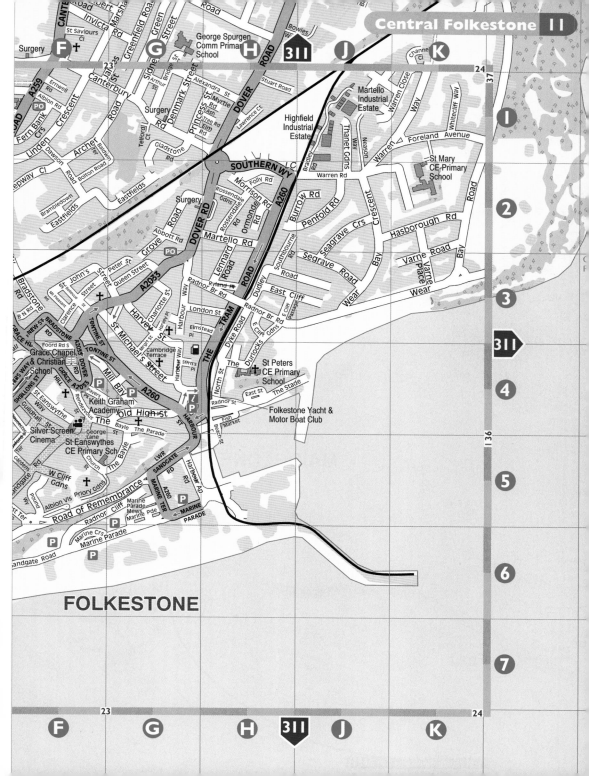

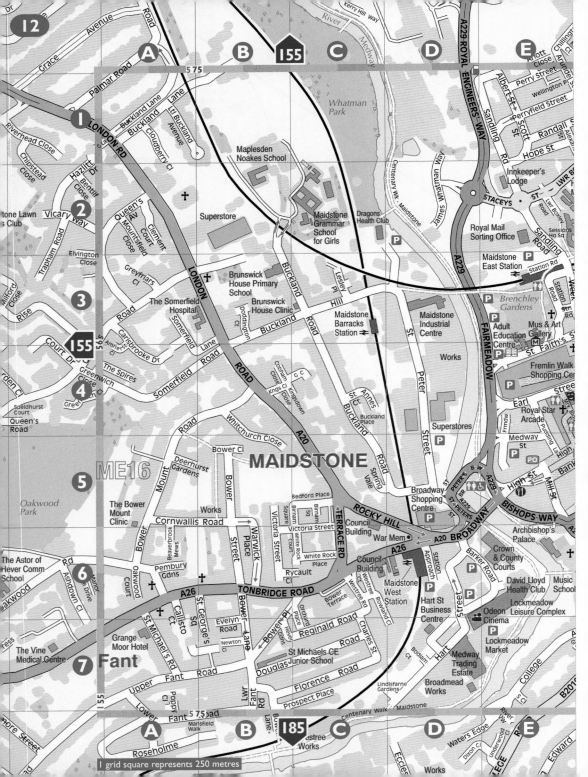

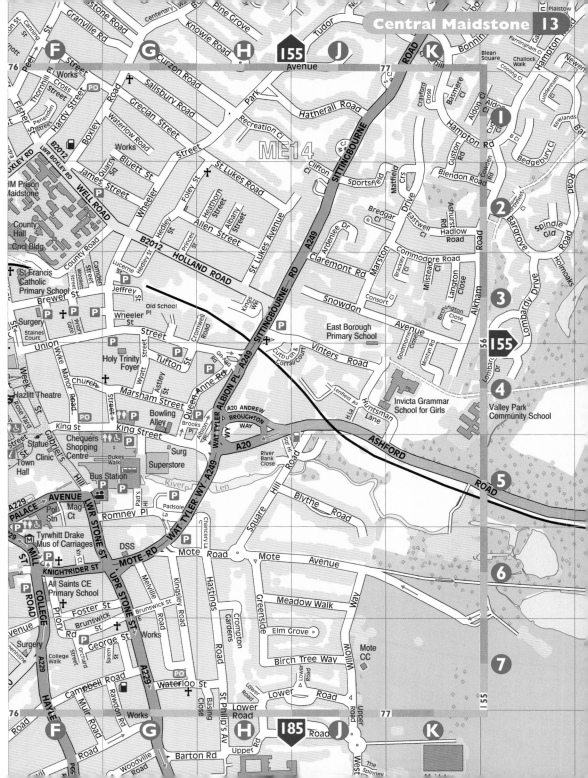

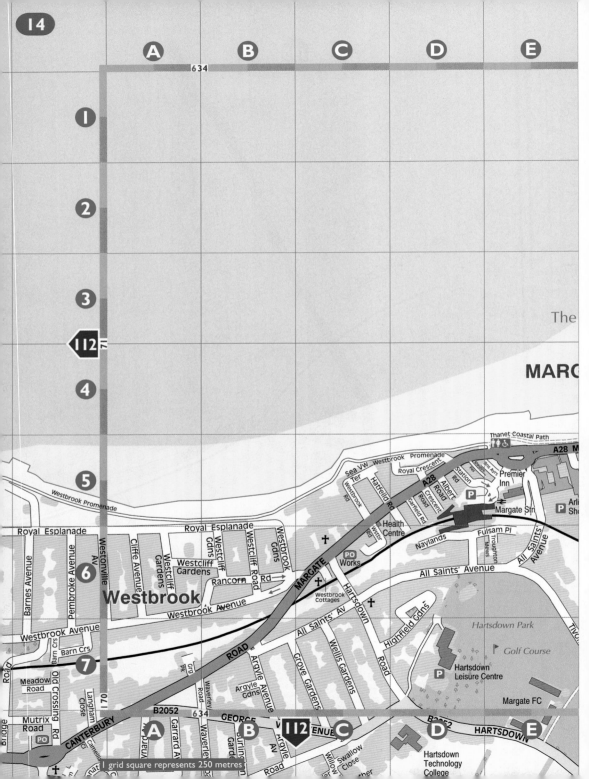

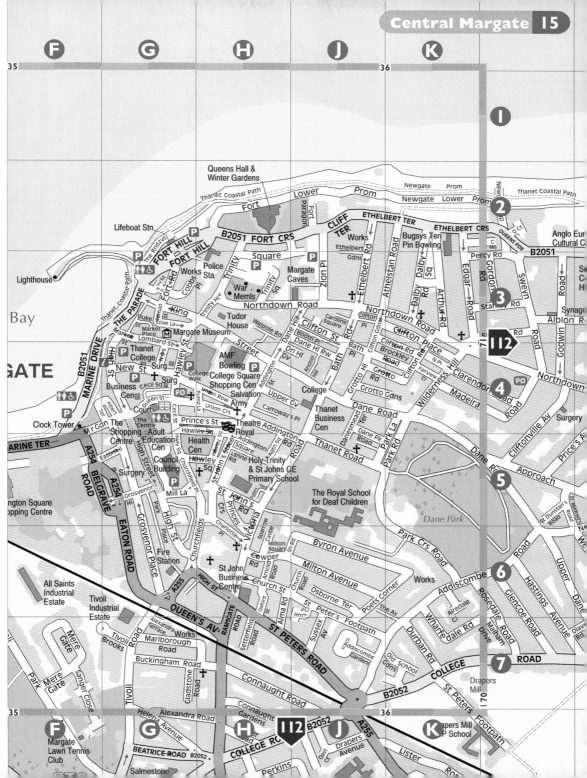

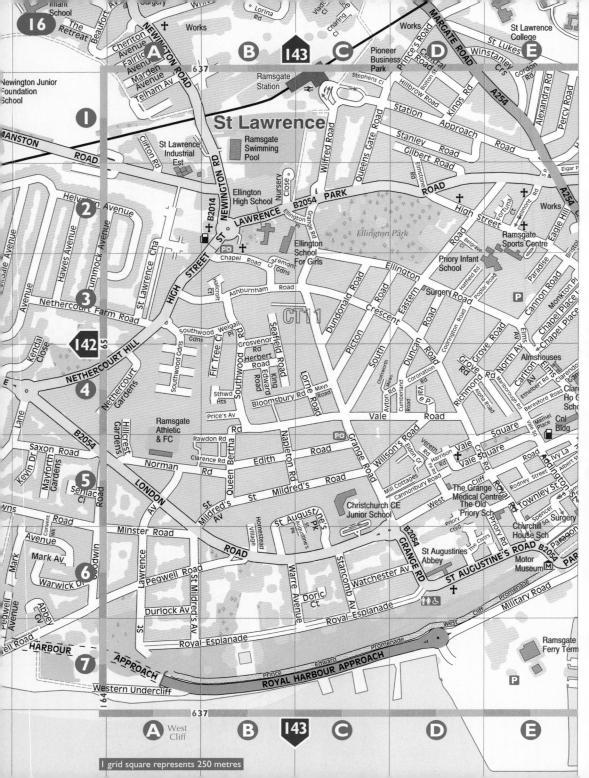

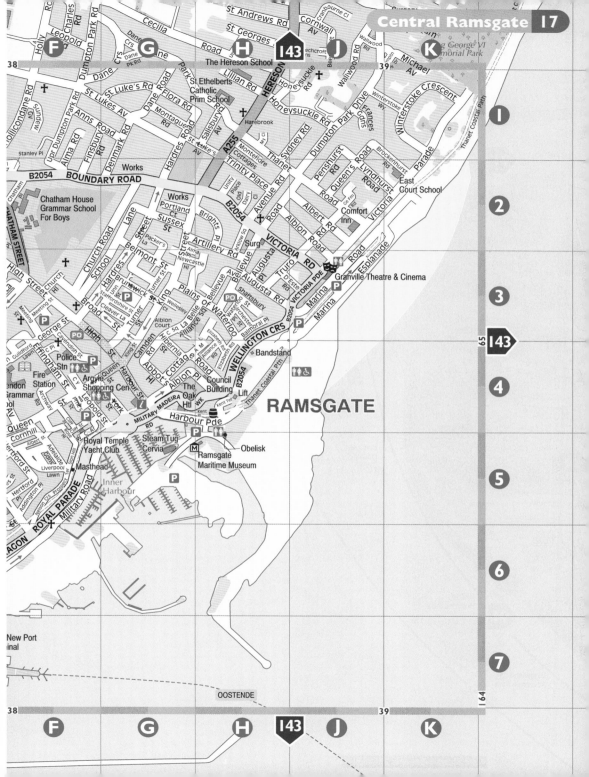

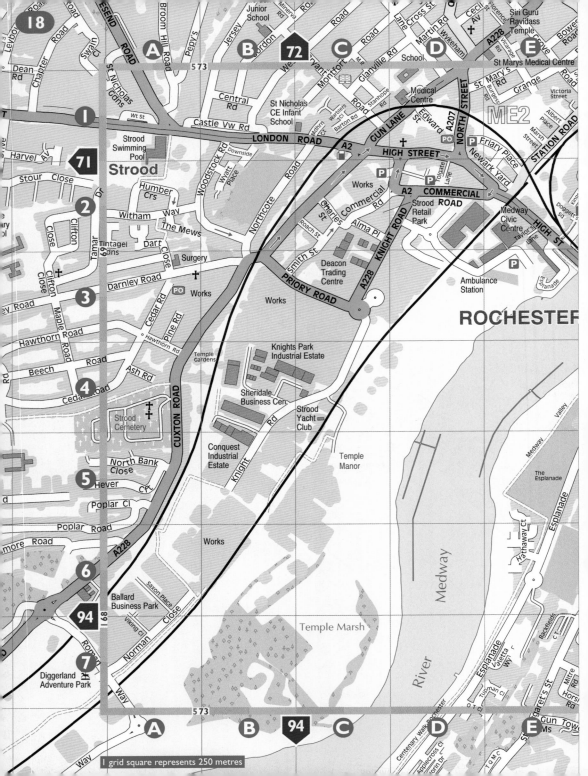

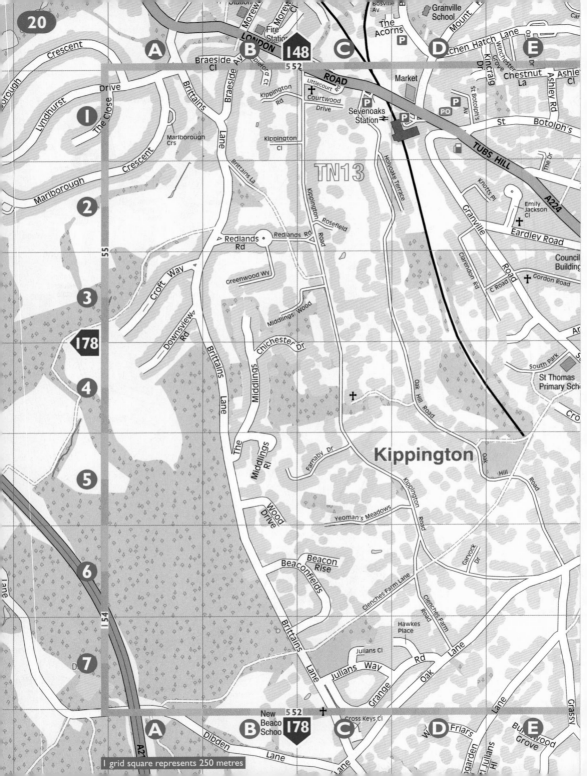

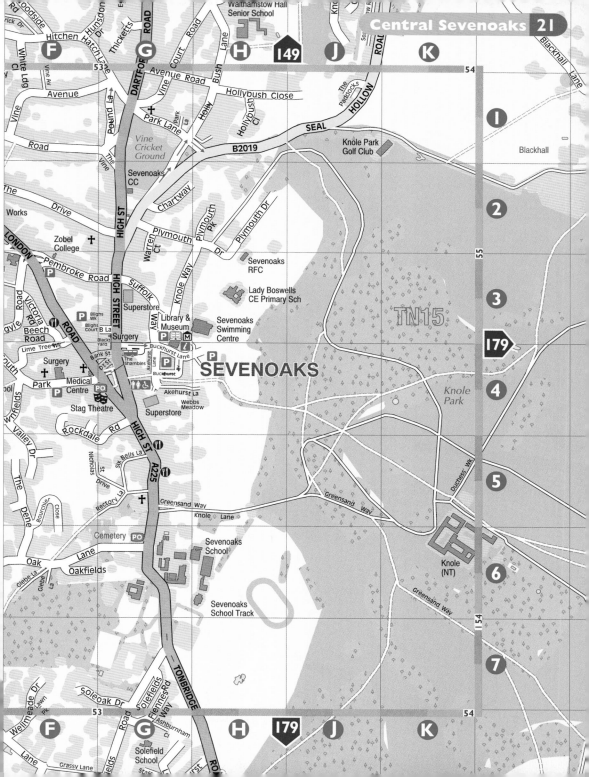

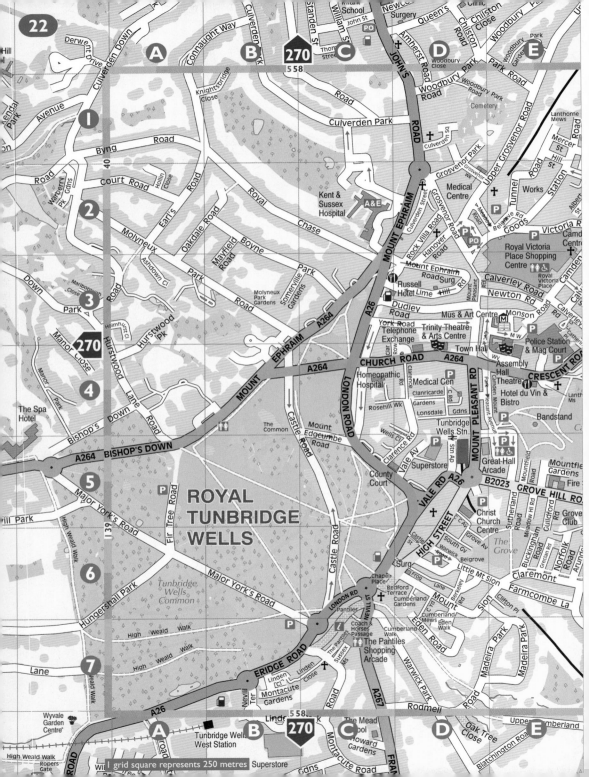

ROYAL TUNBRIDGE WELLS

1 grid square represents 250 metres

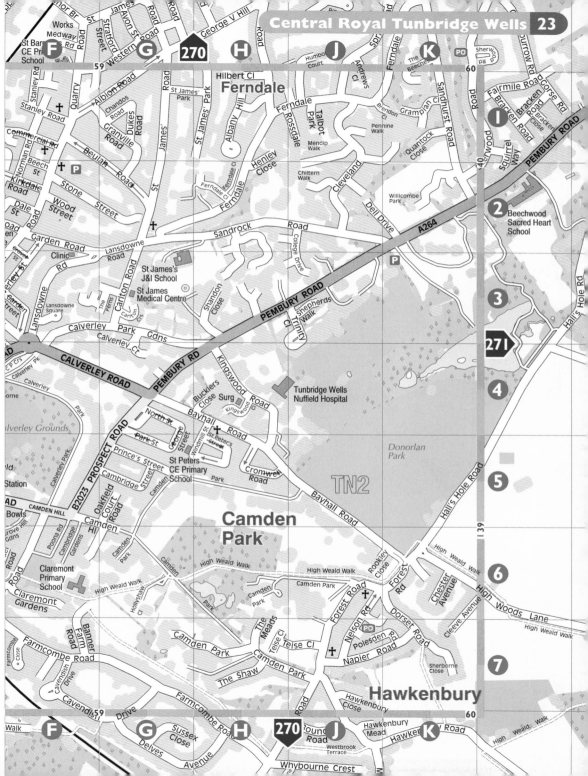

Works
Medway
Rd

F

St Barn
CE Pri
School

Stanley Rd

Stanley Road

Quarry

Commercial Rd

Norman Rd

Beech
St

Kirkdale
Road

Dale
Road

Garden Road

Lansdowne

Garden
Street

Grove
St

Clinic

Lansdowne
Square

The
Ferns

Carlton

Carlton Road

Calverley Park Gdns

Calverley Ct

CALVERLEY ROAD

PEMBURY RD

Calverley
Pk

Calverley Park

Calverley Grounds

Camden HILL

CAMDEN HILL

Bowls

Grove Hill
Gdns

Poona Rd

Cambridge
Gardens

Claremont
Primary
School

Claremont
Gardens

Farmcombe
Close

Banner
Farm
Road

Farmcombe Road

Cavendish Drive

Cavendish Dr

59

Walk

F

G

James
St

Stratford
Street

Avon St

Medway Rd

Western

59

Albion Road

Granville
Road

Chandos
Road

Dukes Road

Beulah Road

Stone
Street

Wood
Street

Lansdowne
Road

Carlton Road

North St

Park St

Prince's Street

Cambridge
Street

Oakfield
Court
Road

Camden
HILL

Camden

Hollyshaw
Cl

High Weald Walk

Camden Park

Camden Park

The Shaw

Farmcombe Road

G

Sussex
Close

Delves
Avenue

George V Hill

Road

270

James
Road

Road

James
St

St James'
Park

St James Park

Ferndale Cl

Ferndale

Ferndale

Sandrock
Road

Prospect Road

George
Street

Windmill St

St Peter's
Street

Bayhall

St Peters
CE Primary
School

Camden Park

High Weald Walk

Camden
Park

High Weald Walk

Park

270

Round

Hilbert Cl

H

Ferndale

Albany Hill

Henley
Close

Ferndale Cl

Sandrock

Road

College Drive

Shandon
Close

Kingswood Road

Bucklers
Close Surg

Kingswood

Road

Cromwell
Road

Park

The
Meads

Teise Cl

Teise Cl

H

Humbolt
Court

Ferndale
Rossdale

Talbot
Park

Mendip
Walk

Chiltern
Walk

Cleveland

Road

College Drive

Trinity

Shepherds
Walk

Tunbridge Wells
Nuffield Hospital

Bayhall Road

**Camden
Park**

Camden Park

270

J

Andrews
Ct

Brendon
Cl

Pennine
Walk

Dell Drive

A264

P

Road

Camden Park

Rookley
Close

Forest
Rd

Forest Road

Nelson Rd

Napier Road

Dorset Road

Polesden
Rd

PO

TN2

*Donorlan
Park*

High Weald Walk

High Weald Walk

Chester
Avenue

Cleeve Avenue

Hawkenbury
Close

Hawkenbury
Mead

Road

Hawkenbury

Westbrook
Terrace

Whybourne Crest

K

J

The
Beeches

PO

Sherwood
Rd

Grampian Close

Willicombe
Park

Sandhurst Road

Quantock
Close

2
Beechwood
Sacred Heart
School

3

271

4

5

I 39

6

High Woods Lane

High Weald Walk

7

Sherborne
Close

Hawken
Road

K

High Weald Walk

Fairmile Road

Gorse Rd

Bracken
Road

Bracken
Close

Squirrel
Way

Hall's Hole Rd

Sherwood

I

PEMBURY ROAD

A 40

PEMBURY ROAD

Hall's Hole Road

59

60

60

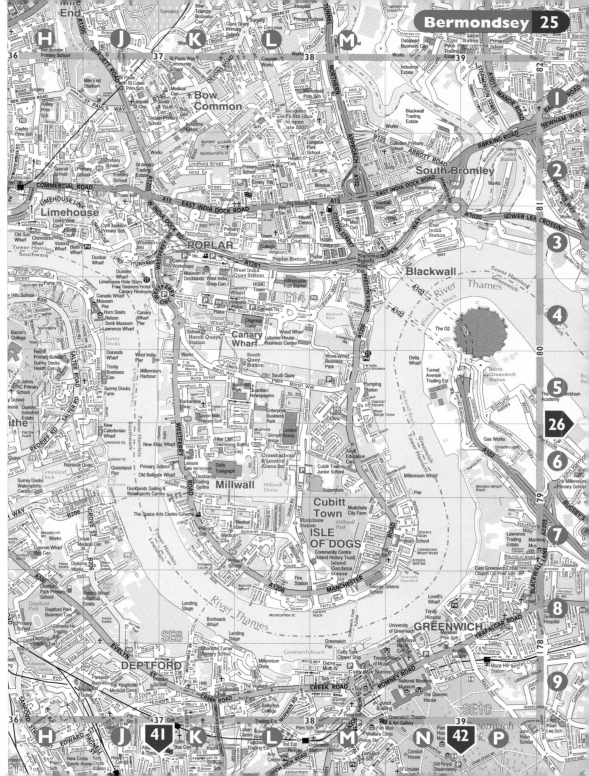

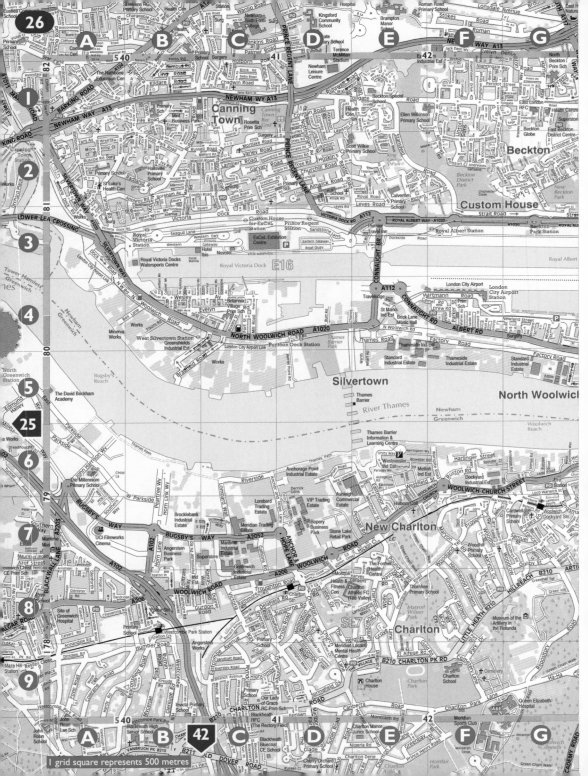

I grid square represents 500 metres

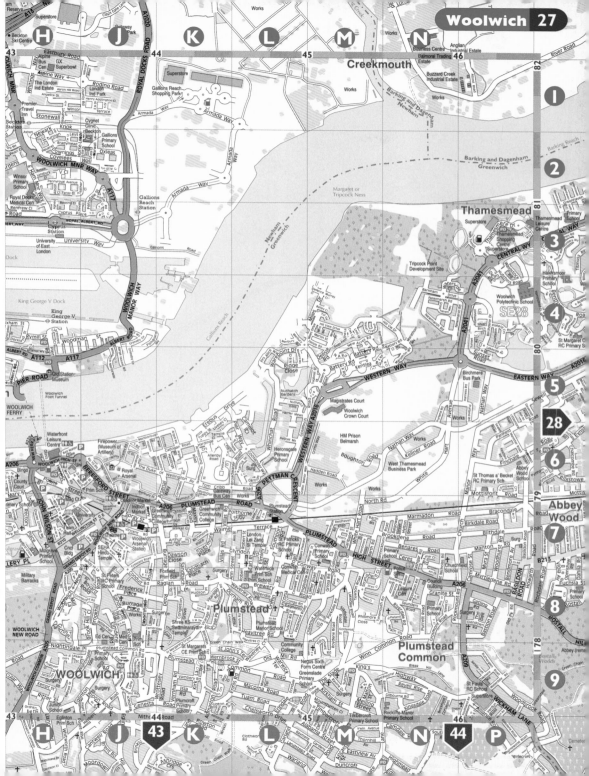

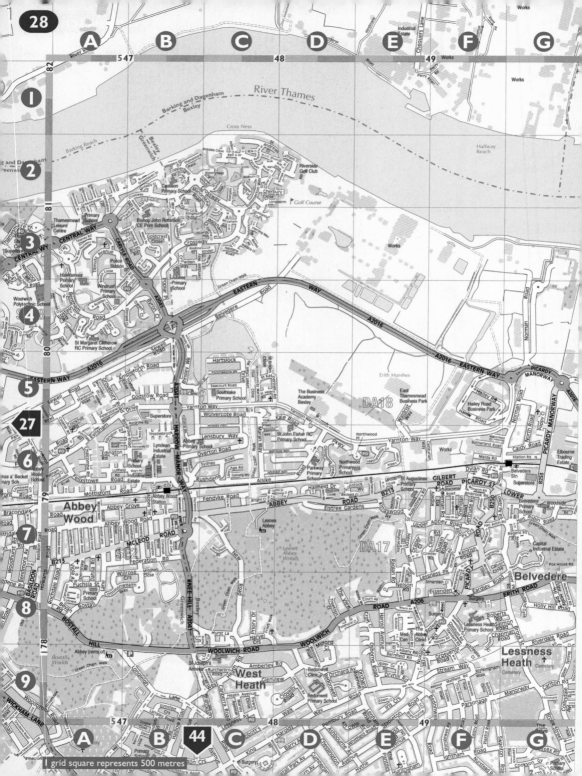

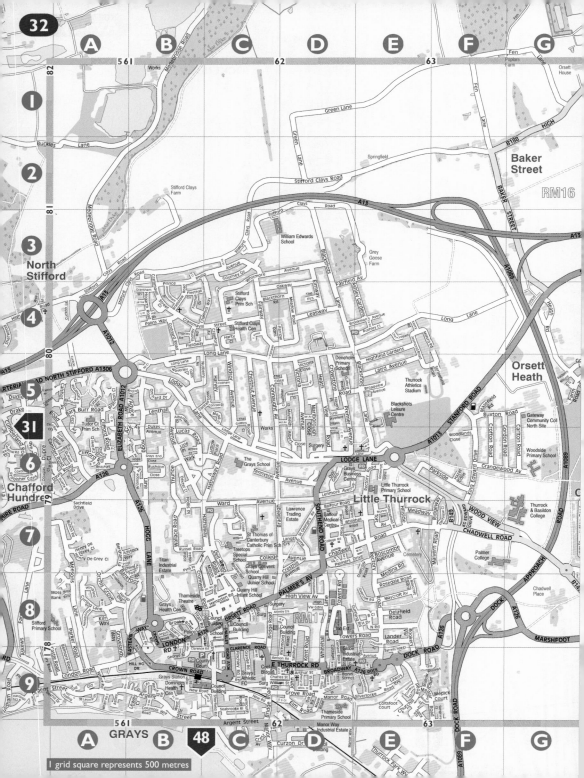

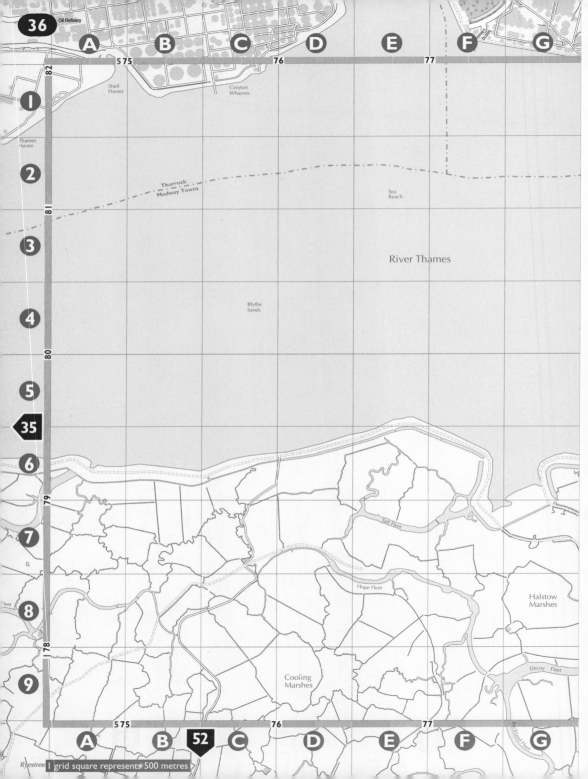

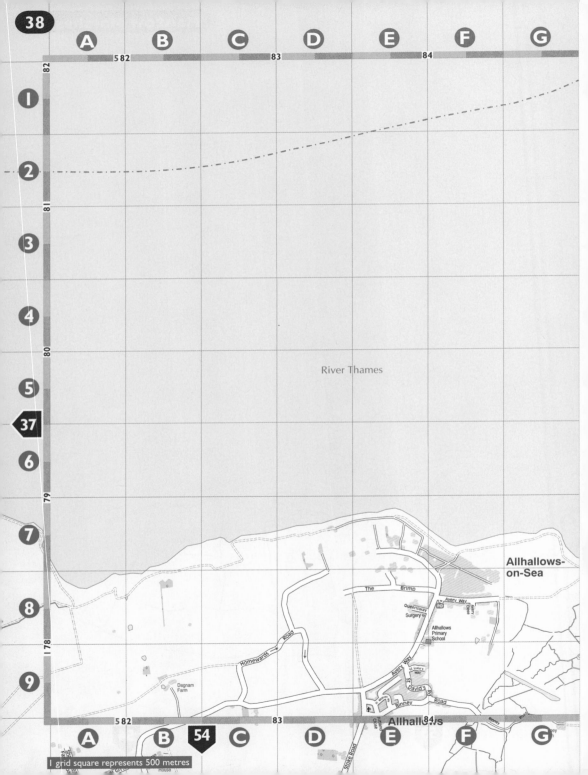

Ⓐ Ⓑ Ⓒ Ⓓ Ⓔ Ⓕ Ⓖ

5 82   83   84

82

Ⓘ

Ⓔ 2

81

Ⓔ 3

Ⓔ 4

80

Ⓔ 5

37

Ⓔ 6

79

Ⓔ 7

River Thames

Allhallows-
on-Sea

Ⓔ 8

The   Brimp

Avery Way

Queensway
Surgery

Allhallows
Primary
School

78

Homewards   Road

Avery Way

St. Luke's Way

Ⓔ 9

Dagnam
Farm

David's

Binney   Road

5 82   83   84

Allhallows

Ⓐ Ⓑ 54 Ⓒ Ⓓ Ⓔ Ⓕ Ⓖ

I grid square represents 500 metres

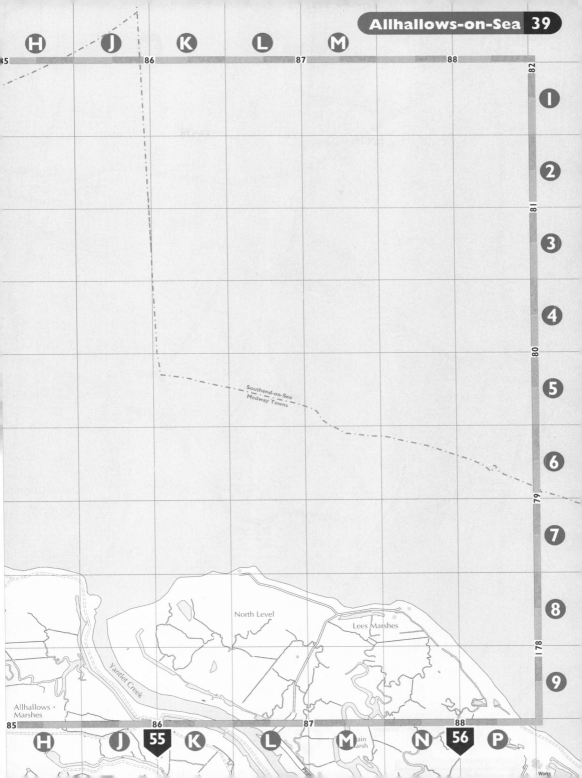

Southend-on-Sea
Medway Towns

North Level

Lees Marshes

Yantlet Creek

Allhallows
Marshes

ain
arsh

Works

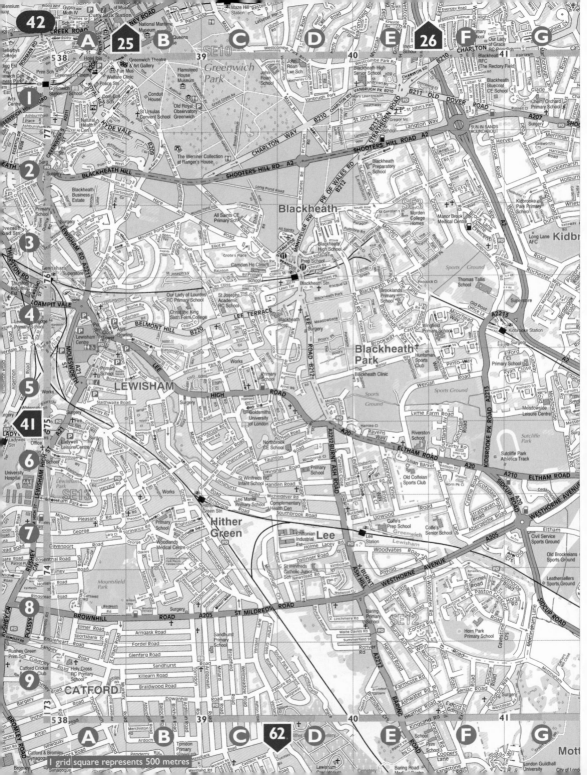

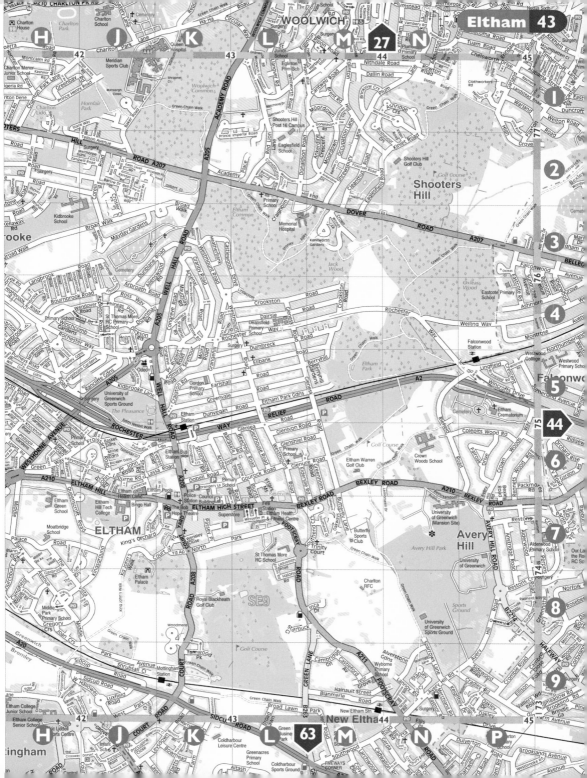

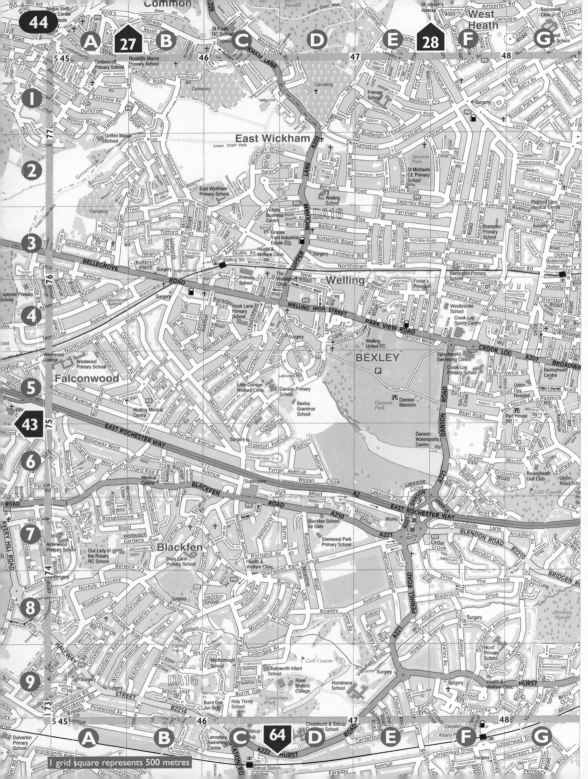

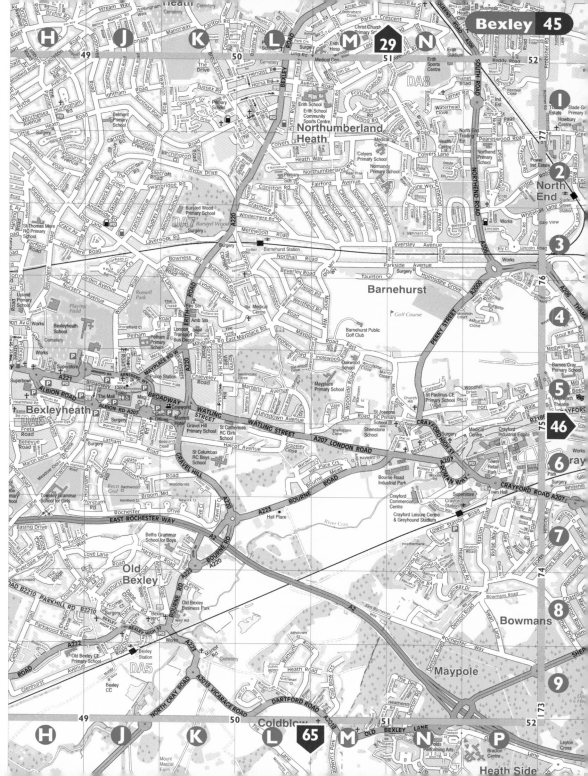

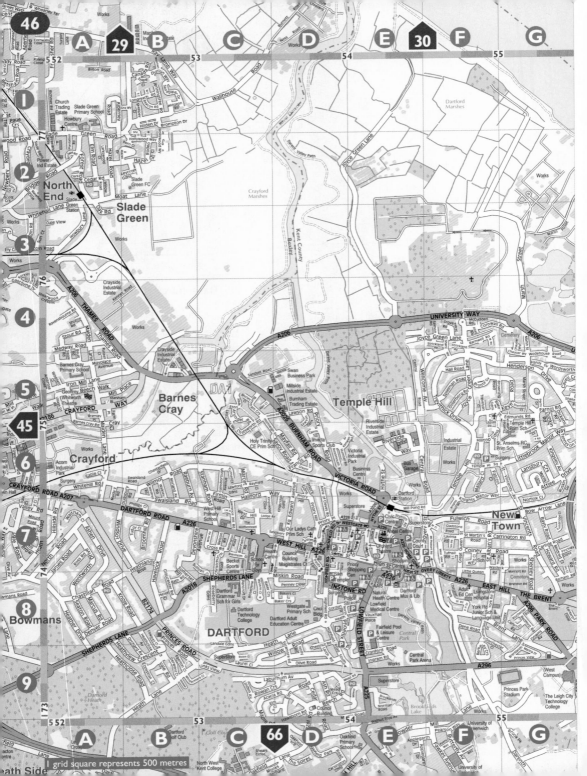

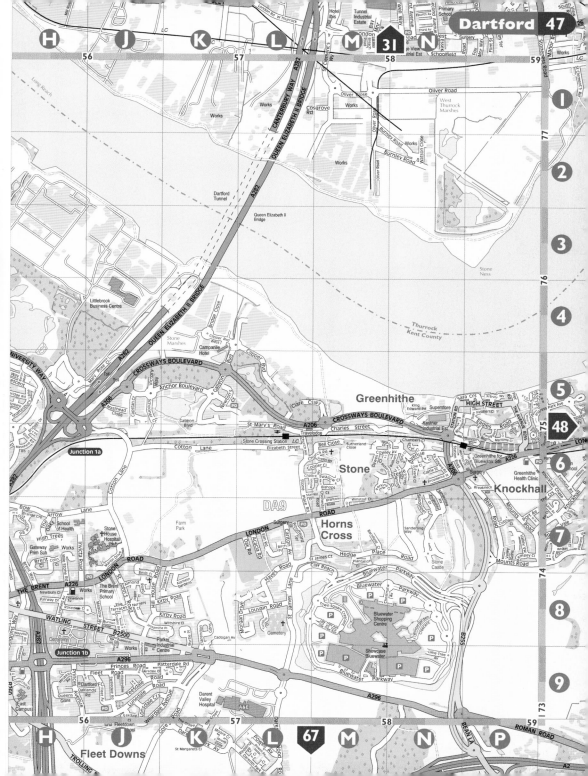

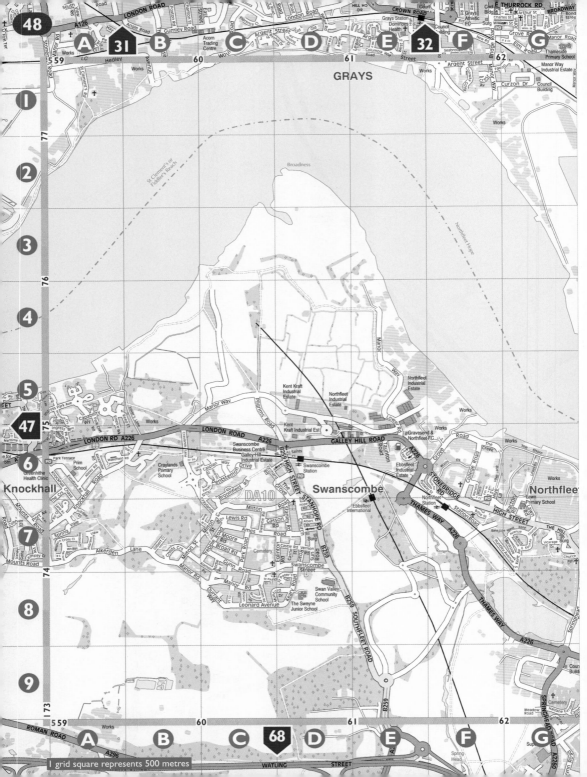

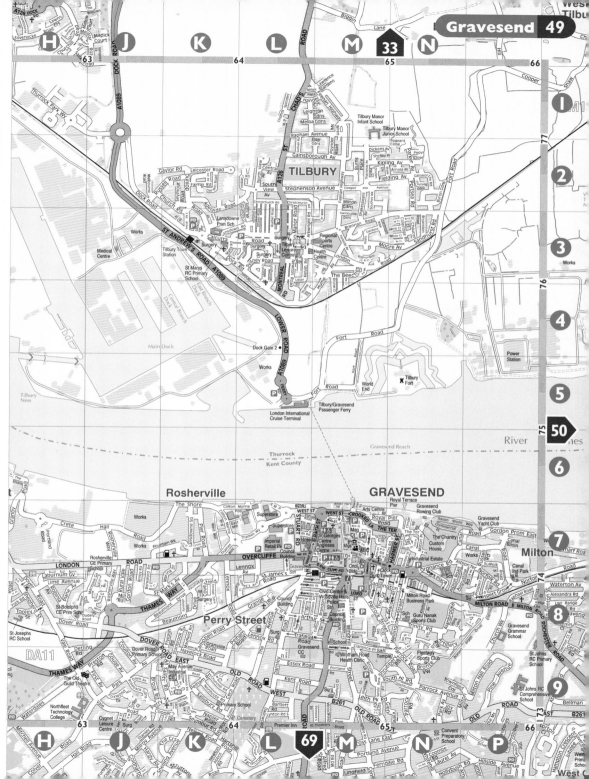

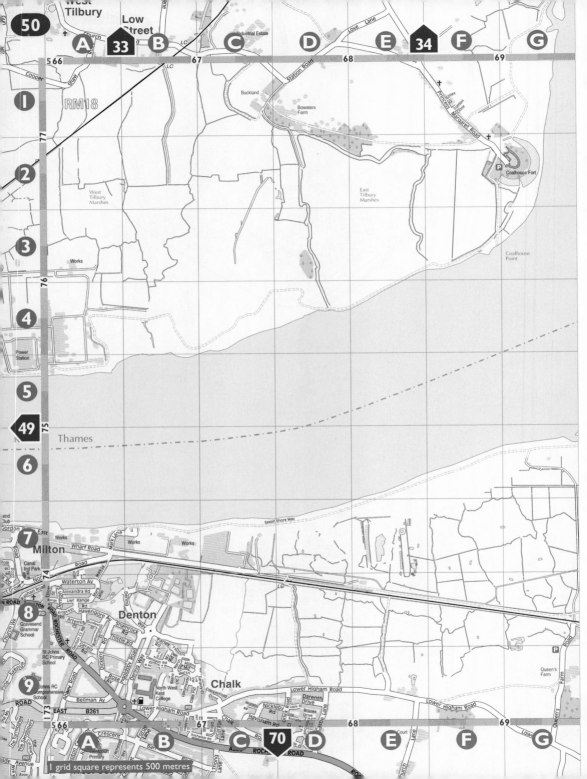

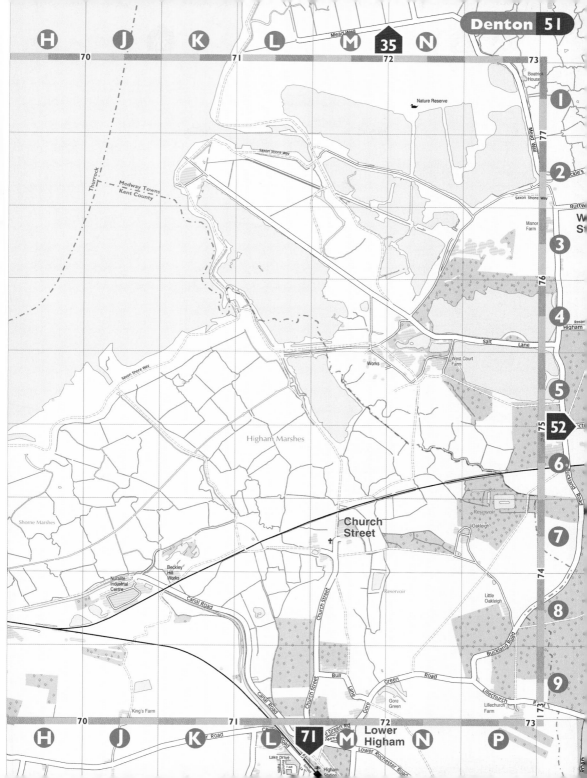

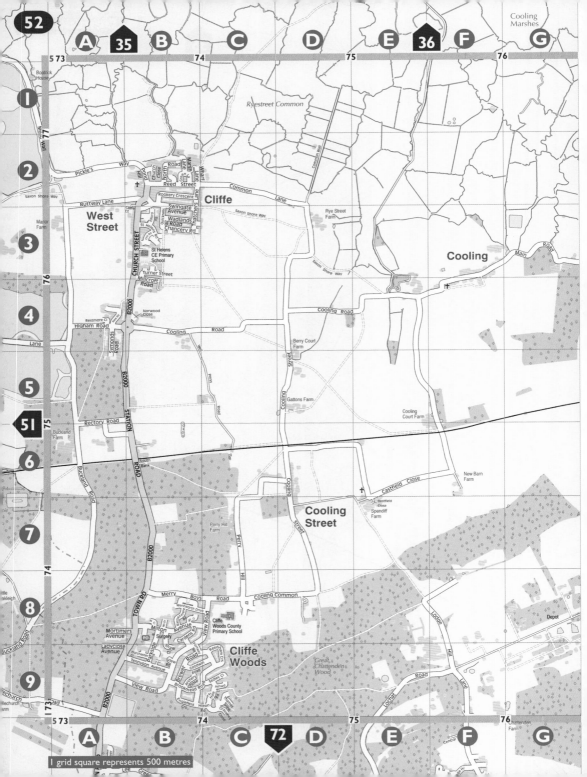

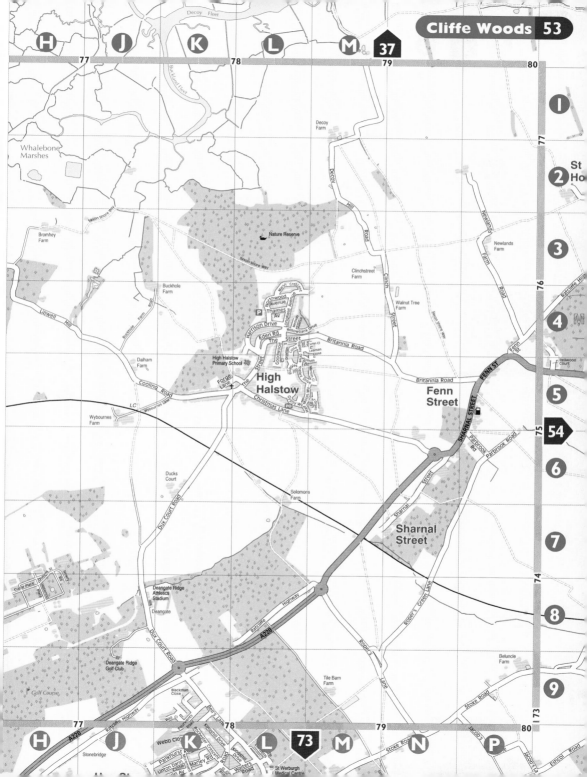

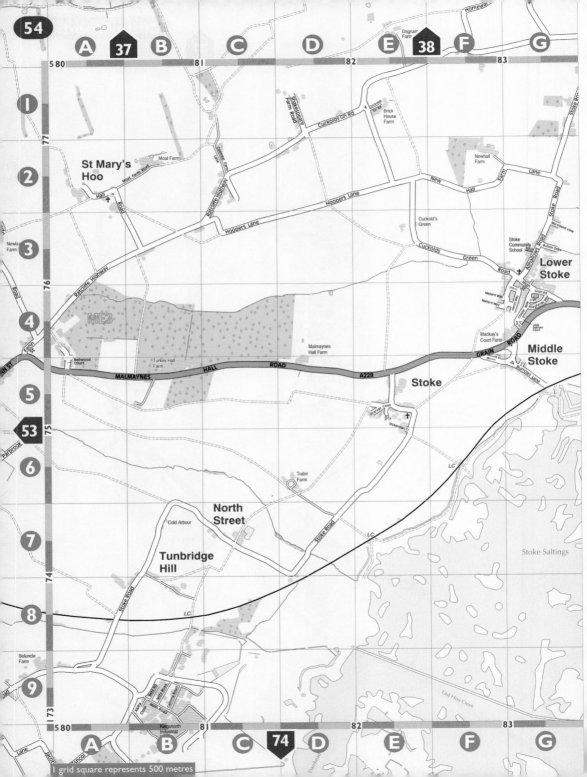

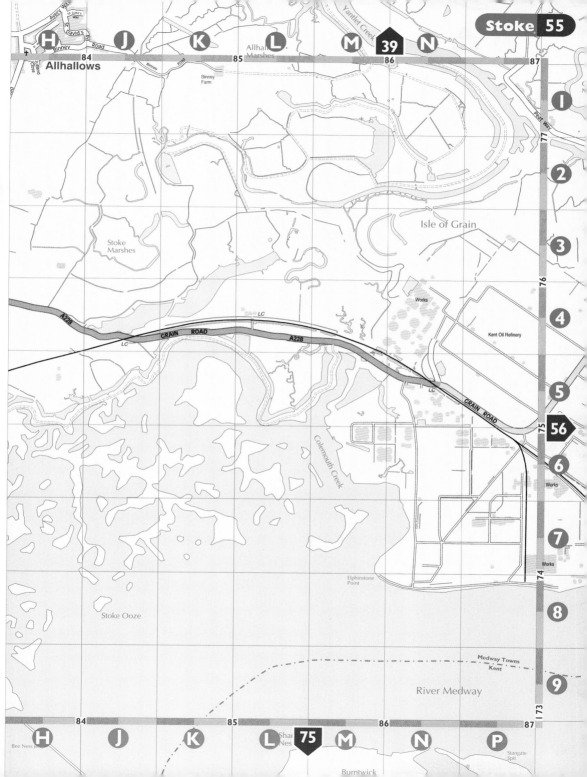

Allhallows

Isle of Grain

Stoke Marshes

Binney Farm

Allhallows Marshes

Yantlet Creek

Works

Kent Oil Refinery

GRAIN ROAD

A228

A228

GRAIN ROAD

LC

LC

LC

Stoke Ooze

Colemouth Creek

Elphinstone Point

Works

Works

Medway Towns
Kent

River Medway

Bee Ness

Sharfleet Ness

Burntwick

Stangate Spit

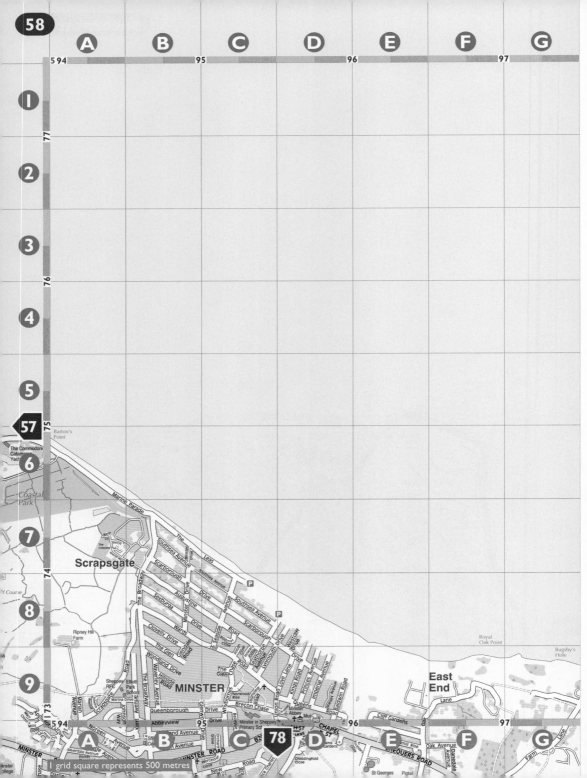

A   B   C   D   E   F   G

5 94   95   96   97

1

77

2

3

76

4

5

57 75

Barton's
Point

The Commodore
Cattani
Yacht

Coastal
Park

6

7

Scrapsgate

Marine Parade

The Crescent

The Esplanade

Southsea Avenue

Scarborough

Seaburn

The Broadway

Augustine

The Leas

Southsea Avenue

Minster Drive

P

74

8

Ripney Hill
Farm

Of Course

Clovelly Drive

The Glen

Woodland Drive

Wards

Cundale Road

Waverley Avenue

Village Road

The Glen

Seaside

Scarborough Road

Minster Road

P

Royal
Oak Point

Bugsby's
Hole

9

Sheppey
RFC

Elliott
Park
School

Marina Drive

The Broadway

Scrapsgate Road

Kent Avenue

Queenborough

Abbeyview

Glenway

Drive

Norwood
Rise

MINSTER

The Glen
Chase

Brecon Chase

Love Lane

Imperial Avenue

Princes Avenue

Queens
Minster
Abbey
Mus

Baldwin Road

King's Road

Cliff Gardens

East
End

Lane

Oak Avenue

Danesdale
Avenue

Farm Lane

5 94   95   96   97

A   B   C   D   E   F   G

MINSTER

Silverdale Avenue

Porter

Noreen Avenue

Kent Avenue

MINSTER ROAD

New

Worcester
Close

Norcester
Road

Road

CHAPEL
ST

Chiddingfold
Close

CHEQUERS ROAD

St Georges

Pigtail

1 grid square represents 500 metres

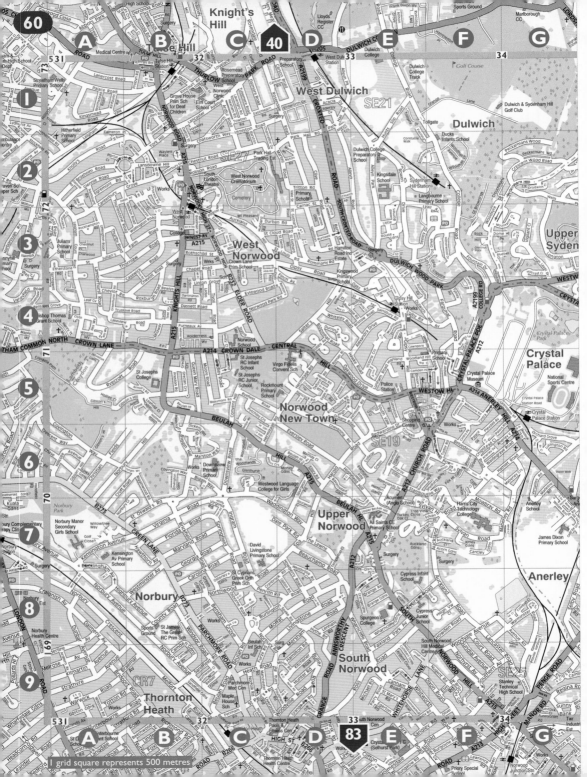

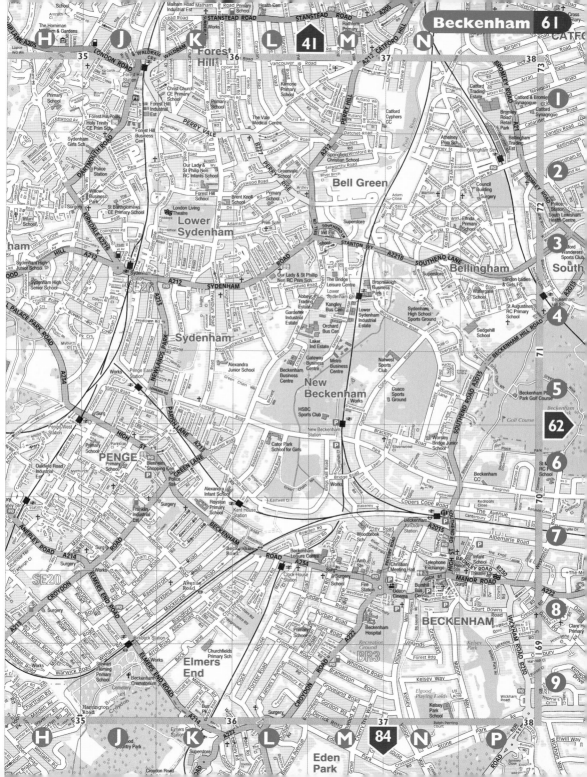

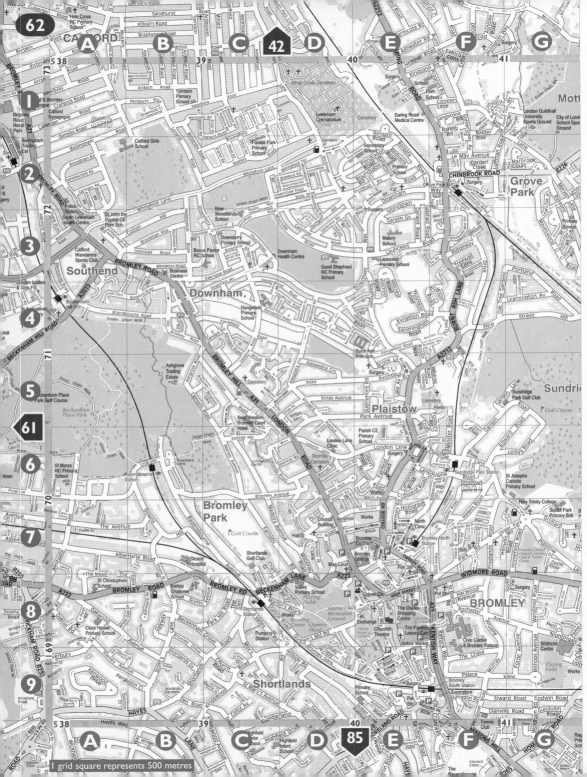

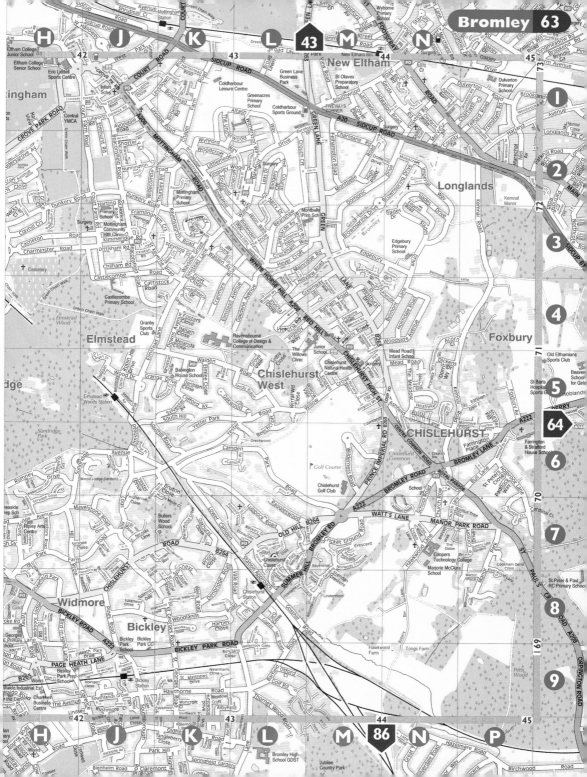

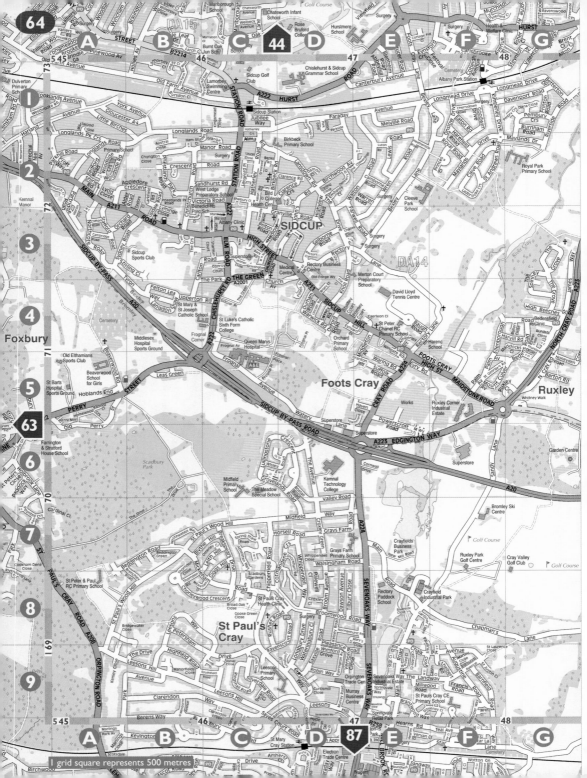

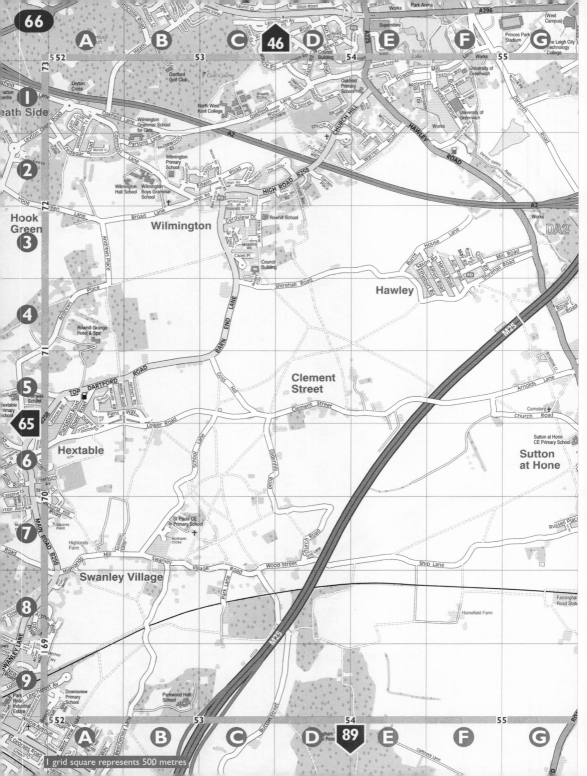

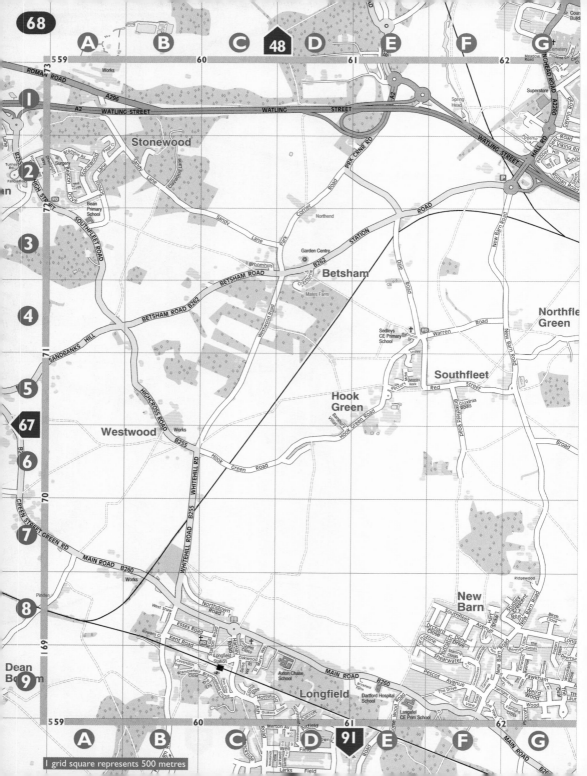

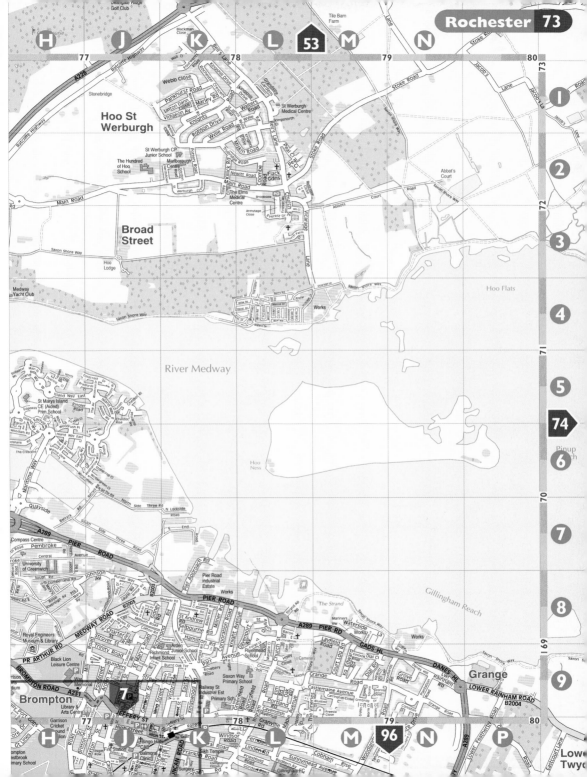

A **B** **C** **54** **D** **E** **F** **G**

East Hoo

73 80 **81** **82** **83**

I

Jacob's La.

Eshcol Road

Tatson Road

Kingsnorth Industrial Estate

Kingsnorth

Damhead Creek

Oakham Ness Jetty

Oakham Marsh

72

Kingsnorth Power Station

Slede Ooze

3

Medway

oo Flats

Long Reach

4

River

71

5

Darnet Fort

Bishop Ooze

73

South Yantlet Creek

6

Pinup Reach

70

7

RSPB Reserve

Nor Marsh

8

69

Saxon Shore Way

9

AINHAM ROAD B2004

East Court Farm

Bartlett Creek

RSPB Reserve

Works

Motney Hill

Lower

urt Lane

WER RAINHAM

Shurls Green

Riverside Country Park

Rainham C

ham Creek

1 grid square represents 500 metres

H J K L 55 M N

84 85 86 87

Bee Ness Jetty

Sharp Ness

Burntwick Island

Stangate Spit

Oakham Ness

Kethole Reach

Bishop Spit

Sharfleet Creek

Greenborough Marshes

Ham Ooze

Slayhills Marsh

Medway Towns Kent

Half Acre

Millfordhope Marsh

Twinney Creek

Halstow Creek

Bayford

Shoregate Lane

Pool Lane

Saxon Shore Way

Saxon Shore Way

Ham Green

84 85 86 87

H J K L M 98 N P

Wetham Green

Horsham

River Medway

I 1
2
3
4
5
76
6
70
7
169
8
9

73
72
71

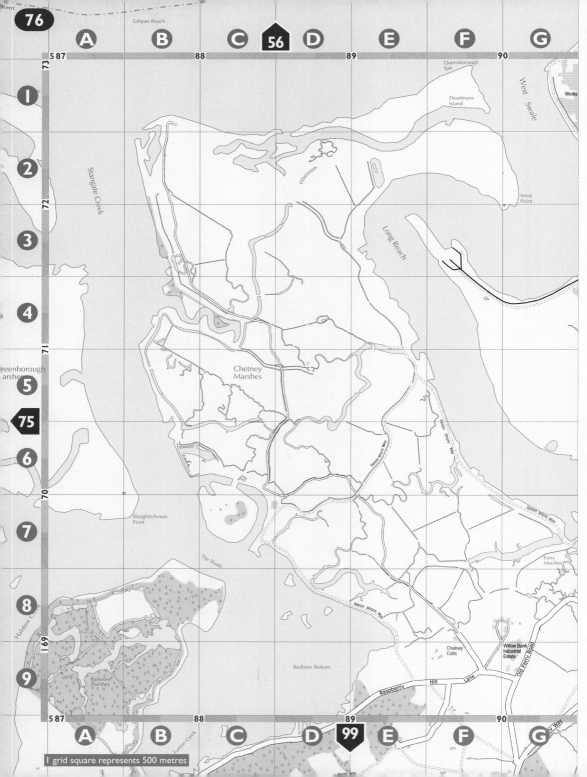

Kent

Saltpan Reach

5 87
88
89
90

73

Queenborough
Spit

Deadmans
Island

West Swale

Works

I

Stangate Creek

West
Point

2

72

3

Long Reach

4

71

Greenborough
Marshes

Chetney
Marshes

5

75

6

70

Slaughterhouse
Point

Saxon Shore Way

Saxon Shore Way

7

The Shade

Saxon Shore Way

Ferry
Marshes

8

69

Barksore
Marshes

Saxon Shore Way

Chetney
Cotts

Willow Bank
Industrial
Estate

Old Ferry Road

Halstow Creek

9

Bedlams Bottom

Raspberry
Hill Lane

5 87
88
89
90

Ferry Way

I grid square represents 500 metres

Saxon Shore Way

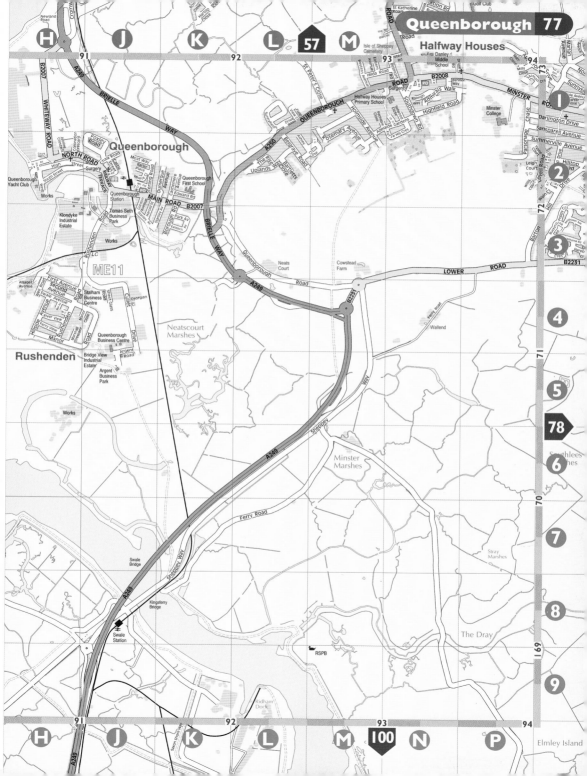

Halfway Houses

Queenborough

Rushenden

Minster Marshes

Neatscourt Marshes

The Dray

Elmley Island

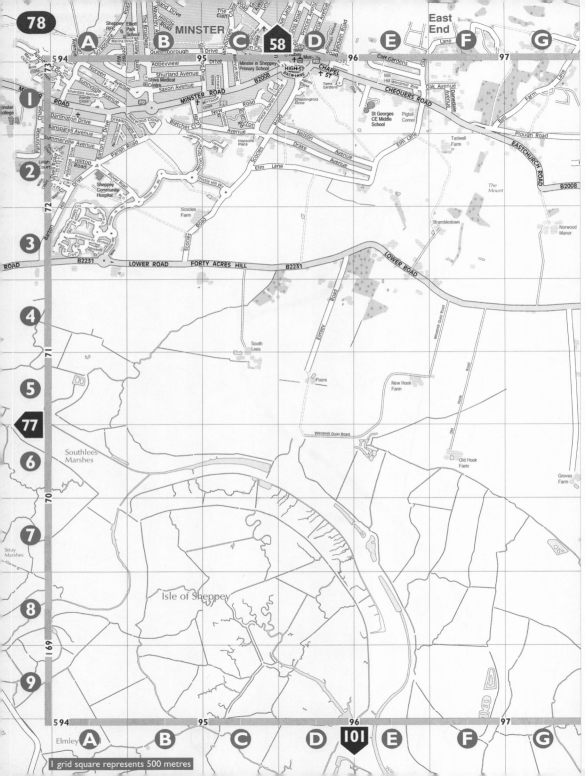

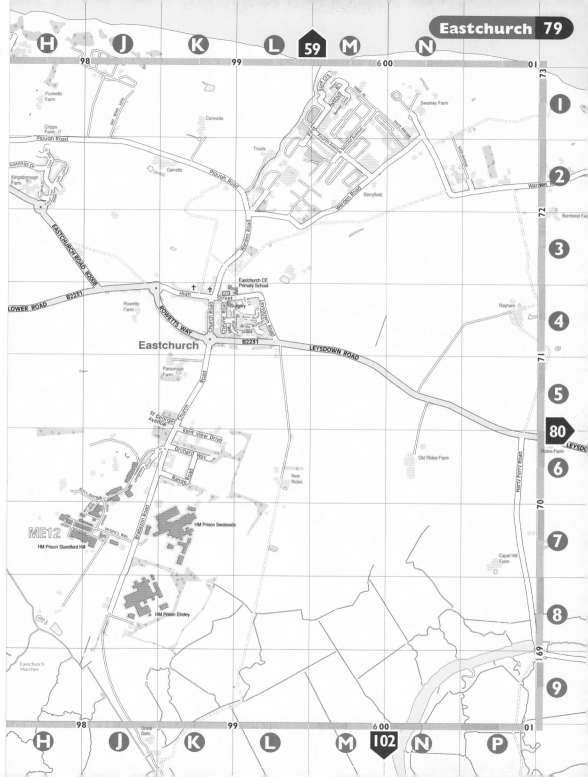

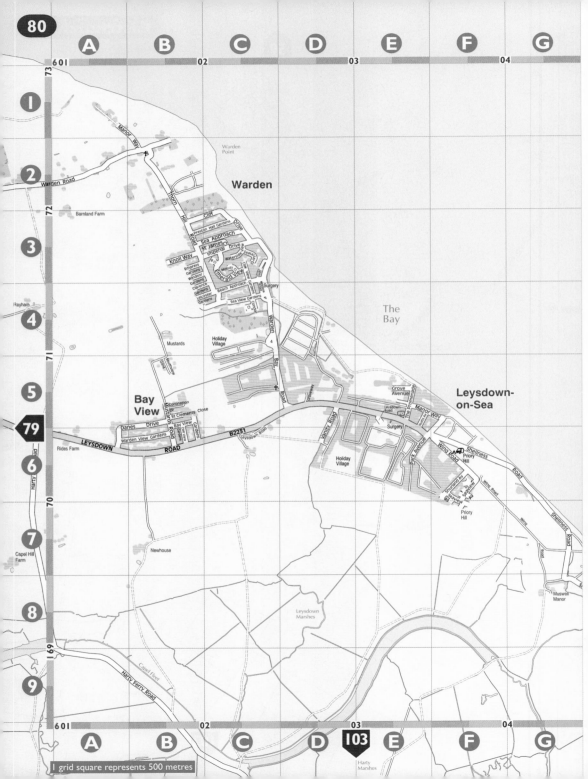

601   02   03   04

73

1

Manor Way

Warden
Point

2
Warden Road

Warden

72

Barnland Farm

Thorn Hill Road

Cliff Drive

Preston Hall Gardens

3
Knoll Way

Sea Approach
St James
Imperial Drive

Waterside

Empress
Gardens
Windsor
Gardens
Clarence
Gardens
Leicester
Gardens

Emerald View

Beach Approach

Surgery

Rayham

Sea View Gardens

4

Mustards

Holiday
Village

Warden Road

The
Bay

71

Southmoor Close

5
**Bay
View**

Coronation
Avr
St Clements Close

Grove
Avenue

**Leysdown-
on-Sea**

Danes Drive
Bay View Gardens
Warden View Gardens

Mustards Road

Leysdown Road

Bay Road

The Promenade

Manor Way

Leysdown
Road

Surgery

79

LEYSDOWN   **ROAD**
B2251

Harty Road

Vanity Road

Park Avenue

Wing Road

Shellness
Priory
Hill

Rides Farm

6

70

Holiday
Village

Spurland Rd
Seaview
Seaview
Av

Wing Road

Priory
Hill

Wing Road

Shellness Road

7
Capel Hill
Farm

Newhouse

69

8

Leysdown
Marshes

Muswell
Manor

Harty Ferry Road

Capel Fleet

9

Harty
Marshes

1 grid square represents 500 metres

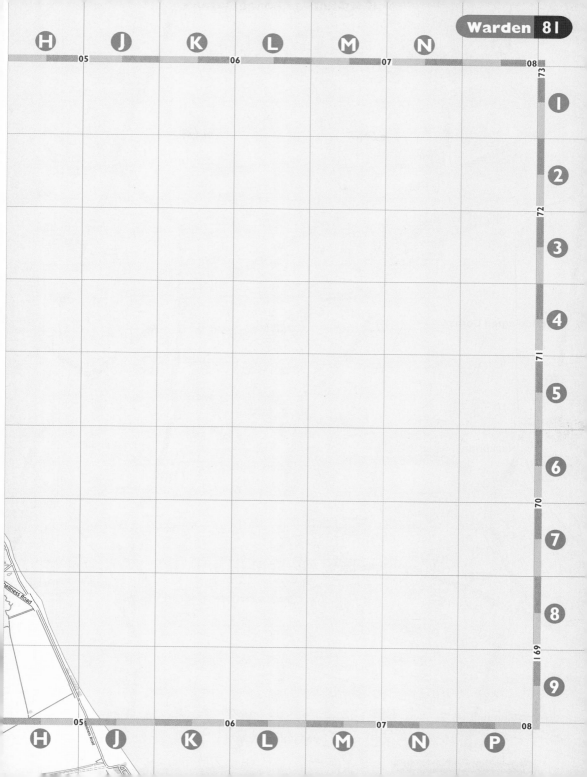

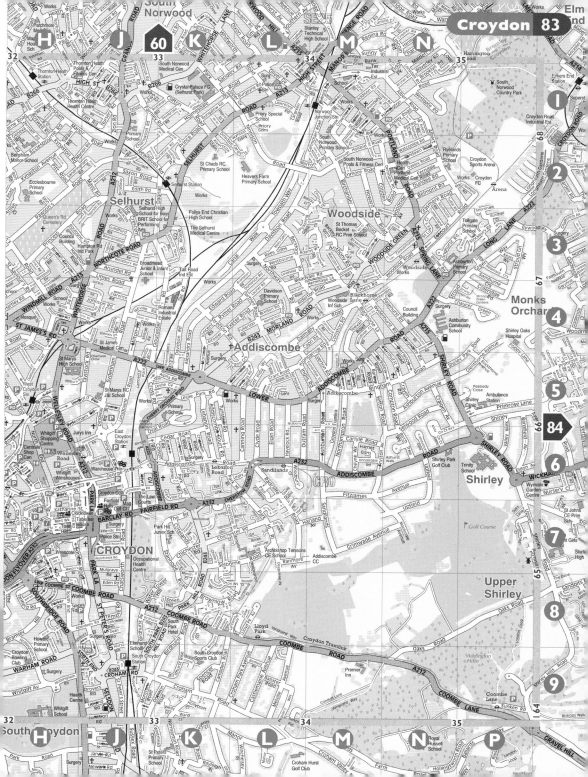

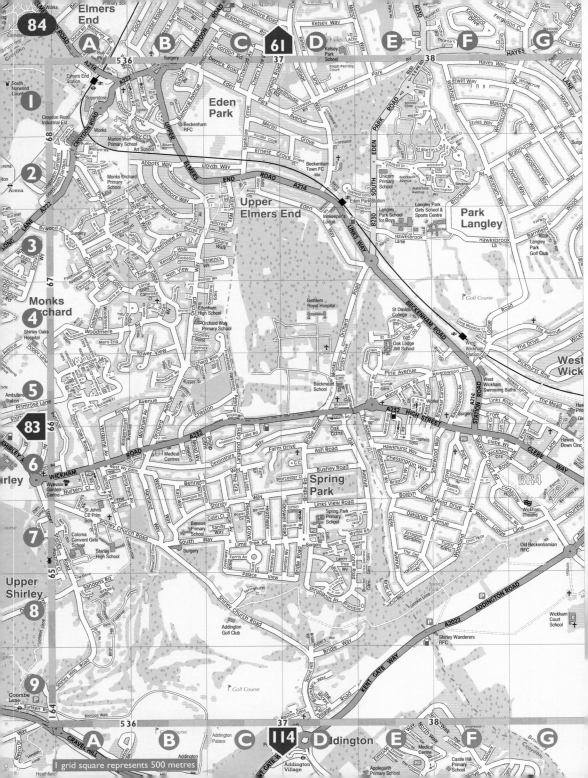

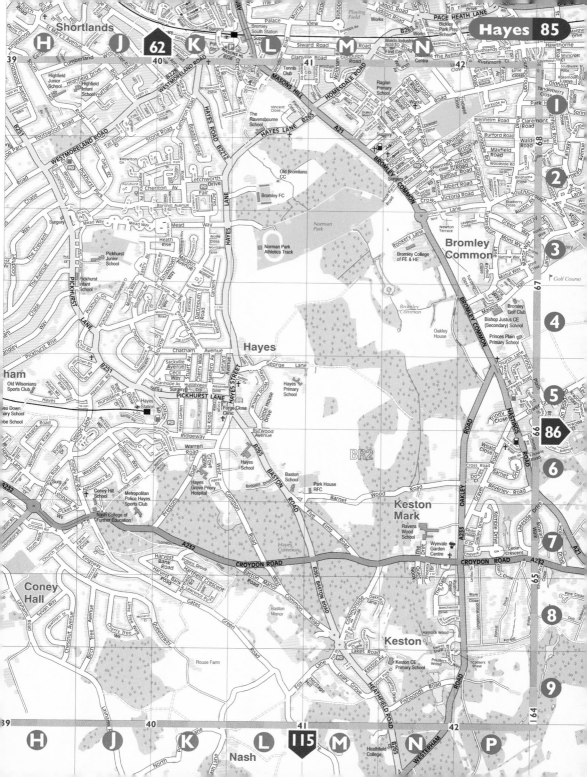

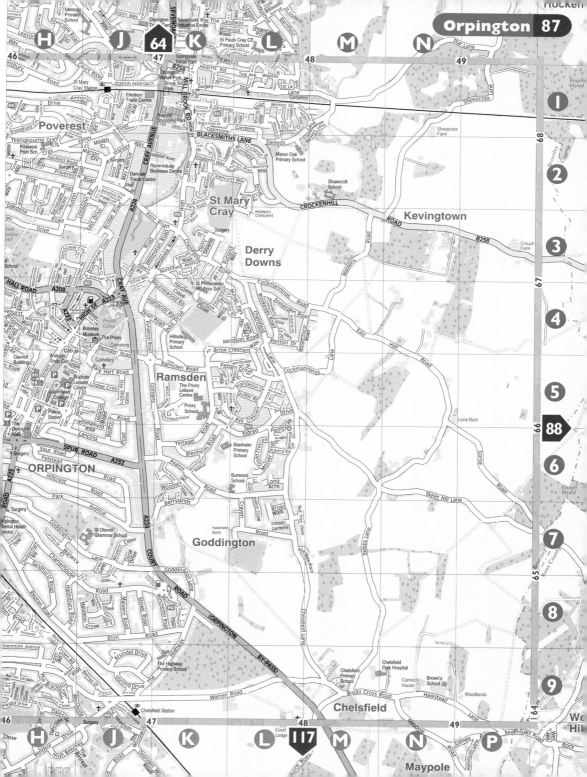

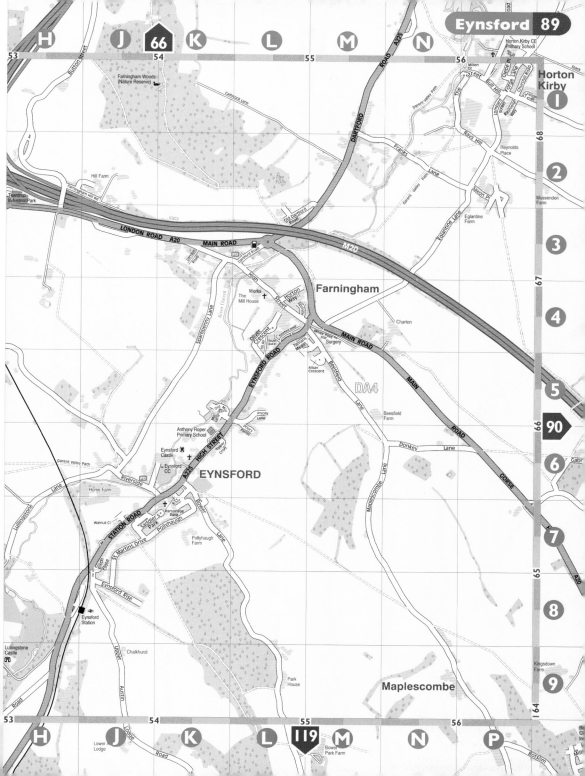

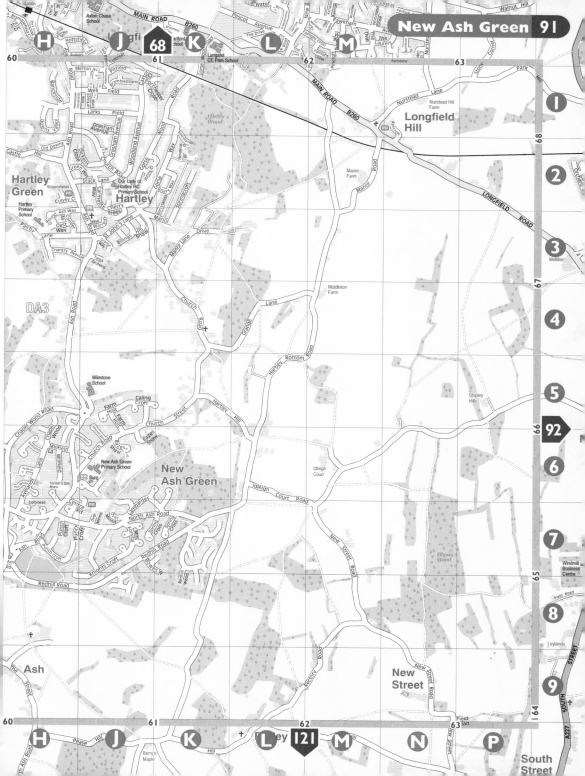

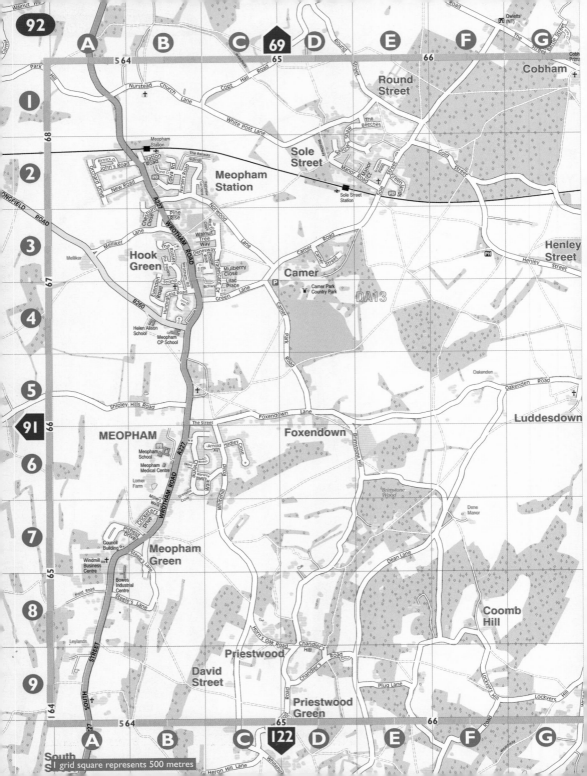

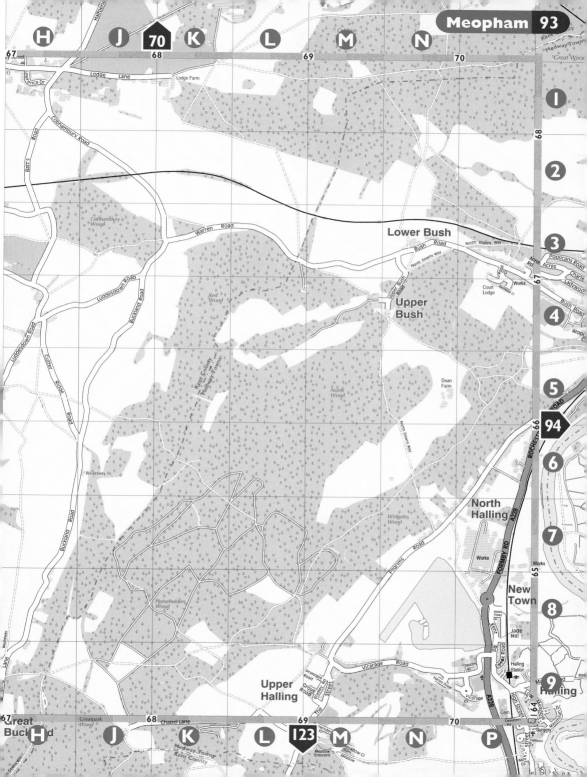

H J **70** K L M N

68

I

2

3

4

5

94

6

7

8

9

Lower Bush

Upper Bush

North Halling

New Town

Halling

Upper Halling

123

H J K L M N P

67 68 69 70

Lodge Lane
Lodge Farm

Cobnambury Road

Warren Road

Bush Road

North Downs Way

North Downs Way

Poplicans Road

Nine Acres

Charle

Court Lodge

Works

Ladywoo

Bush Road

Wood C

Cobhambury Wood

Red Wood

Luddesdown Road

Buckland Road

Curtter Ridge Road

Kent County Medway Towns

North Wood

Dean Farm

Wealdway

Wingate Wood

Buckland Road

Horseholders Wood

Pilgrims Road

Rochester 66

FORMBY RD

A228

Works

Works

65

Kent Rd

Jade Hill

Stake

Vicarage Road

Primrose Road

Grove Road

The Street

Halling Station

Cem

Vicarage Cl

A228

High Street

Low Street

A64

Surgery

Meadow Crescent

Chapel Lane

Great Buckland

Greatpark Wood

Medway Towns Kent County

67 68 69 70

Great Wood

Medway Town

Kent

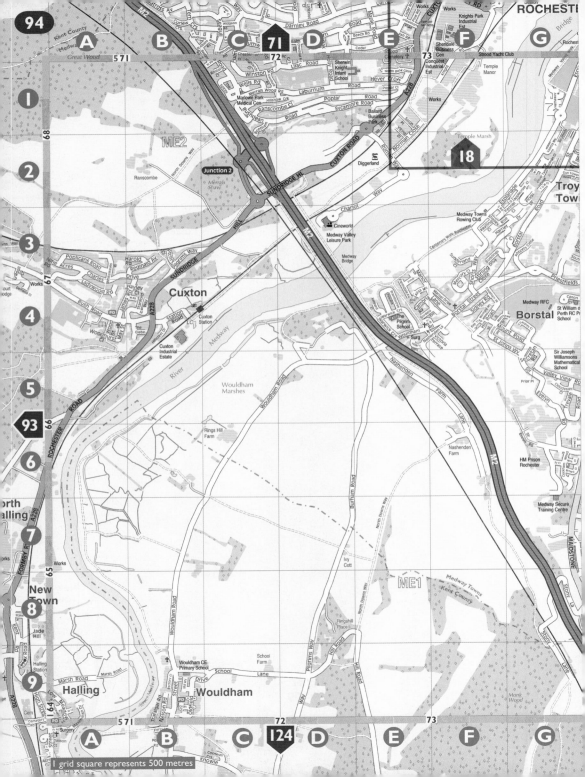

A B C 75 D E F G

5 85   86   87

I

Wetham Green

68

2

Upchurch

67

Holywell Prim Sch

3

Holywell Lane

4

Gore Farm

5

97

66

6

Gore House

Breach

Boxted Lane

The Green

Lapwing Drive

Lower Halstow

Callum Park

Barksore

Saxon Shore Way

Elm Farm

Lower Halstow School

School Lane

Wardwell Lane

Vicarage Lane

Funton Brickworks

Barksore Marshes

Funton Creek

Hawes Wood

High Oak Hill

Oak Hill

Great Norwood

Little Norwood

Bedior Avenue

Cemetery

Newington CE Primary School

7

HARTLIP HILL   Hartlip Hill

65

A2

Newington Industrial Estate

8

Lower Hartlip Road

9

64

Lower Hartlip

5 85

Newington Station

School Lane

London Rd

Orchard Drive

Bull Lane

HIGH STREET

Newington Manor

Station Rd

Church St

St Mary's View

Newington

BOYCES HILL

A2

Keycol

KEYCOL HILL

Cold Harbour

Cold Harbour

Coll Harb

MAIDSTONE ROAD

Chestnut

A B C 128 D E F G

86   87

1 grid square represents 500 metres

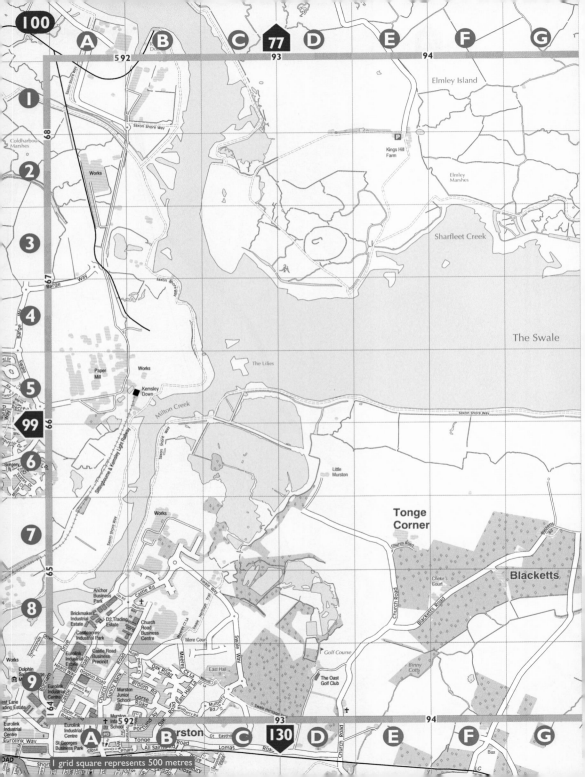

A B C 77 D E F G

592 93 94

I

Coldharbour
Marshes

2 Works

3

Barge Way

4 Barge

5 Kemsley
Down

99 Works

6

7

8

9

Elmley Island

Kings Hill
Farm

Elmley
Marshes

Sharfleet Creek

The Swale

The Lilies

Saxon Shore Way

Little
Murston

**Tonge
Corner**

Church Road

Blacketts

Choke's
Court

Binny
Cotts

Golf Course

The Oast
Golf Club

Anchor
Business
Park

Brickmakers
Industrial
Estate

Castlefields
Industrial Park

D2 Trading
Estate

Castle Rd

Church
Road
Business
Centre

Mere Court

Swale Way

Swale Heritage Trail

Eurolink
Industrial
Estate

Castle Road
Business Precinct

Dolphin Road

Eurolink
Industrial
Centre

Dolphin
Sawmills

Works

Murston
Junior
School

Oak Road

Broom Rd

Gorse
Road

East Hall

Mulberry Rd

St Georges
Business Park

Eurolink
Industrial
Centre

Eurolink Way

A 592 B Urston C 130 D E F G

Tonge
All Saints Rd

Gt Easthall
Lomas Rd

Church Road

93 94

Bax

LC

H J **78** K L M N

95 96 97 98

Eastchurch
Marshes

Great
Bells

I

68

Bells

2

Windmill Creek

Nature
Reserve

3

Dutchman's
Island

Wellmarsh
Creek

Spitend
Marshes

67

4

Spitend Point

Peg Fleet

5

66 **102**

Saxon Shore Way

Fowley Island

6

South Deep

Conyer Creek

7

Swale Heritage Trail

65

Conyer

Teynham Level

8

Saxon Shore Way

9

64

Burwick
Field

Conyer Road

Conyer Road

95 96 97 98

H J K L **131** M N P

Teynham
Stre

Luddenham
Marshes

Teynham
Court

A   B   C   79   D   E   F   G

599   600   01

I

68

Great
Bells

Bells Creek

2

67

3

tchman's
nd

4

Spitend Point

5

101   66

6

7

65

8

9

64

599   600   01

A   B   C   132   D   E   F   G

Luddenham
Marshes

Poplar Hall

Uplees

Howletts

Uplees Road

Nature
Reserve

Mocketts

Harty Ferry Road

Harty Ferry Road

Harty Ferry Road

The Ferry
Inn

Capel Fleet

Court

H J **80** K L M

02 03 04 05

I

68

2

Nature
Reserve

3

67

4

Isle of
Harty

Elliots
Farm

5

104

66

6

Sayes
Court

7

The Swale

65

8

Cleve
Marshes

9

64

Nagden
Marshes

Saxon Shore Way

02 03 04 05

H J K L **133** M N P

Graveney
Marshes

Saxon Shore Way

Endless Road

A   B   C   81   D   E   F   G

6 06   07   08

1

68

2

3

67

4

5

103   66

6

7

65

Seasalter
Sailing Club

Faversham Road

8   PH

Graveney
Marshes

9

64

6 06   07   08

A   B   C   134   D   E   F   G

Preston
Parade
St. Mary's   Grove
Foxdene Rd.
Alan Road   Kimberley Gr.

Lucerne Drive
Seasalter Cross   Faversham Road
Bridge J
Country
Leisure Club

Seasalter
Level

1 grid square represents 500 metres

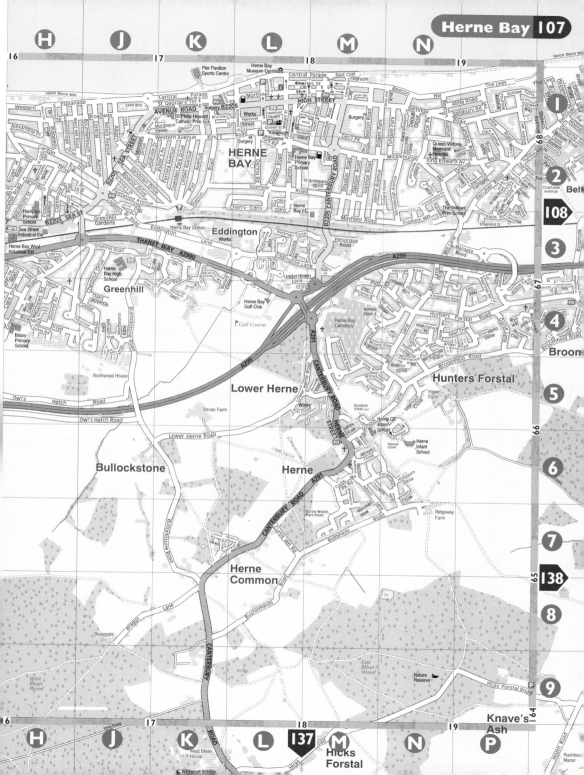

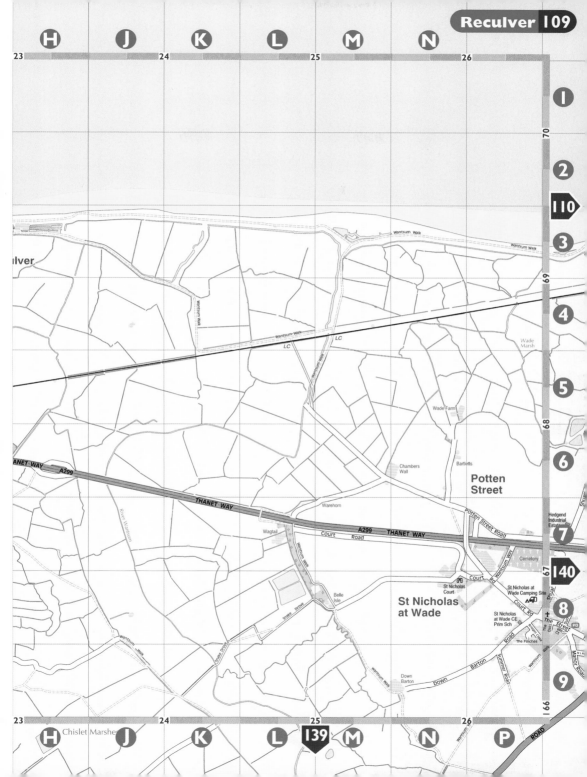

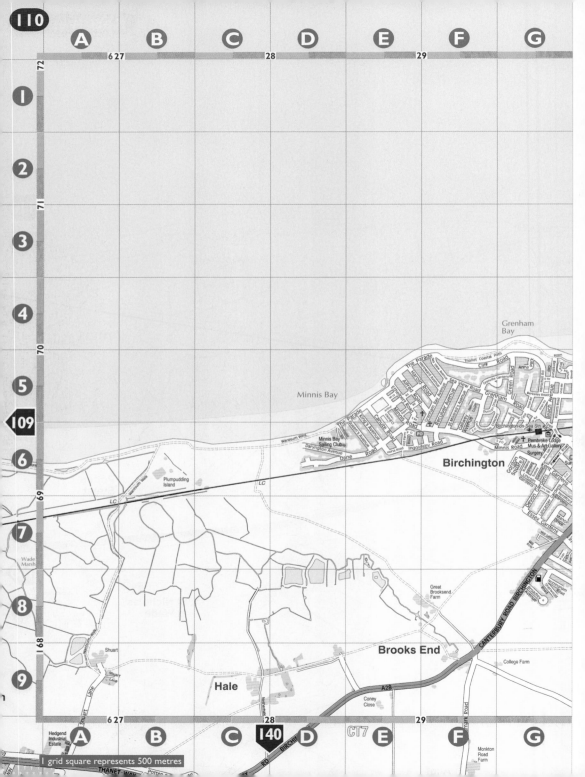

6 27 28 29

72

1

71

2

3

4

70

5

109

Minnis Bay

Grenham Bay

The Parade Thanet Coastal Path Cliff Road Anna Road

Green Road

Grenham Road

Minnis Bay Sailing Club

Darryngton Avenue

Dane

Birchington-on-Sea Stn

Minnis Road

Pembroke Lodge Mus & Art Gallery Surgery

6

Birchington

69

Plumpudding Island

Wantsum Walk

LC

LC

7

Wade Marsh

Canterbury Road Birchington

8

68

Shuart

Great Brooksend Farm

College Farm

9

Hale

Brooks End

A28

Coney Close

Monkton Road Farm

6 27 28 29

Hedgend Industrial Estate

THANET WAY

1 grid square represents 500 metres

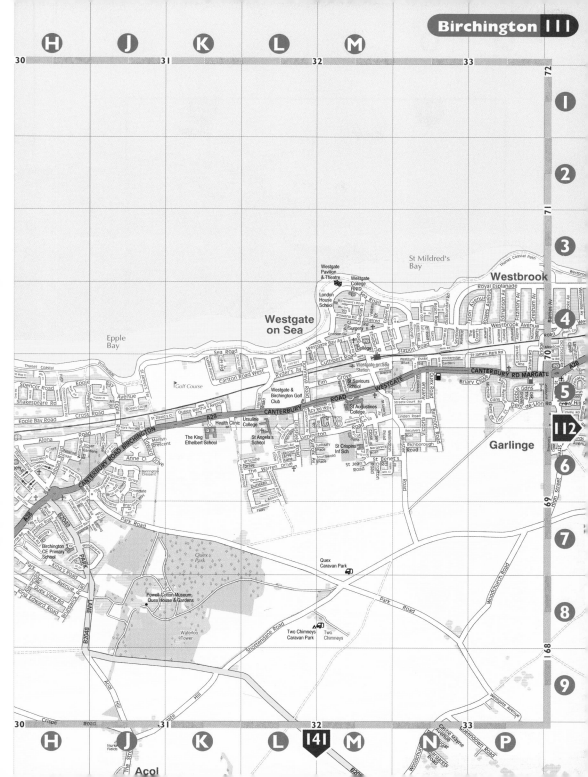

H   J   K   L   M

30   31   32   33

72

1

71

2

3

St Mildred's Bay

Westbrook

Westgate Pavilion & Theatre

Westgate College RNID

London House School

Thanet Coastal Path

Westbrook

Royal Esplanade

Westbrook Avenue

Tyson Avenue
Bowes Avenue
Edmanson Av
Fitzroy Av
Cresham Av
Barnet Av

4

70

Westgate on Sea

Epple Bay

Golf Course

Sea Road

Carlton Road West

Ryder's Avenue

Domneva Road

Cuthbert Road

Elm Grove

St Saviours School

Station Road

Westbury Road
Essex Road

Briary Close

WESTGATE

Canterbury Rd Margate

CANTERBURY RD MARGATE

A28

5

Crow Hill

Epple Bay Road
Cross Road
Shakespeare Rd
Spencer Road
Alpha

Ocean Close
St David's Cl
Queen Bertha's Avenue

Health Clinic

CT8

St Augustines College

Linden Road

Belmont Road

Minster Road
Richborough Road

Garlinge

112

CANTERBURY ROAD BIRCHINGTON

The King Ethelbert School

Ursuline College

St Angela's School

Lymington

Linksfield Road

St Crispins Inf Sch

Wellington Road

Margaret Road

St Benet's Road

St Jean Road

6

69

Anne Cl
Marilyn Crescent

Barrington Crescent

Dovedale

Ursuline Drive

The Warren Drive

Dundan Avenue

Allen Avenue

Southwold Place

High Street

7

Park Road

Birchington CE Primary School

King's Road

Quex Park

Quex Caravan Park

Park Road

Woodchurch Road

8

68

Avenue
Quex View Rd
King Edward Road

Powell-Cotton Museum, Quex House & Gardens

Waterloo Tower

ACOL LANE

Two Chimneys Caravan Park

Two Chimneys

Shottendane Road

Westgate Avenue

9

30   31   **141**   32   33

H   J   K   L   **141**   M   N   P

Crispe   Road

Nurse Fields

The Street

Acol

Castle Mayne Avenue

Woodnesborough Road

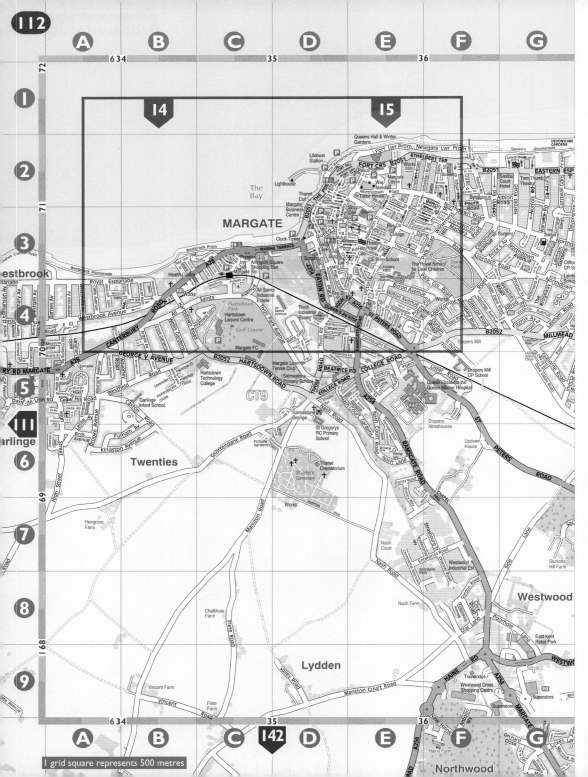

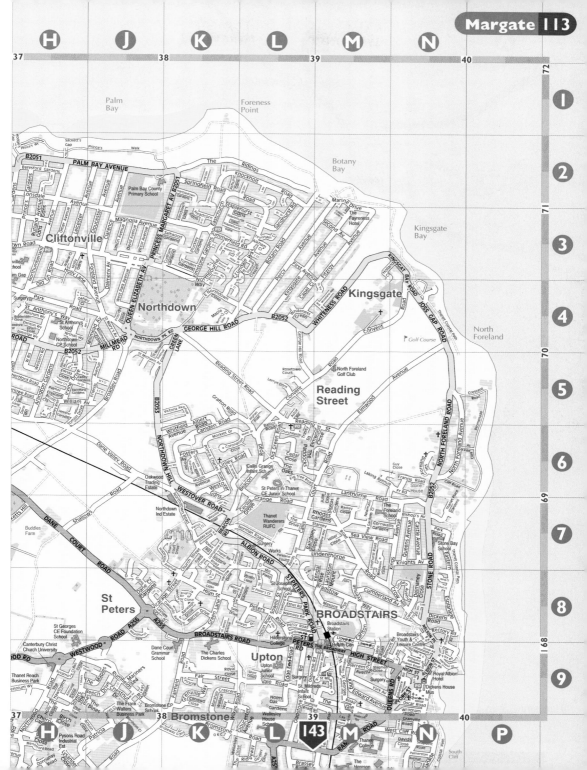

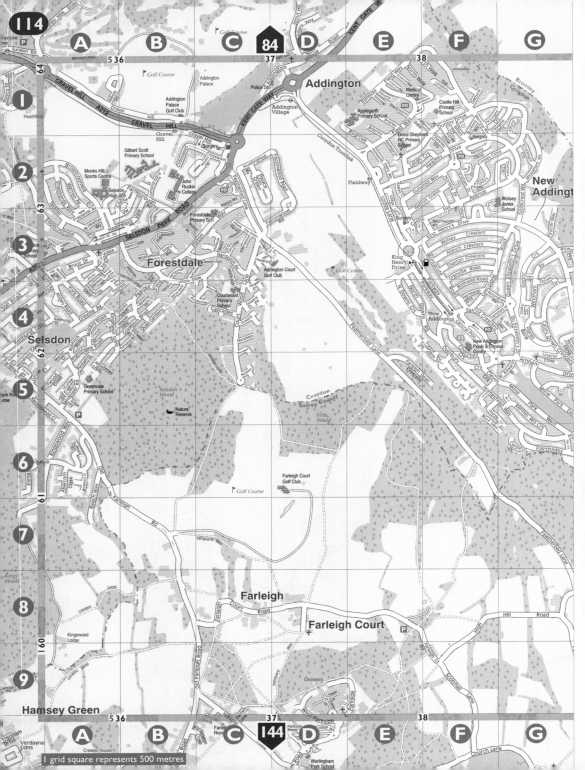

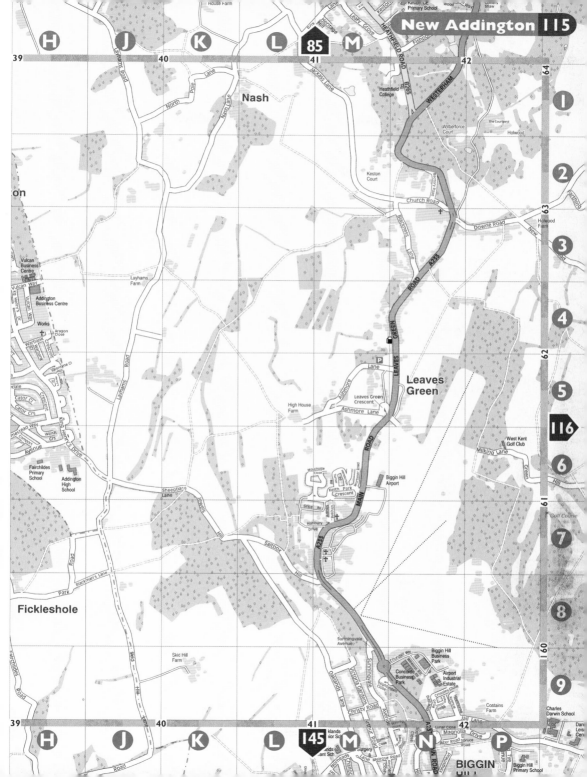

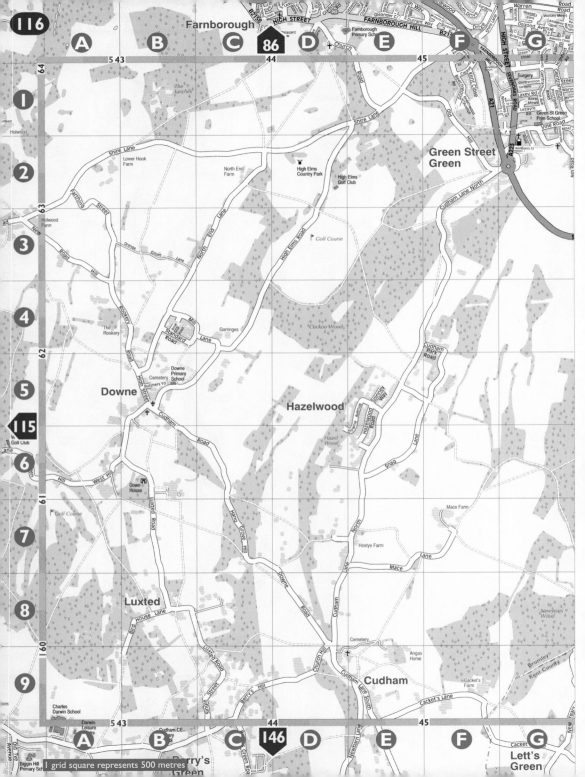

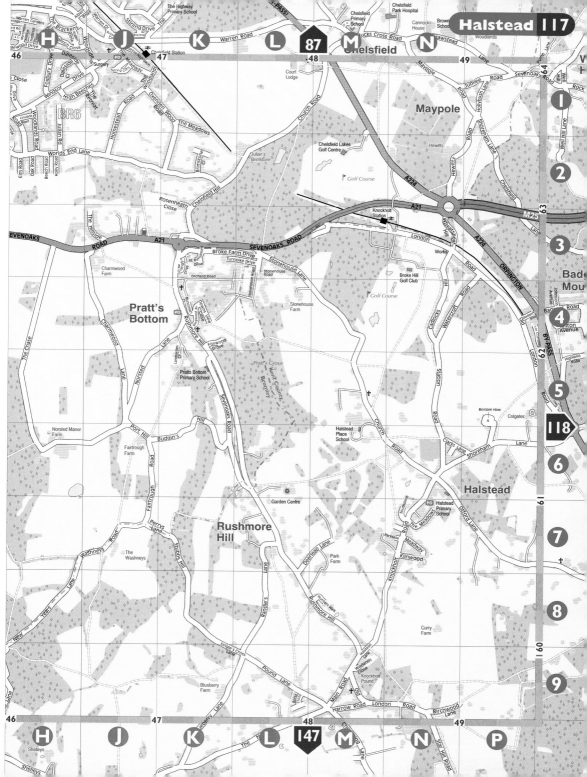

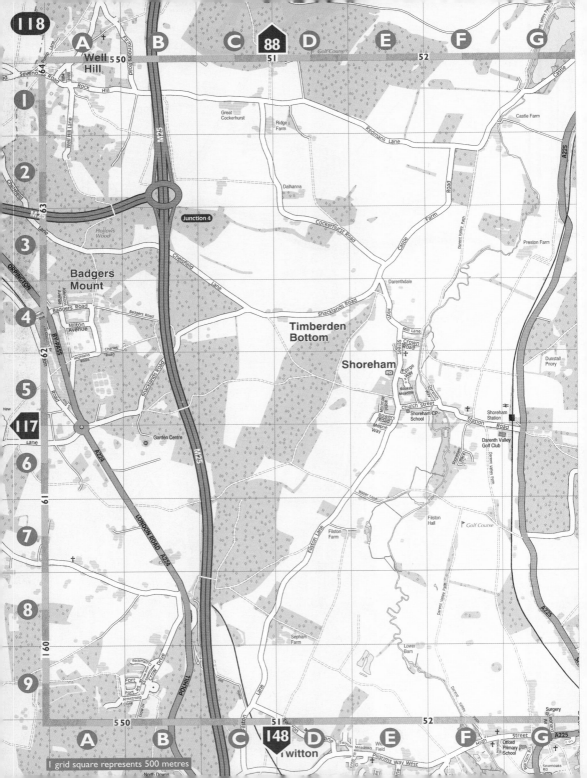

A   B   C   88   D   E   F   G

Well Hill

550   51   52

Firmingers Road

Well Hill Lane

Rock Hill

Sevenoaks

1

2

M26

Chelsfield

Great Cockerhurst

Ridge Farm

Golf Course

Redmans Lane

Castle Farm

Dalhanna

M25

Preston Farm

Junction 4

Cockerhurst Road

Darenth Valley Path

3

Hollows Wood

Chelsfield Lane

Badgers Mount

Darenthdale

Shacklands Road

Castle Farm Road

Dunstall Priory

Orpington

Badgers Road

Johnsons Avenue

Milton Avenue

Charles Road

Highland Road

4

By-Pass

Timberden Bottom

High

Mill Lane

Crown Road

Forge Way

Shoreham

PO

Bakers
Milk Way

Darent

Church Street

Shoreham CP-School

Shoreham Station

5

117

Lane

Haw

A224

Shacklands Road

Garden Centre

Bowers Road

Mane Way

Station Road

Darenth Valley Golf Club

Darent Valley Path

6

161

M25

7

London Road A224

Water Lane

Filston Lane

Filston Farm

Filston Hall

Golf Course

A225

8

160

Polhill

Sepham Farm

Lower Barn

Darent Valley Path

9

Beckmans

Fort

Crow Drive

Fort

Armstrong Close

Drow Dr

Surgery

Otford Primary School

Sevenoaks

A225

550   51   52

A   B   C   148   D   E   F   G

Twitton

Wells Meadows

Pilgrims Way West

North Downs

1 grid square represents 500 metres

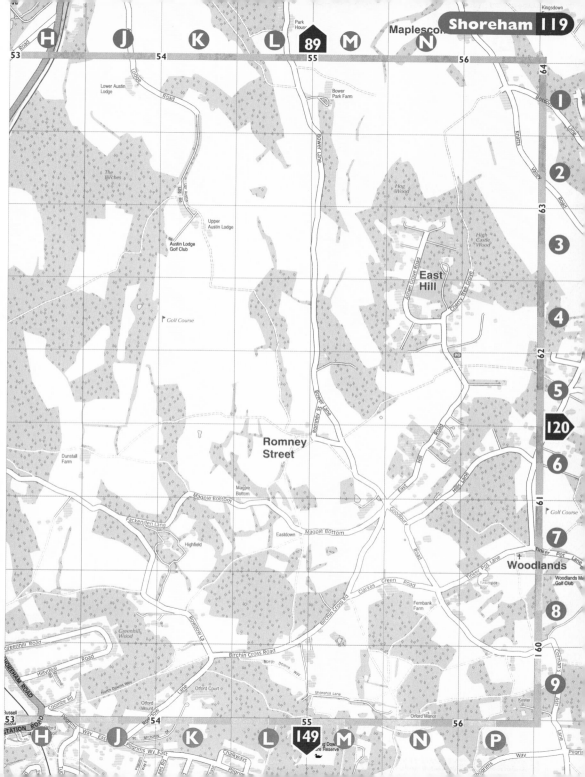

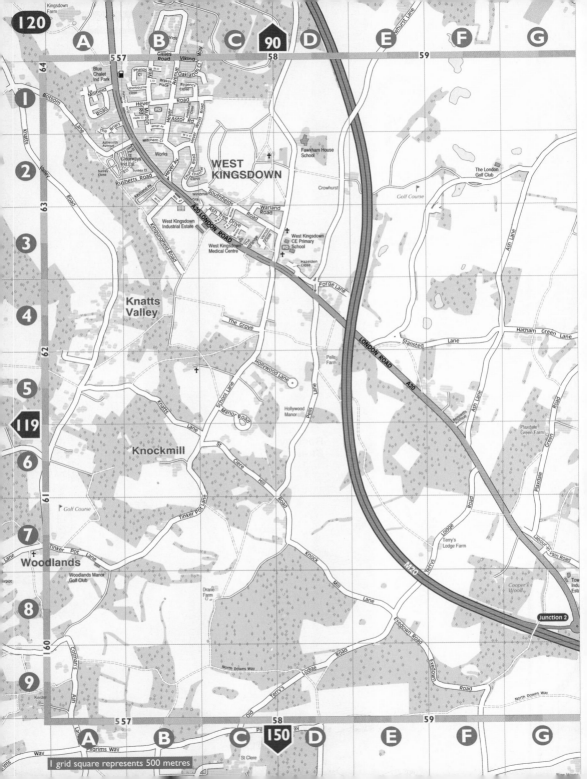

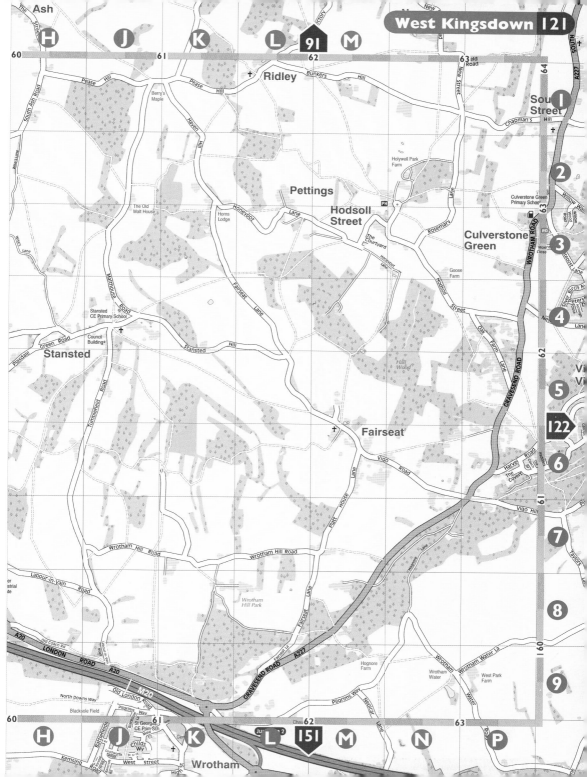

Ash

H J K L 91 M

Ridley

Pease Hill

Berry's Maple

Bunkers Hill

New Street

Pettings

Hodsoll Street

Holywell Park Farm

Culverstone Green Primary School

Culverstone Green

Goose Farm

The Old Malt House

Horns Lodge

Honeypot Lane

The Courtyard

Rosemary Lane

Hodsoll Street

Oak Farm Lane

Stansted CE Primary School

Malthouse Road

Council Building

Green Road

Stansted

Stansted Hill

Fairseat Lane

Hill Wood

Fairseat

Vigo Road

Timberfield Road

Platt House Lane

Wrotham Hill Road

Wrotham Hill Road

Wrotham Hill Park

Labour-in-Vain Road

The Covert

Vigo Hill

Harvel Road

GRAVESEND ROAD

WROTHAM ROAD

A20 LONDON ROAD A20

Old Coach Rd

Old London Road

M20

North Downs Way

Blacksole Field

Pilgrims Way

St George's CE Prim Sch

Childs Way

West Street

Wrotham

GRAVESEND ROAD A227

Pilgrims Way

Hognore Farm

Wrotham Water

Wrotham Water La

West Park Farm

South Ash Road

Wessex Lane

West Lane

Plaxdale

Peter's

Silver Birch Av

Mounts Close

Willow Walk

South Street

Chapman's Hill

I 2 3 4 5 122 6 7 8 9

H J K L 151 M N P

60 61 62 63 64

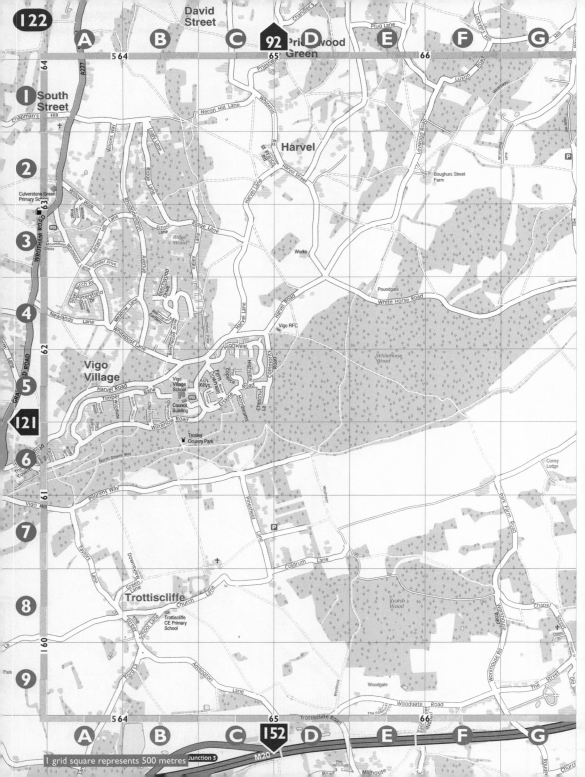

SITTINGBOURNE

Borden

Harman's Corner

Hearts Delight

Tunstall

Grove End

Woodstock

Highsted

Bredgar

Bexon

Chalkwell

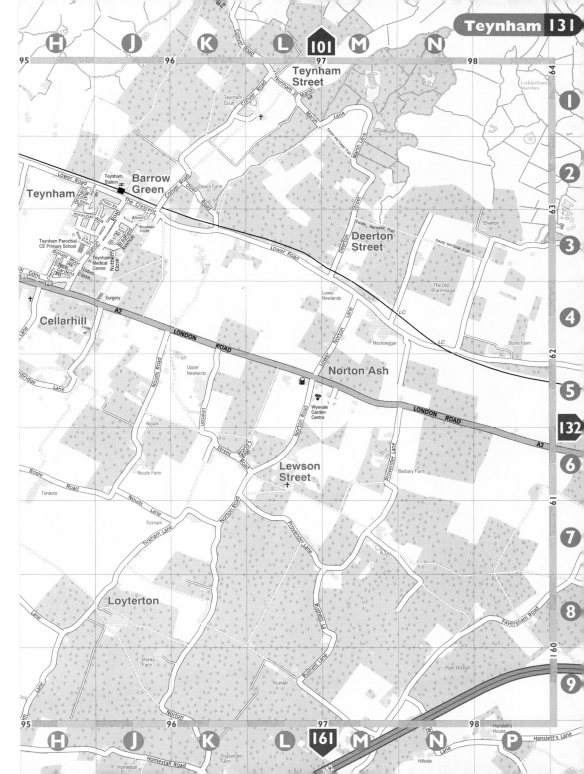

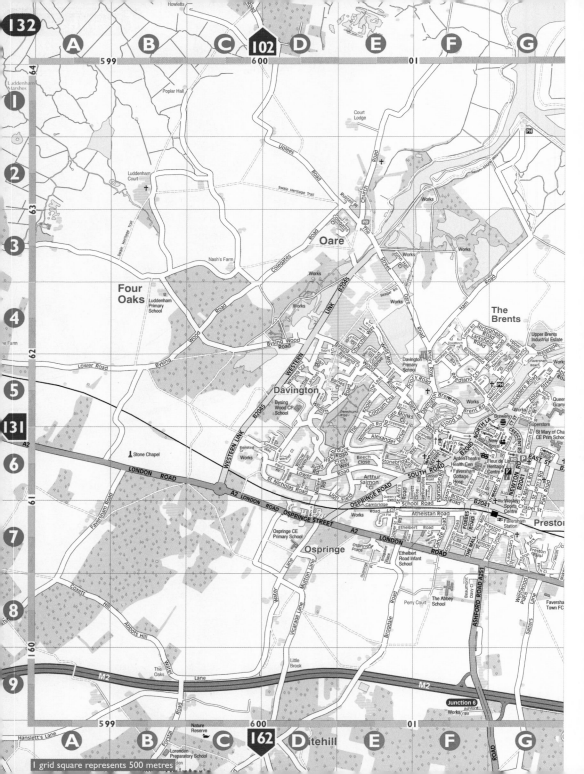

A B C 102 D E F G

599 600 01

64

Luddenham
Marshes

I

Poplar Hall

Court
Lodge

Howletts

PH

2

63

Luddenham
Court

Uplees

Swale Heritage Trail

Church Road

The

Works

Oare

3

Nash's Farm

Swale Heritage Trail

Coulters

Works

Works

Works

Works

Works

Four
Oaks

Luddenham Primary
School

Wood Road

Bysing Wood
Road

WESTERN LINK B2045

Davington
Primary
School

Priory Row

The Brents

Larksfield
Road

Upper Brents
Industrial Estate

Faversham Reach

4

62

Lower Road

Bysing

WESTERN LINK

B2045

Davington

Bysing
Wood CP
School

Brent Hill

Works

Brent Rd

North La

B2040

PH

Queen

Bowdere Road

Abbey St

Church

Superstore

5

131

A2

Stone Chapel

LONDON ROAD

Benstead
Gr
Works

Alexander Drive

Stonebridge

Arden Theatre

Fleur de Lis
Heritage
Centre

Faversham
Cottage
Hosp

St Mary of Cha
CE Prim Scho

EAST ST

6

61

A2 LONDON ROAD OSPRINGE STREET

St Nicholas Road

Arthur
Salmon

Beech
Close

South Road

Plantation

School Road

Newton Road

Wesley
Sports
Centre

Chapel St

A2

Cambridge

Works

Atheistan Road

Faversham
Station

Preston

7

Ospringe CE
Primary School

Ospringe

LONDON ROAD A2

Ospringe's
Place

Ethelbert Road

Ethelbert
Road Infant
School

Smeed Road

FORBES ROAD

The Mall

Preston
Park

8

60

Corett Hill

Abbots Hill

The
Oaks

Water Lane

Vicarage Lane

Minton Lane

Broddale

Perry Court

The Abbey
School

Beaumont
Davy Cl

ASHFORD ROAD A251

Westwood
Place

Faversham
Town FC

9

M2

Water Lane

Little
Brook

M2

Junction 6
Ashford

Works
Rd

599 600 01

A B C 162 D Ditehill E F G

Hanslett's Lane

Forstal Road

Nature
Reserve

Lorenden
Preparatory School

I grid square represents 500 metres

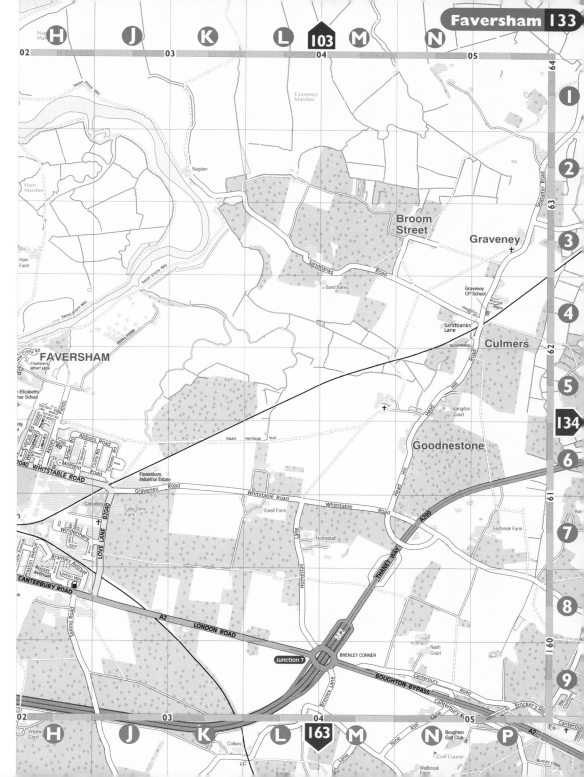

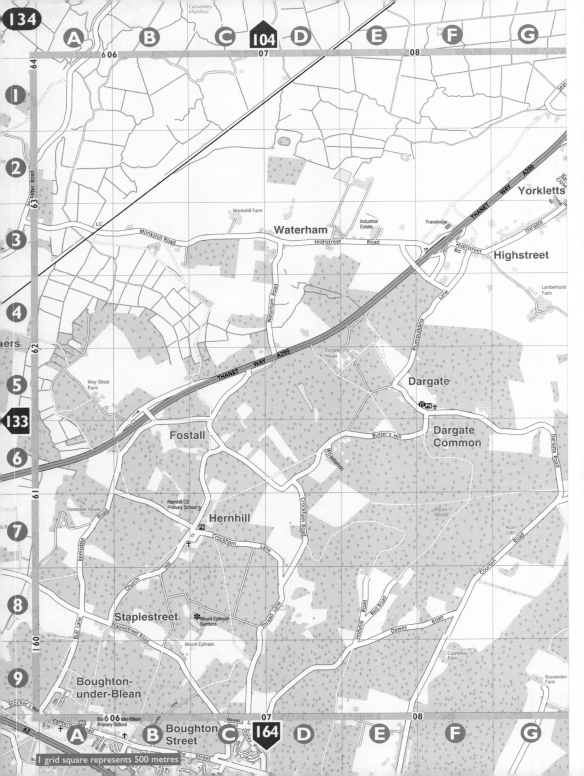

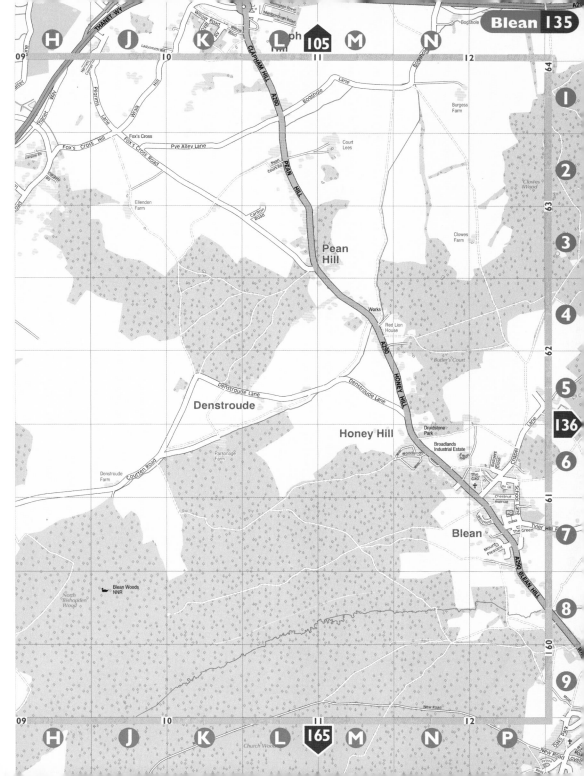

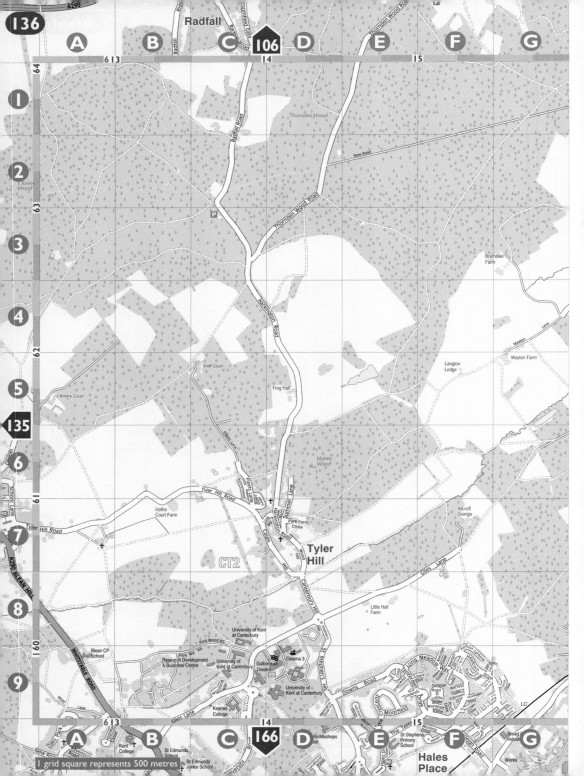

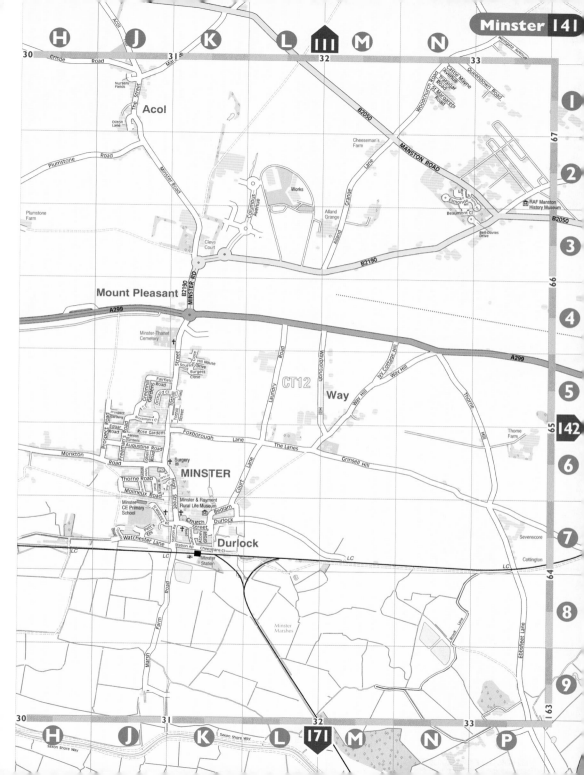

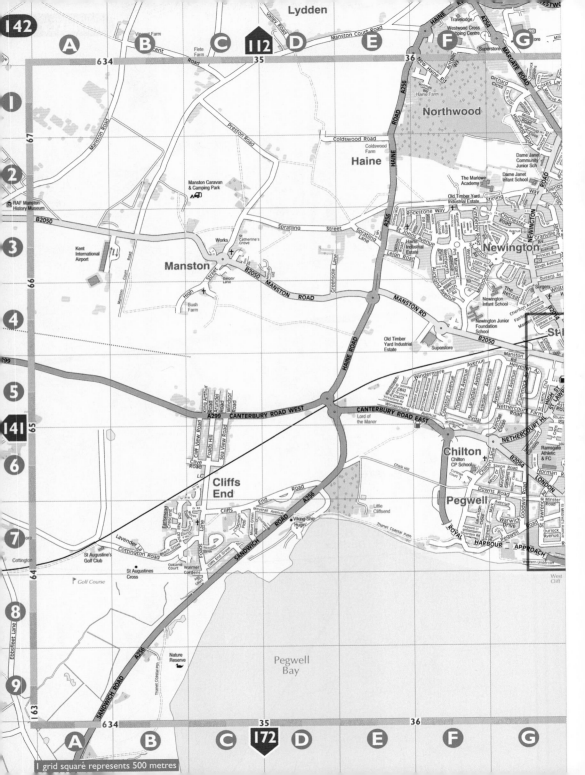

A **B** **C** **112** **D** **E** **F** **G**

Lydden

Vincent Farm
Fitete Farm

634

Valley Road
Manston Court Road
New Haine Rd
Westwood Cross Shopping Centre

Margate Road

I

67

Preston Road

Manston Road

Northwood

Coldswood Road
Coldswood Farm

Haine Road

Haine

2

RAF Manston History Museum

B2050

Manston Caravan & Camping Park

The Marlowe Academy

Old Timber Yard Industrial Estate

Dame Janet Community Junior Sch
Dame Janet Infant School

Stirling Way

Newington

3

66

Kent International Airport

Manston

Works
St Catherine's Grove

Spratling Street
Spratling Lane

B2050 MANSTON ROAD

Greensole Lane

A256

Rockstone Way

St Johns Avenue

Haine Industrial Estate
Leigh Road

Chichester Road
Granville Av

Princes Avenue
Kings Avenue
Queens Avenue

Newington
The Retreat

4

High Street
Dalgor Lane

Bush Farm

MANSTON RD

HAINE ROAD

Old Timber Yard Industrial Estate

Superstore

B2050

Manston Rd
Helvellyn Av

St

5

299

King Arthur
Arundel Road
Windsor Road

A299 CANTERBURY ROAD WEST

Windermere Avenue
Coniston Avenue
Thirlmere Avenue
Estdale Avenue
Rydal

Windermere

CANTERBURY ROAD EAST

Nethercourt Farm

Crummock

High St

St Lawr

Nethercourt Hill

141

65

Cliff View Road
Foads Hill
Sea View Road

Clive Road
LCf

Lord of the Manor

Chilton
Chilton CP School

Chilton Lane

Leicester Circle
Rydal

Ramsgate Athletic & FC

LONDON ROAD
Horman

6

Cliffs End

Chalk Hill

B2054

Downs Road

Pegwell

Minster

7

64

Lavender
Cottington Road

St Augustines Golf Club
St Augustines Cross

Oakland Court
Walmer Gardens

Beech Grove
Foads
Nichols

Cliffs End Grove
Cliff End Road

Cottington Road

Cliffs
Meyerall Avenue

SANDWICH ROAD

A256

Viking Ship Hugin

Thanet Coastal Path

Little Cliffsend

ROYAL HARBOUR APPROACH

Goodwin Road
Warwick Drive

Durlock Road

West Cliff

8

Ebbsfleet Lane

A256

Golf Course

Cottington

Nature Reserve
Thanet Coastal Path

Pegwell
Bay

9

163

634

SANDWICH ROAD

A **B** **C** **172** **D** **E** **F** **G**

1 grid square represents 500 metres

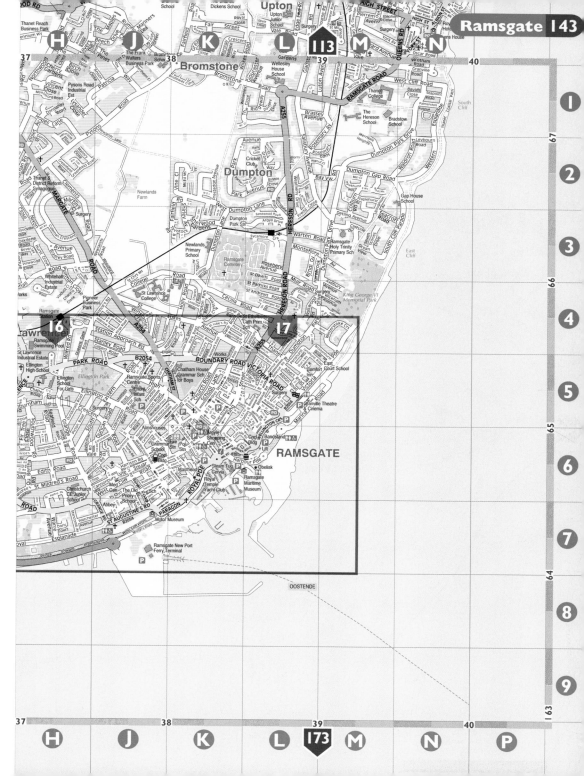

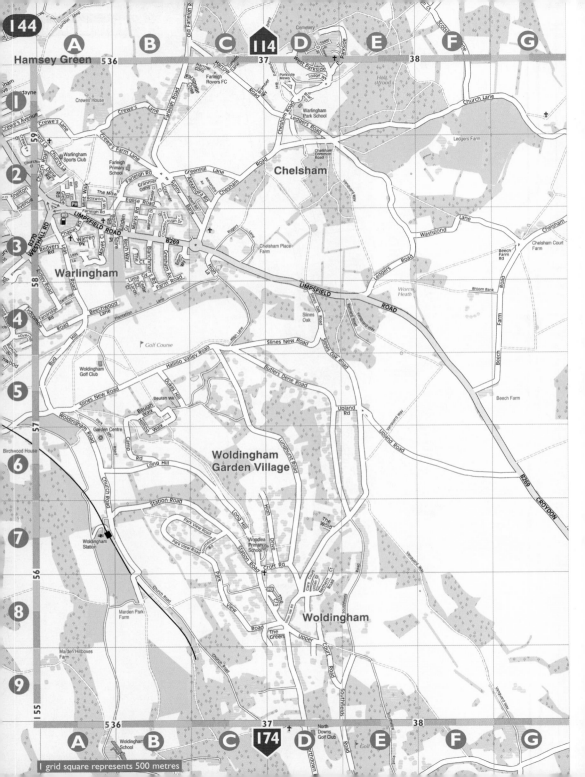

H   J   K   L   **117**   M

46   47   48   49

I

59

2

3

58

4

5

57   **148**

Junction 5

6

56

7

8

9   55   Dryhill

H   J   K   L   **177**   M   N   P

46   47   48   49

Knockholt

Shelleys

Shelleys Lane

Main Road

The Mount

Brasted Lane

Brasted Hill Farm

Brasted Hill

Hogtrough Hill

Station Road

Church Road

Rectory Lane

Coles Lane

St Martins Mdw

Pym Orchd

Brasted

The Mill Works

Works

Works

High Street

Chart Lane

The Carriageway

Westerham Road

Blueberry Farm

Blueberry Lane

St Katharines Knockholt CE Primary School

Sundridge Lane

Sundridge Hill

Sundridge Hill Farm

Sheetfield

Combe Bank Farm

Court Lodge Farm

Braisted Hill Road

Combe Bank Senior School

The Nower

Ivy Lane

TN14

Ovenden Road

M25

Combe Bank Drive

B2211

PO

Manor Road

Woodside Road

Chapmans Road

Main Road

Sundridge

Sundridge & Brasted CE Primary School

St Mary's Church Road

Sundridge Place

Round Lane

Way Close

Knockhill Pound

Main Road Old

Harrow Road

Chevening Lane

London Road

Birchwood Lane

North Downs Way

Lord Chatham's Ride

Lord Chatham's Ride

Chevening Road

Chevening Park

Chevening

Chevening Cross

Chevening Road

M25

B2211

Westerham Road A25

Star Hill Road

North Downs Way

Star Hill Road

Star House

Turvins Farm

Morants Cou Farm

Sundridge Road

Chevening Primary School

Willow Farm

M25

Dryhill Lane

Creystop Park

Birchfield

Heverswood

Westerham Road

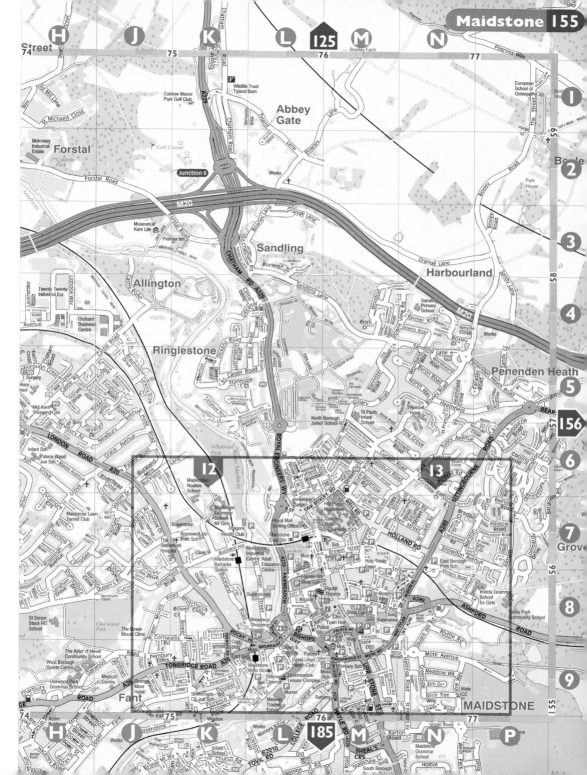

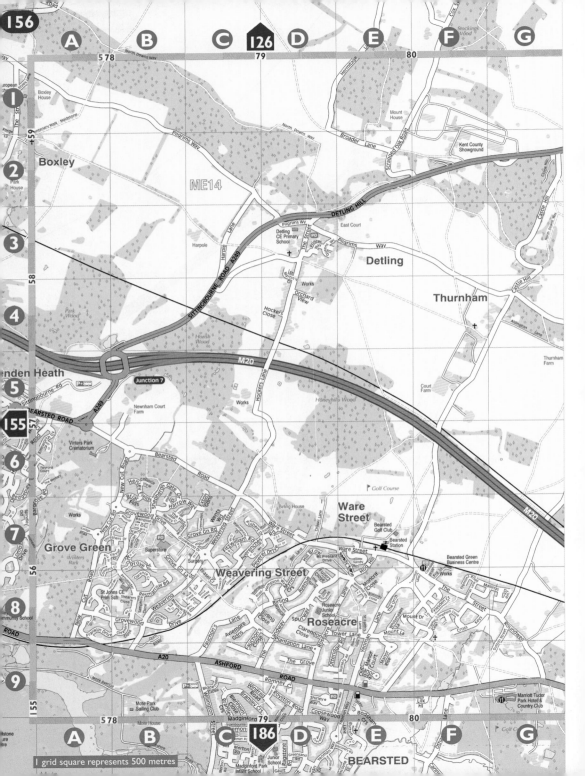

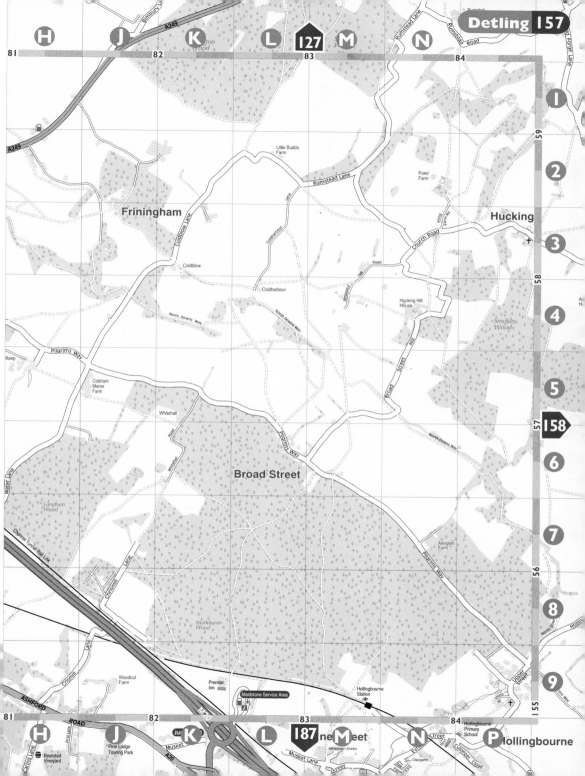

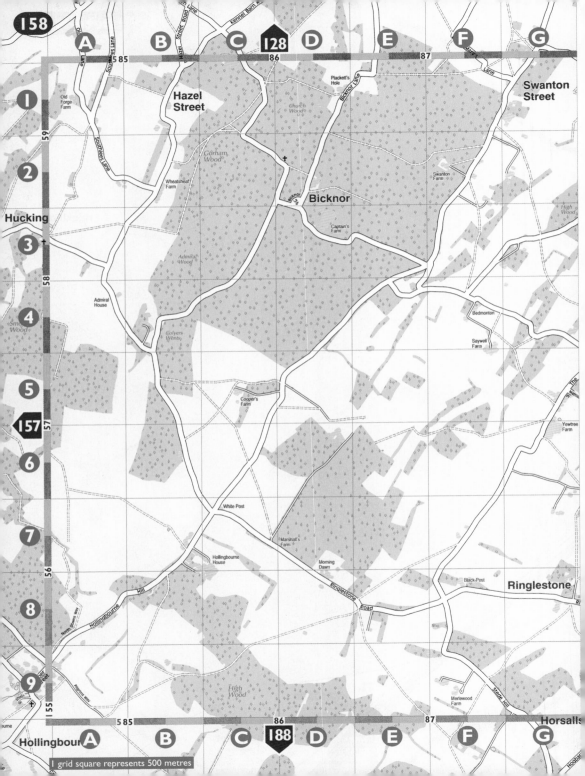

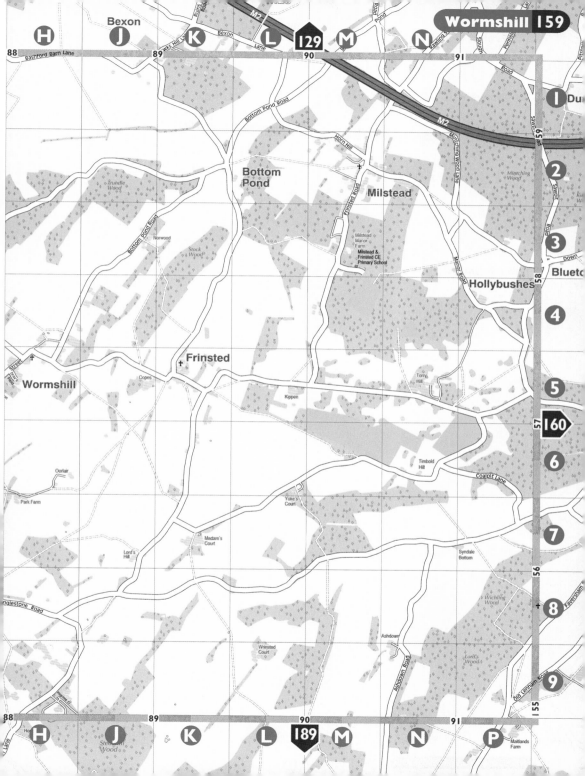

Bexon

(H) (J) (K) (L) **129** (M) (N)

88 Bashford Barn Lane   89   WKS Hill Lo   Bexon   Lane   90   91

(I) Du

M2

Bottom Pond Road

Bottom
Pond

Horn Hill

Frinsted Road

Milstead

Mintching Wood Lane

Mintching
Wood

(2)

Trundle
Wood

Norwood

Stock
Wood

Milstead
Manor
Farm

Milstead &
Frinsted CE
Primary School

Manor Road

(3)

Blueto

Hollybushes

58

Bottom Pond Road

(4)

Street

Wormshill

Copes

Frinsted

Kippen

Torry
Hill

(5)

57

160

Oorlair

Timbold
Hill

Coalpit Lane

(6)

Park Farm

Yoke's
Court

(7)

Madam's
Court

Syndale
Bottom

56

nglestone Road

Lord's
Hill

Ashdown Road

Wichling
Wood

(8)

Faversham

Ashdown

Wormsted
Court

Lord's
Wood

Old Lenham Road

(9)

155

Lane

(H) (J) (K) (L) **189** (M) (N) (P)

88   89   90   91

Steed
Wood

Maitlands
Farm

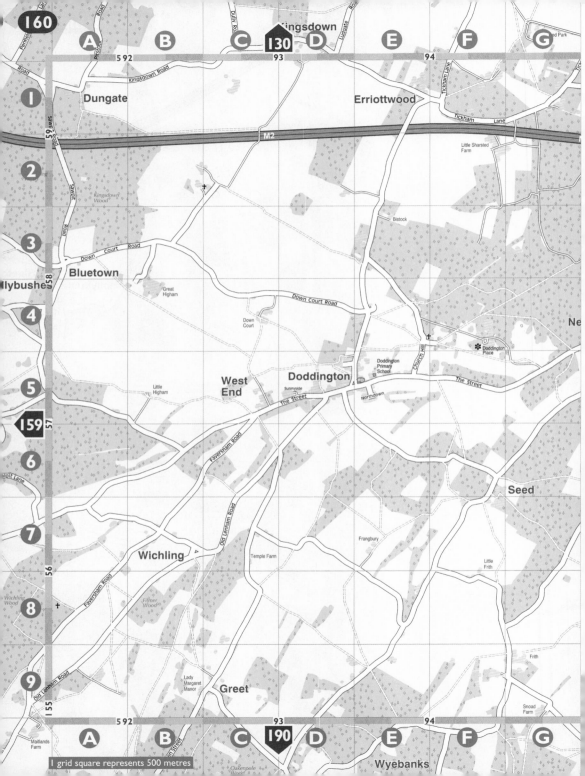

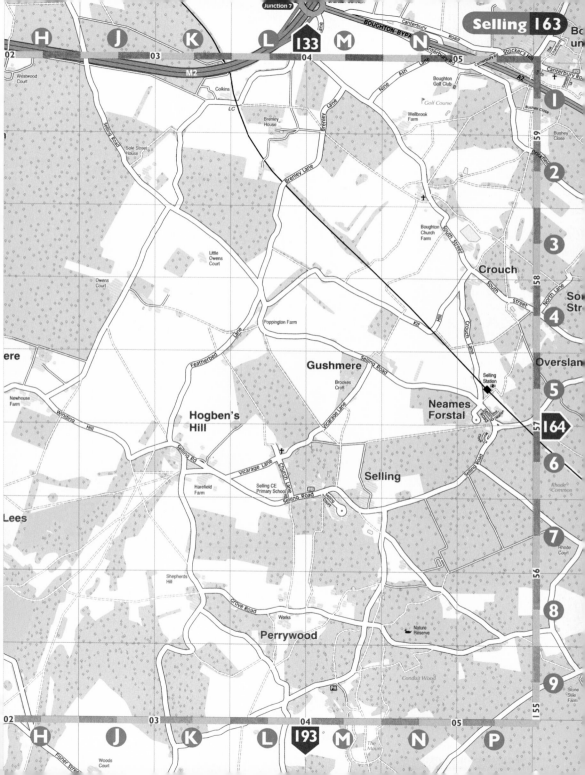

Junction 7

BOUGHTON BYPASS

Canterbury
Road

H   J   K   L   **133**   M   N

02   03   04   05

M2

A2

Canterbury Rd

Interbury Rd

Stocker's Hill

Westwood
Court

Selling Road

Sole Street
House

Colkins

LC

Brenley
House

Brenley Lane

Brenley Lane

Nine Ash
Lane

Wellbrook
Farm

Boughton
Golf Club

Golf Course

Boughton
Church
Farm

Busney Close

Bushey
Close

Brockled

1

59

2

3

Little
Owens
Court

Owens
Court

Poppington Farm

Featherbed Lane

Selling Road

Kit Hill

South Street

Crouch

South
Street

Crouch Lane

North Lane

Sou
Stre

58

4

ere

Newhouse
Farm

Winding Hill

Gushmere

Brookes
Croft

Selling Road

**Neames
Forstal**

Selling Station

Selling Rd

Overslan

Oversland

164

57

5

6

**Hogben's
Hill**

Selling Rd

Vicarage Lane

Church Lane

Vicarage Lane

Selling CE
Primary School

Selling Road

Selling Court

Selling

Selling Road

Rhode
Common

Rhode
Court

7

Harefield
Farm

PO

Lees

Shepherds
Hill

Grove Road

Works

Perrywood

PH

Nature
Reserve

Conduit Wood

Stone
Stile
Farm

56

8

9

155

H   J   K   L   **193**   M   N   P

02   03   04   05

Fisher Street

Woods
Court

The
Mount

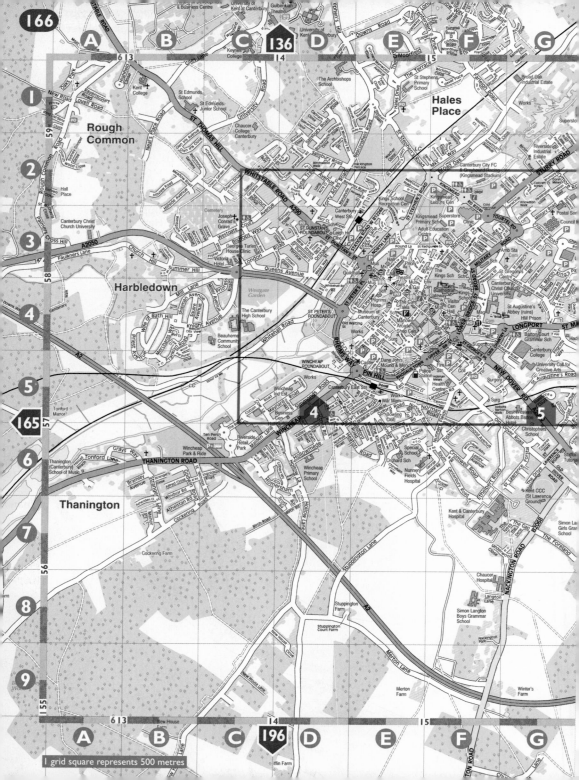

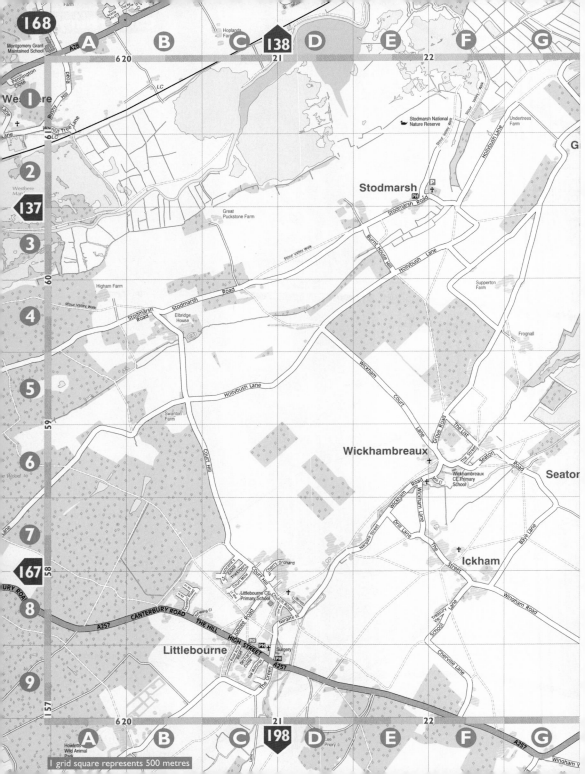

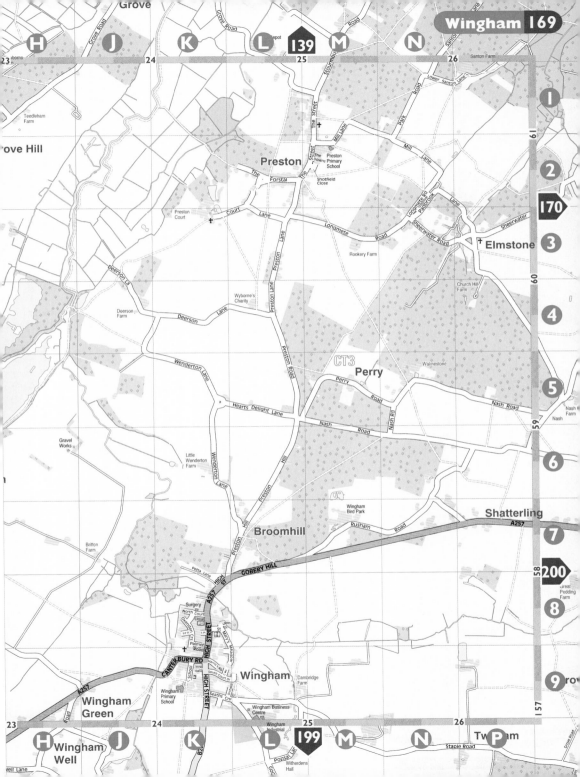

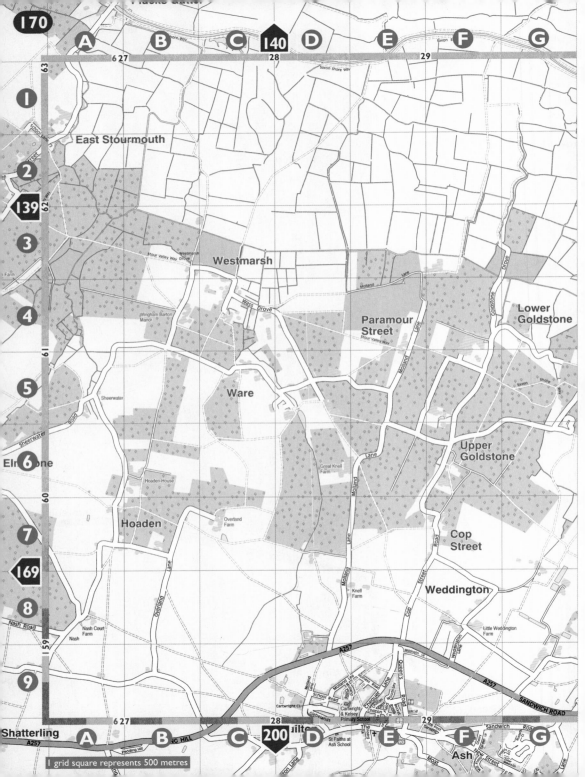

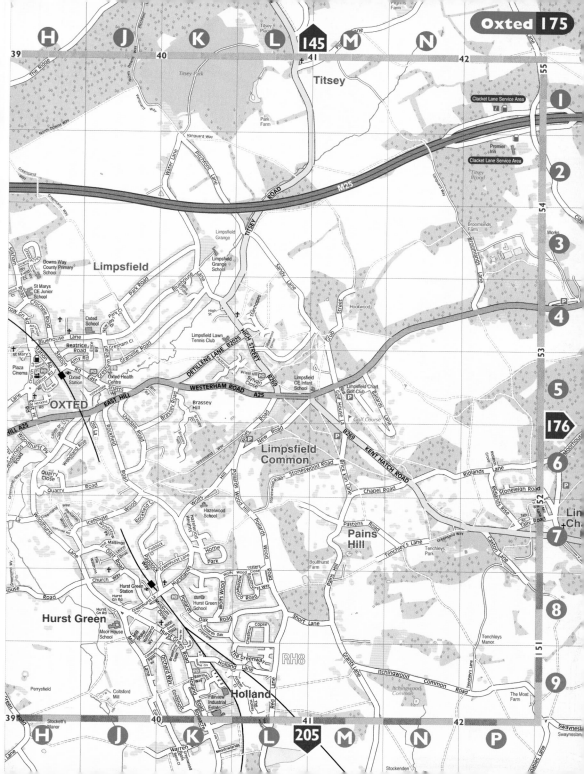

Oxted 175

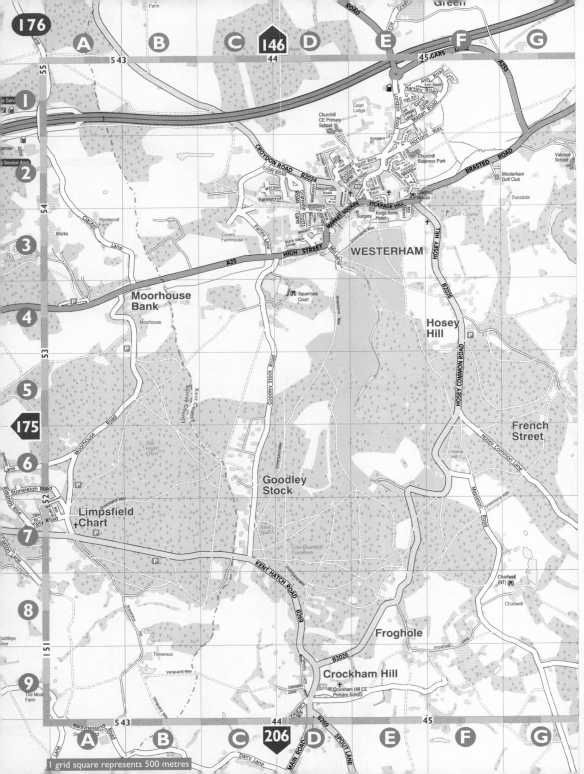

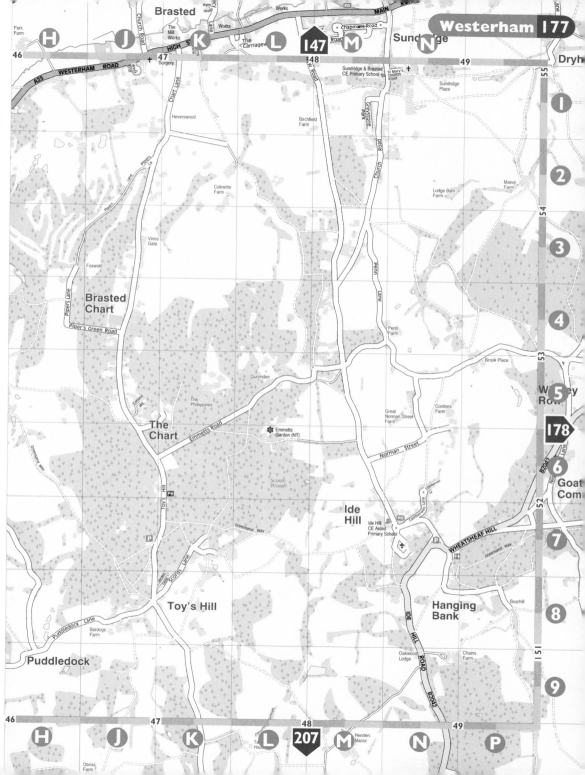

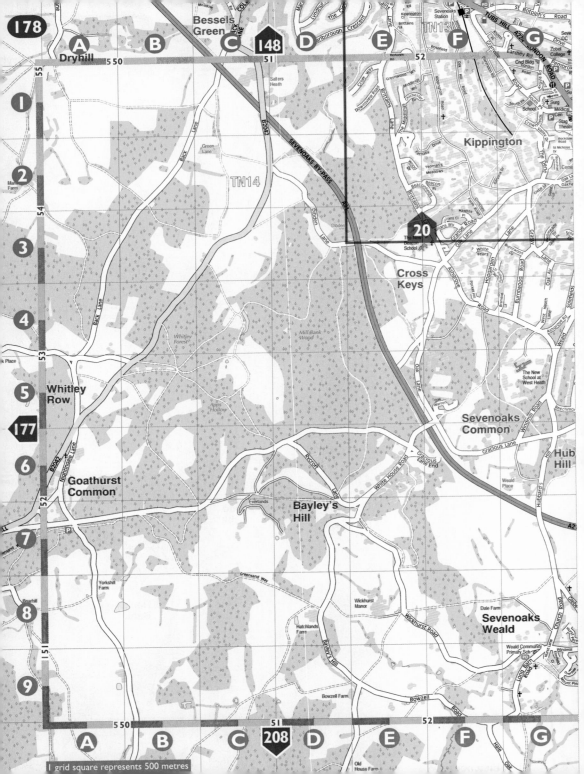

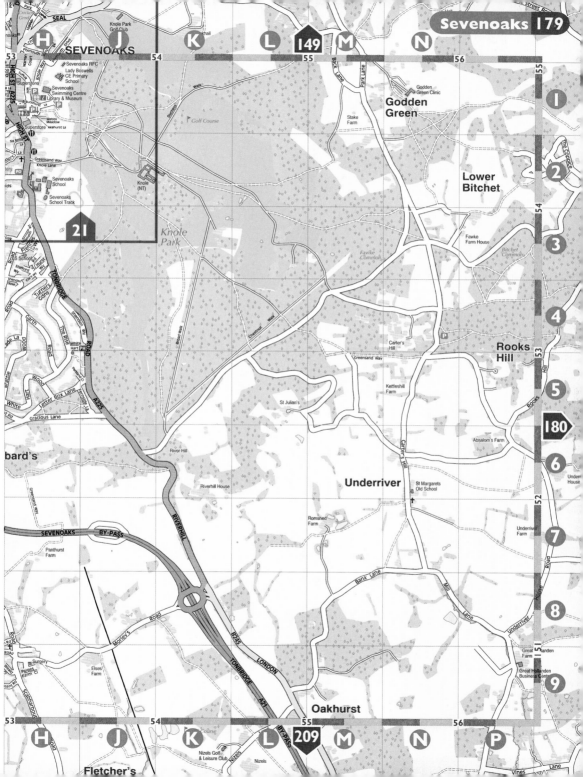

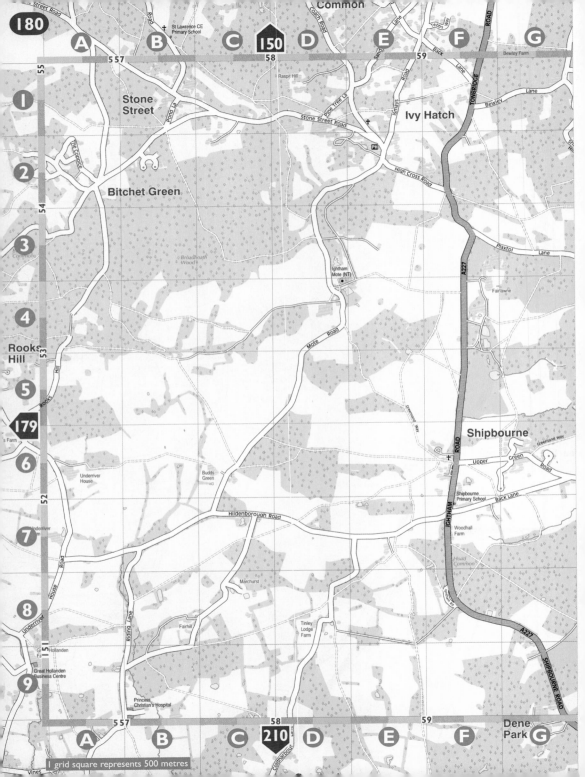

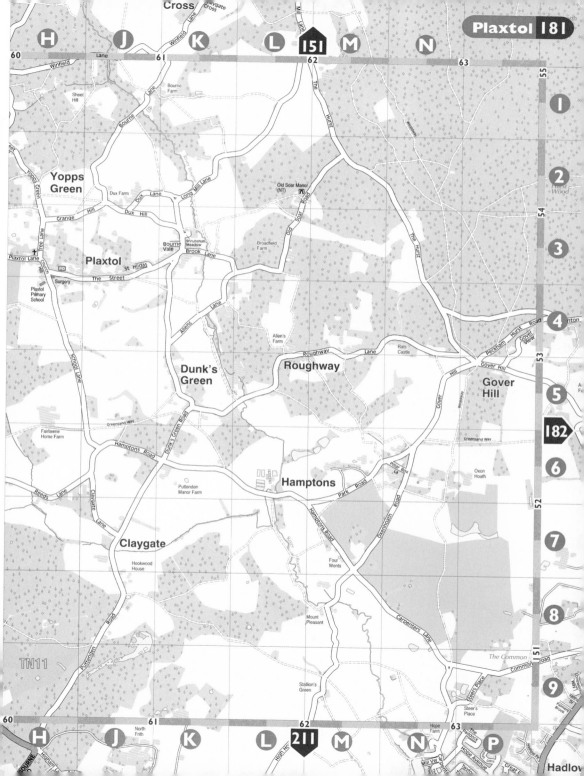

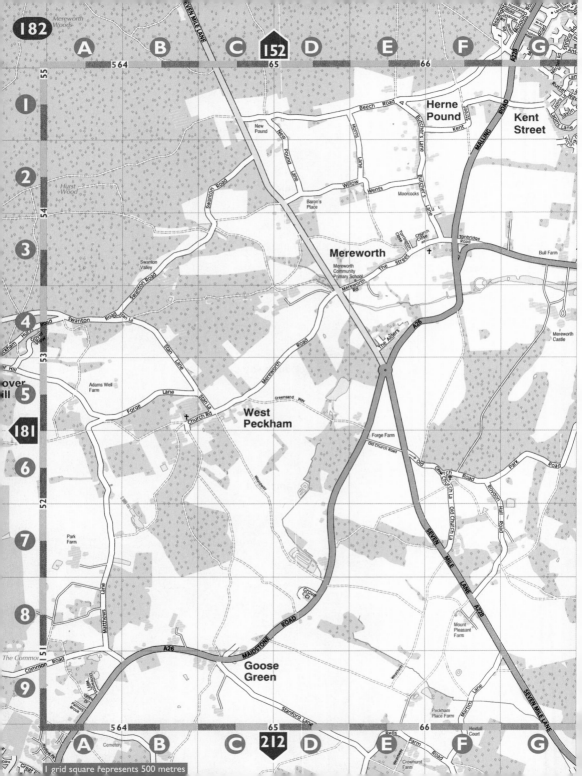

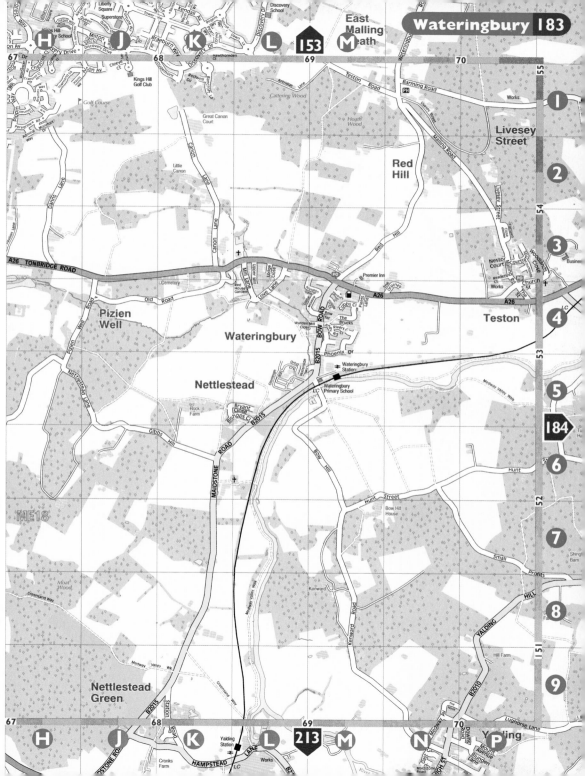

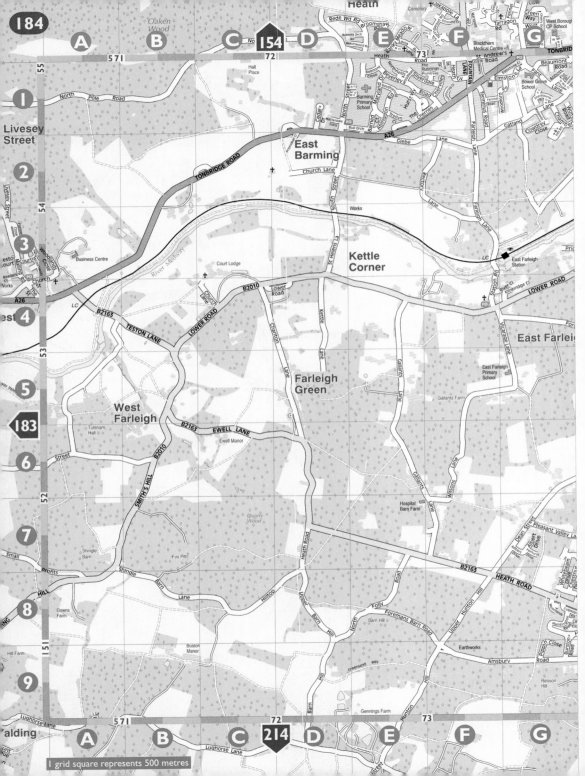

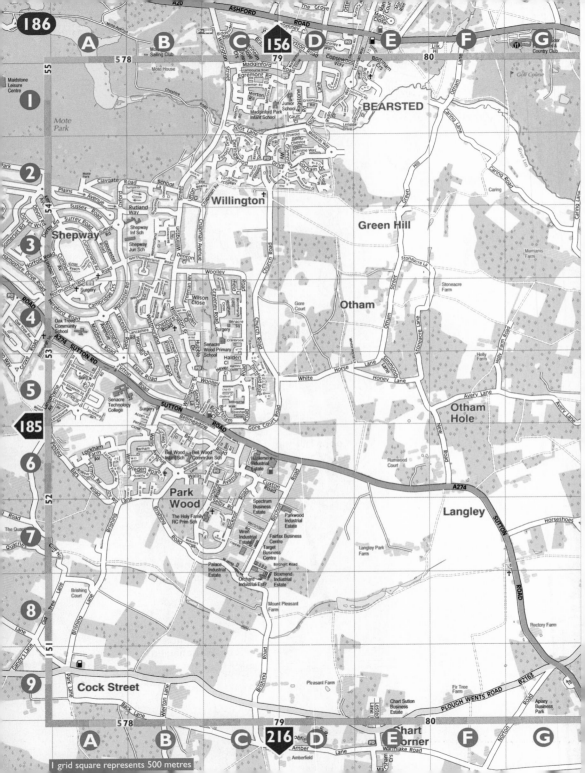

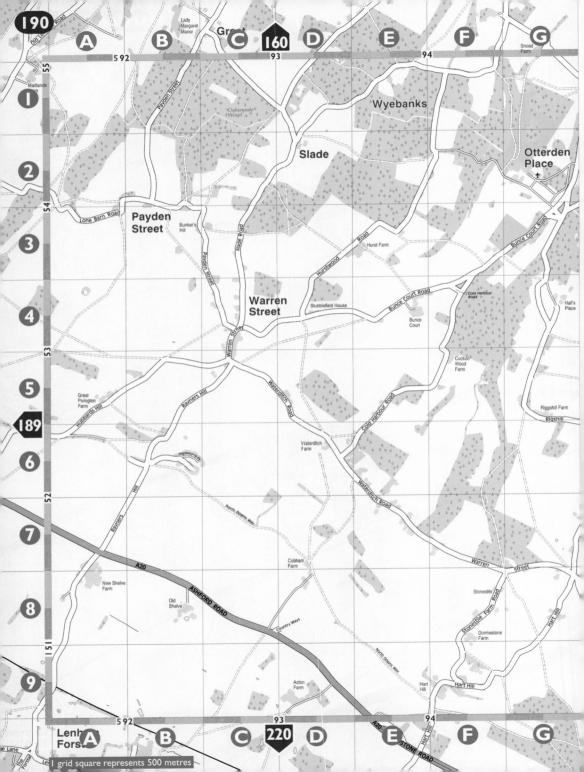

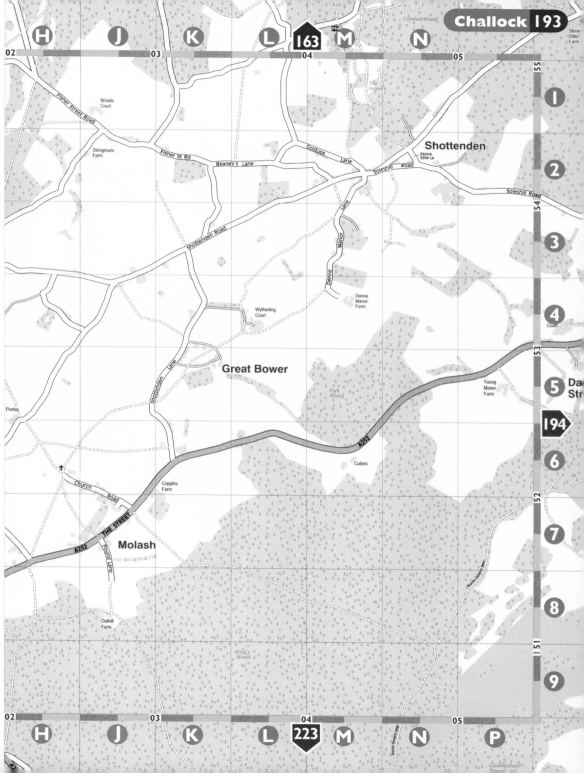

H   J   K   L   **163**   M   N

02   03   04   05

Conduit Wood

Stone Stile Farm

PH

The Mount

Fisher Street Road

Woods Court

Stringmans Farm

Fisher St Rd

Beaney's Lane

Goldups Lane

Shottenden

Soleshill Road

Stone Stile La

Soleshill Road

Shottenden Road

Denne Manor Lane

Wytherling Court

Denne Manor Farm

Great Bower

Shottenden Lane

Park Wood

Young Manor Farm

Da Str

194

Pontus

A252

Cutlers

Church Road

Coppins Farm

THE STREET

Molash

A252

Pound Lane

Oathill Farm

King's Wood

North Downs Way

Godmersham Downs

I

2

3

4

5

6

7

8

9

55

54

53

52

51

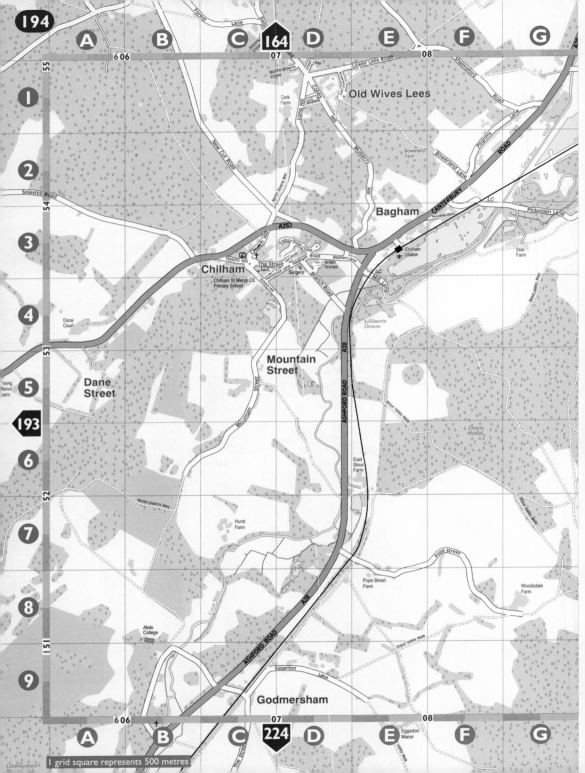

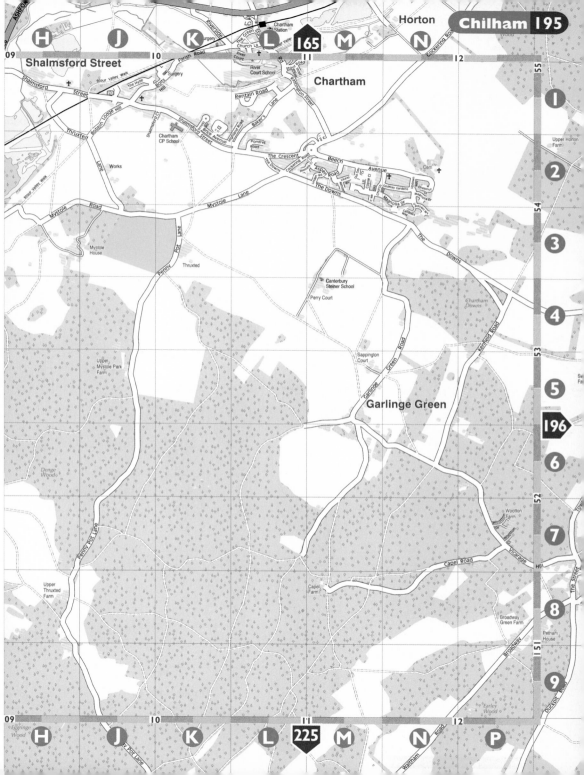

Horton

Shalmsford Street

Chartham

Garlinge Green

196

225

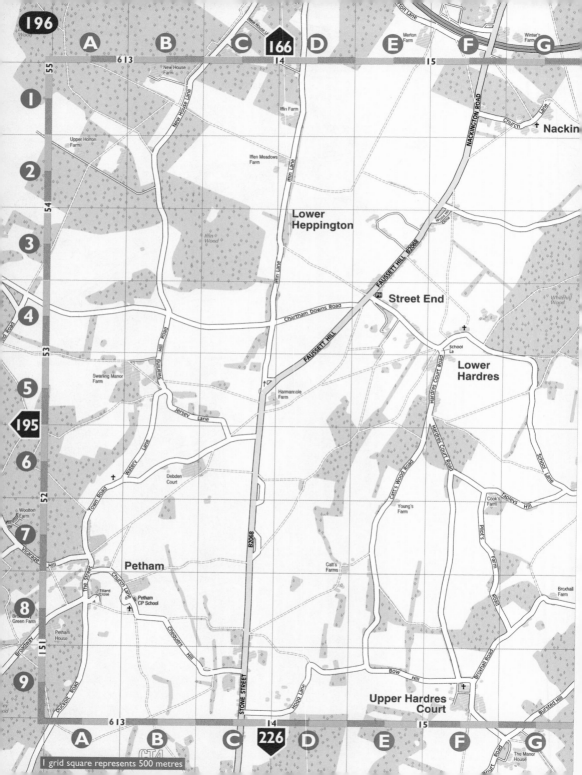

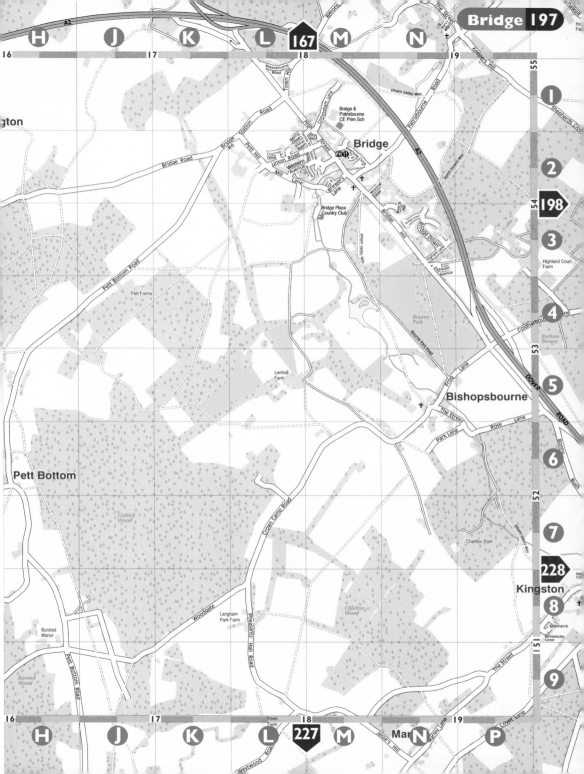

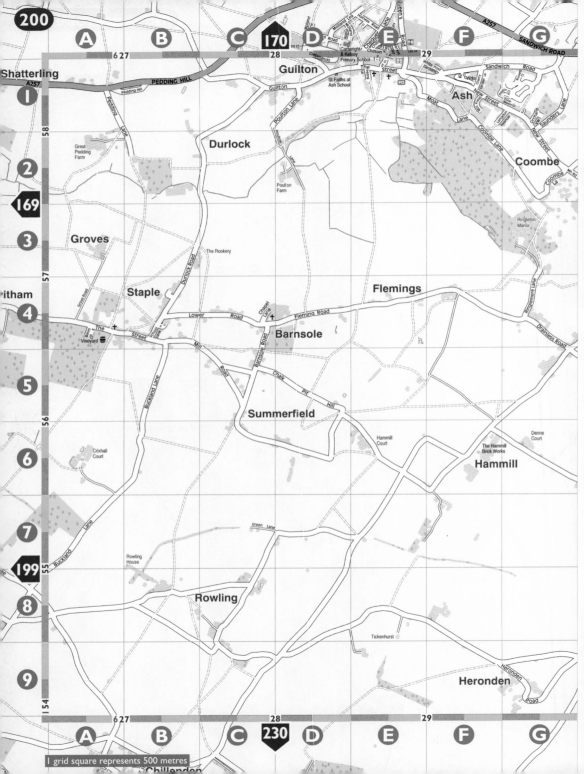

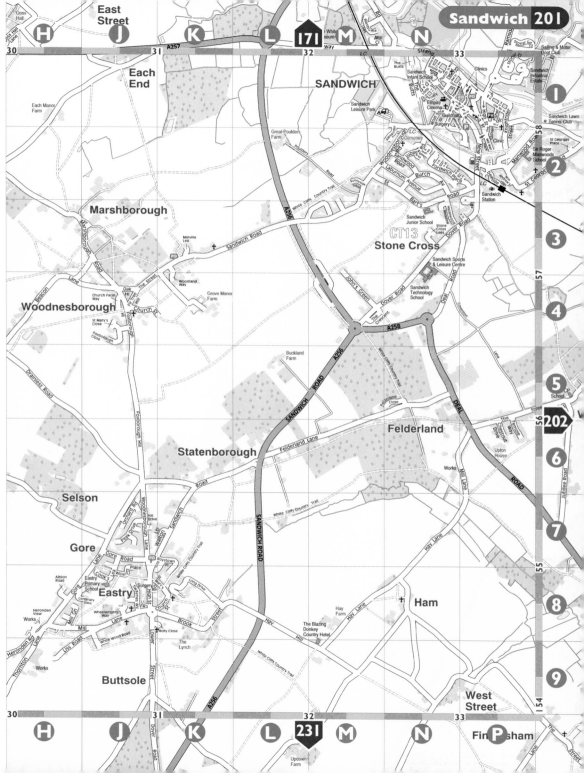

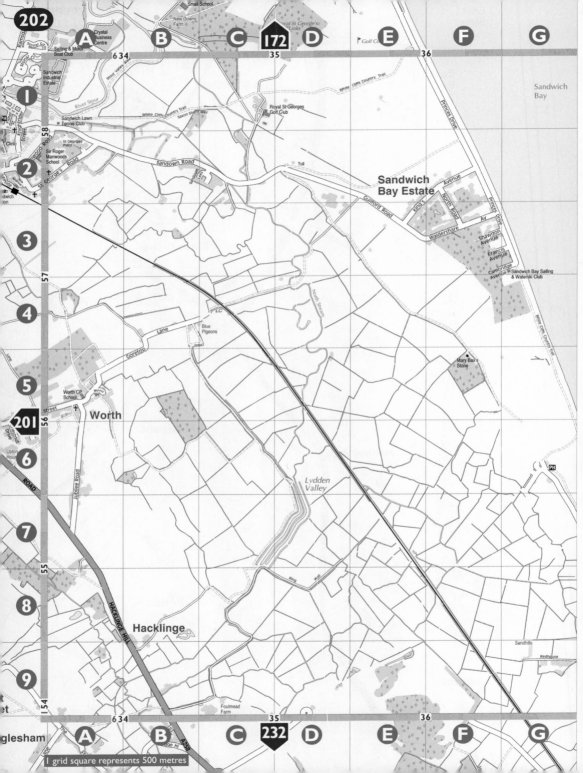

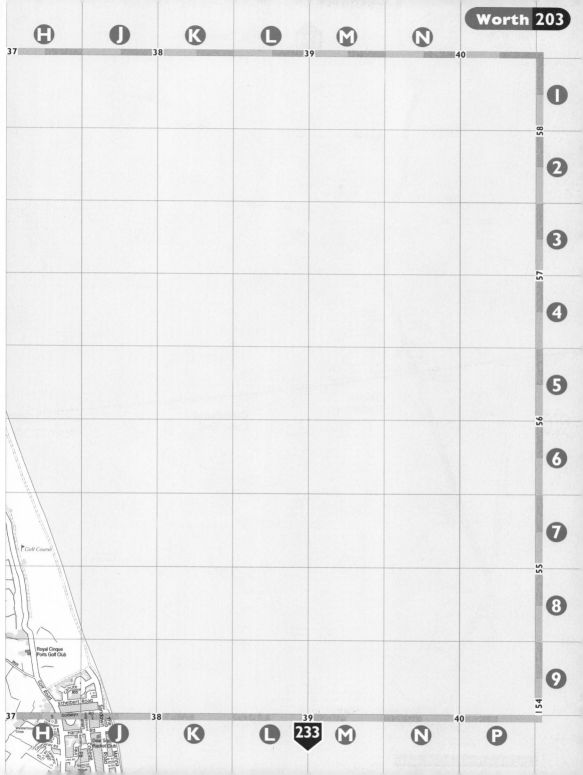

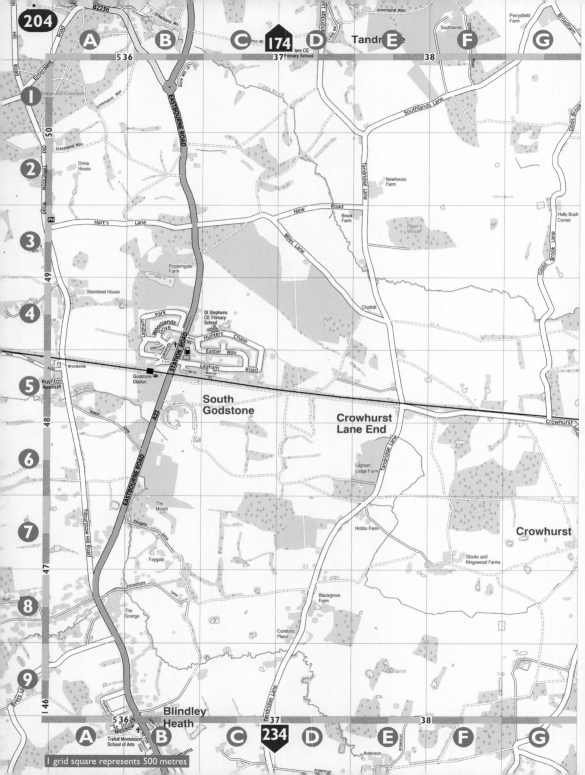

174

Tandridge

37 Primary School

234

Blindley Heath

1 grid square represents 500 metres

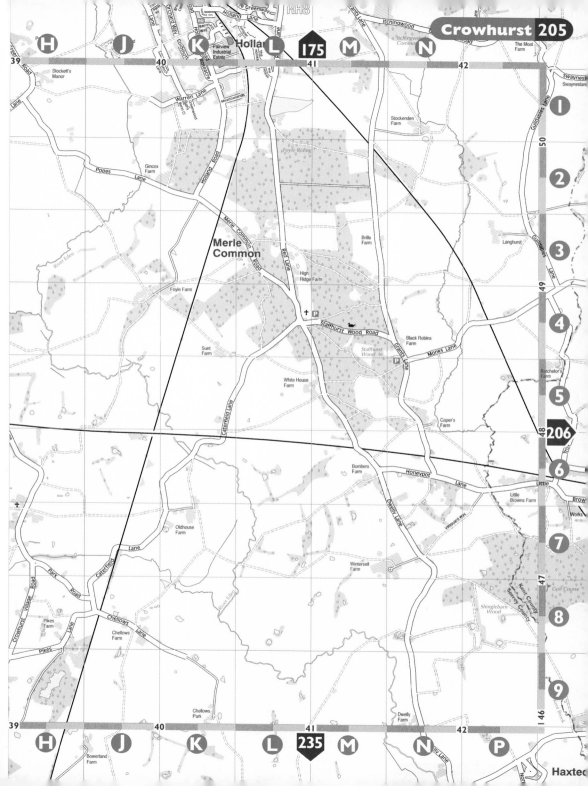

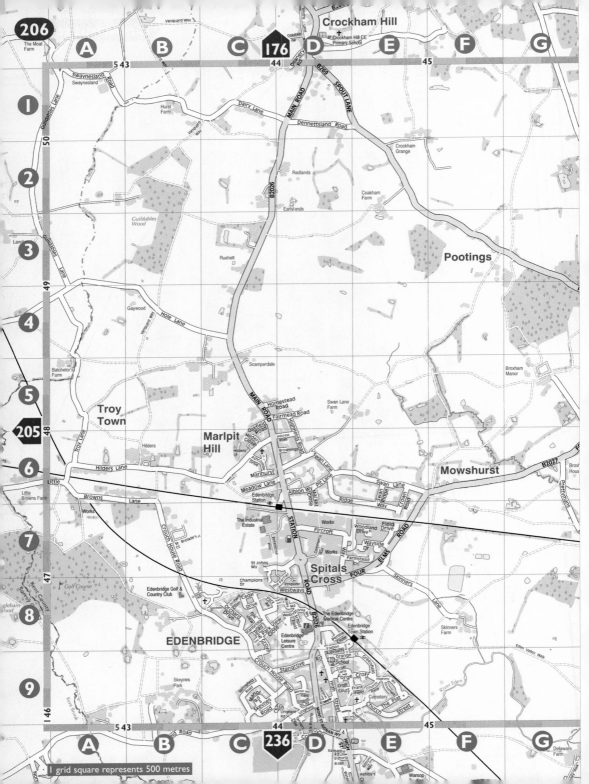

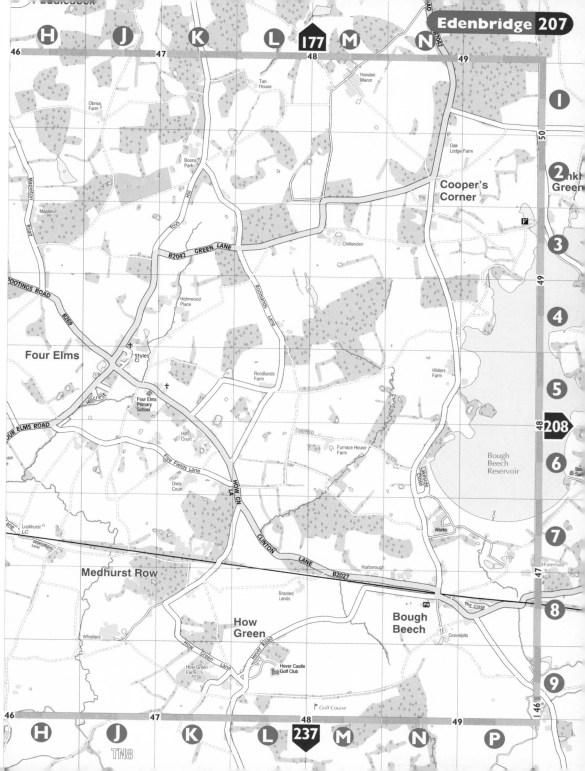

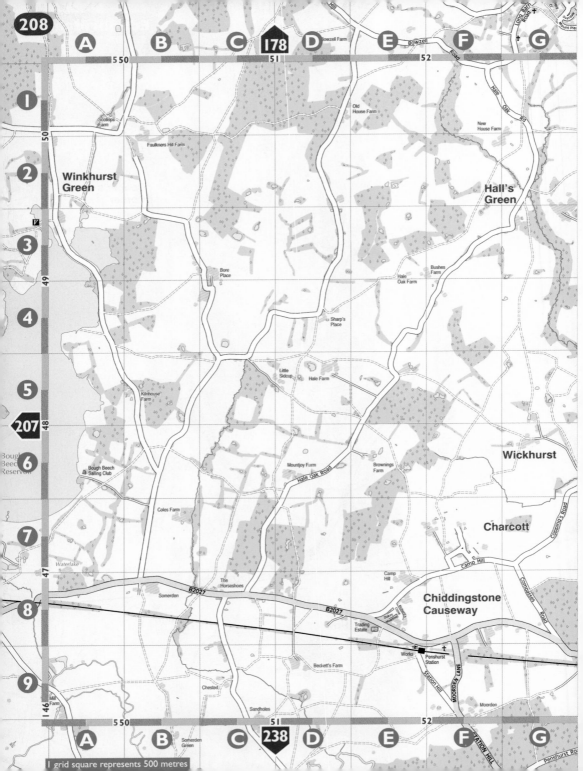

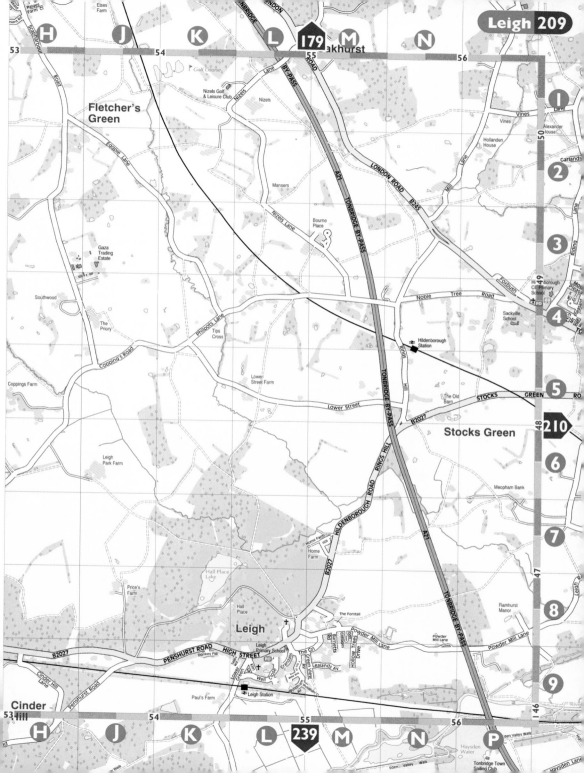

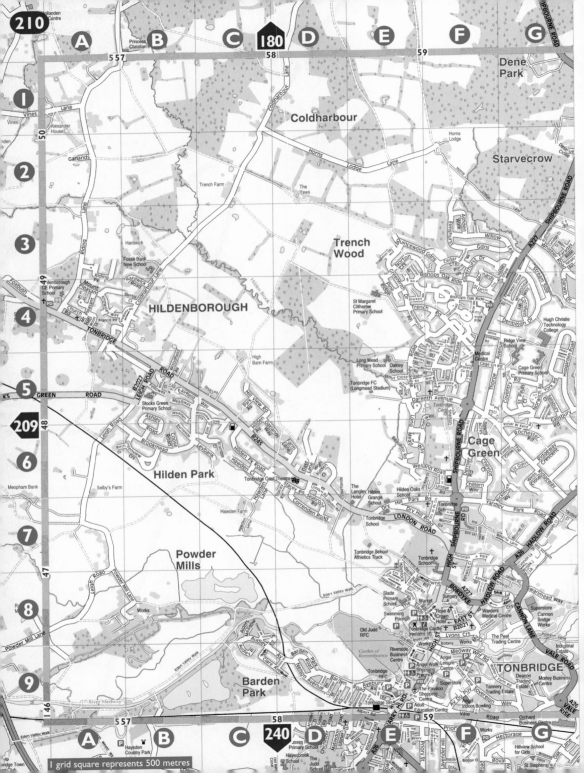

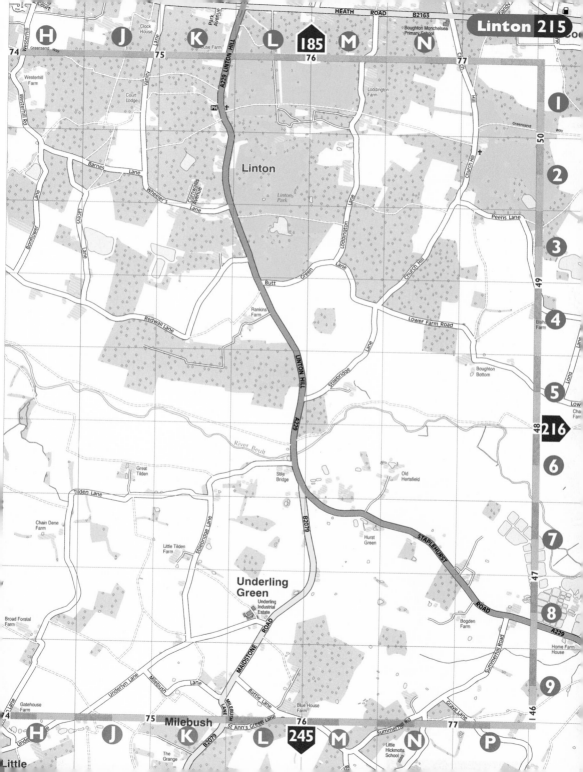

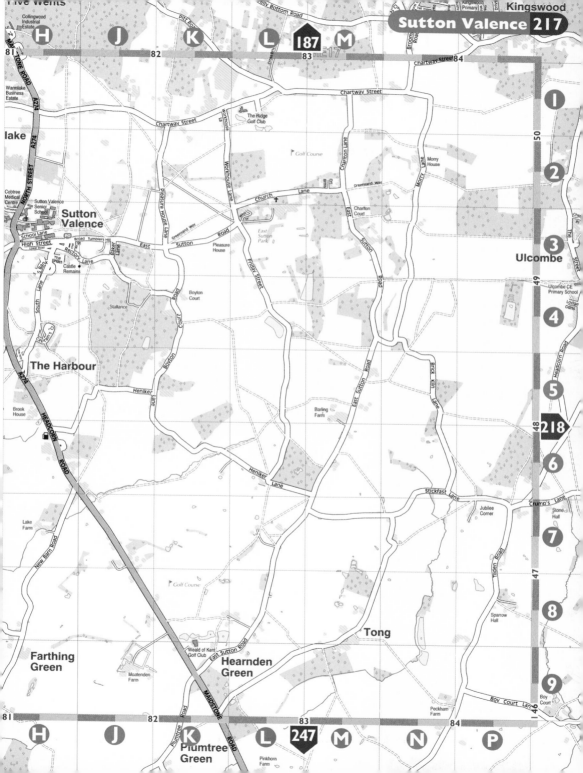

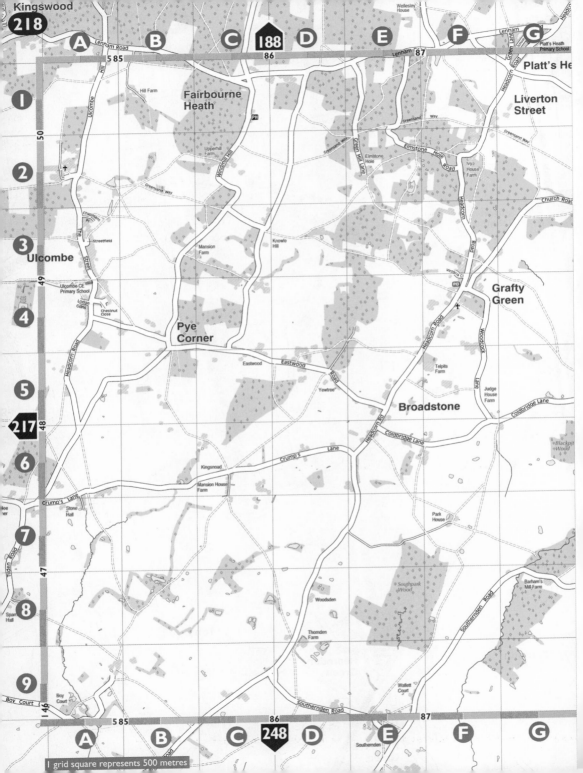

H J K L **191** M N

95 96 97 98

I

Stocker's Head

Charing Hill

Crows Hole Farm

CANTERBURY ROAD A252

2

Squids Gate Farm

50

FAVERSHAM ROAD

Bowl Road

CHARING HILL

The Wind

3

A252 NORTHERN BY-PASS

Sayer Road

Charing

Pilgrims

Way

49

Cem

Downs View

Charing CE Primary School

Surgery

School Road

High St

Drive

Pett Lane

Woodbrook

Works

4

Toll Lane

Burnham Road

MAIDSTONE ROAD A20

Pett Lane

Wicken Lane

Pett Place

Burnt House Farm

5

Westwell Lane

Kent County Crematorium

Wicken Lane

Lacton Manor

North Downs Way

48

222

A20

Summerlands Special School

Wootton Manor

Digges Court

6

Westwell Lane

MAIDSTONE ROAD

Westwell Lane

Westwell Lane

Leacon Farm

Westwell Leacon

Park House Farm

Cemetery

7

47

M20

M20

8

Westwell

Maidstone Rd

Ram Lane

Premier Inn

Nash Court

Chapel Road

Common Road

Tutt Hill

MAIDSTONE ROAD

9

146

Works

95 96 97 98

H J K **251** L M N P

Little Chart Forstal

Ram Lane

Hothfield Common

Greensand

Hothfield Bogs

Apple Court

Works

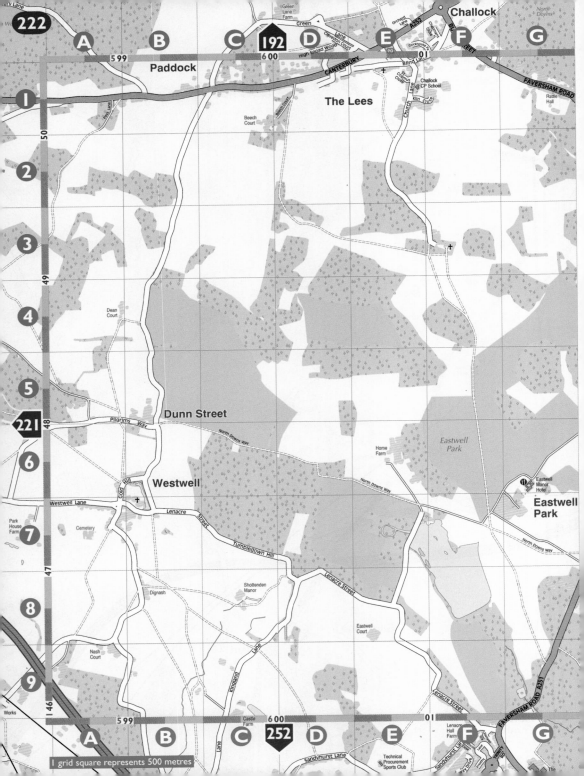

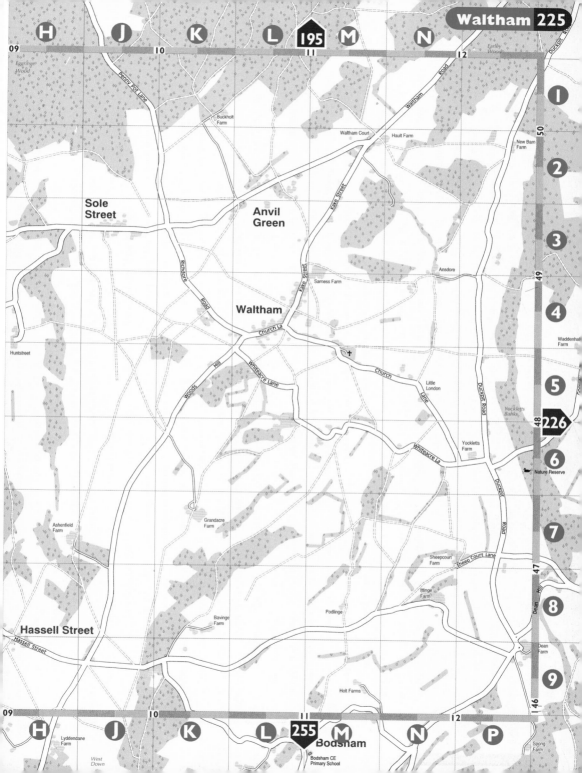

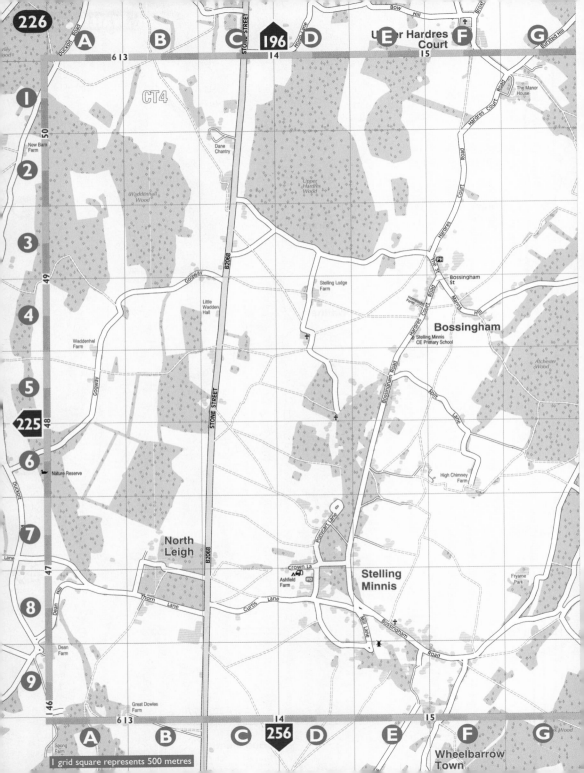

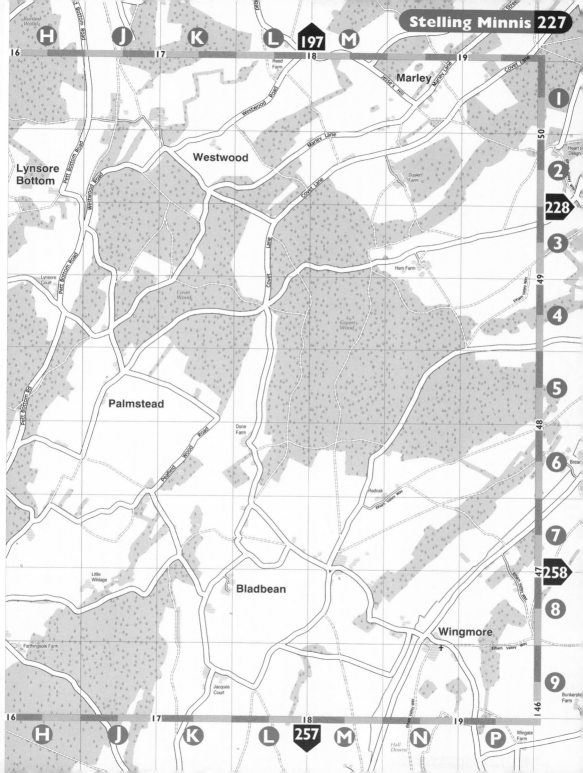

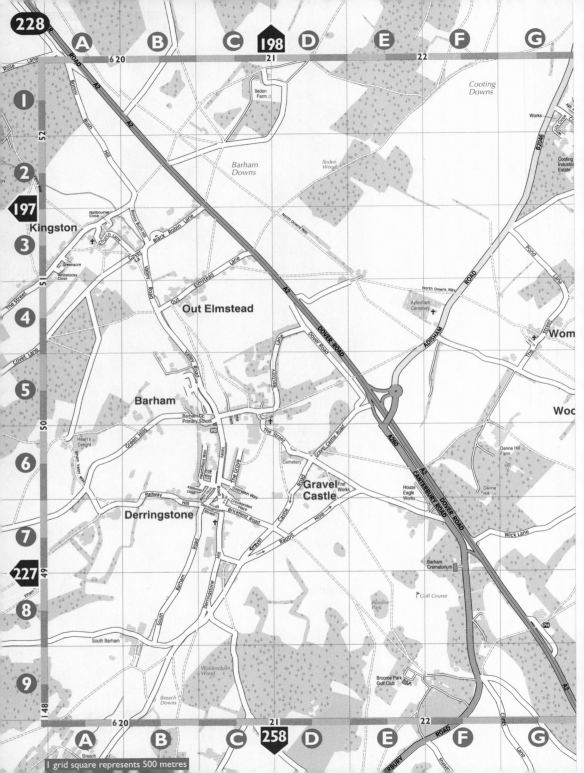

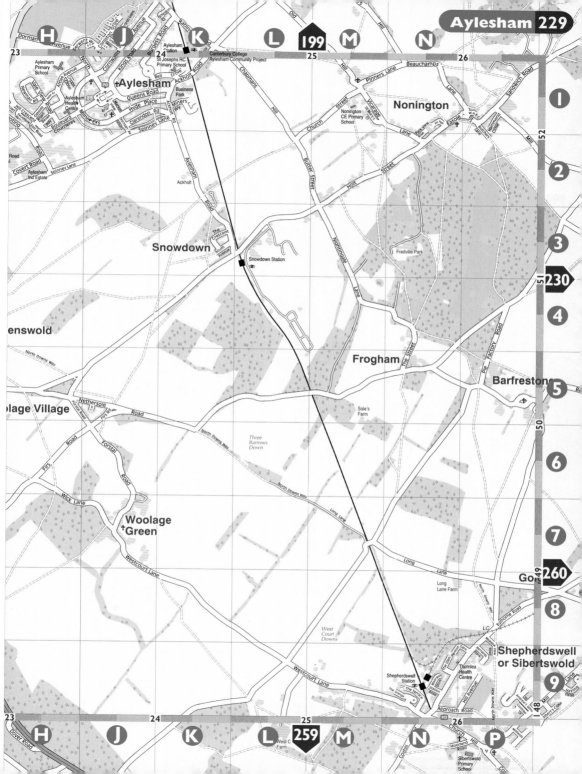

A   B   C   200   D   E   F   G

Heronden

1

Chillenden

Knowlton

2

199

Knowlton Park

3

Shingleton Farm

Thornton Lane

Venson Farm

4

Thornton Farm

Mill Lane

5

Kittington Farm

The Downs

School Road

Dane Court

6

Beeches Farm

Pike Road

7

229

Works

8

Barfrestone

Barfrestone Road

Works

Barville Road

Elmton Lane

Wigmore Lane

Elvington

9

Lower Eythorne

Barfrestone Road

Church Hill

Wigmore Lane

Eythorne Elvington Primary School

Sandwich Road

Green Lane

Cherry W'ks

A   B   C   260   D   E   F   G

1 grid square represents 500 metres

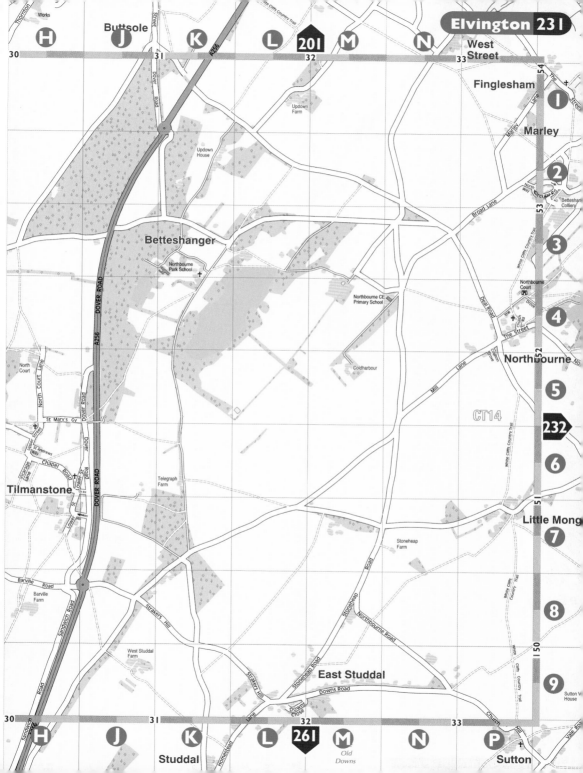

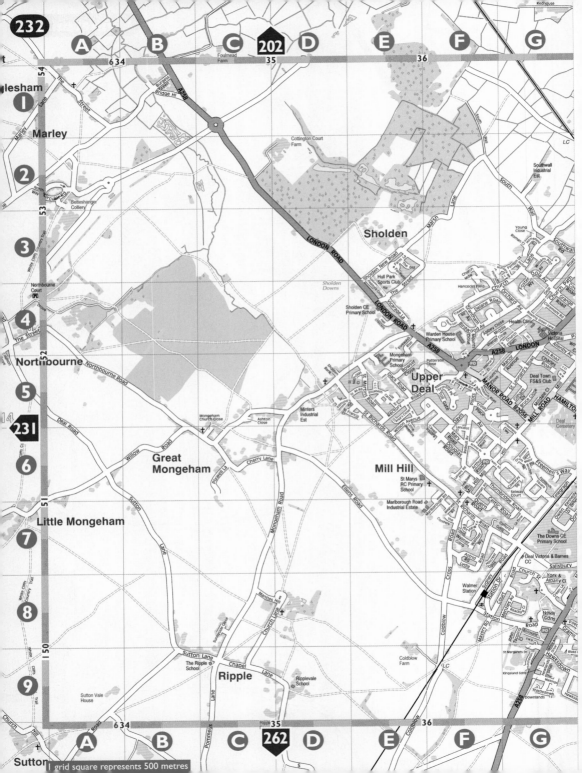

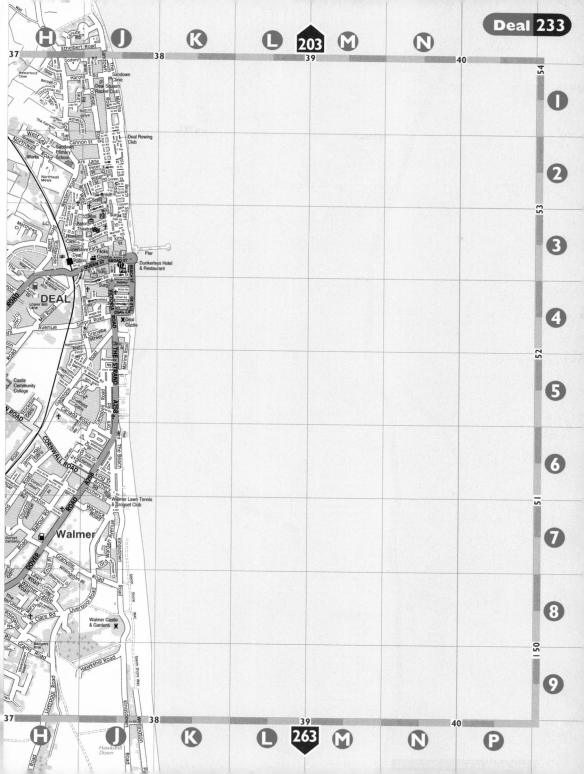

Deal 233

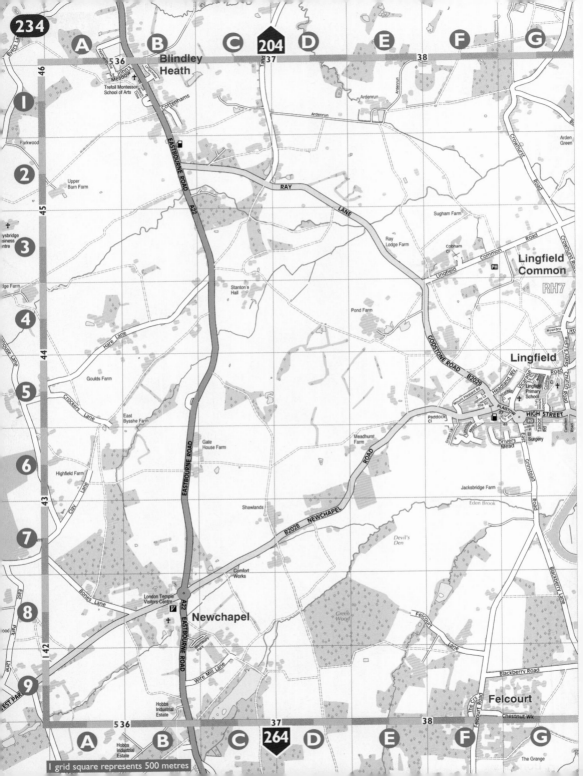

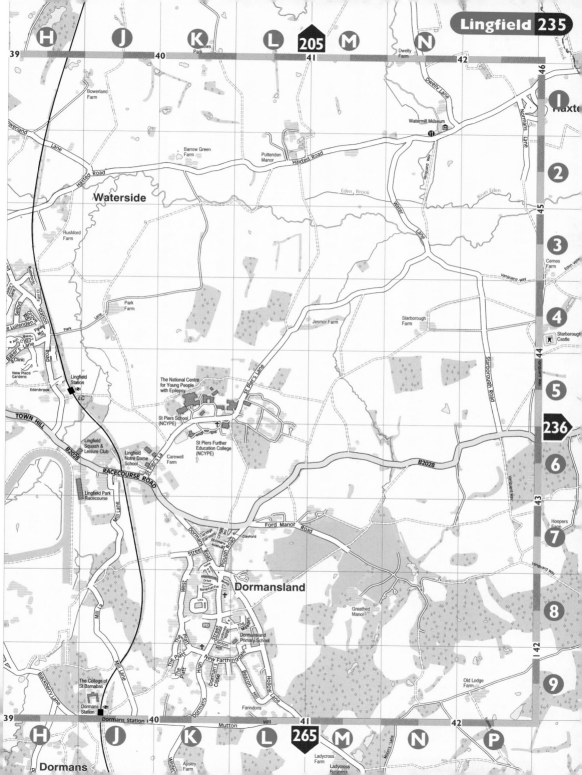

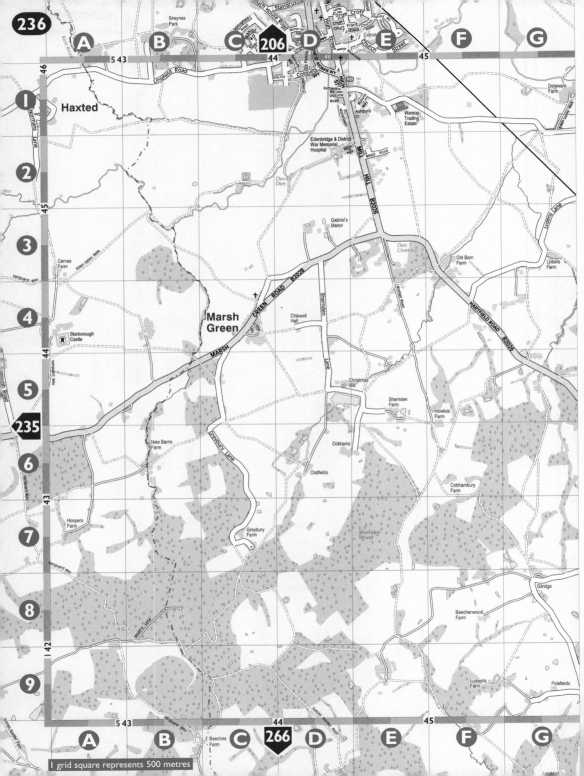

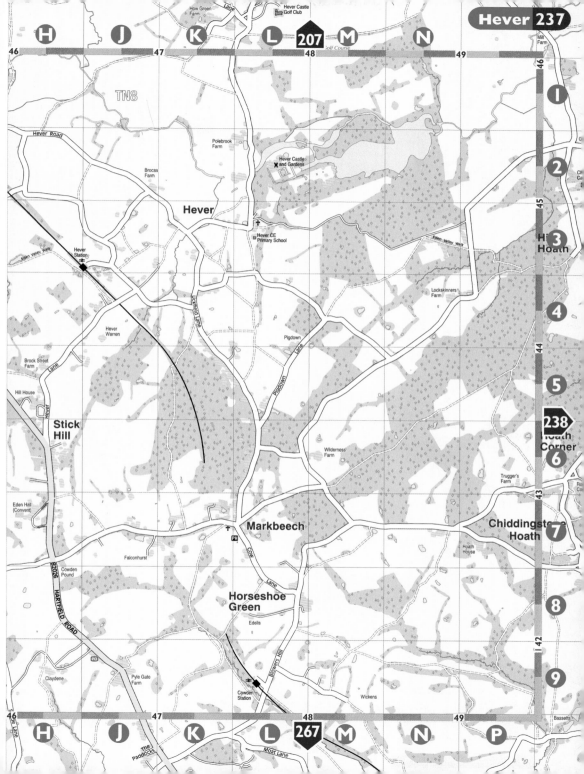

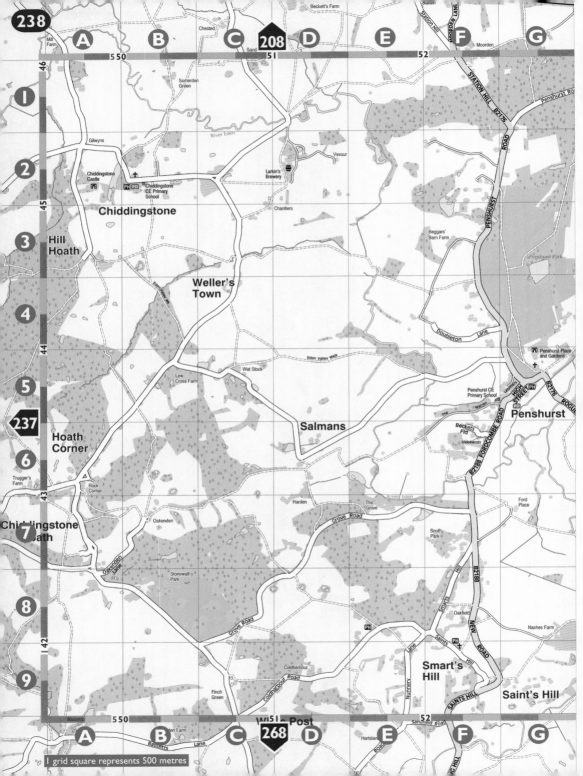

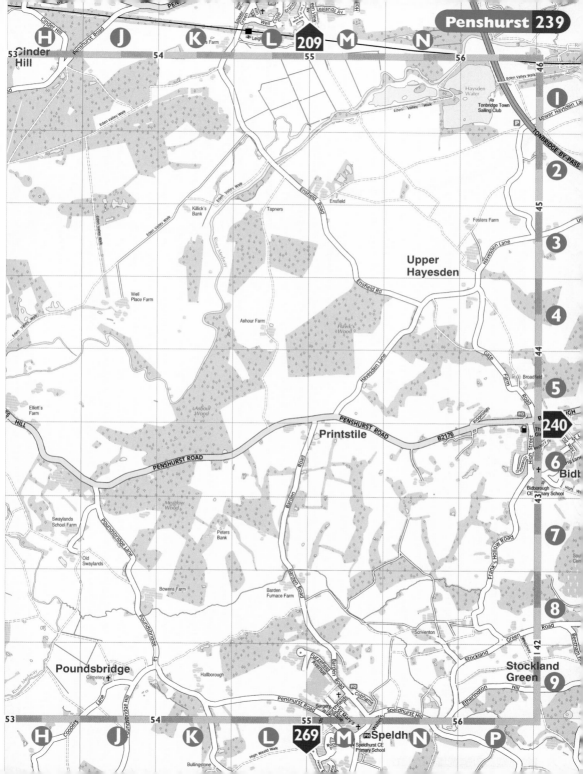

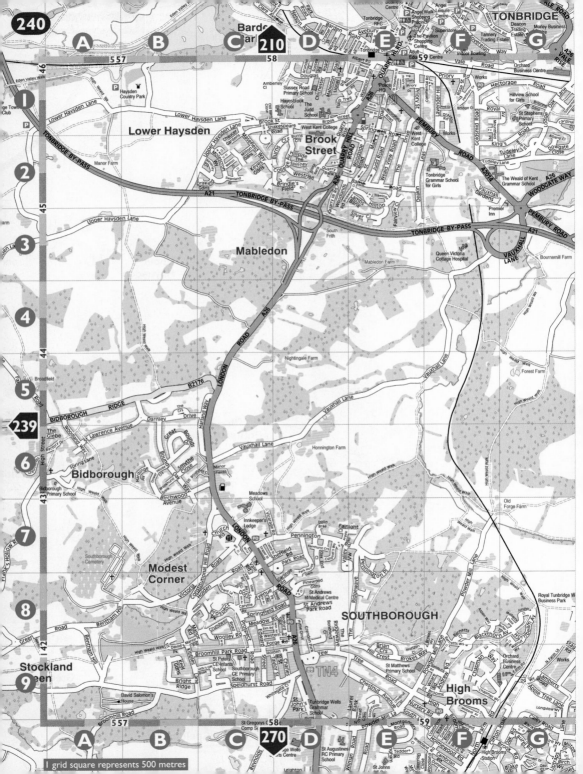

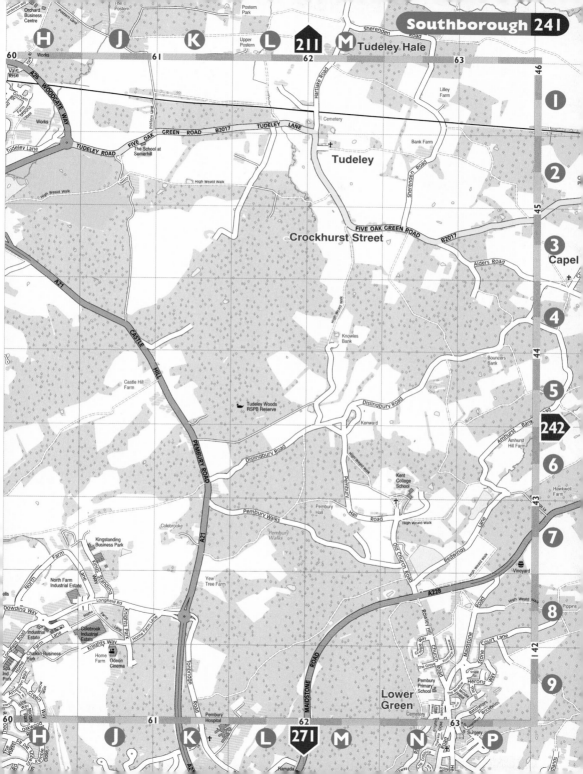

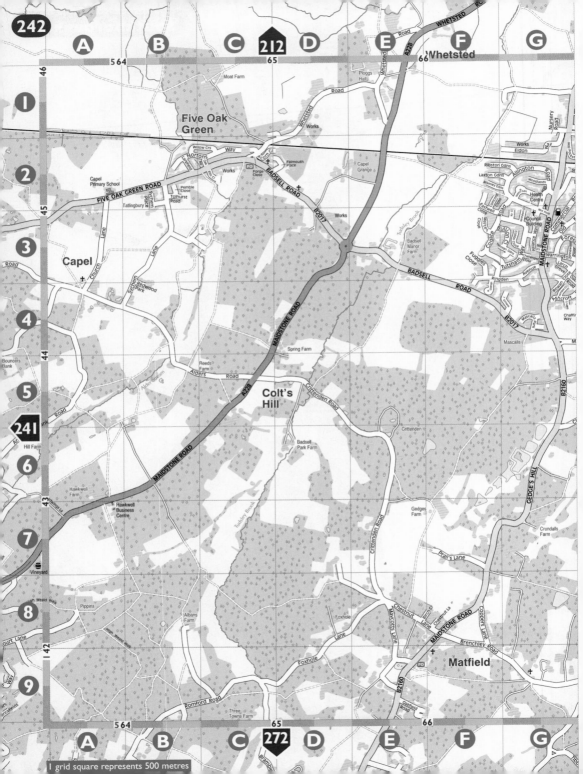

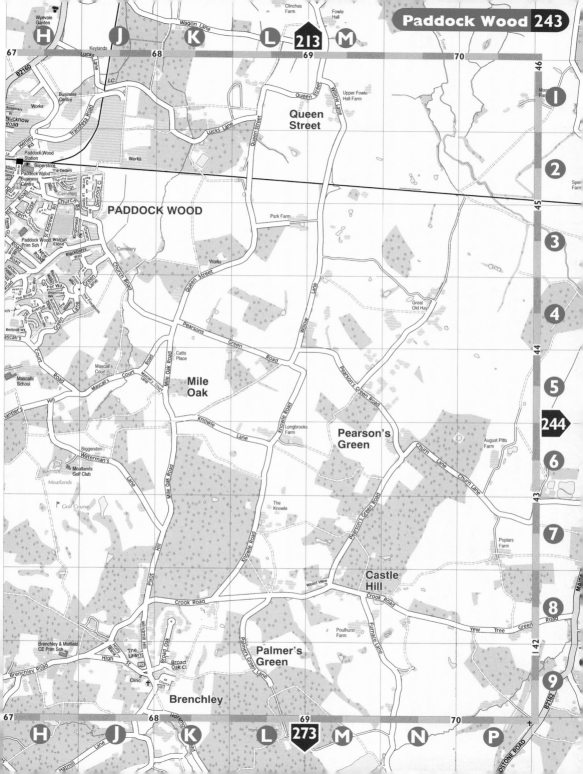

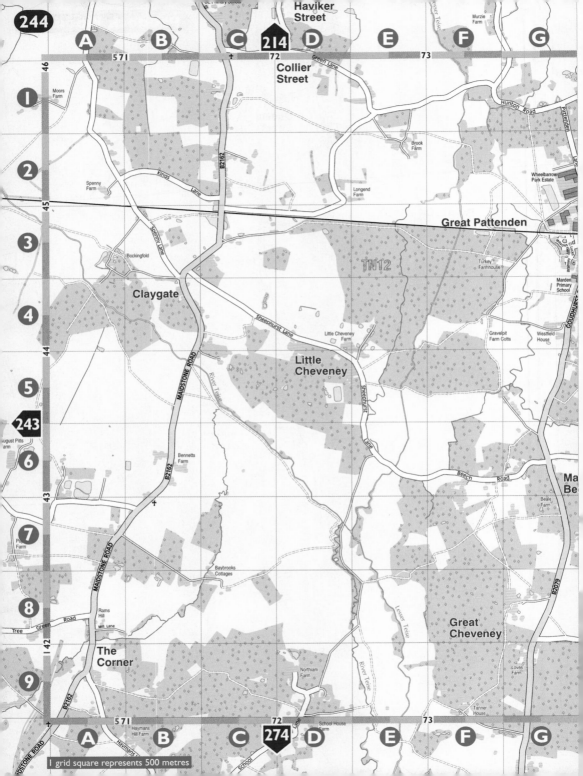

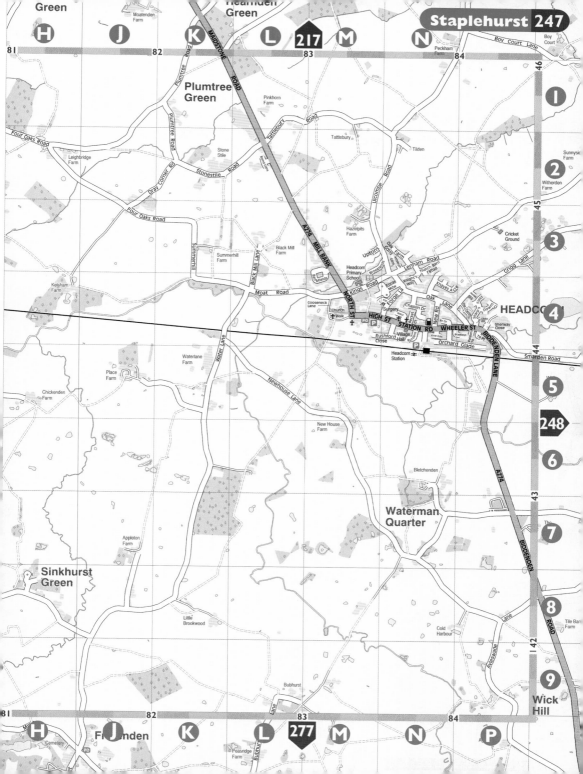

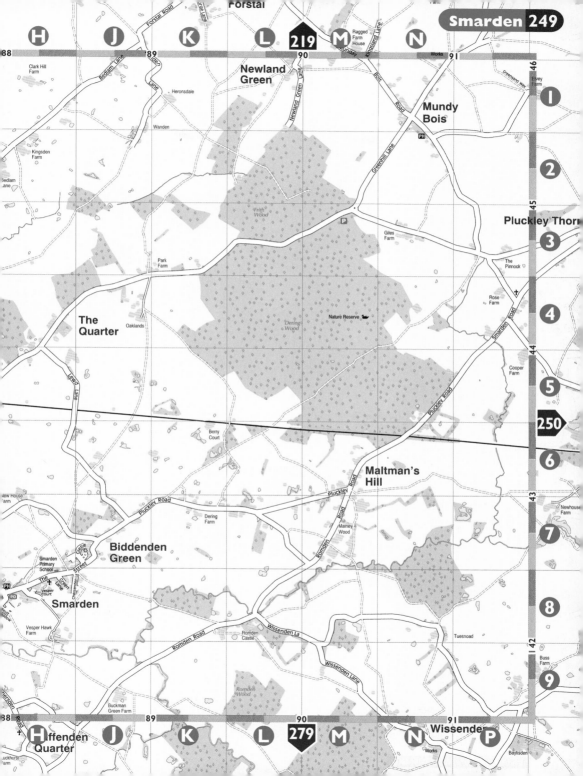

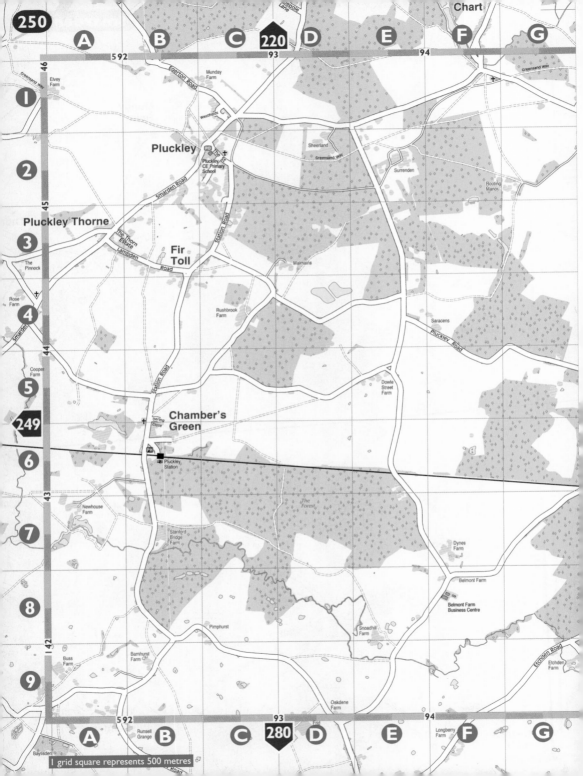

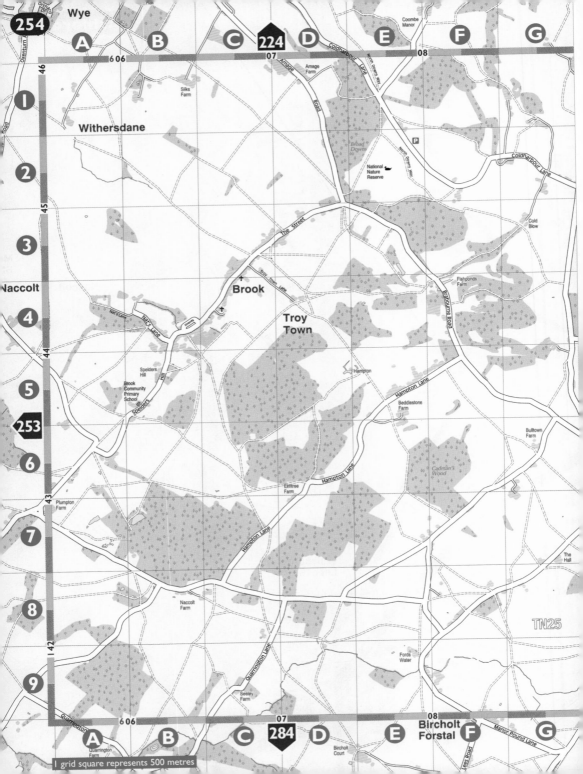

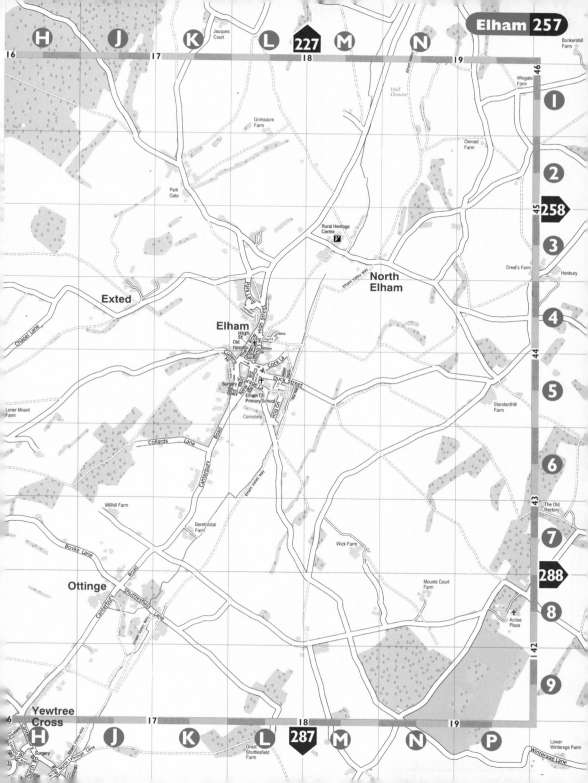

H J K L **227** M N

16 17 18 19

Jacques Court

Bunkershill Farm

Wingate Farm

I

46

Grimsacre Farm

Oxroad Farm

2

45 **258**

Park Gate

Rural Heritage Centre

3

Dreal's Farm

Henbury

Exted

Chapel Lane

Park La

The High Street

Elham

High St

Old Hospital

Clonei

Hidden

Gardens

North Elham

Elham Valley Way

Hall Bourne

4

44

Cock La.

Duck Street

5

Standardhill Farm

Loner Mount Farm

Cullens Hill

Surgery

Vicarage La

New Rd

Elham CE Primary School

Cemetery

Old Rd

Hog La

Elham Valley Way

6

43 The Old Rectory

Collards Lane

Canterbury Lane

Millhill Farm

Bereforstal Farm

Wick Farm

7

288

Boyke Lane

Canterbury Road

Mounts Court Farm

Acrise Place

8

42

Ottinge

Shuttlesfield Lane

Elham Valley Way

9

Yewtree Cross

Surgery

H J K L **287** M P

6 17 18 19

Great Shuttlesfield Farm

North Lyminge Lane

Lower Winterage Farm

Winterage Lane

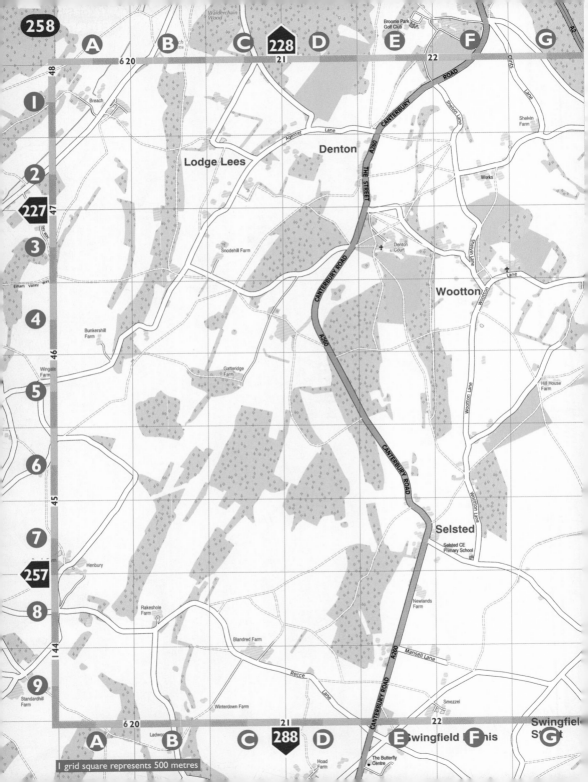

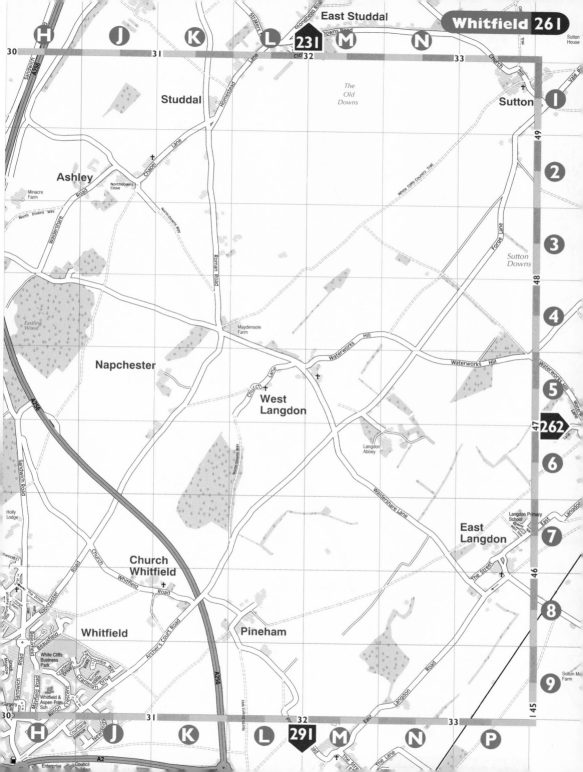

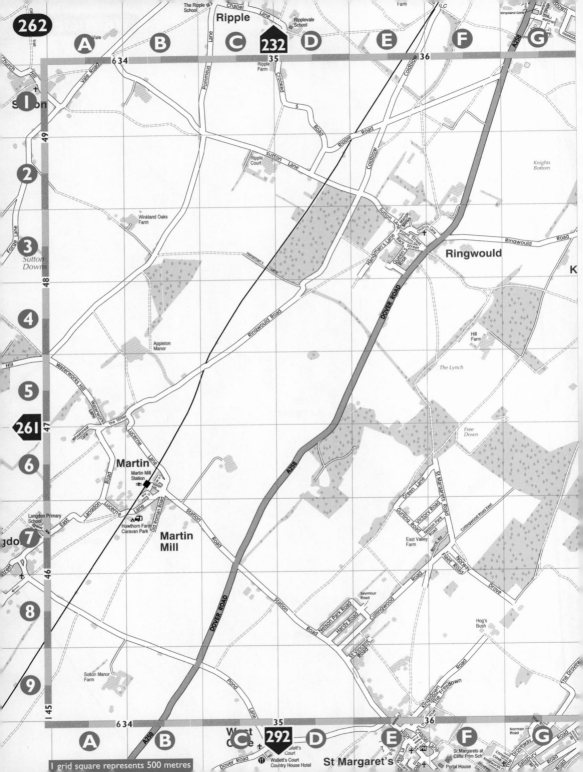

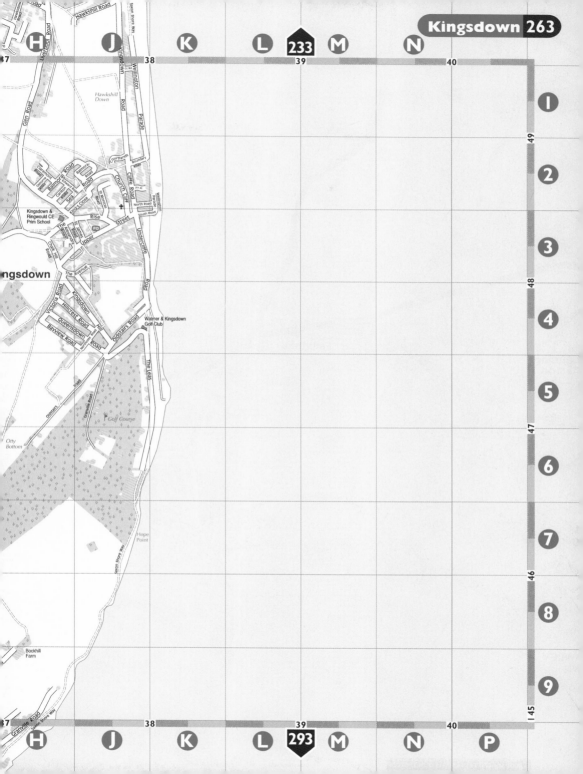

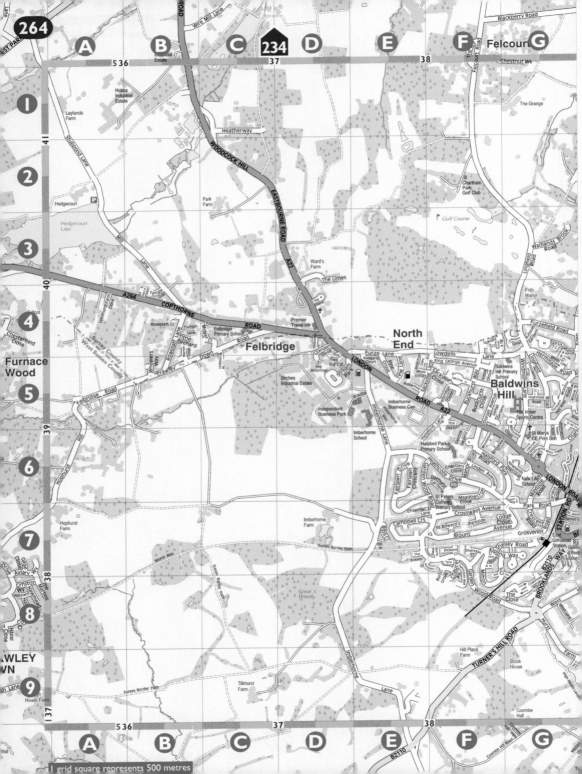

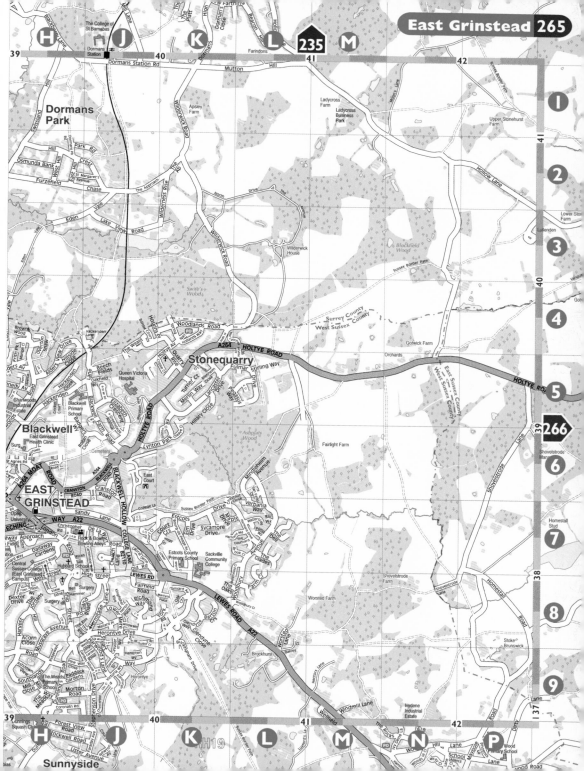

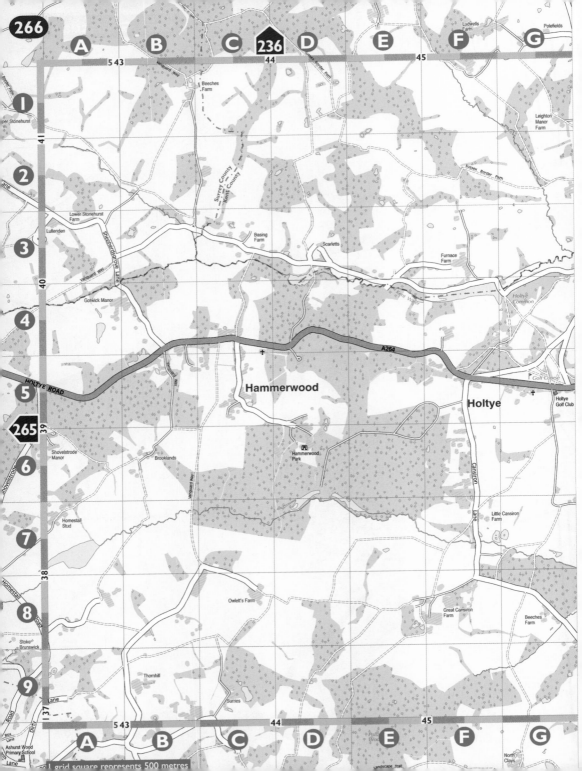

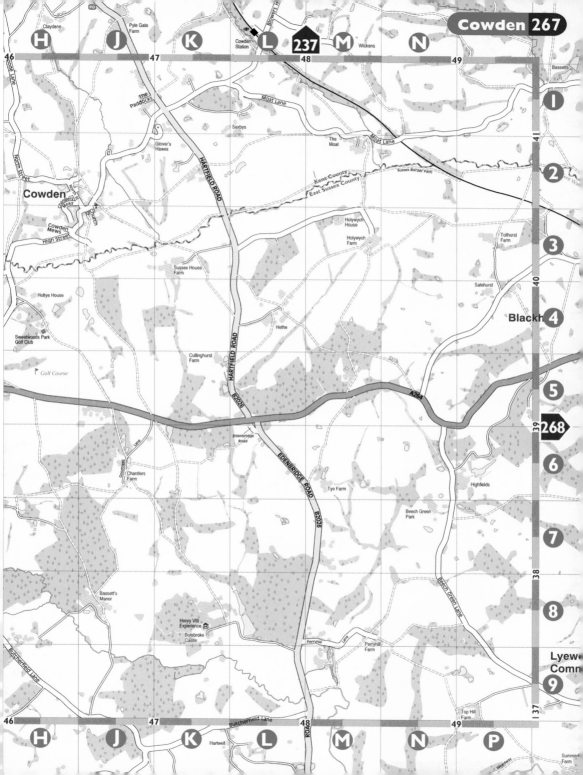

H J K L 237 M N

46 47 48 49

Bassetts

1

41

2

Kent Wal

3

40

Blackh 4

5

268

6

7

38

8

Lyewe
Comm

9

137

46 47 48 49

H J K L M N P

Claydene
Pyle Gate
Farm

Blowers H

Cowden
Station

Wickens

The Paddocks

Moat Lane

Saxbys

Moat Lane

The
Moat

Glover's
Hawes

Sussex Border Path

Kent County
East Sussex County

Cowden

North Street

Cowden Mead

Church

Holywych
House

Cowden
Mews

Holywych
Farm

High Street

Tollhurst
Farm

Sussex House
Farm

Salehurst

Holtye House

Hothe

HARTFIELD ROAD

Sweetwoods Park
Golf Club

Cullinghurst
Farm

A264

Golf Course

B2026

Edenbridge
Road

Chantlers
Farm

Coombers
Lane

EDENBRIDGE ROAD

Highfields

Tye Farm

Beech Green
Park

B2026

Bassett's
Manor

Beech Green Lane

Henry VIII
Experience

Bolebroke
Castle

Perryview

Lane

Perryhill
Farm

Butchersfield Lane

ROAD

Top Hill
Farm

Summer

Butchersfield Lane

Hartwell

Waterway

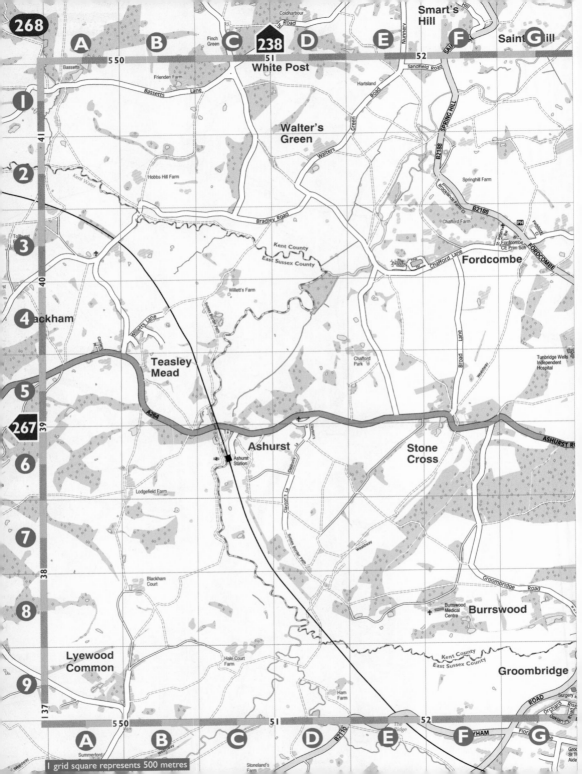

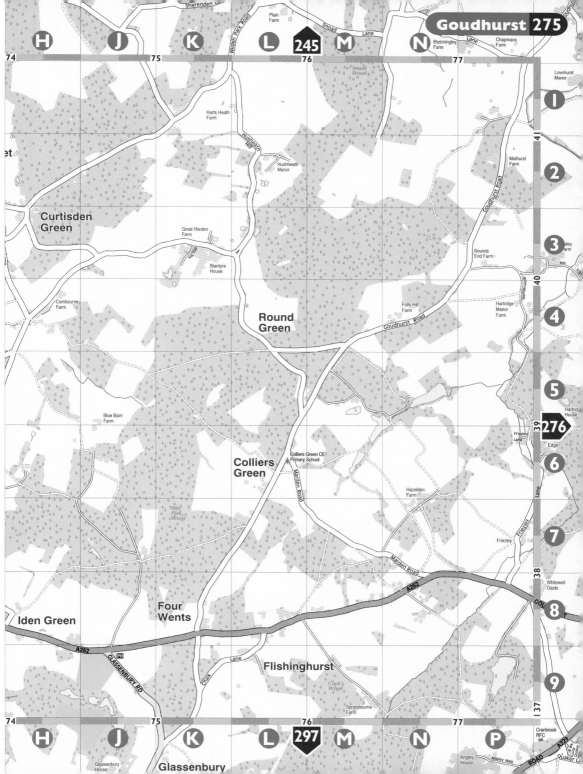

H J K L **245** M N

74 75 76 77

I

Lovehurst Manor

Plain Farm

Snoad Lane

Bletchingley Farm

Chapmans Farm

Snoad Wood

Wilden Park Road

Harts Heath Farm

Hushheath Hill

Hushheath Manor

Mathurst Farm

2

41

3

...sley Farm

Hill

Curtisden Green

Great Horden Farm

Blantyre House

Combourne Farm

Round Green

Bounds End Farm

Folly Hill Farm

Hartridge Manor Farm

Goudhurst Road

4

40

5

Blue Barn Farm

Friezley Lane

Hartridge House

39

276

Edge

6

Colliers Green CE Primary School

Colliers Green

Marden Road

Hazelden Farm

Old Park Wood

Friezley

Friezley

Lane

7

38

Iden Green

Four Wents

A262

Marden Road

Whitewell Oasts

GOU...T

8

A262

Glassenbury Rd

PH

Chalk Lane

Flishinghurst

Cook's Wood

Spratsbourne Farm

9

37

H J K L **297** M N P

74 75 76 77

Glassenbury House

Glassenbury

Angley House

Angley Walk

Cranbrook RFC

ROAD

A229

Quaker L...

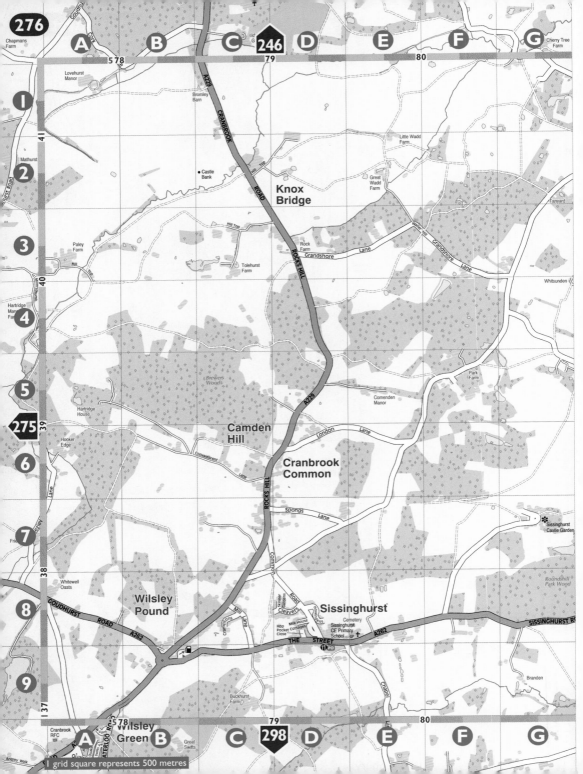

A B C 246 D E F G

5 7 8   7 9   8 0

41

I

Lovehurst
Manor

Chapmans
Farm

Bromley
Barn

2

Mathurst

Castle
Bank

CRANBROOK ROAD A229

Knox
Bridge

Little Wadd
Farm

Great
Wadd
Farm

Tanyard

3

Paley
Farm

Hill Top

Hill Top

Rock
Farm
Grandshore

Grandshore Lane

Grandshore Lane

Whitsunden

Tolehurst
Farm

40

Hartridge
Manor
Farm

4

ROCKS HILL

Park
Farm

5

Brewers
Woods

A229

Comenden
Manor

Hartridge
House

39

Camden
Hill

London   Lane

Hooker
Edge

6

Convalescent Lane

Cranbrook
Common

ROCKS HILL

Spongs   Lane

Lane

Sissinghurst
Castle Garden

7

Friezley Lane

Common Road

Roundshill
Park Wood

38

Whitewell
Oasts

Wilsley
Pound

Mill Lane

Cleavers

Hop
Pocket Cottages
Close

Sissinghurst

Cemetery
Sissinghurst
CE Primary
School

SISSINGHURST RD

8

GOUDHURST ROAD A262

Milk House

THE STREET

A262

9

WATERLOO RD

Buckhurst
Farm

Chapel

Branden

1 3 7

A 578 Wilsley B 298 C D E F G
Cranbrook   Green
RFC

Angley Walk

7 9   8 0

1 grid square represents 500 metres

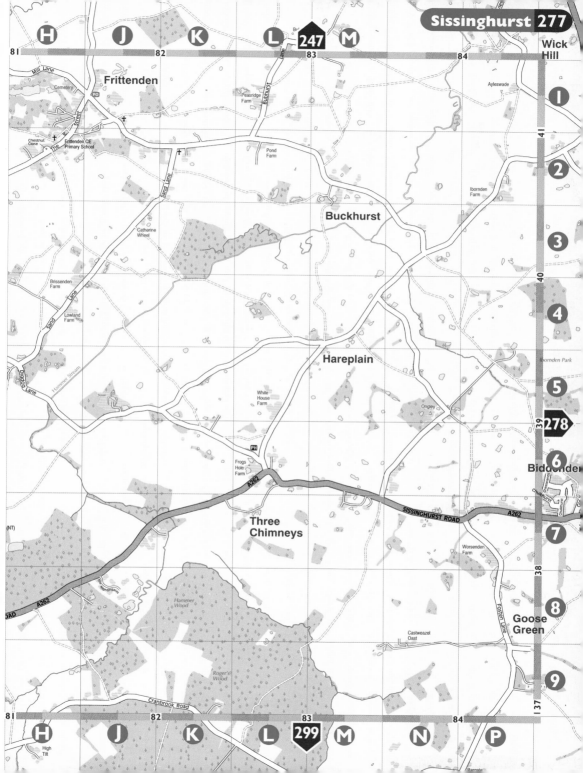

Wick Hill

Frittenden

Mill Lane

Cemetery

PO

Chestnut Close

The Street

Frittenden CE Primary School

Sand Lane

Peasridge Farm

Buckhurst Lane

Pond Farm

Ayleswade

Ibornden Farm

Buckhurst

Catherine Wheel

Brissenden Farm

Sand Lane

Lowland Farm

Hummer Stream

Diggood Lane

Sand Lane

Hareplain

White House Farm

Ibornden Park

Ongley

278

Biddenden

Frogs Hole Farm

PH

A262

Churn Lane

SISSINGHURST ROAD

A262

Three Chimneys

Nightingale

Hammer Wood

Worsenden Farm

Foster Lane

Goose Green

(NT)

A262

ROAD

Castweazel Oast

Roger's Wood

Cranbrook Road

High Tilt

299

Barnate

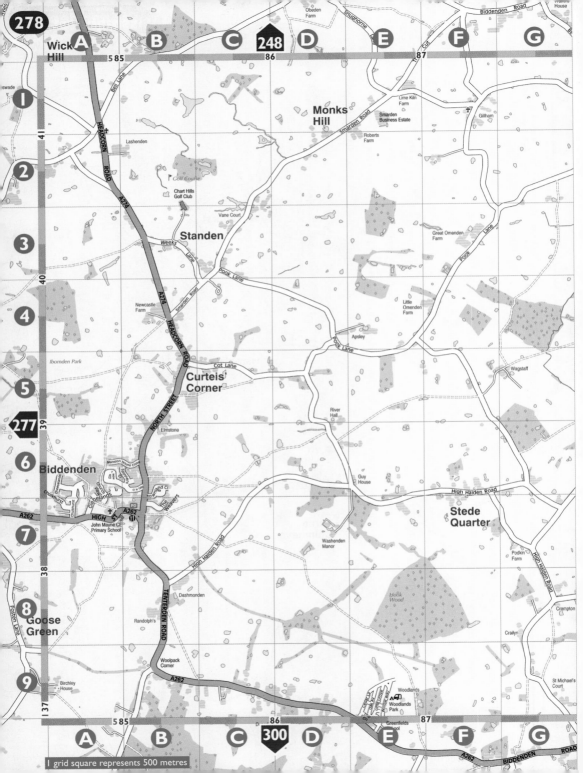

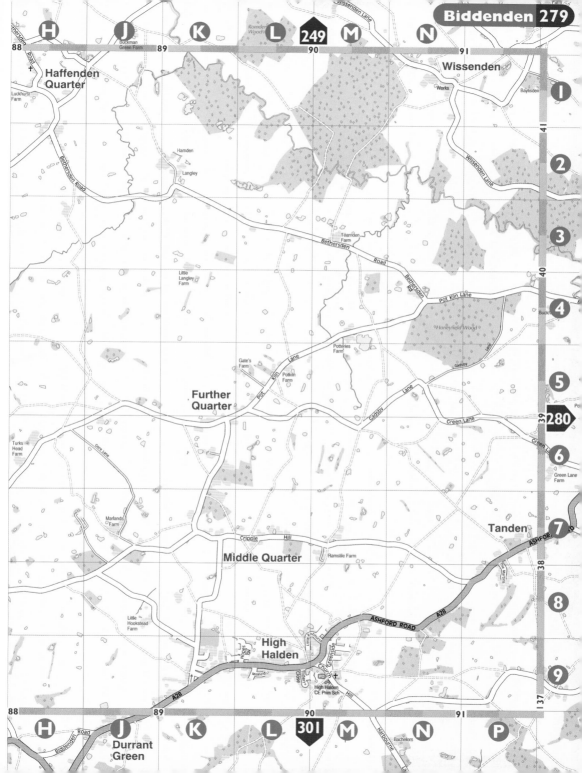

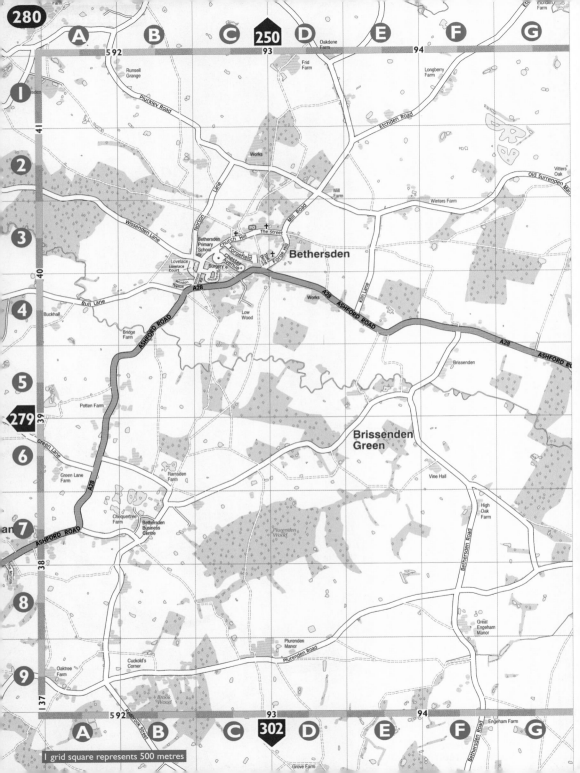

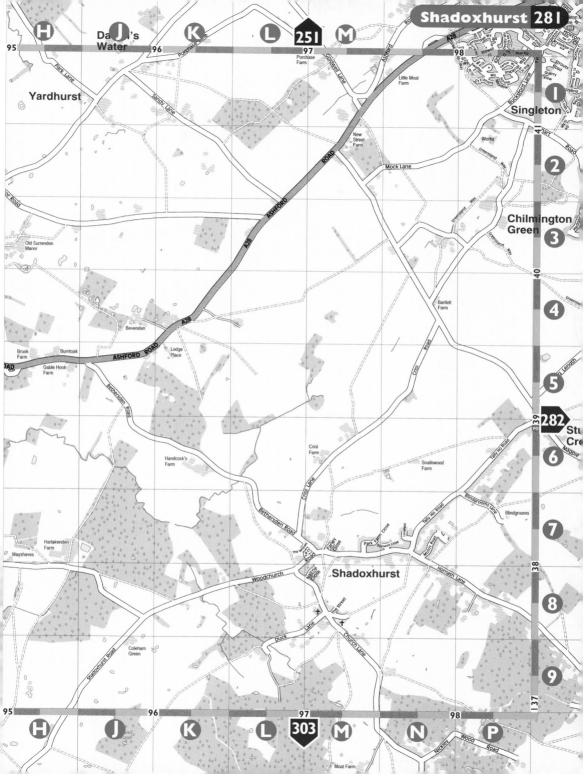

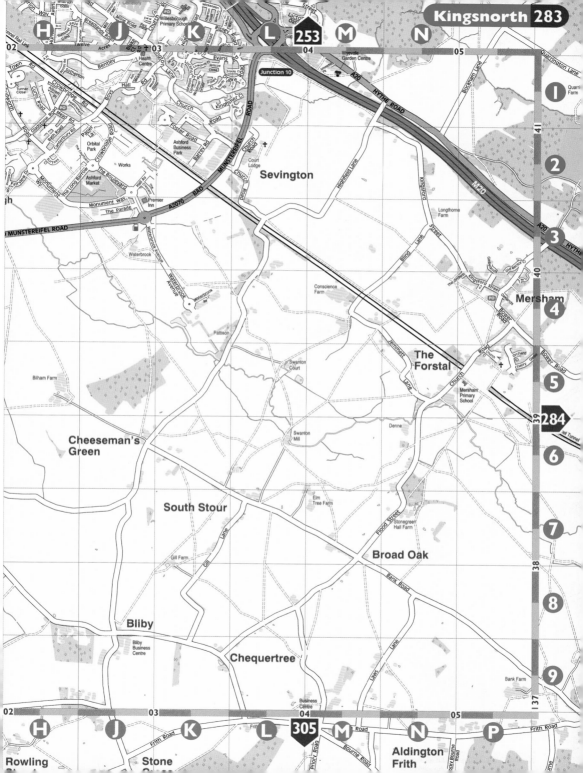

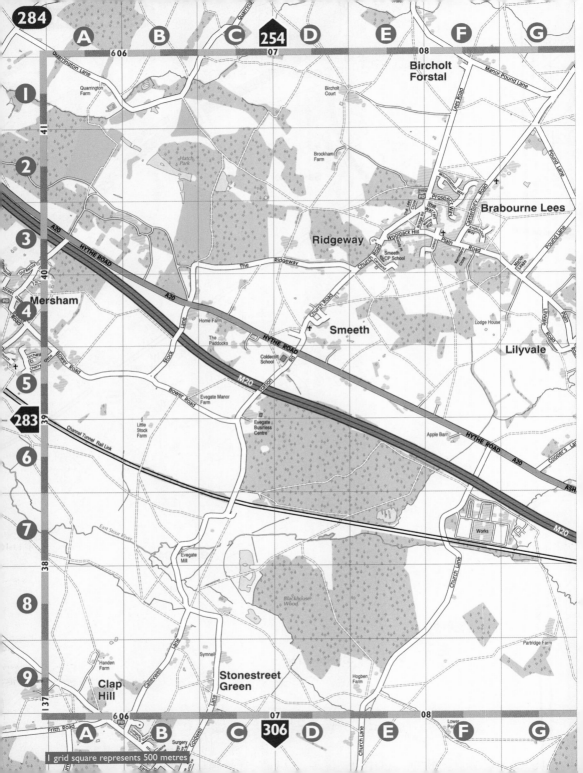

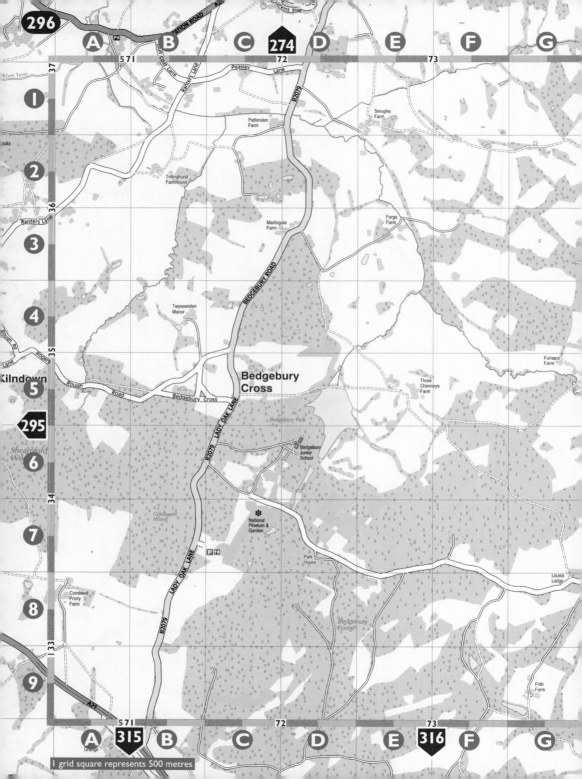

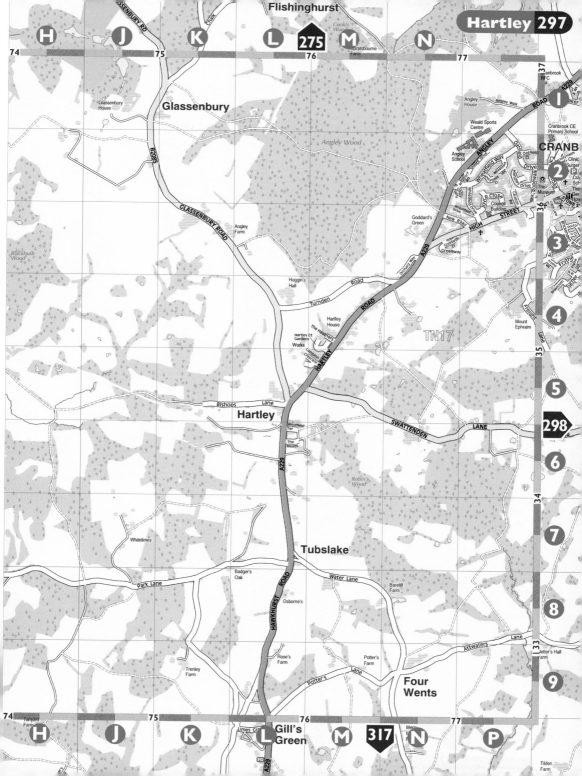

Flishinghurst

H J K L **275** M N

74 75 76 77

Glassenbury House

Glassenbury

Angley Wood

GLASSENBURY ROAD

B2085

Angley Farm

Huggin's Hall

Blackbush Wood

Turnden

Hartley House

HARTLEY ROAD

Hartley Ct Gardens Works

The Heathers

TN17

Bishops Lane

Hartley

Westfield Ter

The Meads

A229

SWATTENDEN LANE

Robin's Wood

298

Whitelimes

Tubslake

Park Lane

Badger's Oak

Water Lane

Barehill Farm

HAWKHURST ROAD

Osborne's

Attwaters Lane

Jetter's Hall Farm

Rose's Farm

Trenley Farm

Potter's Farm

Potter's Lane

Four Wents

Tolhurst Farm

74 75 76 77

H J K L M **317** N P

Gill's Green

Limes Gr

A229

Tilden Farm

Cranbrook RFC

A229

ROAD

ANGLEY

Angley House

Angley Walk

Weald Sports Centre

Cranbrook CE Primary School

Angley School

Wheatfield Way

Oatfield Cl

Oatfield Drive

Rodwell

Clinic Surger

Cra Sch

CRANB

2

Crane Hotel

The Museum

STONE ST

HIGH STREET

Council Building

New Road

Goddard's Green

Gossams Greenway

Orchard Way

A229

3

Glebe

Mount Ephraim

4

Freight Lane

5

6

34

7

8

33

9

37

36

35

I

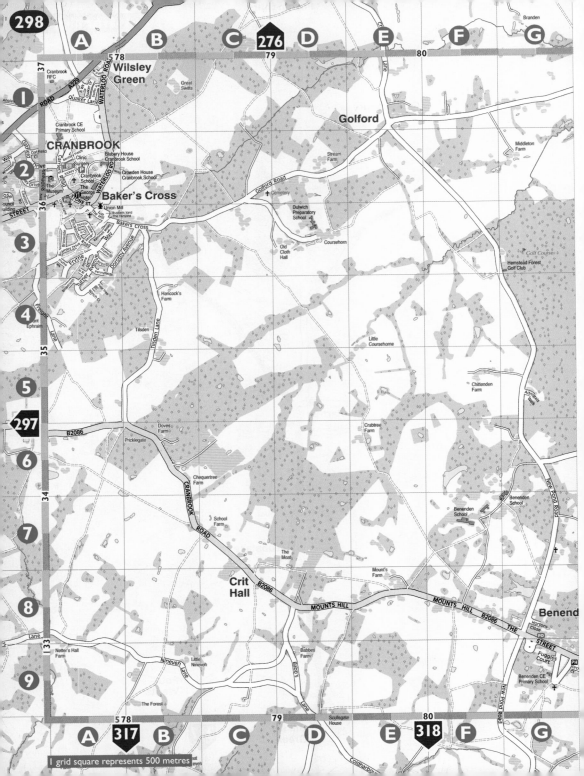

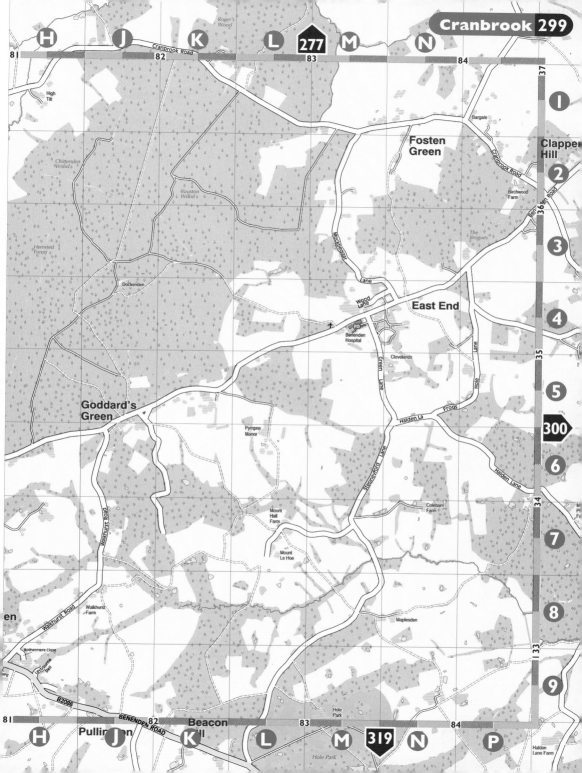

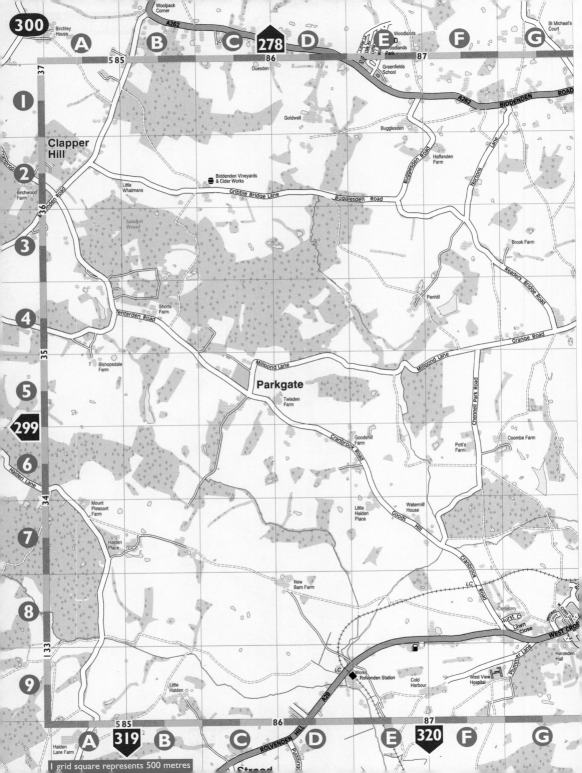

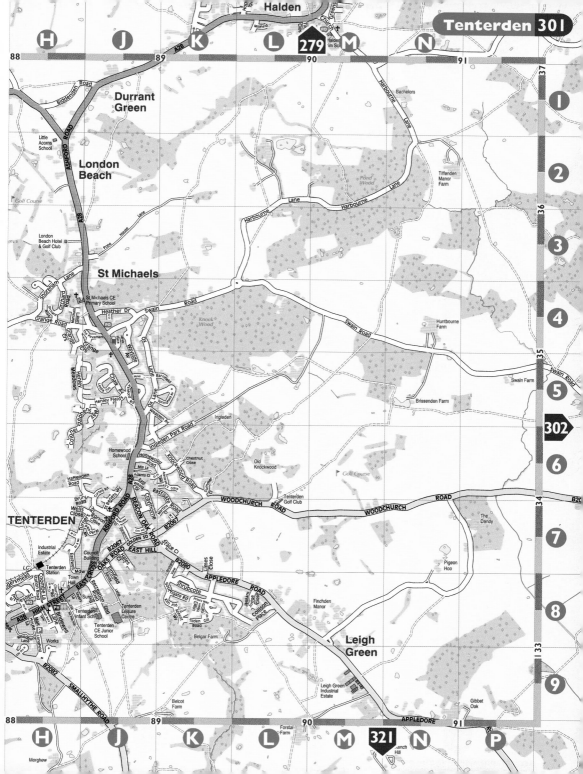

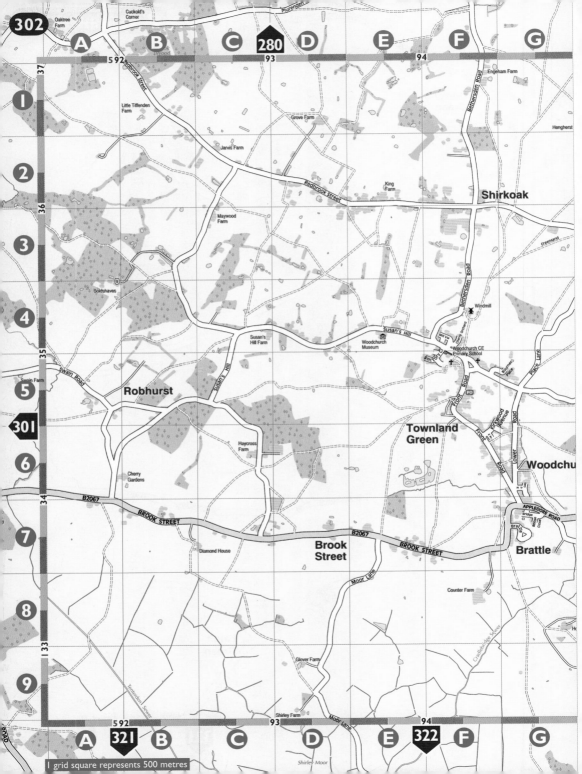

I grid square represents 500 metres

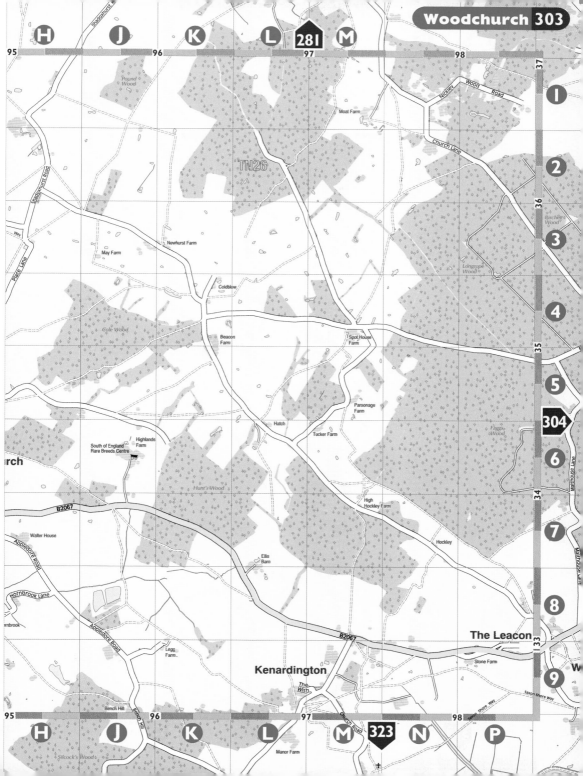

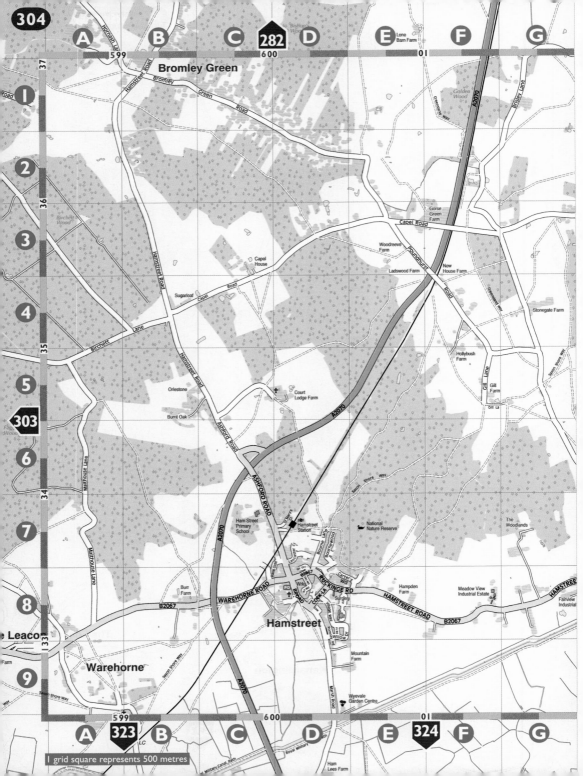

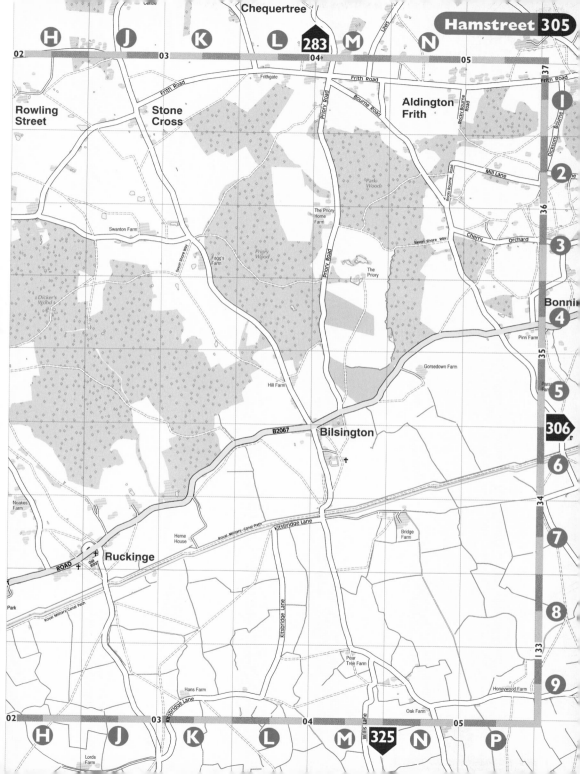

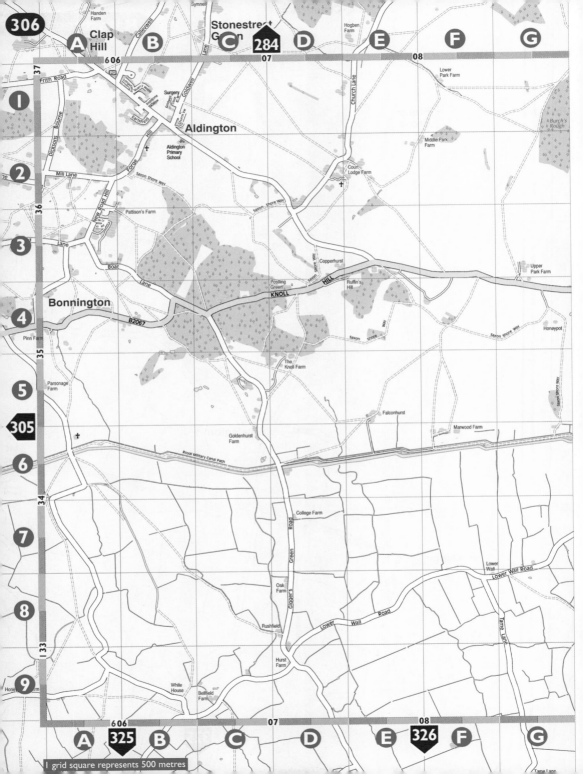

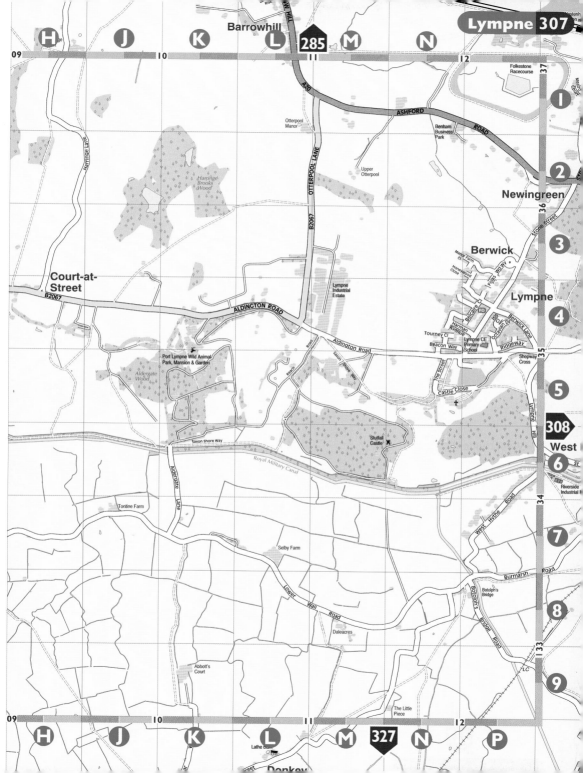

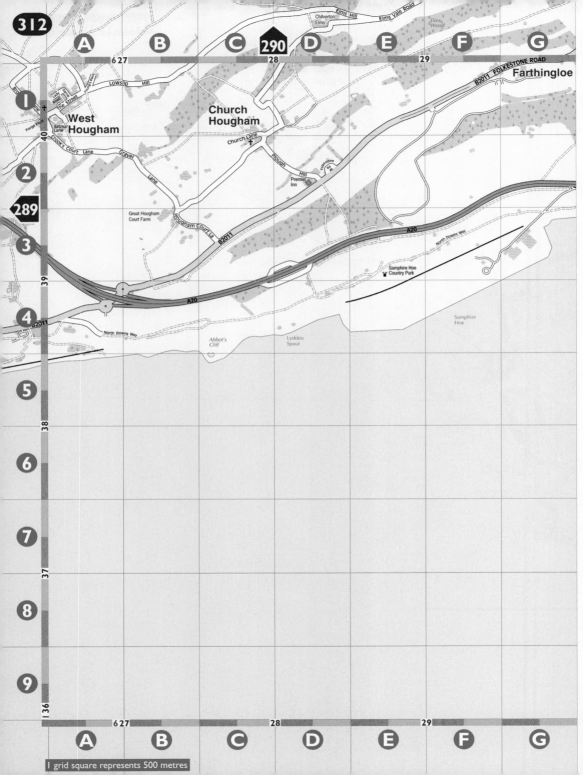

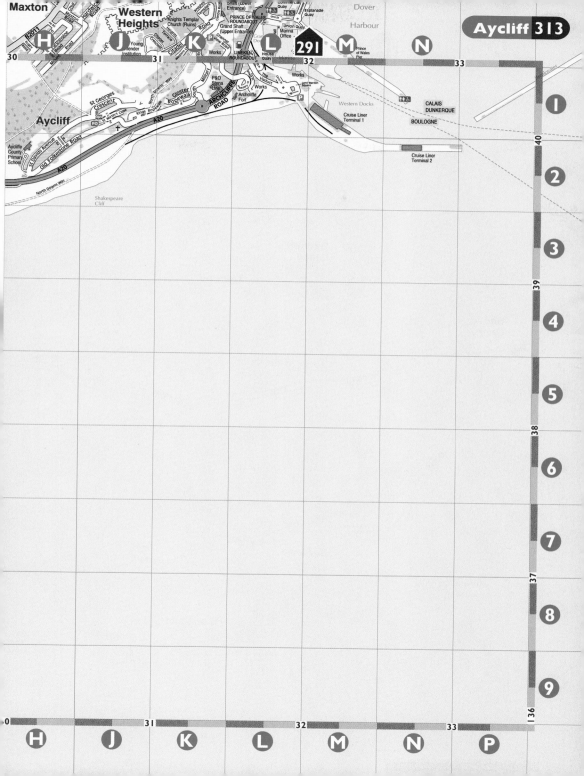

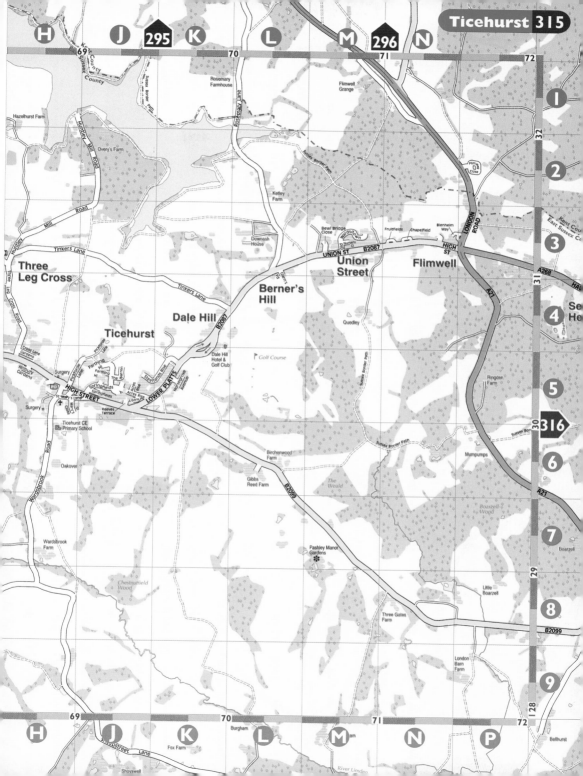

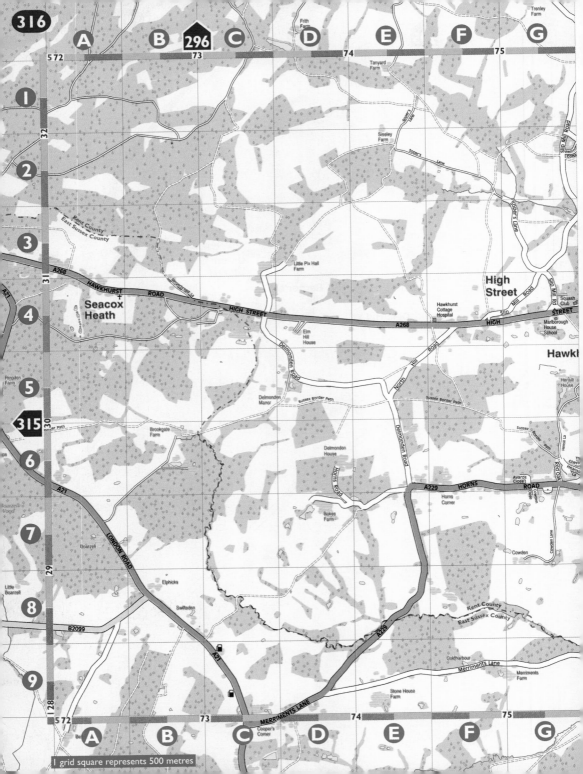

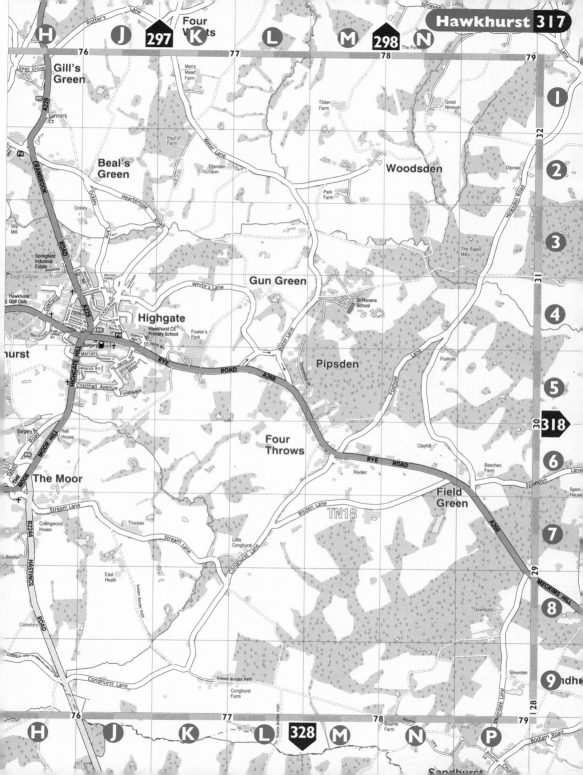

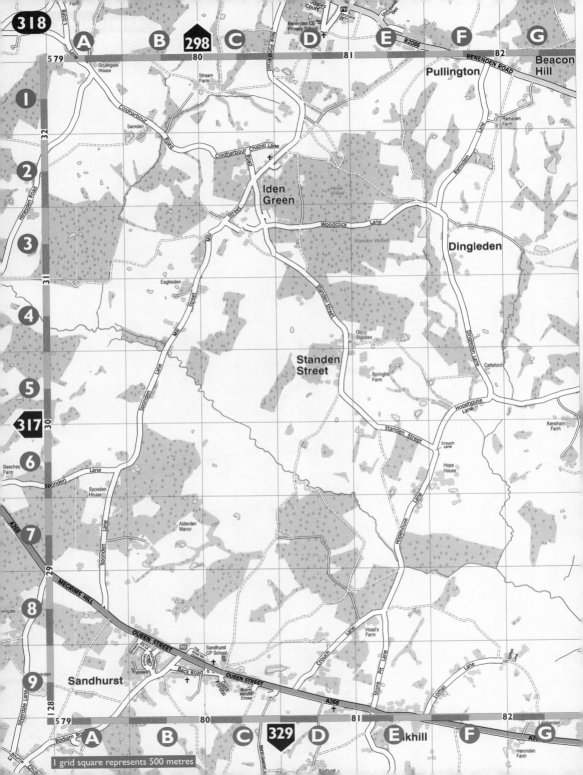

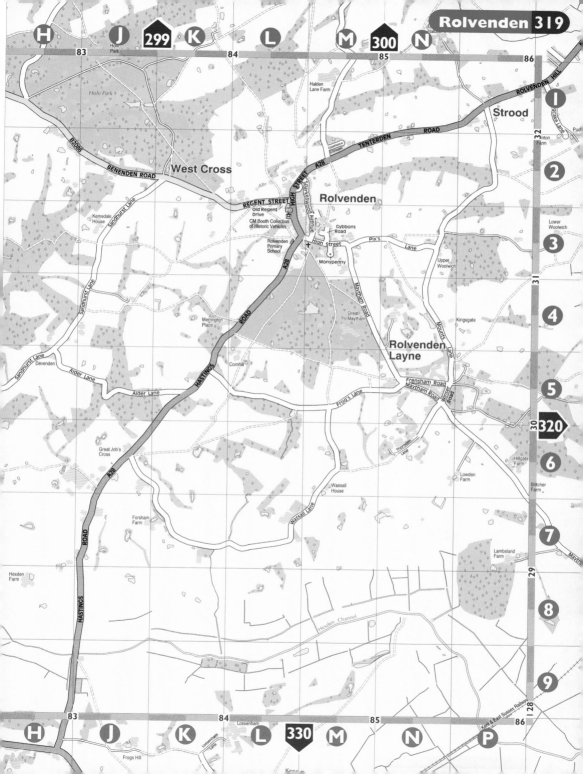

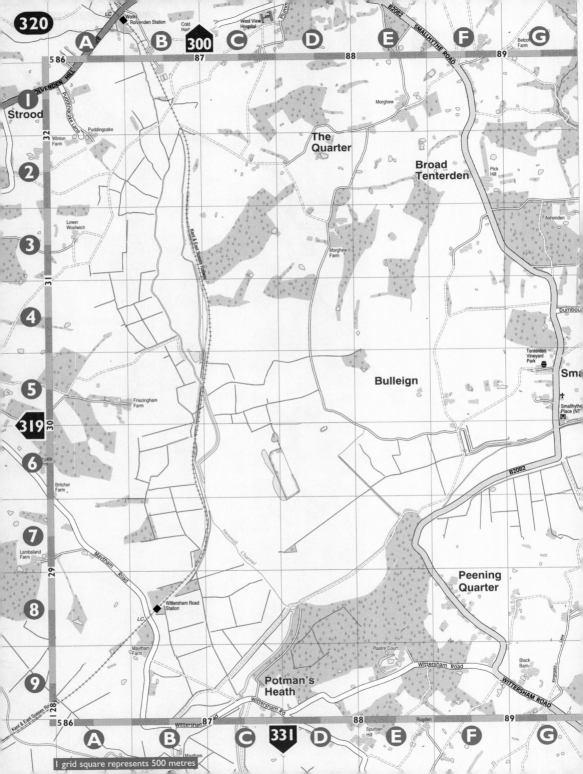

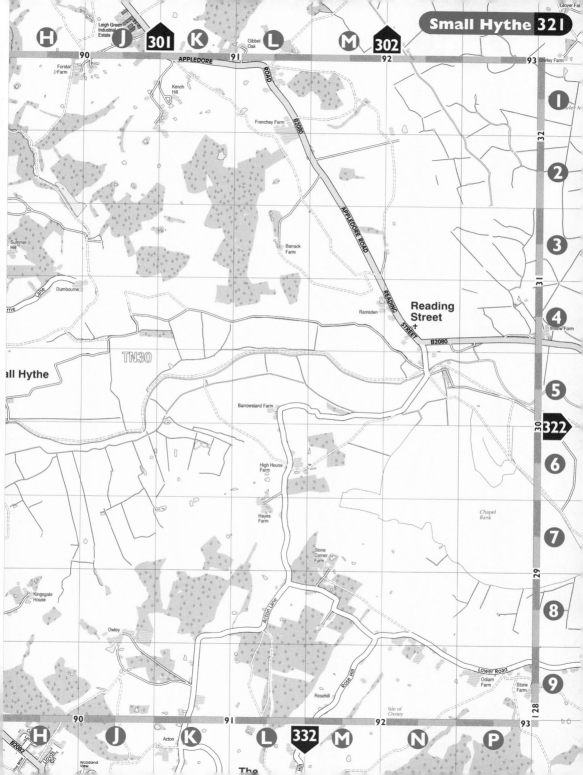

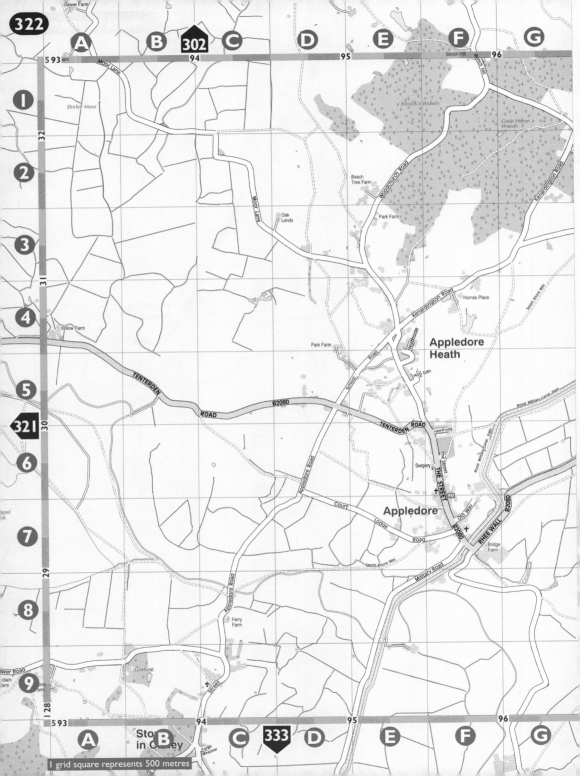

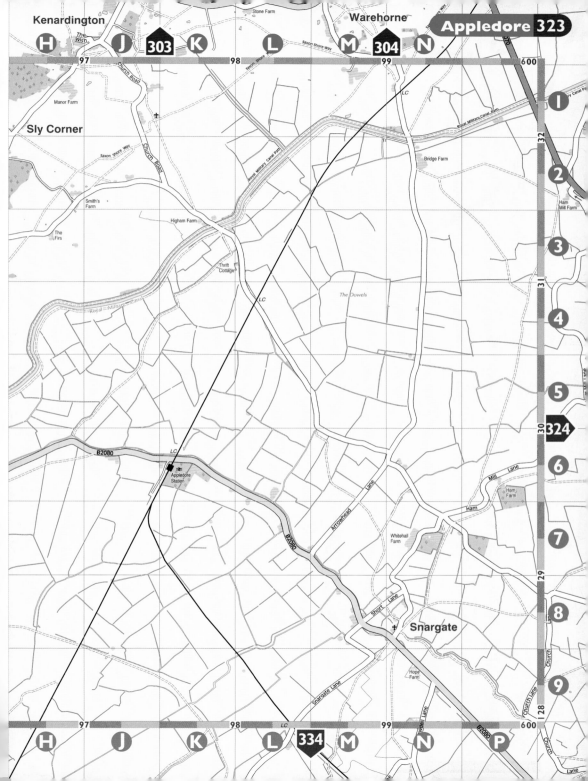

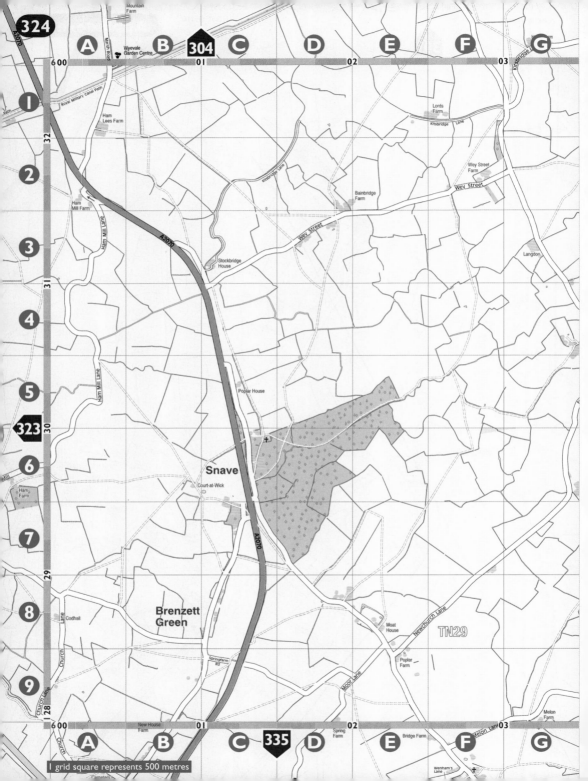

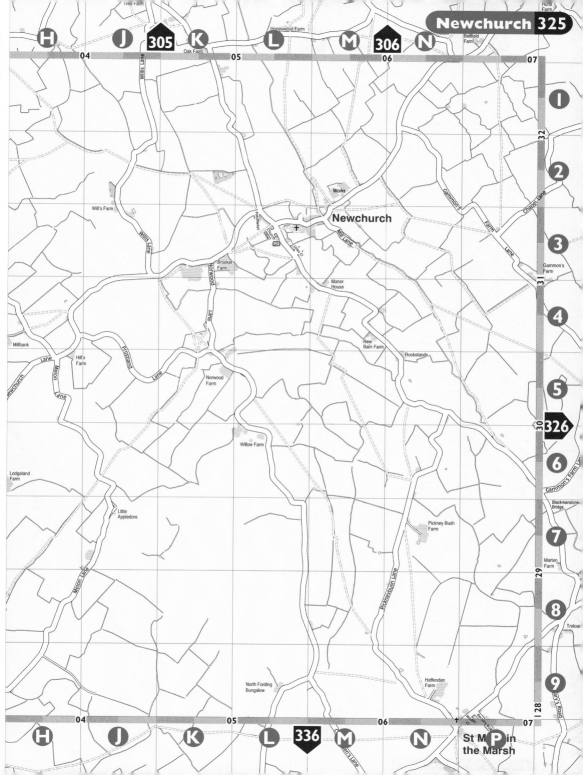

H   J   305   K   L   M   306   N

04   05   06   07

I   1

32

2

Chapel Lane

3

Gammon's Farm   31   Gammon's Farm

4

5

30   326

6

Gammon's Farm Lane

Blackmanstone Bridge

7

Marten Farm

29

8

Treloar

9

St Mary's Road

I   28

Hurst Farm

Bellfield Farm

Tree Farm

Honeywood Farm

Oak Farm

Willis Lane

Works

Newchurch

Patchways View

Church View

P

Mill Lane

Brooker Farm

Norwood Lane

Manor House

New Barn Farm

Rookelands

Millbank

Newchurch Lane

Marion Lane

Hill's Farm

Frostland Lane

Norwood Farm

Will's Farm

Willow Farm

Lodgeland Farm

Little Appledore

Pickney Bush Farm

Pickney Bush Lane

North Fording Bungalow

Haffenden Farm

H   J   04   K   05   L   336   M   06   N   07   P

St Mary in the Marsh

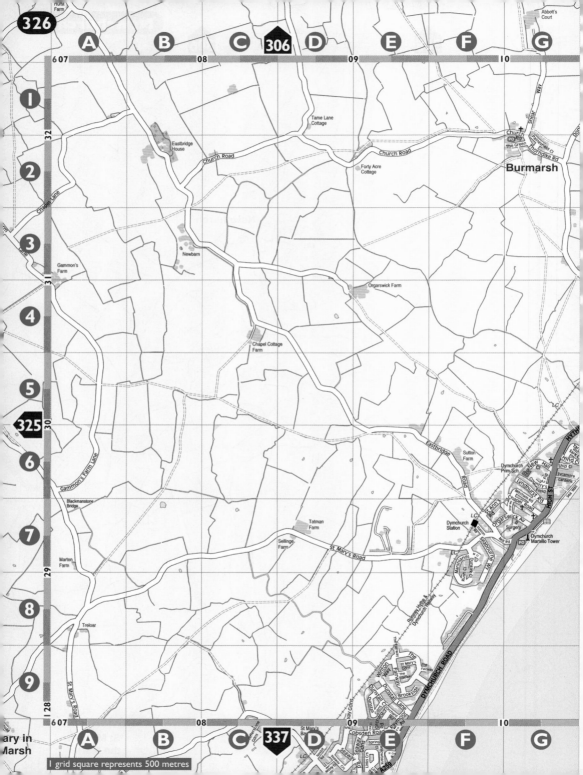

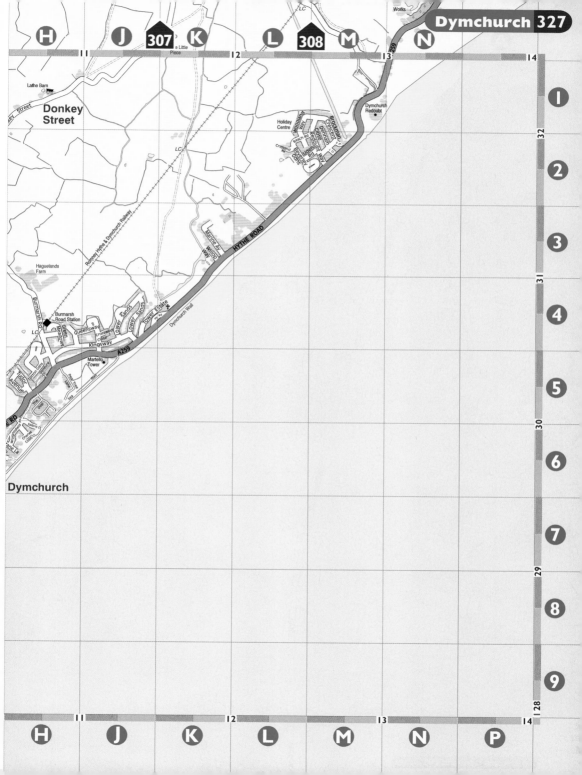

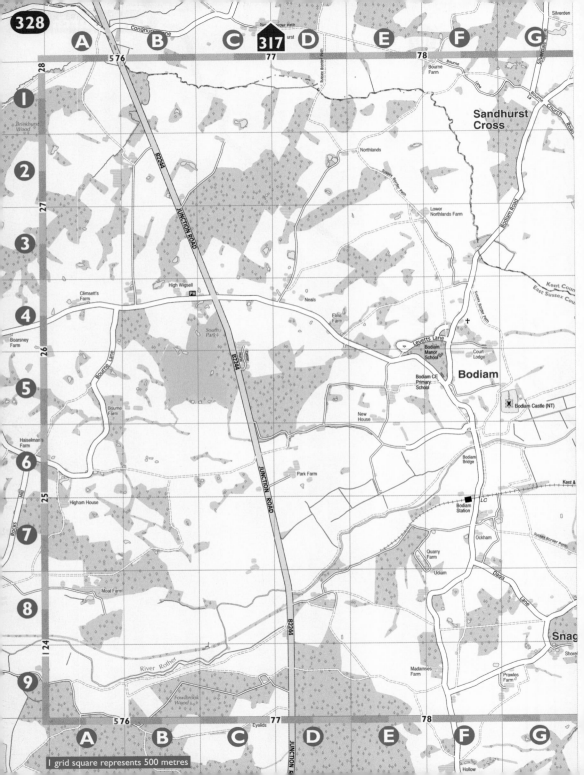

317

Sandhurst
Cross

Bodiam

Bodiam Castle (NT)

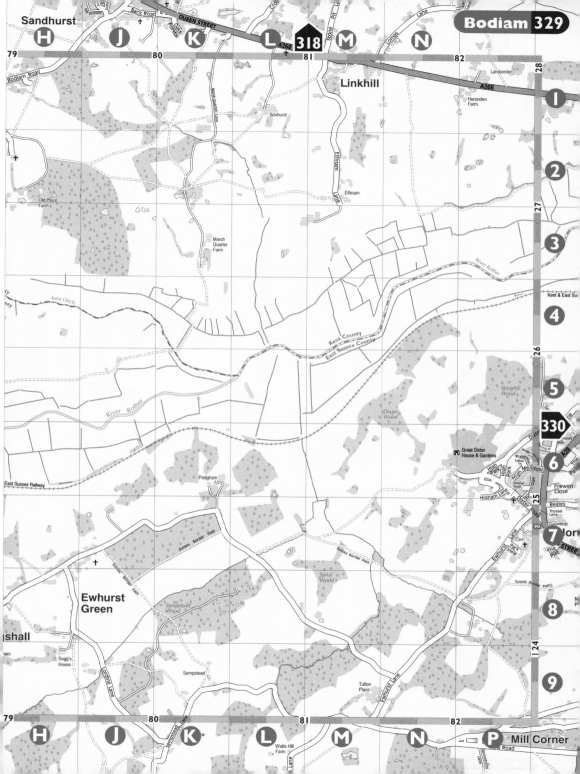

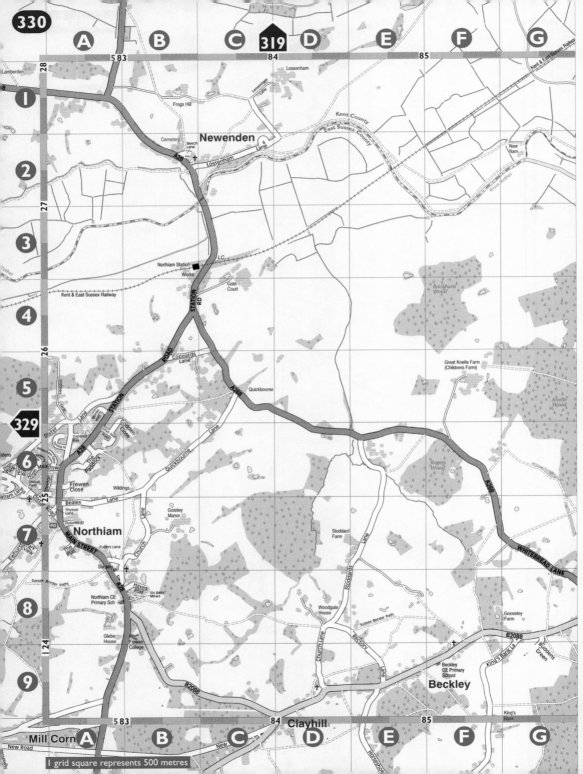

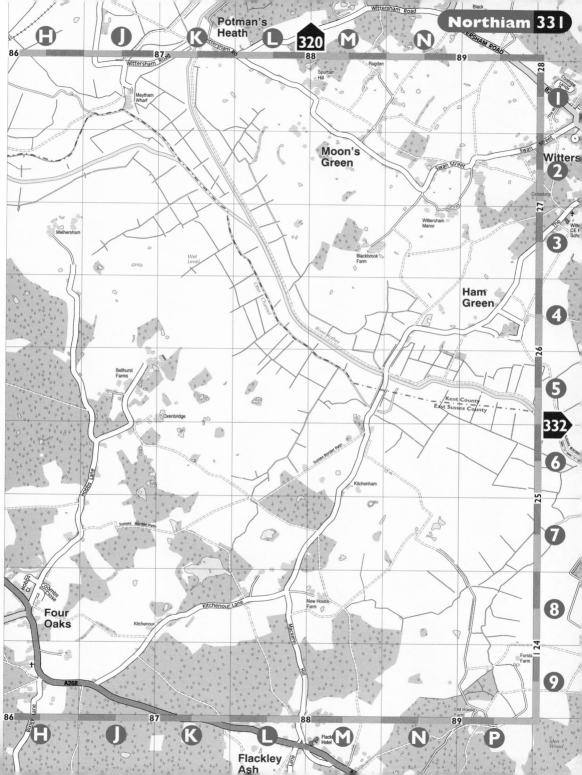

Wittersham Road

Black

ERSHAM ROAD

86   87   88   89   28

H   J   K   L   320   M   N   I

Potman's Heath

Wittersham Road

Maytham Wharf

Spurban Hill

Rugden

Coombe Lands

Witters

Swan Street

2

Methersham

Wet Level

Moon's Green

Wittersham Manor

The

27

Witter CE P Scho

3

Otter Channel

Blackbrook Farm

Ham Green

4

River Rother

26

Kent County
East Sussex County

5

Bellhurst Farms

Oxenbridge

Sussex Border Path

332

6

25

Hobbs Lane

Sussex Border Path

Kitchenham

Sussex Border

7

8

Four Oaks

Coombs Close

Kitchenour Lane

Kitchenour

New House Farm

Mackerel Hill

Forsta Farm

24

9

A268

Old House Farm

86   87   88   89

H   J   K   L   M   N   P

Flackley Ash

Flacki Hotel

Iden Wood

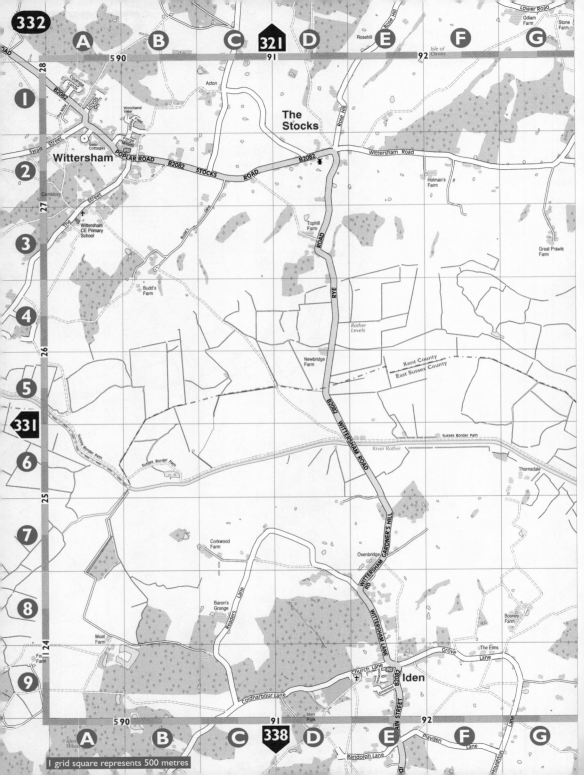

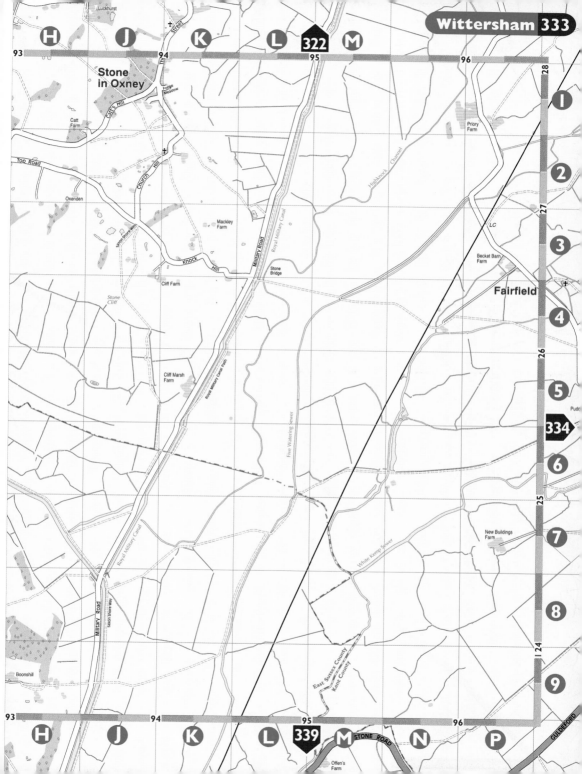

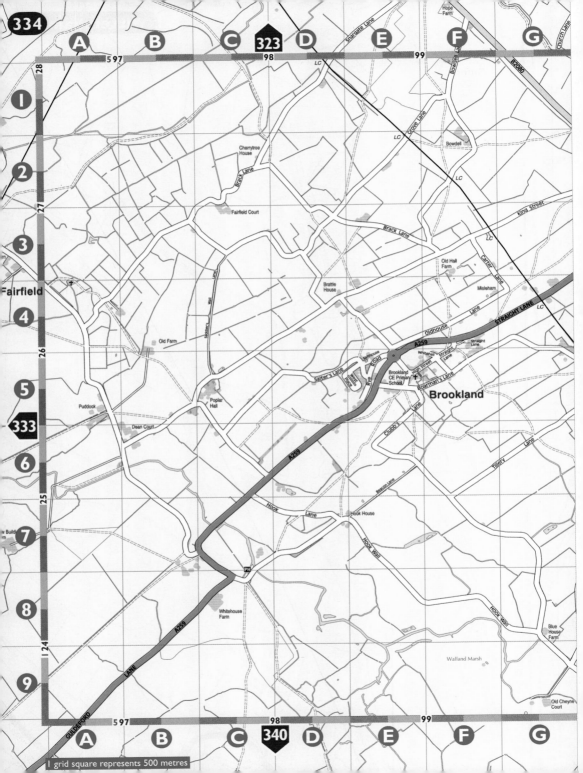

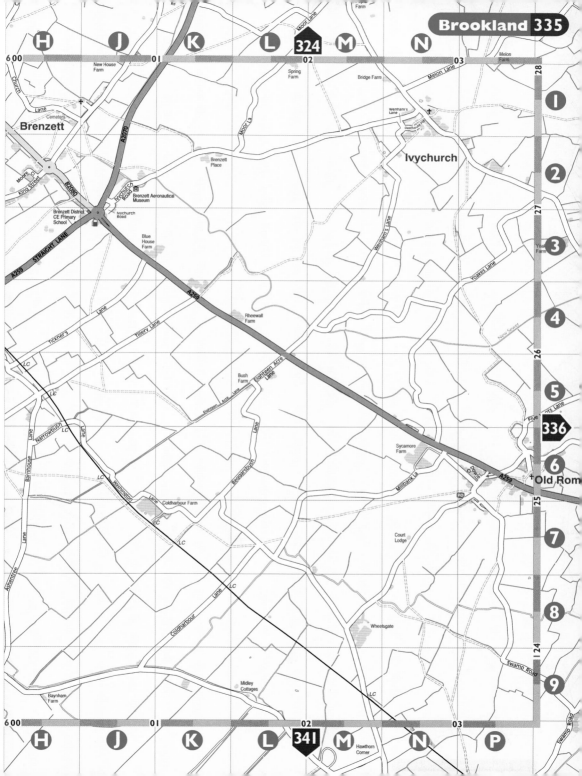

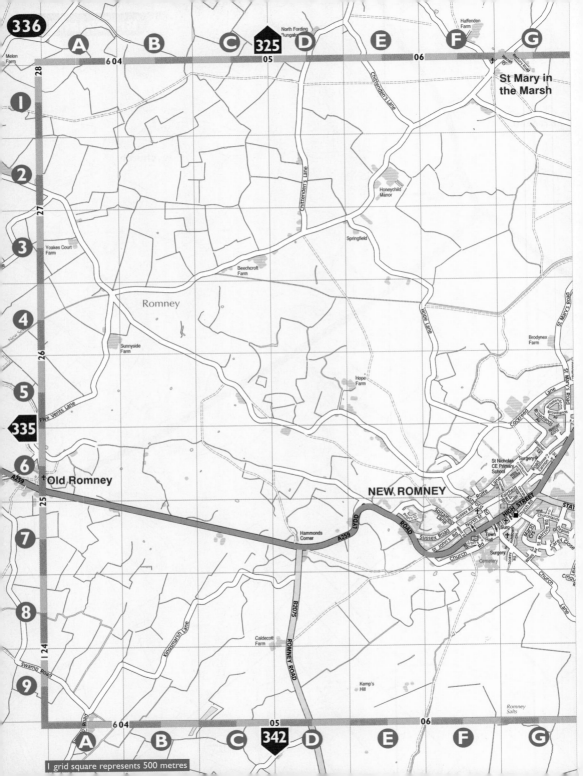

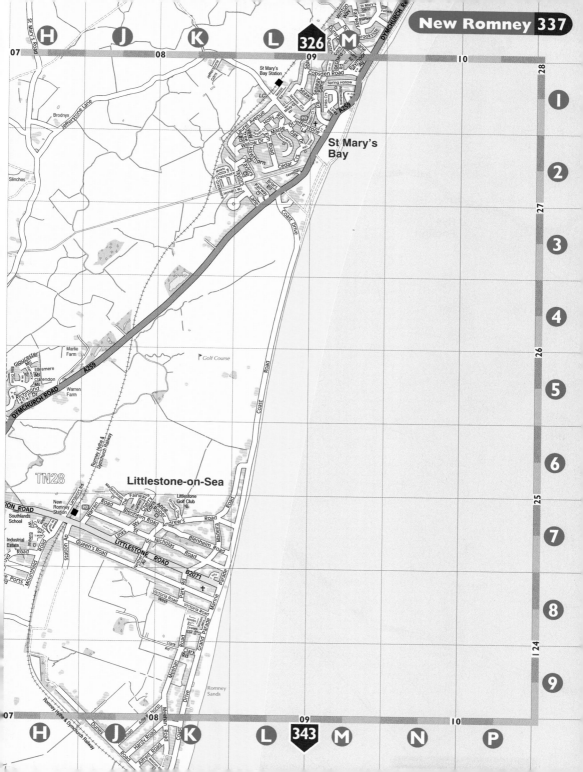

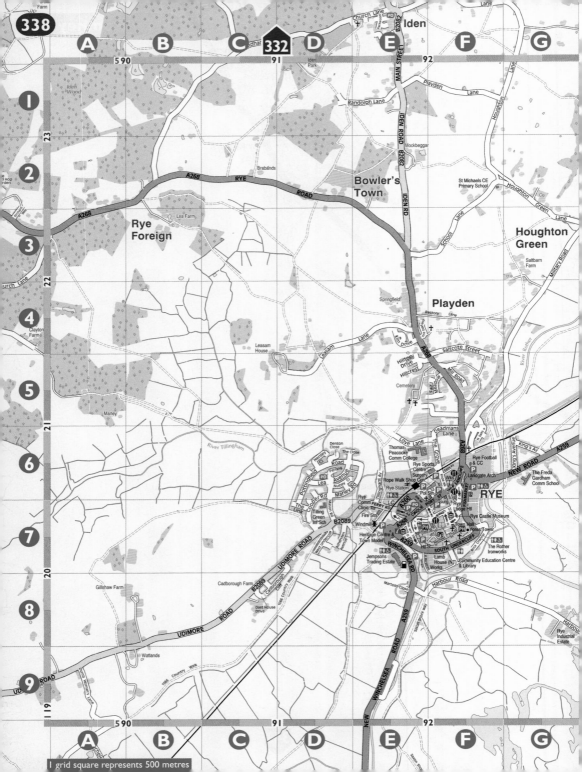

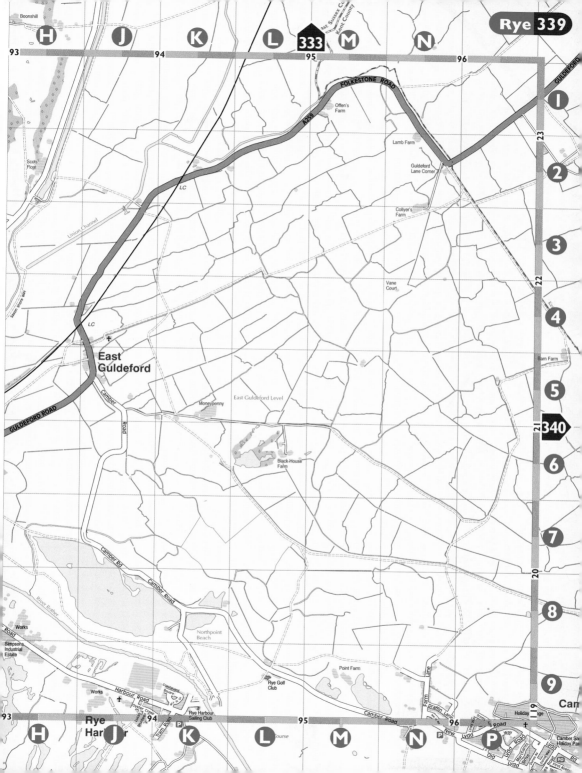

H J K L **335** M N

Haynham Farm

Midley Cottages

Hawthorn Corner

LC

I

23

Marsh

LC

2

Swamp Road

Swamp Road

Westbro Farm

Newland Farm

3

Newland

Horse Bones Farm

22

4

Little Scotney

5

21

342

LYDD

Red House

6

Kent County
East Sussex County

Pigwell

High St

+

Lydd

7

Jury's

Gap

Road

20

Scotney Court

Jury's

Gap

Road

8

West Ripe

Jury's Gut Sewer

The Forelands

9

119

Jury's Road

Maplestone

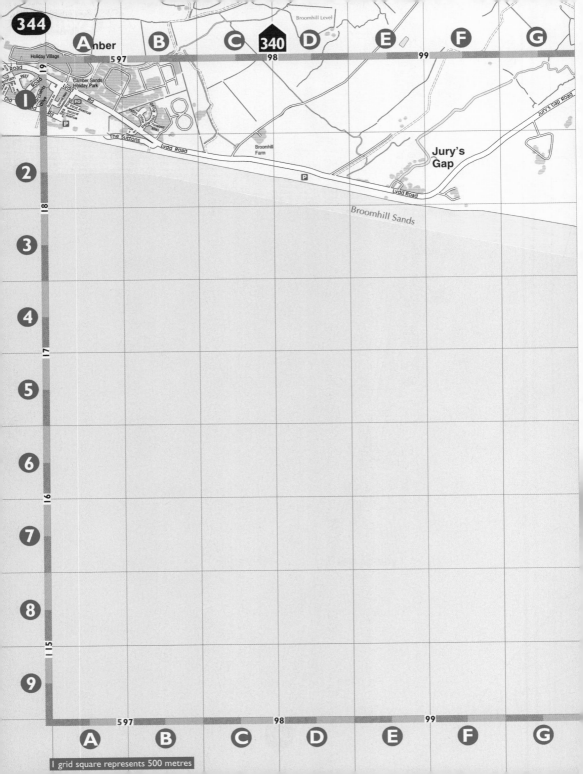

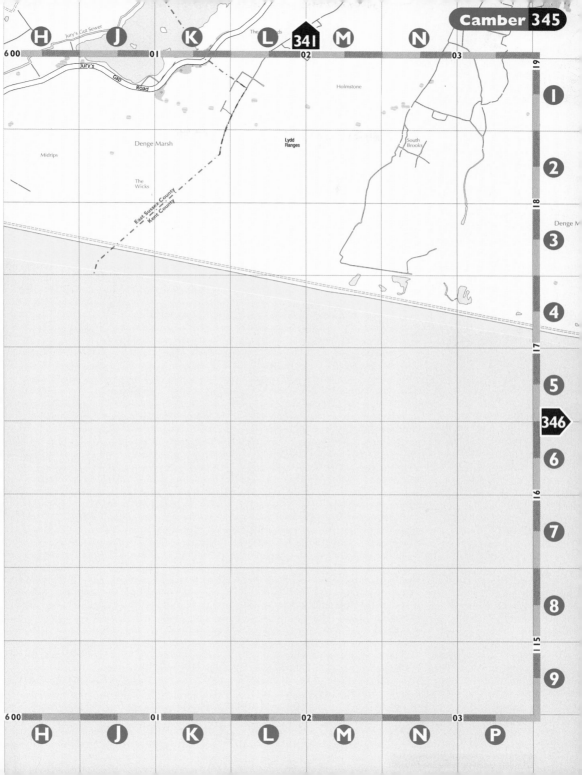

341

346

Jury's Cut Sewer

Jury's Gap Road

Holmstone

Denge Marsh

Lydd Ranges

South Brooks

Midrips

The Wicks

East Sussex County
Kent County

Denge M

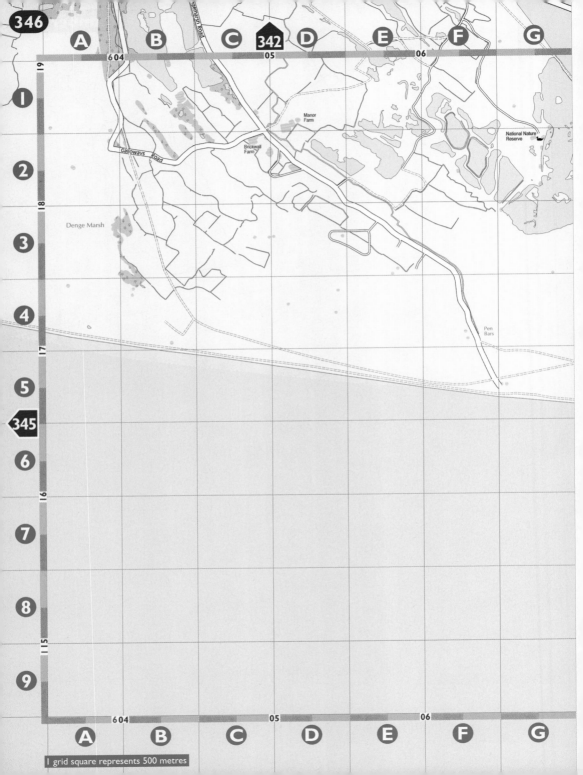

346

A B C 342 D E F G

604   05   06

19

1

18

2

Denge Marsh

3

17

4

5

345

6

16

7

8

115

9

604   05   06

A B C D E F G

Ivychurch Road

Galloways Road

Brickwall Farm

Manor Farm

National Nature Reserve

Pen Bars

1 grid square represents 500 metres

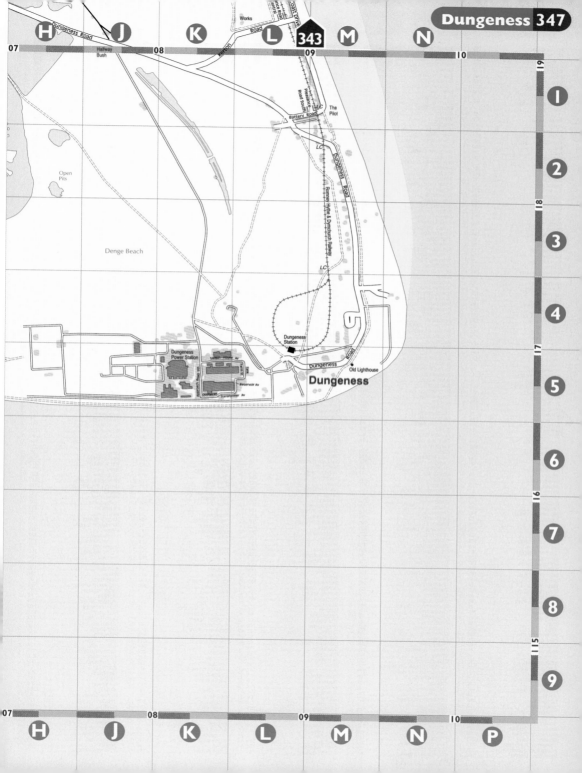

H Dungeness Road J K L 343 M N

07 08 09 10

Halfway
Bush

Works

Kerton Road

Coast Drive

Prince Road

Pleasance Road South

Battery Road

LCC

The Pilot

LC

Dungeness Road

19
I
18
2
3
17
4
5
16
6
7
15
8
9

Romney Hythe & Dymchurch Railway

LC

Open Pits

Denge Beach

Dungeness Power Station

Switch House Av

Reservoir Av

Penn St

Dungeness Station

Dungeness Road

Dungeness

Old Lighthouse

Southlands Av

Transformer Av

Abbey Gate.....155 L1	Boughton-under-Blean.....134 A9	Cinder Hill.....209 H9	East Guldeford.....339 J5	Great Buckland.....123 H1
Abbey Wood.....28 A7	Bow Common.....25 K1	Clapham Hill.....105 L9	East Hill.....119 N3	Great Chart.....251 P8
Acol.....141 J1	Bowler's Town.....338 E2	Clap Hill.....284 A9	East Langdon.....261 P7	Great Cheveney.....244 F8
Addington.....152 E2	Bowmans.....45 P8	Clapper Hill.....300 A2	Eastling.....161 K6	Great Mongeham.....232 B6
Addiscombe.....83 L4	Boxley.....156 A2	Claygate.....244 B4	East Malling.....154 A6	Greatness.....149 K5
Adisham.....198 C7	Boyden Gate.....138 F1	Claygate.....181 J7	East Malling Heath.....153 M9	Great Pattenden.....244 F5
Aldington.....306 B1	Brabourne.....255 K9	Claygate Cross.....151 K9	East Peckham.....212 G4	Great Stonar.....171 N8
Aldington Frith.....305 N1	Brabourne Lees.....284 F3	Claypits.....199 M3	Eastry.....201 J8	Greatstone-on-Sea.....343 J2
Alkham.....289 M3	Bramling.....198 G1	Clement Street.....66 D5	East Stourmouth.....170 A2	Green Hill.....186 E3
Allhallows.....38 C7	Branbridges.....213 J4	Cliffe.....52 C2	East Street.....171 J9	Greenhill.....107 J4
Allhallows-on-Sea.....155 J4	Brasted.....147 J9	Cliffe Woods.....52 C9	East Studdal.....231 M9	Greenhithe.....47 M5
Allington.....60 G8	Brasted Chart.....177 J4	Cliffs End.....142 C6	East Tilbury.....34 A7	Green Street Green.....116 F2
Anerley.....60 C8	Brattle.....302 C7	Cliftonville.....113 H3	Eastwell Park.....222 G7	Green Street Green.....67 N5
Anvil Green.....225 L3	Breach.....98 A6	Cobham.....92 C1	East Wickham.....44 B4	Greenwich.....27 H3
Aperfield.....146 A2	Bredgar.....129 H8	Cock Street.....186 A9	Eccles.....124 F8	Greet.....160 C9
Appledore.....322 E7	Bredhurst.....125 N8	Coldblow.....65 L1	Eddington.....107 K3	Grigg.....248 B3
Appledore Heath.....322 E7	Brenchley.....243 K9	Coldharbour.....210 D1	Edenbridge.....206 B8	Groombridge.....268 F9
Arpinge.....287 P5	The Brents.....132 G4	Cold Harbour.....98 F8	Eden Park.....84 C1	Grove.....139 J9
Ash.....200 F1	Brenzett.....335 H1	Coldharbour.....29 M7	Egerton.....219 M7	Grove End.....129 K6
Ash.....91 H9	Brenzett Green.....324 B8	Coldred.....260 A5	Egerton Forstal.....219 L9	Grove Ferry.....139 J7
Ashbank.....187 L4	Bridge.....197 M2	Colliers Green.....275 L6	Elham.....257 K4	Grove Green.....156 A7
Ashford.....3 F6	Brissenden Green.....280 E6	Collier Street.....244 D1	Elmers End.....61 K9	Grove Hill.....168 G2
Ashley.....261 H2	Brixton.....40 A5	Colt's Hill.....242 C5	Elmstead.....65 J4	Grove Park.....62 C2
Ashurst.....268 C6	Broad Ford.....274 B4	Comp.....153 A6	Elmsted.....255 P3	Groves.....200 A3
Aveley.....30 C3	Broad Green.....82 C4	Coney Hall.....85 H8	Elmstone.....169 P3	Grubb Street.....67 P7
Avery Hill.....43 N7	Broadham Green.....174 F8	Congelow.....213 M3	Eltham.....43 J7	Guilton.....200 D1
Aycliff.....313 H1	Broad Oak.....137 J6	Conyer.....101 K8	Elvington.....230 D8	Gun Green.....317 L4
Aylesford.....154 E1	Broad Oak.....283 M7	Cooling.....52 F3	Erith.....29 L8	Gushmere.....163 H5
Aylesham.....229 J1	Broad Street.....157 L6	Coolinge.....310 C7	Erriottwood.....160 D1	Guston.....291 M1
Badgers Mount.....118 A3	Broad Street.....285 N5	Cooling Street.....52 D7	Etchinghill.....287 H5	Hackbridge.....82 A6
Badlesmere.....192 F2	Broad Tenterden.....320 E2	Coombe.....200 G2	Evington.....255 L2	Hacklinge.....202 B8
Bagham.....194 E3	Broadwater Down.....270 C8	Coomb Hill.....92 F8	Ewell Minnis.....259 P9	Hadlow.....211 J2
Baker's Cross.....298 A2	Brockley.....41 M6	Cooper's Corner.....207 N2	Ewhurst Green.....329 J8	Hadlow Stair.....211 K6
Baker Street.....32 G2	Bromley.....62 F8	Cooper Street.....171 H7	Exted.....257 J4	Haffenden Quarter.....279 H1
Baldwins Hill.....264 F5	Bromley Common.....85 N3	Coppins Corner.....220 F4	Eyhorne Street.....187 L1	Haine.....142 E2
Bandonhill.....82 C9	Bromley Green.....304 B1	Cop Street.....170 F7	Eynsford.....89 K6	Hale.....96 A6
Bapchild.....130 D2	Bromley Park.....62 C7	Copton.....162 G2	Eythorne.....260 C1	Hale.....207 J9
Barden Park.....210 C9	Brompton.....7 J1	The Corner.....244 A9	Fairbourne Heath.....218 B1	Hales Place.....166 F1
Bardown.....314 C7	Bromstone.....143 K1	Court-at-Street.....307 H4	Fairfield.....333 P4	Hale Street.....213 H3
Barfrestone.....229 P5	Brook.....254 C4	Cousley Wood.....294 D8	Fairseat.....121 M6	Halfway Houses.....57 N9
Barham.....228 B5	Brookland.....334 F5	Cowden.....267 H2	Falconwood.....44 A5	Halfway Street.....259 N2
Barming Heath.....154 E9	Brooks End.....110 E9	Coxheath.....185 J8	Fant.....219 M7	Halling.....94 A9
Barnehurst.....45 M4	Brook Street.....240 D2	Crabble.....290 F5	Farleigh.....114 C8	Hall's Green.....208 F2
Barnes Cray.....46 B5	Brook Street.....302 D7	Cranbrook.....298 A2	Farleigh Court.....114 D8	Halstead.....117 P6
Barnes Street.....212 B6	Broomfield.....108 A8	Cranbrook Common.....276 D6	Farleigh Green.....184 D5	Ham.....201 N8
Barnfield.....220 B6	Broomfield.....187 M6	Crayford.....46 A5	Farnborough.....86 B9	Ham Green.....75 K9
Barnsole.....200 C4	Broom Hill.....86 G4	Creekmouth.....27 M1	Farningham.....89 M4	Ham Green.....331 P4
Barrow Green.....131 J2	Broomhill.....169 L7	Crit Hall.....298 C3	Farthing Corner.....127 H2	Ham Hill.....125 P7
Barrowhill.....225 K9	Broomhill Bank.....269 P1	Crockenhill.....88 B3	Farthing Green.....217 H9	Hammerwood.....266 C5
Basted.....151 J8	Broom Street.....133 N3	Crockham Hill.....176 D9	Farthingloe.....312 C1	Hammill.....200 F6
Bayley's Hill.....178 D7	Buckhurst.....277 M5	Crockhurst Street.....241 L3	Faversham.....133 H5	Hampton.....106 C1
Bay View.....80 B5	Buckland.....291 K5	Crofton.....86 C7	Fawkham Green.....90 E7	Hamptons.....181 L6
Beacon Hill.....318 C1	Buckland Valley.....291 J5	Cross-at-Hand.....216 B9	Felbridge.....264 C4	Hamstreet.....304 C8
Beal's Green.....317 J2	Bulleign.....320 E5	Cross Keys.....178 E3	Felcourt.....234 F9	Hanging Bank.....177 N8
Bean.....67 P2	Bullockstone.....107 J6	Crouch.....151 L8	Felderland.....201 N6	Harbledown.....166 A4
Bearsted.....186 E1	Burham.....124 E4	Crouch.....163 P5	Fenn Street.....53 H5	Harbourland.....155 N3
Beckenham.....61 N8	Burham Court.....124 C4	Crowdleham.....149 P1	Ferndale.....23 H1	The Harbour.....217 H5
Beckley.....330 F9	Burmarsh.....326 C2	Crowhurst.....204 C9	Fickleshole.....115 H8	Hareplain.....277 M5
Beckton.....26 G2	Burswood.....268 F8	Crowhurst Lane End.....204 D5	Field Green.....129 J3	Harman's Corner.....129 J3
Beddington.....82 D6	Buttsole.....201 J9	Croydon.....83 J7	Finglesham.....231 P1	Harrietsham.....188 E5
Bedgebury Cross.....296 C5	Bybrook.....252 F4	Crundale.....224 E3	Fir Toll.....250 B3	Hartley.....91 J2
Bekesbourne.....198 A3	Cage Green.....213 H1	Crystal Palace.....60 G5	Five Oak Green.....242 B1	Hartley.....297 L5
Bekesbourne Hill.....167 N7	Calcott.....137 K5	Cubitt Town.....25 M7	Five Wents.....187 H9	Hartley.....91 H2
Bell Green.....61 M2	Camber.....340 A9	Cudham.....115 K4	Fleet Downs.....47 J1	Hartley Green.....91 J2
Bellingham.....61 N3	Camberwell.....40 F7	Culmers.....135 H4	Flemings.....200 E4	Hartlip.....97 N9
Beltinge.....108 A6	Camden Hill.....276 C6	Culverstone Green.....121 P3	Fletcher's Green.....209 J1	Harvel.....122 D2
Beltring.....213 J6	Camden Park.....271 J8	Curteis' Corner.....278 B5	Flimwell.....315 N3	Hassell Street.....225 H8
Belvedere.....28 G8	Camer.....92 D3	Curtisden Green.....275 H3	Flishinghurst.....275 L9	Hastingleigh.....255 J3
Benenden.....298 C8	Canary Wharf.....25 M7	Custom House.....26 C1	Folkestone.....11 F6	Hawker Street.....216 F2
Benover.....214 A5	Canning Town.....26 C1	Custon.....94 B4	Foots Cray.....64 D5	Hawkenbury.....246 F2
Bermondsey.....24 C5	Canterbury.....5 J1	Dale Hill.....315 K4	Force Green.....146 F9	Hawkenbury.....23 J7
Berner's Hill.....315 L4	Capel.....242 A3	Danaway.....128 D3	Ford.....138 B1	Hawkhurst.....316 G5
Berry's Green.....146 B1	Capel Cross.....274 B5	Dane Street.....194 A5	Fordcombe.....268 F3	Hawkinge.....288 E2
Berwick.....307 P3	Capel-le-Ferne.....311 L1	Daniel's Water.....251 J9	Fordwich.....137 M9	Haxted.....236 A1
Bessels Green.....146 C1	Capstone.....96 A7	Darenth.....67 J4	Forestdale.....114 B3	Hayes.....85 L4
Bethersden.....280 D3	Castle Hill.....243 M8	Dargate.....134 E5	Forest Hill.....41 M9	Hazel Street.....158 B1
Betsham.....68 D3	Catford.....42 A9	Dargate Common.....134 F6	Forstal.....155 H2	Hazel Street.....275 M5
Betteshanger.....225 L4	Cellarhill.....131 H4	Dartford.....65 C8	The Forstal.....275 M5	Hazelwood.....116 D5
Bexley.....44 E5	Chadwell St Mary.....32 G6	Davington.....132 G8	Fosten Green.....299 N2	Headcorn.....247 P4
Bexleyheath.....45 H5	Chafford Hundred.....31 P6	David Street.....132 D5	Four Elms.....207 H5	Hearnden Green.....217 K9
Bexon.....129 J9	Chainhurst.....214 F6	Davington.....132 D5	Four Oaks.....132 B4	Hearts Delight.....128 G6
Bickley.....63 J8	Chalk.....50 C9	Deal.....233 H4	Four Oaks.....331 H8	Heath Side.....65 P1
Bicknor.....158 D2	Chalksole.....259 L9	Dean Bottom.....67 P9	Four Throws.....317 K8	Heaverham.....150 B2
Bidborough.....240 A6	Chalkwell.....129 K1	Deans Bottom.....128 D8	Four Wents.....275 K8	Hempstead.....96 B9
Biddenden.....277 P6	Challock.....192 F9	Deans Hill.....128 E7	Four Wents.....297 N9	Hemsted.....256 C9
Biddenden Green.....249 J7	Chamber's Green.....250 B5	Dean Street.....185 J5	Foxbury.....63 P4	Henhurst.....70 A7
Biggin.....33 K9	Charcott.....208 F7	Deerton Street.....131 M3	Foxendown.....91 P6	Henley Street.....92 C5
Biggin Hill.....145 N1	Charing.....221 J2	Dene Park.....210 C1	French Street.....176 C6	Henwood Green.....272 A2
Bilsington.....305 M6	Charing Heath.....220 E1	Denny Bottom.....270 A5	Frindsbury.....72 C7	Herne.....107 L6
Bilting.....223 P2	Charing Hill.....221 J1	Densole.....288 D4	Friningham.....157 J3	Herne Bay.....107 K2
Birchett's Green.....314 C3	Chariton.....26 E8	Denstroude.....135 K5	Frinsted.....159 K5	Herne Common.....107 J7
Birchington.....110 F6	Chart Corner.....216 E1	Denton.....50 A8	Frittenden.....277 J1	Herne Hill.....40 C7
Bircholt Forstal.....284 E1	Chartham.....195 M1	Denton.....258 D2	Frogham.....229 M5	Herne Pound.....182 F1
Birling.....123 J7	Chartham Hatch.....165 L6	Deptford.....25 N7	Froghole.....176 E8	Hernhill.....134 C7
Bishopsbourne.....197 N5	Chart Hill.....216 D2	Derringstone.....228 B7	Frogholt.....287 K8	Heronden.....200 F9
Bishopstone.....108 C5	Chart Sutton.....216 D5	Derry Downs.....87 L3	Further Quarter.....279 K5	Hersden.....138 C9
Bitchet Green.....180 A2	The Chart.....177 J6	Detling.....156 E3	Gadshill.....71 L5	Hever.....237 K3
Blacketts.....100 G8	Chatham.....6 D4	Dingleden.....314 F2	Garlinge.....111 P6	Hextable.....66 A6
Blackfen.....44 B7	Chattenden.....72 E2	Ditton.....154 D2	Garlinge Green.....195 M5	Hickmans Green.....164 B2
Blackham.....267 P4	Cheeseman's Green.....283 H6	Doddington.....160 D5	Gibraltar.....288 C9	Hicks Forstal.....137 M1
Blackheath.....42 E5	Chegworth.....188 A5	Donkey Street.....327 H1	Gillingham.....7 F1	Higham.....71 L3
Blackheath Park.....42 E5	Chelsfield.....87 M9	Dormansland.....205 H1	Gill's Green.....317 H1	Higham Wood.....211 J4
Blackwall.....25 N3	Chelsham.....144 D2	Dormans Park.....265 H1	Glassenbury.....297 K1	High Brooms.....240 F9
Blackwell.....265 H6	Chequertree.....283 L9	Dover.....9 F5	Goathurst Common.....178 A6	Highgate.....317 J4
Bladbean.....227 L8	Cheriton.....309 P1	Downe.....116 A5	Goddard's Green.....299 J5	High Halden.....279 J9
Blean.....135 N7	Chesley.....128 B2	Downham.....62 B4	Godden Green.....179 J7	High Halstow.....53 L5
Bilby.....283 J8	Chestfield.....106 C6	The Down.....294 G4	Goddington.....87 K7	Highstead.....108 D9
Blindley Heath.....204 B9	Chestnut Street.....128 F1	Drellingore.....289 K5	Godinton Park.....252 A7	Highsted.....129 N6
Blue Bell Hill.....125 H4	Chevening.....147 N4	Dryhill.....146 C3	Godmersham.....194 C9	High Street.....316 F4
Bluetown.....160 A3	Chiddingstone.....238 A3	Dulwich.....60 F1	Golden Green.....212 A5	Highstreet.....134 C5
Blue Town.....57 H5	Chiddingstone Causeway.....208 E8	Dulwich Village.....40 E8	Golford.....298 D1	Hildenborough.....210 B4
Bobbing.....99 J7	Chiddingstone Hoath.....237 P7	Dumpton.....143 K2	Golgotha.....229 P8	Hilden Park.....210 B6
Bockhanger.....252 E3	Childsbridge.....144 C3	Dungate.....160 A1	Goodley Stock.....176 C6	Hillborough.....108 D6
Bodiam.....328 F5	Chilham.....194 C3	Dungeness.....347 M5	Goodnestone.....133 N6	Hill Green.....127 M4
Bodsham.....255 M1	Chillenden.....201 J5	Dunkirk.....164 E2	Goodnestone.....190 E6	Hill Park.....146 C8
Bonnington.....306 A4	Chillmill.....273 H2	Dunk's Green.....152 A8	Goose Green.....182 C9	Hill Street.....255 N1
Borden.....129 H3	Chilmington Green.....281 P5	Dunn's Green.....222 B5	Goose Green.....277 P8	Hinxhill.....253 H8
Borough Green.....151 K4	Chilton.....202 G8	Dunn Street.....126 D5	Gore.....201 H7	Hither Green.....42 B8
Borstal.....94 C4	Chipstead.....148 B7	Dunton Green.....148 D4	Gore Street.....140 B5	Hoaden.....170 A7
Bossingham.....225 J8	Chislehurst.....63 N6	Durlock.....200 C2	Gosmere.....162 F4	Hoath.....138 C4
Bossington.....198 G4	Chislehurst West.....63 L5	Durrant Green.....297 P3	Goudhurst.....274 E8	Hoath Corner.....238 A6
Bottom Pond.....159 L2	Chislet.....138 G4	Dymchurch.....327 H6	Gover Hill.....181 P5	Hockenden.....65 K9
Bough Beech.....207 N8	Chislet Forstal.....138 F3	Each End.....201 J1	Grafty Green.....218 F4	Hockley.....161 P9
Boughton Aluph.....223 L5	Chitty.....138 G3	East Barming.....184 D2	Grain.....56 E2	Hodsoll Street.....121 M5
Boughton Corner.....223 M5	Church Hougham.....312 C1	East Dulwich.....79 J4	Grange.....79 J4	Hogben's Hill.....163 K5
Boughton Green.....185 M1	Church Street.....51 M7	East End.....40 G6	Gravel Castle.....228 D6	Holborough.....123 P3
Boughton Lees.....223 J7	Church Whitfield.....261 J7	East End.....248 B5	Graveney.....133 N3	Holland.....175 K9
Boughton Malherbe.....219 H2		East End.....58 E9	Gravesend.....49 M6	Hollingbourne.....187 P1
Boughton Monchelsea.....185 M8		East End.....299 N4	Grays.....48 D1	
Boughton Street.....164 B1		East Farleigh.....184 G4	Great Bower.....193 K5	
		East Grinstead.....265 H6		

Hollow Street................138 F4
Hollybushes................159 P4
Holt Hill................154 C4
Holtye................266 F5
Honey Hill................135 M6
Honor Oak................41 K7
Honor Oak Park................41 L7
Hoo................140 C6
Hook Green................92 B3
Hook Green................68 D5
Hook Green................294 E3
Hook Green................65 P3
Hoo St Werburgh................73 J1
Horns Cross................47 M7
Horns Green................146 F2
Horn Street................123 M7
Horn Street................309 N3
Horsalls................188 C1
Horseshoe Green................237 K8
Horsmonden................273 M2
Horton................165 N9
Horton Kirby................90 A1
Hosey Hill................176 F4
Hothfield................251 M2
Houghton Green................338 G3
How Green................207 L8
Howt Green................99 L5
Hubbard's Hill................178 C6
Hucking................157 P3
Hulberry................88 G6
Hungershall Park................270 B6
Hunter's Forstal................107 N5
Hunton................214 D2
Hurst Green................175 H8
Hythe................309 H6
Ickham................168 F7
Ide Hill................177 M7
Iden................332 E9
Iden Green................318 C2
Iden Green................275 H8
Ightham................150 G6
Ightham Common................150 D9
Isle of Dogs................25 M7
Istead Rise................69 J6
Ivychurch................335 N2
Ivy Hatch................180 E1
Iwade................99 K1
Joyden's Wood................65 P3
Jury's Gap................344 F2
Kearsney................290 D3
Kempe's Corner................223 L8
Kemsing................149 L2
Kemsley................99 N6
Kemsley Street................126 F4
Kenardington................303 L9
Kennington................253 H3
Kent Street................182 G1
Keston................85 N8
Keston Mark................85 M7
Kettle Corner................184 E3
Kevington................87 N3
Keycol................98 F8
Key's Green................272 D4
Key Street................99 H9
Kidbrooke................42 G5
Kilndown................295 P5
Kingsdown................130 C9
Kingsdown................262 C5
Kings Farm................69 N2
Kingsgate................113 M4
Kings Hill................153 J8
Kingsnorth................74 B1
Kingsnorth................282 D5
Kingston................197 P8
Kingswood................187 P9
Kipping's Cross................272 B4
Kippington................32 C5
Kit's Coty................125 H5
Knatts Valley................120 B4
Knave's Ash................107 P9
Knight's Hill................40 C9
Knockhall................47 P6
Knockholt................147 H2
Knockmill................120 B6
Knowlton................230 D2
Knox Bridge................276 C2
Laddingford................231 K9
Lade................343 K6
Ladywell................41 N5
Lakeside................31 K7
Lamberhurst................295 J2
Lamberhurst Quarter................272 E6
Lamb's Cross................216 C4
Lane End................67 K4
Langley................67 P6
Langley Heath................187 J7
Langton Green................269 L4
Larkfield................153 P2
The Leacon................303 P8
Leadingcross Green................189 K8
Leaveland................192 D5
Leaves Green................115 N5
Lee................42 D7
Leeds................187 K4
The Lees................187 J4
Leigh................209 L8
Leigh Green................301 M8
Lenham................189 K6
Lenham Forstal................190 A5
Lenham Heath................220 A2
Lessness Heath................28 C9
Lett's Green................146 G1
Lewes Heath................273 P5
Lewisham................42 A5
Lewson Street................131 L6
Leybourne................153 M1
Leysdown-on-Sea................80 F5
Lidsing................126 B4
Lilyvale................284 C5
Limehouse................25 H5
Limpsfield................175 J3
Limpsfield Chart................176 A7
Limpsfield Common................175 L6
Linford................33 N5
Lingfield................234 G3
Lingfield Common................234 G3
Linkhill................329 M1
Linton................214 C1
Little Bayham................294 A3
Littlebourne................168 B9

Little Chart................220 F9
Little Chart Forstal................251 H1
Little Cheveney Fm................244 D5
Little Mill................212 E5
Little Mongeham................245 P7
Little Pattenden................245 H1
Little Preston................154 F3
Littlestone-on-Sea................337 J6
Little Thurrock................32 D7
Liverton Street................218 G1
Livesey Street................183 P1
Lockesbottom................86 C7
Lodge Lees................258 B2
London Beach................301 H7
Longfield................68 D9
Longfield Hill................91 N1
Longford................148 C5
Longlands................63 N2
Loose................185 L7
Loose Hill................185 L6
Lords Wood................125 P5
Lower Bitchet................179 P2
Lower Bush................93 N3
Lower Cousley Wood................294 F7
Lower Cox Street................126 G7
Lower Eyrthorne................230 C9
Lower Goldstone................107 G4
Lower Green................24 N9
Lower Green................269 P3
Lower Halstow................98 D3
Lower Hardres................196 F5
Lower Hartlip................127 P1
Lower Haysden................240 B1
Lower Heppington................196 C7
Lower Herne................107 L5
Lower Higham................71 M1
Lower Island................105 K5
Lower Rainham................97 H5
Lower Stoke................54 C3
Lower Sydenham................61 K3
Lower Twydall................96 F1
Lower Upnor................72 F4
Low Street................33 N9
Loyterton................131 J8
Luddesdown................92 C5
Lunsford................123 M9
Luton................95 N5
Luxted................116 B8
Lydd................342 A6
Lydden................112 D9
Lydden................259 P5
Lydd-on-Sea................343 K7
Lyewood Common................268 A9
Lymbridge Green................226 A5
Lympne................286 G2
Lympne................307 P4
Lynsore Bottom................227 H2
Lynsted................130 C7
Mabledon................240 C5
Maidstone................12 B5
Maitman's Hill................249 M6
Manston................142 B3
Maplescombe................89 N9
Marden................263 H4
Marden Beech................244 G6
Marden Thorn................245 M7
Margate................14 E4
Marine Town................21 N3
Markbeech................237 L7
Marley................227 N1
Marley................231 P1
Marlpit Hill................206 C6
Marlborough................201 J3
Marsh Green................236 C4
Marshside................108 E9
Martin................262 A6
Martin Mill................262 C7
Matfield................242 F9
Maxted Street................256 A3
Maxton................291 H9
Maypole................138 B3
Maypole................45 N9
Maypole................207 J8
Meopham................92 A6
Meopham Green................92 B7
Meopham Station................92 C2
Meresborough................97 K9
Mereworth................182 D3
Merle Common................205 K3
Mersham................285 N3
Middle Quarter................279 K7
Middle Stoke................54 G4
Milebush................245 K1
Mile Oak................243 K5
Mile Town................21 H3
Millbank................57 J6
Millbank................138 C2
Mill Hill................232 E6
Mill Street................153 M5
Millwall................25 K6
Milstead................159 M2
Milton................49 P7
Milton Regis................99 J9
Minster................93 L5
Minster................141 K6
Mockbeggar................72 A2
Modest Corner................240 B7
Molash................194 C3
Monks Hill................278 D1
Monks Orchard................83 P4
Monkton................140 E5
Moon's Green................331 M2
Moorhouse Bank................76 B4
Moorstock................285 K6
Moor Street................97 L7
The Moor................317 H6
Morehall................310 C5
Mottingham................42 C5
Mountain Street................194 C5
Mount Pleasant................141 J4
Mowshurst................206 F6
Mucking................42 G1
Muckingford................33 N6
Mundy Bois................249 N1
Murston................253 P4
Nackington................196 G1
Napchester................261 J5
Nash................115 L1

Nash Street................69 K8
Neames Forstal................163 N5
Nettlestead................183 K5
Nettlestead Green................183 J9
New Addington................114 G2
New Ash Green................91 K6
New Barn................68 F8
Newbarn................286 G4
New Beckenham................61 L5
Newchapel................234 B8
New Charlton................26 G7
Newchurch................325 M5
New Cross................41 L3
New Cross Gate................41 L2
New Eltham................65 M1
Newenden................330 C2
New House................69 J1
New Hythe................124 A9
Newington................307 P2
Newington................98 D8
Newington................142 F3
Newington................287 L8
Newland Green................249 L1
Newnham................160 C4
New Romney................336 E6
New Town................91 N9
New Town................46 F7
New Town................153 J3
New Town................93 P8
Noah's Ark................149 M4
Noke Street................72 C3
Nonington................229 N1
Norbury................60 B8
Northbourne................231 P5
North Cray................65 J2
Northdown................113 J4
North Elham................257 M4
North End................264 E4
North End................45 P2
Northfleet................46 B5
Northfleet Green................68 C4
North Halling................93 P7
Northiam................330 A7
North Leigh................226 B7
North Stifford................47 L3
North Street................54 C7
North Street................162 G3
Northumberland Heath................45 L1
Northwood................142 F1
North Woolwich................26 F5
Norton Ash................131 M5
Norwood New Town................60 D5
Nunhead................41 J3
Oad Street................128 F4
Oakhurst................179 M9
Oare................132 D3
Offham................152 E4
Old Bexley................45 J8
Oldbury................150 E6
Old Cryals................272 E5
Old Romney................336 A6
Old Tree................138 D2
Old Wives Lees................194 D1
Orpington................87 H6
Orsett................33 J1
Orsett Heath................32 G5
Ospringe................132 D7
Otford................148 F2
Otham................186 D4
Otham Hole................186 F5
Otterden Place................190 G2
Otterham Quay................97 M4
Ottinge................257 H8
Out Elmstead................228 B4
Overland................164 A5
Oxted................174 H5
Paddlesworth................123 L4
Paddlesworth................287 P4
Paddock................222 B1
Paddock Wood................243 J3
Pains Hill................175 M7
Painter's Forstal................162 B1
Palmarsh................308 B7
Palmer's Green................243 L9
Palmstead................227 J5
Paramour Street................59 K4
Parker's Green................211 K4
Park Farm................282 F4
Parkgate................300 C5
Park Langley................84 F3
Park Wood................186 B6
Park Wood................126 F2
Parrock Farm................69 P7
Patrixbourne................167 N9
Payden Street................190 B3
Pean Hill................105 H5
Pearson's Green................243 M6
Peckham................41 H3
Peckham Bush................212 E2
Pedlinge................308 C5
Pene................287 N7
Peening Quarter................320 F8
Pegwell................142 F7
Pell Green................294 C8
Pembles Cross................219 K7
Pembury................271 M2
Penenden Heath................155 P5
Penge................60 E6
Pennypot................308 F6
Penshurst................238 C5
Perry................169 M5
Perry Street................49 K8
Perrywood................163 L7
Pested................192 E7
Pett Bottom................196 B7
Petteridge................272 C2
Pettings................121 L2
Petts Wood................86 E5
Pineham................261 L8
Pipsden................317 M5
Pittswood................211 K2
Pizien Well................168 G6
Plaistow................35 N6
Platt................151 M5
Platt's Heath................218 G1
Plaxtol................180 F3
Playden................338 F4
Pluckley................250 B2
Pluckley Thorne................249 P5

Plucks Gutter................140 B9
Plumford................162 D2
Plumstead................27 K8
Plumstead Common................27 N9
Plumtree Green................247 K1
Pollhill................188 G3
Pootings................206 F3
Poplar................25 K3
Posting................286 D6
Potman's Heath................320 C9
Potten Street................109 P6
Potters Corner................252 B5
Potter's Forstal................219 J8
Poundsbridge................239 H9
Poverest................87 H1
Powder Mills................210 B7
Pratling Street................124 C9
Pratt's Bottom................117 J4
Preston................132 C7
Preston................169 L2
Priestwood................92 D9
Priestwood Green................92 D9
Printstile................239 M6
Puddledock................177 H9
Puddledock................65 M5
Pullington................318 F1
Purfleet................30 D8
Pye Corner................218 B4
The Quarter................320 D2
The Quarter................249 J4
Queenborough................77 J2
Queen Street................243 L1
Rabbit's Cross................216 B6
Radfall................106 B9
Radfield................130 F3
Rainham................97 K7
Ram Lane................221 K8
Ramsden................87 K5
Ramsgate................17 H4
Ramsye................270 A7
Ratling................199 J7
Reading Street................113 M5
Reading Street................321 N4
Reculver................108 G3
Red Hill................185 N2
Rhodes Minnis................256 F6
Richborough Port................172 A3
Ridge Row................288 C3
Ridgeway................284 D5
Ridley................121 C1
Ringlestone................158 G8
Ringlestone................155 J5
Ringwould................262 F5
Ripper's Cross................251 J5
Ripple................252 C9
Riseden................295 P2
River................290 E4
Riverhead................148 C7
Riverview Park................70 C3
Robhurst................302 B5
Rochester................18 D3
Rodmersham................130 C5
Rodmersham Green................130 A6
Rolvenden................319 M2
Rolvenden Layne................319 N4
Romford................272 A1
Romney Street................119 L6
Rooks Hill................179 P4
Roseacre................156 D8
Rosherville................24 G6
Rotherhithe................24 C6
Rough Common................166 A1
Roughway................181 L5
Round Green................275 L4
Round Street................92 E1
Rowling................200 B8
Rowling Street................305 H1
Royal British Legion Village................154 B4
Royal Tunbridge Wells................22 A5
Ruckinge................305 J7
Rushenden................77 H5
Rushmore Hill................117 K7
Rusthall................269 P4
Ruxley................64 C5
Ryarsh................123 H9
Rye................338 F6
Rye Foreign................338 B3
St George in the East................24 D5
St John's................270 C2
St John's................148 F7
St Johns................41 P5
St Lawrence................16 B1
St Leonard's Street................153 H5
St Margaret's at Cliffe................292 D1
St Mary Cray................87 K2
St Mary in the Marsh................335 J5
St Mary's Bay................337 M2
St Mary's Hoo................54 A2
St Mary's Island................72 C5
St Michaels................301 J3
St Nicholas at Wade................109 N8
St Paul's Cray................87 J2
St Peters................113 J8
Saint's Hill................238 C9
Salmans................238 D6
Saltwood................308 F3
Sandgate................310 B8
Sandhurst................318 A9
Sandhurst Cross................328 F1
Sandling................155 L3
Sandown Park................189 J8
Sandway................189 J8
Sandwich................201 M1
Sandwich Bay Estate................202 E2
Sarre................139 N2
Satmar................289 N9
Scragged Oak................126 C6
Scrapsgate................58 A7
Seabrook................309 M5
Seacox Heath................316 A4
Seal................149 M6
Seasalter................105 H7
Seaton................168 C6
Seed................160 G6
Selgrove................162 F2
Selhurst................60 B6
Sellindge................285 K7
Selling................163 M6
Selson................201 H7
Selsted................258 E7

Sevenoaks................21 H4
Sevenoaks Common................178 F5
Sevenoaks Weald................178 F8
Sevington................283 L2
Shadoxhurst................281 M8
Shadwell................24 F3
Shalmsford Street................195 H1
Sharnal Street................53 N7
Shatterling................169 P7
Sheerness................37 L5
Sheldwich................162 F6
Sheldwich Lees................162 G7
Shelvingford................138 D2
Shepherdswell................281 J9
Shepway................185 P3
Sherwood Park................271 H2
Shipbourne................180 F6
Shirkoak................302 F2
Shirley................83 P6
Sholden................232 E5
Shooters Hill................43 N2
Shoreham................118 D5
Shorncliffe Camp................310 A7
Shorne................70 G4
Shorne Ridgeway................70 F6
Shortlands................62 C9
Shottenden................193 N2
Shover's Green................314 A4
Shuttlesfield................257 H7
Sibertswold................281 J9
Sidcup................64 D3
Silver Street................65 M4
Silvertown................26 D5
Singleton................281 P1
Singlewell................69 N5
Sinkhurst Green................247 H8
Sissinghurst................276 D8
Sittingbourne................129 P3
Sixmile................256 C4
Skeete................286 C1
Slade................190 D2
Slade Green................46 A3
Sly Corner................323 H1
Small Hythe................320 C5
Smarden................249 H8
Smarden Bell................248 F7
Smart's Hill................238 E9
Smeeth................284 D4
Snagshall................328 G8
Snargate................323 N6
Snave................324 C6
Snipeshill................130 B2
Snodland................123 M4
Snowdown................229 J3
Sole Street................92 D2
Sole Street................225 J3
South Alkham................289 L4
South Ashford................2 A7
South Ashford................252 C9
Southborough................263 L8
Southborough................240 D8
South Bromley................25 N2
South Darenth................90 K7
Southend................62 A3
Southfields................33 J3
Southfleet................68 F5
South Godstone................204 C5
South Green................128 B6
South Norwood................60 C9
South Stifford................47 N4
South Stour................283 K7
South Street................146 A4
South Street................158 A8
South Street................127 N6
South Street................121 P7
South Street................105 P7
South Willesborough................282 G2
Speed Gate................90 C6
Speldhurst................269 M1
Spitalfields................24 D1
Spitals Cross................206 D7
Spring Park................84 C3
Stalisfield Green................191 J5
Standen................278 B3
Standen Street................318 D5
Stanford................286 A7
Stanhope................283 C7
Stansted................121 H5
Staple................200 B4
Staplehurst................246 C5
Staplestreet................134 A9
Starvecrow................181 J4
Statenborough................201 K6
Stede Quarter................278 E7
Stelling Minnis................226 E8
Stepney................24 E4
Stick Hill................237 H6
Stiff Street................128 G6
Stockbury................127 P5
Stocker's Head................221 L4
Stockland Green................239 N6
Stocks Green................209 N6
Stodmarsh................168 E2
Stoke................54 E5
Stonebridge Green................219 P6
Stone Cross................268 C6
Stone Cross................305 J1
Stonecouch................273 N3
Stonegate................314 E8
Stonehall................260 D8
Stone Hill................285 H6
Stonein Oxney................333 J1
Stonequarry................265 K5
Stone Street................180 B1
Stonestreet Green................284 C9
Stonewood................68 D9
Stowting................255 P9
Stowting Common................255 P9
Strawberry Hill................270 A8
Street End................196 E4
Strood................17 K2
Strood................319 H1
Stubb's Cross................282 A6
Studdal................261 K1
Studd Hill................106 F5
Sturry................137 K7
Styants Bottom................150 C6

Summerfield	200	C5
Sundridge	62	G5
Sundridge	147	N9
Sutton	261	P1
Sutton at Hone	66	G6
Sutton Valence	217	H3
Swalecliffe	106	D3
Swanley	65	N7
Swanley Village	66	A8
Swanscombe	48	D6
Swanton Street	158	G1
Swift's Green	248	F4
Swingfield Minnis	288	E1
Swingfield Street	288	C1
Sydenham	61	K4
Tanden	279	P7
Tandridge	174	D9
Tankerton	105	D5
Tatsfield	145	N5
Teasley Mead	268	B5
Temple Ewell	290	F2
Temple Hill	46	D5
Tenterden	301	H7
Teston	183	P4
Teynham	131	H2
Teynham Street	131	L1
Thamesmead	27	N3
Thanington	166	A7
The Rocks	153	P7
The Stocks	332	D1
The Valley	191	J3
The Warren	252	C4
Thong	70	C5
Thornton Heath	60	B9
Three Chimneys	277	L7
Three Leg Cross	315	H3
Throwley	162	A8
Throwley Forstal	191	P2
Thurnham	156	F4
Ticehurst	315	J4
Tilbury	49	L2
Tilmanstone	231	H6
Timberden Bottom	118	D4
Titsey	175	M1
Tolhurst	314	D4
Tonbridge	210	F9
Tong	217	M8
Tonge Corner	100	E7
Tong Green	191	N2
Tovil	185	K2
Tower Hamlets	291	H7
Townland Green	302	E6
Toy's Hill	177	K8
Trench Wood	210	D3
Trottiscliffe	122	B8
Troy Town	206	A5
Troy Town	254	D4
Troy Town	19	G7
Tubslake	297	L7
Tudeley	241	M2
Tudeley Hale	211	M9
Tulse Hill	40	B9
Tunstall	129	L5
Tutt Hill	221	M9
Twenties	112	B6
Twitham	199	P1
Twitton	148	D1
Twydall	96	E4
Tyler Hill	136	D7
Ulcombe	217	P3
Underling Green	215	L8
Underriver	179	M6
Under the Wood	108	E8
Union Street	315	M3
Upchurch	98	A2
Upper Bush	93	N4
Upper Deal	232	E5
Upper Elmers End	84	C2
Upper Goldstone	170	F6
Upper Halling	93	L9
Upper Harbledown	165	N3
Upper Hardres Court	196	E9
Upper Hayesden	239	N3
Upper Norwood	60	D7
Upper Rodmersham	130	B7
Upper Shirley	83	P8
Upper Sydenham	60	C3
Upper Upnor	72	E6
Upstreet	138	F6
Upton	113	L9
Vigo Village	122	A5
Waddon	82	D6
Wainscott	72	C5
Walderslade	125	L2
Wallcrouch	314	D5
Wall End	139	J5
Wallington	82	A9
Walmer	233	H7
Walter's Green	268	D1
Waltham	225	L4
Wandle Park	82	F6
Wanshurst Green	245	M2
Wapping	24	E4
Warden	80	C2
Ware	170	C5
Warehorne	304	A9
Ware Street	156	E7
Warlingham	144	A3
Warmlake	216	C2
Warren Street	190	C4
Waterham	134	D3
Wateringbury	183	K4
Waterman Quarter	247	N7
Waterside	82	F6
Way	141	M5
Wayfield	95	N7
Weavering Street	156	C8
Weddington	170	H8
Welches's Town	238	B4
Well Hill	88	A9
Welling	44	D4
Well Street	153	M6
Wennington	137	P6
Westbere	111	P3
Westbrook	292	C1
West Cliffe	82	H6
West Court	70	H1
West Cross	319	K2
West Dulwich	60	D1
Wested	88	D4
West End	160	C5
West End	106	F6
Westenhanger	308	A1
Westerham	176	E3
Western Heights	291	J9
West Farleigh	184	A5
Westfield Sole	125	P6
Westgate on Sea	111	L4
West Heath	28	C9
West Hougham	312	A1
West Hythe	308	A6
West Kingsdown	120	C2
West Langdon	261	L5
West Malling	153	J5
Westmarsh	170	C5
West Minster	57	H8
West Norwood	60	C3
West Peckham	182	C5
West Stourmouth	139	N7
West Street	52	A3
West Street	189	M2
West Street	201	P9
West Thurrock	31	K8
West Tilbury	33	M9
Westwell	222	B6
Westwell Leacon	221	J7
West Wickham	84	C5
Westerham	68	A6
Westwood	112	G8
Westwood	227	K2
West Yoke	90	C7
Wetham Green	98	A1
Whatsole Street	255	N5
Wheelbarrow Town	256	F1
Whetsted	212	F9
Whitfield	162	D1
White Oak	65	N8
White Post	268	C1
Whitfield	261	J8
Whitley Row	178	A5
Whitstable	105	L3
Wichling	160	B7
Wickhambreaux	168	D6
Wick Hill	248	A9
Wickhurst	208	G6
Widmore	63	H8
Wierton	216	C2
Wigmore	126	F1
Wilderness	149	K7
Wilgate Green	162	C6
Willesborough	176	B4
Willesborough Lees	253	L7
Willington	186	C2
Wilmington	66	B3
Wilsley Green	298	A1
Wilsley Pound	276	B8
Winchet Hill	274	G2
Windmill Hill	97	M3
Wingham	169	L9
Wingham Green	169	J9
Wingham Well	199	H1
Wingmore	227	N8
Winkhurst Green	208	A2
Winterbourne	164	B4
Wissenden	279	N1
Withersdane	254	A1
Wittersham	332	A2
Woldingham	144	D8
Woldingham Garden Village	144	C6
Wolverton	290	A5
Womenswold	228	C4
Woodchurch	302	C6
Woodland	286	D1
Woodlands	119	P7
Woodnesborough	201	H4
Woodsden	317	N2
Wood's Green	294	A7
Woodstock	83	M3
Woodside	94	B9
Woodside Green	189	M3
Woodstock	129	M7
Woodside	229	J7
Woolage Green	228	G5
Woolwich	27	H9
Wootton	258	F4
Worms Hill	274	G4
Wormshill	159	H5
Worten	251	M6
Worth	202	A5
Wouldham	94	B9
Wrotham	151	K1
Wrotham Heath	151	P5
Wye	224	A9
Wyebanks	190	E1
Yalding	213	P1
Yardhurst	281	H1
Yelsted	127	K4
Yewhedges	161	L8
Yewtree Cross	257	H9
Yopps Green	181	H2
Yorkletts	134	G2

USING THE STREET INDEX

Street names are listed alphabetically. Each street name is followed by its postal town or area locality, the Postcode District, the page number, and the reference to the square in which the name is found.

Standard index entries are shown as follows:

Aaron Hill Rd *EHAM* E6 ....27 H1

Street names and selected addresses not shown on the map due to scale restrictions are shown in the index with an asterisk:

Abbey Pl *DART* DA1 * 46 D6

GENERAL ABBREVIATIONS

ACC....ACCESS	CTYD....COURTYARD	HLS....HILLS	MWY....MOTORWAY	SE....SOUTH EAST
ALY....ALLEY	CUTT....CUTTINGS	HO....HOUSE	N....NORTH	SER....SERVICE AREA
AP....APPROACH	CV....COVE	HOL....HOLLOW	NE....NORTH EAST	SH....SHORE
AR....ARCADE	CYN....CANYON	HOSP....HOSPITAL	NW....NORTH WEST	SHOP....SHOPPING
ASS....ASSOCIATION	DEPT....DEPARTMENT	HRB....HARBOUR	O/P....OVERPASS	SKWY....SKYWAY
AV....AVENUE	DL....DALE	HTH....HEATH	OFF....OFFICE	SMT....SUMMIT
BCH....BEACH	DM....DAM	HTS....HEIGHTS	ORCH....ORCHARD	SOC....SOCIETY
BLDS....BUILDINGS	DR....DRIVE	HVN....HAVEN	OVAL....OVAL	SP....SPUR
BND....BEND	DRO....DROVE	HWY....HIGHWAY	PAL....PALACE	SPR....SPRING
BNK....BANK	DRY....DRIVEWAY	IMP....IMPERIAL	PAS....PASSAGE	SQ....SQUARE
BR....BRIDGE	DWGS....DWELLINGS	IN....INLET	PAV....PAVILION	ST....STREET
BRK....BROOK	E....EAST	IND EST....INDUSTRIAL ESTATE	PDE....PARADE	STN....STATION
BTM....BOTTOM	EMB....EMBANKMENT	INF....INFIRMARY	PH....PUBLIC HOUSE	STR....STREAM
BUS....BUSINESS	EMBY....EMBASSY	INFO....INFORMATION	PK....PARK	STRD....STRAND
BVD....BOULEVARD	ESP....ESPLANADE	INT....INTERCHANGE	PKWY....PARKWAY	SW....SOUTH WEST
BY....BYPASS	EST....ESTATE	IS....ISLAND	PL....PLACE	TDG....TRADING
CATH....CATHEDRAL	EX....EXCHANGE	JCT....JUNCTION	PLN....PLAIN	TER....TERRACE
CEM....CEMETERY	EXPY....EXPRESSWAY	JTY....JETTY	PLNS....PLAINS	THWY....THROUGHWAY
CEN....CENTRE	EXT....EXTENSION	KG....KING	PLZ....PLAZA	TNL....TUNNEL
CFT....CROFT	F/O....FLYOVER	KNL....KNOLL	POL....POLICE STATION	TOLL....TOLLWAY
CH....CHURCH	FC....FOOTBALL CLUB	L....LAKE	PR....PRINCE	TPK....TURNPIKE
CHA....CHASE	FK....FORK	LA....LANE	PREC....PRECINCT	TR....TRACK
CHYD....CHURCHYARD	FLD....FIELD	LDG....LODGE	PREP....PREPARATORY	TRL....TRAIL
CIR....CIRCLE	FLDS....FIELDS	LGT....LIGHT	PRIM....PRIMARY	TWR....TOWER
CIRC....CIRCUS	FLS....FALLS	LK....LOCK	PROM....PROMENADE	U/P....UNDERPASS
CL....CLOSE	FM....FARM	LKS....LAKES	PRS....PRINCESS	UNI....UNIVERSITY
CLFS....CLIFFS	FT....FORT	LNDG....LANDING	PRT....PORT	UPR....UPPER
CMP....CAMP	FTS....FLATS	LTL....LITTLE	PT....POINT	V....VALE
CNR....CORNER	FWY....FREEWAY	LWR....LOWER	PTH....PATH	VA....VALLEY
CO....COUNTY	FY....FERRY	MAG....MAGISTRATE	PZ....PIAZZA	VIAD....VIADUCT
COLL....COLLEGE	GA....GATE	MAN....MANSIONS	QD....QUADRANT	VIL....VILLA
COM....COMMON	GAL....GALLERY	MD....MEAD	QU....QUEEN	VIS....VISTA
COMM....COMMISSION	GDN....GARDEN	MDW....MEADOWS	QY....QUAY	VLG....VILLAGE
CON....CONVENT	GDNS....GARDENS	MEM....MEMORIAL	R....RIVER	VLS....VILLAS
COT....COTTAGE	GLD....GLADE	MI....MILL	RBT....ROUNDABOUT	VW....VIEW
COTS....COTTAGES	GLN....GLEN	MKT....MARKET	RD....ROAD	W....WEST
CP....CAPE	GN....GREEN	MKTS....MARKETS	RDG....RIDGE	WD....WOOD
CPS....COPSE	GND....GROUND	ML....MALL	REP....REPUBLIC	WHF....WHARF
CR....CREEK	GRA....GRANGE	MNR....MANOR	RES....RESERVOIR	WK....WALK
CREM....CREMATORIUM	GRG....GARAGE	MS....MEWS	RFC....RUGBY FOOTBALL CLUB	WKS....WALKS
CRS....CRESCENT	GT....GREAT	MSN....MISSION	RI....RISE	WLS....WELLS
CSWY....CAUSEWAY	GTWY....GATEWAY	MT....MOUNT	RP....RAMP	WY....WAY
CT....COURT	GV....GROVE	MTN....MOUNTAIN	RW....ROW	YD....YARD
CTRL....CENTRAL	HGR....HIGHER	MTS....MOUNTAINS	S....SOUTH	YHA....YOUTH HOSTEL
CTS....COURTS	HL....HILL	MUS....MUSEUM	SCH....SCHOOL	

POSTCODE TOWNS AND AREA ABBREVIATIONS

ABYW....Abbey Wood	BGR/WK....Borough Green/West Kingsdown	BRXS/STRHM....Brixton south/Streatham Hill	CAR....Carshalton	CROY/NA....Croydon/New Addington
ASH....Ashford (Kent)	BH/WHM....Biggin Hill/Westerham	BUR/ETCH....Burwash/Etchingham	CAT....Catford	CTHM....Caterham
BANK....Bank	BKHTH/KID....Blackheath/Kidbrooke	BXLY....Bexley	CDW/CHF....Chadwell St Mary/Chafford Hundred	CVI....Canvey Island
BARB....Barbican	BMLY....Bromley	BXLYHN....Bexleyheath north	BXLY....Bexley	DAGW....Dagenham west
BARK....Barking	BOW....Bow	BXLYHS....Bexleyheath south	CHARL....Charlton	DART....Dartford
BECK....Beckenham	BRCH....Birchington	CAN/RD....Canning Town/Royal Docks	CHAT....Chatham	DEAL....Deal
BELV....Belvedere	BRDST....Broadstairs	CANST....Cannon Street station	CHST....Chislehurst	DEPT....Deptford
BERM/RHTH....Bermondsey/Rotherhithe	BROCKY....Brockley	CANT....Canterbury	CITYW....City of London west	DIT/AY....Ditton/Aylesford
BFN/LL....Blackfen/Longlands	BRXN/ST....Brixton north/Stockwell	CANTW/ST....Canterbury west/Sturry	CMBW....Camberwell	DUL....Dulwich
			CRAWE....Crawley east	DVE/WH....Dover east/Whitfield
			CRBK....Cranbrook	

DVW Dover west
E/WMAL East & West Malling
EDEN Edenbridge
EDUL East Dulwich
EGRIN East Grinstead
EHAM East Ham
ELTH/MOT Eltham/Mottingham
ERITH Erith
ERITHM Erith Marshes
EYN Eynsford
FAV Faversham
FENCHST Fenchurch Street
FOLK Folkestone
FOLKN Folkestone north
FSTH Forest Hill
GDST Godstone
GILL Gillingham
GNWCH Greenwich
GRAYS Grays
GVE Gravesend east
GVW Gravesend west
HART Hartley
HAWK Hawkhurst
HAYES Hayes
HB Herne Bay
HDCN Headcorn
HDTCH Houndsditch
HNHL Herne Hill
HOO/HM Hoo St Werburgh/Higham
HRTF Hartfield
HYTHE Hythe
IOS Isle of Sheppey
KEN/WIL Kennington/Willesborough
LBTH Lambeth
LEE/GVPK Lee/Grove Park
LEW Lewisham
LING Lingfield
LOTH Lothbury
LVPST Liverpool Street
LYDD Lydd
MAID/BEAR Maidstone/Bearsted
MAID/SHEP Maidstone/Shepway
MAIDW Maidstone west
MANHO Mansion House
MARG Margate
MEO Meopham
MON Monument
MSTR Minster
MTCM Mitcham
NROM New Romney
NRWD Norwood
NWCR New Cross
OBST Old Broad Street
ORP Orpington
OXTED Oxted
PECK Peckham
PGE/AN Penge/Anerley
PLSTW Plaistow
POP/IOD Poplar/Isle of Dogs
PUR Purfleet
QBOR Queenborough
RAIN Rainham (Gt Lon)
RAM Ramsgate
RASHE Rural Ashford east
RASHW Rural Ashford west
RBTBR Robertsbridge
RCANTE Rural Canterbury east
RCANTW Rural Canterbury west
RDART Rural Dartford
RDV Rural Dover
RFOLK Rural Folkestone
RHAM Rainham (Kent)
RMAID Rural Maidstone
ROCH Rochester
RRTW Rural Royal Tunbridge Wells
RSEV Rural Sevenoaks
RSIT Rural Sittingbourne
RTON Rural Tonbridge
RTW Royal Tunbridge Wells
RTWE/PEM Royal Tunbridge Wells east/Pembury
RYE Rye
SAND/SEL Sanderstead/Selsdon
SBGH/RUST Southborough/Rusthall
SCUP Sidcup
SDTCH Shoreditch
SEV Sevenoaks
SIT Sittingbourne
SLH/COR Stanford-le-Hope/Corringham
SNOD Snodland
SNWD South Norwood
SOCK/AV South Ockendon/Aveley
SOS Southend-on-Sea
STHWK Southwark
STLK St Luke's
STMC/STPC St Mary Cray/St Paul's Cray
STPH/PW Staplehurst/Paddock Wood
STRD Strood
STRHM/NOR Streatham/Norbury
SWCH Sandwich
SWCM Swanscombe
SWLY Swanley
SYD Sydenham
TENT Tenterden
THHTH Thornton Heath
THMD Thamesmead
TIL Tilbury
TON Tonbridge
TONN Tonbridge north
TWRH Tower Hill
VX/NE Vauxhall/Nine Elms
WADH Wadhurst
WALD Walderslade
WALW Walworth
WAP Wapping
WARL Warlingham
WBY/YAL Wateringbury/Yalding
WCHPL Whitechapel
WELL Welling
WGOS Westgate on Sea
WLGTN Wallington
WNWD West Norwood
WOOL/PLUM Woolwich/Plumstead
WOS/PRIT Westcliff-on-Sea/Prittlewell
WSEA Winchelsea
WSTB Whitstable
WTHK West Thurrock
WWKM West Wickham

Index - streets

A

Aaron Hill Rd *EHAM* E6 **27** H1
Abbess Cl *BRXS/STRHM* SW2 **40** B9
Abbey Brewery Ct
E/WMAL ME19 * **153** K4
Abbey Cl *DEAL* CT14 **232** F4
IOS ME12 **78** D1
Abbey Ct *WGOS* CT8 **111** L6
Abbey Crs *BELV* DA17 **28** F7
Abbey Dr *RDART* DA2 **65** N1
Abbeyfield Est
BERM/RHTH SE16 **24** F7
Abbeyfield Rd
BERM/RHTH SE16 **24** F7
Abbey Flds *FAV* ME13 **133** H6
Abbey Gdns *CANTW/ST* CT2 **166** F1
CHST BR7 **63** L7
STHWK SE1 **24** D7
Abbey Gv *ABYW* SE2 **28** A7
MSTR CT12 **141** K7
RAM CT11 **142** G7
Abbeyhill Rd *BFN/LL* DA15 **44** E9
Abbey La *BECK* BR3 **61** N6
Abbey Mt *BELV* DA17 **28** E8
Abbey Pk *BECK* BR3 **61** N6
Abbey Pl *DART* DA1 * **46** D6
FAV ME13 **132** G5
Abbey Rd *BELV* DA17 **28** C7
BXLYHN DA7 **44** G5
CROY/NA CR0 **82** G7
DVE/WH CT16 **290** E3
DVW CT17 **290** F6
FAV ME13 **132** G5
GVE DA12 **50** A9
RDV CT15 **290** C6
RHAM ME8 **96** D4
SAND/SEL CR2 **114** A4
STRD ME2 **71** P7
SWCM DA10 **48** A6
Abbey St *FAV* ME13 **132** G5
STHWK SE1 **24** C6
Abbey Ter *ABYW* SE2 **28** B6
Abbeyview Dr *IOS* ME12 **78** B1
Abbey Wy *KEN/WIL* TN24 **253** K7
Abbey Wood Rd *ABYW* SE2 **28** A7
E/WMAL ME19 **153** H7
Abbots Barton Wk *CANT* CT1 **5** G7
Abbotsbury Ms *PECK* SE15 **41** J4
Abbotsbury Rd *WWKM* BR4 **85** J6
Abbots Cl *STMC/STPC* BR5 **86** D5
Abbots Ct *HOO/HM* ME3 * **73** N2
Abbots Court Rd
HOO/HM ME3 **73** M3
Abbots Fld *MAIDW* ME16 **184** G1
Abbots Gn *CROY/NA* CR0 **114** A1
Abbotshade Rd
BERM/RHTH SE16 * **24** G4
Abbotshall Rd *CAT* SE6 **42** B9
Abbots Hl *FAV* ME13 **132** B8
Abbot's Hl *RAM* CT11 **17** G4
Abbots La *STHWK* SE1 **24** B4
Abbots Pk *BRXS/STRHM* SW2 **40** A9
Abbots Pl *CANT* CT1 **4** E3
Abbots Rd *FAV* ME13 **133** H6
The Abbots *DVW* CT17 **8** A3
Abbots Wk *RASHE* TN25 **223** P7
Abbots Wy *BECK* BR3 **84** B2
Abbotswell Rd *BROCKY* SE4 **41** M6
Abbotswood Cl *BELV* DA17 **28** D6
Abbotswood Rd *EDUL* SE22 **40** E5
Abbott Dr *RSIT* ME9 **129** L7
Abbott Rd *BGR/WK* TN15 **151** J5
FOLK CT20 **11** G2
POP/IOD E14 **25** M1
Abbotts Cl *ROCH* ME1 **94** G3
SWLY BR8 **88** F1
THMD SE28 **28** B3
Abbotts Rd *MTCM* CR4 **82** B1
Abbott's Wk *BXLYHN* DA7 **44** F1
Abbott Wy *TENT* TN30 **301** K8
Abchurch La *MANHO* EC4N **24** A3
Abercorn Cl *SAND/SEL* CR2 **114** A6
Abercorn Wy *STHWK* SE1 **24** D8
Aberdare Cl *WWKM* BR4 **84** F6
Aberdeen Cl *RCANTE* CT3 **138** G6
Aberdeen Rd *CROY/NA* CR0 **83** H8
Aberdeen Ter *BKHTH/KID* SE3 **42** B3
Aberdour St *STHWK* SE1 **24** B7
Aberfeldy St *POP/IOD* E14 **25** M2
Aberford Gdns
WOOL/PLUM SE18 **43** J2
Abergeldie Rd *LEE/GVPK* SE12 **42** F7
Abernethy Rd *LEW* SE13 **42** C5
Abery St *WOOL/PLUM* SE18 **27** M7
Abigail Crs *WALD* ME5 **125** M4
Abingdon Cl *STHWK* SE1 * **24** C8
Abingdon Gv *RCANTE* CT3 **138** G6
Abingdon Rd *MAIDW* ME16 **184** E1
Abingdon Wy *ORP* BR6 **87** J8
Abinger Cl *BMLY* BR1 **63** J9
CROY/NA CR0 **114** F1
WLGTN SM6 **82** D9
Abinger Dr *NRWD* SE19 **60** C6
WALD ME5 **126** A3
Abinger Gv *DEPT* SE8 **25** J9
Ablett St *BERM/RHTH* SE16 **24** F8
Acacia Av *RCANTE* CT3 **138** A9
Acacia Cl *DEPT* SE8 **25** H7
STMC/STPC BR5 **86** E2
Acacia Gdns *WWKM* BR4 **84** F6
Acacia Gv *DUL* SE21 **60** D1
Acacia Rd *BECK* BR3 **61** M9
DART DA1 **46** C9
RDART DA2 **47** L7
Acacia Wy *BFN/LL* DA15 **44** B8
Academy Dr *GILL* ME7 **96** C6
Academy Gdns *CROY/NA* CR0 **83** L5
Academy Pl
WOOL/PLUM SE18 **43** K2
Academy Rd
WOOL/PLUM SE18 **43** K1
Acanthus Dr *STHWK* SE1 **24** D8
Acer Av *RTWE/PEM* TN2 **270** F8
Acer Rd *BH/WHM* TN16 **145** N1
Achilles Cl *STHWK* SE1 **24** D8
Achilles Rd *WALD* ME5 **125** P3
Achilles St *NWCR* SE14 **41** L1
Ackholt Rd *RCANTE* CT3 **229** K1
Ackroyd Dr *BOW* E3 **25** J1
Ackroyd Rd *FSTH* SE23 **41** K8
Acland Cl *WOOL/PLUM* SE18 **43** P1
Acland Crs *CMBW* SE5 **40** D5
Acol Hl *BRCH* CT7 **111** J9
Acorn Cl *ASH* TN23 **282** F5
CHST BR7 **63** N4
EGRIN RH19 **265** H8
STPH/PW TN12 **242** C2
Acorn Gdns *NRWD* SE19 **60** F7
Acorn Gv *DIT/AY* ME20 **154** C4
Acorn Pde *PECK* SE15 * **41** H1
Acorn Pl *MAID/SHEP* ME15 **186** B5
Acorn Rd *DART* DA1 **45** P6
GILL ME7 **96** C2
The Acorns *HDCN* TN27 **248** G8
SEV TN13 **148** F8
WADH TN5 **314** D8
Acorn St *IOS* ME12 **57** L7
Acorn Wy *BECK* BR3 **84** F2
FSTH SE23 **61** K2
ORP BR6 **86** C8
Acorn Wharf Rd *ROCH* ME1 **19** G3
Acott Flds *WBY/YAL* ME18 **213** N1
Acre Cl *ROCH* ME1 **95** K5
Acre Dr *EDUL* SE22 **40** G5
Acre Gv *STRD* ME2 **123** P1
Acres Ri *WADH* TN5 **315** J5
The Acre *DVE/WH* CT16 **260** G8
Acton La *TENT* TN30 **321** L8
Acton Rd *WSTB* CT5 **105** L5
Acworth Pl *DART* DA1 * **46** C7
Ada Gdns *POP/IOD* E14 **25** N2
Adair Cl *SNWD* SE25 **61** H9
Adam Cl *CAT* SE6 **61** M3
FSTH SE23 **61** J1
RMAID ME17 **185** J8
Adams Cl *TENT* TN30 **301** J6
Adams Ct *WALD* ME5 * **95** N8
Adamson Rd *CAN/RD* E16 **26** B2
Adamson Wy *BECK* BR3 **84** F2
Adamsrill Rd *SYD* SE26 **61** K3
Adams Rd *BECK* BR3 **84** B2
Adams Sq *BXLYHS* DA6 **44** G4
Adams Wy *CROY/NA* CR0 **83** L3
Ada Rd *CANT* CT1 **166** C6
CMBW SE5 **40** E1
Adbert Dr *MAID/SHEP* ME15 **184** G7
Addelam Cl *DEAL* CT14 **232** F5
Addelam Rd *DEAL* CT14 **232** F5
Adderley Gdns *ELTH/MOT* SE9 **63** L3
Adderley St *POP/IOD* E14 **25** M2
Addington Gv *SYD* SE26 **61** L3
Addington La *E/WMAL* ME19 **122** B9
Addington Pl *RAM* CT11 **17** F5
Addington Rd *CROY/NA* CR0 **82** F5
MARG CT9 **15** H4
SIT ME10 **129** M2
WWKM BR4 **84** F8
Addington Sq *CMBW* SE5 **40** C1
MARG CT9 **15** H5
Addington St *MARG* CT9 **15** H4
RAM CT11 **16** E5
Addington Village Rd
CROY/NA CR0 **114** C1
Addiscombe Av *CROY/NA* CR0 **83** M4
Addiscombe Court Rd
CROY/NA CR0 **83** K5
Addiscombe Gdns *MARG* CT9 **15** J7
Addiscombe Gv *CROY/NA* CR0 **83** J6
Addiscombe Rd
CROY/NA CR0 **83** K6
MARG CT9 **15** K6
Addison Cl *E/WMAL* ME19 **153** N3
STMC/STPC BR5 **86** D3
Addison Dr *LEE/GVPK* SE12 **42** F6
Addison Gdns *GRAYS* RM17 **32** D7
Addison Rd *HAYES* BR2 **85** N2
SNWD SE25 **83** M1
Addison's Cl *CROY/NA* CR0 **84** C6
Addlestead Rd
STPH/PW TN12 **212** F4
Adelaide Av *BROCKY* SE4 **41** N5
Adelaide Dr *SIT* ME10 **129** K1
Adelaide Gdns *IOS* ME12 **77** M1
RAM CT11 **17** F5
Adelaide Pl *CANT* CT1 **4** D5
Adelaide Rd *CHST* BR7 **63** M4
GILL ME7 **7** J5
RDV CT15 **230** C8
TIL RM18 **49** K2
The Adelaide *HOO/HM* ME3 **71** L1
Adelina Gv *WCHPL* E1 **24** F1
Adenmore Rd *CAT* SE6 **41** N8
Adie Rd *NROM* TN28 **343** J1
Adie Rd North *NROM* TN28 **343** J1
Adisham Downs Rd
RCANTE CT3 **198** E5
Adisham Dr *MAIDW* ME16 **154** G5
Adisham Gn *SIT* ME10 **99** N6
Adisham Rd *RCANTW* CT4 **198** A4
RCANTW CT4 **228** F4
Adisham Wy *MARG* CT9 **113** H4
Adler St *WCHPL* E1 **24** D1
Admaston Rd
WOOL/PLUM SE18 **43** N1
Admers Wy *MEO* DA13 **122** C5
Admiral Cl *STMC/STPC* BR5 **87** L1
Admiral Moore Dr
DIT/AY ME20 **154** E3
Admiral Pl *BERM/RHTH* SE16 **25** H4
Admiral Seymour Rd
ELTH/MOT SE9 **43** K5
Admiral's Ga *GNWCH* SE10 **41** P2
Admiral St *DEPT* SE8 **41** N2
Admiral's Wk *CHAT* ME4 **72** F8
Admirals Wk *CRBK* TN17 **298** G5
HYTHE CT21 * **309** H6
IOS ME12 **77** N1
RDART DA2 **47** P6
TENT TN30 **301** K6
Admirals Wy *POP/IOD* E14 **25** K5
Admiralty Cl *DEPT* SE8 * **41** N2
FAV ME13 **132** E5
Admiralty Ms *DEAL* CT14 **233** J5
Admiralty Rd *STRD* ME2 **72** F6
Admiralty Ter *STRD* ME2 **72** F6
Admiralty Wk *WSTB* CT5 **105** H7
Admiral Wy *E/WMAL* ME19 **183** H2
Adolf St *CAT* SE6 **61** N3
Adolphus St *DEPT* SE8 **41** M1
Adrian Ct *WGOS* CT8 * **111** M4
Adrian Ms *WGOS* CT8 * **111** N4
Adrian Sq *WGOS* CT8 **111** M4
Adrian St *DVW* CT17 **8** D5
Adstock Wy *GRAYS* RM17 **32** A7
Advance Rd *WNWD* SE27 **60** C3
Advice Av *CDW/CHF* RM16 **32** B5
Adys Rd *PECK* SE15 **40** F4
Aerodrome Rd *RCANTW* CT4 **198** B4
RFOLK CT18 **288** B8
Afghan Rd *BRDST* CT10 **113** L5
CHAT ME4 **6** A5
Afton Dr *SOCK/AV* RM15 **31** L2
Agate Cl *CAN/RD* E16 **26** E2
Agate Ct *SIT* ME10 **99** L8
Agatha Cl *WAP* E1W **24** E4
Agaton Rd *ELTH/MOT* SE9 **63** N1
Agester La *RCANTW* CT4 **258** D2
Agnes Cl *EHAM* E6 **27** H3
Agnes St *POP/IOD* E14 **25** J2
Agnew Rd *FSTH* SE23 **41** L8
Ailsa Cft *ROCH* ME1 **94** E4
Ailsa Ms *ROCH* ME1 **94** E4
Ailsa St *POP/IOD* E14 **25** M1
Ailsworth La *RYE* TN31 * **338** F6
Ainsborough Av *MARG* CT9 **113** H5
Ainsdale Cl *FOLKN* CT19 **310** D4
ORP BR6 **86** E5
Ainsdale Dr *STHWK* SE1 **24** D8
Ainsty St *BERM/RHTH* SE16 * **24** F5
Ainsworth Cl *CMBW* SE5 * **40** E3
Ainsworth Rd *CROY/NA* CR0 **82** G6
Aintree Cl *GVE* DA12 **69** M2
Aintree Rd *WALD* ME5 **125** P2
Airedale Cl *MARG* CT9 **15** K6
RDART DA2 **47** J9
Airfield Vw *IOS* ME12 **79** J7
Aisher Rd *THMD* SE28 **28** B3
Aisher Wy *SEV* TN13 **148** D6
Aislibie Rd *LEE/GVPK* SE12 **42** C5
Aisne Dr *CANT* CT1 **167** J3
Aitken Rd *CAT* SE6 **61** P1
Ajax Rd *ROCH* ME1 **95** H7
Akabusi Cl *CROY/NA* CR0 **83** M3
Akehurst La *SEV* TN13 **21** G4
Akerman Rd *BRXN/ST* SW9 **40** B2
Alabama St *WOOL/PLUM* SE18 **43** P1
Alamein Av *WALD* ME5 **95** L7
Alamein Cl *RDV* CT15 **291** N5
Alamein Gdns *RDART* DA2 **47** K8
Alamein Rd *SWCM* DA10 **48** B7
Alanbrooke *GVE* DA12 **49** N8
Alan Cl *DART* DA1 **46** C5
Alanthus Cl *LEE/GVPK* SE12 **42** D7
Albacore Crs *LEW* SE13 **41** P7
Alban Crs *EYN* DA4 **89** M5
Albany Cl *BXLY* DA5 **44** E8
TON TN9 **240** G2
Albany Dr *HB* CT6 **107** J1
Albany Hl *RTWE/PEM* TN2 **23** H1
Albany Ms *BMLY* BR1 **62** E5
Albany Pl *DVW* CT17 **8** D4
Albany Rd *BELV* DA17 **28** E9
BXLY DA5 **44** E8
CHAT ME4 **95** N4
CHST BR7 **63** M4
RFOLK CT18 **311** L2
ROCH ME1 **95** H3
SIT ME10 **129** M1
TIL RM18 **49** L2
WALW SE17 **24** A9
Albany St *MAID/BEAR* ME14 **13** H2
Albany Ter *CHAT* ME4 **6** A5
Albatross Av *STRD* ME2 **71** L9
Albatross Gdns
SAND/SEL CR2 **114** A5
Albatross St *WOOL/PLUM* SE18 **44** A1
Albemarle Cl *GRAYS* RM17 **32** B5
Albemarle Pk *BECK* BR3 * **61** P7
Albemarle Rd *BECK* BR3 **61** P7
KEN/WIL TN24 **253** J9
WALD ME5 **125** P3
Alberta Cl *DVE/WH* CT16 **291** J4
Alberta Rd *ERITH* DA8 **45** L2
Albert Cl *CDW/CHF* RM16 **32** D6
Albert Cots *RTW* TN1 * **23** F2
WCHPL E1 * **24** D1
Albert Ct *RAM* CT11 * **17** F4
WSTB CT5 * **105** L4
Albert Dr *MAID/SHEP* ME15 **184** G7
Albert Gdns *WCHPL* E1 **24** G2
Albert La *HYTHE* CT21 **308** G6
Albert Ms *BROCKY* SE4 * **41** M5
POP/IOD E14 * **25** H3
Albert Murray Cl *GVE* DA12 **49** N8
Albert Pl *STRD* ME2 **18** E1
Albert Reed Gdns
MAID/SHEP ME15 **185** K1
Albert Rd *BELV* DA17 **28** E8
BRDST CT10 **113** K6
BXLY DA5 **45** J7
CAN/RD E16 **26** F4
CANT CT1 **5** H5
CHAT ME4 **6** D7
DEAL CT14 **233** H3
DVE/WH CT16 **8** C1
ELTH/MOT SE9 **63** J2
FOLKN CT19 **10** E1
GILL ME7 **7** H4
HAYES BR2 **85** N2
HYTHE CT21 **308** G6
KEN/WIL TN24 **2** D2
MARG CT9 **14** D5
ORP BR6 **87** H9
PGE/AN SE20 **61** K6
RAM CT11 **17** J2
RDART DA2 **66** C2
RFOLK CT18 **311** M2
ROCH ME1 **95** H3
SNWD SE25 **83** N1
STMC/STPC BR5 **87** J3
SWCM DA10 **48** D7
TON TN9 **210** E9
WARL CR6 **144** B2
Albert St *MAID/BEAR* ME14 **12** E1
RAM CT11 **16** E5
RTW TN1 **22** E2
WSTB CT5 **105** L4
Albert Ter *IOS* ME12 * **78** G2
MARG CT9 **15** F4
Albert Wy *PECK* SE15 **41** H1
Albion Cl *HB* CT6 **107** M6
Albion Ct *RAM* CT11 **17** G3
Albion Est *BERM/RHTH* SE16 * **24** F5
Albion La *HB* CT6 **107** M6
Albion Ms *RAM* CT11 **17** H4
Albion Mews Rd *FOLK* CT20 **10** E5
Albion Pl *CANT* CT1 **5** G3
FAV ME13 **132** F6
IOS ME12 **57** L6
KEN/WIL TN24 **283** H1
MAID/BEAR ME14 **13** H4
MARG CT9 * **15** H3
RAM CT11 **17** G4
SNWD SE25 **60** G9
Albion Rd *BRCH* CT7 **111** H6
BRDST CT10 **113** L7
BXLYHS DA6 **45** H5
DEAL CT14 **233** J1
FOLKN CT19 **11** F1
GVE DA12 **49** N8
MARG CT9 **112** F2
RAM CT11 **17** H2
RTW TN1 **23** F1
STPH/PW TN12 **245** J4
SWCH CT13 **201** H8
WALD ME5 **125** N3
Albion St *BERM/RHTH* SE16 **24** F5
BRDST CT10 **113** N9
CROY/NA CR0 **82** G5
Albion Ter *GVE* DA12 **49** N7
SIT ME10 * **99** M8
Albion Vls *FOLK* CT20 **11** F5
Albion Villas Rd *SYD* SE26 **61** J2
Albion Wy *EDEN* TN8 **206** D6
LEW SE13 **42** A5
Albrighton Rd *EDUL* SE22 **40** E4
Albuhera Sq *CANT* CT1 **167** J3
Albury Av *BXLYHN* DA7 **44** G3
Albury Cl *WALD* ME5 **126** A3
Albury St *DEPT* SE8 **25** K9
Albyfield *BMLY* BR1 **63** K9
Albyn Rd *DEPT* SE8 **41** N2
Alcester Rd *WLGTN* SM6 **82** A8
Aldbridge St *WALW* SE17 **24** B8
Aldeburgh St *GNWCH* SE10 **26** B8
Alder Cl *IOS* ME12 **57** J8
PECK SE15 **24** C9
SBGH/RUST TN4 **240** F8
Aldergate La *HYTHE* CT21 **307** K6
Alderholt Wy *PECK* SE15 * **40** E1
Alder La *CRBK* TN17 **319** H5
Alderman Cl *DART* DA1 **45** N8
Aldermary Rd *BMLY* BR1 **62** E7
Aldermoor Rd *CAT* SE6 **61** M2
Aldernay Wy *KEN/WIL* TN24 **252** F2
Alderney Ms *STHWK* SE1 **24** A6
Alderney Rd *ERITH* DA8 **46** A1
Alder Rd *FOLKN* CT19 **10** C1
SCUP DA14 **64** A2
Alders Av *EGRIN* RH19 **264** G5
Aldersford Cl *BROCKY* SE4 **41** K5

Aldersgrove Av ELTH/MOT SE9 ...62 G2
Aldershot Rd WALD ME5..............95 M7
Aldershot Ter
  WOOL/PLUM SE18 * 43 L1
Aldersmead Av CROY/NA CRO ...84 A3
Alders Meadow TON TN9 ....210 C8
Aldersmead Rd BECK BR3...........61 L6
Alders Rd RTON TN11................241 P5
  STPH/PW TN12 ....242 B5
The Alders WBY/YAL ME18........182 E4
  WWKM BR4 ....84 E5
Alders View Dr EGRIN RH19 ....265 H5
Alderton Rd CDW/CHF RM16 .....33 L2
  CROY/NA CRO...........................83 L4
  HNHL SE24................................40 C4
Alder Wy SWLY BR8....................65 M8
Alderwood Rd ELTH/MOT SE9 ...43 P7
Aldgate FENCHST EC3M..............24 B2
Aldgate Barrs WCHPL E1 * 24 C2
Aldgate High St TWRH EC3N * ...24 C2
Aldham Dr SOCK/AV RM15..........31 L1
Aldington Cl WALD ME5................95 P8
Aldington La
  MAID/BEAR ME14..................156 G4
Aldington Rd CHARL SE7............63 L6
  HYTHE CT21.............................307 K4
  MAID/BEAR ME14..................156 C8
Aldon Cl MAID/BEAR ME14..........15 K1
Aldon La E/WMAL ME19.............152 C4
Aldred Rd FAV ME15...................132 F2
Aldrich Crs CROY/NA CRO.........114 F3
Aldridge Cl HB CT6.....................106 G3
Aldwick Cl ELTH/MOT SE9 ....63 P2
Aldwick Rd CROY/NA CRO............82 A7
Alec Pemble Cl KEN/WIL TN24 ..253 H4
Alefe Wy RSIT ME9.......................99 L3
Alen Sq STPH/PW TN12 ....246 C5
Alers Rd BXLYHS DA6...................66 F6
Alestan Beck Rd CAN/RD E16 ......26 E2
Alexander Cl BFN/LL DA15...........44 A6
  FAV ME13 ....132 E5
  HAYES BR2 ....85 K5
  SWCH CT13 ....201 N2
Alexander Ct SIT ME10 * 99 M9
Alexander Dr FAV ME13.............132 E6
Alexander Evans Ms
  FSTH SE23.................................61 K1
Alexander Gv E/WMAL ME19 ....153 H9
Alexander PI OXTED RH8............175 H4
Alexander Rd BXLYHN DA7..........44 F5
  CHST BR7 ....188 A2
  SWCM DA10 ....68 A6
Alexander Ter ABYW SE2 * 28 A8
Alexandra Av GILL ME7.................96 B2
  WARL CR6 ....114 A2
Alexandra Cl CDW/CHF RM16 .....33 J5
  SIT ME10 ....99 M7
  SWLY BR8 ....65 M8
Alexandra Corniche
  HYTHE CT21...........................309 P5
Alexandra Cots NWCR SE14 * 41 M2
Alexandra Crs BMLY BR1..............62 D5
Alexandra Dr NRWD SE19 ....60 E4
Alexandra Gdns FOLK CT20 ....115 P5
Alexandra Gln WALD ME5...........125 M4
Alexandra Homes MARG CT9 * ...15 G7
Alexandra PI CROY/NA CRO..........83 K5
  DVW CT17 ....291 H6
  SNWD SE25 ....60 B4
Alexandra Rd BH/WHM TN16....145 L4
  BRCH CT7 ....111 H8
  BRDST CT10 ....113 N9
  CHAT ME4 ....95 N4
  CROY/NA CRO...........................84 A1
  DEAL CT14 ....263 H5
  ERITH DA8 ....29 L9
  GVE DA12 ....50 A8
  IOS ME12 ....53 N2
  MARG CT9 ....112 D5
  PGE/AN SE20 ....61 K5
  RAM CT11 ....16 E1
  RFOLK CT18 ....311 H1
  TIL RM18 ....49 K3
  WARL CR6 ....144 B2
  WSTB CT5 ....105 K6
Alexandra St CAN/RD E16 ....26 B1
  FOLKN CT19 ....11 C1
  MAID/BEAR ME14...................48 A7
  NWCR SE14 ....41 L1
Alexandra Ter MARG CT9.............15 G7
Alexandra Wk FNY DA4 * 67 K8
Alexandra Wy TIL RM18 ....34 A2
Alexandria Dr HB CT6.................107 H1
Alex Hughes Cl SNOD ME6.........123 N7
Alexis St BERM/RHTH SE16 ....24 D7
Alfan La RDART DA2 ....65 K8
Alford Dr CROY/NA CRO.............114 C1
Alford Rd ERITH DA8 ....29 H8
Alfred Cl CANT CT1 ....166 B6
  CHAT ME4 ....95 N4
Alfred PI DVW CT17 ....28 E8
Alfred Rd BELV DA17 ....28 E8
  BRCH CT7 ....110 E5
  CANT CT1 ....166 B6
  DVE/WH CT16 ....291 J5
  KEN/WIL TN24 ....282 O1
  MARG CT9 ....112 C4
  SNWD SE25 ....83 M2
  SOCK/AV RM15 ....30 F4
Alfred Sq DEAL CT14 ....233 J2
Alfred St GRAYS RM17 ....32 D9
Afriston Av CROY/NA CRO 82 C8
Alfriston Cl DART DA1.................145 N7
Alfriston Gv E/WMAL ME19 ....153 K9
Algernon Rd LEW SE13.................41 P4
Algiers Rd LEW SE13.....................41 N5
Alice St STHWK SE1 ....24 A4
Alice Thompson Cl
  LEE/GVPK SE12 ....62 G1
Alice Walker Cl HNHL SE24 * 40 B5
Alicia Av MARG CT9 ....111 P5
Alison St WCHPL E1 ....24 C2
Alison Cl BRCH CT7 ....111 J5
  CROY/NA CRO...........................84 A5
  DVE/WH CT16 ....291 H1
  EHAM E6 ....27 H2

Alison Crs DVE/WH CT16...........291 H1
Alkerten La SWCM DA10..............48 A7
Alkham Cl MARG CT9..................113 L3
Alkham Rd DVE/WH CT16...........290 E9
  MAID/BEAR ME14....................13 K3
  RDV CT15 ....290 C3
Alkham Valley Rd
  RFOLK CT18 ....310 F1
Allan Cl SBGH/RUST TN4 ....269 P4
Allandale PI ORP BR6 ....87 L7
Allandale Rd RTWE/PEM TN2 ....270 G2
Alland Grange La MSTR CT12.....141 M3
Allan Rd WSTB CT5 ....104 F7
Allard Cl STMC/STPC BR5.............87 K4
Allen Av WGOS CT8 ....111 K6
Allenby Dr DEAL CT14................232 C4
Allenby Rd GRAYS RM17..............32 C8
Allenby Rd BH/WHM TN16........145 P2
  FSTH SE23.................................61 L2
Allen Cl WALD ME5.......................95 P8
Allen Ct IOS ME12........................78 A2
Allendale Cl CMBW SE5................40 D3
  RDART DA2 ....47 P9
  SYD SE26...................................61 J5
Allendale St FOLKN CT19..............10 E1
Allen Fld ASH TN23 ....252 C9
Allen Rd BECK BR3 ....61 K8
  CROY/NA CRO...........................82 E4
Allens CI STPH/PW TN12 * 245 J4
Allens La RTON TN11...................181 K4
Allens Md GVE DA12.....................50 B9
Allen St MAID/BEAR ME14..........15 G2
Allenswood Rd ELTH/MOT SE9 ...43 J4
Allerford Rd CAT SE6.....................61 N3
  HOO/HM ME3...........................54 G3
Alleyn Crs DUL SE21.....................60 D1
Alleyn Pk DUL SE21 ....60 D1
Alleyn Rd DUL SE21 ....60 D2
Alleyn Rd DUL SE21 ....60 D1
Allhallows La CANST EC4R............24 A3
Allhallows Rd EHAM E6 ....26 F2
  HOO/HM ME3...........................54 C3
Allhallows Rd PLSTW E13 ....26 D1
  RAM CT11 ....17 H4
  WOOL/PLUM SE18 ....77 P9
Alliance Wy STPH/PW TN12 ......242 G3
Allington Dr STRD ME2 ....7 N7
  TONW TN10 ....211 K5
Allington Gdns
  WBY/YAL ME18 ....183 L4
Allington Rd ORP BR6 ....86 F5
  RHAM ME8 ....96 D5
  STPH/PW TN12 ....242 G2
Allison Av MAIDW ME16.............154 C6
Allison Rd CHNCH SE10................40 E9
Allison Cv DUL SE21 ....60 E1
Allnutt Mill Cl
  MAID/SHEP ME15 ....185 K1
Alloa Rd DEPT SE8 ....24 G8
Allotment La SEV TN13 ....149 H7
Allport Ms WCHPL E1 * 24 E1
All Saints' Av MARG CT9...............14 C7
All Saints Cl SWCM DA10.............48 D6
All Saints' Cl WSTB CT5 ....105 M5
All Saints Dr BKHTH/KID SE3......42 D5
All Saints La CANT CT1 ....4 E4
All Saints Ri BSGH/RUST TN4 *..270 D1
All Saints' Rd GVW DA11..............49 M9
All Saints' Rd HAWK TN18..........317 J5
  SBGH/RUST TN4 ....270 D2
  SIT ME10 ....130 F1
Allsworth Cl RSIT ME9..................98 C8
Allwood Cl SYD SE26....................61 K3
Alma Gv STHWK SE1 ....1 G2
Alma PI CANT CT1 * 1 G2
  NRWD SE19 ....60 F6
  RAM CT11 ....17 G3
  STRD ME2 ....7 J2
  THHTH CR7 ....82 F2
Alma Rd BFN/LL DA15.................44 C2
  DIT/WAL ME20 * 124 E7
  E/WMAL ME19 ....153 H4
  FOLK CT20 ....310 A6
  HB CT6 ....107 N1
  IOS ME12 ....57 L6
  MARG CT9 ....15 H7
  RAM CT11 ....17 H5
  STMC/STPC BR5........................87 L6
  SWCM DA10 ....48 C6
Alma St CANT CT1 ....5 G2
  IOS ME12 ....57 M6
The Alma GVE DA12 * 70 B3
Almond Cl BRDST CT10 ....113 H9
  CDW/CHF RM16 ....33 M4
  HAYES BR2 ....86 B4
  PECK SE15 ....40 C3
  RASHE TN25 ....252 C4
  WSTB CT5 ....105 C5
Almond Dr SWLY BR8...................65 M9
Almond Gv GILL ME7..................126 D1
Almond Rd BERM/RHTH SE16 .....24 E7
  RDART DA2 ....47 J8
The Almonds
  MAID/BEAR ME14..................156 D8
Almond Tree Cl IOS ME12............57 J8
Almond Wy HAYES BR2 ....86 B4
  MTCM CR4 ....82 C2
Almon PI ROCH ME1 ....8 H6
Almshouse Rd FAV ME13............191 N6
  HDCN TN27 ....194 D7
Alnwick Rd CAN/RD E16 ....26 D2
  LEE/GVPK SE12 ....42 F8
Alnwick Ter LEE/GVPK SE12 * 42 F8
Alpha Cl HOO/HM ME3.................54 B9
Alpha Cv POP/IOD E14..................25 K5
Alpha Rd BRCH CT7 ....111 H6
  CROY/NA CRO...........................83 K5
  NWCR SE14 ....41 M2
  RAM CT11 ....16 D4
Alpine Cl CROY/NA CRO...............83 K7
Alpine Cv HOM E9.........................45 C4
Alpine Copse BMLY BR1...............63 L8
Alpine Rd BERM/RHTH SE16 ....24 F7
Alpine Wy EHAM E6 ....27 J1
Alsace Rd WALW SE17 ....14 B8
Alsager Av QBOR ME11.................77 H4
Alscot Rd STHWK SE1 ....24 C6
Alscot Wy STHWK SE1 ....24 C7

Alsike Rd ERITHM DA18................28 C6
Alsops Rd KEN/WIL TN24...........283 H1
Alston Cl IOS ME12.......................58 C9
Altash Wy ELTH/MOT SE9.............63 K1
Alton Av E/WMAL ME19...............183 J1
Alton Cl BXLY DA5.........................44 G9
Alton Rd BRCH CT7 ....61 N6
Alton Ms GILL ME7 * 7 J5
Alton Rd CROY/NA CRO................82 F7
Alton St POP/IOD E14....................25 L1
Altyre Cl BECK BR3 ....83 J6
Altyre Rd CROY/NA CRO...............84 A1
Altyre Wy BECK BR3 ....83 J6
Aluric Cl CDW/CHF RM16 ....33 J7
Alverstone Gdns
  ELTH/MOT SE9 ....43 M9
Alverston Gdns SNWD SE25 ....83 K2
Alverton St DEPT SE8 ....24 G9
Alvey St WALW SE17 ....24 B8
Alvis Av WB CT6 ....106 F2
Alwen Gv SOCK/AV RM15 ....31 L1
Alwold Crs LEE/GVPK SE12 ....42 G7
Alwyn Cl CROY/NA CRO..............114 C2
Amage Rd RASHE TN25 ....254 D1
Amanda Cl WALD ME5.................125 K2
Amar Ct WOOL/PLUM SE18 ....27 N7
Amardeep Ct
  WOOL/PLUM SE18 ....27 N8
Amazon St WCHPL E1 ....24 E2
Ambassador Gdns EHAM E6..........26 G5
Ambassador Sq POP/IOD E14 ....25 L7
Amber Cl RSIT ME9 ....131 J5
Amber La MAID ME17 ....216 D1
Amberleaze Dr
  RTWE/PEM TN2 ....271 N2
Amberley Cl ORP BR6 ....86 G9
  TON TN9 ....240 C1
Amberley Cv SCUP DA14...............64 E4
Amberley Cv CROY/NA CRO..........83 L8
  SYD SE26...................................61 H5
Amberley Rd ABYW SE2................28 C9
  SIT ME10 ....99 M9
Amberwood Cl WLGTN SM6..........82 D9
Ambiecote Cl LEE/GVPK SE12 ......62 F2
Ambcote Mdw
  LEE/GVPK SE12 * 62 F2
Ambleside Rd BXLYHN DA7..........45 J3
Ambleside Bn RHAM ME8..............96 B6
Ambley Cn RHAM ME8...................96 B6
Ambley Rd RHAM ME8 ....96 D5
Ambrook Rd BELV DA17................28 F6
Ambrose Cl DART DA1 ....45 P5
  ORP BR6 ....87 P9
Ambrose Hl CHAT ME4..................95 P4
Ambrose St BERM/RHTH SE16 .....24 E7
Ameis Hl RSIT ME9 ....128 A5
America Sq TWRH EC3N 4 C4
Amershan Rd NWCR SE14............41 M1
  NWCR SE14 ....41 M2
Amersham Rd CROY/NA CRO........83 H5
  NWCR SE14 ....41 M2
Amersham V NWCR SE14............41 M1
Ames Av MAID/BEAR ME14.........156 D8
Amesbury Rd BMLY BR1...............63 J3
Ames Cots POP/IOD E14 * 25 H1
Amethyst La WALD ME5................95 K8
Amethyst Cl ORP BR6 ....116 F1
Amethyst Dr SIT ME10...................99 L8
Amherst Cl MAIDW ME16............12 A3
  MARG CT9 ....113 H4
  STMC/STPC BR5........................87 H1
Amherst Dr STMC/STPC BR5.........86 G1
Amherst Hl GILL ME7 ....7 K5
  SEV TN13 ....148 D1
Amherst PI SEV TN13 ....148 D1
Amherst Rd ROCH ME1 ....95 J3
  SBGH/RUST TN4.....................270 D3
  SEV TN13 ....148 C1
Amhurst Bank Rd
  RTWE/PEM TN2 ....241 P6
Amina Wy BERM/RHTH SE16 ....24 D6
Amos Cl FAV ME13 ....162 F7
  HB CT6 ....107 P5
Amott Rd PECK SE15.....................40 G4
Ampere Wy CROY/NA CRO...........82 D4
Ampleforth Cl ORP BR6 ....87 K8
Ampleforth Rd ABYW SE2 ....28 A5
Amroth Cl FSTH SE23.....................41 H9
Amsbury Rd
  MAID/SHEP ME15 ....184 F9
Amsterdam Rd POP/IOD E14 ....25 M6
Amy Rd OXTED RH8....................175 M4
Amyruth Rd BROCKY SE4..............41 N6
Amy Warne Cl EHAM E6................26 F1
Anatase Cl SIT ME10 ....99 K7
Ancaster St BECK BR3 ....61 K9
Ancaster St WOOL/PLUM SE18 ....27 L8
Anchorage Cl HOO/HM ME3 ....54 G5
Anchor Bay Est CANT CT1...........136 F9
Andace Park Gdns BMLY BR1 * 62 G7
Anderson Wy BELV DA17..............28 G5
Andover Cl CAN/RD E16 ....26 E2
Andover Rd ORP BR6....................86 F5
Andrew Av CDW/CHF RM16..........32 A5
Andrew Broughton Wy
  MAID/BEAR ME14....................48 A2
Andrew St DART DA1 ....45 M6
Andrewes Gdns EHAM E6..............26 G3
Andrews Rd SBGH/RUST TN4......240 F9
Andrews Ct RTWE/PEM TN2........270 G3
  STMC/STPC BR5........................87 M6
Andrews PI RDART DA2.................66 A3
Andrew St POP/IOD E14 ....25 M2

Andwell Cl ABYW SE2 ....28 A5
Anerley Cl MAIDW ME16.............155 J5
Anerley Cv NRWD SE19.................60 F6
Anerley Hl NRWD SE19.................60 F6
Anerley Pk PGE/AN SE20..............61 H6
  PGE/AN SE20 ....61 H6
Anerley Park Rd PGE/AN SE20 .....61 H6
Anerley Rd PGE/AN SE20...............60 G7
  PGE/AN SE20 ....61 H7
Anerley Station Rd
  PGE/AN SE20 ....61 H7
Anerley V NRWD SE19..................60 F6
Anerley Vale NRWD SE19..............60 F7
Angel Cl WCHPL E1.......................24 C2
Angel Ct LOTH EC2R.....................24 A2
Angel Hts RFOLK CT18................288 B9
Angelica Dr EHAM E6...................27 H1
Angelica Gdns CROY/NA CRO........84 A5
Angel La TON TN9 ....210 E9
Angel Park Gdns
  BRXN/ST SW9 ....40 A4
Angell Town Est
  BRXN/ST SW9 ....40 A4
Angel Ms WCHPL E1 ....24 E3
Angel Pas CANST EC4R.................24 A3
Angle Rd MTHK RM20....................31 N9
Anglesea Ms
  WOOL/PLUM SE18 ....27 J9
Anglesea PI GVW DA11..................49 M7
Anglesea Rd STMC/STPC BR5 ....87 K3
  WOOL/PLUM SE18 ....27 J7
Anglesey Av
  MAID/BEAR ME14..................185 M5
Anglesey Cl WALD ME5..................95 M7
Angley Cl CRBK TN17 ....275 P3
Angley Rd CRBK TN17 ....297 N2
Angley Wk CRBK TN17 ....297 P2
Angus Dr KEN/WIL TN24............252 F2
Angus Rd NWCR SE14...................41 L1
Anisa Cl E/WMAL ME19 ....153 J9
Ankerdine Crs
  WOOL/PLUM SE18 ....43 M2
Annabel Cl POP/IOD E14...............25 L2
Annabell Av CDW/CHF RM16........31 L5
Annalee Gdns SOCK/AV RM15......31 L1
Annalee Rd SOCK/AV RM15..........31 L1
Annandale Rd BFN/LL DA15..........44 A6
  CROY/NA CRO...........................83 M6
  GNWCH SE10.............................26 A8
Anna Pk BRCH CT7 ....110 C5
Anne Boleyn Cl IOS ME12.............79 L4
Anne Cl BRCH CT7......................111 H6
Anne Compton Ms
  LEE/GVPK SE12 ....42 D8
Anne Figg Ct ROCH ME1 * 19 C7
Anne Green Wk CANT CT1.............5 H1
Anne Heart Cl CDW/CHF RM16.....31 N7
Anne of Cleves Rd DART DA1........46 D6
Anne Roper Cl NROM TN28 ....337 J7
Annesley Dr CROY/NA CRO..........84 C8
Annesley Rd BKHTH/KID SE3 ....42 F2
Annesmere Gdns
  BKHTH/KID SE3 ....43 H4
Annes Rd BRDST CT10................113 N6
Annetts Hall BGR/WK TN15 ....151 K4
Annexe Market WCHPL E1 * 24 C1
Annie Rd SNOD ME6....................116 B6
Annison St TON TN9 ....210 E8
Ann Moss Wy
  BERM/RHTH SE16 ....24 F6
Ann St WOOL/PLUM SE18 ....27 L7
Annsworthy Av THHTH CR7 ....60 D3
Annsworthy Crs SNWD SE25 ....60 D9
Ansdell Rd PECK SE15 ....41 K4
Anselm Cl CROY/NA CRO..............83 L7
  SIT ME10 ....129 M1
Anselm Rd DVW CT17 ....291 H7
Ansford Rd BMLY BR1...................61 M9
Anson Av E/WMAL ME19.............152 G9
Anson Cl BRDST CT10 ....143 H1
  WALD ME5 ....95 P8
Anstee Rd DVW CT17 ....233 H5
Anstey Rd PECK SE15 ....40 G4
Anstridge Rd ELTH/MOT SE9........43 P7
Antelope Rd
  WOOL/PLUM SE18 ....28 G6
Anthony Cl SEV TN13 ....148 D6
Anthony Crs WSTB CT5 ....105 J8
Anthony Rd SNWD SE25 ....83 M3
  WELL DA16 ....44 C2
Anthonys La WAP E1W..................24 F4
Anthonys La SWLY BR8.................65 M8
Anthonys St WCHPL E1 ....24 E2
Anthonys Wy STRD ME2 ....19 K2
Antill Ter WCHPL E1 ....24 G2
Antolin Wy MSTR CT12...............142 F1
Antonius Ct ASH TN23 ....282 D3
Anvil Cl BRCH CT7......................111 H7
Anvil Ct RDART DA2 ....65 N1
Anzio Crs RDV CT15....................291 M5
Aostie Wy THHTH CR7...................82 E3
Apart St BECK BR3 ....61 P7
Apollo Av BMLY BR1 ....63 J3
Apollo Wy CHAT ME4 ....73 J5
  ERITH DA8 ....29 J8
  THMD SE28 ....27 L6
Apple Cl STPH/PW TN12.............242 G3
Applecross Cl ROCH ME1..............94 G2
  IOS ME12 ....57 K8
Appledore Av BXLYHN DA7..........45 L2
  RAINE RM13 ....31 L8
Appledore Cl HAYES BR2..............85 J2
  MARG CT9 ....112 C4
Appledore Crs FOLKN CT19.........310 A4
  SCUP DA14 ....64 A3
Appledore Rd RASHW TN26........322 D6
  RHAM ME8 ....96 D5
  TENT TN30 ....301 K8
Appledown Wy CANT CT1...........167 J2
Appleford Dr IOS ME12.................57 P9

Applegarth CROY/NA CRO...........114 E2
Applegarth Dr DART DA1..............45 J8
Applegarth Pk WSTB CT5 * 105 H8
Applegarth Rd THMD SE28............28 A4
Apple Orch SWLY BR8...................88 C1
Appleshaw Cl GVW DA11..............69 L4
Appleton Cl BXLYHN DA7.............45 K3
Appleton Dr RDART DA2...............66 B2
Appleton Rd ELTH/MOT SE9.........43 M1
Appletons RTON TN11.................212 A2
Apple Tree Cl MAIDW ME16........184 E1
Apple Tree La PGE/AN SE20..........61 H7
Apple Tree La RTWE/PEM TN2....240 D9
Appold St ERITH DA8....................29 L9
  LVPST EC2M 24 B1
  SDTCH EC2A 24 B1
Approach Rd DVW CT17.............291 H9
  MARG CT9 ....112 F3
  RDV CT15 ....229 N9
Approach Rd South
  LYDD TN29..............................347 K5
The Approach EGRIN RH19 ....265 J2
  ORP BR6 ....86 G6
April Cl GIN FSTH SE23.................61 J2
  ORP BR6 ....86 A8
April Ri WSTB CT5 ....105 J7
Apsley Rd SNWD SE25 ....83 N1
  SBGH/RUST TN4.......................2 C4
Arabin Rd BROCKY SE4 ....270 A4
Aragien Av SOCK/AV RM15..........31 L1
Aragon Cl ASH TN23...................282 B1
  CROY/NA CRO.........................115 H4
  HAYES BR2 ....86 A5
Arbor Cl BECK BR3.......................61 P8
Arbour Sq WCHPL E1 ....24 G2
Arbroath Cl ELTH/MOT SE9..........43 J4
Arbrook Cl STMC/STPC BR5..........64 C9
Arbuthnot La BXLY DA5.................44 C7
Arbuthnot Rd NWCR SE14............41 K3
Arcade Chambers
  ELTH/MOT SE9 * 43 L7
The Arcade ELTH/MOT SE9 * 43 L7
  LVPST EC2M * 24 B1
Arcadian Av BXLY DA5...................44 C5
Arcadian Cl BXLY DA5...................44 C5
Arcadian Rd BXLY DA5...................44 C8
Arcadia Rd MEO IOS ME12.............69 K7
Arcadia St POP/IOD E14................25 K2
Archangel St
  BERM/RHTH SE16 ....24 G5
Archates Av CDW/CHF RM16........32 A4
Archcliffe Rd DVW CT17.............313 K1
Archdale Rd EDUL SE22................40 F5
Archer Fld FOLKN CT19.................11 F1
  SNWD SE25 ....83 H3
  STMC/STPC BR5........................87 H5
  WALD ME5 ....95 N8
Archer's Court Rd
  DVE/WH CT16 ....291 H1
Archery Cl MAIDW ME16.............155 H9
Archer's Wk BRM 65 H8
Archery Cl HOO/HM ME3..............52 B8
Archery Rd ELTH/MOT SE9...........43 K6
Archery La CANT CT1 ....233 J6
Archway Cl WLGTN SM6 * 82 D7
Archway Rd IOS ME12...................57 J5
  RAM CT11 ....17 H4
Arcon Cl ASH TN23.....................282 D1
Arcon Rd ASH TN23....................282 D1
Arcus Rd BMLY BR1.......................62 C5
Ardbeg Rd HNHL SE24...................40 D7
Arden CI THMD SE28....................28 C8
Arden Ct CANT CT1 ....5 C6
Arden Ct CRS POP/IOD E14...........25 K7
Arden Dr KEN/WIL TN24 ....252 F2
Arden Gra RCANTW CT4..............194 D3
Arden Gv ORP BR6.......................86 C8
Ardenham St DEPT SE8.................24 G8
Arden Rd FAV ME13.....................153 H6
  HB CT6 ....107 N4
Ardenrun LING RH7 ....234 D1
Arden St GILL ME7 ....7 H1
Ardent Cl SNWD SE25 ....60 A8
Ardent Cl SNWD SE25 ....60 A9
Ardfern Av STRHM/NOR SW16.....60 A9
Ardfillan Rd CAT SE6 ....42 B7
Ardgowan Rd CAT SE6 ....42 C6
Ardingly Cl CROY/NA CRO.............84 A7
Ardley Cl CAT SE6 ....61 P7
Ardleigh Gdns MARG CT9 * 14 D6
Ardmere Rd LEW SE13..................42 B7
Ardoch Rd CAT SE6 ....62 B1
Ardross PI SWCM DA10 * 7 H1
Arethusa Rd ROCH ME1 ....95 H6
Argent Rd QBOR ME11 ....77 J5
Argent St GRAYS RM17..................31 P9
Argent Wy SIT WALD ME5 ....95 J8
Argles Rd RDART DA2 ....47 N6
Argyle Av MARG CT9 ....14 B7
Argyle Cl ROCH ME1 ....95 K7
Argyle Gdns MARG CT9 * 14 B7
Argyle Rd CAN/RD E16 ....26 C2
  SBGH/RUST TN4....................240 D7
  SEV TN13 ....20 E3
  WSTB CT5 ....105 J5
Argyle Wy BERM/RHTH SE16 ....24 D5
Argyll St RAM CT11.....................143 L3
Argyll Rd GRAYS RM17..................32 B8
  WOOL/PLUM SE18 ....27 K6
Archie St STHWK SE1 ....24 B5
Ariel Cl MARG CT9 ....18 B7
Ariel Ct UVD12 * 70 B3
Arisdale Av SOCK/AV RM15..........31 L1
Ark Av CDW/CHF RM16................32 B6
Arkell Gv NRWD SE19...................60 C8
Arkindale Rd CAT SE6 ....62 A3
Ark La DEAL CT14 ....233 J2
Arklow Rd NWCR SE14...................25 J9
Arklow Sq RAM CT11....................17 H3
Arklow St BROCKY SE4..................41 L3
Arlingford Rd
  BRXS/STRHM SW2 ....40 A7
Arlington ASH TN23 ....252 C8
Arlington Cl BFN/LL DA15.............44 A8
  LEW SE13..................................42 B6
Arlington Gdns MARG CT9 ....113 H5
  LEW SE13..................................41 M7
Arlott Cl MAID/BEAR ME14.........155 L6

Armada Cl *NROM* TN28.....337 K8
Armada Ct *CHAT* ME4 *.....95 K5
Armadale Vls *RAM* CT11 *.....16 B4
Armada St *DEPT* SE8.....25 K9
Armada Wy *CHAT* ME4.....6 B6
  EHAM E6.....27 J1
  EHAM E6.....27 K1
Armistice Gdns *SNWD* SE25.....60 C9
Armitage Rd *GNWCH* SE10.....26 A7
Armor Rd *PUR* RM19.....30 C7
Armoury Dr *GVE* DA12.....49 N8
Armoury Rd *DEPT* SE8.....41 P5
Armstrong Cl *BMLY* BR1.....63 J9
  EHAM E6.....26 C2
  RSEV TN14.....118 A9
Armstrong Rd
  MAID/SHEP ME15.....185 M2
  WOOL/PLUM SE18.....27 K6
Armstrong Sq *HB* CT6.....106 F3
Arne Cl *TONN* TN10.....211 H4
Arne Rd *WELL* DA16.....86 G7
Arne Wk *LEW* SE13.....42 G5
Arngask Rd *CAT* SE6.....42 B8
Arnheim Pl *POP/IOD* E14.....25 K4
Arnhem Av *SOCK/AV* RM15.....30 F4
Arnhem Dr *CROY/NA* CRO.....114 C5
  WALD ME5.....6 E4
Arnold Av *MEO* DA15.....92 C6
Arnolde Cl *STRD* ME2.....19 K2
Arnold Est *STHWK* SE1 *.....24 C5
Arnold Pl *TIL* RM18.....19 N2
Arnold Rd *GVE* DA12.....69 N1
  MARG CT9.....15 H6
  RCANTW CT4.....195 K1
Arnolds Ct *TONN* TN10.....210 F5
Arnolds La *EYN* DA4.....66 D5
Arnott Cl *THMD* SE28.....28 B4
Arnould Av *CMBW* SE5.....42 A4
Arnsberg Wy *BXLYHN* DA7.....45 J5
Arnside Rd *BXLYHN* DA7.....45 J2
Arnside St *WALW* SE17.....24 E6
Arnulf St *CAT* SE6.....61 P3
Arnull's Rd *STRHM/NOR* SW16...60 B5
Arolla Rd *HB* CT6.....107 P2
Arragon Gdns *WWKM* BR4.....64 E1
Arran Cl *ERITH* DA8.....29 J9
  WLGTN SM6.....82 B8
Arran Rd *CAT* SE6.....61 J9
  MAID/SHEP ME15.....185 M5
Arrol Rd *BECK* BR3.....61 J9
Arrowhead La *RASHW* TN26.....323 H7
Arsenal Rd *ELTH/MOT* SE9.....43 K3
Arsenal Wy *CANL RD* E16.....27 H5
  WOOL/PLUM SE18.....27 H5
Artemis Cl *GVE* DA12.....50 A8
Arterial Road Purfleet
  PUR RM19.....30 F7
Arterial Road North Stifford
  CDW/CHF RM16.....31 N5
Arterial Road West Thurrock
  WTHK RM20.....31 L9
Arthurdon Rd *BROCKY* SE4.....41 N4
Arthur Gv *WOOL/PLUM* SE18....27 K7
Arthur Kennedy Cl *FAV* ME13..164 A1
Arthur St *BH/WHM* TN16.....115 M9
  BRCH CT7.....110 E5
  DEAL CT14.....232 F6
  HYTHE CT21.....309 H6
  MARG CT9.....3 K5
  RHAM ME8.....97 H6
  ROCH ME1.....95 J3
Arthur Salmon Cl *FAV* ME13..132 E6
Arthur St *CANST* EC4R.....24 A5
  ERITH DA8.....45 P1
  FOLKN CT19.....11 G1
  GRAYS RM17.....32 D9
  GVW DA11.....13 J5
  SIT ME10.....129 M1
Arthur St West *GVW* DA11.....49 L8
Artichoke Hl *WAP* E1W.....24 E3
Artichoke Pl *CMBW* SE5 *.....42 D1
Artillery Gdns *CANT* CT1 *.....5 G3
Artillery La *LVPST* EC2M.....24 B1
Artillery Pas *WCHPL* E1 *.....24 B1
Artillery Pl *WOOL/PLUM* SE18..26 C8
Artillery Rd *RAM* CT11 *.....17 G2
Artillery Rw *GVE* DA12.....49 N8
Artillery St *CANT* CT1.....5 G3
Artington Cl *ORP* BR6.....86 D8
Arundel Av *CHDH/MOT* SE9 *..43 N8
Arun *TIL* RM18.....34 B7
Arundel Av *SIT* ME10.....129 M4
Arundel Cl *BXLY* DA5.....45 H7
  CROY/NA CRO *.....82 G7
  TON TN9.....140 D8
  WALD ME5.....126 A4
Arundel Dr *ORP* BR6.....87 J9
Arundel Rd *CROY/NA* CRO.....83 J5
  DART DA1.....46 C5
  MAID/BEAR ME14.....155 J9
  MSTR CT12.....142 C5
  RTW TN1.....143 G6
Arundel St *MAID/BEAR* ME14..155 L6
Aschurch Rd *CROY/NA* CRO.....83 J5
Ascot Cl *BGR/WK* TN15.....151 L5
  WALD ME5.....125 P3
Ascot Gdns *WCOS* CT8.....111 M6
Ascot Rd *GVW* DA11.....69 M2
  STMC/STPC BR5.....64 B1
Ashbee Cl *SNOD* ME6.....123 P6
Ashbee Gdns *HB* CT6.....107 P1
Ashborne Cl *KEN/WIL* TN24....252 C3
Ashbourne Av *BXLYHN* DA7.....44 G1
Ashbourne Gv *EDUL* SE22.....42 A6
Ashbourne Rd *BRO* ME8.....86 E8
Ashbrittle Av *CROY/NA* CRO.....83 J5
Ashburnham Cl *SEV* TN13.....179 H3
Ashburnham Gv *GNWCH* SE10..41 P1
Ashburnham Pl *GNWCH* SE10..41 P1
Ashburnham Retreat
  GNWCH SE10.....41 P1
Ashburnham Rd *BELV* DA17.....29 H7
  MAID/BEAR ME14.....155 N4
  RAM CT11.....4 D2
  TONN TN10.....210 F7
Ashburton Ms *GILL* ME7 *.....96 B3
Ashburton Av *CROY/NA* CRO....83 N5
Ashburton Cl *CROY/NA* CRO....83 M5
  KEN/WIL TN24.....3 K4
Ashburton Gdns *CROY/NA* CRO.83 M6

Ashburton Rd *CAN/RD* E16.....26 B2
  CROY/NA CRO.....83 M6
Ashby Cl *CDW/CHF* RM16.....33 M2
  STRD ME2 *.....123 P1
Ashby Ms *BROCKY* SE4.....41 M4
Ashby Rd *BROCKY* SE4.....41 M4
Ashby's Cl *EDEN* TN8.....236 E1
Ashby Wk *CROY/NA* CRO.....83 H3
Ash Cl *BRDST* CT10.....113 H9
  DIT/AY ME20.....154 D5
  DVW CT17.....290 F4
  EDEN TN8.....206 C9
  EDEN TN8.....206 C9
  HB CT6.....107 L5
  LING RH7.....235 H4
  PGE/AN SE20.....61 J8
  RAM CT11.....4 F2
  RTWE/PEM TN2.....270 C8
  SCUP DA14.....64 D2
  STMC/STPC BR5.....64 B8
  SWLY BR8.....65 L8
  WALD ME5.....95 P5
Ash Close Vls *DEAL* CT14 *.....201 L6
Ashcombe Dr *DEN* TN8.....206 C6
Ash Ct *MSTR* CT12.....142 C6
Ash Crs *HOO/HM* ME3.....71 K4
Ashcroft *CANT* CT1.....138 B8
Ashcroft Av *BFN/LL* DA15.....44 C7
Ashcroft Crs *BFN/LL* DA15.....44 C7
Ashcroft Rd *HOO/HM* ME3.....72 B5
  STPH/PW TN12.....242 C4
Ashdale Rd *LEE/GVPK* SE12....42 F9
Ashden Wk *TONN* TN10.....210 F3
Ashdon Cl *SOCK/AV* RM15.....31 L2
Ashdown Cl *BECK* BR3.....61 P8
  BXLY DA5.....45 L8
  HB CT6.....106 E8
  MAIDW ME16.....155 J9
  SBGH/RUST TN4.....22 A3
Ashdown Crs *NROM* TN28.....336 C7
Ashdown Fld *RCANTW* CT4.....195 J3
Ashdown Rd *RMAID* ME17.....188 N2
Ashdown Vw *EGRIN* RH19.....265 H9
Ashen *EHAM* E6.....26 F7
Ashenden *HDCN* TN27.....248 G7
Ashenden Av *EYN* DA4.....79 N7
Ashenden Cl *CANT* CT1.....166 B7
Ashend ME2.....72 C5
Ashenden Wk
  RDART DA1.....241 H9
Ashen Dr *DART* DA1.....46 A7
Ashen Grove Rd
  BGR/WK TN15.....119 N4
Ashentree La *DVE/WH* CT16.....8 E5
Ashentree La *LYDD* TN29.....335 H8
Ashen V *SAND/SEL* CR2.....114 A3
Ashers Reeds *RRTW* TN3.....269 M4
Ashers La *RTON* TN1.....211 H1
Ashfield Cl *BECK* BR3.....61 N8
Ashfield La *CHST* BR7.....63 N5
Ashfield St *WCHPL* E1.....24 E1
Ashfield Yd *WCHPL* E1 *.....24 F1
Ashford Dr *RMAID* ME17.....187 M8
Ashford Rd *ASH* TN23.....281 N1
  FAV ME13.....192 E3
  HYTHE CT21.....307 N1
  MAID/BEAR ME14.....13 J3
  NROM TN28.....336 F7
  RASHE TN25.....284 C6
  RASHW TN26.....279 M8
  RASHW TN26.....281 L3
  RASHW TN26.....282 C8
  RASHW TN26.....339 H6
  RMAID ME17.....187 N5
  TENT TN30.....301 N2
Ashgrove *RSEV* TN14 *.....117 M9
Ash Gv *LYDD* TN29.....342 C5
  MAIDW ME16.....155 H6
  PGE/AN SE20.....61 J8
  RDV CT15.....230 C7
  SEV TN13.....292 F1
  WWKM BR4.....84 F5
Ashgrove Rd *BMLY* BR1.....62 B5
Ash Keys *MEO* DA13.....112 C8
Ashla *BGR/WK* TN15.....120 F5
Ashlar Pl *WOOL/PLUM* SE18....27 J7
Ashleigh Cl *MEO* DA13.....122 A4
Ashleigh Gdns *RMAID* TN27....247 N3
Ashleigh Rd *PGE/AN* SE20.....61 J7
Ashley Av *CROY/NA* CRO.....310 B5
  IOS ME12.....77 L2
  MSTR CT12.....142 C2
  SEV TN13.....179 J3
Ashley Dr *WSTB* CT5.....105 H7
Ashley Gdns *CDW/CHF* RM16..32 C4
  ORP BR6.....86 F9
  SBGH/RUST TN4.....269 P5
Ashley La *CROY/NA* CRO.....82 G8
Ashley Mill Cots *FOLKN* CT19..310 B4
Ashley Park Cl
  SBGH/RUST TN4.....22 C5
Ashley Rd *RHAM* ME8.....96 H6
  RTON TN1.....210 B5
  SEV TN13.....20 E1
  THHTH CR7.....82 E1

RDART DA1.....66 F3
STRD ME2.....18 A4
Ash Rw *HAYES* BR2.....86 D3
Ashstead Dr *RSIT* ME9.....130 C3
Ashton Cl *DEAL* CT14.....232 C5
Ashton Ms *BRDST* CT10 *.....113 N9
Ashton St *POP/IOD* E14.....25 M3
Ashton Wy *E/WMAL* ME15.....153 H7
Ashtree Cl *ORP* BR6.....86 C8
Ash Tree Cl *BGR/WK* TN15 *...120 C5
  CROY/NA CRO.....84 B3
  LYDD TN29.....337 L2
Ash Tree Dr *BGR/WK* TN15.....120 C5
Ash Tree La *WALD* ME5.....76 A5
Ash Tree Rd *FOLKN* CT19.....11 H1
Ash Tree Wy *CROY/NA* CRO....84 B2
Ashurst Av *WSTB* CT5.....105 K7
Ashurst Dr *CDART* DA1.....46 A9
  PGE/AN SE20.....61 H7
Ashurst Gdns
  BRXS/STRHM SW2 *.....40 A9
  MARG CT9.....113 K2
Ashurst Rd *MAID/BEAR* ME14..13 J4
  RRTW TN3.....268 G6
Ashurst Wk *CROY/NA* CRO.....83 N6
Ashwater Rd *LEE/GVPK* SE12..42 E9
Ashwell Cl *EHAM* E6.....26 C9
Ashwood Cl *HOO/HM* ME3.....52 G9
Ashwood Gdns *CROY/NA* CRO.114 E1
Ashworth Av *BGR/WK* TN15....120 A2
Ashworth Cl *CMBW* SE5.....40 D5
Askers Cl *BXLYHS* DA6.....44 F5
Askes Ct *ASH* TN23.....252 A9
Askews Farm La *GRAYS* RM17...31 P9
Aspdin Rd *GVW* DA11.....69 H2
Aspen Cl *LYDD* TN29.....337 L2
  ORP BR6.....87 H9
  SWLY BR8.....65 M7
Aspen Copse *BMLY* BR1.....63 K8
Aspen Dr *ASH* TN23.....252 A6
  DVE/WH CT16.....291 H2
Aspen Gn *ERITHM* DA18.....28 E6
Aspen Rd *HB* CT6.....107 K7
Aspen Wy *POP/IOD* E14.....25 M5
  SBGH/RUST TN4.....240 F8
Aspian Dr *RMAID* ME17.....185 J9
Aspinall Cl *RCANTW* CT4.....167 N8
Aspinall Rd *BROCKY* SE4.....41 M4
  NWCR SE14.....41 M4
Aspinden Rd *BERM/RHTH* SE16.24 E7
Asprey Ms *BECK* BR3.....84 C2
Asquith Rd *RHAM* ME8.....96 F8
Assam St *WCHPL* E1.....24 C1
Assembly Pas *WCHPL* E1.....24 F1
Astbury Rd *PECK* SE15.....41 J2
Aster Rd *HOO/HM* ME3.....73 L4
Astley *GRAYS* RM17.....32 A9
Astley Cl *DVE/WH* CT16.....291 K5
Astley Dr *DVE/WH* CT16.....291 K5
Astley St *MAID/BEAR* ME14.....13 C4
Aston Cl *SCUP* DA14.....64 D4
  WALD ME5.....125 M3
Astonplace *STRHM/NOR* SW16.60 B3
Aston St *POP/IOD* E14.....25 H2
Astor Av *WCHPL* E1.....24 C1
Astor Dr *DEAL* CT14.....232 A2
Astoria Wk *BRXN/ST* SW9.....40 A4
Astor Rd *BGR/WK* TN15.....120 B1
Astra Dr *GVE* DA12.....70 A4
Astrid Rd *DEAL* CT14.....232 F7
Asylum Rd *PECK* SE15.....41 K2
Atcost Rd *BARK* IG11.....27 P1
Atheleney St *CAT* SE6.....61 N2
Athelstan Gn *RMAID* ME17.....187 M1
Athelstan Pl *DEAL* CT14.....232 A3
Athelstan Rd *CANT* CT1.....166 B7
  CHAT ME4.....95 K4
  FAV ME13.....132 E7
  FOLKN CT19.....310 C4
Athelstan Wy *STMC/STPC* BR5..64 C1
Athenlay Rd *PECK* SE15.....41 K6
Atherton Gdns
  CDW/CHF RM16.....33 K7
Athol Pl *FAV* ME13.....132 D5
Athol Rd *ASH* TN23.....282 C1
  ERITH DA8.....29 H8
Athol Sq *POP/IOD* E14.....25 M3
Athol Ter *DVE/WH* CT16.....9 K3
Atkins Dr *WWKM* BR4.....84 G7
Atkinson Cl *ORP* BR6.....87 H9
Atkinson Rd *CAN/RD* E16.....26 D1
Atkinson Wk *KEN/WIL* TN24...252 A9
Atlanta Ct *CHAT* ME4.....95 J3
Atlantic Cl *SWCM* DA10.....48 C6
Atlantic Rd *BRXN/ST* SW9.....40 A5
Atlas Gdns *CHARL* SE7.....26 D7
Atlas Rd *DART* DA1.....46 D8
Atterbury Ct *BH/WHM* TN16...176 E2
Attlee Av *RCANTE* CT3.....229 H1
Attlee Cl *THHTH* CR7.....83 H5
Attlee Ct *GRAYS* RM17.....32 B6
Attlee Dr *DART* DA1.....46 D4
Attlee Rd *THMD* SE28.....28 A5
Attlee Wy *SIT* ME10.....99 M6
Attwaters La *HAWK* TN18.....297 P9
Atwell Rd *PECK* SE15.....41 J3
Auburn Cl *NWCR* SE14.....41 L1
Aubyn Hl *WNWD* SE27.....60 D3
Aubyn Sq *PUT/ROE* SW15 *.....40 D1
Auckland Cl *MSTR* CT12.....142 F3
Auckland Cl *NRWD* SE19.....60 F6
  TIL RM18.....19 L7
Auckland Crs *DVE/WH* CT16...291 K4
Auckland Dr *SIT* ME10.....129 K2
Auckland Gdns *NRWD* SE19....60 E7
Auckland Rd *BMLY* BR1.....62 C5
  NRWD SE19.....60 F7
Auckland Ri *NRWD* SE19.....60 E7
  RTW TN1.....270 F2
Aucuba Vls *WELL* DA16 *.....44 D4
Audley Av *GILL* ME7.....96 B5
Audley Dr *CAN/RD* E16.....26 G4
  MARG CT9.....111 P4
  TON TN9.....210 C8
Audley Ri *TON* TN9.....210 C9

Audley Rd *FOLK* CT20.....310 C6
Audrey Cl *BECK* BR3.....84 E5
Auger Cl *RSIT* ME9.....130 D4
Augusta Cl *GILL* ME7.....75 J8
Augusta Gdns *FOLK* CT20.....10 C6
Augusta Pl *RAM* CT11.....17 H5
Augusta Rd *RAM* CT11.....17 H5
Augustine Rd *GVE* DA12.....49 N8
  IOS ME12.....58 B8
  MSTR CT12.....142 F1
  STMC/STPC BR5.....64 F9
Augustus Wk *ASH* TN23.....282 C5
Aurelia Gdns *CROY/NA* CRO....82 E2
Aurelia Rd *CROY/NA* CRO.....82 D3
Aurelie Wy *WSTB* CT5.....105 N7
Aurellus Cl *ASH* TN23.....282 D4
Austen Cl *EGRIN* RH19.....264 E7
  SWCM DA10 *.....48 A7
  THMD SE28.....28 A4
  TIL RM18.....49 N3
Austen Rd *ERITH* DA8.....45 L1
Austens Orch *TENT* TN30 *....301 H8
Austen Wy *DIT/AY* ME20.....123 N9
Austin Av *HAYES* BR2.....85 P5
  HB CT6.....106 E2
Austin Cl *FSTH* SE23.....99 P6
  SIT ME10.....99 P6
Austin Friars *OBST* EC2N.....24 A2
Austin Friars Sq *OBST* EC2N *..24 A2
Austin Rd *ASH* TN23.....282 E8
  STMC/STPC BR5.....87 H5
Austins La *SWCH* CT13.....201 J7
Austral Cl *BFN/LL* DA15.....64 B2
Autumn Gld *WALD* ME5.....126 A5
Autumn Gv *BMLY* BR1.....62 E3
Avalon Cl *ORP* BR6.....87 L6
Avalon Rd *ORP* BR6.....87 L6
Avard Gdns *ORP* BR6.....86 D8
Avards Cl *HAWK* TN18.....316 C6
Avebury Av *RAM* CT11.....16 G4
  TON TN9.....210 E9
Avebury Rd *ORP* BR6.....86 E7
Aveley By-Pass *SOCK/AV* RM15.31 J3
Aveley Cl *ERITH* DA8.....30 C4
Aveling *HOO/HM* ME3.....73 K1
Avenons Rd *PLSTW* E13.....26 D3
Avent Wk *RSIT* ME9.....130 D2
Avenue Du Puy *TON* TN9.....210 F9
Avenue Gdns *MARG* CT9.....113 H2
  SNWD SE25.....60 G8
Avenue Le Puy *TON* TN9.....210 F9
Avenue Ldg *GRAYS* RM17.....32 C8
Avenue of Remembrance
  SIT ME10.....129 N2
Avenue Park Rd *WNWD* SE27...60 D3
Avenue Rd *BH/WHM* TN16.....176 C2
  BXLYHN DA7.....45 J1
  ERITH DA8.....45 L1
  HB CT6.....107 J8
  PGE/AN SE20.....61 J7
  RAM CT11.....17 H2
  SEV TN13.....178 A4
  RTON TN1.....180 F7
  SEV TN13.....145 G9
  STPH/PW TN12.....229 J2
  WTHK RM20.....31 L6
Averenches Rd
  MAID/BEAR ME14.....156 C7
Avereng Gdns *FOLKN* CT19.....10 A2
Avereng Rd *FOLKN* CT19.....10 A3
Averil Gv *STRHM/NOR* SW16....60 B5
Avery Cl *HOO/HM* ME3.....38 F8
  MAID/SHEP ME15.....185 L2
Avery Hill Rd *ELTH/MOT* SE9....43 N9
Avery La *MAID/SHEP* ME15.....185 N9
  RMAID ME17.....186 G5
Avery Wy *DART* DA1.....47 H4
Aviary Cl *CAN/RD* E16.....26 E1
Aviemore Cl *BECK* BR3.....84 C2
Aviemore Gdns
  MAID/BEAR ME14.....156 C6
Aviemore Wy *BECK* BR3.....84 B2
Avignon Rd *BROCKY* SE4.....41 K4
Avington Cl *MAID/SHEP* ME15.185 L2
Avington Gv *PGE/AN* SE20.....61 J6
Avis Sq *WCHPL* E1.....25 H2
Avocet Cl *STHWK* SE1 *.....24 C8
Avocet Ms *THMD* SE28.....37 J3
Avon Cl *CANT* CT1.....167 H4
  GVE DA12.....50 C4
Avondale Cl *WSTB* CT5.....105 P6
Avondale Pavement
  STHWK SE1 *.....24 C8
Avondale Rl *HOO/HM* ME3.....54 G4
Avondale Rd *PECK* SE15.....40 D7
Avondale Rd *BMLY* BR1.....62 C5
  CAN/RD E16.....25 P1
  ELTH/MOT SE9.....63 J1
  GILL ME7.....96 A4
Avondale Sq *STHWK* SE1.....24 D4
Avon Gn *SOCK/AV* RM15.....31 L3
Avonley Rd *NWCR* SE14.....41 J1
Avonmouth Rd *DART* DA1.....46 D6

Avon Rd *BROCKY* SE4.....41 N4
Avonstowe Cl *ORP* BR6.....86 D7
Avon St *RTW* TN1.....270 F3
Awliscombe Rd *WELL* DA16....44 B3
Axis Ct *GNWCH* SE10.....25 P6
Axminster Crs *WELL* DA16.....44 C2
Axtane Rd *STMC/STPC* BR5.....87 L4
Axtane *MEO* DA13 *.....68 A8
Axtane Cl *EYN* DA4.....67 J8
Aycliffe Cl *BMLY* BR1.....86 A1
Ayelands *HART* DA3.....91 H6
Ayelands La *HART* DA3.....91 H6
Aylesbury Rd *HAYES* BR2.....62 E4
  WALW SE17.....24 A8
Aylesford Av *BECK* BR3.....84 B2
Aylesford Crs *RHAM* ME8.....96 D3
Aylesford Rl *KEN/WIL* TN24...283 H1
Aylesham Rd *ORP* BR6.....86 F4
  RDV CT15.....229 K2
Ayleswade La *SNWD* SE25.....83 N1
Aylewyn Gn *SIT* ME10.....130 A3
Aylton Est *BERM/RHTH* SE16 *.24 F5
Aylward Rd *FSTH* SE23.....61 K1
Aylward St *WCHPL* E1.....24 G2
Aylwin Est *STHWK* SE1 *.....24 B6
Aynscombe Angle *ORP* BR6...87 H4
Ayrshire Cl *KEN/WIL* TN24.....252 F2
Aysgarth Rd *DUL* SE21.....42 D7
Ayton Rd *RAM* CT11.....16 C4
Azalea Dr *SWLY* BR8.....65 J5
Azenby Rd *PECK* SE15.....41 G4
Azof St *GNWCH* SE10.....25 P7

B

Babbacombe Rd *BMLY* BR1.....62 F6
Babb's La *DEAL* CT14.....298 D9
Babs Oak Hl *CANTW/ST* CT2..137 N7
Babylon La *RMAID* ME17.....216 E7
  STPH/PW TN12.....171 J4
Back Church La *WCHPL* E1.....24 D2
Backfields *ROCH* ME1.....18 D6
Back La *BGR/WK* TN15.....149 M9
  BGR/WK TN15.....150 F9
  BXLY DA5.....45 J8
  CDW/CHF RM16.....31 M4
  CRBK TN17.....274 D8
  IOS ME12.....78 D1
  PUR RM19.....31 H7
  RMAID ME17.....216 B5
  RSEV TN14.....178 A4
  RTON TN1.....180 F7
  STPH/PW TN12.....229 J2
  WTHK RM20.....31 L6
Backley Gdns *CROY/NA* CRO....83 M5
Back Rd *SCUP* DA14.....64 C3
Back St *DEAL* CT14.....187 H5
  RMAID ME17.....187 H5
Bacon Gv *STHWK* SE1.....24 C6
Baddlesmere Rd *WSTB* CT5....105 P5
Baden Pl *STHWK* SE1 *.....24 A5
Baden Powell Rd *SEV* TN13...148 D7
Baden Rd *GILL* ME7.....75 K8
Bader Crs *WALD* ME5.....95 M7
Bader Wk *GNWCH* SE10 *.....25 P6
Badger Rd *WALD* ME5.....125 P4
Badgers Cl *CANTW/ST* CT2...135 P6
Badgers Cft *ELTH/MOT* SE9....63 L2
Badgers Den *ASH* TN23.....282 A1
Badgers Holt
  RTWE/PEM TN2.....271 H3
Badgers Mt *CDW/CHF* RM16...32 C5
Badgers Rl *DEAL* CT14.....233 H9
  DVW CT17.....290 D9
  RSEV TN14.....117 N4
Badgers Rd *RSEV* TN14.....118 A4
Badgers Wy *EGRIN* RH19.....265 H5
Badlow Cl *ERITH* DA8.....45 N1
Badminton Ms *CAN/RD* E16....26 B4
Bad Munstereifel Rd
  ASH TN23.....282 E3
Badsell Rd *STPH/PW* TN12.....242 C1
Badsworth Rd *CMBW* SE5.....40 C1
Baffin Cl *CHAT* ME4.....95 L4
Bafton Ga *HAYES* BR2.....85 H8
Bagham La *RCANTW* CT4.....194 D3
Bagham Rd *RCANTW* CT4.....194 D3
Bagley House
  WOOL/PLUM SE18 *.....43 J1
Bagshill Rd *FAV* ME13.....162 B8
Bagshaw Ct
  WOOL/PLUM SE18 *.....43 L2
Bagshot St *WALW* SE17.....24 B8
Baildon St *DEPT* SE8.....41 M1
Bailey Cl *PUR* RM19.....30 G7
  RHAM ME8.....96 D5
Bailey Cots *POP/IOD* E14 *.....25 H1
Bailey Dr *RHAM* ME8.....96 D5
Bailey House
  WOOL/PLUM SE18 *.....43 L2
Bailey Ms *BRXS/STRHM* SW2....40 A6
Bailey Pl *SYD* SE26.....61 J6
Baileys Fld *ASH* TN23.....282 C8
Baillemore Ct *RAM* CT11 *.....143 L3
Baillie Cl *RAIN* RM13 *.....29 N1
Baird Gdns *NRWD* SE19.....60 F3
Bairds Hi *BRDST* CT10.....113 L7
Bairdsley Cl *BRDST* CT10.....113 L7
Baizdon Rd *BKHTH/KID* SE3...42 C5
Baker Cl *RSIT* ME9.....131 H2
Baker Crs *DART* DA1.....46 C3
Baker Hill Cl *GVW* DA11.....69 K3
Baker La *HDCN* TN27.....248 A2
Baker Ms *ORP* BR6.....217 J3
Baker Rd *WOOL/PLUM* SE18...43 H3
Baker Ms *ORP* BR6.....116 C1
Baker Rd *WOOL/PLUM* SE18...310 D5
  WOOL/PLUM SE18 *.....43 J1
Bakers Av *BGR/WK* TN15.....120 B2
Bakers Cl *CANTW/ST* CT2.....166 B5
  DART DA1.....46 D8

Baker's Cl *LING* RH7 ....235 H4
Bakers Cross *CRBK* TN17 ....298 A3
Baker's La *LING* RH7 ....235 H5
  RCANTW CT4 ....195 L1
Baker St *CDW/CHF* RM16 ....32 F2
  ROCH ME1 ....95 H5
  ROCH ME1 ....124 E4
Baker's Wk *ROCH* ME1 ....19 F4
Balaclava La *WADH* TN5 ....294 A8
Balaclava Rd *STHWK* SE1 ....24 C7
Balantyne Cl *ELTH/MOT* SE9 ....63 J3
Balas Dr *SIT* ME10 ....99 H6
Balcaskie Rd *ELTH/MOT* SE9 .....63 K6
Balchier Rd *EDUL* SE22 ....41 H7
Balcomb Crs *MARG* CT9 ....113 H5
Balcombe Cl *BXLYHS* DA6 ....45 H5
Balcombes Hl *CRBK* TN17 ....274 D8
Balcomb Ms *MARG* CT9 ....113 H5
Balder Ri *LEE/GVPK* SE12 ....62 F1
Baldric Rd *FOLK* CT20 ....310 C6
Baldwin Crs *CMBW* SE5 ....42 D7
Baldwin Rd *IOS* ME12 ....58 D9
  NROM TN28 ....343 J3
Baldwins Fld *ECRIN* RH19 ....264 F4
Baldwin's Pl *RMAID* ME17 ....188 E5
Baldwin Ter *FOLKN* CT19 ....13 M1
Baldwyn's Pk *BXLY* DA5 ....65 M1
Baldwyn's Rd *BXLY* DA5 ....65 M1
Bale Rd *WCHPL* E1 ....25 H1
Balfour Rd *CHAT* ME4 ....9 H4
  DEAL CT14 ....233 H7
  DVE/WH CT16 ....291 K6
  GRAYS RM17 ....32 D7
  HAYES BR2 ....85 J2
  SNWD SE25 ....83 M1
Balfour St *STHWK* SE1 ....24 A7
Balgowan Rd *BECK* BR3 ....61 L9
Balgowan St
  WOOL/PLUM SE18 ....27 N7
Baliol Rd *WSTB* CT5 ....105 M4
Balkan Wk *WAP* E1W * 24 E3
Balladier Wk *POP/IOD* E14 ....25 L1
Ballamore Rd *BMLY* BR1 ....62 E2
Ballard Cl *STPH/PW* TN2 ....245 H5
Ballard Rd *NROM* TN28 ....343 J5
Ballards La *OXTED* RH8 ....175 M5
Ballard Wy *STPH/PW* TN2 ....245 J2
Ballater Rd *SAND/SEL* CR2 ....25 N9
Ballens Rd *WALD* ME5 ....125 P2
Ballina St *FSTH* SE23 ....41 K8
Balliol Rd *BRDST* CT10 ....113 L6
  WELL DA16 ....64 D5
Ball La *RASHE* TN25 ....253 H2
Balloch Rd *CAT* SE6 ....42 B9
Ballow Cl *CMBW* SE5 * 40 C7
Balmer Cl *RHAM* ME8 ....60 C1
Balmoral Av *BECK* BR3 ....84 B1
Balmoral Gdns *BXLY* DA5 ....45 H8
Balmoral Pl *RAM* CT11 ....17 H3
Balmoral Rd *DEAL* CT14 ....263 H2
  EYN DA4 ....51 N1
  GILL ME7 ....7 J3
  MARG CT9 ....112 A5
Baltic Rd *TON* TN9 ....240 E2
Baltimore Pl *WELL* DA16 ....48 A4
Bamber Rd *PECK* SE15 ....40 F2
Bamford Rd *BMLY* BR1 ....62 B7
Bamford Wy *DEAL* CT14 ....233 H5
Bampfylde Cl *WLGTN* SM6 ....62 B7
Bampton Rd *FSTH* SE23 ....41 K2
Banavie Gdns *BECK* BR3 ....61 P7
Banbury Vls *MEO* DA13 ....68 D5
Banchory Rd *BKHTH/KID* SE3 ...42 F1
Banckside *HART* DA3 ....70 A6
Bancroft Gdns *ORP* BR6 ....86 C5
Bancroft La *E/WMAL* ME19 ......183 K1
Bancroft Rd *BGR/WK* TN15 .....151 J1
Banfield Rd *WLGTN* SM6 ....82 C9
Bangor Rd *STRD* ME3 ....71 M9
Bankfields *HDCN* TN27 ....247 M4
Bankfield Wy *CRBK* TN17 ....274 C9
Bankfoot *GRAYS* RM17 ....52 A1
Bankfoot Rd *BMLY* BR1 ....62 C3
Bankhurst Rd *CAT* SE6 ....41 M8
Bank La *BGR/WK* TN15 ....179 M8
Bank Rd *RASHE* TN25 ....266 D4
Bank Side *RASHW* TN26 ....304 C8
  SEV TN13 ....148 C6
  WALD ME5 ....95 N6
Bankside Av *LEW* SE13 ....42 A4
Bankside Cl *BH/WHM* TN16 ....136 A5
  BXLY DA5 ....65 M3
Banks La *BXLYHS* DA6 ....45 H5
Banks Rd *ASH* TN23 ....282 D1
  STRD ME3 ....71 J7
The Banks *BRDST* CT10 ....113 L7
Bank St *ASH* TN23 ....2 D4
  CHAT ME4 ....7 F6
  CRBK TN17 ....298 D7
  FAV ME13 ....132 F6
  GVW DA11 ....49 M7
  HB CT6 ....107 M1
  HYTHE CT21 ....309 H5
  MAID/BEAR ME14 ....14 C2
  SEV TN13 ....148 C6
  TON TN9 ....210 B8
Bankton Rd *BRXS/STRHM* SW2 .40 A4
Bankwell Rd *LEW* SE13 ....42 C5
Banky Fields Cl *RHAM* ME8 ....45 J2
Banky Meadow *MAID* ME15 .....154 E9
Bann Cl *SOCK/AV* RM15 ....31 L3
Banner Cl *PUR* RM19 ....30 C7
Banner Farm Rd
  RTWE/PEM TN2 ....23 J7
Banner Wy *IOS* ME12 ....77 N1
Banning St *GNWCH* SE10 ....25 P8
  STRD ME2 ....72 A7
Bannister Cl *BRXS/STRHM* SW2 .40 A9
Bannister Gdns
  STMC/STPC BR5 ....64 E9
Bannister Hl *RSIT* ME9 ....129 J3
Bannister Rd
  MAID/BEAR ME14 ....155 M5
Bannockburn Rd
  WOOL/PLUM SE18 ....27 M7
Banstead St *PECK* SE15 ....41 M4
Banstead Wy *WLGTN* SM6 ....82 D9

Bantry St *CMBW* SE5 ....40 D1
Banwell Rd *BXLY* DA5 ....44 F7
Banyard Rd *BERM/RHTH* SE16 ...24 E6
Bapchild Pl *STMC/STPC* BR5 .....87 K1
Barberry Av *WALD* ME5 ....95 J9
Barchester Wy *POP/IOD* E14 .....25 L1
Barchester Wy *TONN* TN10 ....211 J3
Barclay Av *TONN* TN10 ....211 J5
Barcombe Cl *STMC/STPC* BR5 ...64 C9
Barclay Rd *CROY/NA* CR0 ....83 J7
Barclay Wy *WTHK* RM20 ....31 J8
Barcombe Cl *STMC/STPC* BR5 ...64 C9
Bardell Ter *ROCH* ME1 ....19 H6
Barden Park Rd *TON* TN9 ....210 D9
Barden Rd *RRTW* TN3 ....239 L7
  TON TN9 ....210 D9
Barden St *WOOL/PLUM* SE18 ....28 A1
Bardolph Av *CROY/NA* CR0 ....114 C5
Bardon Rd *WADH* TN5 ....314 B6
Bardsey Pl *WCHPL* E1 ....24 F1
Bardsley Cl *CROY/NA* CR0 ....83 L7
  STPH/PW TN1 ....213 H5
Bardsley La *GNWCH* SE10 ....25 M9
Barfield *EYN* DA4 ....67 H7
Barfield Rd *BMLY* BR1 ....63 L9
Barfleur Mnr *GILL* ME7 * 72 C9
Barfleur St *FAV* ME15 ....41 H4
Barfreston Cl
  MAID/SHEP ME15 ....185 L1
Barfreston Rd *RDV* CT15 ....230 A8
Barfreston Wy *PGE/AN* SE20 * ...61 H7
Bargate Cl
  WOOL/PLUM SE18 ....27 N8
Bargates *ASH* TN23 ....282 B2
Barge House Rd *CAN/RD* E16 ....27 J5
Bargery Rd *CAT* SE6 ....41 P9
Bargrove Wy *SIT* ME10 ....99 P4
Bargrove Cl *PGE/AN* SE20 ....60 C6
Bargrove Rd *CAT* SE6 ....41 N1
Bargrove Rd
  MAID/BEAR ME14 ....156 A7
Barham Cl *CHST* BR7 ....63 H4
  GVE DA12 ....50 B9
  HAYES BR2 ....85 L6
  MAID/SHEP ME15 ....186 B6
Barham Rd *CHST* BR7 ....63 H4
  DART DA1 ....46 C8
  SAND/SEL CR2 ....83 J7
Barham's Mill Rd *HDCN* TN27 ...219 J8
Baring Cl *LEE/GVPK* SE12 ....62 E1
Baring Rd *CROY/NA* CR0 ....83 M5
  LEE/GVPK SE12 ....62 E1
Bark Burt Rd *CDW/CHF* RM16 ...52 A5
Barker Rd *MAIDW* ME16 ....12 D6
Barkers Cl *SIT* ME10 ....129 L1
Bark Hart Rd *ORP* BR6 ....87 J5
Barking Rd *CAN/RD* E16 ....26 F1
  POP/IOD E14 ....25 P2
Barkis Cl *ROCH* ME1 ....95 J7
Barkway Dr *ORP* BR6 ....86 B8
Barkworth Rd
  BERM/RHTH SE16 ....24 E8
Barlborough St *NWCR* SE14 .....41 K1
Barle Gdns *SOCK/AV* RM15 ....31 L2
Barler Pl *QBOR* ME11 ....77 J2
Barley Cl *HB* CT6 ....108 A8
  RDV CT15 ....262 B6
Barleycorn Cl *MAID/BEAR* ME19 .153 M3
Barleycorn Dr *RHAM* ME8 ....97 H8
Barley Flds *MAID/BEAR* ME14 ...95 P8
Barley Wy *ASH* TN23 ....282 A3
Barling Cl *WALD* ME5 ....125 H4
Barlow Cl *RHAM* ME8 ....97 H9
  WOOL/PLUM SE18 ....43 J2
Barlow St *WALW* SE17 ....24 A7
Barlow Wy *RAIN* RM13 ....29 J2
Barlow Wy South *RAIN* RM13 ....29 J2
Barmeston Rd *CAT* SE6 ....41 P2
Barming Rd *WBY/VAL* ME18 .....183 N1
Barmouth Rd *CROY/NA* CR0 ......84 A6
Barnaby Ter *ROCH* ME1 ....95 H4
Barnard Cl *CHST* BR7 ....63 P7
  WOOL/PLUM SE18 ....43 H1
Barnardo Gdns *WCHPL* E1 * 24 G2
Barnardo St *WCHPL* E1 ....24 G2
Barnard Rd *MARG* CR6 ....144 E4
Barnberry Cl *ASH* TN23 ....282 B3
Barn Cl *RCANTE* CT3 ....138 B4
  RSIT ME9 ....129 H3
  WSTB CT5 ....134 C2
Barn Crs *MARG* CT9 ....113 J6
Barncroft Cl
  MAID/BEAR ME14 ....156 C8
Barncroft Dr *GILL* ME7 ....126 C1
Barndale Ct *GVE* DA12 ....70 C4
Barnehurst Av *BXLYHN* DA7 ......46 A4
Barnehurst Cl *ERITH* DA8 ....45 L2
Barnehurst Rd *BXLYHN* DA7 .....45 L3
Barn End Dr *DART* DA2 ....66 C5
Barn End La *RDART* DA2 ....66 C5
Barnes Av *MARG* CT9 ....112 A4
Barnes Cray Rd *DART* DA1 ....46 A5
Barnesdale Crs
  STMC/STPC BR5 ....87 H3
Barnes La *RMAID* ME17 ....215 J2
Barnes St *POP/IOD* E14 ....25 N3
Barnes Wk *STPH/PW* TN12 ......245 J4
Barnet's La *CANTW/ST* CT2 .....137 J5
Barnett Cl *ERITH* DA8 ....45 P3
Barnett Flds *ASH* TN23 ....252 C9
Barnett Cl *SBCH/RUST* TN4 ....240 E8
Barnetts Rd *RTON* TN19 ....209 M8
Barnett's Shaw *OXTED* RH8 .....174 C3
Barnetts Wy *OXTED* RH8 ....174 C4
  SBCH/RUST TN4 ....240 F8
Barnet Wood Rd *HAYES* BR2 ....85 M6
Barney Cl *CHARL* SE7 ....26 C8
Barnfield *GVW* DA11 ....69 L1
  RTWE/PEM TN2 ....270 C9
  TENT TN30 ....301 J5
  WALD ME5 ....95 M6
Barnfield Av *CROY/NA* CR0 ....85 P5
  MTCM CR4 ....82 A1

Barnfield Cl *HART* DA3 ....69 H9
  RDART DA2 ....67 M7
  SWLY BR8 ....68 B3
Barnfield Gdns
  WOOL/PLUM SE18 * 27 J9
Barnfield Pl *POP/IOD* E14 ....25 K7
Barnfield Rd *BELV* DA17 ....28 F7
  BH/WHM TN16 ....145 N5
  FAV ME13 ....132 F5
  FOLKN CT19 ....310 F4
  SEV TN13 ....148 C8
  STMC/STPC BR5 ....64 F9
  WOOL/PLUM SE18 ....27 J9
Barnfields Ct *SIT* ME10 ....100 D9
Barnmead *MAID/BEAR* ME14 .13 J6
Barnmead Cl *MAID/BEAR* ME14 .13 J6
Barnmead Wy *OXTED* RH8 ....175 K9
Barnmead Wood Cl *BECK* BR3 ...84 G3
Barnham Dr *THMD* SE28 ....27 N4
Barnham St *STHWK* SE1 ....24 C8
Barn Hl *MAID/SHEP* ME15 ....184 D9
Barnhill Av *HAYES* BR2 ....85 K2
Barnhouse La *LYDD* TN29 ....335 H6
Barnlea La *RFOLK* CT18 ....288 D7
Barnhurst Rd
  MAID/BEAR ME14 ....155 M4
  STRD ME2 ....123 M1
Barnmead Rd *BECK* BR3 ....61 P7
Barnock Cl *DART* DA1 ....45 N8
Barn Platt *SIT* ME10 ....252 D9
Barnsley Cl *IOS* ME12 ....57 N6
Barnsole Rd *GILL* ME7 ....96 B4
  RCANTE CT3 ....200 C5
Barnstaple La *LEW* SE13 ....42 A5
The Barn *GRAYS* RM17 * 32 C7
Barn Ct *DIT/AY* ME20 ....291 M1
Barnwell Pl *GILL* ME7 ....96 B2
Barnwell Rd *BRXS/STRHM* SW2 .40 A6
  DART DA1 ....46 B3
Barnwood Cl *ROCH* ME1 ....96 A4
Baron Cl *GILL* ME7 ....73 L8
Baron Rd *MAID/BEAR* ME14 .....156 C7
Barrack Hl *HYTHE* CT21 ....308 F5
Barrack Rd *CHAT* ME4 ....73 H7
Barrack Rw *GVW* DA11 ....49 M7
Barrel Arch Cl *STPH/PW* TN2 ...245 H3
Barretts Rd *HAWK* TN18 ....317 J4
  SEV TN13 ....148 C5
Barrey Rd *KEN/WIL* TN24 ....291 M1
Barriedale *NWCR* SE14 ....41 L2
Barrie Dr *DIT/AY* ME20 ....123 N9
Barrier Point Rd *CAN/RD* E16 ...27 H4
Barrier Rd *CHAT* ME4 ....6 C2
Barrington Crs *BRCH* CT7 ....111 J6
Barrington Rd *BRXN/ST* SW9 ....40 B4
  BXLYHN DA7 ....45 H4
Barrington Vls
  WOOL/PLUM SE18 ....43 L2
Barrington Wk *NRWD* SE19 * 60 E5
Barrowfields *WALD* ME5 ....126 A4
Barrow Green Rd *OXTED* RH8 ...174 D6
Barrow Gv *SIT* ME10 ....129 L2
Barrow Hl *ASH* TN23 ....2 C3
Barrow Hill Cots *ASH* TN23 ....2 B3
Barrow Hill Rd *RASHE* TN25 ....285 L9
Barrow Hill Ter *ASH* TN23 ....2 C2
Barrows Cl *BRCH* CT7 ....111 H7
Barr Rd *GVE* DA12 ....70 B1
Barry Av *BXLYHN* DA7 ....45 M9
  BRCH CT7 ....111 H7
Barry Rd *CDW/CHF* RM16 ....33 H6
  ORP BR6 ....86 F7
Barry Pde *EDUL* SE22 * 40 G5
Barry Rd *EDUL* SE22 * 40 F5
Barser Rd *PECK* SE15 ....41 J4
Barsons Cl *PGE/AN* SE20 ....61 J6
Barston Rd *WNWD* SE27 ....60 C1
Barth Ms *WOOL/PLUM* SE18 * ...27 M7
Bartholomew Cl *HYTHE* CT21 ...308 G4
Bartholomew Gdns
  HYTHE CT21 * 308 G5
Bartholomew La *HYTHE* CT21 ...308 F4
  LOTH EC2R * 24 A2
Bartholomew St *DVE/WH* CT16 ...8 B7
Bartholomew St *HYTHE* CT21 ...308 G5
  STHWK SE1 ....24 A6
Bartholomew Wy *SWLY* BR8 ......65 N9
Barth Rd *WOOL/PLUM* SE18 ....27 P7
Bartlett Cl *POP/IOD* E14 ....25 M2
  WALD ME5 ....125 P4
Bartlett Rd *BH/WHM* TN16 ......137 D2
  GVW DA11 ....49 L9
Bartlett St *SAND/SEL* CR2 ....77 J2
Bartley Mill Rd *WADH* TN5 ......294 B6
Barton Cl *BXLYHS* DA6 ....45 H6
  EHAM E6 ....26 G2
  PECK SE15 ....41 J4
Barton Crs *ECRIN* RH19 ....265 K8
Barton Fld *RFOLK* CT18 ....286 C1
Barton Mill Rd *CANTW/ST* CT2 .156 G2
Barton Rd *CANT* CT1 ....167 H6
  CDW/CHF RM16 ....291 K5
  EYN DA4 ....67 H7
  MAID/SHEP ME15 ....185 M1
  SCUP DA14 ....64 G4
  STRD ME2 ....18 C1
Barton View Ter *DVW* CT17 * ...291 K6
Bartram Rd *BROCKY* SE4 ....41 L6
Barts Cl *BECK* BR3 ....84 D1
Barville Rd *RDV* CT15 ....230 F8
Barwick Rd *CDW* CT17 ....290 G6
Barwood Av *WWKM* BR4 ....84 C9
Bascombe Gv *DART* DA1 ....45 H8
Bascombe St *BRXS/STRHM* SW2 ...40 A2
Baseing Cl *EHAM* E6 ....27 H3
Basevi Wy *DEPT* SE8 ....41 P5
Bashford Barn La *RSIT* ME9 .....159 H1
Basi Cl *STRD* ME2 ....72 C6

Basildon Rd *ABYW* SE2 ....27 P7
Basil Gdns *CROY/NA* CR0 ....84 A5
  WNWD SE27 ....60 C4
Basilon Rd *BXLYHN* DA7 ....44 G3
Basil Ter *MAID/SHEP* ME15 * 185 M2
Basin Ap *POP/IOD* E14 ....25 K3
Basing Ct *MAID/SHEP* ME15 ....15 H7
Basing Cr *PECK* SE15 ....42 A1
Basingdon Wy *CMBW* SE5 ....40 D5
Basing Dr *BXLY* DA5 ....45 J6
Basinghall Av *CITYW* EC2V 24 A2
Basinghall St *CITYW* EC2V 24 A2
Baskerville *KEN/WIL* TN24 ....2 J1
Basket Gdns *ELTH/MOT* SE9 .....43 J6
Basmere Cl *MAID/BEAR* ME14 ...13 J5
Bassano St *EDUL* SE22 ....40 F6
Bassant Rd *WOOL/PLUM* SE18 ...27 N9
Bassett Cl *HYTHE* CT21 ....309 J3
Bassett Gdns *HYTHE* CT21 ......309 J2
Bassett St *MAID* ME10 ....129 L1
Bassetts Cl *ORP* BR6 ....86 C8
Bassetts Hl *LING* RH7 ....235 K7
Bassetts La *EDEN* TN8 ....268 B1
Bassetts St *PECK* SE15 ....41 H4
Basswood Cl *PECK* SE15 ....41 J4
Basted La *BGR/WK* TN15 ....151 H4
Basted Mi *BGR/WK* TN15 ....151 J7
Bastion Rd *ABYW* SE2 ....27 P6
Batavia Ms *NWCR* SE14 ....41 L1
Batavia Rd *NWCR* SE14 ....41 L1
Batchelors Rd *RTWE/PEM* TN2 ...241 P9
Batchelor St *CHAT* ME4 ....6 D5
Bates Cl *DIT/AY* ME20 ....123 P9
  RCANTE CT3 ....200 A4
Bates Crs *CROY/NA* CR0 ....82 F9
Bates Hl *BGR/WK* TN15 ....150 F7
Bate St *POP/IOD* E14 ....25 M3
Bath Cl *PECK* SE15 ....41 H1
Bath Hard *ROCH* ME1 ....19 J6
Bath House Rd *CROY/NA* CR0 ....82 D5
Bath Ms *KEN/WIL* TN24 ....283 H2
Bath Pl *MARG* CT9 ....15 J4
Bath Rd *DART* DA1 ....46 B8
  KEN/WIL TN24 ....283 H2
  MARG CT9 ....15 J4
Bathurst Cl *MSTR* CT12 ....142 G3
  STPH/PW TN2 ....246 B5
Bathurst Rd *FOLK* CT20 ....310 D6
  STPH/PW TN2 ....246 B5
Bathway *WOOL/PLUM* SE18 ....28 H7
Baton Cl *PUR* RM19 ....30 C7
Batten Cl *EHAM* E6 ....26 G2
Batten Cots *POP/IOD* E14 * 25 N1
Battenhurst Rd *WADH* TN5 ....314 F9
Batteries Cl *RSIT* ME9 ....130 C5
Battersby Rd *CAT* SE6 ....62 B1
Battery Rd *LYDD* TN29 ....344 C1
  THMD SE28 ....27 M5
Battle Bridge La *STHWK* SE1 ...24 B4
Battlefields *BGR/WK* TN15 ....151 J7
Battle La *STPH/PW* TN12 ....245 M1
Battle of Britain Flats
  CDW CT17 * 8 D4
Battle Rd *ERITH* DA8 ....9 P2
Battlesmere Rd *HOO/HM* ME3 ...52 B8
Battle St *GVE* DA12 ....70 B9
Batt's Rd *CHAT* ME4 ....9 J1
Batty St *WCHPL* E1 ....24 D2
Baudwin Rd *CAT* SE6 ....62 C1
Baugh Rd *SCUP* DA14 ....64 G6
Bavent Rd *CMBW* SE5 ....40 C6
Bawdale Rd *EDUL* SE22 ....40 F6
Bawden Cl *CANTW/ST* CT2 .....136 F9
Bawtree Rd *NWCR* SE14 ....41 L1
Baxendale Ct *KEN/WIL* TN24 ...282 C1
Baxter Rd *CAN/RD* E16 ....26 D2
Baxter Wy *E/WMAL* ME19 ....153 K9
Baye La *RCANTE* CT3 ....171 N6
Bayfield *FAV* ME13 ....162 B2
Bayfield Rd *ELTH/MOT* SE9 ....43 H5
Bayford Rd *SIT* ME10 ....129 P1
Bayhall Rd *RTWE/PEM* TN2 ....23 L7
Bayham Rd *RTWE/PEM* TN2 ....23 J8
  SEV TN13 ....149 H8
Bay Hl *RDV* CT15 ....2 B2
Bayle St *FOLK* CT20 ....11 G4
The Bayle *FOLK* CT20 ....11 G4
Bayley's Hl *RSEV* TN14 ....178 D8
Bayliss Av *THMD* SE28 ....27 M6
Bay Manor La *WTHK* RM20 ....31 J9
Bay Rd *FAV* ME15 ....41 H4
Baynham Cl *BXLY* DA5 ....45 H7
Bays Cl *SYD* SE26 ....61 J4
Bayswater Dr *RHAM* ME8 ....127 H1
Baythorne St *BOW* E3 ....25 J1
Baytree Cl *BFN/LL* DA15 ....64 B4
  BMLY BR1 ....85 M1
Bay View Gdns *IOS* ME12 ....80 B6
Bay View Hts *BRCH* CT7 ....110 E5
Bay View Rd *BRDST* CT10 ....113 K2
Bayview Rd *DEAL* CT14 ....263 H4
Baywell *RYE* TN31 ....2 B2
Bazeham Rd *ASH* TN23 ....83 M6
Bazes Shaw *HART* DA3 ....91 J6
Beacham Cl *CHARL* SE7 ....26 E9
Beach Ap *IOS* ME12 ....57 J4
Beach Av *BRCH* CT7 ....110 G5
Beachborough Rd *BMLY* BR1 ....61 N1
  FOLKN CT19 ....310 E1
Beach Ct *CRBK* TN17 * 298 G6
Beach Houses *MARG* CT9 * 14 C5
Beachmont Cl *NROM* TN28 .....343 K4
Beach Rd *LYDD* TN29 ....327 L5
  SIT ME10 ....111 L4
  WGOS CT8 ....111 N4
Beach St *DEAL* CT14 ....233 J5
  FOLKN CT19 ....310 G3
  HB CT6 ....107 L1
  IOS ME12 ....57 K6

Beach Ter *IOS* ME12 * 57 K6
The Beach *DEAL* CT14 ....233 J6
Beach Wk *WSTB* CT5 ....105 M3
Beacon Av *HB* CT6 ....107 N1
Beacon Cl *RHAM* ME8 ....96 G7
Beacon Dr *RDART* DA2 ....68 A2
Beaconfields *SEV* TN13 ....30 B6
Beacon Ga *NWCR* SE14 ....41 K4
Beacon Hl *HB* CT6 ....107 N1
  LING RH7 ....235 L9
Beacon Hill La *HOO/HM* ME3 ...72 F3
Beacon La *LYDD* TN29 ....334 E6
  SWCH CT13 ....201 H4
Beacon Oak Rd *TENT* TN30 ......301 J7
Beacon Ri *SEV* TN15 ....20 C6
Beacon Rd *BRDST* CT10 ....113 K7
  ERITH DA8 ....107 M2
  HB CT6 ....107 M2
  LEW SE13 ....42 E7
  RMAID ME17 ....189 K6
  WALD ME5 ....95 P4
Beaconsfield Av
  DVE/WH CT16 ....291 K6
  GILL ME7 ....96 A1
Beaconsfield Cl
  BKHTH/KID SE3 ....26 J3
Beaconsfield Gdns
  BRDST CT10 ....113 L8
Beaconsfield Rd
  BKHTH/KID SE3 ....26 B9
  BMLY BR1 ....63 H9
  BXLY DA5 ....65 N1
  CANTW/ST CT2 ....166 E2
  CHAT ME4 ....9 J3
  CROY/NA CR0 ....83 J5
  DEAL CT14 ....233 J4
  DVE/WH CT16 ....8 A1
  ELTH/MOT SE9 ....63 J2
  MAID/SHEP ME15 ....185 K1
  SIT ME10 ....130 B2
  WALD ME5 ....95 P4
The Beacons *RMAID* ME17 ....185 H9
Beacon Wk *HB* CT6 ....107 M1
Beacon Wy *RTWE/PEM* TN2 ....307 N4
Beadles La *OXTED* RH8 ....174 G6
Beadman Pl *WNWD* SE27 * 60 B3
Beadman St *WNWD* SE27 ....60 B3
Beadnell Rd *FSTH* SE23 ....41 K9
Beadon Rd *HAYES* BR2 ....85 J5
Beagles Cl *STMC/STPC* BR5 ......87 L6
Beagles Wood Rd
  RTWE/PEM TN2 ....271 N1
Beales La *RYE* TN31 ....44 C2
Beaman St *CRBK* TN17 ....274 E8
Beamish Rd *STMC/STPC* BR5 ....87 K4
The Beams *MAID/SHEP* ME15 ...186 B2
Bean Cl *ASH* TN23 ....251 P8
Beaney's La *FAV* ME13 ....193 K2
Bean La *RDART* DA2 ....50 G9
Bean Rd *BXLYHS* DA6 ....47 P7
  SWCM DA10 ....47 P5
Beanshaw *ELTH/MOT* SE9 ....63 J5
Beardell Rd *NRWD* SE19 ....60 E5
Beard's Hl *MARG* CT9 ....112 A5
Beardsted La *RASHW* TN26 .....251 K5
Bearsted Cl *BRXS/STRHM* SW2 ...41 M6
Bearsted Cl *RHAM* ME8 ....96 E3
Bearsted Rd
  MAID/BEAR ME14 ....155 P5
Beaton Cl *SWCM* DA10 ....47 P5
Beatrice Hills Cl
  KEN/WIL TN24 ....253 H4
Beatrice Ms *NROM* TN28 * 343 K5
Beatrice Rd *MARG* CT9 ....112 D5
  OXTED RH8 ....175 H4
  RFOLK CT18 ....311 M1
  STHWK SE1 ....24 E6
Beatty Av *GILL* ME7 ....96 C3
Beatty Cl *FOLKN* CT19 ....310 G3
Beatty Rd *FOLKN* CT19 ....310 G4
  ROCH ME1 ....32 J6
Beauchamp Av *DEAL* CT14 ....232 F6
Beauchamp Cl *KEN/WIL* TN24 ...253 H4
Beauchamp Rd *NRWD* SE19 ......60 D7
Beauchamps La *RDV* CT15 ....229 N1
Beaufighter Rd
  E/WMAL ME19 ....152 F9
Beaufort *EHAM* E6 ....27 H1
Beaufort Cl *MSTR* CT12 ....142 G4
Beaufort Ct *CDW/CHF* RM16 ....32 A6
Beaufort Rd *STRD* ME2 ....18 C1
Beaufort Rd *STRD* ME2 ....71 N7
Beaufort Wy
  MAID/SHEP ME15 ....186 B5
Beaufoy Rd *DVW* CT17 ....291 H6
Beaufoy Ter *DVW* CT17 ....290 G6
  SYD SE26 ....61 L5
Beaulieu Cl *CMBW* SE5 ....40 D4
Beaulieu Ri *ROCH* ME1 ....95 J3
Beaulieu Rd *TON* TN10 ....210 D9
Beaulieu Wk *MAIDW* ME16 ......155 H5
Beaumanor *HB* CT6 ....107 L2
Beaumanor Rd *CVW* DA11 ....141 M9
Beaumont Davy Cl *FAV* ME13 ...132 F4
Beaumont Dr *CVW* DA11 ....49 J8
Beaumont Rd *MAID/SHEP* ME15 .184 G1
  NRWD SE19 ....60 C5
  STMC/STPC BR5 ....86 E5
Beaumont Sq *WCHPL* E1 ....25 H1
Beaumont St *RTWE/PEM* TN2 ...52 H1
  LEW SE13 ....42 F2
Beauval Rd *EDUL* SE22 ....40 F7
Beauvoir Dr *SIT* ME10 ....111 N9
Beaworth Pk
  MAID/SHEP ME15 ....186 B5
Beauxfield *DVE/WH* CT16 ....261 H8
Beaverbank Rd *ELTH/MOT* SE9 .345 P9
Beaverbrook Ms *MAID/BEAR* ME16 .12 A6
Beaver Cl *PGE/AN* SE20 * 60 G6
Beaver Ct *ASH* TN23 ....282 D1
Beaver La *ASH* TN23 ....252 B9
Beaver Rd *ASH* TN23 ....2 D7
  MAIDW ME16 ....154 C6

Beaverwood Rd *CHST* BR7 ....64 A4
Beazley Ct *KEN/WIL* TN24 ...282 C1
Bebbington Rd
   WOOL/PLUM SE18 * 27 M7
Beblets Cl *ORP* BR6 ....86 C9
Beccles St *POP/IOD* E14 .....25 J2
Beck Cl *LEW* SE13 ....41 P2
Beckenham Dr *MAIDW* ME16 ..155 J5
Beckenham Gv *HAYES* BR2 ....62 B8
Beckenham Hill Rd *BECK* BR3 ...61 P5
Beckenham La *HAYES* BR2 .....62 C8
Beckenham Pk *RHAM* ME8 * ...97 L3
Beckenham Place Pk
   BECK BR3..........................
Beckenham Rd *BECK* BR3 ......84 E4
Becket Av *CANTW/ST* CT2 ...166 C5
Becket Cl *DEAL* CT14 ....233 H1
   RCANTE CT5..................170 E4
   SNWD SE25 ....83 M5
Becket Ct *RTON* TN27 ....247 N4
Becket's Cl *RASHE* TN25 .....255 J3
Beckets Fld *RTON* TN11 ......238 F6
Becket St *STHWK* SE1 ....24 B6
Beckett Cl *BELV* DA17 ....28 D6
Becketts Cl *ORP* BR6 ....86 G7
Beckett St *FAV* ME13 ....132 E6
Beckett Wy *RCANTE* CT3 .....139 H6
Beckett Wy *BECK* BR3 ....61 L5
Beckett Wy *EGRIN* RH19 .....265 J8
Beckford Dr *STMC/STPC* BR5....86 E4
Beckford Rd *CROY/NA* CRO ...83 L3
Beck La *BECK* BR3 ....61 K9
Beckley Cl *ORP* BR6 ....70 D1
Beckley Ms *WALW* SE17 ....95 L9
Beckley Pl *RASHE* TN25 ......286 A8
Beckley Rd *IOS* ME12 ....57 N6
Beckman Cl *RSEV* TN14 ....118 B9
Beck River Pk *BECK* BR3 ....61 M7
Becksbourne Cl
   MAID/BEAR ME14............155 M4
Beckton Rd *SCUP* DA14 ....86 G2
Bexton Rd *CAN/RD* E16 ....26 A1
Beck Wy *BECK* BR3 ....61 M9
Beckway St *WALW* SE17 ....95 L6
Beckwith Gn *FOLK* CT20 * ...310 B6
Beckwith Rd *NHNL* SE24 ....42 A4
Beckworth Pl *MAIDW* ME16 * .154 C9
Becondale Rd *NRWD* SE19 .....60 E4
Becton Pl *ERITH* DA8 ....45 K2
Bedale St *STHWK* SE1 ....24 A4
Beddington Cross
   CROY/NA CRO....................82 C5
Beddington Farm Rd
   CROY/NA CRO....................82 D5
Beddington Gn
   STMC/STPC BR5................64 B7
Beddington La *WLGTN* SM6....82 C9
Beddington Pk
   STMC/STPC BR5................64 A7
Beddington Ter
   CROY/NA CRO....................82 E4
Beddlestead La *WARL* CR6 ...145 J2
Bedlow Wy *DIT/AY* ME20 .....154 C2
Bedens Rd *STMC/STPC* BR5 ...87 J8
Bedgebury Sq *FAV* ME13 * ...132 C6
Bedlow Wy *CROY/NA* CRO 82 A8
Bedonwell Rd *BELV* DA17 .....28 D9
   BXLYHN DA7....................
Bedser Cl *THHTH* CR7 ....
Bedson Wk *RHAM* ME8 ....97 L5
Bedwardine Rd *NRWD* SE19 ...60 E6
Bedwell Rd *BELV* DA17 ....28 F8
Bedwin Cl *ROCH* ME1 ....95 J7
Beeby Rd *CAN/RD* E16 ....26 B5
Beecham La *TONN* TN10 ......211 H4
Beech Av *BFN/LL* DA15 ....44 C8
   CANT CT1..........................
   SWLY BR8..........................
Beech Cl *DEPT* SE8 ....25 J9
   EGRIN RH19 * 264 C6
   FAV ME13.......................132 E6
   FOLKN CT19.....................10 C1
   LING RH7.........................234 B1
Beech Copse *BMLY* BR1 ....63 K8
   SAND/SEL CR2..................83 K9
Beech Ct *CANT* CT1 * 5 F7
   ELTH/MOT SE9..................43 J7
   RASHE TN25 ....222 D1
Beechcroft *CHST* BR7 ....63 L6
   WSTB CT5 ....
Beechcroft Av *BXLYHN* DA7 ...45 M1
   SLH/COR SS17...................33 P7
Beechcroft Cl *ORP* BR6 ....86 E8
Beechcroft Gdns *RAM* CT11 ..143 L3
Beechcroft Rd *ORP* BR6 ....86 E8
Beech Dell *HAYES* BR2 ....
Beech Dr *BRDST* CT10 ....113 H9
   MAIDW ME16....................155 H7
   RASHW TN26 ....279 P7
   RDV CT15........................230 C7
Beechen Bank Rd *WALD* ME5 ..125 N8
Beechenlea La *SWLY* BR8 ....88 F1
Beechen Pl *FSTH* SE23 ....
Beeches Cl *PGE/AN* SE20 ....61 J7

The Beeches *DIT/AY* ME20.....154 D3
   HART DA3...........................68 G8
   LYDD TN29......................342 C5
   MEO DA13 ....92 E1
   RTWE/PEM TN2 ....270 C5
   SWLY BR8..........................65 P6
   TIL RM18...........................49 M3
   WALD ME5 ....125 M1
Beech Farm Rd *WARL* CR6 ...144 C5
Beechfield Rd *BMLY* BR1 ....62 G8
   CAT SE6.............................61 N1
   ERITH DA8 ....45 N1
Beech Flds *EGRIN* RH19 ......265 J5
Beech Green Cl *RDV* CT15 ...266 D8
Beech Green La *HRTF* TN7 ....267 N8
Beech Gv *HOO/HM* ME3..........71 K4
   MSTR CT12......................142 B7
   MTCM CR4 ....82 C2
   SOCK/AV RM15...................30 B3
Beech Hl *RCANTW* CT4 ....197 N5
Beechhill Rd *ELTH/MOT* SE9 ...43 L6
Beech House Rd *CROY/NA* CRO ..83 J7
Beech Hurst *RTWE/PEM* TN2 ...271 N1
Beech Hurst Cl
   MAID/SHEP ME15............185 M1
Beechings Gn *RHAM* ME8 ....96 F2
Beechings Wy *RHAM* ME8 ....96 C5
Beechings Wy *EGRIN* RH19 ...264 C7
Beechin Wood La
   BGR/WK TN15...................151 M7
Beechlands Cl *HART* DA3 ....91 K1
Beech La *HAWK* TN18 ....330 B2
   STPH/PW TN12 ....272 D5
Beech Mast *MEO* DA13 ....122 C5
Beechmont Cl *BMLY* BR1 ....62 C4
Beechmont Ri *TONN* TN10 ....210 B5
Beechmont Rd *SEV* TN13 .....178 G5
Beechmore Dr *WALD* ME5 ....125 M3
Beecholme Dr *KEN/WIL* TN24 ..252 F4
Beech Rd *BH/WHM* TN16 ......145 M2
   CAT SE6.............................46 D9
   E/WMAL ME19 ....153 N5
   HOO/HM ME3 ....55 L4
   ORP BR6..........................117 H2
   SEV TN13...........................21 F3
   STPH/PW TN12 ....244 F6
   STRD ME2 ....51 P9
   WBY/YAL ME18 ....182 E1
Beech St *RTW* TN1 ....3 K3
Beech St *STPH/PW* TN12 * ...?..?
Beech Wk *DART* DA1 ....46 A5
Beechway *BXLY* DA5 ....44 F7
   MEO DA13 ....92 C4
Beech Wy *SAND/SEL* CR2 .....114 A7
Beechwood Av *DEAL* CT14 ...233 H4
   ORP BR6..........................116 F1
   SIT ME10...........................99 M8
   THHTH CR7........................82 C1
   WALD ME5 ....125 J9
Beechwood Cl *DVE/WH* CT16 ..260 C2
   LYDD TN29......................337 L2
Beechwood Ct *DEAL* CT14 ...233 H4
Beechwood Dr *HAYES* BR2 .....85 N8
   MEO DA13 ....122 B5
Beechwood Gdns *MEO* DA13 ..122 B4
   RAIN RM13........................30 B1
Beechwood La *WARL* CR6 ....144 A4
Beechwood Ms
   RTWE/PEM TN2 ....271 H4
Beechwood Ri *CHST* BR7 ....63 M3
Beechwood Rd
   MAIDW ME16....................154 E9
Beechy Lees Rd *RSEV* TN14 ...149 J2
Beecroft Cl *CANTW/ST* CT2 ...136 F9
Beecroft Rd *BROCKY* SE4 ....41 L6
Beecroft Rd *BROCKY* SE4 ....41 L6
Beehive Pi *BRXN/ST* SW9 ....42 A4
Beehive Dene *ORP* BR6 ....?
Beer Cart La *CANT* CT1 ....4 D5
Beesfield La *EYN* DA4 ....79 M2
Begbie Rd *BKHTH/KID* SE3 ......43 L2
Beggarsbush La *LYDD* TN29 ..335 L6
Beggars La *BH/WHM* TN16 ...176 E1
Begonia Av *RHAM* ME8 ....96 F4
Begonia Cl *EHAM* E6 ....26 F1
Beke Rd *RHAM* ME8 ....126 C1
Bekesbourne Hl *RCANTW* CT4 ..167 N5
Bekesbourne La *RCANTE* CT3 ..167 K5
   RCANTE CT3....................198 C2
   RCANTW CT4....................167 P7
Bekesbourne Rd
   RCANTW CT4....................197 L1
Bekesbourne St
   POP/IOD E14 * 25 L7
Belcaire Cl *HYTHE* CT21 ......307 P4
Belcroft Cl *BMLY* BR1 ....62 C1
Beldam Haw *RSEV* TN14 ......117 P5
Belfast Rd *SNWD* SE25 ....83 P9
Belfield Rd *RTWE/PEM* TN2 ..271 N2
Belford Gv *WOOL/PLUM* SE18 ..27 H7
Belfort Rd *PECK* SE15 ....41 J3
Belfry Cl *BERM/RHTH* SE16 ....96 B7
   BMLY BR1..........................86 C1
Belgrave Cl *RAM* CT11 ....58 D2
   STMC/STPC BR5..................87 K1
Belgrave Rd *DVW* CT17 ....291 J8
   IOS ME12...........................77 J2
   MARG CT9..........................15 D5
   RTW TN1.............................22 E2
   SNWD SE25 ....83 L1
Belgrave St *DIT/AY* ME20 ....124 E1
   WCHPL E1..........................
Belgravia Gdns *BMLY* BR1 .....62 C5
Belgrove *RTW* TN1 ....22 D6
Belinda Ct *FOLK* CT19 ....310 E4
Belinda Rd *BRXN/ST* SW9 ......40 B4
Bellamaine Cl *THMD* SE28 ......27 N5
Bell Chapel Cl *ASH* TN23 .....282 F4
Bell Cl *BAPT* DA11 * 47 M6
Bell Cots *RTON* TN27 ....212 A5
Bell Crs *ROCH* ME1 ....95 L9
Bell-Davies Dr *RCANTE* CT3 ..141 P5
Belle Friday Cl *RSIT* ME9 .....131 H5
Bellegrove Cl *WELL* DA16 ......44 B5

Bellegrove Rd *WELL* DA16 .....44 A3
Bellenden Rd *PECK* SE15 ....40 F3
Bellevue Av *RAM* CT11 ....17 H3
Bellevue Pk *THHTH* CR7 ....82 B5
Bellevue Rd *IOS* ME12 ....58 C9
   RAM CT11..........................17 H3
   WSTB CT5 ....105 N6
   BXLYHS DA6......................45 H6
Belle Vue Rd HB CT6 ....107 N1
   ORP BR6..........................116 B4
Bell Farm Gdns *MAIDW* ME16 ..184 E1
Bell Farm La *IOS* ME12 ....72 F1
Bellfield *CROY/NA* CRO 11 F5
Bellfield Cl *BKHTH/KID* SE3 ....42 F1
Bellflower Av *IOS* ME12 ....78 A3
Bell Gdns *STMC/STPC* BR5 .....87 K2
Bell Gn *SYD* SE26 ....61 M3
Bell Green La *SYD* SE26 ....61 M4
Bell Gv *RCANTE* CT3 ....229 J1
Bellgrove Ct *WALD* ME5 ......125 M5
Bell Hammer *EGRIN* RH19 ....265 H8
Bellingham Av *DIT/AY* ME20 ..154 A1
Bellingham Rd *CAT* SE6 ....61 N2
Bellingham Wy *DIT/AY* ME20 ..154 A1
Bell La *CAN/RD* E16 ....26 A4
   DIT/AY ME20...................154 A2
   HDCN TN27......................278 A1
   MAID/BEAR ME14............125 M6
   MAID/BEAR ME14............124 B3
   ROCH ME1.......................124 E5
   STPH/PW TN12 ....246 B6
   SWCH CT13......................201 P1
   WCHPL E1..........................24 C1
Bellman Av *GVE* DA12 ....50 A9
Bellmeadow
   Bell Meadow *NRWD* SE19 ..186 B5
Bello Cl *HNHL* SE24 ....60 B3
Bellot St *GNWCH* SE10 ....25 P8
Bell Pde *WWKM* BR4 * 84 F6
Bellring Cl *BELV* DA17 ....45 H1
Bell Rd *MAID/SHEP* ME15 ....186 B6
   SIT ME10...........................129 M3
Bells Farm La *RTON* TN11 ....212 D2
Bellegrove Ct *WALD* ME5 ....125 M5
Bell's La *HOO/HM* ME3 ....53 N9
Bells Lane *HART* TN30 ....301 H8
Bell St *WOOL/PLUM* SE18 ......27 M5
Bell Water Ga
   WOOL/PLUM SE18 ....27 H6
Bell Wy *RMAID* ME17 ....187 P9
Bellwood Ct *HOO/HM* ME3 ......53 N9
Bellwood Rd *PECK* SE15 ....41 K5
Bell Yard Ms *STHWK* SE1 ....24 B5
Belmont Cl *WARL* CR6 ....232 C6
Belmont Ct *MAIDW* ME16 ......46 A3
Belmont Gv *LEW* SE13 ....41 P1
Belmont Hl *LEW* SE13 ....41 P1
Belmont Park Cl *LEW* SE13 .....42 A1
Belmont Pk *LEW* SE13 ....42 B5
Belmont Park Cl *LEW* SE13 ....42 C5
Belmont Rd *BECK* BR3 ....61 P1
   BRDST CT10.....................
   CHST BR7..........................63 M4
   ERITH DA8 ....45 J1
   FAV ME13.......................132 F7
   GILL ME7...........................42 G4
   GRAYS RM17......................32 A8
   IOS ME12...........................77 N1
   RAM CT11..........................16 E2
   SIT ME10.........................129 M2
   SNWD SE25 ....83 N2
   WSTB CT5 ....105 L5
Belmont St *RAM* CT11 ....16 E2
Belmont Vls *BRDST* CT10 * ...113 K7
Belmore Pk *KEN/WIL* TN24 ......2 C1
Belnor Av *RSIT* ME9 ....98 F5
Belsey La *RDV* CT15 ....230 G8
Belson Rd *WOOL/PLUM* SE18 ..26 G7
Beltana Dr *GVE* DA12 ....70 A3
Beltinge Dr *HB* CT6 ....108 B4
Beltinge Rd *HB* CT6 ....107 N1
Belton Cl *WSTB* CT5 ....105 M6
Belton Gv *BECK* BR3 ....84 E5
Belton Wy *BOW* E3 ....25 K1
Beltring Rd *SBCH/RUST* TN4 ..270 D2
   STPH/PW TN12 ....213 J6
Beltwood Rd *BELV* DA17 ....29 J8
Beluncle Halt *HOO/HM* ME3 * ..54 A8
Belvedere Cl *GVE* DA12 ....49 N9
   GVE DA12............................49 N9
Belvedere Ct *BELV* DA17 * 28 C4
Belvedere Ms *PECK* SE15 ....41 J4
Belvedere Rd *ABYW* SE2 ....28 C4
   BH/WHM TN16 ....146 A5
   BRDST CT10.....................113 N9
   BXLYHN DA7......................45 J4
   FAV ME13.......................132 C5
   NRWD SE19 ....60 E9
Belvoir Rd *EDUL* SE22 ....60 D1
Bembridge Cl *HB* CT6 ....105 L8
Benares Rd *WOOL/PLUM* SE18 ..27 N7
Benbow St *DEPT* SE8 ....25 K9
Benbury Cl *BMLY* BR1 ....45 H4
Benchfield Cl *EGRIN* RH19 ....265 H6
Bench Rd *CROY/NA* CRO 3 F4
Bencurtis Pk *WWKM* BR4 ....84 D1
Benden Cl *STPH/PW* TN12 ....246 B4
Bendmore Av *ABYW* SE2 ....27 P8
Benedan Cl *HART* DA3 ....53 M7
Benedict Cl *ORP* BR6 ....86 F7
   STRD ME2 ....124 A1
Beneden Gn *HAYES* BR2 ....85 K2
Benenden Rd *CRBK* TN17 ....318 F1
   HDCN TN27......................299 P5
   WOOL/PLUM SE18 ....28 A8
Bengal Rd *MSTR* CT12 ....142 F5
Bengeworth Rd *DENM* ME8 .....85 K2
Benhall Mill Rd *RRTW* TN3 ....271 H8
   RTWE/PEM TN2 ....270 F8
Benhill Rd *CMBW* SE5 ....95 H3
Benhurst Cl *SAND/SEL* CR2 ..114 A4

Benhurst La
   STRHM/NOR SW16 ....60 A4
Benin St *LEW* SE13 ....42 B8
Ben Jonson Rd *WCHPL* E1 ......25 N1
Benledi St *POP/IOD* E14 ....26 C1
Benn Cl *OXTED* RH8 ....205 K1
Bennells Av *WSTB* CT5 ....106 A4
Bennett Cl *WELL* DA16 ....44 C3
Bennett Cv *LEW* SE13 ....41 P2
Bennett Pk *BKHTH/KID* SE3 ....41 P3
Bennett Rd *BRXN/ST* SW9 ......42 A3
Bennetts Av *BGR/WK* TN15 ...120 F6
   CROY/NA CRO....................83 N2
Bennetts Copse *CHST* BR7 .....63 J2
Bennetts Wy *CROY/NA* CRO 84 B6
Bennetts Wy *RDART* DA2 ....67 H7
Benover Rd *WBY/YAL* ME18 ..213 N2
Bensham Cl *THHTH* CR7 ....83 K1
Bensham Gv *THHTH* CR7 ....60 C8
Bensham La *CROY/NA* CRO 82 G5
   THHTH CR7..........................82 G5
Bensham Manor Rd
   THHTH CR7........................83 H1
Ben Smith Wy
   BERM/RHTH SE16...............24 D6
Benson Cl *RFOLK* CT18 ....288 C8
Benson Quay *WAP* E1W 24 E5
Benson Rd *CROY/NA* CRO 82 F7
   FSTH SE23.........................41 J9
   GRAYS RM17......................32 C9
Bensted ASH TN23 ....
Bentham Cl *MAID/SHEP* ME15 ..186 F2
Bentham Gv *FAV* ME13 ....132 D6
Bentham Hl *RRTW* TN3 ....240 A8
Ben Tillet Cl *CAN/RD* E16 * 26 A4
Bentley Av *HB* CT6 ....106 G2
Bentley Cl *DIT/AY* ME20 ......154 E3
   HART DA3...........................68 G9
   WALD ME5 ....126 A3
Bentley Rd *KEN/WIL* TN24 ....283 J1
Bentley's Meadow
   BGR/WK TN15...................149 L5
Bentley St *GVE* DA12 ....49 N7
Bentlif Cl *MAID/SHEP* ME15 ..186 C7
Benton's La *WNWD* SE27 ....60 C3
Benton's Ri *WNWD* SE27 ....60 D4
Berwick Cl *BERM/RHTH* SE16 ..96 C7
   THHTH CR7..........................82 F4
Berber Pde
   WOOL/PLUM SE18 * 43 J1
Berber Rd *STRD* ME2 ....72 B7
Bercta Rd *ELTH/MOT* SE9 ....63 N1
Bere Cl *SWCM* DA10 ....48 F5
Berengrave La *RHAM* ME8 ....97 H5
Berens Rd *STMC/STPC* BR5 .....87 K2
Berens Wy *CHST* BR7 ....86 G1
Beresford Av *ROCH* ME1 ....95 K4
Beresford Ct *BRCH* CT7 ....110 C5
Beresford Dr *BMLY* BR1 ....85 H9
   BMLY BR1..........................64 C5
Beresford Gap *BRCH* CT7 .....110 C5
Beresford Gdns *MARG* CT9 ...113 H2
Beresford Rd *CRBK* TN17 .....319 J3
   DIT/AY ME20...................125 H6
   DVW CT17.......................290 F4
   GILL ME7.............................7 A4
   RAM CT11..........................49 J8
   STRD ME2 ....51 M5
Beresford Sq
   WOOL/PLUM SE18 ....27 J7
Beresford St
   WOOL/PLUM SE18 ....27 J7
Bere Rd *WAP* E1W 24 E3
Bergamot Cl *SIT* ME10 ....129 N3
Berger Cl *STMC/STPC* BR5 .....86 E5
Bergland Pk *STRD* ME2 * 7 J2
Bering Cl *POP/IOD* E14 ....25 K9
Bering Wk *CAN/RD* E16 ....26 E2
Berkeley Av *BXLYHN* DA7 ....44 F2
   MAID/SHEP ME15............164 C1
   FOLKN CT19 *..................310 D4
   ROCH ME1.........................51 P9
   RTWE/PEM TN2 ....271 P1
Berkeley Cl *SIT* ME10 ....129 L2
   WLGTN SM6.......................
Berkeley Crs *DART* DA1 ....46 F2
Berkeley Mt *CHAT* ME4 * 6 B5
Berkeley Pl *RTW* TN1 *............22 C6
Berkeley Rd *BRCH* CT7 ....110 C5
   RTW TN1..............................22 C6
The Berkeleys *SNWD* SE25 * ..88 M1
Berkeley Ter *TIL* RM18 ....49 L1
Berkhampstead Rd *BELV* DA17 ..28 F4
Berkley Rd *GVE* DA12 ....49 M7
Berkley Rw *GVE* DA12 * 49 N7
Berkshire Cl *WALD* ME5 ....95 L1
Berkshire Wy *MTCM* CR4 ....82 D1
Bermondsey St *STHWK* SE1 ...24 D5
Bermondsey Wall East
   BERM/RHTH SE16...............24 D5
Bermondsey Wall West
   STHWK SE1..........................24 C5
Bermuda Rd *TIL* RM18 ....49 L3
Bernal Cl *THMD* SE28 ....28 B1
Bernard Ashley Dr *CHARL* SE7 ..26 C8
Bernard Cassidy St
   CAN/RD E16.......................26 A1
Bernard Rd *WLGTN* SM6 ....82 A9
Bernards Gdns *RDV* CT15 ....229 P9
Bernard St *GVE* DA12 ....49 M7
Bernel Dr *CROY/NA* CRO 84 D4
Berne Rd *THHTH* CR7 ....83 L5
Berner Ter *WCHPL* E1 * 24 E2
Berney Rd *CROY/NA* CRO 3 H1
Berridge Rd *IOS* ME12 ....57 N6
   NRWD SE19 ....60 E5
Berries Rd *FOLK* CT18 ....288 E8
Berry Cots *POP/IOD* E14 * 25 H2
Berryfield Cl *BMLY* BR1 ....85 J5
Berryhill *ELTH/MOT* SE9 ....43 H5
Berryhill Gdns *ELTH/MOT* SE9 ..43 H5
Berrylands *HART* DA3 ....91 K3
Berry La *DUL* SE21 ....60 D3
Berryman's La *SYD* SE26 ....61 K3
Berry Rd *HOO/HM* ME3 ....73 L4
Berry's Green Rd
   BH/WHM TN16 ....146 C1

Berry's Hl *BH/WHM* TN16 .....116 C9
Berry St *SIT* ME10 ....129 N1
Bersham La *GRAYS* RM17 ......32 A7
Berthon St *DEPT* SE8 ....41 N1
Bertie Rd *SYD* SE26 ....61 L5
Bertrand St *LEW* SE13 ....41 P1
Bert Rd *THHTH* CR7 ....83 H2
Berwick Crs *BFN/LL* DA15 ....44 A7
Berwick La *HYTHE* CT21 ......307 P4
Berwick Rd *CAN/RD* E16 ....26 C3
   WELL DA16........................44 D2
Berwick Wy *RSEV* TN14 ....118 C6
   STRD ME2 ....72 D6
Berwyn Av *HSLW TN13 ....
Berwyn Rd *HNHL* SE24 ....60 B9
Beryl Av *EHAM* E6 ....26 F1
Bessels Green Rd *SEV* TN13 ..148 C5
Bessels Meadow *SEV* TN13 ...148 C5
Bessemer Rd *CMBW* SE5 ....40 C3
Bessie Lansbury Cl *EHAM* E6 ..27 H2
Best La *CANT* CT1 ....4 E3
Best St *CHAT* ME4 ....6 B2
Best Ter *SWLY* BR8 * 88 B2
Bestwood St *DEPT* SE8 ....24 G7
Beta Rd *HOO/HM* ME3 ....54 B9
Betchley Cl *EGRIN* RH19 ......265 H6
Betchworth Wy
   CROY/NA CRO..................114 C3
Betenson Av *SEV* TN13 ....148 E7
Bethany Cl *DEAL* CT14 ....233 H1
Bethel Rd *SEV* TN13 ....149 H8
   WELL DA16...........................44 D4
Bethersden Cl *BECK* BR3 ....61 M6
Bethersden Rd *HDCN* TN27 ...279 H1
   RASHW TN26 ....281 J5
   RASHW TN26 ....250 B2
Bethwin Rd *CMBW* SE5 ....40 B1
Betjeman Cl *DIT/AY* ME20 ....153 N1
Betsham Rd *ERITH* DA8 ....45 P1
   MAID/SHEP ME15............185 C5
   MEO DA13 ....48 C3
   SWCM DA10 ....48 C8
Betterton Dr *SCUP* DA14 ....64 G3
Bettescombe Rd *RHAM* ME8 ...96 C7
Betts Cl *BECK* BR3 ....61 C6
Betts Rd *CAN/RD* E16 ....26 C1
Betts St *WAP* E1W 24 E3
Betts Wy *PGE/AN* SE20 ....61 H8
Beulah Av *THHTH* CR7 ....82 C8
Beulah Crs *THHTH* CR7 ....82 C8
Beulah Gv *CROY/NA* CRO 83 H3
Beulah Hl *NRWD* SE19 ....60 B5
Beulah Rd *RTW* TN1 ....23 F1
   THHTH CR7..........................82 C8
Beulah Wk *CTHM* CR5 ....144 B5
Beult Meadow *HDCN* TN27 ...248 C1
Bevan Cl *DEAL* CT14 ....46 A4
Bevan Ct *CROY/NA* CRO 82 D4
Bevan Pl *SWLY* BR8 ....88 E1
Bevan St *EMPK* RM11 ....28 A8
Bevan Wy *RCANTE* CT3 ....229 H1
Beverley Cl *CDW/CHF* RM16 * ..33 J8
   RHAM ME8............................97 J3
Beverley Crs *TON* TN3 ....260 C6
Beverley Gdns *LYDD* TN29 ....327 C2
Beverley Rd *BXLYHN* DA7 ....45 L3
   CANTW/ST CT2 ....
   HAYES BR2 ....85 P6
   MAIDW ME16....................184 C1
   MTCM CR4 ....82 F2
   PGE/AN SE20 ....61 H8
Beverley Wy *MSTR* CT12 ......143 H3
Beverley Cl *BRCH* CT7 * ....
Beverstone Rd *THHTH* CR7 .....82 C1
Bevill Cl *SNWD* SE25 ....60 D9
Bevington Rd *BECK* BR3 ....61 P1
Bevington St *BERM/RHTH* SE16 ..24 D6
Bevis Cl *RDART* DA2 ....
Bevis Marks *HDTCH* EC3A 24 B2
Bewick Ms *PECK* SE15 ....41 H1
Bewl Bridge Cl *WADH* TN5 ....315 M3
Bewlbridge La *RRTW* TN5 .....295 K6
Bewley La *BGR/WK* TN15......180 F1
Bewley St *WCHPL* E1 * 24 E3
Bewlys Rd *WNWD* SE27 ....60 B4
Bewsbury Cross La
   DVE/WH CT16..................260 C9
Bexhill Dr *GRAYS* RM17 ....31 P9
Bexhill Rd *BROCKY* SE4 ....41 M7
Bexley High St *BXLY* DA5 ....45 J8
Bexley La *DART* DA1 ....46 N6
   SCUP DA14...........................64 E3
Bexley Rd *ELTH/MOT* SE9 ......43 L7
   ERITH DA8 ....45 L3
Bexon La *RSIT* ME9 ....129 H8
Bhutan Rd *HB* CT6 ....107 P2
Bianca Rd *PECK* SE15 ....24 G9
Bibury Cl *PECK* SE15 ....24 E9
Bickley Vw STHWK SE1 * ....?
Bickley Crs *BMLY* BR1 ....85 J5
Bickley Park Rd *BMLY* BR1 .....63 K9
Bickley Rd *BMLY* BR1 ....63 K8
Bickmore Wy *TON* TN3 ....210 F7
Bicknell Rd *CMBW* SE5 ....40 C4
Bicknor Cl *CANTW/ST* CT2 ....136 C9
Bicknor La *RSIT* ME9 ....158 D1
Bicknor Rd *MAID/SHEP* ME15 ..186 C7
   ORP BR6............................86 C2
Bidborough Cl *HAYES* BR2 .....85 J2
Bidborough Rdg *RRTW* TN3 ..243 A5
Biddenden Cl
   MAID/SHEP ME15............156 C9
   MARG CT9..........................113 H4
Biddenden La *HDCN* TN27 .....247 P4
Biddenden Rd *HDCN* TN27 ....277 P7
   RASHW TN26 ....301 H1
   TENT TN30..........................
Biddenden Wy *ELTH/MOT* SE9 ..63 L3
   MEO DA13 ....69 J7

Bidder St CAN/RD E16....25 P1
Bideford Rd BMLY BR1....62 D2
  WELL DA16....44 D1
Bidwell St PECK SE15 *....41 H2
Bifrons HI RCANTW CT4....167 M9
Bifrons Rd RCANTW CT4....167 M8
Bigbury Rd RCANTW CT4....165 M5
Biggin HI NRWD SE19....60 B6
Biggin La CDW/CHF RM16....33 J9
Biggin St DVE/WH CT16....8 C5
Biggins Wood Rd FOLKN CT19....310 A4
Biggin Wy NRWD SE19....60 B6
Bigginwood Rd
  STRHM/NOR SW16....60 B6
Bigland St WCHPL E1....24 E2
Bignell Rd WOOL/PLUM SE18....27 J8
Bilberry Rd MAID/BEAR ME14....156 B7
Billet HI BGR/WK TN15....90 F8
Bill Hamling Cl ELTH/MOT SE9....63 K1
Billingford Cl BROCKY SE4....41 K5
Billings HART DA3....91 J3
Billing Gdns
  KEN/WIL TN24....253 H5
Billington HI CROY/NA CR0....83 J6
Billington Rd NWCR SE14....41 K1
Billiter Sq FENCHST EC3M *....24 B3
Billiter St FENCHST EC3M....24 B3
Bilsdon Cl POP/IOD E14....25 M7
Bill Street Rd STRD ME2....72 B7
Bilsington Cl MAID/BEAR ME14....127 J9
Bindon Blood Rd
  DVE/WH CT16....291 H2
The Bines STPH/PW TN12....243 H4
Binfield Rd SAND/SEL CR2....63 M6
Bingham Cl SOCK/AV RM15....31 L2
Bingham Rd CROY/NA CR0....83 M5
  STRD ME2....72 C6
Bingley Cl SNOD ME6....125 N5
Bingley Ct CANT CT1....4 C6
Bingley Rd CAN/RD E16....26 D2
  ROCH ME1....19 K7
Binland Gv WALD ME5....95 J9
Binnacle Rd ROCH ME1....95 M1
Binney Rd HOO/HM ME3....55 J1
Binnie Cl BRDST CT10....143 L2
Binsey Wk ABYW SE2....28 B4
Birbetts Rd ELTH/MOT SE9....63 K3
Birchanger Rd SNWD SE25....83 M2
Birch Cl BRDST CT10....143 H1
  CAN/RD E16....26 C9
  EYN DA4....89 J7
  HART DA3....68 G8
  KEN/WIL TN24....3 K5
  RTON TN11....210 A6
  RTWE/PEM TN2....270 C1
  SEV TN13....148 G8
  STPH/PW TN12....243 G8
Birch Ct RAM CT11 *....16 D1
  RCANTW CT4....228 C7
  WLGTN SM6....82 A8
Birchden Dr THMD SE28....27 H4
Birch Dr WALD ME5....126 A4
Birchen La BANK EC3V....24 A2
The Birches CHARL SE7....26 C9
  CMBW SE5 *....40 E4
  ORP BR6....86 B8
  SWLY BR8....80 A5
  TON TN9....240 E1
Birchett La RASHW TN26....304 A5
Birchetts Av RRTW TN3....269 K5
Birchetts Green La
  WADH TN5....314 C3
Birchfield CDW/CHF RM16....31 N5
Birchfield Cl
  MAID/SHEP ME15....185 N3
Birchfields WALD ME5....125 M2
Birchfield St POP/IOD E14....25 J3
Birch Gv GILL ME7....90 D9
  LEE/GVPK SE12....42 E8
  WELL DA16....44 C4
Birch HI CROY/NA CR0....84 A9
Birch HI Ct BRCH CT7....111 J9
Birchin Cross Rd RSEV TN14....119 K9
Birchington Cl BXLYHN DA7....45 K2
  MAID/BEAR ME14....13 K3
Birch Md ORP BR6....86 B6
Birchmere Rw BKHTH/KID SE3....42 A3
Birchott Forstal
  RASHE TN25 *....284 F1
Birchott Rd MAID/SHEP ME15....186 C2
Birch Pl RDART DA2....47 L7
Birch Rd CANT CT1....166 C7
  HOO/HM ME3....75 L4
  STPH/PW TN12....243 H5
  WSTB CT5....105 P6
Birch Rw HAYES BR2....86 A4
Birch Tree Av WWKM BR4....85 J1
Birch Tree Gdns EGRIN RH19....264 E5
Birch Tree Wy CROY/NA CR0....85 N6
  MAID/SHEP ME15....13 H7
Birch Vls FOLK CT20....310 A8
Birchway HYTHE CT21....130 C3
Birch Wy RTWE/PEM TN2....270 C1
  WARL CR6....144 B3
Birchwood Av BECK BR3....84 C1
  SBCH/RUST TN4....260 D2
Birchwood Dr RDART DA2....66 D2
Birchwood La RSEV TN14....117 N9
Birchwood Park Av SWLY BR8....65 N5
Birchwood Rd MAID/SHEP ME16....155 H7
  STMC/STPC BR5....86 E1
  SWLY BR8....65 L6
Birchwood Wk
  CANTW/ST CT2....166 D2
Birdbrook Rd BKHTH/KID SE3....42 G4
Birdham Cl BMLY BR1....85 P2
Bird House La ORP BR6....116 B8
Birdhurst Av SAND/SEL CR2....83 J8
Birdhurst Gdns SAND/SEL CR2....83 J8
Birdhurst Ri SAND/SEL CR2....83 K9
Birdhurst Rd SAND/SEL CR2....83 K8
Bird In Bush Rd PECK SE15....40 F6
Bird-in-Hand La BMLY BR1....63 H8
Bird-in-Hand Ms FSTH SE23....61 J1

Bird-in-Hand Pas FSTH SE23....61 J1
Bird in Hand St RRTW TN3....268 G8
Birds Av MARG CT9....112 A6
Birdwood Av DEAL CT14....232 F4
Birdwood Cl SAND/SEL CR2....114 A5
Birkbeck HI DUL SE21....60 B1
Birkbeck Pl DUL SE21....40 B9
Birkbeck Rd BECK BR3....61 K9
  SCUP DA14....64 C2
Birkdale Ct BERM/RHTH SE16....24 F8
  ORP BR6....86 E4
  THMD SE28....28 B2
  WSTB CT5....106 C6
Birkdale Cl MAIDW ME16 *....87 K2
Birkdale Dr FOLKN CT19....310 D5
Birkdale Gdns CROY/NA CR0....84 A8
  HB CT6....107 J4
Birkdale Rd ABYW SE2....27 P7
Birken Rd RTWE/PEM TN2....270 C1
Birkhall Cl WALD ME5....95 M9
Birkhall Rd CAT SE6....42 B9
Bir La RSIT ME9....129 L8
Birling Av MAID/BEAR ME14....156 D8
  RHAM ME8....96 C5
Birling Cl MAID/BEAR ME14....156 C8
Birling Dr RTWE/PEM TN2....270 D8
Birling Pk RE/WMAL ME19....123 H8
Birling Park Av
  RTWE/PEM TN2....270 E8
Birling Rd E/WMAL ME19....123 H8
  ERITH DA8....45 M1
  KEN/WIL TN24....253 K7
  RTWE/PEM TN2....270 D8
  SNOD ME6....123 N6
Birling Road Rookery HI
  SNOD ME6....123 N5
Birnam Sq MAIDW ME16....12 B5
Birtrick Dr MEO ME6....12 A2
Biscoe Wy LEW SE13 *....42 B5
Bisenden Rd CROY/NA CR0....83 K6
Bishop Butt Cl ORP BR6....86 C7
Bishop Ct SIT ME10 *....99 M9
Bishopden Ct
  CANTW/ST CT2 *....136 B9
Bishop Jenner Ct
  RCANTE CT3 *....169 M2
Bishop La RSIT ME9....97 P3
Bishops Av BMLY BR1....62 C9
Bishops Av BRDST CT10....113 N7
Bishops Ct ELTH/MOT SE9....63 N1
  WBY/VAL ME18....183 K5
Bishop's La MAID/SHEP ME15....214 C3
Bishops Md CMBW SE5 *....40 C1
Bishops Ms TON TN9....240 F1
Bishops Oak Ride TONN TN10....210 E4
Bishops Rd CROY/NA CR0....83 H3
Bishops Ter
  MAID/BEAR ME14 *....12 E1
Bishopsthorpe Rd SYD SE26....61 J3
Bishopstone Rd CAT SE6....108 C4
Bishopstone La HB CT6....108 C5
Bishops Wk CHST BR7....63 N7
  CROY/NA CR0....119 C6
  ROCH ME1....19 G6
Bishops Wy CANTW/ST CT2....166 C3
  MAID/BEAR ME14....12 D5
Bishopswood ASH TN23....282 F3
Bismuth Dr SIT ME10....99 L8
Bittern Cl RFOLK CT18....288 D7
Blackberry Fld
  STMC/STPC BR5....64 C7
Blackberry La LING RH7....234 F8
Blackberry Rd EGRIN RH19....234 F9
Blackberry Wy
  STPH/PW TN12....243 H3
  WSTB CT5....106 A6
Blackbrook La HAYES BR2....86 D2
Black Bull Rd FOLKN CT19....10 E2
Blackburn Rd HB CT6....106 C4
Blackdown Dr KEN/WIL TN24....252 E5
Blackdown Ter
  WOOL/PLUM SE18 *....43 K2
Black Eagle Cl BH/WHM TN16....176 D3
Blacketts Rd RSIT ME9....100 C8
Blackfen Pde BFN/LL DA15 *....44 C7
Blackfen Rd BFN/LL DA15....44 B6
Blackfriars St CANT CT1....4 D4
Black Griffin La CANT CT1....4 D4
Blackhall La BGR/WK TN15....149 N8
Blackheath Av GNWCH SE10....41 P2
Blackheath Gv
  BKHTH/KID SE3....42 A4
Blackheath HI GNWCH SE10....41 P3
Blackheath Pk
  BKHTH/KID SE3....42 A6
Blackheath Ri LEW SE13....42 A3
Blackheath V BKHTH/KID SE3....42 A4
Black Horse Cl STHWK SE1....24 A6
Blackhorse La CROY/NA CR0....83 P3
Black Horse Ms BGR/WK TN15....151 K5
Blackhorse Rd DEPT SE8....25 H9
Black Horse Rd SCUP DA14....64 D3
Blackhouse HI HYTHE CT21....309 J4
Blackhouse La RFOLK CT18....309 J4
Blackhurst La RTWE/PEM TN2....271 J2
Blacklands E/WMAL ME19....153 H4
Blacklands Dr E/WMAL ME19....153 H4
Blacklands Rd CAT SE6....62 A3
Blackman Ct HOO/HM ME3....53 K9
Blackmans Cl DART DA1....66 A4
Blackman's La RTON TN11....211 N3
  WARL CR6....115 H8
Blackmanstone Br
  LYDD TN29....326 A7
Blackmanstone Wy
  MAIDW ME16....154 G5

Blackmead SEV TN13....148 D6
Black Mill La HDCN TN27....247 L3
Blackmore Rd GRAYS RM17....52 D8
Blackness Cots HAYES BR2 *....115 N5
Blackness La HAYES BR2....115 N5
Blackpool Rd PECK SE15....41 H5
Black Robin La RCANTW CT4....228 B5
Black Rock Gdns GILL ME7....126 E1
Blackshots La CDW/CHF RM16....32 D1
Blacksmith Dr
  MAID/BEAR ME14....156 A7
Blacksmiths La
  STMC/STPC BR5....87 K2
Blacksole La BGR/WK TN15....151 J1
Blacksole Rd BGR/WK TN15....151 J1
Black Swan Yd STHWK SE1....24 B5
Blacks Yd SEV TN13....21 F5
Blackthorn Av
  SBCH/RUST TN4....240 F8
  WALD ME5....125 M2
Blackthorn Cl BGR/WK TN15....120 C3
Blackthorn Dr DIT/AY ME20....154 A1
Blackthorne Av CROY/NA CR0....83 P5
Blackthorne Rd RHAM ME8....97 K6
Blackthorn Gv BXLYHN DA7....44 G4
Blackthorn Wy ASH TN23....282 F5
Blacktree Ms BRXN/ST SW9 *....40 B4
Blackwall La GNWCH SE10....25 P8
Blackwall Rd RASHE TN25....253 L5
Blackwall North
  KEN/WIL TN24....253 K7
Blackwall Rd South
  KEN/WIL TN24....253 K7
Blackwall Tunnel Ap
  POP/IOD E14....25 M3
Blackwall Tunnel Northern Ap
  POP/IOD E14....25 M3
Blackwall Wy POP/IOD E14....25 N4
Blackwater Cl RAIN RM13....29 J1
Blackwater St EDUL SE22....40 F6
Blackwell Farm Rd
  EGRIN RH19....265 J5
Blackwell Hollow EGRIN RH19....265 J6
Blackwood St WALW SE17 *....24 A8
Bladindon Dr BXLY DA5....44 F8
Blagdon Rd CAT SE6....41 P7
Blair Cl BFN/LL DA15....44 B3
Blair Dr SEV TN13....148 C8
Blair St POP/IOD E14....25 M2
Blake Cl DEAL CT14....232 C9
  WELL DA16....44 A2
Blake Ct KEN/WIL TN24....253 J9
Blake Dr DIT/AY ME20....153 P1
Blake Gdns DART DA1....46 F5
Blakemore Rd THHTH CR7....82 E2
Blakemore Wy BELV SE2....27 N5
Blakeney Av BECK BR3....61 L8
Blakeney Cl MAID/BEAR ME14....156 E8
Blaker Av ROCH ME1....95 K5
Blake Rd CROY/NA CR0....83 K6
  CAN/RD E16....26 D8
Blakes Gn WWKM BR4....84 F4
Blake's Rd PECK SE15....40 E1
Blake Wy RTWE/PEM TN2....270 C1
Blanchard Cl ELTH/MOT SE9....63 H4
Blanch Cl PECK SE15....41 J1
Blanchedowne CMBW SE5....60 D5
Blanchman's Rd WARL CR6....144 B5
Blandford Dr RFOLK CT18....309 J4
Blandford Rd BECK BR3....61 L8
Blandford Gdns SIT ME10....129 M4
Blandford Rd BFN/LL DA15....44 B3
Blanmerle Rd ELTH/MOT SE9....63 M9
Blann Cl ELTH/MOT SE9....63 H4
Blashford St LEW SE13....61 H1
Blatchington Rd
  RTWE/PEM TN2....270 D7
Blaxland Cl FAV ME13....132 E4
Bleak Hill La WOOL/PLUM SE18....27 N9
Bleakwood Rd WALD ME5....95 L9
Blean Gv PGE/AN SE20....61 J6
Blean HI CANTW/ST CT2....135 P8
Blean Rd RHAM ME8....96 F4
Blean View Rd HB CT6....106 C4
Bledlow Cl THMD SE28....28 B3
Blendon Dr BXLY DA5....44 F7
Blendon Rd BXLY DA5....44 F7
Blendon Ter
  WOOL/PLUM SE18....43 K8
Blenheim Av CANT CT1....167 J5
  CHAT ME4....95 K4
  FAV ME13....133 H8
Blenheim Cl BRDST CT10....143 K2
  DART DA1....46 D3
  EGRIN RH19....265 K5
  HB CT6....107 M5
  MAID/SHEP ME15....156 C9
  MEO ME6....12 B3
Blenheim Ct BFN/LL DA15....64 A3
Blenheim Dr DVE/WH CT16....291 K4
  RFOLK CT18....288 D7
  WELL DA16....44 E4
Blenheim Gdns SOCK/AV RM15....30 E4
Blenheim Gv PECK SE15....40 F5
Blenheim Pl FOLK CT20....310 C7
Blenheim Rd BFN/LL DA15....44 B7
  BMLY BR1....85 P3
  DART DA1....46 C7
  DEAL CT14....233 H4
  E/WMAL ME19....152 G2
  NROM TN28....337 J7
  PGE/AN SE20....61 K6
  PECK SE15....87 K6
Blenheim Wy WADH TN5....315 N3
Blessington Rd LEW SE13....42 B5

Bletchingley Cl THHTH CR7....82 G1
Bligh Rd GVW DA11....49 L7
Blighs Ct WLGTN SM6 *....21 F3
Blighs Wk SEV TN13....21 F3
Bligh Wy STRD ME2....71 J9
Blindgrooms La RASHW TN26....281 P7
Blindhouse La RASHE TN25....285 P5
Blind La CRBK TN17....274 D7
  GILL ME7....126 C4
  RASHE TN25....222 E1
  RASHE TN25....253 L5
Blissett St GNWCH SE10....42 A2
Bliss Wy TONN TN10....211 H5
Blithdale Rd ABYW SE2....27 L3
Blockhouse Rd GRAYS RM17....52 D9
Blockmakers Ct CHAT ME4....95 N5
Blomfield St LVPST EC2M....24 A1
Bloomfield Rd HAYES BR2....85 N2
  WOOL/PLUM SE18....27 J8
Bloom Gv WNWD SE27....60 B2
Bloomhall Rd NRWD SE19....60 D4
Bloomsbury Rd RAM CT11....16 B4
Bloomsbury Wk
  MAID/BEAR ME14....13 G3
Bloomsbury Wy
  KEN/WIL TN24....252 E5
Bloors La RHAM ME8....96 C5
Bloors Wharf Rd RHAM ME8....96 F1
Blossom Cl SAND/SEL CR2....83 J2
Blossom La RASHE TN25....252 B4
Blossom St WCHPL E1....24 B1
Blount Av EGRIN RH19....264 B4
Blount St POP/IOD E14....25 H2
Blowers HI EDEN TN8....237 J9
Blowers Wood Gv GILL ME7....126 E2
Bloxam Gdns ELTH/MOT SE9....43 J6
Bloxworth Cl WLGTN SM6....82 B7
Blucher Rd CMBW SE5....40 C1
Blue Anchor La
  BERM/RHTH SE16....24 D7
  TIL RM18....33 H7
Blue Anchor Yd WCHPL E1....24 D3
Bluebell Cl ASH TN23....282 E4
  EGRIN RH19....264 E7
  GILL ME7....73 M9
  ORP BR6....86 C5
  SYD SE26....60 F3
  SWLY BR8....82 A5
Bluebell Dr SIT ME10....129 N5
Bluebell Rd ASH TN23....282 E4
Bluebell Wks STPH/PW TN12....243 H5
Blueberry Cl BRDST CT10....143 L2
Blueberry La RSEV TN14....147 K1
Bluebird Wy THMD SE28....27 L5
Blue Coat La CRBK TN17....274 D6
Blue Fld ASH TN23....251 P9
Bluehouse Gdns OXTED RH8....175 K4
Blue House La OXTED RH8....175 H4
Blue Line La KEN/WIL TN24....252 B1
Blue Riband Est
  CROY/NA CR0....82 G6
Bluett St MAID/BEAR ME14....13 J2
Bluewater Pkwy RDART DA2....47 M9
Blunden La WBY/VAL ME18....213 P1
Blunt Rd SAND/SEL CR2....83 J9
Blunts Rd ELTH/MOT SE9....43 M8
Blythe Cl CAT SE6....41 M8
Blythe HI CAT SE6....41 M8
  STMC/STPC BR5....64 B7
Blythe Hill La CAT SE6....41 M8
Blythe Hill Pl FSTH SE23 *....41 L8
Blythe Rd MAID/SHEP ME15....13 J5
Blythe V CAT SE6....41 M9
Blyth Rd BMLY BR1....63 N2
  THMD SE28....28 B5
Blyths Wk POP/IOD E14....25 H3
The Blytons EGRIN RH19....264 A3
Boakes Meadow RSEV TN14....118 E5
Boarders La WADH TN5....314 C3
Boarley La MAID/BEAR ME14....155 L3
Boarman's Rd LYDD TN29....334 E3
Boathouse Rd IOS ME12....57 H5
Boathouse Wk PECK SE15....40 F7
Boat La RASHE TN25....306 A3
Boat Lifter Wy
  BERM/RHTH SE16....25 H7
Boat Quay CAN/RD E16....26 D3
Bob Amor Cl FAV ME13....133 H6
Bob Harvey Wy SIT ME10....99 H9
Bobbin Lodge HI
  RCANTW CT4....195 J2
Bob Marley Wy HNHL SE24....40 A5
Bockham La RASHE TN25....283 P1
Bockhanger La
  KEN/WIL TN24....252 F3
Bockingford La
  MAID/SHEP ME15....185 K3
Bodell Cl CDW/CHF RM16....32 C5
Bodenham Rd FOLK CT20....310 D7
Bodiam Br RBTBR TN32....328 F6
Bodiam Cl RHAM ME8....96 F4
Bodiam Rd RBTBR TN32....328 G3
Bodkins Cl RMAID ME17....186 A6
Bodle Av SWCM DA10....48 C7
Bodmin Cl STMC/STPC BR5....87 K5
Bodsham Crs
  MAID/SHEP ME15....156 C9
Bofors House CHARL SE7 *....43 J5
Bogarde Dr HOO/HM ME3....72 B5
Bognor Dr HB CT6....107 L2
Bognor Rd WELL DA16....44 F2
Bogshole La HB CT6....108 A4
  WSTB CT5....135 L1
Boham's Rd WCHPL E1....25 H1
Bolden St DEPT SE8....41 P3
Bolderwood Wy WWKM BR4....84 C7
Boley HI ROCH ME1....19 H4
Boleyn Av EW KT17....111 P4
Boleyn Cl CROY/NA CR0....83 L5
Boleyn Ct BERM/RHTH SE16 *....25 H6
Boleyn Gdns WWKM BR4....84 C7
Boleyn Rd BGR/WK TN15....149 K5

Boleyn Wy SWCM DA10....48 C8
Bolina Rd BERM/RHTH SE16....24 F8
Bolner Cl WALD ME5....125 L3
Bolton Crs CMBW SE5....40 A1
Bolton Gdns BMLY BR1....62 D5
Bolton Rd FOLK CT19....11 G2
Bolton St RAM CT11....16 D1
Bolts HI RCANTW CT4....195 K1
Bombay St BERM/RHTH SE16....24 E7
Bombers La BH/WHM TN16....146 E4
Bonar Pl CHST BR7....63 J6
Bonar Rd PECK SE15....40 C1
Bonaventure Ct GVE DA12....70 B3
Bonchester Cl CHST BR7....63 L6
Bond Cl RSEV TN14....117 L9
Bond Rd SBCH/RUST TN4....240 C8
Bondfield Rd E/WMAL ME19....153 N4
Bond Gdns WLGTN SM6....82 B8
Bond La ASH TN23....282 D6
Bond Rd ASH TN23....252 D9
  RHAM ME8....127 H1
  WARL CR6....144 A3
Bond St GRAYS RM17....32 D9
Boneashe La BGR/WK TN15....151 N6
Bone Mill La GDST RH9....204 B1
Boneta Rd WOOL/PLUM SE18....26 G6
Bonetta Ct IOS ME12....57 K8
Bonfield Rd LEW SE13....42 A5
Bonflower La RMAID ME17....215 H5
Bonham Dr CDW/CHF RM16....33 H1
  SIT ME10....99 P9
Bonita Ms PECK SE15....41 K4
Bonner Rd BGR/WK TN15....32 A6
Bonner Wy SWLY BR8....65 J6
Bonnington Rd
  MAID/BEAR ME14....155 P6
Bonny Bush HI RCANTW CT4....228 A1
Bonsor Rd FOLKN CT19....10 D7
Bonsor St CMBW SE5....40 C1
Bonville Rd BMLY BR1....62 D4
Boones Rd LEW SE13....42 C5
Boone St LEW SE13....42 C5
Boord St GNWCH SE10....25 P6
Boormans Ms
  WBY/VAL ME18....183 M4
Bootham Cl STRD ME2....94 C2
Booth Cl SNOD ME6....123 P5
  THMD SE28....28 A4
Booth Rd CHAT ME4....95 L4
  CROY/NA CR0....2 A5
Borden La RSIT ME9....129 L5
Border Ct EGRIN RH19....265 J4
Border Crs SYD SE26....61 H4
Border Gv CROY/NA CR0....84 E8
Border Rd SYD SE26....61 H4
Bordyke TON TN9....210 F8
Boreham Av CAN/RD E16....26 E2
Boresisle TENT TN30....301 J5
Borgard House CHARL SE7 *....43 J1
Borgard Rd WOOL/PLUM SE18....26 G6
Borkwood Pk ORP BR6....86 D5
Borkwood Wy ORP BR6....86 F8
Borland Cl RDART DA2....47 N6
Borland Rd PECK SE15....41 J5
Bornefields ASH TN23....282 D1
Borough CANT CT1....5 F3
Borough Green Rd
  BGR/WK TN15....150 C5
Borough High St STHWK SE1....24 A5
Borough Rd CROY/NA CR0....82 G7
  BH/WHM TN16....145 N6
  GILL ME7....7 K5
  QBOR ME11....7 K5
Borrowdale Av RAM CT11....142 F5
Borstal HI WSTB CT5....105 K6
Borstal Ms ROCH ME1....94 C3
Borstal St ROCH ME1....94 H4
Borstwick St DEPT SE8....25 L9
Bosbury Rd CAT SE6....62 A2
Boscobel Cl BMLY BR1....63 K8
Boscombe Av GRAYS RM17....32 E7
Boscombe Rd FOLKN CT19....10 D2
Bosney Banks RDV CT15....260 B2
Bossingham Rd RCANTW CT4....226 E8
Bossingham St RCANTW CT4....226 F4
Bossington Rd RCANTE CT3....198 G6
Boss St STHWK SE1....24 C5
Bostall Heath ABYW SE2....27 P6
Bostall HI ABYW SE2....28 A8
Bostall La ABYW SE2....28 A8
Bostall Manorway ABYW SE2....28 A8
Bostall Park Av BXLYHN DA7....27 P6
Bostall Rd STMC/STPC BR5....64 D6
Boston Cl DVE/WH CT16....291 H4
Boston Gdns RHAM ME8....96 F5
Boston Rd CROY/NA CR0....82 E3
  WALD ME5....125 N5
Bosville Dr SEV TN13....148 F8
Bosville Rd SEV TN13....148 F8
Boswell Cl STMC/STPC BR5....87 K3
Boswell Rd THHTH CR7....82 G6
Botany TON TN9....210 F9
Botany Bay La CHST BR7....63 N6
Botany Rd BRDST CT10....113 L3
Botany Ter RAM CT11 *....5 H?
Botany Wy PUR RM19....30 D8
Botha Rd PLSTW E13....26 E3
Bothwell Cl CAN/RD E16....26 E7
Bothwell Rd CROY/NA CR0....114 F4
Botolph Aly MON EC3R *....24 B3
Botolph La MON EC3R....24 B3
Botolph's Bridge Rd
  HYTHE CT21....307 P8
Bottom La BGR/WK TN15....119 P5
Bottlescrew HI RMAID ME17....187 N7
Bottles La RSIT ME9....129 P8
Bottom Pond Rd RSIT ME9....159 J3
Boucher Dr GVW DA11....69 K2
Boughton Av BRDST CT10....143 M3
  HAYES BR2....85 J4
Boughton By CANTW/ST CT2....165 K2
Boughton La....133 M9
Boughton Pde
  MAID/SHEP ME15 *....185 M4

Boughton Rd *RMAID* ME17 ....219 H2
  THMD SE28 ....27 M6
Boulcott St *WCHPL* E1 ....24 C2
Boulevard Courrieres
  RCANTE CT3 ....229 H2
The Boulevard *DIT/AY* ME20 ....283 J2
Boulogne Rd *CROY/NA* CR0 ....83 H3
Boulthurst Wy *OXTED* RH8 ....175 L8
Boultwood Rd *EHAM* E6 ....26 G2
Boundary Chs *WSTB* CT5 ....106 A6
Boundary Ct *IOS* ME12 ....78 E1
Boundary St *CANT* CT1 *...........166 C6
Boundary Rd *BFN/LL* DA15 ....44 A6
  CHAT ME4 ....95 L3
  DEAL CT14 ....233 J2
  HYTHE CT21 ....308 F6
  RAM CT11 ....17 F2
  RTWE/PEM TN2 ....270 C7
Boundary St *ERITH* DA8 ....45 P1
The Boundary *CANT* CT1 ....166 C6
  RRTW TN3 ....93 K2
Boundary Wy *CROY/NA* CR0 ....84 D9
Boundfield Rd *CAT* SE6 ....62 C2
Bounds La *FAV* ME13 ....164 B1
Bounds Oak Wy
  SBGH/RUST TN4 ....240 B6
The Bounds *DIT/AY* ME20 ....154 D3
Bourchier Cl *SIT* TN13 ....21 F5
Bourdon Rd *PGE/AN* SE20 ....61 J8
Bourg-de-Peage Av
  EGRIN RH19 ....265 K7
Bournbrook Rd
  BKHTH/KID SE3 ....43 H4
Bourne Cl *TON* TN9 ....210 G7
Bourne Grange La
  RTON TN11 ....211 N2
Bourne Gv *SIT* ME10 ....99 K5
Bourne La *BGR/WK* TN15 ....181 J1
  HAWK TN18 ....328 F1
  RASHW TN26 ....304 D7
  RBTBR TN32 ....328 A5
  TON TN9 ....210 F7
Bourne Lodge Cl
  CANTW/ST CT2 ....135 P6
Bourne Md *BXLY* DA5 ....45 L6
Bournemouth Cl *PECK* SE15 ....43 G3
Bournemouth Dr *HB* CT6 ....107 J1
Bournemouth Gdns
  FOLKN CT19 ....10 D2
Bournemouth Rd *FOLKN* CT19 ...10 D3
  PECK SE15 ....43 G2
Bourne Pde *BXLY* DA5 * 45 K8
Bourne Park Rd *RTON* TN11 ......212 A6
Bourne Park Rd *RCANTW* CT4 ...197 N4
Bourne Place Ctyd
  RTON TN11 * 209 M3
Bourne Place Mdw
  RTON TN11 ....209 M3
Bourne Rd *BXLY* DA5 ....45 K7
  GVE DA12 ....17 L9
  HAYES BR2 ....85 N1
  RASHE TN25 ....305 M1
Bournes Cl *CANTW/ST* CT2 ......137 L2
Bourneside Gdns *CAT* SE6 ....64 A4
Bourneside Ter *RMAID* ME17 *..187 N1
Bournes Pl *RASHW* TN26 ....304 D5
Bourne St *CROY/NA* CR0 ....82 C6
Bourne V *BGR/WK* TN15 ....181 K3
  HAYES BR2 ....85 K5
Bourne Wy *HAYES* BR2 ....85 L9
  SWLY BR8 ....65 L9
Bournewood *RASHW* TN26 ....304 D7
Bournewood Cl
  MAID/SHEP ME15 ....186 C2
Bournewood Rd
  STMC/STPC BR5 ....87 J4
  WOOL/PLUM SE18 ....44 C1
Bournville Av *CHAT* ME4 ....95 L5
Bournville Rd *CAT* SE6 ....41 N8
Bousfield Rd *NWCR* SE14 ....61 K3
Boutique Hall *LEW* SE13 * 42 A5
Bouverie Rd West *FOLK* CT20 ....10 B6
Bouverie Sq *FOLK* CT20 ....10 C6
Boveney Rd *E/WMAL* ME19 ....153 K9
Bovey Rd *FSTH* SE23 ....41 K8
Bovey Wy *SOCK/AV* RM15 ....31 L1
Bovill Rd *FSTH* SE23 ....41 K8
Bow Arrow La *DART* DA1 ....46 C7
Bowater Pl *BKHTH/KID* SE3 ....42 F1
Bowater Rd *WOOL/PLUM* SE18 ..26 F6
Bowdell La *LYDD* TN29 ....334 F1
Bowden Crs *FOLK* CT20 ....309 P1
Bowditch *DEPT* SE8 ....25 J5
Bowen Dr *DUL* SE21 ....60 E2
Bowen Rd *FOLK* CT19 ....310 B5
  SBGH/RUST TN4 ....269 N3
Bowers Fld *ASH* TN23 ....2 C6
Bowen St *POP/IOD* E14 ....25 L2
Bowenswood *CROY/NA* CR0 ......114 C3
Bowens Wd *CROY/NA* CR0 * 114 C3
Bower Av *GNWCH* SE10 ....42 C2
Bower Cl *MAIDW* ME16 ....41 N8
Bowerland La *LING* RH7 ....234 C1
  RCANTW CT4 ....194 D1
Bower La *BGR/WK* TN15 ....119 N5
  EYN DA4 ....119 M2
  MAIDW ME16 ....12 B6
Bowerman Av *NWCR* SE14 ....61 K3
Bowerman Rd *CDW/CHF* RM16 ..33 H7
Bower Mount Rd
  MAIDW ME16 ....12 A4
Bower Pl *MAIDW* ME16 ....12 B7
Bower Rd *RASHE* TN25 ....283 P4
  SWLY BR8 ....66 A6
Bowers Av *GVW* DA11 ....69 K3
Bowes Av *RSEV* TN14 ....118 E5
Bower St *MAIDW* ME16 ....12 B5
  WCHPL E1 * 24 G1
Bower Ter *MAIDW* ME16 ....12 C6
Bowes Av *MARG* CT9 ....111 P4
Bowes Cl *BFN/LL* DA15 ....44 B5
Bowesden La *GVE* DA12 ....71 H6
Bowes Rd *STRD* ME2 ....9 G7
Bowes Vls *DEAL* CT14 * 201 M6
Bow Hart *WALD* ME5 * 91 J7
Bowford Av *BXLYHN* DA7 ....44 A7
Bow Hl *RCANTW* CT4 ....196 F9
Bowhill Cl *BRXN/ST* SW9 ....40 A1
Bowland St *HB* CT6 ....107 P4

Bowles Well Gdns
  FOLKN CT19 ....311 J4
Bowley Cl *NRWD* SE19 ....60 F4
Bowley La *NRWD* SE19 ....60 F4
Bowl Hill *KEN/WIL* TN24 ....283 J2
Bowley St *POP/IOD* E14 ....25 J3
Bowl Rd *RASHE* TN25 ....255 J5
Bowling Green La *DEAL* CT14 ...232 C4
Bowling Green Pl *STHWK* SE1 ....24 A5
Bowling Green Rw
  WOOL/PLUM SE18 * 26 G7
Bowling Green Ter *DVW* CT17 ......8 C4
Bowling St *SWCH* CT13 ....201 N1
Bowl Rd *HDCN* TN27 ....221 J1
Bowman Pl *STPH/PW* TN11 ....243 H2
Bowman Av *CAN/RD* E16 ....66 E2
Bowman Cl *WALD* ME5 ....95 P9
Bowmans Lea *FSTH* SE23 ....41 J8
Bowmans Meadow
  WLGTN SM6 ....82 A7
Bowmans Rd *DART* DA1 ....45 P8
Bowmead *ELTH/MOT* SE9 ....63 K1
Bow Meadow Cots
  WBY/YAL ME18 *...................183 M5
Bown Cl *TIL* RM18 ....49 M5
Bowness Rd *BXLYHN* DA7 ....45 K3
Bowser Cl *DEAL* CT14 ....232 E5
Bow Rd *WBY/YAL* ME18 ....183 M4
Bow Ter *WBY/YAL* ME18 ....183 M4
Bowyer Cl *EHAM* E6 ....26 G1
Bowyer Pl *CMBW* SE5 ....40 C1
Bowyer Rd *WSTB* CT5 ....104 G7
Bowyer St *CMBW* SE5 ....40 C1
Bowzell Rd *RSEV* TN14 ....178 E9
Boxall Rd *DUL* SE21 ....60 E7
Boxford Ct *SAND/SEL* CR2 ....114 A6
Boxgrove Rd *ABYW* SE2 ....28 A5
Box La *FAV* ME13 ....162 A5
Boxley La *SIT* TN13 ....252 C9
Boxley Cl *IOS* ME12 ....57 K9
  MAID/BEAR ME14 ....155 N4
Boxley Rd *MAID/BEAR* ME14 .....113 F1
  WALD ME5 ....125 M5
Boxley St *CAN/RD* E16 ....26 C4
Boxted La *RSIT* ME9 ....98 B5
Boxwood Wy *WARL* CR6 ....144 A2
Boyard Rd *WOOL/PLUM* SE18 ....27 J8
Boyces Hl *RSIT* ME9 ....98 E8
Boy Court La *HDCN* TN27 ....217 P9
Boyden Gate Hl *RCANTE* CT3 ...138 E1
Boyd St *WCHPL* E1 ....24 D2
Boyes La *RCANTE* CT3 ....199 N5
Boyke La *RCANTW* CT4 ....257 H7
Boyland Rd *BMLY* BR1 ....62 C6
Boyle Wy *STPH/PW* TN12 ....213 J2
Boyne Pk *SBGH/RUST* TN4 ....22 B2
Boyne Rd *LEW* SE13 ....42 B4
  IOS ME12 ....57 K9
Boys Hall Rd *KEN/WIL* TN24 .....283 J1
Boystown Pl *SWCH* CT13 ....185 L8
Boyton Court Rd
  RMAID ME17 ....217 K5
Brabazon Rd *IOS* ME12 ....79 J7
Brabner Cl *POP/IOD* E14 ....25 H3
Brabner Cl *FOLKN* CT19 ....311 H5
Brabourne Av *RCANTW* CT2 .....136 F9
  NRWD SE19 ....60 E4
Brabourne Crs *BXLYHN* DA7 ....28 F8
Brabourne Gdns *FOLK* CT20 .....310 B6
Brabourne La *RASHE* TN25 ....255 N7
Brabourne Rd *BECK* BR3 ....84 G2
Brabourne Rd *RASHE* TN25 ....254 F4
Brabourn Gv *PECK* SE15 ....41 J5
Bracewood Gdns
  CROY/NA CR0 ....83 L7
Bracken Av *CROY/NA* CR0 ....84 C7
Bracken Cl *EHAM* E6 ....26 C1
  KEN/WIL TN24 ....252 F5
  RTWE/PEM TN2 ....271 H5
Bracken Ct *BRDST* CT10 * 115 K8
Brackendene *RDART* DA2 ....65 N3
Bracken Hl *WALD* ME5 ....125 M4
Bracken Hill La *BMLY* BR1 ....62 D7
Bracken Lea *WALD* ME5 ....95 P5
Bracken Rd *RTWE/PEM* TN2 .....271 H5
The Brackens *DBR* BR6 ....87 H9
Bracken Wk *TONN* TN10 ....210 E4
Brack La *LYDD* TN29 ....334 C2
Brackley Av *PECK* SE15 ....41 J4
Brackley Cl *MAID/BEAR* ME14 ...13 K5
Brackley Rd *BECK* BR3 ....61 M6
Bracklyn Av *EGRIN* RH19 * 265 K2
Brackondale *RHAM* ME8 ....96 C9
Bracondale Rd *ABYW* SE2 ....27 P7
Bracton La *RDART* DA2 ....65 H5
Bradbourne La *DIT/AY* ME20 .....154 A3
Bradbourne Park Rd
  E/WMAL ME19 ....153 P3
  SEV TN13 ....148 F8
Bradbourne Rd *BXLY* DA5 ....45 J8
  GRAYS RM17 ....32 C9
  SEV TN13 ....148 E7
Bradbourne Vale Rd
  SEV TN13 ....148 E7
Bradbridge Gn *ASH* TN23 ....252 A9
Braddick Cl *MAID/SHEP* ME15 ..185 N6
Braddon Cl *SWCH* CT13 ....25 P5
Bradenham Av *WILL* DA16 ....44 C5
Bradenham Cl *WALW* SE17 ....23 N9
Bradfield Av West *WALD* ME5 .....95 L8
Bradfield Rd *CAN/RD* E16 ....26 D6
  RASHE TN25 ....252 E4
Bradfields Av *WALD* ME5 ....95 L8
Bradfields Av West *WALD* ME5 ...95 L8
Bradford Cl *HAYES* BR2 ....86 A5
  SYD SE26 ....61 H5
Bradfords Cl *CHAT* ME4 ....95 H7
Bradford St *TON* TN9 ....210 B3
Bradgate Rd *CAT* SE6 ....41 P7
Bradheigh Rd *CROY/NA* CR0 ......82 E8
Bradleigh Av *GRAYS* RM17 ....32 D7
Bradley Dr *SIT* ME10 ....129 M3
Bradley La *FOLKN* CT19 ....11 J2
  MSTR CT12 ....143 H3
  NRWD SE19 ....60 C5

  RRTW TN3 ....268 C3
  STRD ME2 ....93 M9
Bradley Stone Rd *EHAM* E6 ....26 G2
Bradshaw Cl *RSIT* ME9 ....97 P3
Bradshaw Cots *POP/IOD* E14 * 25 H2
Bradshaw Rd *CDW/CHF* RM16 ....32 D4
Bradshaws Cl *SNWD* SE25 ....60 G9
Bradstow Av *FOLKN* CT19 ....10 E2
Bradstone Rd *FOLK* CT20 ....11 F5
Bradstow New Rd *FOLK* CT20 ....11 F5
Bradstow Wy *BRDST* CT10 ....113 L8
Brady Dr *BMLY* BR1 ....63 L9
Bradymead *EHAM* E6 ....26 H2
Brady Rd *RFOLK* CT18 ....286 F2
Braeburn Wy *E/WMAL* ME19 .....153 J9
Braemar Av *BXLYHN* DA7 ....45 L1
  SEV TN13 ....60 A9
Braemar Gdns *BFN/LL* DA15 ....63 P2
  WWKM BR4 ....84 F5
Braeside *BECK* BR3 ....61 N4
Braeside Av *SEV* TN15 ....167 M9
Braeside Cl *SEV* TN13 ....20 D1
Braeside Crs *BXLYHN* DA7 ....45 L5
The Braes *HOO/HM* ME3 ....71 L4
Braesyde Cl *BELV* DA17 ....28 F2
Brafferton Rd *CROY/NA* CR0 ....83 H8
Braggs La *HB* CT6 ....107 J8
Brake Av *WALD* ME5 ....95 K9
Brakefield Rd *MEO* DA13 ....83 F5
Brakes Pl *BGR/WK* TN15 ....120 B1
Bramber Wy *WARL* CR6 ....144 C1
Bramble Av *RDART* DA2 ....68 A2
Bramble Bank *MEO* DA13 ....122 A6
Bramblebury Rd
  WOOL/PLUM SE18 ....27 L8
Bramble Cl *BECK* BR3 ....84 F2
  CROY/NA CR0 ....85 J3
  MAIDW ME16 ....154 D9
  RASHE TN25 ....223 N7
  RTON TN11 ....210 C6
Bramble Cft *ERITH* DA8 ....29 H7
Brambledown *FOLKN* CT19 ....11 J1
  HART DA3 ....91 J1
  WALD ME5 ....95 M5
Brambledown Cl *WWKM* BR4 ......85 H5
Bramblefield Cl *HART* DA3 ....68 B9
Bramblefield La *RSIT* ME9 ....99 L5
Bramblefields *HB* CT6 ....107 N4
Bramblehill Rd *FAV* ME13 ....132 F5
Bramble La *RASHE* TN25 ....223 N7
  SEV TN15 ....178 C4
Bramble Reed La
  STPH/PW TN12 ....272 C1
Brambles Cl *IOS* ME12 ....78 A2
Brambletree Crs *ROCH* ME1 ....94 E4
Brambletree Whf *ROCH* ME1 * 94 D4
Bramble Wk
  RTWE/PEM TN2 ....270 C2
Brambley Crs *FOLK* CT20 ....310 B6
Brambling Ri *SIT* ME10 * 99 M8
Bramcote Gv
  BERM/RHTH SE16 ....43 H4
Bramdean Crs *LEE/GVPK* SE12 ..42 F8
Bramdean Gdns
  LEE/GVPK SE12 ....42 E9
Bramerton Rd *BECK* BR3 ....61 M9
Bramford La *CHARL* SE12 ....26 C9
Bramley Av *CANT* CT1 ....166 B6
Bramley Cl *IOS* ME12 ....69 K6
  MEO DA13 ....86 C5
  ORP BR6 ....86 C5
  RHAM ME8 ....97 J6
Bramley Ct *STPH/PW* TN12 ....244 C3
Bramley Crs
  MAID/SHEP ME15 ....156 C9
Bramley Gdns *ASH* TN23 ....282 D2
  DVE/WH CT16 * 260 C9
  HB CT6 ....108 A8
  RMAID ME17 ....185 J8
Bramley Hl *SAND/SEL* CR2 ....83 H9
Bramley Hyrst *SAND/SEL* CR2 *..83 H9
Bramley Pl *DART* DA1 ....46 A5
Bramley Ri *STRD* ME2 ....46 A5
Bramley Rd *SNOD* ME6 ....125 P5
  STPH/PW TN12 ....212 G4
Bramleys *HDCN* TN27 ....247 N4
Bramley Wy *E/WMAL* ME19 ....183 H1
  IOS ME12 ....79 K4
  WWKM BR4 ....84 F1
Bramling Gv *RCANTE* CT3 ....198 E3
  RCANTW CT4 ....198 D3
Brampton Bank *RTON* TN11 * 241 P5
Brampton Rd *BXLYHN* DA7 ....44 G3
  CROY/NA CR0 ....83 L4
Bramshaw Av *CANTW/ST* CT2 ...266 D2
Bramshaw Cl *MAIDW* ME16 ....155 H6
Bramshot Av *BKHTH/KID* SE3 ....42 E3
Bramshott Rd *IOS* ME12 ....78 C1
Bramston Rd *STRD* ME2 ....198 B2
Branbridges Rd
  STPH/PW TN12 ....213 H7
Branch Rd *POP/IOD* E14 ....25 H2
  RCANTW CT4 ....194 D3
Branch St *CMBW* SE5 ....40 E1
Brandon Cl *CDW/CHF* RM16 ......32 A5
Brandon Ms *BARB* EC2Y * 24 A1
Brandon Rd *DART* DA1 ....46 A5
Brandon St *CANT* CT1 ....142 F5
  GVW DA11 ....49 M8
Brandon Wy *BRCH* CT7 ....111 J7
Brandram Ms *LEW* SE13 * 42 C5
Brandram Rd *LEW* SE13 ....42 C4
The Brandries *WLGTN* SM6 ....82 D7
Brands Hatch Pk *HART* DA5 * 90 D7
Brands Hatch Rd *HART* DA3 ....90 D7
Brand St *GNWCH* SE10 ....42 D1
Brangbourne Rd *BMLY* BR1 ....62 A4
Branscombe St *LEW* SE13 ....41 P4
Bransell Cl *SWLY* BR8 ....66 A3

Bransgore Cl *RHAM* ME8 ....96 C7
Branston Crs *STMC/STPC* BR5 ....86 E5
Brantingham Cl *TON* TN9 ....240 C2
Branton Rd *RDART* DA2 ....47 M7
Brantwood Av *ERITH* DA8 ....45 L1
Brantwood Rd *BXLYHN* DA7 ....45 K3
  HNHL SE24 ....40 C6
Brantwood Wy
  STMC/STPC BR5 ....64 E9
Brasenose Rd *GILL* ME7 ....96 B3
Brasier Ct *IOS* ME12 ....78 A2
Brassey Av *BRDST* CT10 ....143 L1
Brassey Cl *OXTED* RH8 ....175 K5
Brassey Dr *DIT/AY* ME20 ....154 C4
Brassey Hl *OXTED* RH8 ....175 K5
Brassey Rd *OXTED* RH8 ....175 K5
Brasted Cl *BXLYHS* DA6 ....44 F6
  SYD SE26 ....61 J3
Brasted Ct *STRD* ME2 ....72 A6
Brasted La *RSEV* TN14 ....147 H5
Brasted Hill Rd
  BH/WHM TN16 ....147 K7
Brasted La *RSEV* TN14 ....147 H4
Brasted Rd *BH/WHM* TN16 ....176 F2
  ERITH DA8 ....45 N1
Brattle Asfield *SEV* TN26 ....302 G7
Brattle Wd *SEV* TN15 ....179 H5
Braundton Av *BFN/LL* DA15 ....44 B9
Braunstone Dr *MAID/SHEP* ME15 .12 B6
Braxfield Rd *BROCKY* SE4 ....41 L5
Brayard's Rd *PECK* SE15 ....41 H5
Braybrooke Gdns *NRWD* SE19 ....60 E6
Bray Crs *BERM/RHTH* SE16 ....43 J5
Bray Dr *CAN/RD* E16 ....26 A3
Brayford Sq *WCHPL* E1 * 24 F2
Bray Gdns *MAID/SHEP* ME15 ....185 L6
Braywood Rd *ELTH/MOT* SE9 .....43 P5
Brazil Cl *CROY/NA* CR0 ....82 D9
Breach La *RSIT* ME9 ....98 A6
Breach Rd *WTHK* RM20 ....31 J9
Breadlands Cl *KEN/WIL* TN24 ....252 A5
Breadlands Rd *KEN/WIL* TN24 ...253 J9
Breakneck Hl *RDART* DA2 ....47 P6
Breakspears Dr
  STMC/STPC BR5 ....64 C7
Breakspears Ms *BROCKY* SE4 .....41 M4
Breakspears Rd *BROCKY* SE4 .....41 M4
Bream Cl *DIT/AY* ME20 ....123 P8
Brecon Cha *IOS* ME12 ....58 C9
Brecon Rd *MTCM* CR4 ....82 D1
Brecon Ri *KEN/WIL* TN23 * 142 F5
Bredgar Cl *ASH* TN23 ....282 C2
  MAID/BEAR ME14 ....13 J2
Bredgar Rd *RHAM* ME8 ....96 D2
Bredhurst Cl *IOS* ME12 ....79 J7
  PGE/AN SE20 ....61 J5
Bredhurst Rd *CROY/NA* CR0 ....84 D1
Bredon Av *SBGH/RUST* TN4 ......240 B8
Breezer's Hl *WAP* E1W * 24 D3
Bremner Cl *SWLY* BR8 ....88 F1
Brenchley Av *DEAL* CT14 ....232 E5
Brenchley Cl *ASH* TN23 ....282 B2
  CHST BR7 ....63 J7
  HAYES BR2 ....85 J6
  MAID/SHEP ME15 ....41 J7
Brenchley Gdns *EDUL* SE22 ....41 J7
Brenchley Rd
  MAID/SHEP ME15 ....185 L1
  RHAM ME8 ....96 E4
  SIT ME10 ....99 P7
  STMC/STPC BR5 ....64 A2
  STPH/PW TN12 ....242 F8
  STPH/PW TN12 ....273 N3
Brendon Av *ELTH/MOT* SE9 ....63 P1
Brendon Cl *ASH* TN23 * 282 A5
Brendon Cl *ERITH* DA8 ....125 M1
Brendon Ct *ERITH* DA8 ....45 N1
Brendon Dr *KEN/WIL* TN24 ....23 J1
Brentfield Rd *DART* DA1 ....46 C7
Brent Hl *FAV* ME13 ....132 F5
Brentlands Dr *DART* DA1 ....46 D8
Brent La *DART* DA1 ....46 C8
Brent St *RDART* DA2 ....46 B2
Brent Rd *CAN/RD* E16 ....26 B5
  FAV ME13 ....132 F5
  WOOL/PLUM SE18 ....43 M1
The Brent *DART* DA1 ....46 D8
  TONN TN10 ....210 F4
Brent Wy *RDART* DA2 ....47 H7
Brentwood Ash *TN23 ....282 B5
Brentwood Cl *ELTH/MOT* SE9 .....43 N9
Brentwood Rd *IOS* ME12 ....57 K8
Bretland Rd *SBGH/RUST* TN4 ....270 A4
Bretton Rd *ROCH* ME1 ....94 B6
Brettell St *WALW* SE17 * 23 N9
Brevet Cl *PUR* RM19 ....30 C7
Brewers Fld *RDART* DA2 ....66 C5
Brewers Hl *RCANTW* CT4 ....258 B2
Brewers Pl *RCANTE* CT5 * 170 F6
Brewer St *DART* DA1 ....46 C4
Brewery Dr *MAID/BEAR* ME14 ....13 J2
  RTW TN3 ....285 P8
Brewery La *RCANTW* CT4 ....197 M2
  SEV TN13 ....21 G3
Brewery Rd *HAYES* BR2 ....85 P5
  WOOL/PLUM SE18 ....27 M8
Brewery Sq *RCANTE* CT3 ....139 N2
  STHWK SE1 ....24 C4
Brewhouse La *RASHE* TN25 ....223 J6
  WAP E1W * 24 E4
Brewhouse Rd
  WOOL/PLUM SE18 ....26 G7
Brewhouse Wk
  BERM/RHTH SE16 ....25 H4

Brewhouse Yd *DA12* 49 M7
Brian Crs *SBGH/RUST* TN4 ....240 E9
Briant St *NWCR* SE14 ....41 K2
Briar Cl *DIT/AY* ME20 ....153 P2
  DVW CT17 ....290 G5
  KEN/WIL TN24 ....252 F5
  RASHE TN25 * 229 N7
  RCANTE CT3 ....229 J2
  WARL CR6 ....144 D1
Briar Dl *HOO/HM* ME3 ....71 K1
Briarfield Cl *BXLYHN* DA7 ....45 J1
Briar Flds *MAID/BEAR* ME14 .....156 B7
Briar Gdns *HAYES* BR2 ....85 J5
Briar La *CROY/NA* CR0 ....84 E8
  RAM CT11 ....143 H6
Briarlea *CROY/NA* CR0 ....114 E8
The Briars *BGR/WK* TN15 ....120 A1
  WSTB CT5 ....105 K8
Briars Wy *LYDD* TN29 ....337 L2
Briars Wd *CROY/NA* CR0 ....81 K2
Briarswood Wy *ORP* BR6 ....86 E9
Briar Wk *TONN* TN10 ....210 F4
Briary Cl *WGOS* CT8 ....111 N5
Briary Ct *SCUP* DA14 ....64 H7
Briary Gdns *BMLY* BR1 ....62 F4
Brice Cl *RCANTW* CT4 ....195 K1
Brice Rd *HOO/HM* ME3 ....71 K1
Brick Ct *GRAYS* RM17 * 32 B9
Brickenden Rd *CRBK* TN17 ....298 A3
Brickfield Cots
  WOOL/PLUM SE18 ....27 N9
Brickfield Farm *HART* DA3 ....91 N1
Brickfield Farm Gdns *ORP* BR6 ...86 D8
Brickfield La *FAV* ME13 ....183 L5
Brickfield Rd *RCANTW* CT4 ....228 C7
  THHTH CR7 ....60 B7
Brickfields *E/WMAL* ME19 ....153 P3
  RTWE/PEM TN2 ....241 P9
Brick Field Vw *STRD* ME2 ....72 A6
Brick Kiln La *OXTED* RH8 ....175 M6
  RMAID ME17 ....217 N5
  STPH/PW TN12 ....275 P7
Brick La *WCHPL* E1 ....24 C2
Brickwood Cl *SYD* SE26 ....61 H2
Brickwood Rd *CROY/NA* CR0 ....83 K6
Brickworks Cl *TON* TN9 ....240 D2
Brideale Cl *PECK* SE15 ....24 C9
Bridewain St *STHWK* SE1 ....24 C5
Bridewell La *TENT* TN30 ....301 H8
Bridewell Pk *WSTB* CT5 ....105 P5
Bridewell Pl *WAP* E1W * 24 E4
The Bridge Ap *WSTB* CT5 ....105 M6
Bridge La *STPH/PW* TN12 ....308 F5
  RASHW TN26 ....302 G7
  RDART DA2 ....47 G4
  TON TN9 ....240 F4
Bridge Cl *GRAYS* RM17 * 32 C9
Bridge Down *RCANTW* CT4 ....197 N3
Bridgefield Rd *CROY/NA* CR0 ......83 K6
Bridge Hl *DEAL* CT14 ....232 B1
  RCANTW CT4 ....197 M2
Bridge House App
  DA11 ....25 M4
Bridge House Quay
  POP/IOD E14 ....25 M4
Bridgelands Rd *CAN/RD* E16 ....81 M6
Bridgelands Cl *BECK* BR3 ....61 M6
Bridgeman Ct *HYTHE* CT21 * 308 C5
Bridge Mdw *NWCR* SE14 ....24 G9
Bridge Mill Wy
  MAID/SHEP ME15 ....185 J1
Bridgen Rd *BXLY* DA5 ....44 G8
Bridge Pl *CROY/NA* CR0 ....83 J5
  DIT/AY ME20 ....154 E2
Bridgeport Pl *WAP* E1W * 24 F4
Bridge Rd *ASH* TN23 ....252 C7
  BECK BR3 ....61 M6
  BXLYHN DA7 ....44 G4
  DEAL CT14 ....233 J2
  ERITH DA8 ....45 J2
  FAV ME13 ....132 F5
  GILL ME7 ....73 J8
  GRAYS RM17 ....32 C9
  IOS ME12 ....57 K5
  MARG CT9 ....112 A2
  RASHE TN25 ....284 E5
  RCANTW CT4 ....197 K2
  ROCH ME1 ....95 H4
  STMC/STPC BR5 ....87 J3
  WLGTN SM6 ....82 C6
Bridge Rw *CROY/NA* CR0 ....83 J5
Bridges Cl *BRCH* CT7 ....109 P8
Bridges Dr *DART* DA1 ....47 H5
Bridges La *CROY/NA* CR0 ....233 H5
Bridges La *CROY/NA* CR0 ....81 N7
Bridge St *DVE/WH* CT16 ....8 B1
  FOLKN CT19 ....11 C1
  MAID/SHEP ME15 ....185 L6
Bridge Ter *LEW* SE13 * 42 B5
Bridgetown Cl *NRWD* SE19 ....60 E4
Bridge Vw *SWCM* DA10 ....31 P5
Bridgewater Pl
  E/WMAL ME19 ....153 M2
Bridgewater Rd *IOS* ME12 ....57 K8
Bridgewood Cl *PGE/AN* SE20 .....61 H6
Bridle Mth *CROY/NA* CR0 ....82 D7
Bridle Cl *CROY/NA* CR0 ....84 D9
  HB CT6 ....107 J3
  HYTHE CT21 ....308 B5
  ORP BR6 ....86 D8
Bridleway Gdns *BRDST* CT10 ....143 J1
Bridleway La *ASH* TN23 ....282 E4
The Bridle Wy *WLGTN* SM6 ....82 B8
Bridge Rd *RASHE* TN25 ....223 J6
Bridgat Cl *STRD* ME2 ....92 A8
Bridstow Rd *LEE/GVPK* SE12 * 42 C6
Brier Ct *RTW* TN3 ....28 C7
Brightfield Rd *LEE/GVPK* SE12 ...42 C6
Brightlands *GVW* DA11 ....69 J3
Brightling Rd *BROCKY* SE4 ....41 M7

Brightlingsea Pl POP/IOD E14....25 J3
Brightlingsea Rd SWCH CT13...201 N2
Bright Rdg SBGH/RUST TN4....240 B9
Bright Rd CHAT ME4....95 N4
Brightside Rd LEW SE13....42 B7
Brights Pl RAM CT11....17 H2
Brights St POP/IOD E14....25 J3
Brightwell Cl CROY/NA CRO....82 F5
Brig Ms DEPT SE8....25 K9
Brigstock Rd BELV DA17....28 G7
THHTH CR7....4 E2
Brimfield Rd PUR RM19....30 F7
Brimpsfield Cl ABYW SE2....28 A6
The Brimp HOO/HM ME3....38 E8
Brimstone Cl ORP BR6....117 K2
Brimstone HI MEO DA13....92 D6
Brindle Ga BRN/LL DA15....44 A6
Brindle Gv RAM CT11....143 L3
Brindles Cl SLH/COR SS17....35 P7
Brindle's Fld TON TN9....240 D2
Brindle Wy MAID ME15....125 M4
Brindley Cl BXLYHN DA7....45 J4
Brindley St NWCR SE14....41 M2
Brindley Wy BMLY BR1....62 E4
Brinkburn Cl ABYW SE2....27 P7
Brinklow Crs
WOOL/PLUM SE18....43 M1
Brinsley St WCHPL E1 *....24 E2
Brionne Gdns TON TN9....240 C8
Brisbane Dr MSTR CT12....142 F3
Brisbane Rd CHAT ME4....6 D7
Brisbane St CMBW SE5....40 D1
Bristed Rd ELTH/MOT SE9....43 H4
Brishing Cl MAID/SHEP ME15...186 A6
Brishing La MAID/SHEP ME15..186 B7
RMAID ME17....186 A8
Brisley Cl ASH TN23....282 A2
Brisley Ct ASH TN23....282 A2
Brisley La RASHW TN26....304 G1
Brissenden Cl NROM TN28....235 L7
STRD ME2 *....72 C4
Bristol Cl STRD ME2....94 C1
Bristol Pl RAM CT11....16 E5
Bristol Rd CANT CT1....4 F5
GVE DA12....69 P2
Bristowe Cl BRXS/STRHM SW2...40 A7
Bristowe Dr CDW/CHF RM16....33 L2
Bristow Rd BXLYHN DA7....44 C2
CROY/NA CRO....82 D8
NRWD SE19....60 E4
Britannia Av WSTB CT5....105 J7
Britannia Cl ERITH DA8....29 J9
SIT ME10....99 N7
Britannia Dr GVE DA12....70 B4
Britannia Ga CAN/RD E16....26 B4
Britannia La ASH TN23....282 C5
Britannia Rd DEAL CT14....233 J1
HOO/HM ME3....53 M4
POP/IOD E14....25 K7
Briton Ct IOS ME12....57 K7
Briton Rd FAV ME13....132 F6
Brittains La SEV TN13....20 A1
Britten Cl HYTHE CT21....308 F4
TONN TN10....211 J4
Brittenden Pde ORP BR6 *....116 C1
Britton Cl CAT SE6....42 B8
Britton St GILL ME7....7 G2
Brixham Rd WELL DA16....44 F2
Brixham St CAN/RD E16....26 G4
Brixton Ov BRXS/STRHM SW2...40 A5
Brixton Rd BRXS/STRHM SW2....40 A5
Brixton Station Rd
BRXN/ST SW9....40 A4
Brixton Water La
BRXS/STRHM SW2....40 A6
Broad RASHW TN26....304 D8
Broadacre RDV CT15....260 A8
RSIT ME9....131 J5
Broad Bridge Cl
BKHTH/KID SE3....42 E1
Broadcloth CRBK TN17....298 D4
Broadcoombe SAND/SEL CR2....114 A2
Broadcroft RTWE/PEM TN2....270 C8
Broadcroft Rd STMC/STPC BR5...63 K4
Broad Ditch Rd MEO DA13....68 C6
Broadeaves Cl SAND/SEL CR2....83 K9
Broader La MAID/BEAR ME14...196 C2
Broadfield Crs FOLK CT20....310 D6
Broadfield Rd CAT SE6....42 C9
FOLK CT20....310 D6
MAID/SHEP ME15....185 M3
Broad Green Av CROY/NA CRO..82 G4
Broad Gv RTWE/PEM TN2....270 C8
Broadham Green Rd
OXTED RH8....174 C9
Broadham Pl OXTED RH8....174 C9
Broadheath Dr CHST BR7....63 K4
Broadhoath BGR/WK TN15 *...180 B2
Broadhope Av SLH/COR SS17....35 B1
Broadhurst Dr KEN/WIL TN24...252 G2
Broadlands CANTW/ST CT2....137 L2
GRAYS RM17....32 A8
Broadlands Av NROM TN28....336 G5
Broadlands Crs NROM TN28....336 G5
Broadlands Dr WALD ME5....125 N1
Broadlands Rd BMLY BR1....62 F3
Broad La DEAL CT14....231 P5
RDART DA2....66 B3
RRTH TN5....268 F5
Broad Lawn ELTH/MOT SE9....43 L9
Broadley Av BRCH CT7....110 C8
Broadley Rd MART CT9....113 J5
Broadmead ASH TN23....282 B2
CAT SE6....61 N2
RTWE/PEM TN2....270 D8
Broadmead Av
RTWE/PEM TN2....270 C8
Broadmead Rd FOLKN CT19....10 D3
Broadmere Rd MAIDW ME16 *..12 A6
Broadoak E/WMAL ME19....153 L2
Broad Oak STPH/PW TN12....243 K9
Broadoak Av
MAID/SHEP ME15....185 M3
Broadoak Cl EYN DA4....66 C6
Broad Oak La RTWE/PEM TN2...270 C8
STMC/STPC BR5....64 C8
STPH/PW TN12....243 K9
Broad Oak Rd CANTW/ST CT2..137 H9
Broadoak Rd ERITH DA8....45 M1
RSIT ME9....129 L6
Broad Oaks Wy HAYES BR2....85 J2
Broad Rd SWCM DA10....68 C7
Broadsole La RDV CT15....289 P7
Broadstairs Rd BRDST CT10....113 K8
Broad St CANT CT1....5 F5
DEAL CT14....233 J5
IOS ME12....57 K6
MARG CT9....15 G5
RAM CT11....17 F3
RASHE TN25....285 M3
RMAID ME17....217 H3
Broad Street Av LVPST EC2M....24 B1
Broad Street Hl RMAID ME17..157 N5
Broad Street Pl LVPST EC2M....24 A1
Broadview FOLK CT20....309 P1
Broadview Av CDW/CHF RM16...32 E5
RHAM ME8....97 H6
Broad Wk BGR/WK TN15....179 K4
BKHTH/KID SE3....42 G3
ORP BR6....87 L7
Broadwater Down
RTWE/PEM TN2....270 D4
Broadwater Forest La
RRTW TN5....269 P9
Broadwater Gdns ORP BR6....86 C8
Broadwater La
RTWE/PEM TN2....270 C7
Broadwater Ri
RTWE/PEM TN2....270 C7
Broadwater Rd
E/WMAL ME19....153 L6
THMD SE28....27 L6
Broadway BXLYHS DA6....44 G5
GRAYS RM17....32 B7
IOS ME12....57 L6
MAIDW ME16....12 D6
RCANTW CT4....195 P9
RHAM ME8....88 B3
SWLY BR8....88 B3
TIL RM18....49 K3
Broadway Av CROY/NA CRO....83 J1
The Broadway BRDST CT10....113 M9
HB CT6....107 H1
IOS ME12....58 B9
RTON TN11....211 P2
Broadwood GVW DA11....69 M4
Broadwood Rd HOO/HM ME3....72 E5
Brockbank Cl WALD ME5....125 M4
Brockdene Dr HAYES BR2....85 N8
Brockenhurst Av
MAID/SHEP ME15....185 N2
Brockenhurst Cl
CANTW/ST CT2....166 D2
RHAM ME8....96 F7
Brockenhurst Dr
SLH/COR SS17....34 B1
Brockenhurst Rd
CROY/NA CRO....83 N4
RAM CT11....17 F1
Brockett Rd CDW/CHF RM16...33 H6
Brock Gn SOCK/AV RM15....31 L2
Brockham Crs CROY/NA CRO..114 G2
Brockhill Rd HYTHE CT21....308 C4
Brockill Crs BROCKY SE4....41 L5
Brocklebank Rd CHARL SE7....26 D7
Brocklehurst St NWCR SE14....41 K1
Brocklestby Rd SNWD SE25....83 N6
Brockley Av BROCKY SE4....41 M6
Brockley Cross BROCKY SE4....41 L5
Brockley Gv BROCKY SE4....41 M6
Brockley Hall Rd BROCKY SE4..41 L6
Brockley Ms BROCKY SE4....41 L6
Brockley Pk FSTH SE23....41 L7
Brockley Ri FSTH SE23....41 L7
FSTH SE23....41 L8
Brockley Vw FSTH SE23....41 L6
Brockley Vw FSTH SE23....41 K6
Brockman Crs LYDD TN29....327 N1
Brockman Rd FOLK CT20....10 D4
Brockman's Cl MSTR CT12....141 J5
Brock St PLSTW E15....26 C5
Brock Wy BGR/WK TN15....151 K6
Brockwell Av BECK BR3....84 E2
Brockwell Cl STMC/STPC BR5...86 C2
Brockwell Park Gdns
HNHL SE24....40 B8
Brockwell Park Rw
BRXS/STRHM SW2....40 A8
Brodie St STHWK SE1 *....24 C8
Brodlove La WAP E1W....24 G3
Brodrick Gv ABYW SE2....28 A7
Brogdale Pl FAV ME13....132 E7
Brogdale Rd FAV ME13....132 E8
Brogden Crs RMAID ME17....187 J4
Brograve Gdns BECK BR3....61 P8
Brokes Cr RAM CT11 *....16 C1
Brokes Wy SBGH/RUST TN4...240 E9
Bromar Rd CMBW SE5....40 E4
Bromehead St WCHPL E1 *....24 F2
Brome House CHARL SE7 *....43 J1
Brome Rd ELTH/MOT SE9....43 K4
Bromford Cl OXTED RH8....175 K2
Bromhedge ELTH/MOT SE9....43 J5
Bromholm Rd ABYW SE2....28 A6
Bromley Av BMLY BR1....62 C6
Bromley Cl WALD ME5....125 N4
Bromley Common HAYES BR2..85 P4
Bromley Ct BMLY BR1....62 C6
Bromley Crs HAYES BR2....62 D9
Bromley Gdns HAYES BR2....62 D9
Bromley Green Rd
RASHW TN26....304 B1
Bromley Gv HAYES BR2....62 B6
Bromley Hall Rd POP/IOD E14..25 M1
Bromley Hl BMLY BR1....62 C5
Bromley La CHST BR7....63 N6
Bromley Pk BMLY BR1 *....62 C8
Bromley St WCHPL E1 *....24 G1
Brompton Dr ERITH DA8....46 B1
Brompton Farm Rd
STRD ME2....71 P6
Brompton HI CHAT ME4....6 C7
Brompton La STRD ME2....72 A7
Brompton Rd GILL ME7....7 F1
Brompton Ter
WOOL/PLUM SE18 *....43 L2
Bromstone Rd BRDST CT10....143 K1
Bromington Cl WALD ME5....95 N3
Bronte Cl DIT/AY ME20....153 N1
ERITH DA8....45 K1
TIL RM18....49 N3
Bronte Dw DART DA1....46 F5
The Brontes EGRIN RH19 *....266 C2
Bronze Vw GVE DA12....49 N9
Bronze St DEPT SE8....25 K9
Brook CHAT ME4 *....95 N1
Brookbank MAID/BEAR ME14..155 M4
Brookbank Rd LEW SE13....41 N4
Brook Cl EGRIN RH19....265 L7
HB CT6....107 H5
HYTHE CT21....309 M4
Brookdale Rd BXLY DA5....44 G7
CAT SE6....41 P8
Brookdene Rd
WOOL/PLUM SE18....27 M7
Brooke Av MARG CT9....112 A6
Brooke Dr GVE DA12....50 D9
Brooke End OXTED RH8 *....175 K9
Brookehowse Rd CAT SE6....61 N1
Brookend Rd BFN/LL DA15....44 A9
Brooker Cl POP/IOD E14....25 J1
RMAID ME17....186 A6
Brooke Rd GRAYS RM17....32 D1
KEN/WIL TN24....9 G4
Brookes Pl RSIT ME9....98 C8
Brookfield Av DIT/AY ME20....123 P9
DVE/WH CT16....291 J5
Brookfield Pl DVE/WH CT16....291 J5
Brookfield Rd DVE/WH CT16...291 H4
Brookfields SNWD SE25....83 N3
Brookfields Av MTCM CR4....61 H9
Brookhill Cl EBED/NFELT *....291 J5
Brookhurst Gdns
SBGH/RUST TN4....240 B6
Brooklands DART DA1....46 E9
HDCN TN27....247 M3
RTWE/PEM TN2....270 C1
Brooklands Av BFN/LL DA15....63 N1
Brooklands Cl CANTW/ST CT2..137 L2
Brooklands Farm Cl
RRTW TN5....268 F2
Brooklands Pk BKHTH/KID SE3..42 F2
Brooklands Rd DIT/AY ME20...153 P1
Brooklands Wy EGRIN RH19...264 C8
Brook La BGR/WK TN15....181 K5
BKHTH/KID SE3....42 F3
BMLY BR1....62 F1
BXLY DA5....44 F7
HB CT6....108 E5
MSTR CT12....141 M8
RASHE TN25....285 M6
SNOD ME6....123 P7
Brooklyn Av SNWD SE25....83 N1
Brooklyn Gv SNWD SE25....83 N1
Brooklyn Paddock GILL ME7....7 F9
Brooklyn Rd HAYES BR2....85 N2
SNWD SE25....83 N1
Brookmead Av HAYES BR2....86 A2
Brookmead Cl STMC/STPC BR5..87 J3
Brookmead Rd CROY/NA CRO..82 B9
HOO/HM ME3....52 B9
Brookmill Rd DEPT SE8....41 N2
Brook Pk DART DA1....66 D4
Brook Rd DIT/AY ME20....123 M9
FAV ME13....132 F5
GVW DA11....49 J9
RTWE/PEM TN2....270 F1
SEV TN13....65 M9
THHTH CR7....83 H1
WSTB CT5....106 B3
Brooks Cl STPH/PW TN12....246 E1
Brookscroft CROY/NA CRO....114 B4
Brookside CRBK TN17....296 D8
GDST RH9....190 D2
HOO/HM ME3....73 L2
LYDD TN29....326 E9
ORP BR6....86 C4
STPH/PW TN12 *....243 J4
Brookside Av
MAID/SHEP ME15....185 N1
Brookside Rd CROY/NA CRO....84 A3
Brookside Pl MAID/BEAR ME14..5 G1
Brook St BELV DA17....28 G8
ERITH DA8....45 K1
RASHW TN26....304 B5
SNOD ME6....124 A5
SWCH CT13....201 K8
TON TN9....240 C1
Brooks Wy LYDD TN29....342 B7
The Brook CHAT ME4....6 D4
Brockway BKHTH/KID SE3....42 E4
RAIN RM13....29 N1
Brookwood Cl HAYES BR2....85 J1
Broom Av STMC/STPC BR5....64 C6
Broom Bank WARL CR6....144 F4
Broom Cl HAYES BR2....86 A5
Broomcroft Rd RHAM ME8....97 J4
Broome Pl SOCK/AV RM15....30 G4
Broomfield KEN/WIL TN24 *....253 L3
Broomfield Crs MARG CT9....113 L5
Broomfield Ga WSTB CT5....106 C3
Broomfield Rd BECK BR3....45 J6
BXLYHS DA6....45 J6
FAV ME13....132 F4
FOLKN CT19....310 B5
HB CT6....107 H5
RMAID ME17....187 M8
SEV TN13....148 E7
SWCM DA10....68 C7
Buckingham Gdns
THHTH CR7....60 A8
Broomfields HART DA3....91 H2
Broomfield St POP/IOD E14....25 K1
Broom Gdns CROY/NA CRO....84 D7
Broomhill Park Rd
SBGH/RUST TN4....240 B9
Broomhill Ri BXLYHS DA6....45 J6
Broomhill Rd DART DA1....46 B7
ORP BR6....87 H1
RTWE/PEM TN2....270 A2
Broom Hill Rd STRD ME2....71 P7
Broomhurst Av WALD ME5....68 C3
Broomlands La OXTED RH8....175 P5
Broommead Rd BXLY DA5....45 J7
Broomshaw Rd MAIDW ME16.154 E9
Broomwood Cl BXLY DA5....65 N1
CROY/NA CRO....84 D2
Broomwood Rd
STMC/STPC BR5....64 D8
Broseley Gv SYD SE26....61 K4
Broster Gdns SNWD SE25....60 F9
Broughton Ct ASH TN23....252 B8
Broughton Dr BRXN/ST SW9....40 A5
Broughton Rd ORP BR6....86 E6
RSEV TN14....148 F1
THHTH CR7....82 F3
Brow Cl STMC/STPC BR5....87 L4
Brow Crs STMC/STPC BR5....87 L4
Browndens Rd STRD ME2....123 N4
Brownelow Copse WALD ME5..125 N4
Brownhill Rd CAT SE6....41 P9
Brownhill St POP/IOD E14....25 M1
Browning Cl DIT/AY ME20....123 N9
WELL DA16....44 A2
Browning Pl FOLKN CT19....311 H4
Browning Rd DART DA1....46 F5
Brownings EDEN TN8....206 D6
Brownings Orch RSIT ME9....129 P6
The Brownings EGRIN RH19...264 C2
Brown Rd GVE DA12....70 A1
Brownspring Dr
ELTH/MOT SE9....63 M2
Brown St RHAM ME8....97 H5
Broxbourne Rd ORP BR6....86 C5
Broxburn Dr SOCK/AV RM15....31 K5
Broxhall Rd RCANTW CT4....196 F9
Broxholm Rd WNWD SE27....60 A2
Broxted Rd FSTH SE23....41 K9
Bruce Cl DEAL CT14....232 G5
WELL DA16....44 D1
Bruce Dr SAND/SEL CR2....114 A3
Bruce Gv ORP BR6....87 H5
Bruce Rd SNWD SE25....83 J9
Bruces Wharf Rd GRAYS RM17..32 B9
The Brucks WBY/YAL ME18....183 H4
Bruford Ct DEPT SE8....25 L9
Brundell Ter RCANTW CT4 *..195 J3
Brunel Cl CHAT ME4 *....72 C8
TIL RM18....49 M3
Brunel Ct NRWD SE19....60 E9
Brunel House
WOOL/PLUM SE18 *....43 J1
Brunel Rd BERM/RHTH SE16....24 F3
CAN/RD E16....26 A2
CHAT ME4....72 C7
Brunel St CAN/RD E16....26 A2
Brunswick Cl BXLYHS DA6....44 G5
STHWK SE1....24 C1
Brunswick Fld RSIT ME9....101 K9
Brunswick Gdns
DVE/WH CT16....291 J4
Brunswick Pk CMBW SE5....40 D2
Brunswick Pl NRWD SE19....60 G6
Brunswick Quay
BERM/RHTH SE16....24 G4
Brunswick Rd BXLY DA5....45 J7
BRCH CT7....111 H8
BXLYHS DA6....44 F5
Brunswick Sq HB CT6....107 K1
Brunswick St MAID/SHEP ME15..13 F7
RTW TN1 *....17 G3
RAM CT11....17 G3
Brunswick St East
MAID/SHEP ME15....13 G6
Brunswick Ter DEAL CT14 *....232 G5
RTW TN1 *....17 G3
Brunswick Wk GVE DA12....49 P7
Brunton Pl POP/IOD E14....25 H2
Brushfield St WCHPL E1....24 C1
Brushwood Cl POP/IOD E14....25 L1
Bruton Cl CHST BR7....63 K6
Bryan Rd BERM/RHTH SE16....25 K1
Bryanston Rd TIL RM18....49 N3
Bryant Cl E WBY/YAL ME18....183 L5
Bryant Rd STRD ME2....7 L2
Bryant St CHAT ME4....6 D7
Bryces Aly WSTB CT5....105 L4
Bryden Cl SYD SE26....61 L4
Brymore Cl DART DA1....46 F5
Brymore Rd CANT CT1....5 J1
Bryony Dr ASH TN23....282 F5
Bubblestone Rd RSEV TN14...148 C1
Bubhurst La CRBK TN17....277 L1
Buchanan Cl SOCK/AV RM15...31 K5
Buchan Rd PECK SE15....41 J4
Buckden Cl LEE/GVPK SE12....42 D7
Buckham Thorns Rd
BH/WHM TN16....176 D2
Buckhole Farm Rd
HOO/HM ME3....53 J4
Buckhurst Av SEV TN13....21 G4
Buckhurst Cl EGRIN RH19....264 F5
Buckhurst Dr MARG CT9....113 L5
Buckhurst La SEV TN13....21 G5
Buckhurst Rd BH/WHM TN16..146 C5
Buckingham Cl
STMC/STPC BR5....86 F4
Buckingham Dr CHST BR7....63 M4
EGRIN RH19....265 K9
Buckingham Hill Rd
SLH/COR SS17....35 P3
Buckingham La FSTH SE23....41 L8
Buckingham Rd BRDST CT10 *.113 N9
GILL ME7....96 A1
GVW DA11....49 H8
MARG CT9....82 D2
MTCM CR4....61 K4
RTW TN1....17 L2
WSTB CT5....106 A4
Buckingham Rw
MAID/SHEP ME15....186 A8
Buckingham La FSTH SE23....41 L8
Buckland Cl MALD W5 *....125 M3
Buckland HI MAIDW ME16....12 B3
Buckland La MAIDW ME16....12 B1
RCANTE CT3....200 A2
Buckland Pl MAIDW ME16....12 C4
Buckland Rd HOO/HM ME3....51 P9
MAIDW ME16....12 B5
MEO DA13....86 F8
Buckleigh Wy NRWD SE19....60 F7
Bucklersbury MANHO EC4N....24 A2
Bucklers Cl IOS ME12....80 C5
RTWE/PEM TN2....17 G4
Buckles La SOCK/AV RM15....31 N1
Buckle St WCHPL E1....24 C2
Buckley Cl DART DA1....45 M3
FSTH SE23....41 J5
Bucknall Ct BRXN/ST SW9 *....40 A4
Bucknall Wy BECK BR3....84 E1
Bucks Cross Rd GVW DA11....69 K2
Buck Pl ABYW SE2....87 M9
Bucksford La ASH TN23....281 P1
Buckstone Cl FSTH SE23....41 J5
Buck St RASHE TN25....192 F9
Buckters Rents
BERM/RHTH SE16....25 H4
Buckthorne Rd BROCKY SE4....41 L7
IOS ME12....78 A3
Buddens Gn RYE TN31....330 C9
Buddle Dr IOS ME12....57 N9
Budd's La TENT TN30....332 B3
Budgin's Hl ORP BR6....117 J6
Budleigh Crs WELL DA16....44 E2
Buenos Ayres MARG CT9....14 D6
Buffs Av FOLK CT20....309 N1
Buggleden Rd HDCN TN27....300 D2
Bugi Hl WARL CR6....144 A5
Bugsby's Wy CNWCH SE10....26 A7
Builders Sq RCANTE CT3 *....168 D8
Bulganak Rd THHTH CR7....83 H1
Bullace Rw CMBW SE5....40 D2
Bull Aly WELL DA16....44 D4
Bullbanks Rd BELV DA17....29 H7
Bull Cl CDW/CHF RM16....32 A5
Bulldog Rd WALD ME5....125 N3
Bulleid Pl KEN/WIL TN24....282 C1
Buller Cl PECK SE15....40 C1
Buller Rd CHAT ME4....95 L4
Buller's Av HB CT6....107 K2
Buller's Cl SCUP DA14....64 C4
Bullers Wood Dr CHST BR7....63 J7
Bull Flds SNOD ME6....125 L5
Bullfinch Cl SEV TN13....148 C7
STPH/PW TN12....243 H4
Bullfinch Dene SEV TN13....148 D7
Bullfinch La SEV TN13....148 D7
Bullfinch and SAND/SEL CR2...114 A4
Bull Hl EYN DA4....89 P1
RMAID ME17....219 P1
Bullingstone La RRTW TN5....269 L1
Bullion Cl STPH/PW TN12....242 F5
Bullivant Cl RDART DA2....47 M8
Bullivant St POP/IOD E14....25 M3
Bull La BGR/WK TN15....151 K1
CHST BR7....63 P6
DIT/AY ME20....48 E8
FAV ME13....134 A8
HOO/HM ME3....51 M9
RMAID ME17....216 C1
RSIT ME9....127 P4
Bullockstone Rd HB CT6....107 J3
Bull Orch MAIDW ME16....184 E1
Bull Rd E/WMAL ME19....153 L1
Bullrush Cl CROY/NA CRO....83 K3
Bull's Bridge RTWE/PEM TN2..271 J1
Bulwark St DEAL CT14....313 L1
Bull Yd GVE DA12 *....49 M7
PECK SE15....40 C2
The Bull Yd KEN/WIL TN24 *....9 L2
Bulrushes La ASH TN23....125 L2
The Bulrushes ASH TN23....251 P9
Bulwark Rd DEAL CT14....233 J2
Bumbles Cl ROCH ME1....95 J6
Bunce Court Rd FAV ME13....134 B9
Bungalow Rd SNWD SE25....83 K1
The Bungalows SWCH CT13 *..201 J5
WTHK RM20 *....31 K9
The Bungalow BRDST CT10 *..112 G7
Bunham La RMAID ME17....188 F7
Bunker's Hl BELV DA17....28 G8
Bunker's Hl BGR/WK TN15....121 L1
Bunkers Hl SCUP DA14....65 H2
Bunkers Hl All DVW CT17....291 H5
Bunkers Hill Rd DVW CT17....291 H6
Bunkley Meadow
RASHW TN26....304 D8
Bunkley Ter RASHW TN26....304 D8
Bunkley Hl GVE DA12 *....49 L7
Bunters Hill Rd HOO/HM ME3..72 A3
Bunton St WOOL/PLUM SE18...27 M4
Burbage Cl STHWK SE1....24 A6
Burberry Cl RMAID ME17....187 L6
Burcharbro Rd ABYW SE2....28 D5
Burcham St POP/IOD E14....25 L2
Burchell Rd PECK SE15....41 J3
Burcher Gale Gv PECK SE15....40 E1
Burdens Cl RMAID ME17....247 N4
Burdett Av GVE DA12....70 G3
Burdett Cl SCUP DA14....64 G4
Burdett Rd CROY/NA CRO....83 J5
POP/IOD E14....25 J2
SBGH/RUST TN4....269 N6

Burdock Cl CROY/NA CRO 84 A5
Bure TIL RM18 ....34 B6
Burford Rd BMLY BR1 ....85 P1
  CAT SE6 ....165 J5
Burford Wy CROY/NA CRO 114 F1
Burgate CANT CT1 ....5 F5
Burgate Cl DART DA1 ....45 P4
Burgate La CANT CT1 ....5 F5
Burgess Cl DVE/WH CT16 ......232 B1
  MSTR CT12 ....141 K5
Burgess Gv GNWCH SE10 ......129 M1
Burgess Hall Dr RMAID ME17 ..187 J5
Burgess Rd RCANTE CT5 ....199 J3
  STRD ME2 ....18 E1
Burgess St POP/IOD E14 ....25 E1
Burge St STHWK SE1 ....24 A6
Burghclere Dr MAIDW ME16 ..184 C1
Burghfield Rd MEO DA15 ....69 K6
Burghill Rd SYDE SE26 ....61 K3
Burghley Rd CDW/CHF RM16 ...31 M6
Burgos Gv GNWCH SE10 ....129 M1
Burgoyne Hts RDV CT15 ....291 M5
Burgoyne Rd SNWD SE25 ....63 L1
Burham Cl PGE/AN SE20 ....61 J4
Burham Rd ROCH ME1 ....94 D7
Burial Ground La
  MAID/SHEP ME15 ....185 K2
Burkestoon Cl SIT ME10 ....99 P6
Burke St CAN/RD E16 ....26 A1
Burleigh Av BFN/LL DA15 ....44 B6
Burleigh Cl STRD ME2 ....71 N7
Burleigh Dr MAID/BEAR ME14 ..155 L3
Burleigh Rd HDCN TN27 ....221 H3
Burleigh Wk CAT SE6 ....42 A9
Burley Rd CAN/RD E16 ....26 D2
  SIT ME10 ....99 K1
Burlings La RSEV TN14 ....146 G2
Burlington Cl EHAM E6 ....26 F2
  ORP BR6 ....86 C6
Burlington Dr RTW TN1 ....108 A5
Burlington Gdns MARG CT9 ...112 B5
Burlington House
  DVE/WH CT16 * 8 E4
Burlington Rd THHTH CR7 ....60 C8
Burman Ct DART DA1 ....167 J8
Burman Rd RDART DA2 * 31 L3
Burmarsh Cl MAID ME5 ....95 N9
Burmarsh Rd LYDD TN29 ....327 H6
Burma Ter SNWD SE19 * 60 E4
Burma Wy WALD ME5 ....95 L8
Burnaby Rd GVW DA11 ....49 J8
Burnan Rd WSTB CT5 ....106 B4
Burnell Av WELL DA16 ....44 C3
Burnell St STHWK SE1 * 24 E3
Burnett Rd ERITH DA8 ....30 A9
Burney St GNWCH SE10 ....42 A1
Burnham Cl SIT ME10 ....99 H6
  SIT ME10 ....54 C7
Burnham Crs DART DA1 ....46 C5
Burnham Gdns CROY/NA CRO ...63 J7
  SCUP DA14 ....64 G1
Burnham Ter DART DA1 ....46 D6
Burnham Wk RHAM ME8 ....127 H2
Burnham Wy SYDE SE26 ....61 N4
Burnhill Rd BECK BR3 ....51 N8
Burnley Rd WTHK RM20 ....47 P2
Burns Av BFN/LL DA15 ....44 D7
  WELL DA16 ....44 A2
Burns Crs TON TN9 ....240 D2
Burnside Cl BERM/RHTH SE16 ..24 G4
Burns Pl TIL RM18 ....49 M3
Burns Rd GILL ME7 ....73 J8
Burns Wy MAIDW ME16 ....185 H1
Burnt Ash Hll LEE/GVPK SE12 ...42 D7
Burnt Ash La BMLY BR1 ....52 E5
Burntash Rd DIT/AY ME20 ......154 D4
Burnt House Cl HAWK TN18 ....318 C9
Burnt House Hl RDART DA2 * 51 K5
Burnt House La HDCN TN27 ....248 E6
Burnt House La RDART DA2 ......32 E9
  RRTW TN3 ....269 L3
Burnt Lodge La WADH TN5 ....314 F5
Burnt Oak La BFN/LL DA15 ......44 C6
Burnt Oak Ter GILL ME7 ....73 K9
Burnt Oast Rd FAV ME13 ....146 B4
Burnthouse La RSIT ME9 ....98 C3
Burntwood Gv SEV TN13 ....178 D5
Burntwood Rd SEV TN13 ....178 G4
Burntwood Vw NRWD SE19 * 60 F4
Buross St WCHPL E1 ....24 F4
Burrage Gv WOOL/PLUM SE18 ...28 K7
Burrage Pl WOOL/PLUM SE18 ...27 J8
Burrage Rd WOOL/PLUM SE18 ...27 K7
Burrard Rd CAN/RD E16 ....26 B2
Burr Bank Ter RDART DA2 * 66 C3
Burr Cl BXLYHN DA7 ....45 H4
  WAP E1W 24 D4
Burrell Cl CROY/NA CRO 64 B3
Burrell Rw BECK BR3 ....51 N8
Burrells Whf POP/IOD E14 ....25 F2
Burrfield Dr STMC/STPC BR5 ....87 L2
Burroughs Cps
  POP/IOD E14 * 25 H1
Burrow Rd EDUL SE22 ....40 F1
  FOLKN CT19 ....11 H2
Burrows La HOO/HM ME3 ....54 C5
The Burrs SIT ME10 ....129 N1
Burrstock Wy RRTW TN3 * 269 H9
Bursar St STHWK SE1 ....24 B4
Bursdon Cl BFN/LL DA15 ....64 A1
Bursill Crs MSTR CT12 ....142 C3
Burslem St WCHPL E1 ....24 E2
Bursted Rd RCANTW CT4 ....196 G9
Burston Gdns ECRIN RH19 ......264 G4
Burston Rd RMAID ME17 ....184 D4
Burston Cl FOLKN CT19 ....310 D4
  HOO/HM ME3 ....72 C4
  THHTH CR7 ....60 D9
Burton Flds THHTH CR7 ....107 N2
Burton La WALW SE17 ....24 H8
Burton Rd BRXN/ST SW9 ....40 A3
Burton Rd BRXN/ST SW9 ....40 A3
  KEN/WIL TN24 ....252 G3

Burt Rd CAN/RD E16 ....26 D4
Burtwell La WNWD SE27 ....60 D3
Burwash Ct STMC/STPC BR5 ....87 K2
Burwash Rd WOOL/PLUM SE18 ..27 L8
Bury Cl WCHPL E1 ....24 D2
Burwood Av HAYES BR2 ....85 L6
Bury Ct BERM/RHTH SE16 ....24 C4
Bury Ct HDTCH EC3A 24 B2
Bury Rd HDTCH EC3A 24 B2
Busbridge Rd
  MAID/SHEP ME15 ....185 K6
  SNOD ME6 ....123 M6
Bush Av MSTR CT12 ....142 C3
Bushbaby Cl STHWK SE1 ....24 B8
Bush Cl RSIT ME9 ....128 C8
Bushell Wy CHST BR7 ....63 K8
Bushey Av STMC/STPC BR5 ......86 E4
Bushey Av STMC/STPC BR5 ......86 E4
Bushey Cl WULT SE17 ....163 P1
Bushey Cft OXTED RH8 ....174 F6
Busheyfields Rd HB C6 ....107 L8
Bushey Hill Rd CMBW SE5 ....40 F2
Bushey Lees BFN/LL DA15 * 44 B7
Bushey Rd CROY/NA CRO 65 J2
Bushey Wy BECK BR3 ....84 C5
Bush House
  WOOL/PLUM SE18 * 43 J1
Bush La CANST EC4R 24 A3
Bushmeadow Rd RHAM ME8 ....97 J4
Bushmoor Crs
  WOOL/PLUM SE18 ....43 M1
Bush Rd DEPT SE8 ....25 P6
  STPH/PW TN12 ....212 F2
  STRD ME2 ....93 N3
Bush Rw DIT/AY ME20 ....154 F2
Bushwood Dr STHWK SE1 * 24 C8
Bushy Gill HART DA3 ....269 M5
Bushy Gv RMAID ME17 ....187 N9
Bushy Hill Rd CANTW/ST CT2 ...137 P6
Bushy Royds CANTW/ST CT2 ...282 C2
Buston Manor Farm Cots
  WBY/VAL ME18 * 184 A9
Busty La BGR/WK TN15 ....90 G6
Butcher La WBY/VAL ME18 ......182 E1
Butcherfield La HRTF TN7 ....267 H9
Butcher Rw POP/IOD E14 ....25 H2
  WAP E1W 24 D2
Butchers La BGR/WK TN15 ....90 C6
  RDV CT15 ....229 P1
Butchery La CANT CT1 * 5 H4
Butchers Rd CAN/RD E16 ....26 B2
Butchers Yd ORP BR6 ....116 B5
The Butchery SWCH CT13 * 201 P1
Bute Gdns WLGTN SM6 ....82 B9
Bute Gdns West WLGTN SM6 ...82 B9
Bute Rd CROY/NA CRO 63 F5
  WLGTN SM6 ....82 B9
Butler's & Colonial Whf
  STHWK SE1 * 24 C5
Butlers Dene Rd CTHM CR3 .....144 C5
Butler's Hi FAV ME13 ....134 E6
Butlers Pl BGR/WK TN15 * 91 H7
Butler's Ct GRAYS RM17 ....32 B2
Buttercup Cl STPH/PW TN12 ...243 H4
Butterfield ECRIN RH19 ....264 E5
Butterfield Cl
  BERM/RHTH SE16 ....24 D6
Butterfield House CHARL SE7 * ..43 J1
Butterfield Sq EHAM E6 ....26 G2
Butterfly Av DART DA1 ....45 K9
Butterfly La ELTH/MOT SE9 ......43 M7
Butterfly Wk CMBW SE5 * 40 D2
Buttermere Av DART DA1 * 66 F1
Buttermere Cl FOLKN CT19 ......10 D1
  GILL ME7 ....96 C1
Buttermere Gdns
  RCANTE CT5 ....199 J9
Buttermere Rd
  STMC/STPC BR5 ....87 L1
Butternut Copse ASH TN23 ....252 A6
Butterside Rd ASH TN23 ....252 B9
Butter St RDV CT15 ....229 L2
Butt Field Rd ASH TN23 ....252 B9
Butt Green La RMAID ME17 ....215 L4
Butt Haw Cl HOO/HM ME3 ....54 C5
Buttmarsh Cl
  WOOL/PLUM SE18 ....27 J8
Button Dr HOO/HM ME3 ....45 P4
Button La MAID/SHEP ME15 ....186 E1
Button Rd GRAYS RM17 ....32 A7
Button St SWLY BR8 ....89 H1
Butts La SLH/COR SS17 ....34 B1
  WADH TN5 ....294 D8
Butts Rd BMLY BR1 ....52 E4
The Butts RSEV TN14 ....148 C2
  SIT ME10 ....99 K4
  SWCH CT13 ....201 N1
Buttway La HOO/HM ME3 ....52 A2
Buxted Rd EDUL SE22 ....40 E1
Buxton Cl MAID/SHEP ME15 ...185 M3
  WALD ME5 ....95 J8
Buxton Rd CDW/CHF RM16 ......32 F5
  ERITH DA8 ....45 H1
  MSTR CT12 ....142 G2
  THHTH CR7 ....60 A3
Bybrook La KEN/WIL TN24 ......252 F5
Bycliffe Ms CVW DA11 ....49 K8
Bycliffe Rd CVW DA11 ....49 K8
Bycroft St PGE/AN SE20 ....61 K6
Byelands Cl BERM/RHTH SE16 ..25 H5
Byfield Cl BERM/RHTH SE16 ......25 H5
Bygrove CROY/NA CRO 114 E1
Bygrove St POP/IOD E14 ....25 N3
Byland Cl ABYW SE2 ....28 F3
Byllan Rd DVW CT17 ....290 F4
Byne Rd SYD SE26 ....61 K6
Byng Rd SBGH/RUST TN4 ....270 D4
Bynon Av BXLYHN DA7 ....45 J5
Byrneside RTON TN11 ....210 B6
Byron Av CAT CT1 ....5 K7
Byron St POP/IOD E14 ....25 K5
  PGE/AN SE20 ....61 N9

SYD SE26 * 61 L3
THMD SE28 ....28 B4
Byron Dr ERITH DA8 ....45 K1
Byron Gdns TIL RM18 ....49 M3
Byron Gv ERITH DA8 ....264 F8
Byron Rd DART DA1 ....47 H5
Byron St POP/IOD E14 ....25 M6
  MAID/BEAR ME14 ....155 N5
Bysing Wood Rd FAV ME13 ....132 B5
Bythorne St RHAM ME8 ....97 L5
Bywater St BERM/RHTH SE16 ..25 H4
Bywood Av CROY/NA CRO 83 P3

C

Cabbage Stalk La
  SBGH/RUST TN4 ....270 B6
Cabborns Crs SLH/COR SS17 ....34 C1
Cable Pl GNWCH SE10 ....42 A2
Cables Cl ERITH DA8 ....29 H6
Cable St WCHPL E1 ....24 D5
Cabot Sq POP/IOD E14 ....25 K4
Cackett's La RSEV TN14 ....116 E9
Cactus Cl CMBW SE5 * 40 E3
Cadborough Cliff RYE TN31 ....338 C8
Cadbury Wy BERM/RHTH SE16 ..24 C4
Cade La SEV TN13 ....179 M4
Cade Rd ASH TN23 ....282 D1
  GNWCH SE10 ....42 B2
Cades Orch FAV ME13 ....162 B1
Cadet Dr STHWK SE1 ....24 C8
Cadet Pl GNWCH SE10 ....25 P8
Cadlocks HI RSEV TN14 ....117 N4
Cadman Cl BRXN/ST SW9 ....40 B3
Cadman Cl CANTW/ST CT2 ......166 D1
  STRD ME2 ....72 A7
Cadogan Av RDART DA2 ....47 K8
Cadogan Gdns RTW TN1 ....7 L5
Cadogan Rd WOOL/PLUM SE18 ..27 K9
Cadvalton Rd ELTH/MOT SE9 ...63 M1
Caerleon Cl SCUP DA14 ....64 E4
Caernarvon Dr
  MAID/SHEP ME15 ....185 L2
Caesar's Wy FOLKN CT19 ......310 D4
Cage Farm Cots OXTED RH8 * ..204 E1
Cage Green Rd TONN TN10 ....210 F5
Cage La HDCN TN27 ....248 G8
Cagney Cl HOO/HM ME3 ....72 C4
Cahir St POP/IOD E14 ....25 M7
Cairndale Cl BMLY BR1 ....52 B5
Cairns Rd DART DA1 ....46 D6
Cairo New Rd CROY/NA CRO 82 C6
Caistor Rd TON TN9 ....240 E4
Caithness Gdns BFN/LL DA15 ...44 B7
Calais HI CANTW/ST CT2 ....136 C7
Calais St CMBW SE5 ....40 B2
Calcraft Ms CANT CT1 ....5 H1
Calcroft Av SWCM DA10 ....48 A6
Calcutta Rd TIL RM18 ....49 K3
Caldecote Cl RHAM ME8 ....97 L5
Caldecote La CLDD TN29 ....342 C2
Caldecot Rd CMBW SE5 ....40 C3
Calder Rd MAID/BEAR ME14 ....155 H3
Calderwood GVE DA12 ....70 A5
Calderwood St
  WOOL/PLUM SE18 ....27 H7
Caldew Av RHAM ME8 ....96 F5
Caldew St CMBW SE5 ....40 D2
Caldew Wv MAID/SHEP ME15 ...186 B2
Caldy Cl CMBW SE5 ....40 D1
Caldy Rd BELV DA17 ....28 G6
Caledonian Wharf Rd
  POP/IOD E14 ....25 N7
Caledon Ter CANT CT1 * 5 F7
Calehill Cl MAID/BEAR ME14 ...155 F6
Calehill La RTW TN1 * 240 C9
Calfstock La RTW TN1 ....89 J4
Calgary Crs FOLKN CT19 ....311 H5
Calgary Ter DVE/WH CT16 * 291 J4
Caling Cft HART DA3 ....91 J5
Caliph Cl GVE DA12 ....70 B1
Callaghan Cl LEW SE13 ....42 A1
Callaghan Cots WCHPL E1 * 24 F1
Callander Rd CAT SE6 ....41 P7
Callis New Rd CXTH SE14 ....41 M3
Callaways La RSIT ME9 ....98 C8
Calley Down Crs
  CROY/NA CRO 114 G4
Calleywell La RASHE TN25 ......284 D6
Callis Court Rd BRDST CT10 ....113 J7
Callisons Pl GNWCH SE10 ....26 B8
Callisto Cl MAIDW ME16 ....12 A6
Callonfield Jn CMBW SE5 ....24 D9
Calmont Rd BMLY BR1 ....52 B4
Calshot Av CDW/CHF RM16 ......31 P5
Calton Av DUL SE21 ....40 E7
Calverden Rd SWCH CT12 ....142 F3
Calverley Cl BECK BR3 ....51 N5
Calverley Pk RTW TN1 ....23 L5
Calverley Park Crs RTW TN1 .....23 L6
Calverley Park Gdns RTW TN1 ..23 L5
Calverley Rd RTW TN1 ....23 L5
Calvert Cl BELV DA17 ....29 H7
  SCUP DA14 ....64 G5
Calvert Rd GNWCH SE10 ....26 C8
Calydon Rd CHARL SE7 ....42 B5
Calypso Crs PECK SE15 ....41 F5
Camberley Av RYE TN31 ....339 J7
Camber Rd RYE TN31 ....339 J7
Cambert Wy BKHTH/KID SE3 ....42 F5
Camberwell Church St
  CMBW SE5 ....40 D2
Camberwell Gv CMBW SE5 ......40 D2
Camberwell Gn CMBW SE5 ......40 D2
Camberwell Gv CMBW SE5 ......40 D2
Camberwell La CMBW SE5 ......40 D2
Camberwell La RSEV TN14 ......177 N6
Camberwell New Rd
  CMBW SE5 ....40 B1

Camberwell Station Rd
  CMBW SE5 ....40 C2
Camborne Rd CROY/NA CRO 83 M4
  SCUP DA14 ....64 E2
  WELL DA16 ....44 A3
Cambourne Av WGOS CT8 ......111 L5
Cambrai Ct CANT CT1 ....167 J5
Cambray Rd ORP BR6 ....86 C4
Cambria Av ROCH ME1 ....94 E4
Cambria Cl BFN/LL DA15 ....45 M9
Cambria Crs GVE DA12 ....70 A3
Cambria Rd CMBW SE5 ....40 C3
Cambridge Av RSIT ME9 ....98 C8
Cambridge Av SBGH/RUST TN4 ..270 F1
Cambridge Barracks Rd
  WOOL/PLUM SE18 ....26 G7
Cambridge Cl BRCH CT7 ....111 J6
Cambridge Gdns
  CDW/CHF RM16 ....33 H7
  FOLK CT20 ....10 E4
  RTWE/PEM TN2 ....23 F7
Cambridge La ELTH/MOT SE9 ...43 M9
Cambridge La MAID/BEAR ME14 ..155 M9
Cambridge La RSIT ME9 ....130 G5
  CANT CT1 ....4 D7
Cambridge Pl DEAL CT14 ....233 J6
  DVW CT17 ....7 F3
  FAV ME13 ....132 C2
  PGE/AN SE20 ....61 J8
  RAM CT11 ....88 G6
  SCUP DA14 ....64 C3
  SIT ME10 ....130 A3
  STRD ME2 ....72 A7
Cambridge Rw
  WOOL/PLUM SE18 ....27 J8
Cambridge St
  RTWE/PEM TN2 ....23 H5
  FOLK CT20 ....10 C4
  MARG CT9 ....112 G4
Cambridge Ter CHAT ME4 ....6 A7
Cambridge Wy CANT CT1 ....166 E6
Cambus Rd CAN/RD E16 ....26 B1
Camdale Rd
  WOOL/PLUM SE18 ....44 B1
Camden Av RTWE/PEM TN2 ....271 M2
Camden Cl CDW/CHF RM16 .....33 J7
Camden Cl CHST BR7 ....63 H7
  CVW DA11 ....48 C9
  WALD ME5 ....95 L8
Camden Crs DVE/WH CT16 ....8 E2
Camden Gv CHST BR7 ....63 H5
Camden Hill Rd NRWD SE19 ....60 E6
Camdenhurst St POP/IOD E14 ..25 F2
Camden Pk RTW TN1 ....22 E4
Camden Pk CHST BR7 ....63 K6
Camden Park Rd CHST BR7 ......63 H6
  CVW DA11 ....48 C9
Camden Rd BRDST CT10 ....113 K6
  BXLY DA5 ....45 H9
  CDW/CHF RM16 ....31 P9
  GILL ME7 ....73 J6
  LING RH7 ....254 G8
  RAM CT11 ....17 G4
  RTW TN1 ....22 E3
  SEV TN13 ....148 G2
Camden Rw BKHTH/KID SE3 ....42 C5
Camden St RAM CT11 * 17 G4
Camden St KEN/WIL TN24 ....3 J6
Camden Wy CHST BR7 ....63 K6
  THHTH CR7 ....60 B4
Camellia Cl MARG CT9 ....112 A5
  RHAM ME8 ....96 E7
Camelot Cl BH/WHM TN16 ....145 M1
  THMD SE28 ....27 L5
Camel Rd CAN/RD E16 ....26 E4
Cameron Cl BXLY DA5 ....65 M2
Cameron Pl STRHM/NOR SW16 ..60 H1
Cameron Rd CAT SE6 ....41 M1
  CROY/NA CRO 63 K5
  HAYES BR2 ....85 K1
Cameron Ter LEE/GVPK SE12 * ..62 F2
Camer Park Rd MEO DA13 ....92 C4
Camer St MEO DA13 ....92 C4
Cam Gn SOCK/AV RM15 ....31 L2
Camilla Rd BERM/RHTH SE16 ..24 G6
Camille Cl SNWD SE25 ....63 H6
Camilla Rd BMLY BR1 ....85 L1
Camomile Cl LVPST EC2M 24 B1
Campbell Cl HB C6 ....107 P3
  WOOL/PLUM SE18 ....43 J3
Campbell Cl ECRIN RH19 ....264 D7
Campbell Rd CROY/NA CRO 82 C4
  DEAL CT14 ....233 J6
  GVW DA11 ....49 H8
  MAID/BEAR ME14 ....155 H3
  SBGH/RUST TN4 ....270 D2
Campden Sand SEAL/SEL CT20 ..85 K9
Camperdown St WCHPL E1 ....24 C3
Campfield Rd ELTH/MOT SE9 ....43 K5
Camp Hill RTON TN11 ....208 H7
Campion Cl CROY/NA CRO * 82 C2
  EHAM E6 ....26 G4
Campion Pl THMD SE28 ....28 C9
Campleshon Rd RHAM ME8 ......96 D9
Campshill Pl LEW SE13 ....42 A6
Campshill Rd LEW SE13 ....42 A6
Campus Wy MAID/SHEP ME15 ..185 M6
Camrose Av ERITH DA8 ....28 G9
Camrose Cl CROY/NA CRO 64 D3
Camrose St WOOL/PLUM SE18 ..27 P7
Canada Cl FOLKN CT19 ....309 P1
Canada Farm Rd HART DA3 ......90 B4

Canada Ms DEAL CT14 ....233 H6
Canada Rd DEAL CT14 ....233 H5
  ERITH DA8 ....45 J4
Canada Sqaure POP/IOD E14 ....25 L4
Canada St BERM/RHTH SE16 ....25 H6
Canadian Av CAT SE6 ....41 P9
  GILL ME7 ....73 J8
Canal Ap DEPT SE8 ....25 H8
Canal Basin GVE DA12 ....49 P7
Canal Gv PECK SE15 ....24 D9
Canal Rd GVE DA12 ....49 N7
  HOO/HM ME3 ....39 K8
  STRD ME2 ....19 F2
Canal St CMBW SE5 ....24 A9
Canal Wk CROY/NA CRO 63 J4
  CROY/NA CRO 63 J4
Canberra Gdns SIT ME10 ....129 K1
Canberra Rd ABYW SE2 ....28 C9
  CHARL SE7 ....42 C6
Canbury Ms SYD SE26 ....61 L5
Canbury Pth STMC/STPC BR5 ...87 L1
Cancell Rd BRXN/ST SW9 ....40 A2
Cander Wy SOCK/AV RM15 ......31 L3
Candle Gv PECK SE15 ....41 H4
Candover Rd BXLYHN DA7 ....45 N4
Canham Rd SNWD SE25 ....60 E9
Canning Crs CMBW SE5 ....40 C3
Canning Rd CROY/NA CRO 83 L6
Cannings La MAID/BEAR ME14 ..155 N6
Cannonbury Rd RAM CT11 ....16 D5
Cannon Dr POP/IOD E14 ....25 K3
Cannongate Av HYTHE CT21 ...309 J4
Cannongate Ci HYTHE CT21 ...309 K5
Cannongate Gdns
  HYTHE CT21 ....309 J4
Cannongate Rd HYTHE CT21 ...309 J4
Cannon La TON TN9 ....210 C8
Cannon Pl CHARL SE7 ....42 C6
  RAM CT11 ....16 E3
Cannon St DEAL CT14 ....233 H2
  DVE/WH CT16 ....342 B6
  LYDD TN29 ....327 J5
  MANHO EC4N 24 A3
  NROM TN28 ....336 C6
Cannon Street Rd WCHPL E1 ....24 E2
Canon Beck Rd
  BERM/RHTH SE16 ....24 G5
Canonbie Rd FSTH SE23 ....41 J8
Canon Cl CANT CT1 ....94 C4
Canon Gn RCANTE CT5 * 169 K9
Canon La MAID/SHEP ME15 ....183 K2
Canon Murnane Rd
  STHWK SE1 * 24 C6
Canon Rd BMLY BR1 ....52 E4
Canons Gate Rd DVE/WH CT16 ..9 F7
Canons Rd BH/WHM TN16 ......177 J5
Canon's Wk CROY/NA CRO 84 A7
Canon Woods Wy
  KEN/WIL TN24 ....253 J3
Cansiron La EDEN TN8 ....266 E1
Cantelupe Ms EGRIN RH19 * 265 H7
Cantelupe Rd EGRIN RH19 ......265 J7
Canterbury Av BECK BR3 ....64 E1
Canterbury Cl BECK BR3 ....51 P1
  EHAM E6 ....26 G3
Canterbury Gv BRXN/ST SW9 ....40 G5
Canterbury Gv WNWD SE27 ....60 A3
Canterbury Hl CANTW/ST CT2 ..136 D6
  RHAM ME8 ....97 H5
Canterbury Rd CROY/NA CRO ...82 C4
  FAV ME13 ....133 H8
  FAV ME13 ....162 E2
  FAV ME13 ....164 E2
  FOLKN CT19 ....11 F1
  GVE DA12 ....70 B2
  KEN/WIL TN24 ....3 G4
  RASHE TN25 ....222 D1
  RCANTE CT3 ....167 F4
  RCANTE CT5 ....169 K9
  RCANTW CT4 ....194 F5
  RCANTW CT4 ....257 J8
  RDV CT15 ....258 E6
  RDV CT15 ....259 L6
  RDV CT15 ....288 E1
  RFOLK CT18 ....287 J5
  RYE TN31 ....337 J7
  SIT ME10 ....130 A2
  WSTB CT5 ....105 L6
Canterbury Road Birchington
  BRCH CT7 ....110 F3
Canterbury Rd East
  MARG CT9 ....142 E5
Canterbury Rd West
  MSTR CT12 ....142 C5
Canterbury Road Westgate
  WGOS CT8 ....111 L5
Canterbury St GILL ME7 ....7 H3
Canterbury Wy WTHK RM20 ......47 L1
Cantley Gdns NRWD SE19 ....60 F1
Canton St POP/IOD E14 ....25 L3
Cantwell Rd WOOL/PLUM SE18 ..43 M1
Canute Rd BRCH CT7 ....110 F2
  DEAL CT14 ....203 H9
  FAV ME13 ....132 C5
Capability Wy SWCM DA10 ......48 A5
Capel Av WLGTN SM6 ....82 G9
Capel Cl ASH TN23 ....253 F8
  BRDST CT10 ....113 L4
  HAYES BR2 ....84 E5
  RHAM ME8 ....96 G5
Capel Court Pk RFOLK CT18 * ..311 N1
Capel Rd FAV ME13 * 132 E6
  RASHW TN26 ....304 C4
  RCANTW CT4 ....195 N7
  SIT ME10 ....129 M3

Capel St RFOLK CT18 311 L2
Cape Yd WAP E1W 24 D4
Capri Rd CROY/NA CR0 83 L4
Capstan Ct RDART DA2 47 J5
Capstan Dr RAIN RM13 29 M1
Capstan Rd DEPT SE8 25 J7
Capstan Rw DEAL CT14 233 J2
Capstan Sq POP/IOD E14 25 M5
Capstan Wy BERM/RHTH SE16 25 H4
Capstone Rd BMLY BR1 62 D3
GILL ME7 96 B7
WALD ME5 95 P5
Captain's Cl RMAID ME17 217 H4
Capulet Ms CAN/RD E16 26 B4
Caradoc St GNWCH SE10 25 P8
Caravel Cl CDW/CHF RM16 32 A6
Caravel Ms DEPT SE8 * 25 K9
Caraway Cl PLSTW E13 26 C1
Caraway Pl WLGTN SM6 82 A7
Carberry Rd NRWD SE19 60 E5
Carbis Rd POP/IOD E14 25 J2
Cardale St POP/IOD E14 25 M6
Carden Rd PECK SE15 41 H4
Cardens Rd HOO/HM ME3 52 B8
Cardiff St WOOL/PLUM SE18 44 A1
Cardigan Cl HOO/HM ME3 53 M5
Cardigan Pl LEW SE13 * 42 B3
Cardinal Bourne St
STHWK SE1 * 24 A6
Cardinal Cl CHST BR7 63 P7
IOS ME12 58 D9
TON TN9 240 C1
Cardinal Rd CDW/CHF RM16 31 P6
Cardinal Wk E/WMAL ME19 153 J9
Cardine Cl SIT ME10 99 M7
Cardine Ms PECK SE15 41 H1
Carew Cl CDW/CHF RM16 31 P5
Carew Rd THHTH CR7 60 B9
Carew St CMBW SE5 40 C3
Carew Wy STMC/STPC BR5 87 K5
Carey Cl NROM TN28 336 G7
Carey's Fld SEV TN13 148 D5
The Carfax SYD SE26 * 61 J2
Cargreen Rd SNWD SE25 83 L1
Carholme Rd FSTH SE23 41 M9
Caring La MAID/SHEP ME15 186 F1
Caring Rd RMAID ME17 186 F2
Carisbrooke Av BXLY DA5 44 F9
Carisbrooke Dr MAIDW ME16 12 A3
Carisbrooke Gdns PECK SE15 * 40 F1
Carisbrooke Rd HAYES BR2 85 M1
MTCM CR4 82 D1
STRD ME2 71 N7
Carleton Pl EYN DA4 89 P1
Carleton Rd DART DA1 46 G8
Carlisle Av TWRH EC3N 24 B2
Carlisle Rd DART DA1 46 G7
Carlsden Cl DVW CT17 291 H4
Carlton Av BRDST CT10 113 M8
GILL ME7 96 B2
IOS ME12 57 K7
RAM CT11 16 E4
RDART DA2 47 L7
Carlton Crs RTW TN1 23 G3
WALD ME5 96 A6
Carlton Gdns
MAID/SHEP ME15 185 N3
Carlton Gn SCUP DA14 * 64 B3
Carlton Gv PECK SE15 41 H2
Carlton Hl HB CT6 107 H2
Carlton Ldg RTW TN1 * 23 G3
Carlton Pde SEV TN13 * 149 H7
Carlton Ri WGOS CT8 111 K5
Carlton Rd ASH TN23 252 C6
CDW/CHF RM16 32 G5
DEAL CT14 263 H2
ERITH DA8 28 C9
RTW TN1 23 G3
SCUP DA14 64 B4
WELL DA16 44 D4
WSTB CT5 135 L3
Carlton Rd East WGOS CT8 111 L5
Carlton Rd West WGOS CT8 111 K5
Carlton Ter SYD SE26 61 J3
Carlyle Av BMLY BR1 63 H9
Carlyle Rd CROY/NA CR0 83 M6
THMD SE28 28 A3
Carlys Cl BECK BR3 61 K8
Carmel Cl RCANTW CT4 * 195 J1
Carmelite Wy HART DA3 91 J2
Carmen St POP/IOD E14 25 L2
Carmichael Rd SNWD SE25 83 M2
Carnach Gn SOCK/AV RM15 31 L3
Carnac St WNWD SE27 60 D3
Carnation Cl E/WMAL ME19 153 P3
Carnation Crs E/WMAL ME19 153 N4
Carnation Rd STRD ME2 71 M8
Carnation St ABYW SE2 28 B8
Carnbrook Rd BKHTH/KID SE3 43 H4
Carnecke Gdns
ELTH/MOT SE9 43 J6
Carnet Cl DART DA1 45 N8
Carnoustie Cl WSTB CT5 106 D6
Carnoustie Cl THMD SE28 28 C2
Caroland Cl RASHE TN25 284 E3
Carolina Rd THHTH CR7 60 B8
Caroline Cl CROY/NA CR0 83 K8
WSTB CT5 105 J8
Caroline Crs BRDST CT10 113 K7
MAIDW ME16 155 J5
Caroline Gdns PECK SE15 * 41 H1
Caroline Sq MARG CT9 15 J3
Caroline St WCHPL E1 24 G2
Carolyn Dr ORP BR6 87 H7
Carp Cl DIT/AY ME20 123 P9
Carpeaux Cl CHAT ME4 6 E5
Carpenters Cl ROCH ME1 95 K4
Carpenters La RTON TN11 211 P2
STPH/PW TN12 245 P2
Carpinus Cl WALD ME5 125 N4
Carre Ms CMBW SE5 40 B2
Carr Gv WOOL/PLUM SE18 26 F7
Carriage Ms CANTW/ST CT2 4 D3
The Carriageway
BH/WHM TN16 147 L9
Carrick Dr SEV TN13 148 G8
Carrick Ms DEPT SE8 25 K9
Carriers Pl RRTW TN3 268 A4
Carriers Rd CRBK TN17 298 A2
Carrill Wy BELV DA17 28 C6
Carrington Cl CROY/NA CR0 84 B4
GILL ME7 73 M9
Carrington Rd DART DA1 46 F7
Carroll Cl STRD ME2 123 P1
Carroll Gdns DIT/AY ME20 153 N1
Carronade Pl THMD SE28 27 K6
Carron Cl POP/IOD E14 25 L2
Carroway's Pl MARG CT9 15 H4
Carr St POP/IOD E14 25 H1
Carsington Gdns DART DA1 66 D1
Carson Rd CAN/RD E16 26 B1
DUL SE21 60 C1
Carstairs Rd CAT SE6 62 A2
Carston Cl LEE/GVPK SE12 42 D6
Carswell Rd CAT SE6 42 A8
Cartel Cl PUR RM19 30 G7
Carter Av BGR/WK TN15 * 120 B2
Carteret Wy DEPT SE8 25 H7
Carter La LYDD TN29 334 F3
Carter's Hl BGR/WK TN15 179 N6
Carters Hill Cl ELTH/MOT SE9 42 G9
Carters Hill La MEO DA13 122 A3
Carter's Rd FOLK CT20 310 C6
Carter's Wd RASHW TN26 304 D8
Cart La GRAYS RM17 32 C8
Cartmel Rd BXLYHN DA7 45 J2
Carton Cl ROCH ME1 95 J4
Carton Rd HOO/HM ME3 71 K4
Cartwright Cl RCANTE CT3 170 D9
Cartwright St WCHPL E1 24 C3
Carver Dr RSIT ME9 129 M7
Carver Rd HNHL SE24 40 C7
Carville Av SBGH/RUST TN4 240 C8
Carvoran Wy RHAM ME8 96 F9
Cascade Cl STMC/STPC BR5 64 E9
Cascades CROY/NA CR0 114 C4
Casella Rd NWCR SE14 41 K1
Casewick Rd WNWD SE27 60 B4
Casino Av HNHL SE24 40 C6
Caslocke St FAV ME13 132 F6
Caspian St CMBW SE5 40 D1
Caspian Wk CAN/RD E16 26 E2
Caspian Wy PUR RM19 30 D8
SWCM DA10 48 B6
Cassini Cl CDW/CHF RM16 33 H1
Cassilda Rd ABYW SE2 27 P7
Cassilis Rd POP/IOD E14 25 K5
Cassino Sq RDV CT15 291 M5
Cassland Rd THHTH CR7 83 J1
Casslee Rd CAT SE6 41 M8
Casson St WCHPL E1 24 D1
Casstine Cl SWLY BR8 65 P7
Casterbridge Rd
BKHTH/KID SE3 42 E4
Castfield Cl HOO/HM ME3 52 E6
Castile Rd WOOL/PLUM SE18 27 H7
Castillon Rd CAT SE6 62 C1
Castlands Rd CAT SE6 61 M1
Castle Av BRDST CT10 113 N7
DVE/WH CT16 291 L6
HYTHE CT21 308 G4
ROCH ME1 95 H2
Castle Bay FOLK CT20 309 P4
Castle Cl HAYES BR2 62 C9
HYTHE CT21 307 N5
Castlecombe Rd
ELTH/MOT SE9 63 J4
Castle Ct BANK EC3V * 24 A2
SYD SE26 61 L3
Castle Dene
MAID/BEAR ME14 155 K4
Castledine Rd PGE/AN SE20 61 H6
Castle Dr BGR/WK TN15 149 K2
DVE/WH CT16 260 G9
Castle Farm Rd RSEV TN14 118 E3
Castle Fld TON TN9 * 210 E8
Castlefields MEO DA13 69 K7
Castleford Av ELTH/MOT SE9 43 M9
Castle Hl FOLKN CT19 310 D3
HART DA3 90 G2
MAID/BEAR ME14 156 G4
ROCH ME1 19 F4
RTON TN11 241 J4
Castle Hill Av CROY/NA CR0 114 E3
FOLK CT20 10 C4
Castle Hill Ct ROCH ME1 19 F4
Castle Hill Rd DVE/WH CT16 8 E3
Castle Hurst RBTBR TN32 328 C5
Castle La GVE DA12 70 D1
Castlemaine Av GILL ME7 73 L9
SAND/SEL CR2 83 L9
Castlemaine St WCHPL E1 24 E1
Castle Mayne Av BRCH CT7 141 N1
Castle Md CMBW SE5 * 40 C1
Castlemere Av QBOR ME11 77 K2
Castle Ms DEAL CT14 * 232 G5
Castlemount Rd DVE/WH CT16 8 D1
Castle Rd CHAT ME4 95 M4
EYN DA4 118 G1
FOLK CT20 310 C8
GRAYS RM17 31 P9
HYTHE CT21 308 G3
MAIDW ME16 155 H5
SBGH/RUST TN4 22 B4
SIT ME10 100 A9
SWCM DA10 48 D7
WSTB CT5 105 M4
Castle Rough La SIT ME10 99 N5
Castle Rw CANT CT1 4 D6
Castle St CANT CT1 4 D5
DVE/WH CT16 8 E4
KEN/WIL TN24 2 D3
QBOR ME11 77 J2
RDART DA2 47 N6
ROCH ME1 124 B1
RTW TN1 22 D6
SBGH/RUST TN4 240 C7
STRD ME2 72 E6
SWCM DA10 48 D7
TON TN9 210 F8
Castle Ter RTON TN11 * 211 P2
Castleton Av BXLYHN DA7 45 M2
Castleton Cl CROY/NA CR0 84 B3
Castleton Rd ELTH/MOT SE9 63 H3
MTCM CR4 82 C1
Castle Vw RTON TN11 * 211 P2
Castle View Rd STRD ME2 18 A1
Castle Wy E/WMAL ME19 153 L2
Castlewood Dr ELTH/MOT SE9 43 K3
Castor La POP/IOD E14 25 L3
Catalina Av CDW/CHF RM16 32 A5
Catalpa Ct LEW SE13 42 B7
Caterfield La LING RH7 205 J8
Caterham Rd LEW SE13 42 A4
Catesby St WALW SE17 24 A7
Catford Broadway CAT SE6 41 P8
Catford Hl CAT SE6 41 M9
Catford Island CAT SE6 * 41 P8
Catford Rd CAT SE6 41 N9
Catharine Cl CDW/CHF RM16 32 A5
Cathay St BERM/RHTH SE16 24 E5
Cathcart Dr ORP BR6 86 F6
Cathedral St STHWK SE1 * 24 A4
Catherine Cl MAIDW ME16 154 F9
Catherine Gv GNWCH SE10 41 P2
Catherine Pl RTW TN1 22 E3
Catherine St ROCH ME1 95 J3
Catherine Wy BRDST CT10 113 M7
Catherine Wheel Aly
LVPST EC2M 24 B1
Catkin Cl WALD ME5 125 L4
Catling Cl FSTH SE23 61 J2
Catlin St BERM/RHTH SE16 24 D8
Catlyn Cl E/WMAL ME19 153 P4
Cator Cl CROY/NA CR0 115 H5
Cator Crs CROY/NA CR0 115 H5
Cator La BECK BR3 61 M8
Cator Rd SYD SE26 61 K5
Cator St PECK SE15 24 C9
Catsole Hl RCANTE CT3 199 N5
Catterick Rd WALD ME5 126 A3
Cattistock Rd ELTH/MOT SE9 63 J4
Cattle Market SWCH CT13 201 N1
Cattle Aly SNOD ME6 123 P6
Catt's Hl TENT TN30 333 J1
Catts Pl STPH/PW TN12 * 243 K5
Catt's Wood Rd RCANTW CT4 196 E6
Cauldham Cl RFOLK CT18 311 K2
Cauldham La RFOLK CT18 311 L1
Caulfield Rd PECK SE15 41 H3
Causeway Br PUR RM19 31 H6
The Causeway CANTW/ST CT2 4 E2
SWCH CT13 171 L9
Causton Cots POP/IOD E14 * 25 H1
Causton Rd CRBK TN17 297 P2
Cavalier Wy EGRIN RH19 265 J9
Cave Hl MAID/SHEP ME15 185 L2
Cave La RCANTE CT3 199 N4
Cavell Crs DART DA1 46 G5
Cavell Sq DEAL CT14 232 F6
Cavell St WCHPL E1 24 E1
Cavell Wy SIT ME10 99 L9
Cavenagh Rd RDV CT15 292 G1
Cavendish Av BFN/LL DA15 44 C8
ERITH DA8 29 H9
GILL ME7 73 L9
SEV TN13 148 F7
WELL DA16 44 B4
Cavendish Cl TONN TN10 210 G3
Cavendish Dr RTWE/PEM TN2 23 F7
Cavendish Pl BMLY BR1 63 K9
RAM CT11 17 F4
Cavendish Rd CROY/NA CR0 82 G5
HB CT6 107 M2
ROCH ME1 95 J3
Cavendish Sq HART DA3 68 B9
Cavendish St RAM CT11 17 F3
Cavendish Wy
MAID/SHEP ME15 156 D9
WWKM BR4 84 E5
Caversham Cl RHAM ME8 97 J5
Cavour Rd FAV ME13 132 F6
IOS ME12 57 L6
Cawdor Av SOCK/AV RM15 31 K3
Cawnpore St NRWD SE19 60 E4
Caxton Cl HART DA3 91 J1
TENT TN30 300 G8
Caxton La OXTED RH8 175 P7
RTON TN11 211 P2
Caxton Rd MARG CT9 112 B5
The Caxtons BRXN/ST SW9 * 40 B1
Caxton St North CAN/RD E16 26 A2
Cayenne Ct STHWK SE1 24 B4
Caygill Cl HAYES BR2 85 J1
Cayser Dr RMAID ME17 187 P9
Caysers Cft STPH/PW TN12 212 F4
Cazeneuve St ROCH ME1 19 G7
Cdiamond Ter GNWCH SE10 42 A1
Cecil Av CDW/CHF RM16 32 A5
IOS ME12 57 K7
RHAM ME8 96 D4
STRD ME2 72 B7
Cecil Ct HB CT6 107 M2
KEN/WIL TN24 2 D2
Cecilia Gv BRDST CT10 113 L7
Cecilia Rd RAM CT11 143 K4
Cecil Pk HB CT6 107 M2
Cecil Rd CROY/NA CR0 82 D3
DEAL CT14 263 J1
GVW DA11 49 K9
ROCH ME1 95 H3
Cecil Sq MARG CT9 15 G4
Cecil St MARG CT9 15 G4
Cecil Wy HAYES BR2 85 K5
Cedar Av BFN/LL DA15 44 C8
GVE DA12 69 N3
Cedar Cl ASH TN23 252 B6
BRDST CT10 113 L6
DIT/AY ME20 154 C4
DUL SE21 40 C9
HAYES BR2 85 P7
MARG CT9 112 G4
MEO DA13 92 B3
SIT ME10 130 A3
SWLY BR8 65 L8
WARL CR6 144 B3
Cedar Copse BMLY BR1 63 K8
Cedar Ct CHARL SE7 * 26 D9
ELTH/MOT SE9 * 43 J7
Cedar Crs HAYES BR2 85 P7
LYDD TN29 337 L2
TONN TN10 210 F3
Cedar Dr EDEN TN8 206 C8
EYN DA4 67 H8
MAIDW ME16 184 D1
Cedar Gdns RSIT ME9 * 127 P5
Cedar Gv BXLY DA5 44 F7
GILL ME7 96 D9
Cedarhurst BMLY BR1 * 62 C6
Cedarhurst Dr ELTH/MOT SE9 42 G6
Cedar La HDCN TN27 278 E9
Cedar Mt ELTH/MOT SE9 43 H9
Cedar Pl CHARL SE7 26 D8
Cedar Rdg RTWE/PEM TN2 270 G2
Cedar Rd BMLY BR1 62 G8
CANTW/ST CT2 137 L7
CDW/CHF RM16 33 H6
CROY/NA CR0 83 K6
DART DA1 46 D9
ERITH DA8 46 A2
STRD ME2 18 A3
Cedars Cl LEW SE13 42 B4
Cedars Rd BECK BR3 61 L8
CROY/NA CR0 82 D7
The Cedars RASHE TN25 285 L8
SIT ME10 * 100 B9
STPH/PW TN12 243 H2
Cedar Ter DVE/WH CT16 * 291 K4
FAV ME13 * 132 D9
Cedar Terrace Rd SEV TN13 149 H8
Cedar Tree Gv WNWD SE27 60 B4
Cedarview CANTW/ST CT2 166 B3
Cedric Rd ELTH/MOT SE9 63 N2
Ceil Vis DEAL CT14 * 202 A6
Celandine Cl POP/IOD E14 * 25 K1
Celandine Dr THMD SE28 28 A4
Celedon Cl CDW/CHF RM16 31 P5
Celestial Gdns LEW SE13 42 B5
Celestine Cl WALD ME5 125 M4
Celia Av BGR/WK TN15 120 B2
Cellar Hl RSIT ME9 131 H4
Celt Cl SIT ME10 99 N6
Celtic Av HAYES BR2 62 C9
Celtic Rd DEAL CT14 232 F7
Celtic St POP/IOD E14 25 L1
Cement Block Cots
GRAYS RM17 32 D8
Cemetery La CHARL SE7 26 F9
KEN/WIL TN24 252 F5
RTON TN11 212 B2
Cemetery Rd ABYW SE2 28 A9
SNOD ME6 123 N4
STRD ME2 123 P1
Centenary Cl HDCN TN27 221 H2
Centenary Gdns SWCH CT13 201 H8
Centenary Wk CANTW/ST CT2 4 A3
Centenary Walk Canterbury
RCANTW CT4 165 M6
Centenary Walk-Maidstone
MAID/BEAR ME14 12 D1
Centenary Walk-Rochester
ROCH ME1 94 F3
Central Av CHAT ME4 73 H7
GVE DA12 69 M1
HB CT6 107 J1
RSIT ME9 129 L7
SIT ME10 129 N2
SOCK/AV RM15 30 F5
TIL RM18 49 L2
WELL DA16 44 C3
WLGTN SM6 82 D9
WTHK RM20 31 J8
Central Hl NRWD SE19 60 C4
Central Ldg BGR/WK TN15 * 121 P7
Central Pde BFN/LL DA15 * 64 C2
CROY/NA CR0 114 F4
HB CT6 107 K1
PGE/AN SE20 * 61 K6
Central Park Gdns CHAT ME4 95 K4
Central Pl SNWD SE25 * 83 M1
Central Rd DART DA1 46 E6
DIT/AY ME20 154 A1
RAM CT11 143 J4
STRD ME2 18 B1
Central Ter BECK BR3 * 61 K9
HOO/HM ME3 72 F1
Central Wy OXTED RH8 174 G3
THMD SE28 27 P3
Centre Common Rd CHST BR7 63 N6
Centre Ct STRD ME2 * 19 K2
Centre Rd DVW CT17 8 B6
HART DA3 91 H7
The Centre HB CT6 * 107 L1
MARG CT9 15 G4
Centurian Wy ERITHM DA18 28 E6
Centurion Cl RHAM ME8 96 C5
Centurion Ct WLGTN SM6 * 82 A6
Centurion Sq CHARL SE7 * 43 J1
Centurion Wk ASH TN23 282 E4
Centurion Wy PUR RM19 30 C7
Century Rd FAV ME13 133 H6
RHAM ME8 96 G6
Ceres Rd WOOL/PLUM SE18 27 N7
Cerise Rd PECK SE15 40 G2
Cerne Rd GVE DA12 70 A3
Cervia Wy GVE DA12 70 B2
Chabot Dr PECK SE15 41 H4
Chada Av GILL ME7 96 B3
Chadbourn St POP/IOD E14 25 L1
Chadd Dr BMLY BR1 63 J9
Chadfields TIL RM18 49 L1
Chadwell By-Pass
CDW/CHF RM16 33 H8
Chadwell Hl CDW/CHF RM16 33 J8
Chadwell Rd GRAYS RM17 32 D7
Chadwick Cl GVW DA11 69 J1
Chadwick Rd PECK SE15 40 F3
Chadwick Wy THMD SE28 28 C3
Chadwin Rd PLSTW E13 26 C1
Chaffe's La RSIT ME9 97 P4
Chaffes Ter RSIT ME9 * 97 P4
Chaffinch Av CROY/NA CR0 84 A3
Chaffinch Cl CROY/NA CR0 84 A2
WALD ME5 95 M7
Chaffinch Ct ORP BR6 87 H4
Chaffinch Dr ASH TN23 282 F5
Chaffinch Rd BECK BR3 61 L7
Chaffinch Wy STPH/PW TN12 242 G4
Chafford La RRTW TN3 268 F3
Chafford Wy CDW/CHF RM16 32 B4
The Chain SWCH CT13 201 P2
Chalcombe Rd ABYW SE2 28 A6
Chalcroft Rd FOLK CT20 310 B7
LEW SE13 42 C6
Chalet Cl BXLY DA5 65 M3
Chalfont Dr HB CT6 108 A8
RHAM ME8 96 G8
Chalfont Rd SNWD SE25 60 F9
Chalford Rd DUL SE21 60 D3
Chalgrove Ms STRD ME2 93 P9
Chalice Wy RDART DA2 47 L6
Chalk Av TENT TN30 301 J5
Chalk Cl FOLKN CT19 310 D4
Chalk Ct GRAYS RM17 * 32 B9
Chalkenden Av RHAM ME8 96 D4
Chalkenden Cl PGE/AN SE20 61 H6
Chalket La RTWE/PEM TN2 271 M3
Chalk Hl RAM CT11 142 E6
Chalk Hill Rd DEAL CT14 263 H3
Chalk La CRBK TN17 275 K9
Chalk Pit Av STMC/STPC BR5 64 E9
Chalk Pit Hl CHAT ME4 6 D7
RCANTE CT3 200 C5
Chalkpit Hl RCANTW CT4 198 A4
Chalkpit La OXTED RH8 174 F3
Chalkpit Wd OXTED RH8 174 G3
Chalk Rd GVE DA12 50 C9
HOO/HM ME3 71 L1
PLSTW E13 26 C1
QBOR ME11 77 J2
Chalksole Green La RDV CT15 289 K2
Chalkstone Cl WELL DA16 44 C2
Chalkways BGR/WK TN15 149 K1
Chalkwell Rd SIT ME10 129 L1
Chalky Bank GVW DA11 69 L3
Chalky Bank Rd RHAM ME8 97 J4
Chalky Rd RSIT ME9 127 M7
Challenge Cl GVE DA12 70 B3
Challenger Cl SIT ME10 99 M7
STPH/PW TN12 242 G3
Challin St PGE/AN SE20 61 J7
Challock Cl BH/WHM TN16 145 M1
Challock Ct MARG CT9 113 L3
Challock Wk
MAID/BEAR ME14 * 155 P6
Chalmers Wy RHAM ME8 96 D2
Chalsey Rd BROCKY SE4 41 M5
Chamberlain Av MAIDW ME16 184 G1
Chamberlain Cl THMD SE28 27 L6
Chamberlain Cots CMBW SE5 * 40 D2
Chamberlain Ct RHAM ME8 96 E9
Chamberlain Crs WWKM BR4 84 E5
Chamberlain Dr HB CT6 106 G2
Chamberlain Rd CHAT ME4 95 N4
DVW CT17 291 H7
Chambers Ct RDART DA2 47 N6
Chambers St
BERM/RHTH SE16 24 D5
Chamber St WCHPL E1 24 C3
Chambers Wharf La
FAV ME13 133 H5
Champion Crs SYD SE26 61 L3
Champion Gv CMBW SE5 40 D4
Champion Hl CMBW SE5 40 D4
Champion Pk CMBW SE5 40 D3
Champion Rd SYD SE26 61 L3
Champions Dr EDEN TN8 206 C8
Champness Cl WNWD SE27 60 D3
Chance Cl CDW/CHF RM16 32 A6
Chancel Cl BGR/WK TN15 120 B2
Chancellor Gv DUL SE21 60 C1
Chancelot Rd ABYW SE2 28 A7
Chance Meadow RDV CT15 291 N1
Chancery La BECK BR3 61 P8
MAID/SHEP ME15 13 H5
Chancery Rd HOO/HM ME3 52 B3
Chanctonbury Cha WSTB CT5 105 H8
Chanctonbury Cl
ELTH/MOT SE9 63 M2
Chandler Av CAN/RD E16 26 B1
Chandlers Cl LEE/GVPK SE12 * 62 F1
Chandlers Dr ERITH DA8 29 J7
Chandler's Hl MEO DA13 92 D8
Chandlers Ms POP/IOD E14 25 K5
Chandler's Rd MEO DA13 92 D9
Chandler St WAP E1W 24 E4
Chandler Wy PECK SE15 40 F1
Chandos Rd RTW TN1 23 G1
Chandos Sq BRDST CT10 113 N9
Chandos Ter RAM CT11 * 17 F2
Chanlock Pth SOCK/AV RM15 31 L3
Channel Cl FOLKN CT19 311 J4
Channel Lea DEAL CT14 233 H8
Channel Rd MARG CT9 112 F7
Channel View Ct RAM CT11 * 17 J3
Channel View Rd DVW CT17 8 B7
Channon Rd NROM TN28 343 K5
Chantlers Cl EGRIN RH19 264 F6
Chantler's Hl STPH/PW TN12 242 G6
Chantlers Md EDEN TN8 267 H3
Chantrey Cl SCUP DA14 64 G4
Chantry Av HART DA3 91 H3
Chantry Cl ABYW SE2 28 B6
Chantry Ct CANT CT1 * 4 E3
Chantry La HAYES BR2 85 N2
Chantry Pk BRCH CT7 139 M2
Chantry Pl SEV TN13 148 E7
STPH/PW TN12 245 H4
Chantry Rd STPH/PW TN12 245 H4
The Chantry HDCN TN27 247 P4
Chapel Cl DART DA1 45 N6
E/WMAL ME19 122 G8
WTHK RM20 31 L9
Chapel Ct STHWK SE1 24 A5
WOOL/PLUM SE18 27 N9
Chapel Farm Rd
ELTH/MOT SE9 63 K1
Chapel Fld RYE TN31 329 P6
Chapelfield WADH TN5 315 N3
Chapel Hl DART DA1 45 N5
MARG CT9 112 F6
RDV CT15 260 D1
Chapel Hill Cl MARG CT9 112 E6
Chapel House St POP/IOD E14 25 L7
Chapel La CANTW/ST CT2 135 P6
CANTW/ST CT2 137 J6
CRBK TN17 276 E9
CRBK TN17 318 C2
DEAL CT14 232 C9
GILL ME7 126 D3
HDCN TN27 219 J7
LYDD TN29 325 P3
MAID/BEAR ME14 156 D7
RCANTE CT3 138 F1
RCANTE CT3 200 C4
RCANTW CT4 257 H4
RDV CT15 261 J2
RDV CT15 292 E1
STPH/PW TN12 246 C6
STRD ME2 123 K1

Chapel Pk SIT ME10 * ...100 B8
Chapel Pl DVW CT17 ...8 D4
RAM CT11 ...16 E4
RTW TN1 ...22 C6
Chapel Place La RAM CT11 ...16 E3
Chapel Rd BLYHN DA7 ...45 J5
DEAL CT14 ...231 H6
DVE/WH CT16 ...261 H8
HOO/HM ME3 ...56 C3
LYDD TN29 ...326 C6
OXTED RH8 ...175 M6
RAM CT11 ...16 E3
RASHW TN26 ...221 L9
RMAID ME17 ...217 H3
SNOD ME6 ...123 P5
WARL CR6 ...144 A5
WNWD SE27 ...60 B3
Chapel Rw BGR/WK TN15 ...150 E6
HOO/HM ME3 ...56 G4
Chapel St DEAL CT14 ...233 J3
E/WMAL ME19 ...122 C8
E/WMAL ME19 ...153 P6
FAV ME15 ...132 C2
HYTHE CT21 ...308 C5
IOS ME12 ...57 J5
IOS ME12 ...78 D1
The Chapel MAIDW ME16 * ...154 C9
Chapel Wd HART DA3 ...91 H6
Chapel Wood Rd HART DA3 ...91 H6
Chaplains Wk RCANTW CT4 ...195 M2
Chaplin Cl HOO/HM ME3 ...72 C4
Chaplin Dr HDCN TN27 ...247 N4
Chapman Av
MAID/SHEP ME15 ...186 B3
Chapman Flds MSTR CT12 ...142 C7
Chapman Rd BELV DA17 ...28 F8
CROY/NA CRO ...82 F5
Chapmans Cl RASHE TN25 ...192 F9
Chapman's Hl MAID DA13 ...121 P1
Chapmans Hl RCANTE CT3 ...229 L1
Chapmans La EGRIN RH19 ...264 E7
STMC/STPC BR5 ...64 D5
SWLY BR8 ...65 J5
Chapmans Pl RMAID ME17 ...218 A3
Chapmans Rd RSEV TN14 ...147 M9
Chapman Sq WCHPL E1 ...28 C5
Chapman Wy E/WMAL ME19 ...153 N4
RTWE/PEM TN2 ...240 F9
Chappell Wy SIT ME10 ...99 L8
Chapter Rd STRO ME2 ...71 P8
Chardwell Cl EHAM E6 ...26 F2
Charford Rd CDW/CHF ME16 ...26 F1
Chargrove Cl
BERM/RHTH SE16 ...24 G5
Charing Cl MSTR CT12 ...143 H4
ORP BR6 ...86 G8
Charing Crs WGOS CT8 ...111 L6
Charing Heath Rd HDCN TN27 ...220 D3
Charing Hl HDCN TN27 ...221 K1
Charing Rd RHAM ME8 ...94 D5
Chariot Wy STRO ME2 ...71 P8
Charlbury Cl MAIDW ME16 ...155 H9
Charldane Rd ELTH/MOT SE9 ...63 M2
Charlecote Av SYD SE26 ...61 N7
Charles Cl SCUP DA14 ...64 D5
SNOD ME6 ...123 P5
Charles Cobb Cl LYDD TN29 ...327 H6
Charles Cobb Gdns
CROY/NA CRO ...82 F9
Charles Coveney Rd
CMBW SE5 * ...40 F2
Charles Crs FOLKN CT19 ...310 B4
Charles Dickens Av
HOO/HM ME3 ...71 L5
Charles Dickens Ter
PGE/AN SE20 * ...61 J6
Charles Drayton Ct FAV ME13 ...133 H4
Charles Dr STRD ME2 ...94 A3
Charlesfield ELTH/MOT SE9 ...62 C2
Charles Flemwell Ms
CAN/RD E16 * ...26 D4
Charlesford Av RMAID ME17 ...187 N8
Charles Grinling Wk
WOOL/PLUM SE18 ...27 H7
Charles Haller St
BRXS/STRHM SW2 ...40 A8
Charles Rd DEAL CT14 ...232 C5
RAM CT11 ...143 K4
RSEV TN14 ...118 A4
Charles St CAN/RD E16 ...26 D4
CHAT ME4 ...6 A6
CROY/NA CRO ...83 H7
GRAVS RH17 ...32 C9
HB CT6 ...107 L1
IOS ME12 ...57 D7
MAIDW ME16 ...155 H9
RDART DA2 ...47 M6
SBGH/RUST TN4 ...240 D9
STRD ME2 ...18 C2
Charles Whincup Rd
CAN/RD E16 ...26 C4
Charlesworth Dr BRCH CT7 ...49 K6
Charleville Circ SYD SE26 ...60 C4
Charleville Rd ERITH DA8 ...45 J1
Charlock Cl MAIDW ME16 ...155 J4
Charlock Dr RIS ...78 A3
Charlotte Cl BXLYHS DA6 ...44 G6
WALD ME5 ...95 N8
Charlotte Dr RHAM ME8 ...96 F5
Charlotte Ms CANT CT1 * ...6 C6
Charlotte Pde FSTH SE23 * ...61 L1
Charlotte Pk Av BMLY BR1 ...63 J9
Charlotte Pl MARG CT9 ...15 G5
Charlotte Sq MARG CT9 ...15 H5
Charlotte St SIT ME10 ...99 H9
SIT ME10 ...99 H9
Charlton Av DVE/WH CT16 ...291 K6
Charlton Church La CHARL SE7 ...26 B5
Charlton Cl KEN/WIL TN24 ...293 K9
MSTR CT12 ...142 C2
Charlton Dene CHAT ME4 ...6 A6
Charlton Dr BH/WHM TN16 ...145 N2
Charlton Gn DVE/WH CT16 ...291 K6
Charlton La CHARL SE7 ...26 C5
MAID/SHEP ME15 ...184 C4
RMAID ME17 ...217 H3
Charlton Park La CHARL SE7 ...26 C6
Charlton Park Rd CHARL SE7 ...26 C6
Charlton Rd BKHTH/KID SE3 ...26 C9

CHARL SE7 ...26 D9
The Charltons FAV ME13 ...134 A4
Charlton St MAIDW ME16 ...185 H1
WTHK ME20 * ...31 N9
Charlton's Wy
SBGH/RUST TN4 ...270 B7
Charlton Wy BKHTH/KID SE3 ...42 D1
GNWCH SE10 ...42 C2
Charlwood CROY/NA CRO ...114 C3
Charlwoods Pl EGRIN RH19 ...265 H5
Charlwoods Rd EGRIN RH19 ...264 G6
Charminster ASH TN23 ...282 B2
Charminster Rd ELTH/MOT SE9 ...63 H3
Charmouth Rd WELL DA16 ...44 C2
Charnwood La ORP BR6 ...117 J4
The Charne RSEV TN14 ...146 D3
Charnock SWLY BR8 ...88 D1
Charnwood WSTB CT5 ...106 C5
Charnwood Gdns
POP/IOD E14 ...25 K7
Charnwood Rd HB CT6 ...107 N5
SNWD SE25 ...82 J2
Charollais Cl CANTW/ST CT2 ...166 F2
Charrington Rd CROY/NA CRO ...82 G6
Charsley Rd CAT SE6 ...61 P7
Chart Cl CROY/NA CRO ...83 P3
FAV ME13 ...132 E6
HAYES BR2 ...62 C7
Charter Dr BXLY DA5 ...44 G8
Charterhouse Dr SEV TN13 ...148 F8
Charterhouse Rd ORP BR6 ...117 H7
Charters Cl SNWD SE19 ...42 A1
Chart St CHAT ME4 ...95 L4
GILL ME7 ...73 J8
Chartham Downs Rd
RCANTW CT4 ...196 D4
Chartham Rd SNWD SE25 ...60 A2
Chartham Ter RAM CT11 ...16 D6
Chart Hills Cl THMD SE28 ...28 D2
Chart La BH/WHM TN16 ...177 K1
Charton Cl BELV DA17 ...28 E9
Chart Pl RHAM ME8 ...126 F2
Chart Rd ASH TN23 ...252 A8
FOLKN CT19 ...310 C5
RMAID ME17 ...216 F3
Chart Vw BGR/WK TN15 ...149 M2
Chartway SEV TN13 ...21 C2
Chartway St RMAID ME17 ...217 J1
Chartwell Av HB CT6 ...106 A8
Chartwell Cl CROY/NA CRO ...63 D1
ELTH/MOT SE9 ...63 J1
STRD ME2 ...72 B6
Chartwell Ct CHAT ME4 ...6 A6
Chartwell Dr MAIDW ME16 ...154 C8
ORP BR6 ...86 E9
Chartwell Gv SIT ME10 ...129 K2
Chartwell Wy PGE/AN SE20 ...61 H2
Charwood STRHM/NOR SW16 ...60 A3
Chaseley Sq POP/IOD E14 * ...25 H2
Chasemore Gdns
CROY/NA CRO ...82 F9
Chase Sq GVW DA11 * ...49 M7
The Chase BGR/WK TN15 ...149 K1
BMLY BR1 ...63 J4
BXLYHN DA7 ...45 K4
CHAT ME4 ...95 J4
ORP BR6 ...117 H5
RAM CT11 * ...16 A3
RHAM ME8 ...96 D4
TONN TN10 ...210 F5
WLGTN SM6 ...82 D9
RAM CT11 ...31 N9
Chastilian Rd DART DA1 ...46 A8
Chater Cl ASH TN23 ...251 P9
DEAL CT14 ...233 H5
Chatfield Rd CROY/NA CRO ...82 G5
Chatfield Wy E/WMAL ME19 ...154 A3
Chatham Av HAYES BR2 ...83 J4
Chatham Gv CHAT ME4 ...95 L5
Chatham Hl WALD ME5 ...7 F6
Chatham Hill Rd RSEV TN14 ...146 D5
Chatham Market CHAT ME4 * ...6 D5
Chatham Pl RAM CT11 ...17 F2
Chatham Rd DIT/AY ME20 ...125 J1
MAID/BEAR ME14 ...155 K1
WALD ME5 ...125 J4
Chatham St RAM CT11 ...16 E2
WALW SE17 ...24 A7
WOOL/PLUM SE18 ...27 J8
Chatsworth Av BFN/LL DA15 ...44 C9
MAID/BEAR ME14 ...155 N5
WWKM BR4 ...85 J6
Chatsworth Dr SIT ME10 ...99 J9
STRD ME2 ...72 A6
Chatsworth Ms RAM CT11 ...16 C4
Chatsworth Rd CROY/NA CRO ...83 J8
DART DA1 ...45 M5
GILL ME7 ...73 J9
Chatsworth Wy WNWD SE27 ...60 B8
Chattenden Cl
MAID/BEAR ME14 ...155 N5
Chattenden La HOO/HM ME3 ...72 F3
Chatterton Rd HAYES BR2 ...85 N2
Chaucer Av EGRIN RH19 ...264 F8
Chaucer Cl CANT CT1 ...106 A5
STRD ME2 ...19 K1
TIL RM18 ...49 N3
Chaucer Crs DVE/WH CT16 ...291 J4
Chaucer Dr STHWK SE1 ...24 C8
Chaucer Gdns TON TN9 ...240 C2
Chaucer Ms CANTW/ST CT2 ...165 N5
Chaucer Pk DART DA1 ...46 F8
Chaucer Rd BFN/LL DA15 ...44 E9
BRDST CT10 ...143 M1
CANT CT1 ...5 L2
GILL ME7 ...73 J9
CROY/NA CRO ...83 H7
HNHL SE24 ...40 A6
RDV CT15 ...230 C8
SIT ME10 ...129 L2
WELL DA16 ...44 B2
Chaucer Rbt CANT CT1 ...5 J6
Chaucer Wy DART DA1 ...46 G5
DIT/AY ME20 ...125 N9
Chaundrye Cl CAN/RD E16 ...26 C2
Chauntler Rd CAN/RD E16 ...26 D4

Chave Rd RDART DA2 ...66 E2
Cheam St PECK SE15 * ...41 H4
Cheesemans HDCN TN27 ...220 C3
Cheesmans Cl MSTR CT12 ...141 K7
Chegwell Rd WALD ME5 ...125 N1
Chegworth Gdns SIT ME10 ...129 M4
Chegworth La RMAID ME17 ...188 A5
Chegworth Rd RMAID ME17 ...188 A1
Cheldoc Ri CHAT ME4 ...75 J5
Chelford Rd BMLY BR1 ...62 B4
Chellows La LING RH7 ...264 G6
Chelmer Dr SOCK/AV RM15 ...31 M3
Chelmer Rd CDW/CHF RM16 ...33 H8
Chelmsford Cl EHAM E6 ...26 C2
Chelmsford Rd STRD ME2 ...71 M9
Chelsea Rd DEAL CT14 ...137 H9
Chelsfield Gdns SYD SE26 ...61 J2
Chelsfield Hl ORP BR6 ...117 K3
Chelsfield La ORP BR6 ...87 L8
STMC/STPC BR5 ...87 J4
Chelsfield Rd STMC/STPC BR5 ...87 K3
Chelsham Common Rd
WARL CR6 ...144 D2
Chelsham Court Rd
WARL CR6 ...144 G3
Chelsworth Dr
WOOL/PLUM SE18 ...27 L9
Cheltenham Cl GVE DA12 ...69 H4
MAID/SHEP ME15 * ...186 C5
PECK SE15 ...41 J5
Cheney Cl RHAM ME8 ...96 C9
Cheney Hl RSIT ME9 ...129 P8
Cheney Rd FAV ME13 ...133 J6
Chenies Cl RTWE/PEM TN2 ...270 C8
The Chenies ORP BR6 ...86 F5
RDART DA2 ...66 E2
Chennell Park Rd TENT TN30 ...300 F5
Chepstow Ri CROY/NA CRO ...83 K7
Chepstow Rd CROY/NA CRO ...83 K7
Chequer Rd EGRIN RH19 ...265 J7
Chequers Cl MEO DA13 ...85 L5
Chequers Ct STRD ME2 ...72 A6
Chequers Orch RASHE TN25 ...223 P9
Chequers Rd IOS ME12 ...78 D2
Cherbourg Crs WALD ME5 ...95 L7
Cherbury Cl THMD SE28 ...28 C2
Cheriton Av HAYES BR2 ...85 J2
MSTR CT12 ...142 C4
Cheriton Court Rd FOLK CT20 ...309 H1
Cheriton Dr WOOL/PLUM SE18 ...43 P1
Cheriton Gdns FOLK CT20 ...10 D4
Cheriton High St RFOLK CT18 ...309 H1
Cheriton Pl FOLK CT19 ...309 H1
Cheriton Rd DEAL CT14 ...233 J5
FOLK CT20 ...10 E5
FOLKN CT19 ...310 C5
RHAM ME8 ...96 C7
Cheriton Wy MAIDW ME16 ...155 H5
The Cherries MAIDW ME16 ...184 E1
Cherry Amber Cl RHAM ME8 ...97 J6
Cherry Av CANTW/ST CT2 ...166 C2
SWLY BR8 ...65 M9
Cherrybrook Rd FOLK CT20 ...310 A8
Cherry Cl BRXS/STRHM SW2 * ...40 A8
MAID/BEAR ME14 ...189 K6
RCANTE CT3 ...99 L8
SIT ME10 ...99 L8
Cherrycot Ri ORP BR6 ...86 D8
Cherrydown CDW/CHF ME16 ...33 P6
Cherrydown Rd SCUP DA14 ...64 F1
Cherry Dr CANTW/ST CT2 ...166 C2
Cherry Flds SIT ME10 ...99 L8
Cherry Garden Av FOLKN CT19 ...310 D5
Cherry Garden Crs
RASHE TN25 ...224 A8
Cherrygarden La RCANTE CT3 ...199 P7
Cherry Garden La
FOLKN CT19 ...310 C4
RASHE TN25 ...224 A8
RCANTE CT3 ...200 F1
Cherry Garden Rd
CANTW/ST CT2 ...166 C2
Cherry Gdns ASH TN23 ...282 D3
BRDST CT10 ...143 H1
HB CT6 ...107 K3
NROM TN28 ...313 K6
RCANTW CT4 ...257 L4
Cherry Garden St
BERM/RHTH SE16 ...24 C5
Cherry Glebe RASHE TN25 ...283 E5
Cherry Gv RDV CT15 ...230 D7
TONN TN10 ...211 H5
Cherry Hill Ct RSIT ME9 ...98 B8
Cherry Hill Gdns CROY/NA CRO ...82 D2
Cherry La DEAL CT14 ...232 C6
Cherry Orch CHARL SE7 ...26 D9
RASHW TN26 ...302 F4
RCANTE CT3 ...233 H7
RCANTW CT4 ...194 D1
TENT TN30 ...301 H9
WSTB CT5 ...106 B6
Cherry Orchard Cl
STMC/STPC BR5 ...87 K2
Cherry Orchard Gdns
CROY/NA CRO ...83 J5
Cherry Orchard La
RASHE TN25 ...305 P5
Cherry Orchard Rd
CROY/NA CRO ...83 J5
HAYES BR2 ...85 P6
The Cherry Orch RTON TN5 ...211 P1
Cherry Orchard Wy
MAIDW ME16 ...154 G9
Cherry Rd HOO/HM ME3 ...73 H4
Cherry Tree Av DVE/WH CT16 ...291 H6
Cherry Tree Cl RSIT ME9 ...131 J5
Cherry Tree Ct CHARL SE7 * ...26 D9
Cherry Tree Gdns MSTR CT12 ...142 G1
Cherry Tree Gv BGR/WK TN15 ...119 N4

Cherry Tree La RDART DA2 ...65 P2
Cherry Tree Rd HDCN TN27 ...220 D3
RHAM ME8 ...97 J6
RTWE/PEM TN2 ...270 C8
TONN TN10 ...210 G5
Cherry Trees HART DA3 ...91 H6
Cherry Tree Ter STHWK SE1 * ...24 B5
Cherry Vw BGR/WK TN15 ...149 K5
Cherry Wk CDW/CHF ME16 ...33 H6
HAYES BR2 ...85 K5
Cherry Waye RDV CT15 ...260 D3
Cherrywood Av GVW DA11 ...69 H3
Cherrywood Ri RASHE TN25 ...292 C5
Chertsey Crs CROY/NA CRO ...114 F4
Cherville La RCANTE CT3 ...168 F9
Chervilles MAIDW ME16 ...184 E1
Cherwell Ms THMD SE28 ...28 A4
Cherwell Cl STMC/STPC BR5 ...87 L1
Cheseman St SYD SE26 ...61 K2
Chesfield Cl RTON TN11 ...212 A2
Chesham Av STMC/STPC BR5 ...86 F1
Chesham Crs PGE/AN SE20 ...61 J7
Chesham Dr RHAM ME8 ...97 H8
Chesham Rd PGE/AN SE20 ...61 J8
WARL CR6 ...144 D2
Cheshire Rd
MAID/SHEP ME15 ...186 B5
Cheshunt Cl MEO DA13 ...92 B3
Chesley Cr CROY/NA CRO ...114 F2
Chessel Cl THHTH CR7 ...82 C1
Chessenden La HDCN TN27 ...249 H8
Chessington Av BXLYHN DA7 ...45 H6
Chessington Wy WWKM BR4 ...84 G6
Chester Av RASHW TN26 ...280 C3
Chester Cl CDW/CHF RM16 ...31 P6
STRD ME2 ...71 M9
Chesterfield Cl
STMC/STPC BR5 ...87 L1
Chesterfield Dr DART DA1 ...46 B3
SEV TN13 ...148 C7
Chesterfield Gdns
GNWCH SE10 ...42 B1
Chesterfield Gv EDUL SE22 ...40 F6
Chesterfield Wy PECK SE15 ...41 J1
Chester Rd BFN/LL DA15 ...45 M4
GILL ME7 ...36 A5
WGOS CT8 ...111 N5
Chesterton Cl EGRIN RH19 ...265 J9
Chesterton Rd DIT/AY ME20 ...123 N9
HOO/HM ME3 ...56 C3
Chesterton Wy SIT ME10 ...129 K3
Chestfield Cl RHAM ME8 ...97 H4
Chestfield Rd WSTB CT5 ...106 D6
Chestnut Av CANTW/ST CT2 ...135 P7
CDW/CHF ME4 ...32 C5
RDART DA2 ...47 M5
SBGH/RUST TN4 ...240 D9
STPH/PEW TN2 ...246 B5
WALD ME5 ...125 K2
WWKM BR4 ...85 J9
Chestnut Cl ASH TN23 ...252 B6
BFN/LL DA15 ...64 C1
CAT SE6 ...62 A3
CRBK TN17 ...277 H2
DVE/WH CT16 ...261 H4
E/WMAL ME19 ...153 H9
EDEN TN8 ...206 C8
EGRIN RH19 ...265 K7
ORP BR6 ...87 H9
RMAID ME17 ...195 N2
RMAID ME17 ...184 E9
STRHM/NOR SW16 ...60 A3
TENT TN30 ...301 K6
Chestnut Copse OXTED TN8 ...184 A1
Chestnut Ct DEAL CT14 ...164 A1
RTWE/PEM TN2 ...270 D8
Chestnut Dr BRDST CT10 ...113 J9
BXLYHN DA7 ...44 F4
CANTW/ST CT2 ...137 M7
DEAL CT14 ...107 J4
HB CT6 ...107 J4
RMAID ME17 ...184 D4
RMAID ME17 ...187 N9
Chestnut Gv MTCM CR4 ...82 C2
MEO DA13 ...92 B3
Chestnut La ASH TN23 ...282 F4
MEO DA13 ...122 C6
STPH/PEW TN2 ...242 E8
Chestnut Ri WOOL/PLUM SE18 ...27 M8
Chestnut Rd DART DA1 ...46 D9
DVW CT17 ...291 J8
STRD ME2 ...71 P8
WNWD SE27 ...60 B2
Chestnuts RASHE TN25 ...284 E5
The Chestnuts BECK BR3 * ...61 K9
E/WMAL ME19 ...153 H9
HAWK TN18 ...316 C6
RASHE TN25 ...284 E5
Chestnut St HYTHE CT21 ...128 F1
Chestnut Vw RSIT ME9 ...99 H2
Chettle Cl STHWK SE1 ...24 A8
Chevalier Rd DVW CT17 ...291 H8
Cheval St POP/IOD E14 ...25 K6
Cheveney Wk HAYES BR2 ...62 E9
Chevening La RSEV TN14 ...147 M1
Chevening Rd GNWCH SE10 ...26 F9
NRWD SE19 ...60 E8
The Chevenings SCUP DA14 ...64 D2
Cheviot Cl BXLYHS DA6 ...45 N2
TON TN9 ...210 F6

Cheviot Ct BRDST CT10 ...113 N8
Cheviot Gdns
MAID/SHEP ME15 ...186 D3
Cheviot Rd WNWD SE27 ...60 A4
Cheviot Wk KEN/WIL TN24 ...252 F5
Chevron Cl CAN/RD E16 ...26 E2
Chevy Rd ...
Cheyne Cl HAYES BR2 ...85 P7
Cheyne Rd IOS ME12 ...57 J5
Cheyne Wk CROY/NA CRO ...83 M6
MEO DA13 ...92 B6
Chicago Av GILL ME7 ...96 B1
Chichele Gdns CROY/NA CRO ...83 M6
Chichele Rd OXTED RH8 ...175 N4
Chichester Cl ASH TN23 ...282 F4
BKHTH/KID SE3 ...42 C1
CDW/CHF RM16 ...31 N7
EHAM E6 ...26 F2
RHAM ME8 ...97 K6
SOCK/AV RM15 ...30 F4
Chichester Dr SEV TN13 ...20 B4
Chichester Ri GVE DA12 ...69 K4
Chichester Rd CROY/NA CRO ...83 K7
FOLK CT20 ...310 B7
MSTR CT12 ...142 G3
RDART DA2 ...67 K6
TON TN9 ...240 D1
Chichester Whf ERITH DA8 ...29 K8

Chickenden La
Chickfield Gdns WALD ME5 ...95 P4
Chicksand St WCHPL E1 ...24 C1
Chicks La CRBK TN17 ...295 P5
Chiddingfold Cl IOS ME12 ...57 L2
Chiddingstone Av BXLYHN DA7 ...45 H1
Chiddingstone Cl
MAID/SHEP ME15 ...186 C5
Chidley Cross Rd
STPH/PEW TN2 ...212 F4
Chieftain Cl RHAM ME8 ...96 E5
Chieftain Dr PUR RH19 ...30 D7
Chieveley Dr RTWE/PEM TN2 ...270 F7
Chieveley Pde BXLYHN DA7 ...45 K4
Chieveley Rd BXLYHN DA7 ...45 K4
Chiffinch Gdns CROY/NA CRO ...69 J2
Chigwell Hl WAP E1W ...24 E3
Chilberic Rd NWCR SE14 ...41 L4
Childers St DEPT SE8 ...25 H9
Childgate Rd WSTB CT5 ...134 G2
Child La GNWCH SE10 ...26 A6
Childsbridge La
BGR/WK TN15 ...149 K3
Childsbridge Wy
BGR/WK TN15 ...149 L3
Childs Crs SWCM DA10 ...48 B7
Childscroft Rd RHAM ME8 ...97 J4
Childs La NRWD SE19 * ...60 E5
Childs Wy BGR/WK TN15 ...151 J1
Chilham Av WGOS CT8 ...111 L6
Chilham Cl BXLY DA5 ...45 H8
CHAT ME4 ...6 A6
IOS ME12 ...57 L2
Chilham Rd ELTH/MOT SE9 ...63 J3
FOLKN CT19 ...310 A5
RHAM ME8 ...96 D5
Chilham Wy HAYES BR2 ...85 K4
Chillington St
MAID/BEAR ME14 ...155 L6
Chillwack Rd HOO/HM ME3 ...72 F2
Chilston Cl SBGH/RUST TN4 ...270 D3
Chilston Rd RMAID ME17 ...189 L6
SBGH/RUST TN4 ...270 D3
Chiltenhurst EDEN TN8 ...206 B8
CROY/NA CRO ...83 K7
MAID/SHEP ME15 ...186 C2
Chiltern End KEN/WIL TN24 ...2 C1
Chiltern Gdns HAYES BR2 ...85 J1
Chiltern Rd GVW DA11 ...211 J5
Chiltern Wy TON TN9 ...23 J2
Chiltern Wy TON TN9 ...210 F6
Chilthorne Cl CAT SE6 ...61 M1
Chilton Av DVE/WH CT16 ...290 D4
SIT ME10 ...99 H5
Chilton Ct RHAM ME8 ...97 H5
Chilton Dr HOO/HM ME3 ...71 K4
Chilton Fld RCANTE CT3 ...170 E9
Chilton Gdns RCANTE CT3 ...170 E9
Chilton Gv DEPT SE8 ...25 M5
Chilton La RAM CT11 ...142 F6
Chilton Pl RCANTE CT3 ...170 E9
Chilton Rd CDW/CHF RM16 ...33 H6
Chilton Sq RCANTE CT3 ...200 E1
Chilton Wy CHAT ME4 ...39 H4
Chilver St GNWCH SE10 ...26 A8
The Chimes KEN/WIL TN24 ...2 D1
China Hall Ms BERM/RHTH SE16 ...25 H8
Chinbrook Crs LEE/GVPK SE12 ...62 F2
Chinbrook Rd LEE/GVPK SE12 ...62 F2
Chineham Wy CANT CT1 ...166 E6
Chingley Cl BMLY BR1 ...62 C5
Chipka St POP/IOD E14 ...25 L6
Chipley St NWCR SE14 ...41 L4
Chipman's Wy MSTR CT12 ...140 F5
Chippendale Cl WALD ME5 ...125 L4
Chippendale Dr
RMAID ME17 ...188 E5
Chipperfield Rd
STMC/STPC BR5 ...64 C3
Chipstead Av THHTH CR7 ...82 C1
Chipstead Cl MAIDW ME16 ...155 J7
NRWD SE19 ...60 G6
Chipstead La SEV TN13 ...148 C7
Chipstead Pk SEV TN13 ...148 D5
Chipstead Park Cl SEV TN13 ...148 C5
Chipstead Place Gdns
SEV TN13 ...148 B7
Chipstead Rd ERITH DA8 ...45 N1
RHAM ME8 ...126 C1
Chipstead Sq CROY/NA CRO ...83 K6
Chislehurst Cl

Cliff View Rd MSTR CT12 .... 142 C6
Cliff Wk CAN/RD E16 .... 26 A1
Clifton Cl MAID/BEAR ME14 ...... 13 J2
ORP BR6 .... 86 D9
STRD ME2 .... 9 D9
Clifton Cots RTWE/PEM TN2 * .. 240 C9
Clifton Ct BECK BR3 * 61 P7
Clifton Crs FOLK CT20 .... 10 B7
PECK SE15 .... 41 H1
Clifton Gdns CANTW/ST CT2 ..... 4 A1
FOLK CT20 .... 10 D6
Clifton Gr GVW DA11 .... 49 M8
Clifton Lawn RAM CT11 * 16 E6
Clifton Marine Pde GVW DA11 ... 49 K7
Clifton Ms WSTB CT5 .... 83 K1
Clifton Pl BERM/RHTH SE16 ...... 24 F5
MARG CT9 .... 15 J3
RTW TN1 .... 22 E6
Clifton Ri NWCR SE14 .... 41 L1
Clifton Rd CAN/RD E16 .... 25 P7
FOLK CT20 .... 10 C6
GILL ME7 .... 73 J8
GVW DA11 .... 49 L7
MARG CT9 .... 15 J3
RAM CT11 .... 16 E6
RTWE/PEM TN2 .... 270 F1
SCUP DA14 .... 64 A3
SNWD SE25 .... 83 K1
WELL DA16 .... 44 E4
WLGTN SM6 .... 62 A9
WSTB CT5 .... 105 L6
Clifton St MARG CT9 .... 15 J3
SDTCH EC2A 24 J1
Cliftonville Av MARG CT9 .... 112 F5
MSTR CT12 .... 142 C5
Clifton Wy PECK SE15 .... 41 L1
Clinch St HOO/HM ME3 .... 53 M3
Clink St STHWK SE1 .... 24 H1
Clinton Av STRD ME2 .... 71 M7
WELL DA16 .... 44 C5
Clinton Cl RMAID ME17 .... 184 G8
Clinton La LEDEN TN8 .... 207 L7
Clinton Ter DEPT SE8 * 25 K9
Clints La RCANTW CT4 .... 228 F9
Clipper Bvd RDART DA2 .... 47 L6
Clipper Bvd West RDART DA2 .... 47 L6
Clipper Cl BERM/RHTH SE16 .... 24 G5
STRD ME2 .... 72 E8
Clipper Ct STRD ME2 * 72 E8
Clipper Crs GVE DA12 .... 70 B3
Clipper Wy LEW SE13 .... 42 A5
Clive Av DART DA1 .... 45 P7
Cliveden Cl MAIDW ME16 .... 155 J5
Clive Dennis Ct KEN/WIL TN24 .. 3 K5
Clive Rd BELV DA17 .... 28 F7
DUL SE21 .... 60 D2
GVW DA11 .... 49 M7
MARG CT9 .... 112 F8
MSTR CT12 .... 142 C6
ROCH ME1 .... 95 H5
SIT ME10 .... 39 M3
Clivers Cots RRTW TN3 * 240 A8
Clockhouse RTWE/PEM TN2 ... 271 J2
Clockhouse La CDW/CHF RM16 . 31 P6
Clockhouse Pk RASHE TN25 .... 192 E9
Clock House Rd BECK BR3 .... 61 L9
Clock Tower Ms THMD SE28 ..... 28 F1
Cloister Gdns SNWD SE25 .... 83 N3
Cloisterham Rd ROCH ME1 ...... 95 J7
Cloisters SIT ME10 * 129 M1
Cloisters Av HAYES BR2 .... 86 A2
The Cloisters RAM CT11 .... 16 D6
Cloonmore Av ORP BR6 .... 86 C6
The Close ASH TN23 .... 282 B1
BECK BR3 * 86 B1
BGR/WK TN15 .... 150 C6
BH/WHM TN16 * 146 C1
BXLY DA5 .... 45 J7
CANTW/ST CT2 .... 136 C5
CDW/CHF RM16 .... 32 C5
E/WMAL ME19 .... 123 J8
EDEN TN8 .... 207 P8
ERITH RH19 .... 264 G8
FAV ME13 .... 133 F7
FOLKN CT19 .... 311 H3
HART DA3 .... 57 P8
HYTHE CT21 .... 308 G3
RASHE TN25 .... 223 P9
RCANTW CT4 * 64 C2
RDART DA2 .... 66 C2
RDV CT15 .... 260 A8
ROCH ME1 .... 19 F7
RYE TN31 .... 338 D6
SCUP DA14 .... 64 D4
SEV TN13 .... 148 D9
SNWD SE25 .... 83 M3
STMC/STPC BR5 .... 86 F3
Cloth Hall Gdns HDCN TN27 ... 178 C8
Clothier St HDTCH EC3A 24 J2
Clothworkers Rd
  WOOL/PLUM SE18 .... 43 N1
Cloudberry Cl MAIDW ME16 .... 12 A1
Cloudesley Cl ROCH ME1 .... 54 F8
Cloudesley Rd BXLYHN DA7 ..... 45 H2
ERITH DA8 .... 45 J3
Clouston Cl FOLK CT18 .... 288 E7
WLGTN SM6 .... 62 B9
Clove Crs POP/IOD E14 .... 25 M3
Clovelly Dr IOS ME12 .... 58 B8
Clovelly Rd BXLYHN DA7 .... 28 D9
WSTB CT5 .... 105 L7
Clovelly Wy ORP BR6 .... 86 G5
WCHPL E1 .... 24 F2
Clover Bank Vw WALD ME5 ..... 95 N8
Cloverdale Gdns BFN/LL DA15 .. 44 F8
Clover Ct HAYES BR2 * 97 L4
Clover Ri WSTB CT5 .... 106 A8
Clover Rd HOO/HM ME3 .... 75 L4
The Clovers GVW DA11 .... 69 J3
Clover St CHAT ME4 .... 6 C4
Clover Ter MAID/SHEP ME15 * . 186 A3
Clover Wy STPH/PW TN12 ..... 243 H4
WLGTN SM6 .... 62 B9
Clowders Rd CAT SE6 .... 61 L4
Cloysters Gn WAP E1W * 24 E4
Club's La LYDD TN29 .... 334 E6
Club Gardens Rd HAYES BR2 .... 85 K4

Cluny Est STHWK SE1 .... 24 B6
Cluny Pl STHWK SE1 .... 24 B6
Cluny Rd FAV ME13 .... 133 J6
Clutton St POP/IOD E14 .... 25 L1
Clyde Ter RM18 .... 34 B7
Clyde Rd CROY/NA CR0 .... 83 L6
TONN TN10 .... 210 F5
WLGTN SM6 .... 82 B9
Clyde St CANT CT1 * 5 G2
DEPT SE8 .... 25 J9
IOS ME12 .... 57 M4
Clyde V FSTH SE23 .... 61 J1
Clyde V FSTH SE23 .... 61 J1
Clydon Cl ERITH DA8 .... 45 J1
Clynton Wy ASH TN23 .... 282 D1
Coach Dr MARSH TN26 .... 251 M2
The Coach Dr MEO DA13 .... 121 P6
Coach & Horses Pas
  RTWE/PEM TN2 * 22 C7
Coach House Ms FSTH SE23 * ... 61 J1
Coach Rd BGR/WK TN15 .... 150 D9
HDCN TN27 .... 178 H4
RFOLK CT18 .... 288 C4
SBGH/RUST TN4 .... 269 P5
The Coachyard MAIDW ME16 .. 154 C9
Coalpit La RSIT ME9 * 159 P6
Coal Post Cl ORP BR6 * 116 G2
Coast Dr LYDD TN29 .... 337 L3
LYDD TN29 .... 343 L9
NROM TN28 .... 343 K1
Coastguard Cots BRCH CT7 * .. 110 E5
HYTHE CT21 * 308 G6
Coastguard Sq RYE TN31 ...... 339 K9
Coast Rd NROM TN28 .... 337 L5
Coates CI THMTH CR7 .... 60 C9
Coates Hill Rd BMLY BR1 * 63 J1
Coats Av IOS ME12 .... 57 J8
Cobalt Cl BECK BR3 .... 86 A1
Cobay Cl HYTHE CT21 .... 309 J5
Cobb Cl STRD ME2 .... 71 M7
Cobbets Wy EDEN TN8 .... 236 D1
Cobbett Cl E/WMAL ME19 ...... 153 N4
Cobbett Rd ELTH/MOT SE9 ...... 43 J4
Cobbett's Ride
  RTWE/PEM TN2 * 270 C7
Cobblers Bridge Rd HB CT6 .... 107 J2
Cobblestone Pl CROY/NA CR0 .. 85 H9
Cobblestones GILL ME7 .... 96 C9
Cobbs Cl STPH/PW TN12 .... 242 G5
WBY/WAL ME18 .... 183 M4
Cobbs Hl RCANTW CT4 .... 194 D1
Cobbs Ms FOLK CT20 .... 10 D5
Cobbs Pl MARG CT9 .... 15 G5
Cobb St WCHPL E1 .... 24 J2
Cobden Ms SYD SE26 .... 61 H4
Cobden Pl CANT CT1 * 5 F3
Cobden Rd CHAT ME4 .... 95 N4
FOLKN CT19 .... 308 G6
ORP BR6 .... 86 D8
SEV TN13 .... 149 H8
SNWD SE25 .... 83 M2
Cobdown Cl DIT/AY ME20 ...... 154 A2
Cobdown Gv RHAM ME8 .... 97 K4
Cob Dr GVE DA12 .... 70 G4
Cobfield RMAID ME17 .... 216 D1
Cobham Cl BFN/LL DA15 .... 64 C2
Cobham Av RSIT ME9 * 159 N3
Cobhamhurst Rd GVE DA12 ...... 93 H1
Cobham Cha HAY ME13 .... 132 E5
Cobham Cl BFN/LL DA15 .... 44 D7
  CANT CT1 .... 167 H6
  HAYES BR2 * 86 A2
  LING RH7 .... 234 F5
  MAIDW ME16 .... 12 B4
  STRD ME2 .... 71 N8
  SWCM DA10 .... 47 P7
Cobham Dr E/WMAL ME19 ..... 153 K9
Cobham Pl BXLYHS DA6 .... 44 G6
Cobham Ri GILL ME7 .... 96 B1
Cobhams RRTW TN3 .... 239 M9
Cobham St GVW DA11 .... 49 L9
Cobham Ter GVW DA11 .... 49 K9
  SWCM DA10 * 47 P6
Cobland Rd LEE/GVPK SE12 .... 62 C5
Cobourg Rd CMBW SE5 .... 25 L8
Cobs Cl BGR/WK TN15 .... 150 F6
Cobsden Cl LYDD TN29 .... 337 M1
Cobsdene GVE DA12 .... 69 P5
Cobsden Rd LYDD TN29 .... 337 L1
Cobtree Cl WALD ME5 .... 95 P6
Cobtree Rd RMAID ME17 .... 197 N2
Coburg Dwellings WCHPL E1 * .. 24 F3
Cockerhurst Rd RSEV TN14 .... 118 C3
Cockering Rd CANT CT1 .... 166 B7
  RCANTW CT4 .... 195 L2
Cock La RASHW TN26 .... 304 D8
  RCANTW CT4 .... 257 L5
Cockmannings La
  STMC/STPC BR5 .... 87 L5
Cockmannings Rd
  STMC/STPC BR5 .... 87 L4
Cockreed La NROM TN28 .... 336 G6
Cocksett Av ORP BR6 .... 116 F1
Cocksure La SCUP DA14 .... 65 J3
Codling Cl WAP E1W * 24 F5
Codrington Crs GVE DA12 .... 69 N4
Codrington Gdns GVE DA12 ..... 69 N4
Codrington Rd RAM CT11 .... 16 D4
Coe Av SNWD SE25 .... 83 M3
Coe's Gn HOO/HM ME3 .... 72 C3
Coffey St DEPT SE8 .... 41 N1
Cogans Ter CANT CT1 .... 166 D6
Cogate Rd STPH/PW TN12 ..... 242 F5
Coinston Av RAM CT11 .... 142 F5
Cokers La DUL SE21 .... 60 C9
Coke St WCHPL E1 .... 24 D2
Colburn Rd BRDST CT10 .... 143 M5
Colby Rd NRWD SE19 .... 60 E4
Colchester Cl CHAT ME4 .... 95 L7
Colchester St WCHPL E1 .... 24 C2
Cold Arbor Rd SEV TN13 .... 148 C9
Coldbath St LEW SE13 .... 41 P2
Coldblow DEAL CT14 .... 262 C1
Cold Blow Crs BXLY DA5 .... 45 M9
Coldblow La
  MAID/BEAR ME14 .... 157 K3
Cold Blow La NWCR SE14 .... 41 K1
Coldbridge La HDCN TN27 ...... 219 H5
  RMAID ME17 .... 218 E6

Cold Harbour CANT CT1 .... 5 G1
Coldharbour POP/IOD E14 .... 25 M4
Coldharbour Crest
  ELTH/MOT SE9 * 63 L2
Coldharbour La RSIT ME9 .... 98 G8
Coldharbour La BRXN/ST SW9 . 40 A5
  DIT/AY ME20 .... 154 F3
  LYDD TN29 .... 335 K8
  MAID/BEAR ME14 .... 157 L3
  RAIN RM15 .... 28 M7
  RASHE TN25 .... 254 G2
  RTON TN11 .... 210 B4
  RYE TN31 .... 339 J6
  SIT ME10 .... 99 N5
Coldharbour Pl CMBW SE5 .... 40 C5
Cold Harbour Rd FAV ME13 ..... 190 F4
  RMAID ME17 .... 190 E6
Coldharbour Rd CRBK TN17 ... 318 A1
  CROY/NA CR0 .... 82 F9
  EDEN TN8 .... 238 C9
  GVW DA11 .... 69 J1
Coldharbour Wy
  CROY/NA CR0 .... 82 F9
Coldred Hl RDV CT15 .... 206 B8
Coldred Rd MAID/SHEP ME15 . 186 C7
  RDV CT15 .... 206 C8
Coldrum La E/WMAL ME19 ..... 122 D8
Coldshott OXTED RH8 .... 175 K9
Coldswood Rd HART DA3 .... 142 G2
Cole Av CDW/CHF RM16 .... 33 K2
Colebrook Rd HAYES BR2 .... 62 G8
Colebrook St
  SBGH/RUST TN4 .... 270 F1
Colebrook St ERITH DA8 * 45 L9
Coleby Pth CMBW SE5 * 40 D3
Coledale Dr STAN HA7 .... 28 A4
Colegate Dr
  MAID/BEAR ME14 .... 156 F8
Colegates Cl FAV ME13 .... 132 D3
Colegates Ct FAV ME13 .... 132 E3
Colegates Rd FAV ME13 .... 132 D3
Colegrove Rd PECK SE15 .... 25 K8
Coleman Cl SNWD SE25 .... 83 N1
Coleman Crs SIT ME10 .... 143 H5
Coleman Dr MSTR CT12 .... 143 M3
Coleman Rd BELV DA17 .... 28 G3
  CMBW SE5 .... 40 E1
Colemans Cl LYDD TN29 .... 342 C6
Colemans Heath
  ELTH/MOT SE9 .... 63 L2
Coleman's Stable Rd
  BRCH CT7 .... 111 H5
Coleman St LOTH EC2R 24 H1
Colenso Rd CROY/NA CR0 .... 83 N1
Colemso Wy STPH/PW TN12 * . 245 H3
Colepits Wood Rd
  ELTH/MOT SE9 .... 43 P6
Coleraine Rd BKHTH/KID SE3 .. 26 A9
  CROY/NA CR0 .... 123 P9
Coleridge Gdns RCANTE CT3 ... 199 H3
Coleridge Rd CROY/NA CR0 ...... 83 P1
  DART DA1 .... 46 C3
  TIL RM18 .... 49 N5
Coleridge Wy ORP BR6 .... 87 H1
Cole Rd FAV ME13 .... 133 H6
Colesburg Rd BECK BR3 .... 61 M9
Coleshall Cl MAID/SHEP ME15 . 186 C5
Coles La BH/WHM TN16 .... 147 K8
Cole Ter RMAID ME17 * 216 B8
Colets Orch RSEV TN14 .... 148 C1
Colette Cl BRDST CT10 .... 113 M3
Coleville Crs NROM TN28 .... 343 K5
Colewood Dr STRD ME2 .... 71 K7
Coleworth Rd EDUL SE22 .... 60 D1
Coley Cl ELTH/MOT SE9 .... 63 M1
Coley Rd GVW DA11 .... 69 H1
Colyers Cl ERITH DA8 .... 45 L2
Colyers La ERITH DA8 .... 45 L3
Colyton Cl WALL SM6 .... 62 G4
Colyton La STRHM/NOR SW16 . 60 A3
Colyton Rd EDUL SE22 .... 60 E1
Combe Av BKHTH/KID SE3 ...... 42 D1
Combe Bank Dr RSEV TN14 .... 147 M8
Combedale Rd GNWCH SE10 .... 26 B8
Combermere Cl WALL SM6 .... 62 C4
Combeside WOOL/PLUM SE18 . 43 P2
Combwell Crs ABYW SE2 .... 28 F1
Comerford Rd BROCKY SE4 ...... 41 M5
Comet Cl PUR RM19 .... 30 D7
Comet Pl DEPT SE8 .... 41 N1
Comet St DEPT SE8 .... 41 N1
Comforts Farm Av
  OXTED RH8 .... 175 J9
Comfrey Ct GRAYS RM17 .... 32 E9
Commerce Rd CROY/NA CR0 ... 82 G1
  EDEN TN8 .... 206 D7
Commercial Rd DIT/AY ME20 ... 154 D2
Commercial Quay DVW CT17 .... 8 F4
Commercial Rd POP/IOD E14 ... 25 P1
  RTW TN1 .... 23 F1
  STPH/PW TN12 .... 242 G3
  STRD ME2 .... 72 B8
  TON TN9 .... 240 F1
  WCHPL E1 .... 24 C2
Commercial Wy CMBW SE5 ...... 40 F2
Commercial Pl GNWCH SE10 ... 26 A8
Commercial St CHAT ME4 .... 6 E6
Commissioners Ct CHAT ME4 ... 6 D5
Commissioner's Rd STRD ME2 ... 72 C7
Commodore Rd
  MAID/BEAR ME14 .... 13 K2
Commodore St WCHPL E1 .... 24 G1
Common La DVW CT17 .... 290 F4
  HOO/HM ME3 .... 52 C2
  RDART DA2 .... 67 J8
Common Rd BGR/WK TN15 .... 150 B8
  CRBK TN17 .... 276 C7
  HOO/HM ME3 .... 34 G4
  RTON TN11 .... 181 P9
  SWLY BR8 .... 65 N6
Commonside HAYES BR2 .... 85 J5
Commonside East MTCM CR4 ... 82 B1
The Common ROCH ME1 .... 19 G3
  SBGH/RUST TN4 .... 22 A4
Common Wall HOO/HM ME3 .. 269 H4
Common Wall Rd MEO DA13 .... 52 D2
Commonwealth Wy ABYW SE2 . 28 H8
Commonwealth Cl SIT ME10 .. 130 A6
Commority Rd MEO DA13 .... 122 C5
Como Rd FSTH SE23 .... 61 L1

Collie Dr TN23 .... 282 B3
Collier Cl EHAM E6 .... 27 J5
Colliers Shaw HAYES BR2 .... 85 P9
Colliers Water La THHTH CR7 ... 82 F2
Collindale Av BFN/LL DA15 ...... 44 C9
  ERITH DA8 .... 45 P9
Collingbourne ASH TN23 .... 282 B2
Collington Cl GVW DA11 .... 49 K9
Collington St GNWCH SE10 * ... 25 N8
Collington Ter
  MAID/SHEP ME15 .... 186 C7
Collingtree Rd SYD SE26 .... 61 J3
Collingwood Cl PGE/AN SE20 .. 61 H7
Collingwood Ct BRDST CT10 .. 113 K9
  EGRIN RH19 .... 266 B5
  WGOS CT8 .... 111 L6
Collingwood Ri
  RDV CT15 .... 262 E8
  WSTB CT5 .... 105 K5
Collingwood Rd East
  RDV CT15 .... 262 F7
Collins Rd HB CT6 .... 107 H4
Collins Sq BKHTH/KID SE3 ...... 42 A9
Collins St BKHTH/KID SE3 .... 42 C5
Collison Pl TENT TN30 .... 301 L8
Collis St STRD ME2 .... 72 A7
Collyer Av CROY/NA CR0 .... 82 D8
Collyer Pl PECK SE15 .... 40 G1
Collyer Rd CROY/NA CR0 .... 82 D8
Colman Pde
  MAID/BEAR ME14 * 13 H4
Colman Rd CAN/RD E16 .... 26 F1
Colmore Ms PECK SE15 .... 41 J2
Colne TIL RM18 .... 34 B6
Colne Cl SOCK/AV RM15 .... 31 M3
Colne Rd TONN TN10 .... 210 E5
Colney Rd DART DA1 .... 46 D3
Colombo Sq MSTR CT10 .... 142 F5
Colomb St GNWCH SE10 .... 25 P8
Colonel's La FAV ME13 .... 164 B1
Colonel Stephens Wy
  TENT TN30 .... 301 H6
Colonel's Wy SBGH/RUST TN4 240 D7
The Colonnade DEPT SE8 * 25 P9
Colorado Cl DVW CT16 .... 291 J4
Colson Dr RSIT ME9 .... 99 L3
Colson Rd CROY/NA CR0 .... 83 M9
Coltness Crs ABYW SE2 .... 28 A8
Coltsfoot Ct DVE/WH CT16 .... 291 J3
Coltsfoot Dr GRAYS RM17 .... 32 E9
Coltsfoot Dr
  MAID/BEAR ME14 .... 156 C6
Coltsfoot La OXTED RH8 .... 175 J9
Coltsfoot Rd HENM/HW ME15 . 153 N5
Coltstead HART DA3 .... 57 P9
Columbia Av WSTB CT5 .... 105 J7
Columbia Wharf Rd
  GRAYS RM17 .... 33 H8
Columbine Av EHAM E6 .... 26 F1
Columbine Cl E/WMAL ME19 . 153 N5
  STRD ME2 .... 71 N8
  WSTB CT5 .... 105 K8
Columbine Rd E/WMAL ME19 153 N5
  STRD ME2 .... 71 N8
Columbine Wy LEW SE13 .... 42 A5
Columbus Av MSTR CT12 ...... 141 L3
Colveiw Ct ELTH/MOT SE9 * 43 H9
Colvin Cl SYD SE26 .... 61 J4
Colvin La BH/WHM TN16 .... 147 K8
Colwell Rd EDUL SE22 .... 60 D1
Colworth Rd CROY/NA CR0 ...... 83 P9
Colyer Cl ELTH/MOT SE9 .... 63 M1
Colyer Rd GVW DA11 .... 69 H1

Compass Cl ROCH ME1 .... 95 H5
Compasses Rd RTON TN11 .... 208 G8
The Compasses
  HOO/HM ME3 * 52 B2
Comp La BGR/WK TN15 .... 151 M6
Comport Gn CROY/NA CR0 .... 115 H6
Compton Cl PECK SE15 .... 40 C1
Compton Ct PECK SE15 .... 41 J1
  WALD ME5 .... 126 A5
Compton Pl ERITH DA8 .... 29 L8
Compton Rd CROY/NA CR0 .... 83 N5
  HOO/HM ME3 * 24 B7
Comus Pl WALW SE17 * 24 B7
Comyns Cl CAN/RD E16 .... 26 A1
Conant Ms WCHPL E1 * 24 D3
Concord Cl RTWE/PEM TN2 * ... 23 H2
Concord Ct RTWE/PEM TN2 * . 242 F3
  STPH/PW TN12 * 242 F3
Concorde Dr EHAM E6 .... 26 G1
Conder St BERM/RHTH SE16 ... 24 H2
Condor Cl IOS ME12 .... 80 C4
Condover Crs
  WOOL/PLUM SE18 .... 43 M1
Conduit Hl RYE TN31 .... 338 F6
Conduit La SAND/SEL CR2 .... 83 M9
Conduit Rd WOOL/PLUM SE18 . 43 M1
Conduit St FAV ME13 * 132 C5
Coney Banks FAV ME13 * 133 L3
Coneyburrow Rd
  RTWE/PEM TN2 .... 271 K3
Coney Hall Pde WWKM BR4 * ... 85 H7
Coney Hill Rd WWKM BR4 .... 85 H6
Coney Ms CHAT ME4 .... 95 M5
Coneygar Rd HAYES BR2 .... 62 B7
Congnurst La HAWK TN18 ..... 317 J9
Congleton Gv
  WOOL/PLUM SE18 .... 27 K8
Congo Rd WOOL/PLUM SE18 ... 27 L8
Congress Rd ABYW SE2 .... 28 F7
Congreve Rd ELTH/MOT SE9 .... 43 K4
Congreve St WALW SE17 .... 24 B7
Conifer Av HART DA3 .... 91 H3
Conifer Cl ORP BR6 .... 86 E8
Conifer Dr WOOL/PLUM SE18 . 43 L4
Conifer Dr MEO DA13 .... 122 A3
  WALD ME5 .... 126 A4
The Conifers DEAL CT14 .... 232 F7
Conifer Wy SWLY BR8 .... 65 L7
Conisborough Crs CAT SE6 .... 62 A2
Coniscliffe Cl CHST BR7 .... 63 L7
Coniston Av PUR RM19 .... 30 F9
  SBGH/RUST TN4 .... 270 B3
  WELL DA16 .... 44 A2
Coniston Cl BXLYHN DA7 .... 45 L2
  DART DA1 .... 46 B9
  ERITH DA8 .... 45 M1
  SIT ME10 .... 99 N3
Coniston Dr RCANTE CT3 ...... 199 J3
Coniston Rd BMLY BR1 .... 62 C5
  BXLYHN DA7 .... 45 L2
  CROY/NA CR0 .... 83 M4
  FOLKN CT19 .... 10 A1
Conker Cl ASH TN23 .... 282 F5
Conley St GNWCH SE10 .... 25 P8
Connaught Av CDW/CHF RM16 . 32 C5
Connaught Br CAN/RD E16 .... 26 E3
Connaught Cl
  MAID/SHEP ME15 .... 186 C7
Connaught Gdns MARG CT9 ..... 15 H7
Connaught Ms CHAT ME4 .... 95 N4
Connaught Rd
  CHAT ME4 .... 95 N4
  FOLK CT20 .... 291 L6
  GILL ME7 .... 6 K2
  MARG CT9 .... 15 H7
  SIT ME10 .... 27 H8
Connaught Wy
  SBGH/RUST TN4 .... 270 C3
Conrad Av CANT CT1 .... 167 H1
Conrad Ct CDW/CHF RM16 ...... 32 C5
  RHAM ME8 .... 76 A5
Conrad Gdns CDW/CHF RM16 . 32 B5
Conroy Ct SCUP DA14 .... 64 C5
Consort Cl MAID/BEAR ME14 .. 13 J3
Consort Rd PECK SE15 .... 41 H3
Constable Av CAN/RD E16 .... 26 E3
Constable Rd BRCH CT7 .... 111 H5
Constable Wk DUL SE21 .... 60 J2
  TONN TN10 .... 211 H5
Constable's Rd DVE/WH CT16 .... 9 F1
Constance Rd CROY/NA CR0 .... 82 G4
Constance St CAN/RD E16 .... 26 F4
Constantine Rd ASH TN23 ...... 282 C3
Constitutional Hill Rd
  SBGH/RUST TN4 .... 240 B8
Constitution Hl CHAT ME4 .... 95 N4
  DEAL CT14 .... 49 N9
  SNOD ME6 .... 123 N5
Constitution Ri
  WOOL/PLUM SE18 .... 43 L2
Constitution Hl WALD ME5 .... 7 J2
Consul Gdns SWLY BR8 * 66 A6
Contessa Cl ORP BR6 .... 116 D4
Continental Ap MARG CT9 ...... 112 E7
Convalescent La CRBK TN17 ... 276 B6
Convent Cl BECK BR3 .... 62 A6
  RDV CT15 .... 292 F3
Convent Hl NRWD SE19 .... 60 C6
Convent Rd BRDST CT10 .... 113 L5
Conway Cl BRCH CT7 .... 110 F6
  STRD ME2 .... 71 N6
Conway Gdns GRAYS RM17 ...... 48 F1
  MTCM CR4 .... 82 E2
Conway Ms GILL ME7 .... 6 D1
Conway Rd BGR/WK TN15 ...... 154 G6
  WOOL/PLUM SE18 .... 27 L2
Conway Rd BGR/WK TN15 ...... 154 G6
Conyer End RSIT ME9 .... 100 A7
Conyer Rd RSIT ME9 .... 131 J2
Conyngham La MSTR CT12 .... 142 G2
Conyngham La RCANTW CT4 . 197 M3
Conyngham Rd HB CT6 .... 108 A4
  MSTR CT12 .... 142 G2
Cooden Cl BMLY BR1 .... 62 F6
  RHAM ME8 .... 97 K4
Cook Cl WALD ME5 .... 95 P8

Cooke Cl CDW/CHF RM16 .....31 P6
Cookham Dene Cl CHST BR7 ....63 P7
Cookham Hl ROCH ME1 .....94 F4
Cookham Rd SCUP DA14 .....45 J7
Cookham Wood Rd ROCH ME1 ..94 C6
Cookhill Rd ABYW SE2 .....28 A5
Cooks La SIT ME10 .....99 M8
Cook's Lea SWCH CT13 .....201 J8
Cookson Gv ERITH DA8 .....45 K1
Cooks Whf ROCH ME1 .....19 K7
Coolfin Rd CAN/RD E16 .....26 B2
Cooling Cl MAID/BEAR ME14 ...155 P6
Coolinge La FOLK CT20 .....310 C6
Coolinge Rd FOLK CT20 .....10 D4
Cooling Rd HOO/HM ME3 .....52 B4
STRD ME2 .....72 B5
Cooling St HOO/HM ME3 .....52 C6
Coombe Av CROY/NA CR0 .....3 K8
RSEV TN14 .....148 C5
Coombe Cl DVW CT17 .....291 H6
SNOD ME6 .....123 P6
WALD ME5 .....125 N2
Coombe Dr RDV CT15 .....229 P9
SIT ME10 .....130 B1
Coombe Farm La
HOO/HM ME3 .....52 C8
Coombe Cl RASHW TN26 .....221 L8
Coombe Lands TENT TN30 ....332 A1
Coombe La CROY/NA CR0 ....83 N9
RCANTE CT3 .....200 F1
SWCH CT13 .....200 G2
TENT TN30 .....301 H8
Coombe Lea BMLY BR1 .....63 J9
Coombe Ldg CHART SE7 .....26 D9
FOLKN CT19 .....310 C5
GVE DA12 .....69 N1
HOO/HM ME3 .....73 L2
MAID/SHEP ME15 .....185 L1
TENT TN30 .....119 H9
SAND/SEL CR2 .....83 K8
SYD SE26 .....61 H3
Coomber Wy CROY/NA CR0 ....82 C4
Coombe Valley Rd DVW CT17 ..291 H7
Coombe Wy RFOLK CT18 ....288 F9
Coombe Wood La
RFOLK CT19 .....288 E8
Coomb Fld EDEN TN8 .....236 C1
Coombfield Dr RDART DA2 ....67 K3
Coombs Cl RYE TN31 .....331 H8
Cooper Rd RDART DA2 .....47 L6
RYE TN31 .....338 D2
SNOD ME6 .....123 N7
WALD ME5 .....125 M2
Coopers Cl EYN DA4 .....67 J7
Coopers Dr RDART DA2 .....65 N1
Cooper Shaw Rd TIL RM18 ....49 P5
Coopers La LEE/GVPK SE12 ....62 F1
Cooper's La RRTW TN5 .....284 C6
Coopers Ms BECK BR3 .....47 K1
Coopers Rd GVW DA11 .....49 J9
STHWK SE1 .....24 C8
Cooper's Rw TWRH ECN 24 C2
Cooper St CAN/RD E16 .....26 A1
Cooper Street Dro
RCANTE CT3 .....171 H8
Coote Rd BXLYHN DA7 .....160 E5
Cooting La RCANTE CT3 .....198 G8
Cooting Rd RCANTE CT3 .....228 G1
Copeland Rd PECK SE15 .....40 G3
Copeman Cl SYD SE26 .....61 J4
Copenhagen Pl POP/IOD E14 ...25 J2
Copenhagen Rd GILL ME7 .....7 F5
Copers Cope Rd BECK BR3 ....46 M5
Cope St BERM/RHTH SE16 ....24 G7
Copinger Cl CANTW/ST CT2 ..136 F7
Copland Av IOS ME12 .....7 L6
Coplands Ri RYE TN31 .....350 A6
Copleston Rd PECK SE15 .....40 F4
Copley Dene BMLY BR1 .....63 K1
Coppards La RYE TN31 .....330 B5
Coppelia Rd BKHTH/KID SE3 ..42 D5
Copperas St DEPT SE8 .....41 M2
Copper Beech Cl GVE DA12 ....49 P8
STMC/STPC BR5 .....87 K2
Copperfield Cl NRWD SE19 ....50 O9
Copperfield Cl GVE DA12 ....50 C9
KEN/WIL TN24 .....112 C3
RMAID ME17 .....187 H9
Copperfield Crs HOO/HM ME3 ..71 L5
Copperfield Dr RMAID ME17 ....187 H7
Copperfield Rd ROCH ME1 ....95 H4
Copperfield St STHWK SE1 ....18 C1
Copperfields BGR/WK TN15 ..149 L2
LYDD TN29 .....342 A6
The Copperfields ROCH ME1 *..18 D7
Copperfields Wk
BGR/WK TN15 .....149 L2
Coppergate CANTW/ST CT2 ....4 D1
GILL ME7 .....96 C9
Copperhouse La GILL ME7 ...73 P9
Copperhouse Rd STRD ME2 ....71 J8
Copper La STPH/PW TN12 ...245 K4
Copperpenny Dr GILL ME7 ....126 C1
Coppers La STPH/PW TN12 ...242 F8
Copper Tree Ct
MAID/SHEP ME15 .....185 M6
Copperwood KEN/WIL TN24 *..352 F5
Coppice Cl BECK BR3 .....84 E1
Coppice Ct GILL ME7 .....126 E1
Coppice Rd WALD ME5 .....125 P3
The Coppice BGR/WK TN15 ..150 A2
BXLY DA5 .....65 M2
CANTW/ST CT2 .....157 L7
DIT/AY ME20 .....154 D3
MEO DA13 .....122 C5
TENT TN30 .....271 N1
Coppice Vw
MAID/BEAR ME14 .....156 B6
Copping Cl CROY/NA CR0 ....83 K8
Copping's Rd RTON TN11 ....208 D2
Coppins Cl RSIT ME9 .....129 J3

The Coppins CROY/NA CR0 ...114 E1
Coppin St DEAL CT14 .....233 J3
Coppock Cl MSTR CT12 .....142 G3
Copse Av WWKM BR4 .....84 E7
Copse Bank BGR/WK TN15 ...149 L5
Copse Cl CHARL SE7 .....26 C7
EGRIN RH19 .....265 J5
ROCH ME1 .....95 K5
Copsehill E/WMAL ME19 ....153 M2
Copse Rd RTON TN11 .....210 B6
Copse Side HART DA3 .....68 C7
The Copse ASH TN23 .....252 B6
HOO/HM ME3 .....73 L4
Copse Vw SAND/SEL CR2 ....114 A2
Copsewood Cl BFN/LL DA15 ...44 A7
Copsewood Wy
MAID/SHEP ME15 .....156 D9
Cop Street Rd RCANTE CT3 ..170 E8
Copt Cl CANTW/ST CT2 .....137 L6
Coptefield Dr BELV DA17 ....28 C6
Copthall HAWK TN18 * 330 C2
Copthall Av HAWK TN18 ....317 H5
LOTH EC2R 24 A2
Copthall Gdns FOLK CT20 ...10 E4
Copt Hall Rd BGR/WK TN15 ..150 D8
MEO DA13 .....92 C1
Copthorne Av HAYES BR2 ....86 A6
Copthorne Rd EGRIN RH19 ..264 B4
Copton Cl BOW E3 .....25 L2
Copyhold Rd EGRIN RH19 ...264 G8
Coralline Wk ABYW SE2 ....28 B5
Corben Cl MAIDW ME16 ....154 F6
Corbett Cl CROY/NA CR0 ...114 C6
Corbett's La BERM/RHTH SE16 ..24 F7
Corbylands Rd BFN/LL DA15 ...44 A8
Cordelia Cl HNHL SE24 .....40 B5
Cordelia Crs ROCH ME1 .....94 E4
Cordelia St POP/IOD E14 ....25 L2
Cordingham Rd WSTB CT5 ..105 H8
Cording St POP/IOD E14 ....25 L1
Cordwell Rd LEW SE13 .....42 G5
Corelli Rd BKHTH/KID SE3 ....43 J2
Corianda Dr MAIDW ME16 ...154 F6
Coriander St DEPT SE8 .....41 M2
Corinthian Manorway
ERITH DA8 .....29 J7
Corinthian Rd ERITH DA8 ....29 J7
Cork La STPH/PW TN12 .....246 A9
Corkscrew Hl WWKM BR4 ....84 F6
Cork Sq WAP E1W * 24 D4
Cork St DIT/AY ME20 .....124 E7
Corkwell St CHAT ME4 .....6 A7
Cormont Rd CMBW SE5 ....40 B2
Cormorant Cl STRD ME2 ....71 L8
Cormorant Rd GILL ME7 ....99 M3
Cormorant Wy HB CT6 .....108 C5
Cornbrook Rd HYTHE CT21 ..308 C7
Cornelis Dr MSTR CT12 .....141 J7
Corneli Ct SCUP DA14 .....64 C5
Corner Farm Rd
STPH/PW TN12 .....246 B5
Corner Fld ASH TN23 .....282 E5
Corner Gn BKHTH/KID SE3 ....42 A5
Corner House Blds
HYTHE CT21 .....308 G5
Cornes Cl KEN/WIL TN24 ...253 K8
Cornfield Wy TONN TN10 ...210 C4
Cornflower Ct
MAID/BEAR ME14 *.....156 B8
Cornflower La CROY/NA CR0 ..84 A5
Cornflower Ter EDUL SE22 ....41 H7
Cornford Cl HAYES BR2 .....85 K2
RTWE/PEM TN2 .....271 L2
Cornford La STPH/PW TN2 ...271 H4
Cornford Rd BRCH CT7 .....111 H7
Cornforth Cl STPH/PW TN12 ..246 C5
Cornforth Dr RSIT ME9 .....129 N7
Cornhill BANK EC3V 24 A3
RAM CT11 .....17 F5
The Cornhill FOLK CT20 ....309 P4
Cornish Cv PCE/AN SE20 ....61 H7
Corn Mill Dr ORP BR6 .....86 G4
Cornmill La LEW SE13 .....41 P4
Cornwall Av RAM CT11 .....143 L4
WELL DA16 .....44 A4
Cornwall Cl MAID/SHEP ME15 ..186 A8
Cornwall Crs ROCH ME1 ....124 C1
Cornwall Dr STMC/STPC BR5 ..64 E6
Cornwall Gdns CANT CT1 ....167 G5
EGRIN RH19 .....265 J3
MARC CT9 .....112 C3
SNWD SE25 .....45 L1
Cornwallis Av CHAT ME4 ....95 P5
ELTH/MOT SE9 .....63 P1
FOLKN CT19 .....10 C1
GILL ME7 .....96 C2
HB CT6 .....107 P3
RCANTE CT3 .....229 J1
RMAID ME17 .....215 G2
TONN TN10 .....211 H6
Cornwallis Cl WSTB CT5 ....105 K5
Cornwallis Cl ERITH DA8 ....29 L9
FOLKN CT19 .....10 B1
KEN/WIL TN24 .....283 L1
Cornwallis Gdns BRDST CT10 ..113 M7
Cornwallis Rd MAIDW ME16 ...12 A3
WOOL/PLUM SE18 .....27 J6
Cornwallis Wk ELTH/MOT SE9 ..43 N1
Cornwall Rd CROY/NA CR0 ....82 G6
DART DA1 .....54 C1
DEAL CT14 .....233 H6
GILL ME7 * 73 J9
HB CT6 .....108 A6
ROCH ME1 .....95 H5
Cornwall St WCHPL E1 .....24 E3
Cornwall Av GVE DA12 .....69 N2
Cornwood Dr WCHPL E1 .....24 F2
Corona Rd LEE/GVPK SE12 ...42 F5
Corona Ter SNOD ME6 .....123 N7
Coronation Av TIL RM18 ....30 A7
Coronation Cl BRDST CT10 ..113 K6
BXLY DA5 .....44 F7
Coronation Cots
FOLKN CT19 .....77 H2
Coronation Crs MARC CT9 ....112 A5
QBOR ME11 .....77 H2
Coronation Dr ASH TN23 ....251 P2
IOS ME12 .....80 B5

Coronation Flats CHAT ME4 *...6 C6
Coronation Rd EGRIN RH19 ..265 H9
HOO/HM ME3 .....56 D3
IOS ME12 .....57 L7
RAM CT11 .....17 H3
WALD ME5 .....95 P4
Coronation St LYDD TN29 ...342 B6
Corone Cl FOLKN CT19 .....310 D4
Coronation Rd GILL ME7 ....73 K9
Corporation Rd GILL ME7 ....73 K9
Corporation St ROCH ME1 ....19 G4
Corral Cl WALD ME5 .....96 A4
Corrance Gn
MAID/SHEP ME15 .....185 M3
Corran Wy SOCK/AV RM15 ....31 L3
Correnden Rd TONN TN10 ...210 D7
Corry Dr BRXN/ST SW9 .....40 B5
Cortland Cl DART DA1 .....45 N7
Cortland Ms SIT ME10 .....99 M8
Corunna Cl HYTHE CT21 ....308 C5
Corunna Pl RDV CT15 .....291 M4
Corve La SOCK/AV RM15 ....31 L3
Corylus Dr WSTB CT5 .....105 H7
Cory's Rd ROCH ME1 .....19 G3
Cosbycote Av HNHL SE24 ....40 C5
Cosedge Crs CROY/NA CR0 ...82 F9
Cosgrove Rd WTHK RM20 ....47 L1
Cossack St ROCH ME1 .....95 H5
Cossall Wk PECK SE15 .....41 H3
Cossar Ms BRXS/STRHM SW2 ..40 A7
Cossington Rd CANT CT1 .....5 G6
WALD ME5 .....125 N4
Costa St PECK SE15 .....40 G3
Costells Meadow
BH/WHM TN16 .....176 A2
Cotall St POP/IOD E14 .....25 K2
Cotelands CROY/NA CR0 .....83 K7
Cotford Rd THHTH CR7 .....83 H1
Cot La HDCN TN27 .....278 C5
Cotleigh Av BXLY DA5 .....64 F1
Cotmandene Crs
STMC/STPC BR5 .....64 D8
Cotman's Ash La
BGR/WK TN15 .....150 A1
Cotman Wy STPH/PW TN12 ..212 F4
Coton Rd WELL DA16 .....44 C4
Cotswold Cl BXLYHN DA7 ....45 N2
KEN/WIL TN24 .....252 C5
Cotswold Gdns
MAID/SHEP ME15 .....186 D2
Cotswold Ri ORP BR6 .....86 G3
Cotswold Rd GVW DA11 .....69 J2
Cotswold St WNWD SE27 ....60 B5
Cottage Av HAYES BR2 .....85 P5
Cottage Field Cl SCUP DA14 ..44 G9
Cottage Gn CMBW SE5 .....40 D3
Cottage Rd CHAT ME4 .....72 F9
Cottage Rd RAM CT11 .....17 G4
Cottage St POP/IOD E14 ....25 L3
Cottall Av CHAT ME4 .....95 J4
Cottenham Cl
E/WMAL ME19 .....153 N5
Cottenhams LING RH7 .....234 B1
Cottesbrock St NWCR SE14 ...41 L1
Cottingham Rd PGE/AN SE20 ..61 K6
Cottington Rd MSTR CT12 ...141 K7
Cottongrass Cl CROY/NA CR0 ..84 A5
Cotton Hill BMLY BR1 .....62 G3
Cotton La RDART DA2 .....54 F4
Cotton Rd CANT CT1 .....4 A1
Cottons Centre STHWK SE1 *..24 A6
Cotton St POP/IOD E14 ....25 M3
Couchman Green La
STPH/PW TN12 .....246 C2
Coulgate St BROCKY SE4 ....41 L4
Coulman St GILL ME7 .....96 B9
Coulson Cv DEAL CT14 .....231 P4
Coulter Rd ASH TN23 .....282 A3
HB CT6 .....106 G4
Coulters Cl MAID/BEAR ME14 ..156 A8
Coulton Av GVW DA11 .....68 J2
Couldrip Cl IOS ME12 .....79 H2
Council Av GVW DA11 .....48 C9
Councillor St CMBW SE5 ....40 C1
Counter St STHWK SE1 .....36 B4
Counters La RYE TN31 .....351 P6
Country Wk ASH TN23 .....280 E5
Country Ways RMAID ME17 ...190 C8
County Ga ELTH/MOT SE9 ....63 N2
County Gv CMBW SE5 .....40 C2
County Rd RHAM ME6 .....13 F5
THHTH CR7 .....60 B8
County Sq ASH TN23 * 2 D3
County Wy DEAL CT14 .....233 H4
Coupland Pl WOOL/PLUM SE18 ..27 K4
The Course ELTH/MOT SE9 ....63 L2
Court Ap FOLK CT20 .....10 C5
Courtaulds Cl THMD SE28 ....28 D7
Court Av BELV DA17 .....28 G4
Court Bromes RMAID ME17 ...217 M2
Court Cl EGRIN RH19 .....265 K7
Court Crs EGRIN RH19 .....265 K7
SWLY BR8 .....88 D1
Court Downs Rd BECK BR3 ....61 P9
Court Dr CROY/NA CR0 .....82 G6
MAIDW ME16 .....154 A6
Courtenay Dr BECK BR3 .....62 B8
ROCH ME1 * 94 D5
Courtenay Rd DEAL CT14 ...233 H1
MAID/SHEP ME15 .....185 L1
PGE/AN SE20 .....46 D8
Courteney Rd RHAM ME8 ....96 D6
Court Farm La ELTH/MOT SE9 ..63 H1
Courtfield Av MAID/SHEP ME15 ..186 A8
Court Hall QBOR ME11 .....77 H2
Court Hl RCANTE CT3 .....168 C7
Courthill Rd LEW SE13 .....42 A5
Courthope Rd RHAM ME8 ....96 D6
Courtland Av DVE/WH CT16 ..291 H5
Courtland Dr ELTH/MOT SE9 ...63 H1
Courtland Gv THMD SE28 ....28 G6
Courtlands CHST BR7 .....63 H6
DEAL CT14 .....232 C9
TONN TN10 .....210 D7
WBY/YAL ME18 .....183 P3

Courtlands Av HAYES BR2 ....85 H5
LEE/GVPK SE12 .....42 F6
Courtlands Cl MSTR CT12 ...142 C7
Courtlands Wy WGOS CT8 ..111 H4
Court La DUL SE21 * 40 F8
MAID/BEAR ME14 .....126 F8
RCANTE CT3 .....169 K3
RTON TN11 .....212 B2
Court La Gdns DUL SE21 ....40 F8
Courtleet Dr BXLYHN DA7 ....45 K2
Court Ldg GVE DA12 .....70 C5
Court Lodge Farm
WBY/YAL ME18 * 183 M4
Court Lodge Rd GILL ME7 ....73 M9
RASHW TN26 .....322 D2
Courtmead Cl HNHL SE24 ....40 C7
Court Meadow RHAM ME8 ....96 F4
Court Mdw RCANTE CT3 ....168 C8
Court Mt BRCH CT7 * 111 H7
Courtney Cl NRWD SE19 .....60 E1
Courtney Pl CROY/NA CR0 ....82 F7
Courtney Rd CDW/CHF RM16 ..33 K5
CROY/NA CR0 .....82 F7
Court Rd BRCH CT7 .....109 H7
DEAL CT14 .....232 F8
RDART DA2 .....67 L4
ROCH ME1 .....124 C4
SBGH/RUST TN4 .....270 B4
SIT ME10 .....99 M7
SNWD SE25 .....45 M1
Court Road (Orpington By-Pass)
ORP BR6 .....87 J7
Courtside SYD SE26 * 61 J2
The Courts MARC CT9 .....111 P4
Courtstreet BMLY BR1 .....62 C8
Court St FAV ME13 .....132 C3
WCHPL E1 .....24 D1
The Court WARL CR6 .....144 B5
Court Tree Dr IOS ME12 .....79 H2
Courtwood Dr SEV TN13 ....82 C7
Court Ldg GVE DA12 .....82 F7
Courtwood Vis RFOLK CT15 *..259 N1
Court Wurtin Beaver La ASH TN23 .....282 D1
Court Yd ELTH/MOT SE9 .....43 J7
The Courts MARC CT9 .....111 P4
Courtyard Ms STMC/STPC BR5 ..64 C7
The Courtyard BGR/WK TN15 ..149 M3
BH/WHM TN16 .....176 E2
EGRIN RH19 .....115 P1
HAYES BR2 .....283 P1
RCANTE CT3 .....200 L4
RHAM ME8 * 96 F4
The Court Yd RHAM ME8 ....97 J5
Cousin La CANST EC4R 24 A3
Cousley Wood Rd WADH TN5 ..294 B9
Couthurst Rd BKHTH/KID SE3 ..42 B2
Coutts Av GVE DA12 .....70 C5
Covelees Wall EHAM E6 .....27 K1
Coventon La DEAL CT14 ....201 P5
Coventry Cl EHAM E6 .....26 G2
STRD ME2 .....71 M9
Coventry Gdns HB CT6 .....108 A5
Coventry Rd SNWD SE25 ....83 M1
TONN TN10 .....210 C5
Coverack Cl CROY/NA CR0 ...84 D4
Coverdale Av
MAID/SHEP ME15 .....186 A5
Coverdale Cl WALD ME5 .....95 N7
Coverdale Gdns CROY/NA CR0 ..83 L7
Coverley Cl WCHPL E1 .....24 D1
Covert Rd RCANTE CT3 .....229 H2
The Covert BGR/WK TN15 ...121 P6
NRWD SE19 * 60 E2
ORP BR6 .....86 F5
WALD ME5 .....125 M4
Covesfield GVW DA11 .....49 K8
Covet La RCANTW CT4 .....227 L4
Cover Wood Cl
STMC/STPC BR5 .....86 G3
Covey Wall Rd SNOD ME6 ...123 P5
Covington Gdns
STRHM/NOR SW16 .....61 P2
Covington Wy
STRHM/NOR SW16 .....60 N3
Cowbeck Cl RHAM ME8 .....96 C8
Cowden Cl HAWK TN18 .....316 C6
Cowden La HAWK TN18 .....316 C6
Cowden Ms EDEN TN8 .....267 H5
Cowden Rd MAID/BEAR ME14 ..157 P7
ORP BR6 .....86 G7
Cowdray Rd DEAL CT14 .....232 F6
Cowdray Sq DEAL CT14 .....232 G6
Cowdrey Cl MAID/SHEP ME15 ..283 K1
MAIDW ME16 .....184 C2
ROCH ME1 .....94 C4
Cowdrey Ct DART DA1 .....46 A5
Cowgate Hl DVW CT17 .....166 C6
Cowgate La RFOLK CT18 ....288 F6
Cow La CANT CT1 .....4 F1
DVW CT17 .....291 H8
EDEN TN8 .....291 H8
Cow Leaze EHAM E6 .....27 L2
Cowley Av RDART DA2 .....47 M6
Cowley Ri MARC CT9 .....113 H5
Cowley Rd BRXN/ST SW9 ....40 B7
Cowper Av TIL RM18 .....49 M2
Cowper Cl HAYES BR2 .....85 N1
WELL DA16 .....44 B5
Cowper Rd BELV DA17 .....28 F4
DEAL CT14 .....232 G4
DVW CT17 .....291 J8
GILL ME7 .....7 K6
HAYES BR2 .....85 P1
MARC CT9 .....113 J4
SIT ME10 .....130 A1

Cox's Cl SNOD ME6 .....123 N5
Cox Cots WARL CR6 * 115 H8
Coxson Wy STHWK SE1 .....24 C8
Cox St MAID/BEAR ME14 ...126 F8
RSIT ME9 * 127 J4
Coxwell Rd NRWD SE19 .....60 E6
WOOL/PLUM SE18 .....27 L8
Cozenton Cl RHAM ME8 .....97 H5
Crabble Av DVW CT17 .....291 H5
Crabble Cl DVW CT17 .....290 G5
Crabble Hl DVW CT17 .....291 H4
Crabble La DVW CT17 .....290 G5
Crabble Mdw DVW CT17 ....291 H5
Crabble Rd DVW CT17 .....291 H5
Crabbs Croft Cl ORP BR6 ....86 D9
Crab Hl BECK BR3 .....62 B6
Crabtree Cl E/WMAL ME19 ...183 H1
Crabtree La RMAID ME17 ...220 A2
Crabtree Manorway North
BELV DA17 .....29 H5
Crabtree Manorway South
BELV DA17 .....29 H5
Crabtree Rd RHAM ME8 .....96 C6
Craddock Dr CANT CT1 * 5 H1
Craddock Rd CANT CT1 .....5 H1
Craddock Wy RHAM ME8 ....96 C6
Cradducks La STPH/PW TN12 ..246 E5
Cradle Bridge Dr
KEN/WIL TN24 .....3 K4
Cradles Rd RSIT ME9 .....43 P9
Cradley Rd ELTH/MOT SE9 ...63 P3
Crafford St DVW CT16 .....8 C2
Craigen Av CROY/NA CR0 ....83 N5
Craigerne Rd BKHTH/KID SE3 ..42 F1
Craigholm WOOL/PLUM SE18 ..43 L5
Craigton Rd ELTH/MOT SE9 ....43 K5
Crail Rw WALW SE17 .....24 A7
Crammavill St CDW/CHF RM16 ..32 B3
Crampton Rd PGE/AN SE20 ....61 J5
Cramptons CRBK TN17 .....276 C8
Crampton's Rd RSEV TN14 ..148 C5
Cranborne Av
MAID/SHEP ME15 .....185 N3
Cranbrook Cl RHAM CT11 ...143 L4
Cranbrook Dr HAYES BR2 ....85 K3
MAID/SHEP ME15 .....186 C4
MARC CT9 .....113 K4
RHAM ME8 .....96 G8
Cranbrook Dr SIT ME10 .....129 L4
Cranbrook Rd BXLYHN DA7 ...45 H2
CRBK TN17 .....274 C6
CRBK TN17 .....277 J9
DEPT SE8 .....41 N2
HAWK TN18 .....317 H2
STPH/PW TN12 .....276 C1
TENT TN30 .....300 F7
THHTH CR7 .....60 C1
Crandalls RTON TN11 .....209 L9
Crandon Wk EYN DA4 * 67 L3
Crane La CRBK TN17 .....298 C2
Cranell Gn SOCK/AV RM15 ...31 L4
Crane Md BERM/RHTH SE16 ...25 J2
Crane St PECK SE15 .....40 F2
Cranfield Rd BROCKY SE4 ....41 M4
Cranford St WAP E1W 24 G3
Cranford Cots WAP E1W * 24 G3
Cranford Rd DART DA1 .....46 E9
TONN TN10 .....211 K5
Cranham Rd RHAM ME8 .....96 G5
Cranham St WAP E1W * 24 C3
Cranmam Sq STPH/PW TN12 ..245 H4
Cranleigh Cl BXLY DA5 .....87 K7
ORP BR6 .....61 H8
PGE/AN SE20 .....61 H8
Cranleigh Dr DVE/WH CT16 ..261 H9
SNWD SE25 .....60 D1
Cranleigh Gdns CHAT ME4 ...95 J3
MAIDW ME16 .....155 H5
SNWD SE25 .....60 D1
WSTB CT5 .....105 M6
Cranley Rd PLSTW E13 .....26 B1
Cranmer Cl RCANTW CT4 ...167 N8
Cranmer Ct MAID/SHEP ME15 ..185 N3
Cranmere Ct STRD ME2 .....72 C7
Cranmer Gdns WARL CR6 ...144 B2
Cranmer Rd BRXN/ST SW9 ...40 A1
CROY/NA CR0 .....82 G7
SEV TN13 .....148 G2
Cranmore Rd BMLY BR1 .....62 C2
CHST BR7 .....63 K4
Cranston Rd EGRIN RH19 ...265 H5
FSTH SE23 .....41 L9
Cranswick Rd
BERM/RHTH SE16 .....24 E8
Crantock Rd CAT SE6 .....61 M2
Cranwell Rd SBGH/RUST TN4 ..269 L8
Cranworth Gdns BRXN/ST SW9 ..40 A2
Crathie Rd LEE/GVPK SE12 ...42 F7
Craufurd Gn FOLK CT20 ....310 A6
Craufurd Ri MARC CT9 .....112 B5
Craven Rd CROY/NA CR0 ....83 N5
ORP BR6 .....87 H6
Crawford Av CDW/CHF RM16 ..32 C4
Crawford Gdns MARC CT9 ...113 L2
Crawford Rd BRDST CT10 ...113 L8
CMBW SE5 .....40 C3
Crawfords SWLY BR8 .....65 N6
Crawford Rd EGRIN RH19 ...265 J5
Crawley Down Rd
EGRIN RH19 .....264 B5
Crawshay Cl SEV TN13 .....148 F6
Crawthew Gv EDUL SE22 ....40 F2
Cray Av STMC/STPC BR5 ....87 J2
Craybrooke Rd SCUP DA14 ..64 D3
Crayburne SEV TN13 * 147 P4
Craybury End ELTH/MOT SE9 ..63 N1
Crayford Cl MAID/BEAR ME14 ..13 H1
Crayford High St DART DA1 ...45 N5
Crayford Rd DART DA1 .....45 M5
Craylands STMC/STPC BR5 ....65 H7
Craylands La SWCM DA10 ....48 B6
Craylands Sq SWCM DA10 ....48 B6
Crayleigh Ter SCUP DA14 * ...64 F5
Cray Rd BELV DA17 .....46 A1
SCUP DA14 .....88 B3
SWLY BR8 .....88 B3

Crays Pde STMC/STPC BR5 *......64 E8
Craythorne TENT TN30......301 J6
Craythorne Cl HYTHE CT21...309 N5
  NROM TN28......337 H5
Craythorne La NROM TN28...336 G6
Cray Valley Rd
  STMC/STPC BR5......87 H2
Creasy Est STHWK SE1 *......24 B6
Crebor St EDUL SE22......40 G7
Credenhall Dr HAYES BR2......86 A5
Credon Rd BERM/RHTH SE16...24 E8
Credo Wy WTHK RM20......19 L9
Creechurch La HDTCH EC3A...24 B2
Creechurch Pl HDTCH EC3A *...24 B2
Creek Rd DEPT SE8......25 K9
Creekside DEPT SE8......25 K9
The Creek DUW DA11......48 F6
Creeland Gv CAT SE6......41 M9
Cremer Cl RCANTW CT4......195 K1
Cremer Pl FAV ME13......132 C5
Cremers Rd SIT ME10......100 A9
Cremorne Rd GVW DA11......49 K8
Crescent Pk SBGH/RUST TN4...240 D8
Crescent TWRH EC3N......24 C3
Crescent Av CNWCH SE10......25 M9
Crescent Av GRAYS RM17......32 E8
Crescent Cots SEV TN15......148 D5
Crescent Ct GRAYS RM17 *......32 E9
Crescent Dr STMC/STPC BR5...86 D3
Crescent Gdns SWLY BR8......65 L8
Crescent Rd BECK BR3......61 P8
  BFN/LL DA15......64 B2
  BGR/WK TN15......151 K4
  BMLY BR1......62 F6
  BRCH CT7......111 H6
  BRDST CT10......113 P5
  EGRIN RH19......264 C7
  ERITH DA8......29 L9
  FAV ME13......132 C6
  MARG CT9......14 C3
  RAM CT11......5 H3
  RTW TN1......14 C3
  SOCK/AV RM15......30 F5
  WOOL/PLUM SE18......27 J8
The Crescent BECK BR3......61 N7
  BGR/WK TN15......151 K4
  BXLY DA5......64 B2
  CANTW/ST CT2......166 E1
  CHAT ME4......73 H6
  CROY/NA CRO......3 J3
  CTHM CR3......144 D8
  EGRIN RH19......234 C8
  FAV ME13......164 B1
  FOLK CT20......310 B8
  GVW DA11......69 K1
  HART DA3......68 G2
  IOS ME12......77 N1
  KEN/WIL TN24......283 J2
  MAID/BEAR ME14......155 L4
  RCANTW CT4......195 L2
  RDV CT15 *......229 K5
  RDV CT15 *......260 D1
  RDV CT15 *......292 F2
  RSIT ME9......131 J2
  SBGH/RUST TN4......240 B5
  SCUP DA14......64 B5
  SEV TN13......149 J7
  SIT ME10......99 N5
  SWCH CT13......201 M4
  SWCM DA10......48 A5
  TON TN9......210 E8
  WWKM BR4......85 H3
Crescent Wk SOCK/AV RM15...30 F5
Crescent Wy BROCKY SE4......41 N4
  ORP BR6......87 J5
  SOCK/AV RM15......30 G5
  WALD ME5......95 J9
Crescent Wood Rd SYD SE26...60 C2
Cressey Ct CHAT ME4......6 A5
Cressfield ASH TN23......252 C8
Cressingham Rd LEW SE13......42 A4
Cress Wy FAV ME13......132 D6
Cresswell Pk BKHTH/KID SE3...43 J2
Cresswell Rd SNWD SE25......83 M1
Cressy Cl WCHPL E1 *......24 F1
Cressy Houses WCHPL E1 *...24 F1
Crest Av GRAYS RM17......48 F1
Crest Cl RSEV TN14......118 A5
Cresthill Av GRAYS RM17......32 D8
Crest Rd HAYES BR2......85 N5
  ROCH ME1......95 H5
Crest Vw RDART DA2......47 H5
Crest View Dr STMC/STPC BR5...86 A3
Crestway WALD ME5......95 N6
Creswell Dr BECK BR3......84 F4
Crete Hall Rd GVW DA11......49 H7
Crete Rd East RFOLK CT18......310 F2
Crete Rd West RFOLK CT18...310 D2
Creteway Cl FOLKN CT19 *......311 H3
Creve Coeur Cl
  MAID/BEAR ME14......156 D7
Crewdson Rd BRXN/ST SW9...40 A1
Crewe's Farm La WARL CR6...144 A1
Crewe's Cl WARL CR6......144 A1
Crews St POP/IOD E14......25 K7
Crichton Av WLGTN SM6......82 C9
Cricket Ct EGRIN RH19......265 H5
Cricketers Dr MEO DA13......92 D7
Cricket Field Rd ASH TN23......282 D6
  RFOLK CT18......288 E6
  RMAID ME17......187 H8
  SIT ME10......99 N6
Cricketers Dr MEO DA13......92 D7
Cricketers Wk SYD SE26......60 G2
Cricket Ground Rd CHST BR7...63 M4
Cricket La BECK BR3......61 L5
Crimond Av LYDD TN29......327 L2
Crimscott St STHWK SE1......24 B6
Crinan Ct RAM CT11 *......143 J4
Criol La RASHW TN26......281 L7
Criol Rd ASH TN23......281 N5
Cripple Hl RASHW TN26......279 L7
Cripple St MAID/SHEP ME15...185 M4
Cripps Cl RCANTE CT3......229 H1
Cripps La RDV CT15......292 E6
Crismill La RMAID ME17......157 H9
Crispe Cl RHAM ME8......97 H2
Crispe Park Cl BRCH CT7......111 J6
Crispe Rd BRCH CT7......141 H1
Crispin Cl FAV ME13......132 G5
Crispin Ct RMAID ME17......185 H8
Crispin Crs CROY/NA CRO......82 C6
Crispin Rd ERITH DA8......71 N7
Crispin St WCHPL E1......24 C1
Crispin Wy E/WMAL ME19......153 H9
Crittenden Rd STPH/PW TN12...242 D5
Crockenhall Wy MEO DA13...109 J7
Crockenhill Hl STMC/STPC BR5...87 L2
Crockenhill La SWLY BR8......88 F4
Crocken Hill Rd HDCN TN27...219 K8
Crockenhill Rd
  STMC/STPC BR5......87 L3
Crockers La LING RH7......234 A5
  RYE TN31......330 A5
Crockham La FAV ME13......134 C7
Crockham Rd FAV ME13......134 D7
Crockham Wy ELTH/MOT SE9...63 L3
Crockshard Hl RCANTE CT3...199 L3
Crockshard La RCANTE CT3...199 J3
Crocus Cl CROY/NA CRO......84 A5
Crocus Dr SIT ME10......129 N4
Croft Av ABYW SE2 *......28 E8
  CHST BR7......63 K4
  TONN TN10......211 J5
  WALD ME5......125 P4
Croft Cl EDEN TN8......206 D9
Croft Cl HYTHE CT21......308 D7
Crofters Ct DEPT SE8......25 L4
Crofters Md CROY/NA CRO *...114 C3
The Crofters RHAM ME8......97 J7
Croft Gdns RMAID ME17......189 L6
Croft La EDEN TN8......206 D9
  FOLK CT20......310 C6
Crofton Av BXLY DA5......64 F8
  ORP BR6......86 D6
Crofton Cl KEN/WIL TN24......252 F5
Crofton Gate Wy BROCKY SE4...41 L9
Crofton La STMC/STPC BR5......86 E5
Crofton Park Rd BROCKY SE4...41 M7
Crofton Rd CDW/CHF RM16...32 F7
  CMBW SE5......40 E2
  ORP BR6......86 B7
  WGOS CT8......111 M6
Croft Rd BH/WHM TN16......176 C2
  BMLY BR1......62 C5
  CTHM CR3......144 C7
  KEN/WIL TN24......3 G4
  STRHM/NOR SW16......60 A4
Croft Road Flats KEN/WIL TN24...3 G4
Croftside MEO DA13......122 B5
Crofts Pl BRDST CT10......113 N9
Croft St DEPT SE8......25 H7
  WCHPL E1......24 D1
The Croft E/WMAL ME19......153 M2
  SWLY BR8......65 L9
Croft Wy BFN/LL DA15......63 N6
  SEV TN13......20 A3
Croftwood ASH TN23......282 A2
Crohan Park Av
  SAND/SEL CR2......83 L9
Croham Rd SAND/SEL CR2......83 J9
Croindene Ct IOS ME12 *......78 A1
Crombie Rd BFN/LL DA15......43 P9
Cromer Rd RCANTW CT4......84 B5
  SNWD SE25......83 J3
  STRD ME2......72 D7
Cromer St TON TN9......210 D9
Cromford Cl ORP BR6......86 F1
Cromlix Cl CHST BR7......63 M8
Crompton Gdns
  MAID/SHEP ME15......13 H6
Cromwell Av HAYES BR2......62 F9
Cromwell Cl HAYES BR2......85 L1
Cromwell Park Pl FOLK CT20...310 A7
Cromwell Pl EGRIN RH19......265 J9
Cromwell Rd BECK BR3......61 L8
  BRXN/ST SW9......40 B2
  CROY/NA CRO......166 F6
  GRAYS RM17......32 E7
  IOS ME12......77 H9
  MAID/BEAR ME14......13 G5
  RTWE/PEM TN2......223 H5
  WSTB CT5......105 L5
Cromwell Ter CHAT ME4......6 D6
Cronin Cl DIT/AY ME20......123 N9
Cronin St PECK SE15......40 F1
Crooked La GVW DA11......49 M7
Crooked S Rd DEAL CT14......262 D1
Crookenden Rd RCANTW CT4...228 C7
Crooke Rd DEPT SE8......25 H8
Crook Log BXLYHS DA6......44 F4
Crook's Court La RDV CT15......312 A2
Crookston Rd ELTH/MOT SE9...43 L4
Coombs Rd CAN/RD E16......26 D7
Croom's Hl GNWCH SE10......25 N9
Croom's Hill Gv GNWCH SE10...42 A1
Crosby La BXLY DA5 *......64 F8
Crosby Rd STHWK SE1......24 B3
Crosby Sq OBST EC2N......24 B2
Cross Ct BKHTH/KID SE3......43 J3
Crosier Ct RSIT ME9......97 P3
Crosley Rd GILL ME7......95 P4
Crossbrook Rd BKHTH/KID SE3...43 J3
Cross Dr RMAID ME17......217 L1
Crossfield Est DEPT SE8......25 L4
Crossfield St DEPT SE8......41 N1
Crossfield Wk SNOD ME6......123 M6
Cross Keys MAID/BEAR ME14...156 F8
Crossland Rd THHTH CR7......82 C5
Cross La BXLY DA5......64 B3
  FAV ME13......191 P4
  MON CE3R......24 B3
  SIT ME10......99 M8
Cross Lane East GVE DA12......69 M1
Cross Lanes CROY/NA CRO......3 J5
Cross La West GVW DA11......69 M2
Crosslet St WALW SE17......24 A7
Crosslet V GNWCH SE10......41 P2
Crossley Cl BH/WHM TN16...176 C9
Crossmead ELTH/MOT SE9......43 L9
Cross Rd BRCH CT7......111 H5
  CMBW SE5......40 E3
  CROY/NA CRO......83 G5
  DART DA1......46 C7
  DEAL CT14......203 J6
  GVW DA11......49 K7
  HAYES BR2......85 P6
  RDART DA2......66 F3
  ROCH ME1......64 D5
  STMC/STPC BR5......87 J2
Cross St CANTW/ST CT2......4 B3
  CHAT ME4......8 A8
  ERITH DA8......29 K9
  HB CT6......107 J3
  MAID/BEAR ME14......13 F1
  STRD ME2......72 B7
Crosswaite Av HNHL SE24......40 D5
Crosswall TWRH EC3N......24 C3
Crosswall Quay DUW CT17......8 D7
Cross Wy ROCH ME1......94 C3
Crossway EDEN TN8......206 E7
Crossways BH/WHM TN16......145 M5
  CANTW/ST CT2......166 D1
  SAND/SEL CR2......114 B2
Crossways Av EGRIN RH19......266 F7
  MARG CT9......112 F8
Crossways Bvd RDART DA2...47 J5
Crossways Cl LYDD TN29......327 J4
  SBGH/RUST TN4......84 D1
  STPH/PW TN12......242 B8
The Crossway ELTH/MOT SE9...63 K4
  SBGH/RUST TN4......270 A6
Crothall Hvn KEN/WIL TN24 *...2 D2
Crouch Cl BECK BR3......61 N5
Crouch Cl RCANTW CT4......168 D3
Crouch Hill Cl RSIT ME9......98 D3
Crouch House Rd EDEN TN8...206 B7
Crouch La BGR/WK TN15......151 K6
  HAWK TN18......318 D9
Crouchman Cl CDW/CHF RM16...32 D5
Crouchmans Cl SYD SE26......60 F2
Crouch Rd CDW/CHF RM16...35 H8
Crowborough Pl WARL CR6...144 B3
Crowborough Rd WARL CR6...144 B3
Crowbridge Rd
  KEN/WIL TN24......283 J2
Crowden Wy THMD SE28......28 B3
Crowder St WCHPL E1......24 E1
Crow Dr RSEV TN14......118 B9
Crowfoot Cl THMD SE28......28 C7
Crow Hl BRDST CT10......113 N8
  MARG CT9......116 A4
Crow Hill Rd BGR/WK TN15...151 K3
  MARG CT9......112 A5
Crowhurst Cl BRXN/ST SW9...40 B1
Crowhurst La BGR/WK TN15...90 E9
  OXTED RH8......204 C5
Crowhurst Rd BGR/WK TN15...151 H8
  LING RH7......234 C3
Crowhurst Village Rd
  LING RH7......205 H8
Crowhurst Wy STMC/STPC BR5...87 K2
Crowland Rd THHTH CR7......83 J1
Crowle Rd ASH TN23......282 E4
Crowley Crs CROY/NA CRO......82 D7
Crowmarsh Gdns FSTH SE23...41 J8
Crown Acres STPH/PW TN12...213 H4
Crown Cl ORP BR6......87 H8
  RSEV TN14......118 A4
  SIT ME10......99 M9
Crownfields
  MAID/BEAR ME14......156 B8
  SEV TN13......20 E4
Crown Gn GVE DA12......70 C4
Crown Hl CROY/NA CRO *......2 A5
Crown Hill Rd HB CT6......107 H2
Crown La CHST BR7......63 N7
  GVE DA12......70 C3
  HAYES BR2......85 N2
  RCANTW CT4......226 D8
  STRHM/NOR SW16......60 A4
Crown Lane Gdns
  STRHM/NOR SW16 *......60 A4
Crown Quay La SIT ME10......129 N1
Crown Rd EDEN TN8......206 E7
  ORP BR6......87 H9
  RSEV TN14......118 A4
  SIT ME10......99 M9
Crownstone Rd
  BRXS/STRHM SW2......40 A6
Crown St CMBW SE5......40 E1
  GILL ME7......7 K1
Crown Whf STRD ME2 *......19 K1
Crown Woods La
  WOOL/PLUM SE18......43 P6
Crown Woods Wy
  ELTH/MOT SE9......43 P6
Crows Camp Rd RCANTW CT4...197 L7
Crowstone Rd CDW/CHF RM16...32 D5
Crowther Cl STPH/PW TN12...246 B5
Crowther Rd SNWD SE25......83 M1
Crowton Ct SNOD ME6 *......124 A5
Croxley Cl STMC/STPC BR5......64 D8
Croxley St STMC/STPC BR5......64 D8
Croxted Cl DUL SE21......40 D8
Croxted Rd DUL SE21......60 D1
Croydo Cl BFN/LL DA15 *......125 P1
The Croydon F/O
  CROY/NA CRO......82 G8
  WALD ME5......95 M6
Croydon Gv CROY/NA CRO......82 G5
Croydon Rd BECK BR3......84 A2
  BH/WHM TN16......176 C2
  CROY/NA CRO......82 A2
  MTCM CR4......61 J7
  PGE/AN SE20......61 H8
  RCANTW CT4......144 C7
Crucifix La STHWK SE1......24 B5
Cruden Rd GVE DA12......70 B2
Cruick Av SOCK/AV RM15......31 H4
Crumpsall St ABYW SE2......28 E7
Crump's La RMAID ME17......217 P7
Crundale La RCANTE CT3......197 M1
Crundale Cl ASH TN23......282 C2
Crundale Rd RHAM ME8......96 F3
Crundale Wy MARG CT9......113 K3
Crundwell Rd
  SBGH/RUST TN4......240 C8
Crusader Cl PUR RM19......30 D7
  RHAM ME8......96 D6
Crusader Gdns CROY/NA CRO...83 K7
Crusoe Rd ERITH DA8......29 J8
Crutched Friars TWRH EC3N...24 C3
Crutches La HOO/HM ME3......71 K6
  STRD ME2......71 K7
Crutchley Rd CAT SE6......62 C1
  SIT ME10......129 K1
Cryals Rd STPH/PW TN12......272 D4
Cryol Rd ASH TN23......282 C1
Crystal Palace NRWD SE19 *...60 G6
Crystal Palace Pde NRWD SE19...60 G6
Crystal Palace Park Rd
  SYD SE26......61 H5
Crystal Palace Rd EDUL SE22...40 G7
Crystal Palace Station Rd
  NRWD SE19......60 G6
Crystal Ter NRWD SE19......60 D5
Cuba St POP/IOD E14......25 K8
Cuckmere Wy STMC/STPC BR5...87 L5
Cuckolds Green Rd
  HOO/HM ME3......54 D1
Cuckoo La ASH TN23......282 D1
  CDW/CHF RM16......32 A4
  HYTHE CT21......211 K5
  RTON TN11......211 K3
  STPH/PW TN12......273 H6
Cuckoowood Av
  MAID/BEAR ME14......155 L3
Cudham Cl MAID/BEAR ME14...155 P6
Cudham Dr CROY/NA CRO......114 C4
Cudham Gdns MARG CT9......113 K4
Cudham La North ORP BR6...116 F3
  RSEV TN14......116 E5
Cudham La South RSEV TN14...116 E5
Cudham Park Rd RSEV TN14...116 E5
Cudham Rd BH/WHM TN16...145 P4
  ORP BR6......116 B5
Cudham St CAT SE6......41 P8
Cudworth Rd KEN/WIL TN24...282 G7
Cuff Crs ELTH/MOT SE9......43 H8
Cugley Rd RDART DA2......47 J8
Cuilfail Rd FAV ME13......34 C1
Culford Rd CDW/CHF RM16...32 D5
Cullens Hl RCANTW CT4......257 K5
Cullen Sq SOCK/AV RM15......31 K5
Culloden Cl BERM/RHTH SE16...24 D2
Culloden St POP/IOD E14......25 N1
Cullum St FENCHST EC3M......24 B2
Culmers Ter FAV ME13 *......133 P4
Culmore Rd PECK SE15......41 H1
Culpeper Cl RMAID ME17......187 N1
Culpeper Cl ELTH/MOT SE9...43 H8
Culpepers CRBK TN17......274 D9
Culpepper Cl CANTW/ST CT2...136 F9
Culpepper Rd RHAM ME8......126 A1
  RMAID ME17......184 C8
Culverden Av
  SBGH/RUST TN4......270 C2
Culverden Down
  SBGH/RUST TN4......270 C1
Culverden Pk
  SBGH/RUST TN4......270 C2
Culverden Park Rd
  SBGH/RUST TN4......270 C2
Culverden Sq SBGH/RUST TN4...22 C1
Culverden St SBGH/RUST TN4...22 C2
Culver Dr OXTED RH8......204 A8
Culverley Rd CAT SE6......41 P9
Culver's La LYDD TN29......342 C7
Culverstone Cl HAYES BR2......85 J3
Culvey Cl HART DA3......68 G4
Cumberland Av BRDST CT10...113 M8
  CANT CT1......167 J5
  GVE DA12......49 N8
  MAID/SHEP ME15......186 A5
  WELL DA16......64 A4
Cumberland Dr BXLYHN DA7...44 G1
  DART DA1......46 F8
  RSIT ME9......98 D3
Cumberland Gdns RTW TN1...22 C5
Cumberland Ms RTW TN1......22 C6
Cumberland Rd
  CDW/CHF RM16......31 P5
  CHAT ME4......73 H8
  GILL ME7......7 J2
  HAYES BR2......85 H1
  MARG CT9......112 G2
  PLSTW E13......26 C1
  RAM CT11......16 D4
  SNWD SE25......83 N5
Cumberland Ter
  PGE/AN SE20 *......61 H6
Cumberland Wd
  RTWE/PEM TN2......22 C7
Cumberland Yd RTW TN1......22 C6
Cumberlow Av SNWD SE25......60 G8
Cumbrian Av BXLYHN DA7......45 N3
Cumdy Rd CAN/RD E16......26 F2
Cunningham Cl
  SBGH/RUST TN4......270 A1
  WWKM BR4......85 M6
Cunningham Crs
  BRCH CT7......110 F5
  WALD ME5......95 M6
Cunningham Rd
  SBGH/RUST TN4......270 C1
  WWKM BR4......84 D6
Cunningham Ter
  PGE/AN SE20 *......61 H6
Cupar Pl HOO/HM ME3......53 H8
Cupola Cl BMLY BR1......62 E4
Curates Wk RDART DA2......66 D2
Curlew Av RSIT ME9......98 C3
Curlew Cl SAND/SEL CR2......114 A5
  THMD SE28......28 C3
Curlew Crs STRD ME2......72 C1
Curlew Pl RFOLK CT18......288 C6
The Curlews GVE DA12......69 P1
Curnick's La WNWD SE27......60 C3
Curran Av BFN/LL DA15......44 B5
Currie Rd SBGH/RUST TN4...270 C2
Curtis La TENT TN30......301 J4
Curtis La RCANTW CT4......226 E1
Curtismill Cl STMC/STPC BR5...64 D9
Curtismill Wy STMC/STPC BR5...64 D9
Curtis Rd KEN/WIL TN24......283 H1
Curtis St STHWK SE1......24 C7
Curtis Wy FAV ME13 *......132 F6
  ROCH ME1......95 H7
  STHWK SE1......24 C7
Curtis Wood Rd HB CT6......107 K7
Curtis Wood Rd HB CT6......107 L7
Curton Av CHAT ME4......233 H6
  ORP BR6......86 E8
Curzon Dr GRAYS RM17......48 C9
Curzon Rd CHAT ME4......6 C7
  MARG CT9......291 J7
  MAID/BEAR ME14......155 M6
  THHTH CR7......82 B7
Cushman Ct CANT CT1......4 B7
Custom House Quay DUW CT17...8 C7
Custom House Reach
  BERM/RHTH SE16 *......25 J6
Custom House Rd
  BERM/RHTH SE16 *......25 J6
Cutbush Cl RMAID ME17......188 C5
Cutbush & Corrall Ct
  MAID/BEAR ME14 *......13 H4
Cutcombe Rd CMBW SE5......40 D2
Cuthbert Gdns SNWD SE25......60 E9
Cuthbert Rd CROY/NA CRO......82 C6
  WGOS CT8......111 M5
Cutlers Gardens Ar
  LVPST EC2M......24 B1
Cutler St HDTCH EC3A......24 B2
Cutmore St GVW DA11......49 M8
Cutter Cl STRD ME2......72 F4
Cutter Ridge Rd MED CT3......72 F4
The Cut HDCN TN27......278 E1
The Cuttings MSTR CT12......143 H3
Cutty Sark Ct RDART DA2 *...47 N6
Cuxton Cl BXLYHS DA6......64 A6
Cuxton Rd MAID/SHEP ME15...186 C6
  STRD ME2......18 A3
Cyclamen Rd SWLY BR8......88 E1
Cygnet Cl DIT/AY ME20......153 P2
Cygnet Rd WALD ME5......125 P3
Cygnet Vw WTHK RM20......31 J6
Cygnet Wy ASH TN23......252 C8
Cylinder Rd HYTHE CT21......308 C3
Cypress Av ASH TN23......252 B7
  HOO/HM ME3......73 L4
Cypress Cl GILL ME7......73 M9
  WSTB CT5......105 K7
Cypress Gdns BROCKY SE4......41 L6
Cypress Gv RDV CT15......230 C7
  RTWE/PEM TN2......270 F8
Cypress Rd SNWD SE25......60 E8
  STRD ME2......72 C6
Cypress Tree Cl BFN/LL DA15...44 B6
Cyprus Pl EHAM E6......27 H3
  RYE TN31......338 F7
Cyprus Rd FAV ME13......133 H6
Cyrena Rd EDUL SE22......40 F7
Cyril Rd BXLYHN DA7......44 G3
  ORP BR6......87 H4
Czar St DEPT SE8......25 K9

D

Dabbling Cl ERITH DA8 *......46 B1
Dabin Crs GNWCH SE10......42 A2
Dacca St DEPT SE8......25 J9
Dacre Crs SOCK/AV RM15......30 G4
Dacre Gdns LEW SE13......42 C5
Dacre Pk LEW SE13......42 C4
Dacre Rd CROY/NA CRO......82 D4
Dacres Est FSTH SE23......61 K2
Dacres Rd FSTH SE23......61 K2
Dartwood Cl HAYES BR2......86 A5
Daffodil Cl CROY/NA CRO......84 A5
Daffodil Rd STRD ME2......71 N9
Dagg La RBTBR TN32......328 F8
Daglish Cl NROM TN28......336 G7
Dagmar Rd CHAT ME4......95 N4
  CMBW SE5......41 K1
  SNWD SE25......83 K1
Dagnall Pk SNWD SE25......83 K2
Dagnall Rd SNWD SE25......83 K2
Dahlia Dr SWLY BR8......88 E1
Dahlia Gdns MTCM CR4......82 C1
Dahlia Rd ABYW SE2......28 A8
Daiglen Dr SOCK/AV RM15......31 K3
Dailmer Av HB CT6......106 G3
Dainford Cl BMLY BR1......62 F6
Dairsie Rd ELTH/MOT SE9......43 L4
Dairy Cl BMLY BR1......62 F6
  EYN DA4......60 C8
  THHTH CR7......60 C8
Dairy La EDEN TN8......206 C1
  WOOL/PLUM SE18......214 E6
Dairy Pl STPH/PW TN12 *......214 E6
Daisy Cl CROY/NA CRO......84 A5
Dakin Cl WCHPL E1......25 H1
The Dakins EGRIN RH19......265 J8
Dalberg Rd BRXS/STRHM SW2...40 A6
Dalberg Wy ABYW SE2......28 G6
Dalby Rd MARG CT9......15 K3
Dalby Sq MARG CT9......15 K3
Dale Cl WALD ME5......125 M3
Dale Park Rd NRWD SE19......60 D8
Dale Rd CHAT ME4......6 B1
  MEO DA13......68 E3
  ROCH ME1......95 H3
  SWLY BR8......65 L8
Daleside ORP BR6......117 H1
Daleside Cl ORP BR6......117 H1
Dale St CHAT ME4......6 B7
  RTW TN1......23 F2
The Dale HAYES BR2......85 N8
Dale Vw ERITH DA8......46 A3

Dale Wk KEN/WIL TN24.....252 F2
Dalewood SIT ME10.....129 P5
Dale Wood Rd ORP BR6.....86 F4
Dalison Ct STRD ME2.....124 A1
Dalkeith Rd DUL SE21.....40 C9
Dallas-Brett Crs FOLKN CT19.....311 H3
Dallas Rd SYD SE26.....
Dallaway Gdns EGRIN RH19.....265 H7
Dallinger Rd BRCH CT7.....110 C5
    LEE/GVPK SE12.....42 D7
Dallin Rd BXLYHS DA6.....45 H1
    WOOL/PLUM SE18.....43 M1
Dalmain Rd FSTH SE23.....41 K9
Dalmally Rd CROY/NA CR0.....83 L4
Dalmeny Av MARG CT9.....113 J4
    STRHM/NOR SW16.....62 A8
Dalmeny Rd ERITH DA8.....45 K2
Dalmeny Ter HYTHE CT21 *.....308 F5
Dalmore Rd DUL SE21.....60 C1
Dalroy Cl SOCK/AV RM15.....31 K2
Dalrymple Rd BROCKY SE4.....41 L5
Dalton Cl ORP BR6.....86 F7
Daltons Rd SWLY BR8.....88 B6
Daltons Shaw CDW/CHF RM16.....33 H1
Dalton St GILL ME7.....7 J1
    WNWD SE27.....40 B1
Dalwood St CMBW SE5.....40 E2
Damerham Cl CANTW/ST CT2.....166 D7
Damiani Cl CHAT ME4.....95 M4
Damien St WCHPL E1.....24 E1
Damigos Rd GVE DA12.....50 B9
Damon Cl SCUP DA14.....64 D2
Damsel Ct BERM/RHTH SE16 *.....24 D8
Damson Dr HOO/HM ME3.....73 K4
Danbury Crs SOCK/AV RM15.....31 L2
Danbury Ms WLGTN SM6.....82 A8
Danby St PECK SE15.....42 F4
Danebury CROY/NA CR0.....114 E1
Daneby Rd CAT SE6.....62 A2
Dane Cl BXLY DA5.....45 J8
    ORP BR6.....86 E9
    RSIT ME9.....97 N9
Dane Ct DEAL CT14.....230 C5
    RMAID ME17.....185 H9
Danecourt Gdns
    CROY/NA CR0.....83 L7
Dane Court Rd BRDST CT10.....113 H3
Dane Crs RAM CT11.....17 F1
Danecroft Rd HNHL SE24.....40 H7
Danedale Av SIT ME10.....129 M3
Dane End Rd WOOS CT8.....111 L5
Dane Gdns MARG CT9.....112 C5
Dane Hl MARG CT9.....15 H4
Dane Hill Rw MARG CT9.....15 J3
Danehurst WOOS CT8 *.....111 M4
Dane John Ct CANT CT1.....4 D6
Dane John Ms CANT CT1.....4 D6
Dane La RSIT ME9.....97 M9
Danemore TENT TN30.....301 J7
Dane Mt MARG CT9.....15 H4
Dane Park Rd MARG CT9.....15 J4
    RAM CT11.....17 H1
Dane Park Vils MARG CT9 *.....15 H4
Dane Ri MARG CT9.....113 H5
Dane Rd BRCH CT7.....110 D6
    MARG CT9.....15 J4
    RAM CT11.....17 G1
    RSEV TN14.....148 D2
    WARL CR6.....144 A2
Danes Cl GILL ME7.....68 C2
Danescombe LEE/GVPK SE12.....42 E8
Danes Ct DVE/WH CT16.....291 K5
Danes Dr IOS ME12.....16 A9
Danes Hl GILL ME7.....73 N9
Danes Me RSIT ME9.....99 M4
Danesmead Ter MARG CT9.....15 J5
Danes Vw CAT SE6.....62 A2
Dane Valley Rd MARG CT9.....112 G5
Daniel Bolt Cl POP/IOD E14.....25 L1
Daniel Cl CDW/CHF RM16.....33 J6
    CDW/CHF RM16.....33 J6
Daniel Gdns PECK SE15.....42 D1
Daniels Ct HRSTD CT5.....105 K5
Daniels La WARL CR6.....144 C1
Daniel's Rd PECK SE15.....43 J4
Daniel Wy RYE TN31.....347 N9
Danns La WBY/YAL ME18.....183 H5
Dansington Rd WELL DA16.....45 N4
Danson Crs WELL DA16.....45 D4
Danson La WELL DA16.....45 N4
Danson Md WELL DA16.....44 F6
Danson Rd BXLYHS DA6.....45 G5
Danson U/P BFN/LL DA15.....44 F7
Danson Wy RHAM ME8.....96 G5
Danton La RFOLK CT18.....287 P7
Danvers Rd TON TN9.....210 D9
Daphin St WCHPL E1.....24 D1
Darby Gdns HOO/HM ME3.....71 K4
Darby Pl FOLK CT20.....10 E3
Darby Rd FOLK CT20.....10 E3
D'arcy Av MARG CT9 *.....15 M6
D'Arcy Pl HAYES BR2.....85 K1
Darent Cl SEV TN13.....148 B7
Darenth Dr TONN TN10.....210 D2
Darenth Gdns BH/WHM TN16.....176 E2
Darenth Hl RDART DA2.....67 H4
Darenth La SEV TN13.....148 C6
    SOCK/AV RM15.....31 K2
Darenth Pk Av RDART DA2.....67 K1
Darenth Ri RDART DA2.....67 H4
Darenth Rd WALD ME5.....125 N2
Darenth Rd DART DA1.....66 E4
    WELL DA16.....44 C2
Darenth Rd South RDART DA2.....67 H3
Darenth Wy RSEV TN14.....118 E5
Darenth Wood Rd RDART DA2.....47 L9
Darent Md SEV TN13.....148 A7
Darent Valley Pth ERITH DA8.....46 D2
    EYN DA4.....88 C9

SEV TN13.....148 A6
Darfield Rd BROCKY SE4.....41 M6
Dargate Cl MAIDW ME16.....155 H5
    NRWD SE19.....60 F6
Dargate Rd FAV ME13.....134 C6
Dargets Rd WALD ME5.....125 M2
Dark Hl FAV ME13.....132 E5
Darland Av GILL ME7.....96 B4
Darley Cl CROY/NA CR0.....84 A5
Darlinghurst Rd FOLKN CT19.....310 B4
Darling Rd BROCKY SE4.....41 N4
Darlington Dr IOS ME12.....77 P1
Darlington Rd WNWD SE27.....60 B8
Darnach Cl WNWD SE27.....60 H7
Darnhills RAM CT11.....8 A9
Darnley Dr SBGH/RUST TN4.....240 B5
Darnley Rd GRAYS RM17.....32 C9
    GVE DA12.....13 J8
    STRD ME2.....18 A3
Darnley St GVW DA11.....49 L8
Darracott Cl DEAL CT14.....232 C4
Darrell Cl HB CT6.....107 H3
Darrell Rd EDUL SE22.....40 G6
Darren Gdns BRDST CT10.....143 L2
Darrick Wood Rd ORP BR6.....86 E6
Dart Cl STRD ME2.....18 A2
Dartford Rd BXLY DA5.....46 A7
    DART DA1.....5 L7
Dart Gn SOCK/AV RM15.....31 L2
Dartmoor Wk POP/IOD E14 *.....25 K7
Dartmouth Gv GNWCH SE10.....42 A2
Dartmouth Hl GNWCH SE10.....42 A2
Dartmouth Pl FSTH SE23.....61 J1
Dartmouth Rd GNWCH SE10.....42 A1
Dartmouth Rw GNWCH SE10.....42 B2
Dartmouth Rd HAYES BR2.....85 K4
    SYD SE26.....61 H2
Dartnell Rd CROY/NA CR0.....83 P4
Dartview Rd GRAYS RM17.....32 F7
Darwin Cl ORP BR6.....86 E9
Darwin Ct ROCH ME1 *.....19 H6
Darwin Dr TONN TN10.....210 C4
Darwin Rd BRCH CT7.....110 C5
    TIL RM18.....49 K3
    WELL DA16.....44 B4
Darwin St WALW SE17.....24 A7
Darryngton Av BRCH CT7.....110 D6
Dashmonden Cl STRD ME2.....72 C5
Dashwood Cl BXLYHS DA6.....45 H1
Dashwood Rd GVW DA11.....49 L9
Dassett Rd WNWD SE27.....60 D4
Datchelor Pl CMBW SE5 *.....40 D2
Datchet Rd CAT SE6.....61 M3
Davema Cl CHST BR7.....63 L7
Davenant Rd WCHPL E1.....24 D1
Davenport Av GILL ME7.....73 L9
Davenport Rd CAT SE6.....41 P7
    SCUP DA14.....64 F1
Davern Cl GNWCH SE10.....26 A7
Davey Cl ROCH ME1.....19 H6
Davey St PECK SE15.....24 C9
David Av MARG CT9.....113 J5
Davids Cl BRDST CT10.....143 N1
Davidson Rd CANTW/ST CT2.....83 K5
    CROY/NA CR0.....83 P6
David's Rd FSTH SE23.....41 M1
Davie Cl IOS ME12.....57 K8
Davies Cl CROY/NA CR0.....83 P6
Davington Cots FAV ME13 *.....132 F5
Davington Rd FAV ME13.....132 E5
Davis Av DEAL CT14.....232 F5
    GVW DA11.....49 J9
Davis Cl SEV TN13.....149 H7

Davis Farm Cots
    RMAID ME17 *.....215 K4
    SOCK/AV RM15.....31 P6
Davy's Pl GVE DA12.....70 A5
Dawell Dr BH/WHM TN16.....145 M2
Dawes Cl RDART DA2.....47 M6
Dawes Rd CANTW/ST CT2.....134 G8
    FAV ME13.....164 C1
Dawes St WALW SE17 *.....24 A7
Dawley Gn SOCK/AV RM15.....31 K2
Dawn La E/WMAL ME19.....153 K9
Dawn Ri IOS ME12.....79 M4
Dawson Av STMC/STPC BR5.....64 D8
Dawson Cl WOOL/PLUM SE18.....27 K7
Dawson Rd FOLKN CT19.....11 N1
Dawson's La BFN/LL DA15.....153 F2
Dayona Wy HB CT6.....106 H9
Days La BFN/LL DA15.....44 A8
Dayton Dr ERITH DA8.....30 A9
Dayton Gv PECK SE15.....41 J2
Deacon Cl STRD ME2.....162 E9
Deacon Ct SBGH/RUST TN4.....N7
Deacon Ct LING RH7 *.....234 F5
Deacons Leas ORP BR6.....86 F7
Deadmans La RYE TN31.....338 F6
Deakin Leas TON TN9.....240 E2
Deakins Ter ORP BR6.....87 H4
Deal Castle Rd DEAL CT14.....233 J4

Deal Porters Wy
    BERM/RHTH SE16.....24 F6
Deal Rd DEAL CT14.....231 P4
Deals Gtwy LEW SE13.....41 P2
The Deals RYE TN31.....338 E7
Deal St WCHPL E1.....24 D1
Dean Av IOS ME12.....57 H4
Dean Cl BERM/RHTH SE16.....24 F4
Dean Cft HB CT6.....107 N4
Deancross St WCHPL E1.....24 E2
Deane Cl WHSTB CT5.....105 M7
Deanery Rd EDEN TN8.....206 D1

Deanfield Gdns
    CROY/NA CR0.....83 J9
Dean Hl RCANTW CT4.....226 A8
Dean La MEO CT12.....92 E7
Dean Md FOLKN CT19.....310 E4

Dean Rd CROY/NA CR0.....83 J8
    SIT ME10.....99 M8
    STRD ME2.....71 N7
    THMD SE28.....27 H4
Dean's Blds WALW SE17.....24 A6
Deans Cl CROY/NA CR0.....83 L7
Deans Ct TON TN9 *.....240 E1
Deans Gate Hl FSTH SE23.....61 K2
Deans Hill Rd RSIT ME9.....128 C8
Dean St MAID/SHEP ME15.....184 G7
Dean's Wk RSIT ME9.....128 C4
Deansway Av CANTW/ST CT2.....137 K6
Deanwood Dr RHAM ME8.....126 C2
Deanwood Rd DVW CT17.....290 F6
Debnams Rd
    BERM/RHTH SE16.....24 F7
Deborah Cl WSTB SE16.....105 N1
Debrabant Cl ERITH DA8.....29 J9
De Burgh Hl DVW CT17.....8 A7
De Burgh St DVW CT17.....8 A2
Decima St STHWK SE1.....24 B6
Decimus Cl THHTH CR7.....85 J1
Deck Cl BERM/RHTH SE16.....24 G4
Decoy Hill Rd HOO/HM ME3.....53 M2
De Crespigny Pk CMBW SE5.....40 D5
Deedes Cl HYTHE CT21.....309 H4
Deepdale Av HAYES BR2.....85 J1
Deepdene WADH TN5.....394 A9
Deepdene Av CROY/NA CR0.....84 A6
Deerdale Rd HNHL SE24.....40 C5
Deerhurst Cl MAIDW ME16.....12 A5
Deerhurst Gdns MAIDW ME16 *.....12 A5
Deering La RSEV TN14.....117 L7
Deer Park Wy WWKM BR4.....85 J6
Deerson La RCANTE CT3.....169 J5
Deerton St RSIT ME9.....131 M3
De Frene Rd FSTH SE23.....61 K2
Defiant Cl WALD ME5.....95 M4
Defoe Cl WALD ME5.....95 N8
Defoe Pde CDW/CHF RM16.....33 J6
Defoe Rd BERM/RHTH SE16.....25 H5
De Frene Rd SYD SE26 *.....61 K3
Degema Rd CHST BR7.....63 M4
De Haviland Dr
    WOOL/PLUM SE18.....27 J8
De Havilland Cl RFOLK CT18.....288 E6
De Havillands RCANTW CT4.....198 B4
Dekker Rd DUL SE21.....40 E7
Delacourt Cl MSTR CT12.....142 G7
Delacourt Rd BKHTH/KID SE3.....42 A1
Delafield Rd CHARL SE7.....26 C5
Delaford Rd BERM/RHTH SE16.....24 D6
Delagarde Rd BH/WHM TN16.....176 D2
Delamare Crs CROY/NA CR0.....83 P5
Delamark Rd IOS ME12.....57 L6
Del Amere Gdns SNOD ME6 *.....123 P5
De l'Angle Rw RCANTW CT4 *.....165 J3
De Lapre Cl STMC/STPC BR5.....87 J4
Delargy Cl CDW/CHF RM16.....33 J6
Delarue Cl RTON TN11.....210 C2
Delaware Cl CANTW/ST CT2.....137 L2
De La Warr Rd EGRIN RH19.....265 D7
Delawyk Crs HNHL SE24.....40 D8
Delce Rd ROCH ME1.....19 H7
Delfside SWCH CT13.....201 P2
Delius Dr TONN TN10.....211 J4
Delisle Rd THMD SE28.....27 N4
Della Wy RTWE/PEM TN2.....23 J2
Dellfield Cl BECK BR3.....61 K8
Dellow St WCHPL E1.....24 E3
Dell Rd GRAYS RM17.....32 C7
The Dell ABYW SE2.....27 P8
    BECK BR3.....61 N6
    BXLY DA5.....45 J8
    EGRIN RH19.....265 L9
    NRWD SE19.....60 F7
    RCANTW CT4.....197 L2
    RDART DA2.....67 H9
Delmamey Cl BRDST CT10.....113 N8
Delme Crs BKHTH/KID SE3.....42 A2
Delmey Cl CROY/NA CR0.....83 L7
Delmonden Rd HAWK TN18.....316 D6
Delne St DEPT SE8.....41 N2
De Luci Rd ERITH DA8.....29 N8
De Lucy St ABYW SE2.....28 A3
Delves Av RTWE/PEM TN2.....270 F7
Demelza Cl SNOD ME6 *.....123 P5
De Mere Cl RHAM ME8.....96 G8
Demesne Rd WLGTN SM6.....82 D7
Demozay Cl RFOLK CT18.....288 D6
Denbeigh Dr TONN TN10.....210 C4
Denberry Dr SCUP DA14.....64 F2
Denbigh Cl CHST BR7.....63 K5
    SIT ME10.....129 M3
Denbigh Pl ASH TN23.....252 E9
Denbigh Rd MSTR CT12.....142 F3
    SBGH/RUST TN4.....270 F1
Denbridge Rd BMLY BR1.....63 N1
Dence Cl HB CT6.....107 N2
Dence Pk HB CT6.....107 N2
Dencorra Wy RHAM ME8.....96 F6
Dene Av BFN/LL DA15.....45 J5
Dene Cl BECK BR3.....85 J4
    BXLYHN DA15.....66 H3 (?)
    EGRIN RH19.....265 L9
    RASHE TN25.....252 F1
Denecroft Gdns GRAYS RM17.....32 E6
Dene Dr HART DA3.....90 B7
    ORP BR6.....87 H2
Denecroft Gdns GRAYS RM17.....32 E6
Dene Farm La RCANTE CT3.....199 K3
Dene Holm Rd GVW DA11.....49 K9
Dene Lodge Cl BGR/WK TN15.....151 J3
Dene Pth SOCK/AV RM15.....31 N7
Dene Rd BROCKY SE4.....41 L6
    HAYES BR2 *.....85 J4
Denesway ABYW SE2.....28 A3
The Dene CANT CT1.....166 C7
    CROY/NA CR0.....83 H8
    HYTHE CT21.....309 H5
    RASHW TN26.....215 P5
    SEV TN13.....21 F5
Dene Wk HART DA3.....68 G7

MARG CT9.....112 E6
Dene Wy RRTW TN3.....269 M1
Dengemarsh Rd LYDD TN29.....342 B9
Dengrove Pk
    CANTW/ST CT2 *.....137 J7
Denham Cl DVW CT17.....327 M1
Denham Rd RSIT ME9.....98 C7
Denison Ms HOO/HM ME3.....54 C4
Deniston Av BXLY DA5.....45 J4
Den La STPH/PW TN12.....214 B7
Denman Rd PECK SE15.....42 E1
Denmark Hl HNHL SE24.....40 D5
    CMBW SE5.....40 C2
    RAM CT11.....17 G2
    SNWD SE25.....83 N2
Denmark St FOLKN CT19.....11 G1
    PLSTW E13.....26 C1
Denmark Ter ASH TN23.....2 E7
Denmead Rd CROY/NA CR0.....82 G5
Denne Cl CANTW/ST CT2.....137 L6
Denne Manor La RCANTW CT4.....193 M4
Dennes La LYDD TN29.....342 A3
Dennes Mill Cl RASHE TN25.....223 N8
Denness Rd ASH TN23.....282 E1
Dennett Cl CROY/NA CR0.....82 F4
Dennett's Gv NWCR SE14.....41 L3
Dennett's Rd NWCR SE14.....41 J2
Denning Av CROY/NA CR0.....82 G6
Denning Cl MAIDW ME16.....154 C9
Dennis Rd GVW DA11.....69 G2
Dennis Wy CROY/NA CR0.....310 D4
Dennis Wilcocks Cl RSIT ME9.....98 C8
Den Rd HAYES BR2.....61 L7
Densole Cl BECK BR3.....61 M7
Densole La RFOLK CT18.....288 D4
Densole Wy RFOLK CT18.....288 D4
Denstead Ct CANTW/ST CT2.....136 B9
Denstead La CANTW/ST CT2.....165 J5
    RCANTW CT4.....165 K5
Denstead Oast RCANTW CT4 *.....165 J4
Denstroude La
    CANTW/ST CT2.....135 K5
Dent Cl SIT ME10.....129 H1
Dental St HYTHE CT21.....309 H5
Dent Cl SOCK/AV RM15.....31 K2
Dent-de-Lion Ct MARG CT9.....111 P5
Dent-de-Lion Rd MARG CT9.....111 M4
Denton Cl MAID/SHEP ME15.....186 B5
    RYE TN31.....338 D6
Denton Court Rd GVE DA12.....50 A9
Denton Gv WALD ME5.....45 N9
    DART DA1.....50 A9
    WELL DA16.....44 E1
Denton St GVE DA12.....50 A8
Denton Ter BXLY DA5 *.....46 B6
Denton Wy GILL ME7.....73 L9
Denver Cl ORP BR6.....86 F7
Denver Rd DART DA1.....66 B3
Depot St CMBW SE5 *.....24 A9
Deptford Br DEPT SE8.....41 N2
Deptford Broadway
    NWCR SE14.....41 M3
Deptford Church St DEPT SE8.....25 K9
Deptford High St DEPT SE8.....25 K9
Deptford Whrf DEPT SE8.....25 M7
De Quincey Ms CAN/RD E16.....26 A6
Derby Cl RTON TN11.....210 B4
Derby Hl FSTH SE23.....61 J1
Derby Hill Crs FSTH SE23.....61 J1
Derby Rd CROY/NA CR0.....82 G6
    MAID/SHEP ME15.....185 P3
    SWCH CT13.....96 B4
Derby Road Br GRAYS RM17.....32 C8
Derek Av WLGTN SM6.....82 A7
Derek Wallcott Cl HNHL SE24 *.....40 B6
Derifall Cl EHAM E6.....26 E8
Dering Cl HDCN TN27.....250 B5
    RCANTW CT4.....197 L2
Dering Pl CROY/NA CR0.....83 H8
Dering Rd CROY/NA CR0.....83 H8
    HB CT6.....3 H4
    KEN/WIL TN24.....197 L2
Dering Wy GVE DA12.....50 A8
Deringwood Dr
    MAID/SHEP ME15.....186 C2
Deringwood Pde
    MAID/SHEP ME15 *.....186 C2
Dermody Gdns LEW SE13.....42 B9
Dermody Rd LEW SE13.....42 A8
Deronda Rd HNHL SE24.....40 B9
Derrick Gdns CHARL SE7.....26 B5
Derrick Rd BECK BR3.....61 M9
Derringstone Hl RCANTW CT4.....198 D2
Derringstone St RCANTW CT4.....198 D2
Derry Av SOCK/AV RM15.....31 K1
Derry Downs STMC/STPC BR5.....87 K3
Derry Rd CROY/NA CR0.....82 G5
Derville Rd NROM TN28.....348 G5
Derwent Av RAM CT11.....142 F5
Derwent Cl DART DA1.....66 A4
Derwent Dr SBGH/RUST TN4.....270 B5
    STMC/STPC BR5.....87 H4
Derwent Gv EDUL SE22.....40 F5
Derwent Pde SOCK/AV RM15.....31 N8
Derwent Rg PGE/AN BR20.....61 L9
    TONN TN10.....210 P5
Derwent St GNWCH SE10.....26 A5
Derwent Wy RCANTE CT3.....199 H9
    RHAM ME8.....96 F6
Desenfans Rd DUL SE21.....40 E7
Desmond Crs FAV ME13.....133 K8
Desmond St NWCR SE14.....41 L9
Desmond Tutu Dr FSTH SE23.....61 L1
D'Este Rd RAM CT11.....17 H5
Detling Cl OXTED RH8.....143 H5
Detling Av BRDST CT10.....143 M3
Detling Cl IOS ME12.....57 K9
Detling Hl MAID/BEAR ME14.....156 D3
Detling Rd BMLY BR1.....62 F1
    ERITH DA8.....45 M1
    GVW DA11.....49 H9

Devalls Cl EHAM E6.....27 H3
Devenish Rd ABYW SE2.....27 P5
Deverell St STHWK SE1.....24 B6
Devereux Rd CDW/CHF RM16.....32 A6
Deveron Gdns SOCK/AV RM15.....31 K1
Devon Cl RHAM ME8.....96 F7
    WALD ME5.....95 P7
Devon Gdns BRCH CT7.....110 C2
Devonport St WCHPL E1.....24 F2
Devon Rd CANT CT1.....167 J4
    EYN DA4.....6 F7
    FOLKN CT19.....10 E3
    MAID/SHEP ME15.....185 P2
Devonshire Av DART DA1.....46 B7
Devonshire Cl
    RTWE/PEM TN2.....270 C6
Devonshire Dr GNWCH SE10.....41 P2
    SLH/COR SS17.....33 P5
Devonshire Gv PECK SE15.....24 E9
Devonshire Rd BXLYHS DA6.....44 G5
    CAN/RD E16.....26 C2
    CDW/CHF RM16.....31 P7
    DART DA1.....66 C2
    DVW CT17.....291 J7
    ELTH/MOT SE9.....63 J1
    FSTH SE23.....41 K8
    GILL ME7.....73 J8
    ORP BR6.....87 H5
Devonshire Rw LVPST EC2M.....24 B1
Devonshire Sq HAYES BR2.....85 L1
    LVPST EC2M.....24 B1
Devonshire Ter BRDST CT10.....113 N8
    EDUL SE22 *.....40 G5
Devons Rd BOW E3.....25 K1
Devon St PECK SE15.....24 G4
Dewar St PECK SE15.....42 G4
Dewberry Cl CHAT ME4.....73 H6
Dewberry Gdns EHAM E6.....26 F1
Dewberry St POP/IOD E14.....25 M2
Dewey La BRXS/STRHM SW2.....42 A1
Dewlands Av RDART DA2.....47 H8
Dexter Cl CANTW/ST CT2.....166 E2
    MAID/SHEP ME15 *.....32 B6
    RASHE TN25.....252 F1
Dexter Dr EGRIN RH19.....265 H8
Deyley Wy ASH TN23.....251 P9
D'Eynsford Rd CMBW SE5.....40 D2
Dhekelia Cl MAID/BEAR ME14.....155 M5
Dial Cl GILL ME7.....74 A4
    SWCM DA10.....48 A6
Dial Rd GILL ME7.....73 M9
Diameter Rd STMC/STPC BR5.....86 C4
Diamond Cl CDW/CHF RM16.....32 A6
    FOLKN CT19.....310 C2
Diamond Ct IOS ME12.....57 K8
Diamond Rd WSTB SE23.....105 M4
Diamond St PECK SE15.....42 E1
Diamond Vls NROM TN28 *.....336 E7
Diana Cl CDW/CHF RM16.....32 A6
    DEPT SE8.....25 J9
    SCUP DA14.....65 K5
Diana Gdns DEAL CT14.....232 F4
Diana Rd CHAT ME4.....95 M4
Dianthus Cl ABYW SE2.....28 A3
Dibden La RSEV TN14.....178 D3
Dibdin Rd DEAL CT14.....233 J2
Dickens Av CANT CT1.....167 J4
    DART DA1.....46 C5
    TIL RM18.....49 M2
Dickens Ct EGRIN RH19.....264 F7
    DART DA1.....46 C5
Dickens Dr CHST BR7.....63 N5
    E/WMAL ME19.....153 N5
Dickens Rd
    BERM/RHTH SE16.....24 D6
Dickenslan Cl HOO/HM ME3.....54 E5
Dickenson's Pl SNWD SE25.....83 M5
Dickens Rd BRDST CT10.....113 N8
    GVE DA12.....50 A9
    MAID/BEAR ME14.....155 K5
    ROCH ME1.....95 H4
Dickens Wk BRDST CT10 *.....113 N8
    HOO/HM ME3 *.....52 F4
Dickens Wood Cl NRWD SE19.....60 B6
Dickley La RMAID ME17.....189 M5
Dickson House CHARL SE7 *.....43 J1
Dickson Rd ELTH/MOT SE9.....43 J4

Dicksons Bourne
    RASHE TN25.....306 A2
Dieu Stone La DVE/WH CT16.....85 E3
Digby Cl RMAID ME17.....8 E3
Digby Rd FOLK CT20.....310 B9
Digdog La CRBK TN17.....277 H5
Diggon St WCHPL E1.....24 C1
Dignals Cl RHAM ME8.....96 F7
Dilhorne Cl LEE/GVPK SE12.....62 F2
Diligent Dr SIT ME10.....99 N7
Dillon Wy RTWE/PEM TN2.....270 G2
Dilly Rd RCANTW CT4.....195 L3
Dilly Wood Rd HOO/HM ME3.....71 L9
Dillywood La HOO/HM ME3.....71 K9
Dilton La BRCH CT7.....141 J1
Dimmock Cl PUR/KEN ME17.....243 J3
Dingleden La CRBK TN17.....318 F4
Dingle Gdns POP/IOD E14 *.....25 K3
Dingle Rd CROY/NA CR0.....83 H6
Dingwall Av CROY/NA CR0.....83 J6
Dingwall Rd CROY/NA CR0.....83 J6
Dinsdale Gdns SNWD SE25.....83 H4
Dinsdale Rd BKHTH/KID SE3.....26 A9
Dippers Cl BGR/WK TN15.....149 L3
Discovery Dr E/WMAL ME19.....153 N9

Discovery Rd
    MAID/SHEP ME15.....186 A5
Discovery Wk CANT CT1.....167 K3
    WAP E1W.....24 E4
Dislingbury Rd RTON TN11.....241 L6
Disraeli Cl MAID/SHEP ME15.....186 B6
    THMD SE28.....27 J8
Ditchburn St POP/IOD E14.....25 M3
Dittisham Rd ELTH/MOT SE9.....63 J3

Harbourland Cl
  MAID/BEAR ME14 ....155 N4
Harbour Ms *WSTB* CT5 * 105 L4
Harbourne La *RASHW* TN26 ...301 L3
Harbour Pde *RAM* CT11 ....17 C4
Harbour Rd *DVW* CT17 ....40 C4
  RYE TN31 ....358 F8
Harbour St *BRDST* CT10 ....113 N9
  FOLK CT20 ....11 C4
  RAM CT11 ....17 C4
  WSTB CT5 ....105 L4
The Harbour *RMAID* ME17 ....217 H5
Harbour View Rd *DVW* CT17 ...291 J7
Harbour Wy *FOLK* CT20 ....11 C3
Harcourt Av *BFN/LL* DA15 ....44 E7
  WLCTN SM6 ....
Harcourt Dr *CANTW/ST* CT2 ....4 A1
  HB CT6 ....106 C2
Harcourt Fld *WLCTN* SM6 ....82 A8
Harcourt Gdns *RHAM* ME8 ....127 H1
Harcourt Rd *BROCKY* SE4 ....41 M5
  BXLYHS DA6 ....
  FOLKN CT19 ....310 C4
  THHTH CT7 ....82 E3
  WLCTN SM6 ....
Harcourt Wy *GDST* RH9 ....204 B4
Hardcastle Cl *CROY/NA* CRO ...83 M3
Hardcourts Cl *WWKM* BR4 ....84 E8
Hardes Street *NWCR* SE14 ....
Hardie Cl *E/WMAL* ME19 * ...153 N5
Harding Cl *CROY/NA* CRO 83 L7
Harding Av *SBCH/RUST* TN4 ...240 B6
Hardinge Cl *RHAM* ME8 ....126 F1
Hardinge Rd *KEN/WIL* TN24 ...2 E2
  WOOL/PLUM SE18 ....27 J6
Harding Rd *BXLYHN* DA7 ....45 H1
  CDW/CHF RM16 ....33 H6
Hardings La *PGE/AN* SE20 ....61 K5
Hardinge Crs
  WOOL/PLUM SE18 ....27 K6
Hardman Rd *CHARL* SE7 ....26 C8
Hardres Court Rd
  RCANTW CT4 ....226 E4
Hardres Rd *RAM* CT11 ....17 G2
Hardres St *RAM* CT11 ....17 G2
Hardres Ter *STMC/STPC* BR5 *...87 L6
Hardwick Av *EHAM* E6 ....6 E5
Hardwick Crs *RDART* DA2 ....
Hardwicke Rd *DVW* CT17 ....291 J9
Hardwick Rd *FOLK* CT20 ....310 D7
  RTON TN11 ....210 B4
Hardwidge St *STHWK* SE1 ....24 B5
Hardy Av *CAN/RD* E16 ....26 B4
  GVW DA11 ....
Hardy Cl *BERM/RHTH* SE16 ....24 G5
  CANTW/ST CT2 ....166 B3
  KEN/WIL TN24 ....283 K1
  MAID ME15 ....95 N8
Hardy Cots *GNWCH* SE10 * ...25 N9
Hardy Gv *DART* DA1 ....46 C5
Hardy Rd *BKHTH/KID* SE3 ....26 A9
  NROM TN28 ....345 J1
  RDV CT15 ....
Hardy St *MAID/BEAR* ME14 ...113 F1
Harebell Cl *IOS* ME12 ....78 A3
  MAID/BEAR ME14 ....156 B7
Harebell Dr *EHAM* E6 ....
A & Billet Rd
  BKHTH/KID SE3 ....42 B2
Harebrook *RAM* CT11 ....17 H1
Haredale Cl *ROCH* ME1 ....
Haredale Rd *HNHL* SE24 ....40 C5
Haredon Cl *FSTH* SE23 ....41 J8
Harefield Ms *BROCKY* SE4 ....41 M4
Harefield Rd *BROCKY* SE4 ....41 M4
  SCUP DA14 ....64 F1
Hare La *LING* RH7 ....
Hares Bank *CROY/NA* CRO ...114 C4
Harescroft *RTWE/PEM* TN2 ...270 C9
Hare St *WOOL/PLUM* SE18 ...27 H6
Hare Ter *WTHK* RM20 * ....
Harfield Gdns *CMBW* SE5 * ...40 E6
Harfst Wy *SWLY* BR8 ....65 L7
Hargate Cl *RTWE/PEM* TN2 ...270 C9
Hargood Rd *BKHTH/KID* SE3 ...42 G2
Harkness Dr *CANTW/ST* CT2 ....4 A1
Harland Av *BFN/LL* DA15 ....63 P2
  CROY/NA CRO 83 L7
Harland Rd *LEE/GVPK* SE12 ...42 G7
Harlands Gv *ORP* BR6 ....86 C8
Harland Wy *SBCH/RUST* TN4 ...240 C6
Harlech Cl *ERID* ME2 ....71 P6
Harlequin Cl *HB* CT6 ....107 K4
Harlescott Rd *PECK* SE15 ....41 K5
Harleyford *BMLY* BR1 ....62 C7
Harley Gdns *ORP* BR6 ....86 F8
Harlinger St
  WOOL/PLUM SE18 ....26 F6
Harlington Rd *BXLYHN* DA7 ...44 C4
Harman Av *GVW* DA11 ....69 M4
  HYTHE CT21 * 307 N4
Harman Cl *STHWK* SE1 * 24 B7
Harman Dr *BFN/LL* DA15 ....44 B7
Harman Dr *EGRIN* RH19 ....265 L7
Harmans Md *EGRIN* RH19 ...265 K7
Harmer Rd *SWCM* DA10 ....48 D7
Harmer St *GVE* DA12 ....49 N7
Harmers Wy *HDCN* TN27 ...219 N7
Harmony Cl *SIT* ME10 ....129 L2
Harmony Pl *STHWK* SE1 ....24 C8
Harmony St *SBGH/RUST* TN4 ...270 A4
Harmony Wy *BMLY* BR1 ....62 E8
Harmsworth Gdns
  BRDST CT10 ....113 M8
Harness Rd *THMD* SE28 ....27 P5
Harnet St *SWCH* CT13 ....201 N1
Harnetts Cl *SWLY* BR8 * 88 C4
Harold Cl *FAV* ME13 ....28 B8
  GILL ME7 ....
  WGOS CT8 ....111 M5
Harold Ct *FAV* ME13 * ....
Harold Est *STHWK* SE1 * 24 B6

Harold Rd *BRCH* CT7 ....110 E5
  DEAL CT14 ....233 H1
  MARG CT9 ....
  NRWD SE19 ....112 C3
  RDART DA2 ....86 F5
  SIT ME10 ....130 A1
  STRD ME23 ....94 A3
Harold's Rd *DVE/WH* CT16 ...9 F2
Harold St *DVE/WH* CT16 ....8 D2
  QBOR ME11 ....77 J3
Harpenden Rd *WNWD* SE27 ...60 B1
Harper Cl *CDW/CHF* RM16 ...31 M8
Harper Rd *EHAM* E6 ....26 C2
Harp Farm Rd
  MAID/BEAR ME14 ....125 P7
Harp La *MON* CC3R 24 B3
Harple La *MAID/BEAR* ME14 ...156 C5
Harps Av *IOS* ME12 ....78 B1
Harpswood La *HYTHE* CT21 ...308 F4
Harptree Dr *WALD* ME5 ....95 L5
Harraden Rd *BKHTH/KID* SE3 ...42 C2
Harrap Cha *GRAYS* RM17 ...52 A8
Harrier Dr *SIT* ME10 ....129 P5
Harrier Ms *THAM* E6 ....26 C1
Harrier Wy *EHAM* E6 ....26 G1
Harries Rd *RTWE/PEM* TN2 ...270 C9
Harriet Dr *ROCH* ME1 ....94 F3
Harriet Gdns *CROY/NA* CRO ...83 M6
Harriets Cnr *WSTB* CT5 ....135 H1
Harriet Tubman Cl
  BRXS/STRHM SW2 ....40 A8
Harringe La *HYTHE* CT21 ...307 J2
Harrington Cl *CROY/NA* CRO ...82 D6
Harrington Crs
  CDW/CHF RM16 ....31 N4
Harrington Rd *SNWD* SE25 ...83 M1
Harrington Wy
  WOOL/PLUM SE18 ....26 E6
Harriot Cl *FOLKN* CT19 ....310 E4
Harriott Cl *GNWCH* SE10 ....26 A7
Harris Cl *GVW* DA11 ....69 J2
Harris Ct *GILL* ME7 ....96 C4
Harrison Dr *HOO/HM* ME3 ...53 L4
  RMAID ME17 ....188 F5
Harrison Rd *BGR/WK* TN15 ...151 P3
  RAM CT11 ....16 D5
Harrison's Ri *CROY/NA* CRO ...83 H2
Harrison's Whf *PUR* RH19 ...30 D8
Harrison Ter *FAV* ME13 * ...132 E3
Harrison Wy *SEV* TN15 ....148 F7
Harris Pl *MAID/SHEP* ME15 ...185 K2
Harris Rd *BXLYHN* DA7 ....44 C2
  IOS ME12 ....57 L6
Harris's Aly *RCANTE* CT3 ...169 K9
Harris St *CMBW* SE5 ....40 F2
Harrowby Gdns *GVW* DA11 ...69 J1
Harrow Cl *MAID* ME15 ....127 N5
Harrow Dene *BRDST* CT10 ...113 K8
  WARL CR6 ....87 J8
Harrow Gdns *ORP* BR6 ....86 C2
  WARL CR6 ....
Harrow Manor Wy *ABYW* SE2 ...28 B6
Harrow Pl *WCHPL* E1 ....24 B2
  RSEV TN14 ....117 M9
  WARL CR6 ....114 C9
Harrow Wy *ASH* TN23 ....282 B3
  MAID/BEAR ME14 ....
Harry Pay Cl *KEN/WIL* TN24 ...253 H5
Harrys Rd *RSIT* ME9 ....131 H2
Harry Wells Rd *HB* CT6 ....106 G3
Hart Cl *FOLK* CT18 * 288 D7
Hart Cnr *WLTN* RM20 * 31 N8
Hart Dyke Rd *STMC/STPC* BR5...87 K6
  SWLY BR8 ....65 M9
Hartfield Cl *TONN* TN10 ....211 H5
Hartfield Crs *WWKM* BR4 ....85 K7
Hartfield Pl *PGE/AN* SE20 ....61 H7
Hartfield Rd *EDEN* TN8 ....267 L5
  WWKM BR4 ....85 K8
Hartford Rd *BXLY* DA5 ....45 J7
Harting Rd *ELTH/MOT* SE9 ...63 J9
Hartington Cl *ORP* BR6 ....86 D8
Hartington Rd *CAN/RD* E16 ...26 C2
Hartington St *CHAT* ME4 ....6 D6
Hartlake Rd *RTON* TN11 ....241 M1
Hartlands Cl *BXLY* DA5 ....45 H7
Hartland Wy *CROY/NA* CRO ...84 B6
Hartley Bottom Rd *HART* DA3...91 L5
Hartley Cl *BMLY* BR1 ....63 K8
  MAID/BEAR ME14 ....186 C5
Hartley Court Gdns
  CRBK TN17 ....297 L4
Hartley Hl *HART* DA3 ....91 K5
Hartley Ms *RHAM* ME8 ....96 E3
Hartley Rd *BXLYHN* DA7 ....176 E1
  CRBK TN17 ....297 M5
  CROY/NA CRO 83 H1
  HART DA3 ....68 C8
  WELL DA16 ....44 E1
Hartlip Cl *IOS* ME12 ....56 G2
Hartlip Hl *RSIT* ME9 ....97 P7
Hartmann Rd *CAN/RD* E16 ...26 E4
Hartnokes *HAWK* TN18 ....317 J4
Hartnup St *MAIDW* ME16 ....185 H1
Harton Cl *BMLY* BR1 ....63 H7
Harton St *DEPT* SE8 ....41 N2
Hartpiece Cl *RHAM* ME8 ....97 J4
Hartsdown Pk *MARG* CT9 * ...14 C7
Hartsdown Rd *MARG* CT9 ...14 C6
Hart Shaw *HART* DA3 ....68 F8
Hartshill Rd *GVW* DA11 ....69 K1
Hartsland Rd *SEV* TN13 ....149 H8
Hart's La *GDST* RH9 ....204 A3
  NWCR SE14 ....41 L2
Hartstock Dr *ABYW* SE2 ....41 L5
Hartsmead Rd *ELTH/MOT* SE9...63 K1
Hartswood *SWCM* DA10 ....48 A5
Hart St *MAIDW* ME16 ....12 D7
  MON EC3R 24 B3
Hartville Rd *WOOL/PLUM* SE18...27 M7
Harty Av *RHAM* ME8 ....126 E2
Harty Ferry *IOS* ME12 ....102 C6
Harty Ferry Vw *WSTB* CT5 ...105 K8
Harty Ter *IOS* ME12 * 78 D1
Harvard Rd *LEW* SE13 ....42 A6
Harvel Av *STRD* ME2 ....71 N8

Harvel Cl *CHST* BR7 ....64 C9
Harvel Crs *ABYW* SE2 ....28 C8
Harvel La *MEO* DA13 ....122 C4
Harvel Rd *BGR/WK* TN15 ...121 P6
  MEO DA13 ....122 A5
Harvel St *MEO* DA13 ....122 D2
Harvest Bank Rd *WWKM* BR4...85 K7
Harvest Ct *HB* CT6 ....107 P4
Harvesters Cl *RHAM* ME8 ....97 H8
Harvesters Wy
  MAID/BEAR ME14 ....156 A8
Harvest Hl *EGRIN* RH19 ....265 H8
Harvest Rdg *E/WMAL* ME19 ...153 L2
Harvest Rd *TONN* TN10 ....210 G4
Harvest Wy *ASH* TN23 ....282 A1
  RFOLK CT18 ....288 E8
  SWLY BR8 ....88 B4
Harvey Cl *CDW/CHF* RM16 ...32 C5
Harvey Av *DEAL* CT14 ....233 H6
Harvey Dr *SIT* ME10 ....129 P3
Harvey Ct *HB* CT6 ....106 A5
Harvey Gdns *CHARL* SE7 * ...26 C8
Harvey Pl *FOLK* CT20 ....11 C3
Harvey Rd *CMBW* SE5 ....40 G2
  KEN/WIL TN24 ....253 J7
  MAID ME15 ....97 H6
Harvey St *FOLK* CT20 ....11 C3
Harville Rd *RASHE* TN25 ....223 M8
Harvill Rd *SCUP* DA14 ....64 F4
Harwich St *WSTB* CT5 ....105 L6
Harwick Dr *NROM* TN28 ....337 H5
Harwood Av *BMLY* BR1 ....62 F7
Harwood Rd *RHAM* ME8 ....97 L5
Harwoods Cl *EGRIN* RH19 ...265 J9
Harwood's La *EGRIN* RH19 ...265 J9
Hasborough Rd *FOLKN* CT19...11 K2
Hascombe Ter *CMBW* SE5 * ...40 D3
Haseley End *FSTH* SE23 * 41 J8
Haseltine Rd *SYD* SE26 ....61 M3
Haskard Cl *RFOLK* CT18 ....288 C8
Haslam St *PECK* SE15 ....40 F2
Haslemere Cl *WLGTN* SM6 ....82 D2
Haslemere Rd *BXLYHN* DA7 ...45 H3
  THHTH CR7 ....82 C2
Hasler Cl *THMD* SE28 ....28 B3
Hasletts Cl *RTW* TN1 ....270 E2
Haslewood Cl *HDCN* TN27 ...249 J7
Hassall Reach *CANT* CT1 ...166 A6
Hassell St *RASHE* TN25 ....225 H9
Hassendean Rd
  BKHTH/KID SE3 ....26 C9
Hassocks Cl *SYD* SE26 ....61 H2
Hassock Wd *HAYES* BR2 ....85 H2
Hasted Cl *SWCM* DA10 ....48 A7
Hasted Rd *CHARL* SE7 ....26 E8
  HOO/HM ME3 ....71 K6
  HOO/HM ME3 ....72 C4
  RSIT ME9 ....99 K8
Hasteds *RMAID* ME17 ....187 M1
Haste Hill Cl *RMAID* ME17 ...185 M8
Haste Hill Rd *RMAID* ME17 ...185 M8
Hastings Av *MARG* CT9 ....15 H4
Hastings Cl *GRAYS* RM17 ....51 P9
  PECK SE15 * 40 G1
Hastings Pl *CROY/NA* CRO ...83 L5
  CROY/NA CRO 85 L5
  HAWK TN18 ....317 H7
  HAYES BR2 ....85 P5
  MAID/SHEP ME15 ....13 H1
  RTWE/PEM TN2 ....271 N2
Hastings Rd *CRBK* TN17 ....319 J8
  CROY/NA CRO 85 L5
  HAWK TN18 ....317 H7
  HAYES BR2 ....85 P5
  MAID/SHEP ME15 ....13 H1
  RTWE/PEM TN2 ....271 N2
Hastings St *WOOL/PLUM* SE18...27 K6
Hatcham Park Ms *NWCR* SE14...41 K3
Hatcham Park Rd *NWCR* SE14...41 K3
Hatcham Rd *PECK* SE15 ....24 F9
Hatchers Ms *STHWK* SE1 * ...24 B3
Hatches La *STPH/PW* TN12 ...212 E4
Hatch La *RCANTW* CT4 ....165 J7
Hatch Rd *RMAID* ME17 ....189 K6
Hatcham Gv *MARG* CT9 * 14 B4
Hatcliffe Cl *BKHTH/KID* SE3 ...42 D4
Hatcliffe St *GNWCH* SE10 ...26 B7
Hatfeild Rd *CDW/CHF* RM16...31 N8
Hatfield Cl *BKHTH/KID* SE3 * ...42 E1
  RAM CT11 ....16 D3
  STRD ME2 ....72 A7

Haven Pl *CDW/CHF* RM16 ....32 D5
Havens Ms *BOW* E5 ....25 J1
Haven St *HOO/HM* ME3 ....72 C2
The Haven *CDW/CHF* RM16 ...32 G7
  DEAL CT14 * 263 J2
  HYTHE CT21 ....308 B7
Haventhorpe *KEN/WIL* TN24 ...2 D1
Haven Wy *CHAT* ME4 ....6 A4
Havering Cl *RTWE/PEM* TN2 ...271 J2
Havering St *WCHPL* E1 ....24 G2
Haverthwaite Rd *ORP* BR6 ....86 E7
Havil St *CMBW* SE5 ....40 E2
Havisham Cl *ROCH* ME1 ....95 J4
Havisham Pl *NRWD* SE19 ....60 B1
Havisham Rd *GVW* DA11 ....50 C9
Hawarden Gv *HNHL* SE24 ....60 C3
Hawarden Pl *RCANTE* CT3 * ...169 K9
Hawbeck Rd *RHAM* ME8 ....126 F7
Hawden Cl *RTON* TN11 ....210 C6
Hawden La *RTON* TN11 ....210 C7
Hawden Rd *TON* TN9 ....210 E8
Hawe Cl *CANTW/ST* CT2 ....136 F9
Hawe La *RCANTE* CT3 * 137 M6
Hawes Av *RAM* CT11 ....142 G5
Hawes Rd *BMLY* BR1 ....62 F7
Hawes Rd *BMLY* BR1 ....62 F7
Hawfield Bank *ORP* BR6 ....87 K7
Hawgood St *BOW* E5 ....25 K1
Hawk Cnr *WTHK* RM20 * 31 N8
Hawkenbury Cl
  RTWE/PEM TN2 ....23 J7
Hawkenbury Md
  RTWE/PEM TN2 ....270 C7
Hawkenbury Ri *STRD* ME23 ...72 B5
Hawkenbury Rd *RRTW* TN3 ...271 H7
  STPH/PW TN12 ....246 F3
Hawkenbury Vls
  STPH/PW TN12 * 246 F3
Hawke Pl *BERM/RHTH* SE16 * ...24 G5
Hawke Rd *NRWD* SE19 ....60 B6
Hawkesbury Dr *DVW* CT17 ...313 L1
Hawkes Cl *GRAYS* RM17 ....32 C9
Hawkesfield Rd *FSTH* SE23 ...61 L1
Hawkes Pl *SEV* TN13 ....
Hawkes Rd *DIT/AY* ME20 ....124 F8
Hawkhurst Cl *BRCH* CT7 ....111 J5
Hawkhurst Rd *HAWK* TN18 ...297 L8
  RHAM ME8 ....
  WADH TN5 ....316 A4
Hawkhurst Wy *BRDST* CT10 ...143 M2
  WWKM BR4 ....84 E6
Hawkinge Wy *HYTHE* CT21 ...290 G8
Hawkins Cl *GILL* ME7 ....96 C5
  SIT ME10 ....
Hawkins Dr *CDW/CHF* RM16...31 N5
Hawkins Rd *FOLKN* CT19 ....310 A5
Hawkins Ter *CHARL* SE7 ....26 F8
Hawkins Wy *LEW* SE13 ....61 N4
Hawkley Gdns *WNWD* SE27 ...60 B1
Hawkridge Dr *GRAYS* RM17 ...52 C9
Hawksbrook La *BECK* BR3 ....84 E5
Hawksdown Rd *DEAL* CT14 ...232 G9
Hawksdown Rd *DEAL* CT14 ...233 H9
Hawkshead Cl *BMLY* BR1 ....62 C5
Hawks Hill La *RSIT* ME9 ....129 K9
Hawks La *CANT* CT1 ....4 D4
Hawks Ms *GNWCH* SE10 * 42 A1
Hawksmoor Cl *EHAM* E6 ....26 F2
  WOOL/PLUM SE18 ....27 M8
Hawks Rd *WCHPL* E1 ....24 E3
Hawkstone Est
  BERM/RHTH SE16 ....24 F7
Hawkstone Rd
  BERM/RHTH SE16 ....24 F7
Hawks Wy *ASH* TN23 ....282 B1
Hawkwood *MAIDW* ME16 ....154 G7
Hawkwood Cl *CHST* BR7 ....63 N7
Hawkwood La *CHST* BR7 ....63 N7
Hawley Cl *HPTN* TW12 ....
Hawley Rd *DART* DA1 ....66 E1
Hawley Sq *MARG* CT9 ....15 G4
Hawley St *MARG* CT9 ....15 G4
Hawley Ter *RDART* DA2 * 66 E1
Hawser V *RDART* DA2 * 66 C4
Hawser Rd *ROCH* ME1 ....95 H5
Hawstead La *ORP* BR6 ....87 N9
Hawstead Rd *CAT* SE6 ....41 P7
Hawthorn Av *CANTW/ST* CT2...166 F2
  IOS ME12 ....57 J8
  THHTH CR7 ....60 B7
Hawthorn Cl *DVW* CT17 ....290 F5
  EDEN TN8 ....206 G8
  GVE DA12 ....69 M3
  HYTHE CT21 * 308 F1
  LYDD TN29 ....337 L2
  RAM CT11 ....143 G3
  STMC/STPC BR5 ....86 E5
Hawthorn Cl
  E/WMAL ME19 * 153 K9
Hawthorndene Cl *HAYES* BR2 *...85 J6
Hawthorndene Rd *HAYES* BR2...85 J6
Hawthorn Dr *WWKM* BR4 ....85 H8
Hawthorne Av
  BH/WHM TN16 ....115 N9
  RHAM ME8 ....96 F4
Hawthorne Cl *BMLY* BR1 ....63 K9
  WSTB CT5 ....260 E1
Hawthorne Rd *BELV* DA17 * ...28 E7
Hawthorn Gv *PGE/AN* SE20 ...61 H7
Hawthorn La *SEV* TN13 ....148 C7
Hawthorn Pl *ERITH* DA8 ....29 H8
Hawthorn Rd *ASH* TN23 ....282 E4
  BXLYHS DA6 * 45 J6
  SIT ME10 ....129 M1
  STRD ME2 ....18 A3
  WALD ME5 * ....
Hawthorns *HART* DA3 ....91 H1
  WALD ME5 * 125 L4
The Hawthorns *BRDST* CT10 ...113 H9
  DIT/AY ME20 ....154 D3
  WOOL/PLUM SE18 ....175 K7
Hawthorn Ter *BFN/LL* DA15...44 B7
Hawthorn Wk
  RTWE/PEM TN2 ....241 N9
  TONN TN10 ....210 F3
Haxted Rd *BMLY* BR1 ....62 F7
  LING RH7 ....235 H2

Hay Currie St *POP/IOD* E14 ...25 L2
Hayday Rd *CAN/RD* E16 ....26 B1
Haydens Ct *STMC/STPC* BR5...87 K4
Haydens Ms *TON* TN9 ....210 F7
The Haydens *TON* TN9 ....210 F7
Haydon Cl *MAIDW* ME16 ....154 C8
Haydon St *TWRH* EC3N 24 C3
Haydon Wk *TWRH* EC3N 24 C2
Hayes Cha *WWKM* BR4 ....84 C3
Hayes Cl *HAYES* BR2 ....85 K6
  HOO/HM ME3 ....71 L4
  WTHK RM20 ....31 M9
Hayesden La *RTW* TN3 ....239 M5
Hayesford Park Dr *HAYES* BR2...85 J2
Hayes Gdn *HAYES* BR2 ....85 K5
Hayes Gv *EDUL* SE22 ....40 F8
Hayes Hl *HAYES* BR2 ....85 H5
Hayes Hill Rd *HAYES* BR2 ....85 J5
Hayes La *BECK* BR3 ....62 B9
  HAYES BR2 ....85 K2
  RSIT ME9 ....128 A3
Hayes Mead Rd *HAYES* BR2...85 H5
Hayes Plat *RYE* TN31 ....330 B8
Hayes Rd *HAYES* BR2 ....85 K1
  RDART DA2 ....47 L8
Hayes Ter *GVE* DA12 * 70 C4
Hayes Wk *E/WMAL* ME19 ....183 H1
Hayes Wy *BECK* BR3 ....84 B3
Hayes Wood Av *HAYES* BR2...85 L5
Hayfield *E/WMAL* ME19 ....153 L2
Hayfield Rd *STMC/STPC* BR5...87 H2
Hayfields *WALD* ME5 ....126 A3
Hay Hl *SWCH* CT13 ....201 L8
Hay La *DEAL* CT14 ....201 M8
Hayle *TIL* RM18 ....34 B6
Hayle Mill Rd
  MAID/SHEP ME15 ....185 L3
Hayle Rd *MAID/SHEP* ME15 * ...185 L3
Hayley Cl *CDW/CHF* RM16 ...31 N6
Haymakers La *ASH* TN23 ....282 B3
Haymans Hl *STPH/PW* TN12 ...274 A1
Hayman Wk *DIT/AY* ME20 * ...124 E7
Haymen St *CHAT* ME4 ....
Haymerle Rd *PECK* SE15 ....24 H7
Haynes Cl *BKHTH/KID* SE3 ....42 C4
Haynes La *NRWD* SE19 ....60 E5
Haynes Rd *GVW* DA11 ....69 L4
Hay Pl *SWLY* BR8 * ....
Hayrick Cl *MAID/BEAR* ME14 ...156 B7
Haysel *SIT* ME10 ....129 P3
Hayslenge St *MAID* ME15 ....13 G8
Hays Rd *SNOD* ME6 ....127 N1
Hayton Rd *RASHE* TN25 ....285 P7
Haywain Cl *ASH* TN23 ....282 B3
  MAID/BEAR ME14 ....156 C8
  STPH/PW TN12 ....283 H4
The Haywain *DVE/WH* RH8 ...174 G6
Hayward Av *STRD* ME2 ....72 B7
Hayward Cl *DART* DA1 ....45 M6
  DEAL CT14 ....252 F5
  KEN/WIL TN24 ....253 K9
Hayward Dr *DART* DA1 ....66 E2
Haywardens *LING* RH7 ....234 C4
Hayward Rd *RAM* CT11 ....
Hayward's Hl *FAV* ME13 ....161 N8
Haywood Pl *CDW/CHF* RM16 *...33 K5
Haywood Ri *ORP* BR6 ....86 E3
Haywood Rd *HAYES* BR2 ....85 N1
Hazelbrook Rd *FAV* ME13 ....132 D6
Hazel Av *HOO/HM* ME3 ....
  MAIDW ME16 ....
Hazelbank *RRTW* TN3 ....269 L5
Hazelbank Rd *CAT* SE6 ....62 B1
Hazel Cl *CROY/NA* CRO 84 C1
  MTCM CR4 ....
  RDV CT15 ....260 D1
Hazelden Cl *BGR/WK* TN15 ...120 D3
Hazelden Rd *BROCKY* SE4 ....44 L6
Hazeldown Cl *DVW* CT17 ....290 F5
Hazel Dr *ERITH* DA8 ....46 A2
Hazel End *SWLY* BR8 ....88 D2
Hazel Gdns *CDW/CHF* RM16 ...32 F6
Hazel Gv *ORP* BR6 ....85 K3
  SYD SE26 ....61 K3
  WALD ME5 ....95 N6
Hazel Hts *RASHE* TN25 ....252 B4
Hazelhurst *BECK* BR3 ....62 B7
Hazelmere Rd *STMC/STPC* BR5...87 J3
Hazelmere Wy *HAYES* BR2 ....85 K3
Hazel Rd *DART* DA1 ....66 D1
  ERITH DA8 ....46 A2
Hazel Shaw *TONN* TN10 ....210 F4
The Hazels *RHAM* ME8 ....
Hazel Street Rd *RSIT* ME9 ....128 B9
Hazel Wk *HAYES* BR2 ....86 B3
Hazel Wy *STHWK* SE1 * 24 C7
Hazelwood
  RTWE/PEM TN2 ....240 C9
Hazelwood Dr *MAIDW* ME16...154 C8
Hazelwood Cl *CHST* BR7 ....
Hazelwood Dr *DVE/WH* RH8 ...175 K7
Hazelwood Meadow
  SWCH CT13 ....201 N3
  OXTED RH8 ....175 L8
  RSEV TN14 ....116 B6
Hazen Rd *E/WMAL* ME19 ....153 K9
Hazledean Rd *CROY/NA* CRO...83 J6
Hazlemere Dr *GILL* ME7 ....96 D1
Hazlitt Cl *HB* CT6 ....108 A5
Hazlitt Dr *MAIDW* ME16 ....155 J7
Headcorn Dr *CANTW/ST* CT2...136 F9
Headcorn Gdns *MARG* CT9 ...112 G4
Headcorn Rd *BMLY* BR1 ....62 C4
  HDCN TN27 ....278 A1
  RHAM ME8 ....188 D2
  RMAID ME17 ....188 D2
  RMAID ME17 ....217 H5
  STPH/PW TN12 ....214 C1
  THHTH CR7 ....82 E6
Head Hl *FAV* ME13 ....133 N5
Head Hill Rd *FAV* ME13 ....133 N5
Headingley Rd *MAIDW* ME16...154 G6

Headland Wy LING RH7......234 F5
Headley Av WLGTN SM6......82 E9
Headley Dr CROY/NA CR0......114 F2
The Head Race
  MAID/SHEP ME15......185 J1
Head St WCHPL E1......24 C2
Heald Gdns DIT/AY ME20 *......154 E3
Heald St NWCR SE14......41 M2
Healy Dr DART SE2......86 C8
Heansill La HAWK TN18......316 C6
Heard Wy SIT ME10......100 A9
Hearn's Blds WALW SE17 *......24 A7
Hearns Cl STMC/STPC BR5......87 K1
Hearnshaw St POP/IOD E14......25 H1
Hearns Rd STMC/STPC BR5......87 K1
Heartenoak Rd HAWK TN18......317 J2
Heart in Hand Rd HB CT6......108 C8
Hearts Delight La
  RCANTE CT3......169 L5
Hearts Delight Rd RSIT ME9......129 J4
Heartwood Dr ASH TN23......252 D6
Heath Av BXLYHN DA7......28 C9
Heath Cl CAN/RD ME16 *......137 L6
  STMC/STPC BR5......87 J1
  SWLY BR8......65 N8
Heathclose Av DART DA1......46 B8
Heathclose Rd DART DA1......46 A9
Heathcote Cl DIT/AY ME20......46 E2
Heathcote Dr EGRIN RH19......264 E6
Heathdene Dr BELV DA17......28 C7
Heathedge SYD SE26......61 N1
Heathend Rd BXLY DA5......45 N9
Heather Av RAM CT11 *......5 J3
Heather Bank STPH/PW TN12......243 J3
Heatherbank CHST BR7......63 L8
Heatherbank Cl DART DA1......45 N7
Heather Cl EHAM E6......27 K2
  LEW SE13 *......
  MARC CT9......112 B5
  SIT ME10......129 P2
  WALD ME5......125 L1
Heather Dr DART DA1......46 A8
  MAID/SHEP ME15......185 N1
  TENT TN30......301 J4
Heather End SWLY BR8......88 C2
Heather Rd LEE/GVPK SE12......62 E1
Heatherside Rd SCUP DA14......62 C2
The Heathers CRBK TN17......297 M4
Heather Wk TONN TN10......210 G6
Heatherway EGRIN RH19......264 C5
Heather Wy SAND/SEL CR2......114 A3
Heatherwood Cl RMAID ME17......187 P9
Heathfield CHST BR7......63 N5
  RMAID ME17......
Heathfield Av DVE/WH CT16......291 J5
  MAID/BEAR ME14......155 P5
Heathfield Cl CAN/RD E16......26 E1
  HAYES BR2......85 M9
  MAID/BEAR ME14......155 P5
  WALD ME5......95 N7
Heathfield Cots GRAYS RM17 *......31 P9
Heathfield Gdns
  CROY/NA CR0 *......83 H8
Heathfield La CHST BR7......63 N5
Heathfield Rd BMLY BR1......62 D6
  BXLYHS DA6......45 H5
  HAYES BR2......85 M9
  KEN/WIL TN24......155 N5
  SAND/SEL CR2......83 J8
  SEV TN13......148 D7
Heathfield Ter SWLY BR8 *......27 M9
  WOOL/PLUM SE18......
Heathfield V SAND/SEL CR2......114 A3
Heathfield Wy RCANTW CT4......228 C6
Heath Gdns DART DA1 *......46 C9
Heath Gv MAIDW ME16......184 F1
  PGE/AN SE20......
Heathlands Ri DART DA1......46 B8
Heath La BKHTH/KID SE3......42 B3
  DART DA1......46 B9
Heathlee Rd BKHTH/KID SE3......42 D5
  DART DA1......45 N7
Heathley End CHST BR7......63 N5
Heathorn St MAID/BEAR ME14......13 H2
Heath Park Dr BMLY BR1......63 J9
Heath Ri HAYES BR2......85 K3
Heath Rd BXLY DA5......45 J8
  CDW/CHF RM16......32 C5
  DART DA1......46 D7
  MAID/SHEP ME15......184 D1
  MAIDW ME16......154 E9
  RMAID ME17......187 H7
  THHTH CR7......60 C9
Heathside RASHW TN26......322 E5
Heath Side STMC/STPC BR5......86 D5
Heathside Av BXLYHN DA7......44 C1
  RMAID ME17......185 H7
Heath St DART DA1......46 D8
The Heath E/WMAL ME19......153 M7
Heathview Av DART DA1......45 N7
Heathview Crs DART DA1......46 A8
Heath View Dr ABYW SE2......28 C9
Heath View Gdns
  CDW/CHF RM16......32 D5
Heathview Rd THHTH CR7......60 C9 *
Heath Vw WOOL/PLUM SE18......82 D5
Heath Vls WOOL/PLUM SE18 *......27 N8
Heathway BKHTH/KID SE3......42 E1
  CROY/NA CR0......
Heath Wy ERITH DA8......45 L2
Heathwood Dr RAM CT11......143 K3
Heathwood Gdns CHARL SE7......26 F7
  SWLY BR8......65 L8
Heathwood Pde SWLY BR8 *......65 L8
Heathwood Wk BXLY DA5......65 L8
Heaton Rd CANT CT1......166 D6
  PECK SE15......41 H4
Heaverham Rd BGR/WK TN15......149 N2
Heavitree Cl WOOL/PLUM SE18......27 J8
Heavitree Rd
  WOOL/PLUM SE18......27 L8
Heber Rd EDUL SE22......40 F7
Heckford St WAP E1W......24 D4
Hectorage Rd TON TN9......240 F1
Hectors La EGRIN RH19......265 M9
Hector St WOOL/PLUM SE18 *......27 M7
Hedgecourt Pl EGRIN RH19......264 B4
Hedge Place Rd RDART DA2......47 M7

Hedgerows ASH TN23......282 A1
The Hedgerows GVW DA11......69 J1
The Hedgerow
  MAID/BEAR ME14......156 B7
Hedgers Wy ASH TN23......282 A3
The Hedges MAID/BEAR ME14......155 M4
Hedgley St LEE/GVPK SE12......42 D6
Hedingham Rd CDW/CHF RM16......31 M8
Hedley Av WTHK RM20......31 M9
Hedley St MAID/BEAR ME14......13 C2
Hedley Ct RSIT ME9......129 M7
Heela La CANTW/ST CT2......137 H5
Heel Rd FAV ME13......191 N4
Hegarty Ct SNOD ME6......123 N4
Hegarts Gdns CROY/NA CR0......82 C9
Heights Ter DVW CT17......8 A7
The Heights BECK BR3 *......62 A6
  CHARL SE7......26 D8
  SEV TN13 *......148 D7
  WSTB CT5......105 K7
Helder Gv LEE/GVPK SE12......42 D8
Helding Cl HB CT6......107 N4
Helegan Cl ORP BR6......86 E3
Helena Av MARG CT9......112 D5
Helena Corniche FOLK CT20......309 P4
Helena Rd RFOLK CT18......311 M1
Helena Sq BERM/RHTH SE16......25 H3
Helen Cl DART DA1......46 B8
Helen Keller Cl TONN TN10 *......210 G6
Helen St WOOL/PLUM SE18 *......27 J7
Helen Thompson Cl RSIT ME9......99 M2
Helenmore Rd MSTR CT12......32 A8
Hellings St WAP E1W......24 D4
Hellyar Ct ROCH ME1 *......95 H2
Helmdon Cl MSTR CT12......143 H2
Helsinki Sq BERM/RHTH SE16......25 H6
Helvellyn Av RAM CT11......142 C5
Helvetia St CAT SE6......61 M1
Hemley Rd CDW/CHF RM16......53 L2
Hemmings Cl SCUP DA14......64 D3
Hempstead La RSIT ME9......130 D2
Hempstead Rd GILL ME7......126 C2
Hempstead Valley Dr
  GILL ME7......126 D2
Hempsted Dr ASH TN23 *......2 D4
Hemp Wk WALW SE17 *......24 A7
Hemstead Rd ERITH DA8......45 N1
Henbane Cl MAID/BEAR ME14......156 B7
Henderson Dr DART DA1......46 A8
Henderson Rd BH/WHM TN16......115 M6
  CROY/NA CR0......
Hendley Dr CRBK TN17......297 P2
Hendre Rd STHWK SE1......24 B7
Hendy Rd SNOD ME6......124 A3
Heneage Crs CROY/NA CR0......114 F4
Heneage La HDTCH EC3A......24 B2
Heneage St WCHPL E1......24 D2
Henfield Cl BXLY DA5......45 J7
Hengest Rd DEAL CT14......233 J2
Hengist Av MARG CT9......112 C4
Hengist Ct MAID/BEAR ME14 *......13 G4
Hengist Rd BRCH CT7......110 D6
  ERITH DA8......45 L1
Hengrave Rd FSTH SE23......41 J8
Hengrove Ct BXLY DA5......44 G9
Henham Gdns STPH/PW TN12......213 H4
Henhurst Rd IGH DA3......68 P8
Heniker La RMAID ME17......217 J5
Henley Cl BERM/RHTH SE16 *......25 H3
  RHAM ME8......96 G6
  RTWE/PEM TN2......23 H2
  RYE TN31 *......338 D6
  WALD ME5......95 M8
Henley Deane GVW DA11......69 J3
Henley Dr STHWK SE1......24 C7
Henley Fds MAID/BEAR ME14......156 B6
  TENT TN30......301 J5
Henley Rd CAN/RD E16......26 G5
  STPH/PW TN12......243 H2
Henley St MEO DA13......92 G3
Hennel Ct FSTH SE23......41 J2
Henrietta Cha CHAT ME4......75 H5
Henrietta Ct DEPT SE8......25 J9
Henriques St WCHPL E1......24 D3
Henry Addlington Cl EHAM E6......27 J1
Henry Cooper Wy
  ELTH/MOT SE9......63 J2
Henry Ct CANT CT1......7 H1
Henry De Grey Cl GRAYS RM17......32 A7
Henry Dent Cl CMBW SE5......40 D4
Henryson Rd BROCKY SE4......41 N6
Henry St BMLY BR1......62 F7
  CHAT ME4......7 F7
  GRAYS RM17......32 D9
Henry Tate Ms
  STRHM/NOR SW16......60 A4
Hensford Gdns SYD SE26......61 H3
Henshaw St WALW SE17......24 A7
Hensil La HAWK TN18......316 C6
Henslowe Rd EDUL SE22......40 G6
Henson Cl ORP BR6......86 C6
Henville Rd BMLY BR1......62 F7
Henwick Rd ELTH/MOT SE9......43 H4
Henwood Green Rd
  RTWE/PEM TN2......271 N1
Henwoods Crs
  RTWE/PEM TN2......271 N2
Henwoods Mt
  RTWE/PEM TN2......271 P2
Hepburn Cl CDW/CHF RM16......31 N7
Hepburn Gdns HAYES BR2......85 J5
Hepplewhite Ms WALD ME5......125 L4
Herald Gdns WLGTN SM6......82 E9
Herbert Ms BRXS/STRHM SW2......40 A2
Herbert Pl WOOL/PLUM SE18......27 J9
Herbert Rd BXLYHN DA7......44 G3
  CHAT ME4......7 G7
  HAYES BR2......85 N2
  KEN/WIL TN24......146 E1
  RAM CT11......16 B4
  RHAM ME8......97 H6
  SWCM DA10......49 J8
  SWLY BR8......66 B5
  WOOL/PLUM SE18......43 M1

Herbert St HOO/HM ME3 *......54 G4
Herbert Sreet DVW CT17......291 J6
Herdsden HOO/HM ME3......73 K2
Herdson Rd FOLK CT20......310 D6
Hereford Cl KEN/WIL TN24......252 F2
Hereford Gdns BRCH CT7......110 G6
Hereford Pl NWCR SE14 *......41 M1
Hereford Retreat PECK SE15......40 G1
Hereford Rd
  MAID/SHEP ME15......185 P4
Hereson Rd BRXN/ST SW9......143 L2
  RAM CT11......17 H1
Heretage Cl BRXN/ST SW9......40 B4
Hereward Av BRCH CT7......110 E5
Herga Hyll CDW/CHF RM16......33 H1
Heritage Cl WSTB CT5......105 H8
Heritage Dr GILL ME7......96 C5
Heritage Gdns DVE/WH CT16......8 C2
Heritage HI HAYES BR2......85 M9
Heritage Rd FOLK CT20......310 A5
  WALD ME5......95 M8
Herman Ter CHAT ME4......6 C5
Hermitage Cl MAIDW ME16......154 E7
  HYTHE CT21......308 G5
Hermitage La MAIDW ME16......154 E7
  NRWD SE19......60 C6
  RMAID ME17......216 B4
Hermitage Rd EGRIN RH19......264 L6
  HOO/HM ME3......54 A4
  NRWD SE19......60 C6
The Hermitage FSTH SE23......41 J9
  LEW SE13 *......42 A3
Hermitage Wall WAP E1W......24 D4
Hermit Rd CAN/RD E16......26 A1
Hernaby Cl CANTW/ST CT2......137 K6
  RCANTE CT3......171 K4
  WSTB CT5......105 J5
Herndon Dr HB CT6......107 M2
Herne Bay Rd CANTW/ST CT2......137 K6
  RCANTE CT3......171 K3
Herne HI HNHL SE24......40 C6
Herne Hill Rd HNHL SE24......40 D4
Herne PI HNHL SE24......40 B6
Herne Rd RHAM ME8......96 F4
Herne St HB CT6......107 M5
Herneville Gdns HB CT6......107 N2
Heron Cl RSIT ME9......98 C3
Heron Ct HAYES BR2......85 M4
  RCANTE CT3......171 N8
Heron Crs SCUP DA14......64 A3
Herondale SAND/SEL CR2......114 A3
Heronden Rd
  MAID/SHEP ME15......186 C7
  SWCH CT13......200 F8
Heronden Wy SWCH CT13......201 H8
Heron Dr IOS ME12......78 B2
Heron Forstal Av RFOLK CT18......288 E8
Herongate Rd SWLY BR8......65 N5
Heron HI BELV DA17......28 E7
Heron Hill La MEO DA13......122 C1
Heron Rd EGRIN RH19......265 J8
Heron Quays POP/IOD E14......25 J8
Heron Rd CROY/NA CR0 *......83 K5
  DIT/AY ME20......153 N3
  NHNL SE24......40 C5
Heronsbank HOO/HM ME3......53 L4
Herons Brook RASHE TN25......233 N3
Herons Cl RCANTW CT4......229 M3
Heron's Wy HYTHE CT21......308 D7
Herons Wy RTWE/PEM TN2......241 P9
Herontye Dr EGRIN RH19......264 E6
Heron Wk ASH TN23......252 B9
Heron Wy HOO/HM ME3......54 G4
  WALD ME5......95 M8
  WTHK RM20......31 M2
Herringham Rd CHARL SE7......26 D6
Herschell Rd BRCH CT7......110 G5
  FSTH SE23......41 L2
Herschell Rd East DEAL CT14......233 H6
Herschell Rd West DEAL CT14......233 H6
Herschell Sq DEAL CT14......233 H6
Hertford Pl RAM CT11......17 H1
Hertford Rd MARG CT9......112 C5
Hertford St RAM CT11......16 E5
Hertford Wy MTCM CR4......82 D1
Herts Crs MAID/SHEP ME15......185 L8
Hertsmere Rd POP/IOD E14......25 K3
Herying Cl STRD ME2......124 A1
Hesiers Hill WARL CR6......145 H2
Hesiers Rd WARL CR6......145 H1
Hesketh Av RDART DA2......47 H9
Heskett Pk RTWE/PEM TN2......271 P2
Hesperus Crs POP/IOD E14......25 J8
Hessel St WCHPL E1......24 E2
Hesterman Wy CROY/NA CR0......82 D5
Hestia Wy ASH TN23......282 B5
Heston St DEPT SE8......41 M2
Hevelius Cl GNWCH SE10......26 A8
Hever Av BGR/WK TN15......120 B1
Hever Cl MAID/SHEP ME15......186 C5
Hever Court Rd GVE DA12......69 N5
Hever Crt ELTH/MOT SE9......63 L3
Hever Gdns BMLY BR1......64 L8
  MAIDW ME16......12 B7
Heverham Rd
  WOOL/PLUM SE18......27 M7
Hever La EDEN TN8......237 H5
Hever Pl CANTW/ST CT2......166 F1
  SIT ME10......129 K2
Hever Rd BGR/WK TN15......120 B5
  EDEN TN8......237 H2
Heversham Rd BXLYHN DA7......44 G3
Hever Wood Rd
  BGR/WK TN15......120 B1
Hewett Pl SWLY BR8......88 C1
Hewitt Cl CROY/NA CR0......84 D7
  GILL ME7......95 M9
  MAIDW ME16......155 G5
Hewitt Rd DVE/WH CT16......8 C2
Hewitt Sq KEN/WIL TN24......253 J8
Hewitts Rd ORP BR6......117 N2
Hew Watt Cl CDW/CHF RM16......62 G2
Hexal Rd CAT SE6......62 C2
Hexham Rd WNWD SE27......60 C1
Hextable La MTN TN23......282 C2
  MAIDW ME16......155 H5

Heyford Cl RFOLK CT18......288 E8
High Oak HI RSIT ME9......98 F8
High Pk RYE TN31......329 P6
High Point ELTH/MOT SE9......63 M2
High Rdg ASH TN23......281 P1
  CRBK TN17......274 C9
Highridge GILL ME7......96 C5
  HYTHE CT21......309 M4
Highridge Cl MAID/BEAR ME14......156 C7
High Rd CDW/CHF RM16......31 P4
  CDW/CHF RM16......32 C1
  RDART DA2......66 B2
High Rocks La RRTW TN3......269 P7
Highshore Rd PECK SE15......40 F3
High Snoad Wd RASHE TN25......192 D9
Highstead Crs ERITH DA8......45 N2
Highsted Rd SIT ME10......129 N6
High St BECK BR3......61 N7
  BH/WHM TN16......149 L6
  BH/WHM TN16......176 D3
  BMLY BR1......62 F4
  BRDST CT10......113 K8
  CANT CT1......4 C4
  CANTW/ST CT2......137 L8
  CHAT ME4......224 D8
  CRBK TN17......297 P5
  CRBK TN17......319 L3
  CROY/NA CR0......83 H7
  DART DA1......46 D8
  DIT/AY ME20......154 E1
  DVE/WH CT16......8 E3
  E/WMAL ME19......153 M2
  EDEN TN8......206 D9
  EDEN TN8......267 H5
  EGRIN RH19......265 J8
  EYN DA4......89 K6
  GILL ME7......7 J1
  GRAYS RM17......32 B9
  GVW DA11......48 F7
  HAWK TN18......316 C4
  HB CT6......107 M2
  HDCN TN27......247 M4
  HDCN TN27......278 A7
  HOO/HM ME3......54 C4
  HOO/HM ME3......56 D2
  HYTHE CT21......309 J5
  IOS ME12......79 J5
  IOS ME12......78 D1
  KEN/WIL TN24......2 D3
  LING RH7......326 G7
  LYDD TN29......336 C7
  LYDD TN29......334 E5
  LYDD TN29......342 A6
  MAID/BEAR ME14......12 E5
  MARG CT9......115 L5
  MSTR CT12......141 K6
  MSTR CT12......142 G2
  NROM TN28......336 D7
  ORP BR6......86 B6
  ORP BR6......116 D1
  OXTED RH8......174 G6
  PGE/AN SE20......61 J6
  PUR RM19......30 D8
  OBOR ME11......16 D2
  RASHE TN25......223 P8
  RCANTE CT3......168 C3
  RCANTE CT3......169 K9
  RCANTW CT4......257 L4
  RDART DA2......67 P2
  RDV CT15......292 E1
  RFOLK CT18......286 C2
  RHAM ME8......96 E8
  RMAID ME17......189 L7
  RMAID ME17......217 H5
  ROCH ME1......19 F4
  ROCH ME1......24 L6
  RRTW TN3......239 P6
  RRTW TN3......295 H3
  RSEV TN14......148 F1
  RSIT ME9......98 E3
  RTON TN11......211 H4
  RTON TN11......211 P2
  RTON TN11......238 G5
  RTW TN1......22 D6
  RTWE/PEM TN2......271 M2
  RYE TN31......338 F7
  SCUP DA14......64 D3
  SEV TN13......21 G4
  SIT ME10......99 M8
  SNOD ME6......123 P5
  SOCK/AV RM15......30 F4
  STMC/STPC BR5......87 K3
  STPH/PW TN12......243 J9
  STPH/PW TN12......271 M2
  STPH/PW TN12......246 C6
  STRD ME2......18 C1
  STRD ME2......93 P9
  SWCH CT13......201 J8
  SWCH CT13......201 P1
  SWLY BR8......66 B5
  TENT TN30......301 H8
  THHTH CR7......45 D6
  TON TN9......210 F9
  WADH TN5......314 B5
  WADH TN5......315 N3
  WBY/YAL ME18......213 N1
  WSTB CT5......105 L4
  WWKM BR4......84 D5
Highstreet Rd FAV ME13......134 C5
High Street St Gregory's
  CANT CT1......5 F2
High Street St Lawrence
  ......16 A3
The High St HDCN TN27......221 H4
High Tor Cl BMLY BR1......62 F6
High Trees BRXS/STRHM SW2......40 A3
  CROY/NA CR0......83 J8
  RDART DA2......67 K8
High Trees Cl KEN/WIL TN24......253 K8
High Vw HOO/HM ME3......71 L3
Highview MEO DA13......122 C6
High View Av GRAYS RM17......32 C9
  HB CT6......106 G1
  WLGTN SM6......82 E9

Highmore Rd BKHTH/KID SE3......42 C1
High Highmore Rd BKHTH/KID SE3......98 F8
High Oak HI RSIT ME9......329 P6
High Beeches ORP BR6......117 H1
  ME12......59 J5
  IOS ME12......78 D1
  KEN/WIL TN24......2 D3
  LING RH7......326 G7
  LYDD TN29......336 C7
  LYDD TN29......334 E5
  LYDD TN29......342 A6
  MAID/BEAR ME14......12 E5
  MARC CT9......115 L5
  MSTR CT12......141 K6
  MSTR CT12......142 G2
  NROM TN28......336 D7
  ORP BR6......86 B6
  ORP BR6......116 D1
  OXTED RH8......174 G6
  PGE/AN SE20......61 J6
  PUR RM19......30 D8
  OBOR ME11......16 D2
Highfield Gdns
  CDW/CHF RM16......32 C5
  MARC CT9......14 C7
Highfield HI NRWD SE19......60 D6
Highfield La RASHE TN25......283 M2
Highfield Rd BGR/WK TN15......145 M2
  BH/WHM TN16......86 A1
  BMLY BR1......64 E7
  BXLYHS DA6......44 D8
  CHST BR7......63 N5
  DART DA1......46 C8
  EGRIN RH19......264 C5
  IOS ME12......77 N1
  KEN/WIL TN24......253 K9
  MSTR CT12......142 C1
  RSIT ME9......130 C3
  RHAM ME8......97 H9
  RTWE/PEM TN2......271 N2
Highfield Rd North DART DA1......46 D7
Highfield Rd South DART DA1......46 D7
Highfields Av HB CT6......107 P2
Highfields Rd EDEN TN8......206 D5
Highfields Vw HB CT6......107 P2
High Firs SWLY BR8......88 D1
Highgate HI TOWN TN10......317 H6
Highgate Rd WSTB CT5......106 A5
Highgate Wk FSTH SE23......61 J1
High Gv BMLY BR1......62 F5
Highgrove ELTH/MOT SE9......43 P8
Highgrove Ct BECK BR3......62 A9
Highgrove Rd WALD ME5......95 M9
High Halden Rd HDCN TN27......278 B7
  RASHW TN26......278 D7
High Hilden Cl TONN TN10......210 D6
High Hill Wd WARL CR6......114 F8
High House La RTON TN11......211 L5
  TIL RM18......33 L6
Highland Cl FOLK CT20......310 C7
Highland Cots WLGTN SM6 *......82 E9
Highland Dft BMLY BR1......62 D7
Highland Rd BMLY BR1......62 D7
  BXLYHS DA6......45 J5
  HAYES BR2......85 H5
  MAID/SHEP ME15......186 B4
  NRWD SE19......60 E5
  RCANTW CT4......195 K2
  RSEV TN14......118 A5
Highlands Cl STRD ME2......71 M9
Highlands Crs LYDD TN29......337 M1
Highlands Gdns MSTR CT12......142 G2
Highlands HI SWLY BR8......66 A8
Highlands Pk BGR/WK TN15......149 M8
  SEV TN13......149 H3
Highland Ter LEW SE13 *......41 P4
High La CTHM CR3......144 C2
  WARL CR6......144 C2
High Level Dr SYD SE26......60 G1
High Limes NRWD SE19 *......60 E5
Highmead WOOL/PLUM SE18......28 B1
High Md WWKM BR4......84 B9
High Meadow DVW CT17......329 P6
  RASHW TN26......278 B7

Highview CI FAV ME13 * 164 C1
High View Rd FAV 60 F8
Highview Dr WALD 95 J9
High View Gdns GRAYS RM17 ..32 D8
Highview Pk RFOLK CT18 .....311 K3
Highview Rd IOS ME12 .....58 C9
High View Rd SCUP DA14 .....64 D3
High View Rd DART DA1 * 66 D6
The Highway ORP BR6 .....87 J9
  WAP E1W 24 F3
  WCHPL E1 .....24 F3
High Weald Landscape Trail
  EGRIN RH19 .....264 C9
High Weald Wk RRTW TN3...269 H9
  RRTW TN3 .....269 L1
  RRTW TN3 .....271 H7
  RTON TN11 .....240 F4
  SBGH/RUST TN4 .....22 A7
  SBGH/RUST TN4 .....240 F6
  SBGH/RUST TN4 .....269 P3
Highwood CI FSTH SE23 .....40 C9
  ORP BR6 .....86 D6
Highwood Dr ORP BR6 .....86 D6
Highwoods CI HOO/HM ME3 ..71 K3
High Woods La RRTW TN5 .....271 J6
  RTWE/PEM TN2 .....23 K6
Hilary CI ERITH DA8 .....45 K2
  HB CT6 .....107 P2
Hilary Gdns ROCH ME1 .....94 E4
Hilbert CI RTW TN1 .....23 H1
Hilbert Rd RTWE/PEM TN2 .....270 F2
Hilborough Wy ORP BR6 .....86 C9
Hilda Lockert Wk
  BRXN/ST SW9 .....40 B3
Hilda May Av SWLY BR8 .....65 N8
Hilda Rd CHAT ME4 .....6 D7
  IOS ME12 .....77 M1
Hilda Ter BRXN/ST SW9 * 40 A3
Hilda Vale Rd ORP BR6 .....86 B8
Hilden Av RTON TN11 .....210 C6
Hildenborough Crs
  MAIDW ME16 .....154 C5
Hildenborough Gdns
  BMLY BR1 .....62 C5
Hildenborough Rd
  RTON TN11 .....180 C7
  RTON TN11 .....209 M7
Hilden Dr ERITH DA8 .....46 B1
Hildenlea PI HAYES BR2 .....62 C8
Hilden Park Rd RTON TN11 .....210 C6
Hildersham CI EDEN TN8 .....206 A6
Hildershaw La EDEN TN8 .....206 A6
Hillary Av GVW DA11 .....69 J2
Hillary CI EGRIN RH19 .....265 K6
Hillary Rd MAID/BEAR ME14 .....155 M5
Hill Av RDV CT15 .....229 P9
Hillbeck CI PECK SE15 .....41 J1
Hillborough Dr HB CT6 .....108 C4
Hillborough Gv WALD ME5 .....125 M2
Hill Brow BMLY BR1 .....63 H7
  DART DA1 .....45 P7
  MAID/BEAR ME14 .....156 D7
  SIT ME10 .....129 L3
Hillbrow Av CANTW/ST CT2 .....137 L6
  HB CT6 .....107 N4
Hillbrow La ASH TN23 .....252 C8
Hillbrow Rd ASH TN23 .....2 A6
  BMLY BR1 .....62 E8
  RAM CT11 .....16 D1
Hillbury Gdns WADH TN5 .....315 H5
Hill Cha WALD ME5 .....125 K2
Hill CI CHST BR7 .....63 M4
  MEO DA13 .....69 J6
Hill Cnr RRTW TN3 .....268 C5
Hillcote Av STRHM/NOR SW16..60 A6
Hill Ct HOO/HM ME3 .....72 F3
Hillcourt Rd EDUL SE22 .....41 H7
Hill Crs BXLY DA5 .....45 L9
  RCANTE CT3 .....229 H1
Hill Crest BFN/LL DA15 .....44 C8
  EGRIN RH19 .....265 H2
  SBGH/RUST TN4 .....240 E9
  SEV TN13 .....148 F7
Hillcrest ASH TN23 .....251 N9
  EDEN TN8 .....207 J5
  HNHL SE24 * 40 D5
  RYE TN31 .....338 E5
Hillcrest Av WTHK RM20 .....31 K9
Hillcrest CI BECK BR3 .....84 C3
  KEN/WIL TN24 .....253 H5
  SYD SE26 .....62 G3
Hillcrest Dr RDART DA2 .....47 N6
  RTWE/PEM TN2 .....270 C3
  STRD ME2 .....94 B4
Hillcrest Gdns DEAL CT14 .....232 F7
  RAM CT11 .....16 A4
Hillcrest Rd BH/WHM TN16 .....145 N1
  BMLY BR1 .....62 G2
  CHAT ME4 .....95 L4
  DART ME4 .....5 N8
  DEAL CT14 .....263 H4
  HYTHE CT21 .....308 C4
  ORP BR6 .....87 H6
  RCANTE CT3 .....168 B2
Hillcrest Vw BECK BR3 .....84 C3
Hillcroft Rd RHAM E6 .....27 J1
  HB CT6 .....107 N3
Hillden Shaw
  MAID/SHEP ME15 .....185 M3
Hilldown Rd HAYES BR2 .....85 H5
Hill Dr SWCH CT13 .....201 J7
Hilldrop Rd BMLY BR1 .....62 F5
Hill End ORP BR6 .....86 D4
  WOOL/PLUM SE18 .....43 L2
Hilley CI BRDST CT10 .....113 M7
Hillery CI WALW SE17 .....24 A7
Hillfield PI SEV TN13 .....148 C5
Hillfield Rd SEV TN13 .....148 C5
Hillgarth SBGH/RUST TN4 .....240 D9
Hill Green Rd RSIT ME9 .....127 M5
Hill House Dr CDW/CHF RM16..33 J8
  GRAYS RM17 .....32 B9
Hillhouse Rd DART DA1 .....66 C5
Hilliard's Ct WAP E1W * 24 F3
Hillier Gdns CROY/NA CR0 .....82 F9

Hillier's La CROY/NA CR0.........82 D7
Hillingdale BH/WHM TN16 .....145 L3
Hillingdon Av SEV TN13 .....149 H6
Hillingdon Ri SEV TN13 .....149 J7
Hillingdon Rd BXLYHN DA7 .....45 L4
  GVW DA11 .....69 M1
Hill La RFOLK CT18 .....287 N7
Hillman Av HB CT6 .....106 F2
Hillman CI BRXN/ST SW9 .....40 B5
Hillmore Gv SYD SE26 .....61 K4
Hillreach WOOL/PLUM SE18 .....26 C8
Hill Ri FSTH SE23 .....41 H9
  RASHE TN25 .....252 B4
  RDART DA2 .....67 K4
Hill Rd FOLKN CT19 .....310 B8
  RDART DA1 .....66 E1
  ROCH ME1 .....94 A5
  WALD ME5 .....124 E2
Hillsboro Rd EDUL SE22 .....40 E6
Hillsgrove CI WALD DA16 .....44 E1
Hill Shaw HART DA3 .....91 J3
Hillshaw Crs STRD ME2 .....94 C1
Hillside AYN DA4 .....89 L4
  FOLK CT20 .....310 B8
  GRAYS RM17 .....32 E7
  RDART DA2 .....67 L4
  TON TN9 .....240 D2
Hillside Av CANTW/ST CT2 .....166 B3
  GVE DA12 .....69 P1
  QBOR ME11 .....77 H4
  STRD ME2 .....72 B7
Hillside CI EGRIN RH19 .....265 H5
Hillside CI STRD ME2 * 18 E1
  SWLY BR8 .....88 F1
Hillside Dr GVE DA12 .....69 P1
Hillside Gdns
  BRXS/STRHM SW2 * 60 A1
  HAYES BR2 .....85 K6
Hillside Rd BGR/WK TN15 .....149 L2
  BH/WHM TN16 .....145 P4
  CHAT ME4 .....6 E5
  CROY/NA CR0 .....82 A6
  DART DA1 .....46 A7
  DVW CT17 .....291 H5
  FAV ME13 .....191 J4
  HAYES BR2 .....62 D9
  IOS ME12 .....58 B9
  SEV TN13 .....149 J8
  WSTB CT5 .....105 P5
Hillside St HYTHE CT21 .....308 C5
Hillside Ter FAV ME13 * 132 F6
  GVE DA12 * 49 M9
The Hillside ORP BR6 .....117 J3
Hills La BGR/WK TN15 .....119 N6
Hills PI STRD ME2 * 93 M9
Hills Ter CHAT ME4 .....6 B6
Hillstead Rd RASHE TN25 .....255 N3
  RTW TN1 .....23 N1
Hill St RASHE TN25 .....255 N3
Hill Top CRBK TN17 .....298 A3
  GVW DA11 .....48 G7
  HDCN TN27 .....221 H2
  RCANTE CT3 .....168 B8
Hill Top CRBK TN17 .....275 K3
Hilltop MAID/SHEP ME15 .....184 C8
  TON TN9 .....240 E2
  WSTB CT5 .....105 L7
Hilltop Cots SYD SE26 * 61 H3
Hilltop Dr RYE TN31 .....338 E5
Hilltop Gdns DART DA1 * 86 F6
  ORP BR6 .....86 D5
Hilltop Rd IOS ME18 .....78 A2
  STRD ME2 .....72 A9
  WTHK RM20 .....31 K9
Hilltop Wk CTHM CR3 .....144 B5
Hill Vw BGR/WK TN15 .....151 K5
  KEN/WIL TN24 .....3 F1
Hill View CI DEAL CT14 .....287 M4
Hillview Crs ORP BR6 .....86 F5
Hill View Dr THMD SE28 .....27 M4
  WELL DA16 .....44 A3
Hillview Rd WSTB CT5 .....105 L6
  CANTW/ST CT2 .....166 B2
  CHST BR7 .....63 L4
Hill View Rd HART DA3 .....68 F7
  ORP BR6 .....86 G5
  RTON TN11 .....210 C5
  SBGH/RUST TN4 .....269 P4
Hill View Wy WALD ME5 .....95 K9
Hillworth BECK BR3 * 61 P7
Hillworth Rd
  BRXS/STRHM SW2 * 60 A1
Hillyard St BRXN/ST SW9 .....40 A2
Hillydeal Rd RSEV TN14 .....119 H9
Hillyfield CI STRD ME2 .....71 P6
Hillyfield Rd ASH TN23 .....252 C7
Hilly Fields BROCKY SE4 * 41 N5
Hilly Fields Crs BROCKY SE4..41 N4
Hilton CI FAV ME13 .....132 G7
Hilton Dr SIT ME10 .....99 J8
Hind Crs ERITH DA8 .....45 L1
Hinde CI SIT ME10 .....99 N7
Hind Gv POP/IOD E14 .....25 K2
Hindhead Wy WLGTN SM6 .....82 D9
Hindmans Rd EDUL SE22 .....24 D5
Hindmarsh CI WCHPL E1 * 24 D5
Hindsley's PI FSTH SE23 .....61 L1
Hind Ter WTHK RM20 * 31 N9
Hines Ter WALD ME5 * 95 P5
Hinksden Rd CRBK TN17 .....317 P3
Hinksey PI ABYW SE2 .....28 A5
Hinstock Rd WOOL/PLUM SE18..43 H3
Hinton CI ELTH/MOT SE9 .....43 J9
Hinton Crs GILL ME7 .....96 D8
Hinton Rd BRXN/ST SW9 .....40 B4
Hinxhill Rd KEN/WIL TN24 .....253 H3
Hirst CI DVE/WH CT16 .....291 J3
Hitcham Hatch La SEV TN13 .....148 F8
Hither Chantlers RRTW TN3..269 M5
Hither Farm Rd
  BKHTH/KID SE3 .....42 C4
Hither Fld HDCN TN27 .....220 G3
Hither Green La LEW SE13 .....42 A6
Hitherwood Dr NRWD SE19 .....60 F3
Hive La GVW DA11 .....48 F6

Hoaden Rw RCANTE CT3 *.......170 A7
Hoades Wood Rd
  CANTW/ST CT2 .....137 M6
Hoads Wood Gdns
  RASHE TN25 .....252 B3
Hoath CI RHAM ME8 .....96 D7
Hoath La RHAM ME8 .....96 E7
Hoath Meadow
  STPH/PW TN12 * 273 P2
Hoath Rd CANTW/ST CT2 .....137 N6
Hoath Wy GILL ME7 .....126 C2
  RHAM ME8 .....96 A3
Hobart Crs DVE/WH CT16 .....291 J4
Hobart Gdns SIT ME10 .....129 K1
  THHTH CR7 .....60 D9
Hobart Rd MSTR CT12 .....142 F3
  TIL RM18 .....49 L2
Hobbs CI RYE TN31 .....331 H8
Hobbs La RYE TN31 .....331 J7
Hobbs Rd WNWD SE27 .....60 C3
Hobday St POP/IOD E14 .....25 L2
Hoblands End CHST BR7 .....64 A5
Hobsons PI WCHPL E1 * 24 D1
Hockenden La SWLY BR8 .....65 J9
Hockeredge Gdns WGOS CT8 ..111 N5
Hockers La MAID/BEAR ME14..156 D4
Hockers La MAID/BEAR ME14..156 C5
Hoddesdon Rd BELV DA17 .....28 F8
Hodges CI CDW/CHF RM16 .....31 N8
Hodge's Gap MARG CT9 .....23 H7
Hodgkins CI THMD SE28 .....28 C3
Hodgson Crs SNOD ME6 .....123 P5
Hodgson Rd WSTB CT5 .....104 F7
Hodister CI CMBW SE5 .....40 C1
Hodsoll St BGR/WK TN15 .....121 L5
Hodson Crs STMC/STPC BR5 ..87 L3
Hogarth CI CAN/RD E16 .....26 E1
  HB CT6 .....108 B5
Hogarth Crs CROY/NA CR0.......83 H4
Hogarth Rd CDW/CHF RM16..32 B4
Hogbarn La RMAID ME17 .....188 G1
Hogben CI RFOLK CT18 .....286 C1
Hogbrook Hill La RDV CT15 ..289 N5
Hogg La CDW/CHF RM16 .....32 B7
Hog Hl MAID/BEAR ME14 .....294 F5
Hog Hole La RRTW TN3 .....294 F5
Hognore La BGR/WK TN15 .....121 N7
Hogshead Pas WAP E1W * 24 E3
Hogtrough HI BH/WHM TN16..147 H7
Hogtrough La OXTED RH8 .....174 J4
Holbeach Gdns BFN/LL DA15..44 A7
Holbeach Rd CAT SE6 .....41 N8
Holbeam Rd FAV ME13 .....191 J4
Holbeck Rw PECK SE15 .....40 C1
Holborn La CHAT ME4 .....6 B3
Holborn Rd PLSTW E13 .....26 C5
Holbrough Rd SNOD ME6 .....123 N5
Holbrook CI CHST BR7 .....63 P6
Holbrook Dr MSTR CT12 .....142 C3
Holbrook Wy HAYES BR2 .....63 N6
Holburne CI BKHTH/KID SE3..42 G2
Holburne Gdns BKHTH/KID SE3..43 H2
Holburne Rd BKHTH/KID SE3..42 G2
Holcombe CI BH/WHM TN16..176 A2
  ROCH ME1 .....95 H3
Holcote CI BELV DA17 .....28 D6
Holdenby Rd BROCKY SE4 .....41 L6
Holdenhurst Ash TN23 .....282 B2
Holden Park Rd
  SBGH/RUST TN4 .....240 C9
Holden Rd SBGH/RUST TN4..240 C8
Holder CI WALD ME5 .....95 P8
Holderness Wy WNWD SE27..60 A6
Holding St RHAM ME8 .....97 H5
Hole La EDEN TN8 .....206 B4
Holford Rd TIL RM18 .....33 L7
Holford St TON TN9 .....210 E9
Holgate St CHAT ME4 .....5 K6
Holiday Sq MARG CT9 .....15 C3
Holland CI BRDST CT10 .....113 M3
  HAYES BR2 .....85 J6
  IOS ME12 .....57 K7
Holland Crs OXTED RH8 .....175 K9
Holland Dr FSTH SE23 .....61 L2
Holland Gv BRXN/ST SW9 .....40 A1
Holland La OXTED RH8 .....175 K9
Holland Rd MAID/BEAR ME14..13 G3
  OXTED RH8 .....205 K2
  SNWD SE25 .....83 M2
  WALD ME5 .....125 K1
Hollands Av FOLKN CT19 .....311 J4
Hollands CI GVE DA12 .....70 C4
Hollands Wy EGRIN RH19 .....265 K4
Holland Wy HAYES BR2 .....85 J6
Hollicondane Rd RAM CT11 .....17 F1
Hollies Av BFN/LL DA15 .....64 B1
Hollies CI STRHM/NOR SW16..60 A5
The Hollies GVE DA12 .....69 P5
  HART DA3 .....91 J3
  OXTED RH8 .....175 J5
Holligrave Rd BMLY BR1 .....62 G7
Hollin CI SBGH/RUST TN4 .....22 A2
Hollingbourne Av BXLYHN DA7..45 H2
Hollingbourne HI RMAID ME17..158 A8
Hollingbourne Rd HNHL SE24..40 C6
  RHAM ME8 .....96 F3
Hollington Rd KEN/WIL TN24..2 D2
Hollingworth Rd
  MAID/SHEP ME15 .....186 C6
  STMC/STPC BR5 .....86 C4
Hollis Wy BH/WHM TN16 .....176 B2
Hollis PI GRAYS RM17 .....32 B6
Hollman Gdns
  STRHM/NOR SW16 .....60 E2
Hollow Down Rd
  MAID/SHEP ME15 .....186 C6
Hollow La CANT CT1 .....166 D6
  LING RH7 .....235 L2
Hollow St RCANTE CT3 .....138 D5
The Hollow
  MAID/SHEP ME15 * 184 D5

Hollow Trees Dr RTON TN11 ..209 M9
Hollow Wood Rd DVW CT17 ..290 F7
Holly Bank STPH/PW TN12 .....243 J9
Hollybrake CI CHST BR7 .....63 P6
Hollybush La SEV TN13 .....21 H1
Hollybush La ORP BR6 .....117 P1
  RCANTE CT3 .....168 C5
Holly Bush La SEV TN13 .....25 H1
Hollybush Rd GVE DA12 .....69 N1
Hollybush Ter NRWD SE19 .....60 E5
Holly CI BECK BR3 .....84 B6
  BRDST CT10 .....143 H1
  FOLKN CT19 .....311 H4
  GILL ME7 .....96 C4
  HYTHE CT21 * 309 J4
  SWCH CT13 .....201 K8
  WALD ME5 .....95 P5
Holly Crs BECK BR3 .....84 C2
Hollycroft STRD ME2 .....94 B1
Hollycroft CI SAND/SEL CR2 ..83 K9
Hollydale Dr HAYES BR2 .....86 A8
Hollydale Rd PECK SE15 .....41 J3
Hollydene Rd WADH TN5 .....294 A9
Holly Farm Rd
  MAID/SHEP ME15 .....186 P5
Holly Gdns BXLYHN DA7 .....45 L5
  MAID/BEAR ME14 * 12 E2
  MARG CT9 .....113 H5
Holly Gv PECK SE15 .....41 H3
Holly Hedge Ter LEW SE13 .....42 A6
Holly HI MEO DA13 .....122 G2
Holly Hill Rd BELV DA17 .....28 G8
Hollyhill Rd CANTW/ST CT2 ..134 E8
Holly La MARG CT9 .....113 H3
Holly Mdw ASH TN25 .....252 A6
Hollymount CI GNWCH SE10 ..42 A2
Holly Rd DART DA1 .....66 E3
  LYDD TN29 .....337 L1
  ORP BR6 .....117 K2
  RAM CT11 .....143 K4
  STRD ME2 .....71 N9
Hollyshaw CI RTWE/PEM TN2..129 J3
Hollytree Av SWLY BR8 .....65 K7
Holly Tree CI RMAID ME17 ..187 P9
Hollytree Dr SCUP DA14 * 64 A8
Holly Vis MAID/SHEP ME15 ..184 D5
  STPH/PW TN12 * 272 D1
Holly Wy MTCM CR4 .....82 C1
Hollywood La BGR/WK TN15..120 C5
  HOO/HM ME3 .....72 C5
Holman Ms
  CROY/NA CR0 .....114 C3
Holmbury Gv CROY/NA CR0..114 C2
Holmbury Mnr SCUP DA14 * ..64 C3
Holmbury Pk BMLY BR1 .....63 J4
Holmdene Av HNHL SE24 .....40 C5
Holmdene CI BECK BR3 .....62 A8
Holmdene CI BMLY BR1 .....63 J9
Holmesdale
  LEE/GVPK SE12 .....42 D7
Holme Oak CI CANT CT1 .....166 E6
Holmes CI EDUL SE22 .....40 G5
  HOO/HM ME3 .....53 L5
Holmesdale CI
  MAID/SHEP ME15 .....185 L8
  SNWD SE25 .....60 P9
Holmesdale HI EYN DA4 .....64 K7
  CROY/NA CR0 .....83 J2
  EYN DA4 .....64 K7
  SNWD SE25 .....83 K1
Holmesdale Ter FOLK CT20 ..10 E5
Holmesley Rd FSTH SE23 .....41 L7
Holmestone Rd DVW CT17 ..290 F6
Holmes Wy MSTR CT12 .....142 F1
Holmewood Rd RRTW TN3..269 L5
  SBGH/RUST TN4 .....270 C1
  SNWD SE25 .....83 K1
Holmhurst CI SBGH/RUST TN4..270 B4
Holmhurst Rd BELV DA17 .....28 G8
Holmleigh Av DART DA1 .....46 C5
Holm Mill La RMAID ME17 ..158 C8
Holm Oak Gdns BRDST CT10..113 L9
Holmoaks MAID/BEAR ME14..156 C5
  RHAM ME8 .....97 H4
Holmscroft Rd HB CT6 .....108 A5
Holmshaw CI SYD SE26 .....62 A3
Holmshaw CI SYD SE26 .....61 L5
Holmside GILL ME7 .....96 N3
Holmside Av IOS ME12 .....77 M1
Holmside Rd ASH TN23 .....282 B1
Holmstall Av EDGW HA8 * 28 C6
Holness Rd RCANTE CT3 .....139 P8
Holstein Wy ERITHM DA18 .....28 C6
Holt CI ASH TN23 .....251 P9
Holt Hill STHWK SE1 .....24 B5
Holton Ct BRCH CT7 .....111 H7
Holt Rd CAN/RD E16 .....26 F4
Holt St RDV CT15 .....229 M2
The Holt WLGTN SM6 .....82 B8
Holt Wood Av RDV CT15 * 229 M2
Holtwood CI RHAM ME8 .....96 G2
Holtye Av EGRIN RH19 .....265 K5
Holtye Crs MAID/SHEP ME15..185 N1
Holtye Rd EGRIN RH19 .....265 L5
Holwood Park Av ORP BR6 ..86 A8
Holyoake Ct BERM/RHTH SE16..25 H5
Holyoake Ter SEV TN13 .....20 C1
Holyrood Dr IOS ME12 .....78 A2
Holyrood Ms CAN/RD E16 .....26 D6
Holyrood St STHWK SE1 .....24 D4
Holywell CI BERM/RHTH SE16..26 B9
  BKHTH/KID SE3 .....26 B9
  ORP BR6 .....87 H1
Holywell La RSIT ME9 .....98 A4
Homecourt Rd SYD SE26 .....61 J4
Homedean Rd RTON TN11 ..209 L7
Home Farm La
  RTWE/PEM TN2 .....241 H8

Homefield CI STMC/STPC BR5 .....87 J1
  SWLY BR8 .....65 P9
Homefield Dr RHAM ME8 .....97 L4
Homefield Ms BECK BR3 * 61 N7
Homefield Ri ORP BR6 .....87 H5
Homefield Rd BMLY BR1 .....62 G7
  SEV TN13 .....148 D7
Home HI SWLY BR8 .....65 P6
Home Gdns DART DA1 .....8 A8
Home Md 85 P6
Homelands Dr NRWD SE19 .....60 E6
Home Lea ORP BR6 .....86 G9
Homeleigh Rd MSTR CT12..142 G1
  PECK SE15 .....41 K6
Home Mead MEO DA13 * 92 B3
Home Mead CI GVE DA12 .....49 M8
Homemead Rd CROY/NA CR0..82 D3
  HAYES BR2 .....86 A2
Home Pk OXTED RH8 .....175 K7
Homer CI BXLYHN DA7 .....45 P5
Homer Dr POP/IOD E14 .....25 K7
Homer Rd CROY/NA CR0 .....84 A3
Homersham CANT CT1 .....166 C6
Homesdale Rd HAYES BR2 .....85 M1
  ORP BR6 .....86 F4
Homeside Farm RCANTE CT4..226 E4
Homestall CI CANTW/ST CT2 *..136 E4
Homestall La FAV ME13 .....133 L8
Homestall Rd EDUL SE22 .....41 J6
  EGRIN RH19 .....265 P8
  RSIT ME9 .....161 J1
Homestead ASH TN23 .....252 A9
Homestead CI MARG CT9 .....15 J6
Homestead CI DEAL CT14 .....232 A5
Homestead CI RDV CT15 .....261 K1
Homestead La
  RHAM ME8 * 97 J6
  RRTW TN3 .....269 H9
The Homestead DART DA2 .....67 N3
Homestead Vw RSIT ME9 .....129 J3
Homestead Village RAM CT11..16 B5
Homestead Wy CROY/NA CR0..114 B9
Homeview SIT ME10 .....130 A1
Homewards Rd HOO/HM ME3..38 C9
Homewood Av SIT ME10 .....129 L2
Homewood Crs CHST BR7 .....64 A5
Homewood Gdns
  SNWD SE25 .....83 K2
Homewood Rd
  CANTW/ST CT2 .....137 M2
  RRTW TN3 .....269 L5
  TENT TN30 .....301 J6
Homoeland Rd
  MAID/BEAR ME14 .....155 N6
Hone St STRD ME2 .....72 B7
Honeyball Wk RSIT ME9 .....131 H3
Honey Bee Gld RHAM ME8 .....97 H8
Honeybourne Wy
  STMC/STPC BR5 .....86 D5
Honey CI GILL ME7 .....96 D9
Honeycrock HI RSIT ME9 .....128 A5
Honeyden Rd SCUP DA14 .....64 G5
Honey Hl WSTB CT5 .....135 N5
Honey La MAID/SHEP ME15 ..185 N5
Honeypot CI STRD ME2 .....72 B7
Honeypot La BGR/WK TN15 ..121 K3
  BGR/WK TN15 .....149 P4
Honeysuckle CI DEAL CT14 ..205 L6
  GILL ME7 .....95 N8
Honeysuckle CI GILL ME7 .....112 B5
  CROY/NA CR0 .....84 A4
Honeysuckle Wy RE RAM CT11..1 H1
Honeysuckle Wy HB CT6 .....108 A3
Honeywood CI CANT CT1 .....5 H1
  DVE/WH CT16 .....291 H1
  HYTHE CT21 .....307 N3
Honeywood Pkwy
  DVE/WH CT16 .....291 J2
Honeywood Rd DVE/WH CT16..291 H1
Honfleur Rd SWCH CT13 .....201 N2
Honiton Gdns PECK SE15 * 41 J3
Honiton Rd WELL DA16 .....44 B2
Honley Rd CAT SE6 .....41 P8
Honner Rd RFOLK CT18 .....288 C9
Honor Oak Pk FSTH SE23 .....41 J8
Honor Oak Ri FSTH SE23 .....41 J7
Honor Oak Rd FSTH SE23 .....41 J9
Honywood Rd RMAID ME17..189 K6
Hoo Common HOO/HM ME3..72 G3
Hood Av STMC/STPC BR5 .....87 J2
Hood CI CROY/NA CR0 .....83 J9
Hook CI FOLK CT20 .....310 C6
  WALD ME5 .....95 K9
Hook Farm Rd HAYES BR2 .....85 N2
Hookfields GVW DA11 .....48 F9
Hook Green La DART DA2 .....67 J2
Hook Green Rd MEO DA13 .....68 C6
Hook HI WADH TN5 .....295 H9
Hook La HDCN TN27 .....220 F3
  LYDD TN29 .....334 C7
  RMAID ME17 .....188 D5
  WELL DA16 .....44 B3
Hook Rd SNOD ME6 .....123 N5
Hook Wall LYDD TN29 .....338 F8
Hookwood Cnr OXTED RH8 ..175 L4
Hoo Marina Pk HOO/HM ME3 *..75 L9
Hooper CI CAN/RD E16 .....68 C6
Hoopers La HB CT6 .....108 A8
Hoopers PI ROCH ME1 .....54 C3
Hooper's Ri ROCH ME1 * 19 C7
Hooper St WCHPL E1 .....24 D3
Hope Av RTON TN11 .....211 P1
Hope CI LEE/GVPK SE12 .....63 J1
Hopedale Rd CHARL SE7 .....26 C6
Hopehouse La HAWK TN18 ..318 E7
Hope La ELTH/MOT SE9 .....63 J3
Hope Pk BMLY BR1 .....62 D6
Hope Rd DEAL CT14 .....233 J4
  SWCM DA10 .....48 D7
Hopes Gv RASHW TN26 .....279 J6
Hopes La MSTR CT12 .....143 H1
Hope St CHAT ME4 .....6 E1
  IOS ME12 .....57 K6
  MAID/BEAR ME14 .....12 E1

Hope Ter *HOO/HM* ME3 * 51 M9
WTHK RM20 * 31 N8
Hopetown St *WCHPL* E1..........24 C1
Hopeville Av *BRDST* CT10 ......113 J7
Hopewell Cl *CDW/CHF* RM16.....31 N8
Hopewell Dr *GVE* DA12 ....70 B4
WALD ME5........................95 P6
Hopewell St *CMBW* SE5 ....40 C5
Hopewell Yd *CMBW* SE5..........40 D1
Hop Gdn *RASHW* TN26 ....322 E5
Hopgarden La *RYE* TN31.........178 F4
Hopgarden Rd *TONN* TN10 ......210 G5
Hop Garden Wy *CANT* CT1.......166 D6
Hophurst Hl *CRAWE* RH10.......264 A6
Hoppers Wy *ASH* TN25...........252 A9
Hop Pocket Cl *CRBK* TN17......276 D8
Hop Pocket La
STPH/PW TN12...................242 G2
Hopsons Pl *IOS* ME12 ....78 C2
Hop St *GNWCH* SE10.............26 A7
Hopwood Rd *WOOL/PLUM* SE18...27 J6
Hopwoods
SBGH/RUST TN4.................270 D2
Hopwood Rd *WALW* SE17........24 A9
Horatio Pl *POP/IOD* E14........25 M5
ROCH ME1 *......................34 C2
Hordle Prom East *PECK* SE15...40 F1
Hordle Prom North *PECK* SE15...40 F1
Hordle Prom West *PECK* SE15...40 E1
Horizon Cl *SBGH/RUST* TN4....240 E9
Horley Cl *BXLYHS* DA6 ....45 J6
Horley Rd *ELTH/MOT* SE9 ....63 J3
Hornash La *RASHW* TN26.......281 N8
Hornbeam Av
SBCH/RUST TN4.................240 C8
WALD ME5.......................125 N3
Hornbeam Cl *ASH* TN23.........252 C6
DIT/AY ME20....................74 A2
STPH/PW TN12..................242 G4
Hornbeam Dr *ASH* TN23........122 C5
Hornbeam La *HAYES* BR2........86 B5
Hornbrook La *RASHW* TN26.....303 H8
Hornbrook La *RASHW* TN26 * ...42 E8
Horncastle Rd *LEE/GVPK* SE12...42 E8
Horne House *CHARL* SE7 * 43 J1
Hornfair Rd *CHARL* SE7 ....43 J1
Horn Hl *RSIT* ME9.................159 M2
Horning Cl *ELTH/MOT* SE9.......63 J5
Horn La *GNWCH* SE10.............26 B6
Horn Link Wy *GNWCH* SE10.....26 B6
Horn Park Cl *LEE/GVPK* SE12...42 F6
Horn Park La *LEE/GVPK* SE12...42 F6
Hornsby La *CHAF* RM16...........33 H8
Hornshay St *PECK* SE15...........9 N9
Horns La *WBY/YAL* ME18.........182 C1
Horns Oak Rd *MEO* DA13.........92 C8
Horns Rd *HAWK* TN18.............316 D6
Horn St *HYTHE* CT21.............309 N4
Horsa Rd *BRCH* CT7..............110 E6
ERITH DA8.......................233 J1
LEE/GVPK SE12.................42 G8
Horsebridge Rd *WSTB* CT5......105 K4
Horsecroft Cl *ORP* BR6...........87 P5
Horseferry Pl *GNWCH* SE10.....25 M9
Horseferry Rd *POP/IOD* E14.....25 H3
Horsegrove Av *WADH* TN5......315 N5
Horse Leaze *EHAM* E6.............27 J2
Horseleees Rd *FAV* ME13.......164 B4
Horsell Rd *STMC/STPC* BR5.....64 C7
Horselydown La *STHWK* SE1.....24 C4
Horseshoe Cl *GILL* ME7..........96 C5
MAID/BEAR ME14...............135 N8
Horseshoes La *RMAID* ME17....186 G7
Horsewash La *ROCH* ME1........19 F3
Horsfield Rd *ELTH/MOT* SE9....43 H6
Horsfield Cl *RDART* DA2 *........47 J8
Horsham Hl *RSIT* ME9.............97 N3
Horsham Rd *BXLYHS* DA6.........45 H7
The Horshams *HB* CT6...........108 A5
Horsley Cl *RFOLK* CT18..........288 D9
Horsley Dr *CROY/NA* CR0.......114 F2
Horsley Rd *BMLY* BR1............18 E7
ROCH ME1 *......................34 A9
Horsley St *WALW* SE17...........24 A9
Horsmans Pl *DART* DA1 * 4 E4
Horsmonden Cl *ORP* BR6.........86 F4
Horsmonden Rd *BROCKY* SE4....41 M6
STPH/PW TN12..................273 K1
Horsted Av *CHAT* ME4............95 K5
Horsted Wy *CHAT* ME4...........95 J7
Horton Downs
MAID/SHEP ME15...............186 C2
Horton Pl *ELTH/MOT* SE9.......176 E2
Horton Rd *CRBK* TN17...........298 C8
Horton St *LEW* SE13..............41 P4
Hortons Wy *BH/WHM* TN16.....176 E2
Horton Wy *CROY/NA* CR0.........84 A2
EYN DA4.........................89 L4
Horwood Cl *ROCH* ME1............94 C6
Hoselands Vw *HART* DA3.........91 H1
Hoser Av *LEE/GVPK* SE12.........62 E1
Hoser Gdns *BRCH* CT7...........111 H6
Hosey Common La
BH/WHM TN16..................176 F6
Hosey Common Rd
BH/WHM TN16..................176 F5
Hosey Hl *BH/WHM* TN16.........176 F5
Hoskins Cl *CAN/RD* E16...........26 G9
Hoskins Rd *EGRIN* RH19.........265 J4
Hoskins Wk *OXTED* RH8.........175 H5
Hoskins St *GNWCH* SE10.........25 N8
Hospital Ct *HYTHE* CT21........309 N4
Hospital La *CANT* CT1 *............4 D5
ROCH ME1 *......................19 K7
Hospital Rd *RMAID* ME17........187 P5
SEV TN13.......................154 B4
Hospital Wy *LEW* SE13............62 A7
Hostier Cl *STRD* DA12...........124 A1
Hotel Rd *RDV* CT15..............292 C1
RHAM ME8.......................96 D4

Hotham Cl *EYN* DA4...............66 C6
SWLY BR8........................66 C6
Hothfield Pl *BERM/RHTH* SE16...24 F6
Hothfield Rd *RHAM* ME8...........97 J5
Hottsfield *HART* DA3..............68 C9
Hougham Court La *RDV* CT15...312 B3
Houghton Av *GILL* ME7..........126 E2
Houghton Green La
RYE TN31.......................338 G2
Houghton La *RYE* TN31..........338 F1
Houlder Crs *CROY/NA* CR0.......82 G9
Houndsditch *HDTCH* EC3A........24 B2
House Fld *KEN/WIL* TN24........253 J8
Housefield Rd *FAV* ME13........191 N5
Houselands Rd *TON* TN9.........210 E8
Houseman Wy *CMBW* SE5.......40 D1
House Meadow *ASH* TN23.......281 P1
Houston Rd *FSTH* SE23...........61 L1
Hove Cl *GRAYS* RM17.............32 B9
Hovenden Cl *CANTW/ST* CT2...136 F9
Hovendens *CRBK* TN17...........276 D8
Hoveton Rd *THMD* SE28.........28 B2
Howard Av *BXLY* DA5..............44 E9
ROCH ME1 *......................34 C3
SIT ME10.........................99 L8
Howard Cl *IOS* ME12..............58 C9
Howard Dr *MAIDW* ME16.........154 G6
Howard Rd *BMLY* BR1.............62 E6
CDW/CHF RM16..................31 M6
DART DA1........................46 G7
E/WMAL ME19..................153 N4
PGE/AN SE20....................30 A7
SNWD SE25.......................83 M2
Howards Crest Cl *BECK* BR3.....82 A8
Howarth Rd *ABYW* SE2...........27 P8
Howberry Rd *THHTH* CR7.........60 D7
Howbury La *ERITH* DA8...........46 C4
Howbury Rd *PECK* SE15..........41 J4
Howden Cl *THMD* SE28...........28 C3
Howden Rd *SNWD* SE25..........60 F8
Howden St *PECK* SE15.............40 G4
Howe Barracks *CANT* CT1......167 H5
Howells Cl *BGR/WK* TN15.......120 B1
Howerd Wy *WOOL/PLUM* SE18...43 J2
Howfield La *RCANTW* CT4......165 M7
How Green La *EDEN* TN8.........207 K9
Howick Cl *CDW/CHF* RM16 ......30 A3
Howland Cl *DIT/AY* ME20........154 E4
Howland Ms *CANT* CT1...........166 D6
Howland Rd *STPH/PW* TN12....245 L3
Howland St *STPH/PW* TN12 *...245 J4
Howland Wy
BERM/RHTH SE16...............25 M5
Howletts Rd *NHNL* SE24.........40 C7
Howley Rd *CROY/NA* CR0.........82 C7
Howismere Cl *STRD* ME2.......124 A2
Howson Rd *BROCKY* SE4..........41 L5
Howt Gn *RSIT* ME9.................99 L5
Hoxton Cl *ASH* TN23............252 A9
Hoyland Ct *PECK* SE15 * 41 H1
The Hoystings Cl *CANT* CT1 * ...5 F7
Hoy St *CAN/RD* E16...............26 A2
Hoy Ter *WTHK* RM20 * 31 N8
Hubbard Rd *WNWD* SE27.......60 C5
Hubbards Hl *RMAID* ME17......185 M8
Hubbards Hl *RSEV* TN14.........178 C7
Hubbard's La *RMAID* ME17.....185 M8
Hubble Dr *MAID/SHEP* ME15...186 B4
Hubert Wy *BRDST* CT10.........113 K7
Huckleberry Cl *WALD* ME5.......125 N2
Hucksteps Rw *RYE* TN31 *......338 F7
Huddart St *BOW* E3................25 L2
Hudson Cl *CANTW/ST* CT2......137 L7
ROCH ME1 *......................34 D9
RHAM ME8........................96 F5
Hudson Pl *WOOL/PLUM* SE18...27 K8
Hudson Rd *BXLYHN* DA7..........45 H5
CANT CT1 *.......................5 J1
Huggens College *GVW* DA11 * ...48 F6
Hughes Dr *STRD* ME2.............72 D5
Hughes Rd *CDW/CHF* RM16......33 H6
Hughes Ter *CAN/RD* E16 *.......26 A1
Hugin Av *BRDST* CT10...........113 K6
Hugin Rd *BRDST* CT10...........113 K6
Huguenot Pl *WCHPL* E1..........24 C1
Hulkes La *ROCH* ME1..............19 K7
Hull Cl *BERM/RHTH* SE16 * 24 C4
Hull Rd *LYDD* TN29..............343 K6
Hulsewood Cl *RDART* DA2........66 B2
Humber Av *HB* CT6...............106 E2
SOCK/AV RM15..................31 J2
Humber Crs *STRD* ME2.............8 A1
Humber Rd *BKHTH/KID* SE3....26 B9
DART DA1........................46 D6
Humboldt Cl *RTWE/PEM* TN2..270 G3
Hume Av *TIL* RM18.................49 M4
Humes Rd *ASH* TN23..............21 M8
Humphrey St *STHWK* SE1........24 C8
Humphreys Cl *WGOS* CT8........111 L8
Hungerford St *WCHPL* E1 *.......24 C1
Hunger Hatch La *HDCN* TN27...220 D5
Hungershall
SBGH/RUST TN4.................270 B6
Hunsdon Dr *SEV* TN13...........148 G8
Hunsdon Rd *NWCR* SE14.........41 K1
Hunstanton Cl *RHAM* ME8......127 H2
Hunt Cl *BKHTH/KID* SE3 *.......42 E5
RFOLK CT18....................288 D8
Hunter Av *KEN/WIL* TN24.......255 H9
Hunter Cl *KEN/WIL* TN24.......253 H9
Hunter Cl *CMBW* SE5 * 24 A6
Hunter Ct *CMBW* SE5 * 40 D5
Hunter Rd *KEN/WIL* TN24 * 3 K6
THHTH CR7......................60 D9
Hunters Bank *RCANTW* CT4....257 K5
Hunters Cha *GDST* RH9.........204 C4
HB CT6..........................106 D2
Hunters Cl *BXLY* DA5..............65 N2
Huntersfield Cl *WALD* ME5.....125 N3
Hunters Forstal Rd *HB* CT6.....107 N4
Hunter's Gv *ORP* BR6.............86 G6
Hunters Meadow *NRWD* SE19...60 E3
Hunters Wk *DEAL* CT14.........232 F5
RSEV TN14.....................117 M8
Hunters Wy *CROY/NA* CR0.......83 K8
FAV ME13......................162 F7

GILL* ME7..........................96 B5
RTWE/PEM TN2..................270 C2
Hunters Wy West *WALD* ME5....96 A4
Huntingdon Cl *MTCM* CR4.......82 D1
Huntingdon St *CAN/RD* E16.....26 A2
Huntingdon Wk
MAID/SHEP ME15 * 186 B4
Huntingfield *CROY/NA* CR0.....114 C2
Huntingfield Rd *MEO* DA13......92 B4
Hunting Ga *BRCH* CT7...........110 G5
Hunting Rd *BRCH* CT7...........110 G6
Huntington Cl *CRBK* TN17......298 A3
Huntington Rd *RMAID* ME17....184 G8
Huntland Cl *RAIN* RM13..........29 N1
Huntley Av *GVW* DA11 *..........48 C7
Huntley Mill Rd *WADH* TN5....315 H3
Huntleys Pk *SBGH/RUST* TN4...270 C2
Huntly Rd *SNWD* SE25............60 E9
Hunton Gdns *CANTW/ST* CT2...136 F9
Hunton Hl *RMAID* ME17.........165 L1
Hunton Rd *STPH/PW* TN12.....214 C6
Hunton St *WCHPL* E1.............24 C1
Hunt Rd *GVW* DA11..............211 H4
Hunts Cl *BKHTH/KID* SE3.......43 H1
Hunts Farm Cl *BGR/WK* TN15...151 K5
Huntsman La *BGR/WK* TN15.....151 P5
MAID/BEAR ME14................13 J4
Huntsmans Cl *ROCH* ME1.........95 J5
Huntsman St *WALW* SE17 *......23 H8
Hunts Medde *CHST* BR7...........63 J6
Hunts Mede Cl *CHST* BR7........63 K6
Hunts Slip Rd *DUL* SE21...........60 E1
Hunt St *MAID/SHEP* ME15......183 P6
WBY/YAL ME18.................183 M7
Hurley Crs *BERM/RHTH* SE16...24 G4
Hurlfield *RDART* DA2..............66 C2
Hurlingham Rd *BXLYHN* DA7....45 H1
Hurlstone Rd *SNWD* SE25........83 J2
Huron Cl *ORP* BR6................116 F1
Huron Ter *DVE/WH* CT16 *.....291 J4
Hurst Cl *BKHTH/KID* SE3.........42 C4
Hurricane House
WOOL/PLUM SE18 * J1
Hurricane Rd *E/WMAL* ME19...152 G9
Hurstbourne Rd *FSTH* SE23.....41 L9
Hurst Cl *HAYES* BR2................85 J5
STPH/PW TN12..................246 C5
TENT TN30.......................300 F8
WALD ME5........................95 K8
Hurst Ct *IOS* ME12................58 A8
Hurstdene Av *HAYES* BR2........85 J5
Hurst Farm Rd *EGRIN* RH19....264 C8
RSEV TN14......................178 C4
Hurstfield *HAYES* BR2.............85 J5
Hurstford La *HDCN* TN27........220 C8
Hurst Green Cl *OXTED* RH8....175 K8
Hurst Green Rd *OXTED* RH8....175 J8
Hurst Gv *MSTR* CT12............143 H3
Hurst Hl *CHAT* ME4...............95 J4
Hurst La *BKHTH/KID* SE3.........42 C4
HDCN TN27......................220 D4
RFOLK CT18....................289 L8
RSEV TN14.....................178 G9
SIT ME10.........................99 K4
Hurst Pl *ABYW* SE2................28 A8
DART DA1 *......................46 C7
RHAM ME8........................97 J6
Hurst Rd *BFN/LL* DA15...........64 D1
BXLY DA5........................44 G9
CROY/NA CR0....................83 J9
ERITH DA8........................45 L1
KEN/WIL TN24..................252 E2
Hurst Springs *BXLY* DA5.........44 G9
Hurst St *HNHL* SE24...............40 C2
The Hurst *BGR/WK* TN15.......181 M4
Hurst Vls *STPH/PW* TN12 *.....245 J4
Hurst Wy *MAIDW* ME16..........184 F1
SEV TN13......................148 G6
Hurstwood *WALD* ME5...........125 K1
Hurstwood Av *BXLY* DA5.........44 G9
ERITH DA8........................45 N2
Hurstwood Dr *BMLY* BR1.........63 K9
Hurstwood La
SBGH/RUST TN4.................270 B5
Hurstwood Pk
SBGH/RUST TN4.................270 B5
Hurstwood Rd *FAV* ME13........190 D5
GILL ME7.......................126 E5
MAID/BEAR ME14...............126 A6
Husheath Hl *STPH/PW* TN12...275 L2
Husseywell Crs *HAYES* BR2......85 K5
Hustings Dr *HB* CT6 *.............78 G2
Hutchinson's Rd
CROY/NA CR0...................114 F5
Hutching's St *POP/IOD* E14......25 P4
Hutchins Rd *THMD* SE28..........27 P5
Hutsford Ct *RHAM* ME8...........60 C6
Huxbear St *BROCKY* SE4.........41 M6
Huxley Ct *FOLK* CT20 * 19 H7
Huxley Rd *WELL* DA16.............44 B4
Hyacinth Rd *STRD* ME2...........84 C5
Hybrid Cl *ROCH* ME1 * 95 J5
Hyde Cl *CDW/CHF* RM16..........31 N6
Hyde Dr *STMC/STPC* BR5........87 J1
Hyde Pl *RCANTE* CT3.............229 J1
MAIDW ME16...................154 G6
Hyder Rd *BXLYHN* DA7...........155 J5
Hydes Orch *HDCN* TN27.........247 P4
Hyde St *DEPT* SE8.................26 A9
The Hyde *RCANTW* CT4.........195 J1
Hylands Cl *RYE* TN31.............330 A7
Hylton St *WOOL/PLUM* SE18....27 N7
Hyndewood *FSTH* SE23 * 61 L4
Hyndford Crs *SWCM* DA10......48 A6
Hyndman St *PECK* SE15..........24 E9
Hyperion Dr *STRD* ME2...........71 P6
Hyrstdene *SAND/SEL* CR2.......82 G8
Hyson Rd *BERM/RHTH* SE16....24 E4
Hythe Av *BXLYHN* DA7............44 G1
Hythe Cl *FOLK* CT20..............310 C6
SBGH/RUST TN4.................240 D8
STMC/STPC BR5.................87 K1
Hythe Pl *SWCH* CT13............201 P2

Hythe Rd *HYTHE* CT21...........308 B3
KEN/WIL TN24....................3 H7
LYDD TN29.......................326 G6
RASHE TN25.....................284 A3
SIT ME10.........................99 L9
THHTH CR7........................60 D8
Hythe St *DART* DA1................46 E6
Hyton Dr *DEAL* CT14.............232 D2

I

Ian's Wk *HYTHE* CT21............309 M4
Ibbotson Av *CAN/RD* E16.........26 A3
Iberia Av *WLGTN* SM6..............82 C8
Ibis Cl *WSTB* CT5.................105 J8
Icehouse Wd *OXTED* RH8.......175 H7
Ickleton Rd *ELTH/MOT* SE9......63 J4
Ida St *POP/IOD* E14................25 M2
Ide Hill Rd *RSEV* TN14...........177 N8
Iden Cl *HAYES* BR2.................82 C9
Iden Crs *STPH/PW* TN12.........246 B7
Iden La *HDCN* TN27..............219 P6
Iden Rd *RYE* TN31................338 E2
STRD ME2........................72 C6
Idenwood Cl *RHAM* ME8.........96 C8
Idleigh Court Rd *HART* DA3.....91 L6
Idmiston Rd *WNWD* SE27........60 C3
Idol La *MON* EC5R..................24 B3
Idonia St *DEPT* SE8................25 M1
Iffin La *RCANTW* CT4.............196 D4
Ifield Cl *MAID/SHEP* ME15......186 C3
Ifield Wy *GVE* DA12...............69 P5
Ightham By-Pass
BGR/WK TN15...................150 F6
Ightham Rd *ERITH* DA8...........45 J1
RTON TN11......................180 F8
Ildersly Gv *DUL* SE21..............60 D1
Ilderton Rd *PECK* SE15..........158 F9
Ilex Rd *FOLKN* CT19..............310 C5
Ilex Wy *STRHM/NOR* SW16.....60 A4
Ilfracombe Rd *BMLY* BR1.........62 D2
Ilkley Cl *NRWD* SE19..............60 D5
Ilkley Rd *CAN/RD* E16.............26 C1
Illustrious Cl *WALD* ME5.........95 M9
Imberhorne La *EGRIN* RH19....264 C9
Imberhorne Wy *EGRIN* RH19...264 D9
Imbert Cl *NROM* TN28............337 H7
Impala Gdns *SBGH/RUST* TN4...270 C2
Imperial Av *IOS* ME12..............58 D9
Imperial Cl *E/WMAL* ME19......153 J9
Imperial Dr *GVE* DA12.............70 B4
IOS ME12.........................58 D9
Imperial Pl *CHST* BR7.............63 J7
Imperial Rd *GILL* ME7...............7 H7
Imperial Wy *ASH* TN23..........281 P1
CHST BR7........................82 N2
Impton La *WALD* ME5............125 L5
Inca Dr *ELTH/MOT* SE9............43 H6
Ince Rd *CANTW/ST* CT2.........137 L6
Inchmery Rd *CAT* SE6.............61 P1
Inchwood *CROY/NA* CR0..........84 E8
Independents Rd
BKHTH/KID SE3..................42 D4
Indescon Ct *POP/IOD* E14.......25 K5
India St *TWRTH* EC3N............24 C2
Indigo Ms *POP/IOD* E14 *........25 M3
Indus Rd *CHARL* SE7..............42 G1
Infant House
WOOL/PLUM SE18 * 43 J1
Inglefield Sq *WAP* E1W * 25 E4
Inglemere Rd *FSTH* SE23.........61 K2
Ingleside Cl *BECK* BR3.............61 N6
Ingleside Gv *BKHTH/KID* SE3...26 A9
Ingles La *FOLK* CT20..............10 C5
Ingles Rd *FOLK* CT20..............10 B5
Ingleton Av *WELL* DA16..........44 C6
Ingleton St *BRXN/ST* SW9........40 A5
Inglewood *CROY/NA* CR0........114 B3
SWLY BR8........................65 N8
Inglewood Cl *POP/IOD* E14.....25 K7
Inglewood Copse *BMLY* BR1.....63 J8
Inglewood Rd *BXLYHN* DA7.....45 M5
Inglis Rd *CROY/NA* CR0............83 L5
Inglis St *CMBW* SE5................40 B3
Ingoldsby Rd *BRCH* CT7.........111 H4
CANT CT1.......................166 A4
FOLKN CT19.....................311 H4
GVE DA12........................70 A8
Ingram Cl *RFOLK* CT18...........288 C9
Ingram Rd *DART* DA1 * 46 B8
GILL ME7.........................96 B1
GRAYS RM17....................32 D7
THHTH CR7......................60 D7
Ingress Park Av *SWCM* DA10...47 P5
Ingress Ter *MEO* DA13 *..........58 B8
Inigo Jones Rd *CHARL* SE7......43 H1
Inner Lines *GILL* ME7..............72 C9
Innes St *PECK* SE15................40 E1
Innes Yd *CROY/NA* CR0............82 A2
Institute Rd *CHAT* ME4.............8 E5
FAV ME13.......................132 C6
Instone Rd *DART* DA1.............46 D8
Inverary Ct *RAM* CT11 *.........143 K3
Inverine Rd *CHARL* SE7............26 C8
Invermore Pl
WOOL/PLUM SE18 * 27 K7
Inverness Ter *BRDST* CT10.....143 H1
Inverton Rd *PECK* SE15...........41 M1
Invicta Cl *CHST* BR7................63 L4
Invicta Gv *NHLT* UB5...............99 H7
Invicta Pde *SCUP* DA14 * 64 D3
Invicta St *BKHTH/KID* SE3......42 E1
FOLKN CT19....................310 G4
IOS ME12..........................57 L6

MARG* CT9.......................112 C5
RDART DA2........................47 H7
WSTB CT5......................105 N5
Inville Rd *WALW* SE17............24 A8
Inwood Cl *CROY/NA* CR0.........84 B6
Iona Cl *CAT* SE6....................41 N8
WALD ME5......................126 A4
Iona Wk *MAID/SHEP* ME15.....185 M4
Ionia Wk *GVE* DA12................70 B2
Irchester St *RAM* CT11 * 17 H3
Irchester Vls *RAM* CT11 *.........17 H3
Ireland Cl *EHAM* E6.................27 H2
Irene Rd *ORP* BR6...................86 D8
Ireton Pl *GRAYS* RM17............32 D7
Iris Av *BXLY* DA5.....................44 C7
Iris Cl *CROY/NA* CR0................84 A5
EHAM E6.........................27 H2
Iris Crs *BXLYHN* DA7...............45 H4
Iron Bar La *CANT* CT1...............5 F5
Iron Mill La *DART* DA1.............45 P5
Iron Mill Pl *DART* DA1..............45 P5
Ironmonger La *LDTH* EC2R.......24 A2
Ironmongers Pl *POP/IOD* E14...25 K7
Ironside Cl *BERM/RHTH* SE16...24 C5
WALD ME5.......................95 M6
Ironstones *RRTW* TN5............269 N5
Irvine Dr *MARG* CT9..............112 A2
Irvine Gdns *SOCK/AV* RM15.....31 J3
Irvine Ms *MARG* CT9..............113 H5
Irvine Rd *HOO/HM* ME3............71 K4
Irving Pl *WALD* ME5.................86 E9
Irving Wy *SWLY* BR8................65 N8
Irwell Est *BERM/RHTH* SE16....24 F5
Irwin Av *WOOL/PLUM* SE18.....44 A4
Isabella Dr *ORP* BR6................86 D8
Isambard Ms *POP/IOD* E14......25 M6
Isambard Pl *BERM/RHTH* SE16...24 F4
Isis Cl *HYTHE* CT21...............307 P4
Island Rd *BERM/RHTH* SE16....24 E8
BRCH CT7......................139 M4
CANTW/ST CT2.................137 M7
RCANTE CT3...................138 B9
Island Rw *POP/IOD* E14...........25 J2
Island Wall *WSTB* CT5...........105 K5
Island Wy East *CHAT* ME4........73 H5
Island Wy West *CHAT* ME4.......73 H5
Isla Rd *WOOL/PLUM* SE18.......27 K9
Islay Whf *POP/IOD* E14 * 25 M1
Isledon Rd *HOLWY* N7.............J1
Islingham Farm Rd
HOO/HM ME3.....................72 C4
Ismays Rd *BH/WHM* TN15......180 E1
Istead Ri *MEO* DA13.................69 K6
Itchingwood Common Rd
OXTED RH8......................175 M9
Ivanhoe Rd *CMBW* SE5...........40 E6
HB CT6...........................107 M2
WGOS CT8......................111 M4
Ivedon Rd *WELL* DA16.............44 E3
Ivens Wy *RMAID* ME17...........188 E5
Iverhurst Cl *BXLYHS* DA6.........44 F6
Iversgate Cl *RHAM* ME8............97 J2
Ivers Wy *CROY/NA* CR0..........114 E2
Ives Rd *CAN/RD* E16................25 P1
TON TN9.........................210 C9
Ivory Gv *ELTH/MOT* SE9..........43 M9
Ivory Cl *FAV* ME13.................132 D4
Ivorydown *BMLY* BR1...............62 E3
Ivy Bower Cl *RDART* DA2..........47 P6
Ivychurch Cl *PGE/AN* SE20.......60 C9
Ivychurch Gdns *MARG* CT9.....113 K3
Ivy Church La *MAID/SHEP* ME15 * ...J8
Ivychurch Rd *LYDD* TN29.......335 J2
Ivy Cl *DART* DA1....................63 G7
GVE DA12........................70 C5
RFOLK CT18....................289 J5
RMAID ME17...................187 M9
Ivy Cottage Hl *MSTR* CT12.....141 M5
Ivy Ct *BERM/RHTH* SE16 *.......24 D8
CANTW/ST CT2.................136 D7
Ivydale Rd *PECK* SE15.............41 K6
Ivy House La *SEV* TN13..........148 C2
Ivy House Rd *WSTB* CT5.........105 N5
Ivy La *CANT* CT1......................5 G5
RAM CT11........................16 C5
RSEV TN14.....................147 M1
Ivymount Rd *WNWD* SE27.......60 A2
Ivy Pl *CANT* CT1 *....................4 C7
ROCH ME1 *......................94 F4
Ivy Rd *BROCKY* SE4................41 M5
CAN/RD E16......................26 B2
Ivy St *RHAM* ME8....................97 J6
Ivy Wy *FOLKN* CT19..............311 H4
Izane Rd *BXLYHS* DA6.............45 H5

J

Jaarlen Rd *LYDD* TN29...........342 A6
Jacinth Dr *SIT* ME10................99 K8
Jackass La *GDST* RH9.............174 C7
HAYES BR2........................85 L7
Jack Bailey Rw *FAV* ME13 * 154 B7
Jack Evans Ct *SOCK/AV* RM15...31 K2
Jacklin Cl *WALD* ME5.............125 L2
Jackson Av *ROCH* ME1.............95 K6
Jackson Cl *RDART* DA2............47 M6
RHAM ME8........................96 F5
Jackson Rd *CANT* CT1..............85 B6
HAYES BR2........................85 P6
Jackson's La *TENT* TN30.........301 H8
Jackson's Pl *CROY/NA* CR0.......83 J5
Jackson St *WOOL/PLUM* SE18...27 H9
Jackson's Wy *CROY/NA* CR0....84 B7
Jacob Cl *MARG* CT9...............112 D6
Jacob St *STHWK* SE1...............23 P1
Jacobs Oak *KEN/WIL* TN24.....282 G2
Jacob St *STHWK* SE1...............24 C5
Jacob Yd *FAV* ME13...............132 C6
Jade Cl *CAN/RD* E16................26 E2
WALD ME5.........................96 B6
Jade Ms *HB* CT6......................79 J6
Jaffray Rd *HAYES* BR2..............85 N1
Jaggard Wy *STPH/PW* TN12...246 B6
Jagger Cl *RDART* DA2..............27 K9
Jago Cl *WOOL/PLUM* SE18.......27 K9
Jago Wk *CMBW* SE5.................40 D1

Jail La BH/WHM TN16...............115 N9
Jamaica Rd STHWK SE1.............24 C5
THHTH CR7.........................82 G3
Jamaica St WCHPL E1................24 F1
Jamaica Ter
  MAID/BEAR ME14.................155 M5
James Ailchin Gdns
  KEN/WIL TN24....................253 J5
James Av BER/WK TN15 *..........120 B2
James Cl RCANTE CT3...............170 E9
  RFOLK CT18......................286 C1
James Hall Gdns DEAL CT14.........233 H6
James Haney Dr
  KEN/WIL TN24....................253 H5
James Joyce Wk BRXN/ST SW9......40 B5
James Rd DART DA1..................46 A8
  STRD ME2.........................94 A4
James St ASH TN23...................2 B3
  CHAT ME4..........................6 C5
  FOLKN CT19.......................11 G1
  GILL ME7...........................7 J1
  IOS ME12..........................57 M6
  MAID/BEAR ME14...................13 F2
  RAM CT11..........................6 E7
  ROCH ME1.........................19 G7
Jamestown Wy POP/IOD E14.........25 N3
James Watt Wy ERITH DA8...........29 K9
James Whatman Ct
  MAID/BEAR ME14 *................12 D2
James Whatman Wy
  MAID/BEAR ME14..................12 D2
Jamuna Cl POP/IOD E14.............25 H1
Jane St WCHPL E1....................24 E1
Janet St POP/IOD E14...............25 K6
Janeway Pl BERM/RHTH SE16 *......2 A5
Janeway St BERM/RHTH SE16.......24 D5
Japonica Cl WALB TN15.............125 P3
Jardine Rd WAP E1W.................24 G3
Jarman's Fld RASHE TN25...........224 A8
Jarrah Cots PUR RM19 *.............30 C9
Jarrett Av STRD ME2.................72 C5
Jarrett Cl BRXS/STRHM SW2........40 B9
Jarrett's EYE TN31................338 F7
Jarrow Rd BERM/RHTH SE16........24 E5
Jarvis Dr KEN/WIL TN24...........283 K1
Jarvis La CRBK TN17...............274 C7
Jarvis Pl TENT TN30...............301 J4
Jarvis Rd EDUL SE22................40 E5
Jarvist Pl DEAL CT14...............263 J2
Jasmine Cl E/WMAL ME19...........153 N4
  ORP BR6..........................86 C6
  RCANTW CT4......................195 L2
Jasmine Ct LEE/GVPK SE12..........42 F9
Jasmine Gdns CROY/NA CRO.........84 C2
Jasmine Gv PGE/AN SE20............61 H7
Jasmine Pl RCANTE CT5 *...........169 K8
Jasmine Rd E/WMAL ME19...........153 N4
Jasmine Wy STPH/PW TN12 *.......245 H4
Jason Cl CDW/CHF RM16.............33 M2
Jason Wk ELTH/MOT SE9.............63 L3
Jasper Av RDART DA2................46 A1
Jasper Rd CAN/RD E16...............26 E2
  NRWD SE19.......................60 F5
Javelin Rd E/WMAL ME19...........152 C9
Jay Gdns CHST BR7..................63 K3
Jayne Wk WSTB CT5.................105 J8
Jefferson Cl ASH TN23.............252 C8
Jefferson Rd IOS ME12..............57 M7
Jefferstone Gdns LYDD TN29......337 K1
Jefferstone La LYDD TN29.........337 H2
Jeffery St GILL ME7 *................7 H1
Jeffrey Cl STPH/PW TN12 *.......245 J4
Jeffrey Rd MAID/BEAR ME14.........13 G3
Jeken Rd BRXS/STRHM SW2...........42 C5
Jellicoe Av GVE DA12................69 N2
Jellicoe Cl KEN/WIL TN24.........283 K1
Jemmett Av RASHE TN25............283 N4
Jemmett Rd ASH TN23.................2 B7
Jenkins' Dl CHAT ME4...............95 N4
Jenkins Dr MAID/SHEP ME15.......186 B6
Jenner Cl SCUP DA14................64 C3
Jenner Rd ROCH ME1.................95 H2
Jenner's CI LING RH7...............234 C5
Jenners Wy LYDD TN29.............337 K2
Jennett Rd CROY/NA CRO............87 H1
Jennifer Cl MARG CT9..............113 H5
Jennifer Rd BMLY BR1...............62 D2
Jenningham Dr
  CDW/CHF RM16....................32 B4
Jennings Rd EDUL SE22.............40 F7
Jennings Rd ERITH DA8..............28 B1
Jenningtree Wy BELV DA17.........29 H5
Jenny La LING RH7.................234 C5
Jenson Wy NRWD SE19...............60 F6
Jenton Av BXLYHN DA7..............44 C2
Jephson St CMBW SE5...............40 D2
Jeremiah St POP/IOD E14...........25 L2
Jerningham Rd NWCR SE14...........41 L3
Jerome Rd DIT/AY ME20............123 N9
Jerome St WCHPL E1................24 F4
Jerrard St LEW SE13...............41 P4
Jersey Cl KEN/WIL TN24...........252 F1
Jersey La RCANTW CT4.............196 B5
Jersey Rd CAN/RD E16..............26 D1
  STRD ME2.........................72 A7
Jerviston Gdns
  STRHM/NOR SW16..................60 A5
Jervois House
  WOOL/PLUM SE18 *.................43 J1
Jeskyns Rd CDW/CHF RM16...........32 E4
Jesmond Cl
  CROY/NA CRO.....................83 L4
Jesmond St SFOLKN CT19............10 D2
Jessamine Pl RDART DA2............27 J8
Jessamine Ter SWLY BR8............65 L7
Jesse's Hl RCANTW CT4............227 M1
Jessett Cl ERITH DA8...............29 J7
Jessica Ms CANT CT1................5 G2
Jessica Rd WAND/EARL SW18 *......99 M7
Jesson Cl LYDD TN29..............337 M1
Jessops Wy CROY/NA CRO............82 B3
Jessups Mdw MAID/SHEP ME15......17 J8
Jesuit Cl CANTW/ST CT2.............56 F9
Jesus Hospital CANT CT1 *..........5 G1
Jetty Rd HOO/HM ME3................54 B9

IOS ME12...........................57 H5
IOS ME12...........................80 C3
Jetty Wk GRAYS RM17................32 B9
Jevington Wy LEE/GVPK SE12.......42 F9
Jewell Gv STPH/PW TN12...........245 J4
Jewels Hl WARL CR6................115 K6
Jewry La CANT CT1...................4 E4
Jewry St TWRH GC5N................24 C2
Jews Wk SYD SE26...................61 H5
Jeyes Rd GILL ME7...................7 H5
Jezreels Rd GILL ME7 *..............7 H5
Jim Bradley Cl
  WOOL/PLUM SE18..................27 H7
Jinlwin Rd ROCH ME1...............95 J4
Joan Crs ELTH/MOT SE9.............43 H8
Jocelyn St PECK SE15...............40 A2
Jockey La CRBK TN17...............298 C3
Jodane Rd DEPT SE8.................6 C3
Jodrell Wy WTHK RM20..............31 J8
Johannesburg Rd
  DVE/WH CT16.....................291 K3
John Badger Cl
  KEN/WIL TN24....................253 H4
John Dutton Wy
  KEN/WIL TN24....................253 H5
John Felton Rd
  BERM/RHTH SE16 *................24 D3
John Fisher St WCHPL E1...........24 D5
John Hall Cl FAV ME13.............132 E3
John Harrison Wy
  BERM/RHTH SE16 *................24 D6
John Maurice Cl WALW SE17........24 A7
John McKenna Wk
  BERM/RHTH SE16..................24 C7
John Newington Ct
  KEN/WIL TN24....................253 H4
John Penn St LEW SE13..............41 P2
John Rennie Wk WAP E1W *..........24 F3
John Roll Wy
  BERM/RHTH SE16..................24 D6
John Ruskin St CMBW SE5..........40 B1
Johns Cl HART DA3..................91 J7
Johnsdale OXTED RH8...............175 J5
John's Gn SWTCH CT13.............201 M4
John Silkin La DEPT SE8............24 C8
John Smith Ms POP/IOD E14........25 N3
Johnson Av GILL ME7................73 J8
Johnson Cl DIT/AY ME20.............69 H2
  KEN/WIL TN24....................285 K1
Johnson Ct FAV ME13..............132 E4
Johnson Rd CROY/NA CRO............83 J4
  HAYES BR2........................85 N2
Johnsons Dr HPTN TW12............129 L1
Johnson St RSEV TN14.............118 A4
Johnson St WCHPL E1................24 F2
Johnsons Wk SWCM DA10............48 A7
Johnsons Wtrf RDART DA2 *.........47 N7
Johnson Wy GILL ME7 *.............58 A9
John's Pl WCHPL E1.................24 E2
John St CROY/NA CRO................83 K5
  MEO DA13.........................92 A2
John St POP/IOD E14...............25 N3
John's Ter CROY/NA CRO............83 K5
  STPH/PW TN12....................243 H1
Johnston Cl CMBW SE5..............40 A2
Joiner St STHWK SE1................24 B9
Jointon Rd FOLK CT20...............10 B5
Jonson Cl MTCM CR4.................44 A1
Jordan Cl MAID/SHEP ME15 *.......186 B6
The Jordans EGRIN RH19...........265 H8
Joseph Hardcastle Cl
  NWCR SE14.......................41 K1
Joseph St BOW E3...................25 J1
Joshua St POP/IOD E14.............25 N2
Josling Cl GRAYS RM17.............32 A9
Joslin Rd PUR RM19.................30 F9
Joss Gap Rd BRDST CT10...........113 N4
Jowett St PECK SE15.................40 F7
Joyce Cl CRBK TN17...............297 P3
Joyce Green La ERITH DA8..........47 J1
Joyden's Wood Rd BXLY DA5........65 N2
Joyes Cl DVE/WH CT16.............261 H9
  FOLKN CT19.......................11 H1
Joyes Rd DVE/WH CT16.............311 H4
  FOLKN CT19.......................11 H1
Joy La WSTB CT5...................105 H7
Joy Rd GVE DA12....................49 N9
Joy Wd RMAID ME17................186 A6
Jubilee Cl HYTHE CT21............322 D4
  SWCM DA10........................48 A7
Jubilee Crs BGR/WK TN15..........150 F6
  GVE DA12.........................70 A1
  OBOM ME11........................77 H2
Jubilee Ct DEAL CT14..............233 L8
Jubilee Fld TENT TN30............332 B1
Jubilee Rd BGR/WK TN15...........149 L6
Jubilee Ri DEAL CT14.............202 A7
Jubilee St WCHPL E1................24 F1
Jubilee Ter DEAL CT14.............233 L8
The Jubilee CNWCH SE10 *..........9 H3
Jubilee Wy DVE/WH CT16.............9 J1
  SCUP DA14........................64 C1
Judd Rd FAV ME13...................13 D6
  TON TN9..........................240 E2
Jude St CAN/RD E16..................26 A2
Judeth Gdns GVE DA12..............69 N8
Judges Ter EGRIN RH19............265 H8
Judge's Wk HAMP NW3 *..............unclear
Judkins Cl WALD ME5................95 P8
Jugans Rd ORP BR6.................87 H5
Julian Pl POP/IOD E14..............25 L8

Julian Rd FOLKN CT19..............10 B3
  ORP BR6..........................117 H1
Julians Cl SEV TN13................20 C7
Julians Wy SEV TN13................20 C7
Julian Tayler Pth FSTH SE23 *.....61 H1
Julie Cl BRDST CT10...............113 M7
Julien Pl KEN/WIL TN24............253 N9
Juliette Wy SOCK/AV RM15.........30 C4
Junction Rd DART DA1..............46 D7
  GILL ME7..........................96 A2
Juniper Cl ASH TN23...............252 B7
  BH/WHM TN16.....................145 P2
  CANT CT1........................166 F6
  MAIDW ME16.......................154 G6
  OXTED RH8.......................180 C8
  SBGH/RUST TN4....................240 C8
  WALD ME5.........................125 M1
  WSTB CT5........................105 N5
Juniper La EHAM E6.................26 F1
Juniper St WCHPL E1 *..............24 F1
Juno Wy NWCR SE14.................41 J7
Jupiter La ASH TN23...............282 B5
Jurgens Rd PUR RM19...............30 F7
Jury's Gap Rd LYDD TN29.........341 M8
Jury St GVW DA11...................49 M7
Jutland Cl HOO/HM ME3.............55 H1
Jutland Rd CAT SE6.................42 A8

K

Kake St RCANTW CT4...............225 L4
Kale Rd ERITHM DA18................28 C5
Kangley Bridge Rd SYD SE26.......61 M4
Karen Ct BMLY BR1..................62 D7
  ELTH/MOT SE9.....................43 N4
Karloff Wy HOO/HM ME3..............54 A9
Kashgar Rd WOOL/PLUM SE18........27 N8
Katharine Cl DEAL CT14.............43 H1
Katharine St CROY/NA CRO..........83 H7
Katherine St BERM/RHTH SE16......24 G4
Katherine Ct WALD ME5 *..........125 N3
Katherine Gdns
  ELTH/MOT SE9.....................43 H5
Katherine Rd EUDL TN24..........236 D1
Kavelin Wy KEN/WIL TN24............3 J2
Kaysland Rd BGR/WK TN15.........120 B2
Kearney Rd CAN/RD E16..............44 D2
Kearsney Abbey Vis
  DVE/WH CT16.....................290 E3
Kearsney Dr DVE/WH CT16.........290 D3
Keary Rd SWCM DA10................48 B8
Keat Farm Cl HB CT6...............108 C5
Keating Cl ROCH ME1................94 F5
Keats Av CAN/RD E16................26 C4
Keats Cl STHWK SE1 *...............24 C7
Keats Gdns TIL RM18...............49 H8
Keats Pl EGRIN RH19..............264 D7
Keats Wy CROY/NA CRO.............153 N1
  DIT/AY ME20.....................unclear
  WELL DA16........................44 A4
Keats Wy CROY/NA CRO..............83 P3
Kechill Gdns HAYES BR2.............85 K4
Keddow's Cl HYTHE CT21...........308 C7
Kedleston Dr STMC/STPC BR5........86 C3
Kedleston Rd DVE/WH CT16........291 K2
Keeble Cl WOOL/PLUM SE18 *.......43 L1
Keedonwood Rd BMLY BR1............62 C5
Keefe Cl WALD ME5.................125 J4
Keel Cl BERM/RHTH SE16............24 G4
Keeley Ms GILL ME7 *...............96 B3
Keeley Rd CROY/NA CRO..............83 H6
Keel Gdns SBGH/RUST TN4.........240 B9
Keeling Rd ELTH/MOT SE9...........43 H6
Keemor Cl WOOL/PLUM SE18 *.......43 L1
Keens Rd CROY/NA CRO..............83 H8
Keepers Hl RCANTW CT4............167 P9
The Keep ELTH/MOT SE9.............42 E3
Keesey St WALW SE17................24 A9
Keetons Rd
  BERM/RHTH SE16..................24 E6
Keeton's Rd BERM/RHTH SE16......24 D6
Keightley Dr ELTH/MOT SE9.........43 N9
Keith Av EYN DA4....................67 H5
Keith Park Crs BH/WHM TN16......115 N6
Kelbrook Rd BKHTH/KID SE3.........43 J5
Kelchers La RTON TN11.............212 A5
Kellaway Rd BKHTH/KID SE3.........42 C3
  WALD ME5........................125 M3
Kellerton Rd LEW SE13.............42 C6
Kellett Rd BRXS/STRHM SW2........40 C9
Kelling Gdns CROY/NA CRO..........82 C4
Kellner Rd THMD SE28...............27 N6
Kelly Av PECK SE15.................40 E7
Kelly Dr GILL ME7...................77 J1
Kelmore Gv EDUL SE22..............40 D5
Kelsail Cl BKHTH/KID SE3..........42 F3
Kelsey Av BECK BR3.................61 N7
Kelsey Park Av BECK BR3...........61 N6
Kelsey Park Rd BECK BR3...........61 N6
Kelsey Sq BECK BR3.................61 N6
Kelso Dr GVE DA12..................70 B1
Kelvedon Rd DEAL CT14............233 H7
Kelvin Cl BRDST CT10...............113 J7
Kelvin Gdns CROY/NA CRO...........82 D4
Kelvington Cl CROY/NA CRO.........61 H2
Kelvington Rd PECK SE15...........41 K6
Kelvin Pde ORP BR6.................86 F5
Kelvin Rd TIL RM18..................49 H8
  WELL DA16........................44 C4
Kemble Pl RTWE/PEM TN2...........271 H1
Kemerton Rd BECK BR3..............61 N1
  CMBW SE5.........................40 C4
  CROY/NA CRO.....................46 G9
Kennal Rd CHST BR7.................63 J3
Kemp Cl WALD ME5.................125 K1
Kempes Pl RASHE TN25 *..........223 P8
Kemp Gdns CROY/NA CRO............83 H3
Kemp Rd WSTB CT5.................106 B4

Kemps Dr POP/IOD E14..............25 K3
Kempthorne Rd DEPT SE8...........25 P7
Kempton Cl ERITH DA8..............29 P9
  WALD ME5........................125 P2
Kempton Wk CROY/NA CRO...........84 B5
Kempt St WOOL/PLUM SE18.........27 J9
Kemsdale Rd FAV ME13.............134 A7
Kemsing Cl BXLY DA5................45 H1
  THHTH CR7........................83 H1
Kemsing Gdns CANTW/ST CT2.......136 G9
Kemsing Rd BGR/WK TN15..........150 D2
  GNWCH SE10.......................26 B8
Kemsley Cl GVW DA11................26 B8
  SWCM DA10........................47 P7
Kemsley Gdns GVW DA11.............49 K3
Kemsley Street Rd GILL ME7......126 C1
Kenardington Rd
  RASHW TN26......................322 E4
Kenbrook KEN/WIL TN24............252 F2
Kenbury St CMBW SE5...............40 C3
Kendal Cl BRXN/ST SW9.............40 D3
  RAM CT11........................142 G6
Kendal Dr TON TN9.................210 F8
Kendale CDW/CHF RM16..............33 J6
Kendale Rd BMLY BR1...............62 C4
  E/WMAL ME19....................153 K9
Kendall Av BECK BR3................61 J2
  SAND/SEL CR2.....................63 M8
Kendall Gdns GVW DA11.............49 K8
Kendall Rd BECK BR3................61 K1
  WOOL/PLUM SE18...................43 J2
Kendal Meadow WSTB CT5...........106 C5
Kendal Pk SBGH/RUST TN4.........270 B3
Kendal Rd BRDST CT10.............113 M8
Kendal Wy RHAM ME8................96 C6
Kender St NWCR SE14................41 J1
Kendrick Rd RCANTW CT4..........195 P5
Kenilworth Av
  STMC/STPC BR5...................86 C3
Kenilworth Cl SEV TN13............86 E5
Kenilworth Gdns
  WOOL/PLUM SE18..................43 M3
Kenilworth Rd PGE/AN SE20.........61 K7
  STMC/STPC BR5....................86 C3
Kenilworth Rd
  RASHW TN26......................unclear
Kenley Cl BXLY DA5.................45 J8
  CHST BR7.........................64 A9
Kenley Gdns THHTH CR7.............82 C1
Kenmare Rd THHTH CR7..............82 F3
Kenmere Rd WELL DA16..............44 E3
Kennacraig Cl CAN/RD E16..........26 C4
Kennard Cl RANT E16................94 E4
Kennard St CAN/RD E16.............26 G4
Kennedy Av EGRIN RH19............266 A3
Kennedy Cl FAV ME13..............132 C5
  STMC/STPC BR5....................86 E5
Kennedy Wk WALW SE17 *...........24 A7
Kennel Barn Rd RSIT ME9.........128 C9
Kennel Hl RDV CT15...............260 F2
Kennelling Rd FAV ME13...........191 J7
Kennel Wood Crs
  CROY/NA CRO.....................114 C5
Kennet Dr DART DA1.................46 A4
Kennet Rd DART DA1.................46 A4
Kennet Tnl WAP E1W................25 H4
Kennet St WAP E1W..................24 D4
Kennett La RASHE TN25............285 P7
Kenning St BERM/RHTH SE16........24 F1
Kennington Rd
  MAID/SHEP ME15..................186 C3
  RHAM ME8.........................96 E2
Kensal Rd NKENS W10...............unclear
Kensington Av THHTH CR7..........60 A7
Kensington Gdns GRAYS RM17 *......32 D9
Kensington Rd CANT CT1...........137 H9
Kent Av CANT CT1..................167 H4
  KEN/WIL TN24.....................78 B1
  MAID/SHEP ME15..................185 P2
  SIT ME10.........................129 L2
  WELL DA16........................44 B6
Kent Cl BGR/WK TN15 *...........120 B2
  MTCM CR4.........................60 B4
  ORP BR6..........................116 F1
  ROCH ME1.........................95 H6
  STPH/PW TN12....................243 H3
Kent Cotts BRCH CT7...............110 C5
Kent Gate Wy CROY/NA CRO.........114 C1
Kent Hatch Rd OXTED RH8.........175 M6
Kent House La BECK BR3............61 L4
Kent House Rd BECK BR3............61 K6
Kentish Dr DVE/WH CT16............28 F7
Kentish Gdns RTWE/PEM TN2 *.....271 P8
Kentish Rd BELV DA17...............29 H4
Kentish Wy BMLY BR1................62 B3
Kentlea Rd THMD SE28..............27 N7
Kentmere Rd WELL DA16 *..........142 E5
Kentmere Rd
  WOOL/PLUM SE18..................27 M7
Kenton Gdns MSTR CT12...........141 J4
Kent Pl RAM CT11..................142 F4
Kent Rd DART DA1...................47 H4
  FOLKN CT19.......................11 H2
  GRAYS RM17.......................32 B9
  GVW DA11.........................49 J9
  HART DA3.........................91 K5
  SBGH/RUST TN4....................270 B3
  SNOD ME6.........................94 E8
  STMC/STPC BR5....................87 H1
  STRD ME2.........................93 J9
  WWKM BR4.........................61 P8
Kent St WBY/YAL ME18.............182 F1
  WSTB CT5........................105 L6
Kent Ter HOO/HM ME3...............55 J2
  MEO DA13.........................92 B7
  RAM CT11........................142 G4
  RHAM ME8.........................95 G9
Kent Vw SOCK/AV RM15..............30 D5
Kent View Dr SIT ME10..............unclear
Kentwell Cl BROCKLY SE4 *.........41 M5
Kenward Cl RTON TN11.............211 P2
Kenward Rd ELTH/MOT SE9...........43 L8
  MAIDW ME16.......................unclear
  WBY/YAL ME18....................183 M8
Kenwood Av HART DA3...............68 G9
  WALD ME5........................125 M1
Kenwood Dr BECK BR3...............62 A9

Kenwyn Rd DART DA1.................46 D6
Kenya Rd CHARL SE7.................43 H1
Kenya Ter MAID/BEAR ME14........155 M5
Kerbey St POP/IOD E14..............25 L2
Kerfield Crs CMBW SE5.............40 D2
Kerfield Pl CMBW SE5...............40 D2
Kerry Av SOCK/AV RM15.............30 C5
Kerry Cl CAN/RD E16................26 C2
Kerry Hill Wy
  MAID/BEAR ME14..................155 K6
Kerry Pth NWCR SE14................25 J9
Kerry Rd CDW/CHF RM16.............32 E4
  NWCR SE14........................25 J9
Kershaw Cl CDW/CHF RM16..........31 M6
Kerton Rd LYDD TN29..............347 K1
Kesteven Cl STRD ME2..............93 P9
Keston Av HAYES BR2................85 M9
Keston Cl WELL DA16................44 E2
Keston Ct RHAM ME8 *..............96 D4
Keston Gdns HAYES BR2.............85 M8
Keston Park Cl HAYES BR2..........86 A8
Keston Rd PECK SE15................40 F4
  THHTH CR7........................60 A4
Kestrel Av EHAM E6.................26 F1
  HNHL SE24........................40 B6
Kestrel Cl ASH TN23...............282 F5
  SIT ME10.........................129 M9
Kestrel Pl NWCR SE14 *.............25 H9
Kestrel Pl WALD ME5...............125 P5
Kestrel Wy CROY/NA CRO...........114 C3
Keswick Av SIT ME10...............130 B2
Keswick Cl TON TN9................210 C8
Keswick Dr MAIDW ME16............155 H7
Keswick Gdns PUR RM19.............30 F9
  ORP BR6..........................86 H6
  WWKM BR4.........................85 H6
Ketridge La E/WMAL ME19.........183 L1
Kettle Dr RFOLK CT18.............288 E2
Kettle Hl FAV ME13................161 J4
Kettle Hill Rd FAV ME13..........161 K7
Kettle La MAID/SHEP ME15.........184 D4
Kettlewell Ct SWLY BR8............65 P8
Kevin Dr RAM CT11................142 G5
Kevington Ct STMC/STPC BR5.......86 C1
Kevington Dr CHST BR7.............86 C1
Kewlands MAID/BEAR ME14.........155 P6
Keycol Hl RSIT ME9.................98 H3
Keyes Av CHAT ME4..................95 L9
Keyes Cl DVE/WH CT16.............291 H7
Keyes Gdns TIL RM18...............49 J8
Keyes Pl FOLKN CT19..............311 H4
Keyes Rd DART DA1..................46 F6
Keymer Cl BH/WHM TN16...........145 M1
Keynsham Gdns
  ELTH/MOT SE9.....................43 J6
Keynsham Rd ELTH/MOT SE9.........43 H6
Keyse Rd STHWK SE1.................24 D8
The Keys RFOLK CT18..............288 F7
Key St SIT ME10....................99 H9
Keyworth Cl STPH/PW TN12........242 G3
Keyworth Ms CANT CT1...............5 H5
Kezia St DEPT SE8..................25 P8
Khalsa Av GVE DA12................49 N8
Khartoum Pl GVE DA12..............49 N7
Khartoum Rd CHAT ME4...............6 C1
Khartoum Sq DVE/WH CT16.........291 H7
Khyber Rd GILL ME7.................73 H9
Kibbles La SBGH/RUST TN4........240 B9
Kidbrooke Gdns
  BKHTH/KID SE3....................42 E2
Kidbrooke Gv BKHTH/KID SE3.......42 E2
Kidbrooke La ELTH/MOT SE9.........43 J5
Kidbrooke Park Cl
  BKHTH/KID SE3....................42 E2
Kidbrooke Park Rd
  LEE/GVPK SE12....................42 F3
Kidbrooke Wy BKHTH/KID SE3.......42 F3
Kidderminster Pl
  CROY/NA CRO.....................82 G5
Kidderminster Rd
  CROY/NA CRO.....................82 G5
Kidd Pl CHARL SE7..................26 F8
Kilbride Ct CHAT CT11 *..........143 L3
Kildare Rd CAN/RD E16..............26 A1
Kilgour Rd FSTH SE23..............41 L7
Kilburns Mill Rd WLGTN SM6........82 A6
Kilgearn Rd CAT SE6................42 B9
Killewarren Wy
  STMC/STPC BR5....................87 K4
Killick Cl SEV TN15...............148 D6
Killick Rd HOO/HM ME3.............73 K2
Killip Cl CAN/RD E16...............26 A2
Kilmartin Av
  STRHM/NOR SW16..................60 B2
Kilmorie Rd FSTH SE23.............41 L9
Kiln Av CHST BR7...................63 K4
Kiln Barn Rd DIT/AY ME20.........134 B5
Kilnbridge Cl
  MAID/SHEP ME25 *................184 G4
Kiln Cl RASHW TN26...............222 E1
  SIT ME10.........................129 P2
Kilndown CVE DA12.................62 G9
Kilndown Cl ASH TN23.............282 B2
Kilndown Gdns
  CANTW/ST CT2....................136 F9
  MARG CT9........................113 K3
Kilner St POP/IOD E14.............338 K4
Kiln Fld TENT TN30...............301 K8
Kiln La RASHW TN26...............280 L4
  RTON TN11........................unclear
Kiln Wy GRAYS RM17.................306 A3
  STPH/PW TN12....................243 H4
Kilnwood RSEV TN14...............117 N7
Kimbell Pl BKHTH/KID SE3.........43 J4
Kimberley Av PECK SE15............41 K1
Kimberley Cl DVE/WH CT16........291 K4
Kimberley Dr SCUP DA14............64 F1
Kimberley Gv WSTB CT5............104 G3
Kimberley Rd BECK BR3.............61 K8
  CROY/NA CRO......................82 G3
  GILL ME7..........................unclear
  MSTR CT12........................unclear
Kimbolton Cl LEE/GVPK SE12.......42 D7
Kime Gdns
  ELTH/MOT SE9.....................43 J5
Kimmeridge Gdns
  ELTH/MOT SE9....................63 J3
Kimmeridge Rd ELTH/MOT SE9......63 J3
Kimpton Rd CMBW SE5...............40 D2

Kinburn St BERM/RHTH SE16 *...24 G5
Kincaid Rd PECK SE15................41 H1
Kincraig Dr SEV TN13............148 F8
Kinder CI THMD SE28 ....28 C5
Kindersley Ct EGRIN RH19 .....265 L5
Kinder St WCHPL E1 ....24 E2
Kinfauns Rd BRXS/STRHM SW2..60 A1
King Alfred Av CAT SE6..............61 L5
King Arthur CI PECK SE15 ....41 J1
King Arthur Rd HYTHE CT21 .....142 C5
King Charles Ter WAP E1W *.......24 E5
Kingcup CI CROY/NA CR0 ....83 J4
King David La WCHPL E1............24 E5
King Edward Av BRDST CT10......113 M9
 DART DA1...............................46 D7
 HB CT6..................................107 N2
King Edward Dr GRAYS RM17....32 F7
King Edward III Ms
 BERM/RHTH SE16 *...................24 E5
King Edward St BRCH CT7 ....111 H8
 CHAT ME5..............................95 L4
 DEAL CT14............................203 J9
 GILL ME7................................73 M9
 MAID/SHEP ME15....................185 L1
 RAM CT11...............................16 B4
 RDART DA2 ....47 N5
 ROCH ME1 ....19 F6
King Edward's Rd
 SLH/COR SS17 ....34 C1
King Edward St WSTB CT5 ....105 L5
Kingfield St POP/IOD E14 ....25 M7
Kingfisher Av HYTHE CT21 ....308 C7
Kingfisher CI KEN/WIL TN24.....283 K1
 MARG CT9..............................112 A5
 RSIT ME9...............................95 L4
 STMC/STPC BR5.......................87 L1
 THMD SE28............................28 B3
 WSTB CT5..............................105 K7
Kingfisher CI HB CT6................107 J3
Kingfisher Dr RDART DA2..........40 A5
 WALD ME5..............................95 P7
Kingfisher Gdns
 SAND/SEL CR2......................114 A4
Kingfisher Ms LEW SE13 ....41 P6
Kingfisher Rd EGRIN RH19 ......265 J6
Kingfisher Rd DIT/AY ME20.......153 N2
Kingfisher St EHAM E6...............26 F1
Kingfisher Wk BRDST CT10 *.....113 L8
Kingfisher Wy BECK BR3...........84 A2
King Gdns CROY/NA CR0 ....82 C9
King Garth Ms FSTH SE23...........61 J1
King George Av CAN/RD E16......26 E2
 EGRIN RH19..........................264 F5
King George Rd WALD ME5.......125 K1
King George St GNWCH SE10.....42 A1
King George VI Hi TN1..............270 F3
King George W Av TIL RM18.......34 A7
King Harolds Wy BXLYHN DA7....46 F1
King Henry Ms ORP BR6..............86 D9
King Henry's Dr CROY/NA CR0..114 F3
King Henry Ter WAP E1W *.........24 E5
King Hi E/WMAL ME9 ....152 C8
King John St WCHPL E1..............24 E2
King John's Wk ELTH/MOT SE9..43 J8
Kinglake Est WALW SE17 *..........9 M4
Kinglake St WALW SE17..............19 M7
Kingland La RASHE TN25...........222 C9
King Lear's Wy DVW CT17 ....313 J1

King & Queen CI
 ELTH/MOT SE9........................63 J3
King & Queen Whf
 BERM/RHTH SE16 *...................24 C4
Kings Acre MAID/SHEP ME15.....186 D2
Kingsand Rd LEE/GVPK SE12 ....62 E1
King's Arms Yd LOTH EC2R........24 A2
Kings Av ASH TN23 ....62 D5
 BMLY BR1..............................62 D5
King's Av BRCH CT7 ....110 E5
 BRDST CT10..........................113 M8
Kings Av ROCH ME1 ....95 H5
King's Av ROCH ME1 ....338 C6
 RYE TN31...............................338 C6
 SWCH CT13...........................202 E3
 WSTB CT5..............................105 M5
Kings Bank La RYE TN31..........338 F9
King's Bastion GILL ME7............88 E2
Kingsbridge Ct POP/IOD E14......25 K6
Kings Cha KEN/WIL TN24..........253 K7
Kings Ci DART DA1....................45 L5
Kings Ci DEAL CT14.................203 H5
Kings Copse EGRIN RH19 *.......265 J8
Kingscote Rd CROY/NA CR0.......83 N4
Kingsdale Rd PCE/AN SE20........61 K6
 WOOL/PLUM SE18..................27 N9

Kingsdown Chambers
 WSTB CT5..............................105 N3
Kingsdown CI
 BERM/RHTH SE16 *...................24 E6
 MARG CT9..............................126 D1
 GVE DA12..............................50 B9
 MAIDW ME16..........................12 B4
Kingsdown HI DEAL CT14..........263 H4
Kingsdown Pk DEAL CT14 *.......263 J3
 WSTB CT5..............................105 N4
Kingsdown Rd DEAL CT14.........233 J9
 RDV CT15..............................262 E9
 RSIT ME9...............................160 B3
Kingsdown Wy HAYES BR2.........85 K3
Kings Dr GVE DA12 ....69 M2
Kingsferry Br RSIT ME9.............77 J8
Kingsfield Rd HB CT6...............107 N4
Kingsfield Ter DART DA1 *..........5 M8
Kingsford St RASHE TN25........283 N2
Kingsford Yd ASH TN23 *..........282 D2
Kingsford Wy EHAM E6...............26 C1
Kingsgate Av BRDST CT10.......115 L4

Kingsgate Bay Rd
 BRDST CT10..........................113 M3
Kingsgate CI BXLYHN DA7.........44 G2
 MAIDW ME16..........................155 H8
 STMC/STPC BR5.......................64 E9
Kingsgate La TENT TN30...........320 C9
Kingsground ELTH/MOT SE9.......43 H5
King's Gv PECK SE15.................41 H1
Kings Hall Ms LEW SE13 *...........42 A4
Kings Hall Rd BECK BR3.............61 K6
Kings Hwy WOOL/PLUM SE18....27 M9
Kings Hill Av E/WMAL ME9........153 H8
Kingshill Dr HOO/HM ME3..........73 K1

Kingsholm Gdns
 ELTH/MOT SE9........................43 H5
Kingshurst Rd
 LEE/GVPK SE12......................62 E8
Kingsingfield Ct
 BGR/WK TN15.......................120 B2
Kingsingfield Rd
 BGR/WK TN15.......................120 B3
Kings Keep HAYES BR2 *...........62 C9
Kingsland Gdns HCDN TN27.....232 G9
Kingsland Gv HCDN TN27.........247 N4
Kingsland Hollow LYDD TN29....337 M1
Kingsland La HDCN TN27.........219 M9
 RASHE TN25..........................252 C2
Kings La STPH/PW TN12..........244 B2
Kingsleigh Wk HAYES BR2.........85 J1
Kingsley Av DART DA1................46 C6
Kingsley Ms CHST BR7 ....63 N5
 WAP E1W *..............................24 E5
Kingsley Rd CROY/NA CR0..........82 F5
 MAID/SHEP ME15...................164 C6
 ORP BR6................................86 C9
 WSTB CT5.............................105 M6
Kingsley Wk CDW/CHF RM16.....33 H7
Kingsley Wood Dr
 ELTH/MOT SE9........................63 K2
Kingsmead Ct CRS NRWD SE19....60 E7
Kingsman Dr CDW/CHF RM16.....32 C5
Kingsman St
 WOOL/PLUM SE18....................26 C7
Kingsmarsh La LYDD TN29.........336 B9
Kingsmead Dr WHM TN16.........145 N1
 FOLKN CT19..........................310 E3
Kingsmead CI BFN/LL DA15........64 C1
Kingsmead Cr
 CANTW/ST CT2 *....................166 F2
Kings Meadow RASHE TN25.....253 H2
Kingsmead Pk
 STPH/PW TN12......................243 H3
Kingsmead Rd
 BRXS/STRHM SW2....................60 A1
 CANTW/ST CT2 *......................5 F1
Kings Ms CANT CT1 *..................5 F2
 RAM CT11................................5 F2
Kings Mill Ct SIT ME10................99 M9
Kingsnorth CI HOO/HM ME3........73 L1
Kingsnorth Gdns FOLK CT20.......10 B4
Kingsnorth Rd ASH TN23..........282 D2
 FAV ME13..............................132 F7
 RHAM ME8............................96 F2
Kings Oak HB CT6 *.....................85 L1
Kings Orch ELTH/MOT SE9.........43 J7
 ROCH ME1..............................19 G5
Kings Pde KEN/WIL TN24 *..........5 D3
Kings's Pk CANT CT1...................5 J5
King's Prospect
 KEN/WIL TN24.......................282 G2
Kings Reach
 MAID/SHEP ME15..................186 A3
Kingsridge Gdns DART DA1........46 D7
Kings Rd BH/WHM TN16...........145 M2
Kings Rd BRCH CT7 ....291 H8
Kings Rd DVW CT17 ....291 H3
Kings Rd FAV ME13 ....132 F6
Kings Rd FOLK CT20 ....310 A5
Kings Rd HB CT6......................107 J2
Kings Rd HDCN TN27 ....247 N4
 IOS ME12................................58 D9
 ORP BR6................................86 C8
Kings's Rd RAM CT11 ....16 D1
Kings's Rd RCANTE CT5...........229 J1
Kings's Rd SNWD SE25.............60 D9
 TON TN9...............................240 F2
 WALD ME5.............................96 A5
Kings Ropewalk DVW CT17......313 J1
Kings Rw MAID/SHEP ME15 *...185 M2
Kings Standing Wy
 RTWE/PEM TN2.....................241 J7
Kings Stairs CI
 BERM/RHTH SE16....................24 E5
Kingsthorpe Rd SYD SE26.........61 K5
Kings Toll Rd RTWE/PEM TN2...272 B2
Kingston Av MARG CT9.............112 A6
Kingston CI DVW CT17.............290 G4
 HB CT6..................................98 B4
 MSTR CT12............................142 C5
Kingston Crs CGVW DA11 ....41 H7
Kingston Crs BECK BR3.............61 M7
 WALD ME5.............................125 N1
Kingston Dr
 MAID/SHEP ME15..................185 M5
Kingston Gdns CROY/NA CR0.....82 D7
Kingston Pde GRAYS RM17 *.....32 C7
Kingston Rd SNWD SE19...........60 D4
King St CANT CT1 *......................4 E5
 CANTW/ST CT2.......................137 L9
 CHAT ME5................................6 D4
 DEAL CT14............................233 J6
 DVW CT17..............................11 H6
 E/WMAL ME9.........................153 J4
 EGRIN RH19..........................265 H7
 GILL ME7.................................7 J1
 GVE DA12...............................49 M7
 IOS ME12...............................58 D9
 LYDD TN29............................334 C5
 MAID/BEAR ME14....................13 G4
 MARG CT9...............................15 Q3
 RAM CT11................................17 G2
 ROCH ME1...............................19 F9
 SIT ME10................................99 M9
Kings Wk MAID/BEAR ME14 ....13 H5
Kings Wy CROY/NA CR0............82 D6
Kingsway LYDD TN29................327 J4
 STMC/STPC BR5......................86 E2
 WALD ME5...............................96 A5
 WWKM BR4............................85 J7
Kingswear Gdns STRD ME2........18 E1
Kingswood AV BELV DA17...........28 E7
 CHAT ME5................................95 H4
 HAYES BR2.............................62 C9
 SWLY BR8...............................87 F1
 THHTH CR7.............................82 F1
Kingswood CI DART DA1............46 C2
 RTWE/PEM TN2.......................23 H4
 STMC/STPC BR5......................86 E4
Kingswood Ct DUL SE21...........60 E3
Kingswood PI LEW SE13............42 C5

Kingswood DIT/AY ME20..........125 J5
 GILL ME7..................................7 K1
 HAYES BR2..............................62 C9
 PGE/AN SE20..........................61 J5
 RTWE/PEM TN2.......................23 H4
 SEV TN13..............................148 D6
Kingswood Vls DVW CT17 *......291 H5
Kingswood Wy SAND/SEL CR2..114 A6
 WLGTN SM6............................82 D9
Kingsworth CI BECK BR3............84 B2
King William La GNWCH SE10....25 P8
Kingsway Av BRDST CT10 *........82 F2

King William CI GILL ME7............73 J8
King William St STHWK SE1........24 A4
King William Wk GNWCH SE10..25 M9
Kinlet Rd WOOL/PLUM SE18.......45 N1
Kinnaird Av BMLY BR1...............62 D5
Kinnaird CI BMLY BR1................62 D5
Kinnimburgh Dr LING RH7.........235 K8
Kinnings Rw TON TN9...............210 F8
Kinross CI WALD ME5.................95 N7
Kinsale Rd PECK SE15................41 J3
Kinveachy Gdns CHARL SE7.......26 F8
Kinver Rd SYD SE26...................61 J5
Kipling Av TIL RM18...................49 M2
Kipling Dr ELTH/MOT SE20........123 N9
Kipling Est STHWK SE1..............2 C5
Kipling Rd ASH TN23...................2 C3
 BXLYHN DA7............................47 N1
 DART DA1...............................47 H6
Kipling St STHWK SE1.................2 A5
Kipling Wy EGRIN RH19............265 H7
Kipping CI RFOLK CT18.............288 D8
Kippington CI SEV TN13..............20 B1
Kippington Dr ELTH/MOT SE9.....43 H8
Kippington Rd SEV TN13............20 B1
Kirby CI CRBK TN17..................298 A3
Kirby St BERM/RHTH SE16 *.......24 E6
Kirby Gv STHWK SE1 ....24 B5
Kirby Rd HOO/HM ME3...............73 J8
 RDART DA2 ....47 J8
Kirby's La CANTW/ST CT2 ....4 D5
Kirkdale CI WALD ME5...............126 A4
Kirkdale Cnr SYD SE26...............61 J5
Kirkdale Rd MAID/SHEP ME15...185 L5
 RTW TN1.................................11 F2
Kirkham Rd EHAM E6..................26 F2
Kirkham St WOOL/PLUM SE18....27 M9
Kirkins CI STPH/PW TN12.........273 P2
Kirkland CI BFN/LL DA15............63 M7
Kirkland Ter BECK BR3...............61 N5
Kirk La HOO/HM ME3 *................27 K9
Kirklees Rd THHTH CR7 ....82 F2
Kirkmichael Rd POP/IOD E14.....25 M3
Kirkstone Av RAM CT11 ....142 E5
Kirkstone Wy BMLY BR1.............62 A1
Kirk Vw ASH TN23....................281 P1
Kirkwood Av RASHW TN26........302 F6
Kirkwood Rd PECK SE15.............41 J3
Kirtley Rd SYD SE26...................61 L5
Kirton CI RFOLK CT18...............288 C8
Kirwyn Wy CMBW SE5................40 C1
Kitchener Av CRANT ME4............26 E7
 GVE DA12................................69 N3
Kitchener Rd DVW CT17............291 H5
 HOO/HM ME3............................72 F5
 THHTH CR7.............................82 A7
Kitchener Sq FOLKN CT19........311 H3
Kitchenour La RYE TN31...........331 K8
Kite Farm WSTB CT5................106 C5
Kite La STPH/PW TN12.............273 H2
Kitewell La LYDD TN29.............342 C4
Kither Rd ASH TN23.................282 D1
Kit HI FAV ME13.......................165 N4
Kitley Gdns NRWD SE19...........60 F7
Kitsbridge La RASHW TN26.......324 C2
Kitson Rd CMBW SE5 ....40 C1
Kittiwake CI HB CT6..................108 C6
 SAND/SEL CR2......................114 A6
Kitto Rd NWCR SE14..................41 K3
Knapdale CI FSTH SE23.............61 H1
Knapmill Rd CAT SE6..................61 N1
Knapmill Wy CAT SE6.................61 N1
Knatchbull Rd CMBW SE5...........40 B3
Knatchbull Wy RASHE TN25......284 F5
Knatts La BGR/WK TN15............120 B5
Knatts Valley Rd
 BGR/WK TN15........................119 P1
Knaves Acre HDCN TN27..........247 N4
Knave Wood Rd
 BGR/WK TN15.......................149 K2
Knee HI ABYW SE2.....................28 B8
Knee Hill Crs ABYW SE2.............28 B8
Kneller Bd BROCKY SE4..............41 L5
Knight Av CANTW/ST CT2.........166 B4
 GILL ME7................................73 K9
Knighten St WAP E1W................24 E4
Knighthead Point
 POP/IOD E14 *..........................25 K5
Knighton Park Rd SYD SE26.......61 K4
Knighton Rd RSEV TN14............148 E2
Knightrider Ct
 MAID/SHEP ME15....................13 F6
Knightrider St
 MAID/SHEP ME15....................13 F6
 SWCH CT13............................201 P2
Knight Rd STRD ME2..................18 D2
 TONN TN15............................211 H4
Knights Av BRDST CT10...........113 N7
Knightsbridge La
 RTWE/PEM TN2.......................22 A1
Knights CI HOO/HM ME3 ....73 L2
 RTWE/PEM TN2.....................271 N1
Knights Cft HART DA3.................91 J8
Knightsfield Rd SIT ME10............99 L1
Knights Hi WNWD SE27..............60 B5
Knights Hill Sq WNWD SE27 *.....60 B5
Knights Manor Wy DART DA1......46 F7
Knights Pk RTWE/PEM TN2........241 J8
Knights Rd CAN/RD E16.............26 B4
Knights Rdg RTWE/PEM TN2....271 N1
Knight's Rd DVE/WH CT16............9 F2

Knights Rd HOO/HM ME3............73 K1
Knights Templars DVW CT16 *...291 H4
Knights Wy DVW CT16..............291 H4
Knight's Wy HDCN TN27...........247 N4
Knights Wy RTWE/PEM TN2.......241 J9
Knockhall Cha DA10...................48 A5
Knockhall Rd SWCM DA10..........48 A7
Knock HI TENT TN30.................333 K3
Knockholt Rd ELTH/MOT SE9.....43 H5
 MARG CT9.............................113 K2
 RSEV TN14...........................130 D7
Knock Mill La BGR/WK TN15.....120 D7
Knock Rd ASH TN23..................282 E1
Knockwood Rd TENT TN30........301 K6
Knoll Pk MARG CT9..................112 D5
Knole CI CROY/NA CR0 *...........83 P2
Knole Gv EGRIN RH19..............264 F5
Knole La SEV TN13....................21 H5
Knole Rd DART DA1...................46 A8
 SEV TN13..............................149 J8
 WALD ME5.............................125 P9
The Knole ELTH/MOT SE9..........63 L3
 FAV ME13..............................153 P5
 MEO DA15...............................69 J6
The Knoll BECK BR3...................61 P7
 HAYES BR2.............................85 K6
Knoll Wy IOS ME12....................58 B8
Knollys CI STRHM/NOR SW16 *..60 B2
Knollys CI STRHM/NOR SW16.....60 A2
Knolly's Rd STRHM/NOR SW16...60 A2
Knott CI MAID/BEAR ME14........155 M6
Knott Crs KEN/WIL TN24...........283 L1
Knott's La CANT CT1 *.................F5
Knotts La RDV CT15..................292 E1
Knotts PI SEV TN13....................20 D3
Knowle Av BXLYHN DA7.............44 A1
Knowle CI BRXN/ST SW9 ....40 A3
 RRTW TN3............................269 K5
Knowle La STPH/PW TN12.........243 K5
Knowle Rd HAYES BR2...............85 P6
 MAID/BEAR ME14...................155 M6
 ROCH ME1............................124 D1
 STPH/PW TN12.....................243 L7
Knowler Wy HB CT6..................107 P1
Knowles Gdns HDCN TN27........247 N4
Knowles Hill Crs LEW SE13 *......42 B6
Knowlton Gdns MAIDW ME16....184 G1
Knowlton Gn HAYES BR2............85 J2
Knowlton Wk CANT CT1 *.............5 J5
Knowsley Wy RTDN TN11...........210 G4
Knowle St NWCR SE14...............41 H3
Kohima PI RDV CT15...................95 P3
Koonowla CI BH/WHM TN16......115 N9
Kossuth St GNWCH SE10 ....25 P9
Kydbrook CI STMC/STPC BR5......86 D4
Kyetop Wk RHAM ME8................96 G8
Kymbeline Ct DEAL CT14...........232 G5
Kynaston Av THHTH CR7.............82 F4
Kynaston Crs THHTH CR7...........83 H2
Kynaston Rd BMLY BR1..............62 E4
 STMC/STPC BR5......................87 J4
 THHTH CR7............................83 H2

L

La Belle Alliance Sq RAM CT11...17 G3
Labour-in-Vain Rd
 BGR/WK TN15.......................120 G7
Laburnum Av DART DA1..............46 C9
 SWCH CT13...........................201 N2
 SWLY BR8...............................65 M9
Laburnum CI DVE/WH CT16.......290 F3
 PECK SE15..............................41 J1
Laburnum Dr DIT/AY ME20........153 P2
Laburnum Gdns CROY/NA CR0...84 A4
Laburnum Gv GVW DA11...........49 H8
Laburnum La CANTW/ST CT2....137 L6
 SIT ME10................................129 M6
Laburnum PI ELTH/MOT SE9 *....43 L6
Laburnum Rd DART DA1.............46 D7
Laburnum Wy HAYES BR2...........86 B4
Labworth CI IOS ME12................77 H1
Lacebark CI BFN/LL DA15...........44 B8
Lacey CI RMAID ME17...................7 H7
Laceys La RMAID ME17..............215 H5
Lachlan Wy FOLK CT20.............310 C8
Lackington St SDTCH EC2A 4 A1
Lacock Gdns
 MAID/SHEP ME15..................185 M2
Lacon Rd EDUL SE22..................40 G5
Lacton Oast KEN/WIL TN24.......253 K9
Lacton Wy KEN/WIL TN24.........253 K9
Ladas Rd WNWD SE27................60 C4
Ladbroke Hurst LING RH7..........235 K8
Ladbrooke Crs SCUP DA14..........64 C7
Ladbrook Rd SNWD SE25............60 D3
Ladds La SNOD ME6..................123 P3
Ladds Wy SWLY BR8 ....88 C1
Lade Fort Crs LYDD TN29...........343 L6
Ladham Rd CRBK TN17.............274 F4
Ladyclose Av HOO/HM ME3.........52 A9
Ladycroft Gdns ORP BR6.............86 B9
Ladycroft Rd LEW SE13...............41 P4
Ladycroft Wy ORP BR6................86 B9
Ladyfields GVW DA11..................69 K3
Ladyfield CI RSIT ME9.................98 C9
 WALD ME5.............................126 A5
Ladyfields La RSIT ME9...............98 C9
Lady Garne Rd RDV CT15...........312 A1
Ladygrove CROY/NA CR0...........114 B9
Ladymount WLGTN SM6..............82 C8
Lady Oak La CRBK TN17............296 E5
Lady's Gift Rd
 SBGH/RUST TN4....................271 H8
Ladyship Ter EDUL SE22 *...........41 H8
Ladysmith Gv WTHK ME20 ....104 D8
Ladysmith Rd ELTH/MOT SE9.....43 L7
 WSTB CT5..............................105 J1
Ladywell DVE/WH CT16................8 C2

Ladywell CI BROCKY SE4...........41 N6
Ladywell Rd LEW SE13...............41 N4
Ladywood Av STMC/STPC BR5....86 F2
Ladywood Rd CANTW/ST CT2....137 L6
 RDART DA2.............................94 A4
 STRD ME2...............................18 A3
Lady Wootton's La CANT CT1........5 G4
Lafone St STHWK SE1..................24 C5
Lagado Ms BERM/RHTH SE16.....24 G4
Lagham Ct GDST RH9................204 B5
Lagham Dr GDST RH9...............204 B4
Lagham Rd GDST RH9...............204 B4
Lagonda Wy DART DA1................46 J5
Lagoon Rd STMC/STPC BR5........87 J2
Lagos Av MSTR CT12.................142 F3
Lairdale CI DUL SE21..................40 C9
Lake Av CDW/CHF RM16.............32 E3
Lake Av BMLY BR1......................62 E5
Lakedale Rd WOOL/PLUM SE18..27 M8
Lake Dr HOO/HM ME3.................71 L1
Lake Gdns WLGTN SM6...............82 G2
Lakehall Gdns THHTH CR7..........82 G2
Lakehall Rd THHTH CR7..............82 G2
Lakelands MAID/SHEP ME15......185 M4
 RMAID ME17..........................188 F5
Lakemead ASH TN23.................252 B9
Lake Ri WTHK RM20....................31 K7
Lake Rd CROY/NA CR0................84 C6
 DIT/AY ME20..........................154 D4
 SBGH/RUST TN4....................270 D4
Laker Rd ROCH ME1....................95 H8
Lakeside ASH TN23...................252 B8
 BECK BR3................................61 P9
 RTWE/PEM TN2.....................271 H2
 SNOD ME6..............................123 N7
 WLGTN SM6............................82 A8
Lakeside Av THMD SE28.............27 P4
Lakeside CI BFN/LL DA15............44 E6
 EDEN TN8.............................207 N6
 SNWD SE25.............................60 G8
Lakeside Dr HAYES BR2..............85 P9
Lakes Rd HAYES BR2.................85 M9
The Lakes DIT/AY ME20.............123 P9

Lakewood Rd
 STMC/STPC BR5......................86 C3
Lakeview CI SNOD ME6.............123 P7
Lake View Rd EGRIN RH19.........265 J5
 SEV TN13..............................148 F8
Lakeview Rd WELL DA16............44 D5
 WNWD SE27............................60 A4
Lakewood Dr RHAM ME8.............96 F8
Laking Av BRDST CT10..............113 M6
Laleham Gdns MARG CT9..........112 G3
Laleham Rd CAT SE6 ....42 A8
 MARG CT9.............................112 G4
Laleham Wk MARG CT9.............112 G4
Lamberde Av ELTH/MOT SE9......63 L3
Lambarde CI STRD ME2.............123 P1
Lambarde Dr SEV TN13..............148 F8
Lambarde Rd SEV TN13.............148 F7
Lambarde Sq HART DA3..............91 J7
Lambardes CI ORP BR6................87 L3
Lamb CI TIL RM18........................49 N3
Lambden Rd HDCN TN27............250 A3
Lambe CI SNOD ME6.................123 P3
Lamberhurst CI
 STMC/STPC BR5......................87 L5
Lamberhurst Gn RHAM ME8.........96 K4
Lamberhurst Rd
 STPH/PW TN12......................273 K7
 WNWD SE27............................60 B3
Lambersart Ct
 SBGH/RUST TN4....................240 G9
Lambert Ct BH/WHM TN16.........145 N1
Lambert Ms SNOD ME6..............126 P5
Lambert Rd CAN/RD E16.............26 C2
Lamberts PI CROY/NA CR0..........83 J5
Lamberts PI STPH/PW TN12.......274 A1
Lamberts Rd RTWE/PEM TN2.....240 E9
Lambert's Yd TON TN9...............210 E9
Lambeth CI WALD ME5...............125 N1
Lambeth Rd CANT CT1 *.............167 H1
 CROY/NA CR0..........................82 F5
Lambeth Wk PECK SE15.............40 F3
Lambfrith Gv HELE ME7 *...........126 E2
Lambourn CI EGRIN RH19..........265 H5
Lambourne Dr E/WMAL ME19....182 C1
Lambourne Gv
 BERM/RHTH SE16....................24 G8
 RHAM ME8...............................97 K4
Lambourne Rd
 MAID/SHEP ME15..................186 C1
Lambourne Wk CANT CT1.............5 K5
Lambourn Wy
 RTWE/PEM TN2.....................270 P3
 WALD ME5.............................125 P3
Lambs Bank TON TN9................240 E2
Lambscroft Av ELTH/MOT SE9.....62 C2
Lambsfrith Gv GILL ME7.............126 E2
Lamb's La South RAIN RM13.......29 P1
Lamb's Pas STLK EC1Y...............24 A1
Lamb St WCHPL E1.....................24 C1
Lamb Wk STHWK SE1................105 K8
Lamb Wk DVW CT17..................291 H6
Lamerock Rd BMLY BR1..............62 D3
Lamerton St DEPT SE8.................25 K9
Laming Rd BRCH CT7................111 J7
Lammas Dr SIT ME10...................99 N8
Lammas Ga HART DA3...............132 C5
Lamorbey CI BFN/LL DA15..........64 B1
Lamorbey Pk BFN/LL DA15 *........44 B8
Lamorna Av GVW DA11................69 P1
Lamorna CI ORP BR6...................87 H8
Lampington Rw RTWE/PEM TN2..23 H4
Lamplighters CI DART DA1...........46 F7
 GILL ME7................................126 C1
Lampmead Rd LEE/GVPK SE12...42 C8
Lamport CI WOOL/PLUM SE18....26 G7
Lamson Rd RAIN RM13................29 K1
Lanbury Rd PECK SE15................41 K5
Lancashire Rd
 MAID/SHEP ME15..................186 B4
Lancaster Av MTCM CR4.............82 D1
 RFOLK CT18...........................311 H1
 WNWD SE27............................60 B1
Lancaster CI HAYES BR2.............85 J1

MSTR CT12 ....142 G3
RASHW TN26 ....304 D7
Lancaster Ct *RHAM* ME8 ....96 F7
Lancaster Dr *EGRIN* RH19 ....265 K5
POP/IOD E14 ....25 M4
Lancaster Gdns *BARN* BR1 ....85 P2
Lancaster House
WOOL/PLUM SE18 * 43 J1
Lancaster Rd *CANT* CT1 ....166 E6
CDW/CHF RM16 ....31 N7
DVW CT17 ....8 D3
SNWD SE25 ....60 F8
Lancaster Wy *E/WMAL* ME19 ....152 C9
Lance Cl *SIT* ME10 ....99 N6
Lancelot Av *STRD* ME2 ....71 N8
Lancelot Cl *DEAL* CT14 ....232 F6
STRD ME2 ....71 J9
Lancelot Rd *WELL* DA16 ....44 C5
Lances Cl *RASHW* DA13 ....92 B4
Lancaster House
WOOL/PLUM SE18 * 43 P1
Lanchester Ter *HAYES* BR2 ....85 J4
Landau Av *BLY* ERITH DA8 ....30 A8
Landbury Wk *RASHE* TN25 ....252 C5
Landcroft Rd *EDUL* SE22 ....40 F7
Landells Rd *EDUL* SE22 ....40 F7
Lander Rd *GRAYS* RM17 ....32 E8
Landgate *RYE* TN31 ....338 F6
Landmann Wy *NWCR* SE14 ....24 C9
Landon Rd *HB* CT6 ....107 P1
Landons Cl *POP/IOD* E14 ....25 M4
Landor Ct *GILL* ME7 ....126 D2
Landrail Rd *RSIT* ME9 ....98 C3
Landseer Av *GVW* DA11 ....69 H2
Landstead Rd
WOOL/PLUM SE18 ....43 P1
Landway *BGR/WK* TN15 ....149 L5
Land Wy *HOO/HM* ME3 ....71 M2
The Landway *BGR/WK* TN15 ....149 M2
BGR/WK TN15 ....151 J5
MAID/BEAR ME14 ....156 D9
STMC/STPC BR5 ....
Lane Av *SWCM* DA10 ....48 A7
Lane End *BXLYHN* DA7 ....45 K4
HB CT6 ....107 J1
Lanercost Rd
BRXS/STRHM SW2 ....60 A1
Lanes Av *GVW* DA11 ....69 K3
Laneside *CHST* BR7 ....
The Lanes *MSTR* CT12 ....141 L6
The Lane *BKHTH/KID* SE3 ....42 E4
TN9 TN11 ....269 H3
RRTW TN3 ....269 H3
Lanfranc Gdns *CANTW/ST* CT2 ....166 B3
Lanfranc Rd *DEAL* CT14 ....233 F1
Langafel Cl *HART* DA3 ....68 C8
Langbrook Rd *BKHTH/KID* SE3 * 43 H4
Lang Ct *WSTB* CT5 ....106 B5
Langdale Ash *TN23* 252 B9
Langdale Av *RAM* CT11 ....142 F5
ORP BR6 ....86 C7
RHAM ME8 ....96 F5
Langdale Crs *BXLYHN* DA7 ....45 K2
Langdale Rd *MAIDW* ME16 ....155 H7
Langdale Rd *GNWCH* SE10 ....42 A1
THHTH CR7 ....87 F1
Langdale St *WCHPL* E1 * 24 C2
Langdon Av *CANT* CT1 ....166 C4
Langdon Cl *RDV* CT15 ....292 E2
Langdon House
WOOL/PLUM SE18 * 43 J1
Langdon Rd *FOLKN* CT19 ....310 A4
HAYES BR2 ....62 F9
Langdon Shaw *SCUP* DA14 ....64 B4
Langdon Wy *STHWK* SE1 ....24 D7
Langdon Wy *CDW* SE5 ....40 B1
Langford Cl *GVW* DA14 ....64 C2
Langham Cl *MARG* CT9 ....112 L4
Langham Gv *MAIDW* ME16 ....155 H8
Langham Park Pl *HAYES* BR2 ....85 J1
Langham Rd *ASH* TN23 ....282 D1
RRTW TN3 ....269 L5
Langhorne Gdns *FOLK* CT20 ....10 D6
Langland Gdns *CROY/NA* CR0 ....64 C6
Langlands Dr *RDART* DA2 ....69 L4
Langley Ct *BECK* BR3 * ....
Langley Gdns *MARG* CT9 ....113 K2
STMC/STPC BR5 ....86 C3
Langley Rd *BECK* BR3 ....85 A1
SAND/SEL CR2 ....114 A3
SIT ME10 ....99 N8
WELL DA16 ....28 B9
Langley Wy *WWKM* BR4 ....85 J5
Langley Wd *BECK* BR3 ....85 H2
Langmead St *WOOL* SE27 ....60 B3
Langney Dr *ASH* TN23 ....282 A2
Langport Rd *NROM* TN28 ....337 H7
Langridge Dr *EGRIN* RH19 ....265 H8
Langsmead *LING* RH7 ....234 B1
Langston Hughes Cl
HNHL SE24 * ....
Langthorn Ct *LOTH* EC2R 24 A2
Langton Cl *CROY/NA* CR0 ....13 C0
Langton Dr *MAID/BEAR* ME14 ....13 C0
Langton La *RCANTW* CT4 ....166 F8
Langton Ri *EDUL* SE22 ....41 H8
DEAL CT14 ....233 H1
Langton Wy *BKHTH/KID* SE3 ....42 E1
CDW/CHF RM16 ....31 K8
CROY/NA CR0 ....83 K8
Langton Wy *RDART* DA2 ....69 L4
Lanier Rd *LEW* SE13 ....42 A7
Lankester Parker Rd
ROCH ME1 ....95 H8
Lankton Cl *BECK* BR3 ....62 A7
Lannoy Rd *ELTH/MOT* SE9 ....44 B1
Lanrick Rd *POP/IOD* E14 ....25 N1
Lanridge Rd *ABYW* SE2 ....28 C1
Lansbury Crs *DART* DA1 ....32 B9
Lansbury Gdns *POP/IOD* E14 * 25 N2
Lansdowne Av *BXLYHN* DA7 ....44 E1

MAID/SHEP ME15 ....185 P5
ORP BR6 ....86 C5
Lansdowne La *CHARL* SE27 ....60 B2
Lansdowne Ms *CHARL* SE27 ....26 E8
Lansdowne Pl *NRWD* SE19 ....60 F8
STHWK SE1 ....24 A6
Lansdowne Rd *BMLY* BR1 ....62 A4
CHAT ME4 ....95 K4
CROY/NA CR0 ....83 J5
RTW TN1 ....149 J7
SEV TN13 ....149 J7
TON TN9 ....210 E7
Lansdowne Sq *GVW* DA11 ....69 K7
RTW TN1 ....23 F5
Lansdowne Wood Cl
WNWD SE27 ....60 B2
Lansdown Pl *GVW* DA11 ....49 K9
Lansdown Rd *CANT* CT1 ....5 F7
SCUP DA14 ....64 D2
SIT ME10 ....130 B1
TIL RM18 ....49 K3
Lantern Cl *ORP* BR6 ....86 C6
Lanterns Ct *POP/IOD* E14 ....25 M3
Lanthorne Ct *BRDST* CT10 * 113 N7
Lanthorne Ms *RTW* TN1 ....22 C3
Lanthorne Rd *BRDST* CT10 ....113 M6
Lanvanor Rd *PECK* SE15 ....41 J3
Laplins La *ELTH/MOT* SE9 ....182 G1
Lapis Cl *GVE* DA12 ....50 D9
La Providence *ROCH* ME1 ....6 D1
Lapse Wood Wk *FSTH* SE23 ....41 H9
Lapwing Cl *ERITH* DA8 * 46 B1
IDS ME12 ....78 B2
RFOLK CT18 ....288 D9
SAND/SEL CR2 ....114 B4
Lapwing Dr *ASH* TN23 ....282 C5
RSIT ME9 ....98 C3
Lapwing Rd *HOO/HM* ME3 ....56 D5
Lapwings *HART* DA3 ....68 F9
Lapworth Cl *ORP* BR6 ....87 K6
Larch Cl *LEW* SE13 ....42 B3
Larch Cl *BRDST* CT10 ....113 J9
DEPT SE8 ....26 A9
DIT/AY ME20 ....154 A2
RCANTE CT3 ....138 B9
WARL CR6 ....144 B4
Larch Crs *HOO/HM* ME3 ....73 L4
Larch Dene *ORP* BR6 ....86 B6
The Larches *EGRIN* RH19 ....265 K4
FAV ME13 ....132 D5
HOO/HM ME3 ....71 L4
WSTB CT5 ....105 K6
Larch Gv *BFN/LL* DA15 ....44 M9
STPH/PW TN12 ....242 C3
Larch Rd *DART* DA1 ....46 D9
Larch Ter *IOS* ME12 * 57 J8
Larch Tree Wy *CROY/NA* CR0 ....64 D7
Larch Wk *KEN/WIL* TN24 ....252 F7
Larch Wy *HAYES* BR2 ....86 B4
Larch Wood Cl *WALD* ME5 ....128 A3
Larchwood Rd *ELTH/MOT* SE9 ....44 B3
Larcombe Cl *CROY/NA* CR0 ....83 L8
Larissa St *WALW* SE17 * 24 A8
Larkbere Rd *SYD* SE26 ....61 L3
Larkey Vw *RCANTW* CT4 ....195 M2
Larkfield *STPH/PW* TN12 ....242 B2
Larkfield Av *GILL* ME7 ....96 B2
SIT ME10 ....99 M8
Larkfield Rd *DIT/AY* ME20 ....153 P3
Larkfield Rd *DIT/AY* ME20 ....153 P5
SCUP DA14 ....64 B2
SEV TN13 ....148 B8
Larkfields *GVW* DA11 ....50 A6
Larkhill Ter
WOOL/PLUM SE18 * 43 L1
Larkin Cl *STRD* ME2 ....72 B5
Larking Dr *MAIDW* ME16 ....155 J5
Larkscliff Ct *BRCH* CT7 * 110 E5
Larks Fld *HART* DA3 ....31 J1
Larkfield Rd *FAV* ME13 ....132 F4
Larkspur Ct *E/WMAL* ME19 ....153 P5
ORP BR6 ....87 K6
Larkspur Rd *E/WMAL* ME19 ....153 K1
Larkstore Pk
STPH/PW TN12 ....246 B4
Larkswood Cl *ERITH* DA8 ....46 A2
Larkwell La *HART* DA3 ....91 J1
Larkfield Cl *CHART* ME5 ....45 N1
Lascelles Rd *DVW* CT17 ....291 H9
Laser Quay *STRD* ME2 ....19 J3
Lassa Rd *ELTH/MOT* SE9 ....43 J6
Lassell St *GNWCH* SE10 ....25 M8
Lasseter Pl *BKHTH/KID* SE3 ....25 P9
La-terne *DEAL* CT14 ....232 C7
Latham Cl *BH/WHM* TN16 ....145 M1
EHAM E6 ....26 F2
RDART DA2 ....67 L1
Latham Rd *BXLYHS* DA6 ....45 N5
Latham's Wy *CROY/NA* CR0 ....83 H9
Latimer Cl *HB* CT6 ....107 M6
Latimer Pl *GILL* ME7 ....73 J8
Latimer Rd *CROY/NA* CR0 ....83 H9
Latona Dr *GVE* DA12 ....70 D4
Latona Rd *PECK* SE15 ....24 F9
La Tourne Gdns *ORP* BR6 ....86 F7
Latymers *RTON* TN11 ....238 C5
Laud St *CROY/NA* CR0 ....83 F9
Launcelot Rd *BMLY* BR1 ....62 E5
Launch St *POP/IOD* E14 ....25 N3
Launder's La *RAIN* RM13 ....30 B1
Laundry Rd *MSTR* CT12 ....141 L5
Laura Dr *SWLY* BR8 ....66 A3
Laura Pl *ROCH* ME1 ....94 E4
Laureate Ct *MARG* CT9 ....112 C3
Laurel Av *GVE* DA12 ....229 N1
LYDD TN29 ....337 L2
Laurel Bank *SBCH/RUST* TN4 ....240 F9
Laurel Cl *BFN/LL* DA15 ....44 D1
DART DA1 ....46 C9
FOLK CT20 ....310 B5
Laurel Crs *CROY/NA* CR0 ....64 F1
Laurel Dr *OXTED* RH8 ....175 J7
Laurel Gv *PGE/AN* SE20 ....61 H6
RMAID ME17 ....187 N9

SYD SE26 ....61 K4
Laurel Pl *FAV* ME13 * 134 A8
Laurel Rd *GILL* ME7 ....72 J8
RTWE/PEM TN2 ....270 G1
The Laurels *BRXN/ST* SW9 * 40 B1
HART DA3 ....68 G9
RDART DA2 * 86 F8
Laurel Vls *STPH/PW* TN12 * 245 H4
Laurel Wy *RCANTW* CT4 ....195 M2
Laurence Pountney Hl
CANST EC4R 24 A3
Laurensfield *MSTR* CT12 ....141 K5
Laureston Pl *DVE/WH* CT16 ....8 E2
Laurie Gray Av *WALD* ME5 ....125 J4
Laurie Gv *NWCR* SE14 ....41 J2
Laurier Rd *CROY/NA* CR0 ....83 L4
Lauriston Cl *RAM* CT11 ....142 M7
Lauriston Mt *BRDST* CT10 ....113 M8
PECK SE15 ....41 H5
Lausanne Ter *MARG* CT9 * 15 H5
Lavenda Cl *SIT* ME10 ....100 B1
Lavender Cl *E/WMAL* ME19 ....153 N4
Lavender Cl *WADH* TN5 ....315 J5
Lavender Hl *SWLY* BR8 ....65 M9
TON TN9 ....240 F1
Lavender La *MSTR* CT12 ....142 B7
Lavender Ms *CANT* CT1 ....4 C1
Lavender Rd *BERM/RHTH* SE16 ....25 H4
PECK SE15 ....82 E3
E/WMAL ME19 ....153 N4
Lavenders Rd *E/WMAL* ME19 ....153 N8
Lavender Wy *CROY/NA* CR0 ....84 A3
Lavengro Rd *WNWD* SE27 ....60 C1
Lavernock Rd *BXLYHN* DA7 ....45 J3
Laverstoke Rd *MAIDW* ME16 ....155 M9
Lavidge Rd *ELTH/MOT* SE9 ....63 J1
Lavinia Av *WFD* IG8 ....71 N2
Lavinia Rd *DART* DA1 ....46 E7
Law Cl *CANTW/ST* CT2 ....166 B4
Lawdon Gdns *CROY/NA* CR0 ....82 C6
Lawford Gdns *DART* DA1 ....46 G6
Lawless St *POP/IOD* E14 * 25 L3
Lawley Cl *MSTR* CT12 ....143 H5
Lawn Cl *BMLY* BR1 ....62 F6
CHAT ME4 ....95 M4
SWLY BR8 ....66 A2
TENT TN30 ....305 L8
Lawn House Cl *POP/IOD* E14 ....25 M5
Lawn Pk *SEV* TN13 ....178 C3
Lawn Rd *BECK* BR3 ....61 N1
BRDST CT10 ....113 M9
DEAL CT14 ....233 H8
GVW DA11 ....49 L9
TON TN9 ....240 F1
Lawns Crs *GRAYS* RM17 ....32 G8
Lawns Pl *GRAYS* RM17 * 32 E9
The Lawns *BKHTH/KID* SE3 * 42 D4
NRWD SE19 ....60 C1
SCUP DA14 ....64 D1
STPH/PW TN12 ....243 J9
Lawn Ter *BKHTH/KID* SE3 ....42 D4
Lawn Vls *RAM* CT11 * 17 F4
Lawrance Sq *GVW* DA11 * 69 K2
Lawrence Cl *FOLKN* CT19 ....310 C5
MAID/SHEP ME15 ....186 F6
Lawrence Ct *FOLKN* CT19 ....11 H1
Lawrence Dr *GVE* DA12 ....93 H1
Lawrence Gdns *HB* CT6 ....107 P2
TIL RM18 ....49 K8
Lawrence Hill Gdns *DART* DA1 ....46 B8
Lawrence Hill Rd *DART* DA1 ....46 B8
Lawrence Rd *ERITH* DA8 ....45 K1
SNWD SE25 ....83 L1
TONN TN10 ....211 H4
WWKM BR4 ....85 K8
Lawrence St *CAN/RD* E16 ....26 A1
GILL ME7 ....7 K3
IOS ME12 ....79 H2
Lee Ter *BKHTH/KID* SE3 ....42 C4
Leeward Rd *ROCH* ME1 ....95 H5
Leeway *DEPT* SE8 ....26 B9
Leewood Cl *LEE/GVPK* SE12 * 42 D7
Leewood Pl *SWLY* BR8 ....88 C1
Legatt Rd *ELTH/MOT* SE9 ....43 H6
Legge La *E/WMAL* ME19 ....153 H4
Legge St *LEW* SE13 ....42 A6
Leggs' La *RRTW* TN3 ....269 K3
Leghorn Rd *WOOL/PLUM* SE18 ....27 L8
TIL RM18 ....49 K8
Leicester Av *MARG* CT9 ....113 H3
MTCM CR4 ....
Leicester Dr *RTWE/PEM* TN2 ....270 C8
Leicester Rd *CROY/NA* CR0 ....83 K8
MAID/SHEP ME15 ....186 A4
TIL RM18 ....49 K7
WSTB CT5 ....106 B2
Leigham Ct *STRHM/NOR* SW16 ....60 A3
Leigham V *STRHM/NOR* SW16 ....60 A2
Leigh Av *MAID/SHEP* ME15 ....185 N5
Leigh Crs *CROY/NA* CR0 ....114 C2
Leigh Gn *RASHE* TN25 ....
Leigh Pl *RDART* DA2 ....66 C2
WELL DA16 ....44 C3
Leigh Place La *GDST* RH9 ....176 C8
Leigh Rd *GVW* DA11 ....69 M1
HOO/HM ME3 ....72 C4
MSTR CT12 ....142 E5
RTON TN11 ....210 A8
Leigh Ter *STMC/STPC* BR5 * 64 D9
Leighton Cl *SBGH/RUST* TN4 ....270 D1
Leighton Gdns *TIL* RM18 ....49 L1
Leighton Rd *ELTH/MOT* SE9 ....291 K6
Leighton Rd *CROY/NA* CR0 ....82 G5
Leighville Dr *HB* CT6 ....107 J2
Leila Parnell Pl *CHAT* ME4 ....
Leith Av *RCANTW* CT4 ....179 H4
Leith Cl *STMC/STPC* BR5 ....64 C7
Leith Park Rd *GVE* DA12 ....49 M9
Leivers Rd *DEAL* CT14 ....232 F6
Leman St *WCHPL* E1 ....24 C2
Le May Av *LEE/GVPK* SE12 ....63 L4
Lemmon Rd *GNWCH* SE10 ....25 P9
Lemonwell Dr *ELTH/MOT* SE9 ....44 B3
Lenacre Av *DVE/WH* CT16 ....260 C9
Lenacre La *DVE/WH* CT16 ....260 D8
Lenacre St *RASHE* TN25 ....222 B7

Lendon Rd *BGR/WK* TN15 ....151 J6
Lendrim Cl *GILL* ME7 * 72 F9
Leneda Dr *RTWE/PEM* TN2 ....270 B8
Leney Rd *WBY/YAL* ME18 ....183 M4
Lenfield Av *MAID/BEAR* ME14 ....13 J4
The Length *BRCH* CT7 ....140 A2
Lenham Cl *BRDST* CT10 ....143 M2
Lenham Forstal Rd
RMAID ME17 ....219 P1
Lenham Gdns *MARG* CT9 ....112 A5
Lenham Heath Rd
RMAID ME17 ....219 N1
Lenham Rd *BXLYHN* DA7 ....28 E9
HDCN TN27 ....247 N3
LEE/GVPK SE12 ....247 N3
RMAID ME17 ....218 C1
THHTH CR7 ....60 D8
Lenmead *RMAID* ME17 ....188 D5
Lenmore Av *GRAYS* RM17 ....32 D6
Lennard Av *WWKM* BR4 ....85 H6
Lennard Rd *CROY/NA* CR0 ....83 H5
FOLK CT20 ....11 H3
HAYES BR2 ....
PGE/AN SE20 ....61 K5
SEV TN13 ....148 D5
The Leas *DEAL* CT14 ....263 J5
FAV ME13 ....132 E5
FOLK CT20 ....10 C7
IOS ME12 ....58 B7
WADH TN5 ....294 B9
WSTB CT5 ....106 B5
Leasway *CDW/CHF* RM16 ....
Leathercote Av *SOCK/AV* RM15 * ....
Leathercote Gn
ERITH DA8 ....28 E6
Leather Cl *EDEN* TN8 ....236 D1
Leathermarket Ct *STHWK* SE1 ....24 B5
Leathermarket St *STHWK* SE1 ....24 B5
Leather Sq *WAP* E1W 24 C3
Leathwell Rd *DEPT* SE8 ....41 P5
Leatt Cl *BRDST* CT10 ....113 J6
Lea V *DART* DA1 ....45 M3
Leaveland Cl *ASH* TN23 ....282 C2
BECK BR3 ....
Leaves Green Crs *HAYES* BR2 * 115 M4
Leaves Green Rd *HAYES* BR2 ....115 N4
Lebanon Gdns *BH/WHM* TN16 ....145 N2
Lebanon Rd *CROY/NA* CR0 ....83 K5
Lebrun Sq *BKHTH/KID* SE3 ....42 F5
Leckhampton Pl
BRXS/STRHM SW2 ....40 A8
Leckwith Av *ABYW* SE2 ....28 D8
Lecnnfield Cl *TON* TN9 ....240 C2
Leda Rd *WOOL/PLUM* SE18 ....26 G6
Ledbury Rd *CROY/NA* CR0 ....83 H8
STMC/STPC BR5 ....40 C1
Ledgers Rd *WARL* CR6 ....144 C7
Ledrington Rd *NRWD* SE19 ....60 F5
Leechcroft Av *BFN/LL* DA15 ....44 B6
SWLY BR8 ....
Lee Church St *LEW* SE13 ....42 C3
Leeds Cl *ORP* BR6 ....87 L6
Leeds House Ms *RTON* TN11 * 211 P2
Leeds Rd *RMAID* ME17 ....187 H8
Leeds Sq *RHAM* ME8 ....96 E5
Lee Gn *STMC/STPC* BR5 ....87 H2
Lee Green Rd *HOO/HM* ME3 ....56 B7
Lee High Rd *LEW* SE13 ....42 C3
Lee Pk *BKHTH/KID* SE3 ....42 D5
Lee Rd *BKHTH/KID* SE3 ....42 C5
SNOD ME6 ....125 P5
The Lees Cl *RASHE* TN25 ....284 E3
Lees Court Rd *FAV* ME13 ....162 F6
Leeson Rd *HNHL* SE24 * 40 B1
Leesons Hl *CHST* BR7 ....
Leesons Wy *STMC/STPC* BR5 ....64 B8
Lees Rd *KEN/WIL* TN24 ....253 K8
RASHE TN25 ....284 F1
WBY/YAL ME18 ....213 M3
Lees Rd *CROY/NA* CR0 ....34 B6
HB CT6 ....107 P1
Leet Cl *GILL* ME7 ....73 L9
Le Temple Rd *STPH/PW* TN12 ....243 J2
Letter Box La *SEV* TN13 ....179 H5
Levendale Rd *FSTH* SE23 ....61 L1
Leven Rd *POP/IOD* E14 ....25 M1
Leveret Cl *CROY/NA* CR0 ....114 C5
Leverholme Gdns
ELTH/MOT SE9 ....63 L3
Lever Sq *CDW/CHF* RM16 ....33 M6
Leveson Rd *CDW/CHF* RM16 ....33 N6
Levetts Cl *RBTBR* TN32 ....328 E4
Leviathan Wy *CHAT* ME4 ....72 G6
Lewd La *HDCN* TN27 ....249 H5
Lewes Cl *GRAYS* RM17 ....32 B9
Lewes Rd *BMLY* BR1 ....62 G3
EGRIN RH19 ....265 J3
Lewin Rd *BXLYHS* DA6 ....45 G5
Lewis Av *RHAM* ME8 ....96 E4
Lewis Court Dr *RMAID* ME17 ....188 A5
Lewis Crs *MARG* CT9 ....112 G2
Lewis Gv *LEW* SE13 ....42 A5
Lewisham High St *LEW* SE13 ....41 P6
Lewisham Pk *LEW* SE13 ....42 A8
Lewisham Rd *DVW* CT17 ....290 F4
LEW SE13 ....
Lewisham Wy *NWCR* SE14 ....41 M2
Lewis Ms *SNOD* ME6 ....123 N7
Lewis Rd *MEO* DA13 ....93 K7
SCUP DA14 ....64 D4
WELL DA16 ....44 E4
Lewson Street Rd *RSIT* ME9 ....
Lexden Rd *MTCM* CR4 ....
Leybank Cl *RTON* TN11 ....210 B6
Leybourne Cl *HAYES* BR2 ....85 J1
WALD ME5 ....125 M5
Leybourne Dell *CRBK* TN17 ....299 H4
Leybourne Dr *MARG* CT9 ....112 A5

Long Rede La MAIDW ME16 .....154 E9
Longridge SIT ME10 ....130 A3
Longridge Vls
  STPH/PW TN12 * 245 K6
Long Rock WSTB CT5 ....106 B3
Longsfield RASHE TN25 ....306 B1
Longshaw Rd
  MAID/SHEP ME15 ....186 C6
Longshore DEPT SE8 ....25 J7
Long Slip RRTW TN3 ....206 D5
Longtail Ri HB CT6 ....107 K4
Longton Av SYD SE26 ....60 C5
Longton Gn RTON TN11 ....61 H3
Longtye Dr WSTB CT5 ....106 B7
Longview Wy RTWE/PEM TN2 ...209 P2
Longwalk MEO DA13 ....69 J7
Long Wk STHWK SE1 ....24 B6
Longwood WALD ME5 ....125 N4
Longworth CI FSTH SE23 ....63 H2
Lonsdale Av MARG CT9 ....113 H2
Lonsdale CI ELTH/MOT SE9 .....63 H2
Lonsdale Crs RDART DA2 ....67 J1
Lonsdale Dr RHAM ME8 ....86 C2
Lonsdale Gdns
  SIT ME10 ....99 K9
Lonsdale Gdns
  THHTH CT7 ....22 D4
Lonsdale Rd BXLYHN DA7 ......45 H3
  SNWD SE25 ....
Lookers La HYTHE CT21 ....308 G4
Loop Court Ms SWCH CT13 .....201 N1
Loop Rd CHST BR7 ....63 N5
Loop St SWCH CT13 ....201 N1
The Loop MSTR CT12 * 141 L2
Loose Down Rd FAV ME15 ......192 B4
Loose Rd MAID/SHEP ME15 .....185 M6
Lord Chatham's Ride
  RSEV TN14 ....147 L2
Lord Holland La
  BRXN/ST SW9 * 40 B1
Lordine La RBTBR TN32 ....329 J9
Lords CI DUL SE21 ....60 C1
Lords Wd
  WALD ME5 ....130 D3
Lordship La EDUL SE22 ....43 M4
Lord St CAN/RD E16 ....26 E4
  GVE DA12 ....49 M8
Lordswood CI RDART DA2 ......67 L3
Lords Wood CI WALD ME5 ......125 N3
Lords Wood La WALD ME5 ......125 N3
Lord Warden Av DVW CT17 .....233 J7
Lord Warden Sq DVW CT17 .....313 L1
Lord Warwick St
  WOOL/PLUM SE18 ....26 G6
Lorimar CI SIT ME10 ....99 K7
Lorne La BRXN/ST SW9 ....40 A3
Lorn Ct BRXN/ST SW9 ....40 A3
Lorne Av CROY/NA CR0 ....84 A4
Lorne Gdns DVE/WH CT16 ......291 J6
  RAM CT11 ....166 C6
Lorton CI GVE DA12 ....70 A1
Lossenham La HAWK TN18 ......330 C2
Lothbury LOTH EC2R 4 C4
Lothian Rd BRXN/ST SW9 ......40 B1
Lotus Rd BH/WHM TN16 ....146 A3
Loudon Ct ASH TN23 ....252 B6
Loudon Wy ASH TN23 ....252 A5
Loughborough Pk
  BRXN/ST SW9 * 40 B5
Loughborough Rd
  BRXN/ST SW9 ....40 A3
Louisa St WCHPL E1 ....24 G1
Louis CI CHST BR7 ....63 K3
Louise Bennett CI RHNHL SE24 * ..40 D1
Louisville Av GILL ME7 ....96 A2
Lourdes Manor CI
  RASHE TN25 ....285 L7
Lovage Ap RDART DA2 ....47 L8
Lovage Rd RDART DA2 ....26 F1
Lovat La MON EC3R 24 E1
Lovegrove St STHWK SE1 ....34 G8
Lovelace Av ORP BR6 ....86 C7
Lovelace CI BGR/WK TN15 .....190 D7
  RHAM ME8 ....96 G9
Lovelace Ct RASHW TN26 ....280 F3
Lovelace Gn ELTH/MOT SE9 ....43 K4
Lovelace Rd DUL SE21 ....60 C1
Love La BXLY DA5 ....65 J7
  CANT CT1 ....5 G5
  FAV ME13 ....133 J7
  HDCN TN27 ....248 B1
  IOS ME12 ....15 D9
  MARG CT9 ....15 C3
  RCANTE CT3 ....199 G5
  ROCH ME1 ....19 F5
  RYE TN31 ....338 E6
  SNWD SE25 ....
  SOCK/AV RM15 ....30 F5
  TIL RM18 ....34 B9
  WBY/YAL ME18 ....183 L4
  WOOL/PLUM SE18 ....27 H7
Lovel Av WELL DA16 ....44 C3
Lovelinch CI PECK SE15 ....24 F6
Lovell PI BERM/RHTH SE16 .....25 H6
Lovell Rd CANTW/ST CT2 ......166 A1
  IOS ME12 ....78 A2
Lovers La CRBK TN17 ....274 J7
Lover's La SWCM DA10 ....48 B5
Love Wk CMBW SE5 ....40 D3
Loveibonds Av ORP BR6 ....86 C7
Low CI RDART DA2 ....47 N6
Lowdells CI EGRIN RH19 ....264 F4
Lowdells Dr EGRIN RH19 ......264 G4
Lowdells La EGRIN RH19 ......264 F5
Lowden Rd HNHL SE24 ....42 D6
Lowe Av CAN/RD E16 ....26 E5
Lowell St POP/IOD E14 ....25 H2
Lower Addiscombe Rd
  CROY/NA CR0 ....83 J5
Lower Bell La DIT/AY ME20 ....154 A2
Lower Blackhouse HI
  HYTHE CT21 ....309 J5
Lower Boxley Rd
  MAID/BEAR ME14 ....12 E4
Lower Bridge St CANT CT1 .....5 F5
Lower Camden CHST BR7 ......63 K7
Lower Chantry La CANT CT1 ....5 G6
Lower Church St
  CROY/NA CR0 ....82 G6

Lower Coombe St
  CROY/NA CR0 ....83 H8
Lower Crs SLH/COR SS17 ....33 P6
Lower Cft SWLY BR8 ....88 E1
Lower Dene EGRIN RH19 ....265 K7
Lower Denmark Rd ASH TN23 ...2 E7
Lower Ensden Rd
  RCANTW CT4 ....164 D8
Lower Fant Rd MAIDW ME16 ...12 A7
Lower Farm Rd RMAID ME17 ...215 N4
Lower Featherby Rd GILL ME7 ..96 E1
Lower Gravel Rd HAYES BR2 ....85 P5
Lower Gn RTON TN11 ....209 L9
Lower Green Rd RRTW TN3 ....269 P2
  RTWE/PEM TN2 271
  SBGH/RUST TN4 ....269 P4
Lower Hartlip Rd RSIT ME9 ....127 N1
Lower Haysden La
  RTON TN11 ....240 L1
Lower Hazelhurst WADH TN5 ...314 E2
Lower Herne Rd HB CT6 ....107 K6
Lower Higham Rd GVE DA12 ....50 B9
Lower Lea Crossing
  POP/IOD E14 ....25 P3
Lower Lees Rd RCANTW CT4 ...194 E1
Lower Mere EGRIN RH19 ....265 J8
Lower Mill La DEAL CT14 ......233 H4
Lower Northdown Av
  MARG CT9 ....112 G3
Lower Norton La RSIT ME9 .....131 M5
Lower Park Rd BELV DA17 .....28 F6
Lower Platts WADH TN5 ....315 J5
Lower Rainham Rd GILL ME7 ...96 A7
Lower Range Rd GVE DA12 .....50 A8
Lower Rd BELV DA17 ....29 H5
  BERM/RHTH SE16 ....24 F5
  DVE/WH CT16 ....290 E2
  ERITH DA8 ....29 J7
  FAV ME13 ....133 L8
  GVE DA12 ....70 C1
  GVW DA11 ....48 E5
  HOO/HM ME3 ....71 K1
  IOS ME12 ....13 H7
  MAID/SHEP ME15 ....184 B4
  RASHW TN26 ....302 C6
  RCANTE CT3 ....200 B4
  RMAID ME17 ....217 H5
  RSIT ME9 ....130 E2
  STMC/STPC BR5 ....87 J3
  SWLY BR8 ....66 B6
  TENT TN30 ....321 P9
  TIL RM18 ....49 L4
Lower Rd East DVE/WH CT16 ..292 A7
Lower Rochester Rd
  HOO/HM ME3 ....71 L1
Lower Sandgate Rd FOLK CT20 ..10 E6
Lower Sands LYDD TN29 ....327 L4
Lower Santon La ASHW TN23 * ..3 L9
Lower Station Rd DART DA1 ....45 N7
Lower Stone St
  MAID/SHEP ME15 ....13 F5
Lower St DEAL CT14 ....231 H5
  RMAID ME17 ....187 K4
  RTON TN11 ....209 M5
  SWCH CT13 ....201 J8
Lower Thames St MON EC3R ...24 A1
Lower Tovil MAID/SHEP ME15 ..185 K1
Lower Twydall La RHAM ME8 ...96 E2
Lower Vicarage Rd
  KEN/WIL TN24 ....252 F2
Lower Wall Rd RASHE TN25 ....306 C8
Lower Warren Rd
  DIT/AY ME20 ....125 K7
Lower Woodlands Rd
  GILL ME7 ....73 M9
Lowfield Rd IOS ME12 ....77 N1
Lowfield St DART DA1 ....46 B8
Lowlands Rd SOCK/AV RM15 ...30 F4
Low Meadow STRI ME2 ....95 P9
Lowood St WCHPL E1 ....24 G3
Lowry CI ERITH DA8 ....29 J7
The Lowry TON TN9 ....240 F4
Lowslip HI RDV CT15 ....312 A1
Low Street La TIL RM18 ....33 N9
Lowther HI FSTH SE23 ....41 L8
Lowther Rd DVW CT17 ....291 J7
Lowth Rd CMBW SE5 ....42 D3
Loxford Ldg FOLK CT20 ....310 A9
Loxley CI SYD SE26 ....61 K9
Loxton Rd FSTH SE23 ....41 K9
Loxwood CI DVE/WH CT16 .....261 J9
  STMC/STPC BR5 ....87 L6
Lubbock CI MAID/SHEP ME15 ..186 B6
Lubbock Rd CHST BR7 ....63 J7
Lubbock St NWCR SE14 ....41 J1
Lucas CI EGRIN RH19 ....265 J7
Lucas Dr DEAL CT14 ....47 P6
Lucas Rd GRAYS RM17 ....32 B6
  PGE/AN SE20 ....61 J5
  SNOD 123 M6
Lucas St BROCKY SE4 ....41 N3
Lucerne Dr WSTB CT5 ....104 G8
Lucerne St RDV CT15 ....262 A1
Lucerne Rd ORP BR6 ....86 C5
  THHTH CT7 ....82 G2
Lucilina Dr EDEN TN8 ....236 D1
Luckhurst Av ASH TN23 ....3 L5
Luckhurst Gdns MARG CT9 ....113 K2
Luckhurst Rd DVW CT17 ....290 F4
  KEN/WIL TN24 ....283 K1
Lucknow CI RDV CT15 ....291 N4
Lucknow Rd STPH/PW TN12 ...242 C1
Lucknow St WOOL/PLUM SE18 ..44 A1
Lucks HI KE/WMAL ME19 ......153 L4
Lucks La RMAID ME17 ....216 C4
Ludderham CI ASH TN23 ....282 C2
Luddesdown Rd MEO DA13 .....93 H5
Ludford CI CROY/NA CR0 ......82 D3
Ludgate Rd RSIT ME9 ....130 D9

Ludham CI THMD SE28 ....28 B2
Ludlow CI HAYES BR2 * 62 E9
Ludlow PI GRAYS RM17 ....32 C6
Luffield Rd ABYW SE2 ....28 A6
Luffman Rd LEE/GVPK SE12 ....42 F2
Lugard Rd PECK SE15 ....41 H3
Lughorse La WBY/YAL ME18 ...183 P9
Lukes CI DVW CT17 ....291 H6
Lukin St WCHPL E1 ....24 F3
Lullarook CI BH/WHM TN16 ...145 M1
Lullingstone Av SWLY BR8 .....85 P9
Lullingstone CI GILL ME7 ......126 C2
  STMC/STPC BR5 ....64 D6
Lullingstone Crs
  STMC/STPC BR5 ....64 C6
Lullingstone La EYN DA4 ....89 H7
  MAIDW ME16 ....155 H5
Lullington Garth BMLY BR1 ....62 C6
Lullington Rd PGE/AN SE20 ....61 H9
Lulworth CI SLH/COR SS17 ....34 A1
Lulworth Rd ELTH/MOT SE9 ...43 L1
  PECK SE15 ....41 H3
  WELL DA16 ....44 B3
Lumley CI BELV DA17 ....44 G5
Lumsden Ter CHAT ME4 ....6 A5
Lunar CI BH/WHM TN16 ....145 N1
Lunar Ct THHTH CT7 ....60 C9
Lunedale Rd RDART DA2 ....67 L3
Lunghurst Rd CTHM CR3 ......144 D6
Lunham Rd NRWD SE19 ....60 E5
Lunsford La DIT/AY ME20 .....153 N4
Lupin CI BRXS/STRHM SW2 ....60 B1
  CROY/NA CR0 ....84 A5
Lupton CI LEE/GVPK SE12 .....62 F1
Lurkins Ri CRBK TN17 ....274 C9
Lushington Rd CAT SE6 ....61 N6
  MAID/BEAR ME14 ....155 J5
Lusted Hall La BH/WHM TN16 ..145 M5
Luton CI BRDST CT10 ....143 L1
Luton Ct BRDST CT10 ....143 L1
Luton High St WALD ME5 ......95 P4
Luton PI GNWCH SE10 ....42 A1
Luton Rd CHAT ME4 ....7 F6
  FAV ME13 ....133 H6
  RSIT ME9 ....131 J9
Lutwyche Rd FSTH SE23 ....61 M1
Luxfield Rd ELTH/MOT SE9 ....43 H8
Luxford Rd BERM/RHTH SE16 ..24 C7
Luxmore St BROCKY SE4 ....41 M2
Luxon Rd MEO DA13 ....122 F1
Luxor St CMBW SE5 ....42 D4
Luxted Rd ORP BR6 ....116 B6
Lyall Av DUL SE21 ....60 E5
Lyall Wy RHAM ME8 ....96 G7
Lychfield Dr STRD ME2 ....72 A6
Lych Gate Rd ORP BR6 ....86 B1
Lyconby Gdns CROY/NA CR0 ...84 C1
Lydbrook CI SIT ME9 ....129 L1
Lydd CI BFN/LL DA15 ....64 A3
Lydden HI RDV CT15 ....259 N5
Lydd Rd BXLYHN DA7 ....45 H1
  LYDD TN29 ....336 E2
  RYE TN31 ....344 A1
  WALD ME5 ....95 N9
Lydd Town Crossing
  LYDD TN29 ....342 C4
Lydens La EDEN TN8 ....236 G5
Lydia Rd DEAL CT14 ....232 F7
  ERITH DA8 ....29 J7
Lydos CI LYDD TN29 ....343 K7
Lydstep Rd CHST BR7 ....63 L5
Lyell CI HYTHE CT21 ....308 F1
Lyell Rd BRCH CT7 ....110 C6
Lyford St WOOL/PLUM SE18 ...26 F7
Lyle CI STRD ME2 ....72 B7
Lyle La MAIDW ME16 ....155 H7
Lyle Pk SEV TN15 ....148 G8
Lymden La WADH TN5 ....314 D8
Lyme Farm Rd LEE/GVPK SE12 ..42 E5
Lymer Av NRWD SE19 ....60 F4
Lyme Rd WELL DA16 ....44 D2
Lyminge CI RHAM ME8 ....96 F4
  SCUP DA14 ....64 B3
Lyminge Wy MARG CT9 ....113 H4
Lymington CI
  MAID/SHEP ME15 ....186 C7
Lymington Rd WGOS CT8 ......111 L1
Lympne HI HYTHE CT21 ....307 P5
Lympstone Gdns PECK SE15 ...41 G6
Lynbrook Gv PECK SE15 ....40 G6
Lyncourt BKHTH/KID SE3 * 42 B5
Lyndale Av CHST CT9 ....113 J4
Lyndean Rd ABYW SE2 ....28 E2
Lynden Wy SWLY BR8 ....65 L9
Lyndhurst Av MARG CT9 ....112 G3
  RHAM ME8 ....96 F4
Lyndhurst CI BXLYHN DA7 .....45 K4
  CANTW/ST CT2 ....166 D1
  CROY/NA CR0 ....83 L7
  ORP BR6 ....C8
Lyndhurst Dr SEV TN13 ....148 D9
Lyndhurst Farm CI
  EGRIN RH19 ....264 A1
Lyndhurst Gv PECK SE15 ......40 E3
Lyndhurst Leys HAYES BR2 ....85 H1
Lyndhurst Prior SNWD SE25 * ..60 E8
Lyndhurst Rd BRDST CT10 ....115 M8
  BXLYHN DA7 ....45 K4
  DVW CT17 ....290 F5
  THHTH CR7 ....82 D3
  TOTM N17 ....
Lyndon Av BFN/LL DA15 ....45 M9
Lyndon Rd BELV DA17 ....28 F7
Lyndon Wy RFOLK CT18 ....287 N1
Lynette Av STRD ME2 ....72 B6
Lyngate CI MARG CT9 ....113 J5
Lyngs CI WBY/YAL ME18 ....213 N5
Lynmead CI EDEN TN8 ....206 C6
Lynmere Rd WELL DA16 ....44 D3
Lynmouth Dr IOS ME12 ....13 D9
Lynmouth Ri STMC/STPC BR5 ..87 J1
Lynne CI ORP BR6 ....116 C1
Lynors Av STRD ME2 ....72 A5

Lynstead CI BMLY BR1 ....62 G8
Lynsted CI ASH TN23 ....282 C2
  BXLYHS DA6 ....45 K6
Lynsted Ct BECK BR3 * 61 J1
Lynsted Gdns ELTH/MOT SE9 ..43 J8
Lynsted La RSIT ME9 ....130 C6
Lynsted Rd IOS ME12 ....57 N9
  RHAM ME8 ....96 F6
Lynton Av STMC/STPC BR5 .....87 J1
Lynton CI EGRIN RH19 ....265 K6
Lynton Dr WALD ME5 ....125 N2
Lynton Est STHWK SE1 * 34 D2
Lynton Park Av EGRIN RH19 ...265 J6
Lynton Rd CROY/NA CR0 ....82 C6
  GVW DA11 ....49 L9
  HYTHE CT21 ....309 H1
  STHWK SE1 ....24 C7
Lynton Rd South GVW DA11 ....49 L9
Lynwood Gdns CROY/NA CR0 ...82 E8
Lynwood Gv ORP BR6 ....86 F4
Lyons Ct TON TN9 ....216 D8
Lyoth Rd STMC/STPC BR5 .....86 F3
Lypeatt CI CANTW/ST CT2 * ...136 B9
Lyric Ms SYD SE26 ....61 J3
Lysander CI BRDST CT10 ......143 H1
  RCANTW CT4 ....198 B3
Lysander Rd RFOLK CT18 ......287 H4
Lysander Wk RFOLK CT18 .....288 D8
Lytchet Rd BMLY BR1 ....62 B3
Lytcott Gv EDUL SE22 ....42 F6
Lytham Aveune HB CT6 ....107 J5
Lytham CI THMD SE28 ....28 D2
Lytham Gv RHAM ME8 ....96 F7
Lytham St WALW SE17 ....24 C9
  SIT ME10 ....99 H8
  STPH/PW TN12 ....213 J1
  WALD ME5 ....125 J4
The Malvins RHAM ME8 ....96 F7

M

Mabel Rd SWLY BR8 ....66 A5
Maberley Crs NRWD SE19 ....61 J5
Maberley Rd BECK BR3 ....61 K9
  BMLY BR1 ....62 D7
  NRWD SE19 ....61 H7
Mabledon Av KEN/WIL TN24 ...3 K5
Mabledon CI NROM TN28 ......336 C2
Mabledon Rd TON TN9 ....240 D1
Macarthur Ter CHARL SE7 * ...42 A6
Macaulay CI DIT/AY ME20 .....123 P9
Macbean St WOOL/PLUM SE18 ..27 H6
Macclesfield Rd SNWD SE25 ...83 H2
Macdonald Pde WSTB CT5 .....105 H7
Macdonald Rd DVW CT17 .....291 H6
  GILL ME7 ....97 H4
Mace CI WAP E1W 24 E4
Mace La KEN/WIL TN24 ....116 F7
Macey St GNWCH SE10 * 42 A1
Mackenzie Ter
  DVE/WH CT16 * 291 J4
Mackerel Rd RYE TN31 ....331 L8
Mackie Rd BRXS/STRHM SW2 ..60 A8
Mackintosh CI HOO/HM ME3 ...53 L4
Macklands Wy RHAM ME8 ......97 K4
Macleod Rd BERM/RHTH SE16 ..24 D6
Maclean Rd FSTH SE23 ....61 P4
Maclean Ter GVE DA12 * 70 B1
Macleod CI GRAYS RM17 ....32 C7
Macleod House CHARL SE7 * ...43 J1
Macoma Rd WOOL/PLUM SE18 ..27 L9
Macoma Ter WOOL/PLUM SE18 ..27 L9
Maconochies Rd
  POP/IOD E14 * 25 L8
Macquarie Wy POP/IOD E14 ...25 L7
Madan CI BH/WHM TN16 ....176 A6
Madan Rd BH/WHM TN16 ......176 B6
Mada Rd ORP BR6 ....86 C7
Madden Av WALD ME5 ....95 N9
Maddocks CI SCUP DA14 ......65 H5
Madeira Av BMLY BR1 ....62 C7
Madeira Pk RTWE/PEM TN2 ....22 D7
Madeira Rd MARG CT9 ....15 K4
  NROM TN28 ....337 K7
Madeira Wk RAM CT11 ....17 G4
Madginford CI
  MAID/SHEP ME15 ....186 D1
Madginford Rd
  MAID/SHEP ME15 ....186 C1
Madhurst Ct STRD ME2 ....18 C1
Madison CI ASH TN23 ....44 A1
Madison Gdns BXLYHN DA7 ....45 H1
Madison Wy SEV TN13 ....148 E8
Madron St WALW SE17 * 24 D8
Maesmaur Rd BH/WHM TN16 ..145 N5
Mafeking Rd WALD ME5 ....125 J2
Magazine Rd KEN/WIL TN24 ...3 H4
Magdala Rd BRDST CT10 ....113 K7
  DVW CT17 ....291 J6
Magdalen CI GILL ME7 ....126 D1
Magdalen Rd BRDST CT10 .....113 M8
  CANT CT1 ....7 J2
Magdalen St STHWK SE1 * 24 B4
Magdela Rd BRDST CT10 * 87 J3
Magnet Rd WBLY HA9 ....
Magness Rd DEAL CT14 ....232 F7
Magnet Rd WTHK RM20 ....32 B3
Magnolia Av MARG CT9 ....113 J5
  RHAM ME8 ....96 F9
Magnolia Dr BH/WHM TN16 ...176 A6
  RCANTW CT4 ....195 N2
Magpie Bottom BGR/WK TN15 ..119 H4
Magpie CI DIT/AY ME20 ....153 P5
Magpie Ct IOS ME12 * 78 A1
Magpie Gn RMAID ME17 ....204 D5
Magpie Hall CI HAYES BR2 ....85 P5
Magpie Hall La HAYES BR2 ....85 P4
Magpie Hall Rd CHAT ME4 .....6 E7
  RASHW TN26 ....282 A6

Magpie La MAID/BEAR ME14 ...127 J4
  RCANTW CT4 ....156 C5
  RSIT ME9 ....127 K3
Magpie PI NWCR SE14 * 25 H9
Magri Wk WCHPL E1 ....24 F5
Maguire St STHWK SE1 ....24 C5
Magwitch CI ROCH ME1 * 94 C2
Mahogany CI
  BERM/RHTH SE16 ....25 H4
Maida Rd BELV DA17 ....28 F6
Maida CI
  CHAT ME4 ....95 H4
Maida Vale Rd DART DA1 ....44 A9
Maiden Erlegh Av BXLY DA5 ...65 J6
Maiden La CANT CT1 * 126 C6
  DART DA1 ....146 C1
Maidenstone HI GNWCH SE10 ..42 A2
Maidstone Rd BGR/WK TN15 ...149 N7
  BMLY BR1 ....62 D8
  GILL ME7 ....126 E5
  HDCN TN27 ....217 K9
  HDCN TN27 ....220 E1
  RASHE TN25 ....252 C4
  RASHE TN26 ....221 M9
  RMAID ME17 ....187 H9
  RMAID ME17 ....189 K6
  RSIT ME9 ....131 H3
  RTON TN11 ....182 C9
  RTWE/PEM TN2 ....241 M9
  SCUP DA14 ....64 F5
  SEV TN13 ....148 D7
  SIT ME10 ....99 H8
  STPH/PW TN12 ....213 J1
  STPH/PW TN12 ....215 L9
  WALD ME5 ....125 J4
The Mailyns RHAM ME8 ....96 F7
Main Barracks
  WOOL/PLUM SE18 * 26 G8
Maine CI DVE/WH CT16 ....291 J4
Main Gate Rd CHAT ME4 ....72 F8
Mainridge Rd CHST BR7 ....63 L3
Main Rd BH/WHM TN16 ....145 N1
  EYN DA4 ....67 H5
  HART DA3 ....89 M4
  HOO/HM ME3 ....38 G3
  HOO/HM ME3 ....54 B9
  HOO/HM ME3 ....72 F3
  IOS ME12 ....57 J5
  ORP BR6 ....117 K3
  QBOR ME11 ....77 J2
  RDART DA2 ....68 A7
  RDART DA2 ....24 A2
  STMC/STPC BR5 ....64 D5
  SWLY BR8 ....88 B5
Main Road Gorse HI EYN DA4 ..89 N5
Main St CHAT ME4 ....73 H5
  DVW CT17 ....338 E1
Maismore St PECK SE15 ....24 D9
Maison Dieu Rd DVE/WH CT16 ..8 C2
Maitland CI GNWCH SE10 ....41 P1
Maitland Ct FAV ME13 ....132 E4
Maitland Rd SEV SE20 ....61 K5
Majendie Rd
  WOOL/PLUM SE18 ....27 L8
Major CI BRXN/ST SW9 ....40 B4
  WSTB CT5 ....105 J3
Major Rd BERM/RHTH SE16 * ...24 D7
Makenade Av FAV ME13 ....132 G8
Malabar St POP/IOD E14 ....25 L5
Malam Gdns POP/IOD E14 .....25 L3
Malan CI BH/WHM TN16 ....145 P2
Malcolm CI PGE/AN SE20 * 61 K9
Malcolm Rd PGE/AN SE20 ......61 J6
  SNWD SE25 ....83 J5
Malcolm Sargent Rd
  ASH TN23 ....282 E2
Malden Av SNWD SE25 ....83 N1
Malden Dr MAID/BEAR ME14 ...155 L4
Maldon CI CMBW SE5 ....40 E4
Maley Av WNWD SE27 ....60 E1
Malford St CMBW SE5 ....40 E4
Malham Dr MARG CT9 ....112 F4
Malham Rd FSTH SE23 ....41 K9
Mallams Ms BRXN/ST SW9 .....40 A4
Mallard Ct DART DA1 ....46 F6
  HB CT6 ....107 K4
Mallard Ct FAV ME13 * 78 A1
Mallard Crs RSIT ME9 ....99 L2
Mallard PI EGRIN RH19 ....265 J8
Mallard Rd SAND/SEL CR2 .....114 A4
Mallards KEN/WIL TN24 ....282 C1
Mallards Wy
  MAID/SHEP ME15 ....186 D1
Mallard Wk BECK BR3 ....84 A2
Mallard Wy HOO/HM ME3 ......54 A4
Mallet Rd LEW SE13 ....42 B7
Malling Cl CROY/NA CR0 * 83 P3
Mallingdene Cl HOO/HM ME3 ..52 B8
Malling Rd DIT/AY ME20 ....182 F2
  SNOD 123 N7
  WBY/YAL ME18 ....182 E6
  WBY/YAL ME18 ....183 N2
Malling Ter MAIDW ME16 ......155 H8
Mallings Dr MAID/BEAR ME14 ..156 A1
Mallings La MAID/BEAR ME14 ..156 A1
Malling Ter MAIDW ME16 * 85 J4
Mallinson Rd CROY/NA CR0 ....82 C5
Mallory CI BROCKY SE4 ....41 L5
  MSTR CT12 ....143 H2
Mallow Ct DART DA1 ....44 G5
  GVW DA11 ....69 J3
Mallow Crs GRAYS RM17 ....32 F2
The Mall HAY TN15 ....132 F7
  GILL ME7 ....7 J1
Mallys PI EYN DA4 ....
Malmains CI BECK BR3 ....84 C3
Malmains Wy BECK BR3 ....84 B3
Malmesbury Rd CAN/RD E16 ...26 D4
  CHDW/CHDF RM16 ....88 F1
Malpas Rd BROCKY SE4 ....41 M3
  CDW/CHF RM16 ....
Malta Av WALD ME5 ....95 H7
Malta Rd TIL RM18 ....49 K3

Malta Ter MAID/BEAR ME14 ....155 M5
Maltby Cl ORP BR6 ....87 H5
Maltby St STHWK SE1 ....24 C5
Malthouse La RWAID ME17 ....189 L6
Malthouse Hi HYTHE CT21 ....308 G5
MAID/SHEP ME15 ....185 L7
Malthouse La GVE DA12 ....70 C4
RASHW TN26 ....304 A4
Malt House La TENT TN30 ....301 H8
Malthouse Rd BGR/WK TN15 ....121 J3
CANTW/ST CT2 ....4 E1
Maltings Cl RTON TN19 ....211 P2
Maltings La STHWK SE1 * 24 B5
Maltings Pl STHWK SE1 * 24 B5
The Maltings CANT CT1 * 5 C5
DEAL CT14 ....232 C9
MAID/BEAR ME14 ....156 B7
ORP BR6 ....86 C5
OXTED RH8 ....175 J7
RCANTE CT3 ....168 C9
RHAM ME8 ....97 K6
MAID/BEAR ME14 ....156 B7
RTON TN11 * 211 P2
SNWD SE25 ....60 E9
Malt Ms ROCH ME1 ....19 F5
Malton Ms WOOL/PLUM SE18 ....27 M9
Malton St WOOL/PLUM SE18 ....27 M9
Malton Wy RTWE/PEM TN2 ....271 H1
Malt St STHWK SE1 ....24 D9
Malus Cl WALD ME5 ....125 M4
Malvern Av BXLYHN DA7 ....44 C1
Malvern Meadow
DVE/WH CT16 ....290 F2
Malvern Pk HB CT6 ....108 A6
Malvern Rd DVE/WH CT16 ....290 F2
DVW CT17 ....13 K3
GILL ME7 ....84 B4
GRAYS RM17 ....32 F7
KEN/WIL TN24 ....252 C5
ORP BR6 ....87 J8
THHTH CR7 ....82 F1
Malvina Av GVE DA12 ....69 M1
Malyons Rd LEW SE13 ....41 P6
SWLY BR8 ....45 P6
Malyons Ter LEW SE13 ....41 P6
Mamignot Cl
MAID/BEAR ME14 ....156 C7
Managers St POP/IOD E14 * 25 M4
Manaton Cl PECK SE15 ....41 H4
Manchester Cl CAN/RD E16 ....26 C2
Manchester Gv POP/IOD E14 ....25 M8
Manchester Rd POP/IOD E14 ....25 M8
THHTH CR7 ....60 C9
Manciple Cl CANTW/ST CT2 ....166 B5
Manciple St STHWK SE1 ....18 F2
Mandarin La HB CT6 ....107 K4
Mandela Av BRXN/ST SW9 ....40 A1
Mandela Wy STHWK SE1 ....24 B7
Mandeville Rd CANTW/ST CT2 ....291 H5
Mangers La DVE/WH CT16 ....291 H4
Mangold Wy ERITHM DA18 ....28 C6
Mangravet Av
MAID/SHEP ME15 ....185 P4
Manila St POP/IOD E14 ....25 M8
Manister Rd ABYW SE2 ....27 P6
Manley Bvd SNWD SE25 ....123 P3
Manley Cl DVE/WH CT16 ....261 H9
Mann Cl CROY/NA CR0 ....63 H7
Manning Cl DVW CT17 ....290 C4
Manning La EGRIN RH19 ....264 C6
Manning Rd STMC/STPC BR5 ....87 L2
Manningtree St WCHPL E1 ....24 D2
Mannock Rd DART DA1 ....46 F4
Manns Hi RCANTW CT4 ....226 F4
Mann Sq TON TN9 ....240 G2
Manor Av BROCKY SE4 ....41 M3
Manorbrook BKHTH/KID SE3 ....42 E5
Manor Cl CANT CT1 ....166 B7
DART DA1 ....46 E5
DEAL CT14 ....232 F5
GDST RH9 ....204 C5
GVE DA12 ....70 D1
HB CT6 ....108 C4
MAID/BEAR ME14 ....156 B9
QBOR ME11 ....77 H4
RDART DA2 ....67 J8
SBGH/RUST TN4 ....270 B4
SOCK/AV RM15 ....30 F4
THMD SE28 ....28 B9
WARL CR6 ....144 B2
Manor Ct MAID/BEAR ME14 ....156 B9
MEO DA13 ....92 E2
Manor Court Flats CANT CT1 * 4 E7
Manordene Rd THMD SE28 ....28 B2
Manor Dr BRCH CT7 ....110 G7
HART DA3 ....91 J3
Manor Est BERM/RHTH SE16 ....24 E7
Manor Farm Cl HYTHE CT21 ....307 N5
Manor Farm Rd
STRHM/NOR SW16 ....60 A8
Manorfield ASH TN23 ....252 B9
Manor Fld GVE DA12 ....70 C4
Manor Flds SBGH/RUST TN4 ....240 C6
Manorfields Cl CHST BR7 ....63 N9
Manor Forstal HART DA3 ....91 J7
Manor Gdns WALD ME5 ....125 K2
Manor Gv BECK BR3 ....61 P8
PECK SE15 ....24 F9
SIT ME10 ....129 M2
TONN TN10 ....211 M7
Manor House Dr ASH TN23 ....282 F4
MAIDW ME16 ....155 J9
Manor House Gdns EDEN TN8 ....206 D9
Manor La HART DA3 ....90 F4
LEW SE13 ....42 C6
ROCH ME1 ....94 E3
Manor Lane Ter LEW SE13 ....42 C5
Manor Lea RSIT ME9 ....89 J6
Manor Lea BRCH CT7 ....140 A3
Manor Leaze RASHE TN25 ....284 C6
Manor Ms CHAT ME4 ....9 H2
DEAL CT14 ....262 E3
Manor Mt FSTH SE23 ....41 J9
Manor Pk LEW SE13 ....42 B6
SBGH/RUST TN4 ....270 B5

Manor Park Cl WWKM BR4 ....84 E5
Manor Park Rd CHST BR7 ....63 P8
WWKM BR4 ....84 E5
Manor Ri DART DA1 ....47 H2
Manor Pound La RASHE TN25 ....284 F1
Manor Ri DVW CT17 ....291 H9
MAID/BEAR ME14 ....156 C9
Manor Rd BECK BR3 ....61 N8
BFN/LL DA15 ....64 B2
BGR/WK TN15 ....120 C5
BH/WHM TN16 ....145 P5
BRCH CT7 ....140 A3
BXLY DA5 ....45 K3
CAN/RD E16 ....25 P1
CHAT ME4 ....8 B2
DART DA1 ....45 N5
DEAL CT14 ....232 F5
DVW CT17 ....291 H9
EDEN TN8 ....206 D9
EGRIN RH19 ....264 F6
ERITH DA8 ....29 L9
FOLK CT20 ....10 D4
GRAYS RM17 ....32 D9
GVE DA12 * 91 M7
HART DA3 ....91 J3
HB CT6 ....108 C4
LYDD TN29 ....342 B7
QBOR ME11 ....77 H4
RSEV TN14 ....147 L3
RSIT ME9 ....159 N3
SBGH/RUST TN4 ....240 B8
SBGH/RUST TN4 ....269 P4
SNWD SE25 ....83 M1
SWCM DA10 ....48 B3
TIL RM18 ....49 L3
WLGTN SM6 ....32 A8
WSTB CT5 ....105 P3
WTHK RM20 ....31 M9
WWKM BR4 ....84 E5
Manor North WLGTN SM6 ....82 A8
Manor Rw TENT TN30 ....301 H8
Manor St GILL ME7 ....72 G9
Manor Vw HART DA3 * 91 K3
Manor Wy ASH TN23 ....2 A1
BECK BR3 ....61 N9
BKHTH/KID SE3 ....42 E5
BXLYHN DA7 ....45 M4
GRAYS RM17 ....14 B7
GVW DA11 ....48 E4
HAYES BR2 ....83 J5
IOS ME12 ....80 A1
STMC/STPC BR5 ....86 D1
SWCM DA10 ....48 B3
TIL RM18 ....48 G1
The Manor Wy WLGTN SM6 ....82 A8
Manse Fld RASHE TN25 ....284 E6
Mansel Dr ROCH ME1 ....94 B3
Mansell La RDV CT15 ....258 E9
Mansell St WCHPL E1 ....24 C2
Mansergh Cl SMARD ME9 * 88 B7
Manse Wy SWLY BR8 ....88 F1
Mansfield Cl STMC/STPC BR5 ....87 L4
Mansfield St RSIT ME9 ....99 L3
Mansfield Rd SWLY BR8 ....65 N5
Mansfield Wk MAID/BEAR ME14 ....185 J1
Mansion Cl BRXN/ST SW9 ....40 A1
Mansion Gdns DVE/WH CT16 ....291 H3
Mansion House Cl HDCN TN27 ....278 A6
Mansion House Pl
MAID EC4N 24 A2
Mansion Rw GILL ME7 ....72 G9
Mansion St MARG CT9 ....15 G3
Manstead Gdns RAIN RM13 ....29 N2
Manston Cl PGE/AN SE20 ....61 J7
Manston Court Rd MARG CT9 ....112 D9
Manston Rd DART DA1 ....142 B4
Manston Rd MSTR CT12 ....141 M2
RAM CT11 ....142 G5
Manthorpe Rd
WOOL/PLUM SE18 ....27 K8
Mantle Rd BROCKY SE4 ....41 L4
Mantles Hi CHST BR7 ....232 C8
Manton Rd ABYW SE2 ....27 P7
The Manwarings
STPH/PW TN12 ....273 J2
Manwood Av CANTW/ST CT2 ....166 F4
Manwood Cl SIT ME10 ....129 N3
Manwood Rd BROCKY SE4 ....41 M6
SWCH CT13 ....201 P2
Manwood St CAN/RD E16 ....26 G4
Maple Av GILL ME7 ....96 B1
MAIDW ME16 ....155 H6
Maple Cl ASH TN23 ....252 A7
BRDST CT10 ....113 K4
CANTW/ST CT2 ....165 P2
DIT/AY ME20 ....153 H5
STMC/STPC BR5 ....86 E2
SWLY BR8 ....65 M8
Maple Ct RCANTE CT3 ....138 B8
RSIT ME9 ....129 P6
Maple Crs BFN/LL DA15 ....44 C7
Maplecroft Cl EHAM E6 ....26 E2
Mapledale Av CROY/NA CR0 ....63 N2
Maple Dr EGRIN RH19 ....265 K7
LYDD TN29 ....337 L2
RFOLK CT18 ....288 F7
Maplefield Gdns
RFOLK CT18 ....288 F7
Maple Gdns RCANTE CT3 ....138 B8
Maple Leaf Cl BH/WHM TN16 ....145 N1
Maple Leaf Dr BFN/LL DA15 ....44 B9
Maple Leaf Sq
BERM/RHTH SE16 * 24 G5
Maple Ri DART DA1 ....46 C9
GRAYS RM17 ....32 D9
GVE DA12 ....69 N3
HOO/HM ME3 ....75 L4
PGE/AN SE20 ....61 H7
STMD SE2 ....71 P9
Maplescombe La EYN DA4 ....89 M7
Maplesden Cl EHAM E6 ....26 E2
Maplesden Cl MAIDW ME16 ....154 E9
Maples Pl WCHPL E1 * 24 E2
The Maples BRDST CT10 ....113 H9
HART DA3 ....68 B1
IOS ME12 ....80 A2
Maple St IOS ME12 ....85 H7
Maplethorpe Rd THHTH CR7 ....82 F1
Mapleton Cl HAYES BR2 ....83 K2
Mapleton Rd BH/WHM TN16 ....176 F6

Maple Tree Pl BKHTH/KID SE3 ....43 K7
Maplin Rd CAN/RD E16 ....26 B2
Maplins Cl ERHAM ME8 ....97 J5
Mara Ct CHAT ME4 * 95 L5
Maran Wy ERITHM DA18 ....28 C6
Marathon Paddock GILL ME7 ....96 A2
Marathon Ter THMD SE28 ....27 N4
Marble Quay WAP E1W * 24 C4
Marbrook Ct LEE/GVPK SE12 ....62 G2
Marc Brunel Wy CHAT ME4 ....22 G8
Marcella Rd BRXN/ST SW9 ....40 A3
Marcellina Wy ORP BR6 ....86 F7
Marcet Rd DART DA1 ....46 C6
Marchants STPH/PW TN12 * 242 E9
Marchant St NWCR SE14 ....25 H9
Marchwood Cl CMBW SE5 ....40 E1
Marcia Rd STHWK SE1 ....24 B8
Marconi Rd GVW DA11 ....69 H2
Marconi Wy ROCH ME1 ....95 J7
Marcus Garvey Ms EDUL SE22 ....41 H7
Marcus Garvey Wy HNHL SE24 ....40 A5
Marcus Rd DART DA1 ....66 A1
Mardale Cl RHAM ME8 ....97 K5
Mardell Rd CROY/NA CR0 ....84 A2
Marden Av HAYES BR2 ....85 K3
MSTR CT12 ....16 A1
Marden Crs BXLY DA5 ....45 L6
CROY/NA CR0 ....82 E5
Marden Rd CRBK TN17 ....275 L6
CROY/NA CR0 ....82 E5
STPH/PW TN12 ....245 M4
STRD ME2 ....72 C6
Marden Sq BERM/RHTH SE16 ....24 E6
Marden Rd KEN/WIL TN24 ....252 F4
Mardyke Vw PUR RM19 * 31 H6
Marechal Niel Av BFN/LL DA15 ....63 P2
Marechal Niel Pde
SCUP DA14 * 63 K7
Maresfield CROY/NA CR0 ....63 K7
Maresfield Cl DVW CT16 ....291 J5
Margaret Gardner Dr
ELTH/MOT SE9 ....63 K1
Margaret Rd BXLY DA5 ....44 G7
Margaret St FOLK CT20 ....11 G4
Margate Cl GILL ME7 ....73 L5
Margate Hl BRCH CT7 ....141 J1
Margate Rd HB CT6 ....107 N3
MSTR CT12 ....143 H2
Margetts La ROCH ME1 ....124 C4
Margetts Pl STRD ME2 ....72 C4
Maria Cl STHWK SE1 ....24 D7
Marian Cl CDW/CHP RM16 ....31 N4
Marian Sq STPH/PW TN12 ....246 C5
Maria Ter WCHPL E1 ....24 C1
Marie Manor Wy RDART DA2 * 67 J2
Marigold St BERM/RHTH SE16 ....24 E6
Marigold Wy CROY/NA CR0 ....84 A5
MAIDW ME16 ....154 F9
Marilyn Crs BRCH CT7 ....111 M1
Marina Cl DEAL CT14 * 233 J1
Marina Dr DART DA1 ....46 A6
CVW DA11 ....49 K8
IOS ME12 ....85 J5
WELL DA16 ....44 A3
Marina Esp RAM CT11 ....17 J3
Marina Rd RAM CT11 ....17 J3
The Marina DEAL CT14 ....233 J1
Marine Cl CDW/CHP RM16 ....31 N4
HOO/HM ME3 ....73 L4
MARG CT9 ....15 F4
WOOL/PLUM SE18 ....27 J8
Marine Gap WSTB CT5 ....105 K5
Marine Gdns MARG CT9 ....15 F5
Marine Pde DVE/WH CT16 ....291 J4
FOLK CT20 ....11 K5
IOS ME12 ....57 M6
NROM TN28 ....337 K8
WSTB CT5 ....105 N3
Marine Parade Ms FOLK CT20 ....11 G5
Marine Pk IOS ME12 * 57 M6
Marine Rd DEAL CT14 ....233 J5
Mariners Ct WSTB CT5 ....105 L6
Mariners La BRDST CT10 ....113 J9
Mariners Ms POP/IOD E14 ....25 N7
The Mariners RAM CT11 * 18 E7
Mariners Vw GILL ME7 ....73 M8
Mariners Wy CHAT ME4 ....49 J8
Marine St BERM/RHTH SE16 ....24 D6
Marine Ter RDART DA2 ....67 J2
WSTB CT5 ....105 L6
Marine Vw CHAT ME4 ....73 L4
Marine Walk St HYTHE CT21 * 309 H5
Marion Cl WALD ME5 ....125 M5
Marion Crs MAID/SHEP ME15 ....185 N2
STMC/STPC BR5 ....64 D8
Marion Ms DUL SE21 ....60 D2
Marion Rd BRCH CT7 ....83 H2
Marischal Rd LEW SE13 ....42 A4
Marisco Cl CDW/CHP RM16 ....31 N5
Maritime Av HB CT6 ....107 P2
Maritime Cl ERITH DA8 ....29 L7
Maritime Ga RDART DA2 ....67 P6
STRD ME2 ....72 B7
Maritime Quay POP/IOD E14 ....25 K8
Maritime Wy CHAT ME4 ....72 G7
Marjoram Cl BRCH CT7 ....291 H6
Marjoram Dr SIT ME10 ....129 N3
Mark Av RAM CT11 ....142 G7
Mark Cl BXLYHN DA7 ....44 C2
HAYES BR2 ....84 D6
Market Bldgs MAID/BEAR ME14 ....12 F4
Market Hl HYTHE CT21 * 309 H5
Market Meadow
STMC/STPC BR5 ....87 K1
Market Pde BMLY BR1 * 62 E7
SCUP DA14 ....64 C3
SNWD SE25 ....83 M1
Market Pl BERM/RHTH SE16 * 24 D7
BXLYHN DA6 ....45 J5
DART DA1 ....46 E8
HDCN TN27 ....221 H3
MARG CT9 ....15 G3

RCANTE CT3 ....229 J1
TIL RM18 ....49 L3
Market Rd RYE TN31 ....338 E7
Market Sq BH/WHM TN16 ....176 D5
RTW TN1 * 22 E3
Market St DEAL CT14 ....233 J3
FAV ME13 ....132 C6
HB CT6 ....107 L1
MARG CT9 ....15 G5
RTWE/PEM TN2 * 22 C6
RYE TN31 ....338 F7
STPH/PW TN12 ....246 C4
SWCH CT13 ....201 P1
WOOL/PLUM SE18 ....27 H7
The Market PECK SE15 * 40 G3
Market Vw RCANTE CT3 ....229 J1
Market Wy BH/WHM TN16 ....176 D5
CANTW/ST CT2 ....5 D2
Market Yard Ms STHWK SE1 ....24 B6
Markfield CROY/NA CR0 ....114 C4
Markland Rd DVW CT17 ....290 C8
Mark La GVE DA12 ....50 A7
MON EC3R 24 B3
Marks Rd WARL CR6 ....144 B5
Marks Sq GVW DA11 ....69 K3
Markstone Ter ORP BR6 ....87 H4
Mark St CHAT ME4 ....95 M4
Mark Wy SWLY BR8 ....88 F2
Markwell Cl SYD SE26 ....61 H5
Marlborough Av SEV TN13 ....20 A1
Marlborough Cl BRDST CT10 ....145 K1
CDW/CHP RM16 ....32 D5
NROM TN28 ....337 J6
ORP BR6 ....86 G4
SBGH/RUST TN4 ....270 B4
Marlborough Pde
MAIDW ME16 * 184 E1
Marlborough Park Av
BFN/LL DA15 ....44 C9
Marlborough Rd DART DA1 ....46 C7
DEAL CT14 ....232 F7
DVW CT17 ....290 C8
GILL ME7 ....7 G3
HAYES BR2 ....85 M1
MARG CT9 ....16 E4
WOOL/PLUM SE18 ....27 J6
WSTB CT5 ....105 L9
Marlborough Wy
KEN/WIL TN24 ....253 J2
Marie Place Rd
STPH/PW TN12 ....273 J3
Marler Rd FOLKN CT19 ....310 B5
FSTH SE23 ....41 M9
Marley Av BXLYHN DA7 ....28 C9
Marley Ct CANTW/ST CT2 ....136 B9
Marley La DEAL CT14 ....231 P2
HDCN TN27 ....248 D5
RCANTE CT3 ....210 A4
RCANTW CT4 ....227 L2
Marley Rd BERM/RHTH SE16 * 24 C7
HOO/HM ME3 ....75 K1
MAIDW ME16 ....184 E1
RYE TN31 ....338 D6
Marley Wy ROCH ME1 ....95 H4
Marlhurst EDEN TN8 ....206 C6
Marlings Cl CHST BR7 ....86 F1
Marlings Park Av CHST BR7 ....64 A9
Marling Wy GVE DA12 ....70 A4
Marlow Cl PGE/AN SE20 ....61 H9
WSTB CT5 ....105 L6
Marlow Copse WALD ME5 ....125 L4
Marlow Av CANT CT1 ....4 B6
Marlowe Cl CHST BR7 ....63 P5
Marlowe Rd ASH TN23 * 2 B1
DIT/AY ME20 ....153 N1
DVE/WH CT16 ....291 J4
MARG CT9 ....112 G5
Marlowe Sq MTCM CR4 ....82 B1
The Marlowes DART DA1 ....45 M5
Marlow Mdw CANTW/ST CT2 ....137 L8
Marlow Rd PGE/AN SE20 ....61 H9
Marlowe Wy BERM/RHTH SE16 ....61 H9
Marlpit Cl EDEN TN8 ....206 D6
EGRIN RH19 ....265 H5
Marlton St GNWCH SE10 ....26 A8
Marlwood Cl BFN/LL DA15 ....64 A1
Marmadon Rd
WOOL/PLUM SE18 ....27 N7
Marmion Wy ASH TN23 ....251 P9
Marmont Rd PECK SE15 ....40 F3
Marmora Rd EDUL SE22 ....41 J7
Marne Av WELL DA16 ....44 C4
Marnock Rd BROCKY SE4 ....41 M6
Maroon St POP/IOD E14 ....25 K2
Maroons Wy CAT SE6 ....61 N4
Marquis Dr GILL ME7 ....126 E2
Marrabon Cl BFN/LL DA15 ....44 C9
Marriott Cl EBED/NFELT TW14 ....44 B9
Marriott Rd DART DA1 ....46 C6
Marrose Av MSTR CT12 ....142 C1
Marsala Rd LEW SE13 ....41 N5
Marsden Rd PECK SE15 ....41 H3
Marsden St DART DA1 ....46 C6
Marsh Av SWLY BR8 ....86 G8
Marshall Crs BRDST CT10 ....113 K9
QBOR ME11 ....77 H4
Marshall Gdns RTON TN11 ....211 P1
Marsham Meade HAWK ME8 ....96 F5
Marshalls Pl
WOOL/PLUM SE18 ....24 D6
Marshalls Land TENT TN30 ....301 H4
Marshall's Pl
BERM/RHTH SE16 ....24 C6
Marsham Cl CHST BR7 * 63 M4
Marsham Crs RMAID ME17 ....216 E1
Marsham St MAID/BEAR ME14 ....12 E1
Marsham Wy STRD ME2 ....93 P9
Marshborough Pde
SWCH CT13 ....200 G2
Marshbrook Cl BKHTH/KID SE3 ....48 M3
Marsh Crs HOO/HM ME3 ....53 L4
Marsh Dr STMD SE28 ....28 A1
Marshes Rd RYE TN31 * 336 G7
Marsh Farm Rd MSTR CT12 ....141 J9
Marshfield St POP/IOD E14 ....25 M6
Marshfoot Rd CDW/CHP RM16 ....33 H8

GRAYS RM17 ....32 G8
Marsh Green Rd EDEN TN8 ....236 C4
Marshlands LYDD TN29 ....326 F8
Marshlands Cl LYDD TN29 ....326 F7
Marshland Vw HOO/HM ME3 ....54 D4
Marsh La DEAL CT14 ....232 F5
Marsh Vw GVE DA12 ....50 B8
RAIN RM13 ....49 P2
RSIT ME9 ....131 L1
Marsh Quarter La HAWK TN18 ....329 K1
Marsh Ri SIT ME10 ....99 P5
Marsh Rd RASHW TN26 ....304 D9
STRD ME2 ....94 A9
Marsh St DART DA1 ....46 G4
POP/IOD E14 * 25 L7
STRD ME2 ....18 E1
Marsh Ter STMC/STPC BR5 ....87 L1
Marsh Vw GVE DA12 ....50 B9
HYTHE CT21 ....308 B7
IOS ME12 ....58 A7
Marsh Wall POP/IOD E14 ....25 K5
Marsh Wy DIT/AY ME20 ....123 P9
RAIN RM13 ....29 J2
Marshwood Cl CANT CT1 ....167 H1
Marstan Cl RSIT ME9 ....97 P4
Marston Cl WALD ME5 ....125 K2
Marston Dr MAID/BEAR ME14 ....13 F7
WARL CR6 ....144 B3
Marston Wy NRWD SE19 ....60 B6
Martello Cl RYE TN31 ....338 E8
Martello Cots HYTHE CT21 * 308 C6
Martello Dr HYTHE CT21 ....308 D6
Martello Rd FOLK CT20 ....11 H2
FOLK CT20 ....310 A8
Martello Ter FOLK CT20 ....310 C8
Martens Av BXLYHN DA7 ....45 P5
Martens Cl BXLYHN DA7 ....45 L5
Martha Cl FOLKN CT19 ....310 E4
Martham Cl THMD SE28 ....28 C5
Martha St WCHPL E1 ....24 F2
Martha Bowes Rd
ELTH/MOT SE9 ....43 K4
Martin Cl SAND/SEL CR2 ....114 A5
Martin Ct GILL ME7 ....126 D2
Martin Crs CROY/NA CR0 ....82 E5
ORP BR6 ....87 H9
Martindale Cl CANT CT1 ....4 E7
Martin Dale Crs RDV CT15 ....262 B6
Martin Dene BXLYHS DA6 ....45 L6
Martindown Rd WSTB CT5 ....105 K7
Martin Dr RDART DA2 ....47 J7
Martineau St WCHPL E1 ....24 F3
Martin Hardie Wy TONN TN10 ....211 H5
Martin La CANST EC4R 24 A3
Martin Ri BXLYHS DA6 ....45 H5
Martin Rd DART DA1 ....66 C2
SOCK/AV RM15 ....30 C4
STRD ME2 ....72 B7
Martins Cl HOO/HM ME3 ....71 M1
Martin's Cl MSTR CT12 ....143 H2
Martins Cl STMC/STPC BR5 ....64 F9
TENT TN30 ....301 K7
WWKM BR4 ....84 C5
Martins La STPH/PW TN12 ....182 F9
Martins Pl THMD SE28 ....27 M4
Martin Sq DIT/AY ME20 ....153 P2
Martin's Rd HAYES BR2 ....62 C8
Martin's Shaw SEV TN13 ....148 B7
The Martins RASHW TN26 ....279 P7
SYD SE26 ....61 H8
Martin St THMD SE28 ....27 M4
Martins Wk THMD SE28 ....27 M4
Martin's Wy HYTHE CT21 ....308 C7
Marton Cl CAT SE6 ....61 N2
Martyrs Pl EGRIN RH19 ....265 K8
Martyrs' Field Rd CANT CT1 ....4 B6
Marvels Cl LEE/GVPK SE12 ....62 F1
Marvels La LEE/GVPK SE12 ....62 F1
Marwell BH/WHM TN16 ....176 C2
Marwell Cl WWKM BR4 ....85 J6
Marwood Cl WELL DA16 ....44 D4
Mary Ann Blds DEPT SE8 ....25 N8
Marybank WOOL/PLUM SE18 ....26 G9
Mary Burrows Gdns
BGR/WK TN15 ....149 N2
Mary Ct CHAT ME4 ....95 M4
Mary Datchelor Cl CMBW SE5 ....40 D2
Mary Day's CRBK TN17 ....274 D9
Mary Dukes Pl
MAID/SHEP ME15 * 13 H6
Mayfield Cl BXLY DA5 ....65 N2
Mary Green Wk CANT CT1 ....5 H1
Maryland Cl RHAM ME8 ....97 H9
Maryland Dr MAIDW ME16 ....184 E1
Maryland Rd CANT CT1 ....167 H6
Maryland Rd RTWE/PEM TN2 ....270 G7
THHTH CR7 ....60 B7
Mary Munnion Wy MAID/BEAR ME14 ....156 A9
Mary Rose Cl RYE TN31 ....339 K9
Mary St CAN/RD E16 ....26 A1
Mascall's Court La
STPH/PW TN12 ....243 J5
Mascall's Court Rd
STPH/PW TN12 ....243 J5
Mascalls La STPH/PW TN12 ....242 G4
Mascalls Rd CHARL SE7 ....26 D8
Masefield Cl ERITH DA8 ....45 P2
Masefield Dr HOO/HM ME3 ....53 L4
Masefield Rd CDW/CHP RM16 ....32 F5
DART DA1 ....47 H5
GVW DA11 ....69 K5
Masefield Vw ORP BR6 ....86 D7
Mashmarsh LYDD TN29 ....340 C3
Maskall Cl BRXS/STRHM SW2 * 40 A3
Mason Cl BERM/RHTH SE16 ....24 D8
BXLYHN DA7 ....45 K4
CAN/RD E16 ....26 B3
Mason Rd RYE TN31 ....338 D7
Mason's Av CITYW EC2V 24 A2
CROY/NA CR0 ....83 H5

Masons HI HAYES BR2 ....62 E9
  WOOL/PLUM SE18 ....27 J7
Masons Rd BRDST CT10 ....113 M8
Masons Rd DVW CT17 ....291 H6
Mason Way HOO/HM ME5 ....72 B5
Massinger St WALW SE17 ....24 B7
Master CI OXTED RH8 ....175 H5
Masters Av E/WMAL ME19 ....125 J8
Masters La E/WMAL ME19 ....125 J8
Master's St WCHPL E1 ....24 C1
Masthead CI RDART DA2 ....47 J5
Masthouse Ter POP/IOD E14 ....25 K7
Mast House Ter POP/IOD E14 ....25 K7
Mastmaker Rd POP/IOD E14 ....25 K5
Mast Quay WOOL/PLUM SE18 ....26 G6
Matchless CI
  WOOL/PLUM SE18 ....43 L1
Matfield CI HAYES BR2 ....85 K2
Matfield Crs MAID/BEAR ME14 ....13 K2
Matfield Rd BELV DA17 ....28 F9
Matham Gv EDUL SE22 ....40 F9
  RHAM ME8 ....96 E6
Matlock CI NRWD SE19 ....60 D5
Matlock St POP/IOD E14 ....25 H7
Matterdale Gdns
  MAIDW ME16 ....184 D1
Matthew Ct MTCM CR4 ....82 C2
Matthews CI DEAL CT14 ....233 H5
Matthew's Ct GILL ME7 * 7 K3
Matthew's Gdns
  CROY/NA CRO 114 C5
Matthews La RTON TN11 ....182 A8
Matthews PI DVE/WH CT16 ....8 B1
Matthews Rd HB CT6 ....107 H4
Mattingly Wy PECK SE15 ....40 F1
Mattison PI RSIT ME19 ....158 C5
Matts Hill Rd RSIT ME9 ....127 H3
Maud Cashmore Wy
  WOOL/PLUM SE18 ....26 C6
Maude Rd CMBW SE5 ....40 A5
  SWLY BR8 ....66 A5
Maudlins Gn WAP E1W * 24 D4
Maudslay Rd ELTH/MOT SE9 ....43 K4
Maunder CI CROY/NA CRO 82 D5
Maunders CI WALD ME5 ....105 L6
Maunsell PI KEN/WIL TN24 ....282 C1
Mauritius Rd GNWCH SE10 ....25 P7
Mavelstone Rd BMLY BR1 ....63 H7
Mawbey PI STHWK SE1 ....24 C8
Mawbey Rd STHWK SE1 ....24 C8
Maxey Rd WOOL/PLUM SE18 ....27 K7
Maximfeild Rd ERITH DA8 ....29 L3
Maximilian Dr STRD ME2 ....124 A1
Maxim Rd DART DA1 ....45 N6
  ERITH DA8 ....29 K8
Maxine Gdns BRDST CT10 ....113 L8
Maxted Rd PECK SE15 ....40 G4
Maxton CI MAID/BEAR ME14 ....156 C7
Maxton Rd DVW CT17 ....291 H9
Maxwell CI CROY/NA CRO 82 D5
Maxwell Dr MAIDW ME16 ....154 G6
Maxwell Gdns ORP BR6 ....86 E7
Maxwell PI DEAL CT14 ....233 H5
Maxwell Rd GILL ME7 * 6 D2
  WELL DA16 ....44 C3
Maya CI PECK SE15 ....41 H5
Mayall Rd HNHL SE24 ....40 B6
May Av GVW DA11 ....49 K9
  STMC/STPC BR5 ....87 J1
Maybourne CI SYD SE26 ....61 H4
Maybury Av RDART DA2 ....47 H9
Maybury Rd STMC/STPC BR5 ....86 C2
Maycotts La STPH/PW TN12 ....242 E8
Maycroft Av GRAYS RM17 ....32 E8
Maycroft Gdns BRKHTH/KID SE3 ....43 J3
Mayday Gdns BRKHTH/KID SE3 ......43 J5
Mayday Rd THHTH CR7 ....82 C3
Maydowns Rd WSTB CT5 ....106 C4
Mayefield Rd THHTH CR7 ....82 A3
Mayerne Rd ELTH/MOT SE9 ....43 H6
Mayers Rd DEAL CT14 ....232 F8
Mayes CI SWLY BR8 ....88 F1
  WARL CR6 ....144 A3
Mayeswood Rd
  LEE/GVPK SE12 ....62 G3
Mayfair St ME2 * 72 C7
Mayfair Av BXLYHN DA7 ....44 F2
  MAID/SHEP ME15 ....185 M5
Mayfair CI BECK BR3 ....61 P7
Mayfield BXLYHN DA7 ....45 H4
  LING RH7 ....235 K8
Mayfield Av DVE/WH CT16 ....291 J5
  ORP BR6 ....86 C5
Mayfield CI PGE/AN SE20 ....60 F1
  RHAM ME8 ....97 J3
  WALD ME5 ....125 M4
Mayfield Crs THHTH CR7 ....81 M5
Mayfield Rd BELV DA17 ....29 H7
  BMLY BR1 ....76 E4
  DVE/WH CT16 ....261 H9
  GVW DA11 ....49 K9
  HB CT6 ....107 M3
  RFOLK CT18 ....288 A7
  SBCH/RUST TN4 ....27 J3
Mayfields CDW/CHF RM16 ....32 D5
Mayfield VIs SCUP DA14 * 64 E5
Mayflower
  BERM/RHTH SE16 ....24 G7
Mayflower Rd CDW/CHF RM16 ....31 N8
Mayflower St
  BERM/RHTH SE16 ....24 G7
Mayfly CI STMC/STPC BR5 ....87 L1
Mayford CI RFOLK CT18 ....288 D8
Mayford St BECK BR3 ....61 P7
Mayford Rd WALD ME5 ....126 A3
Mayforth Gdns RAM CT11 ....142 G6
Mayham CI SWT ME3 ....153 D9
Mayhill Rd CHARL SE7 ....42 B5
Maylam Gdns SIT ME10 ....44 C3
Maylands Dr SCUP DA14 ....64 G7
Maymills SWCH CT13 * 201 J8
Maynard Av MARG CT9 ....12 A5
Maynard CI ERITH DA8 ....45 P1

Maynard PI WALD ME5 ....96 A4
Maynard Rd CANT CT1 ....4 A7
Maynards STPH/PW TN12 ....245 H4
Maynards Quay WAP E1W * 24 F3
Mayo Rd CHAT ME4 ....83 J2
Mayors La RDART DA2 ....66 C4
Mayow Rd SYD SE26 ....61 K5
Maypits ASH TN23 ....94 D6
May PI STPH/PW TN12 * 245 L3
Mayplace Av DART DA1 ....45 K4
Mayplace CI BXLYHN DA7 ....45 K4
Mayplace La
  WOOL/PLUM SE18 ....27 J9
Mayplace Rd BXLYHN DA7 ....45 L4
Mayplace Rd East BXLYHN DA7 ......45 K4
Mayplace Rd West
  BXLYHN DA7 ....45 J5
Maypole CI RFOLK CT18 ....288 E6
Maypole Crs ERITH DA8 ....30 A9
Maypole Dr E/WMAL ME19 ....153 K9
Maypole La RFOLK CT18 * 288 E7
Maypole Rd EGRIN RH19 ....264 G6
  GVE DA12 ....50 B9
  ORP BR6 ....117 N1
  RCANTE CT3 ....138 B5
Maytree Wk
  BRXS/STRHM SW2 * 60 A1
Mayville Rd BRDST CT10 ....113 K7
Mayweed Av WALD ME5 ....125 K1
Maywood CI BECK BR3 * 61 P6
Maze HI BKHTH/KID SE3 ....42 D1
  GNWCH SE10 ....25 P9
McAlpine Crs
  MAID/SHEP ME15 ....185 L8
McAuley CI ELTH/MOT SE9 ....43 L6
McCabe CI STPH/PW TN12 ....246 C8
McCall Crs CHARL SE7 ....26 F8
McCarthy Av CANT/W ST CT2 ....137 L6
McClean Wk IOS ME12 ....79 J7
McCudden Rd DART DA1 ....46 F4
McCudden Rw GILL ME7 * 72 G9
McDermott Rd BGR/WK TN15 ....151 J5
  PECK SE15 ....40 G4
McDowall CI CAN/RD E16 ....26 D5
McDowall Rd CMBW SE5 ....40 C2
McIndoe Rd EGRIN RH19 ....264 C5
McIver CI EGRIN RH19 ....264 C5
McKenzie CI DIT/AY ME20 ....154 E4
McKenzie Rd WALD ME5 ....125 N2
McKerrell Rd PECK SE15 ....40 G2
McKillop Wy SCUP DA14 ....64 E6
McKinlay Ct BRCH CT7 ....110 E5
McLeod Rd ABYW SE2 ....28 B7
McMillan CI GVE DA12 ....69 N5
McMillan St DEPT SE8 ....25 N3
McNeil Rd CMBW SE5 ....40 E3
Mead CI CDW/CHF RM16 ....32 C5
  SWLY BR8 ....88 D4
Mead Crs DART DA1 ....46 B2
Meades CI LING RH7 ....235 L8
  STPH/PW TN12 ....244 G3
The Meades LING RH7 ....235 L8
The Meade RFOLK CT18 ....288 C8
Meadfield Rd MEO DA13 ....92 B6
Meadow Av CROY/NA CRO 82 A4
Meadowbank BKHTH/KID SE3 ....42 D4
Meadow Bank E/WMAL ME19 ....153 K4
  RTON TN11 ....209 L9
Meadow Bank CI
  BGR/WK TN15 ....120 C3
Meadowbank Rd CHAT ME4 ....6 E5
Meadowbrook FOLK CT20 ....310 B7
  OXTED RH8 ....174 H6
Meadowbrook CI
  KEN/WIL TN24 ....252 G3
Meadowbrook Rd
  FOLK CT20 * 310 B7
Meadowdown
  MAID/BEAR ME14 ....156 B8
Meadowdown CI GILL ME7 ....72 G8
Meadow Dr CROY/NA CRO 83 L4
Meadow Farm Rd RASHE TN25 ....95 L8
Meadow Hill Rd RTW TN1 ....22 E6
Meadowlands BGR/WK TN15 ....149 L9
  OXTED RH8 ....205 K1
Meadow La EDEN TN8 ....206 C6

LEE/GVPK SE12 ....62 F2
MEO DA13 ....122 A4
Meadow Ri RSIT ME9 ....99 L2
Meadow Rd ASH TN23 ....252 D5
  CANTW/ST CT2 ....137 L7
  CDW/CHF RM16 ....32 D4
  GVW DA11 ....48 C9
  HAYES BR2 ....62 C7
  MARG CT9 ....112 A4
  RRTW TN5 ....268 C9
  RTW TN1 ....22 D2
  SBCH/RUST TN4 ....269 P4
  TON TN9 ....240 D1
Meadowside BKHTH/KID SE3 ....42 G5
  DART DA1 ....46 E9
The Meadows HB CT6 ....107 P4
  HDCN TN27 ....278 A6
  MAID/SHEP ME15 ....185 K1
  NROM TN28 ....337 H7
  ORP BR6 ....117 K1
  RSEV TN14 ....117 K1
  SIT ME10 ....129 N3
  TENT TN30 ....332 A1
  WARL CR6 ....144 A2
Meadow Stile CROY/NA CRO 83 H7
Meadowsweet CI CAN/RD E16 ....26 E1
Meadowsweet Vw CHAT ME4 ....73 H5
The Meadow CHST BR7 ....63 N5
  RTWE/PEM TN2 ....241 N9
Meadow Vw BFN/LL DA15 ....44 F8
  HOO/HM ME5 ....38 F8
  RASHW TN26 ....251 L5
  RSIT ME9 * 98 C5
  STMC/STPC BR5 ....84 E9
  SWLY BR8 ....88 C3
  WALD ME5 ....96 E7
Meadowview Rd BXLY DA5 ....44 C7
  CAT SE6 ....61 L1
Meadow View Rd RDV CT15 ....229 P8
  RMAID ME17 ....187 J3
  THHTH CR7 ....81 K2
The Meads Av SIT ME10 ....99 L7
Meadside CI BECK BR3 ....61 L7
Meadside Wk WALD ME5 ....95 L8
The Meads CRBK TN17 ....297 L6
  EGRIN RH19 ....265 H9
  RTWE/PEM TN2 ....241 N9
Meads Wy LYDD TN29 ....337 K2
The Mead BECK BR3 ....62 A8
  E/WMAL ME19 ....153 M2
  HART DA3 ....49 M1
  WWKM BR4 ....84 C5
Meadvale Rd CROY/NA CRO 83 L4
Mead Wall HOO/HM ME5 ....51 P1
Meadow Wy CHST BR7 ....63 J7
  GRAYS RM17 ....32 D9
  RSEV TN14 ....117 N7
  RTON TN11 ....210 B5
  BECK BR3 ....62 A7
Meadow Wy CANTW/ST CT2 ....137 L8
  CROY/NA CRO 84 B6
  ORP BR6 ....116 B4
  SEV TN13 ....148 E7
Meaford Wy PGE/AN SE20 ....61 H6
Meakin Est STHWK SE1 * 24 B6
Meath CI STMC/STPC BR5 ....87 J2
Medbury Rd GVE DA12 ....50 B9
Medburn St CAMTN NW1 * 24 A1
Medebridge Rd
  CDW/CHF RM16 ....32 A2
Medhurst Crs GVE DA12 ....70 B2
Medhurst Gdns CHAT ME4 ....72 B2
Medick Ct GRAYS RM17 ....32 E9
Medina Av RWSTB CT5 ....105 J7
Medina Rd DIT/AY ME20 ....154 B3
  GRAYS RM17 ....32 E8
  TOWN TN10 ....216 C8
Medlar CI RSIT ME9 ....129 H7
Medlar Gv GILL ME7 ....126 D1
Medlar Rd GRAYS RM17 ....32 E9
The Medlars
  MAID/BEAR ME14 ....156 A6
  MEO DA13 ....92 B5
Medlar St CMBW SE5 ....40 C2
Medusa Rd CAT SE6 ....41 P7
Medway Br STRD ME2 ....94 D3
Medway CI CROY/NA CRO 83 P3
  SIT ME10 ....129 L2
Medway Ct DIT/AY ME20 ....154 C2
Medway Gdns CHAT ME4 ....72 F8
Medway Mdw STPH/PW TN12 .213 H4
Medway Rd DART DA1 ....46 A4
  GILL ME7 ....75 H4
  IOS ME12 ....21 N5
  RTW TN1 ....270 E5
Medway St CHAT ME4 ....6 A6
  MAID/BEAR ME14 ....13 G5
Medway Ter WBY/YAL ME18 * .183 L5
Medway Valley Wk
  STPH/PW TN12 ....212 H6
  WBY/YAL ME18 ....183 J9
Medway Vw RTON TN11 ....212 A6
Medway Wharf Rd TON TN9 ....210 D9
Meehan Rd NROM TN28 ....337 K9
Meehan Rd South
  NROM TN28 ....343 J1
Meerbrook Rd BKHTH/KID SE3 .42 G4

Meeres Court La SIT ME10 ....100 B8
Meeson's CI FAV ME13 ....161 K6
Meesons La GRAYS RM17 ....32 A7
Meeting House Aly WAP E1W * .24 E4
Meeting House La CHAT ME4 ....6 E4
  PECK SE15 ....41 H1
Meeting St RAM CT11 ....17 F5
Megan CI LYDD TN29 ....342 C5
Meggett La RDV CT15 ....289 M5
Megone CI RFOLK CT18 ....288 D8
Megrims HI HAWK SE3 ....318 A8
Melanda CI CHST BR7 ....63 K4
Melba Gdns TIL RM18 ....49 G1
Melbourne Av DVW CT16 ....291 J2
  MSTR CT12 ....142 F4
Melbourne CI ORP BR6 ....86 F4
  WLCTN SM6 ....82 B9
Melbourne Gv EDUL SE22 ....40 E5
Melbourne Ms BRXN/ST SW9 ....40 A2
  CAT SE6 ....61 P1
Melbourne Rd CHAT ME4 ....6 E7
  TIL RM18 ....49 H4
  WLCTN SM6 ....82 A9
Melbourne Sq BRXN/ST SW9 ....40 A2
Melbourne Ter EDUL SE22 * 40 E5
Melbury Ct CHST BR7 ....63 K5
Melbury Dr CMBW SE5 ....40 E1
Melbury Ms NROM TN28 ....337 H5
Melcombe CI ASH TN23 ....281 P1
Meldrum CI OXTED RH8 ....175 J8
  STMC/STPC BR5 ....87 K3
Melfield Gdns CAT SE6 ....61 P5
Melford Dr MAIDW ME16 ....154 C8
Melford Rd EDUL SE22 ....61 H1
Melfort Av THHTH CR7 ....81 M4
Melfort Rd THHTH CR7 ....81 M4
Melior PI STHWK SE1 * 24 B5
Melior St STHWK SE1 ....24 A5
Meliot Rd CAT SE6 ....62 B1
Mellanby CI BRCH CT7 ....111 H7
Mellanby St CROY/NA CRO 82 D7
Melliker La MEO DA13 ....92 B5
Mellish St POP/IOD E14 ....25 K6
Melliker Rw SIRT ME10 ....99 N5
Mells CI ELTH/MOT SE9 ....63 K5
Mell St GNWCH SE10 ....25 P7
Melody CI IOS ME12 ....80 C3
  RHAM ME8 ....126 F1
Melody Rd BH/WHM TN16 ....145 M3
Melon La LYDD TN29 ....335 N1
Melon Rd PECK SE15 ....40 G2
  RASHW TN26 ....325 H5
Melrose Av DART DA1 ....45 N8
Melrose CI LEE/GVPK SE12 ....62 F3
  MAID/SHEP ME15 ....185 M1
Melrose Crs ORP BR6 ....86 E6
Melrose Dr BH/WHM TN16 ....145 M1
Melrose VIs BECK BR3 * 61 K7
Melsetter CI BRCH CT7 * 111 J6
Melthorpe Gdns
  BKHTH/KID SE3 ....43 H2
Melville Av SAND/SEL CR2 ....83 L9
Melville CI CHAT ME4 ....72 F9
  MAID/SHEP ME15 ....185 LG
  SCUP DA14 ....64 E1
Melvin Rd PGE/AN SE20 ....61 H2
Memel PI RAM CT11 ....16 E4
Mendfield St FAV ME13 ....132 F6
Mendip Gdns GVE DA12 ....50 C8
Mendip CI SYD SE26 ....61 J3
Mendip Rd ERITH DA8 ....45 L3
Mendip Wk RTWE/PEM TN2 ....23 J1
Menin Rd RSIT ME9 * 99 N1
Menin Gdns NRWD SE19 ....60 D6
Mentmore Rd MSTR CT12 ....143 H1
Menzies Av SIT ME10 ....78 A2
Menzies Ct IOS ME12 ....78 A2
Meopham St BRXS/STRHM SW2 ....60 A2
Meopham Rd MEO DA13 * 45 J3
Mera Dr BXLYHN DA7 ....45 J5
Merbury CI LEW SE13 * 42 A6
THMD SE28 ....27 L4
Merbury St WOOL/PLUM SE18 ....27 J6
Merbury Rd WOOL/PLUM SE18 ....27 J6
Mercator Rd LEW SE13 ....42 G5
Mercator Rd LEW SE13 ....42 G5
Mercer CI DIT/AY ME20 ....154 C3
Mercer Dr RMAID ME17 ....188 G5
Mercers HAWK TN18 ....317 J5
  RRTW TN5 ....269 M5
Mercers CI GNWCH SE10 ....26 A7
Mercers PI E/WMAL ME19 ....183 H1
Mercer St RTW TN1 ....22 E1
Mercers Wy RMAID ME17 ....216 B4
Mercery La CANT CT1 ....4 D4
Merchant PI STPH/PW TN12 ....245 H4
Merchants CI SNWD SE25 ....81 H1
Merchant St BOW E3 ....25 N2
Merchland Rd ELTH/MOT SE9 ....63 K3
Mercia Gv LEW SE13 * 42 F3
Mercury CI ROCH ME1 ....95 J7
Mercury Wy NWCR SE14 ....24 G9
Mere CI ORP BR6 ....86 C6
Meredith CI RMAID ME17 ....187 J4
Meredith Ms BROCKY SE4 * 41 M5
Meredith Rd CDW/CHF RM16 ....31 M7
Mere Ga MARG CT9 ....15 F7
Meresborough La RHAM ME8 ....97 K9
Meresborough Rd RHAM ME8 .127 J1
Mereside ORP BR6 ....86 A5
Meretone CI BROCKY SE4 ....41 M5
Merewood CI BMLY BR1 ....63 L8
Merewood Rd BXLYHN DA7 ....45 M4
Mereworth Rd CROY/NA CRO 84 A4
Mereworth CI HAYES BR2 ....83 J2
Mereworth Dr
  WOOL/PLUM SE18 ....43 M1

Mereworth Rd
  SBCH/RUST TN4 ....270 D2
  WBY/YAL ME18 ....182 C5
Meriden CI BMLY BR1 ....63 H5
Meridian Pk CHST ME2 * 72 E9
Meridian Rd CHARL SE7 ....43 H1
Merivale Wood Ct STRD ME2 * 265 J5
Merleland Av ELTH/MOT SE9 ....43 L5
Merileys CI HART DA3 ....68 G9
Merino Wy ASH TN23 ....282 B3
Merityn Gv SIT ME10 ....125 N1
Merleburgh Dr SIT ME10 ....99 N6
Merle Common Rd
  OXTED RH8 ....205 K3
Merlewood SEV TN15 ....148 G8
Merlewood Dr CHST BR7 ....63 H7
Merlin Av DIT/AY ME20 ....153 N2
Merlin CI CDW/CHF RM16 ....31 P6
  CROY/NA CRO 83 K8
  SIT ME10 ....129 P2
  THHTH CR7 ....211 H6
Merlin Gv BECK BR3 * 84 C1
Merlin Rd North WELL DA16 ....44 C5
Merlin Rd WELL DA16 ....44 C5
Merlin Vs MARG CT9 * 3 J2
Merlin Wy EGRIN RH19 ....265 K5
  GILL ME7 ....7 K3
Mermaid CI CVW DA11 ....49 H8
  WALD ME5 ....95 M8
Mermaid Ct STHWK SE1 ....24 A5
Mermaid St RYE TN31 ....338 E7
Mermerus Gdns GVE DA12 ....70 B3
Merrals Wood Ct STRD ME2 * 94 C1
Merrals Wood Rd STRD ME2 ....94 C1
Merrick Sq STHWK SE1 ....24 A6
Merrilees Rd BFN/LL DA15 ....44 A8
Merriman Rd BKHTH/KID SE3 ....42 G2
Merrimans Vw WALD ME5 * 95 P4
Merriments La
  BUR/ETCH TN19 ....316 F9
Merrion CI SBCH/RUST TN4 ....270 E1
Merrion Wy SBCH/RUST TN4 ....270 E1
Merritt Rd BROCKY SE4 ....41 N6
  RAM CT11 ....343 J2
Merrivale Hts BRDST CT10 ....143 M1
Merrow St WALW SE17 ....24 A8
Merrow Wy CROY/NA CRO 114 F1
Merry Boys Rd HOO/HM ME5 ....52 B8
Merrydown Wy CHST BR7 ....63 J7
Merryfields CI HART DA3 ....91 J1
Merryfield Gv HART DA3 ....91 J1
Merryhills CI BH/WHM TN16 ....145 N1
Merryweather CI DART DA1 ....46 F7
Mersey Rd TOWN TN10 ....215 N5
Mersham Rd PGE/AN SE20 ....61 H7
  THHTH CR7 ....60 D8
Mersham Rd THHTH CR7 ....60 D8
Merton Av HART DA3 ....91 H1
Merton CI WALD ME5 ....125 M1
Merton Gdns STMC/STPC BR5 ....86 C2
Merton La RCANTW CT4 ....166 E9
Merton PI CDW/CHF RM16 ....31 M7
Merton Rd MAID/SHEP ME15 ....186 C1
  SNWD SE25 ....81 J2
Merttins Rd PECK SE15 ....61 L4
Mervan Rd BRXS/STRHM SW2 ....40 A1
Mervyn Av ELTH/MOT SE9 ....63 N2
Meryl Gdns DEAL CT14 ....233 H8
Mesne Wy RSEV TN14 ....91 L1
Messent Rd ELTH/MOT SE9 ....42 G5
Messeter PI ELTH/MOT SE9 ....43 J7
Meteor Av WSTB CT5 ....105 J7
Meteor Ct SIT ME10 ....125 N1
Meteor Rd E/WMAL ME19 ....153 G9
Methuen Rd BELV DA17 ....28 G7
  BXLYHN DA6 ....45 H5
Metropole Rd East FOLK CT20 ....10 A7
Metropole Rd West FOLK CT20 ......10 A7
Metropolitan CI POP/IOD E14 ....25 M1
Metropolitan Whf WAP E1W * 24 F4
Meverall Av MSTR CT12 ....142 C7
Mews CI GILL ME7 ....96 E5
Mewsend BH/WHM TN16 ....145 N3
Mews St WAP E1W 24 D4
The Mews BECK BR3 * 61 N7
  GVE DA12 ....69 P1
  MARG CT9 ....12 C3
  RTWE/PEM TN2 ....271 M2
  SEV TN13 * 271 D1
  SIT ME10 ....129 N2
Meyer Rd ERITH DA8 ....29 J8
Meyrick Rd IOS ME12 ....57 L6
Miah Ter WAP E1W * 24 D4
Micawber CI WALD ME5 ....125 M4
Michael Av RAM CT11 ....17 K1
Michael Gdns GVE DA12 ....70 B3
Michaels CI LEW SE13 ....42 C4
Michaels La HART DA3 ....90 E6
Michelever Rd
  LEE/GVPK SE12 ....42 G7
Michelle Gdns MARG CT9 ....111 P5
Michleburgh Av HB CT6 ....107 N3
Mickleburgh HI HB CT6 ....107 N2
Micklemarsh CI STMC/STPC BR5 ...64 B8
Micklem Ho
  STMC/STPC BR5 ....64 B7
Mickleham Wy CROY/NA CRO 114 D1
Mickleburgh Rd HB CT6 ....251 P6
Middle Deal Rd DEAL CT14 ....232 F4
Middle Fld RTWE/PEM TN2 ....241 P9
Middle Furlong CHST BR7 * 63 J4
Middle Hill DVW CT16 ....291 K8
Middle La BGR/WK TN15 ....149 L6
Middle Md FOLKN CT19 ....310 E4
Middle Park Av ELTH/MOT SE9 ....63 J4
  ELTH/MOT SE9 ....43 H8
Middle Rw FAV ME13 ....132 C6
  KEN/WIL TN24 ....13 G2
  MAID/BEAR ME14 * 12 E5
Middlesex Rd
  MAID/SHEP ME15 ....186 A4
  MTCM CR4 ....82 D2
Middlesex St WCHPL E1 ....24 B1

Middle St ASH TN23 ....2 D4
  CROY/NA CR0 ....85 H6
  DEAL CT14 ....233 J2
  GILL ME7 ....72 C9
Middleton Av SCUP DA14 ....64 E5
Middleton Cl RHAM ME8 ....127 H1
Middleton Dr
  BERM/RHTH SE16 ....24 C5
Middletune Av LEW SE13 ....42 B5
Middletune Av SIT ME10 ....99 M7
Middle Wk RTWE/PEM TN2 ....241 H9
Middle Wall WSTB CT5 ....105 L1
Middle Yd STHWK SE1 * 24 A4
Middlings Ri SEV TN13 ....20 B5
The Middlings SEV TN13 ....20 B5
Middlings Wd SEV TN13 ....20 B5
Midfield Av BXLYHN DA7 ....45 L4
Midfield Wy STMC/STPC BR5 ....64 D7
Midholm Rd CROY/NA CR0 ....84 B7
Midhurst Av CROY/NA CR0 ....84 C3
Midhurst HI BXLYHS DA6 ....45 J5
Midley Cl MAIDW ME16 ....155 H5
Midship Cl BERM/RHTH SE16 * 24 C4
Midship Point POP/IOD E14 * 25 K5
Midsummer HI KEN/WIL TN24 ....252 C5
Midsummer Rd SNOD ME6 ....123 M5
The Midway SBGH/RUST TN4 ....270 A6
Midwinter Cl HNHL SE24 ....42 A4
Miers Ct RHAM ME8 ....97 K6
Mierscourt Rd RHAM ME8 ....97 H8
Milborough Crs
  LEE/GVPK SE12 ....42 C7
Milbourne Gv SIT ME10 * 99 M7
Milburn Rd GILL ME7 ....73 J8
Mildmay Pl RSEV TN14 ....118 E5
Mildred Cl DART DA1 ....46 C4
Mildred Rd ERITH DA8 ....29 K8
Mile End Rd WCHPL E1 ....24 F1
Mile La CRBK TN17 ....274 C7
Mile Oak Rd STPH/PW TN12 ....243 K6
Mile Rd CROY/NA CR0 ....140 A6
Miles Ct RCANTE CT3 ....169 K8
Miles Dr THMD SE28 ....27 M4
Miles La OXTED RH8 ....260 E8
Miles Pl ROCH ME1 ....95 J3
Milestone Cl FOLKN CT19 ....310 D4
Milestone Rd DVE/WH CT16 ....232 G4
  NRWD SE19 ....60 F5
Mile Stone Rd RDART DA2 ....47 H7
Miles Wy BRCH CT7 ....110 C6
Milford Cl ABYW SE2 ....28 D9
  MAIDW ME16 ....155 H7
Milford Gdns CROY/NA CR0 ....83 P2
Milford Rd CDW/CHF RM16 ....32 E4
Military Rd CANT CT1 * 5 G4
  CHAT ME4 ....6 E8
  DVW CT17 ....13 H4
  FOLK CT20 ....310 B7
  HYTHE CT21 ....308 F5
  RAM CT11 ....16 E6
  RASHW TN26 ....322 E8
  TENT TN30 ....333 L3
Milk House Cots CRBK TN17 ....276 D8
Milking La ORP BR6 ....115 P6
Milk St BMLY BR1 ....61 K6
  CAN/RD E16 ....27 J4
Milkwell Yd CMBW SE5 ....40 C2
Milkwood Rd HNHL SE24 ....40 B6
Milk Yd WAP E1W 24 F3
Millais Pl TIL RM18 ....49 L1
Millais Rd DVE/WH CT16 ....291 K6
Millars Meadow
  BKHTH/KID SE3 ....42 D5
Mill Bank HDCN TN27 ....247 M3
Millbank La LYDD TN29 ....335 N6
Millbank Rd ASH TN23 ....252 E8
Millbank Wy LEE/GVPK SE12 ....42 E6
Mill Bay FOLK CT20 ....11 F4
Millbro SWLY BR8 ....66 A7
Millbrook E/WMAL ME19 ....153 L1
  HYTHE CT21 * 309 J5
Millbrooke Av ELTH/MOT SE9 ....43 P5
Millbrook Cl
  MAID/SHEP ME15 ....185 L1
Millbrook Meadow ASH TN23 ....252 B8
Millbrook Rd BRXN/ST SW9 ....40 D2
Mill Brook Rd STMC/STPC BR5 * 87 L1
Mill Cl DVW CT17 ....290 C5
  EGRIN RH19 ....265 H9
  RCANTE CT3 ....168 F6
  RMAID ME17 ....189 K7
  STRD ME2 ....72 B6
  SWCH CT13 ....171 M9
Mill Cots EGRIN RH19 * 265 H9
  LYDD TN29 ....342 A7
  RAM CT11 ....16 C5
Mill Ct KEN/WIL TN24 ....9 L6
Mill Court Cl HB CT6 ....107 N4
Mill Crs TON TN9 ....210 C8
Millcroft Rd HOO/HM ME3 ....52 B4
Milldale Cl DEAL CT14 ....232 G5
Millen Ct EYN DA4 ....89 P1
Millenium Ter CANT CT1 * 166 B6
Millennium Cl CAN/RD E16 ....26 F4
Millennium Dr POP/IOD E14 ....25 N6
Millennium Sq STHWK SE1 * 24 C5
Millennium Wy BRDST CT10 ....112 G9
  GNWCH SE10 ....25 P6
  IOS ME12 ....57 K6
Millennium Whf POP/IOD E14 * 25 M7
Millens Rw FAV ME15 * 162 E9
Millers Cl STMC/STPC CT2 ....166 F8
Miller Cl BMLY BR1 ....62 E4
  KEN/WIL TN24 ....3 G4
  SIT ME10 ....99 P6
Miller Ct IOS ME12 ....78 A2
Miller Rd CROY/NA CR0 ....70 C1
  GVE DA12 ....70 L1
Millers Ct WSTB CT5 ....106 C1
Millers La MSTR CT12 ....140 D5
Millersthumb CRBK TN17 ....275 M3
Millers Wk GREB TN17 ....92 B6
Millers Rd DIT/AY ME20 ....154 C5
Millers Yd CANT CT1 * 4 C7

Miller Wy STRD ME2 ....72 C5
Mill Fld BRDST CT10 ....113 L8
  RCANTE CT3 ....200 F1
Mill Hall Rd ASH TN23 ....252 A8
  HART DA3 ....91 H6
  RASHW TN26 ....279 L9
  RDV CT15 ....230 C1
  RFOLK CT18 ....288 F6
  SIT ME10 ....129 N2
Millfield Cl RFOLK CT18 ....288 E7
Millfield Dr GVW DA11 ....69 J7
Millfield La HART DA3 ....91 H6
Millfield Mnr WSTB CT5 ....105 M5
  FAV ME15 ....162 G1
  MSTR CT12 ....142 C5
Millfields RDV CT15 ....259 P1
  WALD ME7 ....126 A3
Millfields Cl STMC/STPC BR5 ....87 J1
Mill Fields Rd HYTHE CT21 ....308 E5
Millforthorpe Rd STRD ME2 ....71 L8
Mill Gdns SYD SE26 ....61 H3
Mill Gn SWCH CT13 ....201 M9
Millhall DIT/AY ME20 ....154 A1
Mill Hall Rd DIT/AY ME20 ....154 A1
Millharbour POP/IOD E14 ....25 L6
Mill Hl ASH TN23 * 282 C6
  DEAL CT14 ....232 F6
  EDEN TN8 ....262 G6
Mill Hill La GVE DA12 ....70 F4
Millhouse La E/WMAL ME19 ....152 E1
Millhouse Pl WNWD SE27 ....60 B3
Milligan St POP/IOD E14 ....25 J3
Mill La BGR/WK TN15 ....150 C7
  BGR/WK TN15 ....179 N8
  BH/WHM TN16 ....176 D3
  BRCH CT7 ....110 G7
  CANT CT1 * 4 E5
  CANTW/ST CT2 ....166 B4
  CDW/CHF RM16 ....33 H2
  CRBK TN17 ....246 F8
  CRBK TN17 ....277 H1
  CROY/NA CR0 ....F7
  DEAL CT14 ....201 N6
  DEAL CT14 ....231 N5
  DVE/WH CT16 ....291 J5
  EGRIN RH19 ....264 A3
  EYN DA4 ....89 K5
  HB CT6 ....107 N5
  HDCN TN27 ....247 ...
  KEN/WIL TN24 ....253 J9
  LING RH7 ....235 J7
  LYDD TN29 ....325 M3
  MARG CT9 ....15 G5
  ORP BR6 ....116 B4
  OXTED RH8 ....175 J8
  RASHE TN25 ....305 P2
  RCANTE CT3 ....169 M2
  RCANTW CT4 ....194 E4
  RCANTW CT4 ....197 L2
  RCANTW CT4 ....226 E8
  RCANTW CT4 ....228 D5
  RDV CT15 ....259 G5
  RFOLK CT18 ....288 E7
  RMAID ME17 ....185 J8
  RSEV TN14 ....118 E4
  RSEV TN14 ....149 H6
  RSIT ME9 ....97 P8
  RTON TN11 ....209 N2
  SNOD ME6 ....124 A5
  STPH/PW TN12 ....244 B3
  SWCH CT13 ....201 H8
  TENT TN30 ....333 L5
  TON TN9 ....210 F8
  WALD ME5 ....95 P5
  WALD ME5 ....125 J4
  WBY/YAL ME18 ....183 L3
  WBY/YAL ME18 ....213 P4
  WOOL/PLUM SE18 ....27 N8
  WTHK RM20 ....31 N8
Millmark Gv NWCR SE14 ....41 L3
Millmead MARG CT9 ....113 J4
Millmead Gdns MARG CT9 ....113 J4
Mill Meadow Yd
  MAIDW ME16 * 12 D3
Millmead Rd MAIDW ME16 * 12 C4
Mill Ms DEAL CT14 ....232 C5
Mill Pl CHST BR7 ....63 J4
  DART DA1 ....46 A5
  POP/IOD E14 ....25 H2
Mill Pond Cl RSEV TN14 ....149 J6
Millpond Ct STRD ME2 ....72 B7
Millpond Est
  BERM/RHTH SE16 * 24 E5
Millpond La TENT TN30 ....300 C5
Mill Pond Rd DART DA1 ....46 B4
Mill Race DVW CT17 ....290 C4
Mill Rd CAN/RD E16 ....26 G4
  CANTW/ST CT2 ....137 K9
  DEAL CT14 ....232 G5
  ERITH DA8 ....29 J7
  GILL ME7 ....73 J1
  GVW DA11 ....49 J8
  HYTHE CT21 ....309 J5
  LYDD TN29 ....326 F2
  LYDD TN29 ....342 C6
  PUR RM19 ....30 F9
  RASHW TN26 ....280 D5
  RCANTE CT3 ....199 H1
  RCANTE CT3 ....200 B4
  RDART DA2 ....66 F3
  RYE TN31 ....338 F5
  SEV TN13 ....148 D5
  SOCK/AV RM15 ....30 F5
Mill Rw BXLY DA5 * 45 K8
Mills Cl LYDD TN29 * 77 P1
Mills Crs BGR/WK TN15 ....149 L5

Millstock Ter
  MAID/SHEP ME15 * 185 K1
Mill Stone Ct EYN DA4 ....67 J8
Millstone Ms EYN DA4 ....67 J7
Millstream Cl FAV ME13 ....132 F6
  RRTW TN3 ....268 C6
  WSTB CT5 ....105 M5
Millstream Gn KEN/WIL TN24 ....283 J1
Mill Stream Pl TON TN9 ....210 C7
Millstream Rd STHWK SE1 ....24 C6
Mill St BH/WHM TN16 ....176 E8
  CRBK TN17 ....318 B4
  DVE/WH CT16 ....290 E2
  E/WMAL ME19 ....153 N5
  MAID/SHEP ME14 ....12 E5
  MAID/SHEP ME15 ....185 L8
  SIT ME10 ....99 M9
  STHWK SE1 ....24 C7
Millstrood Rd WSTB CT5 ....105 M6
Mill Ter RCANTW CT4 * 165 L9
Mill Vw HAYES BR2 ....62 E9
Mill Vw KEN/WIL TN24 ....253 J9
  RASHW TN26 ....302 F4
Mill View Gdns CROY/NA CR0 ....84 A7
Mill Vw HB CT6 ....107 N5
Mill Wk MAIDW ME16 ....154 F9
Millwall Dock Rd POP/IOD E14 ....25 K6
Mill Wall Pl SWCH CT13 ....201 P2
Millway RCANTE CT3 ....169 J8
  SIT ME10 ....99 M9
Millwood Ct CHAT ME4 ....6 B5
Millwood Rd STMC/STPC BR5 ....24 D3
Mill Yd WCHPL E1 ....24 F3
Milne Gdns ELTH/MOT SE9 ....43 J6
Milne Pk East CROY/NA CR0 ....114 G5
Milne Pk West CROY/NA CR0 ....114 G5
Milner Crs RCANTE CT3 ....229 H1
Milner Ct KEN/WIL TN24 ....253 J9
Milner Rd CROY/NA CR0 ....60 C9
  WSTB CT5 ....105 H8
Milner Rd GILL ME7 ....73 K8
Milners RMAID ME17 ....187 J5
Rio Rd EDUL SE22 ....46 E4
Milroy Av GVW DA11 ....69 J1
Milstead Cl IOS ME12 ....57 K8
  MAID/BEAR ME14 ....13 K3
Milsted Rd RHAM ME8 ....96 F4
Milton Av CROY/NA CR0 ....83 J4
  HOO/HM ME3 ....52 B9
Milton Cl CANT CT1 * 167 H6
  DVE/WH CT16 ....24 C7
  STHWK SE1 ....24 C7
Milton Ct RCANTW CT4 ....194 G4
Milton Court Rd NWCR SE14 ....25 H9
Milton Crs EGRIN RH19 ....264 F7
Milton Dr RTWE/PEM TN2 ....257 L2
Milton Gdns TIL RM18 ....49 M2
Milton Hall Rd GVE DA12 ....49 P9
Milton La E/WMAL ME19 ....153 J9
Milton Pl GVE DA12 ....49 N7
Milton Rd ASH TN23 ....2 C3
  BELV DA17 ....29 J4
  CANT CT1 ....166 F6
  CROY/NA CR0 ....291 J5
  GILL ME7 ....7 J6
  GRAYS RM17 ....32 C7
  GVE DA12 ....49 M7
  HB CT6 ....107 M4
  RASHW TN26 ....281 N7
  SCUP DA14 ....45 J4
  STMC/STPC BR5 ....
Monk's Wy SWCM DA10 ....171 N8
Monks Well SWCM DA10 ....48 A5
Monk Ter FSTH SE23 ....61 M1

Minters Orch BGR/WK TN15 ....151 L5
Mint Rd WLGTN SM6 ....86 A9
The Mint CANTW/ST CT2 * 166 B3
  RYE TN31 ....338 F7
Mint Wk CROY/NA CR0 ....83 H7
  WARL CR6 ....144 A2
The Mint Yd CANT CT1 * 5 F3
Miranda Cl WCHPL E1 ....24 F1
Miranda Ct IOS ME12 ....57 K7
Mirfield St CHARL SE7 ....26 D6
Miriam Rd WOOL/PLUM SE18 ....27 M8
Miskin Rd DART DA1 ....46 C8
  MAID/BEAR ME14 ....73 K2
Misling La RCANTW CT4 ....256 B3
Mission Pl PECK SE15 ....40 D2
Mistletoe Cl CROY/NA CR0 ....84 A5
Mitali Pas WCHPL E1 ....24 D2
Mitcham Wy CROY/NA CR0 ....82 D3
  LYDD TN29 ....326 C6
Mitchell Av CHAT ME4 ....95 J4
  GVW DA11 ....69 H1
  RFOLK CT18 ....288 E7
Mitchell Cl ABYW SE2 ....28 B8
  DART DA1 ....66 E1
  RMAID ME17 ....189 K6
Mitchell Rd E/WMAL ME19 ....182 G1
  ORP BR6 ....88 G8
Mitchell St FOLKN CT19 * 310 A5
Mitchell Wy BMLY BR1 ....62 F7
Mitchem Cl BGR/WK TN15 ....120 B2
Mitre Ct TON TN9 ....210 F8
Mitre Rd ROCH ME1 ....18 E7
  SEV TN13 ....148 A2
Mitre St HDTCH EC3A 24 B2
The Mitre POP/IOD E14 ....25 J3
Moat Cl ORP BR6 ....116 G1
  SEV TN13 ....148 A8
Moat Ct ELTH/MOT SE9 * 43 K7
Moat Crt WELL DA16 ....45 J4
Moat Farm RTWE/PEM TN2 ....270 D4
Moat Farm Cl FOLKN CT19 ....310 F6
Moat Farm Rd FOLKN CT19 ....310 F4
  HOO/HM ME3 ....54 A2
Moatfield Meadow ASH TN23 ....282 G4
Moat La CANTW/ST CT2 ....167 L1
  EDEN TN8 ....267 J1
  ERITH DA8 ....46 A2
  RCANTE CT3 ....200 E1
Moat Rd EGRIN RH19 ....265 H6
  HDCN TN27 ....247 L4
Moat Sole SWCH CT13 ....201 N1
The Moat HDCN TN27 ....221 H3
Moat Wy QBOR ME11 ....77 J2
Mockbeggar La HDCN TN27 ....299 M3
Mockett Dr BRDST CT10 ....113 K6
Mock La ASH TN23 ....281 N2
Model Farm Cl ELTH/MOT SE9 ....63 J2
Moffat Rd THHTH CR7 ....60 C8
Moiety Rd POP/IOD E14 ....25 K5
Moira Rd ELTH/MOT SE9 ....43 K5
Molash Rd STMC/STPC BR5 ....87 L1
Molehill Rd WSTB CT5 ....106 C7
Molescroft ELTH/MOT SE9 ....63 K2
Molescroft Wy TON TN9 ....240 C2
Moles Md EDEN TN8 ....206 D8
Molesworth St LEW SE13 ....42 A4
Molineaux Rd MSTR CT12 ....141 J6
Molland Cl RCANTE CT3 ....170 D9
Molland La RCANTE CT3 ....170 D9
Molland Lea RCANTE CT3 ....170 D9
Mollison Ri GVE DA12 ....70 A4
Molloy Rd RASHW TN26 ....281 N7
Molyneux Park Gdns
  SBGH/RUST TN4 ....22 B3
Molyneux Park Rd
  SBGH/RUST TN4 ....22 A2
Monarch Cl TIL RM18 ....49 M3
  WALD ME5 ....95 M3
  WWKM BR4 ....85 J8
Monarch Dr CAN/RD E16 ....26 E1
  SIT ME10 ....99 N4
Monarch Ms
  STRHM/NOR SW16 ....60 A4
Monarch Rd BELV DA17 ....28 F6
Mona Rd PECK SE15 ....41 J3
Monastery Av DVE/WH CT16 ....8 D1
Monastery St CANT CT1 ....5 G4
Mona St CAN/RD E16 ....26 E1
Monckton's Av
  MAID/BEAR ME14 ....155 N5
Monckton's Dr
  MAID/BEAR ME14 ....155 N5
Monckton's La
  MAID/BEAR ME14 ....155 N6
Moncrief Cl CAN/RD E16 ....26 F1
Moncrieff Cl CHAM ME6 ....40 E2
Moncrieff Pl PECK SE15 * 41 F3
Moncrieff St PECK SE15 ....156 A1
Mongeham Church Cl
  WADH TN5 ....232 C5
Mongeham Rd DEAL CT14 ....232 C5
Monica Cl FAV ME13 ....133 J8
Monins Rd DVW CT17 ....291 J8
Monivea Rd BECK BR3 ....61 N9
Monk St WOOL/PLUM SE18 ....27 H7
Monks Wk HDCN TN27 ....221 H3
Monkery La HDCN TN27 ....191 P9
Monk Dr CAN/RD E16 ....26 E2
Monkey Cl ABYW SE2 ....28 E4
  CANTW/ST CT2 ....167 J2
  FAV ME15 ....132 C5
Monkshill Rd FAV ME13 ....134 B3
Monks La EDEN TN8 ....205 N4
  WADH TN5 ....294 E3
Monks Orchard Rd BECK BR3 ....84 E1
Monk St WOOL/PLUM SE18 ....27 H7
Monks Wk HDCN TN27 ....221 H3
Monks Wy BECK BR3 ....84 D1
  DVE/WH CT16 ....291 H4
  RYE TN31 ....330 A5
  STMC/STPC BR5 ....86 C1
Monk Ter FSTH SE23 ....61 M1

Monkton Ct WSTB CT5 ....106 C6
Monkton Court La RDV CT15 ....260 E1
Monkton Gdns MARG CT9 ....113 K2
Monkton Pl RAM CT11 ....16 E3
Monkton Rd BGR/WK TN15 ....151 J5
  WELL DA16 ....141 H6
Monkton St MSTR CT12 ....140 E6
Monkwood Rd ROCH ME1 ....94 G6
Monmouth Cl MTCM CR4 ....82 D1
  WELL DA16 ....45 H8
Monnow Rd SOCK/AV RM15 ....30 F5
  STHWK SE1 ....24 D8
Mons Cl SIT ME10 ....99 N5
Monson Rd NWCR SE14 ....41 K1
  RTW TN1 ....22 E3
Monson Wy RTW TN1 ....22 E3
Mons Wy HAYES BR2 ....85 P3
Montacute Gdns
  RTWE/PEM TN2 ....22 B7
Montacute Rd CAT SE6 ....41 M8
  CROY/NA CR0 ....114 F3
  RTWE/PEM TN2 ....270 D7
Montague Av BROCKY SE4 ....41 M5
Montague Cl STMC/STPC SE14 ....24 A4
  SWLY BR8 ....88 E1
Montague Ct IOS ME12 ....57 K7
Montague Pl SWLY BR8 ....88 E1
Montague Rd CROY/NA CR0 ....83 G5
  RAM CT11 ....17 G1
Montague Sq PECK SE15 ....41 J1
Montague St HB CT6 ....107 J1
  RTWE/PEM TN2 * 85 K1
Montagu Gdns WLCTN SM6 ....82 B8
Montana Gdns SYD SE26 ....61 M4
Montbelle Rd ELTH/MOT SE9 ....63 M2
Montbretia Cl STMC/STPC BR5 ....87 K1
Montcalm Rd CHARL SE7 ....43 H1
Montcalm Ter
  DVE/WH CT16 * 291 J4
Monteagle Wy PECK SE15 ....41 H4
Montefiore Av RAM CT11 ....145 L3
Montefiore Cots RAM CT11 * 17 H1
Monteith Cl RRTW TN3 ....269 M5
Montem Rd FSTH SE23 ....61 M1
Monterey Cl BXLY DA5 ....65 L1
Montesquieu Ter
  CAN/RD E16 * 26 A2
Montfort Cl ASH TN23 ....282 C1
  CANTW/ST CT2 ....167 K1
Montfort Dr E/WMAL ME19 ....153 H9
Montfort Rd BGR/WK TN15 ....149 K2
  STRD ME2 ....71 M8
  WALD ME5 ....125 K3
Montgomerie Ms FSTH SE23 ....41 J8
Montgomery Av MAIDS ME15 ....155 M7
Montgomery Cl BFN/LL DA15 ....44 A6
  MTCM CR4 * 82 D1
Montgomery Rd EYN DA4 ....67 K7
  GILL ME7 ....7 J1
  SBGH/RUST TN4 ....22 B1
Montgomery Wy FOLKN CT19 ....310 G3
Monthope Rd WCHPL E1 ....24 D1
Montpelier Av BXLY DA5 ....45 K8
  WSTB CT5 ....105 L8
Montpelier Ga MAIDW ME16 * 154 C7
Montpelier Pl WCHPL E1 ....24 F2
Montpelier Rd PECK SE15 ....41 J3
Montpelier Rw BKHTH/KID SE3 ....42 D5
Montpelier V BKHTH/KID SE3 * 42 D5
Montrave Rd PGE/AN SE20 ....61 H1
Montreal Cl DVE/WH CT16 ....291 J4
Montreal Rd SEV TN13 ....148 D8
  TIL RM18 ....49 L4
Montrose Cl BFN/LL DA15 ....44 C8
  WALD ME5 ....96 B4
  WELL DA16 ....45 P4
Montrose Wy FSTH SE23 ....44 B4
  FSTH SE23 * 41 K9
Mont St Aignan Wy
  EDEN TN8 ....206 D9
Montserrat Cl NRWD SE19 ....60 D4
Monument Av MON EC3R 24 A3
Monument Wy KEN/WIL TN24 ....283 J1
Monypenny CRBK TN17 ....319 M3
Monypenny Cl RTON TN11 ....211 N2
Monza St WAP E1W 24 F3
Moodkee St BERM/RHTH SE16 ....24 F4
Moon Ct LEE/GVPK SE12 ....42 C5
Moonfleet Ct SIT ME10 ....99 P5
Moon HI RDV CT15 ....259 P1
Moon La LING RH7 ....265 N1
Moonstone Dr WALD ME5 ....125 N3
Moonstone Sq SIT ME10 ....99 K8
Moorcroft Gdns HAYES BR2 ....85 M4
Moorden La RTON TN11 ....208 F9
Moordown WOOL/PLUM SE18 ....45 M1
Moore Av TIL RM18 ....49 M1
  WTHK RM20 ....31 P8
Moore Cl LYDD TN29 ....335 L2
  RDART DA2 ....67 K1
Moreland Rd BMLY BR1 ....62 D5
Moorend Rd NRWD SE19 ....60 C5
  SWCM DA10 ....48 C7
Moore St STRD ME2 ....72 A7
Moorfield Cl ERITH DA8 * 136 G9
Moorfield Rd ORP BR6 ....88 G1
Moorfields LVPST EC2M 24 A1
Moorfields Highwalk
  BARB EC2Y 24 A1
Moorgate LVPST EC2M 24 A1
Moorgate Pl LOTH EC2R * 24 A2
Moorhead Wy BKHTH/KID SE3 ....42 F4
Moorhen Cl ERITH DA8 ....46 C3
Moor HI HAWK TN18 ....317 H6
Moorhouse Rd OXTED RH8 ....176 A6
Mooring Rd ROCH ME1 ....95 J5
The Moorings EGRIN RH19 ....264 D5
  MAID/SHEP ME15 * 13 F5
Moor La WEST 101 K9
Moorland Rd BRXN/ST SW9 ....40 B5
Moor La BARB EC2Y 24 A1
  LYDD TN29 ....335 L2
  RASHW TN26 ....302 G8
Moor Park Cl RHAM ME8 ....96 C4
Moor Pl EGRIN RH19 ....264 C6
  LVPST EC2M 24 A1
The Moor Rd RSEV TN14 ....148 G5

Moorstock Rd BMLY BR1 .....62 C3
Moorstock La RASHE TN25 ...285 K6
Moor St RHAM ME8 ....97 J6
The Moor HAWK TN18 ......317 H6
Moorwell Dr RDV CT15 ......229 N9
Morant Rd CDW/CHF RM16 ...33 J6
Morants Court Rd SEV TN13 ..148 B3
Morant St POP/IOD E14 .....25 K5
Moray Av BRCH CT7 ....110 G5
Mordaunt Av WGOS CT8 .....111 M5
Morden Av LEW SE13 ....42 A3
Morden La LEW SE13 ....42 A2
Morden Rd BKHTH/KID SE3 ...42 E5
Morden Road Ms
  BKHTH/KID SE3 ....42 E5
Morden St LEW SE13 ......41 P2
Morden Wharf Rd
  ROCH ME1 * 19 F7
Mordred Rd CAT SE6 ....62 C1
Morecambe Cl WCHPL E1 * ..24 C1
Morecambe St POP/IOD E14 ..25 L8
More Cl CAN/RD E16 ....26 A2
Morehall Av FOLKN CT19 ...310 C5
Morelands Av CDW/CHF RM16 .32 D5
Moret Cl SEV TN13 ....148 G7
Morello Cl RSIT ME9 ......131 H3
  SWLY BR8 ....88 C1
More London Riverside
  STHWK SE1 ....24 B4
Moremead Rd CAT SE6 .....61 M3
Morement Rd HOO/HM ME3 ...73 K1
Moreton St CAT SE6 ....61 N3
Moreton Cl SWLY BR8 ......88 D1
Moreton Rd SAND/SEL CR2 ..85 J9
Moreton Ter RASHW TN26 ...281 M7
Morewood Cl SEV TN13 ....148 E8
Morgan Dr RDART DA2 .....47 L8
Morgan Kirby Gdns
  FAV ME13 * 162 G7
Morgan Kirby's Gdn
  FAV ME13 ....162 G7
Morgan Rd BMLY BR1 ......62 E6
  STRD ME2 ....72 A7
Morgans La STHWK SE1 ....24 B4
Morgan St CAN/RD E16 ....26 A4
Morhen Cl SNOD ME6 ......123 M6
Moriarty Cl BMLY BR1 .....86 C1
Morkyns Wk DUL SE21 * ...60 E2
Morland Av CROY/NA CR0 ...83 K5
  DART DA1 ....46 B6
Morland Dr RRTW TN3 .....295 J2
  STRD ME2 ....72 A6
Morland Rd CROY/NA CR0 ...83 K4
  PGE/AN SE20 ....61 K6
Morley Cl ORP BR6 ....86 C6
Morley Dr STPH/PW TN12 ...273 N2
  LEW SE13 ....61 N7
Morley Rd SWDN TN13 .....210 G9
Morley Sq CDW/CHF RM16 ..33 H7
Morley's Rd RSEV TN14 ....179 J9
Morna Rd CMBW SE5 ......40 C3
Mornington Av HAYES BR2 ..62 G1
Mornington Cl
  BH/WHM TN16 ....145 N2
Mornington Ct BXLY DA5 ...45 M9
Mornington Ms CMBW SE5 ..40 D7
Mornington Rd NWCR SE14 .41 M1
Morocco St STHWK SE1 ....24 B5
Morris Av HB CT6 ....106 E2
Morris Cl CROY/NA CR0 ....84 B3
  E/WMAL ME19 ....153 N3
  ORP BR6 ....86 F7
Morris Ct GILL ME7 ....96 C1
Morris Court Cl RSIT ME9 ..130 C3
Morris Gdns DART DA1 .....46 H6
Morris Rd POP/IOD E14 ....25 L1
Morris St WCHPL E1 ....24 E2
Morra La RMAID ME17 .....217 N1
Mortimer Cl ASH TN23 ....282 E1
Mortimer Rd BH/WHM TN16 .115 M6
  DVE/WH CT16 ....9 G2
  ERITH DA8 ....29 J9
  ORP BR6 ....87 H6
Mortimers Av HOO/HM ME3 .52 A8
Mortimer St HB CT6 ....107 L1
Mortlake Cl CROY/NA CR0 ..83 H6
Mortlake Rd CAN/RD E16 ...26 C6
Mortley Cl TON TN9 ....210 F9
Morton Cl MAID/SHEP ME15 .186 A5
Morton Ms WLGTN SM6 ....82 B9
Morton Rd EGRIN RH19 ....265 H9
Morvale Cl BELV DA17 .....28 E7
Morval Rd BRXS/STRHM SW2 .40 A6
Moselle Rd BH/WHM TN16 ..115 M6
Mosquito Rd E/WMAL ME19 .152 C9
Moss Bank GRAYS RM17 ...32 A8
Mossbank WALD ME5 ......125 M2
Moss Cl WCHPL E1 ....24 D1
Mossdown Cl BELV DA17 ...28 F7
Moss End Ms EHAM E6 * ...13 K2
Moss Gdns SAND/SEL CR2 ..114 A2
Mosslea Rd HAYES BR2 ....85 N2
  ORP BR6 ....86 D7
  PGE/AN SE20 ....61 J5
Moss Rd SOCK/AV RM15 ...31 K1
Moss Wy RDART DA2 ....47 N3
Mossy Gld RHAM ME8 .....97 H8
Mostyn Rd BRXN/ST SW9 ...40 C8
  MAID/BEAR ME14 ....13 K4
Mosul Wy HAYES BR2 ......86 C6
Mosyer Dr STMC/STPC BR5 ..87 L6
Mote Av MAID/BEAR ME14 ..186 A2
  MAID/SHEP ME15 ....13 H6
Mote Pk MAID/SHEP ME15 ..186 A2
Mote Rd BGR/WK TN15 ....180 D4
  MAID/SHEP ME15 ....13 G6
Motherwell Wy WTHK RM20 .31 K8
Moth House
  WOOL/PLUM SE18 * 43 J1
Motney Hill Rd RHAM ME8 ..97 K2
Mottingham Gdns
  ELTH/MOT SE9 ....62 H1
Mottingham La
  LEE/GVPK SE12 ....42 G9
Mottingham Rd
  ELTH/MOT SE9 ....63 J2

Mottisfont Rd ABYW SE2 ...27 P6
Mouat Ct WALD ME5 ....125 M2
Mouchotte Cl BH/WHM TN16 .115 L4
Moultain Hl SWLY BR8 .....88 F1
Mountacre Cl SYD SE26 ....60 F7
Mount Adon Pk EDUL SE22 ..40 G8
Mountague Pl POP/IOD E14 .25 M3
Mountain Cl BGR/WK TN15 *.151 J1
Mountain St RCANTW CT4 ..194 C6
Mount Ash Rd SYD SE26 ...61 H2
Mount Av WBY/YAL ME18 ...213 P1
Mountbatten Av HOO/HM ME3.71 L3
  WALD ME5 ....95 M7
Mountbatten Cl RNWD SE19 .60 E4
  WOOL/PLUM SE18 ....27 M9
Mountbatten Wy
  RASHE TN25 ....284 F2
Mount Castle La RMAID ME17.219 N1
Mount Charles Wk
  RCANTW CT4 * 197 L2
Mount Cl BMLY BR1 ....63 J7
  SEV TN13 ....148 E8
Mount Cots BXLYHS DA6 * ..44 G5
Mount Ct WWKM BR4 ......85 H6
Mount Culver Av SCUP DA14 .64 F5
Mount Dr MAID/BEAR ME14 ..156 E8
Mount Egcumbe Rd
  SBGH/RUST ME4 * 22 C4
Mount Ephraim
  SBGH/RUST ME4 ....22 B4
Mount Ephraim La RTW TN1 .22 D3
Mountfield BGR/WK TN15 ...151 K5
Mount Fld FAV ME13 ......132 K5
  OBOR ME11 ....77 J2
Mountfield Cl CAT SE6 .....42 B8
  MEO DA13 ....121 P5
Mountfield Gdns RTW TN1 ..22 E5
Mountfield Pk TON TN9 ....240 F1
Mountfield Rd NROM TN28 ..337 H7
  RTW TN1 ....22 E5
Mountfield Ter CAT SE6 ....42 B8
Mountfield Wy
  STMC/STPC BR5 ....87 K1
  WGOS CT8 ....111 J7
Mount Gdns SYD SE26 .....61 H2
Mount Green Av MSTR CT12 .142 C7
Mount Harry Rd SEV TN13 ..148 F8
Mountjoy Cl ABYW SE2 ....28 A5
Mount La MAID/BEAR ME14 ..156 E8
  RSIT ME9 ....127 M2
Mount Lodge Ter ROCH ME1 *.94 G5
Mount Pleasant
  BH/WHM TN16 ....145 N2
  CANTW/ST CT2 ....135 P7
  DIT/AY ME20 ....154 F1
  DVW CT17 * 7 G4
  RTON TN11 ....210 A4
  STPH/PW TN12 ....242 C3
  TENT TN30 ....301 K7
  WALD ME5 ....7 F6
  WNWD SE27 ....60 C3
Mount Pleasant Av RTW TN1 .22 E4
Mountpleasant Cl
  RFOLK CT18 ....287 H1
Mount Pleasant Ct
  RTON TN11 * 210 A4
Mount Pleasant Dr
  MAID/BEAR ME14 ....156 D7
Mount Pleasant La RRTW TN3.294 G1
Mount Pleasant Pl
  WOOL/PLUM SE18 ....27 L7
Mount Pleasant Rd DART DA1.46 F3
  FOLK CT20 ....11 F3
  LEW SE13 ....42 A7
  LING RH7 ....234 D6
  RSEV TN14 ....178 G9
Mount Ri FSTH SE23 ......61 J1
Mount Rd BXLYHS DA6 .....44 G6
  CANT CT1 ....167 H6
  CHAT ME4 ....6 C6
  DART DA1 ....45 P7
  DVW CT17 ....313 H1
  NRWD SE19 ....60 D5
  ROCH ME1 * 94 F4
Mounts Cl IDEAL CT14 .....11 H1
Mountsfield Cl MAIDW ME16 .12 A2
Mounts Hl CRBK TN17 .....298 D6
Mount Sion RTW TN1 .....22 D6
Mountsole La CRBK TN17 ...319 N4
Mounts Pond Rd
  BKHTH/KID SE3 ....42 B5
Mounts Rd SWCM DA10 ....47 P7
Mount St HYTHE CT21 .....309 H6
Mount Sq RASHE TN25 ....252 C5
Mount Ter WCHPL E1 ......24 E1
The Mount BMLY BR1 * 63 J7
  BXLYHS DA6 * 45 K6
  CHAT ME4 * 6 C6
  RRTW TN3 * 132 E2
Mountview RSIT ME9 ......129 J3
Mount View Ct CHAT ME4 * .6 D5
Mount View Rd HB CT6 ....107 M4
Mount Vis WNWD SE27 ....60 D2
Mowbray Rd NRWD SE19 ...60 F7
Mowll St BRXN/ST SW9 ....40 A1
Moyes Cl MSTR CT12 ......142 C6
Moyle Cl RHAM ME8 ......126 C1
Moyle Pl HYTHE CT21 * ...309 H6
Moys Cl CROY/NA CR0 .....82 D3
Mozart Ct CHAT ME4 * 6 C7
Muckingford Rd til RTIL RM18.33 L7
Mucking Wharf Rd
  SLH/COR SS17 ....34 B2
Muggeridge Cl SAND/SEL CR2.83 J9
Muirfield Cl BERM/RHTH SE16.28 E4
Muirfield Crs POP/IOD E14 ..25 L6
Muirkirk Rd CAT SE6 ......42 A9
Muir St CAN/RD E16 ......27 H3
Mulberry Cl GILL ME7 .....126 D1
  LYDD TN29 ....337 L1
  MEO DA13 ....92 C3
  RASHW TN26 ....17 H1
  SBGH/RUST ME4 ....240 G8
Mulberry Ct CANT CT1 .....4 D5
  HYTHE CT21 * 309 J4

Mulberry Fld SWCH CT13 ...201 N1
Mulberry Hl RCANTW CT4 ..194 G2
Mulberry La CROY/NA CR0 ..83 L5
Mulberry Ms NWCR SE14 ...41 M2
Mulberry Pl ELTH/MOT SE9 ..43 H7
Mulberry Rd ASH TN23 ....252 A6
Mulberry St WCHPL E1 * ...24 D2
Mulberry Wy DA17 ....29 H5
Mulgrave Rd CROY/NA CR0 ..83 J8
Mullein Ct GRAYS RM17 ...32 E9
Multon Rd BGR/WK TN15 ...120 B1
Mulvaney Wy STHWK SE1 * ..24 B5
Mumford Mills GNWCH SE10 .41 N1
Mumford Rd HNHL SE24 * ..40 B6
Mummery Ct FAV ME13 ....162 B2
Muncies Ms CAT SE6 .....62 A1
Mundania Rd EDUL SE22 ...41 H7
Munday Bois Rd HDCN TN27 .219 M9
Munday Rd CAN/RD E16 ....26 B2
Munford Dr SWCM DA10 ...48 C3
Mungo Park Rd GVE DA12 ..69 P4
Mungo Park Wy
  STMC/STPC BR5 ....87 K4
Munnery Wy ORP BR6 .....86 B7
Munn's La RSIT ME9 ......97 P8
Munsgore La RSIT ME9 ....128 F3
Munton Rd WALW SE17 ....24 A7
Murchison Av BXLY DA5 ...44 F9
Murillo Rd LEW SE13 .....42 B5
Murrain Dr MAID/SHEP ME15.186 D2
Murray Av BMLY BR1 ......62 F8
Murray House
  WOOL/PLUM SE18 * 43 J1
Murray Rd STMC/STPC BR5 ..72 C6
Murray Sq CAN/RD E16 ....26 B3
Murston Rd SIT ME10 .....130 A2
Murston vle IOS ME12 * ...78 A2
Murton-Neale Cl HAWK TN18.317 J4
Murton Pl FAV ME13 * 133 H7
Musbury St WCHPL E1 .....24 F2
Muscal W6 ....51 J8
Muschamp Rd PECK SE15 ..41 H4
Muscovy St MON EC3R 24 C4
Muscovy Wy HB CT6 ......107 K3
Musgrave Av EGRIN RH19 ..265 H9
Musgrave Cl MSTR CT12 ...141 N2
Musgore Rd NWCR SE14 ...41 N1
Musket La RMAID ME17 ....187 K1
Mussenden La EYN DA4 * ..65 N6
Mustang Rd E/WMAL ME19 ..152 G9
Mustards Rd IOS ME12 .....80 B5
Mutrix Gdns MARG CT9 ....111 P4
Mutton Cl MARG CT9 ......111 P4
Mutton Hl LING RH7 ......265 K1
Mutton La WTON TN28 ....132 D6
Mycenae Rd BKHTH/KID SE3 .42 B2
Myddelton Cl RCANTW CT4 ..195 K3
Myers La NWCR SE14 .....41 M1
Mylis Cl SYD SE26 ....61 H3
Mymms Cl WSTB SE9 .....106 B6
Mynn Crs MAID/BEAR ME14 .156 D8
Myra St ABYW SE2 ....28 C3
Myrdle St WCHPL E1 .....24 D2
Myron Pl LEW SE13 ......42 A6
Myrtle Aly WOOL/PLUM SE18.27 H6
Myrtle Cl ERITH DA8 .....45 N1
Myrtle Crs WALD ME5 ....95 M5
Myrtledene Rd ABYW SE2 ..27 P8
Myrtle Gv ASH TN23 .....252 A5
Myrtle Rd CROY/NA CR0 ...84 D7
  DART DA1 ....66 D1
  IOS ME12 ....11 H1
The Myrtles IOS ME12 * ...7 H7
Myrtle Vls NROM TN28 ....336 F7
  STPH/PW TN12 ....245 H4
Mystole La RCANTW CT4 ..195 K3
Mystole Rd RCANTW CT4 ..195 K3
Myton Rd DUL SE21 ......60 D2

N

Nackington Pk RCANTW CT4 .166 F8
Nackington Rd RCANTW CT4 .196 F2
Nag's Head La ROCH ME1 ..19 H7
  WELL DA16 ....44 D4
Nailbourne Cl RCANTW CT4 .228 A3
Naildown Rd HYTHE CT21 ..309 M4
Nairn Ct TIL RM18 * 49 K3
Nairne Cl RASHW TN26 ....281 M8
Nairne Gv HNHL SE24 .....40 D6
Nairn St POP/IOD E14 .....25 M1
Namptonbush La LYDD TN29 .335 H6
Namton Dr THHTH CR7 ....82 E1
Namur Pl RDV CT15 ......291 N4
Nankin St POP/IOD E14 ....25 K2
Nansen Rd GVE DA12 .....69 P3
Napchester Rd DVE/WH CT16.261 H8
Napier Av POP/IOD E14 ....25 K9
Napier Cl DEPT SE8 ......41 M1
  SIT ME10 ....129 K1
Napier Ct LEE/GVPK SE12 * .309 H6
Napier Rd BELV DA17 .....28 E7
  BRDST CT10 ....113 N9
  DVE/WH CT16 ....291 ..
  GILL ME7 ....7 ..
  GVW DA11 ....69 ..
  HAYES BR2 ....124 B1
  RAM CT11 ....16 B4
  RTWE/PEM TN2 ....23 J7
  SNWD SE25 ....83 N1
Napier Ter IOS ME12 * 57 M6
Napleton Rd FAV ME13 ....132 K7
Napoleon Dr STPH/PW TN12 .245 J4
Napwood Cl RHAM ME8 ....96 G8
Nare Rd SOCK/AV RM15 ...30 C3
Nares Rd RHAM ME8 ......126 C1
Nargate Cl RCANTE CT3 ...168 D8
Nargate St RCANTE CT3 ...168 D8
Narrabeen Rd FOLKN CT19 .310 B5
Narrow Boat Cl THMD SE28 .35 L5
Narrow St POP/IOD E14 ...25 K5
Narrow Wy HAYES BR2 ....85 P3
Naseby Av FOLK CT20 ....310 A6
Naseby Rd NRWD SE19 ....60 D5
Nash Cl MAIDE ME5 ......69 K8
Nash Court Gdns MARG CT9.112 C5
Nash Court Rd MARG CT9 ..112 C5
Nash Crt CVW DA15 ......69 J1
Nashenden Farm La
  ROCH ME1 ....94 E5
Nashenden La ROCH ME1 ..94 E6
Nash Gdns BRDST CT10 ...113 N9
Nash Gn BXLY DA5 ....44 F9
Nash Hl RFOLK CT18 .....287 H2
Nash La HAYES BR2 ......99 J5
  MARG CT9 ....112 C5
Nash Rd BROCKY SE4 .....41 M4
  MARG CT9 ....112 D5
  RCANTE CT3 ....169 M5
Nash St MEO DA13 ....69 N8
Nasmyth Rd BRCH CT7 ...111 H5
Natal Rd CHAT ME4 ......95 N4
  DVE/WH CT16 ....291 K3
  THHTH CR7 ....60 D7
Nathaniel Cl WCHPL E1 ...24 C2
Nathan Wy ABYW SE2 ....27 P5
  THMD SE28 ....27 N6
National Ter
  BERM/RHTH SE16 * 24 C6
Nativity Cl SIT ME10 .....129 M1
Nat's La RASHE TN25 ....254 A4
Nautilus Cl IOS ME12 .....78 A2
Nautilus Rd IOS ME12 ....78 A2
Naval Rw POP/IOD E14 ...25 M3
Naylands MARG CT9 ......14 D6
Naylor Rd PECK SE15 ....41 H1
Nazareth Cl PECK SE15 ...41 J4
Neale Cl EGRIN RH19 ....264 E5
Neale St CHAT ME4 ......6 B4
Neal Rd BGR/WK TN15 ...120 B1
Neal's Place Rd
  CANTW/ST CT2 ....166 C1
Neal Ter FSTH SE23 * 41 K9
Neame Rd BRCH CT7 .....111 H6
Neason Wy FOLKN CT19 ..311 H4
Neate St CMBW SE5 .....40 E5
Neath Ct MAID/SHEP ME15 *.186 B5
Neatscourt Rd EHAM E6 ..26 G4
Neb La OXTED RH8 ......274 F7
Nebraska St STHWK SE1 ..24 A5
Neckinger BERM/RHTH SE16.24 D6
Neckinger Est
  BERM/RHTH SE16 ....24 C6
Neckinger St STHWK SE1 ..24 C5
Nectarine Wy LEW SE13 ..41 P3
Needleman St
  BERM/RHTH SE16 ....24 C6
Neills Rd RRTW TN3 .....294 E5
Nelgarde Rd CAT SE6 ....61 N4
Nelldale Rd BERM/RHTH SE16.24 E7
Nellington Rd
  SBGH/RUST ME4 ....269 N4
Nello James Gdns WNWD SE27.60 A3
Nelson Av IOS ME12 .....78 D1
  TON TN9 * 210 D9
Nelson Cl BH/WHM TN16 ..145 P2
  CROY/NA CR0 ....82 C5
  IOS ME12 ....78 D1
  KEN/WIL TN24 ....253 L9
Nelson Ct BRCH CT7 .....110 F5
Nelson Crs RAM CT11 ....17 H5
Nelson Mandela Rd
  BKHTH/KID SE3 ....42 G4
Nelson Ms NROM TN28 ...337 H6
Nelson Park Rd RDV CT15 .262 D8
Nelson Pl BRDST CT10 ...113 N9
Nelson Rd BELV DA17 ....28 G8
  CDW/CHF RM16 ....33 L2
  DART DA1 ....46 C7
  GILL ME7 ....7 K4
  GNWCH SE10 ....25 M9
  CVW DA15 ....69 K1
  HAYES BR2 ....124 B1
  RTWE/PEM TN2 ....23 J7
  SCUP DA14 ....64 E4
  WSTB CT5 ....105 K5
Napier Ter IOS ME12 * 57 M6
Napleton Rd FAV ME13 ....132 K7

Nethern Court Rd CTHM CR3.144 D7
Nethersole Cl CANTW/ST CT2.135 J9
Nethersole Rd RCANTW CT4 .229 H5
Netley Cl CROY/NA CR0 ...114 C2
  MAID/BEAR ME14 ....156 A6
Nettleden Av HDCN TN27 ..253 H4
Nettlefold Pl WNWD SE27 ..60 C1
Nettlepole La HDCN TN27 ..220 B8
Nettlestead Cl BECK BR3 ..61 M6
Nettlestead La
  WBY/YAL ME18 ....183 H5
Nettleton Rd NWCR SE14 ..41 K1
Neuchatel Rd CAT SE6 ....61 K6
Nevada Gdns GNWCH SE10 .42 A1
Nevell Rd CDW/CHF RM16 ..33 J6
Nevill Ct E/WMAL ME19 ...153 K3
  SBGH/RUST ME4 ....22 C6
Neville Cl BFN/LL DA15 ...64 B3
  MAID/BEAR ME14 ....155 N4
Neville Pl NEO DA13 * 92 B2
Neville Rd CHAT ME4 .....95 K4
  CROY/NA CR0 ....83 J4
Nevill Gdns DEAL CT14 ...232 C8
Nevill Ga RTWE/PEM TN2 ..22 E7
Nevill Pk SBGH/RUST TN4 .270 A5
Nevill Pl SNOD ME6 ......123 P8
Nevill St RTWE/PEM TN2 ..22 D7
Nevill Ter RTWE/PEM TN2 ..22 B7
New Acres Rd THMD SE28 ..27 M4
Newark Knok EHAM E6 ....27 H2
Newark St WCHPL E1 .....24 E2
Newark Yd STRD ME2 ....18 D1
Newbarn La RASHW TN26 ..146 E1
New Barn Rd HART DA3 ...68 F9
  RMAID ME17 ....217 H7
  SWLY BR8 ....88 C1
New Barns Av MTCM CR4 ..82 C1
New Barns Rd
  MAID/BEAR ME14 ....155 M4
New Barn St CAN/RD E16 ..26 C1
Newberry Rd ERITH DA8 ...45 P2
Newbold Cots WCHPL E1 * .24 F2
Newbridge Av SIT ME10 ...130 A6
New Broad St LGVST EC2M .24 A1
Newburgh Rd GRAYS RM17 .32 E8
Newburn Av MAIDW ME16 .155 H6
Newbury Cl BRCH CT7 ....111 J7
  FOLK CT20 ....310 A6
  HOO/HM ME3 ....52 B8
  RDART DA2 ....47 H8
Newbury La WADH TN5 ...294 D7
Newbury Rd BRCH CT7 ...111 J7
New Butt La DEPT SE8 * ..41 K6
Newby Pl POP/IOD E14 ...25 M3
Newcastle Hl RAM CT11 ...17 G3
Newchapel Rd LING RH7 ..234 D7
Newchurch La LYDD TN29 .324 E8
New Church St CMBW SE5 *.40 C1
Newchurch Rd
  MAID/SHEP ME15 ....185 M2
Newcomen Rd IOS ME12 ..57 L6
  SBGH/RUST TN4 ....270 C3
Newcomen St STHWK SE1 ..24 A5
New Concordia Whf
  STHWK SE1 ....24 C5
New Covenant Pl ROCH ME1.19 J7
New Crane Pl WAP E1W * ..24 F4
New Creek Rd FAV ME13 ..132 G5
New Cross Rd NWCR SE14 .41 L2
New Cross St MARG CT9 ..15 G4
New Cut CHAT ME4 ......6 B4
  MAID/SHEP ME15 ....185 L4
New Cut Rd FAV ME13 ....164 B6
  MAID/BEAR ME14 ....156 A6
  RCANTW CT4 ....194 C2
Newgate
  STRHM/NOR SW16 * 60 U3
New Dover Rd CANT CT1 ..5 H6
  RFOLK CT18 ....311 L2
Newell St POP/IOD E14 ...25 L3
Newenden Cl ASH TN23 ...236 D2
Newenden Rd STRD ME2 ..72 C5
New England Rd
  SBGH/RUST TN4 ....270 C5
Newent Cl PECK SE15 ....40 E1
New Farm Av HAYES BR2 ..85 K1
New Farthingdale LING RH7.235 K9
New Ferry Ap
  WOOL/PLUM SE18 ....27 H6
New Forest La RCANTW CT4.164 B6
New Gardens Rd RSIT ME9 .131 H5
Newgate CROY/NA CR0 ....83 H5
Newgate Gap MARG CT9 ..112 C2
Newgate Lower Prom
  MARG CT9 ....15 K2
Newgate Prom MARG CT9 ..15 K2
New Goulston St WCHPL E1.24 C2
New Green Pl
  BRXS/STRHM SW2 * 40 A5
  NRWD SE19 ....60 E5
Newhache LING RH7 ......235 K8
New Haine Rd MSTR CT12 .112 F9
New Hall Cl LYDD TN29 ...326 C6
New Hall Farm La
  HOO/HM ME3 ....54 F2
Newham's Rw STHWK SE1 .24 B5
Newham Wy CAN/RD E16 ..26 A1
Newhaven Gdns
  ELTH/MOT SE9 ....43 H5
Newhaven La CAN/RD E16 .26 A1
Newhaven Rd SNWD SE25 .83 J2
Newhouse La RCANTW CT4 .166 C8
Newhouse La FAV ME13 ...162 F5
New House La GVW DA11 ..69 F2
Newhouse La RCANTW CT4 .196 B1
New House Ter LING RH7 ..235 K8
New Hythe La DIT/AY ME20 .153 P2
Newick Cl BXLY DA5 .....45 K7
Newing Cl RCANTE CT3 ...168 D3
Newing Gn BMLY BR1 ....63 J5
Newington Rd MSTR CT12 .142 C6
  RAM CT11 ....16 B2
  RFOLK CT18 ....287 M8
Newington Wk
  MAID/BEAR ME14 * 155 P6

Newitt Rd HOO/HM ME3.....73 K2
New King St DEPT SE8.....25 K9
Newland Green La
  HDCN TN27.....249 L1
Newland Rd IOS ME12.....57 H9
Newlands ASH TN23.....282 E2
Newlands Av SIT ME10.....129 J1
Newlands Cl EGRIN RH19.....264 C6
Newlands Dr DEAL CT14.....232 C9
Newlands Farm Rd
  HOO/HM ME3.....53 P2
Newlands La MEO DA13.....143 J1
  MSTR CT12.....143 J1
Newlands Pk SYD SE26.....61 J5
Newlands Quay WAP E1W.....24 F5
Newlands Ri SBGH/RUST TN4.....270 D2
Newlands Rd HDCN TN27.....220 E5
  MSTR CT12.....143 J3
  SBGH/RUST TN4.....270 E2
Newlands Wy
  SBGH/RUST TN4.....270 D1
Newlands Woods
  CROY/NA CR0.....114 C3
Newling Cl RHAM ME8.....26 G2
New Lodge Dr OXTED RH8.....175 J4
New London St MON EC3R *.....24 B3
New Lydd Rd RYE TN31.....339 N9
New Lydenburg St CHARL SE7.....? L2
Newlyn Cl ORP BR6.....86 G8
Newlyn Dr STPH/PW TN12.....246 C2
Newlyn Rd WELL DA16.....44 B3
Newlyn's Meadow RYC CT14.....289 M3
Newman Dr SIT ME10.....9 P6
Newman Rd BMLY BR1.....62 E7
  CROY/NA CR0.....82 E4
  RCANTE CT3.....229 H1
Newmans Cl BRDST CT10.....113 M7
  HYTHE CT21.....308 C7
Newmarch Rd THMD SE28.....27 N4
New Mill Rd STMC/STPC BR5.....64 E7
Newnham Cl RHAM ME8.....96 F4
  THHTH CR7.....60 C8
Newnham La FAV ME13.....161 K5
Newnham Pl CDW/CHF RH16.....53 H7
Newnhams Cl BMLY BR1.....63 K9
Newnham St CHAT ME4.....7 F6
New Place Gdns LING RH7.....235 H5
New Place Sq
  BERM/RHTH SE16 *.....24 E6
New Pond Rd CRBK TN17.....298 F9
Newport Av POP/IOD E14.....25 N3
Newports SWLY BR8.....88 C4
New Pound La
  WBY/YAL ME18.....182 D1
New Rd ABYW SE2.....28 C7
  CANTW/ST CT2.....165 J2
  CHAT ME4.....6 B5
  CRBK TN17.....297 N3
  DIT/AY ME20.....154 B3
  E/WMAL ME19.....155 P7
  EYN DA4.....67 J8
  GRAYS RM17.....32 E1
  GVW DA11.....49 L7
  HB CT6.....136 E2
  HDCN TN27.....219 P8
  HDCN TN27.....247 N4
  HOO/HM ME3.....52 A4
  HYTHE CT21.....308 C6
  IOS ME12.....57 J8
  IOS ME12.....78 C1
  MEO DA13.....90 C2
  ORP BR6.....87 H4
  OXTED RH8.....175 L6
  OXTED RH8.....204 D3
  RCANTW CT4.....257 L5
  ROCH ME1.....19 J7
  ROCH ME1.....124 E5
  RSEV TN14.....238 F8
  RYE TN31.....338 G6
  SOCK/AV RM15.....30 C4
  STPH/PW TN12.....243 H3
  SWLY BR8.....65 P6
  WCHPL E1.....24 D3
  WELL DA16.....44 D3
New Road Av CHAT ME4.....6 A4
New Road Cots Hl HAYES *.....107 K9
New Road Hl HAYES BR2.....115 P3
  RASHE TN25.....306 A3
New Romney Pl SWCH CT13.....201 N2
New Ruttington La CANT CT1.....5 D2
Newry Rd HOO/HM ME3.....53 H7
New Stairs CHAT ME4.....6 D3
Newstead Av ORP BR6.....86 E7
Newstead Rd LEE/GVPK SE12.....42 D8
New St BGR/WK TN15.....121 N1
  BH/WHM TN16.....176 D5
  CANT CT1.....4 C2
  CANTW/ST CT2.....4 B2
  CHAT ME4.....6 D3
  DEAL CT14.....233 J2
  FOLK CT19.....11 F5
  IOS ME12.....57 K7
  KEN/WIL TN24.....2 C2
  LVPST EC2M.....13 J3
  LYDD TN29.....342 B6
  MARG CT9.....15 G4
  RCANTE CT13.....200 F1
  SWCH CT13.....201 P2
New Street Hl MEO DA13.....62 H4
New Street Rd MEO DA13.....91 M7
New Swan Yd GVW DA11 *.....49 M7
New Tank Hill Rd PUR RM19.....30 D6
Newton Abbot Rd GVW DA11.....69 K1
Newton Av TONN TN10.....12 B7
  WALD ME5.....98 A5
Newton Gdns STPH/PW TN12.....242 G4
Newton Pl POP/IOD E14.....25 K7

Newton Rd FAV ME13.....132 C6
  RTW TN1.....22 D5
  TIL RM18.....46 C4
  WELL DA16.....44 C4
Newton's Ct CT5.....106 A4
Newton's Cr RDART DA2.....47 K5
Newton Ter HAYES BR2.....85 N3
Newton Willows RRTW TN3.....269 H9
New Tower Blds WAP E1W *.....24 E4
New Town Gn KEN/WIL TN24.....252 G9
Newtown Rd ASH TN23.....2 E6
New Town Rd KEN/WIL TN24.....282 G1
New Town St CT14.....1 G1
  RCANTW CT4.....165 K7
New Union Cl POP/IOD E14.....25 M6
New Union St BARB EC2Y.....24 A1
New Wharf Rd TON TN9.....210 E8
New Winchelsea Rd
  RYE TN31.....338 E9
New Years La ORP BR6.....117 H8
  RSEV TN14.....145 K3
Niagara Cl E/WMAL ME19.....153 J9
Nicholas Cl MAIDW ME16.....154 F9
Nicholas Ct MSTR CT12.....142 C7
Nicholas La MANHO EC4N.....24 A3
Nicholas Rd CROY/NA CR0.....252 D2
  RASHE TN25.....252 D2
Nichol La BMLY BR1.....62 E6
Nicholls Av BRDST CT10.....149 L5
Nicholson House CHARL SE7 *.....43 J1
Nicholson Rd CROY/NA CR0.....85 L1
Nickelby Cl THMD SE28.....28 B2
Nicklaus Dr WALD ME5.....125 L2
Nickle Bank RCANTW CT4 *.....165 H8
Nickleby Cl ROCH ME1.....95 H4
Nickleby Rd GVE DA12.....50 C9
Nickle Ga RCANTW CT4 *.....165 G9
Nickley Wood Rd
  RASHW TN26.....303 N1
Nicolson Rd STMC/STPC BR5.....87 K4
Niederwald Rd SYD SE26.....61 P1
Nigel Rd PECK SE15.....40 G4
Nigeria Rd CHARL SE7 *.....42 C1
Nightingale Av HYTHE CT21.....308 C7
  WSTB CT5.....105 J8
Nightingale Cl BH/WHM TN16.....115 M9
  DIT/AY ME20.....154 F9
  EGRIN RH19.....264 G9
  GVW DA11.....69 J3
  KEN/WIL TN24.....283 K1
  RCANTW CT4.....165 K6
  RHAM ME8.....97 H7
Nightingale Cnr
  STMC/STPC BR5 *.....87 L1
Nightingale Ct STRD ME2 *.....71 L9
Nightingale Gv LEW SE13.....41 L3
Nightingale La BMLY BR1.....62 G8
  RDV CT15.....229 M3
  RSEV TN14.....178 A6
Nightingale Pl MARG CT9.....115 H4
  WOOL/PLUM SE18.....27 H9
Nightingale Rd BGR/WK TN15.....149 J2
  DVE/WH CT16.....291 K5
  FAV ME13.....132 F6
  HB CT6.....107 K7
  SAND/SEL CR2.....114 A5
  STMC/STPC BR5.....86 D5
The Nightingales HDCN TN27.....277 J8
Nightingale V
  WOOL/PLUM SE18.....27 H9
Nightingale Wy EHAM E6.....26 F1
  SWLY BR8.....65 N9
Nile Rd GILL ME7.....7 J4
Nile Ter PECK SE15.....25 M8
Nina Vis STPH/PW TN12 *.....245 H4
Nine Acres KEN/WIL TN24.....252 F4
Nine Acres Rd STRD ME2.....93 P3
Nine Ash La FAV ME13.....163 N1
Nine Elms Gv GVW DA11.....49 L8
Ninehams Rd BH/WHM TN16.....145 N6
Nineteenth St MTCM CR4.....82 D1
Nineveh La CRBK TN17.....298 B9
Ninhams Wd ORP BR6.....86 B6
Nine La ASH TN25.....253 M7
Nisbett Wk SCUP DA14.....64 C8
Nithdale Rd WOOL/PLUM SE18.....43 M1
Niven Cl HOO/HM ME3.....72 C4
Niwrim Wy IOS ME12.....58 A7
Nixon Av STRHM/NOR SW16.....148 H5
Nizels La RTON TN11.....209 L3
No1 St WOOL/PLUM SE18.....27 J6
No2 St WOOL/PLUM SE18.....27 J6
Noah's Ark BGR/WK TN15.....149 L5
Noah's Ark Rd DVW CT17.....291 H7
Noakes Meadow ASH TN23.....252 C9
Nobel Cl RSIT ME9.....131 H3
Nobel Ct FAV ME13.....132 E6
Noble Cl MARG CT9.....111 P5
Noble Gdns MARG CT9.....111 P5
Noble Tree Rd RTON TN11.....266 B5
No Name St SWCH CT13.....201 N1
Nonsuch Cl CANT CT1.....167 H4
The Nook WBY/YAL ME18.....183 N9
Norah La HOO/HM ME3.....71 K3
Norbiton Rd POP/IOD E14.....25 J2
Norbury Cl STRHM/NOR SW16.....60 A7
Norbury Crs
  STRHM/NOR SW16.....60 A8
Norbury Hl STRHM/NOR SW16.....60 A6
Norbury Rd THHTH CR7.....60 C6
Norcott Gdns EDUL SE22.....40 G8
Nordenfeldt Rd ERITH DA8.....29 P8
Nore Cl GILL ME7.....96 B5
  IOS ME12.....57 L7
Noreen Av IOS ME12.....78 A1
Norfield Rd RDART DA2.....65 L3
Norfolk Cl DART DA1.....46 C9
  WALD ME5.....125 P2
Norfolk Crs BFN/LL DA15.....44 A8
Norfolk Dr ASH TN23.....2 A4
Norfolk Gdns BXLYHN DA7.....45 N6
Norfolk Pl CDW/CHF RM16.....31 M8
  WELL DA16.....44 D3
Norfolk Rd CANT CT1.....166 D6
  GVE DA12.....49 P7
  MAID/SHEP ME15.....185 P3
  MARG CT9.....112 C5
  RTW TN1.....22 E6
  THHTH CR7.....60 C9
  TON TN9.....210 D9

Norfolk Sq WSTB CT5 *.....142 G2
Norfolk St WSTB CT5.....105 L6
Norheads La BH/WHM TN16.....145 K3
Noryhyrst Av SNWD SE25.....60 H9
Norlands Crs CHST BR7.....63 H7
Norman Cl BGR/WK TN15.....149 J2
  MAID/BEAR ME14.....155 N6
  ORP BR6.....86 D7
  RHAM ME8.....126 E1
  STRD ME2.....18 A7
Normandy Cl EGRIN RH19 *.....265 J8
  SYD SE26.....61 L2
Normandy Rd BRXN/ST SW9.....40 A2
Normandy Ter ERITH DA8.....29 P8
Normanhurst Av WELL DA16.....44 F7
Normanhurst Rd
  BGR/WK TN15.....151 K5
  STMC/STPC BR5.....86 D8
Norman Pde SCUP DA14 *.....64 E8
Norman Rl CRBK TN17.....298 A3
Norman Rd ASH TN23.....282 F1
  BELV DA17.....28 G5
  BRDST CT10.....113 K7
  CANT CT1.....4 E9
  DART DA1.....46 E7
  E/WMAL ME19.....153 H5
  FAV ME13.....132 F6
  RAM CT11.....41 P1
  RDV CT15.....292 G1
  RTW TN1.....23 F2
  SNOD ME6.....123 P7
  THHTH CR7.....82 G2
  WGOS CT8.....111 N4
  WSTB CT5.....105 L6
Normans Ct GVW DA11.....49 L8
Normans La EDEN TN8.....235 P1
Norman St DVW CT17.....8 C3
  RSEV TN14.....177 M6
Normanton Dr SNWD SE25.....61 K1
Normington Cl
  STRHM/NOR SW16.....60 D5
Norreys Rd RHAM ME8.....97 H7
Norrie Rd BRCH CT7.....110 C2
Norrington Rd FOLKN CT19.....310 D4
Norrington Rd
  MAID/SHEP ME15.....185 M5
Norris Cl HAWK TN18.....317 K1
Norris Wy DART DA1.....45 N6
Norstead Gdns
  SBGH/RUST TN4.....270 E1
Norsted La ORP BR6.....117 J3
Northall Rd BXLYHN DA7.....45 L3
Northampton Quay DVW CT17 *.....8 D5
Northampton Rd
  CROY/NA CR0.....83 M6
North Ash Rd HART DA3.....91 P7
North Bank Cl STRD ME2.....18 A5
North Barrack Rd DEAL CT14.....233 J5
North Barracks DEAL CT14.....233 J5
Northbourne Av DVW CT17 *.....291 J7
Northbourne Rd DEAL CT14.....232 A5
  RDV CT15.....231 J6
  RHAM ME8.....96 E2
Northbourne Wy MARG CT9.....113 K4
Northbrooke KEN/WIL TN24.....2 E1
Northbrooke La KEN/WIL TN24.....2 E1
Northbrook Rd CROY/NA CR0.....13 J9
  LEW SE13.....42 B6
North Camber Wy
  DVE/WH CT16.....292 A6
Northcliffe Gdns BRDST CT10.....113 M6
North Cl BXLYHS DA6.....44 F5
  FOLK CT20.....310 A7
North Cnr St MAID/SHEP ME15 *.....185 M2
North Court Cl RCANTE CT3.....169 K8
North Court La DEAL CT14.....231 H5
North Cray Rd BXLY DA5.....65 J1
  SCUP DA14.....64 F2
North Crs RMAID ME17.....185 J7
North Cross Rd EDUL SE22.....40 F6
North Dane Wy WALD ME5.....125 P2
Northdown KEN/WIL TN24.....252 F5
  RSIT ME9.....131 H3
North Down STPH/PW TN12.....186 G5
Northdown Av MARG CT9.....112 G3
Northdown Cl MARG CT9.....112 G3
Northdown Cl
  MAID/BEAR ME14.....155 N5
  RMAID ME17.....189 N6
  STPH/PW TN12.....242 G3
Northdown Hl BRDST CT10.....113 J6
Northdown Pde MARG CT9 *.....112 G3
Northdown Park Rd
  MARG CT9.....112 G4
Northdown Rd BGR/WK TN15.....149 J2
  BRDST CT10.....113 K6
  CTHM CR5.....178 D1
  DART DA1.....68 C8
  MARG CT9.....15 H3
  WELL DA16.....44 D3
North Downs Cl RCANTW CT15.....261 J7
North Downs Crs
  CROY/NA CR0.....114 E4
North Downs Rd
  CROY/NA CR0.....114 E4
North Downs Wy
  BGR/WK TN15.....121 H9
  CANT CT1.....165 P4
  CANTW/ST CT2.....165 P4
  DIT/AY ME20.....125 J7
  DVW CT17.....8 B5
  GDST RH9.....174 C4
  HDCN TN27.....247 N4
  HDCN TN27.....276 B6
  KEN/WIL TN24.....2 E2
  MAIDW ME16.....154 C6
  NROM TN28.....336 F7
  RMAID ME17.....217 H5
  RTWE/PEM TN2.....23 C4
  SIT ME10.....99 H7
  STRD ME2.....18 D1

  MEO DA13.....122 A6
  MEO DA13.....123 H1
  RASHE TN25.....221 N4
  RASHE TN25.....223 N1
  RCANTW CT4.....167 M8
  RCANTW CT4.....193 P8
  RMAID ME17.....119 J9
  RSEV TN14.....148 C3
  WAL CR6.....145 K8
North Downs Way
 & Saxon Shore Wy
  RFOLK CT18.....310 B2
Northdown Ter EGRIN RH19 *.....264 G5
Northdown Vw RMAID ME17.....188 G5
Northdown Wy MARG CT9.....113 H4
North Dr BECK BR3.....84 C1
  EGRIN RH19.....265 K2
  ORP BR6.....86 F8
North Eastling Rd RSIT ME9.....161 K5
North End CROY/NA CR0.....116 C3
  EGRIN RH19.....264 E5
North End La ORP BR6.....116 C5
North Farm Rd
  SBGH/RUST TN4.....270 E5
Northfield HART DA3.....68 D9
Northfield Cl BMLY BR1.....87 K3
Northfields GRAYS RM17.....32 D7
  MAIDW ME16.....154 B6
  RRTW TN3.....239 M9
Northfleet Cl
  MAID/BEAR ME14.....155 P7
North Folly Rd
  MAID/SHEP ME15.....184 E8
North Foreland Av
  BRDST CT10.....113 N6
North Foreland Rd
  BRDST CT10.....113 N6
North Frith RTON TN11 *.....211 J1
Northgate CANT CT1.....5 F2
  ROCH ME1.....6 A2
North Green Rd HAWK TN18.....317 H4
North Hill Rd HAWK TN18.....316 E5
North Holmes Rd CANT CT1.....5 K4
North Kent Av GVW DA11.....48 C5
North Lasham RCANTW CT2 *.....191 M5
Northlands Av ORP BR6.....86 C5
Northlands St CMBW SE5.....40 C3
North La CANTW/ST CT2.....4 B1
  FAV ME13.....132 F6
  FAV ME13.....164 A4
  FOLK CT20.....310 B8
North Lea DEAL CT14.....233 H2
Northleigh Cl
  MAID/SHEP ME15.....185 M5
North Lockside Rd CHAT ME4.....75 K7
North Lyminge La
  RFOLK CT18.....287 H1
North Meadow
  CDW/CHF RM16 *.....32 D6
North Military Rd DVW CT17.....152 E5
Northolme
  CDW/CHF RM16 *.....32 D6
  ORP BR6.....86 F6
Northover BMLY BR1.....62 D5
North Pk ELTH/MOT SE9.....43 K7
North Peckham Est PECK SE15.....40 C1
North Pends KEN/WIL TN24.....253 H6
North Pole La HAYES BR2.....115 K1
North Pole Rd WBY/YAL ME18.....184 A4
North Pondside Rd CHAT ME4 *.....72 C7
North Quay RSIT ME9.....101 K8
North Return Rd DVE/WH CT16.....9 K2
North Riding BRAS TN16.....145 M9
Northridge RYE TN31.....339 H7
Northridge Rd GVE DA12.....69 N2
North Riding HART DA3.....69 H9
North Rd BELV DA17.....28 G6
  BMLY BR1.....62 F7
  CHAT ME4.....6 D2
  CRBK TN17.....274 D7
  DART DA1.....45 P7
  DEAL CT14.....263 J2
  DVW CT17.....8 A3
  HOO/HM ME3.....52 B2
  HYTHE CT21.....309 H5
  PUR RM19.....30 F7
  QBOR ME11.....77 H2
  SWCH CT13.....171 P2
  SWCH CT13.....202 F2
  WOOL/PLUM SE18.....27 M7
  WWKM BR4.....84 E5
North West Hythe HYTHE CT21.....308 F4
North Salts RYE TN31.....338 F6
North Several
  BKHTH/KID SE3 *.....42 B3
North St BMLY BR1.....62 E7
  BRDST CT10.....113 K6
  CTHM CR5.....178 D1
  DART DA1.....291 J8
  EDEN TN8.....267 H2
  FOLKN CT19.....11 H4
  GVE DA12.....69 N1
  HB CT6.....107 L1
  HDCN TN27.....247 N4
  HDCN TN27.....276 B6
  KEN/WIL TN24.....2 E2
  MAIDW ME16.....154 C6
  NROM TN28.....336 F7
  RMAID ME17.....217 H5
  RTWE/PEM TN2.....23 C4
  SIT ME10.....99 H7
  STRD ME2.....18 D1
North Tenter St WCHPL E1.....24 C3
North Trench TONN TN10 *.....210 E9
Northumberland Aly
  FENCHST EC3M.....24 B2
Northumberland Av
  KEN/WIL TN24.....252 C4
  MARG CT9.....113 H4

RHAM ME8.....97 H5
WELL DA16.....44 A5
Northumberland Cl ERITH DA8.....45 L1
Northumberland Ct
  MAID/SHEP ME15 *.....186 A4
Northumberland Gdns
  BMLY BR1.....86 B1
  MTCM CR4.....82 D2
Northumberland Pk
  ERITH DA8.....45 L1
Northumberland Rd EHAM E6.....26 F2
  MAID/SHEP ME15.....186 A3
  MEO DA13.....69 K6
  SLH/COR SS17.....33 N5
Northumberland Wy
  ERITH DA8.....45 L2
Northumbria St POP/IOD E14.....25 L2
North Vw MAID/SHEP ME15.....185 N2
  RCANTE CT5.....138 C8
  RRTW TN3 *.....239 M9
Northview SWLY BR8.....65 M7
North View TIL RM18.....49 H6
North Wk CROY/NA CR0.....149 H6
Northwall Ms DEAL CT14.....233 H2
Northwall Quay DVW CT17.....8 D7
North Wall Rd DEAL CT14.....233 H4
North Wy DEAL CT14.....231 P2
  MAID/BEAR ME14.....155 M5
Northway WLGTN SM6.....82 B8
Northway Rd CMBW SE5.....40 C3
  CROY/NA CR0.....83 L3
Northwood CDW/CHF RM16.....33 J5
Northwood Av HOO/HM ME3.....53 J4
Northwood Dr SIT ME10.....129 N4
Northwood Pl ERITHM DA18.....28 G4
Northwood Rd BRDST CT10.....143 H1
  FSTH SE23.....61 M9
  THHTH CR7.....60 C8
  TONN TN10.....210 E4
  WSTB CT5.....105 M4
North Woolwich Rd
  CAN/RD E16.....26 A4
Norton Av HB CT6.....107 M6
Norton Crs TONN TN10.....210 E5
Norton Dr MSTR CT12.....142 G1
Norton Ov WALD ME5.....125 K1
Norton La RASHW TN26.....280 C3
Norton Rd RMAID ME17.....216 F1
  RSIT ME9.....131 J9
  SBGH/RUST TN4.....240 D8
Nortons La RENT TN30.....300 F2
Nortons Wy STPH/PW TN12.....242 B2
Norval Gn BRXN/ST SW9 *.....40 A3
Norview Rd WSTB CT5.....105 J7
Norway Dro RDV CT15.....262 F7
Norway Gdns BERM/RNTH SE16.....25 H6
Norway Pl POP/IOD E14.....25 J2
Norway St GNWCH SE10.....25 J1
Norway Ter MAID/BEAR ME14.....155 L5
Norwich Av TONN TN10.....210 C5
Norwich Cl STRD ME2.....71 M9
Norwood Cl HOO/HM ME3.....52 B4
Norwood Gdns ASH TN23.....2 C5
Norwood High St WNWD SE27.....60 G3
Norwood La LYDD TN29.....325 K3
  MEO DA13.....92 C2
Norwood Park Rd WNWD SE27.....60 C4
Norwood Ri IOS ME12.....58 D9
Norwood Rd HNHL SE24.....40 B9
North Seal ASH TN23.....2 C5
Notley St CANT CT1.....5 G2
Notre Ter CANT CT1 *.....5 G2
Notson Rd SNWD SE25.....83 N1
Nottidge Rd SBGH/RUST TN4.....270 A7
Nottingham Av CAN/RD E16.....26 C1
Nottingham Rd BRCH CT7.....110 C8
  SAND/SEL CR2.....83 H8
Nouds La RSIT ME9.....131 J6
Nouds Rd RSIT ME9.....131 J5
Novar Cl ORP BR6.....86 G4
Nova Rd CROY/NA CR0.....82 G5
Novar Rd ELTH/MOT SE9.....43 N9
The Nower BH/WHM TN16.....146 C5
Nuaia La RTON TN11.....147 L1
Nubia Wy BMLY BR1.....62 C5
Nuding Cl LEW SE13.....41 N4
Nuffield Rd SWLY BR8.....66 A5
Nugent Rd SNWD SE25.....83 P1
Nunappleton Wy OXTED RH8.....175 P8
Nunhead Crs PECK SE15.....41 J4
Nunhead Gv PECK SE15.....41 K4
Nunhead La PECK SE15.....41 J4
Nunnery Flds CANT CT1.....166 F6
Nunnery La RTON TN11.....238 E9
Nunnington Cl ELTH/MOT SE9.....63 J2
Nunns Wy GRAYS RM17.....32 E7
Nursery Av BXLYHN DA7.....45 H4
  CROY/NA CR0.....85 N6
  MAID/BEAR ME14.....156 D9
  MAIDW ME16.....154 C6
Nursery Cl BROCKY SE4.....41 M3
  CROY/NA CR0.....85 J5
  DART DA1.....46 B5
  DEAL CT14.....233 J2
  DVW CT17.....291 J8
  EDEN TN8.....267 H2
  FOLKN CT19.....11 H4
  GVE DA12.....69 N1
  HB CT6.....107 L1
  HDCN TN27.....247 N4
  HDCN TN27.....276 B6
  KEN/WIL TN24.....252 E2
  RHAM ME8.....96 D6
  SBGH/RUST TN4.....240 D8
Nursery Est HB CT6.....107 H5
Nursery Flds BRCH CT7.....141 J1
  HYTHE CT21.....308 E5
Nursery Gdns BRDST CT10.....113 K4
  CHST BR7.....63 M5
  HOO/HM ME3.....73 L2
Nurserylands HB CT6.....107 L3
Nursery La DVE/WH CT16.....260 D9
  CHST BR7.....73 ?
Nursery Rd SEV TN13.....148 C7
Nursery Rd DIT/AY ME20.....154 B3
  MEO DA13.....92 B2
  RHAM ME8.....96 D6
  SBGH/RUST TN4.....240 D8

STPH/PW TN12 ....242 G1
THHTH CR7 ....83 J1
Nursery Rw WALW SE17 ....24 A7
The Nursery ERITH DA8 ......45 F1
Nursery Wk CANTW/ST CT2 .....4 C1
Nursery Wy OXTED RH8 * 175 H5
Nurstead Av HART DA3 ....69 H9
Nurstead Church La
MEO DA13 ....92 B1
Nurstead La HART DA3 ....91 N1
Nurstead Rd ERITH DA8 ......45 F1
Nutberry Av CDW/CHF RM16 ...32 B5
Nutberry Cl CDW/CHF RM16 ...32 B5
RSIT ME9 ....131 J3
Nutbrook St PECK SE15 ......40 F4
Nutcroft Rd PECK SE15 ......41 N5
Nutfield Cl WALD ME5 ....95 N6
Nutfield Rd EDUL SE22 ......40 G5
THHTH CR7 ....82 C1
Nutfields BGR/WK TN15 .....150 E8
SIT ME10 ....130 A2
Nutfield Wy ORP BR6 ....86 A8
Nuthatch HART DA3 ....68 F9
Nuthatch Gdns THMD SE28 ....27 L1
Nuthatch Cl KEN/WIL TN24
RYE TN31 ....338 D6
SWLY BR8 ....85 P7
Nutmead Cl BXLY DA5 ....45 L9
Nutmeg La POP/IOD E14 ......25 M3
Nut Tree Cl ORP BR6 ....87 L7
Nutts Av IOS ME12 ....40 E5
Nutt St PECK SE15 ....45 H5
Nutwood Cl
MAID/BEAR ME14 ....156 B8
Nuxley Rd BELV DA17 ....28 E9
Nyanza St WOOL/PLUM SE18 ...27 L9
Nynehead St NWCR SE14 ......41 L1
Nyon Gv CAT SE6 ....61 M1

O

Oakapple La MAIDW ME16 ....154 F9
Oak Av CROY/NA CRO 84 D6
GILL ME7 ....73 L9
HDCN TN27 ....278 E9
IOS ME12 ....79 E1
RDV CT15 ....260 E3
SEV TN13 ....178 G4
Oakbank CROY/NA CRO 114 F1
Oakbank Gv HNHL SE24 ....40 B5
Oakbrook Cl BMLY BR1 ....62 F3
Oak Bungalows LYDD TN29 * ..342 B6
Oak Caer RASHE TN25 ....306 A3
Oak Cl DART DA1 ....45 N5
HOO/HM ME3 ....75 L4
Oak Cottage Cl CAT SE6 .....42 C9
Oak Cots ORP BR6 * 88 A9
Oak Crs CAN/RD E16 ....25 P7
Oak Cft EGRIN RH19 ....265 K8
Oakcroft Rd LEW SE13 ....42 B5
Oakdale La EDEN TN8 ....176 D9
Oakdale Rd HB CT6 ....107 M2
PECK SE15 ....41 J4
SBGH/RUST TN4 ....2 A2
Oakdene Av CHST BR7 ....63 L4
ERITH DA8 ....29 H9
Oakdene Rd MSTR CT12 ......143 H5
SEV TN13 ....87 H3
STMC/STPC BR5 ....87 K1
Oak Dr DIT/AY ME20 ....153 P2
HOO/HM ME3 ....71 K4
LYDD TN29 ....337 L2
RFOLK CT18 ....288 E7
Oak End Cl SBGH/RUST TN4 ..240 D7
Oakenden La EDEN TN8 ......238 A8
Oakenden Rd MEO DA13 ....92 F5
Oakenpole ASH TN23 ....252 B8
Oak Farm Gdns HDCN TN27 ...247 N3
Oak Farm La BGR/WK TN15 ...121 P4
Oakfield CRBK TN17 * 319 N5
HAWK TN18 ....317 H4
Oakfield Ct MSTR CT12 * ...142 C4
Oakfield Court Rd
RTWE/PEM TN2 ....23 F5
Oakfield Gdns BECK BR3 .....51 M8
Oakfield La DART DA1 ....66 C1
HAYES BR2 ....85 M8
RDART DA2 ....65 P1
Oakfield Park Rd DART DA1 ..66 D1
Oakfield Pl DART DA1 ....66 C1
Oakfield Rd CROY/NA CRO 83 H5
EDEN TN8 ....206 C6
KEN/WIL TN24 ....252 C5
PGE/AN SE20 ....61 H6
STPH/PW TN12 ....242 E9
Oakfields SEV TN13 ....21 F6
SIT ME10 ....129 K2
The Oakfield RH11 TN31 ....338 E4
Oakfield Wy EGRIN RH19 ....265 J5
Oak Gdns CROY/NA CRO 84 D6
Oak Gv RDV CT15 ....260 C7
WWKM BR4 ....84 F6
Oak Grove Rd PGE/AN SE20 ...61 J7
Oakham Cl CAT SE6 * 61 M1
HAYES BR2 ....85 K1
Oak Hl SWCH CT13 ....201 L4
Oakhill Rd BECK BR3 ....51 N1
ORP BR6 ....86 H5
PUR RM19 ....30 E8
Oak Hill Rd SEV TN13 ....76 B8
Oakhouse Rd BXLYHS DA6 .....44 C1
Oakhurst Av BXLYHN DA7 .....44 C1
CHST BR7 ....63 K7
WALD ME5 ....125 L2
Oakhurst Gdns BXLYHN DA7 ...44 C1
EGRIN RH19 ....264 F6
Oakhurst Gv EDUL SE22 ......40 G5
Oakland Ct HB CT6 * 107 K1
MSTR CT12 ....142 B7
Oaklands ASH TN23 ....125 M2
GDST RH9 ....204 B5
RASHE TN25 ....283 P4
Oaklands Av BFN/LL DA15 ....44 B8
BRDST CT10 ....113 K8
THHTH CR7 ....82 B7
WWKM BR4 ....84 A7
Oaklands Cl BGR/WK TN15 ...120 B1

BXLYHS DA6 ....45 H6
STMC/STPC BR5 ....86 F3
Oaklands Dr SOCK/AV RM15 ...31 M1
Oaklands La BFN/HM TN16 ...115 M9
Oaklands Rd BMLY BR1 ....62 C6
BXLYHS DA6 ....45 H5
CVW DA11 ....69 K3
HAWK TN18 ....317 H5
RDART DA2 ....47 P4
Oaklea Rd STPH/PW TN12 ....242 G5
Oakleigh Cl SWLY BR8 ....65 N9
WALD ME5 ....125 K5
Oakleigh Ct OXTED RH8 * ...175 H5
STPH/PW TN12 ....273 N2
Oakleigh Gdns ORP BR6 ......86 F8
Oakleigh La RCANTW CT4 ....167 N7
Oakleigh Park Wy CHST BR7 ..63 L7
Oakley CDW/CHF RM16 ....32 D6
Oakley Cl EGRIN RH19 ......265 L9
EHAM E6 ....26 F2
MAIDW ME16 ....31 M9
Oakley Dr CAT SE6 ....62 B9
ELTH/MOT SE9 ....43 P9
HAYES BR2 ....85 P2
SNWD SE25 ....83 N2
Oak Lodge Dr WWKM BR4 ......84 E4
Oakleigh Pl STHWK SE1 ......24 C8
Oakley Rd HAYES BR2 ....85 P8
SNWD SE25 ....83 K2
Oak Lodge La BH/WHM TN16 ..176 E1
Oak Lodge Rd NROM TN28 ....336 G6
Oakmead MEO DA13 ....92 B6
TONN TN10 ....210 F4
Oakmead Av CROY/NA CRO 82 C5
Oakmere Rd ABYW SE2 ....27 P9
Oakmore Gdns
STMC/STPC BR5 ....87 K1
Oak Rdg RASHW TN26 ....305 J2
Oakridge Rd BMLY BR1 ....62 C5
Oak Rd BH/WHM TN16 ....176 E1
ERITH DA8 ....45 L1
GRAYS RM17 ....32 D9
CVE DA12 ....69 M2
HOO/HM ME3 ....73 L4
ORP BR6 ....117 H2
RDART DA2 ....47 L7
SIT ME10 ....129 J1
STPH/PW TN12 ....242 C2
STRD SE23 ....71 J9
Oaks Av HB CT6 ....107 J4
NRWD SE19 ....60 E4
Oaks Dene WALD ME5 ....125 L4
Oaksford Av SYD SE26 ....61 H2
Oaks Forstal HAWK TN18 ....318 C9
Oakshade Rd BMLY BR1 ....61 P3
Oakshaw OXTED RH8 ....174 G7
Oakside Rd RCANTE CT3 .....229 H1
Oaks La CROY/NA CRO 83 P7
Oaks Pk CANTW/ST CT2 ......166 A1
Oak Rd CROY/NA CRO 83 N9
Oaks Rd CROY/NA CRO 83 N9
FOLK CT20 ....40 E6
TENT TN30 ....301 J8
The Oaks BRCH CT7 ....140 A2
BRDST CT10 ....113 L6
DIT/AY ME20 ....154 D3
EGRIN RH19 ....265 K8
HAYES BR2 ....85 P2
RCANTE CT3 ....138 C8
RDART DA2 ....47 H7
SWLY BR8 ....65 N8
WOOL/PLUM SE18 ....27 K8
WSTB CT5 ....105 J8
Oaks St DEAL CT14 ....233 J3
Oaks Vw HYTHE CT21 ....308 B7
Oak Ter WALD ME5 * 125 M3
Oak Tree Av
MAID/SHEP ME15 ....185 P4
RTWE/PEM TN2 ....270 D7
STPH/PW TN12 ....245 J4
Oak Tree Gdns BMLY BR1 .....62 F4
Oak Tree Gv CROY/NA CRO * ..111 P5
Oak Tree Rd ASH TN23 ......252 C5
Oakum Ct CHAT ME4 ....95 N4
Oakvale Cl DVW CT17 ....291 J8
Oak Vw EDEN TN8 ....206 C8
Oakview Gv CROY/NA CRO 84 H8
Oakview Rd CAT SE6 ....61 P4
Oakway Cl BXLY DA5 ....45 H4
Oak Warren SEV TN13 ....178 F5
Oakway Ct EGRIN RH19 * 309 H6
Oakway Dr CROY/NA CRO 84 A3
Oakway Gv HAYES BR2 ....44 C7
Oakways ELTH/MOT SE9 ....44 C7
Oakwood MARG CT9 * 113 H5
Oakwood Av BECK BR3 ....62 A8
HAYES BR2 ....86 E1
Oakwood Cl CHST BR7 ....63 K5
DART DA1 ....47 J4
LEW SE13 ....42 B7
Oakwood Ct MAIDW ME16 ......12 A6
Oakwood Dr BXLYHN DA7 ......45 L5
NRWD SE19 ....60 D5
WSTB CT5 ....105 P5
Oakwood Gdns ORP BR6 ....86 D6
Oakwood Ms WSTB CT5 * 105 L1
Oakwood Pl CROY/NA CRO 82 F5
Oakwood Ri HART DA3 ....68 C9
RTWE/PEM TN2 ....271 H1
Oakwood Rd CANTW/ST CT2 ...137 M6
CROY/NA CRO 82 F5
MAIDW ME16 ....155 H9
ORP BR6 ....86 D6
Oakwood Vis RAM CT11 * 143 K5
Oare Rd FAV ME13 ....132 E4
Oast Ct RTWE/PEM TN2 .....270 C1
Oast Ct MARG CT9 * 112 E5

SIT ME10 ....129 M3
WBY/YAL ME18 ....213 N1
Oastfield Cl HOO/HM ME3 ....52 E7
Oast House Dr RYE TN31 ....338 C8
Oasthouse Fld LYDD TN29 ...335 N1
Oast House Wy
STMC/STPC BR5 ....87 J1
Oast La HAWK TN18 ....192 B5
TONN TN10 ....210 D6
Oast Meadow KEN/WIL TN24 ..253 J8
Oast Rd OXTED RH8 ....175 J7
The Oast CANT CT1 * 166 C6
Oastview RHAM ME8 ....97 K6
Oast Vw STPH/PW TN12 ......273 P2
Oast Wy HART DA3 ....91 H3
Oaten Hl CANT CT1 ....5 F6
Oaten Hill Pl CANT CT1 * 5 F6
Oates Cl HAYES BR2 ....62 B9
Oatfield Cl CRBK TN17 .....297 P2
Oatfield Dr CRBK TN17 .....297 P2
Odessa Rd BERM/RHTH SE16 ..25 H6
FSTGT E7 ....26 A3
The Oaze WSTB CT5 ....105 K8
Oban Rd THHTH CR7 ....82 A6
Oban St POP/IOD E14 ....25 P2
Oborne Cl HNHL SE24 ....40 A6
Occupation La
WOOL/PLUM SE18 ....43 M2
Ocean Cl BRCH CT7 ....111 J5
Ocean St WHPTL E1 ....24 C1
Ocean Ter IOS ME12 ....58 D9
Ocean Vw BRDST CT10 ....143 M5
Ocelot Ct WALD ME5 ....5 G7
Ockham Dr STMC/STPC BR5 ...64 C6
Ockley La HAWK TN18 ....317 J2
Ockley Rd CROY/NA CRO 82 E4
HAWK TN18 ....317 J4
Ockman La RYE TN31 * 338 F7
Octagon Ar LVPST EC2M 24 B1
Octavia Cl WALD ME5 * 125 N2
Octavia Wy ERITH DA8 * 45 M1
Octavius St DEPT SE8 ....41 N1
Odell Wk LEW SE13 * 45 H5
Odeon Pde ELTH/MOT SE9 * ...43 J5
Odessa Rd BERM/RHTH SE16 ..25 H6
Odiham Dr MAIDW ME16 ......155 H5
Odo Rd DVW CT17 ....291 J7
Offenham Rd ELTH/MOT SE9 ..63 K3
Offen's Dr STPH/PW TN12 ...246 B6
Offenham Rd E/WMAL ME19 ..153 H5
Officers' Rd GILL ME7 ......73 H9
Offley Cl MARG CT9 ....113 H4
Offley Rd BRXN/ST SW9 ......40 A1
Ogilby St WOOL/PLUM SE18 ..35 P3
Oglander Rd PECK SE15 ......40 F5
Okehampton Cl
KEN/WIL TN24 ....253 J2
Okehampton Crs WELL DA16 ..44 D2
Olantigh Rd RASHE TN25 ....224 A6
RCANTW CT4 ....83 B3
Olave Rd MARG CT9 ....112 C4
Old Ash Cl KEN/WIL TN24 ...252 F4
Old Ashford Rd RMAID ME17 .221 H5
RMAID ME17 ....189 M6
Old Badgins Rd FAV ME13 ...162 D6
The Old Bailey RMAID ME17 .188 F5
Old Bakery La LYDD TN29 * ..337 L1
Old Bakery Ms FAV ME13 ....162 B3
Old Barn Cl BGR/WK TN15 ...149 M2
GILL ME7 ....96 C8
TON TN9 ....240 C1
Old Barn Rd E/WMAL ME19 ...153 L2
Old Barn Wy BXLYHN DA7 .....45 N5
Old Belgate Whf POP/IOD E14.25 K6
Old Bexley La BXLY DA5 .....65 M1
Old Billet La IOS ME12 .....79 J1
Old Boundary Rd MARG CT9 ..111 N4
The Old Brewery
MAIDW ME16 * 12 D5
Old Bridge Rd WSTB CT5 ....105 M5
Old Broad St LVPST EC2M 24 B2
OBST EC2N 24 A2
Old Bromley Rd BMLY BR1 ....61 N2
Oldbury Cl STMC/STPC BR5 ...87 L1
Oldbury La BGR/WK TN15 ....150 E7
Oldbury Vis BGR/WK TN15 * .150 E7
The Old Carriageway
GILL ME7 ....126 C2
SEV TN13 ....148 B8
Old Castle St WCHPL E1 .....24 C1
Old Chapel Rd SWLY BR8 .....88 B4
Old Charlton Rd
CHAT ME4 * 6 B4
The Old Ctyd BMLY BR1 ......62 F7
Old Crossing Rd MARG CT9 ..112 A4
Old Dairy Cl RAM CT11 ......17 H2
Old Dartford Rd EYN DA4 ....89 L3
The Old Diary Ms IOS ME12 ..57 M9
Old Dover Rd BKHTH/KID SE3.42 F6
CANT CT1 ....5 F6
RFOLK CT18 ....311 M2
Old Downs HART DA3 ....91 H2
Old Farleigh Rd
SAND/SEL CR2 ....114 A6
Old Farm Av BFN/LL DA15 ....43 P9
Old Farm Cl WSTB CT5 ......105 K8
Old Farm Gdns SWLY BR8 ....88 B5
Old Farm Rd BRCH CT7 ......110 A8
Old Farm Rd East BFN/LL DA15.64 C1
Old Farm Rd West
BFN/LL DA15 ....64 B1
Old Ferry Rd RSIT ME9 ......76 D9
Oldfield Cl BMLY BR1 ....86 A1
MAID/SHEP ME15 ....186 B2
Oldfield Dr ROCH ME1 ....94 B9
Oldfield Gv BERM/RHTH SE16.24 G7

Oldfield Rd BMLY BR1 ....86 A1
BXLYHN DA7 ....44 G3
Old Fold WSTB CT5 ....106 D8
Old Folkestone Rd DVW CT17.313 H2
Old Fordge La ASHF TN23 * .128 A3
Old Forge Wy SCUP DA14 ....65 J5
Old Garden Ct RCANTW CT4 ..195 M2
Old Gardens Cl
RTWE/PEM TN2 ....270 E8
The Old Odn SEV TN13 ......148 C8
Old Gate Rd FAV ME13 ......132 E6
Old George Ct HOO/HM ME3 * .72 F5
Old Green Rd MARG CT9 .....113 H4
Old Hadlow Rd TONN TN10 ...211 H6
Old Hall Dr MSTR CT12 .....142 B7
Old Hall Rd MARG ME17 .....189 J7
Oldhawe Hl RCANTE CT3 .....138 A1
The Old High St FOLK CT20 ..11 F4
Old Hl CHST BR7 ....63 H5
ORP BR6 ....116 F1
Old Hockley Rd FAV ME13 ....85 M1
Old Homesdale Rd HAYES BR2.85 M1
Old Hook Rd IOS ME12 ....78 B2
Oldhouse La LYDD TN29 .....334 F4
Old House La RRTW TN3 .....269 J3
RSIT ME9 ....127 P1
Old Jamaica Rd
BERM/RHTH SE16 ....24 D6
Old James St PECK SE15 .....41 H4
Old Jewry LOTH EC2R 24 A2
Old Kent Rd STHWK SE1 ......24 C7
STPH/PW TN12 ....242 G3
Old Kingsdown Cl
BRDST CT10 ....143 K1
Old Lain RMAID ME17 ....188 D5
Old La BGR/WK TN15 ....150 E8
BH/WHM TN16 ....145 M8
OXTED RH8 ....175 J6
Old Lenham Rd MSTR CT12 * .159 P9
Old London Rd BGR/WK TN15 .121 J9
HYTHE CT21 ....308 D5
RSEV TN14 ....117 M9
TONN TN10 ....210 F7
Old Loose Hl
MAID/SHEP ME15 ....185 L7
Old Maidstone Rd RSIT ME8 ..98 C9
SCUP DA14 ....65 J5
Old Manor Wy BXLYHN DA7 ...45 M3
CHST BR7 ....63 H5
Old Md FOLKN CT19 ....310 D4
Old Mill Cl EYN DA4 ....89 J1
RMAID ME17 ....187 J2
Old Mill Rd RMAID ME17 * ..187 J3
WOOL/PLUM SE18 ....27 P9
The Old Mi RSIT ME9 * 130 D1
Old Montague St WCHPL E1 ..24 D1
Old Oak Rd ASH TN23 ....252 A9
HAWK TN18 ....318 B9
Old Orchard La
E/WMAL ME19 ....153 L3
The Old Orch RHAM ME8 ......97 J4
Old Otford Rd RSEV TN14 ...148 C3
Old Palace STPH/PW TN12 * .283 J9
Old Palace Rd CROY/NA CRO..83 H7
Old Park Av DVE/WH CT16 ...291 H5
Old Park Cl DVE/WH CT16 ...291 H5
Old Park Hl DVE/WH CT16 ...291 H5
Old Park Rd ABYW SE2 ....28 P8
DVW CT17 ....291 J5
Old Pattens La ROCH ME1 ....95 J4
Old Pearson St GNWCH SE10 * .41 H1
Old Perry St CHST BR7 ......64 A6
RDART DA2 ....69 J1
Old Polhill RSEV TN14 .....118 C9
Old Pond Rd ASH TN23 .....252 C8
Old Post Office La
BKHTH/KID SE3 ....42 F4
Old Printworks Cl WSTB CT5.105 L6
Old Rectory Cl RASHE TN25 .283 P3
RFOLK CT18 ....288 B3
Old Regent Dr CRBK TN17 ...319 L3
Old Rd BRCH CT7 ....139 M1
CHAT ME4 ....45 M5
DART DA1 ....232 C4
DIT/AY ME20 ....154 D3
GVW DA11 ....69 M4
STRD SE23 ....71 P6
Old Rd East GVW DA11 ....49 M9
Old Rd West GVW DA11 ....49 L9
Old Roman Rd RDV CT15 .....262 B7
Old Ruttington La CANT CT1 ..5 G1
Old School Cl BECK BR3 .....61 K8
Old School Ct HDCN TN27 ...219 N7
HOO/HM ME3 ....72 F3
SWLY BR8 ....88 B5
Old School Gdns MARG CT9 ..111 N3
Old School La E/WMAL ME19 .122 C9
Old School Ms FOLK CT20 * .310 C8
RCANTW CT4 ....195 L4
Old School Pl CROY/NA CRO..82 F8
LING RH7 ....48 B3
MAID/BEAR ME14 ....13 C5
Old School Rd BRDST CT10 ..113 K8
The Old School WI BRDST CT10.113 K8
RCANTE CT3 ....132 C6
Old Soar Rd BGR/WK TN15 ...150 A2
Oldstairs Rd DEAL CT14 ....263 H5
Oldstead Rd BMLY BR1 ....62 B3
Old Studio Cl CROY/NA CRO..83 J4
Old Surrenden Manor Rd
RASHW TN26 ....280 G2
Old Tannery Cl TENT TN30 ..300 C8
Old Terry's Lodge Rd
RSEV TN14 ....150 C1
The Old Tilmanstone Colliery
RDV CT15 * 230 E7
Old Tovil Rd MAID/SHEP ME15.185 L1
Old Tree La RMAID ME17 ....185 N8
Old Tree Rd RCANTE CT3 ....138 B5
Old Tye Av BH/WHM TN16 ....145 P1

Old Valley Rd RCANTW CT4 ..228 C7
Old Vicarage Gdn
CANTW/ST CT2 ....137 L7
Old Vicarage Gdns
RASHE TN25 ....223 P8
The Old Vicarage SWCH CT13 *.201 K3
The Old Wk RSEV TN14 ......182 C6
Old Walting St CANT CT1 .....4 C4
Old Wardsdown WADH TN5 ...315 M3
Old Watling St STRD ME22 ...71 K7
Old Wy RASHW TN26 ....322 F7
Old Whetsted Rd
STPH/PW TN12 ....212 G8
Old Woolwich Rd GNWCH SE10.25 N9
The Old Yews HART DA3 ......68 F9
Oleander Cl ORP BR6 ....86 E9
O'Leary Sq WCHPL E1 ....24 F1
Olive Gv RAM CT11 * 17 H2
Oliver Av SNWD SE25 ....83 L1
Oliver Cl CHAT ME4 ....40 M1
RM20 ....47 M1
Oliver Crs EYN DA4 ....89 L4
Oliver Gdns EHAM E6 ....26 F1
Oliver Gv SNWD SE25 ....83 L1
Oliver Ms PECK SE15 ....40 G5
Oliver Rd DART DA1 ....46 D9
Oliver St STPH/PW TN12 ....246 B8
STPH/PW TN12 ....85 M9
WTHK RM20 ....47 M1
Oliver Twist Cl ROCH ME1 ...18 D7
Olivier Dr HOO/HM ME3 ......72 B5
Olivine Ct SIT ME10 ....99 K7
WALD ME5 ....5 G7
Olliffe Cl WALD ME5 ....125 L3
Olliffe St POP/IOD E14 ......25 M6
Olmar St STHWK SE1 ....24 D9
Olron Crs BXLYHS DA6 ....44 D3
Olven Rd WOOL/PLUM SE18 ...35 N1
Olyffe Av WELL DA16 ....44 C3
Olyffe Dr BECK BR3 ....62 A3
Omega St NWCR SE14 ....41 M2
Omer Av MARG CT9 ....113 H3
Ommaney Rd NWCR SE14 .....41 L3
Ondine Rd PECK SE15 ....40 F5
Onega Ga BERM/RHTH SE16 ...25 H6
One Tree Cl FSTH SE23 ......41 J7
Onslow Crs CHST BR7 ....63 M7
Onslow Rd CROY/NA CRO 82 F4
Onslow Rd CROY/NA CRO 82 F4
RAM CT11 ....95 J3
Ontario Wy POP/IOD E14 ....25 L6
Onyx Dr SIT ME10 ....99 L8
Opal Cl CAN/RD E16 ....26 C2
Openshaw Rd ABYW SE2 ......28 A7
Ophir Ter PECK SE15 ....40 G2
Oppenheim Rd LEW SE13 .....42 B3
Optima Pk DART DA1 * 46 A4
Orache Dr MAID/BEAR ME14..156 F7
Orange Court La ORP BR6 ...116 B3
Orange Pl BERM/RHTH SE16 ..25 H7
Orangery La ELTH/MOT SE9 ..43 K6
Orange St CANT CT1 * 4 E4
WAP E1W 24 D4
Orange Ter POP/IOD E14 * ...19 H6
Orbit Cl WALD ME5 ....125 M5
Orb St WALW SE17 ....24 B8
Orchard Av BELV DA17 ....28 D9
CROY/NA CRO 84 B6
DART DA1 ....232 C4
DEAL CT14 ....45 M5
DIT/AY ME20 ....154 D3
GVW DA11 ....69 M4
STRD SE23 ....71 P6
Orchard Cl BXLYHN DA7 ......44 G3
DVE/WH CT16 ....136 E9
DVE/WH CT16 ....260 C8
EDEN TN8 ....206 C8
HART DA3 ....41 J7
MAID/SHEP ME15 * 13 F7
MSTR CT12 ....141 J3
RASHE TN25 ....142 G1
RCANTE CT3 ....168 C9
RCANTE CT3 ....169 K3
RMAID ME17 ....185 H8
RSEV TN14 ....187 H7
RSEV TN14 ....149 H6
RTWE/PEM TN2 ....270 C1
STPH/PW TN12 ....273 N2
WSTB CT5 ....105 N3
Orchard Cots FAV ME13 * ...113 H8
Orchard Ct CRBK TN17 ......230 A1
RCANTE CT3 ....230 A1
WLGTN SM6 ....82 A9
Orchard Crs STPH/PW TN12..273 P2
RSEV TN14 ....140 A1
Orchard Dr BKHTH/KID SE3 ..42 C3
DVW CT17 ....290 F4
ORP BR6 ....206 D8
GRAYS RM17 ....32 B5
NROM TN28 ....337 K7
RASHE TN25 ....223 P9
RSIT ME9 ....109 H5
TONN TN10 ....211 H5
Orchard Fld HYTHE CT21 * ..286 D6
RASHW TN26 ....280 C4
Orchard Flats CANT CT1 * ..167 A5
Orchard Gdns MARG CT9 ....111 P4
Orchard Gn HDCN TN27 .....247 N4
Orchard Gv CROY/NA CRO 84 B4
DIT/AY ME20 ....154 A2
IOS ME12 ....78 C1
ORP BR6 ....86 C6
PGE/AN SE20 ....60 G6
Orchard Hts RASHE TN25 ...252 C4
Orchard Hl DART DA1 ....45 N6
LEW SE13 ....41 P2
Orchard La DEAL CT14 ......233 J3
MSTR CT12 ....141 M3
RASHE TN25 ....192 G3
RASHE TN25 ....253 J3
Orchard Lea MEO DA13 * 92 C8
RTON TN11 ....210 C5
Orchard Ms DEAL CT14 ......233 J4
Orchard Pk Rd FOLK CT20 ...108 A6
Orchard Park Homes
HB CT6 * 108 A6

Orchard Pl FAV ME13 132 G6
MAIDW ME16 12 C6
POP/IOD E14 25 P3
SIT ME10 129 P2
STMC/STPC BR5 * 64 E9
Orchard Ri CROY/NA CR0 84 B5
RRTW TN3 268 G9
Orchard Ri East BFN/LL DA15 44 A6
Orchard Ri West BFN/LL DA15 44 A6
Orchard Rd BELV DA17 28 F7
BMLY BR1 62 G7
GVW DA11 68 G1
HB CT6 107 L3
LYDD TN29 326 E9
MAID/BEAR ME14 156 B8
MARG CT9 111 P5
ORP BR6 86 C9
ORP BR6 117 K3
RSEV TN14 148 E1
SCUP DA14 64 A3
SEV TN13 148 D7
SOCK/AV RM15 31 M1
STPH/PW TN12 213 H4
SWCH CT13 201 J7
SWCM DA10 48 C6
TENT TN30 301 H4
WELL DA16 44 D4
Orchard Rw HB CT6 * 107 M6
The Orchards RCANTW CT4 257 L5
Orchard St CANTW/ST CT2 4 B3
DART DA1 46 E7
MAID/SHEP ME15 13 F7
RHAM ME8 97 H7
Orchard Ter RDART DA2 * 47 L6
RYE TN31 * 330 A7
The Orchard BKHTH/KID SE3 42 B3
MAID/BEAR ME14 156 E8
SEV TN13 148 D6
SWLY BR8 65 M8
WSTB CT5 * 105 M7
Orchard Va HYTHE CT21 308 F5
Orchard Vw
MAID/BEAR ME14 156 D4
RCANTE CT3 200 G1
RSIT ME9 131 H2
TENT TN30 301 K8
Orchard Vls SCUP DA14 * 64 E5
Orchard Wy BGR/WK TN15 149 M2
CRBK TN17 297 N3
CROY/NA CR0 84 B4
EGRIN RH19 265 H7
IOS ME12 79 K6
OXTED RH8 175 K9
RDART DA2 66 D2
SNOD ME6 123 N6
STPH/PW TN12 273 P2
Orchid Cl EHAM E6 26 F1
IOS ME12 78 A3
STRD ME2 71 L9
Orchidhurst RTWE/PEM TN2 270 G1
The Orchids RASHE TN25 283 N4
RFOLK CT18 287 J4
Orchis Gv GRAYS RM17 32 A7
Ordnance Crs GNWCH SE10 25 P5
Ordnance Rd CAN/RD E16 26 A1
GVE DA12 49 N7
WOOL/PLUM SE18 27 H9
Ordnance St CHAT ME4 6 A7
Ordnance Ter CHAT ME4 6 A5
Oregano Dr POP/IOD E14 25 N2
Oregon Sq ORP BR6 86 E5
Orford Rd CAT SE6 61 P2
Orgarswick Av LYDD TN29 326 F7
Orgarswick Wy LYDD TN29 326 G7
Oriel Cl MTCM CR4 82 C1
Oriental Rd CAN/RD E16 26 E4
Orient Pl CANTW/ST CT2 4 E1
Oriole Wy DIT/AY ME20 153 N2
THMD SE28 28 A3
Orion Rd ROCH ME1 95 H7
Orion Wy KEN/WIL TN24 3 J7
Orissa Rd WOOL/PLUM SE18 27 M8
Orleans Rd NRWD SE19 60 D5
Orlestone Gdns ORP BR6 87 M9
Orlick Rd GVE DA12 70 D1
Ormanton Rd SYD SE26 60 G3
Orme Cots GDST RH9 * 204 A2
Ormesby Cl THMD SE28 28 C3
Ormiston Rd GNWCH SE10 26 B8
Ormonde Av ORP BR6 86 D6
Ormonde Rd FOLK CT20 11 H2
HYTHE CT21 309 H6
Ormside St PECK SE15 24 F9
Orpheus St CMBW SE5 40 D2
The Orpines WBY/YAL ME18 183 N4
Orpington By-Pass
RSEV TN14 117 P3
Orpington Rd CHST BR7 64 A9
Orpins Cl RASHE TN25 284 E2
Orr Cl RFOLK CT18 288 C8
Orsett Heath Crs
CDW/CHF RM16 33 H6
Orsett Rd GRAYS RM17 32 C8
Orton St WAP E1W 24 D4
Orwell Cl DIT/AY ME20 153 N1
Orwell Spike E/WMAL ME19 153 H7
Osberton Rd LEE/GVPK SE12 42 E6
Osborne Cl BECK BR3 84 B1
Osborne Dr
MAID/BEAR ME14 * 156 F2
Osborne Gdns HB CT6 108 A5
THHTH CR7 60 C8
Osborne Rd BELV DA17 28 E8
DEAL CT14 263 H2
GILL ME7 7 J3
KEN/WIL TN24 3 K7
THHTH CR7 60 C8
Osborne Ter MARG CT9 15 J6
Osborn La FSTH SE23 41 L8
Osborn St WCHPL E1 24 C1
Osborn Ter BKHTH/KID SE3 42 D5
Osbourn Av WGOS CT8 111 M5
Osbourne Rd BRDST CT10 113 L9
RDART DA2 47 H7
Oscar Rd BRDST CT10 113 N9
Oscar St BROCKY SE4 41 N3
DEPT SE8 41 N2
Osgood Av ORP BR6 86 G9
Osgood Gdns ORP BR6 86 G9
Osier Fld RASHE TN25 253 H2
The Osier Fld RASHE TN25 * 253 H2
Osier Rd RSIT ME9 131 K2
Oslac Rd CAT SE6 61 P4
Osmers Hl WADH TN5 294 A8
Osmond Gdns WLGTN SM6 82 B9
Osmunda Bank EGRIN RH19 265 H2
Osney Wy GVE DA12 70 B1
Osprey Av WALD ME5 96 B4
Osprey Cl EHAM E6 26 F1
HAYES BR2 85 P5
WSTB CT5 105 K7
Osprey Ct RFOLK CT18 288 C9
Osprey Est BERM/RHTH SE16 24 G7
Osprey Gdns SAND/SEL CR2 114 A4
Osprey Wk DIT/AY ME20 153 N3
Ospringe Cl PGE/AN SE20 61 J6
Ospringe Pl FAV ME13 132 E7
RTWE/PEM TN2 271 J2
Ospringe Rd FAV ME13 132 E7
Ospringe St FAV ME13 132 D7
Ossory Rd STHWK SE1 24 D8
Osterberg Rd DART DA1 46 F5
Osterley Cl STMC/STPC BR5 64 C7
Osterley Gdns THHTH CR7 60 C8
Ostlers Ct HOO/HM ME3 * 71 L3
SNOD ME6 123 P5
Ostlers La BRCH CT7 139 N3
Oswald Pl DVW CT17 291 J5
Oswald Rd DVW CT17 291 J5
Osward CROY/NA CR0 114 C4
Oswyth Rd CMBW SE5 40 E3
Otford Cl BMLY BR1 63 L9
BXLY DA5 45 K7
PGE/AN SE20 61 J7
Otford Crs BROCKY SE4 41 M7
Otford La RSEV TN14 117 N7
Otford Rd RSEV TN14 148 G5
Otham Cl CANTW/ST CT2 136 F9
Otham St MAID/SHEP ME15 186 E4
Otley Rd CAN/RD E16 26 D2
Otlinge Rd STMC/STPC BR5 87 L1
Ottawa Crs DVE/WH CT16 291 K4
Ottawa Rd TIL RM18 49 L3
Otterbourne Pl EGRIN RH19 264 E7
MAID/SHEP ME15 186 B2
Otterbourne Rd CROY/NA CR0 83 H6
Otterden Cl ASH TN23 282 C2
ORP BR6 86 F8
Otterden Rd FAV ME13 161 K7
Otterden St CAT SE6 61 N3
Otterham Quay La RHAM ME8 97 L6
Otteridge Rd
MAID/BEAR ME14 156 D9
Otterpool La RASHE TN25 307 M2
Otters Cl STMC/STPC BR5 87 L1
Otto Cl CAT SE6 61 M2
SYD SE26 61 H2
Otway St CHAT ME4 6 D7
GILL ME7 7 K1
Otway Ter CHAT ME4 6 E6
Oulton Cl THMD SE28 28 C2
Our Ladys Flats RDV CT15 * 230 C9
Out Elmstead La RCANTW CT4 228 B4
Outfall Av LYDD TN29 347 K5
Outram Rd CROY/NA CR0 83 L6
Outwich St HDTCH EC3A 24 B2
Oval Gdns GRAYS RM17 32 D6
Oval Rd CROY/NA CR0 83 J6
The Oval BFN/LL DA15 44 C8
HART DA3 68 G9
LYDD TN29 327 H5
Ovenden Rd RSEV TN14 147 L5
Overbrae BECK BR3 61 N5
Overbury Av BECK BR3 61 P9
Overbury Crs CROY/NA CR0 114 F4
Overcliffe GVW DA11 49 L7
Overcliff Rd BROCKY SE4 41 N4
GRAYS RM17 32 E8
Overcourt Cl BFN/LL DA15 44 D7
Overdale RSEV TN14 178 G9
Overdown Rd CAT SE6 61 N3
Overhill Rd EDUL SE22 40 G8
Overhill Wy BECK BR3 84 G2
Overland La RCANTE CT3 170 B8
Overmead ELTH/MOT SE9 43 P8
SWLY BR8 88 D2
Over Minnis HART DA3 91 J7
Overstand Cl BECK BR3 84 D2
Overstone Gdns CROY/NA CR0 84 C4
Overton Rd ABYW SE2 28 B6
BRXN/ST SW9 40 A3
Overton Shaw EGRIN RH19 265 H5
Overton's Yd CROY/NA CR0 83 H7
Overy Liberty DART DA1 46 E8
Overy St DART DA1 46 E7
Ovett Cl NRWD SE19 60 E5
Ovex Cl POP/IOD E14 25 M6
Owen Cl CROY/NA CR0 83 J3
E/WMAL ME19 153 N4
THMD SE28 28 B4
Owenite St ABYW SE2 28 A7
Owen's Cl HYTHE CT21 309 M4
Owen Sq DEAL CT14 232 G7
Owens Wy FSTH SE23 41 L8
GILL ME7 73 N9
Owen Wk PGE/AN SE20 60 G6
Owgan Cl CMBW SE5 40 D1
Owl Cl SAND/SEL CR2 114 A4
Owletts Cl MAID/SHEP ME15 186 A3
Owl's Hatch Rd HB CT6 106 G5
Ownsted Hl CROY/NA CR0 114 F4
Oxenden Crs RCANTE CT3 169 K8
Oxenden Park Dr HB CT6 107 K2
Oxenden Rd FOLK CT20 310 B7
Oxenden Wy RCANTW CT4 228 C6
Oxenden Wood Rd ORP BR6 117 J1
Oxenford St PECK SE15 40 F4
Oxenhill Rd BGR/WK TN15 149 K2
Oxenhoath Rd RTON TN11 181 M7
Oxen Lease ASH TN23 252 B9
Oxenturn Rd RASHE TN25 253 P2
Oxestalls Rd DEPT SE8 25 H8
Oxford Av CDW/CHF RM16 33 H7
Oxford Cl GVE DA12 70 B1
Oxford Ct MANHO EC4N * 24 A3
Oxford Ms BXLY DA5 45 J9
Oxford Rd CANT CT1 4 E7
GILL ME7 96 A3
MAID/SHEP ME15 186 A2
NRWD SE19 60 D5
SCUP DA14 64 D4
SLH/COR SS17 34 A1
WLGTN SM6 * 82 B9
Oxford St MARG CT9 15 H6
SNOD ME6 123 P5
WSTB CT5 105 L5
Oxford Ter FOLK CT20 11 F5
Oxhawth Crs HAYES BR2 86 B2
Ox La TENT TN30 301 J5
Ox Lea RRTW TN3 269 M5
Oxleas EHAM E6 27 J2
Oxleas Cl WELL DA16 43 P3
Oxley Cl STHWK SE1 24 C8
Oxley Shaw La E/WMAL ME19 153 M2
Oxney Cl BRCH CT7 110 G6
Oxonian St EDUL SE22 40 F5
Oxted Rd GDST RH9 174 C7
Oyster Catchers Cl
CAN/RD E16 26 C2
Oyster Cl HB CT6 106 G3
SIT ME10 * 99 M8
Oyster Creek RYE TN31 339 J9
Oyster Rw WCHPL E1 24 F2
The Oysters WSTB CT5 * 105 M4
Ozolins Wy CAN/RD E16 26 A2

P

Pablo Neruda HNHL SE24 40 B5
Pace Pl WCHPL E1 24 E2
Pacific Cl SWCM DA10 48 C6
Pacific Rd CAN/RD E16 26 B2
Packer Pl WALD ME5 95 M6
Packer's La RAM CT11 17 G2
Packham Cl ORP BR6 87 K7
Packham Rd GVW DA11 69 K2
Packhorse Rd SEV TN13 148 B8
Packmores Rd ELTH/MOT SE9 43 P6
Padbrook OXTED RH8 175 K5
Padbrook La RCANTE CT3 169 N3
Paddlesworth Rd
E/WMAL ME19 123 K4
Paddock Cl BGR/WK TN15 151 M6
BKHTH/KID SE3 42 E4
CDW/CHF RM16 33 J1
DEAL CT14 232 E4
EYN DA4 67 J7
FOLK CT20 310 C6
LING RH7 234 F5
LYDD TN29 342 A6
ORP BR6 86 C8
OXTED RH8 175 J7
RRTW TN3 268 G3
SYD SE26 61 K3
Paddock Gdns EGRIN RH19 265 H9
NRWD SE19 60 E5
Paddock Rd BRCH CT7 111 H6
BXLYHS DA6 44 G5
Paddocks Cl STMC/STPC BR5 87 L6
The Paddocks ASH TN23 251 P8
BRDST CT10 113 L6
CDW/CHF RM16 33 H1
E/WMAL ME19 122 E9
EDEN TN8 267 J1
GILL ME7 96 D9
HB CT6 108 B5
MARG CT9 113 H4
RFOLK CT18 288 D4
SEV TN13 21 J1
The Paddock BH/WHM TN16 176 D2
CANT CT1 5 J5
CHAT ME4 6 B5
DVE/WH CT16 8 D2
MEO DA13 122 A6
RCANTE CT3 * 169 K8
RRTW TN3 268 E3
RTON TN11 211 P1
RTWE/PEM TN2 271 M2
RYE TN31 330 A6
SIT ME10 * 129 L3
Paddock Vw WSTB CT5 105 L7
Paddock Wy CHST BR7 63 P6
OXTED RH8 175 J7
Padfield Rd BRXN/ST SW9 40 C4
Pad's Hl MAID/SHEP ME15 13 G5
Padsole La MAID/SHEP ME15 13 G5
Padstow Cl ORP BR6 86 G8
Padua Rd PGE/AN SE20 61 J7
Padwell La ASH TN23 251 P9
Paffard Cl CANTW/ST CT2 137 L7
Pageant Cl TIL RM18 49 N2
Pageant Crs BERM/RHTH SE16 25 H4
Pageant Wk CROY/NA CR0 83 K7
Page Cl RDART DA2 68 A2
Page Crs CROY/NA CR0 82 G9
ERITH DA8 45 P1
Page Heath La BMLY BR1 63 H9
Page Heath Vls BMLY BR1 63 H9
Pagehurst Rd CROY/NA CR0 83 M4
STPH/PW TN12 245 P6
Page Pl FOLKN CT19 310 G3
Page Rd RFOLK CT18 288 C9
Pages Wk STHWK SE1 24 B6
Page's Wk STHWK SE1 24 B7
Paget Gdns CHST BR7 63 M7
Paget Ri WOOL/PLUM SE18 43 L1
Paget Rw GILL ME7 7 H2
Paget St GILL ME7 7 G3
Paget Ter WOOL/PLUM SE18 27 J9
Pagette Wy GRAYS RM17 32 B8
Pagitt St CHAT ME4 95 K4
Pagnell St NWCR SE14 41 M1
Pagoda Gdns BKHTH/KID SE3 42 B3
Pagoda Gv WNWD SE27 60 C1
Paiges Farm Cl RSEV TN14 179 H9
Paine Av LYDD TN29 342 B6
Paines Cots RYE TN31 * 339 K9
Painesfield Cl LYDD TN29 326 G2
Pains Hl OXTED RH8 175 M8
Painters Ash La GVW DA11 69 H2
Painter's Forstal Rd
FAV ME13 162 B1
Painters Ms BERM/RHTH SE16 24 D7
Palace Av MAID/SHEP ME15 13 F5
Palace Cl WSTB CT5 106 A4
Palace Gn CROY/NA CR0 114 C2
Palace Gv BMLY BR1 62 F7
NRWD SE19 60 F6
Palace Rd BH/WHM TN16 146 B6
BMLY BR1 62 F7
NRWD SE19 60 F6
Palace Sq NRWD SE19 60 F6
Palace St CANT CT1 5 F3
Palace Vw BMLY BR1 62 F9
CROY/NA CR0 84 C8
LEE/GVPK SE12 62 E1
Palewell Cl STMC/STPC BR5 64 D8
Palins Wy CDW/CHF RM16 32 B4
Pallant Wy ORP BR6 86 B7
Pallet Wy WOOL/PLUM SE18 43 J2
Palliser Dr RAIN RM13 29 M1
Palmar Crs BXLYHN DA7 45 J4
Palmar Rd BXLYHN DA7 45 J3
MAIDW ME16 155 J6
Palmarsh Rd STMC/STPC BR5 87 L1
Palm Av SCUP DA14 64 F5
Palm Bay Av MARG CT9 113 H2
Palm Bay Gdns MARG CT9 113 H2
Palmbeach Av HYTHE CT21 308 C7
Palmeira Rd BXLYHN DA7 44 F4
Palmer Av GVE DA12 69 P3
Palmer Cl HB CT6 107 N6
WWKM BR4 84 G6
Palmer Crs MARG CT9 113 H5
Palmer Dr BMLY BR1 86 C1
Palmer Rd RCANTE CT3 169 K8
Palmer's Av GRAYS RM17 32 D8
Palmers Brook RTON TN11 182 A9
Palmers Cross Hl
CANTW/ST CT2 165 P3
Palmers Dr GRAYS RM17 32 D7
Palmers Green La
STPH/PW TN12 243 L8
Palmers Orch RSEV TN14 118 E5
Palmerston Av BRDST CT10 143 N1
DEAL CT14 233 H6
Palmerston Crs
WOOL/PLUM SE18 27 K9
Palmerston Gdns WTHK RM20 31 N8
Palmerston Rd CHAT ME4 95 L5
CROY/NA CR0 83 J2
DVE/WH CT16 290 G3
ORP BR6 86 D8
WTHK RM20 31 N8
Palmerston St FOLKN CT19 10 E2
Palmers Yd HDCN TN27 247 P4
Palm Tree Cl RDV CT15 260 E1
Palm Tree Wy RFOLK CT18 286 G1
Palting Wy FOLK CT20 10 B5
Panfield Rd ABYW SE2 27 P5
Pankhurst Av CAN/RD E16 26 C4
Pankhurst Cl NWCR SE14 41 K1
Pankhurst Rd HOO/HM ME3 73 K1
Panmure Rd SYD SE26 61 H2
Pannell Cl EGRIN RH19 264 G7
Pannell Dr RFOLK CT18 288 C8
Pannell Rd HOO/HM ME3 56 C2
Panteny La RSIT ME9 130 D3
Panter's SWLY BR8 65 P6
Pantheon Gdns ASH TN23 282 C3
Pantiles RTWE/PEM TN2 22 C6
The Pantiles BMLY BR1 63 J9
BXLYHN DA7 45 H1
RTWE/PEM TN2 22 C7
Panton Cl CROY/NA CR0 82 G5
WALD ME5 125 P1
Paper La KEN/WIL TN24 283 J2
Papillons Wk BKHTH/KID SE3 42 E3
Papion Gv WALD ME5 125 K3
Papworth Cl FOLKN CT19 310 D4
Papworth Wy
BRXS/STRHM SW2 40 A8
Parade Ms BRXS/STRHM SW2 60 B1
Parade Rd FOLK CT20 310 B8
The Parade BH/WHM TN16 * 145 M6
BRCH CT7 110 D6
BROCKY SE4 * 41 M2
CROY/NA CR0 * 82 D3
DART DA1 * 45 P6
EDUL SE22 * 40 E4
EGRIN RH19 * 264 E5
FOLK CT20 11 G4
GVE DA12 * 69 P1
HART DA3 * 91 H2
KEN/WIL TN24 283 J3
MARG CT9 15 G3
MEO DA13 * 92 B4
NROM TN28 343 K4
PGE/AN SE20 * 61 J7
RAM CT11 * 143 K2
SIT ME10 * 129 N3
SOCK/AV RM15 * 30 F5
STRD ME2 71 N7
SWCM DA10 * 48 D6
SYD SE26 * 61 H3
WLGTN SM6 * 82 E9
Paradise RAM CT11 16 E3
Paradise Rw SWCH CT13 201 N1
Paradise St BERM/RHTH SE16 24 E5
Paragon RAM CT11 16 E6
Paragon Cl CAN/RD E16 26 B2
Paragon Ct MARG CT9 * 15 J2
Paragon Ms STHWK SE1 * 24 A7
Paragon Pl BKHTH/KID SE3 42 D3
Paragon St RAM CT11 16 E6
The Paragon BKHTH/KID SE3 42 D3
Paraker Wy HYTHE CT21 309 N4
Parbrook Rd HOO/HM ME3 53 P6
Parbury Rd FSTH SE23 41 L7
Parchmore Rd THHTH CR7 60 B8
Parchmore Wy THHTH CR7 60 B8
Pardoner Cl CANTW/ST CT2 166 B5
Pardoner St STHWK SE1 24 A6
Pardoners Wy DVE/WH CT16 291 H4
Parfett St WCHPL E1 24 D1
Parfitt Wy DVE/WH CT16 291 J5
Parham Cl CANT CT1 166 G2
Parham Rd CANT CT1 166 G2
CHAT ME4 95 L4
Parish Cl BRDST CT10 113 K7
Parish Gate Dr BFN/LL DA15 44 A7
Parish La PGE/AN SE20 61 K5
Parish Rd IOS ME12 78 A2
RCANTW CT4 195 K1
Parish Whf WOOL/PLUM SE18 26 F7
Park Ap BERM/RHTH SE16 * 24 F6
WELL DA16 44 D5
Park Av BMLY BR1 62 E5
BRCH CT7 110 G7
BRDST CT10 143 K2
DEAL CT14 232 G4
EDEN TN8 206 C8
GILL ME7 96 A4
GVW DA11 49 J9
IOS ME12 80 E6
MAID/BEAR ME14 13 H1
ORP BR6 86 A6
QBOR ME11 77 K3
RMAID ME17 185 K9
RTON TN11 210 C5
SIT ME10 129 M3
WSTB CT5 105 N3
WTHK RM20 31 K9
WWKM BR4 84 F6
Park Barn Rd RMAID ME17 187 L6
Park Cha BRDST CT10 143 K2
Park Cliff Rd SWCM DA10 48 A5
Park Cl MARG CT9 * 113 J4
OXTED RH8 175 J4
RFOLK CT18 288 D8
SBGH/RUST TN4 270 B6
Park Corner Rd MEO DA13 68 D3
Park Cots RAM CT11 * 143 K2
Park Ct DUL SE21 * 60 D2
SYD SE26 * 61 H5
Park Crs CHAT ME4 95 L6
ERITH DA8 29 H9
Park Crescent Rd MARG CT9 15 K6
Parkcroft Rd LEE/GVPK SE12 42 D8
Parkdale Rd WOOL/PLUM SE18 27 M8
Park Dr CHARL SE7 26 F8
HART DA3 68 C9
RASHW TN26 251 M3
SIT ME10 129 L4
Park End BMLY BR1 62 D7
Parker Av TIL RM18 49 N2
Parker Cl CAN/RD E16 26 F4
RHAM ME8 97 H9
Parker Pl RFOLK CT18 288 F7
Parker Rd CROY/NA CR0 83 H8
GRAYS RM17 32 A8
Parker's Rw STHWK SE1 24 C5
Parker St CAN/RD E16 26 F4
Parker Ter FSTH SE23 61 M1
Park Farm Cl CANTW/ST CT2 136 D7
FOLKN CT19 310 F3
RASHW TN26 281 M7
Park Farm Rd BMLY BR1 63 H7
E/WMAL ME19 122 F6
FOLKN CT19 310 D3
Parkfield BGR/WK TN15 149 L8
Parkfield Rd FOLKN CT19 10 D2
NWCR SE14 41 M2
RHAM ME8 97 J4
Parkfields CROY/NA CR0 84 C5
STRD ME2 71 L8
Parkfield Wy HAYES BR2 86 A3
Park Gdns ERITH DA8 29 J7
Parkgate BKHTH/KID SE3 42 D4
Park Ga BRDST CT10 143 L2
Parkgate Rd ORP BR6 88 B8
Park Gv BMLY BR1 62 F7
BXLYHN DA7 45 L5
Park Hall Rd DUL SE21 60 D1
Park Hl BMLY BR1 85 P1
FSTH SE23 61 H1
MEO DA13 91 P1
Park Hill Ri CROY/NA CR0 83 K6
Parkhill Rd BFN/LL DA15 64 A2
BXLY DA5 45 H8
Park Hill Rd CROY/NA CR0 83 K8
HAYES BR2 62 C8
RSEV TN14 149 K1
Park House Gdns
SBGH/RUST TN4 240 D7
Parkhouse St CMBW SE5 40 D1
Parkhurst Gdns BXLY DA5 45 J8
Parkhurst Rd BXLY DA5 45 J8
Parkland Cl SEV TN13 179 H5
Parkland Ct BRDST CT10 113 L7
Parkland Md BMLY BR1 63 L9
Parklands OXTED RH8 175 H7
Park La BGR/WK TN15 179 M1
BRCH CT7 111 H7
CRBK TN17 297 J8
CROY/NA CR0 83 J7
LING RH7 235 H4
MAID/BEAR ME14 155 L5
MARG CT9 15 K5
RASHW TN26 281 H1
RCANTW CT4 197 N6
RCANTW CT4 257 L4
RMAID ME17 186 A9
SEV TN13 21 G1
SOCK/AV RM15 30 G4
SWLY BR8 66 C8
Park Lea DEAL CT14 * 233 H4
Park Ley Rd CTHM CR3 144 A5
Park Md BFN/LL DA15 44 C6
Park Ms DVE/WH CT16 8 C2
GNWCH SE10 26 A8
Park Piazza LEW SE13 42 B7
Park Pl ASH TN23 282 E1
BMLY BR1 * 62 F7
DVE/WH CT16 8 C2
GVE DA12 49 N7
KEN/WIL TN24 253 J9
MARG CT9 15 G5
POP/IOD E14 25 K4
SEV TN13 148 C8
Park Rise Rd FSTH SE23 41 L9
Park Rd BECK BR3 61 M6
BMLY BR1 62 F7
BRCH CT7 111 H6
BRDST CT10 113 N7
CHST BR7 63 M5
DART DA1 46 G8
DVE/WH CT16 290 E2
E/WMAL ME19 152 D1
E/WMAL ME19 153 L1
EGRIN RH19 264 G7
FAV ME13 132 G7
FOLKN CT19 310 B5
GVW DA11 69 M1
HB CT6 107 L2
HYTHE CT21 308 G6
IOS ME12 57 M7

KEN/WIL TN24..........252 G3
FOLK RH7..........205 H7
MARG CT9..........9 H5
NROM TN28..........337 K8
OXTED RH8..........175 J4
OBOR ME11..........77 H2
RAM CT11..........16 C2
RCANTE CT5..........169 N1
RTON TN11..........181 M6
SBGH/RUST TN4..........270 E3
SIT ME10..........129 M2
SNWD SE25..........83 K1
STMC/STPC BR5..........87 K3
STPH/PW TN12..........182 C6
SWCM DA10..........88 C1
SWLY BR8..........88 E1
WARL CR6..........115 H8
WLGTN SM6..........82 A9
Park Rd North KEN/WIL TN24..........2 D2
Park Rw GNWCH SE10..........25 N9
Parkside BECK BR3..........61 J8
BKHTH/KID SE3 *..........42 D1
CDW/CHF RM16..........32 E6
DEAL CT14 *..........233 H5
EGRIN RH19..........264 F7
HOO/HM ME3..........52 B9
RSEV TN14..........117 M7
SCUP DA14..........64 D1
Parkside Av BMLY BR1..........65 P1
BXLYHN DA7..........45 M3
TIL RM18..........95 J6
Parkside Cl PGE/AN SE20..........61 J6
Parkside Cross BXLYHN DA7..........45 N3
Parkside Ms WARL CR6..........144 D1
Parkside Pde DART DA1 *..........45 P3
Parkside Pl DART DA1 *..........167 J1
Parkside Rd BELV DA17..........28 C2
Parkside Ter ORP BR6 *..........87 H5
Parkstone Rd PECK SE15 *..........40 C6
Park St CROY/NA CRO..........83 J5
DEAL CT14..........233 J3
DVE/WH CT16..........8 C2
KEN/WIL TN24..........252 C6
LYDD TN29..........342 A6
RTWE/PEM TN2..........23 C5
Park Ter RSEV TN14 *..........147 L3
SWCM DA10..........88 A6
The Park SCUP DA14..........64 D4
Park V KEN/WIL TN24..........252 C3
Park Vw BRCH CT7 *..........141 J7
CANTW/ST CT2..........137 L7
FOLKN CT19..........311 H4
RSIT ME9 *..........131 H8
RYE TN31..........329 P7
SOCK/AV RM15..........30 C4
Park View Cl EDEN TN8..........206 C8
RCANTE CT5..........169 N5
Park View Gdns EGRIN RH19 *..........264 C5
GRAYS RM17..........32 C8
Parkview Ms RAIN RM13..........29 N3
Park View Ri RDV CT15..........229 N2
Parkview Rd CROY/NA CRO..........83 K5
Park View Rd CTHM CR3..........144 B7
ELTH/MOT SE9..........43 M9
WELL DA16..........44 E4
Park Vis RTON TN11 *..........212 A1
SWCH CT13 *..........201 K8
Park Vis GNWCH SE10..........25 N9
Park Wy MAID/SHEP ME15..........185 N2
RMAID ME17..........185 H8
BXLY DA5..........65 P2
Parkway CDW/CHF RM16..........53 H1
CROY/NA CRO..........114 E4
ERITHM DA18..........28 D6
TONN TN10..........210 G5
The Parkway BRCH CT7..........111 J6
Parkwood BECK BR3..........61 N6
RYE TN31..........332 E9
Park Wood Cl ASH TN23..........282 E3
Parkwood Cl BRDST CT10..........143 K2
RTWE/PEM TN2..........270 F2
Park Wood La CRBK TN17..........246 F7
BXLY DA5..........66 D6

Pasley Rd CHAT ME4..........72 G8
Pasley Rd East GILL ME7..........72 G8
Pasley Rd North GILL ME7..........73 H8
The Passage MARG CT9 *..........15 J2
Passey Pl ELTH/MOT SE9..........43 K7
Passfield Dr POP/IOD E14..........25 L1
Passmore Wy
MAID/SHEP ME15..........185 N3
Pastens Rd OXTED RH8..........175 M7
Pastime Cl SIT ME10 *..........99 M6
Paston Cl WLGTN SM6..........82 B7
Paston Crs LEE/GVPK SE12..........42 F8
Pasture Rd CAT SE6..........42 C9
The Pasture KEN/WIL TN24..........252 C5
RFOLK CT18..........288 E8
The Patch SEV TN13..........148 D7
Patchways CDW/CHF RM16 *..........325 L3
The Pathway BRDST CT10..........113 N9
Patmos Rd BRXN/ST SW9 *..........40 F1
Patricia Ct WELL DA16..........44 D1
Patricia Wy BRDST CT10..........143 L6
Patrixbourne Av RHAM ME8..........96 F4
Patrixbourne Rd
RCANTW CT4..........197 N1
Patrol Pl CAT SE6..........41 P7
Pattenden Gdns
STPH/PW TN12..........213 H5
Pattenden La STPH/PW TN12..........244 C1
Pattenden Rd CAT SE6..........41 M9
Pattens Cl SIT CHAT ME4..........95 K6
Pattens La ROCH ME1..........95 K5
Patterdale Cl RAM CT11 *..........62 C5
Patterdale Pl PECK SE15..........41 J1
RDART DA2..........47 J9
Patterson Cl DEAL CT14..........232 F5
Patterson Rd NRWD SE19..........60 F5
Pattina Wk BERM/RHTH SE16..........25 H4
Paulet Rd CMBW SE5..........40 B3
Paul Gdns CROY/NA CRO..........83 L6
Paulinus Cl STMC/STPC BR5..........64 A8
Paul Julius Cl POP/IOD E14..........25 N3
Pauls Md LING RH7..........235 H4
Paul's Pl DVE/WH CT16..........8 C1
Pavement Sq CROY/NA CRO..........83 M5
The Pavement TENT TN30..........301 H4
WNWD SE27 *..........60 C1
Pavilion Cl DEAL CT14..........233 H1
Pavilion Ms SIT ME10..........99 H5
Pavilion La WBY/YAL ME18..........183 H3
Pavilion Meadow DVW CT17..........290 F3
Pavilion Rd FOLKN CT19..........10 E2
Pavilion Wy EGRIN RH19..........265 H6
Pawleyne Cl PGE/AN SE20..........61 J6
Pawson's Rd THHTH CR7..........83 H9
Paxton Av RFOLK CT18..........288 C9
Paxton Pl WNWD SE27..........60 E1
Paxton Rd BMLY BR1..........62 E6
CAT SE6..........61 L2
FSTH SE23..........61 L2
Payden St RMAID ME17..........190 C3
RSIT ME9..........190 B1
Payers Pk FOLK CT20..........11 F4
Paynell Ct BKHTH/KID SE3 *..........42 C4
Paynesfield Rd
BH/WHM TN16..........145 M5
Payne's La MAID/SHEP ME15..........185 M4
Payne St DEPT SE8..........25 J9
Pay St RFOLK CT18..........288 E5
Payton Cl MARG CT9..........112 E7
Payton Ms CANT CT1..........5 H2
Peabody Cl CROY/NA CRO..........85 P5
GNWCH SE10 *..........41 P2
Peabody Cots HNHL SE24 *..........40 C8
Peabody Est CMBW SE5 *..........40 D2
HNHL SE24 *..........40 B8
WALW SE17 *..........24 A7
Peabody Hl DUL SE21..........60 B9
Peace Cl SNWD SE25..........83 K1
Peace Wy WOOL/PLUM SE18..........27 H9
Peach Cft GVW DA11..........69 J2
Peachum Rd BKHTH/KID SE3..........42 A2
Peacock Gdns SAND/SEL CR2..........114 B4
Peacock Ms WALD ME5..........12 D5
Peacock St GVE DA12..........49 N8
Peafield Wood Rd
RCANTW CT4..........227 K6
Peak Dr SWCH CT13..........201 J7
Peak Hl SYD SE26..........61 J5
Peak Hill Av SYD SE26..........61 J5
Peak Hill Gdns SYD SE26..........61 J5
The Peak SYD SE26..........61 J2
Peal Cl HOO/HM ME3..........73 L2
Peal Rd CROY/NA CRO..........82 E5
Pean Hl WSTB CT5..........135 L2
Pearcefield Av FSTH SE23..........41 J9
Pear Cl NWCR SE14..........41 L1
Pearsonwood Rd ERITH DA8..........45 P2
Pearfield Rd FSTH SE23..........61 L3
Pearl Cl EHAM E6..........27 H2
Pearl St WAP E1W *..........24 E4
Pearl Wy E/WMAL ME19..........153 K9
Pearman Cl RHAM ME8..........97 K5
Pearse St RKTW TN5..........295 H2
Pearse St PECK SE15..........24 B8
Pearson's NWCR SE14..........41 N2
Pearsons Green Rd
STPH/PW TN12..........243 K4
Pearson's Green Rd
STPH/PW TN12..........243 K4
Pearson's Wy BRDST CT10..........113 K6
Pearson Wv DART DA1..........66 F1
Pear Tree Av DIT/AY ME20..........154 B4
Pear Tree Cl BRDST CT10..........113 H9
CRBK TN17..........298 A6
Peartree Cl HAYES BR2..........85 N2
Pear Tree Cl SWLY BR8..........65 M8
Pear Tree La LYDD TN29..........327 H5
MAID/SHEP ME15..........185 N5
GILL ME7..........86 F7
Peartree La GVE DA12..........71 J5
WAP E1W *..........24 F1
Peartree Rd HOO/HM ME3 *..........71 K4
Peartree Rd CAT SE6..........107 P5
Pease Hl BGR/WK TN15..........26 B7
Peasley La CRBK TN17..........296 C1

Peatfield Cl BFN/LL DA15..........64 A2
Peat Wy HOO/HM ME3..........55 P1
Peckarmans Wd SYD SE26..........60 G3
Peckford Pl BRXN/ST SW9..........40 A3
Peckham Cl SIT ME10..........99 H6
Peckham Gv PECK SE15..........24 B7
Peckham High St PECK SE15..........40 C1
Peckham Hill St PECK SE15..........40 C1
Peckham Hurst Rd
RTON TN11..........181 D1
Peckham Park Rd PECK SE15..........40 C1
Peckham Rd CMBW SE5..........40 C1
Peckham Rye EDUL SE22..........40 C6
Pecks Yd WCHPL E1 *..........24 C1
Pedding Hl RASHE TN25..........200 A1
Pedding La RCANTE CT3..........200 A1
Peel Dr SIT ME10..........130 B1
Pekin Cl POP/IOD E14..........25 L3
Pelham Cl CMBW SE5..........40 E4
Pelham Cots BXLY DA5 *..........45 K9
Pelham Gdns FOLK CT20..........310 D7
Pelham Rd BALYHN DA7..........45 J4
GVW DA11..........69 K8
RAM CT11..........16 C4
Pelham Rd South GVW DA11..........49 K9
RCANTW CT4..........26 A9
Pelham St STRD ME2..........71 J9
Pelier Rd CAT SE6..........62 C1
Pelham St EDUL SE22..........40 F9
Pell Cl WADH TN5..........294 B9
Pellings Cl HAYES BR2..........62 C9
Pelling St POP/IOD E14..........25 J2
Pellipar Rd WOOL/PLUM SE18..........26 P8
Pells La BGR/WK TN15..........120 D5
Pelton Rd GNWCH SE10..........25 M9
Pelwood Rd RYE TN31..........344 B1
Pemberton Gdns SWLY BR8..........65 N9
Pemberton Rd RYE/WIL TN24..........3 G4
Pemberton Sq STRD ME2..........71 J8
Pemble Cl STPH/PW TN12..........242 B2
Pembroke CHAT ME4..........72 C7
Pembroke Gdns LEE/GVPK SE12..........43 L7
Pembroke Cl ERITH DA8..........28 H7
Pembroke Dr SOCK/AV RM15..........30 E5
Pembroke Gdns RHAM ME8..........127 H1
Pembroke Ms NROM TN28..........337 H5
SEV TN13 *..........148 E7
Pembroke Pde ERITH DA8..........29 H8
Pembroke Ri EYN DA4..........67 H7
Pembroke Ri CHAT ME4..........72 G8
Pembroke Rd BMLY BR1..........62 E4
CHAT ME4 *..........72 G7
EHAM E6..........26 C1
ERITH DA8..........29 H8
RMAID ME17..........185 H8
SEV TN13..........148 D8
SNWD SE25..........83 K1
Pembury Av RTWE/PEM TN2 *..........271 N1
Pembury Cl BRXN/ST SW9..........40 A3
Pembury Crs SCUP DA14..........64 C1
Pembury Gdns MAIDW ME16..........12 A3
Pembury Gra RTWE/PEM TN2..........271 M2
Pembury Hall Rd
RTWE/PEM TN2..........241 H9
Pembury Pl RASHE TN25..........252 C5
Pembury Rd BXLYHN DA7..........45 H2
RTON TN11..........240 D3
RTWE/PEM TN2..........23 C4
TON TN9..........240 D1
Pembury St SIT ME10..........129 M1
Pembury Wy RTON TN11..........147 J2
Pemdevon Rd CROY/NA CRO..........82 F6
Penang St WAP E1W *..........24 E4
Penarth St PECK SE15..........24 F9
Penberth Rd CAT SE6..........42 A8
Pencester Ct DVE/WH CT16 *..........8 E4
Pencester Rd DVE/WH CT16..........8 D4
Pencraig Wy PECK SE15..........24 E6
Pendit Dr DART DA1..........24 E6
Penda Rd ERITH DA8..........45 K1
Pendennis Rd SEV TN13..........148 B2
Penderry Ri CAT SE6..........62 B1
Pendlebury House
CHARL SE7 *..........43 J1
Pendragon Rd BMLY BR1..........62 E2
Pendrell Rd NWCR SE14..........41 L1
Pendrell St WOOL/PLUM SE18..........27 L9
Penenden HART DA3..........91 H9
Penenden Heath Rd
MAID/BEAR ME14..........155 N5
Penenden St MAID/BEAR ME14..........13 F1
Penerley Rd CAT SE6..........41 P9
RAIN RM13..........29 N1
Penfield La RSIT ME9..........129 P9
Penfold Cl CROY/NA CRO..........82 F7
MAID/SHEP ME15..........186 B5
WALD ME5..........95 M1
Penfold Gdns RDV CT15..........229 N8
Penfold Hl RMAID ME17..........187 L3
Penfold La BXLY DA5..........44 F9
Penfold Rd ERITH DA8..........45 M3
Penfolds Cl TONN TN10..........210 F5
Penfold Wy MAID/SHEP ME15..........185 P5
Penford Gdns ELTH/MOT SE9..........43 J5
Penford St CMBW SE5..........40 B1
Pengarth Rd BXLY DA5..........44 F6
Penge La PGE/AN SE20..........61 J6
Pengelly Pl CANTW/ST CT2..........4 C1
Penge Rd SNWD SE25..........60 G9
Penguin Cl STRD ME2..........71 M9
Penhale Cl ORP BR6..........87 H3

Penhall Rd CHARL SE7..........26 E7
Penhill Rd BXLY DA5..........44 E8
Penhurst Cl MAID/BEAR ME14..........156 F3
Peninsular Park Rd CHARL SE7..........26 B8
Penlee Cl EDEN TN8..........206 D8
Penmon Rd ABYW SE2..........27 H5
Pennack Rd PECK SE15..........24 C7
Pennant Rd ROCH ME1..........95 H5
Pennant Cl SIT ME10..........130 A3
Pennethorne Rd PECK SE15..........41 H1
Penn Gdns CHST BR7..........63 M8
Penn Hl ASH TN23..........282 B2
Pennine Wk RTWE/PEM TN2..........23 J1
Pennine Wy BXLYHN DA7..........46 B1
GVW DA11..........69 J2
KEN/WIL TN24..........252 C5
RSEV TN14..........186 D2
Pennington Cl CANTW/ST CT2..........137 P6
Pennington Mnr
SBGH/RUST TN4 *..........240 C7
Pennington Rd
SBGH/RUST TN4..........240 E7
Pennington Wk WAP E1W *..........24 E3
Pennington Wy
LEE/GVPK SE12..........62 F1
Penn La BXLY DA5..........44 F7
RSEV TN14..........177 M1
Penny Cress Rd IOS ME12..........78 A3
Pennycroft CROY/NA CRO..........114 B3
Pennyfields CRBK TN17..........298 A3
Pennyroyal Av EHAM E6..........27 H2
Pennpool La WELL DA16..........44 D4
Penrith Cl BECK BR3..........61 P7
Penrith Pl WNWD SE27..........60 B1
Penrith Rd THHTH CR7..........60 C8
Penry St STHWK SE1 *..........24 C7
Penshurst Av BFN/LL DA15..........44 C7
Penshurst Cl BGR/WK TN15..........120 B1
CANTW/ST CT2..........166 F1
RHAM ME8..........96 C4
Penshurst Gdns MARG CT9..........113 L4
Penshurst Gn HAYES BR2..........85 J2
Penshurst Rd FAV ME13..........132 C5
BXLYHN DA7..........45 H2
RHAM ME8..........96 G2
RTON TN3..........239 L9
THHTH CR7..........82 G2
Penshurst Wy STMC/STPC BR5 *..........87 K1
The Penstocks
MAID/SHEP ME15..........185 J1
The Pentagon CHAT ME4 *..........6 C4
Pentridge St PECK SE15..........40 F1
Pentstemon Dr SWCM DA10..........88 B2
Pent Vale Cl FOLKN CT19..........310 D5
Penventon Cl TIL RM18..........49 L3
Pen wy TONN TN10..........211 H5
Peplis Av DVE/WH CT16..........8 E1
Pepler Ms CMBW SE5 *..........24 C8
Peppercorn Cl THHTH CR7..........60 D8
Pepper Hl GVW DA11..........68 C1
Pepperhill La GVW DA11..........68 C1
Peppermead Sq LEW SE13..........41 N6
Peppermint Cl CROY/NA CRO..........82 D6
Pepys Av POP/IOD E14..........25 L6
Pepys Cl GVW DA11..........69 H2
DART DA1..........67 H2
Pepys Crs CAN/RD E16..........26 B4
Pepys Est DEPT SE8..........25 H7
Pepys Park East DEPT SE8..........25 H6
Pepys Ri ORP BR6..........86 G5
Pepys Rd NWCR SE14..........41 K3
Pepys Wy STRD ME2..........71 J9
Perch Cl DIT/AY ME20..........123 P9
Perch La RRTW TN3..........272 E7
Percival Rd ORP BR6..........86 C5
Percival Ter DVW CT17..........291 J8
Percy Av BRDST CT10..........113 L4
Percy Rd BECK BR3..........113 J8
BXLYHN DA7..........44 G3
CAN/RD E16..........26 P1
MARG CT9..........15 G2
PGE/AN SE20..........61 K6
RAM CT11..........16 E1
SNWD SE25..........83 L2
Percy St GRAYS RM17..........32 D9
Peregrine Cl HYTHE CT21..........308 C7
Peregrine Ct WELL DA16..........44 B2
Peregrine Dr SIT ME10..........129 P5
Peregrine Rd E/WMAL ME19..........153 K9
Peri Ct CANT CT1..........186 H1
Peridot St EHAM E6..........26 F1
Perie Rw GILL ME7 *..........72 C9
Perifield DUL SE21..........60 B2
Perimeter Rd DIT/AY ME20..........154 B1
Periton Rd ELTH/MOT SE9..........43 H5
Periwinkle Cl SIT ME10..........99 M9
Perkins Av MARG CT9..........112 C5
Perkins Cl RDART DA2..........91 J1
Perks Cl BKHTH/KID SE3 *..........42 C5
Perpins Rd ELTH/MOT SE9..........44 A7
Perran Cl HART DA3..........91 J1
Perran Rd BRXS/STRHM SW2..........60 B1
Perries Md FOLKN CT19..........310 G4
Perrot Wy RFOLK CT18..........288 E2
Perry Av EGRIN RH19..........265 M5
Perryfield St MAID/BEAR ME14..........12 E1
Perry Cv DART DA1..........46 C5
Perry Hall Cl ORP BR6..........87 H1
Perry Hall Rd ORP BR6..........86 G1
Perry Hl CAT SE6..........61 M1
Perry La RTON TN11..........200 C6
Perryhill La HRTF TN7..........267 M8
Perry Mnr CHST BR7..........64 A5

Perryn Rd BERM/RHTH SE16..........24 E6
Perry Ri FSTH SE23..........61 L2
Perry Rd DAGW RM9..........28 E1
RCANTE CT5..........169 H5
Perry's Cl FAV ME13..........132 C5
Perry's La ORP BR6..........117 J7
Perry St CHAT ME4..........72 G5
CHST BR7..........64 A5
DART DA1..........45 N4
DART DA1..........49 J9
Perry St Gdns CHST BR7..........64 B5
Perry V FSTH SE23..........61 J1
Perry Wy SOCK/AV RM15..........30 F3
Persant Rd CAT SE6..........62 C2
Perseverance Pl BRXN/ST SW9..........40 A1
Perth Gdns SIT ME10..........129 K1
Perth Rd BECK BR3..........62 A8
DART DA1..........68 D9
Pested Bars Rd
MAID/SHEP ME15..........185 P6
Pested La RASHE TN25..........192 E8
Petchart Cl STRD ME2..........94 B3
Peter Av OXTED RH8..........174 G5
Peterboat Cl GNWCH SE10..........25 P7
Peter Candler Wy
KEN/WIL TN24..........253 H5
Peters Cl WELL DA16..........44 A3
Petersfield RTWE/PEM TN2..........271 N1
Petersfield Cl MAID DA1..........122 A4
Petersham Dr STMC/STPC BR5..........64 B8
Petersham Ter CROY/NA CRO *..........82 D7
Peterstone Rd ABYW SE2..........27 P5
Peter St DEAL CT14..........233 J2
DVE/WH CT16..........8 C3
FOLK CT20..........11 G3
Peterwood Wy CROY/NA CRO..........82 E6
Petfield Cl IOS ME12..........78 C2
Petham Gn RHAM ME8..........96 F4
Peto St North CAN/RD E16..........26 A3
Petrel Cl HB CT6..........108 C6
Petrel Wy FOLK CT19..........288 D9
Petro St South CAN/RD E16..........26 A3
Pettacre Cl THMD SE28..........27 K6
Petta La RCANTE CT3..........169 K7
Pett Bottom Rd RCANTW CT4..........227 H5
Pett Cl RHAM ME8..........96 F5
Pettenden St SIT ME10..........99 N6
Petten Gv STMC/STPC BR5..........87 K5
Petteridge La STPH/PW TN12..........272 F2
Pettfield Hill Rd FAV ME13..........151 P2
Pett Hl RCANTW CT4..........197 L2
Petticoat La LVPST EC2M..........24 B1
Petticoat Sq WCHPL E1 *..........24 C2
Petticoat Tower WCHPL E1 *..........24 C2
Pettits Rw FAV ME13 *..........132 E6
Pett La HDCN TN27..........221 J5
Pettman Cl HB CT6..........107 L3
Pettman Crs THMD SE28..........27 L5
Pettman Ms WSTB CT5 *..........105 K4
Pett's Crs MSTR CT12..........141 J7
Pett St WOOL/PLUM SE18..........26 F7
Petts Wood Rd
STMC/STPC BR5..........86 E2
Petty Wales MON EC3R *..........24 B3
Petworth Rd BXLYHS DA6..........45 J6
Peverel EHAM E6..........27 H2
Peverel Rd MAID/BEAR ME14..........156 C7
Peverill Rd DVE/WH CT16..........291 J2
Pewter Ct CANT CT1..........4 E7
Peyton Pl GNWCH SE10..........42 A1
Phalarop Wy CHAT ME4..........73 J5
Pharos Dr DVE/WH CT16..........8 E1
Pheasant Cl CAN/RD E16..........26 C2
Pheasant Rd
MAID/SHEP ME15..........185 N3
Pheasant Rd CHAT ME4 *..........95 P4
Pheasants' Hall Rd
RCANTW CT4..........197 L3
Phelps Cl BGR/WK TN15..........120 B1
Phelp St WALW SE17..........24 A9
Philchurch Pl WCHPL E1..........24 D2
Philenor Rd WOOL/PLUM SE18..........27 M8
Philip Corby Cl MARG CT9..........112 C3
Philip Gdns CROY/NA CRO..........84 C6
Philippa Gdns ELTH/MOT SE9..........43 H6
Philip Sydney Rd
CDW/CHF RM16..........31 N8
Philip Wk PECK SE15..........40 G4
Phillip Av SWLY BR8..........65 K3
Phillippa Ct SIT ME10..........99 M7
Phillippa Ct SIT ME10..........99 M7
Phillips La RTON TN11..........310 B5
Phillips Cl DART DA1..........46 B7
Phillips Ct RHAM ME8..........87 M1
Phillips Rd BELV DA17..........111 H7
Philpot La FENCHST EC3M..........24 B3
Philpots La RTON TN11..........209 K4
Philpott St WCHPL E1 *..........24 E2
Phineas Pett Rd
ELTH/MOT SE9..........43 J4
Phoebeth Rd LEW SE13..........41 N4
Phoenix Cl WWKM BR4..........84 G6
Phoenix Ct POP/IOD E14..........25 K7
Phoenix Dr HAYES BR2..........85 N7
WBY/YAL ME18..........183 M5
Phoenix Pk
MAID/SHEP ME15..........186 A1
Phoenix Pl DART DA1..........46 D8
Phoenix Rd PGE/AN SE20..........61 J5
WDS ME16 *..........125 N3
Phoenix Wharf Rd STHWK SE1..........24 C5
Picardy Manorway BELV DA17..........28 C6
Picardy Rd BELV DA17..........28 F7
Picardy St BELV DA17..........28 F6
Piccadilly La RCANTW CT4..........194 G3
Pickering Gdns CROY/NA CRO..........83 L5
Pickering St
MAID/SHEP ME15..........185 M5
Pickford Cl BXLYHN DA7..........45 M1
Pickforde La WADH TN5..........315 H5
Pickford La BXLYHN DA7..........45 M1
Pickford Rd BXLYHN DA7..........45 M2
Pickhurst Gn HAYES BR2..........85 J4
Pickhurst La HAYES BR2..........85 J3
Pickhurst Md HAYES BR2..........85 J4
Pickhurst Pk HAYES BR2..........84 G2
Pickhurst Ri WWKM BR4..........84 G5
Pickle's Wy HOO/HM ME3..........52 A2
Pickmoss La RSEV TN14..........148 F1
Pickneybush La LYDD TN29..........325 M8

Pickwick Crs ROCH ME1 ......95 H4
Pickwick Gdns GVW DA11 ......69 H2
Pickwick Rd DUL SE21 ......40 D8
Pickwick Wy CHST BR7 ......63 N5
Picton Rd RAM CT11 ......16 C4
Picton St CMBW SE5 ......40 D1
Piedmont Rd
  WOOL/PLUM SE18 ......27 L8
Pie Factory Rd RDV CT15 ......229 P9
Pier Approach Rd GILL ME7 ......73 K7
Pier Av HB CT6 ......107 K2
  WSTB CT5 ......105 P5
Pierce Mill La RTON TN11 ......212 C5
Pier Head WAP E1W * 24 E4
Piermont Pl BMLY BR1 ......63 M5
Piermont Rd EDUL SE22 ......41 H6
Pierpoint St WSTB CT5 ......105 L7
Pierremont Av BRDST CT10 ......113 M9
Pier Rd CAN/RD E16 ......26 C4
  CHAT ME4 ......7 G7
  ERITH DA8 ......29 K9
  GILL ME7 ......73 K8
  GVW DA11 ......49 K7
  SWCM DA10 ......47 P5
Pier St POP/IOD E14 ......25 M7
The Pier DVE/WH CT16 ......260 C8
Pier Wy THMD SE28 ......27 L6
Pier Whf GRAYS RM17 * 48 E1
Pigdown La EDEN TN8 ......237 L5
Pigeon La HB CT6 ......107 M4
Piggs Cnr GRAYS RM17 * 32 D6
Pigott St POP/IOD E14 ......25 K2
Pike Cl BMLY BR1 ......63 C5
  FOLK CT19 ......310 D4
Pikefish La STPH/PW TN12 ......213 M9
Pike Rd RDV CT15 ......230 F7
Pikey La RLNG RH7 ......205 H5
Pikey La E/WMAL ME19 ......153 L7
Pilckem Cl CANT CT1 ......167 J3
Pile La STPH/PW TN12 ......246 D5
Pilgrimage St STHWK SE1 ......24 A5
Pilgrim Hl WKWD SE27 ......40 C1
Pilgrims Cl RMAID ME17 ......159 H9
Pilgrims Ct DART DA1 ......46 C6
Pilgrims Lakes RMAID ME17 ......188 E4
Pilgrims La CDW/CHF RM16 ......31 M4
  OXTED RH8 ......145 M9
  RCANTW CT4 ......194 F2
Pilgrims Ms POP/IOD E14 ......25 N3
Pilgrims Spring FOLKN CT19 ......310 F5
Pilgrims Rd CANT CT1 ......5 G5
  STRD ME2 ......93 N8
Pilgrims' Rd SWCM DA10 ......48 C5
Pilgrims Wy BGR/WK TN15 ......149 K1
Pilgrims' Wy BH/WHM TN16 ......146 C8
Pilgrims Wy CANT CT1 ......5 J5
  DART DA1 ......47 H9
  DIT/AY ME20 ......124 C7
  DVE/WH CT16 ......291 H4
  E/WMAL ME19 ......152 D8
Pilgrims' Wy EDEN TN8 ......206 E9
Pilgrims Wy HDCN TN27 ......221 K2
  MAID/BEAR ME14 ......125 N9
  MAID/BEAR ME14 ......125 H8
  RASHE TN25 ......222 A5
Pilgrims' Wy RMAID ME17 ......157 L6
Pilgrim's Wy WSTRD ME17 ......188 F3
Pilgrim's Wy STRD ME2 ......94 B3
Pilgrims Wy East RSEV TN14 ......149 H1
Pilgrims Wy West RSEV TN14 ......148 E1
Pilkington Rd ORP BR6 ......85 P3
  PECK SE15 ......41 H5
  RTON TN11 ......181 N6
Pillar Box La BGR/WK TN15 ......150 B7
Pilot Cl DEPT SE8 ......25 J9
Pilot Rd ROCH ME1 ......95 H6
Pilots Av DEAL CT14 ......232 F5
Pilot's Farm Rd RCANTW CT4 ......196 F7
Pilots Pl GVE DA12 ......49 N7
Pimpernel Cl
  MAID/BEAR ME14 ......156 E8
Pimpernel Wy WALD ME5 ......125 K1
Pinchbeck Rd ORP BR6 ......116 C1
Pinchin & Johnsons Yd
  WCHPL E1 * 24 D3
Pinchin St WCHPL E1 ......24 D3
Pincott Pl BROCKY SE4 ......41 K4
Pincott Rd BXLYHS DA6 ......45 J6
Pincroft Wd HART DA3 ......91 M1
Pindar St SDTCH EC2A 13 J1
Pine Av GVE DA12 ......49 P9
  WWKM BR4 ......84 E5
Pine Cl DIT/AY ME20 ......153 P2
  PGE/AN SE20 ......61 J1
  SWLY BR8 ......68 E1
Pine Coombe CROY/NA CRO 84 A8
Pinecrest Gdns ORP BR6 ......86 C8
Pinecroft WOOL/PLUM SE18 ......44 C1
Pinefield Cl POP/IOD E14 * 25 K5
Pine Gv EDEN TN8 ......206 C8
  EGRIN RH19 ......264 E5
  GILL ME7 ......73 J6
  MAID/BEAR ME14 ......155 N6
Pineham Rd RDV CT15 ......291 L1
Pinehurst RSEV TN14 ......149 K6
Pinelands Cl BKHTH/KID SE3 * 42 D1
Pineneedle La SEV TN13 ......168 C8
Pine Pl MAID/SHEP ME15 ......185 K2
Pine Rdg TONN TN9 ......210 B6
Pine Ri MEO DA13 ......92 B3
Pine Rd STRD ME2 ......18 A4
Pinesfield La E/WMAL ME19 ......153 P2
Pineside Rd RCANTE CT3 ......168 B8
Pines Rd BMLY BR1 ......63 J8
The Pines BRDST CT10 ......113 H9
  CDW/CHF RM16 ......32 C4
  NRWD SE19 * 61 J7
Pine Tree La RDV CT15 ......291 J1
Pinetree Cl WSTB CT5 ......105 N3
Pine Tree La BGR/WK TN15 ......180 D1
Pine Vw BGR/WK TN15 ......151 M5
Pine Wk HB CT6 ......108 B5

Pine Wy FOLKN CT19 ......310 A4
Pine Way Cl EGRIN RH19 ......265 H9
Pinewood Av BFN/LL DA15 ......44 A9
  RSEV TN14 ......149 J6
Pinewood Cl CROY/NA CRO 84 B7
  MSTR CT12 ......143 H5
  ORP BR6 ......86 E5
  SLH/COR SS17 ......34 A6
  STPH/PW TN12 ......242 G3
Pinewood Dr ORP BR6 ......86 F9
  WALD ME5 ......126 A5
Pinewood Gdns
  SBGH/RUST TN4 ......240 D8
Pinewood Pl RDART DA2 ......65 N1
Pinewood Rd ABYW SE2 ......28 F7
  HAYES BR2 ......83 K1
  RTWE/PEM TN2 ......270 C3
Pin Hl CANT CT1 ......4 D6
Pinkham STPH/PW TN12 ......213 H5
Pinks Hl SWLY BR8 ......86 D9
Pinnacle Hl BXLYHN DA7 ......45 K5
Pinnacle Hl North BXLYHN DA7 ......45 K4
The Pinnacles CHAT ME4 ......73 J6
Pinnell Rd ELTH/MOT SE9 ......43 H5
Pinners La HDCN TN27 ......199 M9
Pinners La RDV CT15 ......229 M1
Pinnock La STPH/PW TN12 ......246 B8
Pinnock's Av HB CT6 * 107 M4
Pintail Cl RHAM ME8 ......26 F1
  HOO/HM ME3 ......56 D2
Pintail Dr MEO DA13 ......99 M3
The Pintails CHAT ME4 ......73 H6
Pintail Wy HB CT6 ......107 N8
Pinton Hl WADH TN5 ......314 F3
Pinto Wy BKHTH/KID SE3 ......42 F5
Pioneer Rd BKHTH/KID SE16 ......291 H4
Pioneer St PECK SE15 ......40 E2
Pioneer Wy SWLY BR8 ......65 N9
Pipers Gdns CROY/NA CRO 84 B4
Piper's Green Rd
  BH/WHM TN16 ......177 H4
Pipers La BH/WHM TN16 ......177 H4
Pippin Av RCANTW CT4 ......197 N5
Pippin Cl CROY/NA CRO 84 A1
  RCANTE CT3 ......200 F1
  RSIT ME9 ......148 D5
  SIT ME10 ......99 L8
Pippin Cft GILL ME7 ......96 D8
Pippin Rd STPH/PW TN12 ......212 C4
Pippins Ct TONN TN10 ......210 F5
The Pippins MEO DA13 ......92 B9
Pippin Wy E/WMAL ME19 ......183 H1
Piquet Rd PGE/AN SE20 ......61 J8
Pirbright Cl WALD ME5 ......126 A3
Pirbright Crs CROY/NA CRO 114 F1
Pirie St CAN/RD E16 ......26 C4
Pirrip Cl GVE DA12 ......50 B9
Pitchfont La OXTED RH8 ......175 K2
  WARL CR6 ......145 L1
Pitfield HART DA3 ......91 J1
Pitfield Crs THMD SE28 ......27 H4
Pitfield Dr MEO DA13 ......92 A7
Pitfold Rd LEE/GVPK SE12 ......42 E8
Pitlake CROY/NA CRO 2 B3
Pit La EDEN TN8 ......206 D6
Pitman St CMBW SE5 ......40 C1
Pitsea Pl WCHPL E1 ......24 G2
Pitsea St WCHPL E1 ......24 G2
Pitstock Rd RSIT ME9 ......130 H3
Pittlesden TENT TN30 ......301 H8
Pittlesden Pl TENT TN30 ......301 H8
Pitt Rd MAIDW ME16 ......186 A2
  ORP BR6 ......86 D8
  RMAID ME17 ......187 K9
  THHTH CR7 ......83 H2
Pittsmead Av HAYES BR2 ......85 K4
Pittville Gdns SNWD SE25 ......60 G3
Pivington La HDCN TN27 ......220 A8
Pixley St POP/IOD E14 ......25 J2
Pixot Hl STPH/PW TN12 ......243 J8
Pix's La CRBK TN17 ......319 M3
Pixton Wy CROY/NA CRO 114 E8
Pixwell La DEAL CT14 ......232 C6
Pizien Well Rd WBY/YAL ME18 ......183 H4
Place Farm Av ORP BR6 ......86 E5
Place La RASHW TN26 ......302 G5
  RSIT ME9 ......130 D5
The Place RCANTW CT4 ......229 J5
Plain Cots FOLK CT20 ......310 D7
Plain Rd FOLK CT20 ......310 D7
  RASHE TN25 ......284 F3
  STPH/PW TN12 ......245 H6
Plains Av MAID/SHEP ME15 ......185 N2
Plains of Waterloo RAM CT11 ......17 G3
Plaistow Gv BMLY BR1 ......62 F6
Plaistow Sq
  MAID/BEAR ME14 * 155 P6
Plane Av GVW DA11 ......48 G8
Plane St SYD SE26 ......61 H2
Plane Wk TONN TN10 ......210 F3
Plantain Pl STHWK SE1 * 24 B8
Plantation Cl RSIT ME9 ......89 N1
Plantation Dr STMC/STPC BR5 ......87 L3
Plantation La FENCHST EC3M 24 B3
Plantation Rd ERITH DA8 ......46 A2
  FAV ME13 ......132 F7
  GILL ME7 ......73 N9
  SWLY BR8 ......86 A6
  WSTB CT5 ......106 C4
The Plantation BKHTH/KID SE3 ......42 E5
Plassy Rd CAT SE6 ......41 P8
Platt Common BGR/WK TN15 ......151 M5
The Platters RHAM ME8 ......96 F6
The Plat EDEN TN8 ......206 C8
  RYE TN31 ......330 A7
Platt House La BGR/WK TN15 ......121 M7
Platt Mdw TN BGR/WK TN15 * 151 M5
The Platt LING RH7 ......235 K8
  RMAID ME17 ......217 H3
Plawsfield Rd BECK BR3 ......61 K7
Plaxdale Green Rd
  BGR/WK TN15 ......120 G6
Plaxtol Cl BMLY BR1 ......62 G7
Plaxtol La RTON TN11 ......180 F3

Plaxtol Rd ERITH DA8 ......45 J1
Playden La RYE TN31 ......338 E1
Playfield Crs EDUL SE22 ......40 E8
Playgreen Wy CAT SE6 ......61 N5
Playground Cl BECK BR3 * 61 K8
Playing Flds SWCH CT13 * 201 M3
Playstool Cl RSIT ME9 ......98 C8
Playstool Rd RSIT ME9 ......98 B8
Pleasance Rd STMC/STPC BR5 ......64 D8
Pleasance Rd Central
  LYDD TN29 ......343 L9
Pleasance Rd North
  LYDD TN29 ......343 K7
Pleasance Rd South
  LYDD TN29 ......347 L1
Pleasant Gv CROY/NA CRO 84 C7
Pleasant Valley La
  MAID/SHEP ME15 ......184 G7
Pleasant Vw ERITH DA8 ......29 K8
  ORP BR6 ......86 D9
Pleasent Pl IOS ME12 ......77 N1
Pleasure House La
  RMAID ME17 ......217 K2
Plevna St POP/IOD E14 ......25 N6
Pleydel Av NRWD SE19 ......60 F6
Pleydell Gdns FOLK CT20 ......10 D6
  NRWD SE19 * 60 F5
Plimsoll Av FOLKN CT19 ......310 C3
Plimsoll Cl POP/IOD E14 ......25 L2
Plomley Cl RHAM ME8 ......126 C1
Plough Ct HB CT6 ......108 A8
  RDV CT15 ......259 J2
Plough La CROY/NA CRO 82 D8
  EDUL SE22 ......40 F7
Plough Lane Cl WLGTN SM6 ......82 D9
Ploughmans Wy ASH TN23 ......282 A5
  RHAM ME8 ......97 H8
  WALD ME5 ......125 M4
Plough Rd IOS ME12 ......78 C2
  LING RH7 ......235 K7
Plough St WCHPL E1 * 24 D2
Plough Wy BERM/RHTH SE16 ......25 J7
  DEPT SE8 ......25 J7
Plough Wents Rd
  RMAID ME17 ......186 F9
Plover Cl HB CT6 ......108 C5
  WALD ME5 ......126 A4
Plover Rd DIT/AY ME20 ......153 N2
  IOS ME12 ......78 C2
  RFOLK CT18 ......288 C9
Plover Wy BERM/RHTH SE16 ......25 H6
Plowenders Cl E/WMAL ME19 ......152 E1
Pluckley Cl RHAM ME8 ......96 B6
Pluckley Gdns MARG CT9 ......113 K5
Pluckley Rd HDCN TN27 ......249 J7
  HDCN TN27 ......250 F4
  RASHW TN26 ......251 H5
  RASHW TN26 ......280 B1
Plug La MEO DA13 ......92 E9
Plumbers Rw WCHPL E1 ......24 D2
Plumbridge St GNWCH SE10 * 42 A2
Plumford Rd FAV ME13 ......162 D2
Plum La WOOL/PLUM SE18 ......43 M1
Plummer La MTCM CR4 ......300 A1
Plummer Rd CLAP SW4 ......39 N5
Plumpton Av HCH RM12 ......54 F1
Plumpton Cl BELV DA17 ......28 D6
Plumpudding La FAV ME13 ......134 E2
Plumstead Common Rd
  WOOL/PLUM SE18 ......27 J9
Plumstead High St
  WOOL/PLUM SE18 ......27 K7
Plumstead Rd
  WOOL/PLUM SE18 ......27 K7
Plumstone Rd BRCH CT7 ......140 F3
  MSTR CT12 ......141 H4
Plum Tree Gdns RASHW TN26 ......302 G6
Plumtree Gv GILL ME7 ......126 D1
Plum Tree La RSIT ME9 ......127 L5
Plumtree Rd HDCN TN27 ......247 K1
Plumtrees MAIDW ME16 ......184 F1
Plurenden Rd RASHW TN26 ......280 D9
Plymouth Dr SEV TN13 ......21 H2
Plymouth Rd BMLY BR1 ......62 F7
  CAN/RD E16 ......26 B1
Plymouth Whf POP/IOD E14 ......25 N7
Plympton Cl BELV DA17 ......28 D6
Plymstock Rd WELL DA16 ......44 E1
Poachers Cl WALD ME5 ......95 P9
Poachers End RCANTE CT3 ......108 D9
Pochard Crescent HB CT6 ......107 K5
Pocket Hl SEV TN13 ......169 H9
Podkin Wd WALD ME5 ......125 L5
Poets Cnr MARG CT9 ......3 J6
Poets Cl IOS ME12 ......232 G8
Point Cl GNWCH SE10 ......42 A2
Point Cnr RTON TN11 ......181 M9
Pointer Cl THMD SE28 ......28 C2
Pointers Cl POP/IOD E14 ......25 L8
Point Hl GNWCH SE10 ......42 A2
Polebrook Rd BKHTH/KID SE3 ......42 A4
Polecroft La CAT SE6 ......61 M1
Polegate Cots GRAYS RM17 * 31 P9
Polesden Rd RTWE/PEM TN2 ......272 A8
Polesteeple Hl
  BH/WHM TN16 ......145 N2
The Poles RSIT ME9 ......97 N2
Police Station Rd
  E/WMAL ME19 ......153 K4
Pollard Cl ASH TN23 ......252 C5
Pollard Rd WSTB CT5 ......105 K8
Pollards Oak Crs OXTED RH8 ......175 K4
Pollards Oak Rd OXTED RH8 ......175 K4
Pollards Wd OXTED RH8 ......175 K6
Pollards Wood Rd
  OXTED RH8 ......175 L7
Polley Cl RTWE/PEM TN2 ......271 N1
Pollyhaugh EYN DA4 ......89 K7
Polo Wy WSTB CT5 ......106 D5
Polperro Cl ORP BR6 ......86 E1
Polsted Rd CAT SE6 ......41 M8
Polthorne Gv
  WOOL/PLUM SE18 ......27 K7
Polytechnic St
  WOOL/PLUM SE18 ......27 H7

Pomell Wy WCHPL E1 ......24 C2
Pomeroy St PECK SE15 ......41 J1
Pomfret Houses
  RCANTW CT4 * 195 L2
Pomfret Rd CMBW SE5 ......40 B4
Pommeus La DEAL CT14 ......262 D1
Poncia Rd ASH TN23 ......282 D1
Pond Cl BKHTH/KID SE3 ......42 E3
Pond Cottage La BECK BR3 ......84 D5
Pond Dr SIT ME10 ......129 P5
Pond Farm Rd RMAID ME17 ......157 N3
  RSIT ME9 ......128 C4
Pondfield La GVE DA12 ......70 G6
Pondfield Rd HAYES BR2 ......85 H5
  ORP BR6 ......86 C7
Pond Hl HOO/HM ME3 ......52 B2
  RCANTE CT3 ......198 G6
Pond Hill Rd FOLK CT20 ......509 P2
Pond La BGR/WK TN15 ......180 B1
  RDV CT15 ......228 C3
  RDV CT15 ......262 C9
Pondmore Wy RASHE TN25 ......252 C5
Pond Rd BKHTH/KID SE3 ......42 D4
Pond St HAYES BR2 * 85 H1
Pond Wy EGRIN RH19 ......265 J5
Pondwood Ri ORP BR6 ......86 F4
Ponsford Rd RCANTW CT4 ......226 D7
Pontefract Rd BMLY BR1 ......62 E4
Pontoise Cl SEV TN13 ......148 E7
Ponycart La RCANTW CT4 ......226 D7
Pook La HDCN TN27 ......278 C5
Pool Cl BECK BR3 ......61 N6
Pool Ct CAT SE6 ......61 N1
Poolmans St BERM/RHTH SE16 ......24 G5
Poonah St WCHPL E1 ......24 F2
Poona Rd RTW TN1 ......21 F6
Poorhole La BRDST CT10 ......112 F8
Pootings Rd EDEN TN8 ......206 B9
Poot La RSIT ME9 ......75 J9
Pope Dr STPH/PW TN12 ......243 J9
Pope House La TENT TN30 ......301 J3
Pope Rd HAYES BR2 ......85 N2
Popes Gv CROY/NA CRO 84 C7
Popes La CANTW/ST CT2 ......137 K6
  OXTED RH8 ......174 A9
Pope's Rd BRXN/ST SW9 * 40 A5
Pope St MAIDW ME16 ......185 H1
  STHWK SE1 ......24 C8
Popham Rd IOS ME12 ......78 G2
Poplar Av GVE DA12 ......69 N5
  ORP BR6 ......86 C6
Poplar Bath St POP/IOD E14 ......25 L3
Poplar Cl ASH TN23 ......282 D1
  HOO/HM ME3 ......75 L4
  STRD ME2 ......94 E1
Poplar Dr HB CT6 ......107 H4
  RDV CT15 ......259 J2
Poplar Gv MAIDW ME16 ......185 H1
Poplar High St POP/IOD E14 ......25 L3
Poplar La BECK BR3 ......61 N5
  LYDD TN29 ......342 C9
Poplar Mt BELV DA17 ......28 E2
Poplar Pl THMD SE28 ......28 B3
Poplar Rd BRDST CT10 ......113 K7
  HNHL SE24 ......40 C3
  RAM CT11 ......16 D1
  STRD ME2 ......94 E1
  TENT TN30 ......332 A2
Poplars Cl HART DA3 ......68 C9
The Poplars ASH TN23 ......282 D1
  RCANTE CT3 ......138 C8
Poplar Wk CROY/NA CRO 40 C5
  HNHL SE24 ......40 C5
  MEO DA13 ......92 C3
Poplicans Rd STRD ME2 ......83 D2
Poppleton Rd WAN E11 ......243 H4
Poppy Crs IOS ME12 ......78 B3
Poppy La CROY/NA CRO 83 P4
Poppy Meadow
  STPH/PW TN12 ......243 H4
Popsal La RCANTE CT3 ......199 L1
Porchester Md BECK BR3 ......61 N7
Porchfield Cl GVE DA12 ......69 N1
Porcupine Cl ELTH/MOT SE9 ......42 G7
Porrington Cl CHST BR7 ......63 K7
Portal Cl WNWD SE27 ......60 C2
Port Av SWCM DA10 ......47 P7
Portbury Cl PECK SE15 ......40 C2
Portchester Cl HNHL SE24 ......40 C5
Port Cl MAID/BEAR ME14 ......156 C7
  WALD ME5 ......125 N2
Porter Cl IOS ME12 ......78 G4
Porter Rd ENAM E6 ......26 G2
Porters Ct STPH/PW TN12 ......272 C2
Porter's La FAV ME13 ......162 E2
Porters Wk RMAID ME17 ......187 H1
  WAP E1W * 24 E4
Porters Wnt STPH/PW TN12 ......272 C2
Porthallow Cl ORP BR6 ......86 C2
Porthcawe Rd SYD SE26 ......61 L4
Porthkerry Av WELL DA16 ......44 C5
Portland Av BFN/LL DA15 ......44 C7
  SIT ME10 ......130 A1
Portland Cl HYTHE CT21 ......308 D5
  KEN/WIL TN24 ......252 E2
Portland Cots CROY/NA CRO * 82 G4
Portland Ct RAM CT11 ......17 G2
Portland Crs ELTH/MOT SE9 ......42 G6
  GILL ME7 ......73 P3
Portland Pl HART DA3 * 68 C9
  SNOD ME6 ......123 H1
Portland Rd BMLY BR1 ......63 H3
  EGRIN RH19 ......265 H8
  GILL ME7 ......73 P3
  GVE DA12 ......49 M9
  GVW DA11 ......49 H5
  HYTHE CT21 ......308 C5
  ROCH ME1 ......124 B1

SNWD SE25 ......83 N1
Portland Sq WAP E1W 24 E4
Portland St CHAT ME4 ......95 N4
  WALW SE17 ......24 A8
Portland St BXLY DA5 ......45 N9
Portman Pk TON TN9 ......210 F7
Portman Rd RAM CT11 ......44 A8
Portmeadow Wk ABYW SE2 ......28 C5
Portree Ms GILL ME7 * 96 B5
Portree St POP/IOD E14 ......25 N2
Port Ri CHAT ME4 ......4 B6
Portsdown Cl MAIDW ME16 ......185 J1
Portsea Rd TIL RM18 ......49 N1
Portsmouth Cl STRD ME2 ......71 M4
Portsmouth Ms CAN/RD E16 ......26 C3
Portsoken St TWRH EC3N 24 C3
Port Victoria Rd HOO/HM ME3 ......56 D4
Portway WSTB CT5 ......105 K6
Portway Gdns
  WOOL/PLUM SE18 ......43 H2
Portway Rd HOO/HM ME3 ......52 B8
Post Barn Rd CHAT ME4 ......95 L4
Postern La RTON TN11 ......241 J1
  TON TN9 ......210 G8
Postling ASH TN23 ......252 B8
Postling Rd FOLKN CT19 ......310 B4
Postmill Cl CROY/NA CRO 83 N2
Postmill Dr MAID/SHEP ME15 ......185 L2
Post Office Rd RHAM TN18 ......317 H4
Post Office Sq RTW TN1 * 21 D5
Potash La BGR/WK TN15 ......151 M6
Pot Kiln La RASHW TN26 ......279 L5
Potten Street Rd BRCH CT7 ......140 B1
The Potteries RSIT ME9 ......97 P3
Potters Cl CROY/NA CRO 84 C5
  PECK SE15 * 40 E1
  RASHE TN25 ......252 B3
Potters Flds STHWK SE1 ......24 B4
Potter's La HAWK TN18 ......297 M9
Potter St SWCH CT13 ......201 P1
Potters Rd BXLY DA5 ......65 L1
  HOO/HM ME3 ......73 K2
Pottery St BERM/RHTH SE16 * 24 E5
Pottingfield Rd RYE TN31 ......338 D6
Poulders Rd SWCH CT13 ......201 L2
Poulters Wd HAYES BR2 ......85 N9
Poulton La RCANTE CT3 ......290 C2
Poultry CITYW EC2V 24 A2
Pound Bank Cl BGR/WK TN15 ......120 C3
Pound Cl ORP BR6 ......86 E6
Pound Ct ASH TN23 ......282 B8
Pound Court Dr ORP BR6 ......86 E6
Poundfield Rd HAWK TN18 ......318 E9
Poundhurst Rd RASHW TN26 ......304 E3
Pound La ASH TN23 ......282 C4
  CANT CT1 ......4 D3
  RASHE TN25 ......284 C3
  RCANTW CT4 ......195 J7
  RSEV TN14 ......117 L9
Pound Park Rd CHARL SE7 ......26 F7
Pound Pl ELTH/MOT SE9 ......43 L7
Pound Rd STPH/PW TN12 ......212 F4
Poundsbridge Hl RRTW TN3 ......269 J2
Poundsbridge La RTON TN11 ......239 J8
Pound Wy FOLK CT20 ......71 F5
Pounsley Rd SEV TN13 ......148 D6
Pout Rd SNOD ME6 ......123 N6
Poverest Rd STMC/STPC BR5 ......86 G2
Povey Av STRD ME2 ......72 C5
Powdermill Cl
  SBGH/RUST TN4 ......240 F9
Powder Mill La DART DA1 ......66 E1
  RTON TN11 ......209 M8
  SBGH/RUST TN4 ......240 E9
Powell Av RDART DA2 ......67 L1
Powell Cl DIT/AY ME20 ......154 F1
Powell Cotton Dr BRCH CT7 ......111 J7
Powerscroft Rd SCUP DA14 ......64 D5
Power Station Rd IOS ME12 ......79 H8
Powis St WOOL/PLUM SE18 ......27 H6
Powlett Rd BMLY BR1 ......62 E4
Powster Rd BMLY BR1 ......62 E4
Powys Cl BXLYHN DA7 ......28 G9
Poynder Rd TIL RM18 ......49 M9
Poynders Rd CLAP SW4 ......39 N4
Poynings Cl ORP BR6 ......87 K6
Poyntell Crs CHST BR7 ......63 P7
Poyntell Rd STPH/PW TN12 ......246 C5
Prageall Rd LEE/GVPK SE12 ......42 F1
Praill's La STPH/PW TN12 ......242 F7
Pratling St DIT/AY ME20 ......154 C1
The Precincts CANT CT1 * 5 F5
  ROCH ME1 ......15 F5
Premier Av CDW/CHF RM16 ......32 D5
Premiere Pl DIT/AY ME20 ......154 D5
Prendergast Rd
  BKHTH/KID SE3 ......42 C4
Prentis Cl WALW SE17 ......99 H9
Prentis Quay SIT ME10 ......99 H5
Prentiss Ct CHARL SE7 ......26 F7
Prescot St WCHPL E1 ......24 D3
Prescott Av STMC/STPC BR5 ......86 C4
Prescott Cl RDV CT15 ......291 M2
Presidents Dr WAP E1W 24 E4
Prestage Wy POP/IOD E14 ......25 M3
Prestbury Sq ELTH/MOT SE9 ......63 K3
Prested Rd RCANTW CT4 ......63 K3
Prestedge Av FAV ME13 ......143 E9
Prestley Dr TONN TN10 ......210 G3
Preston Av FAV ME13 ......133 H8
  GILL ME7 ......133 H8
Preston Cl WALW SE17 ......24 B8
Preston Dr BXLYHN DA7 ......44 F2
Preston Gv ASH TN23 ......44 F2
Preston Hall Gdns IOS ME12 ......80 E3
Preston Hl RCANTE CT3 ......169 L7
Preston La FAV ME13 ......169 L3
  RCANTE CT3 ......169 L3
Preston Malthouse
  FAV ME13 * 132 G2
Preston Pde WSTB CT5 ......104 C3
Preston Pk FAV ME13 ......132 G7
Preston Rd GVW DA11 ......49 J9

MSTR CT12 ....142 C1
NRWD SE19 ......60 B5
RCANTE CT3 .....169 L4
TON TN9 ....210 D9
Preston's Rd POP/IOD E14 ...25 M4
Prestons Md WWKM BR4 ....85 K7
Preston St FAV ME13 ...132 C1
Prestwood Cl
  WOOL/PLUM SE18 ....44 C1
Prestwood Gdns
  CROY/NA CR0
Pretoria Pde BROCKY SE4 * ...41 N3
Pretoria Rd CANT CT1 ....5 J4
  CHAT ME4 ....95 L4
  GILL ME7 ....7 K6
Prettymans La EDEN TN8 ...206 G6
Price Rd CROY/NA CR0 ...82 C9
Price's Av MARG CT9 ....112 F3
  RAM CT11 ....5 J4
Prickley Wd HAYES BR2 ...85 J5
Priddy's Yd CROY/NA CR0 ...83 H4
Pridham Rd THHTH CR7 ...83 J1
Pridmore Rd SNOD SME6 ...123 N5
Priest Av CANTW/ST CT2 ...166 B4
Priestfield Rd FSTH SE23 ...61 L2
  GILL ME7 ....96 B1
Priest Flds HB CT6 ....108 C5
Priestfields ROCH ME1 ....94 C4
Priest Hl OXTED RH8 ...175 L5
Priestlands Park Rd
  BFN/LL DA15 ...64 B2
Priestley Dr DIT/AY ME20 ...123 N9
Priest Wk WSTB CT5 ...106 A4
Priestwood Rd MEO DA13 ...122 C1
Prima Rd BRXN/ST SW9 ....40 A1
Primmett Cl BGR/WK TN15 ...120 D1
Primrose Av RHAM ME8 ....96 E4
Primrose Cl CAT SE6 ....62 A4
  CHAT ME4 ....95 K7
  WLGTN SM6 ....82 A5
Primrose Dr ASH TN23 ...282 E4
  DIT/AY ME20 ...154 C4
Primrose Hl RCANTW CT4 ...165 H5
Primrose La CROY/NA CR0 ...83 P5
  RSIT ME19 ...
Primrose Rd DVW CT17 ...291 H6
  STRD ME2 ....93 M9
Primrose Ter SDTCH EC2A ...24 B1
Primrose Wk NWCR SE14 ...41 L1
  STPH/PW TN12 ...243 H4
Primrose Wy MSTR CT12 ...142 B7
  WSTB CT5 ....106 B5
Prince Andrew Rd
  BRDST CT10
Prince Arthur Rd GILL ME7 ...73 H9
Prince Charles Av EYN DA4 ...67 K8
  IOS ME12 ....
  SIT ME10 ....130 A3
  WALD ME5 ....125 N1
Prince Charles Rd
  BKHTH/KID SE3 ....42 D2
  BRDST CT10 ....113 K6
Prince Charles Wy
  WLGTN SM6 ....
Prince Consort Dr CHST BR7 ...63 P7
Prince Edward Prom
  RAM CT11 ....16 B7
Prince Henry Rd CHARL SE7 ...43 H1
Prince Imperial Rd CHST BR7 ...63 M6
  WOOL/PLUM SE18 ...43 K2
Prince John Rd ELTH/MOT SE9 ...43 J6
Princelet St WCHPL E1 ...24 C1
Prince of Orange La
  GNWCH SE10 * ...42 A1
Prince of Wales Rd
  BKHTH/KID SE3 ....42 D2
  CAN/RD E16 ....26 D2
Prince of Wales Rbt DVW CT17 ...8 C6
Prince Philip Av
  CDW/CHF RM16 ....32 B2
Prince Regent La CAN/RD E16 ...26 D2
Prince Rd SNWD SE25 ....83 K2
Prince Rupert Rd
  ELTH/MOT SE9 ....43 K5
Princes Av IOS ME12 ....
  MSTR CT12 ....142 C3
  RDART DA2 ....47 H9
  STMC/STPC BR5 ....86 F2
  WALD ME5 ....125 M1
Princes Cl BRCH CT7 ...110 E6
  SCUP DA14 ....
Princes Ct WAP E1W 24 E3
Princes Crs MARG CT9 ...15 H5
Princes Dr SWCH CT13 ...202 F2
Princes Gdns MARG CT9 ...15 H5
Princes Pde HYTHE CT21 ...309 L8
Princes Pln HAYES BR2 ...85 P4
Princes Ri LEW SE13 ....42 A3
Princes Riverside Rd
  BERM/RHTH SE16 ....24 C4
Princes Rd DART DA1 ....46 B8
  GVE DA12 ....69 N3
  PGE/AN SE20 ....61 K5
Prince's Rd RAM CT11 ....16 D4
Princes Rd RDART DA2 ....47 J9
  SWLY BR8 ....66 C5
Princess Alice Wy THMD SE28 ...27 L5
Princess Anne Rd
  BRDST CT10 ....113 K6
Princess Cl TIL RM18 ....34 B7
Princess Cl WSTB CT5 ....106 B3
Princesses Pde DART DA1 * ...45 P6
Princess Margaret Av
  MARG CT9 ....113 J3
  MSTR CT12 ....142 F3
Princess Margaret Rd
  TIL RM18 ....34 A6
Princess Mary Av CHAT ME4 ...73 H8
Princes Rd ORP BR6 * ...
Princess Rd CROY/NA CR0 ...83 H3
  WSTB CT5 ....106 B3
Princess St BXLYHN DA7 ...45 H4
  FOLKN CT19 ....11 G1
Princess St DEAL CT14 ....233 J2
  DVW CT17 ....8 D4
  GVE DA12 ....49 M7
Prince's St LOTH EC2R 24 A2
Prince's St MAID/BEAR ME14 ...13 G3
Prince's St MARG CT9 ...15 G4

RAM CT11 ....17 F4
Princes St ROCH ME1 ....95 H3
Prince's St RTWE/PEM TN2 ...23 G5
Princes Ter HYTHE CT21 * ...308 E2
Prince St DEPT SE8 ....25 J9
Princes Vw DART DA1 ....46 C9
Prince's Wk MARG CT9 ...113 H2
Princes Wy CANTW/ST CT2 ...4 A3
  CROY/NA CR0 ....82 B9
  MAID/BEAR ME14 ....156 D3
  WWKM BR4 ....
Princethorpe Rd SYD SE26 ...61 K3
Prince William Ct DEAL CT14 * ...233 J2
Prinys Dr RHAM ME8 ....126 F1
Priolo Rd CHARL SE7 ....26 D8
Prior Cha GRAYS RM17 ....32 A7
Prioress Rd SWCM DA10 ....48 A5
Prioress St STHWK SE1 ....166 C4
  WNWD SE27 ....60 D2
Prioress St STHWK SE1 ....24 A6
Prior Pl ROCH ME1 ....94 C5
Prior Rd NROM TN28 ....343 K5
Priorsdean Cl MAIDW ME16 ...184 D2
Priorsford Av STMC/STPC BR5 ...87 H1
Prior St GNWCH SE10 ....42 A1
Prior's Wy EDEN TN8 * ...267 H2
Priory Av BY STMC/STPC BR5 ...86 F2
Priory Cl BECK BR3 ....61 L9
  CHST BR7 ....63 K7
  DART DA1 ....46 C6
  MAID/SHEP ME15 ....184 C3
  NROM TN28 ....336 E7
Priory Ctyd RAM CT11 ....16 D6
Priory Crs NRWD SE19 ....60 C6
Priory Dr ABYW SE2 ....28 C3
Priory Flds EYN DA4 ....89 J8
Priory Gdns CANT CT1 * ...166 F6
  DART DA1 ....46 D6
  FOLK CT20 ....11 G5
  SNWD SE25 ....61 L5
Priory Ga MAID/BEAR ME14 ...13 F3
Priory Gate Rd DVW CT17 ....8 B3
Priory Gv DIT/AY ME20 ....154 C3
  RSIT ME19 ....
  TON TN9 ....240 E1
Priory Hl DART DA1 ....46 D7
  DVW CT17 ....8 B3
Priory La EYN DA4 ....89 L5
  HB CT6 ....107 M5
  RASHE TN25 ....
Priory Leas ELTH/MOT SE9 * ...43 J9
Priory of St Jacob CANT CT1 ...166 D6
Priory Pk BKHTH/KID SE3 ....42 D4
  DIT/AY ME20 ....154 B1
Priory PI DART DA1 ....46 D7
Priory Rd BCH CT7 ....88 A7
  DART DA1 ....46 D6
  DVW CT17 ....8 B3
  FAV ME13 ....132 E6
  MAID/SHEP ME15 ....13 F3
  RAM CT11 ....16 A5
  RASHE TN25 ....305 M3
  RHAM ME8 ....96 D4
  STRD ME2 ....18 B3
  TON TN9 ....240 F1
Priory Rw FAV ME13 ....132 F4
Priory Station Approach Rd
  DVW CT17 * 8 B3
Priory St DVW CT17 ....8 B3
  TON TN9 ....240 E1
The Priory BKHTH/KID SE3 ...42 D4
  DVW CT17 ....8 B3
  ORP BR6 * 87 J4
Priory Wk TON TN9 ....240 E1
Priory Wy TENT TN30 ....301 K8
Pristling La STPH/PW TN12 ...245 N9
Pritchard Dr RDART DA2 ....
Priter Rd BERM/RHTH SE16 * ...24 D6
Probert Rd BRXS/STRHM SW2 ...40 A6
Probyn Rd BRXS/STRHM SW2 ...60 B1
Proctor Wk RFOLK CT18 ....288 C8
The Progress Est
  MAID/SHEP ME15 * 186 D1
Progress Wy CROY/NA CR0 ....82 B6
Promenade BRCH CT7 ....110 C5
The Promenade IOS ME12 ....80 E5
Prospect Av STRD ME2 ....72 B7
Prospect Cl BELV DA17 ....28 F7
  SYD SE26 ....61 H3
  WGOS CT8 ....111 M6
Prospect Gdns MSTR CT12 ...141 J5
Prospect Gv GVE DA12 ....49 N8
Prospect Ms BRCH CT7 * ...309 H5
Prospect PI BRCH CT7 ....109 P9
  BRDST CT10 * 113 N9
  CANT CT1 ....
  DVW CT17 ....291 J6
  GRAYS RM17 * 32 C9
  GVE DA12 ....49 P8
  HAYES BR2 ....
  MAIDW ME16 ....12 B7
  ROCH ME1 ....94 F4
  WAP E1W 24 F4
Prospect Rd BRCH CT7 ....110 D6
  BRDST CT10 ....113 N9
  FOLK CT20 ....310 A8
  HYTHE CT21 ....309 H5
  MSTR CT12 ....141 J6
  RTWE/PEM TN2 ....23 G8
  SBGH/RUST TN4 ....240 C8
  SEV TN13 ....149 H8
Prospect Rw CHAT ME4 ....6 D1
Prospect St BERM/RHTH SE16 ...24 D5
Prospect Ter RAM CT11 ....17 F5
Prospect V WOOL/PLUM SE18 ...45 N2
Prospect Wy RASHE TN25 ....284 F2
Provender La FAV ME13 ....131 L2
Provender Wk FAV ME13 * ...132 C5
Provender Wy
  MAID/BEAR ME14 ....156 B8
Providence Sq STHWK SE1 ...24 D5
Providence St ASH TN23 ....252 F9
  RDART DA2 ....
Provincial Ter PGE/AN SE20 * ...61 K6
Prusom St WAP E1W 24 E4
Puckle La CANT CT1 ....166 F6
Pucknells Cl SWLY BR8 ....65 L1
Puddingcake La CRBK TN17 ...320 A1

Pudding La MAID/BEAR ME14 ...12 E4
  MON EC5R 24 A3
  RCANTE CT3 ....200 E1
Pudding La RHAM ME8 ....97 J6
Puddledock La
  BH/WHM TN16 ....177 M8
  RDART DA2 ....65 N4
Puffin Cl BECK BR3 ....84 A2
Puffin Ct RFOLK CT18 ....288 D9
Puffin Rd HB CT6 ....108 B6
  HOO/HM ME3 ....86 D5
Pullman Cl MSTR CT12 ....143 H5
Pullman Ms LEE/GVPK SE12 ...62 F2
Pullman PI ELTH/MOT SE9 ...43 J6
Pump Cha WCHPL E1 ....24 C1
Pump Cl CANT CT1 ....166 C2
Pump House Cl HAYES BR2 ...62 D8
Pump House Ms WCHPL E1 * ...24 D3
Pump La MARG CT9 ....15 J1
  NWCR SE14 ....41 J1
  ORP BR6 ....88 A9
  RHAM ME8 ....96 F4
Punch Ct HART DA3 ....91 H7
Purbeck Rd CHAT ME4 ....95 H6
Purbrook St STHWK SE1 * ...24 B5
Purbrook St STHWK SE1 ....24 B6
Purcell Av TONN TN10 ....211 J4
Purser Wy GILL ME7 * 73 J8
Pursey Cl BGR/WK TN15 ...120 B1
Puttenden Rd RTON TN11 ...181 J9
Puttney Dr SIT ME10 ....99 P6
Pye Alley La WSTB CT5 ....135 K2
Pylon Wy CROY/NA CR0 ....82 D5
Pym Orch BGR/WK TN15 ...147 N9
Pym PI GRAYS RM17 ....32 B7
Pymham Cl ABYW SE2 ....27 P6
Pyott Ms CANT CT1 ....5 J4
Pyrmont Gv WNWD SE27 ...60 B2
Pyrus Cl WALD ME5 ....125 M5
Pysons Rd MSTR CT12 ....143 H2
Pytchley Crs NRWD SE19 ...60 C5
Pytchley Rd EDUL SE22 ....40 E4

Q

Quadrangle Cl STHWK SE1 * ...24 B7
The Quadrangle HNML SE24 * ...40 D1
Quadrant Rd THHTH CR7 ....
The Quadrant BXLYHN DA7 ...44 F1
  PUR RM19 ....30 F7
Quaggy Wk BKHTH/KID SE3 ...42 E5
Quail Gdns SAND/SEL CR2 ...114 D4
Quaker Cl SEV TN13 ....149 J8
Quaker Dr CRBK TN17 ....298 A1
Quaker La CRBK TN17 ....298 A1
Quakers Cl HART DA3 ....68 C9
Quaker's Hall La SEV TN13 ...149 H7
Quakers Gdns MSTR CT12 ...142 C1
Quantock Dr KEN/WIL TN24 ...2 C1
Quantock Gdns MSTR CT12 ...142 C1
Quantock Ms PECK SE15 ....40 C3
Quantock Rd BXLYHN DA7 ...45 N6
The Quarries RMAID ME17 ...185 P7
Quarrington La RASHE TN25 ...254 A9
Quarry Bank TON TN9 ....240 D2
Quarry Cl OXTED RH8 ....175 H6
Quarry Gdns TON TN9 * 240 D2
Quarry Hl BGR/WK TN15 ...149 J8
  GRAYS RM17 ....32 B8
Quarry Hill Rd BGR/WK TN15 ...151 H6
  TON TN9 ....240 D2
Quarry Ms PUR RM19 ....30 F7
Quarry Ri EGRIN RH19 ....265 K5
Quarry Rd GDST RH9 ....174 A3
  HYTHE CT21 ....308 D5
  MAID/SHEP ME15 ....185 M1
  OXTED RH8 ....175 H6
  RTW TN1 ....23 F1
Quarry Sq MAID/BEAR ME14 ...13 F2
Quarry Vw ASH TN23 ....282 A1
  E/WMAL ME19 * 152 D1
Quarry Wk HYTHE CT21 ....309 M4
Quarry Wd RASHE TN25 ....306 B1
Quay House POP/IOD E14 * ...25 K3
Quay La RDART DA2 ....47 P5
  SWCH CT13 ....201 P1
Quayside CHAT ME4 ....73 H7
Quebec Av BH/WHM TN16 ...176 E2
Quebec Rd TIL RM18 ....34 B6
Quebec Sq BH/WHM TN16 * ...176 E2
Quebec Wy BERM/RHTH SE16 ...24 C5
Queen Adelaide Rd
  PGE/AN SE20 ....61 J5
Queen Anne Av HAYES BR2 ...62 B9
Queen Anne Ga BXLYHN DA7 ...44 F4
Queen Anne Rd
  MAID/BEAR ME14 ....13 G4
Queen Anne Ter WAP E1W * ...24 E3
Queen Bertha Rd RAM CT11 ...16 B4
Queen Bertha's Av RECT CT7 ...111 K5
Queenborough Dr IOS ME12 ...58 B9
Queen Borough Gdns
  CHST BR7 ....63 P5
Queenborough Rd IOS ME12 ...77 L3
Queendown Av BRCH CT7 ...141 N1
Queen Elizabeth Av
  MARG CT9 ....113 J4
  TIL RM18 ....34 A6
Queen Elizabeth College
  GNWCH SE10 * 42 A1
Queen Elizabeth II Br

RDART DA2 ....47 J4
Queen Elizabeth Rd
  DVE/WH CT16 ....9 G3
Queen Elizabeth's Dr
  CROY/NA CR0 ....114 C4
Queen Elizabeth's Gdns
  CROY/NA CR0 ....114 C4
Queen Elizabeth Sq
  MAID/SHEP ME15 ....186 A5
Queen Elizabeth St STHWK SE1 ...24 B4
Queen Elizabeth's Wk
  WLGTN SM6 ....82 C8
Queen Mary Av TIL RM18 ...34 B7
Queen Mary Rd NRWD SE19 ...60 B5
The Queen Mother Ct
  ROCH ME1 ....94 C2
Queens Av BRCH CT7 ....110 E6
Queen's Av MAIDW ME16 ...12 A2
  MARG CT9 ....15 G5
Queens Av MSTR CT12 ....142 E3
  SNOD ME6 ....123 P5
Queensbridge Dr HB CT6 ...107 J1
Queens Cl WLGTN SM6 ....82 A9
Queens Ct HAWK TN18 ....317 J4
  KEN/WIL TN24 ....2 C4
Queenscourt Rd
  ELTH/MOT SE9 ....43 H6
Queensdown Rd DEAL CT14 ...263 H4
Queen's Dr RSEV TN14 ....149 H5
Queen's Farm Rd GVE DA12 ...70 G1
Queens Gdns DVW CT17 ....8 D3
Queens Gdns HB CT6 ....107 L1
  RDART DA2 ....47 H9
Queen's Garth FSTH SE23 * ...61 J1
Queens Gate Gdns CHST BR7 ...63 L5
Queens Gate Rd RAM CT11 ...16 C2
Queens House MAIDW ME16 ...154 D9
Queen's Mead Rd HAYES BR2 ...62 B9
Queens Ms DEAL CT14 ....233 J5
  FOLK CT20 ....310 A8
Queens Pde FAV ME13 * ...132 C6
  MARG CT9 ....112 F2
Queen's Rd BRDST CT10 ....113 J9
  BRXS/RUST TN4 ....270 C4
  CROY/NA CR0 ....82 C5
  EGRIN RH19 ....265 N7
Queens Rd ERITH DA8 ....29 K9
Queen's Rd FAV ME13 ....132 E6
  GILL ME7 * 7 J5
Queens Rd GVE DA12 ....69 N7
Queen's Rd HAWK TN18 ....317 J4
Queens Rd IOS ME12 ....58 D9
  KEN/WIL TN24 ....2 C4
  NROM TN28 ....337 H7
  PECK SE15 ....41 J2
  RAM CT11 ....17 J2
Queens Rd RCANTE CT3 ....170 E9
Queen's Rd RCANTE CT3 ....170 E9
  SBGH/RUST TN4 ....270 C4
  SNOD ME6 ....123 P5
  WALD ME5 ....96 A5
  WELL DA16 ....44 G4
  WGOS CT8 ....111 N5
  WLGTN SM6 ....82 A9
Queens Road Upper
  KEN/WIL TN24 ....2 D1
Queen's Rw WALW SE17 ....24 A9
Queens St HOO/HM ME3 ...53 H8
Queensthorpe Rd SYD SE26 ...61 K3
Queensway BRCH CT7 ....141 M1
  EGRIN RH19 ....265 H7
  HOO/HM ME3 ....38 E3
  LYDD TN29 ....327 H4
  STMC/STPC BR5 ....86 D1
  WWKM BR4 ....85 K8
Queenswood Rd BFN/LL DA15 ...46 B6
  DIT/AY ME20 ....125 J6
  FSTH SE23 ....61 L2
Queen Victoria Rw
  MANHO EC4N 24 A3
Queen Victoria Ter WAP E1W * ...24 E3
Quentin PI LEW SE13 ....42 C4
Quentin Rd LEW SE13 ....42 C3
Quentins Dr BRCH CT7 ....110 E5
Quentins Wk
  BH/WHM TN16 * 146 C1
Quernmore Cl BMLY BR1 ...62 B4
Quernmore Rd BMLY BR1 ...62 B5
Quern Rd DEAL CT14 ....232 F7
Querns PI CANT CT1 ....5 J4
Querns Rd CANT CT1 ....5 J4
The Quern MAID/SHEP ME15 ...185 K2

Quested Rd FOLKN CT19 ...310 B5
Quested Wy RMAID ME17 ...188 D5
Questor DART DA1 * 66 F1
Quetta Rd MSTR CT12 ....142 E3
Quex Rd WGOS CT8 ....111 N5
Quex View Rd BRCH CT7 ...111 H8
Quickbourne Cots
  RYE TN31 * 330 C5
Quickbourne La RYE TN31 ...330 B6
Quickrells Av HOO/HM ME3 ...52 B3
Quickstep Cl SIT ME10 ....99 N6
Quilter Rd STMC/STPC BR5 ...87 L3
Quilter St WOOL/PLUM SE18 ...27 N8
Quince Orch RASHW TN26 ...304 D8
Quince Rd LEW SE13 ....41 P3
Quincewood Gdns
  TONN TN10 ....210 E3
Quinion Cl WALD ME5 ....125 L5
Quinnell Gv WOOL/PLUM SE18 ...27 N8
Quinnell St RHAM ME8 ....96 D5
Quinneys PI WSTB CT5 ....106 B4
Quinton Cl BECK BR3 ....62 A9
  WLGTN SM6 ....82 A8
Quinton Rd RTW TN1 * 23 J4
Quixote Crs STRD SE22 * ...62 B6
Quorn Rd EDUL SE22 ....40 E5

R

Rabbit Hole RCANTW CT4 ...228 D7
Rabbits Rd EYN DA4 ....67 M8
Rabus PI EYN DA4 * 89 L3
Raby St POP/IOD E14 * 25 J5
Racecourse Rd LING RH7 ...235 J6
Racefield Cl GVE DA12 ....70 C5
Rackham Cl WELL DA16 ....44 D3
Radcliffe Rd CROY/NA CR0 ...83 L6
  STHWK SE1 ....24 B6
Radfall Ride WSTB CT5 ....106 B9
Radfall Rd WSTB CT5 ....136 C2
Radfield Dr RDART DA2 ....47 J8
Radfield Wy BFN/LL DA15 ...45 P8
Radford Rd LEW SE13 ....42 A7
Radland Rd CAN/RD E16 ...26 B2
Radleigh Gdns ROCH ME1 ...95 K5
Radley Av SYD SE26 ....61 L4
Radley Cl BRDST CT10 ....113 M7
Radley Ct BERM/RHTH SE16 ...24 C5
Radley Ter CAN/RD E16 * ...26 A1
Radnor Av WELL DA16 ....44 D6
Radnor Bridge Rd FOLK CT20 ...11 G5
Radnor Cliff FOLK CT20 ....11 G5
Radnor Cliff Crs FOLK CT20 ...310 C8
Radnor Cl CHST BR7 ....64 A5
  HB CT6 ....107 H5
  MTCM CR4 ....
Radnor Crs WOOL/PLUM SE18 ...44 C1
Radnor Park Av FOLKN CT19 ...10 D2
Radnor Park Crs FOLKN CT19 ...10 D3
Radnor Park Gdns FOLKN CT19 ...10 D2
Radnor Park Rd FOLKN CT19 ...10 D2
Radnor Pk West FOLKN CT19 ...10 D3
Radnor Rd BECK SE15 ....40 C1
Radnor St CROY/NA CR0 ....11 H4
Radnor Wk CROY/NA CR0 ...84 D6
Raeburn Av DART DA1 ....46 B6
Raeburn Cl TONN TN10 ....211 H4
Raeburn Rd BFN/LL DA15 ...45 A7
Rafford Wy BMLY BR1 * 62 E4
Ragge Wy BGR/WK TN15 ...149 L5
Raggleswood CHST BR7 ....63 L7
Rag Hill Rd BH/WHM TN16 ...145 N6
Raglan Cl SAND/SEL CR2 ...
Raglan Rd BELV DA17 ....28 E7
  HAYES BR2 ....85 M1
  WOOL/PLUM SE18 ....27 K8
Ragstone Hollow
  RASHE TN25 * 306 B1
Ragstone Rd
  MAID/SHEP ME15 ....186 D1
Ragstones BGR/WK TN15 ...149 L5
Railton Rd HNHL SE24 ....40 E1
Railway Ap EGRIN RH19 ....264 C7
  STHWK SE1 ....24 A4
Railway Ar BRXN/ST SW9 * ...40 A5
Railway Av BERM/RHTH SE16 ...24 C4
  WSTB CT5 ....105 M5
Railway Cots OXTED RH8 * ...175 K9
  WSTB CT5 ....105 M4
Railway Gv NWCR SE14 ....41 M1
Railway Hl RCANTW CT4 ...228 B6
Railway Pl BELV DA17 ....28 F6
Railway Rd IOS ME12 ....57 K8
The Railway Sidings
  MEO DA13 * 92 A3
Railway St CHAT ME4 ....6 E2
  GILL ME7 ....7 K2
  CVW DA11 ....48 G6
Railway Ter BH/WHM TN16 ...175 J6
  LEW SE13 ....41 P6
  MARG CT9 ....14 E6
  OBOR ME11 ....77 J2
Rainbow Quay
  BERM/RHTH SE16 ....25 H6
Rainbow Rd PUR RM19 ....30 H6
Rainbow St CMBW SE5 ....41 G6
Rainham Cl ELTH/MOT SE9 ...44 A4
  MAID/SHEP ME15 ....185 M2
Rainsborough Av DEPT SE8 ...25 M6
Raistrick Wy POP/IOD E14 * ...25 L8
Raleigh Av WLGTN SM6 ....82 D8
Raleigh Cl ERITH DA8 ....29 K9
  RAM CT11 ....253 K9
  WALD ME5 ....
Raleigh Ms ORP BR6 ....86 C9
Raleigh Rd PGE/AN SE20 ....61 K6
Raleigh Wy IOS ME12 ....77 N1

Ralph Perring Ct *BECK* BR3......84 D1
Ramac Wy *CHARL* SE7..........26 B8
Rama La *NRWD* SE19............95 J9
Ramillies Cl *MAID* ME5..........95 M9
Ramillies Rd *DA15*..............44 D7
Ram La *HDCN* TN27.............251 H1
Rammell Ms *CRBK* TN17........298 A3
Ramones Ter *MTCM* CR4 *.....82 B1
Rampart St *WCHPL* E1..........4 C3
Ramp C *DVE/WH* CT16...........9 M1
Rampion Cl *MAID/BEAR* ME14..156 E2
Ramsay Rd *THHTH* CR7..........82 E3
Ramsgate Cl *DEAL* CT14.......26 C4
Ramsgate Rd *BRDST* CT10.....143 L2
   MARG CT9....................15 H7
   SWCH CT13.................171 P9
Ramslye Rd *SBGH/RUST* TN4..270 A7
Ramstone Cl *RASHE* TN25.....284 F3
Ramus Wood Av *ORP* BR6........86 F9
Rancliffe Gdns *ELTH/MOT* SE9..43 J5
Rancorn Rd *MARG* CT9............9 L4
Randall Cl *ERITH* DA8...........29 H9
Randall Dr *CDW/CHF* RM16.....33 H1
Randall Hill Rd *BGR/WK* TN15..151 J1
Randall St *MAID/BEAR* ME14...12 E1
Randisbourne Gdns *CAT* SE6 *..61 N7
Randlesdown Rd *CAT* SE6........61 N3
Randle Wy *RSIT* ME9...........130 D5
Randolf Rd *BXLYHN* DA7..........7 K3
Randolph Ap *CANF/BAD* E16....26 D2
Randolph Cl *BXLYHN* DA7........45 L4
   CANT CT1.....................166 F6
Randolph Gdns
   KEN/WIL TN24..............253 H4
Randolph La *RYE* TN31.........338 D3
Randolph Rd *DVW* CT17.........291 H6
   GILL ME7........................7 J5
Randolph Sq *MARG* CT9 *.......15 J3
Ranelagh Gdns *GVW* DA11......49 K6
Ranelagh Gv *BRDST* CT10.....143 K8
Ranelagh Rd *DEAL* CT14.......233 J4
   IOS ME12.......................57 L6
Rangefield Rd *BMLY* BR1.........62 C4
Range Rd *GVE* DA12.............89 M9
   HYTHE CT21...................308 G7
   IOS ME12.......................57 L6
Rangeworth Pl *BFN/LL* DA15...64 D2
Rangoon St *TWRH* EC3N *........24 C2
Rankine Rd *RTWE/PEM* TN2...270 C1
Ranleigh Gdns *BXLYHN* DA7....45 M5
Ranmore Av *CROY/NA* CRO......83 L7
Ranmore Pth *STMC/STPC* BR5..87 H1
Ranscombe Ct *WOOL/PLUM* SE18 *87 J1
Ransom Rd *CHARL* SE7..........26 D7
Ranters La *CRBK* TN17.........295 P3
Ranworth Ct *ERITH* DA8.........45 N5
Raphael Av *TIL* RM18...........49 L2
Raphael Rd *GVE* DA12...........49 P8
Rapier Cl *PUR* RM19............30 C7
Rashleigh Wy *EYN* DA4.........89 P1
Raspberry Hill La *RSIT* ME9...72 C6
Ratcliffe Cl *LEE/GVPK* SE12....42 E8
Ratcliffe Cross St *WCHPL* E1 *..5 K1
Ratcliffe Hwy *HOO/HM* ME3....54 A4
   HOO/HM ME3...................72 C2
Ratcliffe La *POP/IOD* E14.......25 P2
Rathbone Market *CAN/RD* E16 *26 A1
Rathbone Sq *CROY/NA* CRO *....83 H8
Rathbone St *CAN/RD* E16........26 A1
Rathfern Rd *CAT* SE6............61 M9
Rathgar Rd *BRXN/ST* SW9......40 B4
Rathmore Rd *CHARL* SE7.........26 B8
   GVW DA11.....................49 L8
Ratling Rd *RCANTE* CT3.........199 J8
Rattington St *RCANTW* CT4....195 L1
Rattray Rd *BRXS/STRHM* SW2..40 A5
Raul Rd *PECK* SE15..............40 G5
Ravel Gdns *SOCK/AV* RM15.....30 F2
Ravel Rd *SOCK/AV* RM15........30 G2
Raven Cl *DIT/AV* ME20.........153 P5
Ravencroft Crs *ELTH/MOT* SE9..43 K2
Ravenlea Rd *FOLK* CT20.......310 D6
Raven Rw *WCHPL* E1.............24 E1
Ravensbourne Av *WCHPL* E1
   CAT SE6........................41 M8
Ravensbourne Pl *LEW* SE13....41 P9
Ravensbourne Park Crs
   CAT SE6........................41 M8
Ravensbourne Pk *CAT* SE6......41 N8
Ravensbourne Rd *BMLY* BR1....62 E9
   CAT SE6........................41 N8
   DART DA1......................46 A4
Ravensbury Rd
   STMC/STPC BR5..............86 G1
Ravenscar Rd *BMLY* BR1.........62 C5
Ravens Cl *HAYES* BR2...........62 D8
Ravenscourt Rd
   CANTW/ST CT2...............166 A1
   DEAL CT14...................233 H4
   STMC/STPC BR5..............86 G1
Ravenscroft Cl *CAN/RD* E16....26 B9
Ravenscroft Rd *BECK* BR3......51 L2
   CAN/RD E16...................26 B9
Ravensdale Gdns *NRWD* SE19..60 D6
Ravens Dane Cl
   MAID/SHEP ME15...........186 D2
Ravenshill *CHST* BR7............63 M7
Ravensleigh Gdns *BMLY* BR1...62 E4
Ravens Ms *LEE/GVPK* SE12 *....42 E6
Ravenswood *BXLY* DA5..........44 C9
Ravenswood Av
   RTWE/PEM TN2..............270 F7
   WWKM BR4....................64 F9
Ravenswood Crs *WWKM* BR4...64 F5
Ravenswood Rd *CROY/NA* CRO..82 G7
Ravensworth Rd
   ELTH/MOT SE9................63 K3
Ravine Gv *WOOL/PLUM* SE18...27 M9
Rawdon Rd *MAID/SHEP* ME15..13 L1
   RAM CT11.....................16 A5

Rawlings Cl *BECK* BR3...........84 F2
   ORP BR6.......................86 G9
Rawling St *RSIT* ME9..........129 N9
Rawlins Cl *SAND/SEL* CR2.....114 C2
Rawlinson Rd *CDW/CHF* RM16..31 M8
Rawsthorne Rd *CAN/RD* E16....26 C4
Ray Bell Ct *BROCKY* SE4 *......41 M3
Rayfield Cl *HAYES* BR2.........85 P5
Rayfield Ct *SNOD* ME6.........123 P4
Rayford Av *LEE/GVPK* SE12.....42 D8
Rayford Cl *DART* DA1...........46 C6
Rayham Rd *WSTB* CT5...........59 M7
Ray Lamb Wy *ERITH* DA8........29 N9
Ray La *LING* RH7...............234 D2
Rayleas Cl *WOOL/PLUM* SE18..43 M2
Rayleigh Cl *MAIDW* ME16.....155 J5
Rayleigh Rd *LEE/GVPK* SE12...42 F6
   WCHPL E16....................26 C4
Raymere Gdns
   WOOL/PLUM SE18...........43 P1
Raymond Av *CANT* CT1 *.........4 E5
Raymond Cl *SYD* SE26...........61 J2
Raymond Fuller Wy
   KEN/WIL TN24..............253 H5
Raymond Rd *BECK* BR3..........84 D1
Raymoor Av *LYDD* TN29........337 M1
Raymouth Rd
   BERM/RHTH SE16............24 E7
Rayners Hi *MAID/BEAR* ME17..190 A7
Rays Hi *EYN* DA4................89 P1
Rays Rd *WWKM* BR4.............84 F4
Reach Cl *RDV* CT15............292 E1
Reachfields *HYTHE* CT21......308 F6
Reach Rd *HYTHE* CT21.........307 L5
   RDV CT15....................292 E2
Readers Bridge Rd
   TENT TN30...................300 C3
Readers St *WBY/YAL* ME18....183 P3
Readers La *RYE* TN31.........332 C8
Reading Cl *DEAL* CT14.........232 G8
Reading Rd *DVW* CT17..........290 G8
Reading St *BRDST* CT10.......113 L5
   TENT TN30...................321 M4
Reading Street Rd
   BRDST CT10..................113 K5
Readscroft Rd *RHAM* ME8......96 C9
Read Wy *GVE* DA12..............49 M8
Realgar Ct *SIT* ME10............99 L8
Reams Wy *SIT* ME10............99 P5
Reardon Pth *WAP* E1W..........24 E4
Reardon St *WAP* E1W............24 E4
The Rear *RTWE/PEM* TN2 *.....22 C6
Reaston St *NWCR* SE14.........41 J1
Recce La *RFOLK* CT18..........258 D9
Record St *PECK* SE15...........24 F9
Recreation Av *SNOD* ME6......123 P5
Recreation Cl
   MAID/BEAR ME14............13 H1
Recreation Ground Rd
   TENT TN30...................301 J8
   SYD SE26......................61 K3
Recreation Wy *SIT* ME10.......99 N5
Rectory Cl *DART* DA1...........45 N5
   RASHW TN26.................302 F5
   ROCH ME1......................94 B9
   SCUP DA14....................64 D5
   SNOD ME6....................123 P5
Rectory Dr *RRTW* TN23........259 P6
Rectory Field Crs *CHARL* SE7..42 C1
Rectory Flds *CREH* TN17......298 A2
Rectory Gdns *BECK* BR3 *......61 N7
   CHST BR7 *....................63 N7
   WSTB CT5....................105 C4
Rectory Gra *ROCH* ME1.........93 P4
Rectory Gn *BECK* BR3...........61 M7
Rectory Gv *CROY/NA* CRO.......82 G6
Rectory La *BGR/WK* TN15.....150 F7
   BH/WHM TN16...............145 P8
   BH/WHM TN16...............145 P9
   HYTHE CT21..................308 C3
   MAIDW ME16.................184 F2
   RASHW TN26.................302 D5
   RFOLK CT18..................287 H2
   RMAID ME17.................188 F6
   RYE TN31....................330 E8
   SCUP DA14....................64 E5
   SEV TN13......................21 C5
   WLGTN SM6...................82 B8
Rectory La North
   WMAL ME19.................153 C2
Rectory La South
   E/WMAL ME19...............153 M2
Rectory Meadow *MEO* DA13....68 A1
Rectory Park Rd
   STPH/PW TN12..............273 P8
Rectory Pk *CHST* BR7 *.........63 N7
Rectory Rd *BECK* BR3...........61 N7
   BGR/WK TN15................113 N8
   CDW/CHF RM16...............33 J1
   DEAL CT14...................232 E5
   GRAYS RM17..................32 E7
   HAYES BR2..................115 N2
   HOO/HM ME3..................53 H9
   LING TN29...................325 P9
   SIT ME10....................130 A2
   SNOD ME6....................48 C8
   TON TN9......................133 J9
Rectory Sq *WCHPL* E1...........24 G1
Rectory Wy *KEN/WIL* TN24...252 F4
Reculver Av *HART* DA3..........77 C6
Reculver Cl *HB* CT6............108 D6
Reculver Dr *HB* CT6............108 D5
Reculver La *HB* CT6............108 B5
Reculver Rd *BERM/RHTH* SE16..24 C8
   HB CT6.......................107 P2
Reculvers Rd *WGOS* CT8......110 H6
Redan Pl *IOS* ME12 *...........57 M6
Redan Ter *CMBW* SE5...........40 B3
Redbank La *RDV* CT15.........289 P1
Red Barracks Rd
   WOOL/PLUM SE18............26 G7
Redberry Gv *SYD* SE26.........61 J2
Redberry Rd *ASH* TN23........282 E3

Redbourne Dr *THMD* SE28......28 C2
Redbridge Cl *WALD* ME5 *......95 N9
Redbridge Gdns *CMBW* SE5....40 E7
Redbrook St *RASHW* TN26.....280 D9
Redbrooks Wy *HYTHE* CT21...308 E4
Redcar St *CMBW* SE5...........40 C1
Redcastle Cl *WAP* E1W..........24 F3
Red Cedars Rd *ORP* BR6........86 F4
Redcliffe La *MAID/BEAR* ME14..155 N5
Redcot Ms *CANT* CT2..........137 N6
Redding Cl *RDART* DA2..........67 L1
Reddins Rd *PECK* SE15...........40 G6
Reddons Rd *BECK* BR3...........61 L6
Reddy Rd *ERITH* DA8............29 L9
Rede Court Rd *STRD* ME2.......71 N7
Rede Wood Rd *MAIDW* ME16..154 D9
Redfern Av *GILL* ME7............1 N7
Redfern Rd *CAT* SE6............42 A8
Redford Av *THHTH* CR7..........82 E1
Redgarth Ct *EGRIN* RH19.....264 E5
Redgate Dr *HAYES* BR2.........85 L8
Redgrave Cl *CROY/NA* CRO......83 L5
Red Hi *CHST* BR7................91 H8
   WBY/YAL ME18..............183 M3
Redhill Rd *HART* DA3............91 H8
   WGOS CT8....................111 L5
Redhill Wd *HART* DA3...........91 H9
Red House Gdns
   WBY/YAL ME18..............183 L4
Red House La *BXLYHS* DA6......44 F5
Redhouse Rd *BH/WHM* TN16..145 N6
Red House Rd *CROY/NA* CRO....82 C5
Redhouse Wall *DEAL* CT14....202 C9
Redland Shaw *ROCH* ME1.......95 K5
Redlands Rd *SEV* TN13..........21 M6
Red La *OXTED* RH8.............205 L3
Redleaf Cl *BXLYHN* DA7........28 F9
Red Lion Ct *EMB* EC4A *........11 P2
   RTWE/PEM TN2..............270 C2
Red Lion La *STMC/STPC* BR5....87 L6
   WALW SE17....................24 A9
Red Lion La *WOOL/PLUM* SE18..43 L2
Red Lion Pl
   WOOL/PLUM SE18 *..........43 L2
Red Lodge Crs *BXLY* DA5........65 M2
Red Lodge Rd *BXLY* DA5.........65 M2
   WWKM BR4....................84 F4
Redmans La *RSEV* TN14........118 E1
Redman's Rd *WCHPL* E1..........24 F1
Redmead La *WAP* E1W...........24 D4
Redmill Cl *FOLK* CT20.........310 B6
Red Oak *HAWK* TN18...........316 C6
Red Oak Cl *ORP* BR6............86 A1
Redoubt Wy *LYDD* TN29........327 L2
Redpoll Wk *STPH/PW* TN12...243 H4
Redpoll Wy *ERITHM* DA18.......28 C6
Red Post Hi *HNHL* SE24........40 D6
Redriff Rd *BERM/RHTH* SE16...24 G6
Redroofs Cl *BECK* BR3..........51 N7
Redsells Cl *MAID/SHEP* ME15..186 D2
Redshank Rd *CHAT* ME4.........72 C6
Redstart Cl *CROY/NA* CRO.....114 C4
   EHAM E6......................26 F1
   NWCR SE14 *..................41 L1
Red St *MEO* DA13................68 F5
Red Tree Orch *ASH* TN23......282 B1
Redvers Rd *CHAT* ME4..........95 M4
   WARL CR6....................144 A3
Redwall La *RMAID* ME17.......174 E9
Redwell Cv *E/WMAL* ME19.....183 K1
Redwell La *BGR/WK* TN15.....150 B5
Redwing Cl *RFOLK* CT18......288 D9
   SAND/SEL CR2...............114 A5
Redwing Rd *ORP* BR6............87 H4
Redwing Ms *CMBW* SE5.........40 C3
Redwings La *RTWE/PEM* TN2..241 N7
Redwood Cl *BERM/RHTH* SE16..25 H4
   BFN/LL DA15..................44 D7
   CANTW/ST CT2...............137 N2
   WALD ME5....................125 N1
Redwood Pk *STPH/PW* TN12..242 B4
Redyear Ct *KEN/WIL* TN24 *..253 K8
Reed Av *CANT* CT1..............167 H2
   ORP BR6.......................86 F7
Reed Cl *CAN/RD* E16............26 A3
   DIT/AV ME20.................123 P8
   LEE/GVPK SE12...............42 E3
Reed Ct *SWCM* DA10............48 A5
Redham Crs *HOO/HM* ME3......52 C9
Reed Pk *PECK* SE15 *............40 C3
Reedland Crs *HART* DA3.........77 C6
Redmace Cl *ASH* TN23.........252 A9
Reeds Cl *HB* CT6...............107 N2
Reeds La *RTON* TN11...........181 H6
Reed St *HOO/HM* ME3...........35 H9
Reeves Cl *CROY/NA* CRO.........83 L5
Reeves Cnr *CROY/NA* CRO *.....82 G6
Reeves Ct *E/WMAL* ME19......153 P5
Reeves Crs *SWLY* BR8...........87 N5
Reeves Rd *WADH* TN5..........315 J5
Reeves Wy *WSTB* CT5..........105 B5
Reform Rd *CHAT* ME4.............7 P7
Regal Cl *WCHPL* E1..............24 D1
Regal Crs *WLGTN* SM6..........82 C1
Regal Dr *EGRIN* RH19..........265 J8
Regal Rw *PECK* SE15.............40 F9
Regency Cl *BH/WHM* TN16....130 A1
   IOS ME12......................57 J9
   RHAM ME8.....................96 B8
Regency Ct *SIT* ME10..........129 L1
Regent Cl *DVW/CHF* RM16....185 M5
Regent Pl *CROY/NA* CRO *.......83 L1
   RTWE/PEM TN2................22 B4
Regent Rd *GILL* ME7..............7 G4
   HNHL SE24....................40 C6
Regents Dr *HAYES* BR2.........85 N9

Regents Pl *ASH* TN23............2 C3
Regent Sq *BELV* DA17..........28 C7
Regent St *CRBK* TN17.........319 L3
   WSTB CT5....................105 L4
Regent Wy *E/WMAL* ME19....153 K9
Reginald Av *STRD* ME2.........94 B3
Reginald Rd *DEPT* SE8.........41 K1
   MAIDW ME16..................12 C7
Reginald Sq *DEPT* SE8.........41 N1
Regina Rd *SNWD* SE25.........60 E4
Regis Crs *SIT* ME10.............99 N7
Reidhaven Rd
   WOOL/PLUM SE18............27 M7
Reigate Rd *BMLY* BR1...........62 B1
Reigate Wy *WLGTN* SM6........82 E3
Reinckendorf Av
   ELTH/MOT SE9................43 N6
Reinden Gv *MAID/SHEP* ME15..186 C2
Relf Rd *PECK* SE15..............40 G4
Reliance Ar *BRXN/ST* SW9 *...40 A5
Rembrandt Cl *POP/IOD* E14....25 N6
   TONN TN10...................211 H4
Rembrandt Dr *GVW* DA11......69 H2
Remington Rd *EHAM* E6........26 B2
Remus Cl *ASH* TN23...........282 C4
Rendezvous St *FOLK* CT20.....11 F4
The Rendezvous *MARG* CT9....15 G3
Rendle Cl *CROY/NA* CRO........60 F8
Renforth St *BERM/RHTH* SE16..24 F5
Renfrew Cl *EHAM* E6............27 H5
Rennell St *LEW* SE13...........42 A4
Rennets Cl *ELTH/MOT* SE9.....43 P5
Rennets Wood Rd
   ELTH/MOT SE9................43 P6
Rennie Est *BERM/RHTH* SE16..24 E7
Renown Rd *WALD* ME5.........125 P5
Renshaw Cl *BELV* DA17........28 C4
Renton Dr *STMC/STPC* BR5....87 L1
Rephidim St *STHWK* SE1........24 B6
Repository Rd
   WOOL/PLUM SE18............26 G9
Repton Cl *BRDST* CT10........113 G9
Repton Ct *BECK* BR3............61 P7
Repton Manor Rd *ASH* TN23....2 F7
Repton Rd *ORP* BR6..............87 H8
Repton St *POP/IOD* E14.........25 N6
Reservoir Av *LYDD* TN29......347 L5
Reservoir Ct *SWCM* DA10......48 C9
   THHTH CR7....................60 D9
Reservoir Rd *BROCKY* SE4.....41 L4
   WSTB CT5....................105 M4
Resolution Cl *WALD* ME5.......95 M9
Resolution Wy *DEPT* SE8.......41 L1
Restell Cl *BKHTH/KID* SE3.....25 P9
Rest Harrow *FAV* ME13.........162 F7
Restharrow Rd
   MAID/BEAR ME14............75 J6
Restharrow Wy *CHAT* ME4......52 A4
Restmore Cl *HOO/HM* ME3......52 A4
Restons Crs *ELTH/MOT* SE9.....43 N4
Reston Wy *CAN/RD* E16.........26 E5
The Retreat *BRCH* CT7.........111 J5
   GRAYS RM17..................32 D2
   MSTR CT12...................142 G4
   ORP BR6......................117 J1
   SEV TN13.....................83 J1
   THHTH CR7....................60 C2
Rettendon Dr *SIT* ME10.........99 N6
Reunion Rw *WAP* E1W...........24 E3
Reveley Sq *BERM/RHTH* SE16..25 H5
Revell Ri *WOOL/PLUM* SE18....27 P7
Revelon Rd *BROCKY* SE4.......41 L5
Revenge Rd *WALD* ME5........125 P4
Reventlow Rd *ELTH/MOT* SE9..43 N9
Reverdy Rd *STHWK* SE1.........24 D7
Reynard Cl *BMLY* BR1...........63 K9
Reynard Dr *NRWD* SE19........60 G9
Reynard Rd *NWCR* SE14 *.......25 H9
Reynola Gdns *CHARL* SE7......26 C8
Reynolds Cl *HB* CT6............107 N6
   TONN TN10...................211 H4
Reynolds Flds *HOO/HM* ME3...71 L1
Reynolds La *RCANTE* CT3......135 P8
   SBGH/RUST TN4.............270 C1
Reynolds Rd *BKHTH/KID* SE3..42 C5
   LEE/GVPK SE12...............41 J6
Reynolds Wy *CROY/NA* CRO....83 K8
Rhee Wall *RASHW* TN26.......322 F7
Rheims Ct *WSTB* CT5..........105 L4
Rheims Wy *CANTW/ST* CT2......4 A3
Rhodaus Cl *CANT* CT1............4 E6
Rhodaus Town *CANT* CT1........4 E6
Rhodes St *CHAT* ME4............95 H5
Rhodeswell Rd *POP/IOD* E14...25 P1
Rhodewood Cl
   MAID/SHEP ME15...........186 D1
Rhododendron Av *MAID* DA13..122 B2
Ribblesdale Rd *RDART* DA2.....47 J9
Ribbon Dance Ms *CMBW* SE5...40 C2
Ribston Cl *HAYES* BR2..........85 N9
Ribston Gdns *STPH/PW* TN12..242 F2
Ribston Wy *ASH* TN23.........281 P9
Ricardo St *POP/IOD* E14........25 N2
Rice Pde *STMC/STPC* BR5 *.....86 E2
Rices Hi *EGRIN* RH19..........265 H7
Richard Cl *WOOL/PLUM* SE18..26 F8
Richard House Dr *CAN/RD* E16..26 F1
Richard's Cl *RTON* TN11.......208 E8
Richardson Cl *RDART* DA2......47 M6
Richardson Rd
   SBGH/RUST TN4.............270 D2
Richardson Wy *MSTR* CT12...142 B6
Richard St *CHAT* ME4...........95 H3
   ROCH ME1.....................95 H3
   WCHPL E1.....................24 E2
Richard Watts Ct *CHAT* ME4 *...6 B3
Richborough Cl
   STMC/STPC BR5..............87 L1
Richborough Dr *STRD* ME2.....71 A6
Richborough Rd *SWCH* CT13..171 L6
   WGOS CT8....................111 J6
Richborough Wy *RASH* TN25..282 B5
Richdore Rd *RCANTW* CT4....225 K3
Richmer Rd *ERITH* DA8.........46 A1
Richmond Av *MARG* CT9.......112 G4

Richmond Cl *BH/WHM* TN16..145 L4
   STRD ME2.....................72 F6
   WALD ME5...................125 N1
Richmond Dr *GVE* DA12.........70 A1
   HB CT6.......................108 B6
   NROM TN28...................337 H5
   IOS ME12......................99 M7
Richmond Gdns
   CANTW/ST CT2...............166 E2
Richmond Gn *CROY/NA* CRO....82 G2
Richmond Pl *RTWE/PEM* TN2..270 E8
   WOOL/PLUM SE18............27 K7
Richmond Rd *CROY/NA* CRO....82 G7
   GILL ME7......................73 J9
   GRAYS RM17..................32 D8
   RAM CT11.....................16 A2
   THHTH CR7....................82 C1
   WSTB CT5....................105 A5
Richmond St *FOLKN* CT19.....310 A5
   HB CT6......................107 L1
   IOS ME12......................57 M6
Richmond Wy *EGRIN* RH19...265 J8
   MAID/SHEP ME15...........185 M3
Richmount Gdns
   BKHTH/KID SE3...............42 E4
Rich St *POP/IOD* E14............25 J3
Rickard Cl *BRXS/STRHM* SW2..40 A9
Ricketts Hill Rd
   BH/WHM TN16...............145 N3
Riddlesdale Av
   SBGH/RUST TN4.............270 D2
Riddles Rd *RSIT* ME9..........129 K2
Riddons Rd *LEE/GVPK* SE12....62 G2
Rideout St *WOOL/PLUM* SE18..26 G8
Ridge Av *DART* DA1.............45 A7
Ridge Cl *BFN/LL* DA15...........44 A7
Ridge Gn *DART* DA1.............45 P7
Ridgecroft Cl *BXLY* DA5........45 L9
Ridgelands *RRTW* TN3.........239 P5
Ridge La *MEO* DA13............122 B2
Ridgemount Av *CROY/NA* CRO..84 A6
Ridgemount Cl *PGE/AN* SE20...60 A9
Ridges Yd *CROY/NA* CRO........82 G7
The Ridge *BXLY* DA5............45 H8
   CHAM CR5....................175 H1
   KEN/WIL TN24..............253 H5
   ORP BR6......................86 C8
Ridge Wy *DART* DA1.............45 P7
   EDEN TN8....................206 D6
Ridgeway *EGRIN* RH19.........265 H9
   GRAYS RM17..................32 F7
   HAYES BR2....................85 K6
   HYTHE CT21..................307 L1
   RDART DA2....................67 L4
   RTWE/PEM TN2..............271 N1
Ridgeway Av *GVE* DA12........49 M2
Ridgeway Cliff *HB* CT6.........107 H1
Ridgeway Crs *ORP* BR6..........86 F7
Ridgeway Crescent Gdns
   ORP BR6.......................86 F6
Ridgeway Dr *BMLY* BR1.........63 K2
Ridgeway East *BFN/LL* DA15...44 B6
The Ridgeway
   SBGH/RUST TN4.............240 D8
Ridgeway Rd *HB* CT6...........107 H1
The Ridgeway *BRDST* CT10...145 K7
   CHAT ME4.....................52 C3
   CROY/NA CRO.................82 E7
   DVW CT17....................291 H1
   FAV ME13....................164 B1
   GILL ME7......................73 J8
   GVE DA12......................70 D6
   MARG CT9...................112 G4
   RASHE TN25.................284 C3
   WSTB CT5....................105 G5
Ridgeway Wk *HB* CT6 *.........107 M7
Ridgeway West *BFN/LL* DA15...44 A6
Ridgewell Cl *SYD* SE26.........61 M3
Ridgewood Rd *HART* DA3.......68 G8
Ridgway *MAIDW* ME16..........12 F8
Ridgway Rd *BRXN/ST* SW9.....40 B4
Ridgwell Rd *CAN/RD* E16.......26 D1
Ridham Av *SIT* ME10............99 P5
Riding Gate Rbt *CANT* CT1 *.....4 E6
   MARG CT9...................113 K2
   RTWE/PEM TN2..............271 J2
   STPH/PW TN12..............243 H2
   WSTB CT5....................105 C5
Ridlands Gv *OXTED* RH8......175 P6
Ridlands La *OXTED* RH8.......175 P6
Ridlands Ri *OXTED* RH8........175 P6
Ridley Cl *HB* CT6...............107 M6
Ridley Rd *HAYES* BR2...........62 D7
   ROCH ME1.....................18 E2
   WAL DA16....................45 N8
Rifle St *POP/IOD* E14...........25 N1
Rigby Cl *CROY/NA* CRO..........82 F7
Rigby Gdns *CDW/CHF* RM16....33 J7
Rigden Rd *ASH* TN23..........282 E1
Rigden St *POP/IOD* E14.........25 N2
Riggall Wy *RMAID* ME17........93 P5
Rigshill Rd *FAV* ME13..........190 G6
Riley Av *HB* CT6...............106 E2
Riley Rd *STHWK* SE1............24 C6
Ring Cl *BMLY* BR1...............62 G6
Ringden Av *STPH/PW* TN12...242 F4
Ringer's Rd *BMLY* BR1...........62 E9
Ringlemere La *SWCH* CT13....200 G2
Ringlestone Crs
   MAID/BEAR ME14...........155 L4
Ringlestone Rd *RMAID* ME17..158 D8
Ringlet Cl *CAN/RD* E16.........26 C1
Ringlet Rd *CHAT* ME4..........123 H5
Ringmer Wy *BMLY* BR1..........63 J4
Ringmore Ri *FSTH* SE23.........41 M8
Ringold Av *MSTR* CT12.........142 D4
Ringshall Rd *STMC/STPC* BR5..64 C9
Rings Hi *RTON* TN11...........209 M6

Ringside *EDEN* TN8..............206 D8
Ringstead Rd *CAT* SE6............41 P8
Ring Wall *DEAL* CT14............202 D8
Ringwold Cl *BECK* BR3............61 L6
Ringwood Av *CROY/NA* CR0......82 D4
ORP BR6.........................117 K4
Ringwood Rd *CANTW/ST* CT2.....166 D1
RHAM ME8........................96 G7
Ringwood Rd
MAID/SHEP ME15................185 P3
Ringwould Rd *RDV* CT15..........262 C4
Ripley Cl *BMLY* BR1..............86 A2
Ripley Rd *DEAL* DA17............114 F1
Ripley Rd *DEAL* DA17.............28 F7
CAN/RD E16......................26 D2
KEN/WIL TN24...................253 K9
Ripleys Market *DART* DA1 *......46 E8
Ripon Cl *RHAM* ME8..............96 G3
Ripon Rd *WOOL/PLUM* SE18.......27 J9
Rippersley Rd *WELL* DA16........44 C2
Ripple Rd *DEAL* CT14............262 D2
Rippolson Rd
WOOL/PLUM SE18................27 N8
Risborough La *FOLK* CT20.......310 A5
Risborough Wy *FOLK* CT20.......310 B5
Risdon La *HAWK* TN18............117 J8
Risdon Cl *CANTW/ST* CT2........137 L7
Risdon St *BERM/RHTH* SE16......24 F5
Risedale Rd *WOOL/PLUM* SE18....27 J9
Riseldine Rd *FSTH* SE23..........41 L7
The Rise *ASH* TN23..............282 B1
SWLY DA5........................44 E8
CHAT ME4........................72 G8
DART DA1........................43 P5
DEAL CT14.......................263 H3
EGRIN RH19......................265 H8
GILL NE2........................126 D2
GVE DA12........................70 A3
IOS ME12........................77 L2
RDV CT15........................189 J5
ROCH ME1........................95 J3
RSIT ME9........................129 J3
SEV TN13........................179 H4

Rising Rd *ASH* TN23.................2 A1
Ritchie Rd *CROY/NA* CR0..........83 N5
Ritch Rd *SNOD* ME6..............123 M5
Ritter St *WOOL/PLUM* SE18.......27 H9
Rivendell Rd *HOO/HM* ME3.........56 D1
River Bank Cl *MAID/BEAR* ME14...13 H5
Riverbank Rd *BMLY* BR1............61 L6
Riverbank Wy *KEN/WIL* TN24.....282 G2
River Barge Cl *POP/IOD* E14......25 M5
RAIN RM13........................29 N1
River Ct *PUR* RM19...............30 D7
RCANTW CT4......................165 L9
River Dl *DVW* CT17..............290 C4
Riverdale Est *TON* TN9 *.........242 C1
Riverdale Rd *BXLY* DA5...........45 H8
MSTR CT12.......................142 F3

Riverdale *CHARL* SE7.............26 C6
CHAT ME4.........................6 B3
CDW/CHF TN4......................77 N8
WOOL/PLUM SE18.................27 N8
EDEN TN8.......................206 D9
EYN DA4..........................89 J6
RCANTW CT4......................165 K9
Riverside Cl *ASH* TN23..........282 D5
RCANTW CT4......................197 M7
STMC/STPC BR5..................64 B8
WLGTN SM6........................82 A7
Riverside Est *STRY* ME2 *........2 D8
Riverside Ms *CROY/NA* CR0 *.....197 M2
SWCH CT13......................171 P2
Riverside Wy *DART* DA1...........46 E6
Rivers Rd *RSIT* ME9.............131 J3
River St *DVW* CT17..............290 F4
GILL ME8........................72 C9
Riverview *ASH* TN23.............252 F9
River Vw *CANTW/ST* CT2..........137 L6
CDW/CHF TN4......................33 H8
MAID/SHEP ME15..................185 L1
OBOR ME11........................77 H4
RHAM ME8.........................96 G3
Riverview Pk *CAT* SE6.............61 N1
Riverview Rd *RDART* DA2..........47 N6
Riverview Ter *PUR* RM19...........9 J2
River Wk *TON* TN9...............210 E9
River Wy *DIT/AY* ME20...........123 P9
CNWCH SE10.....................6 A8
River Whf *BELV* DA17 *...........29 J5
Riverwood La *CHST* BR7...........63 P8
Riviera Rd *FOLK* CT20...........310 C8
Roach St *STRD* ME2..............18 C2
Road of Remembrance
FOLK CT20......................11 F5
Roan Ct *STRD* ME2...............71 P7
Roan St *CNWCH* SE10.............25 M9
Robert Keen Cl *PECK* SE15........40 C2
Robert Lowe Cl *NWCR* SE14.......141 J1
Roberton Dr *BMLY* BR1.............62 C8
Roberts Cl *ELTH/MOT* SE9.........43 P9
SIT ME10.......................99 L7
STMC/STPC BR5..................87 K2
THHTH CR7......................60 D9
Roberts Ct *PGE/AN* SE20..........61 J7
Roberts House
WOOL/PLUM SE18 *...............43 J1
Roberts Orchard Rd
MAIDW ME16....................154 D9

Robert Sq *LEW* SE13..............42 A5
Roberts Rd *BELV* DA17............28 F8
NROM TN28.....................343 K3
RHAM ME8.......................97 H6
SNOD ME6......................123 N5
WSTB CT5......................104 G8
Robert St *CROY/NA* CR0...........83 H7
DEAL CT14.....................233 J2
WOOL/PLUM SE18.................27 L7
Robeson St *BOW* E3...............25 J1
Robina Cl *BXLYHS* DA6............44 G6
Robin Cl *EGRIN* RH19............265 H6
Robin Hill Dr *CHST* BR7...........63 L5
Robinhood Cl *MTCM* CR4...........82 B1
Robin Hood Gdns
POP/IOD E14 *..................25 M3
Robin Hood Gn
STMC/STPC BR5..................87 H2
Robin Hood La *BXLYHS* DA6........44 G6
LYDD TN29.....................342 B7
POP/IOD E14...................125 J4
WALD ME5......................125 J4
Robin Hood Lane (Lower)
WALD ME5......................125 K4
Robin Hood Lane (Upper)
WALD ME5......................125 K4
Robinia Av *GVW* DA11.............49 H8
Robinia Cl *PGE/AN* SE20..........60 C7
Robin La *LYDD* TN29.............342 B6
Robins Av *RMAID* ME17...........189 K7
Robin's Cl *HYTHE* CT21..........308 B7
Robins Cl *RMAID* ME17...........189 K7
Robins Gv *WWKM* BR4..............85 K7
Robin Wy *STMC/STPC* BR5..........64 D9
Robson Cl *EHAM* E6................26 F2
Robson Dr *DIT/AY* ME20..........154 C2
HOO/HM ME3.....................73 K2
Robson Rd *WNWD* SE27.............60 D2
Robus Cl *RFOLK* CT18............287 H1
Robyns Cft *GVW* DA11.............69 J2
Robyns Wy *EDEN* TN8.............236 E1
SEV TN13......................148 E7
Rocastle Rd *BROCKY* SE4..........41 L6
Rocfort Rd *SNOD* ME6............123 P5
Rochdale Rd *ABYW* SE2............28 A8
RTW TN1.......................270 F2
Rochdale Wy *DEPT* SE8............41 N1
Rochester Av *BMLY* BR1...........62 F8
CANT CT1.........................5 J7
ROCH ME1........................95 H2
Rochester Br *STRD* ME2...........19 F3
Rochester Cl *BFN/LL* DA15........64 A5
Rochester Ga *BXLY* DA5...........45 J3
Rochester Crs *HOO/HM* ME3.......73 K1
Rochester Gdns *CROY/NA* CR0......83 K7
Rochester Ga *ROCH* ME1 *........19 H8
Rochester Rd *DART* DA1...........46 G8
DIT/AY ME20.....................154 F1
OVE DA13........................49 N6
ROCH ME1.........................4 D7
STRD ME2........................94 A6
TONN TN10......................210 C6
WALD ME5........................125 H1
Rochester St *CHAT* ME4...........6 E4
Rochester Wk *STHWK* SE1 *........24 A1
Rochester Wy *BKHTH/KID* SE3.....42 F7
DART DA1........................45 M8
Rochester Way Relief Rd
ELTH/MOT SE9..................42 E3
Rochford Wy *CROY/NA* CR0........82 D5
Rock Av *GILL* ME7................7 J1
Rockbourne Ms *FSTH* SE23.........41 K9
Rockbourne Rd *FSTH* SE23.........41 K9
Rock Channel *RYE* TN31..........338 F7
Rockdale Gdns *SEV* TN13 *........21 H4
Rockdale Pleasance
SEV TN13......................21 L4
Rockdale Rd *SEV* TN13............21 F5
Rockell's Pl *EDUL* SE22...........41 H7
Rockfield Cl *OXTED* RH8.........175 J1
Rockfield Rd *OXTED* RH8.........175 J6
Rock Grove Wy
BERM/RHTH SE16.................24 D7
Rockhampton Rd
STRHM/NOR SW16................60 A3
Rock Hl *DUL* SE21...............60 E3
ORP BR6.........................118 A1
Rock Hill Rd *HDCN* TN27.........219 L9
Rockingham Pl *HB* CT6...........107 N4
Rockmount Rd *NRWD* SE19.........60 D5
WOOL/PLUM SE18.................27 N8
Rock Rd *BGR/WK* TN15............151 J5
MAID/BEAR ME14................155 M5
SIT ME10......................129 M1
Rocks Cl *E/WMAL* ME19...........153 P6
Rocks Hl *CRBK* TN17............276 C7
The Rocks Rd *E/WMAL* ME19......153 N6
Rockstone Wy *MSTR* CT12........142 E3
Rock Villa Rd *RTW* TN1...........22 D3
Rockwell Ct
MAID/SHEP ME15................185 K2
Rockwell Gdns *NRWD* SE19.........60 E3
Rocky Bourne Rd
RASHE TN25....................305 N2
Rocky Hill Ter *MAID/ME* ME16....12 C5
Rocombe Crs *FSTH* SE23 *.........41 J8
Rocque La *BKHTH/KID* SE3.........42 D4
Roden Gdns *CROY/NA* CR0..........83 K3
Rodeo Cl *ERITH* DA8..............46 B2
Roding Ms *WAP* E1W...............25 N2
Roding Rd *EHAM* E6...............27 J1
Rodmell Rd *RTWE/PEM* TN2.......272 D7
Rodmer Cl *IOS* ME12..............58 C8
Rodmersham St *CNWCH* SE10........6 D5
Rodney Av *TONN* TN10............211 H6
Rodney Cl *CROY/NA* CR0...........82 G5
Rodney Gdns *WWKM* BR4............85 K8
Rodney St *WALD* ME5..............24 A7
Rodney Rd *CROY/NA* CR0...........82 G5
Rodwell Rd *BMLY* BR1.............62 F7
Rodwell Rd *EDUL* SE22............40 F7
Roebuck Rd *FAV* ME13............132 D6
ROCH ME1........................19 F6
Roedean Cl *ORP* BR6.............117 J2
Roedean Rd *RTWE/PEM* TN2.......270 D7
Roehampton Cl *GVE* DA12..........50 A8
Roehampton Dr *CHST* BR7..........63 N5
Roffen Rd *ROCH* ME1.............95 H4
Roffey St *POP/IOD* E14...........25 M5

Rogers Ct *SWLY* BR8.............88 F1
Rogers La *WARL* CR6............144 C5
Rogersmead *TENT* TN30..........300 G8
Rogers Rough Rd *CRBK* TN17....295 P4
Rogerstown *EDEN* TN8...........266 C4
Rogers Wood La *HART* DA3........90 E2
Rojack Rd *FSTH* SE23.............41 K9
Rokeby Rd *BROCKY* SE4 *.........41 M3
Rokesby Cl *WELL* DA16............43 P3
Rokesley Rd *DVE/WH* CT16.......291 J2
Roland Ms *WCHPL* E1..............24 G1
Roland Wy *WALW* SE17............24 A8
Rolfe La *NROM* TN28.............336 F7
Rolinsden Wy *HAYES* BR2..........85 N8
Rollesby Wy *THMD* SE28...........28 B5
Rolleston Av *STMC/STPC* BR5......86 C5
Rolleston Cl *STMC/STPC* BR5......86 C6
Rollins St *PECK* SE15.............25 K7
Rollo Rd *SWLY* BR8...............65 P6
Roll's Av *IOS* ME12..............79 H6
Rollscourt Av *HNHL* SE24..........60 C1
Rolt St *NWCR* SE14...............24 C8
Rolvenden Av *RHAM* ME8...........96 F5
Rolvenden Gdns *BMLY* BR1.........62 G2
Rolvenden Rd *SIT* ME10...........99 J9
Rolvenden Hl *BMLY* BR1 *.........63 H7
Rolvenden Hl *CRBK* TN17.........319 P1
Rolvenden Rd *STRD* ME2..........72 C5
Roman Cl *DEAL* CT14.............232 G3
WALD ME5......................125 J4
Roman HI *DEAL* CT14.............125 J4
CROY/NA CR0.....................45 N6
DART DA1........................45 N6
FOLKN CT19......................309 P1
RDV CT15........................230 C7
RHAM ME8........................96 F7
Roman Villa Rd *EYN* DA4..........67 J5
Romanby Rd *RHAM* ME8............96 F5
Romanhurst Av *HAYES* BR2........85 H1
Romanhurst Gdns *HAYES* BR2......85 H1
Roman Rd *CANTW/ST* CT2.........165 M3
DVE/WH CT16...................291 L5
EDEN TN8......................236 A4
FAV ME13......................132 F6
GVW DA11......................49 J1
MSTR CT12.....................142 G2
RCANTW CT4....................167 A8
RDART DA2.....................67 P1
RDV CT15........................261 K5
SNOD ME6........................123 N5
Roman Sq *SIT* ME10.............129 N2
THMD SE28.......................27 H4
Roman Villa Rd *EYN* DA4..........67 J5
Roman Wy *ASH* TN23.............282 E4
CROY/NA CR0.....................45 N6
DART DA1........................45 N6
FOLKN CT19......................309 P1
RDV CT15........................230 C7
RHAM ME8........................96 F7
Romany Ri *RHAM* ME8.............86 D5
Romany Rd *RHAM* ME8.............86 D5
Romborough Gdns *LEW* SE13.......42 A6
Romborough Wy *LEW* SE13.........42 A6
Romden Rd *HDCN* TN27...........249 K9
Rome Rd *NROM* TN28.............336 F7
Romero Sq *BKHTH/KID* SE3 *.......42 E4
Rome Ter *CANT* ME4..............271 G4
Romford Rd *RTWE/PEM* TN2.......272 D7
SOCK/AV RM15...................30 F3
Romford St *WCHPL* E1.............24 G1
Romilly Gdns *MSTR* CT12 *.......143 H2
Rommany Rd *WNWD* SE27...........60 D2
Romney Av *FOLK* CT20...........310 C6
Romney Cl *MAID/BEAR* ME14.....156 C6
NWCR SE14......................41 J1
Romney Ct *SIT* ME10.............99 L5
Romney Dr *BMLY* BR1.............63 H6
Romney Gdns *BXLYHS* DA6 *........45 H2
Romney Marsh Rd *ASH* TN23.......2 A4
Romney Rd *MAID/SHEP* ME15......13 P5
Romney Point *ASH* TN23.........252 C5
Romney Rd *CNWCH* SE10...........25 M9
GVW DA11......................69 J2
KEN/WIL TN24...................3 K6
Romney Wy *HYTHE* CT21..........308 D6
TONN TN10.....................211 H5
Romola Rd *HNHL* SE24............60 B8
Romsey Cl *KEN/WIL* TN24........253 K7
ORP BR6.........................86 D8
STRD ME2........................18 C2
Romulus Gdns *ASH* TN23..........282 C4
Ronald Cl *BECK* BR3.............84 C2
Ronalds Ct *SIT* ME10...........129 P1
Ronalds Rd *BMLY* BR1.............62 F7
Ronaldstone Rd *BFN/LL* DA15.....44 A7
Ronfearn Av *STMC/STPC* BR5......87 J2
Ronnagh Ct *SIT* ME10...........129 N2
Ronver Rd *LEE/GVPK* SE12........42 E9
Roodlands La *EDEN* TN8.........207 L4
Rood La *FENCHST* EC3M.............24 D3
Rookery Cl *KEN/WIL* TN24........254 C2
RSIT ME9......................129 H7
Rookery Dr *WTHK* RM20............31 K9
Rookery Crs *HOO/HM* ME3.........52 A2
Rookery Dr *CHST* BR7.............63 L7
Rookery La *HAYES* BR2............85 N3
Rookery Rd *ORP* BR6............116 A4
Rookery Rw
MAID/SHEP ME15...............184 D9
The Rookery *WTHK* RM20...........31 K9
Rookery Vw *GRAYS* RM17...........32 C2
Rookesley Rd *STMC/STPC* BR5......87 K2
Rook La *SIT* ME10...............98 C6
Rookley Cl *RTWE/PEM* TN2.......272 B3
Rooks HI *BOR/WK* TN15...........179 P5
Rooks Vw *RSIT* ME9..............99 J3
Rookwood Av *WLGTN* SM6...........82 C4
Rookwood Cl *GRAYS* RM17..........32 C2
Roopers *RTW* TN5...............269 M1
Ropers *RTTW* TN5...............269 M1
Roosevelt Av *WALD* ME5...........95 L7
Roosevelt Rd *DVE/WH* CT16......291 J4
Ropemaker Rd
BERM/RHTH SE16.................25 H5

Ropemakers Ct *CHAT* ME4..........95 M5
Ropemaker's Flds
POP/IOD E14 *..................25 J3
Ropemaker St *BARB* EC2Y.........24 J1
RHAM ME8......................126 F2
Roper La *STHWK* SE1..............24 E2
Roper Rd *CANTW/ST* CT2...........4 C2
RSIT ME9........................131 J2
Ropers Ga *SBGH/RUST* TN4......270 D7
Ropers Green La
HOO/HM ME3.....................53 N8
Roper's La *HOO/HM* ME5...........53 N8
Roper's Green La
ELTH/MOT SE9...................43 K9
The Ropery *CHAT* ME4 *...........72 F8
Rope St *BERM/RHTH* SE16..........25 H6
Ropewalk *CRBK* TN17.............297 J7
Rope Wk *DART* DA1 *...............6 C3
RYE TN31........................338 F7
Ropewalk Gdns *WCHPL* E1..........24 G2
Rope Yard Rails
WOOL/PLUM SE18.................27 J6
Rosacre Cl *WSTB* CT5.............104 G8
Roseacre Cl *CANTW/ST* CT2 *......4 G2
Roseacre Ct *MARG* CT9...........113 K3
Roseacre Gdns
MAID/BEAR ME14................156 D9
Roseacre La *MAID/BEAR* ME14...156 F9
Rose Acre Rd *RCANTE* CT5.......168 C9
Roseacre Rd *WELL* DA16...........44 D3
Rose Aly *LYPST* EC2N.............24 D1
Rosebank *PGE/AN* SE20............61 H6
Rosebank Gdns *GVW* DA11 *........49 J9
Roseberry Gdns *DART* DA1.........46 C8
ORP BR6.........................86 F7
Roseberry St
BERM/RHTH SE16.................24 E7
Rosebery Av *BFN/LL* DA15........44 A8
HB CT6..........................108 B5
RAM CT11........................143 L3
THHTH CR7.......................60 C8
Rosebery Cl *SIT* ME10...........130 C1
Rosebery Ct *GVW* DA11............49 J9
Rosebery Rd *GILL* ME8............73 K8
GRAYS RM17......................31 P9
Rose Cots *HAYES* BR2 *..........115 M5
Rose Ct *WCHPL* E1...............24 C1
Rosecourt Rd *CROY/NA* CR0........82 E4
Rosecroft *BH/WHM* TN16..........146 A3
Rose Dl *ORP* BR6................116 A1
Rosedale Av *ABYW* SE2............28 A6
RDART DA2.......................47 N8
Rosedale Rd *CROY/NA* CR0.........84 A4
Rosedale Rd *GRAYS* RM17..........15 K6
MARG CT9........................15 K6
Rosedene *CROY/NA* CR0............82 D4
Rosedene Av *GRAYS* RM17.........31 P8
Rosefield *POP/IOD* E14...........25 K3
SEV TN13........................22 D3
Rosefield Gdns *POP/IOD* E14......25 K3
Rose Gdns *BRCH* CT7.............110 C7
HB CT6..........................107 P2
MSTR CT12.......................143 L5
RCANTE CT3......................260 E1
Rosegarth *MEO* DA13.............69 J7
Rose Hl *RAM* CT11...............17 F4
TENT TN30.......................352 D1
Rosehill Rd *BH/WHM* TN16........146 A2
Rosehill Wk *RTW* TN1............22 C4
Roseholme *MAIDW* ME16..........185 J1
Rosehurst Vls
SBGH/RUST TN4.................270 F1
Roselands Cl *CAT* SE6...........232 G8
Roselands Gdns
CANTW/ST CT2..................166 C2
Rose La *CANT* CT1...............197 P6
RMAID ME17......................220 A1
Roselawn Gdns *MARG* CT9........112 A5
Roselea Av *HB* CT6.............107 L5
Roseleigh Av *MAID/ME* ME16......13 H8
Roseleigh Rd *SIT* ME10.........129 L4
Rosemary Av *BRDST* CT10........143 L2
IOS ME12.........................77 M7
Rosemary Cl *CROY/NA* CR0........82 D4
Rosemary Gdns *BRDST* CT10......143 L2
WSTB CT5........................105 N6
Rosemary La *BGR/WK* TN15.......121 N3
CANT CT1........................248 F4
WADH TN5........................315 L1
Rosemary Rd *PJ STPH/PW* TN12...243 H1
Rosemary Rd *E/WMAL* ME19.......153 N3
Rosemary Wy *DVE/WH* CT16........291 L5
PECK SE15.......................40 F1
WELL DA16........................44 B2
Rosemead Gdns *HDCN* TN27.......247 L2
Rosemount Cl
MAID/SHEP ME15................185 L7
Rosemount Rd *STRD* ME2..........72 A6
Rosemount Dr *BMLY* BR1..........86 A1
Rosemount Rd *DUL* SE21..........60 C1
Rosemount Rd *BECK* BR3 *........84 C5
Rosenberg Rd
HNHL SE24......................60 C5
Roseneath Pl
STRHM/NOR SW16.................60 A3
Roseveare Cl *ORP* BR6...........117 J2
Rosemthal Rd *CAT* SE6...........41 P6
Rosenthorpe Rd *PECK* SE15.......61 K6
Roserton St *POP/IOD* E14.........25 M5
The Rosery *CROY/NA* CR0..........84 A3
Rose St *GVW* DA11...............48 F7
IOS ME12........................77 J4
ROCH ME1........................95 J3
TON TN9.........................240 F1
Rose Ter *FAV* ME13.............132 G8
Rosetower Ct *BRDST* CT10 *......115 L5
Rosevear Rd *LEE/GVPK* SE12......42 F9
Rose Vls *DART* DA1 *..............6 E7
STPH/PW TN12 *..................245 H4

Ropemaker Rd
BERM/RHTH SE16.................25 H5

Rose Wk *RFOLK* CT18............288 D8
WWKM BR4........................84 F6
Roseway *DUL* SE21...............40 D7
Rose Wy *LEE/GVPK* SE12...........42 G8
Rosewell Cl *PGE/AN* SE20........61 H6
Rosewood Cl *SCUP* DA14...........64 C6
Rosewood Dr *RASHE* TN25........252 B5
Rosewood Ter *PGE/AN* SE20 *.....61 J6
Rose Yd *MAID/BEAR* ME14.........13 H4
Rosherville Wy *GVW* DA11.........49 J8
Roslin Wy *BMLY* BR1.............62 E4
Rossdale *CHAT* ME4 *.............72 H1
Rosse Ms *BKHTH/KID* SE3..........42 F1
Rossendale Gdns *FOLK* CT20......11 H2
Rossendale Rd *FOLK* CT20........11 H2
Rossetti Rd *BERM/RHTH* SE16.....24 E8
ROCH ME1........................110 G5
Rosslyn Cl *CANTW/ST* CT2.......165 P1
Ross House *CHARL* SE7 *..........43 J1
Rossland Cl *BXLYHS* DA6.........45 J6
Rossland Rd *MSTR* CT12.........142 F4
Rosslare Cl *BH/WHM* TN16.......176 E2
Rosslyn Av *RAIN* RM13...........29 N1
Ross Rd *DART* DA1...............46 G9
SNWD SE25.......................60 E4
Ross St *ROCH* ME1...............19 H7
Ross Wy *ELTH/MOT* SE9............43 J4
Rotary Gdns *GILL* ME7............8 B8
Rothbrook Dr *KEN/WIL* TN24.....252 F2
Rothbury Av *RAIN* RM13..........29 N1
Rothbury Cots *GNWCH* SE10 *......25 P7
Rotherhithe New Rd
BERM/RHTH SE16.................24 E8
Rotherhithe Old Rd
BERM/RHTH SE16.................24 G7
Rotherhithe St
BERM/RHTH SE16.................24 E5
Rotherhithe Tnl
BERM/RHTH SE16.................24 E5
Rothermere Ct *CRBK* TN17.......299 H9
Rothermere Rd *CROY/NA* CR0.......82 E5
Rother Rd *TONN* TN10............210 E5
Rother's Wald Ms *ASH* TN23......125 P1
Rothesay Rd *SNWD* SE25...........83 J1
Rothley Cl *TENT* TN30...........301 J7
Rothsay Ct *RAM* CT11...........143 L3
Rothsay St *STHWK* SE1............24 B6
Rothschild St *WNWD* SE27.........60 B3
Rotterdam Dr *POP/IOD* E14........25 M6
Rouel Rd *BERM/RHTH* SE16........24 D6
Rouge La *GVE* DA12..............49 M9
Rougemont E/WMAL* ME19..........153 J9
Rougin Common Rd
CANTW/ST CT2..................165 P2
Roughetts Rd *E/WMAL* ME19......152 G1
Roughetts Rw
E/WMAL ME19...................152 C1
Rough Fld *EGRIN* RH19...........265 L3
Roughway La *RTON* TN11.........181 L5
Round Ash Wy *HART* DA3..........91 H3
Roundel Ct *BROCKY* SE4..........41 M5
Roundel St *RSIT* ME9............131 J3
The Roundels *RSIT* ME9.........130 F5
Round Gv *CROY/NA* CR0............84 A4
Roundhay *WAP* E1W...............24 G4
Roundhay Cl *FSTH* SE23..........61 K1
Round Hl *SYD* SE26..............61 H1
Roundhill Rd *RTWE/PEM* TN2.....270 C7
Roundlyn Gdns
STMC/STPC BR5..................87 J1
Round St *MEO* DA13..............69 N9
Roundtable Rd *BMLY* BR1.........62 D2
Roundwell *MAID/BEAR* ME14.....156 G8
Roundway *CHST* BR7..............63 H8
Round Wood Cl *WALD* ME5........125 M4
Rouse Gdns *DUL* SE21............60 E8
Routh St *EHAM* E6...............27 J2
Rover Rd *WALD* ME5.............125 N3
Rowan Cl *ASH* TN23.............252 G7
CANTW/ST CT2..................137 L7
DIT/AY ME20...................154 D3
MEO DA13......................92 C5
RCANTE CT3....................200 B4
STPH/PW TN12 *..................244 G9
Rowan Cr *BRDST* CT10 *..........113 M8
Rowan Crs *DART* DA1.............46 C9
Rowan Gdns *CROY/NA* CR0.........83 L7
Rowan La *SOCK/AV* RM15...........30 F3
Rowan Lea *WALD* ME5.............95 N4
Rowan Rd *BXLYHN* DA7.............44 G4
SWLY BR8........................65 M9
Rowans Cl *HART* DA3.............68 B8
Rowan Shaw *TONN* TN10..........210 C4
The Rowans *SIT* ME12 *...........58 C9
RTWE/PEM TN2 *..................271 P2
SOCK/AV RM15.....................30 G7
Rowan Ter *PGE/AN* SE20 *.........61 G7
Rowan Wk *CHAT* ME4..............72 B7
HAYES BR2.......................86 A1
Rowan Wk *EDEN* TN8.............270 B7
Rowanwood Av *BFN/LL* DA15......156 C2
Rowbrook Cl *RHAM* ME8..........126 C2
Rowcross St *STHWK* SE1...........24 C8
Rowden Rd *BECK* BR3.............84 C5
Rowdow La *BGR/WK* TN15.........119 K8
Rowdown Crs *CROY/NA* CR0.......114 C3
Rowe Cl *MARG* CT9..............112 C6
Rowena Rd *WGOS* CT8............111 M4
Rowetts Wy *IOS* ME12.............79 J4
Rowland Av *GILL* ME7............96 E5
Rowland Cl *GILL* ME7............96 E5
MAIDW ME16....................12 C6
Rowland Crs *HB* CT6............108 A3
Rowland Dr *HB* CT6.............107 H4
Rowland Gv *SYD* SE26............61 H2
Rowlatt Cl *RDART* DA2...........66 F2
Rowley Av *BFN/LL* DA15...........44 D8
Rowley Hl *RTWE/PEM* TN2........241 N4
Rowley Rd *IOS* ME12..............77 K2
Rowlplatt Cl *EGRIN* RH19.......264 B4
Rowplatt La *EGRIN* RH19........264 B5

The Row EDEN TN8 * ...206 C6
  RCANTE CT5 * ...170 F6
  RCANTW CT4 ...4 C5
Rowton Rd WOOL/PLUM SE18 ...43 N1
Rowzill Rd SWLY BR8 ...65 P5
Roxburgh Rd WGOS CT8 ...111 N4
  WNWD SE27 ...60 B4
Roxley Rd LEW SE13 ...81 P7
Roxton Gdns CROY/NA CR0 ...84 D9
Royal Albert Rd EHAM E6 ...27 H1
Royal Albert Wy CAN/RD E16 ...26 E3
Royal Arsenal West
  WOOL/PLUM SE18 * ...27 H8
Royal Av TON TN9 ...240 F1
  WSTB CT5 ...105 K9
Royal Blds DEAL CT14 * ...233 J5
Royal Cha SBGH/RUST TN4 ...82 B2
Royal Circ WNWD SE27 ...60 B2
Royal Cl BRDST CT10 ...113 K9
  DEPT SE8 ...25 J9
  ORP BR6 ...86 F5
Royal Ce ELTH/MOT SE9 * ...43 K9
  IOS ME12 * ...57 L6
  LOTH EC2R ...24 A2
Royal Crs MARG CT9 ...14 D5
  RAM CT11 * ...16 E6
Royal Docks Rd EHAM E6 ...27 J1
Royal Eagle Cl STRD SE20 ...19 K1
Royal Engineers' Wy
  MAID/BEAR ME14 ...12 D1
Royal Esp MARG CT9 ...14 A4
  RAM CT11 * ...16 A7
Royal Exchange Blds
  LOTH EC2R * ...24 A2
Royal Harbour Ap RAM CT11...16 B7
Royal Herbert Pavilions
  WOOL/PLUM SE18 * ...43 K2
Royal Hl GNWCH SE10 ...42 A1
Royal Military Av FOLK CT20 ...310 A6
Royal Military Canal Pth
  RASHW TN26 ...305 K7
  RASHW TN26 ...322 C5
  RASHW TN26 ...324 A1
  RENT TN30 ...333 P4
Royal Mint St WCHPL E1 ...24 C5
Royal Mint St WCHPL E1 ...24 C5
Royal Native Wy WSTB CT5 ...105 H8
Royal Naval Pl NWCR SE14 ...41 M7
Royal Oak Pl EDUL SE22 ...63 J1
Royal Oak Rd BXLYHS DA6 ...45 H6
Royal Oak Yd STHWK SE1 * ...24 B5
Royal Pde BKHTH/KID SE3 ...42 D3
  CHST BR7 * ...65 H7
  RAM CT11 * ...17 F6
Royal Pier Rd GVE DA12 ...49 M7
Royal Pl GNWCH SE10 ...42 A1
Royal Rd CAN/RD E16 ...26 C9
  IOS ME12... ...57 L6
  RAM CT11 ...16 E5
  RDART DA2 ...66 C4
  SCUP DA14 ...64 B4
Royal Sovereign Av CHAT ME4...73 H8
Royal Star Ar
  MAID/BEAR ME14 * ...12 E5
Royal Terrace Pier GVE DA12 *...49 N7
Royal Victoria Yd RTW TN1 ...22 E3
Royal West Kent Av
  TONN TN10 ...210 C6
Roycroft Cl
  BRXS/STRHM SW2 * ...40 A9
Roydene Rd WOOL/PLUM SE18...27 M9
Roydon Hall Rd
  STPH/PW TN12 ...182 F6
Royds Rd KEN/WIL TN24 ...282 C2
Roy Sq POP/IOD E14... ...25 L4
Royston Av WLGTN SM6 ...82 C8
Royston Gdns RDV CT15 ...292 E1
Royston Rd DART DA1 ...45 P7
  MAID/SHEP ...156 D9
  PGE/AN SE20 ...61 K2
Roystons Cl RHAM ME8 ...97 J4
Royton Av RMAID ME17 ...189 L6
Rubens St CAT SE6 ...61 M1
Rubery Dro RCANTE CT3 ...171 K5
Ruby Cl SIT ME10 ...51 J5
Ruby St PECK SE15 ...24 E9
Ruby Triangle PECK SE15 * ...24 E9
Ruckinge Rd RASHW TN26 ...304 D8
Ruckinge Wy RHAM ME8 ...96 F3
Ruck La STPH/PW TN12 ...275 M5
Ruddstreet Cl
  WOOL/PLUM SE18 ...27 N8
Rudge Cl WALD ME5 ...126 A3
Rudloe Rd BALHAM DA7... ...45 K4
Ruffets Wd ASH TN23 ...282 F5
  GVE DA12 ...69 N5
Rugby Cl BRDST CT10 ...113 L8
  WALD ME5 ...125 L1
Rugby Gdns ASH TN23 ...282 D2
Rugby Rd DVW CT17 ...291 H9
Ruggles Cl HOO/HM ME3 ...53 L5
Rugg St POP/IOD E14 ...25 K3
Ruins Barn Rd RSIT ME9 ...129 K9
Rum Cl WAP E1W ...24 E3
Rumfields Rd BRDST CT10 ...113 J9
Rumstead La
  MAID/BEAR ME14 ...157 M2
  RSIT ME9 ...127 N9
Runciman Cl ORP BR6 ...86 B1
Runcie Pl CANTW/ST CT2 * ...166 C2
Runham La RMAID ME17 ...188 C7
Running Foxes La ASH TN23 ...282 A1
Runnymede Av FAV ME13 * ...132 F6
Rupack St BERM/RHTH SE16 * ...24 F3
Rupert Gdns BRXN/ST SW9 ...40 B8
Rural Ter RASHE TN25 ...223 P8
Rural V GVW DA11 ...49 J8
Ruscoe Rd CAN/RD E16 ...26 A2
Ruscombe Cl SBCH/RUST TN4 ...240 C7
Rusham Rd RCANTE CT3 ...146 A7
Rushbrook Rd ELTH/MOT SE9 ...63 N1
Rush Cl LYDD TN29 ...326 F7
  WALD ME5 ...125 M2
Rushcroft Rd
  BRXS/STRHM SW2 ...40 A5
Rushdean Rd STRD ME2 ...94 C1
Rushden Cl NRWD SE19 ...60 D6
Rushdene ABYW SE2 ...28 B6

Rushdene Wk BH/WHM TN16 ...145 N2
Rushdon Cl GRAYS RM17 ...32 B6
Rushenden Rd QBOR ME11 ...77 H4
Rushet Rd STMC/STPC BR5 ...64 C8
Rushett La FAV ME13 ...131 L5
Rushetts RRTW TN3 ...269 L4
Rushetts Rd BGR/WK TN15 ...120 A2
Rushey Gn CAT SE6 ...41 P8
Rushey Md BROCKY SE4 ...41 N6
Rushford Cl HDCN TN27 ...247 N4
Rushford Rd BROCKY SE4 ...41 M7
Rushfords LING RH7 ...235 H3
Rushgrove St
  WOOL/PLUM SE18 ...26 G7
Rushley Cl CDW/CHF RM16 ...32 E4
  HAYES BR2 ...85 N8
Rushmead Ct CANTW/ST CT2 ...166 C2
  CROY/NA CR0 ...83 L8
Rushmead Dr
  MAID/SHEP ...185 M4
Rushmere Ct BGR/WK TN15 ...150 C5
Rushmore Cl BMLY BR1 ...63 J9
Rushmore Hl ORP BR6 ...117 K4
  RSEV TN14 ...117 L8
Rusholme Gv NRWD SE19 ...60 E4
Rushout Av WFD/HW TN15 ...149 M5
Ruskin Av WELL DA16 ...44 C4
  RSEV TN14 ...153 N4
Ruskin Dr ORP BR6 ...86 F7
  WELL DA16 ...44 C4
Ruskin Gv DART DA1 ...46 C6
  WELL DA16 ...44 C4
Ruskin Rd BELV DA17 ...28 F7
  CDW/CHF RM16 ...33 J4
  CROY/NA CR0 ...83 G6
Ruskins Vw HB CT6 ...107 M5
Ruskin Wk HAYES ...85 P3
  RSEV TN14 ...40 C6
Rusland Av ORP BR6 ...86 E5
Russel Ct BECK BR3 ...61 P9
Russell Cl BKHTH/KID SE3 ...42 C1
  BXLYHN DA7 ...45 J5
  DART DA1 ...46 A4
  SIT ME10 ...129 K2
Russell Ct CHAT ME4 ...7 F7
Russell Dr WSTB CT5 ...106 C3
Russell Gv BRXN/ST SW9 ...40 A2
Russel Pl RYN DA4 ...66 G7
  RSEV TN14 ...132 E2
Russell Rd CAN/RD E16 ...26 B2
  DIT/AY ME20 ...125 H6
  FOLKN CT19 ...10 D1
  GVE DA12 ...49 J2
  TIL RM18 ...49 J2
Russells Av RHAM ME8 ...97 K6
Russell St DVE/WH CT16 ...8 E3
Russel Ter EYN DA4 * ...89 P1
Russels Yd CRBK TN17 ...298 A5
Russell Ter EYN DA4 ...89 P1
Russet Av GRAYS RM17 ...32 B7
Russet Cl ST STRD ME2 ...71 H7
Russet Dr CROY/NA CR0 ...84 B5
Russet Ct CAT SE6 ...167 H5
The Russets MAIDW ME16 ...154 C7
  MEO DA13 ...92 B3
  WSTB CT5 ...106 C5
Russett Cl ASH TN23 ...281 P1
  DIT/AY ME20 ...154 D4
  ORP BR6 ...87 J9
  RCANTE CT5 ...200 C1
Russett Wy SWLY BR8 ...65 M8
Russet Wy E/WMAL ME19 ...182 C1
Russia Dock Rd
  BERM/RHTH SE16 ...25 H4
Rusthall Cl CROY/NA CR0 ...83 P3
Rusthall Gra SBGH/RUST TN4 ...270 A4
Rusthall High St
  SBGH/RUST TN4 ...269 N4
Rusthall Pk SBGH/RUST TN4 ...270 A4
Rusthall Pl SBGH/RUST TN4 * ...270 A5
Rusthall Rd SBGH/RUST TN4 ...270 A5
Ruston Rd WOOL/PLUM SE18 ...26 F6
Rust Sq CMBW SE5 ...40 D1
Rustwick SBGH/RUST TN4 ...270 A4
Rutherford Rd BRDST CT10 ...252 E4
Rutherford Wy TONN TN10 ...210 G3
Rutherglen Rd ABYW SE2 ...27 P9
Ruthin Rd BKHTH/KID SE3 ...26 B9
Ruth St CHAT ME4 ...95 M4
Rutland Av BFN/LL DA15 ...44 C8
  MARG CT9 ...112 C3
Rutland Cl BXLY DA5 ...44 F7
  CANT CT1 ...167 J5
  DART DA1 ...46 D8
Rutland Ct CHST BR7 ...63 L7
Rutland Gdns BRCH CT7 ...110 C6
  CROY/NA CR0 ...83 K9
  MARG CT9 ...113 H3
Rutland Ga BELV DA17 ...28 G8
  HAYES BR2... ...85 J1
Rutland Pl CHAT SE6 ...65 M1
Rutland Pl RHAM ME8 ...126 F7
Rutland Rd DVE/WH CT16 ...291 J4
Rutland Wk CAT SE6 ...61 M1
Rutland Wy MAID/SHEP ME15...186 B3
  STMC/STPC BR5 ...87 K3
Rutt's Ter NWCR SE14 ...41 M3
Ruxley Cl SCUP DA14 ...64 F5
Ruxton Cl SWLY BR8 ...65 M9
Ruxton Ct SWLY BR8 ...65 S5
Ryan Dr BKHTH/KID SE3 ...42 F5
Ryan Rd MAID/SHEP ME15 ...186 D1
Ryarsh Crs ORP BR6 ...86 C2
Ryarsh La E/WMAL ME19 ...153 J3
Ryarsh Pk E/WMAL ME19 ...152 G1
Ryarsh Rd E/WMAL ME19 ...123 J8
Rycault Cl MAIDW ME16 ...12 B6
Rycault Ct RHAM ME8 ...126 F2
Rycroft La RSEV TN14 ...178 C6
Rycuiff Sq BKHTH/KID SE3 ...42 F3
Rydal Av RAM CT11 ...142 F5
Rydal Cl SBGH/RUST TN4 ...270 B3
Rydal Dr BXLYHN DA7 ...45 J2
  SBGH/RUST TN4 ...270 B3
  WWKM BR4 ...85 H6
Rydal Mt HAYES BR2 * ...85 J1
Ryde St CANTW/ST CT2 ...4 B5
Ryde Dr SLH/COR SS17 ...34 B1

Ryder Dr BERM/RHTH SE16 ...24 E8
Ryders RRTW TN3 ...269 M5
Ryder's Av WGOS CT8 ...111 L5
Ryde St CANTW/ST CT2 ...4 B5
Rye Cl BXLY DA5 ...45 K6
Ryecotes Md DUL SE21 ...40 E9
Ryecroft GVE DA12 ...70 A4
  HART DA3 ...91 N1
Ryecroft Rd LEW SE13 ...87 L5
  LEW SE13 ...148 F2
  STMC/STPC BR5 ...148 F2
  STRHM/NOR SW16 ...60 A5
Ryedale EDUL ...41 H7
Ryedale Ct SEV TN13 ...148 D6
Ryefield Rd NRWD SE19 ...60 C6
Ryegrass Cl IWADE ME5 ...95 P8
Rye Hill Pk PECK SE15 ...41 J5
Ryelands Crs LEE/GVPK SE12 ...42 G7
Rye La PECK SE15 ...40 F3
Rye Rd HAWK TN18 ...317 K5
  LYDD TN29 ...334 E5
  PECK SE15 ...41 K5
  TENT TN30 ...332 D4
Rye Wk HB CT6 ...107 P4
Rykhill CDW/CHF RM16 ...33 K2
Ryland Pl FOLK CT20 ...11 H3
Rylands Rd KEN/WIL TN24 ...252 C5
Rymer Rd CROY/NA CR0 ...83 K4
Rymers Cl RTWE/PEM TN2 ...270 C1
Rymer St HNHL SE24 ...62 B2
Rymill St CAN/RD E16 ...27 H4
Ryngo Cl LYDD TN29 ...342 B7
Rysted La BH/WHM TN16 ...176 D2
Ryswick Ms NROM TN28 ...337 H5

S

Sabbarton St CAN/RD E16 ...26 A2
Sabina Rd CDW/CHF RM16 ...33 K7
Sabre Crs ASH TN23 ...282 A1
Sachfield Dr CDW/CHF RM16 ...32 G2
Sackett's Gap MARG CT9 ...113 J5
Sacketts Hl BRDST CT10 ...112 C7
Sackville Av HAYES BR2 ...85 K5
Sackville Cl EGRIN RH19 ...251 M2
  RASHW TN26 ...201 M2
  SEV TN13 ...148 G7
Sackville Ct EGRIN RH19 * ...265 J8
Sackville La ASH TN23 ...2 A3
Sackville La EGRIN RH19 ...264 E5
Sackville Rd RDART DA2 ...66 D9
Saddington St GVE DA12 ...49 M8
Saddlers Cl BAR EN5 ...49 N8
Saddlers Hall EYN DA4 ...89 J7
Saddlers Ms MSTR CT12 ...142 E5
  WSTB CT5 ...106 C5
Saddler's Pk EYN DA4 ...89 J7
Saddler's Wall La LYDD TN29 ...334 C4
Saddleton Av SEV TN13 ...202 E6
Saddleton Gv WSTB CT5 ...105 L6
Saddleton Rd WSTB CT5 ...105 L6
Sadlers Cl WALD ME5 ...125 J3
Saffron Av POP/IOD E14 ...25 N5
Saffron Cl CROY/NA CR0 ...82 D3
Saffron Rd CDW/CHF RM16 ...31 M7
Saffron's Pl FOLK CT20 ...11 G4
Saffron Wy SIT ME10 ...99 N7
St Catherines Hospital
  ROCH ME1 ...19 H7
Sage Cl DEAL CT14 ...98 G1
Sage Md EDUL SE22 ...26 E6
Sage Rd ROCH ME1 ...94 F5
Sage St WCHPL E1 ...24 E3
Saigasso Cl CAN/RD E16 ...26 E2
Sailmakers Ct CHAT ME4 ...95 N4
Sainsbury Rd NRWD SE19 ...60 E4
St Agnes Gdns IOS ME12 ...80 D2
St Aidan's Rd EDUL SE22 ...62 F4
St Aidan's Wy GVE DA12 ...70 A2
St Albans Cl GILL ME7 ...73 L8
St Alban's Cl GVE DA12 ...69 P2
St Alban's Gdns GVE DA12 ...69 P2
St Alban's Rd DART DA1 ...46 F7
  RCANTE CT3 ...138 B8
St Albans Rd STRD SE20 ...71 J7
St Alfege Pas GNWCH SE10 ...25 M9
St Alfege Rd CHARL SE7 ...26 E9
St Alphege Cl WSTB CT5 ...105 L5
St Alphege Ct WSTB CT5 * ...105 L5
St Alphege Rd DVE/WH CT16...291 K6
St Ambrose Gn RASHE TN25 ...223 P8
St Amunds Cl CAT SE6 ...41 P8
St Andrew Rd GILL ME7 ...73 K8
St Andrew's Cl
  BERM/RHTH SE16 ...24 C8
  CANT CT1 ...4 E4
  FOLKN CT19 ...310 E4
  HB CT6 ...107 J2
  MARG CT9 ...112 D2
  STPH/PW TN12 ...245 H3
  THMD SE28 ...28 E3
St Andrew's Ct
  MAIDW ME16 ...184 F1
  WSTB CT5 ...105 M7
St Andrews Cl
  SBGH/RUST TN4 ...270 B4
St Andrews Dr STMC/STPC BR5...87 J3
St Andrews Gdns RDV CT17 *...291 J5
St Andrew's Lees SWCH CT13 ...201 P2
St Andrews Ms BKHTH/KID SE3...42 E2
St Andrews Pk
  MAIDW ME16 * ...184 F1
St Andrews Park Rd
  SBGH/RUST TN4 ...240 D8
St Andrews Rd DEAL CT14...233 H5
  RAM CT11 ...143 L4
  SCUP DA14 ...64 F2
  STPH/PW TN12 ...245 H3
St Andrew's Rd CROY/NA CR0...83 H8
  RAM CT11 ...143 L4
  SCUP DA14 ...64 F2
St Andrew's Sq
  MAIDW ME16 * ...184 F1
  NROM TN28... ...337 J7

St Dunstan's St CANTW/ST CT2...4 C2
St Dunstan's Ter CANTW/ST CT2...4 B3
St Eanswythe Wy FOLK CT20 ...11 H4
St Edith's Rd BGR/WK TN15 ...149 M3
St Edmunds Cl ERITHM DA18 ...28 C5
St Edmunds Rd CANT CT1 ...4 D5
  DART DA1 ...46 E5
St Edmund's Rd DEAL CT14 ...232 D5
St Edward's Cl CROY/NA CR0 ...114 G5
St Edward's Cl EGRIN RH19 ...264 F7
St Elmos Rd BERM/RHTH SE16 ...25 H5
St Faith's La
  MAID/BEAR ME14 ...156 E8
St Faith's Rd DUL SE21 ...40 B9
St Faith's St MAID/BEAR ME14 ...12 E4
St Fidelis' Rd ERITH DA8 ...29 J7
St Fillans Rd CAT SE6 ...42 A9
St Francis Av GVE DA12 ...70 A3
St Francis Cl DEAL CT14 ...232 D5
  MAID/BEAR ME14 ...155 N5
  MARG CT9 ...86 F5
  ORP BR6 ...86 F5
  STRD ME2 ...71 N9
St Francis Ct ASH TN23 ...282 C1
St Francis Rd EDUL SE22 ...62 E6
  FOLKN CT19 ...310 C5
  MEO DA13 ...122 C2
St Francis Wy CDW/CHF RM16 ...33 K7
St Georges Av
  IOS ME12 * ...79 L5
St George's Av GRAYS RM17...32 D7
  IOS ME12 ...57 K7
St Georges Cl THMD SE28 ...28 C5
St Georges Cl DVW CT17 ...105 M7
St George's Ct BGR/WK TN15...151 J1
St George's Crs DVW CT17 *...291 H5
St George's Crs GVE DA12 ...69 N2
St George's La MON EC3R *...24 A3
St George's Lees SWCH CT13 ...201 P2
St George's Ms DEPT SE8 * ...240 E1
  TON TN9 * ...240 E1
St Georges Pde CAT SE6 *...61 M1
St George's Pk
  RTWE/PEM TN2 ...270 C8
St George's Pl CANT CT1 ...5 F4
  HYTHE CT21 ...308 C7
St Georges Pl RDV CT15 ...292 E1
  SWCH CT13 ...202 A2
St Georges Rd BMLY BR1 ...63 K8
  BRDST CT10 ...113 M9
  RAM CT11 ...143 L4
  STMC/STPC BR5 ...88 E2
  SWLY BR8 ...88 E2
St George's Rd BECK BR3 ...233 J3
  DEAL CT14 ...233 J3
  FOLKN CT19 ...310 C5
  GILL ME7 ...73 J2
  SCUP DA14 ...64 F5
  SEV TN13 ...153 N1
  SWCH CT13 ...201 P2
  WLGTN SM6 ...82 A9
St Georges Rd West BMLY BR1 ...63 J8
St George's Rbt CANT CT1 ...5 F5
St George's Sq MAIDW ME16 ...12 A6
St Georges St CANT CT1 ...4 E4
St George's Ter PECK SE15 ...107 K1
St Georges Ter PECK SE15 *...40 G1
St George's Wy CROY/NA CR0 ...83 H6
St Georges Wy PECK SE15 * ...24 C9
St German's Pl BKHTH/KID SE3 ...42 E2
St German's Rd FSTH SE23 ...41 L1
St Giles Cl CDW/CHF RM16 ...33 H1
  ORP BR6 ...86 E8
St Giles Rd CMBW SE5 ...25 H9
St Giles Wk DVW CT17 ...313 J1
St Gothard Rd WNWD SE27 ...60 D3
St Gregory's CANT CT1 *...5 F3
St Gregory's Cl DEAL CT14 ...232 D5
St Gregory's Crs GVE DA12 ...70 A1
St Helena Rd
  BERM/RHTH SE16 ...24 G7
St Helens Cnr
  MAID/SHEP ME15 * ...184 D3
St Helens La
  MAID/SHEP ME15 ...184 D3
St Helen's Pl IOS OBST EC2N ...24 B2
St Helens Rd ERITHM DA18 ...28 C5
  HOO/HM ME3 ...52 B7
St Helen's Rd IOS ME12 ...57 M7
St Helier's Cl MAIDW ME16 ...184 C1
St Hilda Rd FOLKN CT19 ...310 B5
St Hildas BGR/WK TN15 ...181 J3
St Hilda's Rd HYTHE CT21 ...308 C6
St Hilda's Wy GVE DA12 ...70 A2
St Hugh's Rd PGE/AN SE20 *...61 H7
St Hugh Ter RFOLK CT18 *...288 C2
St Jacob's Pl CANT CT1 *...166 C6
St James Av BRDST CT10 ...113 K8
  MSTR CT12 ...142 G3
St James Cl HOO/HM ME3 ...52 B3
  IOS ME12 ...80 B3
St James Ct RDART DA2 ...47 L8
St James La DVE/WH CT16 ...8 E4
St James Oaks GVW DA11 *...49 H8
St James Pk RTW TN1 ...23 G1
St James Park Rd MARG CT9 ...111 P5
St James Pl DART DA1 ...46 B3
St James Rd DEAL CT14 ...263 H4
  EGRIN RH19 ...264 E2
  HOO/HM ME3 ...56 D2
St James' Rd RTW TN1 ...23 G1
St James's Av BECK BR3 ...61 L9
St James's Cl DART DA1 ...63 N2
St James's
  WOOL/PLUM SE18 ...27 K8
St James's Crs BRXN/ST SW9...40 A4
St James Crs CROY/NA CR0 ...84 C1
St James Sq HART DA3 ...91 J6
St James's Rd
  BERM/RHTH SE16 ...24 D8
  CROY/NA CR0 ...83 H4

GVW DA11 ....49 L8
SEV TN13 ....148 D2
St James Cl GVW DA11 ....49 L7
St James's Ter BRCH CT7 ....111 J5
St James Av DVE/WH CT16 ....8 E4
St James Ter RDAT CT7 * 37 N1
ORP BR6 * 117 K3
SCUP DA14 ....64 G3
Jean's Rd WGOS CT8 ....111 M6
St Johns Av MSTR CT12 ....142 E5
St John's Av SIT ME10 ....150 A2
St John's Church Rd
FOLKN CT19 ....10 D2
St Johns Cl BRCH CT7 ....19 H5
St Johns Cl HOO/HM TN16 * 146 C1
RFOLK CT18 ....71 L4
SWCH CT13 * 288 D5
St Johns Ct GDST RH9 * 204 C5
KEN/WIL TN24 * 283 K2
St Johns Crs CANTW/ST CT2 ....136 C6
St Johns Est STHWK SE1 * 25 H3
St John's Hl SEV TN13 ....149 H8
St Johns Hospital CANT CT1 * 5 F2
St Johns La KEN/WIL TN24 * 4 D5
St Johns La CANT CT1 * 4 D5
HART DA3 ....91 J3
St John's Meadow LING RH7 ....234 A1
St Johns Pde SCUP DA14 * 64 D3
St John's Pk BKHTH/KID SE3 ....42 E1
St John's Pl CANT CT1 * 4 D5
St Johns Ri CDW/CHF RM16 ....146 C1
HOO/HM ME3 ....73 K1
HYTHE CT21 ....266 F4
RDV CT15 ....230 C7
St John's Rd CAN/RD E16 ....26 B2
CROY/NA CRO 82 C7
DVW CT17 ....8 B4
EGRIN RH19 ....265 H6
ERITH DA8 ....29 J8
FAV ME13 ....132 G6
GILL ME7 * 12 H7
GVE DA12 ....49 P8
HOO/HM ME3 ....71 L3
MARG CT9 ....15 H5
NROM TN28 ....336 A3
PGE/AN SE20 ....61 J6
RDART DA2 ....47 J8
SCUP DA14 ....64 C7
SEV TN13 ....148 C7
WELL DA16 ....44 D4
WSTB CT5 ....106 C5
St John's St FOLK CT20 ....11 F3
MARG CT9 ....15 H5
St John's Ter WOOL/PLUM SE18 .....37 K9
MARG CT9 ....15 J5
St John's V BROCKY SE4 ....41 N3
St Johns Wy EDEN TN8 ....206 C7
St Johns Wy RFOLK CT18 ....288 C5
St Johns Wy ROCH ME1 * 80 D5
St Josephs Cl ORP BR6 ....96 B3
St Joseph's V BKHTH/KID SE3 ....42 B1
St Julian's Ct
NROM/SW16 * 60 A3
St Julian's Farm Rd
WNWD SE27 ....60 A3
St Justin Cl STMC/STPC BR5 ....36 H9
St Katharine's Wy WAP E1W 24 C4
St Katherine Rd IOS ME12 ....57 N9
St Katherine's La SNOD ME6 ....123 N6
St Katherines Rd
ERITH DA18 ....28 C5
St Keverne Rd ELTH/MOT SE9 ....63 L2
St Kilda Rd ORP BR6 ....86 C5
St Kitts Ter NRWD SE27 ....60 C3
St Laurence Av DIT/AY ME20 ....154 C4
St Laurence Cl RSIT ME9 ....130 C3
STMC/STPC BR5 ....64 F9
St Lawrence Av RAM CT11 * 16 A7
SBCH/RUST TN4 ....240 A6
St Lawrence Cha RAM CT11 ....16 A3
St Lawrence Cl CANT CT1 * 166 G6
St Lawrence Cots
POP/IOD E14 * 25 M4
St Lawrence Forstal
CANT CT1 ....166 G6
St Lawrence Rd CANT CT1 * 166 G6
St Lawrence St POP/IOD E14 ....25 M4
St Lawrence Ter
DVE/WH CT16 * 291 J4
St Lawrence Wy
BRXN/ST SW9 * 40 A3
St Leonards Cl GRAYS RM17 ....32 A9
WELL DA16 ....44 C4
St Leonards Rd ORP BR6 ....86 F8
St Leonard's Rd HYTHE CT21 ....308 C6
MAIDW ME15 ....155 H4
St Leonard's Rd CROY/NA CRO 82 C7
DEAL CT14 ....232 C5
POP/IOD E14 ....25 M2
St Leonard's St
E/WMAL ME19 ....153 J4
St Louis Gv HB CT6 ....107 H2
St Louis Rd NRWD SE27 ....60 C3
St Lukes Av MAID/BEAR ME14 ....13 H5
RAM CT11 ....16 A8
St Luke's Av WGOS CT8 ....111 M5
St Lukes Cl CAN/RD E16 ....67 L4
St Lukes Cl RDART DA2 ....67 L4
St Lukes Cl SNWD SE25 ....83 N3
St Lukes Cl SWLY BR8 ....85 M1
WSTB CT5 ....105 M7
St Lukes Rd MAID/BEAR ME14 ....13 H2
St Luke's Rd RAM CT11 ....17 G1
SBCH/RUST TN4 ....270 D2
St Luke's Sqn CAN/RD E16 ....67 L4
St Luke's Cl RFOLK CT18 ....288 C5
St Luke's Wy HOO/HM ME3 ....73 N6
St Magnus Cl LBORO CT17 ....111 H5
St Margarets STPH/PW TN12 * 273 P2
St Margarets Av BFN/LL DA15 ....63 P2
BH/WHM TN16 * 146 C1
St Margaret's Av EGRIN RH19 ....265 H4
SLH/COR SS17 ....34 B1

St Margarets Banks
ROCH ME1 * 19 J7
St Margarets CI MAIDW ME16 ....184 C1
ORP BR6 ....42 A2
RDART DA2 ....67 K1
St Margarets Ct
HOO/HM ME3 * 53 L5
St Margaret's Cl GVE DA12 ....24 A2
St Margarets Dr DEAL CT14 ....232 G8
RHAM ME1 ....94 F5
St Margaret's Gv
WOOL/PLUM SE18 ....27 K9
St Margaret's Ms ROCH ME1 ....19 F5
St Margarets Rd BRCH CT7 ....141 N15
RDV CT15 ....262 F6
St Margaret's Rd BROCKY SE4 ....41 M5
EGRIN RH19 ....265 J5
EYN DA4 ....67 L5
RDV CT15 ....292 F2
WGOS CT8 ....111 M6
St Margaret's Ter RYE TN31 ....338 E7
St Margarets Ter
WOOL/PLUM SE18 ....27 K8
St Mark's Av GVE DA12 ....49 J8
St Mark's Cl WSTB CT5 ....105 M6
St Marks Ct DIT/AY ME20 * 124 E7
St Marks Houses DEAL CT14 * 62 F9
St Mark's Rd HAYES BR2 ....62 F9
RTWE/PEM TN2 ....270 C9
SNWD SE25 ....83 M1
St Mark St WCHPL E1 * 24 C2
St Martins Av CANT CT1 * 5 J4
St Martins Cl CANT CT1 * 5 J4
ERITH DA18 ....45 L1
St Martin's Cl DVW CT17 ....313 J1
MAID/BEAR ME14 ....156 D3
St Martins Dr EYN DA4 ....89 J7
St Martins Gdns DVW CT17 * 8 A3
St Martin's Hl CANT CT1 * 5 J4
St Martin's La BECK BR3 ....84 E2
St Martins Meadow
BH/WHM ME3 ....147 K8
St Martin's Pl CANT CT1 * 5 H3
St Martins Rd DEAL CT14 ....232 E5
FOLK CT20 ....310 A5
NROM TN28 ....336 D7
St Martin's Rd CANT CT1 * 5 H4
DART DA1 ....48 F7
RDV CT15 ....291 M3
St Martin's Vw HB CT6 ....107 H6
St Martins Wy MCON EC3A * 24 B3
St Mary Ate HOTCH CA3 * 24 B3
St Marychurch Rd
BERM/RHTH SE16 ....24 F5
St Mary Graces Ct WCHPL E1 * 24 C3
St Mary Newington Cl
WALW SE17 * 24 B8
St Mary's Av SWCH CT13 ....201 N1
St Mary's Av HAYES BR2 ....62 C9
RDV CT15 ....113 J4
St Mary's Church Rd
RSEV TN14 ....177 M1
St Marys Cl GRAYS RM17 ....32 E9
RFOLK CT18 ....287 J3
St Mary's Cl ISGR/WK TN15 ....151 M5
GRAYS RM17 * 32 E9
GVE DA12 ....69 N1
OXTED RH8 ....175 H5
RASHW TN26 ....304 D7
RDV CT15 ....229 M1
STMC/STPC BR5 * 64 D8
SWCH CT13 ....201 J8
WADH TN5 ....315 H5
WBY/YAL ME18 ....213 M6
St Mary's Ct BH/WHM TN16 * 176 E2
St Marys Ct CANT CT1 * 5 J4
E/WMAL ME19 * 153 J4
St Marys Dr RFOLK CT18 ....287 J5
St Mary's Dr SEV TN13 ....148 D8
St Marys Est
BERM/RHTH SE16 * 24 F5
St Mary's Gdns GILL ME7 ....73 H8
LYDD TN29 ....326 E9
St Mary's Gn BH/WHM ME5 ....145 M5
St Marys Gn KEN/WIL TN24 ....253 H2
St Mary's Gv BH/WHM TN16 ....145 M3
DEAL CT14 ....231 H5
WSTB CT5 ....104 G8
St Mary's La RRTW TN3 ....239 M9
WADH TN5 ....315 H5
St Mary's Meadow
RCANTE CT3 ....169 K8
St Marys Ms KEN/WIL TN24 ....253 J9
St Mary's Pth WCHPL E1 * 24 D2
St Marys Pl RCANTE CT3 * 169 K8
St Mary's Rd ISGR/WK TN15 ....151 K2
BRDST CT10 * 113 N9
BXLY DA5 * 33 J7
CDW/CHF RM16 ....33 J7
GILL ME7 ....132 G7
HYTHE CT21 ....308 A6
MSTR CT12 ....141 N9
NROM TN28 ....336 D5
PECK SE15 ....41 J2
RCANTW CT4 ....167 N9
RDART DA2 ....47 L6
SNWD SE25 ....60 E9
STRD ME2 ....18 D1
SWCH CT13 ....201 J8
SWLY BR8 ....88 C1
TON TN9 * 219 M4
St Marys Rw IOS ME12 * 78 A1
St Mary's Sqn KEN/WIL TN24 ....26 C2
St Mary's Sp WOOL/PLUM SE18 .....26 C2
St Mary's Vw RSIT ME9 ....86 B8
St Mary's Wy HART DA3 ....68 C9
St Matthews Dr BMLY BR1 ....63 K9
ROCH ME1 * 94 F4
St Matthew's Wy
HOO/HM ME3 ....38 E9
St Meddens CHST BR7 * 63 P6
St Mellion Cl THMD SE28 ....28 C2
St Merryn Cl WOOL/PLUM SE18 ......43 P1

St Michael's Aly BANK EC3V * 24 A2
St Michaels Av MARG CT9 ....113 J5
St Michael's Cl BMLY BR1 ....63 J9
CAN/RD E16 ....26 E1
CANTW/ST CT2 ....165 P5
DIT/AY ME20 ....155 H1
SOCK/AV RM15 ....30 F3
St Michael's Cl CHAT ME4 ....6 B7
ERITH DA18 * 28 C5
St Michaels Dr RSEV TN14 ....149 J1
St Michaels Pl CANTW/ST CT2 ....166 D2
St Michael's Rd CDW/CHF RM16 ......33 J8
EGRIN RH19 ....265 H6
St Michael's Rd
CANTW/ST CT2 ....166 D1
CROY/NA CRO 83 H5
MAIDW ME16 ....16 A6
SBGH/RUST TN4 ....270 E1
SIT ME10 ....129 M1
WELL DA16 ....44 D4
St Michael's Ter TENT TN30 * 301 H4
St Michaels Wk RFOLK CT18 ....288 C5
St Mildreds Av BRDST CT10 * 113 M9
St Mildred's Av BRCH CT7 ....110 F6
RAM CT11 ....16 A6
St Mildreds Ct DEAL CT14 ....233 H8
St Mildred's Ct LOTH EC2R * 24 A2
St Mildred's Gdns
WGOS CT8 ....111 N4
St Mildreds Pl CANT CT1 * 4 D7
St Mildreds Rd CAT SE6 ....42 C7
LEE/GVPK SE12 ....42 E8
St Mildred's Rd MARG CT9 ....112 F5
MSTR CT12 ....141 J7
RAM CT11 ....16 A6
WGOS CT8 ....111 M4
St Monicas Rd DEAL CT14 ....263 J2
St Nicholas Cl CANTW/ST CT2 ....137 L6
TENT TN30 * 301 H8
St Nicholas Dr SEV TN13 ....71 P7
St Nicholas Rd CANT CT1 * 166 B6
FAV ME13 ....132 D6
HYTHE CT21 ....308 A6
NROM TN28 ....336 F8
WOOL/PLUM SE18 ....27 N8
St Nicholas St DEPT SE8 ....41 M2
St Nicolas La CHST BR7 * 63 J4
St Norbert Rd BROCKY SE4 ....41 L5
St Olaves Est STHWK SE1 * 24 B5
St Oswald's Rd
STRHM/NOR SW16 * 60 B7
St Patricks Cl DEAL CT14 ....233 H3
St Patrick's Cl WSTB CT5 ....105 M7
St Patrick's Gdns GVE DA12 * 69 P3
St Patrick's Pl
CDW/CHF RM16 ....33 J7
St Patricks Rd DVW CT17 ....313 H2
RAM CT11 ....143 L4
St Paul's Av
BERM/RHTH SE16 * 24 C4
FAV ME13 ....132 D6
St Paul's Cl CHARL SE7 ....36 B8
SOCK/AV RM15 ....30 E8
STRD ME2 ....94 C1
St Pauls Cl TONN TN10 ....210 A8
St Pauls Ct RSIT ME10 ....11 H1
St Paul's Cray Rd CHST BR7 ....63 P7
St Pauls Crs FAV ME13 ....164 B1
St Paul's Pl SOCK/AV RM15 ....30 F3
St Paul's Rd FAV ME13 ....164 B1
St Paul's Rd ERITH DA8 ....45 L1
MARG CT9 ....112 F3
RTW TN1 * 99 M9
St Pauls Ter CANT CT1 * 5 F4
St Paul's Wy FOLK CT20 ....310 B7
SIT ME10 ....99 M9
St Paul's Wood Hl
STMC/STPC BR5 * 64 A8
St Peters Av BH/WHM TN16 * 146 C1
St Peter's Br MAIDW ME16 ....12 D5
St Peters Cl CHST BR7 ....63 N6
St Peter's Cl DIT/AY ME20 ....154 A3
St Peter's Ct IOS ME12 ....77 L1
SWCM DA10 ....48 C8
St Peter's Ct BKHTH/KID SE3 * 42 D6
St Peter's Ct BRDST CT10 * 113 M6
FAV ME13 ....132 D6
St Peter's Footpath MARG CT9 .....15 J6
St Peter's Gdns WNWD SE27 ....60 A2
St Peter's La CANT CT1 * 4 D5
St Peter's La CHST BR7 ....63 N6
St Peters Park Rd
BRDST CT10 ....113 L8
St Peters Pth ROCH ME1 ....19 G6
St Peter's Pl CANT CT1 * 4 C4
St Peters Rd BRDST CT10 ....113 H8
DIT/AY ME20 ....154 A3
MARG CT9 ....15 H7
St Peter's Rd CROY/NA CRO 83 J8
FAV ME13 ....164 B1
WSTB CT5 ....105 L4
St Peter's Rbt CANTW/ST CT2 ....4 C5
St Peters Sq RRTW TN3 ....268 C5
St Peter's La CANT CT1 * 4 D5
St Peter's St CANT CT1 * 4 D5
RTWE/PEM TN2 ....23 H5
St Peters St CANT CT1 * 4 D5
SWCH CT13 * 83 J9
St Peter St MAIDW ME16 ....12 D5
ROCH ME1 * 19 H7
St Philip's Av MAID/SHEP ME15 ......13 H7
St Pigas La LING RH7 ....235 J6
St Quentin Rd WELL DA16 ....44 D4
St Radigund's Pl CANT CT1 * 5 F2
St Radigund's Rd DVW CT17 ....291 H6
St Richards Rd DEAL CT14 ....232 F7
St Ronan's Cl
MAID/SHEP ME15 * 185 P4
St Saviour's Cl FAV ME13 ....133 H6

St Saviours Cl FOLKN CT19 ....310 G4
St Saviours Est STHWK SE1 * 24 C6
St Saviour's Rd CROY/NA CRO 83 K5
St Saviours Rd
MAID/SHEP ME15 ....186 A5
Saints Cl WNWD SE27 ....60 B5
Saints Hl RTON TN11 ....238 F9
St Stephen's Cl CHAT ME4 ....6 B7
St Stephens Cots RTW TN1 * 23 F1
St Stephens Cl CANTW/ST CT2 ....4 E2
St Stephens Ct GDST RH9 ....204 B5
RTW TN1 * 23 F1
St Stephen's Crs THHTH CR7 ....60 A8
St Stephen's Flds
CANTW/ST CT2 * 4 E2
St Stephen's Gn
CANTW/ST CT2 * 166 E1
St Stephens Gv LEW SE13 ....42 A4
St Stephen's Hl
CANTW/ST CT2 * 136 D8
St Stephen's Rd BOW E3 ....51 M8
St Stephens Rd CANTW/ST CT2 ....4 E2
St Stephens Sq
MAID/SHEP ME15 ....185 K1
St Stephen's St TON TN9 ....240 E1
St Stephen's Wk ASH TN23 ....282 C2
St Stephens Wk ASH TN23 ....282 C1
St Stephen's Rd FOLK CT20 ....310 C7
St Stephons Ct RTW TN1 * 23 F1
Saint's Wk CDW/CHF RM16 ....33 J7
St Swithin's La MANHO EC4N 24 A3
St Swithin's Rd WSTB CT5 ....105 M7
St Swithun's Rd LEW SE13 * 42 B6
St Swithun's Rd ILEW SE13 * 42 B6
St Teresa Wk CROY/NA CRO 83 J7
St Theresas Cl KEN/WIL TN24 ....4 C7
St Thomas' Dr BXLY DA5 ....45 J8
St Thomas' Dr STMC/STPC BR5 ......86 D5
St Thomas HI CANTW/ST CT2 ....166 B1
St Thomas Rd BELV DA17 ....29 H5
CAN/RD E16 ....26 B2
GVW DA11 * 21 N7
St Thomas's Av DEAL CT14 ....263 J2
St Thomas's Pl GRAYS RM17 ....32 D9
St Thomas's St STHWK SE1 * 24 A4
St Thomas's Wy CHST CT2 * 4 A4
St Vincent Cl WNWD SE27 ....60 A4
St Vincent Rd RDV CT15 ....262 D9
St Vincents Ct DART DA1 ....46 C9
St Vincent's Cl RCANTE CT3 ....168 C8
WSTB CT5 ....105 M7
St Vincents La E/WMAL ME19 ....152 C2
St Vincents St DART DA1 ....46 C9
St Welcume's Wy
RMAID ME17 * 188 F5
St Werburgh Crs HOO/HM ME3 ......73 K2
St William's Wy ROCH ME1 ....95 J3
St Winifred Rd FOLKN CT19 ....310 C5
St Winifred's Rd
WOOL/PLUM SE18 ....146 A3
Saladin Dr PUR RM19 ....30 D7
Salamons Wy RAIN RM13 ....29 K1
Salbris Cl LYDD TN29 ....327 H6
Salcot Crs CROY/NA CRO 114 F4
Salcote Rd GVE DA12 ....70 A5
Salcott Rd BTSEA SW11 ....60 C1
Salehurst Rd BROCKY SE4 ....41 L3
Salem Pl CROY/NA CRO 83 H7
GVW DA11 * 21 N7
Salem St MAID/SHEP ME15 ....13 G8
Salhouse Cl THMD SE28 ....28 B2
Salisbury Av BRDST CT10 ....143 J5
RAM CT11 ....17 H1
RHAM ME8 ....88 F1
SWLY BR8 ....88 F1
Salisbury Cl SIT ME10 ....130 B1
TONN TN10 ....210 A5
WALW SE17 * 24 A7
Salisbury Pl BRXN/ST SW9 ....40 B5
Salisbury Rd BXLY DA5 ....45 J9
CANTW/ST CT2 ....166 D2
CHAT ME4 ....6 C6
DEAL CT14 ....232 H2
DIT/AY ME20 ....125 H5
DVE/WH CT16 ....8 C1
FOLKN CT19 ....310 B4
GVW DA11 ....49 N9
HAYES BR2 ....85 P2
HB CT6 ....107 N1
MAID/BEAR ME14 ....13 J4
RDART DA2 ....47 J9
RDV CT15 ....292 C1
RRTW TN3 ....269 L5
SBGH/RUST TN4 ....240 F9
SNWD SE25 ....269 L5
TOWN TN10 ....210 C6
WSTB CT5 ....105 L6
Salisbury Ter PECK SE15 ....41 J4
Salisbury Vls NROM TN28 * 336 F7
Salix Rd GRAYS RM17 ....32 E9
Sallow Cl CHAT ME4 ....73 J6
Sallows Shaw MEO DA13 ....49 P7
Sally Port GILL ME7 ....72 C9
Sally Port Gdns GILL ME7 ....6 E1
Salmestone Rd MARG CT9 ....113 J5
Salmon Crs IOS ME12 ....77 P1
Salmon La POP/IOD E14 ....25 H2
Salmon Rd BELV DA17 ....28 H8
DART DA1 ....46 F4
St Saviour St POP/IOD E14 * 25 P2
Salomons Rd PLSTW E13 ....26 D1
Saltash Rd WELL DA16 ....44 E2
Saltbox Hl BH/WHM TN16 ....115 L4
Saltcote Cl DART DA1 ....45 N7
Saltcote St RTW TN1 * 23 H3
Salter Rd BERM/RHTH SE16 ....338 F4
Salters Cross
WBY/YAL ME18 * 214 A1
Salters' Hall Ct MANHO EC4N * 24 A4
Salter's La MANHO EC4N 24 B1
Salters La WKENS W14 * 60 D4
Salter's La MAID/SHEP ME15 ....37 J8
Saltford Ct ERITH DA8 ....45 P2
Salthouse Cl LYDD TN29 ....334 E5
Saltings Rd SNOD ME6 ....40 B1
The Saltings NROM TN28 ....337 M8
RSIT ME9 ....99 L2
WSTB CT5 * 105 L4
Salt La HOO/HM ME3 * 51 P4

Saltley Cl EHAM E6 ....26 F2
Saltoun Rd BRXS/STRHM SW2 ....40 A5
Salt's Av MAID/SHEP ME15 ....185 L8
Salts Cl WSTB CT5 ....105 L5
Salts Dr BRDST CT10 ....113 K8
Salts La MAID/SHEP ME15 ....185 M7
Saltwell St POP/IOD E14 ....25 P3
Saltwood Cl ORP BR6 ....87 K8
Saltwood Gdns MARG CT9 ....113 J3
Saltwood Rd WGAL SE17 * 24 A8
Saltwood Rd
MAID/SHEP ME15 ....185 L2
Samara Cl WALD ME5 ....125 M4
Sam Bartram Cl CHARL SE7 ....26 D8
Samian Crs FOLKN CT19 ....309 P1
Samos Rd PGE/AN SE20 ....61 M7
Samphire Cl
MAID/BEAR ME14 ....156 B8
Samphire Ct DVE/WH CT16 ....8 F2
GRAYS RM17 * 32 C6
Samphire Wy GRAYS RM17 * 72 G6
Sampson Cl BELV DA17 ....28 C5
Sampson St WAP E1W * 24 D4
Samuel Cl NWCR SE14 * 41 G9
WOOL/PLUM SE18 ....26 F7
Samuel Dr SIT ME10 * 99 P5
Samuel Lewis Trust Dwellings
CMBW SE5 * 40 C2
Samuel Ms LYDD TN29 ....342 G5
Samuel St WOOL/PLUM SE18 ....26 C7
Sancroft Av CANTW/ST CT2 ....166 B3
Sancroft La BRDST CT10 ....143 L2
DART DA1 ....48 F7
DVW CT17 * 290 E5
Sanctuary Rd RHAM ME8 ....96 D3
The Sanctuary BXLY DA5 ....44 F7
Sandbach Pl
WOOL/PLUM SE18 ....27 N3
Sandbanks Hl RDART DA2 ....68 A5
Sandbanks Rd FAV ME13 ....133 N3
Sandbourne Dr
MAID/BEAR ME14 ....155 L3
Sandbourne Rd NWCR SE14 ....41 L3
Sandcliff Rd ERITH DA8 ....29 J4
Sand End WSTB CT5 ....105 K8
Sanderling Rd HB CT6 ....108 C5
Sanderling Wy RDART DA2 ....47 N6
RSIT ME9 ....99 L2
Sanders Ct IOS ME12 ....99 L2
Sandersons Av WNWD SE14 ....117 P4
Sanderson Wy TON TN9 ....211 H9
Sanderstead Rd
STMC/STPC BR5 ....87 J3
Sandfield Gdns THHTH CR7 ....60 B9
Sandfield Pl THHTH CR7 ....60 B9
Sandfield Rd RTON TN11 ....268 E1
Sandfields AV BXLYHS DA6 ....44 G5
HAYES BR2 ....85 K1
SIT ME10 ....99 P3
Sandford Rd BXLYHS DA6 ....44 G5
HAYES BR2 ....85 K1
SIT ME10 ....99 J9
Sandgate Cl RHAM ME8 ....27 J1
Sandgate Dr RHAM ME8 ....155 L3
Sandgate Hi FOLK CT20 ....310 C6
Sandgate Rd FOLK CT20 ....10 B6
WELL DA16 ....44 E1
Sandgate St PECK SE15 ....24 E9
Sandhawes Hi EGRIN RH19 ....265 K4
Sandhill La RHO ME3 * 71 M1
Sandhills WLGTN SM6 ....82 C8
Sandhurst Av
RTWE/PEM TN2 ....271 J3
Sandhurst Cl CANTW/ST CT2 ....136 F9
RHAM ME8 ....96 F3
RTWE/PEM TN2 ....270 F1
Sandhurst La CRBK TN17 ....319 H5
Sandhurst Market CAT SE6 * 42 A9
Sandhurst Pk
RTWE/PEM TN2 ....270 G2
Sandhurst Rd BFN/LL DA15 ....64 B2
BXLY DA5 ....45 J8
CAT SE6 ....42 B9
MARG CT9 ....113 J3
ORP BR6 ....87 H7
RTWE/PEM TN2 ....270 C1
TIL RM18 ....39 J3
Sandiland Crs HAYES BR2 ....35 J6
Sandilands CROY/NA CRO 83 M7
KEN/WIL TN24 ....3 K5
Sandison St PECK SE15 ....60 F1
Sand La CRBK TN17 ....277 H4
Sandle's Rd BRCH CT7 ....110 G6
Sandlewood Dr BRCH CT7 ....140 F5
Sandling La MAID/BEAR ME14 ....155 K3
Sandling Pl
MAID/BEAR ME14 ....155 L4
Sandling Rd ELTH/MOT SE9 ....63 L2
Sandling Rd HYTHE CT21 ....308 B7
MAID/BEAR ME14 ....13 G2
Sandlings Cl PECK SE15 ....41 H4
The Sandlings HYTHE CT21 * 308 B7
Sandling Wy CHAT ME4 ....73 H6
Sandown Cl DEAL CT14 ....233 H5
Sandown Dr CROY/NA CRO 271 J2
RHAM ME8 ....96 F7
Sandown Gv RTWE/PEM TN2 ....176 C7
RHAM ME8 ....96 F7
Sandown Lees SWCH CT13 ....202 B2
Sandown Pk RTWE/PEM TN2 ....271 J3
Sandown Rd CDW/CHF RM16 ....33 M1
DEAL CT14 ....203 J9
E/WMAL ME19 ....153 J4
GVE DA12 ....69 N5
SNWD SE25 ....202 B2
SWCH CT13 ....202 B2
Sandpiper Cl
BERM/RHTH SE16 ....25 P2
RDART DA2 ....47 N6
Sandpiper Dr ERITH DA8 ....46 B1
Sandpiper Rd RSIT ME9 ....99 M3
Sandpiper Rd RFOLK CT18 ....288 C5
SAND/SEL CR2 ....114 A5
WALD ME5 ....125 P3
The Sandpipers CVE DA12 * 69 P1
Sandpiper Wy STMC/STPC BR5 * 87 L1

Sandpit Hl RCANTE CT3.........138 F4
Sandpit Pl CHARL SE7..............62 C4
Sandpit Rd BMLY BR1................62 C4
  DART DA1..................................46 C5
Sandpits Rd CROY/NA CR0......84 A4
Sandringham Ct
  E/WMAL ME19 *.....................183 H2
Sandringham Dr RDART DA2......65 N3
  WELL DA16.................................44 A3
Sandringham Rd BMLY BR1......62 A4
  RHAM ME8.................................127 H1
  THMTH CR7.................................83 H2
Sand Rd RRTW TN3..................295 H3
Sandrock Dr CROY/NA CR0......84 A4
Sandrock Rd LEW SE13.............41 N4
  RTWE/PEM TN2.......................23 H2
Sandstone Dr SIT ME10.............99 M6
Sandstone La CAN/RD E16.......26 C5
Sandstone Ri WALD ME5..........125 P5
Sandstone Rd LEE/GVPK SE12...62 F1
Sandtoft Rd CHARL SE7.............62 B6
Sandway Rd RMAID ME17.......188 G7
  STMC/STPC BR5.......................87 K1
Sandwich Cl FOLK CT20..........310 C6
Sandwich Rd DVE/WH CT16....261 H9
  MSTR CT12................................142 A9
  RCANTE CT3.............................170 C9
  RDV CT15..................................260 D1
  SWCH CT13...............................155 K3
Sandwood Rd RAM CT11.........143 L3
  SWCH CT13...............................201 N2
Sandy Bank Rd GVE DA12.........49 M9
Sandy Bury ORP BR6.................86 E7
Sandycroft ABYW SE2..............27 P9
Sandycroft Rd STRD ME2..........71 P6
Sandy Dell GILL ME7...............126 D2
Sandy Hill Av
  WOOL/PLUM SE18....................27 J8
Sandy Hill La
  WOOL/PLUM SE18....................27 J7
Sandy Hill Rd
  WOOL/PLUM SE18....................27 J7
Sandyhurst La RASHE TN25....252 B3
Sandy La BGR/WK TN15.........152 A3
  BGR/WK TN15.........................180 E1
  BH/WHM TN16..........................176 E1
  CDW/CHF RM16..........................33 J9
  E/WMAL ME19........................155 H5
  EGRIN RH19..............................265 H7
  FOLK CT20................................309 H4
  HYTHE CT21..............................196 A5
  KEN/WIL TN24..........................253 L8
  MAID/BEAR ME14.....................155 P5
  MEO DA13....................................68 A7
  ORP BR6......................................87 H4
  OXTED RH8................................174 F5
  RASHW TN26.............................281 J2
  RDART DA2.................................68 B2
  SCUP DA14.................................64 F6
  SEV TN15.................................149 H8
  SNOD ME6................................123 M7
  SOCK/AV RM15.........................30 D3
  TENT TN30...............................301 J8
  WTHK RM20................................32 C9
Sandy La North WLGTN SM6......82 D7
Sandy Mt MAID/BEAR ME14....156 E7
Sandy Pl RASHE TN25..............252 B3
Sandy Rdg BGR/WK TN15.......151 K5
  CBIT BR7.....................................63 L5
Sandy's Rw WCHPL E1................24 B1
Sandy Wy CROY/NA CR0...........84 C7
San Feliu Ct EGRIN RH19.........265 L6
Sanford St NWCR SE14..............15 H9
Sanger Cl MARC CT9...................15 F7
Sangley Rd CAT SE6....................41 P8
  SNWD SE25................................83 K1
Sangro Pl CANT CT1................167 J3
San Juan Dr CDW/CHF RM16....31 N7
San Luis Dr CDW/CHF RM16.....31 N7
San Marcos Dr CDW/CHF RM16.31 N7
Sansom St CMBW SE5................40 D1
Sanspareil Av IOS ME12............77 P7
Santers Ct HAWK TN18.............317 H1
Santiago Wy CDW/CHF RM16....31 N8
Santon La RCANTE CT3............139 N9
Sapho Pk GVE DA12...................70 B3
Saphora Cl ORP BR6...................86 E9
Sapphire Cl SIT ME10................99 M7
Sapphire Rd DEPT SE8...............25 H7
Saracen Cl CROY/NA CR0..........83 J3
  RHAM ME8...................................96 D5
Saracen Flds WALD ME5..........125 N5
Saracen's Head Yd
  FENCHST EC3M..........................24 B2
Saracen St POP/IOD E14............25 K2
Sara Crs RDART DA2...................47 N5
Sara Pk GVE DA12......................70 A3
Sark Cl LYDD TN29..................326 G6
Sarre Pl SWCH CT13................201 N2
Sarre Rd STMC/STPC BR5..........87 K2
Sarsen Hts WALD ME5..............125 L4
Sarsens Cl GVE DA12.................70 B9
Sartor Rd PECK SE15...................41 K5
Sassoon Cl DIT/AY ME20.........123 P9
  RFOLK CT18..............................288 D8
Satanita Cl CAN/RD E16............26 E2
Satis Av SIT ME10......................99 J6
Satmar La RDV CT15................312 A1
  RFOLK CT18..............................289 M8
Satmore La RFOLK CT18..........289 M8
  POP/IOD E14 *............................25 N7
Saunders La CVW DA19..............69 J1
  POP/IOD E14 *..........................200 C1
Saunders Ness Rd
  POP/IOD E14..............................25 N7
Saunders Rd SBGH/RUST TN4..270 B8
  WOOL/PLUM SE18......................27 N8
Saunders St CHAT ME4...............6 B1
  GILL ME7....................................73 J9
Saunders Wy DART DA1..............66 F1
  RYE TN31.................................344 B1
  THMD SE28.................................28 A3
Savage Gdns EHAM E6...............26 C2
  TWRH EC3N.................................24 B3
Savage Rd WALD ME5...............125 N2
Savanah Cl PECK SE15................40 F1
Savernake Dr HB CT6................107 N4
Savile Gdns CROY/NA CR0.........83 L6
Saville Rd CAN/RD E16...............26 F4
Saville Rw HAYES BR2................85 J5

Savoy Rd DART DA1...................46 C6
Saw Lodge Fld ASH TN23........282 F4
Sawpit Rd RMAID ME17...........159 P1
Sawyers Ct CHAT ME4................95 N4
Saxby's La LING RH7................234 C5
Saxby Rd BGR/WK TN15..........209 L9
Saxby Wd RTON TN11..............209 L9
Saxon Av IOS ME12....................78 B1
Saxon Cl E/WMAL ME19..........182 G1
  CDW DA11.................................68 C2
  HYTHE CT21.............................309 K5
  RSEV TN14................................148 E2
  STRD ME2...................................71 P6
Saxon HI BH/WHM TN16..........176 E2
Saxon PI EYN DA4.......................18 A6
  STRD ME2...................................71 P6
Saxon Rd BMLY BR1...................62 D6
  FAV ME13.................................132 F7
  RAM CT11.................................142 D6
  RCANTW CT4............................197 M2
  RDART DA2.................................66 E3
  SNWD SE25.................................83 J2
  WGOS CT8................................115 N9
Saxons Dr MAID/BEAR ME14...155 N5
Saxon Shore WSTB CT5..............99 P6
  WSTB CT5..................................105 K6
Saxon Shore Wy DEAL CT14....233 J9
  DVE/WH CT16.............................8 E5
  FAV ME13.................................105 M8
  FAV ME13.................................132 F2
  GILL ME7.......................................6 E1
  GVE DA12...................................49 N7
  HB CT6.....................................106 F2
  HOO/HAM ME3............................51 L2
  MSTR CT12...............................140 P9
  RASHE TN25.............................306 C2
  RASHW TN26............................322 E7
  RCANTE CT3.............................108 F7
  RCANTE CT3.............................139 H4
  RFOLK CT18..............................287 H4
  RSIT ME9.....................................75 K9
  RSIT ME9.....................................97 N9
  RSIT ME9...................................100 P5
  RYE TN31.................................339 H4
  STRD ME2...................................19 F3
  SWCH CT13...............................202 B1
  TENT TN30................................333 J3
  TENT TN30................................333 J5
Saxon St DVW CT17.....................8 C3
Saxon Wk RSIT ME9.....................99 L2
Saxton Cl LEW SE13....................42 B4
Saxton Rd LYDD TN29..............343 K7
Saxton St GILL ME7......................7 J3
Saxville Rd STMC/STPC BR5......64 D9
Sayer Cl RDART DA2...................47 N6
Sayer Rd HDCN TN27...............221 H2
Sayers La TENT TN30................301 H8
The Sayers EGRIN RH19...........264 F7
Sayes Court Rd
  STMC/STPC BR5........................64 C9
Sayes Court St DEPT SE8............25 J8
Scabharbour Rd RSEV TN14....179 H9
Scadbury Gdns
  STMC/STPC BR5........................64 C8
Scads Hill Cl ORP BR6................86 C3
Scandrett St WAP E1W *.............24 E1
Scanlons Bridge Rd
  HYTHE CT21..............................308 F5
Scarborough Cl
  BH/WHM TN16.........................145 M3
Scarborough Dr IOS ME12..........58 B7
Scarborough La ROCH ME1.......124 C4
Scarborough St WCHPL E1..........24 C2
Scarlet Cl STMC/STPC BR5.........87 J1
Scarlet Rd CAT SE6.....................62 C2
Scarlett Cl WALD ME5.................95 P9
Scarsbrook Rd BKHTH/KID SE5..43 H4
Scawen Rd DEPT SE8..................25 H8
Sceales Dr MSTR CT12.............142 C6
Sceptre Wy WSTB CT5...............105 J7
Scholars Ri STRD ME2.................71 L8
Scholey Cl STRD ME2................124 A1
School Ap BGR/WK TN15...........151 J5
School Av GILL ME7....................96 B2
Schoolbank Rd GNWCH SE10.....26 A7
School Cl MEO DA13...................92 B4
The School Cl WGOS CT8..........111 M4
School Crs DART DA1..................45 P5
School Fld EDEN TN8.................206 D8
Schoolfield Rd WTHK RM20........31 K9
School La RCANTW CT4.............194 C4
  RRTW TN3.................................295 J1
School House La
  STPH/PW TN12.........................274 C1
Schoolhouse La WAP E1W *.......24 E2
School Houses
  CDW/CHF RM16 *.......................33 H1
School La BGR/WK TN15..........120 C5
  BGR/WK TN15.........................149 L6
  CANTW/ST CT2.......................135 P6
  CANTW/ST CT2.......................137 M9
  CDW/CHF RM16..........................33 H1
  E/WMAL ME19.........................122 B8
  FAV ME13.................................191 J9
  HART DA3...................................90 C5
  HB CT6.....................................107 M6
  HOO/HAM ME3............................71 L3
  MAID/SHEP ME15....................186 B2
  MEO DA13................................122 B3
  RAM CT11..................................17 F5
  RCANTE CT3.............................138 D5
  RCANTE CT3.............................139 P7
  RCANTW CT4............................167 N8
  RCANTW CT4............................196 F4
  RDART DA2.................................68 A2
  RFOLK CT18..............................287 M9
  RMAID ME17............................188 G9
  RMAID ME17............................217 H5
  ROCH ME1....................................6 A5
  RSIT ME9.....................................98 C7
  RTON TN11...............................181 H5
  RTON TN11...............................211 P2
  RYE TN31.................................338 B3
  SWLY BR8....................................66 B6
  WELL DA16..................................44 D4
School Ms RSIT ME9....................99 M2
School Ri RTWE/PEM TN2.........270 C7
School Rd CHST SE7....................63 N7
  DEAL CT14...............................230 G5

  FAV ME13.................................132 E7
  GVE DA12...................................69 N2
  HDCN TN27..............................221 H2
  HYTHE CT21............................251 M2
  RASHW TN26............................280 C4
  RASHW TN26............................322 J5
  RCANTE CT3.............................170 D9
  RFOLK CT18..............................289 E5
  RFOLK CT18..............................130 A2
  RSIT ME9...................................201 N1
School Sq GNWCH SE10.............26 A6
School Ter HAWK TN18.............317 H4
Schooner Cl BERM/RHTH SE16...25 N6
  POP/IOD E14..............................25 M7
Schooner Ct RDART DA2.............47 J1
Schooner Wk STRD ME2..............72 F4
Schreiber Ms GILL ME7 *............96 B5
Scimitar Cl RHAM ME8................96 D5
Scoles Rd IOS ME12....................78 B3
Scords La BRXS/STRHM SW2.....40 A8
Scotby Av WALD ME5................125 N1
Scotchmen Cl IOS ME12.............57 N9
Scotia Rd BRXS/STRHM SW2.....40 A8
Scotland Common
  MAID/BEAR ME14....................290 D3
Scotland La GVE DA12.................70 C8
Scotney Cl ORP BR6....................86 B8
Scotsdale Cl STMC/STPC BR5.....86 F1
Scotsdale Rd LEE/GVPK SE12....42 F1
Scotshall La WARL CR6.............114 F9
Scott's La RASHE TN25.............255 L9
Scott Av CANT CT1....................166 D7
  IOS ME12...................................58 B7
Scott Cl DIT/AY ME20................154 D2
Scott Crs ERITH DA8....................45 P2
Scottswood Av CHAT ME4...........95 L4
Scott Lidgett Crs
  BERM/RHTH SE16......................25 L7
Scotton St RASHE TN25............224 A8
Scott Rd CDW/CHF RM16............33 H7
  GVE DA12...................................69 P4
  TON TN9...................................240 C1
Scotts Acre RYE TN31...............333 P9
Scotts Av HAYES BR2..................84 A1
Scotts La HAYES BR2...................62 B9
Scotts Pas WOOL/PLUM SE18 *...27 J7
Scotts Ter CHAT ME4....................6 B7
Scott St MAID/BEAR ME14.......122 E1
Scott's Wy RTWE/PEM TN2.......270 B8
Scouting Rd CAN/RD E16............26 A2
Scouler St POP/IOD E14.............25 N7
Scragged Oak Rd
  MAID/BEAR ME14....................156 E2
  RMAID ME17............................157 M4
Scrapsgate Rd IOS ME12.............58 A9
Scraps Hl RSIT ME9...................130 D1
Scratchers La HART DA3.............90 A7
Scratton Rds GVE DA12...............92 E2
Scrooby St CAT SE6.....................41 N6
Scudders Hl HART DA3................90 F5
Scutari Rd EDUL SE22................41 H6
Scylla Rd PECK SE15...................41 M4
Sea Ap IOS ME12..........................80 B3
Seaborough Rd
  CDW/CHF RM16..........................33 K6
Seabourne Wy LYDD TN29.......326 F7
Seabrook Ct HYTHE CT21.........309 N4
Seabrook Dr WWKM BR4............85 H6
Seabrook Gdns HYTHE CT21....309 M5
Seabrook Gv HYTHE CT21.........309 N5
Seabrook Rd TONN TN15..........209 D7
Seabrook V HYTHE CT21...........309 M5
Seacourt Rd ABYW SE2...............28 C5
Seacroft Rd BRDST CT10...........143 M3
Seacroft Cl HYTHE CT21...........309 M3
Seafield Rd BRDST CT10...........113 L9
  RAM CT11...................................16 B3
  WSTB CT5..................................106 A3
Seaford Ct ROCH ME1 *..............18 E7
Seager Rd FAV ME13.................132 E4
Seager Bdns DEPT SE8...............41 N2
Seager Pl BOW E3.......................25 J1
Seager Rd IOS ME12....................77 N8
Seagrave Cl WCHPL E1................24 C1
Seagrave Cv FOLKN CT19...........11 J3
Seagull La CAN/RD E16...............26 B4
Seagull Rd STRD ME2..................71 M9
Sealand Ct ROCH ME1 *..............18 E6
Seal Dr BGR/WK TN15...............149 L6
Seal Hollow Rd SEV TN13...........21 J1
Sealy Rd GRAYS RM17.................32 B8
Seal Rd SEV TN13......................148 G6
Seamark Cl RNTH CT7..............140 E6
Seamark Rd BRCH CT7.............140 E4
  MSTR CT12...............................140 E4
Seapoint Rd BRDST CT10.........143 N1
Searles Dr EHAM E6....................26 A7
Searles St STHWK SE1.................24 A7
Sea Rd DEAL CT14....................263 H2
  HYTHE CT21.............................309 M5
  RYE TN31.................................344 A1
  WGOS CT8................................111 K4
Seasalter Cl SMBW SE5...............40 D1
Seasalter Beach WSTB CT5.......105 H7
Seasalter Cross WSTB CT5.......104 C8
Seasalter La WSTB CT5.............134 C1
Seaside Rd FAV ME13................133 J5
Seaside Av IOS ME12...................58 C8
Sea St HB CT6...........................106 C3
  RCANTE CT3.............................108 C9
Seathorpe Av IOS ME12..............58 C3
Seaths Cnr RCANTE CT3...........169 K9
Seaton Av HYTHE CT21.............308 G4
Seaton Rd DART DA1...................46 A8
  GILL ME7....................................96 B8
  RCANTE CT3.............................108 G8
  WELL DA16..................................44 E1
Seaview HOO/HAM ME3..............56 D5
Sea View Av BRCH CT7.............110 F5
Seaview Av IOS ME12...................80 F6
Sea View Cl RFOLK CT18..........311 L2
Sea View Gdns IOS ME12............80 C4

Sea View Hts BRCH CT7 *..........110 E5
Seaview Hts LYDD TN29...........336 A4
Seaview Rd GILL ME7...................14 C5
  NROM TN28..............................343 J5
Sea View Rd BRCH CT7.............110 F5
  BRDST CT10.............................113 M7
  HB CT6.....................................107 P1
  MARC CT9.................................15 H5
  RDV CT15................................292 E3
Sea View Sq HB CT6 *................107 L1
Sea View Ter FOLK CT20..........310 A8
  MARG CT9...................................77 J2
Seaview Ter OBOR ME11 *...........98 C3
  RSIT ME9...................................338 F7
  RYE TN31..................................338 F7
Seaview Vls BRDST CT10...........113 L4
Seaville Dr HB CT6.....................108 B5
Sea Wall LYDD TN29.................326 G6
  RSIT ME9...................................292 E5
Seaway Cots WSTB CT5.............105 K5
Seaway Crs LYDD TN29.............337 L1
Seaway Gdns LYDD TN29.........326 D9
Seaway Rd LYDD TN29..............337 L1
Second Av BRDST CT10.............113 M3
  CHAT ME4...................................95 P5
  IOS ME12...................................58 B9
  IOS ME12...................................79 M2
  MARC CT9.................................112 G2
  OBOR ME11.................................77 H4
  RYE TN31....................................31 K9
  WTHK RM20.................................31 K9
Secretan Rd ROCH ME1...............94 G5
Sedan Wy WALW SE17.................24 B8
Sedcombe Cl SCUP DA14............64 D3
Sedgebrook Rd
  BKHTH/KID SE5..........................43 H3
Sedge Crs WALD ME5................125 K1
Sedgehill Rd CAT SE6.................61 N4
Sedgemere Rd ABYW SE2............28 B6
Sedgemere Av CAT SE6................62 C1
Sedgewood Cl HAYES BR2..........85 J4
Sedgeworth Rd CMBW SE5.........40 D1
Sedley Cl MEO DA13...................68 A4
Sedley MEO DA13.....................154 D2
Sedley Dr SWLY BR8.....................65 J7
Sedley Cl DIT/AY ME20................65 L7
  RHAM ME8................................126 F2
Sednem Ct PECK SE15.................40 G3
Seeley Dr DUL SE21.....................60 E3
Seething La MON EC3R................24 B3
Sefton Cl STMC/STPC BR5...........86 C1
Sefton Rd CROY/NA CR0.............83 M5
  STMC/STPC BR5........................86 C1
Segrave Rd FOLKN CT19.............11 J3
Selah Dr SWLY BR8.....................65 L7
Selbey Cl HB CT6......................107 P2
Selborne Av BXLY DA5................44 G9
Selborne Rd CMBW SE5..............40 D3
  SCUP DA14.................................83 K7
Selbourne Cl
  MARG CT9.................................112 G4
  RAM CT11...................................64 D3
Selbourne Rd GILL ME7..............73 K8
Selbourne Wy
  MAID/SHEP ME15....................186 C5
Selby Cl CHST BR7......................63 L5
Selby Rd MAID/SHEP ME15......186 C7
  PGE/AN SE20..............................60 C8
  PLSTW E13...................................26 C1
Selbys LING RH7........................235 K7
Selden Rd PECK SE15.................41 J5
Selhurst New Rd SNWD SE25.....83 K5
Selhurst Pl SNWD SE25...............83 K5
Selhurst Rd SNWD SE25..............83 K2
Selkirk Dr ERITH DA8...................45 N2
Selkirk Rd DVE/WH CT16..........291 J4
Selindge Cl BECK BR5................61 M6
Selling Ct FAV ME13..................163 J1
Selling Rd FAV ME13..................163 K6
  RCANTW CT4............................164 C9
Selsdon Park Rd
  SAND/SEL CR2.........................114 A3
Selsdon Rd SAND/SEL CR2.........83 J9
  WNWD SE27................................60 D3
Selsea Av HB CT6......................107 J1
Selsey Crs WELL DA16.................45 J3
Selsey St BOW E3........................25 K1
Selstead Cl RHAM ME8................96 E5
Selway Ct DEAL CT14................232 C6
Selwood Cl IOS ME12..................77 N1
Selwood Rd CROY/NA CR0..........84 D4
Selworthy Rd CAT SE6................61 M2
Selwyn Crs WELL DA16................44 D4
Selwyn Dr BRDST CT10.............113 K8
Semaphore Rd ARCH CT7............77 J2
Semer End RSIT ME9....................99 P3
Semple Rd RI RM18.......................31 M9
Senacre La MAID/SHEP ME15...186 C4
Senacre Sq MAID/SHEP ME15...186 C4
Senacre St PECK SE15..................41 J3
Seneca Rd THMTH CR7................83 H1
Sene Pk HYTHE CT21................309 J4
Senlac Cl RAM CT11...................142 C6
Senlac Rd LEE/GVPK SE12..........42 F9
Senlac Rd LEE/GVPK SE12........269 H9
Senrab St WCHPL E1....................24 D1
Sentamu Cl HNHL SE24...............40 B9
Sequoia Gdns ORP BR6................86 G4
Serenaders Rd BRXN/ST SW9....40 A3
Serene Ct BRDST CT10.............113 N9
Sermon Dr SWLY BR8.................65 J9
Serpentine Rd SEV TN13...........149 H8
Serviden Dr BRDST CT10...........113 M2
Sessions House Sq
  MAID/BEAR ME14....................122 E2
Setchell Rd STHWK SE1...............24 C7
Setchell Wy STHWK SE1..............24 C7
Seth St BERM/RHTH SE16...........25 P8
Settlefield House
  HYTHE CT21............................309 J3
Setterfield Rd MARG CT9.............15 H7
Settington Av WALD ME5.............95 P5
Settles St WCHPL E1....................24 D2
Sevastopol Pl CANT CT1............167 J3
Sevenacre Rd FAV ME13............132 F4
Seven Acres SWLY BR8................88 C3
Seven Mile La BGR/WK TN15....152 B9
Sevenoaks By-Pass
  RSEV TN14................................178 D2

Sevenoaks Cl BXLYHN DA7..........45 L5
Sevenoaks Rd BGR/WK TN15...150 D8
  BROCKY SE4...............................41 M7
  ORP BR6....................................116 G3
  ORP BR6....................................117 P1
  RSEV TN14................................148 G1
Sevenoaks Wy
  STMC/STPC BR5........................64 D9
Sevenscore Farm Cots
  MSTR CT12...............................141 P7
Seven Stars Yd WCHPL E1...........24 C1
Seven Stones Dr BRDST CT10...143 M3
Severn Til RM18............................34 A6
Severnake Cl POP/IOD E14.........25 K7
Severn Cl TONN TN10...............210 F5
Severn Rd SOCK/AV RM15...........30 C3
  WALD ME5...................................95 P9
Sevington La KEN/WIL TN24......253 J9
Sevington Pk
  MAID/SHEP ME15....................185 L5
Seward Rd BECK BR3..................61 K8
Sewell Cl DART DA1...................111 N7
  CDW/CHF RM16..........................31 M8
Sewell Rd ABYW SE2..................27 P5
Sexburga Dr IOS ME12................58 C8
Sextant Av POP/IOD E14.............25 N7
Sextant Pk STRD ME2..................19 K3
Sexton Rd TIL RM18....................49 E2
Seymour Av MARC CT9.............105 N4
  WSTB CT5..................................105 N5
Seymour Cl HB CT6...................107 N5
Seymour Dr HAYES BR2..............86 A5
Seymour Rd BROCKY SE4...........41 K4
Seymour St CVW DA11................49 M9
  RDV CT15................................262 E8
  RHAM ME8...................................97 H6
Seymour Rd CVW DA11...............49 M9
Seymour Ter PGE/AN SE20..........60 H7
Seymour Vls PGE/AN SE20..........60 H7
Seymour Wk SWCM DA10...........48 C8
Seyssel St POP/IOD E14..............25 M7
Shacklands Rd RSEV TN14........118 B3
Shackleton Cl FSTH SE23.............61 H1
  WALD ME5...................................95 P9
The Shades STRD ME2..................71 M8
Shadoxhurst Rd RASHW TN26...303 H3
Shad Thames STHWK SE1...........24 C4
Shadwell Gdns WCHPL E1 *.........24 E3
Shadwell Pierhead WAP E1W *....24 E3
Shaftesbury Av FOLKN CT19.....310 A4
Shaftesbury Cl E/WMAL ME19...153 N3
Shaftesbury Dr MAIDW ME16....155 H8
Shaftesbury La DART DA1.............45 P5
Shaftesbury Rd BECK BR3...........61 M8
  CANTW/ST CT2........................166 D1
  RCANTE CT3............................138 B8
  SBH/RUST TN4.........................270 D8
  WSTB CT5..................................105 L5
Shaftsbury St RAM CT11...............17 H3
Shah Pl RAM CT11.........................16 E2
Shakespeare Av TIL RM18............49 M3
Shakespeare Farm Rd
  HOO/HAM ME3...........................54 D1
Shakespeare Pas MARC CT9......14 D5
Shakespeare Rd BRCH CT7.......111 K6
  BXLYHN DA7...............................45 J5
  DART DA1...................................46 G5
  DVW CT17................................291 J9
  GILL ME7.......................................7 H6
  HNHL SE24..................................40 B1
  MARG CT9...................................15 H6
  SIT ME10...................................129 P1
  TON TN9...................................240 C1
Shakespeare Ter FOLK CT20.......10 D5
Shalfleet Cl WALD ME5................95 L7
Shalford Cl ORP BR6...................86 D8
Shalloak Rd CANTW/ST CT2.......137 J8
Shallons Rd ELTH/MOT SE9........63 H3
Shallows Rd BRDST CT10...........113 H7
Shalmsford Ct RCANTW CT4.....195 J2
Shalmsford Rd RCANTW CT4.....194 A1
Shalmsford St RCANTW CT4.....195 H1
The Shambles SEV TN13..............21 G4
Shamrock Av WSTB CT5.............104 A3
Shamrock Rd CROY/NA CR0........82 E5
  GVE DA12...................................50 A8
Shandon Cl RTWE/PEM TN2.......23 J7
Shand St STHWK SE1...................24 B5
Shandy St WCHPL E1....................24 D1
Shanklin Cl WALD ME5................95 M5
Shannon Wy BECK BR3...............61 P5
  SOCK/AV RM15..........................30 F2
Shapland Cl HB CT6...................107 P5
Shardcroft Av HNHL SE24...........40 B8
Shardeloes Rd NWCR SE14..........41 M3
Shard's Sq PECK SE15..................24 D9
Share & Coulter Rd WSTB CT5...106 C3
Sharfleet Crs RSIT ME9................99 K2
Sharland Cl THHTH CR7................82 F3
Sharland Ct THHTH CR7 *............82 F3
Sharland Rd GVE DA12.................71 M8
Sharman Ct SCUP DA14...............64 C3
Sharnal La SNOD ME6................123 P6
Sharnbrooke Cl WELL DA16.........44 F4
Sharnbrooke Cl WELL DA16.........44 E4
Sharon Crs WALD ME5................125 L1
Sharp's Fld HDCN TN27.............247 P4
Sharps Cn GILL ME7......................96 C1
Sharps Gn DART DA1...................46 F4
Sharratt St PECK SE15..................24 F9
Sharps Gn GILL ME7......................96 C1
Sharsted Hl RSIT ME9.................161 H4
Sharsted Wy GILL ME7...............126 D2
  MAID/BEAR ME14 *.................156 F7
Shawbroke Rd
  ELTH/MOT SE9...........................43 H5
Shawbury Rd EDUL SE22.............40 F5
Shaw Cl HOO/HAM ME3..............52 P9
  MAID/BEAR ME14.......................54 B4
  THMD SE28.................................28 A4
Shaw Crs POP/IOD E14.................49 H2
  TIL RM18....................................49 M2
Shawdene Rd KEN/WIL TN24....252 G4
Shawdon Av SWCH CT13...........202 F3
Shawfield Pk BMLY BR1...............63 H8
Shaw Rd BH/WHM TN16............145 M5
  BMLY BR1...................................62 D2

EDUL SE22 40 E5
Shaws Cots FSTH SE23 * 61 L2
Shaw's Cots FSTH SE23 61 L2
Shawstead Rd WALD ME5 95 P7
Shaws Wy ROCH ME1 94 G3
The Shaw CHST BR7 * 63 N6
RTWE/PEM TN2 23 H7
Shaxton Crs CROY/NA CR0 114 F3
Sheafe Dr CRBK TN17 297 P2
Sheal's Crs MAID/SHEP ME15 185 M1
Shearers Cl MAID/BEAR ME14 156 B8
Shearman Rd BKHTH/KID SE3 42 D5
Shears Cl DART DA1 66 C1
Shearwater HART DA3 68 F9
MAIDW ME16 154 G7
Shearwater Av WSTB CT5 105 K7
Shearwater Cl STRD ME2 71 L8
Shearwater Ct IOS ME12 57 K8
Shear Wy LYDD TN29 326 G1
Shearway Rd FOLKN CT19 310 C4
Shearwood Crs DART DA1 45 P4
Sheenewood SYD SE26 61 H4
Sheen Rd STMC/STPC BR5 86 G1
Sheen Wy WLGTN SM6 82 E9
Sheepbarn La WARL CR6 115 K6
Sheepcote La STMC/STPC BR5 87 P1
Sheep Court La RCANTW CT4 225 P7
Sheepfold La ASH TN23 282 F4
Sheephurst La
STPH/PW TN12 244 C4
Sheepstreet La WADH TN5 314 F8
Sheerness Docks IOS ME12 * 57 K6
Sheerstone RSIT ME9 99 L3
Sheerwater Rd CAN/RD E16 26 E1
RCANTE CT3 169 N3
Sheerways FAV ME13 132 D7
Sheet Glass Rd QBOR ME11 77 J4
Sheet Hl BGR/WK TN15 180 G2
Sheffield Gdns DEAL CT14 233 H5
Sheffield Rd SBGH/RUST TN4 240 C7
The Sheilings BGR/WK TN15 149 L5
Shelbury Cl SCUP DA14 64 C2
Shelbury Rd EDUL SE22 41 H6
Shelden Dr RHAM ME8 97 J6
Sheldon Cl LEE/GVPK SE12 42 F6
PGE/AN SE20 61 H7
RCANTE CT3 199 J9
Sheldon Rd BXLYHN DA7 45 H2
Sheldon St CROY/NA CR0 83 H7
Sheldon Wy DIT/AY ME20 153 P1
Sheldrake Cl CAN/RD E16 26 G4
Shelduck Cl RSIT ME9 99 M2
Sheldwich Cl ASH TN23 282 C2
Sheldwich Ter HAYES BR2 * 85 P3
Shelford Cl CDW/CHF RM16 33 H1
Shelford Ri NRWD SE19 60 E6
Shellbank La RDART DA2 67 P4
Shell Cl HAYES BR2 85 P3
Shelldrake Cl HOO/HM ME3 56 D3
Shelley Av CANT CT1 167 H2
Shelley Cl ORP BR6 86 F7
PECK SE15 41 H3
Shelley Dr WELL DA16 44 A2
Shelley Pl TIL RM18 49 M2
Shelley Ri ROCH ME1 94 F3
Shelley Rd EGRIN RH19 264 F7
MAIDW ME16 185 H1
Shelleys La RSEV TN14 147 H1
Shellness Rd IOS ME12 103 P1
Shellons St FOLK CT20 11 F4
Shell Rd LEW SE13 41 P4
Shelmerdine Cl BOW E3 25 K1
Shelton Cl TONN TN10 210 F5
Shelvin La RCANTW CT4 258 F3
Shenden Cl SEV TN13 179 H4
Shenden Wy SEV TN13 179 H4
Shenley Gv MAID/BEAR ME14 155 L2
Shenley Pk HDCN TN27 * 247 P7
Shenley Rd CMBW SE5 40 E2
DART DA1 46 G7
Shenstone Cl DART DA1 45 M6
Shepherd Cl ASH TN23 282 B3
Shepherd Dr KEN/WIL TN24 283 K1
Shepherds Cl ORP BR6 86 G7
Shepherds Close Rd
RCANTW CT4 198 A5
Shepherdsgate
CANTW/ST CT2 * 4 D2
Shepherds Ga GILL ME7 96 C9
Shepherdsgate Dr HB CT6 107 M6
Shepherds Gate Dr
MAID/BEAR ME14 156 B6
Shepherds Gn CHST BR7 63 P6
Shepherdsgrove La
EGRIN RH19 266 A3
Shepherds La DART DA1 46 A9
THMD SE28 27 M4
Shepherd's Leas
ELTH/MOT SE9 * 43 P5
Shepherd St GVW DA11 49 H8
Shepherds Wk HYTHE CT21 308 D7
RTWE/PEM TN2 23 J3
WSTB CT5 106 B6
Shepherds Wy HOO/HM ME3 54 G4
RMAID ME17 187 H7
SAND/SEL CR2 114 A2
WSTB CT5 106 B6
Shepherdswell Rd RDV CT15 260 A1
Sheppard Dr BERM/RHTH SE16 24 E8
Shepperton Cl WALD ME5 125 P1
Shepperton Rd
STMC/STPC BR5 86 D3
Sheppey Cl BRCH CT7 110 G6
ERITH DA8 46 B1
Sheppey Ct IOS ME12 * 57 M9
Sheppey Rd
MAID/SHEP ME15 185 L4
Sheppey St IOS ME12 57 J6
Sheppey Vw WSTB CT5 105 K8
Sheppey Wy RSIT ME9 77 K8
RSIT ME9 99 K6
Sheppy Pl GVE DA12 49 M8
Shepway KEN/WIL TN24 253 H4
Shepway Cl FOLKN CT19 10 E2
Shepway Ct
MAID/SHEP ME15 * 185 P3
Sherard Rd ELTH/MOT SE9 43 J6
Sheraton Ct WALD ME5 125 L4
Sherborne Cl RTWE/PEM TN2 23 K7
Sherborne Gv BGR/WK TN15 149 M2
Sherborne La MANHO EC4N 24 A3
Sherborne Rd STMC/STPC BR5 86 G2
Sherbourne Cl BGR/WK TN15 120 B1
Sherbourne Dr MAIDW ME16 184 G1
STRD ME2 72 A6
Sherbrooke Cl BXLYHN DA7 45 J5
Sherenden La STPH/PW TN12 245 H9
Sherenden Rd RTON TN11 241 N2
Sherfield Rd GRAYS RM17 32 C9
Sheridan Cl EGRIN RH19 264 F7
MAID/BEAR ME14 155 K4
WALD ME5 95 P7
Sheridan Ct DART DA1 46 G5
Sheridan Crs CHST BR7 63 M8
Sheridan Pl BMLY BR1 63 H8
Sheridan Rd BELV DA17 28 F7
BXLYHN DA7 44 G4
DVE/WH CT16 291 J4
Sheridan St WCHPL E1 24 E2
Sheridan Wy BECK BR3 61 M7
Sheriff Dr WALD ME5 125 M3
Sheriffs Court La MSTR CT12 140 G6
Sheringham Cl MAIDW ME16 155 J5
Sheringham Rd PGE/AN SE20 61 H8
Sherington Rd BKHTH/KID SE3 26 B9
Sherlies Av ORP BR6 86 F6
Sherman Cl RHAM ME8 96 E5
Sherman Rd BMLY BR1 62 E7
Shernden La EDEN TN8 236 D5
Shernolds MAID/SHEP ME15 185 N4
Sheron Cl DEAL CT14 232 F4
Sherway Cl HDCN TN27 247 P4
Sherway Rd HDCN TN27 248 E2
Sherwin Rd NWCR SE14 41 K2
Sherwood CDW/CHF RM16 31 P4
Sherwood Av WALD ME5 125 M3
Sherwood Cl BXLY DA5 44 E7
FAV ME13 132 E5
HB CT6 107 P4
KEN/WIL TN24 252 G2
WSTB CT5 105 K8
Sherwood Ct WGOS CT8 * 111 M4
Sherwood Dr WSTB CT5 105 K8
Sherwood Gdns
BERM/RHTH SE16 24 D8
POP/IOD E14 25 K7
RAM CT11 143 K3
Sherwood Pk
RTWE/PEM TN2 * 271 H3
Sherwood Park Av
BFN/LL DA15 44 C8
Sherwood Park Rd MTCM CR4 82 B1
Sherwood Pl RRTW TN3 269 K5
Sherwood Rd BRCH CT7 110 G8
CROY/NA CR0 83 N4
RTWE/PEM TN2 270 G2
WELL DA16 44 A4
Sherwoods WALD ME5 * 125 J4
Sherwood Wy
RTWE/PEM TN2 270 G2
WWKM BR4 84 F6
Shieldhall St ABYW SE2 28 B7
Shifford Pth FSTH SE23 61 K2
Shillingheld Cl
MAID/BEAR ME14 156 C7
Shimmin Rd RSIT ME9 129 L8
Shingle Barn La
MAID/SHEP ME15 184 A7
Shinglewell Rd ERITH DA8 45 J1
Shinners Cl SNWD SE25 83 M2
Shipbourne Rd TONN TN10 210 F6
Ship Cl LYDD TN29 326 G6
Ship Field Cl BH/WHM TN16 145 M6
Ship Hl BH/WHM TN16 145 M6
Ship La EYN DA4 66 E7
ROCH ME1 19 K7
SOCK/AV RM15 30 G5
SWLY BR8 66 D7
Shipley Hills Rd MEO DA13 92 A5
Shipley Mill Cl ASH TN23 282 F4
Shipman Av CANTW/ST CT2 166 B4
Shipman Rd CAN/RD E16 26 C2
FSTH SE23 61 K1
Shipmans Wy DVE/WH CT16 291 H4
Ship & Mermaid Rw
STHWK SE1 24 A5
Ship St DEPT SE8 41 N2
EGRIN RH19 265 H8
FOLKN CT19 10 E3
Ship Tavern Pas BANK EC3V 24 B3
Shipwright Rd
BERM/RHTH SE16 25 H5
Shipwrights Av CHAT ME4 95 M4
Shipwright Yd STHWK SE1 24 B4
The Shipyard FAV ME13 * 132 G4
Shirburn Cl FSTH SE23 41 J8
Shirbutt St POP/IOD E14 25 K3
Shirebrook Rd BKHTH/KID SE3 43 H3
Shirehall Rd RDART DA2 66 D4
Shire La FAV ME13 191 H5
ORP BR6 116 A2
The Shires STPH/PW TN12 243 H2
Shireway Cl FOLKN CT19 310 D4
Shirley Av BXLY DA5 44 F8
CROY/NA CR0 83 P5
RAM CT11 143 K2
Shirley Church Rd
CROY/NA CR0 84 A7
Shirley Cl DART DA1 46 C5
GVE DA12 70 D1
Shirley Cots SBGH/RUST TN4 * 22 D1
Shirley Crs BECK BR3 84 B1
Shirley Gdns SBGH/RUST TN4 269 P3
Shirley Gv SBGH/RUST TN4 269 P3
Shirley Hills Rd CROY/NA CR0 84 A8
Shirley Oaks Rd CROY/NA CR0 84 A5
Shirley Park Rd CROY/NA CR0 83 N5
Shirley Rd BFN/LL DA15 64 A2
CROY/NA CR0 83 N5
Shirley Rw SNWD SE25 * 60 G8
Shirley St CAN/RD E16 26 A2
Shirley Wy CROY/NA CR0 84 C7
MAID/SHEP ME15 156 D9
Shoebury Ter IOS ME12 * 78 G2
Sholden Bank DEAL CT14 232 D5
Sholden Gdns STMC/STPC BR5 87 K2
Sholden New Rd DEAL CT14 232 E4
Sholden Rd STRD ME2 72 C6
Shooters Cha RSIT ME9 99 L2
Shooter's Hl DVW CT17 8 A1
Shooters Hl RDV CT15 230 D9
Shooters Hill Rd GNWCH SE10 42 C2
Shore Cl BRCH CT7 * 110 E5
HB CT6 106 G3
Shoreditch High St WCHPL E1 24 B1
Shorefields RHAM ME8 97 K4
Shoregate La RSIT ME9 75 K9
Shoreham Cl CROY/NA CR0 83 P3
Shoreham La RSEV TN14 117 P6
SEV TN13 148 E8
TENT TN30 301 H4
Shoreham Pl RSEV TN14 118 F6
Shoreham Rd RSEV TN14 118 G9
STMC/STPC BR5 64 D7
Shoreham Wy HAYES BR2 85 K3
Shorehill La BGR/WK TN15 119 M9
The Shore GVW DA11 49 K7
Shore Wy BRXN/ST SW9 40 A3
Shorland Ct ROCH ME1 * 18 E6
Shorncliffe Crs FOLK CT20 310 B6
Shorncliffe Rd FOLK CT20 10 C4
STHWK SE1 24 C8
Shorndean St CAT SE6 42 A8
Shorne Cl BFN/LL DA15 44 D7
STMC/STPC BR5 87 L1
Shornefield Cl BMLY BR1 63 L9
Shorne Ifield Rd GVE DA12 70 D5
Shorter St TWRH EC3N 24 C3
Shortlands Cl BELV DA17 28 E6
Shortlands Gdns HAYES BR2 62 C8
Shortlands Gv HAYES BR2 62 B9
Shortlands Rd HAYES BR2 62 B9
SIT ME10 129 P1
Short La LYDD TN29 323 M8
OXTED RH8 175 L8
RDV CT15 289 N3
Short's Prospect IOS ME12 79 H7
Shorts Reach ROCH ME1 * 18 E6
Short St CHAT ME4 7 F7
IOS ME12 57 K6
RCANTE CT3 230 B1
SWCH CT13 201 P1
Shorts Wy ROCH ME1 94 F4
Shortway ELTH/MOT SE9 43 J4
Shotfield Cl RCANTE CT3 169 M2
Shottendane Rd BRCH CT7 111 L9
Shottenden La RCANTW CT4 193 J5
Shottenden Rd FAV ME13 192 F4
GILL ME7 73 K8
Shottery Cl ELTH/MOT SE9 63 J2
Shoulder of Mutton Aly
POP/IOD E14 25 H3
Shovelstrode La EGRIN RH19 265 N8
Showfields Rd
RTWE/PEM TN2 270 C7
Shrapnel Cl WOOL/PLUM SE18 43 K1
Shrapnel Rd ELTH/MOT SE9 43 K4
Shrewsbury La
WOOL/PLUM SE18 43 M2
Shrewsbury Rd BECK BR3 61 L9
Shrimpton Cl RCANTW CT4 164 C9
Shroffold Rd BMLY BR1 62 C3
Shropshire Cl MTCM CR4 82 D1
Shropshire Ter
MAID/SHEP ME15 186 B4
Shrubbery Rd EYN DA4 67 K7
GVE DA12 49 M9
The Shrubbery DEAL CT14 233 H8
RCANTW CT4 * 228 C5
Shrubcote TENT TN30 301 K8
Shrub Hill Rd WSTB CT5 106 C7
Shrublands Av CROY/NA CR0 84 D8
Shrublands Cl SYD SE26 61 J2
Shrublands Ct
RTWE/PEM TN2 * 23 H2
Shrubsall Cl ELTH/MOT SE9 43 J9
Shrubshall Meadow
BGR/WK TN15 181 K3
Shrubsole Av IOS ME12 57 L7
Shrubsole Dr
MAID/BEAR ME14 155 K1
Shuart La BRCH CT7 110 A9
Shurland Av IOS ME12 78 B1
IOS ME12 80 F6
SIT ME10 129 N4
Shurland Gdns PECK SE15 * 40 F1
Shurlock Av SWLY BR8 65 M8
Shurlock Dr ORP BR6 86 D8
Shuttle Cl BFN/LL DA15 44 B8
Shuttlemead BXLY DA5 45 H8
Shuttle Rd BRDST CT10 113 N8
DART DA1 46 A4
Shuttlesfield La RCANTW CT4 257 J8
Sibert's Cl RDV CT15 260 A3
Sibley Cl BMLY BR1 85 P2
BXLYHS DA6 44 G6
Sibthorpe Rd LEE/GVPK SE12 42 F8
Sidcup By-Pass Rd SCUP DA14 64 A3
Sidcup Hl SCUP DA14 64 D4
Sidcup Hill Gdns SCUP DA14 * 64 E4
Sidcup Pl SCUP DA14 64 C4
Sidcup Rd LEE/GVPK SE12 42 F6
Siddons Rd CROY/NA CR0 82 F7
FSTH SE23 61 L1
Sidewood Rd ELTH/MOT SE9 43 P9
The Sidings MEO DA13 * 92 B2
RFOLK CT18 287 H1
SEV TN13 148 D5
WSTB CT5 105 M4
Sidmouth Rd PECK SE15 40 F2
STMC/STPC BR5 87 J1
WELL DA16 44 E1
Sidney Cl RTWE/PEM TN2 270 B8
Sidney Gdns RSEV TN14 149 H1
Sidney Rd BECK BR3 61 L8
GILL ME7 73 J8
ROCH ME1 94 F4
SNWD SE25 83 M2
Sidney Sq WCHPL E1 * 24 F1
Sidney St FOLKN CT19 11 G1
MAIDW ME16 185 H1
WCHPL E1 24 E1
Siebert Rd BKHTH/KID SE3 26 B9
Siemens Rd WOOL/PLUM SE18 26 E6
Sienna Ct RHAM ME8 * 126 G1
Signal Ct LING RH7 235 H4
Signpost Fld RTON TN11 * 212 B5
Silchester Ct
MAID/BEAR ME14 155 P5
Silecroft Ct ASH TN23 * 252 B8
Silecroft Rd BXLYHN DA7 45 J2
Silk Cl LEE/GVPK SE12 42 E6
Silkham Rd OXTED RH8 174 G3
Silk Mills Cl RSEV TN14 149 H6
Silk Mills Pth LEW SE13 42 A4
Silver Bank WALD ME5 95 M8
Silver Birch Av MEO DA13 122 A4
Silver Birch Cl CAT SE6 61 M2
RDART DA2 65 N3
THMD SE28 27 P4
Silver Birch Ct RASHW TN26 281 M7
Silver Birches
SBGH/RUST TN4 * 240 E9
WALD ME5 125 M2
Silver Birch Gv ASH TN23 282 E4
Silver Cl NWCR SE14 * 41 L1
TON TN9 240 E3
Silverdale HART DA3 91 J1
MAIDW ME16 184 E1
SYD SE26 61 J3
Silverdale Av IOS ME12 78 A1
Silverdale Dr ELTH/MOT SE9 63 J1
HB CT6 108 A8
RHAM ME8 97 H7
Silverdale Gv SIT ME10 129 K2
Silverdale La HAWK TN18 328 G1
SBGH/RUST TN4 270 E2
Silverdale Rd BXLYHN DA7 45 K3
RAM CT11 142 F7
SBGH/RUST TN4 270 E2
STMC/STPC BR5 86 D1
Silver Hl CHAT ME4 6 C6
ROCH ME1 * 94 E4
Silver Hill Gdns CHAT ME4 6 C6
KEN/WIL TN24 253 K8
Silver Hill Rd KEN/WIL TN24 253 K8
Silverhurst Dr TONN TN10 210 F4
Silverlands Rd RFOLK CT18 286 G1
Silver La WWKM BR4 84 G6
Silverleigh Rd THHTH CR7 82 E1
Silverlocke Rd GRAYS RM17 32 E9
Silvermere Rd CAT SE6 41 N7
Silvermere Rw SNWD SE25 * 60 G8
Silver Rd GVE DA12 70 A1
LEW SE13 41 P4
Silverspot Cl RHAM ME8 97 J7
Silver Spring Cl ERITH DA8 28 G9
Silverstead La BH/WHM TN16 146 F5
Silversted La BH/WHM TN16 146 E6
The Silvers BRDST CT10 113 H9
Silver St DEAL CT14 233 J2
RSIT ME9 128 G8
Silvertown Wy CAN/RD E16 26 A2
Silver Tree Cl WALD ME5 125 M4
Silver Wk BERM/RHTH SE16 25 J4
Silverweed Rd WALD ME5 95 L9
Silverwood Cl BECK BR3 61 N6
CDW/CHF RM16 32 B3
CROY/NA CR0 114 C3
Silvester Rd EDUL SE22 40 F6
Silwood St BERM/RHTH SE16 24 G8
Simcoe Ter DVE/WH CT16 * 291 J4
Simmonds Dr HART DA3 91 K2
Simmonds La
MAID/SHEP ME15 186 E5
Simmonds Rd CANT CT1 4 B7
Simmons Pl CDW/CHF RM16 32 B4
Simmons Rd
WOOL/PLUM SE18 27 J8
Simms Rd STHWK SE1 24 D7
Simnel Rd LEE/GVPK SE12 42 F8
Simon Av MARG CT9 113 J3
Simone Cl BMLY BR1 63 H7
Simone Weil Av
KEN/WIL TN24 252 E5
Simon's Av ASH TN23 282 C1
Simpson Rd SIT ME10 99 K9
SNOD ME6 123 P7
Simpson's Rd HAYES BR2 62 E9
POP/IOD E14 25 L3
Sinclair Cl RHAM ME8 97 H9
Sinclair Wy RDART DA2 67 K3
Singapore Dr GILL ME7 6 E2
Singledge Av DVE/WH CT16 290 G1
Singledge La RDV CT15 260 C5
Singles Cross RSEV TN14 * 117 L9
Single's Cross La RSEV TN14 117 K9
Single St BH/WHM TN16 116 C9
Singleton Cl CROY/NA CR0 83 H4
MSTR CT12 141 J6
Singleton Hl ASH TN23 252 A9
Singleton Rd ASH TN23 251 P8
Singlewell Rd GVW DA11 69 M3
Sion Hl RAM CT11 17 F5
Sion Houses RTW TN1 * 22 D6
Sion Wk RTW TN1 * 22 D6
Sirdar Strd GVE DA12 70 B4
Sir David's Pk
SBGH/RUST TN4 240 B8
Sir Evelyn Rd ROCH ME1 94 G5
Sir John Fogge Av ASH TN23 252 C5
Sir John Hawkins Wy CHAT ME4 6 B4
Sir John Kirk Cl CMBW SE5 40 C1
Sir John Moore Av
HYTHE CT21 308 F5
Sir Thomas Longley Rd
STRD ME2 19 K3
Sir Walter Burke Wy CHAT ME4 72 G7
Sise La MANHO EC4N * 24 A2
Siskin Cl RASHE TN25 252 E2
RFOLK CT18 288 B8
Siskin Gdns STPH/PW TN12 243 H4
Sissinghurst Cl BMLY BR1 62 C4
Sissinghurst Dr MAIDW ME16 154 G8
Sissinghurst Rd CRBK TN17 276 G8
CROY/NA CR0 83 M4
Sister Mabels Wy PECK SE15 * 40 F1
Sisulu Pl BRXN/ST SW9 40 A4
Sittingbourne Rd
MAID/BEAR ME14 13 J2
Siward Rd HAYES BR2 62 F9
Six Bells La SEV TN13 21 G5
Six Bells Ms RYE TN31 330 B8
Six Fields Pth TENT TN30 301 H8
Six Penny Cl EDEN TN8 236 D1
Sixth Av IOS ME12 79 N2
Skeete Rd RFOLK CT18 286 E1
Skeet Hill La STMC/STPC BR5 87 N6
Skeffington St
WOOL/PLUM SE18 27 K6
Skene Cl RHAM ME8 97 K5
Sketchley Gdns
BERM/RHTH SE16 24 G8
Skeynes Rd EDEN TN8 206 C9
Skibbs La ORP BR6 87 M7
Skid Hill La WARL CR6 115 J9
Skiffington Cl
BRXS/STRHM SW2 40 A9
Skinner Gdns CRBK TN17 276 D8
Skinner Rd LYDD TN29 342 B6
Skinners Cl DIT/AY ME20 124 F7
Skinners La EDEN TN8 206 E8
Skinner St CHAT ME4 6 C6
GILL ME7 7 H1
Skinner's Wy RMAID ME17 187 H7
Skinney La EYN DA4 67 K9
Skippers Cl SWCM DA10 47 P6
Skye Cl MAID/SHEP ME15 185 M4
Skylark Wy ASH TN23 282 G5
Skylines Village POP/IOD E14 * 25 M5
Sladebrook Rd BKHTH/KID SE3 43 H4
Slade Cl WALD ME5 125 N3
Sladedale Rd
WOOL/PLUM SE18 27 M8
Slade Gdns ERITH DA8 45 P2
Slade Green Rd ERITH DA8 45 P2
Slade Rd RMAID ME17 190 C3
Slades Cl WSTB CT5 106 B6
Slades Dr CHST BR7 63 N2
ELTH/MOT SE9 63 N3
The Slade RRTW TN3 295 H4
TON TN9 210 E8
WOOL/PLUM SE18 27 M9
Slagrove Pl BROCKY SE4 41 N6
Slaithwaite Rd LEW SE13 42 A5
Slaney Rd STPH/PW TN12 246 C5
Slatin Rd STRD ME2 72 A7
Sleepers Farm Rd
CDW/CHF RM16 33 J5
Sleepers Stile Rd WADH TN5 294 D6
Sleigh Rd CANTW/ST CT2 137 L7
Slicketts Hl CHAT ME4 * 6 D5
Slines New Rd CTHM CR3 144 A5
Slines Oak Rd CTHM CR3 144 D8
Slip La RDV CT15 289 L2
Slip Mill Rd HAWK TN18 316 G4
Slippers Pl BERM/RHTH SE16 24 E6
Slip Rd CHAT ME4 72 G7
The Slip BH/WHM TN16 176 D2
Slipway Rd IOS ME12 57 H5
Sloane Gdns ORP BR6 86 D7
Sloane Sq HART DA3 * 68 C9
Sloane Wk CROY/NA CR0 84 C3
Slocum Cl THMD SE28 28 B3
Sloe La MARG CT9 112 G7
Slough Rd RSIT ME9 129 P9
Sly St WCHPL E1 * 24 E2
Small Bridge Rd
STPH/PW TN12 274 A6
Small Grains HART DA3 90 E7
Small Hythe Cl
MAID/SHEP ME15 186 E1
Smallhythe Rd TENT TN30 300 G8
Small Profits WBY/YAL ME18 183 P7
Smarden Cl BELV DA17 28 F8
Smarden Rd HDCN TN27 247 P5
HDCN TN27 278 B4
Smarts Hl RTON TN11 238 F8
Smarts Rd GVE DA12 69 M2
Smeaton St WAP E1W 24 E4
Smeed Cl SIT ME10 130 A1
Smeeds Cl EGRIN RH19 265 K5
Smetham Gdns STRD ME2 72 B6
Smiles Pl LEW SE13 42 A3
Smith Cl BERM/RHTH SE16 24 G4
Smithers Cl RTON TN11 211 P1
Smithers La STPH/PW TN12 213 H3
Smithfield Rd HOO/HM ME3 56 E3
Smithies Rd ABYW SE2 28 A7
Smith Rd WALD ME5 125 N2
Smith's Hl MAID/SHEP ME15 184 B7
Smiths La EDEN TN8 176 D9
Smiths Orch RSIT ME9 128 G8
Smith St STRD ME2 18 B3
Smithy Dr ASH TN23 282 F4
Smithy St WCHPL E1 24 F1
Smolletts EGRIN RH19 264 F8
Smugglers Leap MSTR CT12 * 141 K4
Smugglers Ms HAWK TN18 317 J5
Smuggler's Wy BRCH CT7 111 H5
Smugglers Whf RDART DA2 47 P6
Smyrk's Rd WALW SE17 24 B8
Smythe Cl SBGH/RUST TN4 240 B6
Smythe Rd EYN DA4 66 G7
Smythe St POP/IOD E14 25 L3
Snag La RSEV TN14 116 E6
Snake Dro BRCH CT7 109 K9
Snakes Hl RCANTE CT3 199 K2
Snargate La LYDD TN29 323 M9
Snargate St DVW CT17 8 C6
Snatts Hl OXTED RH8 175 J5
Snell Gdns HB CT6 106 G4
Snelling Av GVW DA11 69 K1
Snipe Cl ERITH DA8 46 B1
RASHE TN25 252 F2
RTWE/PEM TN2 241 P9
Snoad La STPH/PW TN12 245 M9
Snodhurst Av WALD ME5 95 K9
Snodland Rd E/WMAL ME19 123 K7
Snoggers Hl FAV ME13 164 B5
Snoll Hatch Rd
STPH/PW TN12 212 G5
Snowbell Rd ASH TN23 282 E4
Snowdon Av MAID/BEAR ME14 13 J3
Snowdon Cl WALD ME5 95 N7
Snowdon Pde
MAID/BEAR ME14 * 13 K3
Snowdown Cl PGE/AN SE20 61 J7
Snowdrop Cl FOLKN CT19 310 F3
Snowsfields STHWK SE1 24 A5
Snughorne La HDCN TN27 248 D9
Soames St PECK SE15 40 F4
Sobraon Wy CANT CT1 167 J3
Solander Gdns WCHPL E1 24 E3
Solar Ct RAM CT11 * 16 A7
Solefields Rd SEV TN13 21 G7
Soleoak Dr SEV TN13 21 F7
Soleshill Rd RCANTW CT4 193 M2
Sole St GVE DA12 92 E2
Solomon Rd RHAM ME8 97 J5

Solomons La FAV ME13 ....132 G6
Solomon's Pas PECK SE15 ......41 H5
Solomons Rd CHAT ME4 ....6 C4
Solway TIL RM18 ....34 B6
Solway Rd EDUL SE22 ....40 C5
Somerden Rd STMC/STPC BR5...87 J4
Somerfield Cl MAIDW ME16 * 12 A4
Somerfield La MAIDW ME16 ....12 A3
Somerfield Rd MAIDW ME16........12 A4
Somerfield St
BERM/RHTH SE16..................24 G8
Somerford Wy
BERM/RHTH SE16..................25 H5
Somerhill Av BFN/LL DA15.........44 D8
Somerhill Rd TON TN9 ....240 C1
WELL DA16...........................44 D3
Somerleyton Rd BRXN/ST SW9 ..40 B6
Somerset Av WALD DA16 ....44 B6
Somerset Cl SIT ME10 ....129 K1
WALD ME5.............................95 P6
WSTB CT5 ....105 J9
Somerset Ct MSTR CT12 * 142 G2
Somerset Gdns LEW SE13 ....41 P5
Somerset Rd CANT CT1............167 J5
DART DA1 ....46 B7
DEAL CT14 ....232 G6
FOLKN CT19 ....310 B5
KEN/WIL TN24.........................2 D3
MAID/SHEP ME15 ....185 P9
ORP BR6 ....87 H4
SBGH/RUST TN4 ....270 D2
SLH/COR SS17 ....33 P5
Somerset Street Little
TWRH EC3N * 24 C2
Somersham Rd BXLYHN DA7 ......44 C3
Somerton Rd PECK SE15 ....62 F1
Somertrees Av LEE/GVPK SE12 ..62 F1
Somerville Gdns
SBGH/RUST TN4 ....22 B3
Somerville Rd DART DA1 ....46 F7
PGE/AN SE20 ....50 D9
Somme Ct CANT CT1..............167 J5
Somner Cl CANTW/ST CT2 ....2 A7
Somner Wk MAID/SHEP ME15..186 C1
Sondes Cl HB CT6 ....107 M4
Sondes Rd DEAL CT14 ....233 J4
Sondes St WALW SE17 ....24 A9
Songhurst Cl CROY/NA CRO 82 E5
Sonning Rd SNWD SE25 ....93 K7
Sonning Wy SIT ME10 ....99 K7
Soper Cl FSTH SE23................41 K9
Soper's La HAWK TN18............316 N1
Sophia Rd CAN/RD E16 ....26 C1
Sophia Sq BERM/RHTH SE16....25 H1
Sophurst La POP/IOD E14 ....—
Sophurst Wd
STPH/PW TN12 * 21 K8
Sopwith Cl BH/WHM TN16 ....145 N1
Sorrel Bank CROY/NA CRO 114 B4
Sorrel Cl THMD SE28 ....27 P4
Sorrel Gdns EHAM E6 ....26 F1
Sorrel La POP/IOD E14 ....25 P6
Sorrell Cl BRXN/ST SW9 ....40 A3
NWCR SE14 ....45 L1
Sorrell Rd WALD ME5 ....125 L1
Sorrell Wy GVW RM3 ....69 J3
Sorrento Wy WWKM BR4 ....128 A6
Sotherton Av KEN/WIL TN24.....283 H1
Souberg Cl DEAL CT14.............233 H1
Sounds Ldg SWLY BR8 ....88 B3
Southall Cl MSTR CT12 ....141 K5
Southall Pl STHWK SE1 ....24 C5

Southampton Gdns
MTCM CR4 ....82 D2
Southampton Ms CAN/RD E16...26 C4
Southampton Wy CMBW SE5......43 D1
South Ash Rd BGR/WK TN15....121 H1
South Av RDV CT15 ....83 D3
RHAM ME8.............................96 D4
SIT ME10 ....129 P2
South Bank BH/WHM TN16 ....16 E2
HOO/HM ME3.........................96 C3
RMAID ME7...........................217 H3
STPH/PW TN12 ....246 B7
Southbank SWLY BR8 ....65 P6
South Barham Rd
RCANTW CT4 ....228 B8
Southborough La HAYES BR2....85 P2
Southborough Rd BMLY BR1 ......85 P1
Southbourne ASH TN23 ....282 B3
HAYES BR2..............................85 K4
Southbourne Gdns
LEE/GVPK SE12 ....42 G6
Southbourne Rd FOLKN CT19...11 H4
Southbridge Pl CROY/NA CRO....83 H8
Southbridge Rd CROY/NA CRO...83 H8
Southbrook Rd
LEE/GVPK SE12 ....42 C7
STRD ME2 ....—
Southbury Av RAIN RM13..........29 N1
South Bush La RHAM ME8 ....97 L8
South Camber Wy
DVE/CW CT16 ....292 A7
South Canterbury Rd
CANT CT1 ....166 F6
South Cliff Pde BRDST CT10 ....155 M3
South Cl BXLYHS DA6 ....44 F5
CANT CT1 ....5 F4
The South Colonnade
POP/IOD E14 ....25 K4
Southcote Rd SNWD SE25 ....83 N2
South Court Dr RCANTE CT3 ...169 K9
South Crs E3CN/ME10...............25 N1
RMAID ME7...........................185 H6
Southcroft Rd ORP BR6 ....86 F7
South Croxted Rd DUL SE21.....60 D2
Southdene RSEV TN14 ....117 N7
Southdown Rd CTHM CR3 ....144 C7
IOS ME12 ....77 N1
South Dr ORP BR6 ....86 F9
South Eastern Rd RAM CT11 ....16 C4
STRD ME2 ....18 E1
South Eden Park Rd BECK BR3 ..84 E2
Southenay La RASHE TN25......285 H5
South End CROY/NA CRO...........83 H8
SAND/SEL CR2.........................83 H9
Southend Cl ELTH/MOT SE9.......43 M7

Southend Crs ELTH/MOT SE9......43 L7
Southend La CAT SE6................61 N3
SYD SE26..............................61 M3
Southend Rd BECK BR3.............57 D2
GRAYS RM17 ....32 D7
Southern Av SNWD SE25 ....50 F9
Southernden Rd HDCN TN27....218 D9
Southerngate Wy NWCR SE14...41 L1
Southern Pl SWLY BR8 ....88 D1
Southern Wy FOLK CT20 ....11 H2
GNWCH SE10 ....25 P7
Southernwood Ri FOLK CT20 ...310 D3
Southey Rd BRXN/ST SW9 ....40 A2
Southey St PGE/AN SE20...........61 K6
Southey Wy TIL RM18 ....49 M2
Southey Wy DIT/AY ME20 ....123 N9
Southfield Rd CHST BR7 ....64 B9
SBGH/RUST TN4...................270 D2
Southfields ROCH ME1 ....94 C3
RRTW TN3 ....269 M1
WADH TN5 ....294 A9
Southfield Shaw MEO ME3 ......13 J2
Southfield Shaw Park Homes
MEO DA15 * 122 B4
Southfields Rd BGR/WK TN15...120 C2
CTHM CR3............................174 E1
Southfields Wy
SBGH/RUST TN4 ....240 E9
Southfleet Av HART DA3 ....68 F8
Southfleet Rd GVW DA11...........49 K9
ORP BR6 ....86 F7
RDART DA2............................68 A5
SWCM DA10 ....48 C8
South Ga PUR RM19.................50 F7
Southgate Rd TENT TN30..........301 K8
South Gipsy Rd WELL DA16.......44 D3
South Green La RSIT ME9 ....128 A6
South Gv RSEV TN14 ....22 D6
South Hall Cl EYN DA4 ....89 L4
South Hall Dr RAIN RM13..........29 N1
South Hill CHST BR7 ....63 K5
South Hill Rd GVE DA12 ....49 M9
HAYES BR2.............................62 C9
Southholme Cl NRWD SE19........60 E7
Southill Rd CHAT ME4 ....87 J5
Southill St POP/IOD E14.............25 L2
South Kent Av GVW DA11 ....48 C7
Southland Rd
WOOL/PLUM SE18 ....27 P9
Southlands EGRIN RH19 ....265 N9
Southlands Av ORP BR6 ....86 F8
Southlands Gv BMLY BR1 ....85 J3
Southlands La OXTED RH8.......204 E1
Southlands Rd HAYES BR2 ....85 M4
Southland Ter PUR RM19 ....50 E8
South La RMAID ME7...............217 H4
Southlees La RSIT ME9 ....158 A2
South Lodge Av MTCM CR4 ....82 D1
Southmead Cl FOLKN CT19......310 D5
South Military Rd DVW CT17 ......8 B7
South Molton Rd CAN/RD E16....26 E1
South Motto ASH TN23..............282 E3
South Norwood Hl SNWD SE25..60 E2
Southover BMLY BR1 ....62 E4
South Pk DEV TN13...................20 C4
South Park Crs CAT SE6 ....42 C9
South Park Hill Rd
SAND/SEL CR2........................83 J9
South Park Rd
MAID/SHEP ME15 ....185 N2
South Pl LVPST EC2M 24 A1
South Place Ms LVPST EC2M * ..24 A1
South Pondside Rd CHAT ME4 ...72 G7
Southport Rd
WOOL/PLUM SE18 ....27 L7
South Rd DEAL CT14................263 J3
DVW CT17 ....291 J7
ERITH DA8 ....29 L3
FAV ME13 ....132 E6
FSTH SE23 ....61 K1
GILL ME7 ....72 C8
HB CT6 ....107 M1
HYTHE CT21.........................309 H6
SOCK/AV RM15......................31 M2
STPH/PW TN12 ....245 J4
SWCH CT13 ....171 P3
South Rw BKHTH/KID SE3.........63 E3
Southsea Av IOS ME12..............58 B7
South Sea Dr HB CT6...............107 J2
South Sea St BERM/RHTH SE16..25 H3
South Side Three Rd
CHAT ME4 ....73 H7
Southspring BFN/LL DA15..........43 P8
South Stour Av ASH TN23 ....2 E7
South St BMLY BR1 ....62 E8
CANT CT1 ....7 H2
DEAL CT14 ....233 J4
FAV ME13 ....49 M8
GVE DA12...............................49 M8
LYDD TN29 ....342 B6
MAIDW ME16 ....184 D3
MEO DA15 ....92 A9
OBOR ME11 ....17 H2
WSTB CT5 ....105 P6
South Street Rd MEO ME3 ......186 B4
South Tenter St WCHPL E1 ....24 C3
South Ter EYN DA4 ....89 L4
South Trench TONN TN10 * 210 F5
South Undercliff RYE TN31........338 F7
South V NRWD SE19 ....60 E5
Southview Rd BKHTH/KID SE3...62 E8
South View Bv BMLY BR1 ....62 G8
CDW/CHF RM16 ....33 J1
Southview SWLY BR8 ....88 E1
South View Av IOS ME12............57 L8
South View La BXLY DA5 ....45 H7
South View Cl SWLY BR8 ....88 F1
South View Cl WALD ME5 ....88 E1
South View Gdns IOS ME12 ....57 L8
South View Hts WALW KM20 * 31 M9
Southview Rd BMLY BR1 ....62 B5
CTHM CR3............................174 E6
South View Rd RDART DA2 ....66 D2
SBGH/RUST TN4...................240 E9
WADH TN5 ....294 A9
WSTB CT5 ....105 L8

WTHK RM20...........................31 M9
Southviews SAND/SEL CR2......114 A3
South Wk WWKM BR4................85 H7
South Wall DEAL CT14 ....232 F1
Southwall Rd DEAL CT14 ....232 G5
Southwark Park Est
BERM/RHTH SE16 ....24 E7
Southwark Park Rd
BERM/RHTH SE16 ....24 D7
Southwark Pl BMLY BR1.............63 K9
Southwark Rd STRD ME2 ....71 M9
Southwater Cl BECK BR3 ....61 P6
POP/IOD E14 ....25 M2
South Wy CROY/NA CRO.............84 B7
Southway HAYES BR2................85 K4
PUR RM19 ....31 H6
WLGTN SM6............................82 B8
Southways RMAID ME17...........216 G3
Southwell Cl CDW/CHF RM16....31 M8
Southwell Rd CMBW SE5...........40 C4
CROY/NA CRO 82 F3
STRD ME2 ....71 L9
South West India Dock Entrance
POP/IOD E14 ....25 M5
Southwick Cl EGRIN RH19 ....264 C6
Southwold Pl WGOS CT8..........111 L6
Southwold Rd BXLY DA5 ....45 K7
Southwood MAIDW ME16 ....184 D1
Southwood Av S
BGH/RUST TN4......................270 D2
Southwood Cl BMLY BR1 ....86 A1
Southwood Gdns EHAM E6.......26 B1
Southwood La CHART CT11.......16 A3
RAM CT11 ....16 A3
SBGH/RUST TN4...................269 N3
THMD SE28 ....28 A4
WSTB CT5 ....106 A4
Southy Ms CAN/RD E16 ....26 B4
Sovereign Bvd GILL ME7 ....96 B4
Sovereign Cl WAP E1W 24 E5
Sovereign Crs
BERM/RHTH SE16 ....25 H1
Sovereigns Wy
STPH/PW TN12 ....244 G3
Sovereign Wy TON TN9 ....210 F9
Sowell St BROST CT10.............113 L8
Sowerby Cl ELTH/MOT SE9 ....43 N5
Spade La RSIT ME9 ....97 N8
Spa Hl NRWD SE19 ....60 D7
Spanton Crs HYTHE CT21 ....308 F4
Spar Cl RTON TN11 ....212 A1
Sparepenny La EYN DA4 ....89 K4
Sparkes Cl HAYES BR2...............85 L1
Sparkeswood Av CRBK TN17....319 L2
Sparke Ter CAN/RD E16 ....26 A2
Spa Rd BERM/RHTH SE16 ....24 C6
Sparrow Castle MARC CT9 ....15 H6
Sparrow Dr STMC/STPC BR5.....85 M6
Sparrows La ELTH/MOT SE9......43 N8
Sparrow Rd RCANTE CT3 ....138 C8
Sparta St GNWCH SE10.............42 A2
Speakers Ct CROY/NA CRO.......83 J5
Spearhead Rd
MAID/BEAR ME14...................155 L5
Spearman St
WOOL/PLUM SE18 ....27 H9
Spectrum Pl WALW SE17 ....24 A8
Speedgate Hl HART DA3 ....90 D6
Speedwell Av WALD ME5..........125 K1
Speedwell Cl GILL ME7..............96 B1
MAID/SHEP ME15 ....156 B8
Speedwell Rd WSTB CT5 ....105 J8
Speedwell St DEPT SE8.............41 N1
Spekehill ELTH/MOT SE9...........63 K2
Speke Rd BRDST CT10 ....113 K7
THHTH CR7.............................60 D8
Spekes Rd GILL ME7..................96 D8
Spelders Hl RASHE TN25 ....254 B5
Speldhurst Ct ASH TN23 ....282 J8
Speldhurst Gdns MARC CT9 .....113 J2
Speldhurst La MAIDW ME16 ......155 J8
Speldhurst Gdns HAYES BR2.....15 J8
Speldhurst Rd HI RRTW TN3 ....239 N9
Speldhurst Rd RRTW TN3 ....240 D3
SBGH/RUST TN4....................240 D3
Spelman St WCHPL E1 ....24 D1
Spelmonden Rd
STPH/PW TN12 ....273 N4
Spence Cl BERM/RHTH SE16 .....25 J5
RFOLK CT18..........................288 D8
Spencer Cl ORP BR6.................86 F6
RFOLK CT18 ....95 M9
Spencer Flats WALD ME5 *.........95 N6
Spencer Ms RTW TN1 * 210 D6
Spencer Pl CROY/NA CRO..........83 J4
Spencer Rd BMLY BR1................62 D6
BRCH CT7.............................111 H5
SAND/SEL CR2........................83 K9
Spencer Sq RAM CT11...............16 E5
Spencers Homes SIT ME10 * 129 N2
Spencers Yd CROY/NA CRO 84 A6
Spielman Rd DART DA1 ....46 F5
Spillett Cl FAV ME13.................132 E6
Spencer Wy
MAID/SHEP ME15...................186 B4
Spenlow Dr WALD ME5 ....125 M4
Spenny La STPH/PW TN12 ....244 B8
Spensar Ms DUL SE21................40 D9
Spenser Rd HB CT6..................107 L2
HNHL SE24..............................40 F5
Speranza St WOOL/PLUM SE18..27 N8
Sperl St POP/IOD E14................25 M1
Speyside TONN TN10................210 E5
Spey St POP/IOD E14 ....25 M1
Spicer Cl BRXN/ST SW9 ....40 B3
Spicers Fld HB CT6...................108 A8
Spicers Homes SIT ME10 * 129 N2
Spices Yd CROY/NA CRO 83 J6
Spielman Rd DART DA1 ....46 F5
Spillett Cl FAV ME13.................132 E6
The Spillway
MAID/SHEP ME15...................185 J1
Spindle Cl WOOL/PLUM SE18....26 F6
Spindle Gld MAID/BEAR ME14..155 P7
Spindles TIL RM18 ....49 L1
Spindlewood Cl WALD ME5 ....125 N2
Spindlewood End ASH TN23 .....282 A5
Spindlewood Gdns
CROY/NA CRO 83 K8

Spindrift Av POP/IOD E14 ....25 L7
Spinel Cl WOOL/PLUM SE18......27 N8
Spinnaker Ct ROCH ME1 * 95 H5
Spinners Cl HDCN TN27...........278 A6
Spinney Cl BECK BR3 ....84 E1
Spinney Gdns NRWD SE19 ....60 D8
Spinney La RCANTE CT3 ....229 H2
Spinney Oak BMLY BR1 ....63 J8
The Spinneys BMLY BR1.............62 C9
The Spinney ASH TN23.............252 B6
DVW CT17 ....290 F5
MAID/SHEP ME15 ....185 N1
MARG CT9 ....113 K4
SCUP DA14 ....64 C4
SWLY BR8 ....100 D2
WALD ME5 ....125 N4
Spinney Wy RSEV TN14 ....116 E5
Spire Av WSTB CT5 ....105 N6
Spire Cl GVE DA12 ....144 A3
Spire Pl WARL CT6....................290 F5
The Spires CANTW/ST CT2 * 4 J7
DART DA1 ....66 D1
STRD ME2 ....94 C1
Spirit Quay WAP E1W..................24 E6
Spitalfield La NROM TN28 ....336 F7
Spital Sq WCHPL E1 ....24 B1
Spital St DART DA1 ....46 D7
Spitfire Cl WALD ME5.................24 D1
Spitfire Ct WALD ME5 ....95 M8
Spitfire House
WOOL/PLUM SE18 * 43 J7
Spitfire Rd E/WMAL ME19.........152 C9
Spitfire Wy RFOLK CT18 ....288 E9
Split La RCANTW CT4...............226 F5
Spode La EDEN TN8 ....257 H9
Sponden La HAWK TN18 ....317 P6
Spongs La CRBK TN17 ....270 F2
Spooner Wk WLGTN SM6 ....82 C9
Sportsbank St CAT SE6.............42 E7
Sportsfield MAID/BEAR ME14....13 J2
Sportsman's Cots
E/WMAL ME19 ....153 J7
Spot La MAID/SHEP ME15 ....186 C1
Spout Hl CROY/NA CRO.............84 D7
Spout La EDEN TN8..................54 E9
STPH/PW TN12 ....273 J5
Spratling La MSTR CT12 ....142 E3
Spratling St MSTR CT12............142 D3
Spray Hl RRTW TN3..................295 J3
Spray St WOOL/PLUM SE18 ......27 J9
The Sprig MAID/BEAR ME14......156 D8
Springall St PECK SE15 ....41 H1
Springbank Rd LEW SE13 ....42 C7
Springbourne Ct BECK BR3 ....62 A7
Springcroft HART DA3 ....91 J7
Spring Cross HART DA3.............91 J7
Springfarm Rd LYDD TN29 ....326 D9
Springfield EGRIN RH19 ....264 G4
MAID/BEAR ME14 * 155 L6
OXTED RH8............................174 D6
Springfield Av
MAID/BEAR ME14...................155 K6
SWLY BR8 ....88 D1
TENT TN30 ....301 J5
Springfield Cl RAM CT11 ....143 K2
Springfield Gdns BMLY BR1.......86 B6
WWKM BR4 ....84 E6
Springfield Gv CHARL SE7.........26 D9
Springfield Pl NWMAL KT3.........—
Springfield Ri SYD SE26 ....61 H2
Springfield Rd BMLY BR1...........86 B6
BXLYHN DA7 ....45 K4
CDW/CHF RM16 ....32 F5
DIT/AY ME20............................45 K4
DVE/WH CT16 * 291 J5
EDEN TN8.............................206 C9
GILL ME7 ....96 E5
MARG CT9 ....113 K2
RRTW TN3 ....269 H9
SBGH/RUST TN4 ....240 D3
WELL DA16.............................44 D3
WSTB CT5 ....105 L6
SYD SE26 ....61 H4
THHTH CR7.............................60 B7
Springfields WADH TN5............315 J5
Springfield Ter CHAT ME4 *.........6 B8
Springfield Ter HYTHE CT21.....309 N1
Spring Gdns BH/WHM TN16......145 M5
WLGTN SM6............................82 B9
Spring Gv GVE DA12 ....145 L5
Spring Gv CVE DA12.................49 M8
Springhead Rd ERITH DA8.........29 L9
FAV ME13 ....132 F4
Spring Head Rd
BGR/WK TN15.......................149 J2
Springhead Rd ERITH DA8.........29 L9
Spring Hollow LYDD TN29.........337 M1
Springholm Cl BH/WHM TN16...145 M5
Springhurst Cl CROY/NA CRO....84 C8
Spring La BGR/WK TN15...........150 C7
CANT CT1 ....5 J5
CANTW/ST CT2 ....137 M9
HYTHE CT21 ....309 M1
OXTED RH8............................174 D2
RRTW TN3 ....240 A6
SNWD SE25 ....83 N3
Spring Park Av CROY/NA CRO....84 A6
Springpark Dr BECK BR3 ....84 A6
Spring Park Rd CROY/NA CRO....84 A6
Springrice Rd LEE SE13 ....42 E9
Spring Shaw Rd
STMC/STPC BR5 ....64 C7
Springside Ter RFOLK CT18 .....288 F6
Spring Ter FOLK CT20 ....11 H4
Spring Tide Cl PECK SE15 * 41 H2
Springvale RHAM ME8 ....96 E2
Spring V BXLYHN DA7 ....45 K5
MAIDW ME16..........................12 C5

SWCM DA10 ....48 A7
Spring Vale Cl SWLY BR8 ....65 P6
Springvale Av GVW DA11 *..........48 G1
Spring V North DART DA1 ....46 D8
Spring V South DART DA1 * 46 D8
Springvale Rd STMC/STPC BR5..86 E9
Spring Wk WCHPL E1 ....24 D1
WSTB CT5 ....105 K7
Springwater Cl
WOOL/PLUM SE18 * 43 J7
Spring Wy EGRIN RH19 ....265 K4
Springwell Rd
STRHM/NOR SW16..................60 A3
TON TN9 ....240 F7
Springwood Cl ASH TN23..........252 B6
Springwood Rd MAIDW ME16....154 F9
Sprotlands Av KEN/WIL TN24....253 F8
Sprotshill Cl SIT ME10................99 M8
Spruce Cl DIT/AY ME20.............153 P2
Sprucedale Cl SWLY BR8 ....65 N8
Sprucedale Gdns
CROY/NA CRO 84 A8
Spruce Rd BH/WHM TN16.........145 N1
Sprules Rd BROCKY SE4 ....41 L3
Spurgeon Av NRWD SE19 ....60 D7
Spurgeon Cl GRAYS RM17.........32 D9
Spurgeon Rd NRWD SE19..........60 D6
Spurling Rd EDUL SE22 ....40 F5
Spurrell Av BXLY DA5 ....65 M5
Spur Rd ORP BR6.....................87 H6
Spurway MAID/BEAR ME14.......156 D8
Square Hill MAID/BEAR ME14 ....13 H5
Square Hill Rd
MAID/SHEP ME15....................13 H6
The Square BH/WHM TN16.......176 D3
BRCH CT7.............................111 H6
LING RH7 ....234 F5
MAID/SHEP ME15 * 214 C3
RCANTE CT3 * 169 K9
RCANTW CT4 ....226 A6
RMAID ME17 ....187 J6
RMAID ME17 * 189 L6
RTON TN11 ....211 P2
SEV TN13..............................148 D8
SWLY BR8 ....65 M9
Squerryes Mede
BH/WHM TN16 ....176 D5
Squire Av CANTW/ST CT2 ....166 B4
Squires Cl STRD ME2 ....71 K8
Squires Ct SIT ME12 ....79 L4
Squires Fld SWLY BR8 ....66 A7
Squires Wy DVE/WH CT16.......291 H4
RDART DA2 ....66 M3
Squirrel La RASHE TN25 ....252 C4
Squirrel's Cha CDW/CHF RM16..33 H5
The Squirrels LEW SE13 ....42 B4
Squirrel Wy RTWE/PEM TN2 ....271 H5
Stable Cl WALD ME5 ....95 P9
Stable St FAV ME13 ....132 C7
Stabledene Wy
RTWE/PEM TN2 ....271 N2
Stablemead FOLKN CT19 ....310 D4
Stables End ORP BR6 ....86 D7
Stace Cl TENT TN30...................301 K7
Stacey Cl GVE DA12 ....210 D6
Stacey Rd TONN TN10 ....210 C6
Staceys St MAID/BEAR ME14.....12 E2
Stacklands Rd BGR/WK TN15...120 B1
Stack La HART DA3 ....91 J2
Stace Rd EYN DA4 ....89 A1
Stacy Ph CMBW SE5 *...............40 E1
Staddon Cl BECK BR3................84 B1
Staddon Ct BECK BR3 ....84 B1
Stade St HYTHE CT21 ....309 H5
The Stade FOLKN CT19............11 H4
Stadium Rd WOOL/PLUM SE18...43 K1
Stadium Wy DART DA1 ....45 N7
SIT ME10 ....100 B8
Stadler Cl MAIDW ME16 ....155 J5
Staffa Rd MAID/SHEP ME15 .....185 M4
Staffhurst Wood Rd
OXTED RH8...........................205 M4
Stafford Cl ASH TN23................252 C7
CDW/CHF RM16 ....31 M7
RDART DA2 ....68 A7
SLH/COR SS17.........................33 P6
Stafford Cross CROY/NA CRO....82 E9
Stafford Gdns CROY/NA CRO.....82 E9
Stafford Rd CROY/NA CRO........271 J4
RTWE/PEM TN2 ....271 J4
SCUP DA14 ....64 A3
TON TN9 ....210 E8
WLGTN SM6............................82 B9
Staffordshire St PECK SE15 ....40 G2
RAM CT11 ....17 F3
Stafford St GILL ME7...................7 H3
Stafford Wy SEV TN13..............179 H3
Stag Rd RTWE/PEM TN2 ....240 C8
WALD ME5 ....95 N9
Stagshaw Cl
MAID/SHEP ME15...................185 M1
Stainer Rd TON TN10................211 J4
Stainer St STHWK SE1 * 24 A4
Staines Cl MAIDW ME16 ....13 F3
Staines Hl CANTW/ST CT2 ....137 N7
Stainton Rd CHST BR7................63 P7
Stainsby Pl POP/IOD E14 ....25 K2
Stainsby Rd POP/IOD E14 ....25 K2
Stainton Rd CAT SE6 ....42 B8
Stairfoot La SEV TN13...............148 B7
Staite La SEV TN13 ....211 J6
Stakes La RSIT ME9 ....158 A2
Staleys Rd BGR/WK TN15.........151 H5
Stalham Ct GILL ME7 * 126 C1
Stalham St BERM/RHTH SE16...24 F8
Stalin Av WALD ME5 ....95 N6
Stallisfield Rd FAV ME13...........191 H5
Stambourne Wy NRWD SE19 .....60 E8
WWKM BR4 ....84 D7
Stambourne Woodland Wk
NRWD SE19 ....60 E6
Stamford Dr HAYES BR2.............85 J1
The Stampers
MAID/SHEP ME15...................185 J1
Stanam Rd RTWE/PEM TN2.....271 P3
Stanbridge Rd EDEN TN8.........206 E9

Stanbrook Rd ABYW SE2 .....28 A5
GVW DA11 .....49 K9
Stanbury Crs FOLKN CT19 .311 J5
Stanbury Rd PECK SE15 .....41 H2
Stancomb Av RAM CT11 .....16 C6
Standard Av HB CT6 .....106 F2
ORP BR6 .....116 B4
Standen Cl EGRIN RH19 .....264 C5
RHAM ME8 .....127 H1
Standen La RFOLK CT18 .....288 C7
Standen St CRBK TN17 .....318 D4
SBCH/RUST TN4 .....270 D3
Stane Wy WOOL/PLUM SE18..155 H9
Stanford Dr MAIDW ME16 .....155 H9
Stanford Gdns SOCK/AV RM15..31 H4
Stanford La RTON TN11 .....182 D9
Stanford-le-Hope By-Pass
CDW/CHF RM16 .....33 K2
Stanford Pl WALW SE17 .....24 B7
Stanford Rd CDW/CHF RM16...32 F5
Stanford Wy PL LING RH7 .....234 G6
Stangate Dr RSIT ME9 .....141 K7
Stangate Rd E/WMAL ME19 .123 J5
STRD ME2 .....71 L8
Stanger Rd SNWD SE25 .....83 M1
Stangrove Rd EDEN TN8 .....206 D9
Stanham Pl DART DA1 .....46 C4
Stanham Rd DART DA1 .....46 C6
Stanhope Av HAYES BR2 .....85 K5
SIT ME10 .....129 P2
Stanhope Cl
BERM/RHTH SE16 * 24 G5
MAID/BEAR ME14 .....155 K5
Stanhope Gv BECK BR3 .....84 C2
Stanhope Rd ASH TN23 .....282 C2
BFN/LL DA15 .....44 C3
BXLYHN DA7 .....44 G3
CROY/NA CRO 83 K7
DEAL CT14 .....233 J3
DVE/WH CT16 .....291 K5
RTW TN1 .....270 F5
STRD ME2 .....18 C1
SWCM DA10 .....48 D6
Stanhopes OXTED RH8 .....175 L4
Stanhope Wy SEV TN15 .....148 C7
Stan La WBY/YEL ME18 .....182 A4
Stanley Av BECK BR3 .....62 A9
IOS ME12 .....58 D9
QBOR ME11 .....77 J5
Stanley Cl ELTH/MOT SE9 .....43 N9
LYDD TN29 .....327 H1
RDART DA2 .....47 L6
STPH/PW TN12 .....246 A5
Stanley Ct GILL ME7 .....96 C1
Stanley Crs GVE DA12 .....69 P4
Stanley Gv CROY/NA CRO 83 H8
Stanley Pk RFOLK CT18 .....17 F1
Stanley Rd BRDST CT10 .....113 L7
CROY/NA CRO 82 F4
DEAL CT14 .....233 J4
FOLKN CT19 .....310 B5
GILL ME7 * 5 H5
GRAYS RM17 .....32 C8
GVW DA11 .....69 J1
HAYES BR2 .....62 D3
HB CT6 .....107 L2
ORP BR6 .....116 B4
RAM CT11 .....16 D1
RTW TN1 .....23 F1
SCUP DA14 .....64 A3
SWCM DA10 .....48 C7
WALD ME5 .....95 P8
WSTB CT5 .....105 L7
Stanley St DEPT SE8 .....41 M1
Stanley Sykes Cl MARC CT9 ..112 C5
Stanley Ter BXLYHS DA6 * 45 L7
Stanley Wy STMC/STPC BR5 ...87 K4
Stanmore Cl CANT CT1 .....7 H7
Stanmore Rd BELV DA17 .....29 H7
Stanmore Ter BECK BR3 .....61 N8
Stannet Wy WLGTN SM6 .....82 B8
Stansfeld Rd CAN/RD E16 .....26 E2
Stansfield Cl HARP ME7 * 85 J2
Stanstead Gv CAT SE6 .....62 M5
Stanstead Rd FSTH SE23 .....41 K9
Stansted Cl MAIDW ME16 .....121 K4
Stansted Crs BXLY DA5 .....44 F9
Stansted Hi BGR/WK TN15 ....121 L4
Stansted La BGR/WK TN15 ....120 E4
Stanswood Gdns CMBW SE5 ..40 E1
Stanton Cl STMC/STPC BR5....87 K4
Stanton Rd CROY/NA CRO 83 H4
Stanton St PECK SE15 .....41 J6
Stanton Wy SYD SE26 .....61 M3
Stanworth St STHWK SE1 .....24 C5
Staple Cl BXLY DA5 .....65 M2
SIT ME10 .....90 M8
Staple Dr STPH/PW TN12 .....246 C6
Stapleford Ct SEV TN13 .....20 D1
Staplehurst Av BRDST CT10 .143 M2
Staplehurst Gdns MARC CT9 .113 K2
Staplehurst Rd CRBK TN17 ..246 C7
LEW SE13 .....61 P4
RHAM ME8 .....96 E3
SIT ME10 .....99 K9
STPH/PW TN12 .....215 N7
Staplers Ct RCANTE CT3 .....199 N1
Staplers Ct MAID/BEAR ME14 ..155 N4
Staples Cl BERM/RHTH SE16 ..25 M2
Staple St STHWK SE1 .....24 A5
Stapleton Rd FAV ME13 * 134 A8
Stapleton Gdns CROY/NA CRO ..82 F9
Stapleton Rd BXLYHN DA7 ....45 H1
ORP BR6 .....86 G7
Stapley Rd BELV DA17 .....28 F8
Starboard Av SWCM DA10 ....47 N6
Starboard Wy POP/IOD E14 ....25 N6
Starborough Rd EDEN TN8 ...235 P5
Starbuck Cl ELTH/MOT SE9 ...43 L8
Star Hill DART DA1 .....45 N6
ROCH ME1 .....19 H6
Star Hill Rd RSEV TN14 .....147 N1
Star La FOLKN CT19 .....310 A4
GILL ME7 .....96 D2
MARC CT9 .....112 F8

STMC/STPC BR5 .....87 L1
Starle Cl CANT CT1 .....5 G1
Starling Cl HART DA3 .....68 F9
Starling Rd CROY/NA CRO.....84 B3
Star Mill Ct WALD ME5 * 96 A4
Star Mill La WALD ME5 .....96 A4
Star Pl WAP E1W 2 B3
Star Rd KEN/WIL TN24 .....3 H4
Starts Cl ORP BR6 .....86 B7
Starts Hill Av ORP BR6 .....86 C8
Starts Hill Rd ORP BR6 .....86 C7
State Farm Av ORP BR6 .....86 C8
Station Ap BECK BR3 * 61 L7
BGR/WK TN15 .....151 J5
BKHTH/KID SE3 .....42 F4
BRCH CT7 .....110 C6
BXLYHN DA7 .....46 A4
CHST BR7 .....63 J5
CROY/NA CRO 83 J6
DART DA1 .....46 E7
E/WMAL ME19 * 153 H2
EDEN TN8 .....206 D9
HAYES BR2 .....85 K5
MAIDW ME16 .....12 D6
MSTR CT12 .....141 K7
NROM TN28 .....337 H7
ORP BR6 .....86 G6
OXTED RH8 .....175 H5
RCANTE CT3 .....199 H6
RDV CT15 .....262 B6
RSEV TN14 .....149 H1
RTW TN1 .....22 D5
SEV TN13 .....338 E6
STMC/STPC BR5 .....87 J1
STPH/PW TN12 .....243 H2
STPH/PW TN12 .....246 B4
STRD ME2 .....93 P9
SWLY BR8 .....88 D1
SYD SE26 .....61 N4
WELL DA16 .....44 B5

Station Approach Rd
RAM CT11 .....16 D1
Station Bldgs HAYES BR2 * 85 K5
Station Ct BGR/WK TN15 .....151 J4
Station Crs BKHTH/KID SE3 ..26 B8
Station Dr DEAL CT14 .....232 F8
Station Est BECK BR3 * 84 A1
Station Hill HAYES BR2 .....85 K6
RTON TN11 .....238 F1
Station Ms MSTR CT12 .....143 H3
Station Pde BECK BR3 * 84 A1
BMLY BR1 * 62 E7
BXLYHN DA7 * 44 G5
SEV TN15 * 20 D1
Station Pas PECK SE15 .....41 J2
Station Ri WNWD SE27 .....60 B1
Station Rd ASH TN23 .....2 E4
BELV DA17 .....28 F6
BFN/LL DA15 .....64 C1
BGR/WK TN15 .....151 J5
BH/WHM TN16 .....147 J8
BMLY BR1 .....62 E7
BRCH CT7 .....110 C6
BXLYHN DA7 .....44 G4
CRBK TN17 .....274 B9
CROY/NA CRO 83 H5
CTHM CR3 .....144 B7
DART DA1 .....45 P7
DEAL CT14 .....232 F8
DIT/AY ME20 .....154 B3
EDEN TN8 .....206 D7
EGRIN RH19 .....264 C7
EYN DA4 .....67 H8
EYN DA4 .....89 J7
FOLKN CT19 .....310 C5
GDST RH9 .....204 B5
GVW DA11 .....48 F7
HART DA3 .....68 D3
HAYES BR2 .....62 E8
HB CT6 .....107 K3
HDCN TN27 .....221 H5
HDCN TN27 .....247 N3
HHE ME3 .....52 A5
HYTHE CT21 .....309 J5
LEW SE13 * 42 A4
LING RH7 .....235 H4
LYDD TN29 .....326 F7
LYDD TN29 .....342 C5
MAID/BEAR ME14 .....14 D5
MARC CT9 .....113 G3
MED DA13 .....68 D3
MEO DA15 .....68 D3
MSTR CT12 .....141 K7
NROM TN28 .....336 D2
ORP BR6 .....86 G6
PGE/AN SE20 .....61 J5
RASHE TN25 .....284 C5
RCANTE CT3 .....199 H6
RCANTW CT4 .....165 L9
RCANTW CT4 .....197 L2
RDART DA2 .....47 N6
RDV CT15 .....229 N9
RDV CT15 .....262 B7
RFOLK CT18 .....287 H2
RHAM ME8 .....97 K4
RMAID ME17 .....188 E5
RRTW TN3 .....269 H9
RSEV TN14 .....117 N5
RSEV TN14 .....148 G1
RSIT ME9 .....131 H5
RYE TN31 .....330 A5
SCUP DA14 .....64 C2
SEV TN13 .....148 D5
SNWD SE25 .....83 K1
STMC/STPC BR5 .....87 K1
STPH/PW TN12 .....242 G2
STPH/PW TN12 .....246 C4
STRD ME2 .....18 E2
SWLY BR8 .....88 D1
TENT TN30 .....301 H8
TIL RM18 .....50 D1
WADH TN5 .....314 C9
WAL/WE ME18 .....183 K9
WGOS CT8 .....111 N4
WSTB CT5 .....105 M4
WWKM BR4 .....84 F5
Station Rd East CANT CT1 .....4 D6

OXTED RH8 .....175 H5
Station Rd North BELV DA17 ..28 G6
Station Rd West CANTW/ST CT1..7 H6
OXTED RH8 .....175 H5
Station Sq STMC/STPC BR5 ...86 D2
Station St SIT ME10 .....129 N1
Station Ter CMBW SE5 .....40 C2
St Augustine's Rbt CANT CT1.....5 H5
Staunton St DEPT SE8 .....41 M6
Staveley Cl PECK SE15 .....41 J2
Stave Yard Rd
BERM/RHTH SE16 .....25 H4
St Bartholomews Cl DVW CT17 ...8 H4
Steadman Cl HOO/HM ME3.....71 L2
Stead St WALW SE17 .....24 A7
Stebonheath St POP/IOD E14 ..25 M7
Stedly Cl ASH TN23 .....282 C2
Stede Hi RMAID ME17 .....188 C5
Stedly SCUP DA14 * 64 C3
Stedman Cl BXLY DA5 .....65 N3
Steed Cl HB CT6 .....107 N6
Steeds Cl RASHW TN26 .....282 D1
Steeds La ASH TN23 .....282 D1
Steele Av RDART DA2 .....47 N6
Steele's La MEO DA15 .....92 A4
Steel's Rd STRD ME2 .....72 D1
Steep Cl ORP BR6 .....116 C1
Steep Hl CROY/NA CRO 83 K8
Steeple Heights Dr
BH/WHM TN16 .....145 N2
Steerforth St ROCH ME1 .....95 H4
Steers Pl RTON TN11 .....181 P9
Steers Wy BERM/RHTH SE16 ..25 H5
Stella Cl STPH/PW TN12 .....245 J4
Stelling Rd ERITH DA8 .....45 H1
Stembridge Rd PGE/AN SE20 ..61 H8
Stembrook DVE/WH CT16 .....8 D5
Stempe Cl RFOLK CT18 .....288 E9
Stenning Av SLH/COR SS17 ...34 A7
The Stennings RDV CT15 * ...264 F5
Stephen Cl BRDST CT10 .....113 M9
ORP BR6 .....116 E3
Stephen Rd BXLYHN DA7 .....45 L4
Stephens Cl FAV ME13 .....132 E5
Stephen's Cl MARC CT9 .....112 A6
Stephenson Av DART DA1 ....45 N6
Stephenson Av TIL RM18 .....49 L2
Stephenson Cl WELL DA16 ....44 B3
Stephenson Rd
CANTW/ST CT2 .....7 K1
Stephenson St CAN/RD E16 ..26 D5
Stephen's Rd SBCH/RUST TN4..270 D2
Stepney Cv BXLY DA5 .....65 P1
Stepneyford La CRBK TN17 ...299 M6
Stepney Gn BXLY DA5 .....65 P1
Stepney High St WCHPL E1 ...24 E1
Stepney Wy WCHPL E1 .....24 E1
Step Style SIT ME10 .....130 A3
Sterling Av BXLY DA5 .....65 P1
Sterling Cl BRDST CT10 .....113 K8
Sterling Gdns NWCR SE14 ....25 H9
Sterling Rd QBOR ME11 .....77 J2
SIT ME10 .....129 L4
Sterndale Rd DART DA1 .....46 C8
Sternhall La PECK SE15 .....40 G4
Sterry St STHWK SE1 .....24 A5
Steucers La FSTH SE23 .....41 L9
Steve Biko La CAT SE6 .....61 N3
Stevedale Rd WELL DA16 ....44 D3
Stevedore St WAP E1W 24 E4
Steven Cl CHAT ME4 .....6 E7
Steven Ct RAM CT11 * 142 G7
Stevens Cl BECK BR3 .....61 N5
BXLY DA5 .....65 M3
HDCN TN27 .....219 N7
RDART DA2 .....67 L4
Stevenson Cl ERITH DA8 .....46 B1
MAID/SHEP ME15 .....12 E7
Stevenson Crs
BERM/RHTH SE16 .....24 D8
Stevenson Wy DIT/AY ME20 .123 N9
Stevens Rd DIT/AY ME20 .....124 E7
Stevens St STHWK SE1 .....24 B6
Stewart Cl CHST BR7 .....63 H4
Stewart Rd SBCH/RUST TN4..270 F1
Stewart St POP/IOD E14 .....25 P1
Steyning Gv ELTH/MOT SE9 ...63 K5
Steynton Av BXLY DA5 .....64 C1
Stickens La E/WMAL ME19 ...153 M6
Stickfast La RMAID ME17 ....217 N1
RSIT ME9 .....99 H5
Stickland Rd BELV DA17 .....28 F7
Stifford Clays Rd
CDW/CHF RM16 .....32 A4
Stifford Rd HI SOCK/AV RM15..31 H3
Stifford Rd SOCK/AV RM15....31 J3
Stilebridge La STPH/PW TN12..215 K7
Stiles Cl ERITH DA8 .....28 C8
FOLKN CT19 .....310 D4
HAYES BR2 .....85 J1
IOS ME12 .....78 A1
Still La SBCH/RUST TN4 .....240 C7
Stillness Rd FSTH SE23 .....41 L7
Stillwater Ms CHAT ME4 .....73 H5
Stirling Cl RHAM ME8 .....97 H4
ROCH ME1 .....94 F1
SCUP DA14 .....64 A3
Stirling Dr ORP BR6 .....87 J9
Stirling Rd E/WMAL ME19 ....152 C9
Stirling Wy CROY/NA CRO 82 D2
EGRIN RH19 .....265 L5
MSTR CT12 .....142 E3
Stirnol Rd KEN/WIL TN24 .....282 C1
Stisted Wy HDCN TN27 .....247 N3
Stockbury Dr RHAM ME8 .....155 J5
Stockbury Gdns MARC CT9 ..113 K3
Stockbury Rd CROY/NA CRO ..83 P3
Stockdale Gdns DEAL CT14 ..233 H5
Stockenbury STPH/PW TN12 ..215 L7
Stockers Brow RSIT ME9 .....129 P6
Stocker's Hi FAV ME13 .....133 P9
Stockers La RSIT ME9 .....131 H5
Stockett La RMAID ME17 .....185 H8
Stock Hi BH/WHM TN16 .....145 N1
Stockholm Rd
BERM/RHTH SE16 .....24 F8

Stockholm Wy WAP E1W.....24 D4
Stockland Green Rd
RRTW TN3 .....239 P8
Stock La RASHE TN25 .....284 B5
RDART DA2 .....67 K6
Stocks Green Rd RTON TN11 .209 P6
Stocks Pl POP/IOD E14 .....25 L3
Stocks Rd TENT TN30 .....332 B2
Stockton Cl MAID/BEAR ME14..155 N4
Stockfold Gdns ELTH/MOT SE9..63 H2
Stockwell Cl BMLY BR1 .....62 F8
HOO/HM ME3 .....73 M2
Stockwell Park Rd
BRXN/ST SW9 .....40 A3
Stockwell St GNWCH SE10 ....25 H9
Stodart Rd PGE/AN SE20 .....61 J7
Stoddards La RYE TN31 .....330 D8
Stoddart Rd FOLKN CT19 ....310 B5
Stodmarsh Rd RCANTE CT3 ..167 L3
Stofield Gdns ELTH/MOT SE9 ..63 H2
Stoke Rd HOO/HM ME3 .....73 M2
HOO/HM ME3 .....73 M2
Stokes Rd CROY/NA CRO 84 A3
Stombers La RFOLK CT18 ....288 C7
Stonar Cl RAM CT11 .....15 L5
SWCH CT13 .....201 P7
Stonar Gdns SWCH CT13 ....171 P9
Stone Bank WALD ME5 * 186 E5
Stone Barn Av BRCH CT7 ....111 H7
Stonebridge RASHE TN25 ....254 B4
Stone Br TENT TN30 .....333 L3
Stonebridge Green Rd
HDCN TN27 .....219 P6
Stonebridge Vls
NROM TN28 * 336 F6
Stonechat Av FAV ME13 .....132 E6
Stone Ct La ASH TN23 * 2 E6
Stone Court La
RTWE/PEM TN2 .....241 P8
Stonecroft Rd ERITH DA8.....45 L1
Stonecroft Wy CROY/NA CRO..82 D2
Stonecrop Cl CHAT ME4 .....73 J6
Stone Cross Lees SWCH CT13..201 N5
Stonedane Ct FAV ME13 .....132 F5
Stonefield Cl BXLYHN DA7 ....45 J4
Stonefield CHARL SE7 .....43 H1
Stone Gdns BRDST CT10 .....113 N8
Stonegate RASHE TN25 .....253 P5
Stonegate Rd STMC/STPC BR5..64 E9
Stonegate Rd WADH TN5 ....314 A5
Stonehall Rd RDV CT15 .....260 A8
Stone Hill Rd RDV CT15 .....231 L9
Stone Hl RASHE TN25 .....285 L1
Stone Hill Rd HDCN TN27 ....219 N8
Stonehills Ct DUL SE21 .....60 E2
Stonehill Woods Pk
SCUP DA14 * 65 L1
Stonehorse Ct HOO/HM ME3 ..72 A4
Stonehorse La HOO/HM ME3 ..72 A4
Stone House Cl LVPST EC2M ..24 B2
Stonehouse La PUR RH19 .....31 H8
RSEV TN14 .....117 L3
Stone House Ms
BRDST CT10 * 113 N7
Stonehouse Rd RSEV TN14 ...117 L3
Stonings La HAWK TN18 .....146 C3
Stonelees EGRIN RH19 .....265 J6
Stoneleigh Park Av
CROY/NA CRO 84 A3
Stone Park Av BECK BR3 .....84 D1
Stone Pit La HAWK TN18 .....318 E9
Stone Place Rd RDART DA2 ...47 L6
Stone Rd BRDST CT10 * 113 M9
HAYES BR2 .....85 J2
Stonerock Cl CANTW/ST CT2 .137 N6
Stone Row RRTW TN3 * 268 C3
Stones Cross Rd SWLY BR8 ...88 B2
Stonestile Farm Rd
HDCN TN27 .....190 F8
Stone Stile La RCANTW CT4 ..193 N2
Stonestile Rd HDCN TN27 ....247 K2
Stone St CRBK TN17 .....274 E3
FAV ME13 .....132 F6
GVW DA11 .....49 M7
HYTHE CT21 .....307 P5
RASHE TN25 .....253 M6
RFOLK CT18 .....286 A8
RTW TN1 .....22 D5
Stone Street Rd
BGR/WK TN15 .....149 P9
Stonewall Rd OXTED RH8 ....175 L6
Stonewall Park Rd
Stonewood RDART DA2 .....68 A2
Stonewood Rd
SBCH/RUST TN4 * 240 D7
Stonewood Rd ERITH DA8 ....29 K8
Stoneworks Cots RYE TN31 * .339 J9
Stoney Aly WOOL/PLUM SE18..43 L5
Stoney Bank POP/IOD E14 ....25 L3
Stoney Bank GILL ME7 .....96 C5
Stoneycroft Cl
LEE/GVPK SE12 .....42 D8
Stoney La NRWD SE19 .....60 F5
WCHPL E1 .....24 C2
Stoney Rd FAV ME13 .....164 C1
Stoney St STHWK SE1 .....24 A4
Stoon Cl SEV TN13 .....94 G8
Stopes St PECK SE15 .....40 F6
Stopford Rd GILL ME7 .....7 J5
Storehouse Whf IOS ME12 ....57 H5
Store Rd CAN/RD E16 .....27 H5
Stores Quay POP/IOD E14 ....25 N6
Stories Ms CMBW SE5 .....40 E3
Stories Rd CMBW SE5 .....40 E3
Storks Rd BERM/RHTH SE16 ..24 F1
Stornaway Strd GVE DA12 ....70 B3
Storrington Rd CROY/NA CRO..83 L5
Storway Ct STRD ME2 * 18 C5
Stour KEN/WIL TN24 .....282 G2

Stour Cl ASH TN23 .....252 B8
HAYES BR2 .....85 M8
RCANTW CT4 .....195 L1
STRD ME2 .....71 P8
TONN TN10 .....210 E5
Stour Ct SWCH CT13 .....201 N1
Stour Crs CANT CT1 .....4 D5
Stour Rd CDW/CHF RM16 .....33 H8
DART DA1 .....47 H4
RCANTW CT4 .....195 L1
Stour Valley Cl RCANTE CT3 .138 C6
Stour Valley Wy HDCN TN27 .220 A6
KEN/WIL TN24 .....224 E5
RASHE TN25 .....224 E5
Stour Valley Cl RCANTW CT3 .172 D8
Stowage DEPT SE8 .....25 L9
The Stowage DEPT SE8 .....25 K9
Stowell Av CROY/NA CRO 114 C5
Stowell Cl ASH TN23 * 251 P9
Stowe Rd ORP BR6 .....87 J8
Stowting Hl RASHE TN25 .....255 P8
Stowting Rd ORP BR6 .....86 F8
Stradella Rd HNHL SE24 .....60 A7
Strafford St POP/IOD E14 .....25 K5
Straight La LYDD TN29 .....334 F4
Straightsmouth GNWCH SE10..42 A1
Strait Rd EHAM E6 .....26 F3
Strakers Rd EDUL SE22 .....41 H5
Strand RYE TN31 .....338 E7
Strand Approach Rd GILL ME7..73 L8
Strand Cl MEO DA13 .....92 B4
Strandfield Cl
WOOL/PLUM SE18 .....27 M8
Strand St SWCH CT13 .....171 N9
The Strand DEAL CT14 .....233 K3
Stranger's Cl CANT CT1 .....166 B6
Stranger's La CANT CT1 .....166 B6
Strangford Pl HB CT6 .....107 N5
Strangford Rd WSTB CT5 ....105 N4
Strasbourg St MARC CT9 .....112 F7
Stratford Av RHAM ME8 .....96 E5
Stratford Dr MAID/SHEP ME15..186 A5
Stratford House Av BMLY BR1 ..63 J9
Stratford La RHAM ME8 .....96 E5
Stratford Rd E/WMAL ME19 ..153 H4
THHTH CR7 * 82 F1
Stratford St RTW TN1 .....270 E3
Stratheden Rd BKHTH/KID SE3..42 E2
Strathmore RL RM18 .....50 B2
Strathmore Rd CROY/NA CRO ..83 H4
Strathnairn St STHWK SE1 ....24 D7
Strathyre Av
STRHM/NOR SW16 .....60 E9
Stratton Cl BXLYHN DA7 .....45 G4
Strattondale St POP/IOD E14 ..25 M6
Stratton Rd BXLYHN DA7 .....44 G4
Stratton Ter BH/WHM TN16 ..176 D3
Strawberry Cl RTWE/PEM TN2..270 B8
Strawberry Flds ORP BR6 .....86 C9
RYE TN31 .....329 P6
Strawberry V TON TN9 .....240 F1
Straw Mill Hi
MAID/SHEP ME15 .....185 K2
Streamdale ABYW SE2 .....28 A9
Stream La HAWK TN18 .....317 H7
Streamline Ms EDUL SE22 ....41 H9
Stream Pk EGRIN RH19 .....264 C5
Stream Pit La HAWK TN18 ....317 H7
Streamside DIT/AY ME20 .....154 D3
Stream Side TONN TN10 .....210 G3
Streamside Cl HAYES BR2 ....85 K5
The Stream DIT/AY ME20 .....154 A3
Stream Ws WSTB CT5 .....105 L4
Streamway BELV DA17 .....28 F9
Streatfield EDEN TN8 .....206 E8
Streete Ct WGOS CT8 .....111 N5
Streete Court Rd WGOS CT8 .111 N5
Street End Rd WALD ME5 .....95 N6
Streeters La WLGTN SM6 .....82 C7
Streetfield HB CT6 .....107 N6
Streetfield Ms BKHTH/KID SE3..42 E3
Streetfield Rd RHAM ME8 .....97 J5
The Street ASH TN25 .....251 P9
BGR/WK TN15 .....94 J4
BGR/WK TN15 .....181 J4
BRCH CT7 .....140 A2
CRBK TN17 .....276 D8
DEAL CT14 .....231 P4
E/WMAL ME19 .....122 B8
EYN DA4 .....67 L2
FAV ME13 .....132 E3
FAV ME13 .....162 B1
FAV ME13 .....164 B1
GILL ME7 .....72 D9
HDCN TN27 .....219 H7
HDCN TN27 .....248 A3
HDCN TN27 .....250 C2
HOO/HM ME3 .....53 L4
HYTHE CT21 .....307 N5
KEN/WIL TN24 .....253 H2
MAID/BEAR ME14 .....155 P1
MED DA13 .....68 B8
RASHE TN26 .....251 L3
RASHW TN26 .....251 L3
RCANTE CT3 .....168 F7
RCANTW CT4 .....167 N9
RCANTW CT4 .....196 A8
RCANTW CT4 .....197 N5
RCANTW CT4 .....224 C1
RCANTW CT4 .....228 C5
RCANTW CT4 .....258 E2

RDV CT15 ....291 M1
RDV CT15 ....312 A1
RFOLK CT18 ....287 M9
RFOLK CT18 ....288 C7
RMAID ME17 ....218 A3
RSIT ME9 ....97 P2
RSIT ME9 ....99 M2
RSIT ME3 ....127 N1
RSIT ME2 ....158 G5
STRD ME2 ....93 M9
SWCH CT11 ....201 J4
TENT TN30 ....332 A5
TENT TN30 ....333 J1
WBY/YAL ME18 ....182 E5
WBY/YAL ME18 ....183 P4
Strettitt Gdns STPH/PW TN12 .212 C5
Stretton Rd CROY/NA CR0 ....83 K4
Strickland Av DART CT17 .....46 F4
Strickland St DEPT SE8 ....41 N3
Strickland Wy ORP BR6 ....86 G8
Stringer Dr BRCH CT7 ....111 H7
Strode Crs IOS ME12 ....57 L6
Strode Park Rd HB CT6 ....107 M4
Strond Green Gdns
 CROY/NA CR0 ....83 P4
Strond Green Wy
 CROY/NA CR0 ....83 P4
Strond St DVW CT17 ....85 H2
Strongbow Crs ELTH/MOT SE9 ..43 K6
Strongbow Rd ELTH/MOT SE9 ..43 K6
Stroud Green Wy
 CROY/NA CR0 ....83 N4
Stroud Wood SWCM DA10 .....83 M3
Strouts Rd ASH TN23 ....282 A1
Strover St GILL ME7 ....78 J8
Strumer Cl E/WMAL ME19 .....181 H1
Struttons Av GVW DA11 ....69 K1
Strype St WCHPL E1 ....24 C1
Stuart Av HAYES BR2 ....85 K5
Stuart Cl MAID/BEAR ME14 ....13 K1
 RTWE/PEM TN2 ....270 C8
 SWLY BR8 ....65 P6
Stuart Rd DVW CT17 * 8 B3
Stuart Crs CROY/NA CR0 ....84 C7
Stuart Evans Cl WELL DA16 ....45 E4
Stuart Mantle Wy ERITH DA8 ..45 M1
Stuart Rd FOLKN CT19 ....11 H1
 GILL ME7 ....96 A3
 GRAYS RM17 ....32 C8
 GVW DA11 ....49 J7
 PECK SE15 ....43 J5
 THHTH CR7 ....83 H1
 WELL DA16 ....44 D2
Stuart Wy EGRIN RH19 ....265 J8
Sturdee Av GILL ME7 ....24 E8
Sturdy Cl HYTHE CT21 ....309 J5
Sturdy Rd PECK SE15 ....41 H3
Sturges Fld CHST BR7 ....65 J5
Sturges Rd KEN/WIL TN24 ......2 D2
Sturla Rd CHAT ME4 ....95 M4
Sturmer Cl CANT CT1 ....5 K6
Sturry Court Ms
 CANTW/ST CT2 ....137 K7
Sturry Hl CANTW/ST CT2 ....137 J7
Sturry Rd CANT CT1 ....5 H1
 CANTW/ST CT2 ....137 J9
Sturry Wy POP/IOD E14 ....25 L2
Sturry Wy RHAM ME8 ....96 F4
Stutfield St WCHPL E1 ....24 D2
Styants Bottom Rd
 BGR/WK TN15 ....150 C8
Style Cl RHAM ME8 ....127 H1
Styles Cl EDEN TN8 ....207 J5
Styles Gdns BRXN/ST SW9 .....40 B4
Styles La MAID/BEAR ME14 ....155 P1
Styles Wy BECK BR3 ....84 F1
Sudbury Head HI 4 E4
Sudbury Crs BMLY BR1 ....62 E4
Sudbury Gdns CROY/NA CR0 ...83 K8
Sudbury Pl WGOS CT5 ....111 L6
Suffield Cl SAND/SEL CR2 ......114 A6
Suffield Rd PGE/AN SE20 ....61 K8
Suffolk Av RHAM ME8 ....97 J5
 WGOS CT5 ....111 L6
Suffolk Rd RHAM TN23 ....2 A4
Suffolk La CANST EC4R 4 C4
Suffolk Rd CANT CT1 ....167 J4
 DART DA1 ....46 E7
 GVE DA12 ....49 P7
 MAID/SHEP ME15 ....186 A3
 SCUP DA14 ....64 E5
 SNWD SE25 ....83 L1
Suffolk St FOLKN CT19 ....310 C5
Sugar Loaf Wk FOLKN CT19 ...310 C5
Sullivan Cl DART DA1 ....46 B7
Sullivan Rd TIL RM18 ....49 L2
 TONN TN9 ....211 H5
Sultan Rd MAID ME5 ....125 P5
Sultan St BECK BR3 ....61 K8
 CMBW SE5 ....40 C1
Summer Cl HYTHE CT21 ....308 E5
 TENT TN30 ....301 N6
Summer Cots
 SBGH/RUST TN4 * 269 N4
Summercourt Rd WCHPL E1 ...24 F2
Summerfield Av WSTB CT5 ....105 N5
Summerfield Rd MARG CT9 ....113 K3
Summerhill St CAT/GVPK SE12 ..42 C8
Summerhill CANTW/ST CT2 ...166 B3
 CHST BR7 ....63 L8
Summerhill HDCN TN27 ....247 K5
Summerhill Rd
 SBGH/RUST TN4 * 240 C8

Summerhill Cl ORP BR6 ....86 F8
Summerhill Pk KEN/WIL TN24 .283 M1
Summerhill Rd DART DA1 ....46 C8
 STPH/PW TN12 ....245 N1
Summerhouse Dr RDART DA2 ..65 N4
Summer La CANTW/ST CT2 ....136 D7
Summer Leeze KEN/WIL TN24 .253 H9
Summer Leeze Gdns
 KEN/WIL TN24 ....253 H9
Summer Rd BRCH CT7 ....109 P9
Summerton Wy THMD SE28 ....28 C3
Summervale Rd
 SBGH/RUST TN4 * 270 A7
Summerville Av IOS ME12 ....77 P2
Summer Wy NRWD SE19 ....60 E3
Summer Av PECK SE15 ....40 F2
Sumner Cl ORP BR6 ....86 D8
Sumner Gdns CROY/NA CR0 ...82 E5
Sumner Rd CROY/NA CR0 ......82 G5
 PECK SE15 ....40 F2
Sumner Rd South
 CROY/NA CR0 ....82 F5
Sumpter Wy FAV ME13 ....132 D6
Sunbeam Av IOS ME12 ....106 E2
Sunburst Ct STPH/PW TN12 ...245 J4
Sunbury St WOOL/PLUM SE18 .26 C6
Sun Ct ERITH DA8 ....85 P9
Suncroft Pl SYD SE26 ....61 J2
Sunderland Cl ROCH ME1 ....94 F3
Sunderland Dr RHAM ME8 .....97 K6
Sunderland Mt FSTH SE25 * 41 K1
Sunderland Rd FSTH SE23 .....41 K9
Sundew Cv RAM CT11 ....17 F1
Sundial Av SNWD SE25 ....60 F9
Sundorne Rd CHARL SE7 ....26 C8
Sundridge Av BMLY BR1 ....63 H7
 WELL DA16 ....43 P5
Sundridge Cl CANTW/ST CT2 ..136 F9
 DART DA1 ....46 C7
Sundridge Dr WALD ME5 ......125 M1
Sundridge Hl RSEV TN14 ......147 K3
Sundridge La RSEV TN14 ......147 J2
Sundridge Pde BMLY BR1 * 62 F6
Sundridge Pl CROY/NA CR0 * ..83 L5
Sundridge Rd CROY/NA CR0 ...83 L5
 RSEV TN14 ....147 P5
Sunfields Pl BKHTH/KID SE3 ...42 F1
Sun Hl HART DA3 ....90 D6
Sunhill Pl RTWE/PEM TN2 * ...271 M2
Sun in Sands Rbt
 BKHTH/KID SE3 ....42 F1
Sunken Rd CROY/NA CR0 ....83 P9
Sunland Av BXLYHS DA6 ....44 G5
Sun La BKHTH/KID SE3 ....42 F1
 BRCH CT7 ....140 A2
 GVE DA12 ....50 J1
 HYTHE CT21 ....309 H5
Sunningdale Av FOLKN CT19 ..310 D4
Sunningdale Cl
 BERM/RHTH SE16 ....24 E8
 RHAM ME8 ....69 D2
 THMD SE28 ....28 D2
Sunningdale Dr RHAM ME8 ....96 C8
Sunningdale Rd BMLY BR1 .....85 P1
Sunningdale Wk HB CT6 ....107 J5
Sunninghill GVW DA11 ....35 L8
Sunninghill Rd LEW SE13 ....41 P5
Sunningvale Av
 BH/WHM TN16 ....145 N2
Sunningvale Cl BH/WHM TN16 .145 N1
Sunnybank RDV CT15 * 230 C9
Sunny Bank HYTHE CT21 ......308 E5
Sunnybank Rd
 SIT ME10 ....100 A9
 SNWD SE25 ....60 F9
 WARL CR6 ....144 B2
Sunnycroft Rd SNWD SE25 .....81 M1
Sunnyside ORP BR6 ....86 B6
Sunnydale Rd LEE/GVPK SE12 .42 F6
Sunnydene St SYD SE26 ....61 L3
Sunnyfields Cl RHAM ME8 ......97 H6
Sunnyfields Dr IOS ME12 ....77 L1
Sunnyhill Rd HB CT6 ....107 J5
Sunnymead CANTW/ST CT2 ...136 C6
Sunnymead Av GILL ME7 ....96 M1
Sunnyridge RRTW TN3 * 239 M9
Sunny Side MED DA3 * 43 M2
Sunnyside CAT SE6 * 41 M8
 RSIT ME9 ....160 C5
Sunnyside Av IOS ME12 ....78 A1
Sunnyside Cl DEAL CT14 ....33 H3
Sunnyside Cots DEAL CT14 * ..233 H5
Sunnyside Gdns SWCH CT13 ..201 M2
Sunnyside Rd FOLK CT20 ......309 H4
 THMD SE28 ....28 A2
Sun Pas BERM/RHTH SE16 ......24 D8
Sun Pier CHAT ME4 * 6 B4
Sunray Av HAYES BR2 ....40 D5
 WSTB CT5 ....106 C4
Sunrise Wy E/WMAL ME19 .....153 K9
Sun Rd SWCM DA10 ....48 D7
Sunset Cl ERITH DA8 ....85 P9
 IOS ME12 ....79 M1
 WSTB CT5 ....105 K8
Sunset Gdns SNWD SE25 ....60 E8
Sunset Rd HNHL SE24 ....40 C4
 THMD SE28 ....28 B3
Sunstone Dr SIT ME10 ....99 K7
Sun St CANT CT1 * 4 E4
 LVPST EC2M 24 A1
Sun Ter WALD ME5 * 125 N1
Sun Valley Wy RDV CT15 ....230 D9
Super Abbey Est
 DIT/AY ME20 * 154 C2
Superior Dr ORP BR6 ....116 C1
Surf Crs IOS ME12 ....79 M1
Surlingham Cl THMD SE28 ......28 C3
Surrenden Rd FOLKN CT19 ....310 C4
 STPH/PW TN12 ....246 B6
Surrey Canal Rd PECK SE15 ...41 F9
Surrey Gdns BRCH CT7 ....110 G6
Surrey Gv WALW SE17 ....23 J2
Surrey Ms WNWD SE27 ....60 E3
Surrey Ms WNWD SE27 ....41 H9
Surrey Quays Rd
 BERM/RHTH SE16 ....24 F6

Surrey Rd CANT CT1 ....167 J5
 MAID/SHEP ME15 ....186 A3
 PECK SE15 ....41 K6
Surrey Sq WALW SE17 ....24 B8
Surrey St CROY/NA CR0 ....83 H7
Surrey Ter WALW SE17 ....24 B7
Surrey Water Rd
 BERM/RHTH SE16 ....24 G4
Surridge Gdns NRWD SE19 .....60 D5
Surtees Cl KEN/WIL TN24 ......285 H2
Susannah St POP/IOD E14 ....25 L2
Susan Rd BKHTH/KID SE3 ....42 F5
Susan Hl RASHW TN26 ....302 C5
Sussex Av CANT CT1 ....167 J5
 MTCM CR4 * 2 C2
 SIT ME10 ....15 J7
Sussex Border Pth
 CRAWE RH10 ....264 A9
 EDEN TN8 ....236 D9
 EDEN TN8 ....264 C7
 HAWK TN18 ....317 J8
 RBTBR TN32 ....329 K7
 RYE TN31 ....331 J7
 WADH TN5 ....315 C2
Sussex Cl BGR/WK TN15 ....120 B3
 HB CT6 ....106 C2
 RTWE/PEM TN2 ....270 F7
Sussex Dr WALD ME5 ....125 M1
Sussex Gdns BRCH CT7 ....110 G6
 HB CT6 ....106 C2
Sussex Man WGOS CT8 * 111 N4
Sussex Ms RTWE/PEM TN2 ...270 F7
Sussex Rd DART DA1 ....46 C8
 ERITH DA8 ....45 K1
 FOLKN CT19 ....10 E2
 MAID/SHEP ME15 ....186 A2
 MTCM CR4 * 34 A6
 NROM TN28 ....64 D4
 SCUP DA14 ....87 K3
 STMC/STPC BR5 ....87 K3
 WWKM BR4 ....84 E5
Sussex St PIM SW1V 12 G3
Sussex Ter PGE/AN SE20 * 61 J6
 PUR RM19 * 30 E8
Sussex Wk CANT CT1 ....167 J5
Sutcliffe Rd WELL DA16 ....44 E3
 WOOL/PLUM SE18 ....26 G1
Sutherland Av BH/WHM TN16 .145 N2
 STMC/STPC BR5 ....85 P5
 WELL DA16 ....45 H1
Sutherland Cl GVE DA12 ....70 D1
 HYTHE CT21 ....308 F5
 RDART DA2 ....47 M6
Sutherland Dr ERCH CT7 ......111 J6
Sutherland Rd BELV DA17 ......29 K8
 CROY/NA CR0 ....82 F4
 DEAL CT14 ....233 H5
Suttie Rd CHART SE7 ....42 G1
Sutton Baron Rd RSIT ME9 ....128 C5
Sutton Cl BECK BR3 ....61 P7
 FOLKN CT19 ....310 D4
 RHAM ME8 ....97 K6
Sutton Ct STPH/PW TN12 ......245 H4
Sutton Forge STPH/PW TN12 ..245 H4
Sutton Gdns CROY/NA CR0 ....83 L2
Sutton Hts MAID/SHEP ME15 .186 B5
Sutton La DEAL CT14 ....232 B9
Sutton Rd MAID/SHEP ME15 ..186 A5
 RCANTE CT3 ....138 B8
The Suttons RYE TN31 ....331 N2
Sutton Rd MAID/BEAR ME14 ..156 C9
 WCHPL E1 ....24 F2
Sutton Valence HI
 RMAID ME17 * 216 C4
Swadelands Cl RMAID ME17 ...189 K6
Swaffer Wy ASH TN23 ....281 P1
Swaffield Rd SEV TN13 ....149 H7
Swain Cl STRD ME2 ....71 P7
Swain Rd RHAM ME8 ....96 B8
 TENT TN30 ....301 J4
 THHTH CR7 ....83 H2
Swaisland Rd DART DA1 ....46 B6
Swaislands Dr DART DA1 ....45 P6
Swale Av IOS ME12 ....57 K7
Swale Br RSIT ME9 ....77 H4
Swale Cl RSIT ME9 ....77 J7
Swalecliffe Av HB CT6 ....106 C2
Swalecliffe Court Dr
 WSTB CT5 ....106 C4
Swalecliffe Rd WSTB CT5 ......106 A4
Swale Cl SOCK/AV RM15 ....30 F2
Swaledale Rd RDART DA2 ....47 M6
Swale Heritage Trail
 FAV ME13 ....131 N3
 FAV ME13 ....133 K6
 SIT ME10 ....100 B3
Swale Rd DART DA1 ....46 A4
 STRD ME2 ....71 L8
Swale Wy SIT ME10 ....100 B8
Swallands Rd CAT SE6 ....61 N2
Swallow Av WSTB CT5 ....105 N2
Swallow Cl CDW/CHF RM16 ....31 N7
 ERITH DA8 ....45 N2
 MARG CT9 ....112 D5
 NWCR SE14 ....41 H2
 RDART DA2 ....47 M6
Swallow Cl HB CT6 * 107 J7
Swallowdale SAND/SEL CR2 ..114 A3
Swallow Dr RTWE/PEM TN2 ...271 J2
Swallowfield KEN/WIL TN24 ...283 H1
 LING RH7 ....235 K7
Swallowfield Rd CHARL SE7 ....26 C8
Swallow Rd MAID ME5 ....125 M1
Swallow Ri DIT/AY ME20 ....153 N2
Swallow St EHAM E6 ....26 F1
Swallowtail Cl STMC/STPC BR5 .87 L1
Swamp Rd LYDD TN29 ....335 P9
Swan Ap EHAM E6 * 26 E1
Swanbridge Rd BXLYHN DA7 ...45 J2
Swan Cl CROY/NA CR0 * 83 J8
 SIT ME10 ....130 A1
 STMC/STPC BR5 ....64 C9
Swan Cots TENT TN30 ....332 A2
Swanfield Rd WSTB CT5 ....105 L6

Swan Gn RASHE TN25 ....285 K7
Swanland Dr TON TN9 ....240 C2
Swan La CANST EC4R 4 A5
 CRBK TN17 ....274 D5
 DART DA1 ....45 P8
 EDEN TN8 ....206 D6
 RASHE TN25 ....285 L7
Swanley La SWLY BR8 ....65 P9
Swanley Rd WELL DA16 ....44 E2
Swanley Village Rd SWLY BR8 .66 B4
Swan Md SWTWK SE1 ....24 B6
Swanmead Wy TON TN9 ....210 C8
Swann Wy RFOLK CT18 ....288 D8
Swan Pas WCHPL E1 * 24 C3
Swan Rdg EDEN TN8 ....206 E6
Swan Rd BERM/RHTH SE16 ....24 F4
 WOOL/PLUM SE18 ....26 E3
Swanscombe St SWCM DA10 ..48 D7
Swanstree Av SIT ME10 ....130 A3
Swan St E/WMAL ME19 ....153 H4
 TENT TN30 ....331 N2
Swanton La RCANTE CT3 ....167 P3
 RDV CT15 ....259 M7
Swanton Rd ERITH DA8 ....45 J1
 WBY/YAL ME18 ....148 A4
Swanzy Rd RSEV TN14 ....149 K6
Sward Rd STMC/STPC BR5 .....87 H3
Swarling Hill Rd RCANTW CT4 .196 B5
Swattenden La CRBK TN17 ....297 N5
Swaylands Rd BELV DA17 ....29 J9
Swaynesland Rd EDEN TN8 ....206 A1
Swaynes Wy SWCH CT13 ......201 J8
Swedenbourg Gdns WCHPL E1 .24 D3
Sweden Ga BERM/RHTH SE16 .25 H7
Sweechbridge Rd HB CT6 ......108 C7
Sweechgate CANTW/ST CT2 ..137 K6
Sweeney Crs STHWK SE1 ....24 C5
Sweeps Hill Cl
 RTWE/PEM TN2 ....271 M1
Sweeps La STMC/STPC BR5 ....87 L2
Sweet Bay Crs ASH TN23 ....252 A6
Sweetbriar La RDV CT15 ....230 C7
Sweetings La WADH TN5 ....294 E6
Sweetlands La
 STPH/PW TN12 ....246 D2
Sweetlove Pl RCANTE CT3 .....169 K8
Sweets La E/WMAL ME19 ......153 P8
Sweyne Rd SWCM DA10 ....48 F7
Sweyn Pl BKHTH/KID SE3 ....42 E5
Sweyn Rd MARG CT9 ....112 F2
Swievelands Rd
 BH/WHM TN16 ....145 L4
Swift Cl DIT/AY ME20 ....152 P2
 THMD SE28 ....28 A3
Swift Crs WALD ME5 ....95 N8
Swift Pl STRD ME2 ....72 E7
Swiftsden Wy BMLY BR1 ....63 L3
Swiftshure Rd CDW/CHF RM16 .31 N7
Swifts Vw CRBK TN17 ....298 A1
Swiller's La GVE DA12 ....70 G4
Swinburne Av BRDST CT10 ....143 M1
Swinburne Crs CROY/NA CR0 ..25 H7
Swinburne Gdns TIL RM18 .....49 M5
Swinford Gdns BRXN/ST SW9 ..40 B4
 MARG CT9 ....113 H5
Swingate Av HOO/HM ME3 .....52 G3
Swingate Cl WALD ME5 ....125 N1
Swingate Rd WOOL/PLUM SE18 .44 A1
Swinton Av HOO/HM ME3 ......53 G1
Swires Shaw HAYES BR2 ....85 N6
Swissland Hl EGRIN RH19 ......265 H2
Swiss Wy FOLKN CT19 ....311 J4
Switch House Av LYDD TN29 ...347 K5
Swithland Gdns ELTH/MOT SE9 .63 K5
Sybil Phoenix Cl DEPT SE8 ......24 G8
Sycamore Av BFN/LL DA15 ......64 A8
 RCANTE CT3 ....229 H1
Sycamore Cl BRDST CT10 ......113 H9
 GVE DA12 ....49 P8
 HB CT6 ....107 P1
 HYTHE CT21 ....308 D6
 LYDD TN29 ....342 C5
 MARG CT9 ....112 C6
 SAND/SEL CR2 ....61 J4
Sycamore Crs MAIDW ME16 ...155 H7
Sycamore Dr DIT/AY ME20 ....154 D3
 EGRIN RH19 ....84 H6
 SWLY BR8 ....66 E5
Sycamore Gdns LYDD TN29 ...326 G6
 STPH/PW TN12 ....242 G4
Sycamore Gv CAT SE6 ....42 A7
 PGE/AN SE20 ....60 F8
Sycamore Ms BRITH DA8 * 29 J8
Sycamore Rd DART DA1 ....46 D8
 STRD ME2 ....71 N8
The Sycamores RCANTE CT3 ..138 B9
Sychem La STPH/PW TN12 ....242 B4
Sychem Pl STPH/PW TN12 .....242 B2
Sydcot Dr DEAL CT14 ....233 H1
Sydcote DUL SE21 * 60 C1
Sydenham Cl
 LEE/GVPK SE12 * 62 C1
Sydenham HI SYD SE26 ....60 D2
Sydenham Park Rd SYD SE26 ..61 J1
Sydenham Ri FSTH SE23 ....61 H3
Sydenham Rd CROY/NA CR0 ...83 H6
 DEAL CT14 ....233 J2
Sydenham Station Ap
 SYD SE26 ....61 J3
Sydmons Ct FSTH SE23 * 61 J3
Sydney Av SIT ME10 ....129 K1
Sydney Cooper Cl
 CANTW/ST CT2 ....166 A2
Sydney Rd ABYW SE2 ....28 C5
 BXLYHS DA6 ....44 F5
 CHAT ME4 ....6 D7
 DEAL CT14 ....232 F8
 RAM CT11 ....12 H2
 SCUP DA14 ....64 A3
 TIL RM18 ....49 M5
Sydney St ASH TN23 ....252 P9
Sylewood Cl ROCH ME1 ....94 G6
Sylvan Cl OXTED RH8 ....175 L5

Sylvan Gld WALD ME5 ....125 M5
Sylvan Gv PECK SE15 ....24 E9
Sylvan Hl NRWD SE19 ....60 E7
Sylvan Ms SWCM DA10 ....47 P5
Sylvan Rd NRWD SE19 ....60 F7
 RHAM ME8 ....95 N8
Sylvan Ter PECK SE15 * 41 H1
Sylvan Wy BMLY BR1 ....63 K9
Sylvan Wy WWKM BR4 ....85 H8
Silverdale Rd CROY/NA CR0 ...82 C7
Sylvester Av CHST BR7 ....63 K5
Sylvestre Cl STRD ME2 ....125 P1
Symmonds Dr SIT ME10 ....99 P9
Symonds Cl BGR/WK TN15 ....115 M9
Symonds La WBY/YAL ME18 ..213 M3
Symonds Rd HOO/HM ME3 .....52 A5
Symons Av CHAT ME4 ....95 L4
Symons Cl PECK SE15 ....41 J4

T

Tabard Garden Est STHWK SE1 ..24 A5
Tabard St STHWK SE1 ....24 A5
Tabret Cl KEN/WIL TN24 ....252 C3
Tack Ms BROCKY SE4 ....41 N4
Tadburn On WALD ME5 ....125 N1
Taddington Wood La
 WALD ME5 ....125 N3
Taddy Gdns MARG CT9 ....113 H5
Tadworth Rd KEN/WIL TN24 ..252 C4
Tadley Ct POP/IOD E14 * 25 L2
Taillour Cl SIT ME10 ....99 N7
Tainter Rd RTON TN11 ....211 N1
Tainters Hl EDEN TN8 * 237 L3
Tait Rd CROY/NA CR0 ....83 K4
Talavera Rd DART CT11 ....167 H5
Talbot Av HB CT6 ....106 C3
Talbot Cl BANK EC3V 24 A3
Talbot Pk RTWE/PEM TN2 ......23 J1
Talbot Pl BKHTH/KID SE3 ....42 C5
Talbot Rd EDUL SE22 * 40 E5
 HAWK TN18 ....317 H6
 LING RH7 ....234 G6
 MAIDW ME16 ....13 G5
 THHTH CR7 ....83 J1
Talbot Yd STHWK SE1 * 24 A4
Talcott Pth
 BRXS/STRHM SW2 * 40 A9
Talfourd Pl PECK SE15 ....40 F2
Talfourd Rd PECK SE15 ....40 F2
Talisman Sq SYD SE26 ....60 G3
Tall Elms Cl HAYES BR2 ....85 J2
Talland Cl EYN DA4 ....66 E1
Tallis Cl EHAM E6 ....26 C3
Tallis Gv CHARL SE7 ....26 C9
Tall Trees EGRIN RH19 ....265 J8
Tall Trees Cl RMAID ME17 ....189 N9
Tally Ho Rd RASHW TN26 .....281 N7
Tally Rd OXTED RH8 ....175 P7
Talmage Ct FSTH SE23 ....41 J8
Talma Rd BRXS/STRHM SW2 ...40 A9
Talus Cl PUR RM19 ....30 G7
Tamar Dr SOCK/AV RM15 ....30 F2
Tamar St CHARL SE7 ....26 E1
 STRD ME2 ....71 P9
Tamarind Cl GILL ME7 ....126 C9
Tamarind Yd WAP E1W 24 D4
Tamar Rd HOO/HM ME3 ....53 H2
Tamar St CHARL SE7 ....26 D5
Tamesis Strd GVE DA12 ....70 A4
Tamley La RASHE TN25 ....255 J4
Tampion Cl RAM CT11 ....13 D1
Tamworth Pl CROY/NA CR0 * ...83 H6
Tamworth Pk MTCM CR4 ....82 A1
Tamworth Rd CROY/NA CR0 * ...83 H6
Tandridge Dr ORP BR6 ....86 E5
Tandridgehill La GDST RH9 ....174 C4
Tandridge La LING RH7 ....234 G9
 OXTED RH8 ....174 D9
Tandridge Rd WARL CR6 ....144 A4
Tanfield Rd CROY/NA CR0 ....83 H4
Tangier La DTCH/LGLY SL3 * 6 E1
Tangier Cl RDV CT15 ....291 M4
Tangleberry La BMLY BR1 ....86 A1
Tangle Oak EGRIN RH19 ....264 B4
Tanglewood Cl CROY/NA CR0 ..83 P7
 RHAM ME8 ....96 F8
Tangmere Cl GILL ME7 ....96 C1
Tanhouse Rd OXTED RH8 ......174 C8
Tanker Hl RHAM ME8 ....96 B8
Tankerton Circ WSTB CT5 .....105 N5
Tankerton Rd WSTB CT5 ......105 M3
Tankerton Ter CROY/NA CR0 * .82 G4
Tankerton St STPAN/WC1H 347 L5
Tank Farm St CHST BR7 ....63 K5
Tank Hill Rd PUR RM19 ....30 E7
Tank La PUR RM19 ....30 E7
Tanner's Hl DEPT SE8 ....41 N2
 HYTHE CT21 ....309 H3
Tanners Cl
 STRD ME2 * 309 H3
Tanners Md EDEN TN8 ....206 D3
Tanners Ms DEPT SE8 ....41 M2
Tanners St FAV ME13 ....132 F6
Tanners St STHWK SE1 ....24 C2
Tannery Cl CROY/NA CR0 ....84 A2
Tannery La ASH TN23 ....201 N1
 SWCH CT13 ....201 N1
Tannery Rd TON TN9 ....210 F9
The Tannery STHWK SE1 * 24 C2
Tannsfeld Rd SYD SE26 ....61 K4
Tansy Cl EHAM E6 ....26 H2
Tant Av CAN/RD E16 * 26 C4
Tanyard HAWK TN18 ....318 A5
Tanyard Av EGRIN RH19 ....265 K8
Tanyard Gn HVE DA12 ....22 G2
Tan Yard La RSEV TN14 ....22 G2
Tanyard La SBGH/RUST TN4 ...240 C8
The Tanyard CRBK TN17 ....298 A4
Tapleys Hl RCANTW CT4 ....196 F6
Tappan Dr CHAT ME4 ....73 H5
Tappers Rd PECK SE15 ....41 J4
Tara Ter BROCKY SE4 * 41 N5
Tarbert Rd EDUL SE22 ....40 E6
Tarbert Wk WCHPL E1 ....24 G2
Target Firs DVE/WH CT16 ......290 E2

Tarleton Gdns *FSTH* SE23......41 H9
Tarling Cl *DART* DA1 ....64 D2
Tarling Rd *CAN/RD* E16 ....26 A2
Tarnwood Pk *ELTH/MOT* SE9 ....43 K9
Tarragon Cl *NWCR* SE14 * 41 L1
Tarragon Gv *SYD* SE26 ....61 K5
Tarragon Rd *MAIDW* ME16 .....154 F9
Tarriff Crs *DEPT* SE8 ....25 J7
Tartane La *LYDD* TN29 ....326 G6
Tarves Wy *GNWCH* SE10 ....41 P1
Tasker Cl *MAID/SHEP* ME15 ....156 E9
Tasker Rd *CDW/CHF* RM16 ....33 J6
Tassell Cl *E/WMAL* ME19 ....153 P5
Taswell Ct *DVE/WH* CT16 ....8 E2
Taswell Rd *RHAM* ME8 ....97 K5
Taswell St *DVE/WH* CT16 ....8 E2
Tatchell Dr *HDCN* TN27 ....220 C5
Tate Rd *CAN/RD* E16 ....26 C4
Tates Hawk *TN18 ....317 J5
Tates Orch *HART* DA3 ....91 J3
Tatler Cl *WALD* ME5...............126 A3
Tatnell Rd *FSTH* SE23 ....41 L7
Tatsfield La *BH/WHM* TN16 .....146 A6
Tattersall Cl *ELTH/MOT* SE9 .....43 J6
Tattershall Rd
  MAID/SHEP ME15 ....185 M2
Tattlebury La *CRBK* TN17 ....274 E8
Tattlebury Rd *HDCN* TN27 ....247 L2
Tatum St *WALW* SE17 ....24 A7
Taunton Cl *BXLYHN* DA7 ....189 J1
Taunton Rd *GVW* DA11 ....48 E6
  LEE/GVPK SE12 ....42 C6
Taunton V *GVE* DA12 ....69 P2
Taverners Rd *RHAM* ME8 ....97 H7
Tavern Cl *BGR/WK* TN15 ....151 J5
Tavistock Cl *RHAM* ME8 ....97 H7
  SIT ME10 ....129 L1
  WALD ME5 ....95 N9
Tavistock Crs *MTCM* CR4 ....82 D1
Tavistock Gv *CROY/NA* CR0 ......83 J4
Tavistock Rd *CROY/NA* CR0 ......83 J5
  HAYES BR2 ....
  WELL DA16 ....44 E2
Tavy Br *ABYW* SE2 ....28 B5
Tawney Rd *THMD* SE28 ....28 A3
Tawny Wy *BERM/RHTH* SE16 ....24 J2
Tayburn Cl *POP/IOD* E14 ....25 M2
Tay Cl *WALD* ME5....................95 N9
Taylfield La *STPH/PW* TN12 ....246 C2
Taylor Cl *DEPT* SE8 ....25 J9
  ORP BR6 ....
  RMAID ME17 ....188 E5
Taylor Rd *FOLKN* CT19 ....310 B5
  LYDD TN29 ....343 G6
  MSTR CT12 ....141 J6
  SNOD ME6 ....123 N6
Taylor Rw *RDART* DA2 ....66 C2
Taylor's Blds
  WOOL/PLUM SE18 ....27 J7
Taylors Ci *LYDD* TN29 ....337 L2
  SCUP DA14 ....64 B3
Taylors Hl *RCANTW* CT4 ....194 C5
Taylors La *E/WMAL* ME19 ....122 A7
  STRD ME2 ....57 L2
Taylor's La *STRD* ME2 ....18 E2
  SYD SE26 ....61 H3
Taylors Pas *KEN/WIL* TN24 2
Taylors St *SBCH/RUST* TN4 ....240 C9
Taylors Yd *RASHE* TN25 ....223 P8
Taymount Rl *FSTH* SE23 ....41 L6
Taywood Cl *KEN/WIL* TN24 .....253 J8
Tea Garden La *RRTW* TN4 ....269 P6
Teak Cl *BERM/RHTH* SE16 ....25 H4
Teal Av *STMC/STPC* BR5 ....87 L1
Teal Cl *CAN/RD* E16 ....26 E1
  HOO/HM ME3 ....56 D3
  RFOLK CT18 ....288 C9
  SAND/SEL CR2 ....114 A2
Teal Dr *CHAT* ME4 ....73 H5
  HB CT6 ....107 K4
Teal Wy *RSIT* ME9 ....99 M3
Teapot La *DIT/AY* ME20 ....154 D3
Teasaucer Hl
  MAID/SHEP ME15 ....185 L1
Teasel Cl *CROY/NA* CR0 ....84 A5
  MAID/BEAR ME14 ....156 C8
Teasel Crs *THMD* SE28 ....27 P7
Teasel Rd *WALD* ME5 ....125 L1
Teather St *CMBW* SE5 ....40 E1
Tebbs Wy *BGR/WK* TN15 ....150 F9
Teddars Leas Rd *RFOLK* CT18 ...287 J4
Tedder Rd *SAND/SEL* CR2 ......114 A2
  SBCH/RUST TN4 ....270 E1
Teddington Cl *CANT* CT1 ....5 H1
Teelin Cl *LYDD* TN29 ....337 L9
Teesdale Gdns *SNWD* SE25 ......60 E8
Teesdale Rd *RDART* DA2 ....47 J9
Teevan Cl *CROY/NA* CR0 ....83 M4
Teevan Rd *CROY/NA* CR0 ....83 M4
Teignmouth Rd *WELL* DA16 .....44 E3
Teise Cl *RTWE/PEM* TN2 ....23 H7
Telegraph Hl *HOO/HM* ME3 .....71 L4
Telegraph Pl *POP/IOD* E14 ....25 L7
Telegraph Rd *DEAL* CT14 ....232 C2
Telegraph St *LOTH* EC2R 24 A2
Telford Cl *NRWD* SE19 ....60 F5
Telford Ct *FOLKN* CT19 ....11 G1
Telfords Yd *WAP* E1W * 24 D3
Telham Av *MSTR* CT12 ....16 A1
Tell Gv *EDUL* SE22 ....
Tellson Av *WOOL/PLUM* SE18 ....43 J2
Telscombe Cl *ORP* BR6 ....86 E6
Telston La *RSEV* TN14 ....148 D2
Temeraire Pl *FOLK* CT20 ....309 P4
Temeraire St
  BERM/RHTH SE16 ....24 F5
Tempest Rd *E/WMAL* ME19 .....152 C9
Templar Dr *GVE* DA11 ....48 L4
  THMD SE28 ....28 C2
Templar Rd *DVE/WH* CT16 .....290 E2
Templars Cl *DART* DA1 * 46 C6
Templars St *CMBW* SE5 ....40 B5
  DVW CT17 ....8 A2

  BXLY DA5 ....45 J8
  ERITH DA8 ....45 N1
  MARG CT9 ....15 J3
Temple Av *CROY/NA* CR0 ....84 C7
Temple Boat Yd *STRD* ME2 * 18 B4
Temple Cl *ASH* TN23...............282 C5
Temple Ct *STRD* ME2 * 18 B4
  WSTB CT5 ....290 E1
  THMD SE28 ....27 K6
Temple Gdns *SIT* ME10 ....130 A2
  STRD ME2 ....18 A4
Temple Hl *DART* DA1 ....63 M4
Temple Hill Sq *DART* DA1 ....46 H6
Temple Ms *CANT* CT1 * 4 D5
Templer Av *CDW/CHF* RM16 ....33 H7
Temple Rd *BH/WHM* TN16 .....145 N2
  CANT/W ST CT2 ....4 A2
  CROY/NA CR0 ....78 A4
Temple Side *DVE/WH* CT16 ....290 E2
Templeton Cl *NRWD* SE19 ....60 D7
Temple Wy *DEAL* CT14 ....201 P6
  E/WMAL ME19 ....153 N4
Ten Acre Wy *RAIN* RM8 ....97 L4
Tenby Rd *WELL* DA16 ....44 F2
Tenchley's La *OXTED* RH8 ....175 N7
Tench St *WAP* E1W * 24 E4
Tenda Rd *STHWK* SE1 ....24 E7
Tennison Rd *SNWD* SE25 ....83 L1
Tennis St *STHWK* SE1 ....24 A5
Tennyson Av *CANT* CT1 ....167 J1
  GRAYS RM17 ....32 C6
  HOO/HM ME3 ....52 B9
Tennyson Cl *WELL* DA16 ....44 D3
Tennyson Gdns *RCANTE* CT3 ...199 J9
Tennyson Pl *FOLKN* CT19 ....311 H4
Tennyson Ri *EGRIN* RH19 ....264 F7
Tennyson Rd *ASH* TN23 ....282 D2
  DART DA1 ....46 G6
  GILL ME7 ....7 H6
  PGE/AN SE20 ....
  TIL RM18 ....118 B8
Ten Perch Rd *CANT* CT11 ....166 C6
Tensing Av *GVW* DA11 * 69 J2
Tenterden Cl *ELTH/MOT* SE9 ....63 K3
Tenterden Dr *CANTW/ST* CT2 ..136 E9
Tenterden Gdns *CROY/NA* CR0 ..83 M4
Tenterden Rd *CRBK* TN17 ......319 M2
  CROY/NA CR0 ....83 M4
  HDCN TN27 ....278 B8
  RASHW TN26 ....322 E6
  TENT TN30 ....322 B5
  WALD ME5 ....95 N9
Tenterden Wy *MARG* CT9 ......113 H4
Tenter Gnd *WCHPL* E1 * 24 C1
Tent Peg La *STMC/STPC* BR5 ....86 D2
Terence Butler Av *STRD* ME2 ....2 E1
Teredo St *LEW* SE13 ....41 P3
Terence Cl *CHAT* ME4 ....94 M4
  GVE DA12 ....70 B1
Terlingham La *RFOLK* CT18 ....310 D1
Terminus Dr *HB* CT6 ....108 A5
Terminus Rd *MAIDW* ME16 .....184 F1
Tern Crs *STRD* ME2 ....71 L9
Terrace Rd *MAIDW* ME16 ....12 C5
  RDV CT15 ....230 C8
  SIT ME10 ....130 A2
The Terraces *RDART* DA2 ....47 J8
Terrace St *GVE* DA12 ....49 M7
The Terrace *CANTW/ST* CT2 ....166 E1
  CHAT ME4 ....73 G7
  DEPT SE8 ....25 J7
  FAV ME13 * 132 D6
  FSTH SE23 ....41 L8
  GVE DA12 ....49 J7
  GVE DA12 ....70 B9
  RDV CT15 ....229 N9
  ROCH ME1 ....19 G6
  STHWK SE1 ....211 P2
  SIT ME10 ....148 C7
Terrys Lodge Rd
  BGR/WK TN15 ....120 F7
Terry Wk *E/WMAL* ME19 ....153 M7
Testers Cl *OXTED* RH8 ....175 L7
Teston La *MAID/SHEP* ME15 ...184 B4
Teston Rd *E/WMAL* ME19 ....152 C4
  WBY/YAL ME18 ....183 M1
Tetty Wy *BMLY* BR1 ....62 E8
Teviot Av *SOCK/AV* RM15 ....30 D2
Teviot Cl *WELL* DA16 ....44 D2
Teviot St *POP/IOD* E14 ....25 M1
Tewkesbury Av *FSTH* SE23 ....41 H9
Tewson Rd *WOOL/PLUM* SE18 ..27 M8
Teynham Cl *MARG* CT9 ....113 L3
Teynham Dr *WSTB* CT5 ....105 N4
Teynham Gn *HAYES* BR2 ....85 K2
  RMAID ME8 ....96 D2
Teynham Rd *RDART* DA2 ....47 J9
  WSTB CT5 ....105 N4
Teynham St *RSIT* ME9 ....89 N1
Thackeray Av *TIL* RM18 ....49 M2
Thackeray Rd *DIT/AY* ME20 ....153 N1
Thakeham Cl *SYD* SE26 ....61 H4
Thalia Cl *GNWCH* SE10 ....25 P1
Thames Av *HOO/HM* ME3 ....53 L4
  RAIN RM8 ....57 K7
  RHAM ME8 ....95 L9
Thamesbank Pl *THMD* SE28 .....28 B2
Thames Cir *POP/IOD* E14 ....25 K7
Thames Cl *RAIN* RM13 ....29 N2
Thames Dr *CDW/CHF* RM16 .....33 H8
Thames Ga *DART* DA1 ....63 M4
Thamesmere Dr *THMD* SE28 ....27 P5
Thames Pth *CANST* EC4R 24 A3
Thames Rd *CAN/RD* E16 ....26 E4
  DART DA1 ....46 G2
Thames St *GNWCH* SE10 ....25 L9
Thames Vw *CDW/CHF* RM16 ....33 H8
  HOO/HM ME3 ....52 C9
Thames Wy *GVW* DA11 ....48 E7
  PUR RM19 ....30 D7
Thanescroft Gdns
  CROY/NA CR0 ....83 K7
Thanet Cl *BRDST* CT10 ....113 N8
Thanet Coastal Pth *MARG* CT9 ...4 A1
Thanet Dr *HAYES* BR2 ....85 N7
Thanet Gdns *FOLKN* CT19 ....11 J1
Thanet Ms *CROY/NA* CR0 ....83 H8
Thanet Place Gdns
  BRDST CT10 ....113 N7
Thanet Rd *BRDST* CT10 ....113 N9

  BXLY DA5 ....45 J8
  ERITH DA8 ....45 N1
  MARG CT9 ....15 J3
  RHAM ME8 ....126 F1
  WGOS CT8 ....111 L4
Thanet Ter *RASHW* TN26 * 251 M3
Thanet Wy *RDV* CT15 * 230 C9
  RCANTE CT5 ....105 H3
  WSTB CT5 ....105 J9
  WSTB CT5 ....135 H1
Thanington Rd *CANT* CT11 .....166 B6
Tharp Rd *WLGTN* SM6 ....82 C9
Thatch Barn Rd *HDCN* TN27 ...246 D5
Thatcher Rd *STPH/PW* TN12 ...246 B5
Thatchers La *HOO/HM* ME3 .....52 B5
The Thatchers *MAIDW* ME16 * ..154 C7
Thaxted Rd *ELTH/MOT* SE9 .....63 N1
Thayers Farm Rd *BECK* BR3 .....61 L1
Theatre St *HYTHE* CT21 ....309 H5
Thelma Cl *GVE* DA12 ....70 B4
Theobald Rd *CROY/NA* CR0 ....82 G6
Theobalds Av *GRAYS* RM17 ....32 D8
Theobald St *STHWK* SE1 ....24 A6
Theodore Cl *RTWE/PEM* TN2 ..271 H1
Theodore Pl *GILL* ME7 ....7 H2
Theodore Rd *LEW* SE13 ....42 B7
The Queens Wk *STHWK* SE1 ....24 B4
Therapia La *CROY/NA* CR0 ....82 E6
Therapia Rd *EDUL* SE22 ....42 J1
Theresa Rd *RTWE/PEM* TN2 ...308 C6
Thermopylae Ga *POP/IOD* E14 ..25 L7
Thesiger Rd *PGE/AN* SE20 ....61 K6
Thicket Gv *PGE/AN* SE20 ....60 G6
Thicket Rd *PGE/AN* SE20 ....61 H6
Thicket Rd *PGE/AN* SE20 * 60 G6
Third Av *CHAT* ME4 ....95 P5
  GILL ME7 ....6 B5
  GVW DA11 * 49 K9
  IOS ME12 ....159 M1
  MARG CT9 ....112 C2
  WTHK RM20 ....31 L5
Third St *RRTW* TN3 ....269 L5
Thirlmere Cl *MAIDW* ME16 .....155 J4
Thirlmere Av *RAM* CT11 ....142 F5
Thirlmere Cl *GILL* ME7 ....96 F2
  STRD ME2 ....72 C6
Thirlmere Gdns *RCANTE* CT3 ..199 J9
Thirlmere Ri *BMLY* BR1 ....62 D5
Thirlmere Rd *BXLYHN* DA7 ......45 L5
  SBCH/RUST TN4 ....270 A3
Thirsk Rd *SNWD* SE25 ....83 J1
Thirza Rd *DART* DA1 ....46 J6
Thislefield Cl *BXLY* DA5 ....44 F9
Thistlebank *WALD* ME5 ....125 M2
Thistlebrook *ABYW* SE2 ....28 B6
Thistledown *DEAL* CT14 ....232 C9
  MAID/BEAR ME14 ....156 C8
  STPH/PW TN12 * 242 E7
Thistle Cl *WALD* ME5 ....125 M2
Thistle Dr *WSTB* CT5 ....105 J9
Thistle Hill Wy *IOS* ME12 ....78 A3
Thistlemead *CHST* BR7 ....63 M8
Thistle Rd *GVE* DA12 ....50 A8
Thistlewood Crs
  CROY/NA CR0 ....114 C6
Thomas Bata Av *TIL* RM18 ....34 A7
Thomas Cribb Ms *EHAM* E6 ......26 G2
Thomas Dean Rd *SYD* SE26 * 61 N1
Thomas Dinwiddy Rd
  LEE/GVPK SE12 ....62 F1
Thomas Dr *GVE* DA12 ....69 P1
Thomas La *CAT* SE6 ....41 P7
Thomas Moore St *WAP* E1W 24 D3
Thomas North Ter
  CAN/RD E16 * 26 A1
Thomas Rd *FAV* ME13 ....132 F6
  POP/IOD E14 ....25 J2
  SIT ME10 ....130 A1
Thomas St *ROCH* ME1 ....19 H5
Thompson Av *CMBW* SE5 ....40 C1
Thompson Cl *DEAL* CT14 ....232 C9
  FOLKN CT19 ....10 B3
  RHAM ME8 ....97 K6
Thompson Rd *EDUL* SE22 ....40 F7
Thompson's Av *CMBW* SE5 * 40 C1
Thomson Cl *SNOD* ME6 ....123 P4
Thomson Rd *KEN/WIL* TN24 ...252 E6
Thong La *BGR/WK* TN15 ....151 H7
  GVE DA12 ....70 B3
Thorley Sq *STHWK* SE1 ....24 D7
Thorley Rd *CDW/CHF* RM16 ....32 B4
Thornbridge Rd *DEAL* CT14 ....232 F6
Thorn Cl *HAYES* BR2 ....86 B5
  WALD ME5 ....125 J4
Thorncombe Rd *EDUL* SE22 ......40 E6
Thorndale Cl *WALD* ME5 ....95 J9
Thornden Cl *HB* CT6 ....107 H4
Thornden Ct *CANTW/ST* CT2 * ..136 E9
Thornden La *CRBK* TN17 ....319 H6
Thornden Wood Rd *HB* CT6 ....136 D5
Thorndike Cl *CHAT* ME4 * 95 L6
Thorndike Rd *LYDD* TN29 ....326 G2
Thorndon Rd *STMC/STPC* BR5 ..64 E8
Thorndon Rd *STMC/STPC* BR5 ..64 B8
Thorne Cl *CAN/RD* E16 ....26 D3
  ERITH DA8 ....28 E3
Thorne Hl *MSTR* CT12 ....141 N5
Thorneloe Gdns *CROY/NA* CR0 ..82 G9
Thornes Cl *BECK* BR3 ....61 N3
The Thorn Est *HDCN* TN27 .....250 A5
Thornet Wood Rd *BMLY* BR1 ....63 L4
Thorneycroft Cl *WALD* ME5 .....125 L2
Thorneycroft Rd *RMAID* ME17 .187 N9
Thornfield Gdns
  RTWE/PEM TN2 ....271 J1
Thornford Rd *LEW* SE13 ....42 A6
Thorn Gdns *RAM* CT11 ....143 K5
Thornham Rd *RHAM* ME8 ....96 F5
Thornham St *GNWCH* SE10 ....25 L9

Thornhill Av *WOOL/PLUM* SE18 ..44 A1
Thornhill Pl *MAID/BEAR* ME14 ..13 J7
Thornhill Rd *CROY/NA* CR0 ....83 H4
Thorn Hill Rd *IOS* ME12 ....80 C3
Thorn La *RCANTW* CT4 ....226 D8
Thornlaw Rd *WNWD* SE27 ....60 A3
Thornlea *ASH* TN23 ....282 B8
Thorn Rd *STPH/PW* TN12 ....245 L6
Thornsbeach Rd *CAT* SE6 ....42 A7
Thornsett Pl *PGE/AN* SE20 ....61 H8
Thornsett Rd *PGE/AN* SE20 ......61 H8
Thornsett Ter *PGE/AN* SE20 * ...61 H8
Thorn's Meadow
  BH/WHM TN16 ....147 K8
Thornton Av *CROY/NA* CR0 ......82 E3
Thornton Cl *KEN/WIL* TN24 ....253 K8
Thornton Dene *BECK* BR3 ....61 N8
Thornton Cl *DEAL* CT14 ....233 E3
  SWCH CT13 ....201 H9
Thornton Rd *BELV* DA17 * 29 J7
  BMLY BR1 ....62 E4
  THHTH CR7 ....82 F2
Thornton Rw *THHTH* CR7 ....82 F2
Thornton St *BRXN/ST* SW9 ....40 A3
Thorntree Rd *CHARL* SE7 ....28 B8
Thornville St *DEPT* SE8 ....41 N2
Thornwood Rd *LEW* SE13 ....42 C6
Thorold Cl *SAND/SEL* CR2 ......114 A4
Thorold Rd *WALD* ME5 ....7 F6
Thorpe Av *TONN* TN10 ....210 F5
Thorpe Rd *CROY/NA* CR0 ....114 F5
  ORP BR6 ....86 B6
  SYD SE26 ....61 M3
Thorpe Wk *RHAM* ME8 ....126 F2
Thorpewood Av *SYD* SE26 ....61 H1
Thorsden Wy *NRWD* SE19 * 60 E4
Thrale Wy *RHAM* ME8 ....127 H1
Thrawl St *WCHPL* E1 ....24 C1
Thread La *FAV* ME13 ....134 C8
Threadneedle St *BANK* EC3V 24 A2
Three Colt St *POP/IOD* E14 * 25 J3
Three Corners *BXLYHN* DA7 ......45 K3
Three Elm La *RTON* TN11 ....237 P3
Three Gates Rd *HART* DA3 ....90 D4
Three King's Yd *SWCH* CT15 * ..201 P1
Three Leg Cross Rd
  WADH TN5 ....315 H3
Three Oak La *STHWK* SE1 ....24 C5
Threshers Dr
  MAID/BEAR ME14 ....156 A7
Threshers Fld *EDEN* TN8 * 237 P3
Thriftwood *SYD* SE26 ....61 M4
Thrift Grn *RTON* TN11 ....23 H1
The Thrift *RDART* DA2 ....68 A2
Throckmorten Rd *CAN/RD* E16 ..26 C2
Throgmorton Av *OBST* EC2N 24 A2
Throgmorton St *OBST* EC2N 24 A2
Throwley Cl *ABYW* SE2 ....28 B6
Throwley Dr *HB* CT6 ....107 H2
Throwley Rd *FAV* ME13 ....162 B9
Thrupp Paddock *BRDST* CT10 ..113 M4
Thrush Cl *WALD* ME5 ....95 N7
Thruxted La *RCANTW* CT4 ....195 H2
Thunderland Rd *CAT* SE6 ....42 A7
Thurban Rd *CAT* SE6 ....41 N8
Thurland Rd *BERM/RHTH* SE16 ..24 D8
Thurlby Rd *WNWD* SE27 ....60 A3
Thurlestone Ct
  MAID/BEAR ME14 * 12 E1
Thurlestone Rd *WNWD* SE27 ....32 B6
Thurloe Ms *GRAYS* RM17 ....32 B6
Thurlow Av *WILD* ME5 ....95 J9
Thurlow Hl *DUL* SE21 ....60 B3
Thurlow Park Rd *DUL* SE21 ....60 B1
Thurlow St *WALW* SE17 ....24 B8
Thurlow Wk *WALW* SE17 ....24 B8
Thurrock Park Wy *TIL* RM18 .....49 H1
Thursland Rd *SCUP* DA14 ....64 G4
Thursley Crs *CROY/NA* CR0 .....114 G2
Thursley Rd *ELTH/MOT* SE9 .....63 K2
Thurstan Rd *RYE* TN31 ....29 H9
Thurston Pk *WSTB* CT5 ....105 M5
Thurston Rd *DEPT* SE8 ....41 P7
Thwaite Cl *ERITH* DA8 ....29 H8
Thyer Cl *ORP* BR6 ....86 D8
Thyssel La *RYE* TN31 ....330 C7
Tibbenham Pl *CAT* SE6 ....61 N1
Tibbs Court La
  STPH/PW TN12 ....272 C1
Ticehurst Cl *STMC/STPC* BR5 ....64 C6
Ticehurst Rd *FSTH* SE23 ....61 L1
Tichborne Cl *MAIDW* ME16 .....155 H6
Tickford Cl *ABYW* SE2 ....28 B5
Tickham La *RSIT* ME9 ....133 J7
Tickner's La *LYDD* TN29 ....335 H4
Tidal Basin Rd *CAN/RD* E16 ....26 B4
Tidenham Gdns *CROY/NA* CR0 ..83 K7
Tideswell Rd *CROY/NA* CR0 ......84 D7
The Tideway *ROCH* ME1 ....95 H6
Tidey St *BOW* E3 ....
Tidford Rd *WELL* DA16 ....44 E8
Tieglis La *WWKM* BR4 ....85 H6
Tiger La *HAYES* BR2 ....86 B3
Tilbrook Rd *BKHTH/KID* SE3 ....42 G4
Tilburstow Hill Rd *GDST* RH9 ..204 A3
Tilbury Cl *PECK* SE15 ....40 F7
  STMC/STPC BR5 ....64 D6
Tilbury Rd *RHAM* ME8 ....97 K7
Tilden Cl *LYDD* TN29 ....326 G4
Tilden Gill Rd *TENT* TN30 ....301 K8
Tilden La *STPH/PW* TN12 ....245 M1
Tilden Rd *RMAID* ME17 ....187 N7
Tilebarn Cnr *TONN* TN10 ....211 H6
Tile Farm Rd *ORP* BR6 ....86 E2
Tile Flds *RMAID* ME17 ....187 N1
Tile Fields Cl *ELTH/MOT* SE9 ...187 N1
Tile Kiln La *BXLY* DA5 ....45 K1
  FOLKN CT19 ....310 C4
Tile Kiln Rd *KEN/WIL* TN24 .....252 F2
Tile Lodge Rd *HDCN* TN27 ......220 B3
Tilford Av *CROY/NA* CR0 ....114 G2
Tilghman Wy *SNOD* ME6 ....124 A4
Tillard Cl *RCANTW* CT4 ....196 A8
Tile Av *EYN* DA4 ....65 P8
Tiller Rd *POP/IOD* E14 ....25 K5
Tillery La *LYDD* TN29 ....334 F6
Tilley Cl *HOO/HM* ME3 ....52 A3
Tillingbourne Gn
  STMC/STPC BR5 ....87 H1
Tillingham Av *RYE* TN31 ....338 E6

Tillmans *BGR/WK* TN15 ....151 K5
Tillman St *WCHPL* E1 * 24 E2
Tilmans Md *EYN* DA4 ....89 L4
Tilsden La *CRBK* TN17 ....298 B3
Tilson Cl *CMBW* SE5 ....40 E1
Tilton Rd *BGR/WK* TN15 ....151 H5
Tilt Yard Ap *ELTH/MOT* SE9 .....43 K7
Timber Bank *MEO* DA13 ....122 A5
Timber Cl *MAID/SHEP* ME15 ....185 M5
Timber Ct *CHST* BR7 ....63 L8
Timbercroft La
  WOOL/PLUM SE18 ....27 M9
Timberland Cl *PECK* SE15 * 40 G1
Timberland Rd *WCHPL* E1 * 24 E2
Timber Pond Rd
  BERM/RHTH SE16 ....24 G5
Timbertop Rd *BH/WHM* TN16 ..145 M3
Timber Tops *WALD* ME5 ....126 A1
Timms Cl *BMLY* BR1 ....62 H5
Timothy Cl *BXLYHS* DA6 ....45 G6
Timperley Cl *DEAL* CT14 ....232 C3
Tina Gdns *BRDST* CT10 ....113 M3
Tinbridge Oast *FAV* ME13 * 133 K8
Tindal St *BRXN/ST* SW9 ....40 B2
Tinker Pot La *BGR/WK* TN15 ...119 P7
Tinkerpot Ri *BGR/WK* TN15 ....119 P8
Tinley Cl *SNWD* SE25 ....61 H9
Tinsley Rd *WCHPL* E1 * 24 F1
Tintagel Crs *EDUL* SE22 ....40 E5
Tintagel Rd *ORP* BR6 ....87 K6
Tintern Rd *MAIDW* ME16 ....155 H5
Tinto Rd *CAN/RD* E16 ....26 B1
Tipton Dr *CROY/NA* CR0 ....83 K8
Tirrell Rd *CROY/NA* CR0 ....83 H1
Tirrlingh Pl *WALW* SE17 ....24 A7
Titan Rd *GRAYS* RM17 ....32 B8
Titchfield Rd
  MAID/SHEP ME15 ....186 C5
Tithe Barn La *ASH* TN23 ....252 A9
Tithe Orch *EGRIN* RH19 ....264 B9
Titmuss Av *THMD* SE28 ....28 A3
Titsey Hl *WARL* CT6 ....145 J9
Tiverton Cl *CROY/NA* CR0 ....83 L3
Tivoli Brooks *MARG* CT9 ....15 G7
Tivoli Gdns *WOOL/PLUM* SE18 ..26 F7
Tivoli Park Av *MARG* CT9 ....14 E2
Tivoli Rd *MARG* CT9 ....15 G7
Toad Hall Crs *HOO/HM* ME3 ......72 G3
Tobago St *POP/IOD* E14 ....25 K5
Tobruk Wy *WALD* ME5 ....95 L8
Toby Gdns *RTON* TN11 ....211 P2
Toby Rd *LYDD* TN29 ....343 K6
Todd Crs *SIT* ME10 ....99 P6
Tokenhouse Yd *LOTH* EC2R * 24 A2
Toke Cots *RMAID* ME17 * 215 J2
Toft Av *GRAYS* RM17 ....32 E7
Toledo Paddock *GILL* ME7 * 96 A1
Tolgate Cl *DEAL* CT14 ....232 D2
Tolgate Wy *MAID/BEAR* ME14 ..155 K1
Tolhurst La *WADH* TN5 ....314 E5
Tolhurst Rd *STPH/PW* TN12 ....242 E5
Tollemache Cl *MSTR* CT12 ....141 N2
Tol Ga *DEAL* CT14 ....232 F5
Tollgate Cl *WSTB* CT5 * 105 N6
Tollgate Dr *DUL* SE21 ....60 E1
Tollgate Ms *BGR/WK* TN15 ......151 K5
Tollgate Pl *HDCN* TN27 ....247 P4
Tollgate Rd *EHAM* E6 ....26 C2
  RDART DA2 ....47 K8
Toll La *HDCN* TN27 ....221 K3
Tolsford Cl *FOLKN* CT19 ....310 A5
Tolsford Cl *FOLKN* CT19 ....287 H5
Tomay Cots *HB* CT6 * 108 D7
Tom Cribb Rd
  WOOL/PLUM SE18 ....27 K6
Tom Jenkinson Rd
  CAN/RD E16 ....26 B4
Tom Joyce Cl *SNOD* ME6 ....123 N6
  STPH/PW TN12 ....246 B5
Tomlin Dr *MARG* CT9 ....113 H6
Tomlin's Ter *POP/IOD* E14 ....25 J2
Tom Smith Cl *GNWCH* SE10 .....25 P9
Tonbridge By-Pass
  BGR/WK TN15 ....179 K9
  RTON TN11 ....209 M2
Tonbridge Chambers
  TON TN9 * 240 E1
Tonbridge Rd *BGR/WK* TN15 ...180 E1
  MAIDW ME16 ....210 A4
  RTON TN11 ....210 A4
  RTWE/PEM TN2 ....271 L1
  SEV TN13 ....179 L1
  WBY/YAL ME18 ....183 L6
Tonford La *CANTW/ST* CT2 .....165 N5
Tonge Cl *BECK* BR3 ....61 N4
Tonge Rd *SIT* ME10 ....130 A1
Tong La *STPH/PW* TN12 ....273 J5
Tong Rd *STPH/PW* TN12 ....273 J5
Tongswood Dr *HAWK* TN18 .....317 L5
Tontine St *FOLK* CT20 ....13 F3
Tookey Rd *NROM* TN28 ....336 C9
Tookey St *CHAT* ME4 ....95 J4
  STHWK SE1 ....24 A4
Tootswood Rd *HAYES* BR2 ....85 K2
Topcliffe Dr *ORP* BR6 ....86 A5
Top Dartford Rd *SWLY* BR8 ....66 A5
Toplands Av *SOCK/AV* RM15 .....30 B9
Topley Cl *RHAM* ME8 ....96 A1
Topley St *ELTH/MOT* SE9 ....42 G5
Topmast Point *POP/IOD* E14 * ..25 K5
Top Pk *BECK* BR3 ....85 J3
Top Rd *TENT* TN30 ....301 N2
Torbay Rd *STPH/PW* TN12 ....245 M1
Torcross Dr *FSTH* SE23 ....61 J1
Tor Gv *THMD* SE28 ....28 A1
Tormore Ms *DEAL* CT14 ....232 F5
Tormore Pk *DEAL* CT14 ....232 F5
Tormount Rd
  WOOL/PLUM SE18 ....27 M9
Toronto Cl *DVW* CT17 ....291 J4
Toronto Rd *GILL* ME7 ....49 L3
  TIL RM18 ....49 L3
Torrens Wk *GVE* DA12 ....70 B4

Torres Sq POP/IOD E14............25 K8
Torrey Dr BRXN/ST SW9............40 A3
Torridge Gdns PECK SE15............41 J5
Torridge Rd THHTH CR7............82 C2
Torrington Ct CAT SE6............42 B9
Torrington Rd WBY/YAL ME18..182 E3
Torrington Pl ASH TN23 *............252 F9
WAP E1W............24 D4
Torrington Sq CROY/NA CRO *....83 J4
Tor Rd WELL DA16............44 E2
Torr Rd PGE/AN SE20............61 K6
Torre Rd ORP BR6............86 E7
Tothill St MSTR CT12............141 K5
Totnes Rd WELL DA16............44 D1
Tottan Ter WCHPL E1 *............24 C2
Totton Rd THHTH CR7............60 A9
Toulon St CMBW SE5............40 C1
Tourmaline Dr SIT ME10............99 K8
Tournay Cl ASH TN23............252 C9
Tourney Rd FUL/PGN SW6 *......307 N4
Tourney Rd LYDD TN29............342 A7
Tourtel Rd CANT CT1............5 G2
Toussaint Wk
BERM/RHTH SE16............24 D6
Tovey Sq GILL ME7............73 M9
Tovil Cl PGE/AN SE20............61 J8
Tovil Gn MAID/SHEP ME15......185 K1
Tovil Hl MAID/SHEP ME15......185 K2
Tovil Rd MAID/SHEP ME15......185 L1
Tower Br WAP E1W............24 C4
Tower Bridge Rd STHWK SE1....24 B6
Tower Blds WAP E1W *............24 E4
Tower Cl EGRIN RH19............264 G6
GVE DA20............70 A4
ORP BR6............86 E1
PGE/AN SE20............61 H6
Tower Ct BXRN WK TN15 *......265 H6
Tower Cft EYN DA4............89 K6
Tower Est CUDT TN29............327 J4
Tower Gdns HYTHE CT21......309 H6
MAID/BEAR ME14............156 E9
Tower Hamlets Rd DVW CT17....8 A2
Tower Hamlets Rd DVW CT17....8 A2
Tower Hl E/WMAL ME19............152 E5
TWRH ECN............24 B3
Tower Hill Ter MION EC3R *......24 B3
Tower La MAID/BEAR ME14..156 D8
Tower Mill Rd CMBW SE5............40 E1
Tower Park Rd DART DA1............45 P6
Tower Pl MION EC3R............24 B3
WARL CR6............114 D9
Tower Rd BELV DA17............29 H7
BXLYHN DA7............45 K5
DART DA1............46 C8
ORP BR6............86 E7
WSTB CT5............105 M4
Towers Rd GRAYS RM17............32 D8
Tower St DVW CT17............338 F6
RYE TN31............338 F6
Tower Vw KEN/WIL TN24............252 F2
Towers Wd EYN DA4............67 K7
Tower Vw CROY/NA CRO............84 B5
E/WMAL ME19............153 J9
Tower Wharf CSV DA11 *............48 F5
Town Acres TONN TN10............210 F6
Towncourt Crs
STMC/STPC BR5............85 L8
Towncourt La STMC/STPC BR5..86 E3
Townfield Cnr GVE DA12..........49 N9
Towngate Wood Pk
TONN TN10............210 G3
Town Hill E/WMAL ME19............153 K5
Townland Cl HDCN TN27............278 D7
Town La RCANTW CT4............165 K6
Townley Rd BXLYHS DA6............45 H6
EDUL SE22............16 E5
Townley St RAM CT11............16 E5
WALW SE17 *............24 A7
Town Pier Sq DVW DA11............49 M7
Town Rd HOO/HM ME3............72 A1
RCANTW CT4............196 A7
Townsend Farm Rd RDV CT15..292 E1
Townsend Rd SWDL ME6............123 J9
WOOL/PLUM SE18............27 J6
Townsend Sq E/WMAL ME19..183 H1
Townsend St WALW SE17............24 A7
Townsend Ter DVW CT17 *......313 J1
Townshend Cl SCUP DA14............64 D5
Townshend Rd THMD ME28............63 M4
Town Square Crs RDART DA2..247 M8
Town Wk FOLK CT20............10 E5
Townwall St DVE/WH CT16............8 E4
Towpath Wy CROY/NA CRO............83 L3
Towton Rd WNWD SE27............60 C1
Toynbee Cl CHST BR7............63 M3
Toynbee St WCHPL E1............24 C2
Toy's Hl BH/WHM TN16............177 K7
Toys Hl EDEN TN8............207 K3
The Tracies HART ME19 *............98 D8
Trader Rd EHAM E6............27 J2
Tradescant Rd VX/NE SW8..........H1 K9
Tradewinds WSTB CT5............105 J8
Trafalgar Av PECK SE15............40 F2
Trafalgar Gv GNWCH SE10............25 N9
Trafalgar Ms RAM CT11 *............16 E5
Trafalgar Rd BRCH CT7............141 N1
DART DA1............66 E1
GNWCH SE10............25 N8
GVW DA11............49 L8
ROCH ME1............124 B1
Trafalgar St GILL ME7............7 H3
WALW SE17............24 A8
Trafalgar Wy CROY/NA CRO......82 E6
Trafford Rd THHTH CR7............82 E2
The Tram Rd FOLK CT20............11 H4
Tramway Cl PGE/AN SE20............61 J7
Tramways WALD ME5............94 F4
Tranquil Pas BKHTH/KID SE3 *..42 D3
Tranquil Ri ERITH DA8............30 C5
Tranquil V BKHTH/KID SE3............42 C3

Transfesa Rd STPH/PW TN12..243 H2
Transformer Av LYDD TN29......347 K5
Transmere Rd STMC/STPC BR5..86 D3
Transom Ct BERM/RHTH SE16 ..25 H7
Transom Sq POP/IOD E14............25 L8
Tranton Rd BERM/RHTH SE16....24 E6
Trapfield Cl MAID/BEAR ME14..156 F8
Trapfield La MAID/BEAR ME14..156 F8
Trapham Rd MAIDW ME16............155 J7
Travers Gdns DEAL CT14............128 C8
Travers Rd DEAL CT14............232 F4
Travertine Rd MAID ME15 *......125 N4
Treasury vw RCANTE CT3............168 F8
Trebble Rd SWCM DA10............48 C7
Trebilco Ct RTWE/PEM TN2......270 C1
Tredegar Rd RDART DA2............66 A2
Tredown Rd SYD SE26............61 J4
Tredwell Cl HAYES BR2............85 N1
Tredwell Rd WNWD SE27............60 B3
Treebourne Rd
BH/WHM TN16............145 M2
Tree La BGR/WK TN15............181 H5
Tree Rd CAN/RD E16............26 D2
Treetops BGR/WK TN15............149 M2
GDST RH9............204 B4
TON TN9............69 M4
Treetops Cl ABYW SE2............28 D8
Tree View Cl NRWD SE19............60 E7
Treewall Gdns BMLY BR1............62 F3
Tregony Rd ORP BR6............86 E6
Treherne Ct BRXN/ST SW9 *......42 B2
Trelawn Crs WALD ME5............125 N3
Trelawn Rd BRXS/STRHM SW2..40 A6
Trellyn Cl MAIDW ME16............184 E1
Treloar Gdns NRWD SE19............60 D5
Tremaine Cl BROCKY SE4............41 N3
Tremaine Rd PGE/AN SE20............61 J8
Trenchard Cl KEN/WIL TN24....253 J9
Trench Rd TONN TN10............210 E4
Trenear Cl ORP BR6............87 H8
Trenholme Rd PGE/AN SE20......61 H6
Trenholme Ter PGE/AN SE20......61 H6
Tenley Dr RCANTE CT3............167 L5
Trent TIL RM18............34 B7
Trentham Dr STMC/STPC BR5....87 H1
Trenton Cl MAIDW ME16............154 C5
Trent Rd WALD ME5............95 N9
Tresco Cl BMLY BR1............62 C5
Tresco Rd PECK SE15............41 H5
Tressillian Crs BROCKY SE4......41 N4
Tressillian Rd BROCKY SE4......41 N4
Trevanion Rd ROCH ME1 *............94 C5
Trevano Ter
MAID/SHEP ME15 *............185 K1
Trevelyan Ct DART DA1 *............46 E8
Trevereux Hl OXTED RH8......196 B8
Trevino Dr WALD ME5............125 L3
Treviso Rd FSTH SE23............61 K1
Trevithick Dr DART DA1............46 F5
Trevithick St DEPT SE8............25 K9
Trevor Cl HAYES BR2............167 L5
Trevor Dr MAID/BEAR ME14......155 M4
Trewin Cl DIT/AY ME20............154 C2
Trewsbury Rd SYD SE26............61 L3
The Triangle BFN/LL DA15 *......44 C8
Tribune Ct IOS ME12............57 K8
Tribune Dr SIT ME10............99 N8
Trident Cl STRD ME2............19 K2
Trident St BERM/RHTH SE16......24 G7
Triggs Rw KWT N14 *............131 J3
Trilby Rd FSTH SE23............61 K1
Trilby Vw WSTB CT5............105 J8
Trim St NWCR SE14............25 J9
Trimworth Rd FOLKN CT19......310 C5
Trindad St POP/IOD E14............25 J3
Trinity Buoy Whrf
POP/IOD E14 *............25 N1
Trinity Ci HAYES BR2............85 P5
LEW SE13............41 N3
RTWE/PEM TN2............23 J3
Trinity Ct ELTH/MOT SE9............43 M7
Trinity Crs FOLK CT20............10 B6
Trinity St DEPT SE8............25 J8
Trinity Gdns CAN/RD E16............26 A1
DART DA1............46 E8
FOLK CT20............10 C6
Trinity Gv WCHPL E1 *............24 F1
Trinity Gv GNWCH SE10............42 C2
Trinity Homes DEAL CT14 *......233 H8
Trinity Ms PGE/AN SE20............61 H8
Trinity Pl BXLYHS DA6............45 H5
DEAL CT14............232 F5
RAM CT11............17 H2
Trinity Rd BRXS/STRHM SW2....40 B8
Trinity St WCHPL E1 *............73 J9
GVE DA12............49 N8
IOS ME12............57 L6
KEN/WIL TN24............99 N7
SIT ME10............99 N7
Trinity Sq BRDST CT10............113 L6
MARG CT9............15 H5
TWRH EC3N............24 B3
Trinity St CAN/RD E16............26 A1
Trinity Hl MARG CT9............15 H3
Tristan Gdns SBGH/RUST TN4..269 P4
Tristan Sq BKHTH/KID SE3......42 C4
Tristram Rd BMLY BR1............62 D3
Tritton Av CROY/NA CRO............82 D8
Tritton Fids KEN/WIL TN24......253 J2
Tritton Gdns LYDD TN29............345 H5
Tritton La NROM TN28............336 C7
Tritton Rd DUL SE21............60 D2
Triumph Cl CDW/CHF RM16......31 M6
Triumph Rd EHAM E6............27 K2
Trivett Cl RDART DA2............47 N6
Trojan Wy CROY/NA CRO............82 E7
Trolling Down Hl RDART DA2....64 C4
Trona Cl SIT ME10............99 L8
Troodos Hl MAID/BEAR ME14..155 L4
Troon Cl BERM/RHTH SE16......28 C8
THMD SE28............28 C2
Troon St WCHPL E1............25 H2
Trosley Av GVW DA11............69 M1
Trosley Rd BELV DA17............29 J4
Trossachs Rd EDUL SE22............40 E6

Trothy Rd STHWK SE1............24 D7
Trottiscliffe Rd
E/WMAL ME19............152 D1
Trotts Hall Gdns SIT ME10......129 N2
Trotts La BH/WHM TN16............176 D5
Trotwood Cl WALD ME5............125 M5
Troughton Rd CHARL SE7............42 A1
Troutbeck Rd NWCR SE14............41 L2
Troy La EDEN TN8............206 A6
Troy Rd NRWD SE19............60 D5
Troys Md MAID ME17............187 N1
Troy Town PECK SE15............40 G4
Troy Town La RASHE TN25......254 C5
Trubridge Rd HOO/HM ME3............75 K2
Trueman Cl CANTW/ST CT2....135 P6
Trundleys Rd DEPT SE8............25 H8
Trundley's Rd DEPT SE8............24 G8
Trundley's Ter DEPT SE8............24 F7
Truro Cl RHAM ME8............96 G3
Truro Rd GVE DA12............69 P2
RAM CT11............17 H3
Truro Wk TOWN TN10............210 G5
Trusedale Rd EHAM E6............26 E2
Truslove Rd WNWD SE27............60 A4
Trycevell La BGR/WK TN15......150 G6
Tuann Rd WOOL/PLUM SE18......27 L9
Tubbenden Cl ORP BR6............86 F6
Tubbenden Dr ORP BR6............86 E8
Tubbenden La ORP BR6............86 E9
Tubbenden La South ORP BR6..86 E9
Tubs Hl SEV TN15............20 D1
Tubs Hill Pde SEV TN13 *............20 D1
Tudeley La RTON TN11............241 L1
TON TN9............240 F2
Tudeley Rd RTON TN11............241 H2
Tudor Av LYDD TN29............327 H5
MAID/BEAR ME14............155 N6
Tudor Byway KEN/WIL TN24....252 C4
Tudor Cl BRCH CT7............111 J5
CHST SE7............63 K7
DART DA1............46 B7
ECRIN RH19............265 J9
GVW DA11............49 J9
Tudor Ct CANTW/ST CT2 *......166 B4
Tudor Dr RSEV TN14............149 H2
Tudor Dr RSEV TN14............149 H1
Tudor End KEN/WIL TN24......252 C4
Tudor Farm Cl ASH TN23............282 D5
Tudor Gdns WWKM BR4............84 F7
Tudor Gv HOO/HM ME3............72 F3
RHAM ME8............97 H6
Tudor Pde ELTH/MOT SE9 *......43 J5
Tudor Pl NRWD SE19 *............60 D5
Tudor Rd BECK BR3............62 A9
CANT CT1............4 C7
FOLKN CT19............310 A5
KEN/WIL TN24............252 C4
NRWD SE19............60 C6
PGE/AN SE20............61 J9
SWWD SE25............83 N2
Tudor Wy STMC/STPC BR5............86 E5
Tudway Rd BKHTH/KID SE3......42 C5
Tufa Cl WALD ME5............125 N4
Tufnail Rd DART DA1............46 F7
Tufton Rd KEN/WIL TN24............283 K1
RHAM ME8............97 J5
Tufton St ASH TN23............283 K1
MAID/BEAR ME14............13 G4
Tugboat St THMD SE28............27 M5
Tugela Rd CROY/NA CRO............83 J5
Tugela St CAT SE6............61 M1
Tugmutton Cl ORP BR6............86 C8
Tulip Cl CROY/NA CRO............84 A5
EHAM E6............26 F1
Tulip Tree Cl TON TN9............240 D8
Tulse Cl BECK BR3............62 A9
Tulse Hl BRXS/STRHM SW2......40 A8
Tulsemere Rd WNWD SE27............60 C1
Tumbledown Hl RASHE TN25..222 C7
Tumblefield Rd BGR/WK TN15 ..126 E9
Tunbury Av WALD ME5............125 L5
Tunbury Av South WALD ME5..125 L4
Tunis Ct CANT CT1............167 J3
Tunis Rw BRDST CT10............113 N8
Tunley Gn POP/IOD E14............25 J1
Tunnan Leys EHAM E6............27 K2
Tunnel Av GNWCH SE10............25 N5
Tunnel Rd BERM/RHTH SE16......24 F3
RTW TN1............22 E2
Tunstall Ct ORP BR6............86 F8
Tunstall Rd CANTW/ST CT2......136 F9
CROY/NA CRO............83 K5
RSIT ME9............129 K5
Tunstock Wy BELV DA17............28 G8
Tupman Ct ROCH ME1............18 D7
Tuppy St THMD SE28............27 K6
Turgis Rd RMAID ME17............187 H1
Turketel Rd FOLK CT20............10 D6
Turkey Oak Cl NRWD SE19......60 E7
Turmine St IOS ME12............57 J6
Turmine St IOS ME12............78 A2
Turnagain La CANT CT1............4 A3
Turnberry Cl BERM/RHTH SE16..24 G8
Turnberry Wy ORP BR6............86 E5
Turnbridge Wy ASH TN23......251 P9
Turnbull Cl RDART DA2............47 L8
Turnbury Cl THMD SE28............28 C2
Turnden Gdns MARG CT9............113 K3
Turnden Rd CRBK TN17............297 N4
Turner Av CRBK TN17............298 A4
Turner Cl BRXN/ST SW9............285 H1
KEN/WIL TN24............285 H1
Turner Ct CMBW SE5 *............40 C6
DART DA1............46 C6
ECRIN RH19............265 K5
Turner Rd BH/WHM TN16............115 M6
Turner's Av TENT TN30............301 J7
Turners Gdns SEV TN13............36 B3
Turners Green La WADH TN5..294 A8
Turners Green Rd WADH TN5..294 A8
Turner's Hill Rd EGRIN RH19..264 F9

Turners Meadow Wy
BECK BR3............61 M7
Turner's Oak Shaw HART DA3..91 H6
Turner's Pl DVW DA4 *............67 J7
Turner's Rd BOW E3............25 J1
Turner St CAN/RD E16............26 A2
HOO/HM ME3............72 A1
RAM CT11............17 G3
WCHPL E1............24 E1
Turners Wy CROY/NA CRO............82 B4
Turney Rd DUL SE21............40 C8
Turnham Rd BROCKY SE4............41 M1
Turnpike Dr ORP BR6............117 K3
Turnpike Hl HYTHE CT21......308 F10
Turnpike La TIL RM18............33 L8
Turnpike Link CROY/NA CRO....83 K6
Turnstone HART DA3............68 D9
Turnstone Rd RSIT ME9............99 M2
SAND/SEL CR2............114 B4
Turnstone Rd WALD ME5............125 P5
The Turnstones CVE DA12............69 P1
Turp Av CDW/CHF RM16............32 D5
Turpin Cl WAP E1W *............24 F4
Turpington Cl HAYES BR2............85 P5
Turpington La HAYES BR2............85 P7
Turpin La ERITH DA8............30 C5
Turpins Yd GNWCH SE10............42 A1
Tuscan Dr WALD ME5............125 N3
Tuscan Rd WOOL/PLUM SE18..27 L8
Tuskar St GNWCH SE10............25 P8
Tutsham Wy STPH/PW TN12..242 G3
Tuxford Rd SBGH/RUST TN4..269 N3
Tweed TIL RM18............34 B7
Tweed Rd TONN TN10............210 F5
Tweed Ter HYTHE CT21 *............308 F6
Tweedy Rd BMLY BR1............62 E1
Twelve Acres KEN/WIL TN24..253 H9
Twickenham Cl CROY/NA CRO ..82 E7
Twigg Ct ERITH DA8............45 N1
Twine Ct WCHPL E1............24 F3
The Twins CRBK TN17 *............246 D6
Twin Tumps Wy THMD SE28....27 P3
Twisleton Ct DART DA1............46 D7
Twiss Av HYTHE CT21............309 H9
Twiss Gv HYTHE CT21............309 J5
Twiss Rd HYTHE CT21............309 J5
Twitten La EGRIN RH19............264 G4
The Twitten LING RH7............234 G5
Twitton La HOO/HM ME3............71 P2
Twycross Ms GNWCH SE10......25 P7
Twydall Gn RHAM ME8............96 E3
Twydall La RHAM ME8............96 E4
Twyford Cl MARG CT9............15 L7
Twyford Ct MAID/BEAR ME14..156 A6
Twyford Rd RTON TN11............211 P1
Twyhurst Ct EGRIN RH19......264 G5
Twyne Cl CANTW/ST CT2............137 M7
Tydeman Rd
MAID/SHEP ME15............186 C1
Tye La ORP BR6............86 C1
Tyers Est STHWK SE1 *............24 B5
Tyers Ga STHWK SE1............24 B6
Tyeshurst Cl ABYW SE2............28 D8
Tyland La MAID/BEAR ME14..155 L1
Tyler Cl CANTW/ST CT2............166 E1
E/WMAL ME19............153 N4
ERITH DA8............45 K1
Tyler Dr RHAM ME8............127 H1
Tyler Hill Rd CANTW/ST CT2..135 P7
Tylers Green Rd SWLY BR8............88 B3
Tyler St GNWCH SE10............25 P8
Tyler Wy WSTB CT5............106 D3
Tylney Av NRWD SE19............60 F4
Tylney Rd BMLY BR1............63 H8
Tyndale Pk HB CT6............107 N2
Tyndall Rd WELL DA16............44 B4
Tyne Cl WALD ME5............95 N9
Tynedale Cl RDART DA2............47 K9
Tyne Gdns SOCK/AV RM15......30 F3
Tynemouth Cl EHAM E6............27 J2
Tynemouth Rd
WOOL/PLUM SE18............27 M8
Tyne Rd TONN TN10............210 E5
Tyne St WCHPL E1............24 C2
Typhoon Rd E/WMAL ME19......152 C9
Tyrawley Rd FUL/PGN SW6......307 P6
Tyrell Av WELL DA16............64 A3
Tyrrell Rd EDUL SE22............40 C5
Tyrrells Hall Cl GRAYS RM17....32 E2
Tyrwhitt Rd BROCKY SE4............41 N4
Tysoe Ct IOS ME12............57 J6
Tyson Av MARG CT9............111 P4
Tyson Gdns FSTH SE23............41 J8
Tyson Rd FOLKN CT19............311 H4
FSTH SE23............41 J8

U

Uamvar St POP/IOD E14............25 L1
Uckfield La EDEN TN8............237 K4
Uden Rd LYDD TN29............327 L2
Udimore Rd RYE TN31............338 B8
Uffington Ct RCANTE CT3......199 H5
Uffington Rd WNWD SE27............60 A3
Ufton Cl MAID/SHEP ME15......186 B2
Ufton La SIT ME10............129 M2
Ulcombe Gdns CANTW/ST CT2..166 F1
Ulcombe Hl RMAID ME17............218 A1
Ulcombe Rd HDCN TN27............247 N5
RMAID ME17............187 H8
Ulleswater Rd BMLY BR1............62 C5
Ullswater Gdns RCANTE CT5..199 J9
Ullswater Rd WNWD SE27............60 B1
Ulstan Cl CTHM CR3............136 A9
Ulundi Rd BKHTH/KID SE3......42 C6
Ulverscroft Rd EDUL SE22............40 G6
Undercliffe St WCHPL E1 *............24 C2
Undercliff FOLK CT20............310 D8
Undercliffe Rd DEAL CT14......263 J4

Undercliff Rd LEW SE13............41 N4
Underdown Av CHAT ME4............95 L5
Underdown La HB CT6............107 L3
Underdown Rd DVW CT17............291 J8
HB CT6............107 L1
Underhill Rd EDUL SE22............40 G6
FOLK CT20............309 N2
Underlyn La STPH/PW TN12..245 H1
Underriver House Rd
BGR/WK TN15............179 P8
Undershaft HDTCH EC3A............24 B1
Undershaw Rd BMLY BR1............62 C2
Underwood CROY/NA CRO............114 F1
DART DA1............238 E6
Underwood Cl KEN/WIL TN24..252 G5
MAID/SHEP ME15............185 L1
Underwood St
RPLK CT18............144 F6
The Underwood
ELTH/MOT SE9............63 K1
Undine Rd POP/IOD E14............25 L7
Unicorn Wk RDART DA2............47 M6
Union Ct OBST EC2N............24 B2
Union Crs MARG CT9............15 H4
Union Pk GNWCH SE10............26 A8
Union Rd BXLYHN DA7............45 L5
MAID/SHEP ME15 *............186 C7
CROY/NA CRO............83 H4
DEAL CT14............233 J3
HAYES BR2............85 N2
IOS ME12............58 D9
RAM CT11............143 L4
RCANTW CT4............197 L2
Union Rw MARG CT9............15 H4
Union St BRDST CT10............113 N9
RTWE/PEM TN2............22 C7
Union St CANT CT1............5 G2
CHAT ME4............6 D5
DVW CT17............9 G7
FAV ME13............132 F6
IOS ME12............57 J6
MAID/BEAR ME14............13 F4
RAM CT11............17 G3
RYE TN31............338 E6
WADH TN5............315 M5
Unity Cl CROY/NA CRO............114 E3
NRWD SE19............60 C4
Unity Ct IOS ME12............57 M6
Unity Pl RAM CT11............17 H2
Unity St IOS ME12............57 M6
SIT ME10............129 M2
Unity Wy WOOL/PLUM SE18....26 E6
University Gdns BXLY DA5......45 H8
University Pl ERITH DA8............45 K1
University Rd CANTW/ST CT2..166 C1
University Wy CAN/RD E16......27 H3
Unwin Cl DIT/AY ME20............154 F1
PECK SE15............24 D9
Upbury Wy CHAT ME4............6 E5
Upchat Rd HOO/HM ME3............72 E3
Upchurch Wk MARG CT9............113 K5
Updale Rd SCUP DA14............64 B2
Updown Wy RCANTW CT4......195 N2
Upfield CROY/NA CRO............83 N6
Upfield RFOLK CT18............288 E8
Upland Rd BXLYHN DA7............45 M4
CTHM CR3............144 D5
EDUL SE22............40 G8
SAND/SEL CR2............83 J9
Uplands BECK BR3............61 N8
CANTW/ST CT2............156 E9
Uplands Cl STRD ME2............71 M9
Uplands Rd ORP BR6............87 J5
Uplands Wy IOS ME12............77 L2
SEV TN13............148 E8
Uplees Rd FAV ME13............102 C8
Upnor Rd STRD ME2............72 D7
Upnor Wy WALW SE17 *............24 B8
Upper Abbey Rd BELV DA17......28 E7
Upper Approach Rd
BRDST CT10............143 M1
Upper Austin Lodge Rd
EYN DA4............119 K2
Upper Av RMAID ME17............69 J7
Upper Bank St POP/IOD E14....25 L4
Upper Barn Hl
MAID/SHEP ME15............184 D8
Upper Beulah Hl NRWD SE19....60 E7
Upper Brents FAV ME13............132 G4
Upper Bridge St CANT CT1............5 F6
RASHE TN25............224 A8
Upper Britton Pl GILL ME7............7 G3
Upper Brockley Rd
BROCKY SE4............41 M3
Upper Bush Rd STRD ME2............93 N4
Upper Chantry La CANT CT1......5 G6
Upper Court Rd CTHM CR3......144 D8
Upper Cumberland Wk
RTWE/PEM TN2............270 D2
Upper Dane Rd MARG CT9......112 F4
Upper Dunstan Rd
SBGH/RUST TN4............270 D2
Upper East Rd CHAT ME4............73 H8
Upper Fant Rd MAIDW ME16..185 H1
Upper Fant Rd MAIDW ME16..185 H1
Upper Fld Rd MAIDW ME16......100 A9
Upper Free Down HB CT6............143 G6
Upper Gore La SWCH CT13 *..201 H8
Upper Green Rd RTON TN11..180 F6
Upper Grosvenor Rd RTW TN1..22 D4
Upper Gv MARG CT9............15 H8
Upper Haysden La RTON TN11..240 A3
Upper Holly Hill Rd BELV DA17..29 J4
Upper Hunton Hl
MAID/SHEP ME15............184 F8
Upper Luton Rd WALD ME5............7 H7
Upper Malthouse Hl
HYTHE CT21............308 G5
Upper Mi E/WMAL ME19............153 N5
WBY/YAL ME18............183 L3

Upper Nellington RRTW TN3 * 269 N4
Upper North St POP/IOD E14 ....25 K1
Upper Park Rd BELV DA17 ....28 D7
  BMLY BR1 ....62 F7
Upper Profit RRTW TN3 * 269 M5
Upper Rd DVE/WH CT16 ....9 F1
  MAID/SHEP ME15 ....13 J7
  RDV CT15 ....292 C4
  WLGTN SM6 ....82 C9
Upper St Ann's Rd FAV ME13 ....132 E7
Upper Sheridan Rd BELV DA17 ....28 F7
Upper Shirley Rd
  CROY/NA CRO 83 P7
Upper Stephens RRTW TN3 * 269 M5
Upper Spring La 150 E7
Upper Stone St
  MAID/SHEP ME15 ....13 G6
Upper Strand St SWCH CT13 ....201 P1
Upper St DEAL CT14 ....231 H6
  DEAL CT14 ....263 J3
  RMAID ME17 ....157 P9
  RMAID ME17 ....187 J6
  WALD ME5 ....270 A4
Upperton Rd SCUP DA14 ....64 B4
Upper Vicarage Rd
  KEN/WIL TN24 ....252 G2
Upper Wickham La WELL DA16 ....48 D3
Upstall St CMBW SE5 ....18 E2
Upton Cl BXLY DA5 ....45 H7
  FOLKN CT19 ....310 D4
Upton Rd BRDST CT10 ....113 L8
  BXLYHS DA6 ....48 B5
  THHTH CR7 ....60 D8
  WOOL/PLUM SE18 ....27 K9
Upton Rd South BXLY DA5 ....45 H7
Uptons HDCN TN27 ....247 N3
Upwood Rd LEE/GVPK SE12 ....42 E7
Uridge Crs TONN TN10 ....210 F6
Uridge Rd TONN TN10 ....210 F6
Urwin Wk BRXN/ST SW9 ....40 A2
Urquhart Cl WALD ME5 ....95 M9
Ursuline Dr OXTED RH8 ....175 L6
Usborne Cl STPH/PW TN12 ....246 B6
Usk Rd SOCK/AV RM15 ....30 F2
Uvedale Cl CROY/NA CRO 114 C5
Uvedale Crs CROY/NA CRO 114 C5
Uvedale Rd OXTED RH8 ....175 J3

V

Valance Vw CRBK TN17 * 277 N1
Valan Leas HAYES BR2 ....62 C9
Vale Av RTW TN1 ....22 E5
  SBGH/RUST TN4 ....240 C8
Valebrook Cl FOLK CT20 ....310 E9
Vale Cl ORP BR6 ....86 B8
Vale Dr WALD ME5 ....95 J9
Vale End EDUL SE22 ....40 F5
Valence Rd ERITH DA8 ....48 A1
Valenciennes Rd SIT ME10 ....129 M2
Valentia Pl BRXN/ST SW9 ....40 A3
Valentine Cl DA5 GVE DA12 ....64 C1
Valentine Rd
  MAID/SHEP ME15 ....186 B4
Valentyne Cl CROY/NA CRO 115 N9
Vale Pl RAM CT11 ....16 B3
Valerian Cl WALD ME5 ....125 K1
Vale Ri TON TN9 ....210 C9
Vale Rd BMLY BR1 ....62 B9
  BRDST CT10 ....113 L9
  DART DA1 ....46 B9
  GVW DA11 ....46 D9
  HAWK TN18 ....317 H3
  MAID/SHEP ME15 ....185 K7
  RAM CT11 ....16 C4
  RDV CT15 ....262 A1
  TON TN9 ....210 D5
  SBGH/RUST TN4 ....240 C7
  TON TN9 ....240 F1
  WSTB CT5 ....105 L6
Vale Sq RAM CT11 ....16 B3
Valestone Cl HYTHE CT21 ....309 N3
Vale St DUL SE27 ....42 D2
Valeswood Rd BMLY BR1 ....62 D4
The Vale BRDST CT10 ....113 M9
  CROY/NA CRO 84 A6
Valetta Wy ROCH ME1 * 18 E8
Vale View Rd DVW CT17 ....291 J8
  RCANTE CT3 ....229 H1
Valiant Rd WALD ME5 ....125 P3
Valiant Wy EHAM E6 ....26 C1
Valkyrie Av WSTB CT5 ....105 J6
The Vallance RSIT ME9 ....130 F7
Valley Cl DART DA1 ....45 P7
  MAID/SHEP ME15 ....185 L5
  TON TN9 ....182 A9
  SEV TN13 ....31 F4
Valley Forge Cl TONN TN10 ....211 J6
Valley Gdns SWCM DA10 ....47 P7
Valley Gv CHARL SE7 ....26 B5
Valley La MEO CT13 ....122 B3
Valley Ri WALD ME5 ....125 L3
Valley Rd CANT CT1 ....166 D6
  DART DA1 ....45 P7
  DVW CT17 ....291 K8
  ERITH DA8 ....29 H7
  FOLK CT20 ....310 D7
  GILL ME7 ....96 B2
  HART DA3 ....90 D6
  HAYES BR2 ....62 C8
  MARG CT9 ....112 D9
  RCANTW CT4 ....228 B4
  SBGH/RUST TN4 ....270 A4
  STMC/STPC BR5 ....64 D7
The Valley RMAID ME17 * 185 J8
Valley Vw BH/WHM TN16 ....145 M3
  RDV CT15 ....230 D9
  SBGH/RUST TN4 ....240 C2
  SWCM DA10 ....47 P7
Valley View Rd ROCH ME1 ....94 G5
Valley View Ter EYN DA4 * 67 N4
Valley Wy CROY/NA CRO 83 P6
  HYTHE CT21 ....309 N4

Valliers Wood Rd BFN/LL DA15 ....43 P9
Valmar Rd CMBW SE5 ....40 C2
Vambery Rd WOOL/PLUM SE18 ....27 K9
Vanbrugh Flds BKHTH/KID SE3 ....26 A9
Vanbrugh Hl GNWCH SE10 ....25 P8
Vanbrugh Pk BKHTH/KID SE3 ....42 D1
Vanbrugh Park Rd
  BKHTH/KID SE3 ....42 D1
Vanbrugh Park Rd West
  BKHTH/KID SE3 ....42 D1
Vanbrugh Ter BKHTH/KID SE3 ....42 D2
Vanburgh Cl CAN/RD E16 ....26 E1
  ORP BR6 ....86 F5
Vancouver Cl ORP BR6 ....87 H8
Vancouver Dr RHAM ME8 ....96 F5
Vanessa Cl BELV DA17 ....29 K9
Vandome Cl CAN/RD E16 ....26 C2
Vandyke Cross ELTH/MOT SE9 ....43 J6
Vanessa Cl BELV DA17 * 28 F8
Vanessa Wk GVE DA12 ....70 B4
Vanessa Wy DA5 DA5 ....65 M2
Vange Cottage Ms
  ROCH ME1 * 18 E7
Vange Ms ROCH ME1 * 18 E7
Vanguard Cl CAN/RD E16 ....26 D1
  CROY/NA CRO 82 G5
Vanguard St DEPT SE8 ....41 N2
Vanguard Wy CROY/NA CRO 83 L8
  EDEN TN8 ....206 B1
  EDEN TN8 ....235 N2
  OXTED RH8 ....175 J1
  STRD ME2 ....72 E7
Vanity La RMAID ME17 ....215 J1
Vanity Rd IOS ME12 ....80 D6
Vanoc Gdns BMLY BR1 ....62 E3
Vanquisher Wk GVE DA12 ....70 B2
Vansittart St NWCR SE14 ....41 L1
Varcoe Rd BERM/RHTH SE16 ....24 E4
Varden St WCHPL E1 ....24 E2
Varley Rd CAN/RD E16 ....26 C2
Varne Pl FOLKN CT19 ....11 K3
Varley Rd FOLKN CT19 ....11 K3
Varnes St DIT/AY ME20 ....124 E7
Vassall Rd BRXN/ST SW9 ....40 A1
Vauban Est
  BERM/RHTH SE16 * 24 C4
Vauban St BERM/RHTH SE16 ....24 C4
Vaughan Av TONN TN10 ....211 H4
Vaughan Rd SIT ME10 ....99 N6
Vaughan Rd WELL DA16 * 48 C3
  WELL DA16 ....48 C3
Vaughan St BERM/RHTH SE16 ....25 J5
Vaughan Wy WAP E1W 24 B2
Vaughan Williams Cl DEPT SE8 ....41 N1
Vauxhall Av CANT CT1 ....167 H1
  HB CT6 ....106 F3
Vauxhall Cl GVW DA11 ....49 K8
Vauxhall Crs CANT CT1 * 167 H1
  SNOD ME6 ....123 N7
Vauxhall Gdns RTON TN11 ....240 F2
Vauxhall Industrial Est
  CANT CT1 ....137 H9
Vauxhall La SBGH/RUST TN4 ....240 C6
Vauxhall Pl DART DA1 ....46 E8
Vauxhall Rd CANTW/ST CT2 ....137 H9
Vectis Dr SIT ME10 ....99 N6
Veda Rd LEW SE13 ....41 N5
Venetian Rd CMBW SE5 ....40 C3
Venete Ct RAIN RM13 ....29 N1
Venner Rd SYD SE26 ....61 J5
Venners Cl BXLYHN DA7 ....45 N3
Ventnor Cl WALD ME5 ....95 P6
Ventnor Rd NWCR SE14 ....41 K1
Venture Cl BXLY DA5 ....44 C8
  LYDD TN29 ....327 H5
Venue St POP/IOD E14 ....25 N1
Venus Rd WOOL/PLUM SE18 ....26 G6
Verbania Wy EGRIN RH19 ....265 L1
Verbena Cl CAN/RD E16 ....26 D1
Verdant La CAT SE6 ....62 D2
Verdayne Av CROY/NA CRO 84 A5
Verdun Rd WOOL/PLUM SE18 ....27 P9
Vere Rd BRDST CT10 ....113 M9
Vereth Rd RAM CT11 ....16 D5
Vermont Rd NRWD SE19 ....60 D5
  SBGH/RUST TN4 ....240 A7
Verney Rd BERM/RHTH SE16 ....24 E4
Verney Wy BERM/RHTH SE16 ....24 E5
Vernham Rd
  WOOL/PLUM SE18 ....27 K9
Vernon Cl BGR/WK TN15 ....120 C3
  STMC/STPC BR5 ....64 E4
Vernon Pl CANT CT1 * 233 J1
  DEAL CT14 ....233 J1
Vernon Rd RTW TN1 ....270 F2
  SWM DA10 ....48 D7
Veroan Rd BXLYHN DA7 ....48 A5
Verona Gdns GVE DA12 ....70 A3
Versailles Rd PGE/AN SE20 ....60 C6
Verwood Cl CANTW/ST CT2 ....158 C2
Veryan Cl STMC/STPC BR5 ....87 H1
Vesper Ct HDCN TN27 ....249 H8
Vesta Rd BROCKY SE4 ....41 L3
Vestey St WGOS CT8 ....111 M4
Vesta Rd FSTH SE23 ....61 K1
Vestry Ms CMBW SE5 ....40 D3
Vestry Rd CMBW SE5 ....40 E2
  RSEV TN14 ....148 G4
Vevey St CAT SE6 ....61 M1
Vexil Cl PUR RM19 ....31 N1
Viaduct Cl CANT CT12 ....143 H4
Viaduct Ter EYN DA4 * 67 J8
  RASHW TN26 * 304 C8
The Viaduct DVW CT17 ....313 L1
Vian St LEW SE13 ....41 P4
Via Romana GVE DA12 ....50 D9
Viburnum Cl ASH TN23 ....252 D7
Vicarage Cl BECK BR3 * 61 L9
Vicarage Crs MARG CT9 * 15 H7
Vicarage Dr BECK BR3 ....61 N7
  GVW DA11 ....48 G1
Vicarage Gdn MSTR CT12 ....140 D5
Vicarage Gdns RCANTE CT3 ....169 K9

Vicarage Gv CMBW SE5 ....40 D2
Vicarage Hl BH/WHM TN16 ....176 E2
Vicarage La ASH TN23 ....2 E4
  DEAL CT14 ....231 H6
  DEAL CT14 ....263 J3
  FAV ME15 ....182 D8
  FAV ME15 ....163 L6
  GVE DA12 ....70 C1
  HOO/HM ME3 ....220 B3
  HOO/HM ME3 ....54 E5
  MAID/SHEP ME15 ....184 G4
  RCANTW CT4 ....257 L5
  RCANTW CT4 ....229 M1
  RDV CT15 ....292 E1
  RSIT ME9 ....98 D3
  SEV TN13 ....148 C4
  SWCH CT13 ....201 N1
Vicarage Pk WOOL/PLUM SE18 ....27 K8
Vicarage Rd BXLY DA5 ....45 K9
  CROY/NA CRO 82 F7
  GILL ME7 ....7 G3
  IOS ME12 ....80 C6
  LING RH7 ....234 G5
  SBGH/RUST TN4 ....240 C7
  SEV TN13 ....148 C4
  STRD ME2 ....93 M9
  WBY/YAL ME18 ....213 P1
  WOOL/PLUM SE18 ....27 K7
Vicarage Sq GRAYS RM17 ....32 B9
Vicarage St WAR ME17 ....113 J8
  WARL CR6 ....111 L6
Vicarage Wy RHAM ME8 * 96 E3
Vicars Hl LEW SE13 ....41 P5
Vicars Oak Rd NRWD SE19 ....60 E5
Vicary Wy MAIDW ME16 ....155 J7
Vickers Cl RFOLK CT18 ....288 D8
Vickers Rd ERITH DA8 ....48 C3
Victor Av MARG CT9 ....113 J3
Victoria Av BRDST CT10 ....113 K5
  ELTH/MOT SE9 ....43 L5
  HYTHE CT21 ....308 C5
  MARG CT9 ....112 G4
  RDV CT15 ....292 C1
Victoria Cl CDW/CHF RM16 ....31 J7
  RMAID ME17 ....218 F5
  WALD ME5 ....125 J3
Victoria Cots WCHPL E1 * 24 D1
Victoria Ct HYTHE CT21 ....309 H6
  MAIDW ME16 ....12 C6
Victoria Crs ASH TN23 ....3 D6
  DVE/WH CT16 ....8 B2
  NRWD SE19 ....60 D5
Victoria Dock Rd CAN/RD E16 ....26 A2
Victoria Dr E/WMAL ME19 ....182 C1
  EYN DA4 ....67 K8
  HB CT6 ....107 H1
Victoria Gdns BH/WHM TN16 ....115 M9
Victoria Gv FOLK CT20 ....10 C4
  HYTHE CT21 ....308 G3
Victoria Rd ASH TN23 ....3 D5
  BFN/LL DA15 ....64 B2
  BRDST CT10 ....113 K7
  CANT CT1 ....6 D4
  CHAT ME4 ....95 N4
  CHST BR7 ....63 L4
  DART DA1 ....46 D6
  DEAL CT14 ....233 J4
  EDEN TN8 ....236 D1
  ERITH DA8 ....29 K9
  FOLKN CT19 ....10 D3
  GVW DA11 ....46 D9
  HAYES BR2 ....85 N2
  HYTHE CT21 ....309 H6
  MARG CT9 ....15 H6
  NROM TN28 ....337 K8
  RAM CT11 ....17 J1
  RFOLK CT18 ....311 L1
  RTON TN11 ....212 A4
  RTW TN1 ....22 E2
  SBGH/RUST TN4 ....240 B8
  SEV TN13 ....148 C4
  SIT ME10 ....129 L1
  WALD ME5 ....125 K5
Victoria Rd West NROM TN28 ....337 J8
Victoria Rw CANT CT1 * 5 H4
Victoria St BELV DA17 ....28 C8
  DIT/AY ME20 ....124 E7
  DVW CT17 ....291 J6
Victoria Ter IOS ME12 * 7 J2
  IOS ME12 ....57 K7
  MAIDW ME16 ....12 B5
  NROM TN28 ....336 F7
  ROCH ME1 ....19 G6
  WSTB CT5 ....105 K7
Victoria Ter IOS ME12 * 78 G2
  ROCH ME1 ....94 F4
Victoria Vls RTW TN1 ....23 F5
Victoria Wy CHARL SE7 ....26 C8
  EGRIN RH19 ....265 J9
Victoria Works
  STMC/STPC BR5 ....86 D2
Victoria Yd WCHPL E1 * 24 D2
Victory Rd CDW/CHF RM16 ....31 M7
Victory Pk STRD ME2 ....19 K2
Victory Rd RDV CT15 ....262 E7
  SIT ME10 ....57 K6
Victory Wy BERM/RHTH SE16 ....25 H5
  RDART DA2 ....47 J5
Victory Wd WOOL/PLUM SE18 ....27 P8
View Cl BH/WHM TN16 ....145 M1
View Rd HOO/HM ME3 ....54 E1
Viewfield Rd BFN/LL DA15 ....44 A8
Viewland Rd
  WOOL/PLUM SE18 ....27 N8
Viewlands Av BH/WHM TN16 ....146 F5

View Rd HOO/HM ME3 ....52 B9
The View ABYW SE2 ....28 D8
Vigerons Wy CDW/CHF RM16 ....33 J7
Vigilant Cl SYD SE26 ....60 G3
Vigilant Wy GVE DA12 ....70 B4
Vigo Hl BGR/WK TN15 ....121 P7
Vigo Rd BGR/WK TN15 ....121 P6
Viking Cl BRCH CT7 ....110 E5
  STRD ME2 ....18 A7
Viking Gdns EHAM E6 ....26 E1
Viking Cl GVW DA11 ....48 G4
Viking Wy BGR/WK TN15 ....90 B9
  ERITH DA8 ....29 H6
Villa Cl GVE DA12 ....70 D1
Villacourt Rd
  WOOL/PLUM SE18 ....44 C1
Village Green Av
  BH/WHM TN16 ....145 P2
Village Green Rd DART DA1 ....46 A5
Village Green Wy
  BH/WHM TN16 ....145 P2
The Village CHARL SE7 ....26 D9
Village Vw WALD ME5 ....95 H4
Village Wy BECK BR3 ....61 N3
  DUL SE21 ....42 D7
  RHAM ME8 ....96 A3
Villan Rd
  NROM TN28 ....304 D8
Villa Rd BRXN/ST SW9 ....40 A4
  HOO/HM ME3 ....71 H4
Villas Rd WOOL/PLUM SE18 ....27 K7
Villa St WALW SE17 ....24 A8
Villiers Rd BECK BR3 ....61 K8
  CANT CT1 ....167 J5
Vincennes Est WNWD SE27 * 60 D5
Vincent Cl BFN/LL DA15 ....44 A9
  BRDST CT10 ....143 H1
  FOLK CT20 ....310 B7
  HAYES BR2 ....85 J2
Vincent Gdns IOS ME12 ....57 L7
Vincent Pl KEN/WIL TN24 ....253 J5
Vincent Rd CROY/NA CRO 83 K4
  DIT/AY ME20 ....125 H6
  MARG CT9 ....112 B9
  SIT ME10 ....130 B2
  WOOL/PLUM SE18 ....27 J7
Vincents Cl BERM/RHTH SE16 ....25 H5
Vincents Ct BH/WHM TN16 ....15 M9
Vincent St CAN/RD E16 ....26 D1
Vine Av SEV TN13 ....31 F1
Vine Cl DART DA11 ....143 K2
Vine Cots WCHPL E1 * 24 F2
Vine Ct RHAM ME8 ....96 A4
Vine Cots WCHPL E1 * 24 E2
Vine Court Rd SEV TN13 ....21 C1
Vinegar St WAP E1W 24 E4
Vinegar Yd STHWK SE1 * 24 E4
Vine Lands LYDD TN29 ....342 A6
Vine La STHWK SE1 * 24 E4
The Vineries CAT SE6 ....41 N9
  GILL ME7 ....96 B1
Vine Rd BMLY BR1 ....116 C1
Viners Cl SIT ME10 ....129 M4
Vines La ROCH ME1 ....19 F5
  RTON TN11 ....209 P1
Vine St TWRH EC3N 24 C2
Vine Street Crs TWRH EC3N * 24 C2
The Vine SEV TN13 ....21 C1
Vine Wk STPH/PW TN12 ....246 B6
Vineyard Cl CAT SE6 ....41 N9
Vineyard Crs EHAM E6 * 26 C2
Vineyard La WADH TN5 ....314 F4
Viney Bank CROY/NA CRO 114 C3
Viney Rd LEW SE13 ....41 P4
Viney's Gdns TENT TN30 ....301 K6
Vinson Cl FAV ME13 ....133 N4
  ORP BR6 ....87 H4
Vinten Cl HB CT6 ....107 N6
Vinters Pk
  MAID/BEAR ME14 * 156 A7
Vinters Rd MAID/BEAR ME14 ....13 J4
Vintners Wy
  MAID/BEAR ME14 ....156 B8
Violet Av ORP BR6 ....87 H5
Violet Cl CROY/NA CRO 83 J4
Violet Ct MSTR CT12 ....148 A2
Violet Rd WALD ME5 ....125 J3
Violet Gdns CROY/NA CRO 82 G9
Violet La SAND/SEL CR2 ....82 G9
The Violets STPH/PW TN12 ....243 H4
Virginia Rd GILL ME7 ....73 J8
  THHTH CR7 ....60 B7
  WSTB CT5 ....105 M7
Virginia St WCHPL E1 * 24 D3
Viscount Dr EHAM E6 ....26 C1
Vixen Cl WALD ME5 ....125 N1
The Vista ELTH/MOT SE9 ....43 H7
Vivian Sq PECK SE15 * 41 H3
Vixen Cl WALD ME5 ....125 N1
Vlissingen Dr DEAL CT14 ....233 H1
Voce Rd WOOL/PLUM SE18 ....45 J1
Volante Ct SIT ME10 ....99 M7
Volante Wy CROY/NA CRO 82 G1
Voyagers Cl THMD SE28 * 27 P7
Vulcan Cl EHAM E6 ....26 C2
  MAID/SHEP ME15 ....95 M7
  WSTB CT5 ....105 K7
Vulcan Rd BROCKY SE4 ....41 M7
Vulcan Ter BROCKY SE4 * 41 M7
Vulcan Wy CROY/NA CRO 115 H4
The Vyne BXLYHN DA7 ....48 A5
Wacher Cl CANTW/ST CT2 ....156 E2
Waddington St PECK SE15 * 41 H3
Waddon Cl CROY/NA CRO 82 F7
Waddon Court Rd
  CROY/NA CRO 82 F8
Waddon Marsh Wy
  CROY/NA CRO 82 E5
Waddon New Rd
  CROY/NA CRO 82 F7
Waddon Park Av
  CROY/NA CRO 82 F8
Waddon Rd CROY/NA CRO 82 F7
Wade Av STMC/STPC BR5 ....87 L4
Wade House STHWK SE1 * 24 C5
Wades Cl LYDD TN29 ....325 P9
Wade's Pl POP/IOD E14 ....25 L3

Wadeville Cl BELV DA17 ....28 F8
Wadham Pl SIT ME10 ....130 A3
Wadhurst Cl KEN/WIL SE20 ....61 H8
Wadlands Brook Rd
  EGRIN RH19 ....264 G5
Wadlands Rd HOO/HM ME3 ....52 B3
Wagg G EGRIN RH19 ....265 K7
Waghorn Rd SNOD ME6 ....123 P5
Waghorn St CHAT ME4 ....95 N4
  PECK SE15 ....40 G4
Wagner St PECK SE15 ....41 J1
Wagoners Cl
  MAID/BEAR ME14 ....156 B8
Wagon La STPH/PW TN12 ....213 K9
Wagtail Gdns SAND/SEL CR2 ....114 A4
Wagtail Wk BECK BR3 ....84 F2
Wagtail Wy STMC/STPC BR5 ....87 L1
Waid Cl DART DA1 ....46 F7
Wain Ct IOS ME12 ....78 A2
Wainscott Rd STRD ME2 * 78 A2
Wainscott Wk STRD ME2 ....72 D4
Wainwright Pl KEN/WIL TN24 ....252 C9
Waite Davies Rd
  LEE/GVPK SE12 ....42 B8
Waite St CMBW SE5 ....24 C9
Wakefield Gdns SEV TN13 ....59 E6
Wakefield Rd SWCM DA10 ....48 A6
Wakehurst Cl RMAID ME17 ....184 C8
Wakeley Rd RHAM ME8 ....97 K5
Wakeling St WCHPL E1 * 25 H2
Wakely Cl BH/WHM TN16 ....145 M3
Wake Rd ROCH ME1 ....95 H6
Walbrook MANHO EC4N 24 A3
Walburgh St WCHPL E1 * 24 E2
Walchrenen Cl DEAL CT14 ....233 H1
Walcot Pl HB CT6 ....107 N3
Waldeck Gv NWNWD SE27 ....60 B2
Waldeck Rd DART DA1 ....46 F8
Waldegrave Rd BMLY BR1 ....85 P2
  NRWD SE19 ....60 E5
Waldegrove CROY/NA CRO 83 L7
Walden Av CHST BR7 ....63 K3
Walden Cl BELV DA17 ....28 E8
Walden Ct CANTW/ST CT12 * 166 F1
Walden Gdns THHTH CR7 ....82 E1
Waldenhurst Rd
  STMC/STPC BR5 ....87 L4
Walden Pde CHST BR7 * 87 L3
Walden Rd CHST BR7 ....63 K3
Waldens Cl STMC/STPC BR5 ....87 L4
Waldenshaw Rd FSTH SE23 ....41 J9
Waldens Rd STMC/STPC BR5 ....87 M3
The Waldens RMAID ME17 * 187 P9
Walden St WCHPL E1 * 24 E2
Waldershare Av RDV CT15 ....202 F3
Waldershare Rd CHAT ME3 ....95 K6
  WALD ME5 ....95 L9
Waldron Cl WCHPL E1 * 95 L9
Walderslade Village By Pass
  WALD ME5 ....125 L2
Walderslade Woods
  WALD ME5 ....125 L2
Waldon TIL RM18 ....34 A7
Waldo Rd BMLY BR1 ....62 G9
Waldram Crs FSTH SE23 ....41 J9
Waldrist Wy ERITH DA18 ....28 E5
Waldron Dr MAID/SHEP ME15 ....185 L5
Waldron Gdns HAYES BR2 ....62 B9
Waldron Rd BRDST CT10 ....113 M9
The Waldrons CROY/NA CRO 82 G8
  OXTED RH8 ....175 J7
Waldstock Rd THMD SE28 ....27 P3
Walerand Rd LEW SE13 ....42 A3
Wales Cl PECK SE15 * 24 B1
Waley St WCHPL E1 * 24 G1
Walkden Rd CHST BR7 ....63 L3
Walker Cl DART DA1 ....45 P4
  WOOL/PLUM SE18 ....27 J8
Walker La BRCH CT7 ....110 E5
Walkerscroft Md CAT SE6 ....61 P1
  DUL SE21 ....42 C9
Walkhurst Rd CRBK TN17 ....299 H8
Walkley Rd DART DA1 ....46 E6
The Walk OXTED RH8 ....174 D9
Wallace Cl RTWE/PEM TN2 ....270 D8
  THMD SE28 ....27 N6
Wallace Gdns SWCM DA10 ....48 C7
Wallace Ms FOLKN CT19 ....310 C6
Wallace Rd GRAYS RM17 ....32 B7
  ROCH ME1 ....95 K6
Wallace Wy BRDST CT10 ....113 K9
Wallbridge La RMAID ME17 ....184 A8
Wallbutton Rd BROCKY SE4 ....41 L3
Wall Cl HOO/HM ME3 ....53 K9
Wall End Rd EHAM E6 ....26 E1
Waller Hl CRBK TN17 ....276 E3
Waller Rd MAID/SHEP ME15 * 343 K5
  NWCR SE14 ....41 K2
Wallers RRTW TN3 ....269 N1
Wallers Rd FAV ME13 ....132 D6
Wallhouse Rd ERITH DA8 ....48 D1
Wallis Av MAID/SHEP ME15 ....186 B4
Wallis Cl RDART DA2 ....66 G3
Wallis Ct HB CT6 ....108 C6
Wallis Pk GVW DA11 ....48 F6
Wallis Rd KEN/WIL TN24 ....3 J5
Wall Rd KEN/WIL TN24 ....99 M9
The Wall SIT ME10 ....99 M9
Wallwood Rd RAM CT11 ....17 J1
Wallwood St POP/IOD E14 ....25 J1
Walmer Castle Rd DEAL CT14 ....114 D8
Walmer Cl ORP BR6 ....86 E8
Walmer Ct DEAL CT14 * 232 C8
Walmer Gdns DEAL CT14 ....232 F7
  SIT ME10 ....99 J3
Walmer Rd WSTB CT5 ....105 M6
Walmers Av HOO/HM ME3 ....71 J3
Walmer Ter
  WOOL/PLUM SE18 ....27 K7
Walmer Wy DEAL CT14 ....232 F7
  FOLK CT20 ....310 C6
Walmsley Rd BRDST CT10 ....113 L8
Walner Gdns NROM TN28 ....336 C6
Walner La NROM TN28 ....336 G6

Walnut Cl BRDST CT10 .....143 L2
DEPT SE8 .....25 J9
EYN DA4 .....89 J7
KEN/WIL TN24 .....252 C5
STPH/PW TN12 .....243 H3
WALD ME5 .....91 N6
Walnut Hill Rd MEO DA13 .....69 J9
Walnuts Rd ORP BR6 .....87 H5
Walnut Tree Av DART DA1 .....66 E1
MAID/SHEP ME15 .....185 M6
Walnut Tree Cl
BH/WHM TN16 .....176 E2
CHST BR7 .....63 N7
Walnut Tree Ct DIT/AY DA13 .....154 A3
Walnut Tree St SIT ME10 .....129 L1
Walnut Tree La
CANTW/ST CT2 .....137 P6
MAID/SHEP ME15 .....185 M6
Walnut Tree Ms HYTHE CT21 *.....309 H5
Walnut Tree Rd ERITH DA8 .....29 K8
GNWCH SE10 .....25 P8
Walnut Tree Wy MEO DA13 .....92 B5
Walnut Wy SBGH/RUST TN4 .....240 C9
SWLY BR8 .....65 M8
Walpole Cl E/WMAL ME19 .....153 N1
GRAYS RM17 .....32 D7
Walpole Rd CROY/NA CRO 3 J6
HAYES BR2 .....119 H6
MARG CT9 .....15 H3
Walsby Dr SIT ME10 .....99 P6
Walsham Cl THMD SE28 .....28 C3
Walsham Rd NWCR SE14 .....41 K3
WALD ME5 .....125 L4
Walsh Crs CROY/NA CRO 115 J6
Walsingham Cl RHAM ME8 .....126 C2
Walsingham Pk CHST BR7 .....63 P6
Walsingham Rd
CROY/NA CRO 114 F4
STMC/STPC BR5 .....64 D7
Walsingham Wk BELV DA17 .....28 F9
Walter Burke Av RCANTE ME1 *.....94 B9
Walter's Farm Rd TON TN9 .....210 F9
Walters Green Rd RTON TN11 .....268 D2
Walters Rd HOO/HM ME3 .....73 L1
Walters St SNWD SE25 .....83 K1
Walters Wy FSTH SE23 .....41 K7
Walters Yd BMLY BR1 .....62 E8
Walter Ter WCHPL E1 .....24 C2
Waltham Cl DART DA1 .....46 A7
KEN/WIL TN24 .....253 J7
MARG CT9 .....113 K5
STMC/STPC BR5 .....64 D7
Waltham Rd RCANTW CT4 .....225 N1
RHAM ME8 .....96 E3
Walton Gdns FOLKN CT19 .....310 C4
Walton Gn CROY/NA CRO 114 C5
Walton Manor Cl FOLKN CT19 .....310 C4
Walton Rd FOLKN CT19 .....10 E1
SCUP DA14 .....64 D2
TONN TN10 .....210 D6
Walton's Hall Rd SLH/COR SS17 *.....33 P5
The Waltons FOLKN CT19 .....310 F3
Wambrook Wy MTCM CR4 .....82 B7
Walt Whitman Cl HNHL SE24 *.....40 B5
Walwyn Av BMLY BR1 .....62 G2
Wanden La HDCN TN27 .....219 J9
Wandle Court Gdns
CROY/NA CRO 82 D7
Wandle Rd WLGTN SM6 .....82 A6
Wandle Side CROY/NA CRO 82 C7
WLGTN SM6 .....82 A7
Wanless Rd NHNL SE24 .....40 C4
Wanley Rd CMBW SE5 .....88 D5
Wansbury Wy SWLY BR8 .....88 F2
Wanstead Cl BMLY BR1 .....62 G8
Wanstead Rd BMLY BR1 .....62 G8
Wantage Rd BXLY DA5 .....45 L9
Wantage Rd LEE/GVPK SE12 .....42 D6
Wantsum Cl HB CT6 .....77 M3
Wantsume Lees SWCH CT13 .....171 M9
Wantsum Wk RCANTE CT3 .....189 J2
Wapping Wy WBCH CT7 .....109 P8
Wapping Dock St WAP E1W *.....24 E4
Wapping High St WAP E1W 24 E4
Wapping Wall WAP E1W 24 E3
Warbank Cl CROY/NA CRO 115 H4
Warbank Crs CROY/NA CRO 115 H4
Warberry Park Gdns
SBGH/RUST TN4 .....270 B4
Warblers Cl STRD ME2 .....18 C1
Warburton Cl EGRIN RH19 .....265 K17
Wardalls Gv NWCR SE14 .....41 J1
Ward Av GRAYS RM17 .....32 C7
Ward Rd ERITH DA8 .....29 J3
SAND/SEL CR2 .....83 K9
Warden Bay Rd IOS ME12 .....40 D1
Warden La MAIDW ME16 .....155 H8
Warden House Ms DEAL CT14 .....232 F5
Warden Mill Cl
WBY/HLL SE18 .....183 L4
Warden Point Wy WSTB CT5 .....105 K8
Warden Rd IOS ME12 .....79 L3
ROCH ME1 .....91 J4
Warden Ter WBY/MAL ME18 *.....183 L5
Warden View Gdns IOS ME12 .....80 A6
Wardes WBY/MAL ME18 *.....183 L5
Wardour Cl BRDST CT10 .....113 N9
Wardrobe Pl WADH TN5 .....315 H7
Wards Hill Rd IOS ME12 .....58 B8
Ward's La WADH TN5 .....314 C3
Wards Wharf Ap CAN/RD E16 .....26 E4
Ward's Wy WADH TN5 .....98 D6
Warehorne Rd RASHW TN26 .....304 C8
Wardour St THMD SE28 .....27 L5
Ware St MAID/BEAR ME14 .....186 A6
Warham Rd RSEV TN14 .....148 G1
SAND/SEL CR2 .....83 H9
Warham St CMBW SE5 .....40 B1
Waring Cl ORP BR6 .....116 D1
Waring Dr ORP BR6 .....116 C1
Waring Rd SCUP DA14 .....64 C3
Waring St WNWD SE27 .....60 C5
Warland Rd BGR/WK TN15 .....120 C3
WOOL/PLUM SE18 .....43 P1
Warlingham Cl RHAM ME8 .....97 K5
Warlingham Rd THHTH CR7 .....22 C1
Warmington Rd HNHL SE24 .....40 C7
Warminster Rd SNWD SE25 .....60 G8

Warminster Sq SNWD SE25 .....60 G8
Warmlake Rd RMAID ME17 .....216 E1
Warndon St BERM/RHTH SE16 .....24 F7
Warne Pl BFN/LL DA15 .....44 D7
Warner Rd BMLY BR1 .....62 D6
CMBW SE5 .....40 C2
Warner St CHAT ME4 .....6 C7
Warner Ter POP/IOD E14 *.....25 K1
Warnett Ct SNOD ME6 *.....123 P4
Warnford Gdns
MAID/SHEP ME15 .....185 M5
Warnford Rd ORP BR6 .....86 G9
Warre Av RAM CT11 .....16 D6
Warren Av BMLY BR1 .....62 B8
ORP BR6 .....86 G9
SAND/SEL CR2 .....114 A2
Warren Cl BXLYHS DA6 .....45 J6
EGRIN RH19 .....264 B5
FOLKN CT19 .....11 K1
SIT ME10 .....130 A3
Warren Ct CHARL SE7 .....26 D8
SEV TN15 .....21 G3
Warren Dr BRDST CT10 .....113 K8
ORP BR6 .....87 H9
The Warren Dr WGOS CT8 .....111 L6
Warren Gdns ORP BR6 .....87 H9
Warren Hts CDW/CHF RM16 .....31 P7
Warren La RASHE TN25 *.....284 F3
Warren La CDW/CHF RM16 .....31 N7
KEN/WIL TN24 .....252 D5
OXTED RH8 .....205 K1
RDV CT15 .....199 H3
RSIT ME9 .....127 M2
WOOL/PLUM SE18 .....27 J6
Warren Pk WARL CR6 .....144 A3
Warren Rd BXLYHS DA6 .....45 K6
CHART DA2 .....66 E2
DART DA1 .....66 E2
FOLKN CT19 .....11 J2
HAYES BR2 .....85 K6
NROM TN28 .....337 J7
ORP BR6 .....86 G9
SCUP DA14 .....64 E2
STRD ME2 .....93 K3
WALD ME5 .....125 J5
The Warrens HART DA3 .....91 J3
Warren St HDCN TN27 .....190 F1
RMAID ME17 .....190 C5
Warren Ter CDW/CHF RM16 *.....31 N5
The Warren FAV ME13 .....163 P5
GVE DA12 .....69 P3
RASHE TN25 .....284 F3
RTON TN11 .....238 F5
SLH/COR SS17 *.....34 D2
WADH TN5 .....315 H3
WSTB CT5 .....105 K8
Warren Vw GVE DA12 .....70 C4
RASHE TN25 .....252 C5
Warren Wy FOLKN CT19 .....11 J1
Warren Wood Cl HAYES BR2 .....85 K6
Warren Wood Rd ROCH ME1 .....95 H7
Warrington Rd POP/IOD E14 *.....25 M4
Warrington Rd CROY/NA CRO 82 G7
STPH/PW TN12 .....242 G3
Warrior Av CROY/NA CRO 69 N3
Warspite Rd WOOL/PLUM SE18 .....26 F7
Warwall RAM CT11 .....143 L3
Warwall EHAM E6 .....27 J2
Warwick Cl BXLY DA5 .....45 H8
ORP BR6 .....87 H7
Warwick Crs ROCH ME1 .....94 K9
Warwick Dr RAM CT11 .....142 C7
Warwick Gdns MEO DA13 .....92 B0
THHTH CR7 *.....7 F1
Warwick Pk RTWE/PEM TN2 .....271 J2
Warwick Pl ORP BR6 *.....115 M6
MAIDW ME16 .....12 B6
Warwick Rd CANT CT1 .....167 H4
DEAL CT14 .....233 J7
MARG CT9 .....112 C3
PGE/AN SE20 .....61 H9
RTW TN1 .....271 K2
SCUP DA14 .....64 D4
THHTH CR7 .....22 B1
WELL DA16 .....105 L4

Wateringbury Rd
E/WMAL ME19 .....153 N9
Waterlakes EDEN TN8 .....236 D1
Water La CANT CT1 *.....4 C4
CANTW/ST CT2 .....137 L8
E/WMAL ME19 .....153 N4
EDEN TN8 .....235 N2
FAV ME13 .....132 B9
HAWK TN18 .....297 M8
HDCN TN27 .....247 K5
HDCN TN27 .....248 F7
MAID/BEAR ME14 .....157 H7
MAID/SHEP ME15 .....214 C4
MON EC3R 24 B3
NWCR SE14 .....41 J1
OXTED RH8 .....175 K2
PUR RM19 .....30 F5
RMAID ME17 .....188 B0
RSEV TN14 .....118 G6
SCUP DA14 .....65 H1
Waterloo Crs DVW CT17 .....3 H4
Waterloo Hl IOS ME12 .....78 C1
Waterloo Pl HOO/HM ME3 .....53 H8
RAM CT11 .....4 E3
TON TN9 .....240 E1
Waterloo Rd CRBK TN17 .....298 A1
FOLK CT20 .....310 A6
GILL ME7 .....7 H4
SIT ME10 .....99 N3
TON TN9 .....240 E1
WSTB CT5 .....105 L4
Waterloo St GVE DA12 .....49 N8
MAID/SHEP ME15 .....13 G7
Waterloo Ter IOS ME12 *.....78 G2
Waterlow Rd
MAID/BEAR ME14 .....13 G1
MEO DA13 .....122 B6
Waterman's La
STPH/PW TN12 .....243 J6
Watermans Wy PGE/AN SE20 *.....61 J6
Waterman Wy WAP E1W 24 E4
Watermeadow Ll ERITH DA8 *.....96 C8
GILL ME7 .....96 C8
Water Mdw CANTW/ST CT2 .....137 L9
Watermans St PGE/AN SE20 *.....61 H7
Water Ms PECK SE15 .....41 L6
Watermill Cl MAIDW ME16 .....154 C7
STRD ME2 .....72 C7
Water Mill Wy EYN DA4 .....67 H7
Watermill Wy DART DA1 .....46 G3
STMC/STPC BR5 .....64 A6
Water Slippe RTON TN11 .....211 N1
Watersmeet CHAT ME4 .....73 H6
Watersmeet Cl
MAID/SHEP ME15 .....185 L1
Watersend DVW CT17 .....290 D2
Waterside DART DA1 .....45 L5
Waterside Av
EGRIN RH19 .....265 L7
KEN/WIL TN24 .....253 J9
Waterside Av BECK BR3 .....84 E2
Waterside Cl BERM/RHTH SE16 .....24 D5
FAV ME13 .....132 C5
LEW SE13 .....42 B5
STRD ME2 .....72 A2
Waterside Dr WGOS CT8 .....111 N4
Waterside Ga MAIDW ME16 *.....155 J4
Waterside La GILL ME7 .....7 H8
Waterside Ms WBY/HLL ME18 *.....185 L5
Waterside Vw IOS ME12 .....42 D3
Water Slippe RTON TN11 .....211 N1
Watersmeet CHAT ME4 .....73 H6
Waterstone Pk FAV ME13 *.....132 D7
Water St DEAL CT14 .....233 J2
Waterton Av GVE DA12 .....50 A8
Water Tower Hl CROY/NA CRO 83 J8
Waterworks Cots RSEV TN14 .....149 H5
Waterworks Hl RDV CT15 .....261 M5
Waterworks La RCANTE CT3 .....262 A5
Watery La BGR/WK TN15 .....150 A5
RCANTW CT4 .....196 B6
Watford Rd CAN/RD E16 .....26 G5
Watkin Rd FOLKN CT19 .....10 D1
Watkins Cl STPH/PW TN12 .....246 B4
Watling Av WALD ME5 .....96 A4
Watling Pl SIT ME10 .....129 P2
Watlings Gv SYD SE26 .....61 H9? no
Watling St BXLYHS DA6 .....45 K5
CANT CT1 .....6 E3
GILL ME7 .....7 J3
GVE DA12 .....70 A6
MEO DA13 .....92 A8
PECK SE15 .....24 D9
ROCH ME1 .....91 M7
Watney Market WCHPL E1 .....24 E2
Watney St WCHPL E1 .....24 E2
Watney Wy SWLY BR8 .....88 F5
Watney Cl PUR RM19 .....30 G5
Watson Av WALD ME5 .....91 K9
Watson Cl WTHK RM20 .....47 N2
Watsons Cl RASHE TN25 .....252 F1
Watsons Hl SIT ME10 .....99 M8
Watson's St DEPT SE8 .....41 H1
Watts' Av ROCH ME1 .....6 E3
Watts Cl SNOD ME6 .....124 A5
Watts Cv BOW E3 .....25 M1
Watt's La CHST BR7 .....63 M7
Watts' St CHAT ME4 .....6 A7
Watts St PECK SE15 .....40 G2
Wat Tyler Rd GNWCH SE10 .....42 B5?
Wat Tyler Wy
MAID/SHEP ME15 .....13 G6
Wauchope Rd WSTB CT5 .....104 G8
Wavell Dr BFN/LL DA15 .....64 G1
Waveli Pl SYD SE26 .....60 F3
Waveney Av PECK SE15 .....41 H5

Waveney Cl WAP E1W 24 D4
Waveney Rd TONN TN10 .....210 F5
Waverley Av IOS ME12 .....58 B9
Waverley Cl HAYES BR2 .....85 N2
RMAID ME17 .....185 M1
WALD ME5 .....126 A3
Waverley Crs
WOOL/PLUM SE18 .....27 L9
Waverley Dr RTWE/PEM TN2 .....271 J2
Waverley Gdns CDW/CHF RM16 .....32 B5
EHAM E6 .....26 F1
Waverley Rd MARG CT9 .....15 H1
SNWD SE25 .....83 N1
WOOL/PLUM SE18 .....27 K8
Wayborough Hl MSTR CT12 .....141 L4
Wayfaring Gn GRAYS RM17 .....32 A8
Wayfield Rd WALD ME5 .....95 L7
Way Hl MSTR CT12 .....141 M5
Waylands SWLY BR8 .....88 E1
Waylands Cl RSEV TN14 .....117 M9
Waylett Rd WNWD SE27 .....60 B2
Wayne Cl BRDST CT10 .....113 K8
ORP BR6 .....86 G2
Waynflete Av CROY/NA CRO 82 G7
Wayside CROY/NA CRO *.....114 E1
TENT TN30 .....301 J4
Wayside Av TENT TN30 .....301 J4
Wayside Dr EDEN TN8 .....206 D7
Wayside Gv ELTH/MOT SE9 .....63 K3
Wayville Rd DART DA1 .....47 H8
Way Volante GVE DA12 .....70 A3
Weald Av SEV TN13 .....178 C6
Weald Cl BERM/RHTH SE16 .....24 F4
MAID/SHEP ME15 .....185 P5
MEO DA13 .....92 B6
RSEV TN14 .....178 G3
Weald Rd SIT ME10 .....129 L3
Wealden Av TENT TN30 .....301 J5
Wealden Cl RTON TN11 .....210 B5
Wealden Ct WALD ME5 *.....92 ?
Wealden Forest Pk HB CT6 *.....137 K1
Wealden Wy DIT/AY ME20 .....154 D4
Weald Rd SEV TN13 .....178 C6
The Weald CHST BR7 .....63 K5
EGRIN RH19 .....265 J3
GILL ME7 .....85 M1
Weald View Rd TON TN9 .....240 E2
Wealdway BGR/WK TN15 .....151 N6
WADH TN5 .....294 A9
GVW DA11 .....69 L4
RRTW TN3 .....267 P8
RTON TN11 .....181 P5
WBY/MAL ME18 .....210 F9
Wear Bay Crs FOLKN CT19 .....11 J3
Wear Bay Rd FOLKN CT19 .....11 K3
Weardale Av RDART DA2 .....67 J1
Weardale Rd LEW SE13 .....42 G5
Wearside Rd SBGH/RUST TN4 .....240 F9
Wearside Rd LEW SE13 .....41 P5
Weatherall Cl FAV ME13 .....164 C3
Weatherley Cl BOW E3 .....25 J1
Weatherly Cl ROCH ME1 .....119 J7
Weatherly Dr BRDST CT10 .....143 L2
Weaver Cl CROY/NA CRO 83 L8
EHAM E6 .....27 J3
Weavering Cl STRD ME2 .....72 B5
Weavering St
MAID/BEAR ME14 .....156 B8
Weavers Cl GVW DA11 .....49 L9
STPH/PW TN12 .....246 C5
Weavers La RSEV TN14 .....149 H6
Weaver's La STHWK SE1 *.....24 A3
The Weavers HDCN TN27 .....278 B7
Weavers Wy ASH TN23 .....282 B1
DVE/WH CT16 .....291 H4
Weaver Wk WNWD SE27 .....291 H4
Webb Cl FOLKN CT19 .....310 D6
HOO/HM ME3 .....73 K1
Webber Cl ERITH DA8 .....46 B1
Webbs Meadow SEV TN13 .....21 C4
Webb St STHWK SE1 .....24 B6
Webster Rd BERM/RHTH SE16 .....24 D6
RHAM ME8 .....97 J5
Wedderburn Rd RCANTE CT3 *.....170 E9
Wedgewood Cl MAIDW ME16 .....154 C7
Wedgewood Dr WALD ME5 .....95 M7
Wedgewood Gdns BH/WHM TN16 *.....145 N6
Wedgwood Wy NRWD SE19 .....60 C5
Weeds Wood Rd WALD ME5 .....125 L1
Weekes Ct QBOR ME11 *.....77 J2
Weeks Ct QBOR ME11 .....77 L3
Weeks La HDCN TN27 .....278 B9
Week St MAID/SHEP ME15 .....14 C2
Weigall Pl RAM CT11 .....16 B5?
Weigall Rd LEE/GVPK SE12 .....42 E5
Weighton Rd PGE/AN SE20 .....61 H8
Weird Wd HART DA3 .....68 C2
Weir Rd BXLY DA5 .....45 P5
Welbeck Av BFN/LL DA15 .....64 F1
BMLY BR1 .....62 E3
SBGH/RUST TN4 .....240 F9
Welch Cl CMBW SE5 .....88 D9
Welcomes Cots CTHM CR3 *.....144 D8
Welcome Rd STPH/PW TN12 .....246 B5
Welcomes Rd CTHM CR3 .....144 D8?
Welham Rd TOOT SW17 .....?
Weller Pl ORP BR6 .....116 B5
Weller Rd SBGH/RUST TN4 .....269 P4
Wellers Cl BH/WHM TN16 .....176 D5
Wellesley Av DEAL CT14 .....233 J1
Wellesley Cl BRDST CT10 .....143 K1
CHARL SE7 .....8 ?
WGOS CT8 .....111 M6

Wellesley Ct RAM CT11 .....17 G3
Wellesley Court Rd
CROY/NA CRO *.....83 J6
Wellesley Gv CROY/NA CRO 83 J6
Wellesley Rd CROY/NA CRO 83 H5
DVE/WH CT16 .....8 E4
IOS ME12 .....57 M7
KEN/WIL TN24 .....2 E3
MARG CT9 .....112 C4
WGOS CT8 .....111 M6
Wellesley St WCHPL E1 .....25 J1
Wellesley Vls KEN/WIL TN24 *.....3 F2
Wellfield EGRIN RH19 .....265 M9
Well Fld HART DA3 .....91 J1
Wellfield Rd FOLK CT20 .....310 D6
Wellfit St HNHL SE24 .....40 B4
Well Hall Pde ELTH/MOT SE9 .....43 K5
Well Hl ORP BR6 .....118 A1
Well Hill La ORP BR6 .....118 A2
Wellhouse Rd BECK BR3 .....84 C1
Wellhurst Cl ORP BR6 .....116 G2
Welling High St WELL DA16 .....44 D4
Welling Rd WELL DA16 .....33 L2
Wellington Av BFN/LL DA15 .....44 A2
Wellington Cl WGOS CT8 *.....111 M4
Wellington Cots HAWK TN18 .....316 C2
Wellington Crs RAM CT11 .....17 H4
Wellington Gdns CHARL SE7 .....26 D8
MARG CT9 .....15 J3
Wellington Gv GNWCH SE10 .....42 D1
Wellingtonia Av EDEN TN8 .....206 D8
Wellington Ms CHARL SE7 .....26 D9
EDUL SE22 .....40 C5
HYTHE CT21 *.....309 M5
Wellington Pde BFN/LL DA15 *.....44 C6
DEAL CT14 .....263 J1
Wellington Pl FOLK CT20 .....310 A8
MAID/BEAR ME14 .....12 E1
Wellington Rd BELV DA17 .....28 E8
BXLY DA5 .....44 F7
CROY/NA CRO 82 G4
DART DA1 .....47 H6
DEAL CT14 .....233 J4
DVE/WH CT16 .....290 E2
FOLK CT20 .....310 A6
GILL ME7 .....7 J1
HAYES BR2 .....85 M1
SIT ME10 .....99 J9
STMC/STPC BR5 .....87 J3
TIL RM18 .....51 J5
WALW SE17 .....23 M9
Wellington Sq GVE DA12 *.....49 N8
WOOL/PLUM SE18 .....27 H7
WSTB CT5 .....105 L9
Wellington Ter FOLK CT20 *.....310 A8
WAP E1W 24 E5
Wellington Town Rd
EGRIN RH19 .....264 C5
Wellington Wy E/WMAL ME19 .....152 G9
Welling Wy ELTH/MOT SE9 .....43 K5
Wellis Gdns MARG CT9 .....14 C7
Well La CANTW/ST CT2 .....167 M1
CDW/CHF RM16 .....31 P4
FAV ME13 .....161 N1
RDV CT15 .....292 E1
Wellmeade Dr SEV TN13 .....178 C3
Wellmeadow Rd LEW SE13 .....42 G7
Well Penn Rd HOO/HM ME3 .....52 B4
Well Rd MAID/BEAR ME14 .....173 P2
QBOR ME11 .....77 H4
RFOLK CT18 .....287 H2
RSEV TN14 .....149 H2
Wells Av CANT CT1 .....5 G5
Wells Cl BH/WHM TN16 .....176 D5
NROM TN28 .....337 H7
RTW TN1 .....22 C4
SAND/SEL CR2 .....83 K9
TENT TN30 .....301 H7
TON TN10 .....210 D6
Wells Lea EGRIN RH19 .....264 G5
Wells Meadow EGRIN RH19 .....264 G5
Wellsmoor Gdns BMLY BR1 .....63 L9
Wells Park Rd SYD SE26 .....60 E1
Wells Pl CMBW SE5 .....40 E1
Wells Rd BMLY BR1 .....63 K8
FOLKN CT19 .....310 B5
STRD ME2 .....72 A1
Wells St E/WMAL ME19 .....153 M6
MAID/SHEP ME15 .....185 K7
Wells Wy HART DA3 .....132 A4
WALW SE17 .....23 J7

Wenham's La LYDD TN29 .....335 J2
Wennington Rd RAIN RM13 .....29 N1
Wensley Cl ELTH/MOT SE9 .....43 K5
Wentland Cl CAT SE6 .....62 B1
Wentland Rd CAT SE6 .....62 B1
Wents Wd MAID/BEAR ME14 .....156 C2
Wentworth Av MARG CT9 .....111 P4
Wentworth Cl GVW DA11 .....69 L4
HAYES BR2 .....85 N6
ORP BR6 .....86 F9
RFOLK CT18 .....287 H2
THMD SE28 .....28 B0
Wentworth Crs PECK SE15 .....40 G2
Wentworth Dr DART DA1 .....66 A5
HOO/HM ME3 .....52 B4
MSTR CT12 .....142 D5
RHAM ME8 .....97 H7
Wentworth Gdns HB CT6 .....77 L2
Wentworth Rd CROY/NA CRO 82 C9
Wentworth St WCHPL E1 .....24 C1

Wenvoe Av *BXLYHN* DA7 .... 45 K3
Wenrbrook St
  WOOL/PLUM SE18 .... 27 K9
Werndee Rd *SNWD* SE25 .... 83 M1
Wesley Av *CAN/RD* E16 .... 26 B4
Wesley Cl *WLSDN* NW16 .... 154 E9
  STMC/STPC BR5 .... 64 G9
Wesley School Rd *ASH* TN23 .... 282 A1
Wesley Dr *ERITH* DA8 .... 45 N3
Wessex Wk *RDART* DA2 .... 95 N1
Wessex Ct *BECK* BR3 * 61 L7
Wesson Md *CMBW* SE5 * 40 C1
West Ap *STMC/STPC* BR5 .... 86 D2
West Arbour St *WCHPL* E1 .... 24 F2
West Av *WLGTN* SM6 .... 82 D9
Westbere La *CANTW/ST* CT2 .... 137 N7
Westborough Ms
  MAIDW ME16 .... 154 C9
Westbourne Av *ASH* TN23 .... 282 A2
Westbourne Dr *FSTH* SE23 .... 45 K6
Westbourne Rd *BXLYHN* DA7 .... 44 F1
  CROY/NA CR0 .... 83 L3
  SYD SE26 .... 61 K5
Westbourne St *SIT* ME10 .... 129 M1
Westbrook
  MAIDW ME15 * 185 L6
Westbrook Av *MARC* CT9 .... 14 A7
Westbrook Cots *MARC* CT9 .... 14 C6
Westbrook Dr *STMC/STPC* BR5 .... 87 L5
Westbrooke Cl *CANTW/ST* CT2 .... 135 P7
  SEV TN13 .... 149 H7
Westbrooke Crs *WELL* DA16 .... 44 F4
Westbrooke Rd *BFN/LL* DA15 .... 63 P1
  WELL DA16 .... 44 F4
Westbrook Gdns *MARC* CT9 .... 14 B6
Westbrook Prom *MARC* CT9 .... 14 A6
Westbrook Rd *BKHTH/KID* SE3 .... 42 C2
  MARC CT9 .... 14 C5
  THHTH CR7 .... 60 D7
Westbrook Ter
  RTWE/PEM TN2 .... 270 C4
Westbury Crs *DVW* CT17 .... 291 J9
Westbury Rd *BECK* BR3 .... 61 L9
  BMLY BR1 .... 63 H7
  DVW CT17 .... 291 J9
  PGE/AN SE20 .... 61 K7
  WGOS CT8 .... 111 N5
Westbury Ter *BH/WHM* TN16 .... 176 C2
West Cliff *WSTB* CT5 .... 105 K6
West Cliff Av *RAM* CT11 .... 5 H3
West Cliff Dr *HB* CT6 .... 106 C2
Westcliff Dr *IOS* ME12 .... 58 D9
West Cliff Gdns *FOLK* CT20 .... 15 N5
  HB CT6 .... 106 C3
Westcliff Gdns *MARC* CT9 .... 14 A6
West Cliff Ms *BRDST* CT10 * 143 L4
West Cliff Prom *RAM* CT11 .... 16 D7
West Cliff Rd *BRDST* CT10 .... 143 M1
Westcliff Rd *MARC* CT11 .... 16 D5
Westcliff Terrace Man
  RAM CT11 * 4 F4
West Cross *CROY/NA* CR0 .... 82 D3
Westcombe Hl *BKHTH/KID* SE3.26 B9
Westcombe Park Rd
  BKHTH/KID SE3 .... 25 P9
West Common Rd *HAYES* BR2 .... 85 K6
Westcott Av *GVW* DA11 .... 69 L2
Westcott Cl *BMLY* BR1 .... 85 P2
  CROY/NA CR0 .... 114 E3
Westcott House
  POP/IOD E14 * 25 J2
West Ct *MAID/SHEP* ME15 * 185 M2
Westcourt La *RCANTW* CT4 .... 229 J7
Westcourt St *GILL* ME7 .... 72 F9
West Crescent Rd *GVE* DA12 .... 49 M7
West Cross *TENT* TN30 .... 300 C8
West Cross Ms *TENT* TN30 * 300 C8
Westmarsh Rd
  WOOL/PLUM SE18 .... 27 J9
Westdean Av *LEE/GVPK* SE12 .... 42 F9
Westdean Cl *DVW* CT17 .... 290 F5
Westdown Rd *CAT* SE6 .... 41 N8
West Dr *RMAID* ME17 .... 217 L3
  WALD ME5 .... 19 G1
West Dumpton La *RAM* CT11 .... 143 K2
Wested La *SWLY* BR8 .... 88 F4
West End *BGR/WK* TN15 .... 149 L2
  BH/WHM TN16 .... 177 J1
Westerdale Rd *GNWCH* SE10 .... 26 E8
Westergate Rd *ABYW* SE2 .... 28 D9
  STRD ME2 .... 71 P6
Westerham Dr *CANTW/ST* CT2.156 F9
  MARC CT9 .... 113 K4
  RHAM ME8 .... 96 C2
Westerham Dr *BFN/LL* DA15 .... 44 E7
Westerham Hl *BH/WHM* TN16 .146 C2
Westerham Rd
  BH/WHM TN16 .... 177 H1
  HAYES BR2 .... 115 N1
  OXTED RH8 .... 175 J5
  RSEV TN14 .... 147 P8
  SIT ME10 .... 129 K2
Westerhill Rd *RMAID* ME17 .... 215 F1
Westerhout Cl *DEAL* CT14 .... 233 H5
Westerley Crs *SYD* SE26 * 61 M4
Western Av *ASH* TN23 .... 2 B3
  CHAT ME4 .... 72 C7
  HAWK TN18 .... 317 H4
  HB CT6 .... 107 J2
  IOS ME12 .... 57 M9
  RCANTW CT4 .... 197 J3
  WTHK RM20 * 31 J7
Western Cross Cl *SWCM* DA10.48 A7
Western Esp *BRDST* CT10 .... 143 P4
  HB CT6 .... 107 H1
Western Gdns *KEN/WIL* TN24 .253 H9
Western Gnys *CAN/RD* E16 .... 26 B6
Western Link *FAV* ME13 .... 132 C6
Western Pl *BERM/RHTH* SE16 .24 F1
Western Rd *BGR/WK* TN15 .... 151 J5
  BRXN/ST SW9 .... 40 A4
  DEAL CT14 .... 233 H3
  HAWK TN18 .... 317 H4
  MAIDW ME16 .... 155 H9

  MARC CT9 .... 113 H5
  RTW TN1 .... 270 F3
  SBGH/RUST TN4 .... 240 C8
  WADH TN5 .... 294 A9
Western Undercliff *RAM* CT11..142 G7
Western St *THMD* SE28 .... 27 L6
Westferry Circ *POP/IOD* E14....25 N4
Westferry Rd *POP/IOD* E14 .... 25 K5
Westfield *CANTW/ST* CT2 .... 135 P7
  SEV TN13 .... 149 H7
Westfield Cl *GVE* DA12 .... 69 N5
Westfield La *RFOLK* CT18 .... 288 C2
Westfield Rd *BECK* BR3 .... 61 M8
  BRCH CT7 .... 110 C6
  BXLYHN DA7 .... 45 L4
  CROY/NA CR0 .... 82 G6
  MARC CT9 .... 112 A5
Westfields *HDCN* TN27 .... 250 C1
Westfields Sole Rd
  MAIDW ME14 .... 126 A5
Westfield St *WOOL/PLUM* SE18..26 E6
Westfield Ter *CRBK* TN17 .... 297 L6
Westfield Vls
  STPH/PW TN12 * 244 C4
West Gate Av *BRCH* CT7 .... 111 P9
Westgate Bay Av *WGOS* CT8...111 L4
Westgate Cl *CANTW/ST* CT2...166 B3
Westgate Court Av
  CANTW/ST CT2 .... 166 C3
Westgate Gv *CANTW/ST* CT2 .... 4 C3
Westgate Hall Rd *CANT* CT1 * 4 D5
Westgate Rd *BECK* BR5 .... 62 A7
  DART DA1 .... 46 D7
  FAV ME15 .... 133 H6
Westgate Rbt *CANTW/ST* CT2 .... 4 C5
Westgate Ter *WSTB* CT5 .... 105 L4
West Gn *SIT* ME10 .... 99 N5
West Gv *GNWCH* SE10 .... 42 A2
Westgrove La *GNWCH* SE10....42 A2
West Hallowes *ELTH/MOT* SE9 .. 43 H9
Westharold *SWLY* BR8 .... 65 M9
West Heath Cl *DART* DA1 * 45 P7
West Heath La *SEV* TN15 .... 178 C4
West Heath Rd *ABYW* SE2 .... 28 D5
  DART DA1 .... 45 P7
West Hl *DART* DA1 .... 46 B7
  EGRIN RH19 .... 264 C8
  ORP BR6 .... 116 A6
  OXTED RH8 .... 174 G6
West Hill Bank *OXTED* RH8....174 C6
Westhill Cl *GVE* DA12 .... 49 M9
West Hill Dr *DART* DA1 .... 46 B7
West Hill Ri *DART* DA1 .... 46 C7
West Hill Rd *HB* CT6 .... 107 H1
West Holme *ERITH* DA8 .... 45 L2
Westholme *ORP* BR6 .... 116 A6
West Hl Av *ELTH/MOT* SE9 .... 42 G7
Westhurst Dr *CHST* BR7 .... 63 M4
West Hythe Rd *HYTHE* CT21...307 P7
West India Av *POP/IOD* E14....25 N4
West India Dock Rd
  POP/IOD E14 .... 25 J2
West Kent Av *GVW* DA11 .... 48 C7
Westland Dr *HAYES* BR2 .... 85 J6
Westlands Av *SIT* ME10 .... 129 J1
Westlands Rd *HB* CT6 .... 106 F3
Westlands Wy *OXTED* RH8....174 G5
Westland Vw *CDW/CHF* RM16..32 B4
West La *BERM/RHTH* SE16 .... 24 E5
  EGRIN RH19 .... 264 C8
  HOO/HM ME3 .... 56 C2
  IOS ME12 .... 57 J6
  SIT ME10 .... 129 P1
West Lawn Gdns *FOLK* CT20..310 A8
West Lea *DEAL* CT14 .... 233 H2
West Leigh Gdns *EGRIN* RH19 .265 J9
Westleigh Dr *BMLY* BR1 .... 63 J8
Westleigh Rd *WGOS* CT8 .... 111 L5
Westmarsh Cl
  MAID/SHEP ME15 .... 186 C4
Westmarsh Dr *MARC* CT9 .... 113 K3
Westmarsh Dro *RCANTE* CT3 .. 170 B3
Westmead Dr *DIT/AY* ME20 .... 124 B9
Westmeads Rd *WSTB* CT5 .... 105 M4
West Mersea Cl *CAN/RD* E16.....26 C4
West Mill Cv *GVW* DA11 .... 49 K7
West Mill Rd *DIT/AY* ME20 .... 124 B9
Westminster Cl *THHTH* CR7 .... 60 B8
Westminster Rd *CANT* CT1 .... 137 H9
Westminster Sq *MAIDW* ME16.154 C8
Westminster Wk
  MSTR CT12 * 143 H3
Westmoat Cl *BECK* BR5 .... 62 A6
Westmoors *ASH* TN23 .... 282 A2
Westmoor St *CHARL* SE7 .... 26 C7
Westmoreland Dr *RSIT* ME9 .... 98 C3
Westmoreland Pl *BMLY* BR1 * .. 62 E9
Westmoreland Rd *HAYES* BR2 .. 85 P2
  WALW SE17 * 44 A2
  WWKM BR4 .... 85 H2
Westmoreland Ter
  PGE/AN SE20 * 61 H6
Westmore Rd *BH/WHM* TN16...145 M5
Westmorland Cl
  MAID/SHEP ME15 * 186 B3
Westmorland Gn
  MAID/SHEP ME15 * 186 B4
Westmorland Wy *MTCM* CR4...82 C1
West Motney Wy *RHAM* ME8....97 J3
Westmount Av *CHAT* ME4 .... 95 J5
Westmount Rd *ELTH/MOT* SE9..43 H4
West Norman Rd *DVW* CT16 .... 9 F2
West Oak *BECK* BR3 .... 62 B3
Weston Av *WTHK* RM20 .... 31 J3
Weston Gv *BMLY* BR1 .... 62 G2
Weston Rd *BMLY* BR1 .... 62 D6
  STRD ME2 .... 18 B1
Weston St *STHWK* SE1 .... 24 A5
Westonville Av *MARC* CT9 .... 112 A4
Westover Gdns *BRDST* CT10....113 K6
Westover Rd *BRDST* CT10 .... 113 K6
Westow Hl *NRWD* SE19 .... 60 E5

Westow St *NRWD* SE19 .... 60 E5
West Pde *HYTHE* CT21 .... 308 C2
West Pk *ELTH/MOT* SE9 .... 63 J1
West Park Av *MARC* CT9 .... 113 J4
  SBGH/RUST TN4 .... 240 C8
West Park Rd
  MAID/SHEP ME15 .... 185 N1
West Parkside *GNWCH* SE10 .....25 P5
West Pas *IOS* ME12 * 57 J6
West Pl *LYDD* TN29 .... 334 D5
Westport St *WCHPL* E1 .... 24 G2
West Rd *DVE/WH* CT16 .... 9 J2
Westree Ct *MAIDW* ME16 .... 12 C6
Westree Rd *MAIDW* ME16 .... 12 C6
West Rdg *SIT* ME10 .... 129 L3
Westrise *TON* TN9 .... 240 G8
West Rd *CHAT* ME4 .... 72 C8
  CRBK TN17 .... 295 N4
  FOLK CT20 .... 309 P3
  SWCH CT13 .... 171 P3
West Roman Ditch
  DVE/WH CT16 .... 9 C2
West Shaw *HART* DA3 .... 68 B8
West Side *RDV* CT15 .... 261 P7
West St *ASH* TN23 .... 2 C4
  BGR/WK TN15 .... 151 J1
  BMLY BR1 .... 62 E7
  BXLYHN DA7 .... 45 L4
  CROY/NA CR0 .... 83 H8
  DEAL CT14 .... 233 H2
  DVW CT17 .... 8 A2
  E/WMAL ME19 .... 153 J4
  EGRIN RH19 .... 265 H8
  ERITH DA8 .... 29 J7
  FAV ME13 .... 132 F5
  GILL ME7 .... 7 K1
  GRAYS RM17 .... 32 D7
  GVW DA11 .... 49 L7
  HDCN TN27 .... 251 H1
  IOS ME12 .... 57 J5
  LING RH7 .... 235 K8
  MAID/SHEP ME15 .... 274 J8
  NROM TN28 .... 336 F7
  QBOR ME11 .... 77 H2
  RMAID ME17 .... 188 D5
  RMAID ME17 .... 218 D1
  RYE TN31 .... 338 F7
  SIT ME10 .... 128 A3
  STRD ME2 .... 72 B6
West Street Pl *CROY/NA* CR0 * .83 H8
West Tenter St *WCHPL* E1 .... 24 C2
West Ter *BFN/LL* DA15 * 44 A9
  FOLK CT20 .... 10 E5
West Thurrock Wy
  WTHK RM20 .... 31 K7
West Undercliff *RYE* TN31 .... 338 D7
Westview *CHAT* ME4 .... 73 H5
West Vw *MDTN* TN27 * 247 L2
West View Cl *HB* CT6 .... 107 H4
West View Gdns *EGRIN* RH19...264 B8
West View Rd *DART* DA1 .... 46 F7
  SWLY BR8 .... 88 C3
West Wk *MAIDW* ME16 .... 154 C9
West Wy *CROY/NA* CR0 .... 84 B6
Westway *RMAID* ME17 .... 185 H6
  RTWE/PEM TN2 .... 271 N1
West Wy *STMC/STPC* BR5 .... 86 E2
Westways *BH/WHM* TN16 .... 176 D2
  EDEN TN8 .... 206 D8
West Way Gdns *CROY/NA* CR0...84 A6
Westwell Rd *THMD* SE28 .... 27 L5
Westwood Wy *NRWD* SE19 .... 60 C7
Westwell La *HDCN* TN27 .... 221 K4
Westwood Av *NRWD* SE19 .... 60 C7
Westwood Cl *BMLY* BR1 .... 63 H9
Westwood La *WELL* DA16 .... 44 C5
Westwood Pk *FSTH* SE23 .... 49 M7
Westwood Pl *FAV* ME13 * 132 C8
  SYD SE26 * 60 G4
West Wood Rd *RSIT* ME9 .... 127 L6
Westwood Rd *BRDST* CT10 .... 113 Q3
  MAID/SHEP ME15 .... 185 M4
  MEO DA13 .... 68 C4
  RCANTW CT4 .... 227 J3
  SBGH/RUST TN4 .... 269 N5
Westwood Wy *SEV* TN13 .... 148 E7
Wetheral Dr *WALD* ME5 .... 125 N1
Weybridge Cl *WALD* ME5 .... 125 P1
Weybridge Ct
  BERM/RHTH SE16 * 24 E8
Weybridge Rd *THHTH* CR7 .... 82 F1
Weyburn Dr *MSTR* CT12 .... 142 F3
Weyi Cl *MAID* ME15 * 95 P9
Weyhill Cl *MAID/BEAR* ME14....155 P6
Weyhill Rd *WCHPL* E1 * 24 D2
Weyman Rd *BKHTH/KID* SE3....42 C2
Weymouth Cl *EHAM* E6 .... 27 J2
  FOLKN CT19 * 310 A5
Weymouth Dr *CDW/CHF* RM16..31 N9
Weymouth Rd *FOLKN* CT19 .... 310 A5
Weymouth Ter *FOLKN* CT19 * .. 310 A4
Wharfdale Sq
  MAID/SHEP ME15 .... 185 K2
Wharfedale Gdns *THHTH* CR7 .. 82 E1
Wharfedale Rd *MARC* CT9 .... 15 K6
Wharf La *HOO/HM* ME3 .... 52 B2
  POP/IOD E14 .... 25 J2
Wharf Rd *GILL* ME7 * 73 J8
  GRAYS RM17 .... 32 A7
  GVE DA12 .... 50 A9
  MAID/SHEP ME15 .... 185 K1
  SLH/COR SS17 .... 34 D2
Wharf Rd South *GRAYS* RM17 .. 32 A9
Wharfside Cl *ERITH* DA8 .... 29 L8
Wharfside Rd *POP/IOD* E14 .... 25 P2
Wharf Wy *MEO* DA13 .... 68 G2
The Wharf *RDART* DA2 * 47 P5
Wharncliffe Gdns *SNWD* SE25 .. 60 E8
Wharncliffe Rd *SNWD* SE25 .... 60 E8
Wharton Gdns *KEN/WIL* TN24 ... 3 K7
Wharton Rd *BMLY* BR1 .... 63 H4
Whateley Rd *EDUL* SE22 .... 40 C7
  PGE/AN SE20 .... 61 K6

Whatman Cl
  MAID/BEAR ME14 .... 155 P6
Whatman Rd *FSTH* SE23 .... 41 M8
Whatmer Cl *CANTW/ST* CT2 .. 137 M7
Wheatcroft Cl *SIT* ME10 .... 130 A1
Wheatcroft Gv *RHAM* ME8 .... 95 N7
Wheatear Wv *WALD* ME5 .... 125 N1
Wheatfield *E/WMAL* ME19 .... 153 M3
Wheatfield Dr *CRBK* TN17 .... 297 P3
Wheatfield Dr *CRBK* TN17 .... 297 N3
Wheatfield Lea *CRBK* TN17 .... 297 P2
Wheatfields
  MAID/BEAR ME14 .... 156 A8
  WALD ME5 .... 126 A3
Wheatley Wy *CRBK* TN17 .... 297 P2
Wheathill Rd *PGE/AN* SE20 .... 61 H8
Wheatley La *RDART* DA2 .... 47 N6
Wheatley Rd *MSTR* CT12 .... 143 H5
  WSTB CT5 .... 105 M4
Wheatsheaf Cl *FAV* ME13 .... 164 B1
  MAID/SHEP ME15 .... 185 N3
Wheat Chard Cl *POP/IOD* E14.....12 G7
Wheatsheaf Gdns *IOS* ME12 .... 57 K7
Wheatsheaf Ms *RSEV* TN14 .... 117 N3
  RSEV TN14 .... 177 N7
Wheatshear La *RDV* CT15 .... 262 A6
Wheatsheaf Wy *TONN* TN10....210 G4
Wheeler Av *OXTED* RH8 .... 174 C7
Wheeler La *WCHPL* E1 .... 24 C1
Wheeler Pl *HAYES* BR2 .... 85 L1
Wheeler's La *RMAID* ME17 .... 215 J2
The Wheelers *RHAM* ME8 .... 96 E8
Wheeler St *HDCN* TN27 .... 247 N4
  MAID/BEAR ME14 .... 13 C2
Wheelers Wy *EGRIN* RH19 .... 264 B5
Wheelock Cl *ERITH* DA8 .... 45 L1
The Wheelwrights
  RMAID ME17 .... 188 E5
Wheelwrights Wy *SWCH* CT13..201 J8
Wheelwright Gn *DIT/AY* ME20..153 N2
Wheler Ct *FAV* ME13 * 132 D6
Wheler Rd *HDCN* TN27 .... 221 H2
Whenman Av *BXLY* DA5 .... 65 L1
Whetsted Rd *STPH/PW* TN12 .. 212 F9
Whetstone Rd *BKHTH/KID* SE3..42 C3
Whidborne Cl *DEPT* SE8 .... 41 N5
Whiffen's Av *CHAT* ME4 .... 6 C3
Whiffen's Avenue W
  CHAT ME4 * 6 C3
Whiffen Wk *E/WMAL* ME19 .... 154 A3
Whimbrel Cl *SWCH* CT13 .... 99 N6
Whimbrel Gn *DIT/AY* ME20 .... 153 N2
Whinchat Rd *THMD* SE28 .... 27 L5
Whinfell Av *RAM* CT11 .... 142 E5
Whinfell Wy *GVE* DA12 .... 70 B3
Whinless Rd *DVW* CT17 .... 291 H7
Whippendell Cl
  STMC/STPC BR5 .... 64 D7
Whippendell Wy
  STMC/STPC BR5 .... 64 D7
Whistler Rd *TONN* TN10 .... 210 C5
Whiston Av *RASHW* TN26 .... 280 D4
Whitbourne Ct *WSTB* CT5 .... 105 L6
Whitbread Rd *BROCKY* SE4 .... 41 L5
Whitburn Rd *LEW* SE13 .... 41 P6
Whitby Cl *BH/WHM* TN16 .... 143 J2
  RDART DA2 .... 47 N6
Whitby Rd *WOOL/PLUM* SE18....26 D7
Whitby Ter *DVE/WH* CT16 * 291 J4
Whitcombe Ms *RCH/KEW* TW9..37 M9
White Acre Cl *DEAL* CT14 .... 232 C9
White Beam Wy *MAIDW* ME16...12 A7
Whitebeam Av *HAYES* BR2 .... 86 A4
Whitebeam Cl *ASH* TN23 .... 252 A5
  BGR/WK TN15 .... 149 M2
Whitebeam Dr *RMAID* ME17....184 G8
White Bear Pas *RTW* TN1 * 22 D6
Whitebine Gdns
  STPH/PW TN12 * 213 H4
Whitechapel La *RYE* TN31 .... 330 C7
Whitechapel High St
  WCHPL E1 .... 24 C2
Whitechapel Rd *WCHPL* E1 .... 24 D1
White Church La *WCHPL* E1 .... 24 C2
White Cliffs Country Trail
  DEAL CT14 .... 201 N5
  RDV CT15 .... 261 N2
Whitecliff Wy *FOLKN* CT19 .... 11 H4
White Ct *DVE/WH* CT16 .... 291 J2
White Cottage Rd *TONN* TN10..210 F4
Whitecroft *SWLY* BR8 .... 65 N8
Whitecroft Cl *BECK* BR3 .... 84 A1
Whitecroft Wy *BECK* BR3 .... 84 A1
Whitefield Cl *STMC/STPC* BR5...64 E9
Whitefield Crs *RDART* DA2 .... 47 J8
Whitefield Rd
  SBGH/RUST TN4 .... 240 D7
Whitefoot La *BMLY* BR1 .... 62 B3
Whitefoot Ter *BMLY* BR1 .... 62 D2
White Friars *SEV* TN13 .... 178 F5
Whitefriars *SWCH* CT13 .... 201 N1
Whitefriars Meadow
  SWCH CT13 .... 201 P2
Whitefriars St *CANT* CT1 .... 5 F5
Whitefriars Whf *TON* TN9 .... 210 F9
Whitegate Cl *SBGH/RUST* TN4.240 C9
Whitegates Av *BGR/WK* TN15...149 H2
Whitehall Cl *CANT* CT1 .... 334 D2
Whitehall Bridge Rd
  CANTW/ST CT2 .... 4 B5
Whitehall Cl *CANTW/ST* CT2 .... 4 B5
Whitehall Dr *RMAID* ME17 .... 187 M2
Whitehall Gdns *CANTW/ST* CT2...4 A5
Whitehall La *ERITH* DA8 .... 45 P5
  GRAYS RM17 .... 32 D1
Whitehall Pde *EGRIN* RH19 * .. 265 J8
Whitehall Rd *BMLY* BR1 .... 82 A8
Whitehall Rd *CANTW/ST* CT2 .... 4 A5

  HAYES BR2 .... 85 N2
  MAID/BEAR ME14 .... 157 K6
  MSTR CT12 .... 142 C4
  SIT ME10 .... 129 M3
  THHTH CR7 .... 82 F2
Whitehall Wy *RASHE* TN25 .... 285 L7
White Hart Av
  WOOL/PLUM SE18 .... 27 N6
White Hart La *SEV* TN13 .... 179 N4
White Hart Pde *SEV* TN13 * 148 D7
The White Hart Pde
  SEV TN15 * 148 D7
White Hart Rd *ORP* BR6 .... 87 H4
  WOOL/PLUM SE18 .... 27 M7
White Hart Wd *SEV* TN13 .... 179 H5
White Hart Yd *GVW* DA11 .... 49 M7
  STHWK SE1 * 24 A4
Whitehaven Cl *HAYES* BR2 .... 85 K1
Whitehead Cl *RDART* DA2 .... 66 C2
Whiteheads La
  MAID/BEAR ME14 .... 156 B8
White Hl *RASHW* TN15 .... 151 L1
White Hill Cl *RCANTW* CT4 .... 196 F5
Whitehill La *GVE* DA12 .... 69 P2
Whitehill Pde *GVE* DA12 * 69 N2
White Hill Rd
  MAID/BEAR ME14 .... 127 H4
  RSIT ME9 .... 98 C8
Whitehill Rd *DART* DA1 .... 46 A6
  GVE DA12 .... 68 B8
  HART DA3 .... 68 B8
  MEO DA13 .... 68 B6
  MEO DA15 .... 122 C1
White Horse Hl *CHST* BR7 .... 63 L3
  RFOLK CT18 .... 288 F9
Whitehorse Hl *WALD* ME5 .... 5 G7
White Horse La *CANT* CT1 * 4 E4
  RCANTW CT4 .... 256 F6
Whitehorse La *SNWD* SE25 .... 83 K1
White Horse Rd *MEO* DA13 .... 123 J3
  WCHPL E1 .... 25 H2
Whitehouse Rd *CROY/NA* CR0...83 H4
  WCHPL E1 .... 25 H1
Whitehouse Cl *HOO/HM* ME3 .. 73 L5
Whiteley Lion Ct *LOTH* EC2R * .. 23 J2
White Lion Ct *LOTH* EC2R 24 A2
  PECK SE15 * 24 F9
Whitelocks Cl *RCANTW* CT4 .... 228 A3
White Lodge *NRWD* SE10 .... 60 B6
White Lodge Cl *SEV* TN13 .... 148 C8
White Marsh Ct *WSTB* CT5 * .. 105 M4
Whitenbrook *HYTHE* CT21 .... 309 H4
Whiteness Gn *BRDST* CT10 .... 113 L4
Whiteness Rd *BRDST* CT10 .... 113 N3
White Oak Ct *TON* TN9 * 240 G2
White Oak Br *BECK* BR5 .... 62 A8
White Oak Gdns *BFN/LL* DA15...44 B8
White Oak Sq *SWLY* BR8 * 65 N9
White Post Gdns *RCANTE* CT3..200 E1
White Post Hl *EYN* DA4 .... 89 M4
White Post La *MEO* DA13 .... 92 C1
Whitepost La *PECK* SE15 .... 122 A4
White Post St *NWCR* SE14 .... 41 J1
White Post Ter *RDV* CT15 * 95 M5
White Rock Ct *MAIDW* ME16 .... 12 B8
White Rock Pl *MAIDW* ME16 .... 12 C6
Whites Cl *SWCM* DA10 .... 48 A7
Whites Grounds Est
  STHWK SE1 * 24 B5
Whites Hl *DEAL* CT14 .... 231 H7
Whites La *HAWK* TN18 .... 317 K4
Whites Meadow *BMLY* BR1 * .. 86 B1
White's Rw *WCHPL* E1 .... 24 C1
Whitethorn Gdns
  CROY/NA CR0 .... 83 N6
Whitewall Rd *STRD* ME2 .... 19 J1
Whitewall Wy *QBOR* ME11 .... 77 H1
Whitewebbs Wy
  STMC/STPC BR5 .... 64 D7
White Willow Cl
  KEN/WIL TN24 .... 282 G2
Whitewood Cots
  BH/WHM TN16 .... 145 M5
White Wood Rd *SWCH* CT13 .... 201 J9
Whitfield Rd *ASH* TN23 .... 203 J9
Whitfield Av *BRDST* CT10 .... 113 K6
  DVE/WH CT16 .... 291 J5
Whitfield Ct *DVE/WH* CT16 .... 291 J3
Whitfield Hl *DVE/WH* CT16 .... 290 C5
Whitfield Rd *BXLYHN* DA7 .... 45 J2
  GNWCH SE10 .... 42 B7
Whitgift Av *SAND/SEL* CR2 .... 83 H9
Whitgift St *CROY/NA* CR0 .... 83 H7
Whiting Crs *FAV* ME13 .... 133 J5
Whitings Wy *EHAM* E6 .... 27 H1
Whitmore Av *CDW/CHF* RM16 ...32 C4
Whitmore Cl *CDW/CHF* RM16 .. 33 M2
Whitmore Rd *BECK* BR3 .... 61 L3
Whitnell Wy *PUT/ROE* SW15 * .. 38 A9
Whitstable Cl *BECK* BR3 .... 61 M7
Whitstable Rd *CROY/NA* CR0 .. 83 H8
Whitstable Rd *CANTW/ST* CT2 .... 4 A1
Whitstone La *BECK* BR3 .... 61 M4
Whittaker St *CHAT* ME4 .... 6 E5
Whittell Gdns *SYD* SE26 .... 61 J2
Whittington Av Bank EC3V 24 B2
Whittington College
  EGRIN RH19 * 264 C5
Whittington Ter *CROY/NA* CR15 * .259 N1
Whitworth Rd *SNWD* SE25 .... 60 D1
  WOOL/PLUM SE18 .... 43 H1
Whybornes Cts *IOS* ME12 .... 58 C9
Whybourne Crest
  RTWE/PEM TN2 .... 270 G7

Whyman Av *CHAT* ME4 ....95 M5
Whytecliffs *BRDST* CT10 ....143 M2
Wichling Cl *CANTW/ST* CT2 .....166 F1
  STMC/STPC BR5 ....87 L5
Wickenden Crs *KEN/WIL* TN24...253 K9
Wickenden Rd *SEV* TN15 ....149 H7
Wicken La *HDCN* TN27 ....221 K5
Wickens Meadow
  RSEV TN14 * 148 E4
Wickers Oake *NRWD* SE19 * 60 F3
Wicker St *WCHPL* E1 * 24 D2
The Wickets *KEN/WIL* TN24 * 283 J1
The Wicket *CROY/NA* CR0 ....84 D9
Wicketts End *WSTB* CT5 ....105 L6
Wickham Av *CROY/NA* CR0 ....84 B9
  RAIN CT11 ....143 M4
Wickham Cha *WWKM* BR4 ....84 C4
Wickham Cl *RSIT* ME9 ....98 C8
  WCHPL E1 ....24 F1
Wickham Ct *WWKM* BR4 * 84 A9
Wickham Court La
  RCANTE CT3 ....168 E5
Wickham Court La *WWKM* BR4...84 F6
Wickham Crs *WWKM* BR4 ....84 A9
Wickham Fld *RSEV* TN14 * 148 E1
Wickham Gdns *BROCKY* SE4 * ...41 M3
  SBGH/RUST TN4........................270 A3
Wickham La *ABYW* SE2 * 27 J8
  RCANTE CT3 ....168 E6
Wickham Ms *BROCKY* SE4 * 41 M5
Wickham Rd *CDW/CHF* RM16.......83 K5
  CROY/NA CR0 ....84 D9
  RCANTE CT3 ....168 E7
Wickham St *ROCH* ME1 * 95 J3
  WELL DA16 ....44 A5
Wickhams Wy *HART* DA3 * 11 J2
Wickhurst Rd *RTWE/PEM* TN2 * ...23 K2
Wickhurst Rd *RSEV* TN14 ....178 E8
Wicks La *RCANTW* CT4 ....228 G7
Wicks Cl *LEE/GVPK* SE12 ....63 H3
Wicksteed Cl *BXLY* DA5 ....45 M3
Wickwood St *CMBW* SE5 ....59 M9
Widbury RRTW TN5 * 269 L5
Widbury Pl *RRTW* TN5 ....269 L5
Widcombe Rd *ELTH/MOT* SE9 ....63 J2
Widegate St *WCHPL* E1 ....24 B3
Widgeon Cl *CAN/RD* E16 ....26 C2
Widgeon Rd *ERITH* DA8 ....46 B1
  STRD ME2 ....71 M9
Wife of Bath Hl
  CANTW/ST CT2 ....166 B4
Wigeon Rd *RSIT* ME9 ....99 M3
Wigmore Gld *RHAM* ME8 ....126 E1
Wigmore La *RDV* CT15 ....230 D9
Wigmore Rd *RHAM* ME8 ....126 E1
Wigmore Wd *RDV* CT15 ....230 D9
Wilberforce Rd *BRCH* CT7.........111 H5
Wilfred Rd *RSIT* ME9 ....130 C3
Wilberforce Rd *FOLK* CT20 ....310 B8
  RMAID ME17 ....185 J8
Wife of Bath Hl
  CANTW/ST CT2 ....166 B4
Wilberforce Wy *GVE* DA12 ....69 P4
Wilbrough Rd *BRCH* CT7 ....111 H6
Wilcox Cl *RCANTE* CT3 ....228 G2
Wilde Cl *TIL* RM18 ....49 L3
Wilden Park Rd
  RASHW TN26 ....245 L9
Wilderness Av
  BGR/WK TN15 ....149 K7
Wilderness Mt *SEV* TN13 ....149 J7
Wilderness Gdns *RYE* TN31.......329 P6
Wilderness Rd *MARG* CT9 ....15 L2
Wilderness Ri *EGRIN* RH19 ....265 K3
Wilderness Rd *CHST* BR7 ....63 M6
  OXTED RH8 ....117 N9
Wildfell Rd *ERITH* DA8 ....45 K1
Wilderwick Rd *EGRIN* RH19 .....265 L3
Wildfell Cl *WALD* ME5 ....125 P5
Wildfell Rd *CAT* SE6 ....41 P8
Wild Goose Dr *NWCR* SE14 ....41 J2
Wildish Rd *FAV* ME13 ....132 D5
Wildman Cl *RHAM* ME8 ....126 C2
Wild's Rents *STHWK* SE1 * 24 B3
Wildwood Cl *LEE/GVPK* SE12 .....42 D8
  RMAID ME17 ....187 P9
Wildwood Rd *CANTW/ST* CT2...137 L7
Wiles Av *NROM* TN28 ....336 G2
Wilfred Av *RAIN* RM13 ....29 M1
Wilfred Cl *WSTB* CT5 ....105 M4
Wilfred St *GVE* DA12 ....69 P4
Wilgate Green Rd *FAV* ME13 .....162 B5
Wilkes Rd *BRDST* CT10 ....143 K1
Wilkes St *WCHPL* E1 ....24 C1
Wilkie Rd *BRCH* CT7 ....111 H5
Wilkinson Dr *DEAL* CT14 ....233 J6
Wilkinson Gdns *SNWD* SE25 ......60 E7
Wilkinson Rd *CAN/RD* E16 ....26 D2
Wilks Av *DART* DA1 ....66 F7
Wilks Gdns *CROY/NA* CR0 ....84 B5
Will Adams Wy *RHAM* ME8 ....98 B6
Willan Wall *CAN/RD* E16 ....26 A3
Will Crooks Gdns
  ELTH/MOT SE9 ....43 H5
Willement Rd *FAV* ME13 ....132 G4
Willenhall Rd
  WOOL/PLUM SE18 ....27 J8
Willersley Av *BFN/LL* DA15 ....64 B9
  ORP BR6 ....86 D8
Willersley Ct *BFN/LL* DA15 ....44 B9
Willesborough Ct
  KEN/WIL TN24 ....253 K8
Willesborough Rd
  KEN/WIL TN24 ....253 J6
Willesley Gdns *STMC/STPC* BR5...298 A14
Willett Cl *STMC/STPC* BR5.........86 F3
Willett's Hl *HSTR* CT12 ....
Willetts La *RRTW* TN5 ....268 B4
Willett Wy *STMC/STPC* BR5 ....86 E1
William Av *FOLKN* CT19 ....310 E4
  MARG CT9 ....113 H5

William Barefoot Dr
  ELTH/MOT SE9 ....63 L2
William Booth Rd
  PGE/AN SE20..........................60 C7
William Cl *LEW* SE13 ....42 A4
William Ellis Wy
  BERM/RHTH SE16 * 24 D1
William Foster La *WELL* DA16 .....44 C3
William Gibbs Ct *FAV* ME13 * 132 G6
William Hall Ter *FAV* ME13 * 132 D7
William Judge Cl *TENT* TN30 .....301 L8
William Luck Cl
  STPH/PW TN12 ....212 F4
William Margrie Cl *PECK* SE15 *...40 C9
William Petty Wy
  STMC/STPC BR5 ....87 K5
William Pitt Av *DEAL* CT14 ....232 G3
William Pitt Cl *HYTHE* CT21 .....309 P5
William Rigby Dr *IOS* ME12 ....57 N9
William Rd *ASH* TN23 ....252 E9
  STRD ME2 ....71 P6
Williamson Cl *GNWCH* SE10 ......26 A8
Williamson Rd *LYDD* TN29 ....345 K6
William St *BERM/RHTH* SE16....132 C5
William St *FAV* ME13 * 132 G6
  GRAYS RM17 ....32 C9
  GVE DA12 ....49 M8
  HB CT6 ....107 L1
  RHAM ME8 ....97 K3
  SBGH/RUST TN4........................270 D3
  SIT ME10 ....129 M2
Williams Wy *RDART* DA2 ....65 M1
Willicombe Pk *RTWE/PEM* TN2 ...23 K2
Willingdon Ash TN23 ....282 B3
Willingdon Pl *DEAL* CT14 ....233 H7
Willingdon Rd *DVE/WH* CT16....291 H2
Willington Gn
  MAID/SHEP ME15 ....186 B4
Willington St
  MAID/SHEP ME15 ....186 B5
Willis Cl *IOS* ME12 ....72 F2
Willis La *RASHE* TN25 ....325 J1
Willis Rd *CROY/NA* CR0 ....83 H4
  ERITH DA8 ....46 C3
Willis St *POP/IOD* E14 ....25 L2
Willop Wy *LYDD* TN29 ....345 K6
Willoughby Av *CROY/NA* CR0 ......82 E8
Willoughby Wy *CHARL* SE7 ....26 C7
Willow Av *BFN/LL* DA15 ....44 C7
  BRDST CT10 ....113 J9
  FAV ME13 ....132 D6
  HOO/HM ME3..........................73 L4
  SWLY BR8 ....88 E1
Willowbank Cl *LYDD* TN29 ....337 M1
Willowbank Dr *HOO/HM* ME3 .....73 L4
Willowbrook Est *PECK* SE15 * 40 F1
Willowbrook Rd *PECK* SE15 ....24 C9
Willowby Gdns *RHAM* ME8 ....127 H1
Willow Cl *BXLY* DA5 ....45 H7
  CANTW/ST CT2 ....166 F1
  CAT SE6 ....42 C9
  EGRIN RH19 ....264 C5
  HAYES BR2............................86 A2
  HOO/HM ME3 * 38 F8
  HYTHE CT21 ....308 D6
  MARG CT9 ....113 H5
  RMAID ME17 ....188 E5
  SIT ME10 ....128 B3
Willow Ct *BRDST* CT10 * 113 M8
  WSTB CT5 ....105 M6
Willow Crs *STPH/PW* TN12 ....242 B2
  STPH/PW TN12 ....246 C4
Willow Dr *LYDD* TN29 ....337 L2
  RHAM ME8 ....98 A8
Willow Farm Wy *HB* CT6 ....107 P4
Willowfields Cl
  WOOL/PLUM SE18 ....27 M8
Willow Gra *HOO/HM* ME3 * 73 K2
Willow Gv *CHST* BR7 ....63 L5
Willowherb Cl *CHAT* ME4 ....73 G9
Willow La *STPH/PW* TN12 ....243 L4
  WOOL/PLUM SE18 ....26 G7
Willow Lea *TONN* TN10 ....210 F3
Willowmead *E/WMAL* ME19 ....153 M2
Willow Md *EGRIN* RH19 ....265 J8
Willow Mt *CROY/NA* CR0 ....83 K8
Willow Pk *SEV* TN14 ....149 M1
Willow Ri *MAID/SHEP* ME15......186 C2
Willow Rd *DART* DA1 * 46 C9
  DEAL CT14 ....232 B6
  DIT/AY ME20 ....153 N1
  ERITH DA8 ....46 D6
  STRD ME2 ....71 N9
  WSTB CT5 ....105 K9
Willows Ct *CANTW/ST* CT2 * 166 B4
Willowside *SNOD* ME6 ....123 P4
The Willows *BECK* BR3 * 61 N7
  BGR/WK TN15 ....150 C6
  CANTW/ST CT2 * 137 M9
  GRAYS RM17 ....32 E9
  HB CT6 ....107 J2
  HOO/HM ME3 * 56 D2
  KEN/WIL TN24 ....252 G5
  RASHW TN26 ....281 L7
  RHAM ME8 ....98 C8
  RSIT ME9 ....99 N5
  SIT ME10 ....125 L4
Willow Ter *EYN* DA4 * 89 K6
  PGE/AN SE20 * 61 H7
Willow Tree Cl *HB* CT6 ....108 A5
  KEN/WIL TN24 ....253 L9
Willow Tree Rd
  RTWE/PEM TN2 ....270 B7
Willow Tree Wk *BMLY* BR1 ....62 E7
Willowtree Wy *THHTH* CR7 ....60 A7
Willow Wk *CHST* BR7 ....63 L5
Willow Wk *DART* DA1 * 66 E6
  MEO DA13 ....122 A2
  ORP BR6 ....86 E9
  RTWE/PEM TN2 ....241 H9
  STHWK SE1 ....24 B7
Willow Wy *HDCN* TN27 ....278 E9
  MAID/SHEP ME15 ....18 J7
  RASHW TN26 ....281 L8
  SYD SE26...............................61 H2
  WSTB CT5 ....106 B6
Willow Waye *RDV* CT15 ....260 E1
Willow Wents *WBY/YAL* ME18...182 D2
Willow Wood Crs *SNWD* SE25.....83 K3

Willow Wood Rd *MEO* DA13 .....122 A3
Willrose Crs *ABYW* SE2 ....28 A8
Willson's Rd *RAM* CT11 ....255 J2
Wilman Rd *SBGH/RUST* TN4.....270 D1
Wilmar Gdns *WWKM* BR4 ....84 B5
Wilmar Wy *BGR/WK* TN15 ....149 L5
Wilmington Av *ORP* BR6 ....87 K6
Wilmington Court Rd
  RDART DA2 ....66 A2
Wilmington Wy *RHAM* ME8 ....96 A6
Wilmot Cl *PECK* SE15 * 40 G1
Wilmot Rd *DART* DA1 ....46 B6
Wilmott Pl *SWCH* CT13 ....201 J8
Wilmount St
  WOOL/PLUM SE18 ....27 J7
Wilshaw St *NWCR* SE14 ....41 N2
Wilson Av *DEAL* CT14 ....232 E6
  ROCH ME1 ....95 K7
Wilson Rd *KEN/WIL* TN24 ....255 L8
  MAID/SHEP ME15 ....186 B4
  RTON TN11 ....210 B5
  SAND/SEL CR2........................83 J9
  SLH/COR SS17 ....34 B5
Wilson Sq *BERM/RHTH* SE16.......24 E5
Wilson La *EYN* DA4 ....67 M8
Wilson Rd *CMBW* SE5 ....40 D2
  TONN TN10 ....211 H5
Wilsons La *MAID/SHEP* ME15....184 F7
Wilson's Pl *POP/IOD* E14 ....25 K3
Wilsons St *LVPST* EC2M 24 A1
Wilsons Wy *MEO* DA13 ....122 A2
Wiltie Gdns *FOLKN* CT19 ....10 D5
Wilton Cl *DEAL* CT14 ....232 C4
Wilton Dr *DIT/AY* ME20 ....154 A4
Wilton Rd *ABYW* SE2 ....28 B6
  FOLKN CT19 ....10 A2
  MSTR CT12 ....142 E3
Wilton Ter *SIT* ME10 * 59 J9
Wiltshire Cl *RDART* DA2 ....47 K8
  WALD ME5 ....95 P6
Wiltshire Rd *BRXN/ST* SW9 ....40 A4
  ORP BR6 ....87 H1
  THHTH CR7 ....60 A9
Wiltshire Wy
  MAID/SHEP ME15 ....186 B5
  RTWE/PEM TN2 ....22 C1
Wimborne Av *CANTW/ST* CT2 ....165 G4
Wimborne La *LEE/GVPK* SE12 ....42 D6
Wimborne Pl *MSTR* CT12 ....142 G4
Wimborne Wy *BECK* BR3 ....61 K9
Wimbourne Dr *RHAM* ME8 ....96 G8
Wimpole Cl *HAYES* BR2 ....85 M1
Wimshurst Cl *CROY/NA* CR0 ....82 D5
Winans Wk *BRXN/ST* SW9 ....40 A3
Winant Wy *DVE/WH* CT16 ....291 J4
Winch Cl *CRBK* TN17 ....298 A14
Winchcomb Gdns
  ELTH/MOT SE9 ....43 H4
Winchcroft Rd *RSIT* ME9 ....129 M7
Wincheap *CANT* CT1 ....166 D6
Wincheap Rd *CANT* CT1 ....6 C6
Winchelsea Av *BRXN/ST* DA7 .....45 H1
Winchelsea Dr *DVW* CT17 * 44 A4
Winchelsea Rd *DVW* CT17 ....291 J8
  RYE TN31 ....338 E7
  WALD ME5 ....95 N9
Winchelsea St *DVW* CT17 ....291 J8
Winchelsea Ter *DVW* CT17 ....291 J8
Winchester Av *WALD* ME5 ....125 L1
Winchester Cl *KEN/WIL* TN24....255 M7
Winchester Crs *CVE* DA12 ....69 P2
Winchester Gdns *CANT* CT1 ......166 F6
Winchester Ms *DEAL* CT14 ....232 C6
Winchester Pk *HAYES* BR2 ....62 D9
Winchester Pl
  MAID/BEAR ME14 * 13 G2
  HAWK TN18...........................317 J4
  HAYES BR2 ....62 D9
  ORP BR6 ....87 K8
  TONN TN10 ....210 G5
Winchester Sq *STHWK* SE1 ....24 A4
Winchester St *STHWK* SE1 ....24 A4
Winchester Wy *RHAM* ME8 ....97 K6
Winchfield Rd *SYD* SE26..............61 K3
Wincroft's Garth *STPH/PW* TN12...246 C4
Wincliff Rd *TON* TN9 ....240 E1
Wincrofts Dr *ELTH/MOT* SE9 ......43 P5
Windall Cl *NRWD* SE19 ....60 F2
Windermere FAV ME13 ....133 H7
Windermere Av *RAM* CT11 ....142 E5
Windermere Cl *DART* DA14 * 65 M1
  ORP BR6 ....86 C7
Windermere Dr *RHAM* ME8 ....96 E7
Windermere Gdns
  RCANTE CT3 ....199 J9
Windermere Gv *SIT* ME10 ....129 M7
Windermere Rd *BXLYHN* DA7 .....45 L3
  CROY/NA CR0 ....83 L5
  WWKM BR4............................85 K5
Windfield Cl *SYD* SE26................61 K3
Windham Av *CROY/NA* CR0 ....714 A4
Wind Hl *HDCN* TN27 ....220 D3
Windhover Wy *GVE* DA12 ....70 A3
Winding Hi *FAV* ME13 ....163 H5
Windlass Pl *DEPT* SE8 ....25 M8
Windley Cl *FSTH* SE23 ....41 M1
Windmill Cl *CANT* CT1 ....166 G6
Windmill Cl *MSTR* CT12 ....142 G1
  KEN/WIL TN24 ....255 J6
  LEW SE13 * 42 A3
  RCANTW CT4 ....197 M2
  STHWK SE1 * 24 D7
Windmill Cl *RAMD* ME17..........167 H6
Windmill Gra *BGR/WK* TN15 .....120 B2
Windmill Gv *CROY/NA* CR0 ....60 A8
Windmill Hts
  MAID/BEAR ME14 ....156 E8
Windmill Hl *BGR/WK* TN15 ....151 P4
  RMAID ME17 ....218 C2
  STPH/PW TN12 ....243 J8
Windmill La *BGR/WK* TN15 ....151 P4
  EGRIN RH19 ....265 J7
  FAV ME13 ....85 M1
  HAYES BR2............................85 M8
  WADH TN5 ....294 D7
Windmill La East
  E/WMAL ME19 ....153 J6

Windmill La West
  E/WMAL ME19 ....153 H6
Windmill Pde *RAM* CT11 * 16 C5
Windmill Rd *BGR/WK* TN15.......151 N5
Windmill Rd *RAM* CT11 * 16 C5
Windmill Quay Rd *IOS* ME12 ....78 D6
Windmill Ri *IOS* ME12 ....78 D7
Windmill Rd *CANT* CT1 ....167 H4
  CROY/NA CR0 ....83 H4
  GILL ME7 ....107 M4
  HB CT6 ....107 M4
  MTCM CR4 ....82 B2
  SEV TN13 ....178 G6
  WSTB CT5 ....105 L7
Windmill St *GVE* DA12 ....49 M8
  HYTHE CT21 ....308 D6
  RTWE/PEM TN2 ....22 D2
  STRD ME2 ....71 M9
Windmill Wk *MARG* CT9 * 112 F5
Windmill Wk *MSTR* CT12 ....61 K2
Windsor Av *CDW/CHF* RM16 ....52 C5
  CHAT ME4 ....95 L4
  MARG CT9 ....112 G5
Windsor Cl *BRDST* CT10 ....113 K8
  MAID/BEAR ME14 ....13 J1
  WNWD SE27...........................60 C3
Windsor Ct *MARG* CT9 * 112 G4
  GILL ME7 ....96 A1
Windsor Dr *DART* DA1 ....117 H1
  ORP BR6 ....86 C6
  IOS ME12 ....80 B3
Windsor Gdns *CROY/NA* CR0 ......83 H5
  HB CT6 ....106 C5
  IOS ME12 ....80 B3
Windsor Ms *CAT* SE6 ....42 A9
Windsor Pl *EGRIN* RH19 ....265 K8
Windsor Rd *BXLYHS* DA6 ....44 G5
  CANT CT1 ....166 B7
  GILL ME7 ....96 A1
  MSTR CT12 ....142 C5
  THHTH CR7 ....60 B8
Windsor Wk *CMBW* SE5 ....40 D3
Windspoint Dr *PECK* SE15 ....24 E9
Windstock Cl
  BERM/RHTH SE16.....................25 J3
Windward Rd *ROCH* ME1 ....95 H5
Windy Rdg *BMLY* BR1 ....62 G3
Windyridge *GILL* ME7 ....96 B5
Wine Cl *WAP* E1W 24 F3
Winehouse La *RFOLK* CT18 ....289 M9
Winfield La *BGR/WK* TN15 ....181 H1
Winfield St *DEPT* SE8 ....26 A6
Winforton St *GNWCH* SE10 ....41 G3
Winfreds Cl *CRBK* TN17 ....319 L3
Wingate Crs *CROY/NA* CR0 ....82 D3
Wingate Rd *FOLKN* CT19 ....310 C6
  SCUP DA14 ....64 E4
Wingfield *GRAYS* RM17 ....32 A8
Wingfield Ms *PECK* SE15 ....40 G3
Wingfield Rd *GVW* DA11 ....49 M8
Wingfield St *PECK* SE15 ....40 G3
Wingham Cl
  MAID/SHEP ME15 ....186 C4
  RHAM ME8 ....96 F3
Wingham Rd *RCANTE* CT3 ....168 B5
Wingham Well La
  RCANTE CT3 ....199 J2
Wingmore Rd *HNHL* SE24 ....40 C4
Wingrove Rd *CAT* SE6 ....62 F6
Wingrove Dr *CHAT* ME4 ....290 F5
Wings Cl *BRDST* CT10 ....113 N8
Winifred Av *MSTR* CT12 ....143 H2
Winifred Rd *DART* DA1 ....66 B8
  ERITH DA8 ....29 K8
  MAID/SHEP ME15 ....156 C9
Winifred St *CAN/RD* E16 ....26 C4
Winkle Cl *HB* CT6 ....106 G3
Winlaton Rd *BMLY* BR1 ....61 B3
Winn Common Rd
  WOOL/PLUM SE18 ....27 M9
Winnipeg Dr *ORP* BR6 ....86 C10
Winnipeg Dr *ORP* BR6 ....116 C1
Winn Rd *LEE/GVPK* SE12 ....42 E9
Winser Rd *CRBK* TN17 ....319 N5
Winsley Av *WHM* TN16 ....73 J6
Winstanley Crs *RAM* CT11 ....143 J4
Winstanley Rd *IOS* ME12 ....57 L6
Winston Av *E/WMAL* ME19 ....153 J9
Winston Cl *CANT* CT1 ....167 K5
  RDART DA2 ....47 M7
Winston Ct *DEPT* SE8 ....111 H5
Winston Dr *STRD* ME2 ....72 C6
Winstone Scott Av *RRTW* TN5...269 K4
Winston Gdns *HB* CT6 ....108 A6
Winston Rd *STRD* ME2 ....94 C1
Winterage La *RFOLK* CT18 ....288 C4
Winterbourne Av *ORP* BR6 ....86 C7
Winterbourne Rd *CAT* SE6 ....41 M9
  THHTH CR7 ....82 F1
Winterbrook Rd *HNHL* SE24 ....40 C4
Winterfield La *E/WMAL* ME19....153 K3
Wintergarden Crs *RDART* DA2....47 N8
Wintergreen Cl *CHAT* ME4 ....73 J6
Winters Cft *GVE* DA12 ....70 A3
Winterstoke Crs *RAM* CT11 ....17 K1
Winterstoke Rd *FSTH* SE23 ....41 K5
Winterstoke Wy *RAM* CT11 ....17 J1
Winthorpe St *WCHPL* E1 ....24 E1
Winthrop St *WCHPL* E1 * 24 E1
Winton Cl *SWLY* BR8 ....88 D1
Winton Rd *ORP* BR6 ....86 C6
Winton Wy *LYDD* TN29 ....326 E9
  STRHM/NOR SW16 ....60 A6
Wireless Rd *BH/WHM* TN16......115 N9
Wire Mill La *LING* RH7 ....234 B6

The Wirrals *WALD* ME5 ....125 M1
Wirral Wood Cl *CHST* BR7 ....63 L5
Wisbeach Rd *CROY/NA* CR0 ....83 J2
Wiseacre *RRTW* TN5 ....295 H4
Wise's La *BGR/WK* TN15 ....121 H3
Wises La *SIT* ME10 ....129 H1
Wishart Rd *BKHTH/KID* SE3 ....43 H7
The Wish *RASHW* TN26 ....305 L9
Wish Ward *RYE* TN31 ....338 E7
Wishing Well *STMC/STPC* BR5 ....64 C6
Wissenden La *HDCN* TN27 ....249 L8
  RASHW TN26 ....279 P2
Wisteria Cl *ORP* BR6 ....86 C6
Wisteria Gdns *SWLY* BR8 ....65 M8
Wisteria Rd *LEW* SE13 ....42 B5
Witches La *SEV* TN13 ....148 C8
Witherby Cl *PGE/AN* SE20...........18 A2
Witchell Rd *CROY/NA* CR0 ....83 M5
Witherby Cl *CROY/NA* CR0 ....83 A9
Witherston Wy *ELTH/MOT* SE9 ...63 K1
Witherby Cl *MARG* RI *RRTW* TN5...269 H9
Witley Crs *CROY/NA* CR0 ....114 F1
Witley Wy *FSTH* SE23 ....61 K2
Wittersham Rd *WALD* ME5 ....95 N9
Wittersham La *RYE* TN31 ....332 E8
Wittersham Rd *BMLY* BR1 ....62 A4
  CRBK TN17...........................331 J1
  RYE TN31 ....332 D5
  TENT TN30 ....320 C9
Wivenhoe ASH TN23 ....285 J3
Wivenhoe Cl *PECK* SE15 ....40 G4
  RHAM ME8 ....97 K4
Wiverton Rd *SYD* SE26................61 J5
Woburn Cl *THMD* SE28 ....28 C2
Wodehouse Rd *DART* DA1 ....158 H5
Wodehouse Av *CMBW* SE5 ....40 F2
Wodehouse Cl *DIT/AY* ME20 .....123 N9
Wodeham Gdns *WCHPL* E1 ....24 D1
Wodehouse Av *CMBW* SE5 ....40 F2
Wokindon Rd *CDW/CHF* RM16....53 M4
Woldham Rd *HAYES* BR2 ....85 M1
Woldham Rd *HAYES* BR2 ....85 M1
Wolds Dr *ORP* BR6 ....86 B8
The Wold *CTHM* CR3 ....144 D7
Wolfe Cl *HAYES* BR2 ....85 K3
Wolfe Crs *CHARL* SE7 ....26 E8
Wolfe Rd *MAIDW* ME14 ....184 C1
Wolfe Ter *DVE/WH* CT16 * 291 J4
Wolfington Rd *WNWD* SE27 ....60 B5
Wolfram Cl *LEW* SE13 ....42 C6
Wolfs Cl *OXTED* RH8 ....175 K7
Wolfs Rd *OXTED* RH8 ....175 L6
Wollett St *OXTED* RH8 ....175 L6
Wollaston Cl *RHAM* ME8 ....126 C2
Wollaston Rd *DEAL* CT14 ....233 J5
Wolseley Av *HB* CT6 ....106 C2
Wolseley Pl *KEN/WIL* TN24 ....14 C4
Wolseley Rd *SBGH/RUST* TN4...270 F1
  CROY/NA CR0 ....84 G7
Wolseley St *WCHPL* E1 ....24 C5
Wolsey Ct *ELTH/MOT* SE9 * 43 K7
Wolsey Crs *CROY/NA* CR0 ....114 F3
Wolsey Ms *ORP* BR6 ....86 G9
Wolsey St *WCHPL* E1 ....24 F1
Wolsey Wy *DART* DA1 ....45 N6
Wolvercote Rd *ABYW* SE2 ....28 C5
Wombwell Gdns *GVW* DA11 ....49 J1
Wood Av *FOLK* CT19 ....310 C4
  PUR RM19 ....30 D7
Woodbank Rd *BMLY* BR1 ....62 C2
Woodberry Dr *SIT* ME10 ....150 A2
Woodberry Ct *DART* DA5............65 M2
Woodbine Gv *PGE/AN* SE20 ....61 H6
Woodbine Rd *BFN/LL* DA15 ....44 A9
Woodbridge Dr
  MAID/SHEP ME15 ....185 K2
Woodbrook Rd *HDCN* TN27 ....221 J3
Woodbrook Rd *ABYW* SE2 ....27 J9
Woodbury Av *EGRIN* RH19 ....265 L8
Woodbury Cl *BH/WHM* TN16 .....146 A3
  CROY/NA CR0 ....84 B5
  EGRIN RH19 ....265 L8
  SBGH/RUST TN4........................270 D3
Woodbury Gdns
  LEE/GVPK SE12 ....62 F2
Woodbury La *TENT* TN30 ....301 H8
Woodbury Park Gdns
  SBGH/RUST TN4........................270 E3
Woodbury Park Rd
  RTWE/PEM TN2 ....22 D1
Woodbury Rd *HAWK* TN18 ....317 J3
  WALD ME5 ....125 K4
Woodchurch Cl *SCUP* DA14 ....63 P2
  WALD ME5 ....125 L1
Woodchurch Crs *RHAM* ME8 ......96 F4
Woodchurch Dr *BMLY* BR1 ....63 H6
Woodchurch Rd *BRCH* CT7 ....141 N1
  RASHW TN26 ....281 L8
  TENT TN30 ....301 K7
Wood Cl *BXLY* DA5 ....65 N3
  DIT/AY ME20 ....154 D4
Woodclyffe Dr *CHST* BR7 ....63 L7
Woodcock Hill RFOLK CT18 ....288 C8
Woodcock Hl *EGRIN* RH19 ....264 C2
Woodcock La *CRBK* TN17 ....318 D3
  RMAID ME17 ....218 F4
Woodcocks *CAN/RD* E16 ....26 D1
Woodcombe Crs *FSTH* SE23 ....41 J9
Woodcote Dr *ORP* BR6 ....86 B4
Woodcote Pl *WNWD* SE27 ....60 C4
Woodcote Dr *ORP* BR6 ....86 B4
Wood Cottage La
  FOLKN CT19 ....310 A4
Woodcourt Cl *SIT* ME10 ....129 M3
Woodcroft *ELTH/MOT* SE9 ....63 J2
Woodcroft Ms *DEPT* SE8 ....25 H7
Woodcroft Rd *THHTH* CR7 ....82 E4
Woodcut *MAID/BEAR* ME14.......155 M4
Woodcutters Av
  CDW/CHF RM16 ....32 D5
Wood Dene *PECK* SE15 * 41 H7
Wood Dr *CHST* BR7 ....63 J5
  SEV TN15 ....20 B5
Wooden Bridge Ter
  WNWD SE27 * 60 B2
Woodend *NRWD* SE19 ....60 C5

Wood End SWLY BR8 .... 88 B1
Wooderson Cl SNWD SE25 .... 83 K1
Woodfair Dr DART DA1 .... 45 P5
Woodfarrs CMBW SE5 .... 40 D5
Woodfield Av FOLKN CT19 .. 310 B4
  GVW DA11 .... 49 M9
  RTON TN19 .... 210 B5
Woodfield Cl FOLKN CT19 .. 310 A4
  NRWD SE19 .... 60 C6
Woodfield Rd TON TN9 ...... 240 E1
Woodfields SEV TN13 .... 148 C8
Woodfield Wy HOO/HM ME3 .. 72 D3
Woodford Av MSTR CT12 .... 143 J3
Woodford Ct BRCH CT7 ..... 111 H6
Woodford Gr E/WMAL ME19 .. 153 J9
Woodford Rd MAIDW ME16 .. 184 C1
Woodgate RCANTW CT4 ...... 197 K8
Woodgate Cl FAV ME15 ...... 132 F5
Woodgate La RSIT ME9 ...... 128 C3
Woodgate Wy RTON TN11 ... 240 C2
Woodgers Gv SWLY BR8 ..... 65 P8
Woodget Cl EHAM E6 .... 26 F2
Woodhall Av DUL SE21 ...... 60 F2
Woodhall Dr DUL SE21 ...... 60 F2
Woodhall Ter QBOR ME11 * .. 77 J2
Wooham Rd CAT SE6 .... 42 A2
Woodhatch Cl EHAM E6 ..... 26 F1
Woodhead Dr ORP BR6 ...... 86 F7
Wood Hi CANTW/ST CT2 .... 136 D7
Woodhill WOOL/PLUM SE18 .. 26 F7
Woodhill Pk RTWE/PEM TN2 271 M2
Woodhouse Cl EDUL SE22 ... 40 C5
Woodhurst WALD ME5 .... 125 J1
Woodhurst Av STMC/STPC BR5..86 C5
Woodhurst Cl STRD ME2 ..... 94 A4
Woodhurst La OXTED RH8 ... 175 H1
Woodhurst Pk OXTED RH8 ... 175 H6
Woodhurst Rd ABYW SE2 .... 27 D9
Woodington Cl ELTH/MOT SE9 .43 L7
Woodknoll Dr CHST BR7 .... 63 K7
Woodland Av BRCH CT7 ..... 111 H6
  HART DA3 .... 91 J2
  RCANTE CT3 .... 229 H1
Woodland Cl DVW CT17 ..... 290 F5
  E/WMAL ME19 .... 153 H4
  HART DA3 .... 68 G9
  SWLY BR8 .... 65 H2
  SBGH/RUST TN4 .... 270 F1
Woodland Dr OXTED RH8 .... 174 G4
Woodland Crs
  BERM/RHTH SE16 .... 24 G5
  GNWCH SE10 .... 25 P9
Woodland Gdns EDEN TN8 .. 206 F7
  IOS ME12 .... 58 B9
Woodland Gv GNWCH SE10 .. 25 P8
Woodland Hl NRWD SE19 .... 60 E5
Woodland Ri BGR/WK TN15 .. 149 K8
  HYTHE CT21 * 307 P6
  OXTED RH8 .... 175 H6
Woodland Rd HB CT6 .... 106 C4
  NRWD SE19 .... 60 E4
  RFOLK CT18 .... 50 B8
  SBGH/RUST TN4 .... 270 F1
  THHTH CR7 .... 82 F1
Woodlands BXLYHS DA6 ..... 45 K6
  CANTW/ST CT2 .... 156 N6
  FAV ME15 .... 134 D6
  RMAID ME17 .... 184 D8
  RTWE/PEM TN12 .... 242 G2
  WALD ME5 .... 125 M3
Woodlands Av BFN/LL DA15 .. 44 A9
  SNOD ME6 .... 123 N4
Woodlands Cl BMLY BR1 .... 63 K8
  CDW/CHF RM16 .... 32 F6
  MAID/BEAR ME14 .... 155 N5
  SWLY BR8 .... 65 P8
  WBY/YAL ME8 .... 183 P3
Woodlands Ct
  SBGH/RUST TN4 * 240 D7
Woodlands Dr GDST RH9 ... 204 B4
  HYTHE CT21 .... 309 M3
Woodlands La GVE DA12 .... 70 F6
Woodlands Pde
  DIT/AY ME20 * 154 C4
Woodlands Pk BXLY DA5 .... 65 L3
Woodlands Park Rd
  GNWCH SE10 .... 25 P9
Woodlands Ri SWLY BR8 .... 65 P8
Woodlands Rd BMLY BR1 ... 63 K8
  BXLYHN DA7 .... 44 G4
  DIT/AY ME20 .... 154 B3
  EGRIN RH19 .... 265 K4
  GILL ME8 .... 96 C4
  ISS ME12 .... 53 J7
  KEN/WIL TN24 .... 117 H1
  ORP BR6 .... 117 H1
  RCANTE CT3 .... 198 E7
  SIT ME10 .... 42 B8
  TON TN9 .... 240 D3
Woodlands St LEW SE13 .... 42 B8
Woodlands Ter GILL ME7 * .. 96 C3
  SWLY BR8 .... 88 B3
The Woodlands
  BRXN/ST SW9 * 42 B1
  LEW SE13 .... 42 B8
  NRWD SE19 .... 60 C6
  ORP BR6 .... 117 J1
Woodland Ter CHARL SE7 .. 27 G6
Woodland Vw TENT TN30 ... 332 B1
Woodland Wy ABYW SE2 .... 28 C7
  BRDST CT10 .... 113 M4
  CANTW/ST CT2 .... 84 B5
  CROY/NA CRO 84 B5
  LYDD TN29 .... 327 L1
  MAID/BEAR ME14 .... 155 N5
  RDART DA2 .... 47 N6
  RDART DA2 .... 240 A6
  STMC/STPC BR5 .... 86 D1
  SWCH CT13 .... 233 D1
  WWKM BR4 .... 84 A7
Wood La ASH TN23 .... 282 F5
  CRBK TN17 .... 303 M4
  HART DA3 .... 67 M3
Woodlark Rd CHAT ME4 .... 73 H8
Woodlea E/WMAL ME19 .... 153 M2
  HART DA3 .... 68 G9
  KEN/WIL TN24 .... 3 F1
Woodlea Dr HAYES BR2 .... 85 H3
Woodleas MAIDW ME16 .... 184 E1

Woodley Rd ORP BR6 .... 87 K6
Wood Lodge Gdns BMLY BR1 .. 63 J6
Wood Lodge Gra SEV TN13 * .. 149 H7
Wood Lodge La WWKM BR4 .. 84 F7
Woodman St CAN/RD E16 ... 27 H4
Woodmere ELTH/MOT SE9 ... 43 M1
Woodmere Av CROY/NA CRO .. 84 A4
Woodmere Cl CROY/NA CRO .. 84 A4
Woodmere Gdns
  CROY/NA CRO 84 A4
Woodmere Wy BECK BR3 ... 84 C2
Woodmount SWLY BR8 ...... 88 C4
Woodnesborough La
  SWCH CT13 .... 201 J7
Woodnesborough Rd
  SWCH CT13 .... 201 M2
Woodpecker Dr RSIT ME9 ... 99 M2
Woodpecker Gld RHAM ME8 .. 96 F8
Woodpecker Ms LEW SE13 .. 42 B5
Woodpecker Mt
  CROY/NA CRO 114 B3
Woodquest Av DIT/AY ME20 .. 153 N3
  NWCR SE14 .... 25 H9
Woodquest Av HI/HHL SE24 .. 40 B6
Wood Ride STMC/STPC BR5 .. 86 E1
Wood Rd BH/WHM TN16 .... 145 M3
  HYTHE CT21 .... 308 G5
Woodrow CHARL SE7 .... 26 F7
Woodrow Cha HB CT6 .... 107 M5
Woodruff Cl RHAM ME8 ..... 97 M2
Woodrush Cl NWCR SE14 ... 41 L1
Woodrush Pl CHAT ME4 ..... 73 H6
Woodseer St WCHPL E1 ..... 24 C1
Woodsgate Wy
  RTWE/PEM TN2 .... 271 L2
Woods Hi RCANTW CT4 .... 225 K5
Woods La ASH TN23 .... 282 A2
  FAV ME15 .... 164 C2
  MEO DA13 .... 122 A5
  ORP BR6 .... 87 H9
Woodside Av CHST BR7 .... 86 C6
  SNWD SE25 .... 83 N5
Woodside Cl BXLYHN DA7 .. 45 M5
  DVE/WH CT16 .... 290 F5
  STRD ME2 .... 94 A2
  STMC/STPC BR5 .... 271 P2
Woodside Court Rd
  CROY/NA CRO 83 M4
Woodside Crs BFN/LL DA15 .. 64 A2
Woodside Dr RDART DA2 ... 65 N3
Woodside Gdns SIT ME10 .. 129 L5
Woodside Gn SNWD SE25 .. 83 M3
Woodside La BXLY DA5 ..... 44 F7
Woodside Pde BFN/LL DA15 *.. 64 A2
Woodside Pk SNWD SE25 ... 83 M3
Woodside Rd BFN/LL DA15 .. 64 A2
  BMLY BR1 .... 85 P2
  BXLYHN DA7 .... 45 M5
  CANTW/ST CT2 .... 137 L6
  MAID/SHEP ME15 .... 185 P4
  RSEV TN14 .... 147 L3
  RTWE/PEM TN2 .... 271 P2
  SBGH/RUST TN4 .... 270 A4
  SEV TN13 .... 148 F8
  SNWD SE25 .... 83 N3
  TON TN9 .... 240 F2
Woodside Wy CROY/NA CRO .. 83 P3
Woods Ley RCANTE CT3 .... 170 G9
Woody's Pl DVW CT17 ...... 291 J5
  STHWK SE1 * 24 B6
Wood's Rd PECK SE15 ...... 41 K2
Woodstock EGRIN RH19 .... 264 H6
Woodstock Cl BXLY DA5 .... 65 P7
Woodstock Gdns BECK BR3 .. 61 P7
Woodstock Rd CROY/NA CRO .. 83 J7
  DEAL CT14 .... 233 H5
  SIT ME10 .... 42 B8
  STRD ME2 .... 66 A2
Woodstock St CAN/RD E16 .. 26 A2
Woodstock Ter POP/IOD E14 .. 25 L3
Woodstock Wy
  KEN/WIL TN24 .... 252 F5
Wood St CAN/RD E16 .... 26 C6
  EGRIN RH19 .... 264 C7
  GILL ME7 .... 72 C9
  GRAYS RM17 .... 32 D9
  IOS ME12 .... 57 L6
  RSIT ME9 .... 130 E5
  MEO DA13 .... 122 A4
  STRD ME2 .... 66 C9
  SWLY BR8 .... 66 G2
Woodsyre SYD SE26 .... 60 B2
Wood V FSTH SE23 .... 41 H9
Woodvale Av SNWD SE25 ... 60 F9
  WSTB CT5 .... 106 B6
Wood Vw CDW/CHF RM16 .. 32 F7
Woodview RDART DA2 ...... 67 N5
Wood View Cl BGR/WK TN15 .. 120 D2
Woodview Cl ORP BR6 ...... 86 D6
Woodview Crs RTON TN11 .. 210 H5
Woodview Ri STRD ME2 .... 71 P6
Woodville Rd SWLY BR8 ... 65 L8
Woodville CANTW/ST CT2 * .. 155 N6
  LEE/GVPK SE12 .... 42 E6
Woodville Cots GVE DA12 *.. 50 A7
Woodville Gv WELL DA16 * .. 44 C3
Woodville Pl GVW DA11 .... 49 M8
Woodville Rd
  MAID/SHEP ME15 .... 185 M1
  MSTR CT12 .... 142 G3
  THHTH CR7 .... 82 F1
Woodville St
  WOOL/PLUM SE18 .... 26 F7
Woodward Cl GRAYS RM17 .. 32 C7
Woodward Rd DUL SE21 .... 60 D7
Woodwards Hts GRAYS RM17 .. 32 C7
Woodward Ter RDART DA2 .. 47 L7
Wood Wy ORP BR6 .... 86 B6
Woodyates Rd LEE/GVPK SE12 .. 42 J5
Woolacombe Rd 42 C3
Woolaston Cl
  MAID/SHEP ME15 .... 185 L2
Woolbrook Cl RHAM ME8 ... 97 L4

Woolbrook Rd DART DA1 ... 45 N7
Woolcomber St DVE/WH CT16 * .. 9 F4
Wooldeys Rd RHAM ME8 .... 97 J4
Wooler St WALW SE17 ...... 84 H8
Woolett Cl DART DA1 .... 45 J9
Woolett St SIT ME10 .... 99 J9
Woolf Cl THMD SE28 .... 28 A4
Woollett Cl DART DA1 ...... 45 J5
Woollett St MAID/BEAR ME14 .. 13 F5
Woolley Cl SBGH/RUST TN4 .. 240 C5
Woolmer Dr KEN/WIL TN24 .. 283 K1
Woolmore St POP/IOD E14 .. 25 M3
Woolpack Hl RASHE TN25 .. 284 E5
Woolreeds Rd ASH TN23 ... 282 D1
Woolstaplers Wy
  BERM/RHTH SE16 .... 24 D6
Woolston Cl FSTH SE23 .... 61 L1
Woolwich Church St
  WOOL/PLUM SE18 .... 26 E7
Woolwich Cl MAID ME5 .... 95 M7
Woolwich Common
  WOOL/PLUM SE18 .... 27 H9
Woolwich Foot Tnl C 27 H5
Woolwich High St
  WOOL/PLUM SE18 .... 26 E7
Woolwich Manor Wy
  CAN/RD E16 .... 27 K4
Woolwich Manorway
  CAN/RD E16 .... 27 J5
Woolwich New Rd
  WOOL/PLUM SE18 .... 27 H8
Woolwich Rd ABYW SE2 .... 27 H9
  BXLYHN DA7 .... 45 J4
  GNWCH SE10 .... 26 C5
Wooster Gdns POP/IOD E14 .. 25 N2
Wootton Cl RCANTW CT4 .. 195 P7
Wootton Dr RCANTW CT4 .. 258 F6
Wopsle Cl ROCH ME1 ...... 95 J7
Worbeck Rd PGE/AN SE20 .. 61 H8
Worcester Av E/WMAL ME19 .. 183 H1
Worcester Cl CROY/NA CRO .. 85 C5
  FAV ME15 .... 133 H8
  IOS ME12 .... 78 C1
  MEO DA13 .... 69 K6
  STRD ME2 .... 71 N7
Worcester Dr SIT ME10 .... 99 J8
Worcester La RCANTE CT3 .. 167 K5
Worcester Rd
  MAID/BEAR ME14 .... 186 A4
Wordsworth Cl TIL RM18 ... 49 N3
  WALD ME5 .... 95 N7
Wordsworth Gdns
  RCANTE CT3 .... 199 J9
Wordsworth Ri EGRIN RH19 .. 264 F7
Wordsworth Wy DART DA1 .. 46 C5
Worgan St BERM/RHTH SE16 .. 24 G6
Workhouse La
  MAID/SHEP ME15 .... 185 M1
  RMAID ME17 .... 217 K1
Workhouse Rd E/WMAL ME19 .. 122 F9
  FAV ME15 .... 192 D1
Worlds End RSIT ME9 ...... 131 K5
Worlds End La ORP BR6 ... 117 N1
Worleys Dr ORP BR6 .... 86 E8
Worlingham Rd EDUL SE22 .. 40 F5
Wormdale Hl RSIT ME9 ..... 128 C9
Wormdale Rd RSIT ME9 .... 128 B1
Wormwood St OBST EC2N .. 24 B2
Worsfold Cl
  MAID/SHEP ME15 .... 185 M2
Worships Hl SEV TN13 .... 148 D7
Worship Bridge Rd SYD SE26 .. 61 N4
Worsted La EGRIN RH19 .. 265 L9
Worth Cl ORP BR6 .... 86 F8
Worth Gv WALW SE17 * 84 B8
Worthing Cl GRAYS RM17 .. 31 P9
Worthington Cl MTCM CR4 .. 82 A1
Worthington St DVW CT17 ... 8 C3
Wortley Rd CROY/NA CRO .. 82 J1
Wotton Cl MAID/SHEP ME15 .. 186 B6
Wotton Ct BRCH CT7 ...... 140 A2
Wotton Gn STMC/STPC BR5 .. 87 L1
Wotton Rd ASH TN23 ...... 282 E2
  DEPT SE8 .... 25 J9
Wouldham Rd CAN/RD E16 .. 26 A2
  GRAYS RM17 .... 31 P9
  ROCH ME1 .... 94 B8

Wrights Cl TENT TN30 ..... 301 H7
Wrights Rd SNWD SE25 .... 60 F9
Wright's Wy WLGTN SM6 ... 82 A8
Wright's Wy IOS ME12 ..... 79 J7
Wrotham Hill Rd
  BGR/WK TN15 .... 121 P5
  BRDST CT10 .... 113 N9
  MEO DA13 .... 69 K8
  MEO DA13 .... 121 P5
  WELL DA16 .... 44 E2
Wrotham Water La
  BGR/WK TN15 .... 121 N9
Wrotham Water Rd
  BGR/WK TN15 .... 121 N9
Wrottesley Rd
  WOOL/PLUM SE18 .... 27 K9
Wroxham Rd THMD SE28 ... 28 C3
Wroxton Rd PECK SE15 .... 41 H3
Wulfere Wy STRD ME2 ..... 72 D5
Wulfred Wy BGR/WK TN15 .. 25 J5
Wyatt Cl BERM/RHTH SE16 .. 25 J5
Wyatt Rd STRD ME2 .... 151 J5
Wyatt Pl STRD ME2 .... 18 B2
Wyatt St MAID/BEAR ME14 .. 13 C4
Wybourne Ri RTWE/PEM TN2 .. 270 E7
Wybournes La HOO/HM ME3 .. 53 J5
Wych Elm Wy HYTHE CT21 .. 308 D6
Wycherley Cl BKHTH/KID SE3 .. 42 D1
Wycherley Crs DVE/WH CT16 .. 291 J3
Wychwood Av THHTH CR7 .. 60 B9
Wycliffe Cl WALD ME5 ..... 44 B2
Wycliffe Rw GVW DA11 .... 49 K9
Wydenhurst Rd CROY/NA CRO .. 83 M4
Wydeville Manor Rd
  LEE/GVPK SE12 .... 62 F3
Wye Cl ORP BR6 .... 86 C4
Wye Gdns MARG CT9 ...... 115 L8
Wye Gn HB CT6 .... 107 L4
Wye Rd BGR/WK TN15 .... 151 K4
  GVE DA12 .... 69 P1
  RASHE TN25 .... 223 H7
  TONN TN10 .... 210 P5
Wykeham Cl GVE DA12 .... 70 A5
  QBOR ME11 .... 77 H4
Wykeham Gv RMAID ME17 .. 187 K4
Wykeham La KEN/WIL TN24 .. 130 A1
Wykeham St STRD ME2 .... 72 B7
Wyke Manor Rd
  MAID/BEAR ME14 .... 13 F4
Wyke Rd CHAT ME4 .... 95 H5
Wyles St GILL ME7 .... 18 A3
Wyleu St FSTH SE23 ...... 41 L8
Wylie Rd HOO/HM ME3 .... 73 K2
Wynan Rd POP/IOD E14 .... 25 L8
Wyncham Av BFN/LL DA15 .. 43 N9
Wyncote Wy SAND/SEL CR2 .. 114 A3
Wyncroft Cl BMLY BR1 .... 63 K9
Wyndcliff Rd CHARL SE7 .. 26 C9
Wyndham Av MARG CT9 .. 112 C5
  RTON TN11 .... 209 L9
Wyndham Cl ORP BR6 ..... 86 D5
Wyndham Est CMBW SE5 .. 40 C1
Wyndham Rd CHAT ME4 ... 95 J5
  CMBW SE5 .... 40 C1
  DVW CT17 .... 291 J7
The Wynd RASHE TN25 ... 252 F2
Wyndham La RASHE TN25 .. 221 J1
Wyndham Rd HNHL SE24 .. 40 D6
Wynell Rd FSTH SE23 ..... 61 K2
Wyness Ct STRD ME2 * 72 B7
Wynford Gv STMC/STPC BR5 .. 64 D9
Wynford Pl BELV DA17 .... 29 H5
Wynford Wy ELTH/MOT SE9 .. 63 K2
Wynne Rd BRXN/ST SW9 .. 40 A3
Wynns Av BFN/LL DA15 .... 44 A6
Wynnstow Pk OXTED RH8 .. 175 J7
Wynton Gdns SNWD SE25 .. 83 K2
The Wytchlings RMAID ME17 .. 187 N9
Wytherling Cl
  MAID/BEAR ME14 .... 156 C7
Wythes Cl BMLY BR1 ...... 63 K8
Wythes Rd CAN/RD E16 ... 26 E2
Wythfield Rd ELTH/MOT SE9 .. 43 K7
Wyvern Ct DART DA1 ...... 46 C8
  ORP BR6 * 86 G9
  SIT ME10 .... 99 M7
  SNOD ME6 .... 123 P6
Wyvern Wy KEN/WIL TN24 .. 3 J2
Wyvill Cl HAM ME8 .... 97 H9
Wyvis St POP/IOD E14 ..... 25 L1

Y

Yabsley St POP/IOD E14 ... 25 M4
Yalding Cl MARG CT9 ...... 92 B6
Yalding Gv STMC/STPC BR5 .. 87 L1
Yalding Hl MAID/YAL ME18 .. 183 P8
Yalding Rd BERM/RHTH SE16 .. 24 D6
Yantlet Dr STRD ME2 ...... 71 L8
Yardhurst Gdns MARG CT9 .. 113 L2
Yardley Cl TON TN9 .... 240 B3
Yardley Park Rd TON TN9 .. 210 F7
The Yard RCANTW CT4 .... 228 C5
  WALD ME5 .... 125 N2
Yarnton Wy ABYW SE2 .... 28 E6
  ERITH DA18 .... 28 E6
Yarrow Cl BRDST CT10 .... 143 M1
Yarrow Ct MAID/BEAR ME14 .. 156 C7
Yarrow Rd MAID ME5 ...... 125 N3
Yateley St WOOL/PLUM SE18 .. 26 K5
Yates Cl RYE TN31 .... 344 B1
Yaugher La MARG CT9 .... 127 J2
Yeames Cl MAID/SHEP ME15 .. 185 L2
Yeats Cl LEW SE13 .... 99 P8
Yelsted La MAID/BEAR ME14 .. 126 A6
  RSIT ME9 .... 127 K4
Yelsted Rd RSIT ME9 ...... 127 J3
Yeoman Ct EHAM E6 .... 27 J2
Yeoman Dr CILL ME7 ...... 96 E6
Yeoman Gdns KEN/WIL TN24 .. 253 C6
  STPH/PW TN12 .... 242 F3

Yeoman La MAID/BEAR ME14 .. 156 E9
Yeoman Pk MAID/SHEP ME15 .. 186 D1
Yeomans Dr CANTW/ST CT2 .. 166 B4
Yeoman's Mdw SEV TN13 .. 20 C5
Yeoman St BERM/RHTH SE16 .. 25 H7
Yeoman's Yd WCHPL E1 * .. 24 C3
Yeoman Wy
  MAID/SHEP ME15 .... 186 D1
Yeo St BOW E3 .... 25 L1
Yeovil Cl ORP BR6 .... 86 F6
Yester Dr CHST BR7 .... 63 J6
Yester Pk CHST BR7 .... 63 J6
Yester Rd CHST BR7 .... 63 K6
Yevele Cl QBOR ME11 ..... 77 J2
Yew Cl ASH TN23 .... 252 B7
Yewdale Cl BMLY BR1 ..... 62 C5
Yew La EGRIN RH19 .... 264 E5
Yew Rd HOO/HM ME3 ...... 73 L4
Yew Tree Cl BRDST CT10 .. 113 J9
  DEAL CT14 * 232 F5
  DIT/AY ME20 * 154 D3
  HART DA3 .... 69 H8
  LEW SE13 .... 42 A4
  RASHE TN25 .... 286 A7
  SEV TN13 .... 148 A8
Yew Tree Cl WALD ME5 * .. 3 C2
  CANTW/ST CT2 * 137 M9
Yew Tree Gdns BRCH CT7 .. 111 H6
Yew Tree Green Rd
  STPH/PW TN12 .... 243 P8
Yew Tree Ms DEAL CT14 .. 232 F6
Yew Tree Rd BECK BR3 ... 61 M9
  LYDD TN29 .... 337 L1
  SBGH/RUST TN4 .... 240 D9
Yoakes La LYDD TN29 .... 335 P3
Yoakley Sq MARG CT9 .... 112 C5
Yoke Cl STRD ME2 * 7 H1
Yokosuka Wy RHAM ME8 ... 96 D2
Yolande Gdns ELTH/MOT SE9 .. 43 J6
Yopps Gn BGR/WK TN15 .. 181 H2
York & Albany Cl DEAL CT14 .. 232 C8
York Av BFN/LL DA15 ..... 64 A4
  BRDST CT10 .... 113 M9
  EGRIN RH19 .... 265 K8
  GILL ME7 .... 7 ..
  WALD ME5 .... 125 K2
York Cl CMBW SE5 * 26 C2
  EHAM E6 .... 26 G2
York Gv PECK SE15 .... 41 J2
York Hi CHAT ME4 * 95 P4
  WNWD SE27 .... 60 B2
Yorkland Av WELL DA16 ... 44 B4
York Ms FOLKN CT20 * 310 B4
York Pde TONN TN10 ...... 210 F4
York Ri ORP BR6 .... 71 H1
York Rd BH/WHM TN16 .... 145 L4
  CANT CT1 .... 7 C7
  CROY/NA CRO 82 F4
  DART DA1 .... 46 B8
  GVW DA11 .... 49 H8
  HB CT6 .... 107 J1
  KEN/WIL TN24 .... 252 C4
  MAID/SHEP ME15 .... 95 H5
  ROCH ME1 .... 95 J5
  RTW TN1 .... 22 C3
  SAND/SEL CR2 .... 114 A4
  TONN TN10 .... 210 G5
Yorkshire Rd MTCM CR4 .. 82 D2
  POP/IOD E14 .... 25 H2
York Sq POP/IOD E14 ..... 25 H2
York St BRDST CT10 .... 113 N9
  DVW CT17 .... 8 D4
  RAM CT11 .... 4 C5
York Street Rbt DVW CT17 .. 8 D5
York Ter BRCH CT7 .... 111 J6
  ERITH DA8 .... 45 L2
Young Cl DEAL CT14 ...... 232 G3
Young's Rd CAN/RD E16 ... 26 D2
Young's Pl PDV CT15 ...... 312 A1
Ypres Ct CANT CT1 .... 167 J3
Ypres Dr SIT ME10 .... 99 N5

Z

Zambra Wy BGR/WK TN15 .. 149 L5
Zampa Rd BERM/RHTH SE16 .. 24 F8
Zangwill Rd BKHTH/KID SE3 .. 43 H2
Zarena Ct FOLK CT20 * 310 C8
Zealand Rd CANT CT1 ..... 166 B6
Zelah Rd STMC/STPC BR5 .. 87 J4
Zenoria St EDUL SE22 .... 40 F5
Zermatt Rd THHTH CR7 ... 83 H1
Zetland Av GILL ME7 ...... 96 B4
Zetland St POP/IOD E14 ... 25 M1
Zillah Gdns RHAM ME8 .... 96 E8
Zion Pl GVE DA12 .... 49 M8
  MARG CT9 .... 15 J3
  THHTH CR7 .... 83 J1
Zion Rd THHTH CR7 .... 83 J1

AA Travel Centre
  DVE/WH CT16 .... 9 J3
The Abbey Clinic
  BELV DA17 .... 28 E8
Abbey Court School
  RHAM ME8 .... 126 F1
The Abbey School
  FAV ME13 .... 71 P7
Abbey Primary School
  ABYW SE2 .... 28 B6
The Abbey School
  FAV ME13 .... 132 F8
Abbey Trading Estate
  SYD SE26 .... 61 L4
Abbey Wood School
  ABYW SE2 .... 27 P6
ABC Cinema
  GVE DA12 .... 49 M7
Aberdeen Wharf
  WAP E1W 24 E4
The Academy at Peckham
  PECK SE15 .... 40 F2
Acorn Business Centre
  MAIDW ME16 .... 185 H1
Acorn Industrial Park
  DART DA1 .... 45 P7
Acorn Trading Estate
  WTHK RM20 .... 31 P9
Acumen Anglo School
  NRWD SE19 .... 60 E7
Adamsrill Primary School
  SYD SE26 .... 61 L2
Addey & Stanhope School
  NWCR SE14 .... 41 M2
Addington Business Centre
  CROY/NA CR0 .... 115 H4
Addington Court Golf Club
  CROY/NA CR0 .... 114 C3
Addington Golf Club
  CROY/NA CR0 .... 84 C8
Addington High School
  CROY/NA CR0 .... 115 H6
Addington Palace Golf Club
  CROY/NA CR0 .... 114 B1
Addiscombe CC
  CROY/NA CR0 .... 83 M7
Adisham CE Primary School
  RCANTE CT5 .... 198 F7
Admiral Hyson
  Industrial Estate
  STHWK SE1 .... 24 E7
Agora Shopping Centre
  PECK SE15 .... 40 G3
Airport Industrial Estate
  BH/WHM TN16 .... 115 N9
Albany Centre & Theatre
  DEPT SE8 .... 41 M1
Albany Clinic
  BFN/LL DA15 .... 64 C3
Albion Health Centre
  WCHPL E1 .... 24 E1
Albion J & I School
  BERM/RHTH SE16 .... 24 F5
Albion Street Health Centre
  BERM/RHTH SE16 .... 24 F5
Albright Industrial Estate
  RAIN RM13 .... 29 L1
Alderwood Primary School
  ELTH/MOT SE9 .... 43 P7
Aldington Primary School
  RASHE TN25 .... 306 B2
Alexander McLeod
  Primary School
  ABYW SE2 .... 28 A8
Alexandra Hospital
  WALD ME5 .... 125 L5
Alexandra Infant School
  PGE/AN SE20 .... 61 K6
Alexandra Junior School
  SYD SE26 .... 61 K6
Alfred Salter Primary School
  BERM/RHTH SE16 .... 24 C5
Alleyns Junior School
  EDUL SE22 .... 40 E6
Allhallows Primary School
  HOO/HM ME3 .... 38 F8
Allington Primary School
  MAIDW ME16 .... 154 C5
All Saints CE Junior School
  NRWD SE19 .... 60 E7
All Saints CE Primary School
  BKHTH/KID SE3 .... 42 C3
  CHAT ME4 .... 6 E7
  WSTB CT5 .... 105 L3
All Saints Industrial Estate
  MARG CT9 .... 15 F6
All Souls CE Primary School
  FOLKN CT19 .... 310 B5
Alma Primary School
  BERM/RHTH SE16 .... 24 D7
Alpine Business Centre
  EHAM E6 .... 27 L1
AMF Ashford Ten Pin
  Bowling Centre
  ASH TN23 .... 3 F4
AMF Bowling
  LEW SE13 .... 42 A4
  MARG CT9 .... 15 H4
  WSTB CT5 .... 105 L3
AMF Chatham Ten Pin
  Bowling Centre
  CHAT ME4 .... 6 C4
AMF Maidstone Ten Pin
  Bowling Centre
  MAID/BEAR ME14 .... 13 C2
Amherst School
  SEV TN13 .... 148 D8
Anchorage Point
  Industrial Estate
  CHARL SE7 .... 26 D6
Anchor Bay Industrial Estate
  ERITH DA8 .... 45 P1
Anchor Business Park
  SIT ME10 .... 100 A8
Anchorians All Weather
  Sports Club
  RHAM ME8 .... 97 J5
Anerley School
  NRWD SE19 .... 60 G7
Angel Centre
  DART DA1 .... 46 E7

Angel Indoor Bowling
  TON TN9 .... 210 F9
Angel Leisure Centre
  TON TN9 .... 210 F9
Angel Walk Shopping Precinct
  TON TN9 .... 210 E9
Angerstein Business Park
  GNWCH SE10 .... 26 B7
Anglesea Centre
  GVW DA11 .... 49 M7
Angley School
  CRBK TN17 .... 297 N2
Anthony Roper
  Primary School
  EYN DA4 .... 89 K6
Apiary Business Park
  RMAID ME17 .... 186 G9
Applegarth Primary School
  CROY/NA CR0 .... 114 E1
Aquarius Golf Club
  EDUL SE22 .... 41 J6
Arboricultural Advisory &
  Information Service
  DART DA1 .... 46 E8
The Archbishop Lanfranc
  School
  CROY/NA CR0 .... 82 D7
Archbishop Michael Ramsey
  Technology College
  CMBW SE5 .... 40 B1
Archbishop's Palace
  MAID/SHEP ME15 .... 12 E6
The Archbishops School
  CANTW/ST CT2 .... 166 D1
Archbishop Tenisons CE
  School
  CROY/NA CR0 .... 83 L7
Archcliffe Fort
  DVW CT17 .... 313 L1
Archers Court Maths
  & Computing College
  DVE/WH CT16 .... 291 J2
Archers Court School
  DVE/WH CT16 .... 291 J2
Arches Leisure Centre
  GNWCH SE10 .... 25 N9
Arden Business Park
  STRD ME2 .... 19 K1
Arden Junior School
  GILL ME7 .... 73 K9
Arden Theatre
  FAV ME13 .... 132 F6
Arena Essex
  PUR RM19 .... 31 K5
Argent Business Park
  QBOR ME11 .... 77 J5
Argyle Trading Centre
  RAM CT11 .... 17 F4
Arklow Trading Estate
  NWCR SE14 .... 25 H9
Arlington Square
  Shopping Centre
  MARC CT9 .... 14 E5
Arnhem Wharf
  Primary School
  POP/IOD E14 .... 25 J6
Arnolds Business Park
  STPH/PW TN12 .... 213 H5
Ashburnham Community School
  CROY/NA CR0 .... 83 N4
Ashburton Primary School
  CROY/NA CR0 .... 83 N3
Ashfield Farm Campsite
  RCANTW CT4 .... 226 D8
Ashford Borough Museum
  ASH TN23 .... 2 D4
Ashford Business Park
  KEN/WIL TN24 .... 283 K2
Ashford Civic Centre
  ASH TN23 .... 3 F4
Ashford College
  ASH TN23 .... 2 D4
Ashford International Hotel
  KEN/WIL TN24 .... 252 E5
Ashford (Kent) Golf Club
  RASHE TN25 .... 252 C2
Ashford Market
  KEN/WIL TN24 .... 283 J2
Ashford School
  ASH TN23 .... 3 F3
Ashford South CP School
  ASH TN23 .... 2 A7
Ashford Town FC
  RASHW TN26 .... 282 C8
Ashgrove Trading Estate
  BMLY BR1 .... 62 B5
Ashleigh Commercial Estate
  CHARL SE7 .... 26 D7
Ashmead Primary School
  BROCKY SE4 .... 41 N3
Assembly Hall Theatre
  RTW TN1 .... 22 E4
Associated Newspapers Offices
  BERM/RHTH SE16 .... 24 C6
Association of British
  Dispensing Opticians
  (ABDO) College
  RCANTW CT4 .... 194 B8
The Astor of Hever
  School
  MAIDW ME16 .... 155 H9
Astor Theatre
  DEAL CT14 .... 233 H5
Atheleny Primary School
  CMBW SE5 .... 61 N2
The Atman Clinic
  SBCH/RUST TN4 .... 270 D2
Attlee Youth
  & Community Centre
  WCHPL E1 .... 24 C1
Austin Lodge Golf Club
  EYN DA4 .... 119 K3
Aveley FC
  SOCK/AV RM15 .... 30 F3
Aveley Primary School
  SOCK/AV RM15 .... 31 H4
Aveley School (School House)
  SOCK/AV RM15 .... 31 H4
The Aveley School
  SOCK/AV RM15 .... 30 G3

Avenue Theatre
  SIT ME10 .... 129 N2
Avicenna Medical Centre
  E/WMAL ME19 .... 153 M2
Axton Chase School
  HART DA3 .... 68 D9
Aycliffe CP School
  DVW CT17 .... 313 H2
Aylesford Cemetery
  DIT/AY ME20 .... 154 E2
Aylesford Primary School
  DIT/AY ME20 .... 154 C3
Aylesford Priory
  DIT/AY ME20 .... 154 D2
Aylesford School
  DIT/AY ME20 .... 154 C3
Aylesham Business Park
  RCANTE CT3 .... 229 K1
Aylesham Cemetery
  RCANTW CT4 .... 228 E4
The Aylesham Centre
  PECK SE15 .... 40 G2
Aylesham Health Centre
  RCANTE CT3 .... 229 H1
Aylesham Industrial Estate
  RCANTE CT3 .... 229 H2
Aylesham Primary School
  RCANTE CT3 .... 229 H1
Aylwin Secondary School
  STHWK SE1 .... 24 C7
Babington House School
  CHST BR7 .... 63 K5
Bacon's College
  BERM/RHTH SE16 .... 25 H4
Baldwins Hill Primary School
  EGRIN RH19 .... 264 F5
Balfour Infant School
  ROCH ME1 .... 95 K5
Balfour Junior School
  CHAT ME4 .... 95 K4
Balfour Medical Centre
  GRAYS RM17 .... 32 D7
Balgowan Primary School
  BECK BR3 .... 61 L8
Ballard Business Park
  STRD ME2 .... 18 A6
Balmoral Clinic
  GILL ME7 .... 7 J2
Bandon Hill Cemetery
  WLCTN SM6 .... 82 C9
Bank of England & Museum
  LOTH EC2R 24 A2
Bannockburn Primary School
  WOOL/PLUM SE18 .... 27 N7
Bapchild & Tonge
  CE (Aided) School
  RSIT ME9 .... 130 C2
Barham CE Primary School
  RCANTW CT4 .... 228 B3
Barham Crematorium
  RCANTW CT4 .... 228 F7
Baring Primary School
  LEE/GVPK SE12 .... 42 E8
Baring Road Medical Centre
  BMLY BR1 .... 62 E1
Barkantine Clinic
  POP/IOD E14 .... 25 K5
Barming Primary School
  MAIDW ME16 .... 184 E1
Barnehurst Primary School
  ERITH DA8 .... 45 L2
Barnehurst Public Golf Club
  BXLYHN DA7 .... 45 M4
Barnes Cray Primary School
  DART DA1 .... 46 A3
Barnsole Infant School
  GILL ME7 .... 96 B2
Barnsole Junior School
  GILL ME7 .... 96 B2
Barrington Primary School
  WELL DA16 .... 44 F3
Barrow Grove Junior School
  SIT ME10 .... 129 L1
The Barry Clinic
  SBCH/RUST TN4 .... 270 D2
Barton Business Park
  CANT CT1 .... 167 J5
Barton Court
  Grammar School
  CANT CT1 .... 5 H5
Barton Junior School
  DVE/WH CT16 .... 291 K5
Baston School
  HAYES BR2 .... 85 L6
Bath Factory Estate
  HNHL SE24 .... 40 C7
Bayham Abbey
  RRTW TN3 .... 294 B1
The Bay Museum
  RDV CT15 .... 292 G2
BBC Radio Kent
  CHAT ME4 .... 6 A3
Beacon Hill Industrial Estate
  PUR RM19 .... 30 E7
Beacon Hill School
  SOCK/AV RM15 .... 31 K1
Bean Primary School
  RDART DA2 .... 68 A2
Bearsted Golf Club
  MAID/BEAR ME14 .... 156 C7
Bearsted Green
  Business Centre
  MAID/BEAR ME14 .... 156 F7
Bearsted Vineyard
  MAID/BEAR ME14 .... 187 N1
Beaumerne
  Community School
  CANTW/ST CT2 .... 166 C4
Beaver Industrial Estate
  ASH TN23 .... 282 E1
Beaverwood School for Girls
  CHST BR7 .... 64 A5
Beckenham Business Centre
  BECK BR3 .... 61 L5
Beckenham Crematorium
  BECK BR3 .... 61 J9
Beckenham CC
  BECK BR3 .... 61 P6
Beckenham Hospital
  BECK BR3 .... 61 M8

Beckenham Leisure Centre
  BECK BR3 .... 61 L7
Beckenham Place Park
  Golf Course
  BECK BR3 .... 61 P5
Beckenham RFC
  BECK BR3 .... 84 B1
Beckenham School of Art
  BECK BR3 .... 84 B1
Beckenham Theatre Centre
  BECK BR3 .... 61 P8
Beckenham Town FC
  BECK BR3 .... 84 D2
Becket Sports Centre
  DART DA1 .... 46 C7
Beckley CE Primary School
  RYE TN31 .... 330 F9
Beckmead School
  BECK BR3 .... 84 D5
Beckton Special School
  CAN/RD E16 .... 26 E1
Beddington Infants School
  WLCTN SM6 .... 82 B7
Beddington Medical Centre
  CROY/NA CR0 .... 82 D8
Beddington Park
  Primary School
  CROY/NA CR0 .... 82 C7
Beddington Trading Estate
  CROY/NA CR0 .... 82 D5
Bedensfield Clinic
  SCUP DA14 .... 64 G4
Bedgebury Junior School
  CRBK TN17 .... 296 D6
Bedington Infant School
  WLCTN SM6 .... 82 B8
Bedonwell Clinic
  ABYW SE2 .... 28 D9
Bedonwell Medical Centre
  BELV DA17 .... 28 E8
Bedonwell Primary School
  BXLYHN DA7 .... 28 D9
Beechcroft Farm
  Industrial Estate
  BGR MK TN15 .... 90 G7
Beechings Way
  Industrial Estate
  RHAM ME8 .... 96 E2
Beechwood Sacred Heart
  School
  RTWE/PEM TN2 .... 271 H4
Belhus Golf Club
  & Leisure Centre
  SOCK/AV RM15 .... 31 H2
Bellamys Wharf
  BERM/RHTH SE16 .... 24 C4
Bellenden Primary School
  PECK SE15 .... 40 G4
Bellenden Road
  Business Centre
  PECK SE15 .... 40 F3
Bellenden Road Retail Park
  PECK SE15 .... 40 F2
Bellerbys College
  DEPT SE8 .... 25 L9
Bellingham Trading Estate
  CAT SE6 .... 61 P2
Bell Shopping Centre
  SIT ME10 .... 129 N1
Bell Wood Community
  Junior School
  MAID/SHEP ME15 .... 186 B5
Bell Wood Infant School
  MAID/SHEP ME15 .... 186 B6
Belmont Farm
  Business Centre
  RASHW TN26 .... 250 F8
Belmont House & Gardens
  FAV ME13 .... 162 A7
Belmont Primary School
  ERITH DA8 .... 45 J1
Belvedere Industrial Estate
  BELV DA17 .... 29 J4
Belvedere Link Business Park
  ERITH DA8 .... 29 H6
Belvedere Primary School
  BELV DA17 .... 28 G7
Benedict House
  Preparatory School
  BFN/LL DA15 .... 64 B3
Benenden CE Primary School
  CRBK TN17 .... 298 C9
Benenden Hospital
  CRBK TN17 .... 299 M4
Benenden School
  CRBK TN17 .... 298 F7
Benham Business Park
  HYTHE CT21 .... 307 N1
Bennett Memorial Diocesan
  CE School
  SBCH/RUST TN4 .... 270 B2
Bensham Manor School
  THHTH CR7 .... 83 H2
Benson Primary School
  RHAM ME8 .... 84 B7
Bentley Street
  Industrial Estate
  GVE DA12 .... 49 N7
Bermondsey Trading Estate
  BERM/RHTH SE16 .... 24 F8
Bessemer Grange J & I School
  HNHL SE24 .... 40 D6
Bessemer Park
  Industrial Estate
  BRXN/ST SW9 .... 40 B5
Best Western Abbots Barton
  Hotel
  CANT CT1 .... 5 H7
Best Western Bromley Court
  Hotel
  BMLY BR1 .... 62 C5
Best Western Churchill Hotel
  DVE/WH CT16 .... 8 E5
Best Western Clifton Hotel
  FOLK CT20 .... 10 C6
Best Western Donnington
  Manor Hotel
  SEV TN13 .... 148 C3
Best Western Manor Hotel
  GVE DA12 .... 69 N5

Best Western Rose
  & Crown Hotel
  TON TN9 .... 210 F8
Bethany School
  CRBK TN17 .... 274 C3
Bethersden Business Centre
  RASHW TN26 .... 280 B7
Bethersden Primary School
  RASHW TN26 .... 280 C3
Bethlem Royal Hospital
  BECK BR3 .... 84 D4
Beths Grammar
  School for Boys
  BXLY DA5 .... 45 J7
Beulah Infant School
  THHTH CR7 .... 60 C8
Bewl Water Nature Reserve
  WADH TN5 .... 314 F2
Bewl Water Reservoir
  Visitor Centre
  RRTW TN3 .... 295 J7
Bexley College
  BELV DA17 .... 29 H7
Bexley CC
  BXLY DA5 .... 45 J9
Bexley Grammar School
  BXLYHS DA6 .... 44 D5
Bexleyheath Centre
  BXLYHS DA6 .... 44 C5
Bexleyheath Golf Club
  BXLYHS DA6 .... 44 G6
Bexleyheath Marriott Hotel
  BXLYHS DA6 .... 45 K5
Bexleyheath School
  BXLYHN DA7 .... 45 H4
Bexleyheath Superbowl
  BXLYHS DA6 .... 45 H5
Bexley RFC
  BXLY DA5 .... 45 J8
Bickley Park CC
  BMLY BR1 .... 63 J8
Bickley Park
  Preparatory School
  BMLY BR1 .... 63 H9
Bickley Park School
  BMLY BR1 .... 63 J8
Bidborough CE
  Primary School
  RRTW TN3 .... 239 P6
Biggin Hill Airport
  BH/WHM TN16 .... 115 M6
Biggin Hill Business Park
  BH/WHM TN16 .... 115 N9
Biggin Hill Primary School
  BH/WHM TN16 .... 145 P1
Bigland Green Primary School
  WCHPL E1 .... 24 E2
Billingsgate Fish Market
  POP/IOD E14 .... 25 L4
Birches Industrial Estate
  EGRIN RH19 .... 264 D5
Birchington Primary School
  BRCH CT7 .... 111 H7
Birchington & Westgate
  Health Clinic
  BRCH CT7 .... 111 K5
Birchmere Business Park
  THMD SE28 .... 27 P5
Birchwood Park Golf Club
  RDART DA2 .... 65 L6
Birchwood Primary School
  SWLY BR8 .... 65 M7
Bird College
  SCUP DA14 .... 64 C2
Birkbeck Primary School
  SCUP DA14 .... 64 D2
Bishop Challoner Catholic
  Collegiate School
  WCHPL E1 .... 24 F3
Bishop Challoner Girls School
  WCHPL E1 .... 24 D5
Bishop Challoner School
  HAYES BR2 .... 62 B8
Bishop John Robinson CE
  Primary School
  THMD SE28 .... 28 B3
Bishop Justus CE
  (Secondary) School
  HAYES BR2 .... 85 P4
Bishops Down Primary School
  SBCH/RUST TN4 .... 270 A3
Blackfen Medical Centre
  BFN/LL DA15 .... 44 B6
Blackfen School for Girls
  BFN/LL DA15 .... 44 D7
Blackheath Bluecoat
  CE School
  BKHTH/KID SE3 .... 42 E5
Blackheath Business Estate
  GNWCH SE10 .... 42 A2
The Blackheath Clinic
  BKHTH/KID SE3 .... 42 E5
Blackheath High School GDST
  BKHTH/KID SE3 .... 42 D3
Blackheath High Senior School
  BKHTH/KID SE3 .... 42 E1
Blackheath Hospital
  BKHTH/KID SE3 .... 42 D4
Blackheath
  Preparatory School
  BKHTH/KID SE3 .... 42 E2
Blackheath RFC
  (The Rectory Field)
  BKHTH/KID SE3 .... 42 F1
Blacklands County
  Junior School
  E/WMAL ME19 .... 153 N5
Black Lion Leisure Centre
  GILL ME7 .... 73 H9
Blackshots Leisure Centre
  CDW/CHF RM16 .... 32 C5
Blackthorn Medical Centre
  MAIDW ME16 .... 154 F9
Blackwall Trading Estate
  POP/IOD E14 .... 25 N1
Blackwell Primary School
  EGRIN RH19 .... 265 H5
The Blazing Donkey
  Country Hotel
  DEAL CT14 .... 201 L8

Blean CP School
CANTW/ST CT2 ....136 A9
Blean Wood National
Nature Reserve
RCANTE CT5 ....107 N9
Blenheim Primary School
ORP BR6 ....87 L6
Blenheim Shopping Centre
PGE/AN SE20 ....61 J6
Bleriot Memorial
DVE/WH CT16 ....9 G1
Bilby Business Centre
RASHE TN25 ....283 J9
The Bligh Infant School
STRD ME2 ....71 L8
The Bligh Junior School
STRD ME2 ....71 L8
Blubery House
Cranbrook School
CRBK TN17 ....298 A2
Blue Chalet Industrial Park
BGR/WK TN15 ....120 A1
Blue Gate Fields
Primary School
WCHPL E1 ....24 F3
Bluewater Shopping Cemtre
RDART DA2 ....47 M8
Blyth's Wharf
POP/IOD E14 ....25 H3
Boatman's Hill Cemetery
SWCH CT13 ....201 N2
Bobbing Primary School
RSIT ME9 ....99 J7
The Bob Hope Theatre
ELTH/MOT SE9 ....43 K7
Bodiam Castle (NT)
RBTBR TN32 ....328 G5
Bodiam CE Primary School
RBTBR TN32 ....328 F4
Bodiam Manor School
RBTBR TN32 ....328 F4
Bodsham CE Primary School
RASHE TN25 ....255 M1
Bonnygate Primary School
SOCK/AV RM15 ....31 L1
Bonus Pastor
Roman Catholic School
BMLY BR1 ....62 B3
Borden CE Primary School
RSIT ME9 ....128 G2
Borden Grammar School
SIT ME10 ....129 M2
Borough Cemetery
RTWE/PEM TN2 ....270 F8
Borough Green
Primary School
BGR/WK TN15 ....151 K5
Bough Beech Sailing Club
EDEN TN8 ....208 A6
Boughton Golf Club
FAV ME15 ....163 N1
Boughton Monchelsea
Primary School
RMAID ME17 ....185 N9
Boughton-under-Blean
Primary School
FAV ME13 ....164 A1
Bourne Road industrial Park
DART DA1 ....45 M6
Bower Grove School
MAIDW ME16 ....184 G1
The Bower Mount Clinic
MAIDW ME16 ....12 A5
Bowes Industrial Centre
MEO DA15 ....92 A8
Bow Junior & Youth Centre
BOW E3 ....25 J1
Boxgrove Primary School
ABYW SE2 ....28 B6
Boxmend Industrial Estate
MAID/SHEP ME15 ....186 C8
Boyd Business Centre
STRD ME2 ....19 J1
Brabourne CE Primary School
RASHE TN25 ....255 H9
Bracton Centre
RDART DA2 ....65 P1
Bradbourne School
SEV TN13 ....148 F6
Bradfields School
WALD ME5 ....95 M3
Bradstow School
BRDST CT10 ....143 M1
Brady Primary School
RAIN RM13 ....29 P1
Brady Recreation Centre
WCHPL E1 ....24 D1
Brampton Primary School
BXLYHN DA7 ....44 F3
Branbridges Industrial Estate
STPH/PW TN12 ....213 H5
Brands Hatch
Motor Racing Circuit
HART DA3 ....90 B8
Brandshatch Place Hotel
HART DA3 ....90 D8
Brattle Farm Museum
STPH/PW TN12 ....246 A8
Breaside Preparatory School
BMLY BR1 ....62 G7
Bredgar CE Primary School
RSIT ME9 ....129 H8
Bredhurst CE Primary School
GILL ME7 ....126 E4
Bredinghurst School
PECK SE15 ....41 J5
Brenchley & Matfield CE
Primary School
STPH/PW TN12 ....243 H9
Brent Knoll School
FSTH SE23 ....61 K2
The Brent Primary School
RDART DA2 ....47 J8
Brenzett Aeronautical Museum
LYDD TN29 ....335 J2
Brenzett District CE
Primary School
LYDD TN29 ....335 H3
Brian Johnston Centre
BGR/WK TN15 ....149 L7

Briary Primary School
HB CT6 ....107 H4
Brick Lane Music Hall
CAN/RD E16 ....26 E4
Bricklehurst Manor
Preparatory School
WADH TN5 ....314 C7
Brickmakers Industrial Estate
SIT ME10 ....100 A8
Bridge Country Leisure Club
WSTB CT5 ....104 F8
Bridge Industrial Centre
MAID/SHEP ME15 ....185 K1
The Bridge Leisure Centre
SYD SE26 ....61 M4
Bridge & Patrixbourne CE
Primary School
RCANTW CT4 ....197 M1
Bridge Place Country Club
RCANTW CT4 ....197 M5
Bridge Road Business Centre
ASH TN23 ....252 C7
Bridge View Industrial Estate
OBOR ME11 ....77 J5
WTHK KM20 ....31 K9
Bridgewood Manor Hotel
WALD ME5 ....125 J2
Brigstock Medical Centre
THHTH CR7 ....82 C2
Brindishe Primary School
LEE/GVPK SE12 ....42 D6
Britannia Village
Primary School
CAN/RD E16 ....26 C4
British Air Transport
Association (BATA)
Medical Centre
TIL RM18 ....34 B7
The British School
DEAL CT14 ....233 J2
The British School
for Performing Arts
CROY/NA CR0 ....83 J3
Brittania Business Park
DIT/AY ME20 ....154 D4
Brixton Academy
BRXN/ST SW9 ....40 A4
Brixton Recreation Centre
BRXN/ST SW9 ....40 A4
Broadgate Ice Arena
LVPST EC2M 24 A1
Broad Hembury Holiday Park
RASHW TN26 ....282 E7
Broadlands Industrial Estate
CANTW/ST CT2 ....135 N6
Broadmead J & I School
CROY/NA CR0 ....83 J3
Broad Oak Industrial Estate
CANTW/ST CT2 ....166 G1
Broadstairs CC
BRDST CT10 ....143 L2
Broadstairs Health Centre
BRDST CT10 ....113 M9
Broadstairs Youth
& Leisure Centre
BRDST CT10 ....113 N8
Broadwater Down
Primary School
RTWE/PEM TN2 ....270 C7
Broadway Shopping Centre
MAIDW ME16 ....12 D5
Broadway Square
BXLYHS DA6 ....45 J5
Brockhill Country Park
HYTHE CT21 ....308 E3
Brockhill Park School (Lower)
HYTHE CT21 ....308 F4
Brockhill Park School (Upper)
HYTHE CT21 ....308 F3
Brocklebank Industrial Estate
GNWCH SE10 ....26 B7
Brockley Cross
Business Centre
BROCKY SE4 ....41 L4
Brockley Primary School
BROCKY SE4 ....41 M6
Brockwell Lido
HNHL SE24 ....40 B7
Broke Hill Golf Club
RSEV TN14 ....117 N3
Bromley Cemetery
BMLY BR1 ....62 D6
Bromley College of Further
& Higher Education
BMLY BR1 ....62 E7
HAYES BR2 ....85 N3
Bromley FC
HAYES BR2 ....85 L2
Bromley Golf Club
HAYES BR2 ....85 P4
Bromley High School GDST
BMLY BR1 ....86 B1
Bromley Industrial Centre
BMLY BR1 ....63 H9
Bromley Mall Indoor Market
BMLY BR1 ....62 E8
Bromley Museum
ORP BR6 ....87 J4
Bromley Road Infant School
BECK BR3 ....61 P7
Bromley Road Retail Park
CAT SE6 ....61 L2
Bromley Ski Centre
STMC/STPC BR5 ....64 F7
Bromley Tennis Centre
ORP BR6 ....86 E7
Brompton Medical Centre
GILL ME7 ....72 G9
Brompton Westbrook
Primary School
GILL ME7 ....6 C3
Bromstone CP School
BRDST CT10 ....113 J9
Brook Community
Primary School
RASHE TN25 ....254 A5
Brookfield Industrial Estate
ASH TN23 ....252 C7
Brookfield Infant School
DIT/AY ME20 ....153 P2

Brookfield Junior School
DIT/AY ME20 ....153 P2
Brook Industrial Park
STMC/STPC BR5 ....87 K1
Brookland CE
Primary School
LYDD TN29 ....334 E5
Brooklands Primary School
BKHTH/KID SE3 ....42 E4
Brookmarsh Trading Estate
DEPT SE8 ....41 P1
Brookmead Industrial Estate
CROY/NA CR0 ....82 B3
The Brook Theatre
CHAT ME4 ....6 C3
Broome Park Golf Club
RCANTW CT4 ....228 E9
Broomhill Bank School
RRTW TN3 ....269 P2
Broomsleigh Business Park
SYD SE26 ....61 M4
Brothwick Wharf
DEPT SE8 ....25 K8
Brown's School
ORP BR6 ....87 N9
Brunel Engine House
BERM/RHTH SE16 ....24 F5
Brunswick Centre
Industrial Estate
ASH TN23 ....252 C7
Brunswick House Clinic
MAIDW ME16 ....12 B3
Brunswick House
Primary School
MAIDW ME16 ....12 B3
Brunswick Park
Primary School
CMBW SE5 ....40 D1
Bryony School
RHAM ME8 ....96 F7
Buckland Cemetery
DVE/WH CT16 ....291 L5
Buckland Hospital
DVW CT17 ....291 H6
Bugsys Ten Pin Bowling
MARG CT9 ....15 J2
Bullers Wood School
CHST BR7 ....63 K7
Burgess Business Park
CMBW SE5 ....40 F6
Burham CE Primary School
ROCH ME1 ....124 C5
Burnham Trading Estate
DART DA1 ....46 D5
Burney Street Clinic
GNWCH SE10 ....42 A1
Burnham Business Centre
BECK BR3 ....61 N8
Burnt Ash Primary School
BMLY BR1 ....62 E4
Burnt Oak Junior School
RRTW TN3 ....44 C9
Burrswood Medical Centre
RRTW TN3 ....268 F3
Bursted Wood
Primary School
BXLYHN DA7 ....45 K3
Burwood School
ORP BR6 ....87 L6
The Business Academy Bexley
ERITHM DA18 ....28 D5
The Butterfly Centre
RDV CT15 ....288 E1
Butterfly Sports Club
ELTH/MOT SE9 ....43 M7
Buzzard Creek
Industrial Estate
BARK IG11 ....27 N1
Bygrove Primary School
POP/IOD E14 ....25 L2
Byron Primary School
GILL ME7 ....7 J6
Bysing Wood CP School
FAV ME13 ....132 D5
Cabot Place
POP/IOD E14 ....25 K4
Cage Green Primary School
TONN TN10 ....210 G5
Callis Grange Infant School
BRDST CT10 ....113 L6
Calverton Primary School
CAN/RD E16 ....26 E2
Camber Sands Holiday Park
RYE TN31 ....344 A1
Camberwell Business Centre
CMBW SE5 ....40 D1
Camberwell College of Arts
CMBW SE5 ....40 D2
Camberwell Leisure Centre
PECK SE15 ....41 K7
Camberwell New Cemetery
PECK SE15 ....41 K7
Camberwell Trading Estate
CMBW SE5 ....40 B3
Camden Centre
RTW TN1 ....22 E2
Camden House Clinic
BKHTH/KID SE3 ....42 E5
Camelot Primary School
PECK SE15 ....41 H1
Camer Park Country Park
MEO DA13 ....92 D4
Campanile Hotel
RDART DA2 ....47 K4
Canada Place
POP/IOD E14 ....25 L4
Canada Square
POP/IOD E14 ....25 L4
Canada Water Retail Park
BERM/RHTH SE16 ....24 G6
Canada Wharf Museum
BERM/RHTH SE16 ....25 J4
Canal Industrial Park
GVE DA12 ....49 P7
Canary Riverside
BERM/RHTH SE16 ....25 J4
Canary Wharf Pier
POP/IOD E14 ....25 J4
Cannon Wharf Business Centre
DEPT SE8 ....25 H7

Canterbury
Adult Education Centre
CANT CT1 ....5 F2
Canterbury Bowling Club
CANT CT1 ....4 E7
Canterbury C&CC Site
CANT CT1 ....167 K4
Canterbury Castle
CANT CT1 ....4 D6
Canterbury Cathedral
CANT CT1 ....5 F3
Canterbury Cemetery
CANT CT1 ....166 C3
Canterbury Christ Church
University
BRDST CT10 ....113 H9
CANT CT1 ....5 G4
CANT CT1 ....5 H3
CANTW/ST CT2 ....166 A5
MARG CT9 ....15 J4
CANT CT1 ....167 L3
Canterbury City FC
& Greyhound Racing
(Kingsmead Stadium)
CANTW/ST CT2 ....166 F2
Canterbury City Retail Park
CANT CT1 ....137 J9
Canterbury College
CANT CT1 ....5 H6
Canterbury College Aylesham
Community Project
RCANTE CT3 ....199 K9
Canterbury
Environment Centre
CANT CT1 ....5 F3
Canterbury Golf Club
CANT CT1 ....4 E3
Canterbury Health Centre
CANT CT1 ....167 K4
The Canterbury High School
CANTW/ST CT2 ....4 A4
Canterbury Indoor Market
CANT CT1 ....4 D3
Canterbury Industrial Estate
NWCR SE14 ....24 G9
Canterbury Industrial Park
RCANTE CT3 ....138 D8
Canterbury Pilgrims Hospital
CANT CT1 ....4 D4
Canterbury Road
Health Centre
MARG CT9 ....14 C6
Canterbury Road
Primary School
SIT ME10 ....130 A2
Canterbury Roman Museum
CANT CT1 ....4 E4
Canterbury Steiner School
RCANTW CT4 ....195 M4
Canterbury Tales
CANT CT1 ....4 E4
Canterbury Visitor Centre
CANT CT1 ....5 F4
Canterbury West Gate Towers
CANT CT1 ....4 D4
Cantium Retail Park
STHWK SE1 ....24 D9
Capel Le Ferne
Primary School
RFOLK CT18 ....289 M9
Capel Primary School
STPH/PW TN12 ....242 A2
Capel Road Cemetery
SIT ME10 ....129 N2
Capital Industrial Estate
BELV DA17 ....28 G7
BELV DA17 ....29 H4
Capital Wharf
WAP E1W 24 D4
Capstone Farm Country Park
GILL ME7 ....96 A1
Cardwell Primary School
WOOL/PLUM SE18 ....26 C7
Carew Manor School
WLGTN SM6 ....82 C7
Cartwright & Kelsey
Primary School
RCANTE CT3 ....170 D9
Cascades Leisure Centre
GVE DA12 ....70 C3
Casino Rooms
ROCH ME1 ....19 H5
Castilion Primary School
THMD SE28 ....28 B2
Castleacres Industrial Park
SIT ME10 ....100 A8
Castle Bank
STPH/PW TN12 ....276 C2
Castle Clinic
DVE/WH CT16 ....8 E3
Castlecombe Primary School
ELTH/MOT SE9 ....63 J4
Castle Community College
DEAL CT14 ....233 H5
Castle Hill Primary School
CROY/NA CR0 ....114 F1
Castle Road
Business Precinct
SIT ME10 ....100 A8
Castle Road Industrial Estate
SIT ME10 ....130 A1
Castle View Business Centre
ROCH ME1 ....11 J2
Catford Cricket & Sports Club
CAT SE6 ....41 P9
Catford Cyphers CC
CAT SE6 ....61 M1
Catford Girls School
CAT SE6 ....62 B2
Catford Trading Estate
CAT SE6 ....61 P1
Catford Wanderers
Sports Club
CAT SE6 ....62 A3
Cathedral Gateway
CANT CT1 ....4 E4
Cator Park School for Girls
BECK BR3 ....61 L6
Cavendish School
BERM/RHTH SE16 ....24 F7

Cayley Primary School
WCHPL E1 ....25 H1
Cecil Road Primary School
GVW DA11 ....49 K9
The Cedars School
ROCH ME1 ....95 H2
Central Business Park
STRD SE22 ....19 K2
Central Cinema
Shopping Centre
CROY/NA CR0 ....83 H6
Central Hall Theatre & Cinema
CHAT ME4 ....6 C4
Central Park Arena
CHAT ME4 ....46 E9
Central Sussex College
(East Grinstead Campus)
EGRIN RH19 ....265 H7
Central YMCA
ELTH/MOT SE9 ....63 H1
Chadwell St Mary
Primary School
CDW/CHF RM16 ....33 M7
Chaffinch Business Park
BECK BR3 ....61 K9
Chafford School
RAIN RM13 ....29 P1
Chaffords Sports Complex
RAIN RM13 ....29 P1
Chalkin Business Park
RTWE/PEM TN2 ....241 H9
Challock CP School
RASHE TN25 ....222 E1
Chambers Wharf
BERM/RHTH SE16 ....24 D5
The Channel School
FOLKN CT19 ....310 E1
Channel Tunnel
Exhibition Centre
RFOLK CT18 ....287 N6
Channel Tunnel
Passenger Terminal
RFOLK CT18 ....287 N8
Channel Tunnel Rail Link
HDCN TN27 ....220 E6
KEN/WIL TN24 ....252 C9
MAID/BEAR ME14 ....157 H7
RASHE TN25 ....251 P2
RASHE TN25 ....284 A6
MAID ME17 ....188 E6
Chantry Primary School
GVE DA12 ....49 N9
The Chantry
GVE DA12 ....49 N7
Chapter School
STRD ME2 ....71 M8
Charing CE Primary School
HDCN TN27 ....221 H3
Charles Darwin School
BH/WHM TN16 ....116 A9
The Charles Dickens School
BRDST CT10 ....113 N9
Charles Edward Brooke
School
BRXN/ST SW9 ....40 B2
Charlotte Turner
Primary School
DEPT SE8 ....25 K9
Charlton Athletic FC
(The Valley)
CHARL SE7 ....26 B3
Charlton CE Primary School
DVE/WH CT16 ....291 K5
Charlton Health
& Fitness Centre
CHARL SE7 ....26 D8
Charlton House
CHARL SE7 ....26 E9
Charlton Manor Junior School
CHARL SE7 ....43 H1
Charlton RFC
ELTH/MOT SE9 ....43 M8
Charlton School
CHARL SE7 ....26 F9
Charlton Shopping Centre
DVE/WH CT16 ....8 B2
Charlwoods Industrial Estate
EGRIN RH19 ....265 H5
The Charter School
HNHL SE24 ....40 D6
Chatham Cemetery
RCANTW CT4 ....195 N2
Chatham CP School
RCANTW CT4 ....195 K2
Chatham Park Golf Club
EGRIN RH19 ....264 F2
Chart Hills Golf Club
HDCN TN27 ....278 B2
Chart Sutton Business Estate
RMAID ME17 ....186 E5
Chartwell Business Centre
BMLY BR1 ....63 H9
Chartwell (NT)
BH/WHM TN16 ....176 F8
Chatham Cemetery
CHAT ME4 ....95 L5
Chatham Dockyard
(World Naval Base)
CHAT ME4 ....72 F2
Chatham Gatehouse
CHAT ME4 ....72 F9
Chatham Grammar School
for Boys
CHAT ME4 ....95 K5
Chatham Grammar School
for Girls
WALD ME5 ....95 P4
Chatham House Grammar
School For Boys
RAM CT11 ....17 F2
Chatham South School
CHAT ME4 ....95 K6
Chatsworth Infant School
BFN/LL DA15 ....44 C9
Chaucer Business Park
BGR/WK TN15 ....150 A4
WSTB CT5 ....105 P5
Chaucer College Canterbury
CANTW/ST CT2 ....166 C1
Chaucer Hospital
RCANTW CT4 ....166 F8

Chaucer Technology School
CANT CT1 ....167 H5

Chelsfield Lakes Golf Centre
ORP BR6 ....117 M2

Chelsfield Park Hospital
ORP BR6 ....87 N9

Chelsfield Primary School
ORP BR6 ....87 M9

Chequers Shopping Centre
MAID/SHEP ME15 ....13 F5

Cheriton Primary School
FOLK CT20 ....309 P1

Cheriton Road Cemetery
FOLK CT20 ....310 D6

Cherry Garden Pier
BERM/RHTH SE16 ....24 C5

Cherry Garden Pier
BERM/RHTH SE16 ....24 D7

Cherry Lodge Golf Club
BH/WHM TN16 ....146 B2

Cherry Orchard
Primary School
CHARL SE7 ....42 C1

Chestfield CC
WSTB CT5 ....106 A6

Chestfield Medical Centre
WSTB CT5 ....106 C4

Chestfield (Whitstable)
Golf Club
WSTB CT5 ....106 C6

Chevening Cross
RSEV TN14 ....147 P5

Chevening Primary School
RSEV TN14 ....148 A7

Cheyne Middle School
IOS ME12 ....57 N6

Chiddingstone Castle
EDEN TN8 ....238 A2

Chiddingstone CE
Primary School
EDEN TN8 ....238 B2

Childeric Primary School
NWCR SE14 ....41 L1

Child Health Centre
STRD ME2 ....71 N9

Chilham St Marys CE
Primary School
RCANTW CT4 ....194 C4

Chilston Park
RMAID ME17 ....219 K1

Chilston Park Hotel
RMAID ME17 ....219 L1

Chilton CP School
RAM CT11 ....142 F6

Chiltonian Industrial Estate
LEE/GVPK SE12 ....42 D7

Chinnocks Wharf
POP/IOD E14 ....25 H3

Chislehurst Caves
CHST BR7 ....63 L7

Chislehurst Cemetery
CHST BR7 ....64 A4

Chislehurst Golf Club
CHST BR7 ....63 M6

Chislehurst Natural
Health Centre
CHST BR7 ....63 M5

Chislehurst & Sidcup
Grammar School
BFN/LL DA15 ....64 D1

Chislet CE Primary School
RCANTE CT3 ....138 F4

Chrisp Street Health Centre
POP/IOD E14 ....25 L2

Christchurch CE Junior School
RAM CT11 ....16 C5

Christ Church Centre
RTW TN1 ....22 D5

Christ Church CE
Primary School
BRXN/ST SW9 ....40 A2
FOLK CT20 ....10 D3
FSTH SE23 ....61 K1
WOOL/PLUM SE18 ....43 L2

Christ Church High School
ASH TN23 ....282 C3

Christ Church
Primary School
ERITH DA8 ....29 J9

Christian Meeting Hall
BECK BR3 ....61 N7

Christ the King Sixth Form
College
LEW SE13 ....42 B4

Chunnel Industrial Estate
ASH TN23 ....2 D6

Church Down Adult School
LEE/GVPK SE12 ....62 E1

Churchfield School
WOOL/PLUM SE18 ....27 N7

Churchfields Primary School
BECK BR3 ....61 K9

Churchill Business Park
BH/WHM TN16 ....176 E2

Churchill CE Primary School
BH/WHM TN16 ....176 D1

Churchill Clinic
WALD ME5 ....95 M7

Churchill House School
RAM CT11 ....16 C6

The Churchill School
RFOLK CT18 ....288 D8

Churchill Theatre
BMLY BR1 ....62 E8

Church Road Business Centre
SIT ME10 ....100 B8

Church Stairs
BERM/RHTH SE16 ....24 C5

Church Trading Estate
ERITH DA8 ....46 A1

Cinema 3
CANTW/ST CT2 ....136 D9

Cineworld
RASHE TN25 ....252 F4
STRD ME2 ....94 D3
BXLYHS DA6 ....45 K5

Citigroup Tower
POP/IOD E14 ....25 L4

City Business Centre
BERM/RHTH SE16 ....24 F5

City Business Park
CANT CT1 ....167 H1

City of East London College
WCHPL E1 ....24 D2

City of London Academy
STHWK SE1 ....24 D8

The City of London Academy
EDUL SE22 ....40 G6

City of London College
WCHPL E1 ....24 D2

City of London School
Sports Ground
LEE/GVPK SE12 ....62 G1

City Wall
ROCH ME1 ....19 F4

Civic Centre
& Bromley Palace
BMLY BR1 ....62 F8

Civic Centre & Woodville Halls
GVW DA11 ....49 M8

Civil Service Sports Ground
RTW TN1 ....22 D4

Clanricarde Medical Centre
RTW TN1 ....22 D4

Clare House
E/WMAL KT3 ....153 N4

Clare House Primary School
BECK BR3 ....62 A8

Claremont Primary School
SCUP DA14 ....64 E2

Clarendon House
Grammar School
RAM CT11 ....16 E4

Clarendon & Westbury
Community Centre
DVW CT17 ....291 J8

Clearways Industrial Estate
BCR/WK TN15 ....120 A2

Cleeve Park School
SCUP DA14 ....64 E2

The Cliffe Marshes
Nature Reserve
HOO/HM ME3 ....51 N1

Cliffe Woods CP School
HOO/HM ME3 ....52 C8

Cliftonville CP School
MARG CT9 ....112 C3

Clouster's Green
WAP E1W 24 D4

CM Booth Collection
of Historic Vehicles
CRBK TN17 ....319 L3

Coalhouse Fort
TIL RM18 ....50 G2

Cobbs Wood Industrial Estate
ASH TN23 ....2 B4

Cobham Primary School
GVE DA12 ....70 B9

Cobourg Primary School
CMBW SE5 ....24 C9

Cobtree Manor Park
Golf Club
MAID/BEAR ME14 ....155 J1

Cobtree Medical Centre
RMAID ME17 ....217 H7

Coldcote Centre
RASHE TN25 ....284 C5

Coldharbour Industrial Estate
CMBW SE5 ....40 C3

Coldharbour Leisure Centre
ELTH/MOT SE9 ....63 K1

Coldharbour Sports Ground
ELTH/MOT SE9 ....63 L1

Colebrook Industrial Estate
RTWE/PEM TN2 ....241 H8

Colfe's Preparatory School
LEE/GVPK SE12 ....42 E7

Colfe's Senior School
LEE/GVPK SE12 ....42 E7

The College of St Barnabas
LING RH7 ....235 J9

College Square
Shopping Centre
MARG CT9 ....15 H4

Colliers Green CE
Primary School
CRBK TN17 ....275 L6

Collingwood
Industrial Estate
RMAID ME17 ....187 H9

Collingwood Preparatory
School
WLGTN SM6 ....82 A9

Coloma Convent Girls School
CROY/NA CR0 ....84 A7

Colvers Lane Medical Centre
ERITH DA8 ....45 M2

Colyers Primary School
ERITH DA8 ....45 M2

Combe Bank Senior School
RSEV TN14 ....147 M8

Comber Grove
Primary School
CMBW SE5 ....40 C1

Comelle House
Trading Estate
DEPT SE8 ....25 H8

Comfort Inn
RAM CT11 ....17 J2

The Commodore Catamaran
Yacht Club
IOS ME12 ....57 P6

Community Centre
(Island History Trust)
POP/IOD E14 ....25 M7

Community College & School
GNWCH SE10 ....42 A1

The Community College
Whitstable
WSTB CT5 ....105 N6

Community Education
Centre & Library
DVW CT17 ....338 F7

Community Support Centre
DVW CT17 ....291 J8

Compass Centre
CHAT ME4 ....73 H7

Complementary
Health Centre
LEE/GVPK SE12 ....42 C7

Concorde Business Park
BH/WHM TN16 ....115 N9

Concorde
International School
CANT CT1 ....4 E5

Conduit House
GNWCH SE10 ....42 M7

Coney Hill School
HAYES BR2 ....85 J6

Connaught Barracks (MOD)
RDV CT15 ....291 M5

Connections Business Park
RSEV TN14 ....148 C5

Conquest Industrial Estate
STRD ME2 ....18 B5

Consort Clinic
PECK SE15 ....41 H4

Convent Preparatory School
GVE DA12 ....69 N1

Conway Medical Centre
WOOL/PLUM SE18 ....27 L8

Conway Primary School
WOOL/PLUM SE18 ....27 M7

Coopers Lane Primary School
LEE/GVPK SE12 ....62 E1

Coopers Technology College
CHST BR7 ....63 N7

Cooting Road
Industrial Estate
RCANTE CT3 ....228 G2

Corinthian Sports Club
HART DA3 ....90 G3

Corn Exchange
ROCH ME1 ....19 G4

Cornwallis School
MAID/SHEP ME15 ....185 L8

Cossington House Surgery
CANT CT1 ....5 G7

Cottage Industrial Estate
DIT/AY ME20 ....154 G2

County Square
Shopping Centre
ASH TN23 ....2 D5

Courtwood Primary School
CROY/NA CR0 ....114 C4

Coward Industrial Estate
CDW/CHF RM16 ....33 J8

Cowgate Cemetery
DVW CT17 ....11 H5

Coxheath Primary School
RMAID ME17 ....185 H8

Crabble Corn Mill
DVW CT17 ....290 C4

Cranbrook CE
Primary School
CRBK TN17 ....298 A1

Cranbrook Clinic
CRBK TN17 ....298 A2

Cranbrook Museum
CRBK TN17 ....298 A2

Cranbrook RFC
CRBK TN17 ....298 A1

Cranbrook School
CRBK TN17 ....298 A2

Crawford Primary School
CMBW SE5 ....40 C2

Crayfield Industrial Park
STMC/STPC BR5 ....64 E8

Crayfields Business Park
STMC/STPC BR5 ....64 E7

Crayford Commercial Centre
DART DA1 ....45 N6

Crayford Industrial Estate
DART DA1 ....45 P6

Crayford Leisure Centre
& Greyhound Stadium
DART DA1 ....45 N7

Crayford Medical Centre
DART DA1 ....45 P6

Craylands Primary School
SWCM DA10 ....48 B6

Crayside Industrial Estate
DART DA1 ....46 A4

Cray Valley Golf Club
STMC/STPC BR5 ....64 C7

Creek Road Health Centre
DEPT SE8 ....25 K9

Creek Road Industrial Estate
DEPT SE8 ....25 L9

Crest Industrial Estate
STPH/PW TN12 ....245 H3

Criton Industrial Estate
CDW/CHF RM16 ....33 M2

Crockenhill Primary School
SWLY BR8 ....88 B3

Crockham Hill CE
Primary School
EDEN TN8 ....176 D9

Crofton Leisure Centre
BROCKY SE4 ....41 N7

Crofton School
BROCKY SE4 ....41 N7

Crook Log Primary School
BXLYHS DA6 ....44 F5

Crook Log Sports Centre
WELL DA16 ....44 F4

Crossways Academy
BROCKY SE4 ....41 L3

Crowden House
Cranbrook School
CRBK TN17 ....298 B2

Crown Court Clinic
ROCH ME1 ....19 H6

Crown Lane Primary School
WNWD SE27 ....60 C3

Crown Woods School
ELTH/MOT SE9 ....43 N6

Croydon Bowling Club
SAND/SEL CR2 ....83 H9

Croydon Cemetery
CROY/NA CR0 ....82 E2

Croydon Clocktower Cinema
CROY/NA CR0 ....83 H7

Croydon College
CROY/NA CR0 ....83 J6

Croydon Crematorium
THHTH CR7 ....82 D2

Croydon Fairfield
Halls Cinema
CROY/NA CR0 ....83 J7

Croydon FC
SNWD SE25 ....83 P2

Croydon Road
Industrial Estate
BECK BR3 ....83 P1

Croydon Sports Arena
SNWD SE25 ....83 P2

Cryalls Business Estate
SIT ME10 ....129 K1

Crystal Business Centre
SWCH CT13 ....172 A9

Crystal Palace FC
(Selhurst Park)
SNWD SE25 ....83 K1

Crystal Palace Museum
NRWD SE19 ....60 F5

Cuaco Sports Ground
BECK BR3 ....61 N5

Cubitt Town Junior School
(Adult Education Centre)
POP/IOD E14 ....25 M6

Cubitt Town Primary School
POP/IOD E14 ....25 M6

Cudham CE Primary School
BH/WHM TN16 ....146 B1

Culloden Primary School
POP/IOD E14 ....25 N2

Culverstone Green
Primary School
MEO DA13 ....121 P2

Custom House
GVE DA12 ....49 N7

Customs & Excise Offices
DVW CT17 ....8 A3

Cutty Sark Clipper Ship
GNWCH SE10 ....25 M9

Cuxton Industrial Estate
STRD ME2 ....94 B4

Cygnet Clinic Beckton
EHAM E6 ....27 J1

Cygnet Leisure Centre
GVW DA11 ....49 J9

Cypress Infant School
SNWD SE25 ....60 E8

Cypress Junior School
SNWD SE25 ....60 E8

Cyprus College of Art
WNWD SE27 ....60 B3

Cyril Jackson
Primary School
POP/IOD E14 ....25 J3

D2 Trading Estate
SIT ME10 ....100 A8

Daily Telegraph
Newspaper Offices
POP/IOD E14 ....25 K6

Dajen Business Park
CHAT ME4 ....95 P5

Dale Hill Hotel & Golf Club
WADH TN5 ....315 K5

Dalmain Primary School
FSTH SE23 ....41 L9

Dame Janet Community
Junior School
MSTR CT12 ....142 G2

Dame Janet Infant School
MSTR CT12 ....142 G2

Dame Sybil Thorndike
Health Centre
ROCH ME1 ....95 H2

Damilola Taylor Centre
PECK SE15 ....40 F1

Danecourt Community School
(Special School)
GILL ME7 ....96 C4

Dane Court Grammar School
BRDST CT10 ....113 J9

Dane John Mound
& Monument
CANT CT1 ....4 D6

Danley Middle School
IOS ME12 ....57 N9

Danson Mansion
BXLYHS DA6 ....44 E5

Danson Primary School
WELL DA16 ....44 D5

Danson Watersports Centre
BXLYHS DA6 ....44 E6

Darenth Primary School
RDART DA2 ....67 M5

Darenth Valley Golf Club
RSEV TN14 ....118 F6

Darent Industrial Park
ERITH DA8 ....30 A8

Darent Valley Hospital
RDART DA2 ....47 K9

Darrick Wood
Primary School
ORP BR6 ....86 C8

Darrick Wood School
ORP BR6 ....86 C7

Darrick Wood Sports Centre
ORP BR6 ....86 D7

Darrick Wood
Swimming Pool
ORP BR6 ....86 C7

Dartford Adult Education
Centre
DART DA1 ....46 F8

Dartford FC
RDART DA2 ....47 H9

Dartford Golf Club
DART DA1 ....66 B1

Dartford Grammar School
for Boys
DART DA1 ....46 C7

Dartford Grammar School
for Girls
DART DA1 ....46 C8

Dartford Hospital School
HART DA3 ....68 E9

Dartford Museum & Library
DART DA1 ....46 E8

Dartford Natural
Health Centre
DART DA1 ....46 E8

Dartford Technology College
DART DA1 ....46 C8

Dartford Tunnel
WTHK RM20 ....47 K2

Dartford West Health Centre
DART DA1 ....46 C7

Darwin Leisure Centre
BH/WHM TN16 ....146 A1

The David Beckham
Academy
GNWCH SE10 ....26 A5

David Livingstone
Primary School
THHTH CR7 ....60 C7

David Lloyd Health Club
MAIDW ME16 ....12 E6

David Lloyd Tennis Centre
SCUP DA14 ....64 E4

David Salomon's House
RTW TN3 ....240 A9

Davidson Primary School
CROY/NA CR0 ....83 L4

Davington Primary School
FAV ME13 ....132 E5

Days Lane Primary School
BFN/LL DA15 ....44 B7

Deacon Industrial Estate
DIT/AY ME20 ....154 F2

Deacon Trading Centre
STRD ME2 ....18 C3

Deacon Trading Estate
TON TN9 ....210 G9

Deal Castle
DEAL CT14 ....233 J4

Deal Cemetery
DEAL CT14 ....232 C5

The Deal Maritime
& Local History Museum
DEAL CT14 ....233 J3

Deal Rowing Club
DEAL CT14 ....233 J2

Deal Squash & Racket Club
DEAL CT14 ....233 J1

Deal Town FC
DEAL CT14 ....232 C5

Deal Victoria & Barnes CC
DEAL CT14 ....232 G7

Deal & Walmer Community
Health Clinic
DEAL CT14 ....232 G4

Deangate Ridge
Athletics Stadium
HOO/HM ME3 ....53 J8

Deangate Ridge Golf Club
HOO/HM ME3 ....53 J9

Deansfield Primary School
ELTH/MOT SE9 ....43 L4

Deanwood Primary Education
Technology School
RHAM ME8 ....126 G1

De Bradelei Wharf
Shopping Centre
DVW CT17 ....8 D5

Delce Junior School
ROCH ME1 ....95 H4

Delta Wharf
GNWCH SE10 ....25 N5

Deneholm Primary School
CDW/CHF RM16 ....32 D5

Denture Clinic
SWCH CT13 ....201 P2

Denvale Trade Centre
STMC/STPC BR5 ....87 J2

Denver Industrial Estate
RAIN RM13 ....29 L2

Deptford Business Centre
NWCR SE14 ....24 C8

Deptford Green School
NWCR SE14 ....41 M1

Deptford Park
Business Centre
DEPT SE8 ....25 H8

Deptford Park Primary School
DEPT SE8 ....25 H8

Deptford Trading Estate
DEPT SE8 ....25 H8

Dering Wood Nature Reserve
HDCN TN27 ....249 M4

Derling CE Primary School
RASHW TN26 ....251 L1

Detling CE Primary School
MAID/BEAR ME14 ....156 D3

Dickens House Museum
BRDST CT10 ....113 N9

Diggerland
STRD ME2 ....94 E2

Dilkes Primary School
SOCK/AV RM15 ....31 J2

Diocesan & Payne Smith
CE Primary School
CANT CT1 ....5 F3

Discovery Business Park
BERM/RHTH SE16 ....24 D6

Discovery School
E/WMAL ME19 ....153 L9

Ditton CE Junior School
DIT/AY ME20 ....154 B3

Ditton Infant School
DIT/AY ME20 ....154 B3

Docklands Medical Centre
POP/IOD E14 ....25 K7

Docklands Sailing Centre
POP/IOD E14 ....25 K6

Docklands Sailing
& Watersports Centre
BERM/RHTH SE16 ....25 J6

Dockley Road
Industrial Estate
BERM/RHTH SE16 ....24 C6

Dockmaster's House
POP/IOD E14 ....25 K3

Dockside Outlet Centre
CHAT ME4 ....72 G7

Dockyard Industrial Estate
WOOL/PLUM SE18 ....26 F6

Doddington Place
RSIT ME9 ....160 F4

Doddington Primary School
RSIT ME9 ....160 E5

Dog Kennel Hill
Primary School
EDUL SE22 ....40 E4

Dolphin Sailing Barge
Museum
SIT ME10 ....99 P9

Dombey Primary School
HOO/HM ME3 .... 71 L4
Dominican Priory
CANT CT1 .... 4 E3
Dominoes Health Centre
GRAYS RM17 .... 32 B9
Dormansland Primary School
LING RH7 .... 235 L8
Dorset Road
Industrial Estate
IOS ME12 .... 57 J8
Dorset Road Infant School
ELTH/MOT SE9 .... 63 J1
Dorton College
of Further Education
BGR/WK TN15 .... 149 K7
Dorton House School
BGR/WK TN15 .... 149 L7
The Dover Business Centre
DVW CT17 .... 8 A5
Dover Castle
& Secret Wartime Tunnels
DVE/WH CT16 .... 9 G3
Dover College
DVW CT17 .... 8 E5
Dover Grammar School
for Boys
DVW CT17 .... 291 H7
Dover Grammar School
for Girls
DVE/WH CT16 .... 291 L6
Dover Harbour Board Offices
DVW CT17 .... 8 D3
Dover Health Centre
DVE/WH CT16 .... 8 D2
Dover Leisure Centre
DVE/WH CT16 .... 9 F3
Dover Marina Office
DVW CT17 .... 8 D7
Dover Museum
DVE/WH CT16 .... 8 D4
Dover Pharos
DVE/WH CT16 .... 9 G2
Dover Road Primary School
GVW DA11 .... 49 J9
Dover Water Sports Centre
DVW CT17 .... 8 E5
Downderry Primary School
BMLY BR1 .... 62 C3
Downe Primary School
ORP BR6 .... 116 B5
Downham Health Centre
BMLY BR1 .... 62 C3
Down House
ORP BR6 .... 116 B6
The Downs CE
Primary School
DEAL CT14 .... 232 G7
Downsview Infant School
KEN/WIL TN24 .... 253 H2
Downsview Primary School
NRWD SE19 .... 60 C6
SWLY BR8 .... 66 A9
Downs Way CP School
OXTED RH8 .... 175 H3
Dragons Health Club
MAIDW ME16 .... 12 C2
Drapers Mill CP School
MARG CT9 .... 112 F5
Drew Primary School
CAN/RD E16 .... 26 F4
The Drop Redoubt
DVW CT17 .... 8 C5
Druidstone Park
CANTW/ST CT2 .... 135 N6
Ducks Infants School
DUL SE21 .... 60 F2
Duke of Clarence
Trading Estate
IOS ME12 .... 57 J5
Dulverton Primary School
ELTH/MOT SE9 .... 63 P1
Dulwich College
DUL SE21 .... 40 E9
Dulwich College
Preparatory School
DUL SE21 .... 60 E2
Dulwich College Track
DUL SE21 .... 60 E1
Dulwich Hamlet FC
EDUL SE22 .... 40 E5
Dulwich Hamlet Junior School
HNHL SE24 .... 40 D7
Dulwich Hospital
EDUL SE22 .... 40 E5
Dulwich Leisure Centre
EDUL SE22 .... 40 G5
Dulwich Medical Centre
EDUL SE22 .... 40 G6
Dulwich Picture Gallery
DUL SE21 .... 40 D8
Dulwich Preparatory School
CRBK TN17 .... 298 D3
Dulwich & Sydenham Hill
Golf Club
DUL SE21 .... 60 C1
Dulwich Village CE
Infant School
DUL SE21 .... 40 E7
Dunbar Wharf
POP/IOD E14 .... 25 J3
Dundee Wharf
POP/IOD E14 .... 25 J3
Dungeness National
Nature Reserve
LYDD TN29 .... 346 G2
Dungeness Old Lighthouse
LYDD TN29 .... 347 M5
Dungeness Power Station
LYDD TN29 .... 347 K5
Dunkerheys Hotel
& Restaurant
DEAL CT14 .... 233 J3
Dunkirk CP School
FAV ME13 .... 164 E1
Dunton Green
Primary School
SEV TN13 .... 148 D5
Duppas Junior School
CROY/NA CR0 .... 82 G9

Durands Wharf
BERM/RHTH SE16 .... 25 J5
Dymchurch Martello Tower
LYDD TN29 .... 326 G7
Dymchurch Primary School
LYDD TN29 .... 326 F6
Dymchurch Redoubt
HYTHE CT21 .... 327 M1
Eaglesfield School
WOOL/PLUM SE18 .... 43 L2
Ealdham Primary School
ELTH/MOT SE9 .... 42 G5
East Beckton District Centre
EHAM E6 .... 26 C2
East Borough
Primary School
MAID/BEAR ME14 .... 13 J3
Eastchurch CE
Primary School
IOS ME12 .... 79 L3
Eastcote Primary School
WELL DA16 .... 43 P4
East Court Mansion
EGRIN RH19 .... 265 J6
East Court School
RAM CT11 .... 17 K2
East End Computing
& Business College
WCHPL E1 .... 24 E2
East Farleigh Primary School
MAID/BEAR ME15 .... 184 F5
East Greenwich Christ Church
CE Primary School
GNWCH SE10 .... 25 P7
East Grinstead Health Clinic
EGRIN RH19 .... 265 H6
East Kent Business Centre
RDV CT15 .... 8 E5
East Kent Light Railway
RDV CT15 .... 260 J1
East Kent Retail Park
BRDST CT10 .... 112 C8
Eastling Primary School
FAV ME13 .... 161 K7
East London RFC
EHAM E6 .... 26 C1
Eastmead Trading Estate
ASH TN23 .... 2 E7
East Peckham
Primary School
STPH/PW TN12 .... 212 C3
Eastry Medical Surgery
SWCH CT13 .... 201 J8
Eastry Primary School
SWCH CT13 .... 201 J8
East Stour Primary School
KEN/WIL TN24 .... 282 G2
East Thamesmead
Business Park
ERITHM DA18 .... 28 E5
East Tilbury J & I Schools
TIL RM18 .... 34 B8
Eastwell Manor Hotel
RASHE TN25 .... 222 C6
East Wickham
Primary School
WELL DA16 .... 44 B2
Ebbsfleet Industrial Estate
GVW DA11 .... 48 E6
Ecclesbourne Primary School
THHTH CR7 .... 83 H2
Edenbridge & District
War Memorial Hospital
EDEN TN8 .... 236 D2
Edenbridge Golf
& Country Club
EDEN TN8 .... 206 B8
Edenbridge Leisure Centre
EDEN TN8 .... 206 D8
The Edenbridge
Medical Centre
EDEN TN8 .... 206 D8
Edenbridge Primary School
EDEN TN8 .... 206 D9
Eden Business Centre
ASH TN23 .... 2 E7
Edenham High School
CROY/NA CR0 .... 84 B4
Edgebury Primary School
CHST BR7 .... 63 N3
Edmund Waller
Primary School
NWCR SE14 .... 41 K3
Effra Road Retail Park
BRXS/STRHM SW2 .... 40 A6
Egerton CE Primary School
HDCN TN27 .... 219 M7
Eglinton Junior School
WOOL/PLUM SE18 .... 27 H9
Eglinton Primary School
WOOL/PLUM SE18 .... 43 L1
Elaine Primary School
STRD ME2 .... 71 N8
Elbourne Trading Estate
BELV DA17 .... 28 C6
Electron Trade Centre
STMC/STPC BR5 .... 87 J1
Elfrida Primary School
CAT SE6 .... 61 J3
Elham CE Primary School
RCANTW CT4 .... 257 L5
Eliot Bank Primary School
FSTH SE23 .... 61 H1
Elizabeth Trading Estate
NWCR SE14 .... 24 C9
Ellen Wilkinson
Primary School
CAN/RD E16 .... 26 E1
Ellingham Industrial Centre
ASH TN23 .... 282 D3
Ellington High School
RAM CT11 .... 16 B2
Ellington School For Girls
RAM CT11 .... 16 B2
Elliott Park School
IOS ME12 .... 58 B9
Elm Court Industrial Estate
GILL ME7 .... 126 B2
Elm Court School
WNWD SE27 .... 60 B1

Elmhurst School
SAND/SEL CR2 .... 83 J9
Elmley Marshes
Nature Reserve
IOS ME12 .... 101 K2
The Elms Medical Centre
HAM ME5 .... 73 K2
Elmwood Junior School
CROY/NA CR0 .... 82 G4
Elm Wood Primary School
DUL SE21 .... 60 D2
Eltham Bus Station
ELTH/MOT SE9 .... 43 H6
Eltham CE Primary School
ELTH/MOT SE9 .... 43 K6
Eltham College Junior School
ELTH/MOT SE9 .... 43 H9
Eltham College Senior School
ELTH/MOT SE9 .... 63 H1
Eltham Crematorium
ELTH/MOT SE9 .... 43 P5
Eltham Green School
ELTH/MOT SE9 .... 43 H7
Eltham Health Clinic
ELTH/MOT SE9 .... 43 H7
Eltham Health
& Fitness Centre
ELTH/MOT SE9 .... 43 L7
Eltham Hill
Technology College
ELTH/MOT SE9 .... 43 J7
Eltham Palace
ELTH/MOT SE9 .... 43 J8
Eltham Pools
ELTH/MOT SE9 .... 43 J6
Eltham Warren Golf Club
ELTH/MOT SE9 .... 43 M6
Emery Theatre
POP/IOD E14 .... 25 L2
Emmetts Garden (NT)
RSEV TN14 .... 177 L6
Empire Cinema
SWCH CT13 .... 201 N1
English Martyrs RC
Primary School
STRD ME2 .... 72 B7
Enterprise Business Centre
DVE/WH CT16 .... 291 H1
Enterprise Business Estate
STRD ME2 .... 19 K2
Enterprise Business Park
POP/IOD E14 .... 25 L5
Enterprise Industrial Estate
BERM/RHTH SE16 .... 24 F8
Eric Liddell Sports Centre
ELTH/MOT SE9 .... 63 H1
Erith & District Hospital
ERITH DA8 .... 29 J9
Erith Health Centre
ERITH DA8 .... 29 K9
Erith Library & Museum
ERITH DA8 .... 29 K8
Erith Playhouse
ERITH DA8 .... 29 L8
Erith School
ERITH DA8 .... 45 L1
Erith School Community
Sports Centre
ERITH DA8 .... 45 L1
Erith Small Business Centre
ERITH DA8 .... 29 L9
Erith Sports Centre
ERITH DA8 .... 45 L1
Erith Stadium
ERITH DA8 .... 29 K9
Escots CP School
EGRIN RH19 .... 265 K7
Etchinghill Golf Club
RFOLK CT18 .... 287 J4
Ethelbert Road
Infant School
FAV ME13 .... 132 E7
Eureka Leisure Park
RASHE TN25 .... 252 F4
The Eurogate Business Park
ASH TN23 .... 2 D3
KEN/WIL TN24 .... 252 E4
Eurolink Business Centre
BRXS/STRHM SW2 .... 40 A5
Eurolink Industrial Centre
SIT ME10 .... 129 P1
Eurolink Industrial Estate
SIT ME10 .... 100 A9
Europa Trading Estate
ERITH DA8 .... 29 J8
WTHK RM20 .... 31 N8
European School
of Osteopathy
MAID/BEAR ME14 .... 155 P1
Evegate Business Centre
RASHE TN25 .... 284 C6
Eveline Lowe Primary School
PECK SE15 .... 24 C8
Eversley Medical Centre
CROY/NA CR0 .... 82 F3
ExCeL Exhibition Centre
CAN/RD E16 .... 26 C3
Executive Medical &
Occupational Health Centre
CROY/NA CR0 .... 83 J7
Eynsford Castle
EYN DA4 .... 89 K6
Eynsford CC
EYN DA4 .... 89 K6
Eythorne Elvington
Primary School
RDV CT15 .... 230 D9
Faircham Trading Estate
DEPT SE8 .... 41 P1
Fairchildes Primary School
CROY/NA CR0 .... 115 H6
Fairfax Business Centre
MAID/SHEP ME15 .... 186 C1
Fairfield Pool & Leisure Centre
DART DA1 .... 46 E8
Fairlawn Primary School
FSTH SE23 .... 41 J8
Fairview Community
Primary School
RHAM ME8 .... 96 F9

Fairview Industrial Centre
RAIN RM13 .... 29 J3
Fairview Industrial Estate
OXTED RH8 .... 175 K9
Fairview Industrial Park
RASHW TN26 .... 304 C8
Fairwood Industrial Park
ASH TN25 .... 2 A4
The Family Medical Centre
WALD ME5 .... 125 P3
Fan Museum
GNWCH SE10 .... 42 A1
Farleigh Court Golf Club
WARL CR6 .... 114 D6
Farleigh Primary School
WARL CR6 .... 144 A2
Farleigh Rovers FC
WARL CR6 .... 144 C1
Farleigh Trading Estate
MAID/SHEP ME15 .... 185 K2
Farnborough
Primary School
ORP BR6 .... 86 E9
Farningham Woods
Nature Reserve
SWLY BR8 .... 89 J1
Farrington & Stratford
House School
CHST BR7 .... 63 P6
Faversham Cemetery
FAV ME15 .... 133 H7
Faversham Cottage Hospital
FAV ME13 .... 132 F6
Faversham Golf Club
FAV ME15 .... 162 B6
Faversham Industrial Estate
FAV ME13 .... 133 C8
Faversham Town FC
FAV ME13 .... 132 C8
Fawkham CE Primary School
HART DA3 .... 90 D5
Fawkham House School
BGR/WK TN15 .... 120 D2
Fawkham Manor Hospital
HART DA3 .... 90 F5
The Fayreness Hotel
BRDST CT10 .... 113 M3
Featherby Infant School
RHAM ME8 .... 96 D3
Featherby Junior School
RHAM ME8 .... 96 D3
Felbridge Primary School
EGRIN RH19 .... 264 C4
Fenstanton J & I School
BRXS/STRHM SW2 .... 40 A7
The Ferry Inn
IOS ME12 .... 102 F6
Ferry Lane Industrial Estate
RAIN RM13 .... 29 M1
Financial Times
Newspaper Offices
POP/IOD E14 .... 25 M2
Finchcocks Living
Museum of Music
CRBK TN17 .... 295 P2
Firepower
(Museum of Artillery)
WOOL/PLUM SE18 .... 27 J6
Fisher Athletic FC
BERM/RHTH SE16 .... 24 G4
Five Acre Wood School
MAID/SHEP ME15 .... 185 N5
Flamsteed House Museum
GNWCH SE10 .... 42 B1
Flaxman Sports Centre
CMBW SE5 .... 40 C3
Fleetdown J & I School
RDART DA2 .... 67 J1
Fleetway Sports Club
CVE DA12 .... 49 N9
Fleur de Lis Heritage Centre
FAV ME13 .... 132 F6
Flicks Cinema
DEAL CT14 .... 233 J3
Folkestone C & CC Site
FOLKN CT19 .... 311 K4
Folkestone CC
FOLKN CT19 .... 310 D5
Folkestone Invicta FC
FOLKN CT19 .... 310 D5
Folkestone Racecourse
HYTHE CT21 .... 307 P1
Folkestone RFC
RFOLK CT18 .... 309 K1
Folkestone Rowing Club
FOLK CT20 .... 310 C8
The Folkestone School
for Girls
FOLK CT20 .... 310 C7
Folkestone Sports Centre
& Ski Slope
FOLKN CT19 .... 10 B1
Folkestone Warren
Nature Reserve
FOLKN CT19 .... 311 K4
Folkestone Yacht
& Motor Boat Club
FOLKN CT19 .... 11 H4
Folys End Christian
High School
SNWD SE25 .... 83 K3
Fondu Sports Club
PUR RM19 .... 30 F7
Fordcombe CE
Primary School
RRTW TN3 .... 268 G3
Fordgate Business Park
BELV DA17 .... 29 H5
The Foreland School
BRDST CT10 .... 113 M7
Forestdale Primary School
CROY/NA CR0 .... 114 B3
Forest Hill Business Centre
FSTH SE23 .... 61 J1
Forest Hill Industrial Estate
FSTH SE23 .... 61 J1
Forest Hill Pools
SYD SE26 .... 61 J1
Forest Hill School
FSTH SE23 .... 61 K2

Forge Close Clinic
HAYES BR2 .... 85 K5
The Former Health Centre
CHARL SE7 .... 26 E7
Forster Park Primary School
CAT SE6 .... 62 C2
Fort Amherst Heritage Park
& Caverns
CHAT ME4 .... 6 C2
Fort Luton Museum
CHAT ME4 .... 95 M5
Fort Pitt Grammar School
CHAT ME4 .... 95 K2
Fossdene Primary School
CHARL SE7 .... 26 C8
Fosse Bank New School
RTON TN11 .... 210 B3
Foster's Primary School
WELL DA16 .... 44 E4
Four Elms Primary School
EDEN TN8 .... 207 J5
Four Seasons Hotel
BERM/RHTH SE16 .... 25 J4
Foxfield Primary School
WOOL/PLUM SE18 .... 27 K8
Fox's Cross
WSTB CT5 .... 135 J2
Foxwood Special School
HYTHE CT21 .... 309 L5
Franklin Industrial Estate
PGE/AN SE20 .... 61 J7
The Frank Walters
Business Park
BRDST CT10 .... 113 J9
The Freda Gardham
Community School
RYE TN31 .... 338 G6
Free Trade Wharf
WAP E1W 24 C3
Freight Services Centre
DVE/WH CT16 .... 9 J3
Fremlin Walk
Shopping Centre
MAID/BEAR ME14 .... 12 E4
French Hospital
ROCH ME1 .... 19 G5
Frenchmans Beach
Holiday Village
RYE TN31 .... 339 P9
Frewen College
RYE TN31 .... 330 B8
The Friends of Canterbury
Cathedral
CANT CT1 .... 5 F3
Frittenden CE
Primary School
CRBK TN17 .... 277 H2
Fulston Manor School
SIT ME10 .... 129 N3
Funton Brickworks
RSIT ME9 .... 98 C2
Furley Park Primary School
ASH TN23 .... 282 F6
Furness School
SWLY BR8 .... 65 P5
Furness Swanley FC
SWLY BR8 .... 88 C2
Gads Hill School
HOO/HM ME3 .... 71 L5
Galley Hill Industrial Estate
SWCM DA10 .... 48 C6
Galleywall Primary School
BERM/RHTH SE16 .... 24 E7
Gallions Mount
Primary School
WOOL/PLUM SE18 .... 27 N8
Gallions Primary School
EHAM E6 .... 27 J2
Gallions Reach Shopping Park
EHAM E6 .... 27 J1
Gap House School
BRDST CT10 .... 143 N2
Gardener Industrial Estate
SYD SE26 .... 61 L4
The Garden of England
Crematorium
RSIT ME9 .... 99 K5
Garlinge Infant School
MARG CT19 .... 112 B5
Garrison Cricket Ground
Pavilion
GILL ME7 .... 7 F2
Garrison Sports Stadium
GILL ME7 .... 7 F1
Gate House Wood
Touring Park
BGR/WK TN15 .... 151 P3
Gateway Business Centre
SYD SE26 .... 61 L5
WOOL/PLUM SE18 .... 27 K6
Gateway Community College
North Site
CDW/CHF RM16 .... 32 G5
Gateway Primary School
RDART DA2 .... 47 H7
Gateway to the
White Cliffs (NT)
DVE/WH CT16 .... 9 K1
Gaza Trading Estate
RTON TN11 .... 209 J3
Gemini Business Estate
NWCR SE14 .... 24 C8
Geoffrey Whitworth Theatre
DART DA1 .... 46 A5
George Greens School
POP/IOD E14 .... 25 M8
The George Hotel
CRBK TN17 .... 298 A2
George Spurgen Community
Primary School
FOLKN CT19 .... 311 H4
Georges Turles House Clinic
CANTW/ST CT2 .... 4 A3
Giffin Business Centre
DEPT SE8 .... 41 N1
Gilbert Scott
Primary School
SAND/SEL CR2 .... 114 B2
The Gillingham College
GILL ME7 .... 96 C2

Gillingham FC
(Priestfield Stadium)
GILL ME7 .... 96 B1
Gillingham Golf Club
GILL ME7 .... 96 B4
Gillingham Ice Bowl
RHAM ME8 .... 96 D5
Gillingham Medical Centre
GILL ME7 .... 96 C2
The Glade Business Centre
WTHK RM20 .... 31 J8
The Glades Shopping Centre
BMLY BR1 .... 62 E8
Glebe School
WWKM BR4 .... 84 C5
Glencoe Junior School
CHAT ME4 .... 95 M4
Globe Industrial Estate
GRAYS RM17 .... 32 D9
Globe Wharf
BERM/RHTH SE16 .... 24 C3
Gloucester Primary School
PECK SE15 .... 40 E1
Godden Green Clinic
BGR/WK TN15 .... 179 N1
Godinton House
ASH TN23 .... 251 P5
Godinton Primary School
ASH TN23 .... 252 A6
Godinton Way
Industrial Estate
ASH TN23 .... 2 C4
Golden Hinde
Educational Trust
STHWK SE1 .... 24 A4
Goldsmiths University
BROCKY SE4 .... 41 M4
DEPT SE8 .... 25 K9
LEW SE13 .... 42 C5
Goldsmiths University
Sports Ground
SCUP DA14 .... 65 K2
Goldwyn Community
Special School
ASH TN23 .... 251 N5
Gonville Primary School
THHTH CR7 .... 82 E7
Goodnestone CE
Primary School
RCANTE CT3 .... 199 M5
Goodnestone Park Gardens
RCANTE CT3 .... 199 L6
Goodrich J & I School
EDUL SE22 .... 40 C7
The Good Shepherd
Primary School
ROCH ME1 .... 95 K5
Good Shepherd RC
Primary School
BMLY BR1 .... 62 D3
CROY/NA CR0 .... 114 E2
Goose Green
Primary School
EDUL SE22 .... 40 F5
Goose Green Trading Estate
EDUL SE22 .... 40 G5
Gordonbrock
Primary School
BROCKY SE4 .... 41 N6
Gordon Junior School
STRD ME2 .... 72 C4
Gordon Primary School
ELTH/MOT SE9 .... 43 K5
Gore Court CC
SIT ME10 .... 99 J9
Gore Street Cemetery
MSTR CT12 .... 140 B6
Goudhurst & Kilndown
CE Primary School
CRBK TN17 .... 274 E8
Grace Chapel
& Christian School
FOLK CT20 .... 11 F4
Grain Power Station
HOO/HM ME3 .... 56 D5
Granby Sports Club
CHST BR7 .... 63 J4
Grand Shaft (Lower Entrance)
DVW CT17 .... 8 C6
Grand Shaft (Upper Entrance)
DVW CT17 .... 8 B6
The Grange Medical Centre
RAM ME1 .... 16 D5
Grange Moor Hotel
MAIDW ME16 .... 12 A7
Grange Park College
E/WMAL ME19 .... 153 K2
The Granville School
SEV TN13 .... 148 F8
Granville Theatre & Cinema
RAM CT11 .... 17 J3
Gravel Hill Primary School
BXLYHS DA6 .... 45 K6
Graveney CP School
FAV ME13 .... 133 N4
Gravesend CC
GVW DA11 .... 49 L8
Gravesend Grammar School
GVW DA11 .... 49 P8
Gravesend Museum
GVE DA12 .... 49 M7
Gravesend & Northfleet FC
GVE DA12 .... 48 E6
Gravesend & North Kent
Hospital
GVW DA11 .... 49 L7
Gravesend Rowing Club
GVE DA12 .... 49 N7
Gravesend Yacht Club
GVE DA12 .... 49 P7
Graves Yard Industrial Estate
WELL DA16 .... 44 C3
Grays Athletic FC
GRAYS RM17 .... 32 C9
Grays Business Centre
GRAYS RM17 .... 32 D6
Grays Convent School
GRAYS RM17 .... 32 C7
Grays Farm Primary School
STMC/STPC BR5 .... 64 D7

Grays Health Centre
GRAYS RM17 .... 32 B8
The Grays School
GRAYS RM17 .... 32 C6
Great Chart CC
ASH TN23 .... 251 P8
Great Chart Primary School
ASH TN23 .... 252 A9
Great Comp Garden
BGR/WK TN15 .... 151 P6
Great Dixter House
& Gardens
RYE TN31 .... 329 P6
Greater London Authority
Headquarters (City Hall)
STHWK SE1 .... 24 B4
Great Hall Arcade
RTW TN1 .... 22 D5
Great Hollanden
Business Centre
BGR/WK TN15 .... 179 P9
Great Jubilee Wharf
WAP E1W 24 F4
Greatness Park Cemetery
RSEV TN14 .... 149 J8
Great Oaks Small School
SWCH CT13 .... 172 B9
Greatstone Primary School
NROM TN28 .... 343 J2
Greenacre School
WALD ME5 .... 95 L9
Greenacres Primary School
ELTH/MOT SE9 .... 63 L1
Green Field
Effective Education
EGRIN RH19 .... 264 G2
Greenfields School
HDCN TN27 .... 300 E1
Greenhithe Health Clinic
SWCM DA10 .... 47 P6
Greenland Pier
BERM/RHTH SE16 .... 25 J1
Green Lane Business Park
ELTH/MOT SE9 .... 63 L1
Greenshields
Industrial Estate
CAN/RD E16 .... 26 B5
Greenside Primary School
WOOL/PLUM SE18 .... 27 L9
Green Street Green
Primary School
ORP BR6 .... 116 G1
Greenvale Infant School
CHAT ME4 .... 95 M4
Greenvale Primary School
SAND/SEL CR2 .... 114 A5
Greenvale School
FSTH SE23 .... 61 L2
Greenwich Centre
Business Park
DEPT SE8 .... 41 P1
Greenwich Cinema
GNWCH SE10 .... 42 A1
Greenwich Community
Arts Centre
GNWCH SE10 .... 41 P1
Greenwich
Community College
WOOL/PLUM SE18 .... 27 J7
Greenwich Industrial Estate
CHARL SE7 .... 26 C7
GNWCH SE10 .... 41 P1
Greenwich Natural
Health Centre
GNWCH SE10 .... 42 A1
Greenwich Pier
GNWCH SE10 .... 25 M8
Greenwich School
of Management
GNWCH SE10 .... 42 A1
Greenwich Theatre
& Art Gallery
GNWCH SE10 .... 42 B1
Griffen Manor School
WOOL/PLUM SE18 .... 44 A2
Grinling Gibbons
Primary School
DEPT SE8 .... 25 J9
Grombridge Place Gardens
& Enchanted Forest
RRTW TN3 .... 269 H8
Grosvenor Medical Centre
RTW TN1 .... 22 D2
Grove Bowls Club
RTW TN1 .... 22 E5
Grove Dairy Farm
Business Centre
RSIT ME9 .... 99 H8
Grove Ferry Boat Club
RCANTE CT3 .... 139 J4
Grove House Primary School
for Deaf Children
WWWD SE27 .... 60 B1
Grove Medical Centre
DEPT SE8 .... 25 H7
Grove Park CP School
RTW TN1 .... 99 J8
Guardian Industrial Estate
STPH/PW TN12 .... 245 H2
Guardian Newspapers
POP/IOD E14 .... 25 L5
Guelder Rose Medical Centre
STPH/PW TN12 .... 246 C5
Gulbenkian Theatre
CANTW/ST CT2 .... 136 C9
Guru Nanak Sports Club
GVE DA12 .... 49 N8
Guston CE Primary School
RDV CT15 .... 291 M4
Guy's Hospital
STHWK SE1 .... 24 A4
Gypsy Moth IV
GNWCH SE10 .... 25 M9
Haberdashers Askes
Hatcham College
NWCR SE14 .... 41 K3
Hadlow College
CANT CT1 .... 5 J5

Hadlow College of Agriculture
& Horticulture
RTON TN11 .... 211 N2
Hadlow School
RTON TN11 .... 211 P2
Hailey Road Business Park
ERITHM DA18 .... 28 F5
Haimo Primary School
ELTH/MOT SE9 .... 43 H6
Haine Industrial Estate
MSTR CT12 .... 142 E3
Halfway Houses
Primary School
IOS ME12 .... 77 M1
Halley Primary School
POP/IOD E14 .... 25 H1
Halling Primary School
STRD ME2 .... 124 A2
Hall Place
BXLY DA5 .... 45 L7
Hallsville Primary School
CAN/RD E16 .... 26 B2
Halsford Park
Primary School
EGRIN RH19 .... 264 E6
Halstead Place School
RSEV TN14 .... 117 M6
Halstead Primary School
RSEV TN14 .... 117 N7
Halstow Primary School
GNWCH SE10 .... 26 A8
Hambledon Clinic
CMBW SE5 .... 40 D4
Hamilton Road
Industrial Estate
WNWD SE27 .... 60 D3
Hamlet International
Industrial Estate
ERITH DA8 .... 29 J8
Hammerwood Park
EGRIN RH19 .... 266 D6
Hammonds Corner
LYDD TN29 .... 336 D7
Hampton Pier Yacht Club
HB CT6 .... 106 C1
Hampton Primary School
HB CT6 .... 107 H3
Hampton Road
Industrial Park
CROY/NA CR0 .... 83 H5
Ham Street Primary School
RASHW TN26 .... 304 C7
Hamstreet Woods National
Nature Reserve
RASHW TN26 .... 304 E7
Harbinger Primary School
POP/IOD E14 .... 25 K7
Harbour School
DVW CT17 .... 290 F8
Harcourt CP School
FOLKN CT19 .... 310 B4
Harden Road
Industrial Estate
LYDD TN29 .... 342 C5
Harenc School
SCUP DA14 .... 64 E4
Harrietsham CE
Primary School
RMAID ME17 .... 188 F5
Harris City
Technology College
NRWD SE19 .... 60 F7
Harry Gosling Primary School
WCHPL E1 .... 24 D2
Hartley Primary School
HART DA3 .... 91 H2
Hartlip Endowed CE
Primary School
RSIT ME9 .... 97 N9
Hartsdown Leisure Centre
MARC CT9 .... 14 D7
Hartsdown
Technology College
MARC CT9 .... 112 C5
Hart Street Business Centre
MAIDW ME16 .... 12 D6
Harvey Clinic
FOLK CT20 .... 10 D4
The Harvey Grammar School
FOLKN CT19 .... 310 D5
Haseltine Primary School
SYD SE26 .... 61 M3
Haslemere Industrial Estate
MAID/SHEP ME15 .... 186 C6
Hatcham Mews
Business Centre
NWCR SE14 .... 41 K1
Hawes Down Clinic
WWKM BR4 .... 84 C6
Hawes Down Primary School
WWKM BR4 .... 84 C5
Hawkhurst CE
Primary School
HAWK TN18 .... 317 J4
Hawkhurst Cottage
Hospital
HAWK TN18 .... 316 F4
Hawkhurst Golf Club
HAWK TN18 .... 317 H4
Hawkhurst Squash Club
HAWK TN18 .... 316 C4
Hawkinge Cemetery
RFOLK CT18 .... 288 C7
Hawkinge Crematorium
RFOLK CT18 .... 288 C7
Hawkinge Health Centre
RFOLK CT18 .... 288 E8
Hawkins Clinic
DEAL CT14 .... 233 H1
Hawksmoor Primary School
THMD SE28 .... 28 A3
Hawkwell Business Centre
RTWE/PEM TN2 .... 242 A7
Hawley Health Centre
MARC CT9 .... 15 G5
Hawthorn Farm
Caravan Park
RDV CT15 .... 262 A7
Hayesbrook School
TON TN9 .... 240 D1

Hayes Grove Priory Hospital
HAYES BR2 .... 85 K6
Hayes Primary School
HAYES BR2 .... 85 L5
Hayes School
HAYES BR2 .... 85 L6
Haymerle School
PECK SE15 .... 24 D9
Haysden Country Park
RTON TN11 .... 240 A1
Hays Galleria
STHWK SE1 .... 24 B4
Hazelwood School
OXTED RH8 .... 175 K7
Hazlitt Theatre
MAID/BEAR ME14 .... 13 F4
Headcorn Cricket Club
HDCN TN27 .... 247 P3
Headcorn Primary School
HDCN TN27 .... 247 M3
Heath Farm School
HDCN TN27 .... 220 C3
Heathfield College
HAYES BR2 .... 115 M1
Heath House
Preparatory School
BKHTH/KID SE3 .... 42 D3
Heavers Farm
Primary School
SNWD SE25 .... 83 L2
Heber Primary School
EDUL SE22 .... 40 F7
Heckford Street
Business Centre
WAP E1W 24 G3
Hedgend Industrial Estate
BRCH CT7 .... 140 A1
Helen Alison School
MEO DA13 .... 92 B4
Hempstead House
Country Hotel
RSIT ME9 .... 130 D3
Hempstead Infant School
GILL ME7 .... 96 D9
Hempstead Junior School
GILL ME7 .... 126 D1
Hempstead Valley
Shopping Centre
GILL ME7 .... 126 D1
Hemstead Forest Golf Club
CRBK TN17 .... 298 G3
Henley Business Park
STRD ME2 .... 19 J2
Henry VIII Experience
HRTF TN7 .... 267 K8
Henwick Primary School
ELTH/MOT SE9 .... 43 H4
Henwood Business Centre
KEN/WIL TN24 .... 3 H5
Henwood Industrial Estate
KEN/WIL TN24 .... 3 H2
The Hereson School
BRDST CT10 .... 17 H1
Hermitage Primary School
WAP E1W 24 D4
Herne Bay Cemetery
HB CT6 .... 107 M4
Herne Bay FC
HB CT6 .... 107 L4
Herne Bay Golf Club
HB CT6 .... 107 L4
Herne Bay High School
HB CT6 .... 107 J3
Herne Bay Museum Centre
HB CT6 .... 107 L1
Herne Bay Primary School
HB CT6 .... 107 L2
Herne Bay West
Industrial Estate
HB CT6 .... 107 H3
Herne CE Junior School
HNHL SE24 .... 107 M5
Herne Hill School
HNHL SE24 .... 40 C6
Herne Hill Stadium
(Cycle Centre)
HNHL SE24 .... 40 D7
Herne Infant School
HB CT6 .... 107 N6
Hernhill CE Primary School
FAV ME13 .... 134 B7
Heronsgate Primary School
THMD SE28 .... 27 L6
Herringham Primary School
CDW/CHF RM16 .... 33 J6
Hersden Community
Primary School
RCANTE CT3 .... 138 B8
Hever Castle & Gardens
EDEN TN8 .... 237 L2
Hever Castle Golf Club
EDEN TN8 .... 207 L9
Hever CE Primary School
EDEN TN8 .... 237 L3
Hextable Primary School
SWLY BR8 .... 65 P5
Higgs Industrial Estate
HNHL SE24 .... 40 B4
Higham Primary School
HOO/HM ME3 .... 71 L2
High Elms Country Park
ORP BR6 .... 116 D2
High Elms Golf Club
ORP BR6 .... 116 D2
Highfield Business Centre
CANT CT1 .... 4 B7
Highfield Industrial Estate
FOLKN CT19 .... 11 H1
Highfield Infant School
HAYES BR2 .... 85 J1
Highfield Junior School
HAYES BR2 .... 85 H1
High Firs Primary School
SWLY BR8 .... 88 E1
High Halden CE
Primary School
RASHW TN26 .... 279 H9
High Halstow National
Nature Reserve
HOO/HM ME3 .... 53 L3

High Halstow Primary School
HOO/HM ME3 .... 53 K5
Highshore School
PECK SE15 .... 40 F2
Higsted Grammar School
SIT ME10 .... 129 N3
Highview Primary School
WLGTN SM6 .... 82 D9
The Highway Primary School
ORP BR6 .... 87 K9
The Highway Trading Centre
WAP E1W 24 G3
Highworth Grammar
School for Girls
KEN/WIL TN24 .... 2 B1
Hildenborough CE
Primary School
RTON TN11 .... 209 P4
Hilden Grange School
TONN TN10 .... 210 E7
Hilden Oaks School
TONN TN10 .... 210 E6
Hilderstone College
BRDST CT10 .... 113 L8
Hillborough Business Park
HB CT6 .... 108 C6
Hill Mead Infant School
BRXN/ST SW9 .... 40 B5
Hillmead Primary School
BRXN/ST SW9 .... 40 B5
Hill School
BH/WHM TN16 .... 146 C8
Hills Grove Primary School
WELL DA16 .... 44 E1
Hillside Industrial Estate
FOLK CT20 .... 310 B7
Hillside Primary School
STMC/STPC BR5 .... 87 K4
Hilltop Primary School
STRD ME2 .... 72 C6
Hillview School for Girls
TON TN9 .... 240 C1
Hilly Fields Medical Centre
BROCKY SE4 .... 41 N6
Hilton Business Centre
ASH TN23 .... 282 E2
Hilton Docklands Pier
BERM/RHTH SE16 .... 25 J4
Historical Society Museum
CHAT ME4 .... 6 B2
The Historic Dockyard
Chatham
STRD ME2 .... 72 F7
Hither Green Cemetery
STRHM/NOR SW16 .... 60 M1
Hither Green Cemetery
CAT SE6 .... 62 D1
Hither Green Primary School
LEW SE13 .... 42 B7
HM Prison
CANT CT1 .... 5 H4
IOS ME12 .... 79 H7
IOS ME12 .... 79 J8
IOS ME12 .... 79 K7
MAID/BEAR ME14 .... 12 E2
ROCH ME1 .... 94 G6
THMD SE28 .... 27 M6
HMS Belfast
STHWK SE1 .... 24 B4
HM Young Offender
Institution
DVW CT17 .... 291 J9
Hoath CP School
RCANTE CT3 .... 138 B4
Hobbs Industrial Estate
LING RH7 .... 234 B9
LING RH7 .... 264 A1
Holbeach Primary School
CAT SE6 .... 41 N8
Holborn College
WOOL/PLUM SE18 .... 26 E7
Holborough Marshes
Nature Reserve
SNOD ME6 .... 124 B4
Hollingbourne Primary School
RMAID ME17 .... 187 P1
Holydale Primary School
PECK SE15 .... 41 J3
Hollywood Bowl
BERM/RHTH SE16 .... 24 G6
Holmesdale Technology
College
SNOD ME6 .... 123 P6
Holmewood House School
RRTW TN3 .... 269 M6
Holtye Golf Club
EDEN TN8 .... 266 G5
Holy Cross RC Primary School
CAT SE6 .... 42 A9
SOCK/AV RM15 .... 31 L3
Holy Family RC
Primary School
BKHTH/KID SE3 .... 42 F5
POP/IOD E14 .... 25 K3
The Holy Family RC
Primary School
MAID/SHEP ME15 .... 186 B1
Holy Innocents Catholic
Primary School
ORP BR6 .... 86 G7
Holy Trinity CE Junior School
WLGTN SM6 .... 82 B8
Holy Trinity CE
Primary School
DART DA1 .... 46 C4
GVE DA12 .... 49 N8
SYD SE26 .... 61 J1
Holy Trinity College
BMLY BR1 .... 62 C7
Holy Trinity Foyer
MAID/BEAR ME14 .... 13 G4
Holy Trinity & St Johns
CE Primary School
MARC CT9 .... 15 H5
Holy Trinity School
BFN/LL DA15 .... 44 C9
Holywell Primary School
RSIT ME9 .... 98 A3
Homefarm Estate
DIT/AY ME20 .... 154 E3

Homeopathic Hospital
RTW TN1 ....22 C4
Homewood Infant School
SIT ME10 ....129 L1
Homewood School
TENT TN30 ....301 J6
Homing Park
WSTB CT5 ....105 J8
Honor Oak Crematorium
FSTH SE23 ....41 K6
Honor Oak Gallery
FSTH SE23 ....41 K7
Honor Oak Health Centre
BROCKY SE4 ....41 L5
Hook Lane Primary School
WELL DA16 ....44 C4
The Hope Anchor Hotel
RYE TN31 ....338 E7
Hope Primary School
CMBW SE5 ....40 E1
Hopewell School
ASH TN23 ....282 B1
Hop Farm & Country Park
STPH/PW TN12 ....213 H6
Horizon Industrial Estate
PECK SE15 ....24 D9
The Horniman Museum
& Gardens
FSTH SE23 ....41 H9
Horniman Primary School
FSTH SE23 ....41 H9
Horn Park Primary School
LEE/GVPK SE12 ....42 F8
Horn Stairs
BERM/RHTH SE16 ....25 J4
Horsmonden Primary School
STPH/PW TN12 ....273 P2
Horsted Infants School
WALD ME5 ....95 J9
Horsted Retail Park
WALD ME5 ....95 J8
Horton Kirby CE
Primary School
EYN DA4 ....67 J9
Horton Kirby Trading Estate
EYN DA4 ....67 J8
Hospital Barn Farm
MAID/SHEP ME15 ....184 E1
Hotel du Vin & Bistro
RTW TN1 ....22 E4
Hotel ibis
CAN/RD LE16 ....26 C3
GNWCH SE10 ....25 M9
POP/IOD E14 ....25 M3
WTHK RM20 ....31 J9
Hothfield Village
Primary School
RASHW TN26 ....251 L2
Howard Primary School
SAND/SEL CR2 ....83 H8
The Howard School
RHAM ME8 ....96 C6
Howbury Centre
ERITH DA8 ....46 A1
Howland Quay
BERM/RHTH SE16 ....24 C6
Howletts Wild Animal Park
RCANTW CT4 ....198 A1
HSBC Sports Club
BECK BR3 ....61 L5
HSBC Tower
POP/IOD E14 ....25 L4
Hubbard School
EGRIN RH19 ....265 H7
Hugh Christie
Technology College
TONN TN10 ....210 G4
Hull Park Sports Club
DEAL CT14 ....232 E3
The Hundred of Hoo School
HOO/HM ME3 ....73 J2
Hunton CE Primary School
MAID/SHEP ME15 ....214 C3
Huntsman Sports Club
BKHTH/KID SE3 ....42 E5
Hurst Green School
OXTED RH8 ....175 K8
Hurstmere School
BFN/LL DA15 ....44 D9
Hurst Primary School
BXLY DA5 ....44 F9
Hythe Community Clinic
HYTHE CT21 ....309 H5
Hythe Community School
HYTHE CT21 ....308 C6
Hythe CC
HYTHE CT21 ....309 H5
Hythe Imperial Golf Club
HYTHE CT21 ....309 K5
The Hythe Imperial Hotel
HYTHE CT21 ....309 J4
Hythe Ranges
HYTHE CT21 ....308 D6
Hythe St Leonard CE
Junior School
HYTHE CT21 ....308 C5
Hythe & Saltwood
Sailing Club
HYTHE CT21 ....309 H6
Hythe Swimming Pool
HYTHE CT21 ....309 J6
Ide Hill CE Aided
Primary School
RSEV TN14 ....177 M7
Iden Croft Herbs
STPH/PW TN12 ....246 D7
Ifield School
GVE DA12 ....69 N4
Ightham Mote (NT)
BGR/WK TN15 ....180 D3
Ightham Primary School
BGR/WK TN15 ....150 E7
IKEA Store Croydon
CROY/NA CR0 ....82 E5
IKEA Store Lakeside
WTHK RM20 ....31 L8
Ilderton Primary School
PECK SE15 ....24 D1

Imberhorne Business Centre
EGRIN RH19 ....264 E5
Imberhorne School
EGRIN RH19 ....264 E6
The Imber Sports Centre
EGRIN RH19 ....264 C5
Imperial College London
RASHE TN25 ....223 P8
Imperial Oyster Cinema
WSTB CT5 ....105 K4
Imperial Retail Park
GVW DA11 ....49 L1
Independent Business Park
EGRIN RH19 ....264 D5
Indoor Bowls & Sports Centre
CHAT ME4 ....6 B2
The Industrial Estate
EDEN TN8 ....206 C7
Information, Communications
& Technology Centre
Canterbury College
CANT CT1 ....5 C6
Innkeeper's Lodge
BECK BR3 ....84 D3
IOS ME12 ....167 J8
MAID/BEAR ME14 ....122 C7
SBGH/RUST TN4 ....240 C7
The Integrated Services
Programme (ISP)
Senior School
SIT ME10 ....99 M9
Invicta Grammar School
for Girls
MAID/BEAR ME14 ....13 K4
Invicta Primary School
BKHTH/KID SE3 ....26 B9
Invicta Sports Club
CHAT ME4 ....46 D6
IQRA Independent School
BRXN/ST SW9 ....40 A4
Island Clinic
POP/IOD E14 ....25 M5
Isle of Sheppey Cemetery
IOS ME12 ....57 M9
Isle of Sheppey
Holiday Village
IOS ME12 ....80 C4
Isteed Rise Primary School
MEO DA13 ....69 J7
Ivydale Primary School
PECK SE15 ....41 K5
Ivyclene Industrial Estate
EGRIN RH19 ....265 N9
Iwade Primary School
RSIT ME9 ....99 L2
James Allens Preparatory
Girls School
HNHL SE24 ....40 D6
James Dixon Primary School
PGE/AN SE20 ....60 G7
James Wolfe Primary School
GNWCH SE10 ....41 P1
Jamiatul Ummah School
WCHPL E1 ....24 E2
Jempsons Trading Estate
RYE TN31 ....338 E7
Jenner Health Centre
RYE TN31 ....41 L9
Jessop Primary School
HNHL SE24 ....40 B5
Jewish Community Theatre
HNHL SE24 ....40 D4
John Ball Primary School
BKHTH/KID SE3 ....42 C3
John Dixon Clinic
BERM/RHTH SE16 ....24 E6
John Donne Primary School
PECK SE15 ....41 H2
John Goodhew
Medical Centre
SIT ME10 ....99 M5
John Mayne CE
Primary School
HDCN TN27 ....278 A7
John Orwell Sports Centre
WAP E1W 24 D4
John Roan Lower School
BKHTH/KID SE3 ....42 D1
John Roan School
BKHTH/KID SE3 ....42 C1
John Ruskin College
SAND/SEL CR2 ....114 B2
John Stainer Primary School
BROCKY SE4 ....41 L4
John Wilson Business Park
WSTB CT5 ....106 A5
Joseph Conrad's Grave
CANTW/ST CT2 ....166 C3
Joseph Wilson
Industrial Estate
WSTB CT5 ....105 P7
Joydens Wood Infant School
RDART DA2 ....65 N3
Joydens Wood Junior School
BXLY DA5 ....65 N3
Joy Lane Autism Unit
WSTB CT5 ....105 K7
Jubilee Corner
RMAID ME17 ....217 P7
Jubilee Country Park
BMLY BR1 ....86 C1
Jubilee Hall
CANT CT1 ....4 B7
Jubilee Primary School
BRXS/STRHM SW2 ....40 A7
THMD SE28 ....28 B3
The Judd School
TON TN9 ....240 D1
Julians Primary School
STRHM/NOR SW16 ....60 A3
The Julie Rose Stadium
KEN/WIL TN24 ....253 J5
Junior Kings School
CANTW/ST CT2 ....137 K8
Juno Way Industrial Estate
NWCR SE14 ....24 C9
Jurys Inn
CROY/NA CR0 ....83 H6
Kangley Business Centre
SYD SE26 ....61 M4

Kavanagh Cinema
HB CT6 ....107 L1
Kearsney Abbey
DVE/WH CT16 ....290 E3
Keen Students
Supplementary School
WCHPL E1 ....24 D1
Keir Hardie Primary School
CAN/RD E16 ....26 B1
Keith Graham Academy
FOLK CT20 ....11 F4
Kelsey Park School
BECK BR3 ....61 N9
Kemnal Technology College
STMC/STPC BR5 ....64 D6
Kemsing Down
Nature Reserve
BGR/WK TN15 ....149 M1
Kemsing Primary School
BGR/WK TN15 ....149 N2
Kemsley Primary School
SIT ME10 ....99 N5
Kenden Business Park
STRD ME2 ....72 D7
Kennedy House School
NWGR SE14 ....41 J2
Kengate Industrial Estate
HYTHE CT21 ....308 E6
Kennington CE Junior School
KEN/WIL TN24 ....252 G2
Kennington CC
KEN/WIL TN24 ....252 G2
Kenningtons Primary School
SOCK/AV RM15 ....30 F2
Kensington Avenue
Primary School
THHTH CR7 ....60 A7
Kent & East Sussex
Steam Railway
TENT TN30 ....320 B3
Kent Battle of Britain
Museum
RFOLK CT18 ....288 C9
Kent & Canterbury Hospital
CANT CT1 ....166 F7
Kent CCC
(St Lawrence Ground)
CANT CT1 ....166 C6
Kent College
CANTW/ST CT2 ....166 B1
Kent College School
RTWE/PEM TN2 ....241 N6
Kent County Crematorium
HDCN TN27 ....221 J5
Kent County Showground
MAID/BEAR ME14 ....156 F2
Kent & East Sussex Railway
CRBK TN17 ....330 G3
RBTBR TN32 ....328 G6
RYE TN31 ....330 A4
Kent International Airport
MSTR CT12 ....142 A3
Kent Kraft Industrial Estate
SWCM DA10 ....48 D5
Kent Music School
MAID/SHEP ME15 ....12 E6
Kent Oil Refinery
HOO/HM ME3 ....55 P4
Kent Park Industrial Estate
PECK SE15 ....24 E9
Kent Private Clinic
SWCH CT13 ....201 P1
Kent & Sussex Crematorium
RTWE/PEM TN2 ....270 E8
Kent & Sussex Hospital
SBGH/RUST TN4 ....22 C2
Kestner Industrial Estate
RDART DA2 ....47 N5
Keston CE Primary School
HAYES BR2 ....85 N9
Keynes College
CANTW/ST CT2 ....136 C9
Kidbrooke Park
Primary School
BKHTH/KID SE3 ....42 G3
Kidbrooke School
BKHTH/KID SE3 ....43 H3
Kilmorie Primary School
FSTH SE23 ....61 L1
The King Ethelbert School
BRCH CT7 ....111 K6
Kingfisher Community
Primary School
DEPT SE8 ....25 J9
The Kingfisher Medical Centre
DEPT SE8 ....25 J9
King & Queen Wharf
BERM/RHTH SE16 ....24 G3
Kings Arms Hotel
BR/WHM TN16 ....176 E3
King's College Hospital
CMBW SE5 ....40 C4
Kings College London
CMBW SE5 ....40 D3
Kings College School
of Medicine & Dentistry
CMBW SE5 ....40 D3
Kingsdale School
DUL SE21 ....60 E2
Kingsdown
Industrial Estate
DIT/AY ME20 ....154 A4
Kingsdown & Ringwould
CE Primary School
DEAL CT14 ....263 H5
Kings Farm Infant School
GVE DA12 ....69 N4
Kings Hill Business Park
E/WMAL ME19 ....153 H8
Kings Hill Golf Club
E/WMAL ME19 ....183 J1
Kings Hill Primary School
E/WMAL ME19 ....153 H9
Kingsley Primary School
CROY/NA CR0 ....82 E5
Kingsmead CP School
CANT CT1 ....5 F2
Kingsmead Leisure Centre
CANTW/ST CT2 ....5 F1

Kings North CE
Primary School
ASH TN23 ....282 E5
Kingsnorth Industrial Estate
ASH TN25 ....282 E2
Kingsnorth Power Station
HOO/HM ME3 ....74 B2
Kings Preparatory School
ROCH ME1 ....19 F6
Kings Road Clinic
WALD ME5 ....96 A5
Kings School
ROCH ME1 ....19 F5
Kings School of English
BECK BR3 ....61 M8
Kings School
Recreation Centre
CANTW/ST CT2 ....4 E1
The Kings School
CANT CT1 ....5 F4
Kings Stairs
BERM/RHTH SE16 ....24 E5
Kingstanding Business Park
RTWE/PEM TN2 ....241 J7
Kingswood Primary School
RMAID ME17 ....187 P9
WNWD SE27 ....60 D3
Kitchener Barracks
CHAT ME4 ....6 C1
Kit's Coty House
DIT/AY ME20 ....125 N7
Klondyke Industrial Estate
QBOR ME11 ....77 H3
Knights Park Industrial Estate
STRD ME2 ....18 B4
Knights Templar Church
(Ruins)
DVW CT17 ....8 A7
Knockhall Community
Primary School
SWCM DA10 ....48 A6
Knole (NT)
BGR/WK TN15 ....21 K6
Knole Park Golf Club
BGR/WK TN15 ....21 J1
Kobi Nazrul Primary School
WCHPL E1 ....24 D2
Laban Centre for
Movement & Dance
DEPT SE8 ....41 P1
Laddingford Farm
Industrial Estate
WBY/YAL ME18 ....213 L6
Laddingford St Mary's
CE Primary School
WBY/YAL ME18 ....213 L6
Lady Boswells CE
Primary School
SEV TN15 ....21 H3
Ladycross Business Park
LING RH7 ....265 M1
Lady Joanna Thornhill
(Endowed) Primary School
RASHE TN25 ....223 P8
Ladywell Arena
LEW SE13 ....41 P7
Ladywell Cemetery
BROCKY SE4 ....41 M6
Ladywell Leisure Centre
LEW SE13 ....42 A6
Laker Industrial Estate
BECK BR3 ....61 M4
Lakeside Retail Park
WTHK RM20 ....31 K7
Lakeside Shopping Centre
WTHK RM20 ....31 L7
Lakes View International
Business Park
RCANTE CT3 ....138 D8
Laleham Gap School
MARG CT9 ....112 G3
Lamberhurst CE
Primary School
RRTW TN3 ....295 J1
Lamberhurst Golf Club
RRTW TN3 ....295 J1
Lamberhurst Vineyard
RRTW TN3 ....295 H3
Lamb House (NT)
RYE TN31 ....338 E7
Lambs Court
POP/IOD E14 ....25 H3
Lamont Business Centre
CROY/NA CR0 ....82 D4
Lamorbey Swimming Centre
BFN/LL DA15 ....64 C1
Landgate Arch
RYE TN31 ....338 F6
Langafel CE Primary School
HART DA3 ....68 E9
Langbourne Primary School
DUL SE21 ....60 E2
Langdon Park School
POP/IOD E14 ....25 L2
Langdon Primary School
RDV CT15 ....261 P7
The Langley Hotel
TONN TN10 ....210 G6
Langley Park Girls School
& Sports Centre
BECK BR3 ....84 C2
Langley Park Golf Club
BECK BR3 ....84 G3
Langley Park School for Boys
BECK BR3 ....84 E3
Langton Green CP School
RRTW TN3 ....269 K4
Lansbury Lawrence
Primary School
POP/IOD E14 ....25 L2
Lansdowne Primary School
SIT ME10 ....130 B2
TIL RM18 ....49 K3
Lansdowne Road Clinic
RTW TN1 ....23 F3
Larkfield Leisure Centre
DIT/AY ME20 ....155 P1
Larkfield Trading Estate
DIT/AY ME20 ....124 A8

Larkin's Brewery
EDEN TN8 ....238 C2
Lashenden (Headcorn)
Airfield
HDCN TN27 ....248 B7
Lathe Barn
LYDD TN29 ....327 H1
Launcelot Primary School
BMLY BR1 ....62 E3
Lawn Primary School
GVW DA11 ....48 C7
Lawrence Trading Estate
GNWCH SE10 ....25 P7
GRAYS RM17 ....32 D7
Lawrence Wharf
BERM/RHTH SE16 ....25 J4
Leathersellers Sports Ground
LEE/GVPK SE12 ....42 G8
Leeds & Broomfield CE
Primary School
RMAID ME17 ....187 K4
Leeds Castle
RMAID ME17 ....187 N4
Leeds Castle Golf Club
RMAID ME17 ....187 N3
Lee Manor Primary School
LEW SE13 ....42 C7
Leeside Court
BERM/RHTH SE16 ....24 C4
Leesons Primary School
STMC/STPC BR5 ....64 C9
The Leigh City Technology
College (East Campus)
DART DA1 ....47 H9
The Leigh City
Technology College
DART DA1 ....46 G9
The Leigh City Technology
College (West Campus)
DART DA1 ....46 G9
Leigh Green Industrial Estate
TENT TN30 ....301 M9
Leigh House Clinic
CANTW/ST CT2 ....4 C2
Leigh Primary School
RTON TN11 ....209 L9
Lenham Primary School
RMAID ME17 ....189 K6
Leopold Street Clinic
BOW E3 ....25 J1
Lesnes Abbey (remains of)
ABYW SE2 ....28 A9
Lesnes Abbey
BELV DA17 ....28 C7
Lessness Heath
Primary School
BELV DA17 ....28 F8
Lewisham Bridge
Primary School
LEW SE13 ....41 P4
Lewisham Business Centre
NWCR SE14 ....24 C9
Lewisham Centre
LEW SE13 ....42 A4
Lewisham College
BROCKY SE4 ....41 N3
Lewisham Crematorium
CAT SE6 ....62 D1
Lewisham Lions Centre
BERM/RHTH SE16 ....24 F8
Leybourne Business Centre
E/WMAL ME19 ....153 M2
Leybourne SS
Primary School
E/WMAL ME19 ....153 M2
Leyton Cross
RDART DA2 ....66 A1
Liberty Square
E/WMAL ME19 ....153 J9
Lifeboat Station
MARG CT9 ....15 G2
Lighthouse
MARG CT9 ....15 F3
Limehouse Hole Stairs
BERM/RHTH SE16 ....25 J4
Limpsfield CE Infant School
OXTED RH8 ....175 L5
Limpsfield Chart Golf Club
OXTED RH8 ....175 M5
Limpsfield Grange School
OXTED RH8 ....175 L4
Limpsfield Lawn Tennis Club
OXTED RH8 ....175 K4
Linden Grove Primary School
ASH TN23 ....282 D2
Lingfield Notre Dame School
LING RH7 ....235 J6
Lingfield Park Racecourse
LING RH7 ....235 J6
Lingfield Primary School
LING RH7 ....234 C5
Lingfield Squash
& Leisure Club
LING RH7 ....235 J6
The Link Day Primary School
CROY/NA CR0 ....82 D8
The Link Secondary School
CROY/NA CR0 ....82 E8
Linton Mead Primary School
THMD SE28 ....28 A3
Liongate Clinic
SBGH/RUST TN4 ....270 D3
Little Acorns School
TENT TN30 ....301 N1
Littlebourne CE
Primary School
RCANTE CT3 ....168 C8
Littlebrook Business Centre
DART DA1 ....47 J4
Little Danson Welfare Clinic
WELL DA16 ....44 C5
Little Hickmotts School
STPH/PW TN12 ....245 N1
Little Satmar Holiday Park
RFOLK CT18 ....289 M9
Littlestone Golf Club
NROM TN28 ....337 K7
Little Switzerland Camping
& Caravan Site
RFOLK CT18 ....311 K3

Little Theatre
FOLK CT20 ....310 B8
Little Thurrock
Primary School
GRAYS RM17 ....32 E6
Livesey Museum for Children
PECK SE15 ....24 E9
Livingstone Hospital
DART DA1 ....46 F6
Lloyds of London
BANK EC3V 24 B2
Lloyds of London Office
CANT ME4 ....6 B1
Lloyds Register CC
DUL SE21 ....40 D9
Loaland Business Centre
STRD ME7 ....72 D7
Lockmeadow
Leisure Complex
MAIDW ME16 ....12 E6
Lock Meadow Market
MAIDW ME16 ....12 E7
Locks View Court
POP/IOD E14 ....25 H3
Lombard Business Park
CROY/NA CR0 ....82 E4
Lombard Trading Estate
CHARL SE7 ....26 C7
London Arena
POP/IOD E14 ....25 L6
London Beach Hotel
& Golf Club
TENT TN30 ....301 H3
London Bridge City Pier
STHWK SE1 ....24 B4
London City Airport
CAN/RD E16 ....26 F4
London Dungeon
STHWK SE1 ....24 A4
The London Golf Club
BGR/WK TN15 ....120 F2
London House School
WGOS CT8 ....111 M4
The London Industrial Estate
EHAM E6 ....27 H1
London Industrial Park
EHAM E6 ....27 J1
London International
Cruise Terminal
TIL RM18 ....49 L5
London Islamic School
/ Madrasah
MAIDW ME16 ....24 E2
London Ladies & Girls FC
CAT SE6 ....61 P4
London Lane Clinic
BMLY BR1 ....62 D6
London Living Theatre
SYD SE26 ....61 K3
London Marriott West India
Quay Hotel
POP/IOD E14 ....25 K3
London Metropolitan
University
WCHPL E1 ....24 D2
London Road Medical Centre
CROY/NA CR0 ....82 F3
London Road Trading Estate
SIT ME10 ....129 L1
London Transport Bus Depot
BXLYHN DA7 ....45 K4
Longlands Primary School
BFN/LL DA15 ....64 A2
Long Lane AFC
BKHTH/KID SE3 ....42 C3
Long Mead Primary School
TONW TN10 ....210 E3
Longport Police Station
RFOLK CT18 ....287 N9
Loose Infant School
MAID/SHEP ME15 ....185 M6
Loose Junior School
MAID/SHEP ME15 ....185 M5
Lordswood Health Centre
WALD ME5 ....125 P4
Lordswood Industrial Estate
WALD ME5 ....125 P4
Lordswood Junior School
WALD ME5 ....125 N2
Lordswood Leisure Centre
WALD ME5 ....125 P2
Lorenden Park
Nature Reserve
FAV ME13 ....162 C1
Lorenden Preparatory
School
FAV ME13 ....162 B1
Lorimar Business Centre
RAIN RM13 ....29 K2
Loughborough Primary
School
CMBW SE5 ....40 B3
Lovell's Wharf
GNWCH SE10 ....25 N8
Lower Halstow School
RSIT ME9 ....98 C4
Lower Sydenham
Industrial Estate
SYD SE26 ....61 M4
Lowfield Medical Centre
DART DA1 ....46 E8
Lucas Vale Primary School
DEPT SE8 ....41 N2
Luddenham Primary School
FAV ME13 ....132 B4
Lullingstone Castle
EYN DA4 ....89 H9
Lullingstone Park Golf Club
ORP BR6 ....88 C8
Lullingstone Roman Villa
EYN DA4 ....88 G7
Lunsford Primary School
AYLW ME20 ....153 P2
Lutomer House
Business Centre
POP/IOD E14 ....25 L4
Luton Infant School
CHAT ME4 ....95 P4
Luton Junior School
CHAT ME4 ....95 P4

Luton Medical Centre
WALD ME5 ....95 P5
Lydd Airport
LYDD TN29 ....342 F5
Lydd Camp
LYDD TN29 ....342 A7
Lydden CP School
RDV CT15 ....260 A8
Lydden International
Motor Racing Circuit
RCANTW CT4 ....259 J5
Lydd Golf Club
LYDD TN29 ....342 D3
Lydd Primary School
LYDD TN29 ....342 D3
Lydd Ranges
LYDD TN29 ....342 B6
Lydd Town Museum
LYDD TN29 ....342 A6
Lyminge CE Primary School
RFOLK CT18 ....287 H1
Lympne CE Primary School
HYTHE CT21 ....307 P4
Lympne Industrial Estate
HYTHE CT21 ....307 M4
Lyndean Industrial Estate
ABYW SE2 ....28 B6
Lyndhurst Primary School
CMBW SE5 ....40 D3
Lynsted & Norton
Primary School
RSIT ME9 ....130 F6
Mace International School
KEN/WIL TN24 ....3 F2
Madginford Park
Infant School
MAID/SHEP ME15 ....186 C1
Madginford Park
Junior School
MAID/SHEP ME15 ....186 D1
Madni Girls School
WCHPL E1 ....24 E2
Magnet Estate
WTHM RM20 ....31 M8
Mahatma Gandhi
Industrial Estate
BRXN/ST SW9 ....40 B4
Maidstone General Hospital
MAIDW ME16 ....154 C6
Maidstone Grammar School
MAID/SHEP ME15 ....185 N1
Maidstone Grammar
School for Girls
MAIDW ME15 ....12 C2
Maidstone Industrial Centre
MAIDW ME16 ....12 D3
Maidstone Lawn
Tennis Club
MAIDW ME16 ....155 H7
Maidstone Leisure Centre
MAID/SHEP ME15 ....185 P1
Maidstone Museum
& Bentlif Art Gallery
MAID/BEAR ME14 ....12 E3
Maison Dieu House
DVE/WH CT16 ....8 C2
Malcolm Primary School
PGE/AN SE20 ....61 J6
Malham Road
Industrial Estate
FSTH SE23 ....41 K9
The Mall Bexleyheath
BXLYHS DA6 ....45 J5
The Malling School
E/WMAL ME19 ....153 N5
Malory School
BMLY BR1 ....62 E3
Manford Industrial Estate
ERITH DA8 ....29 N9
Manor Brook Medical Centre
BKHTH/KID SE3 ....42 D5
Manor Clinic
FOLK CT20 ....10 D5
Manorfield Primary School
POP/IOD E14 ....25 L1
Manor Oak Primary School
STMC/STPC BR5 ....87 L2
Manor Park Country Park
E/WMAL ME19 ....153 J6
Manor Way Business Centre
RAIN RM13 ....29 J1
Manor Way Industrial Estate
GRAYS RM17 ....48 G1
Manston Caravan
& Camping Park
MSTR CT12 ....142 C2
Manzoori Clinic
SWLY BR8 ....65 P6
Maple House School
THHTH CR7 ....60 C9
Maplesden Noakes School
MAIDW ME16 ....12 B1
Marden Medical Centre
STPH/PW TN12 ....245 H3
Marden Primary School
STPH/PW TN12 ....244 G4
Margate Adult Education
Centre
MARC CT9 ....15 G5
Margate Business Centre
MARG CT9 ....15 G4
Margate Caves
MARG CT9 ....15 H3
Margate FC
MARG CT9 ....14 E7
Margate Lawn Tennis Club
MARG CT9 ....112 C5
Margate Museum
MARG CT9 ....15 G3
Mariner Clinic
CROY/NA CR0 ....82 E9
Marine Road Clinic
MARG CT9 ....233 J4
Marion Richardson
Primary School
WCHPL E1 ....24 G2
Marion Vian Primary School
BECK BR3 ....84 A2
Maritime Greenwich College
DEPT SE8 ....41 N1

Maritime Industrial Estate
CHARL SE7 ....26 C7
Maritime Museum
GNWCH SE10 ....25 P7
Marjorie McClure School
CHST BR7 ....63 N7
Marlborough Centre
HOO/HM ME3 ....73 K2
Marlborough CC
DUL SE21 ....40 C9
Marlborough House School
HAWK TN18 ....316 C4
Marlborough Road
Industrial Estate
DEAL CT14 ....232 E7
Marlborough School
BFN/LL DA15 ....44 C9
Marle Place
STPH/PW TN12 ....273 K4
The Marlowe Academy
MSTR CT12 ....142 F2
Marlowe Arcade
Shopping Centre
CANT CT1 ....4 E5
Marlowe Business Centre
CANT CT1 ....4 E5
Marlowe Park Medical Centre
STRD ME2 ....41 L1
Marlowe Theatre
CANT CT1 ....4 E3
Marriott Tudor Park Hotel
& Country Club
MAID/BEAR ME14 ....156 C9
Martello Industrial Estate
FOLKN CT19 ....11 J1
Martello Tower
LYDD TN29 ....327 J5
Marvels Lane Primary School
LEE/GVPK SE12 ....62 G3
Mary Bax's Stone
SWCH CT13 ....202 F5
Mascalls School
STPH/PW TN12 ....243 H5
Masthead
RAM CT11 ....17 F5
Matrix Business Centre
DART DA1 ....46 E6
Maudlin's Green
WAP E1W 24 C4
The Maudsley Hospital
CMBW SE5 ....40 D3
Maundene Primary School
WALD ME5 ....95 M9
May Avenue Industrial Estate
GVW DA11 ....49 K9
Maybrook Industrial Estate
CANT CT1 ....167 H1
Mayday University Hospital
THHTH CR7 ....82 G3
Mayflower Primary School
POP/IOD E14 ....25 M3
Mayplace Primary School
BXLYHN DA7 ....45 M5
Maypole Primary School
RDART DA2 ....65 N2
McArthur Glen
Designer Outlet
KEN/WIL TN24 ....282 F1
MDQ Majidiah School
WCHPL E1 ....24 E3
Meadowfield School
SIT ME10 ....130 B2
Meadowgate School
BROCKY SE4 ....41 K4
Meadowside Leisure Centre
BKHTH/KID SE3 ....42 C5
The Meadow Special School
STMC/STPC BR5 ....64 C6
Meadows School
SBN/RUST TN4 ....240 C6
Meadow View
Industrial Estate
RASHW TN26 ....304 F8
Mead Road Infant School
CHST BR7 ....63 N5
The Mead School
RTWE/PEM TN2 ....270 D7
The Meads Primary School
EGRIN RH19 ....265 H9
Medway Adult
Learning Service
GILL ME7 ....7 J2
Medway City Estate
STRD ME2 ....19 K3
Medway Civic Centre
STRD ME2 ....18 E2
Medway Community College
CHAT ME4 ....95 M5
Medway Crematorium
WALD ME5 ....125 K4
Medway Heritage Centre
CHAT ME4 ....6 B2
Medway Little Theatre
ROCH ME1 ....19 H6
Medway Maritime Hospital
GILL ME7 ....7 G5
Medway RFC
ROCH ME1 ....94 C4
Medway Secure
Training Centre
ROCH ME1 ....94 C7
Medway Towns Rowing Club
ROCH ME1 ....94 F3
Medway Trading Estate
MAIDW ME16 ....12 D7
Medway Valley Leisure Park
STRD ME2 ....94 D3
Medway Yacht Club
STRD ME2 ....73 H4
Melbourne CP School
DVE/WH CT16 ....291 K5
Melfish Industrial Estate
WOOL/PLUM SE18 ....26 E6
Memorial Hospital
WOOL/PLUM SE18 ....43 L3
Mental Health Department
(City University)
WCHPL E1 ....24 E1
Meopham CP School
MEO DA13 ....92 B4

Meopham Medical Centre
MEO DA13 ....92 B6
Meopham School
MEO DA13 ....92 B6
Meredale Independent
Primary School
RHAM ME8 ....97 K5
Mereworth Community
Primary School
WBY/YAL ME18 ....182 D3
Meridian Locality Mental
Health Centre
CHARL SE7 ....26 D9
Meridian Primary School
GNWCH SE10 ....25 N8
Meridian Sports Club
CHARL SE7 ....43 J1
Meridian Trading Estate
CHARL SE7 ....26 C7
Merlin Primary School
BMLY BR1 ....62 E2
Mermaid Inn Hotel
RYE TN31 ....338 E7
Mersham Primary School
RASHE TN25 ....283 P5
Merton Court
Preparatory School
SCUP DA14 ....64 E3
Metro Business Centre
SYD SE26 ....61 M5
Metropolitan Police Hayes
Sports Club
HAYES BR2 ....85 J6
Michael Faraday
Primary School
WALW SE17 ....24 A8
Middle Park Primary School
ELTH/MOT SE9 ....43 H8
Middlesex Hospital
Sports Ground
CHST BR7 ....64 B4
Midfield Primary School
STMC/STPC BR5 ....64 C6
Mid Kent Business Park
SNOD ME6 ....124 A5
Mid Kent College of Higher
& Further Education
MAID ME15 ....95 J8
Mid Kent Golf Club
GVW DA13 ....69 M2
Mid Kent Shopping Centre
MAIDW ME16 ....155 H5
Mierscourt Primary School
MAIDW ME16 ....97 J7
The Mildmay Hotel
DVW CT17 ....8 A4
Mile End & Bow
Business Centre
POP/IOD E14 ....24 E1
Mile End Stadium
POP/IOD E14 ....25 J1
Milehams Industrial Estate
PUR RM19 ....30 D6
Milestone School
HART DA3 ....91 J5
Mile Town Industrial Park
IOS ME12 ....57 J7
Military Barracks
WOOL/PLUM SE18 ....27 H8
Millennium Balloon
STHWK SE1 ....24 B4
Millennium Harbour
POP/IOD E14 ....25 J5
The Millennium
Primary School
GNWCH SE10 ....26 A6
Millennium Quay
DEPT SE8 ....25 L9
Millennium Wharf
POP/IOD E14 ....25 N6
Mill Hall Business Estate
DIT/AY ME20 ....154 C2
Millhall Paper Mill
DIT/AY ME20 ....154 B1
Mill Lane Trading Estate
CROY/NA CR0 ....82 E7
Millside Industrial Estate
DART DA1 ....46 D5
Millwall FC (The New Den)
BERM/RHTH SE16 ....24 F8
Milstead & Frinsted CE
Primary School
RSIT ME9 ....159 M1
Milton Court Primary School
SIT ME10 ....99 M8
Milton Road Business Park
GVE DA12 ....49 N8
Minnis Bay Sailing Club
BRCH CT7 ....110 D6
Minster Abbey
IOS ME12 ....58 D9
Minster Abbey
Gatehouse Museum
IOS ME12 ....58 D9
Minster CE Primary School
MSTR CT12 ....141 J7
Minster College
IOS ME12 ....77 P1
Minster in Sheppey
Primary School
IOS ME12 ....78 C1
Minster & Rayment
Rural Life Museum
MSTR CT12 ....141 K7
Minster-Thanet Cemetery
MSTR CT12 ....141 J4
Mint Business Park
CAN/RD E16 ....26 B1
Minterne Junior School
SIT ME10 ....129 L3
Minters Industrial Estate
DEAL CT14 ....232 D5
Moatbridge School
ELTH/MOT SE9 ....43 H7
Moatlands Golf Club
STPH/PW TN12 ....243 H6
Monks Hill Sports Centre
SAND/SEL CR2 ....114 A2

Monks Orchard Primary School
CROY/NA CR0 ....84 A2
Monkton Nature Reserve
MSTR CT12 ....140 D4
Monson Primary School
NWCR SE14 ....41 K1
Montbelle Primary School
ELTH/MOT SE9 ....63 L3
Montgomery Grant
Maintained School
CANTW/ST CT2 ....137 P5
Montpelier Business Park
ASH TN23 ....252 C6
Moor House School
OXTED RH8 ....175 J8
Morden College Homes
BKHTH/KID SE3 ....42 E3
Morden Mount
Primary School
LEW SE13 ....41 P3
Moorehall Primary School
FOLKN CT19 ....310 C5
More Park RC Primary School
E/WMAL ME19 ....153 L4
Moreton Industrial Estate
SWLY BR8 ....88 C1
Morley Business Centre
TON TN9 ....210 G9
Mote CC
MAID/SHEP ME15 ....13 J7
Mote Park Sailing Club
MAID/SHEP ME15 ....156 B9
Motor Museum
RAM CT11 ....16 E6
Motorway Industrial Estate
DIT/AY ME20 ....155 H2
Mottingham Community
Health Clinic
ELTH/MOT SE9 ....63 J3
Mottingham Primary School
ELTH/MOT SE9 ....63 K2
Mudchute City Farm
POP/IOD E14 ....25 M7
Mulberry Business Centre
BERM/RHTH SE16 ....24 C5
Mulberry School for Girls
WCHPL E1 ....24 E2
Mulgrave Primary School
WOOL/PLUM SE18 ....27 H7
Mundella Primary School
FOLKN CT19 ....10 E1
Munroe Centre
STHWK SE1 ....24 A4
Murray Business Centre
STMC/STPC BR5 ....64 D9
Murston Infant School
SIT ME10 ....130 A1
Murston Junior School
SIT ME10 ....100 A9
Museum in Docklands
POP/IOD E14 ....25 K2
Museum of Canterbury
CANT CT1 ....4 D4
Museum of Kent Life
MAID/BEAR ME14 ....155 J3
Museum of the Artillery in
the Rotunda
CHARL SE7 ....26 E7
Myatt Garden Primary School
BROCKY SE4 ....41 M3
Myatts Field Clinic
BRXN/ST SW9 ....40 B2
Napier Primary School
GILL ME7 ....7 K4
Nash College of Further
Education
WWKM BR4 ....85 J7
The National Centre for Young
People with Epilepsy
LING RH7 ....235 K5
National Maritime Museum
GNWCH SE10 ....25 N9
National Pinetum & Garden
CRBK TN17 ....296 C7
National Sports Centre
NRWD SE19 ....60 C5
Natwest Sports Club
BECK BR3 ....61 M5
Negus Sixth Form Centre
WOOL/PLUM SE18 ....27 L9
Nelson Dock Museum
BERM/RHTH SE16 ....25 J4
Neptune Industrial Estate
DEPT SE8 ....72 E8
Nevill Golf Club
RTWE/PEM TN2 ....270 G9
New Addington Pools
& Fitness Centre
CROY/NA CR0 ....114 F4
New Ash Green
Primary School
HART DA3 ....91 J4
New Atlas Wharf
POP/IOD E14 ....25 J9
The New Aylesbury
Medical Centre
WALW SE17 ....24 A8
New Beach Holiday Village
LYDD TN29 ....327 L1
New Brompton College
GILL ME7 ....7 G4
New Caledonian Wharf
BERM/RHTH SE16 ....25 J6
New Century Cinema
SIT ME10 ....129 P1
New Crane Wharf
WAP E1W 24 F4
New Cross Sports Arena
NWCR SE14 ....41 L1
Newham Leisure Centre
PLSTW E13 ....26 D1
New Hythe Business Park
DIT/AY ME20 ....124 B8
Newington CE
Primary School
RSIT ME9 ....98 C2
Newington Industrial Estate
RSIT ME9 ....98 A8
Newington Infant School
MSTR CT12 ....142 F4

Newington Junior Foundation School *MSTR CT12* 142 F4
Newlands Primary School *RAM CT11* 143 K3
New Life School *EGRIN RH19* 264 C6
New Road Business Estate *DIT/AY ME20* 154 A4
New Road Industrial Estate *IOS ME12* 57 J7
New Road Primary School *CHAT ME4* 6 D6
New Royal Cinema *FAV ME13* 132 F6
The New School at West Heath *SEV TN15* 178 C5
News International Offices *WAP E1W* 24 E3
Newstead Wood School for Girls *ORP BR6* 86 E7
New Woodlands School *BMLY BR1* 62 C3
Nightingale Primary School *WOOL/PLUM SE18* 27 J9
Nizels Golf & Leisure Club *RTON TN11* 209 K1
The Noble Clinic *STPH/PW TN12* 243 J9
Nonington CE Primary School *RDV CT15* 229 M1
Norbury Manor Secondary Girls School *STRHM/NOR SW16* 60 A7
Normandy Primary School *BXLYHN DA7* 45 M2
Norman Park Athletics Track *HAYES BR2* 85 L3
North Borough Junior School *MAID/BEAR ME14* 155 L5
Northbourne CE Primary School *DEAL CT14* 231 M4
Northbourne Court *DEAL CT14* 231 P4
Northbourne Park School *DEAL CT14* 231 M4
Northbrook CE School *LEE/GVPK SE12* 42 C6
North Clinic *BMLY BR1* 62 E7
North Croydon Medical Centre *THHTH CR7* 82 G3
Northdown CP School *MARG CT9* 113 H4
Northdown Industrial Estate *BRDST CT10* 113 J7
North Downs Business Park *SEV TN13* 148 B1
North Downs Golf Club *CTRM CR3* 174 D1
Northend Primary School *ERITH DA8* 45 P2
North End Trading Estate *ERITH DA8* 45 N1
North Farm Industrial Estate *RTWE/PEM TN2* 241 H8
Northfleet Cemetery *GVW DA11* 48 G9
Northfleet Industrial Estate *GVW DA11* 48 D5
Northfleet School for Girls *GVW DA11* 69 H1
Northfleet Technology College *GVW DA11* 49 H9
North Foreland Golf Club *BRDST CT10* 113 M5
Northgate Clinic *CANT CT1* 5 G2
Northgate Community & Youth Centre *CANT CT1* 5 G2
Northiam CE Primary School *RYE TN31* 330 A8
North Kent Magistrates Court *CHAT ME4* 6 C3
The North School *KEN/WIL TN24* 3 H5
Northumberland Heath Medical Centre *ERITH DA8* 45 M1
Northumberland Heath Primary School *ERITH DA8* 45 K1
North West Kent College *GVE DA12* 50 B9
RDART DA2 ....66 B1
Northwood Primary School *ERITHM DA18* 28 D6
The Norton Knatchbull School *KEN/WIL TN24* 3 J4
Norwood Heights Shopping Centre *NRWD SE19* 60 E5
Norwood School *NRWD SE19* 60 C4
Notre Dame RC Primary School *WOOL/PLUM SE18* 27 J9
Novotel *CAN/RD E16* 26 C3
GNWCH SE10 ....41 P1
Nugent Shopping Park *STMC/STPC BR5* 87 J1
Nunnery Fields School *CANT CT1* 166 E6
Nuralite Industrial Centre *HOO/HM ME3* 51 J8
The O2 *POP/IOD E14* 25 N4
Oakfield Preparatory School *DUL SE21* 60 D1
Oakfield Primary School *DART DA1* 66 D1
Oakfield Road Industrial Estate *PGE/AN SE20* 61 H6

The Oak Hotel *RAM CT11* 17 G4
Oaklands Infant School *BH/WHM TN16* 145 M1
WALD ME5 ....125 L1
Oaklands Junior School *BH/WHM TN16* 145 M1
Oakley School *RTWE/PEM TN2* 271 K3
TOWN TN1 ....210 E5
Oak Lodge JMI School *WWKM BR4* 84 E4
The Oaks Infant School *SIT ME10* 129 L3
Oak Tree CP School *ASH TN23* 252 C9
Oak Trees Community School *MAID/SHEP ME15* 186 A4
Oakwood Hospital *MAIDW ME16* 154 C8
Oakwood School *BXLYHN DA7* 45 M5
Oakwood Trading Estate *BRDST CT10* 113 J6
Oare Marshes Nature Reserve *FAV ME13* 102 E8
The Oast Golf Club *RSIT ME9* 100 D9
Oasthouse Theatre *RHAM ME8* 97 J6
Oastpark Golf Club *SNOD ME6* 123 M7
Ockendon School *SOCK/AV RM15* 31 K1
Odeon Cinema *BECK BR3* 61 N8
BERM/RHTH SE16 ....24 C6
CANT CT1 ....5 F5
ELTH/MOT SE9 ....43 J5
HAYES BR2 ....62 E8
MAIDW ME16 ....12 E6
RTWE/PEM TN2 ....241 J9
Offham CC *E/WMAL ME19* 152 E5
Offham Primary School *E/WMAL ME19* 152 E4
Old Ashford Cemetery *KEN/WIL TN24* 2 E1
Old Beckenhamian RFC *WWKM BR4* 84 C7
Old Bellgate Wharf *POP/IOD E14* 25 P3
Old Bexley Business Park *BXLY DA5* 45 K8
Old Bexley CE Primary School *BXLY DA5* 45 H9
Oldborough Manor Community School *MAID/SHEP ME15* 185 N4
Old Brocklebians Sports Ground *LEE/GVPK SE12* 42 G7
Old Bromilians CC *HAYES BR2* 85 L2
Oldbury Hill C&C Club Site *BGR/WK TN15* 150 C7
Old Cemetery *EDUL SE22* 41 H7
Old Colfeian Sports Club *LEE/GVPK SE12* 42 G6
Old Elthamians Sports Club *CHST BR7* 64 A5
The Old Guild Theatre *GVW DA11* 49 H9
Old Hospital *RCANTW CT4* 257 L4
Old Jamaica Business Estate *STHWK SE1* 24 C6
Old Judd RFC *TON TN9* 210 E8
The Old Oast Business Centre *DIT/AY ME20* 154 F2
Old Palace School *CROY/NA CR0* 82 G7
The Old Priory School *RAM CT11* 16 D5
Old Royal Naval College *GNWCH SE10* 25 N8
Old Royal Observatory Greenwich *GNWCH SE10* 42 B1
Old St James' Church (ruins) *DVE/WH CT16* 9 F3
The Old School *RFOLK CT18* 289 M8
Old Soar Manor (NT) *BGR/WK TN15* 181 L2
Old Spitalfields Market Hall *LVPST EC2M* 24 E1
Old Station Museum *CAN/RD E16* 27 H5
Old Sun Wharf *POP/IOD E14* 25 H3
Old Timber Yard Industrial Estate *MSTR CT12* 142 E4
Old Town Hall *CANTW/ST CT2* 137 L9
Old Wilsonians Sports Club *WWKM BR4* 85 H5
Oliver Goldsmith Primary School *CMBW SE5* 40 F2
Om Medical Centre *IOS ME12* 57 L6
Open University *EGRIN RH19* 265 H7
Orbital Park *KEN/WIL TN24* 283 J2
Orchard Business Centre *BECK BR3* 61 M4
MAIDW ME16 ....155 H4
RTWE/PEM TN2 ....240 D9
TON TN9 ....240 G1
Orchard Industrial Estate *MAID/SHEP ME15* 186 C8
Orchard Medical Centre *RMAID ME17* 185 H9

Orchard Place Business Centre *BGR/WK TN15* 152 B6
Orchard Primary School *SCUP DA14* 64 D4
Orchard School *CANT CT1* 5 G1
Orchard Shopping Centre *DART DA1* 46 E7
The Orchard Theatre *DART DA1* 46 E7
Orchard Way Primary School *CROY/NA CR0* 84 B4
Orion Business Centre *NWCR SE14* 24 G8
Orpington College of Further Education *ORP BR6* 87 H5
The Orpington Halls *ORP BR6* 87 H6
Orpington Hospital *ORP BR6* 86 C8
Orpington Mental Health Centre *ORP BR6* 86 G7
Orpington Priory *ORP BR6* 87 J4
Orpington Retail Park *STMC/STPC BR5* 87 K1
Orpington Superbowl *ORP BR6* 87 H5
Orpington Trade Centre *STMC/STPC BR5* 64 D9
Orsett CE Primary School *CDW/CHF RM16* 33 H1
Orsett Golf Club *CDW/CHF RM16* 33 M3
Orsett Hospital *CDW/CHF RM16* 33 H1
Orsett Industrial Estate *CDW/CHF RM16* 33 N1
Osmani Primary School *WCHPL E1* 24 D1
Ospringe CE Primary School *FAV ME13* 132 D7
Otford Primary School *RSEV TN14* 148 F1
Our Lady of Grace RC Primary School *CHARL SE7* 26 C9
Our Lady of Hartley RC Primary School *HART DA3* 91 J2
Our Lady of Lourdes RC Primary School *BKHTH/KID SE3* 42 B4
Our Lady of the Rosary RC School *ELTH/MOT SE9* 44 A7
Our Lady RC Primary School *POP/IOD E14* 25 J2
Our Lady & St Philip Neri RC Infants School *FSTH SE23* 61 K2
Our Lady & St Philip Neri RC Primary School *SYD SE26* 61 L3
Our Ladys Catholic Primary School *DART DA1* 46 D7
Oval Primary School *CROY/NA CR0* 83 K5
Owletts (NT) *GVE DA12* 70 B9
Owl House Gardens *RRTW TN3* 272 F9
Oxted Health Centre *OXTED RH8* 175 J5
Oxted & Limpsfield Hospital *OXTED RH8* 174 G4
Oxted School *OXTED RH8* 175 J4

Paddock Wood Business Centre *STPH/PW TN12* 243 H2
Paddock Wood Primary School *STPH/PW TN12* 243 H3
Painters Ash Primary School *GVW DA11* 69 H2
Palace Industrial Estate *MAID/SHEP ME15* 186 C7
Palace Wood Infant School *MAIDW ME16* 155 H4
Palace Wood Junior School *MAIDW ME16* 155 H6
Palmarsh Primary School *HYTHE CT21* 308 C7
Palm Bay CP School *MARG CT9* 113 J2
Palmer College *GRAYS RM17* 32 F7
The Pantiles Shopping Arcade *RTWE/PEM TN2* 22 C7
Parchmore Medical Centre *THHTH CR7* 60 C9
Parish CE Primary School *BMLY BR1* 62 E6
Parish Church CE Primary School *CROY/NA CR0* 82 C7
Parker Industrial Centre *RDART DA2* 47 J8
Park Farm Industrial Estate *FOLKN CT19* 310 E3
Park Farm Primary School *FOLKN CT19* 310 F4
Park Farm Recreation Centre *ASH TN23* 282 D4
Park Farm Retail Park *FOLKN CT19* 310 E3
Park Hall Trading Estate *WNWD SE27* 60 C2
Park Hill Junior School *CROY/NA CR0* 83 J7
Park House RFC *HAYES BR2* 85 M6
Park Mall Shopping Centre *KEN/WIL TN24* 2 D3

Park Medical Centre *BERM/RHTH SE16* 24 G7
Park Mews Small Business Centre *HNHL SE24* 40 C7
Park Road Industrial Estate *SWLY BR8* 65 P9
Parkside Business Estate *DEPT SE8* 25 J9
Parkside Community Primary School *CANT CT1* 167 J2
Parkway Primary School *ERITHM DA18* 28 D6
Park Way Primary School *MAID/SHEP ME15* 185 N2
Park Wood Golf Club *BH/WHM TN16* 145 P7
Parkwood Hall School *SWLY BR8* 66 B9
Parkwood Industrial Estate *MAID/SHEP ME15* 186 D7
Parkwood Infant School *RHAM ME8* 97 H9
Parsonage Farm Rural Heritage Centre *RCANTW CT4* 257 M3
Pashley Manor & Gardens *WADH TN5* 315 M7
Passport Language Schools *BMLY BR1* 62 F7
The Pavilion Leisure Centre *BMLY BR1* 62 E8
The Pavilion Shopping Centre *TON TN9* 210 E9
Paxton Primary School *NRWD SE19* 60 F5
Peall Road Industrial Estate *CROY/NA CR0* 82 E3
Peckham Park Primary School *PECK SE15* 40 C4
The Peckham Pulse Health & Leisure Centre *PECK SE15* 40 G2
Pedham Place Industrial Estate *SWLY BR8* 88 F2
The Peel Trading Centre *TON TN9* 210 E8
Pelham Primary School *BXLYHN DA7* 45 J4
Pembroke Lodge Museum & Art Gallery *BRCH CT7* 110 C4
Pembury Hospital *RTWE/PEM TN2* 241 K9
Pembury Primary School *RTWE/PEM TN2* 241 N9
Pencester Surgery *DVE/WH CT16* 8 D3
Pendragon Secondary School *BMLY BR1* 62 E2
Pennypot Industrial Estate *HYTHE CT21* 308 E6
Penshurst CE Primary School *RTON TN11* 238 F2
Penshurst Place & Gardens *RTON TN11* 238 G5
Pentagon Shopping Centre *CHAT ME4* 6 C4
Pent Valley Technology College *FOLKN CT19* 310 C4
Perry Hall Primary School *ORP BR6* 86 C3
Perrymount Primary School *FSTH SE23* 61 K1
Perry Wood Nature Reserve *FAV ME13* 163 N8
Peter Hills School *BERM/RHTH SE16* 24 C4
Petham CP School *RCANTW CT4* 196 B8
Phoenix Business Centre *POP/IOD E14* 25 K1
Phoenix Community Primary School *KEN/WIL TN24* 252 C4
Phoenix Industrial Estate *STRD ME2* 19 H1
Phoenix Leisure Centre *CAT SE6* 41 P8
Pickford Lane Medical Centre *BXLYHN DA7* 44 G2
Pickhurst Infant School *WWKM BR4* 85 H3
Pickhurst Junior School *WWKM BR4* 85 J3
Pier Pavilion Sports Centre *HB CT6* 107 K1
Pier Road Industrial Estate *ERITH DA8* 73 K8
The Pilgrim School *ROCH ME1* 94 E4
Pilgrims Way CP School *CANT CT1* 5 K7
Pilgrims Way J & I School *PECK SE15* 24 F9
Pilton Estate *CROY/NA CR0* 82 C6
Pine Lodge Touring Park *RMAID ME17* 187 J1
The Pines Garden *RDV CT15* 292 F2
Pioneer Business Park *MSTR CT12* 143 H4
Pioneers Industrial Park *CROY/NA CR0* 82 D5
Platt CE Primary School *BGR/WK TN15* 151 M5
Platt Industrial Estate *BGR/WK TN15* 151 M4
Platt's Heath Primary School *RMAID ME17* 188 G9
Plaxtol Primary School *BGR/WK TN15* 181 H4
Playhouse Theatre *WSTB CT5* 105 L5

Plaza Cinema *OXTED RH8* 175 H5
Pluckley CE Primary School *HDCN TN27* 250 C2
Plumcroft Primary School *WOOL/PLUM SE18* 27 K9
Plumstead Leisure Centre *WOOL/PLUM SE18* 27 N8
Plumstead Manor School *WOOL/PLUM SE18* 27 L8
The Pointer School *BKHTH/KID SE3* 42 E2
Polo Farm Sports Club *RCANTE CT3* 167 L4
Poplar Business Park *POP/IOD E14* 25 K5
POP/IOD E14 ....25 M3
Poplar Coroners Court *POP/IOD E14* 25 L3
Portal House School *RDV CT15* 292 F1
Portland Medical Centre *SNWD SE25* 83 N2
Port Lympne Wild Animal Park, Mansion & Garden *HYTHE CT21* 307 K5
Port Richborough Business Park *SWCH CT13* 171 P2
P&O Stena Line *DVW CT17* 313 K1
Postley Industrial Centre *MAID/SHEP ME15* 185 M2
Poulton Business Park *DVW CT17* 290 C6
Poult Wood Golf Centre *RTON TN11* 211 H1
Pound Farm Nursery School *CHARL SE7* 26 E8
Poverest Primary School *STMC/STPC BR5* 87 H2
Powell-Cotton Museum, Quex House & Gardens *BRCH CT7* 111 J8
The Powell Schooll *DVE/WH CT16* 291 J3
Power Industrial Estate *ERITH DA8* 45 P2
Pratts Bottom Primary School *ORP BR6* 117 K5
Premier Cinema *CHAT ME4* 95 N5
Premier Cinema *PECK SE15* 40 G3
Premier Inn *BGR/WK TN15* 151 P3
BH/WHM TN16 ....175 P2
CAN/RD E16 ....26 E3
CDW/CHF RM16 ....31 M6
CROY/NA CR0 ....83 M9
DVE/WH CT16 ....9 F4
E/WMAL ME19 ....155 M1
EGRIN RH19 ....264 D4
EHAM E6 ....27 H1
FOLKN CT19 ....310 D4
GVE DA12 ....69 N5
KEN/WIL TN24 ....69 L1
MAID/BEAR ME14 ....283 J3
MAIDW ME16 ....155 J3
MARG CT9 ....14 E5
RAIN RM13 ....30 C2
RASHW TN26 ....221 M8
RDV CT15 ....291 N3
RHAM ME8 ....312 D2
RMAID ME17 ....96 C4
RMAID ME17 ....157 K9
RSIT ME9 ....99 J8
RTON TN11 ....240 F3
TON TN9 ....240 F3
WBHM/GYAL SE18 ....183 M3
WSTB CT5 ....105 K8
Prendergast School *BROCKY SE4* 41 N5
Preston Hall Hospital *DIT/AY ME20* 154 E3
Preston Primary School *RCANTE CT3* 169 M2
Prince of Wales Pier *DVW CT17* 9 F7
Princes Court Business Centre *WAP E1W* 24 E3
Princes Golf Club *SWCH CT13* 172 E8
Princes Park Medical Centre *WALD ME5* 95 N8
Princes Park Stadium *DART DA1* 46 G9
Princes Plain Primary School *HAYES BR2* 85 P4
Princess Christian's Hospital *RTON TN11* 180 B9
The Princess Royal University Hospital *ORP BR6* 86 B7
Priory Fields School *DVW CT17* 291 J7
Priory Hill *IOS ME12* 80 F6
Priory Infant School *RAM CT11* 16 D3
The Priory Leisure Centre *STMC/STPC BR5* 87 K5
Priory School *STMC/STPC BR5* 87 K5
Priory Shopping Centre *DART DA1* 46 D7
Priory Special School *SNWD SE25* 83 L1
Progress Business Park *CROY/NA CR0* 82 E6
Pumphouse Educational Museum *BERM/RHTH SE16* 25 H4
Pumping Station Museum *CHAT ME4* 6 C4
Purfleet Industrial Park *SOCK/AV RM15* 30 C5
Purfleet Primary School *PUR RM19* 30 D7

Pysons Road Industrial Estate
BRDST CT10 ....143 H1
Quality Hotel
FOLK CT20 ....10 B7
Quarry Hill Infant School
GRAYS RM17 ....32 C8
Quarry Hill Junior School
GRAYS RM17 ....32 C8
Quarry Wood
Industrial Estate
DIT/FAV ME20 ....154 C1
Quebec House
BH/WHM TN16 ....176 E2
Quebec Industrial Estate
BERM/RHTH SE16 ....25 H5
Queenborough
Business Centre
QBOR ME11 ....77 J4
Queenborough First School
QBOR ME11 ....77 K2
Queenborough Yacht Club
QBOR ME11 ....76 C2
Queen Elizabeth Hospital
WOOL/PLUM SE18 ....28 C9
Queen Elizabeths
Grammar School
FAV ME13 ....132 C6
Queen Elizabeth the
Queen Mother Hospital
MARG CT9 ....112 F5
Queen Marys Hospital
SCUP DA14 ....64 C4
Queens Hall & Winter Gardens
MARG CT9 ....15 H2
The Queens House
GNWCH SE10 ....25 N9
Queen's Road Cemetery
CROY/NA CRO 83 H3
Queen Victoria
Cottage Hospital
RTON TN11 ....240 F3
Queen Victoria Hospital
EGRIN RH19 ....265 G5
Queen Victoria
Memorial Hospital
HB CT6 ....107 N2
Quex Caravan Park
BRCH CT7 ....111 M7
RAF Manston History
Museum
MSTR CT12 ....141 P2
Raglan Primary School
HAYES BR2 ....85 M1
Railton Road Clinic
HNHL SE24 ....40 B6
Rainbow Quay
BERM/RHTH SE16 ....25 H6
Rainham Mark
Grammar School
RHAM ME8 ....96 G4
Rainham School for Girls
RHAM ME8 ....96 F6
Rainham Shopping Centre
RHAM ME8 ....97 J5
Ramac Industrial Estate
CHARL SE7 ....26 B8
Ramada Hotel
DVE/WH CT16 ....290 G1
RMAID ME17 ....187 L2
RTWE/PEM TN2 ....271 L1
Ramsgate Athletic & FC
RAM CT11 ....16 A4
Ramsgate Cemetery
RAM CT11 ....143 K3
Ramsgate Holy Trinity
Primary School
RAM CT11 ....143 M3
Ramsgate Maritime Museum
RAM CT11 ....17 H5
Ramsgate New Port
Ferry Terminal
RAM CT11 ....16 E7
Ramsgate Obelisk
RAM CT11 ....17 H5
Ramsgate Sports Centre
RAM CT11 ....16 E2
Ramsgate Swimming Pool
RAM CT11 ....16 B1
Rangefield Primary School
BMLY BR1 ....62 C4
Range Road Industrial Estate
HYTHE CT21 ....308 F6
The Rathbone
Education Centre
CAN/RD E16 ....26 A1
Rathfern Primary School
FSTH SE23 ....41 M9
Ravensbourne College of
Design & Communication
CHST BR7 ....63 L4
The Ravensbourne School
HAYES BR2 ....85 L1
Ravensquay Business Centre
STMC/STPC BR5 ....87 J2
Ravens Wood School
HAYES BR2 ....85 N7
Raynehurst Junior School
GVE DA12 ....70 B2
Reay Primary School
BRXN/ST SW9 ....40 A1
Rectory Business Centre
SCUP DA14 ....64 D3
Rectory Paddock School
STMC/STPC BR5 ....64 E8
Reculver Country Park
HB CT6 ....108 F4
Reculver Primary CE
Primary School
HB CT6 ....108 D6
Reculver Towers
& Roman Fort
HB CT6 ....108 G3
Red Gates School
CROY/NA CRO 82 F9
Redhill Junior School
CHST BR7 ....63 M4
Red House (NT)
BXLYHS DA6 ....44 G5
Redlands Primary School
WCHPL E1 ....24 F1

Redlibbets Golf Club
BGR/WK TN15 ....90 G6
Redriff Primary School
BERM/RHTH SE16 ....25 H5
Regional Sports Centre
TIL RM18 ....49 M3
Regis Business Park
IOS ME12 ....57 J7
Regis Industrial Estate
IOS ME12 ....57 J7
Regis Manor Community
Primary School
SIT ME10 ....99 M7
Research Development
& Business Centre
CANTW/ST CT2 ....136 B9
Restoration House
ROCH ME1 ....19 G6
Reynolds Performing Arts
RDART DA2 ....65 N1
Richborough
Business Park
SWCH CT13 ....171 P8
Richborough Castle
SWCH CT13 ....171 M6
Rich Industrial Estate
PECK SE15 ....24 E9
Richmond First School
IOS ME12 ....57 M7
Richmond Infant School
GILL ME7 ....73 J9
The Ridge Golf Club
RMAID ME17 ....217 L1
Ridge Meadow
Primary School
WALD ME5 ....95 L8
Ridge View School
TONN TN10 ....210 C4
Riding School
E/WMAL ME19 ....154 A8
Ripley Arts Centre
BMLY BR1 ....63 H7
The Ripple School
DEAL CT14 ....232 B9
Rippleside School
DEAL CT14 ....232 D9
Ritzy Cinema
BRXN/ST SW9 ....40 A5
River Court School
RCANTW CT4 ....195 L1
River CP School
DVW CT17 ....290 F4
Rivermead School
GILL ME7 ....73 L9
Riverside Business Centre
TON TN9 ....210 E9
Riverside Business Park
KEN/WIL TN24 ....3 G3
Riverside Country Park
GILL ME7 ....96 C1
Riverside Golf Club
THMD SE28 ....28 D2
Riverside Industrial Estate
CANT CT1 ....166 C2
DART DA1 ....46 E6
HYTHE CT21 ....308 A6
Riverside Primary School
CANT CT1 ....166 C6
RSEV TN14 ....149 H4
Riverside School
ASH TN23 ....252 C8
Riverside
Swimming Centre
ERITH DA8 ....29 K8
Riverston School
LEE/GVPK SE12 ....42 E6
The River Surgery
DVE/WH CT16 ....290 F3
Riverview Clinic
GVE DA12 ....70 D2
Riverview Primary School
GVE DA12 ....70 A3
Robert Browning
Primary School
WALW SE17 ....24 A8
The Robert Napier School
GILL ME7 ....96 B3
Rochester Adult Education
Centre
ROCH ME1 ....19 H5
Rochester Airport
ROCH ME1 ....95 H7
Rochester Airport
Industrial Estate
ROCH ME1 ....95 H8
Rochester Castle
ROCH ME1 ....19 F4
Rochester Cathedral
ROCH ME1 ....19 F5
Rochester & Cobham
Park Golf Club
STRD ME2 ....70 F9
Rochester Grammar
School for Girls
ROCH ME1 ....95 H4
Rochester Health Centre
ROCH ME1 ....95 J3
Rochester
Independent College
ROCH ME1 ....19 H7
Rock & Bowl Bowling Alley
EGRIN RH19 ....265 H7
Rockliffe Manor
Primary School
WOOL/PLUM SE18 ....27 N9
Rockmount Primary School
NRWD SE19 ....60 C5
Rodmersham Primary School
RSIT ME9 ....A6
Rodmersham Squash Club
RSIT ME9 ....129 F7
Rolvenden Primary School
CRBK TN17 ....319 L3
Roman Industrial Estate
CROY/NA CRO 83 K4
Roman Painted House
DVW CT17 ....8 D4

Romney Hythe
& Dymchurch Railway
HYTHE CT21 ....308 E6
LYDD TN29 ....347 N2
NROM TN28 ....337 H9
Romney Sands
Holiday Village
NROM TN28 ....343 J4
Roper House School
for the Deaf
CANTW/ST CT2 ....4 C2
Ropery Business Park
CHARL SE7 ....26 D7
Rope Walk Shopping Centre
RYE TN31 ....338 E6
Roseacre Junior School
MAID/BEAR ME14 ....156 D8
Rose Bruford College
BFN/LL DA15 ....44 D9
Rose Hill School
SBGH/RUST TN4 ....270 B3
Rosemead Preparatory
School
DUL SE21 ....60 C1
Rosendale Primary School
DUL SE21 ....40 C8
Rose Street School
IOS ME12 ....57 K6
Rosetta Primary School
BOW E16 ....26 C1
Rosherville CE
Primary School
GVW DA11 ....49 J7
Rotherhithe Civic Centre
BERM/RHTH SE16 ....24 F6
Rotherhithe Primary School
BERM/RHTH SE16 ....24 F7
The Rother Ironworks
RYE TN31 ....338 F7
Rowhill Grange Hotel & Spa
RDART DA2 ....66 A4
Rowhill School
RDART DA2 ....66 C3
Royal Albion Hotel
WOOL/PLUM SE18 ....113 N9
Royal Arsenal
WOOL/PLUM SE18 ....27 J6
Royal Blackheath Golf Club
ELTH/MOT SE9 ....43 K8
Royal Cinque Ports Golf Club
DEAL CT14 ....203 H9
Royal Cinque Ports
Yacht Club
DVE/WH CT16 ....8 E5
The Royal Dock
Community School
CAN/RD E16 ....26 D2
Royal Docks Medical Centre
EHAM E6 ....27 H2
Royal Engineers Museum
& Library
GILL ME7 ....73 H8
The Royal London Hospital
WCHPL E1 ....24 E1
Royal Mint Court
TWRH EC3N 24 C3
Royal Museum & Art Gallery
with Buffs Museum
CANT CT1 ....4 C4
Royal National Theatre
CMBW SE5 ....40 A1
Royal Park Primary School
SCUP DA14 ....64 C2
Royal St Georges Golf Club
SWCH CT13 ....202 C1
The Royal School
for Deaf Children
MARG CT9 ....15 J5
Royal Star Arcade
MAID/BEAR ME14 ....12 E4
Royal Terrace Pier
GVE DA12 ....49 N6
Royal Tunbridge Wells
Business Park
SBGH/RUST TN4 ....240 G8
Royal Victoria Docks
Watersports Centre
CAN/RD E16 ....26 B3
Royal Victoria Hospital
FOLKN CT19 ....10 C2
Royal Victoria Place
Shopping Centre
RTW TN1 ....22 E2
Royston Primary School
PGE/AN SE20 ....61 K7
RSPB Reserve
GILL ME7 ....74 B7
LYDD TN29 ....342 E7
LYDD TN29 ....342 G9
RAIN RM13 ....29 N3
RHAM ME8 ....74 F9
RHAM ME8 ....77 M9
Rushey Green Primary School
CAT SE6 ....41 P9
Ruskin House School
HNHL SE24 ....40 C6
Russell Hotel
MAID/BEAR ME14 ....155 N5
RTW TN1 ....22 D3
Russell House School
RSEV TN14 ....118 G9
Rusthall Medical Centre
SBGH/RUST TN4 ....269 N4
Ruxley Corner
Industrial Estate
SCUP DA14 ....64 F5
Ruxley Park Golf Centre
STMC/STPC BR5 ....64 F7
Ryarsh CP School
E/WMAL ME19 ....123 H9
Rye Castle Museum
RYE TN31 ....338 F7
Rye Community Clinic
RYE TN31 ....338 E6
Rye Football & CC
RYE TN31 ....338 F6
Rye Golf Club
RYE TN31 ....339 L1
Rye Harbour Sailing Club
RYE TN31 ....339 K9

Rye Heritage Centre
& Town Model
RYE TN31 ....338 E7
Rye Industrial Estate
RYE TN31 ....338 G8
Ryelands Primary School
SNWD SE25 ....83 N2
Rye Lodge Hotel
RYE TN31 ....338 F7
Rye Sports Centre
RYE TN31 ....338 E6
Rye Oak Primary School
PECK SE15 ....41 H4
Sackville Community College
EGRIN RH19 ....265 K7
Sackville School
RTON TN11 ....209 P4
Sacred Heart RC School
CMBW SE5 ....40 C2
Safari Cinema
CROY/NA CRO 82 C5
Sai Medical Centre
POP/IOD E14 ....25 M3
St Albans Road Infant School
DART DA1 ....46 F7
St Alfege with St Peter
CE Primary School
GNWCH SE10 ....25 M9
St Andrews Arts Centre
GVW DA11 ....49 M7
St Andrews CE School
CROY/NA CRO 82 C6
St Andrews Medical Centre
SBGH/RUST TN4 ....240 D8
St Andrews School
ROCH ME1 ....19 F6
St Anne's Trading Estate
POP/IOD E14 ....25 J2
St Anselms RC Primary School
DART DA1 ....46 F6
St Anselms RC School
CANT CT1 ....167 H1
St Anthonys RC
Primary School
EDUL SE22 ....40 G7
PGE/AN SE20 ....61 H7
St Anthonys School
MARG CT9 ....113 H4
St Augustine of Canterbury
RC Primary School
RHAM ME8 ....126 C2
St Augustines Abbey
CANT CT1 ....16 D6
St Augustine's Abbey (Ruins)
CANT CT1 ....5 H4
St Augustines Business Park
WSTB CT5 ....106 E3
St Augustines College
WGOS CT8 ....111 M5
St Augustines Cross
MSTR CT12 ....142 B7
St Augustines Golf Club
MSTR CT12 ....142 A7
St Augustines Primary School
BELV DA17 ....28 E6
St Augustines RC
Primary School
CAT SE6 ....61 P4
SBGH/RUST TN4 ....270 D1
St Barnabas CE
Primary School
RTW TN1 ....270 E3
St Bartholomews CE
Primary School
SYD SE26 ....61 J3
St Bartholomews Hospital
ROCH ME1 ....19 K7
SWLY BR8 ....65 P9
St Bartholomews RC
Primary School
SWLY BR8 ....65 N9
St Barts Hospital
Sports Ground
CHST BR7 ....63 P5
St Benedicts School
MARG CT9 ....125 P3
St Botolphs CE Primary School
GVW DA11 ....49 H1
St Catherines RC Girls School
BXLYHS DA6 ....45 K6
St Chads RC Primary School
SNWD SE25 ....83 K2
St Christophers School
BECK BR3 ....62 A8
CANT CT1 ....166 C6
St Cleres Hall Golf Club
SLH/COR SS17 ....34 A1
St Cleres School
SLH/COR SS17 ....34 B1
St Columbas RC Boys School
BXLYHS DA6 ....45 K6
St Crispins CP School
WGOS CT8 ....111 M6
St Cyprians Greek Orthodox
Primary School
THHTH CR7 ....60 C8
St Davids College
WWKM BR4 ....84 E4
St Dunstans College
CAT SE6 ....41 M9
St Eanswythes CE
Primary School
FOLK CT20 ....11 F5
St Edmunds CE School
DVE/WH CT16 ....291 K5
St Edmunds Junior School
CANTW/ST CT2 ....166 B1
St Edmunds RC
Primary School
POP/IOD E14 ....25 K7
St Edmunds School
CANTW/ST CT2 ....166 B1
St Edwards RC Primary School
IOS ME12 ....57 K6
St Ethelberts Catholic
Primary School
RAM CT11 ....17 G1
St Faiths Adult
Education Centre
MAID/BEAR ME14 ....12 E3

St Faiths at Ash School
RCANTE CT3 ....200 D1
St Fidelis Catholic
Primary School
ERITH DA8 ....29 H9
St Francesca Cabrini
Primary School
FSTH SE23 ....41 J7
St Francis Catholic
Primary School
MAID/BEAR ME14 ....13 F3
St Francis RC Primary School
PECK SE15 ....24 D9
St George's Business Centre
ASH TN23 ....252 B7
St Georges Business Park
WELL DA16 ....130 A1
St Georges CE
Foundation School
BRDST CT10 ....113 H8
St Georges CE Middle School
CANT CT1 ....78 E1
St Georges Centre
CANT CT1 ....5 G5
GVW DA11 ....49 M7
St Georges CE
Primary School
BGR/WK TN15 ....151 J1
BMLY BR1 ....62 C8
CMBW SE5 ....40 E1
St Georges CE School
GVW DA11 ....69 L1
St Gregorys Catholic
Comprehensive School
SBGH/RUST TN4 ....270 C1
St Gregory's Cemetery
CANT CT1 ....5 H3
St Gregorys Centre
CANT CT1 ....5 G4
St Gregorys College
WGOS CT8 ....111 M4
St Gregorys RC
Primary School
MARG CT9 ....112 D6
St Helens CE Primary School
HOO/HM ME3 ....52 B3
St Helens RC Primary School
BRXN/ST SW9 ....40 B2
St James CE J & I School
BERM/RHTH SE16 ....24 D6
St James CE Primary School
HOO/HM ME3 ....56 D2
NWCR SE14 ....41 L2
St James Infant School
E/WMAL ME19 ....153 M6
St James Medical Centre
CROY/NA CRO 83 J4
RTW TN1 ....23 G3
St James RC Primary School
HAYES BR2 ....86 C2
St James's J & I School
RTW TN1 ....23 G3
St James the Great RC
Primary School
PECK SE15 ....40 F2
THHTH CR7 ....60 B8
St Joachims RC
Primary School
CAN/RD E16 ....26 D2
St John Business Centre
MARG CT9 ....15 H6
St John Fisher Catholic School
CHAT ME4 ....95 K3
CHAT ME4 ....95 L4
St John Fisher RC
Primary School
ERITH DA18 ....28 D6
St Johns Angell Town CE
Primary School
BRXN/ST SW9 ....40 B3
St Johns CE Infant School
CHAT ME4 ....6 A6
St John's Cemetery
MARG CT9 ....112 D6
St Johns CE Primary School
CROY/NA CRO 84 A7
MAID/BEAR ME14 ....156 A6
PGE/AN SE20 ....61 J6
SBGH/RUST TN4 ....270 E1
SEV TN13 ....149 J8
St Johns Infant School
SBGH/RUST TN4 ....270 D3
St Johns RC
Comprehensive School
GVE DA12 ....49 P9
St Johns RC Primary School
BERM/RHTH SE16 ....25 H5
GVE DA12 ....49 P9
St Johns & St Clements CE
J & I School
PECK SE15 ....40 G4
St John the Baptist CE
Primary School
BMLY BR1 ....62 A3
St John the Divine CE
Primary School
CMBW SE5 ....40 B1
St Josephs Academic RC School
BKHTH/KID SE3 ....42 C4
St Joseph's Annexe
ABYW SE2 ....28 B9
St Josephs Catholic
Junior School
CMBW SE5 ....40 C1
St Josephs Catholic
Primary School
BMLY BR1 ....62 G6
St Josephs College
STRHM/NOR SW16 ....60 B5
St Josephs RC Infant School
NRWD SE19 ....60 C5
St Josephs RC Junior School
NRWD SE19 ....60 C5
St Josephs RC Primary School
BERM/RHTH SE16 ....24 F6
DART DA1 ....45 M5
DEPT SE8 ....41 N1
GNWCH SE10 ....25 P8
RCANTE CT3 ....229 J1
STHWK SE1 ....24 D5

Notes

AA **Street by Street** QUESTIONNAIRE

Dear Atlas User
Your comments, opinions and recommendations are very important to us.
So please help us to improve our street atlases by taking a few minutes
to complete this simple questionnaire.

You do not need a stamp (unless posted outside the UK). If you do not want to remove this page from your street atlas, then photocopy it or write your answers on a plain sheet of paper.

Send to: Marketing Assistant, AA Publishing, 14th Floor Fanum House,
Freepost SCE 4598, Basingstoke RG21 4GY

ABOUT THE ATLAS...

Please state which city / town / county you bought:

Where did you buy the atlas? (City, Town, County)

For what purpose? (please tick all applicable)

To use in your local area ☐   **To use on business or at work** ☐

Visiting a strange place ☐   **In the car** ☐   **On foot** ☐

Other (please state)

Have you ever used any street atlases other than AA Street by Street?

Yes ☐   **No** ☐

If so, which ones?

Is there any aspect of our street atlases that could be improved?
(Please continue on a separate sheet if necessary)

continued overleaf

Please list the features you found most useful:

Please list the features you found least useful:

_____

LOCAL KNOWLEDGE...

Local knowledge is invaluable. Whilst every attempt has been made to make the information contained in this atlas as accurate as possible, should you notice any inaccuracies, please detail them below (if necessary, use a blank piece of paper) or e-mail us at *streetbystreet@theAA.com*

_____

_____

_____

ABOUT YOU...

Name (Mr/Mrs/Ms) _____

Address _____

                                       Postcode _____

Daytime tel no _____

E-mail address _____

Which age group are you in?

Under 25 ☐   **25-34** ☐   **35-44** ☐   **45-54** ☐   **55-64** ☐   **65+** ☐

Are you an AA member?   **YES** ☐   **NO** ☐

Do you have Internet access?   **YES** ☐   **NO** ☐

Thank you for taking the time to complete this questionnaire. Please send it to us as soon as possible, and remember, you do not need a stamp (unless posted outside the UK).

We may use information we hold about you to, telephone or email you about other products and services offered by the AA, we do NOT disclose this information to third parties.

Please tick here if you do not wish to hear about products and services from the AA. ☐

ML103y